D1371054

principles of MARKETING

5th canadian edition

philip kotler
Northwestern University

gary armstrong
University of North Carolina

peggy h. cunningham
Queen's University

Toronto

Canadian Cataloguing in Publication Data

Kotler, Philip
Principles of marketing

5th Canadian ed.
Canadian 3rd ed. by Philip Kotler, Gary Armstrong,
Peggy H. Cunningham and Robert Warren.
Includes index.
ISBN 0-13-028641-9

1. Marketing. 2. Marketing – Management. I. Armstrong, Gary.
II. Cunningham, Margaret H. III. Title.

HF5415.K636 2002 658.8 C00-933331-2

0-13-028641-9

Vice President, Editorial Director: Michael Young
Developmental Editor: Paul Donnelly
Production Editor: Mary Ann McCutcheon
Copy Editor: Elaine Freedman
Production Coordinator: Deborah Starks
Page Layout: TechBooks
Permissions and Photo Research: Alene McNeill and Barbara Welling
Art Director: Julia Hall
Interior and Cover Design: Julia Hall
Cover Image: Stone

1 2 3 4 5 06 05 04 03 02

Printed and bound in USA.

About the Authors

As a team, Philip Kotler, Gary Armstrong and Peggy Cunningham provide a blend of skills uniquely suited to writing an introductory marketing text. Professor Kotler is one of the world's leading authorities on marketing. Professor Armstrong and Professor Cunningham are award-winning teachers of undergraduate business students. Together they make the complex world of marketing practical, approachable, and enjoyable.

Philip Kotler is the S. C. Johnson & Son Distinguished Professor of International Marketing at the Kellogg Graduate School of Management, Northwestern University. He received his master's degree at the University of Chicago and his Ph.D. at M.I.T., both in economics. Dr. Kotler is author of *Marketing Management: Analysis, Planning, Implementation, and Control* (Prentice Hall), now in its tenth edition and the most widely used marketing textbook in graduate schools of business. He has authored several successful books and has written over 100 articles for leading journals. He is the only three-time winner of the coveted Alpha Kappa Psi award for the best annual article in the *Journal of Marketing*. Dr. Kotler's numerous major honours include the Paul D. Converse Award given by the American Marketing Association to honour "outstanding contributions to science in marketing" and the Stuart Henderson Britt Award as Marketer of the Year. He was named the first recipient of two major awards: the Distinguished Marketing Educator of the Year Award given by the American Marketing Association and the Philip Kotler Award for Excellence in Health Care Marketing presented by the Academy for Health Care Services Marketing. He has also received the Charles Coolidge Parlin Award, which each year honours an outstanding leader in the field of marketing. In 1995, he received the Marketing Educator of the Year Award from Sales and Marketing Executives International. Dr. Kotler has served as chairman of the College on Marketing of the Institute of Management Sciences (TIMS) and a director of the American Marketing Association. He has received honorary doctorate degrees from DePaul University, the University of Zurich, and the Athens University of Economics and Business. He has consulted with many major U.S. and foreign companies on marketing strategy.

Gary Armstrong is Crist W. Blackwell Distinguished Professor of Undergraduate Education in the Kenan-Flagler Business School at the University of North Carolina at Chapel Hill. He holds undergraduate and masters degrees in business from Wayne State University in Detroit, and he received his Ph.D. in marketing from Northwestern University. Dr. Armstrong has contributed numerous articles to leading business journals. As a consultant and researcher, he has worked with many companies on marketing research, sales management, and marketing strategy. But Professor Armstrong's first love is teaching. His Blackwell Distinguished Professorship is the only permanent endowed professorship for distinguished undergraduate teaching at the University of North Carolina at Chapel Hill. He has been very active in the teaching and administration of Kenan-Flagler's undergraduate program. His recent administrative posts include Chair of the Marketing Faculty, Associate Director of the Undergraduate Business Program, Director of the Business Honors Program, and others. He works closely with business student groups and has received several campus-wide and Business School teaching awards. He is the only repeat recipient of the school's highly regarded Award for Excellence in Undergraduate Teaching, which he won for the third time in 1993.

Peggy Cunningham is Associate Professor of Marketing at Queen's University School of Business. She received her undergraduate degree from Queen's University, completed her MBA at the University of Calgary, and earned her Ph.D. in marketing from Texas A&M University. She is the Co-Chair of the E-Commerce Research Group and the Head of the new MBA program for students with undergraduate business degrees. She has considerable international experience and has been a visiting professor at universities and government training programs in France, Germany, China, the UK, and the US. Her prior industry experience and current consulting practice help her to bring the perspective of the practitioner to the study of marketing. She conducts research in the fields of e-commerce, marketing ethics, strategic alliances, and cause-related marketing. Her work is published in a number of journals including the *Journal of the Academy of Marketing Science*. She is a devoted teacher who tries to inspire her students to realize their full and unique potential. In recognition of these efforts, she has received several teaching and service awards including the Frank Knox award for teaching excellence, a Queen's campus-wide award granted by undergraduate students. She was named as the Academy of Marketing Science Outstanding Teacher in 2001. She has applied her love of teaching to a wide range of courses including marketing management and strategy, principles of marketing, services marketing, international marketing, marketing ethics, and Customer Relationship Management.

(Photo ©2001 Joseph Chan/ARTiculation Group)

Brief Contents

Contents

PART IV Managing Marketing

Preface

Philip Kotler and Gary Armstrong are among the best-known names in marketing and have long been recognized for their expertise and unique perspectives about the field. Peggy Cunningham brings a unique Canadian perspective to the book founded on deep respect for the expertise Canadian marketing academics and practitioners bring to the field. She also thoroughly understands the unique challenges marketing in Canada entails. These challenges include regional and language differences, multiculturalism, population dispersion, different regulatory policies and philosophies, the small domestic marketplace and resulting mandate for global sales, a highly concentrated retail environment, and unique cultural and ethical norms. In addition, many Canadian firms are operating units of large, multinational firms; thus, marketing in Canada often necessitates integrating Canadian strategies with the global programs of the parent firm. Finally, while Canada has one of the most connected populations in the world, our businesses have taken a more conservative approach to marketing on the World Wide Web. Since they have learned from the mistakes of some early movers, many of these on-line ventures have achieved considerable success.

This new edition is more than just words on a page. It is an entryway. A jumping off point. A place to begin a new journey. Phil, Gary and Peggy realized that the marketing revolution is far from finished. They realized that what they were seeing across the globe was so exciting that they had to do more than just write about it: they had to show students, get them involved, get them to participate. The authors re-thought and re-wrote the text from top to bottom. The most important change is, of course, the emphasis and expanded coverage of the revolutionary new marketing technologies. Not only is an entire chapter devoted to the burgeoning use of the Internet, but each chapter provides fresh new material on everything from virtual reality displays to e-commerce databases. Plus, Internet Connections at the end of each chapter provide exercises to reinforce the chapter's highlights.

At the same time, Phil, Gary and Peggy keep their readers abreast of the most current thinking on customer management, assessing customer value, brand equity and value positioning. There is an even greater emphasis on using actual companies to bring concepts to life for students. Each company case in this new edition is new or completely revised.

New to the Fifth Canadian Edition

Let's look at the text changes in more detail. The fifth edition of *Principles of Marketing* retains all of the elements that have made the text a worldwide leader for almost two decades, but has been thoroughly revised around the major marketing theme of the new millennium: connectedness.

Connecting with customers: connecting more selectively, more directly, and for life:

- Relationship marketing—finding, keeping, and growing profitable customers and capturing customer lifetime value by building value-laden customer relationships.
- Delivering superior customer value, satisfaction, and quality—attracting, keeping, and cultivating customers by developing market-centred strategies and "taking care of the customer." Integrated chapter-by-chapter coverage accompanies a full chapter on developing customer value, satisfaction, and relationships.

- Connecting technologies—employing the Internet and other information, computer, communications, and transportation technologies to connect directly with customers and to shape marketing offers tailored to their needs. This edition offers integrated chapter-by-chapter coverage, plus a full chapter on Direct and Online Marketing.
- Connecting with marketing partners: connecting inside and outside the company to jointly bring more value to customers:
- The company value chain—connecting inside the company to create cross-functional, customer-focused teamwork and integrated action.
- Value-delivery networks—connecting with partners outside the company to create effective supply-chains.

Phil, Gary and Peggy guide students through this New World of marketing using a variety of aids.

- *Chapter-opening Examples:* Each chapter starts with a dramatic marketing story that introduces the chapter material and arouses student interest.

You've finally made it through university and you're about to realize a long-held dream—backpacking through Asia. But now you aren't so sure about this adventure. Your travel buddy decided not to come at the last minute, and you've just landed in the crowded Bangkok Airport, only to discover no one speaks English. You are just about ready to climb back on the flight home when you turn around and see a stranger elbowing her way through the crowd wearing a backpack with the distinctive Mountain Equipment Co-op (MEC) logo. A Canadian, for sure, looking just as lost as you, but perhaps the two of you can work together through the maze. Maybe this trip won't be so bad.

As our young traveller discovered, the MEC logo on packs and clothing has come to state "I am Canadian" almost as much as a replica of the Canadian flag. In fact, few companies and brands are as associated with being Canadian as MEC. How has such a young company, born only 29 years ago, developed this level of brand identity, you might ask, especially since MEC has prided itself in shunning such traditional tactics as mass media advertising? Its history is novel, to say the least. MEC's founders began by first recognizing unmet needs in a particular marketplace and then working to fill those needs. In the late 1960s, a small group of students from the University of British Columbia, with a passion for climbing and hiking, discovered that there were no other mountaineering stores in Vancouver. To get the equipment they needed, people were forced to make pilgrimages to the Mecca of gear at the time, REI in Seattle. However, Canada Customs agents were becoming increasingly tough on people who sometimes "forgot" to declare their American purchases. Storm-bound on Mt. Baker one weekend in the spring of 1970, the six original members of MEC came up with the founding concept.

Simply filling a need didn't make MEC what is has become today. It filled this need in a distinct fashion. First, rather than being a traditional retailer, MEC is a cooperative. This means that Mountain Equipment Co-operative is member owned. It has had a narrow and focused approach right from the beginning. MEC provides products and services for self-propelled, wilderness-oriented recreational activities. It prides itself on offering the lowest reasonable price on its products and offering informative, helpful service.

- *Concept Connections:* Each chapter begins with learning objectives that preview the flow of concepts in the chapter.
- *Marketing Highlights:* Additional examples and important information are featured in Marketing Highlight exhibits throughout the text.
- *Key Terms:* Key terms are highlighted within the text, clearly defined in the margins of the pages on which they appear, and listed at the end of each chapter.
- *Review of Concept Connections:* At the end of each chapter, summaries are provided for each chapter objective to reinforce main points and concepts.

marketing highlight 4-2

Single-Source Data Systems: A Powerful Way to Measure Marketing Impact

Information Resources, Inc. (IRI), which operates in 26 countries, is a leader in providing innovative information and marketing software to companies engaged in the marketing, sales, and distribution of Canadian packaged and non-packaged goods. A major competitor of A.C. Nielsen, IRI knows all there is to know about the members of its panel households—what they eat for lunch; what they put in their coffee; and what they use to wash their hair, quench their thirsts, or make up their faces. The research company electronically monitors the television programs that these people watch and tracks the brands they buy, the coupons they use, where they shop, and what newspapers and magazines they read. These households are part of IRI's BehaviorScan service, a single-source data system that links consumers' exposure to television advertising, sales promotion, and other marketing efforts with their store purchases. BehaviorScan and other single-source data systems have revolutionized the way consumer products companies measure the impact of their marketing activities.

The basics of single-source research are straightforward, and the IRI BehaviorScan system provides a good example. IRI maintains a panel of households across Canada. The company meters each home's television set to track who watches what and when, and it quizzes family members to find out what they read. It carefully records important facts about each household, such as family income, age of children, lifestyle, and product and store buying history.

IRI also uses a panel of retail stores in each of its markets. For a fee, these stores agree to carry the new products that IRI wishes to test and they allow IRI to control such factors as shelf location, stocking, point-of-purchase displays, and pricing for these products.

Each BehaviorScan household receives an identification number. When household members shop for groceries in IRI panel stores, they give their identification number to the store checkout clerk. All the information about the family's purchases—brands bought, package sizes, prices paid—is recorded by the store's electronic scanner and immediately entered by computer into the family's purchase file. The system also records any other in-store factors that might affect purchase decisions, such as special competitor price promotions or shelf displays.

Thus, IRI builds a complete record of each household's demographic and psychographic makeup, purchasing behaviour, media habits, and the conditions surrounding purchase. But IRI takes the process a step further. Through cable television, IRI controls the advertisements being sent to each household. It can beam different ads and promotions to different panel households and then use the purchasing information obtained from scanners to assess which ads had more or less impact and how various promotions affected different kinds of consumers. In short, from a single source, companies can obtain information that links their marketing efforts directly with consumer buying behaviour.

BehaviorScan and other single-source systems have their drawbacks, and some researchers are sceptical. One hitch is that such systems produce truckloads of data—more than most companies can handle. Another problem is cost: single-source data can cost marketers hundreds of thousands of dollars a year per brand. Also, because such systems are set up in only a few market areas, usually small cities, the marketer often finds it difficult to generalize from the measures and results. Finally, although single-source systems provide important information for assessing the impact of promotion and advertising, they shed little light on the effects of other key marketing actions.

Despite these drawbacks, more and more companies are relying on single-source data systems to test new products and new marketing strategies. When properly used, such systems can provide marketers with fast and detailed information about how their products are selling, who is buying them, and what factors affect purchase.

Information Resources Inc. used this ad to announce its arrival in the Canadian marketplace.

Sources: See Joanne Lipman, "Single-source ad research heralds detailed look at household habits," *Wall Street Journal*, 16 February 1988:39; Joe Schwartz, "Back to the source," *American Demographics*, January 1989:22–6; Magid H. Abraham and Leonard M. Lodish, "Getting the most out of advertising and promotion," *Harvard Business Review*, May–June 1990:50–60; and Howard Schlossberg, "IRI, Nielsen slug it out in 'scanning wars,'" *Marketing News*, 2 September 1991:1,47.

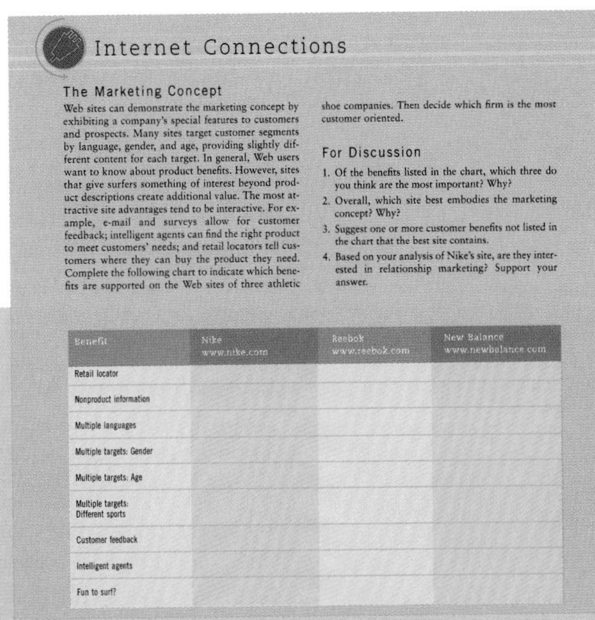

Internet Connections

The Marketing Concept

Web sites can demonstrate the marketing concept by exhibiting a company's special features to customers and prospects. Many sites target customer segments by language, gender, and age, providing slightly different content for each target. In general, Web users want to know about product benefits. However, sites that give surfers something of interest beyond product descriptions create additional value. The most attractive site advantages tend to be interactive. For example, e-mail and surveys allow for customer feedback; intelligent agents can find the right product to meet customers' needs; and retail locators tell customers where they can buy the product they need. Complete the following chart to indicate which benefits are supported on the Web sites of three athletic shoe companies. Then decide which firm is the most customer oriented.

For Discussion

1. Of the benefits listed in the chart, which three do you think are the most important? Why?
2. Overall, which site best embodies the marketing concept? Why?
3. Suggest one or more customer benefits not listed in the chart that the best site contains.
4. Based on your analysis of Nike's site, are they interested in relationship marketing? Support your answer.

Benefit	Nike www.nike.com	Reebok www.reebok.com	New Balance www.newbalance.com
Retail locator			
Nonproduct information			
Multiple languages			
Multiple targets: Gender			
Multiple targets: Age			
Multiple targets: Different sports			
Customer feedback			
Intelligent agents			
Fun to surf?			

- *Issues for Discussion and Marketing Applications:* Each chapter contains a set of discussion questions and application exercises covering major chapter concepts.
- *Internet Connection Exercises:* Each chapter ends with a carefully designed Internet exercise that demonstrates the power of the Web as a marketing tool.
- *Company Cases:* Company Cases for class or written discussion are provided at the end of each chapter, with integrative comprehensive cases included at the end of the text. These cases challenge students to apply marketing principles to companies in real situations.

Company Case 6

Biofoam: Not Just Peanuts!

Like diamonds, polystyrene peanuts are forever. The stash of them is growing at a rate of at least 110 million kilograms annually. Since their introduction in 1970, they have become one of the most popular forms of packaging material. They are lightweight, inexpensive, and resilient. They conform to any shape, protect superbly, resist shifting in transit, and leave no dusty residue on the goods they protect. And, of course, they are indestructible. In fact, that's the problem. Nearly every one of those peanuts used since 1970 is still with us—blowing in the wind or taking up space in a landfill. Worse yet, they will be with us for another 500 years. They're wonderful, but they're just not environmentally sound.

A small firm, Biofoam, believes that it has solved this problem. It sells peanuts made from grain sorghum, which are also known as Biofoam. To make these sorghum peanuts, the company strips the grain of its nutritional value, presses it into pellets, and conveys it through a giant popper. The process creates a product that looks like tan cheese doodles, which is not surprising considering that the inventors originally started out to make a snack food. But since no one wanted to eat these tan cheese doodles, the inventors had to find other uses for them. According to Ed Alfke, Biofoam's CEO, the sorghum peanuts do as good a job as the best foam peanuts but don't cost any more. Moreover, they hold no electrostatic charge, so they won't cling to nylons or other synthetic fibres (like your carpet or clothes). Better yet, they are "absolutely, frighteningly natural," says Tom Schmiegel, a veteran of the plastics industry.

To dispose of a Biofoam peanut, you can throw it in the garbage, toss it on your front lawn; dump it in your compost bin; put it in your dog's or cat's bowl; set it out with salsa at your next party; or simply wash it down your drain. The peanut dissolves in water and has some—although limited—nutritional value. Alfke bought into the company because of its environmentally positive stance. He is convinced that green companies will profit from a global regulatory climate that's increasingly hostile to polluters. "The writing is on the wall for companies that are not environmentally friendly," he says.

Biofoam initially targeted retailers who wanted to send an environmentally friendly message to their customers, and included a Biofoam pamphlet explaining the advantages of the Biofoam peanut. The company targeted the heaviest users of Styrofoam peanuts—organizations like the Home Shopping Network, which consumes 10 to 20 truckloads of loose fill each day at peak volume. To date, Biofoam has signed two major accounts—the Fuller Brush Company and computer reseller MicroAge.

Eventually, Biofoam will have to expand beyond environmentally sensitive firms into a broader market. To convince potential users to use Biofoam peanuts, Alfke has developed a seemingly flawless option: to be environmentally responsible without paying more or sacrificing convenience. He is willing to install machines on the customer's premises to produce peanuts in-house, an arrangement that would give Biofoam rent-free production sites across North America. He'll even provide an employee to operate the machinery. Although this strategy might sound unusual, it has been used by other companies such as Haloid (now Xerox) to sell copies and by Tetra-Pak to sell juice boxes and milk cartons.

The in-house arrangement benefits both the customer and Biofoam. Users receive immediate, reliable, just-in-time delivery combined with on-site service and a five-year price guarantee with no intermediaries involved. With Biofoam on-site, users never run out of packaging and avoid the expense of stockpiling materials. And lower production costs make Biofoam price competitive with that polystyrene. For Biofoam, the arrangement provides a rent-free network of regional manufacturing facilities and an intimacy with each customer. Because the host company will consume only about one-third of the output, Biofoam plans to sell the excess to smaller firms in the host's area.

However, this in-house production arrangement is not without disadvantages. From the host's perspective, the machinery takes up 1500 square feet of space that could be used to produce something else. Furthermore, some of the output of that 1500 square feet goes to other firms, benefiting Biofoam but doing nothing for the host. And the host has a non-employee working in its plant. In addition, the peanut-making machinery is intrusive. It consists of three machines—an extruder, a conditioning chamber, and a de-duster—joined by ducts and conveyor belts. The machines make a lot of noise (like a giant air conditioner), making conversation in the vicinity impossible. The process creates a smell roughly akin to that of the inside of an old barn, and the machines produce heat, which is a potentially troubling

- *Video Cases:* A full selection of written video cases accompanies the fifth edition, supported by exciting and original videos from a number of CBC programs and written case material developed for *Principles of Marketing*. The videos and cases help to bring key marketing concepts and issues to life in the classroom.

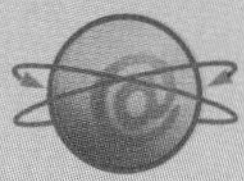

- *Weblinks:* Exciting and useful Web sites are discussed throughout the text and are easily identifiable by the Weblinks icon.

- *Indexes:* Subject and company indexes reference all information and examples in the book.

Supplements

A successful marketing course requires more than a well-written book. Connecting in today's classroom requires a dedicated teacher and a fully-integrated teaching system. *Principles of Marketing,* Fifth Canadian Edition, is supported by an extensive teaching package:

Instructor's Resource Manual with CBC Video Guide Contains chapter objectives, chapter overviews, complete teaching outlines, and lecture notes for each chapter. The manual includes answers to all end-of-chapter questions and comments on the company and comprehensive cases. In addition, it summarizes each video and provides answers to the video case discussion questions. (ISBN 0-13-093184-5)

Test Item File Comprises over 1800 questions (100 per chapter) in a variety of formats, including multiple choice, true/false, and essay. Questions are rated by difficulty and linked by page reference to the text. The Test Item File is also produced in an electronic format. (ISBN 0-13-093183-7)

Test Manager This powerful software program provides fast, simple, and error-free test generation. Entire tests can be previewed on-screen before printing. Test Manager can print multiple variations of the same test, scrambling the order of questions and multiple-choice answers. (ISBN 0-13-093182-9)

PowerPoint Presentations With up to 30 slides per chapter in PowerPoint 97, this disk allows you to present transparencies to your class electronically and also may be used as part of a Presentation Manager lecture. Black-and-white masters are included if you prefer to create your own acetates. (ISBN 0-13-093179-9)

Pearson Education Canada/CBC Video Library Pearson Education Canada and the CBC have worked together to bring you 18 segments from such notable CBC programs as *Venture, Market Place,* and *Undercurrents.* Designed specifically to complement the text, this case collection is an excellent tool for bringing students into contact with the world outside the classroom. These programs have extremely high production quality, present substantial content, and have been chosen to relate directly to chapter content. (Please contact your Pearson Education Canada sales representative for details. These videos are subject to availability and terms negotiated upon adoption of the text.) (ISBN 0-13-0931810).

Companion Web Site The fifth edition's Companion Web Site includes an online study guide with multiple choice, true/false, and short essay questions, and interactive Web exercises. Students can view CBC videos and PowerPoint Presentations online, and instructors have password-protected access to the Instructor's Resource Manual with Video Guide. Additionally, three appendices from the fourth edition—Measuring and Forecasting Demand, Marketing Arithmetic, and Careers in Marketing—have been updated and posted to the site. See www.pearsoned.ca/kotler.

For the Student

Study Guide The Study Guide includes chapter overviews, objectives, key terms and definitions, and detailed outlines for note-taking and review. Short essay questions centre on a case that is designed to illustrate and apply topics in marketing. Each case in the section either is a synopsis of a recent article in marketing or has been drawn from the author's experiences in the field. To reinforce students' understanding of the chapter material, the guide includes a section of multiple-choice and true/false questions. Suggested answers for all short essay, multiple choice and true/false questions are provided for students' self-checking. (ISBN 0-13-060747-9).

Acknowledgments

No book is the work only of its authors. We owe much to the pioneers of marketing who first identified its major issues and developed its concepts and techniques. Our thanks also go to our colleagues at the School of Business, Queen's University, J. L. Kellogg Graduate School of Management, Northwestern University, at the Kenan-Flagler Business School, University of North Carolina at Chapel Hill, for ideas and suggestions. We also thank Steve Arnold of Queen's University who provided insight on the globalization of retailing, Auleen Carson of Wilfrid Laurier University, who wrote some of the CBC video cases, and Mark Smith of Humber College, who provided a unique perspective on positioning. We also wish to express our gratitude to the enthusiastic marketing professionals who granted interviews for the Canadian fourth and fifth editions, including:

Valerie Bell, H.J. Heinz of Canada
Lindsey Davis, Kraft Canada
Peter Elwood, Unilever
Dana Grant, Landmark
Larry Gordon, Metro Credit Union
Scott Hogan, Nortel
Nick Jones, Communiqué
J.J. Lee, H.J. Heinz of Canada
Jeff Norton, Procter & Gamble
Alan Quarry, Quarry Integrated Communications
Jim Shenkman, Brunico Communication Inc.
Arthur Soler, Cadbury Chocolate
Vanessa Vachon, Procter & Gamble

We owe a debt of gratitude to all the professors and instructors who provided suggestions on how to improve the text. Reviewers who gave thoughtful and detailed responses include:

Chris R. Plouffe, University of Western Ontario
Louise Ripley, York University
May Aung, University of Guelph
Daniel Gardiner, The University of British Columbia
Brad Davis, Wilfrid Laurier University
Lee Ann Keple, Athabasca University
Max Winchester, University College of the Fraser Valley
Gordon Fullerton, Saint Mary's University
Scott Colwell, Acadia University

We also owe a great deal to the people at Pearson Education Canada who helped develop this book. Our sincere thanks for the support of the editorial team: Mary Ann McCutcheon, Production Editor, for her enthusiastic and attentive monitoring of a very complex project; Elaine Freeman for her superb copyediting; Julia Hall, designer, who was asked to make a fine design better, and did; and hardworking Paul Donnelly, Developmental Editor. Without their support, hard work, and insightful suggestions, we never could have made the tight deadlines associated with this project.

Finally, we owe many thanks to our students, who make good teaching possible, and to our families—for their constant support and encouragement. To them, we dedicate this book.

Peggy Cunningham
Philip Kotler
Gary Armstrong

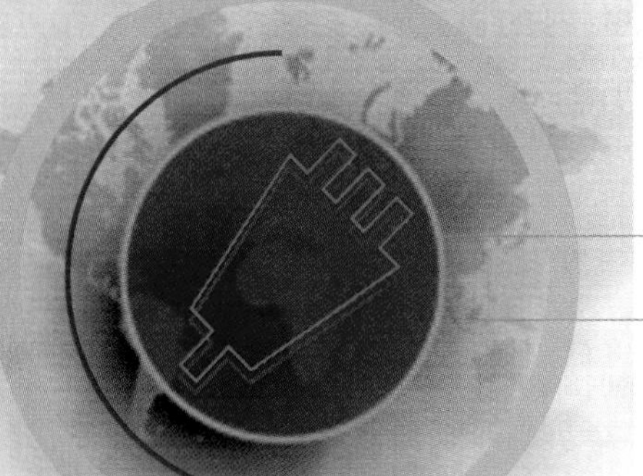

PART 1 2 3 4

Understanding Marketing and the Marketing Process

Concept Connections

After studying this chapter, you should be able to

1. Define marketing and discuss its core concepts.
2. Explain the relationship between customer value, satisfaction, and quality.
3. Discuss marketing management and understand how marketers manage demand and build profitable customer relationships.
4. Compare the five marketing management philosophies.
5. Analyze the major challenges facing future marketers.

chapter 1

Marketing in a Changing World: Creating Customer Value and Satisfaction

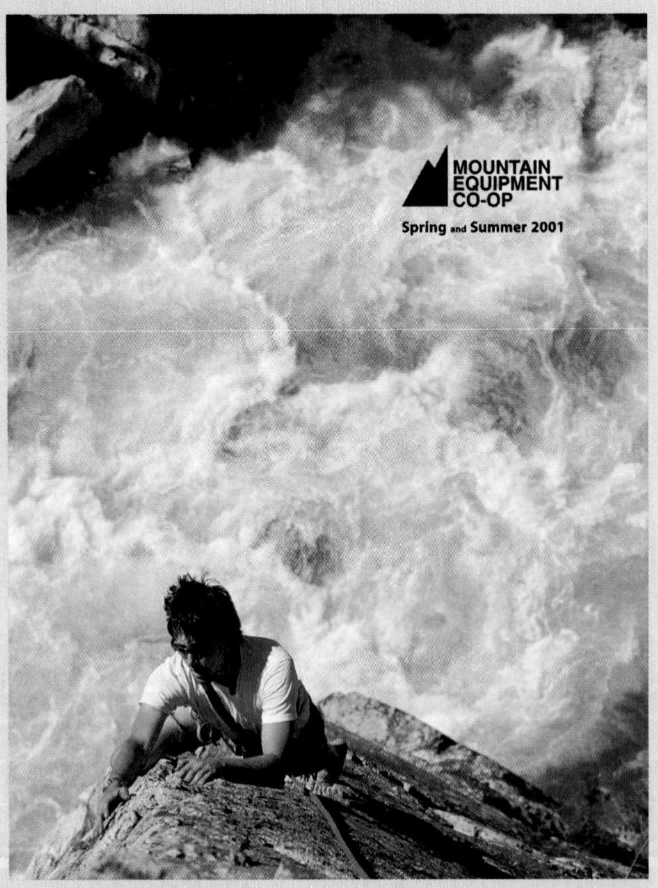

MOUNTAIN EQUIPMENT CO-OP
Spring and Summer 2001

You've finally made it through university and you're about to realize a long-held dream—backpacking through Asia. But now you aren't so sure about this adventure. Your travel buddy decided not to come at the last minute, and you've just landed in the crowded Bangkok Airport, only to discover no one speaks English. You are just about ready to climb back on the flight home when you turn around and see a stranger elbowing her way through the crowd wearing a backpack with the distinctive Mountain Equipment Co-op (MEC) logo. A Canadian, for sure, looking just as lost as you, but perhaps the two of you can work together through the maze. Maybe this trip won't be so bad.

As our young traveller discovered, the MEC logo on packs and clothing has come to state "I am Canadian" almost as much as a replica of the Canadian flag. In fact, few companies and brands are as associated with being Canadian as MEC. How has such a young company, born only 29 years ago, developed this level of brand identity, you might ask, especially since MEC has prided itself in shunning such traditional tactics as mass media advertising? Its history is novel, to say the least. MEC's founders began by first recognizing unmet needs in a particular marketplace and then working to fill those needs. In the late 1960s, a small group of students from the University of British Columbia, with a passion for climbing and hiking, discovered that there were no other mountaineering stores in Vancouver. To get the equipment they needed, people were forced to make pilgrimages to the Mecca of gear at the time, REI in Seattle. However, Canada Customs agents were becoming increasingly tough on people who sometimes "forgot" to declare their American purchases. Storm-bound on Mt. Baker one weekend in the spring of 1970, the six original members of MEC came up with the founding concept.

Simply filling a need didn't make MEC what is has become today. It filled this need in a distinct fashion. First, rather than being a traditional retailer, MEC is a cooperative. This means that Mountain Equipment Co-operative is member owned. It has had a narrow and focused approach right from the beginning. MEC provides products and services for self-propelled, wilderness-oriented recreational activities. It prides itself on offering the lowest reasonable price on its products and offering informative, helpful service.

While it is a retailer that survives by promoting "consumption," it does so in an environmentally responsible manner. One of its initiatives in this regard is MEC's Ecological Footprint Calculator. It developed this educational tool to encourage members to think more about the sustainability of their day-to-day life choices. It was intended to provoke thought and discussion about social values and thoughtful consumption. MEC also encourages its members to use their gear to the full extent of its lifetime. To help them do this, MEC has member education programs on use and care of its products. It has a product repair program and a gear re-use program in addition to its recycling and donation programs for equipment members no longer want or need. It is also working to expand its rental programs for those who need gear only occasionally.

While MEC certainly focused on customer needs, quality products, and high service, it also grew into the realization that many stakeholder groups were critically connected to its long-term success. It is a values-led organization that knows the power of having a motivated network of top-quality suppliers. It is energized by its employees and it is committed to people and their communities, not just to a financial bottom line. This orientation is exemplified in its statement of values:

- We conduct ourselves ethically and with integrity.
- We show respect for others in our words and actions.
- We act in the spirit of community and co-operation.
- We respect and protect our natural environment.
- We strive for personal growth and continual learning.

Mountain Equipment Co-op
www.mec.ca

MEC also knows that simply working to make a one-time sale to a customer isn't enough. Developing lifelong relationships with its members has been another touchstone of the cooperative. As part of its vision, MEC sets the goal of having its members purchase most of their needs for outdoor activities from MEC. It sends members catalogues twice a year. Each is filled with high-quality information as well as product listings. MEC also sends out newsletters and is beginning to rely more and more on its Web site and e-commerce capabilities to maintain the link with people who have paid $5 for their lifetime membership.

Such relationships are critical, since MEC has no doubt that its best marketers are the members themselves. Member-generated word-of-mouth communication has long worked to help the company grow. And grow it has. The six-member organization has become over a million strong and has sales in excess of $139 million a year. MEC currently operates stores in Vancouver, Calgary, Toronto, Ottawa, and Edmonton. It plans to open a new facility in Halifax. But no matter what it does today or in the future, it hopes to always climb the high road and be an exemplar of ethics and integrity in all it undertakes.[1]

Many factors contribute to making a business successful. However, today's successful companies at all levels have one thing in common—like MEC, they are strongly customer focused and heavily committed to marketing. These companies share an absolute dedication to understanding and satisfying the needs of customers in well-defined target markets. They motivate everyone in the organization to produce superior value for their customers, leading to high levels of customer satisfaction.

What Is Marketing?

To create value and satisfaction, marketing, more than any other business function, deals with customers. Although we will explore more detailed definitions of marketing later in this chapter, perhaps the simplest definition is: Marketing is the

Religious orders such as Sisters of Charity are using marketing to overcome outdated stereotypes.

delivery of customer satisfaction at a profit. The two-fold goal of marketing is to attract new customers by promising superior value, and to keep current customers by delivering satisfaction.

Wal-Mart has become the world's largest retailer by delivering on its promise "We sell for less—always." Coca-Cola, long the world's leading soft drink, delivers on the simple but enduring promise "Always Coca-Cola"—always thirst quenching, always good with food, always cool, always a part of your life. These and other highly successful companies know that if they take care of their customers, market share and profits will follow.

Some people believe that only large business organizations operating in highly developed economies use marketing, but sound marketing is critical to the success of every organization—large or small, for-profit or non-profit, domestic or global. Large for-profit firms such as Bell, IBM, Nortel, Zellers, and Marriott use marketing. But so do non-profit organizations such as Halifax's St. Mary's University, Toronto's Hospital for Sick Children, and the Vancouver Public Aquarium. Moreover, marketing is practised throughout the world. Most countries in North and South America, Western Europe, and the Far East have well-developed marketing systems. Even in Eastern Europe and the former Soviet republics, where marketing has long had a bad name, dramatic political and social changes have created new opportunities. Business and government leaders in most of these nations are eager to learn everything they can about modern marketing practices.

You already know a lot about marketing—it's all around you. You see the results of marketing in the abundance of products that line the store shelves in your nearby shopping mall. You see marketing in the advertisements that fill your TV screen, spice up your magazines, add animation to Internet sites, and stuff your mailbox. At home, at school, where you work, where you play—you are exposed to marketing in almost everything you do. Yet, there is much more to marketing than meets the consumer's casual eye. Behind it all is a massive network of people and activities competing for your attention and purchasing dollars.

This book will give you a more complete and formal introduction to the basic concepts and practices of today's marketing. In this chapter, we begin by defining marketing and its core concepts, comparing market orientation with other business perspectives, and discussing some of the major challenges that marketers face as we whirl into the new millennium.

Marketing Defined

What does the term *marketing* mean? Many people think of marketing only as selling and advertising. And no wonder—every day we are bombarded with television commercials, newspaper ads, direct mail, Internet pitches, and sales calls. However, selling and advertising are only the tip of the marketing iceberg. Table 1-1 shows that marketing is one of three key functions that are central to all orga-

TABLE 1-1 Three Functions Required in All Organizations and Sample Decisions Made by People Working in These Functional Areas

Organization	Marketing	Operations	Finance/Accounting
Nike	Develop relationships with new distributors. Manage distributor incentive program. Prepare sales forecast for new product launch. Work with operations on production schedules. Determine prices for new product line. Work with advertising agency on new promotional materials.	Oversee building of new offshore plant. Improve efficiency of basketball-shoe line. Work with marketing to develop production schedules for new product line. Develop specifications for suppliers of materials for new product line.	Develop financing package for new plant. Review supplier payment program to determine if changes required for new supplier. Prepare budgets, and proforma cash flow statements for new product line. Develop repurchase plan stock buyback.

Nike
www.nike.com/canada

nizations. To create customer value and satisfaction, these functions must be coordinated. Marketers act as the customer's voice within the firm and are responsible for motivating people from other functional areas (operations, sales, accounting, etc.) to have a customer focus. They also analyze industries to identify emerging trends. They determine which national and international markets to enter or exit. They conduct research to understand consumer behaviour and use this information to divide markets into the groups that the firm can best serve with its products and services. They design integrated marketing mixes—products, prices, channels of distribution, and promotion programs.

Today, marketing must be understood not in the old sense of making a sale—telling and selling—but in the new sense of satisfying customer needs. Whereas selling occurs only after a product is produced, marketing starts long before a company has a product. Marketing is able to envision a future market only after it has done its homework—assessing needs, measuring their extent and intensity, and determining whether a profitable opportunity exists. Marketing continues throughout the product's life, prospecting for new customers, tracking evolving needs, and always working to retain current customers by learning from product sales results so that product appeal and performance can constantly be improved. The evidence that the marketer has done a good job: Products sell easily and market share and customer loyalty is sustained over time.

Marketing
A social and managerial process by which individuals and groups obtain what they need and want through creating and exchanging products and value with others.

We define **marketing** as a social and managerial process by which individuals and groups obtain what they need and want through creating and exchanging products and value with others.[2] To explain this definition, we examine these important terms: *needs, wants, and demands; products and services; value, satisfaction, and quality; exchange, transactions, and relationships;* and *markets.* Figure 1-1 shows that these core marketing concepts are linked, with each concept building on the one before it.

Needs, Wants, and Demands

Needs
States of felt deprivation.

Wants
The form taken by human needs as they are shaped by culture and individual personality.

The most basic concept underlying marketing is that of human needs. Human **needs** are states of felt deprivation. Humans have many complex needs. These include basic *physical* needs for food, clothing, warmth, and safety; *social* needs for belonging and affection; and *individual* needs for knowledge and self-expression. These needs are not invented by marketers; they are a basic part of the human composition.

Wants are the form taken by human needs as they are shaped by culture and

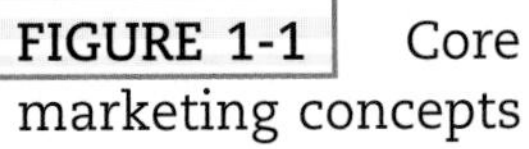
FIGURE 1-1 Core marketing concepts

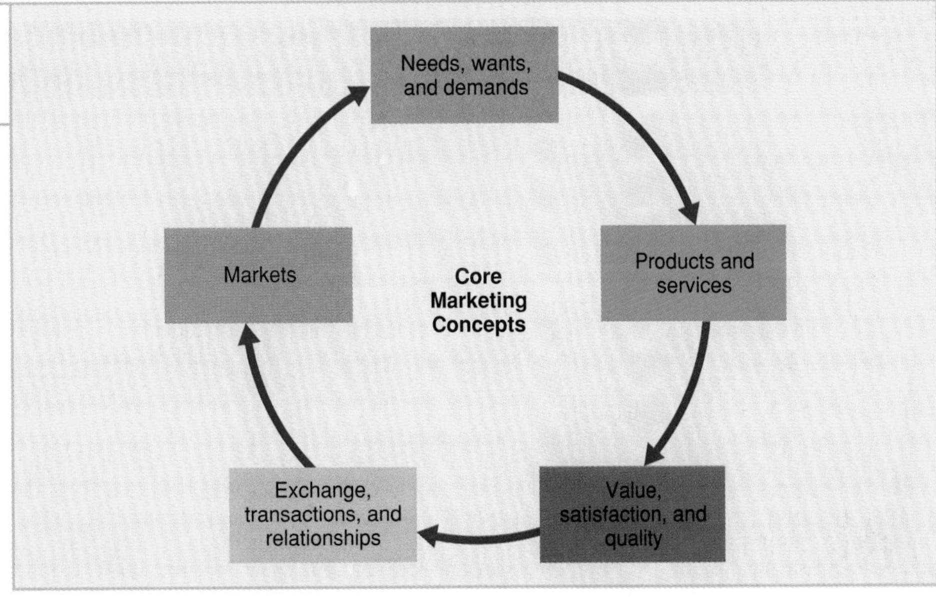

individual personality. A hungry person in Canada may want a hamburger, french fries, and a pop. A hungry person in Bali may want mangoes, suckling pig, and beans. Wants are described in terms of objects that will satisfy needs.

Demands
Human wants that are backed by buying power.

People have almost unlimited wants but limited resources. Thus, they want to choose products that provide the most value and satisfaction for their money. When backed by buying power, wants become **demands.** Consumers view products as bundles of benefits and choose products that give them the best bundle for their money. Thus, one consumer in the market for a car will buy a Honda Civic, since it satisfies the need for reliable transportation and fuel economy and is within his or her limited budget. Another will purchase a Mercedes-Benz, since he or she values and can afford its comfort, luxury, and status.

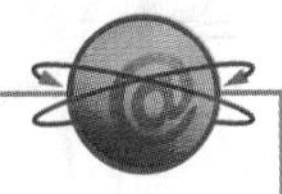

Wal-Mart
www.walmart.com
Marriott Canada
http://go.marriott.com/canada

Outstanding marketing companies go to great lengths to learn about and understand their customers' needs, wants, and demands. They conduct consumer research, focus groups, and customer clinics. They analyze customer complaint, inquiry, warranty, and service data. They train salespeople to watch for unfulfilled customer needs. They observe customers using their own and competing products and interview them in depth about their likes and dislikes. Understanding customer needs, wants, and demands in detail provides important input for designing marketing strategies. (See Marketing Highlight 1-1.)

In these outstanding companies, people at all levels—including top management—stay close to customers in an ongoing effort to understand their needs and wants. For example, top executives from Wal-Mart spend two days each week visiting stores and mingling with customers. At Marriott International Inc., chairman of the board and president Bill Marriott personally reads 10 percent of the 8000 letters and two percent of the 750 000 guest comment cards submitted by customers each year. All in all, understanding customer needs, wants, and demands in detail provides important input for designing marketing strategies.

Products and Services

Product
Anything that can be offered to a market for attention, acquisition, use, or consumption that might satisfy a want or need. It includes physical objects, services, persons, places, organizations, and ideas.

People satisfy their needs and wants with products and services. A **product** is anything that can be offered to a market to satisfy a need or want. The concept of *product* is not limited to physical objects—anything capable of satisfying a need

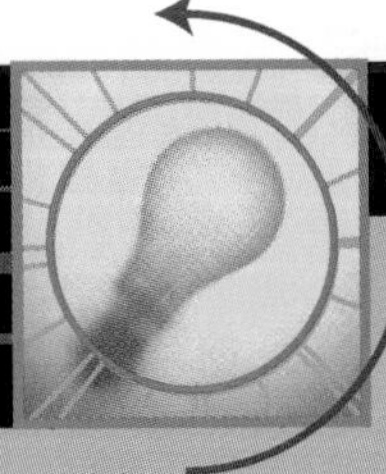

marketing highlight 1-1

No One Knows Better than Mom, Right?

No one knows better than Mom, right? But does she know how much underwear you own? Jockey International does. Or the number of ice cubes you put in a glass? Coca-Cola knows that one. Or which pretzels you usually eat first—the broken ones or the whole ones? Try asking Frito-Lay. Big companies know the whats, wheres, hows, and whens of their customers' needs, wants, and demands. They figure out all sorts of things about us that we don't even know ourselves. To marketers, this isn't a trivial pursuit—knowing all about customer needs is the cornerstone of effective marketing. Most companies research us in detail and amass mountains of facts.

Coca-Cola knows that we put 3.2 ice cubes in a glass, see 69 of its commercials every year, and prefer cans out of vending machines to be at a temperature of 2°C. Did you know that 38 percent of North Americans would rather have a tooth pulled than take their car to a dealership for repairs? For every 10 000 Canadians in 1992, there were 8.13 automated teller machines; while there were only 5.26 for every 10 000 Americans and 3.36 for every 10 000 Germans, according to the Canadian Bankers Association. An Angus Reid poll of Canadian men found that 86 percent believed women spent more time in the bathroom, and that this extra time totalled four minutes. Lever Brothers Co. discovered that 79 percent of women said they didn't trust their husbands to do the laundry. A group called Tidy Britain did a 10-year survey that uncovered that 33 percent of the litter that washed up on Britain's shores originated in Canada. When male readers were surveyed by the Quebec business monthly *Affaires Plus,* 77.6 percent said their families were their top priority, but only 6.8 percent would make a sacrifice in their career to improve their family life. If you send a husband and a wife to the store separately to buy beer, there is a 90 percent chance they will return with different brands.

Nothing about our behaviour is sacred. Procter & Gamble once conducted a study to find out whether most of us fold or crumple our toilet paper; another study showed that 68 percent of consumers prefer their toilet paper to unwind over the spool rather than under. Abbott Laboratories figured out that one in four of us has "problem" dandruff, and Kimberly-Clark, which makes Kleenex, has calculated that the average person blows his or her nose 256 times a year.

People aren't easy to figure out, however. A few years ago, Campbell Soup gave up trying to learn our opinions about the ideal-sized meatball after a series of tests showed that we prefer one so big it wouldn't fit in the can.

Of all businesses, however, the prize for research thoroughness may go to toothpaste makers. Among other things, they know that our favourite toothbrush colour is blue and that only 37 percent of us are using one that's more than six months old. About 47 percent of us put water on our brush before we apply the paste, 15 percent put water on after the paste, 24 percent do both, and 14 percent don't wet the brush at all.

Thus, most big marketing companies have answers to all the what, where, when, and how questions about their consumer demand. Seemingly trivial facts add up quickly and provide important input for designing marketing strategies. But to influence demand, marketers need the answer to one more question: Beyond knowing the whats and wherefores of demand, they need to know the *whys*—what *causes* us to want the things we buy? That's a much harder question to answer.

Sources: John Koten, "You aren't paranoid if you feel someone eyes you constantly," *Wall Street Journal,* 29 March 1985:1, 22; "Offbeat marketing," *Sales & Marketing Management,* January 1990:35; Warren Clements, "Spectrum: Statistical lore for everyday living," *Report on Business,* July 1993:160, July 1994:164, February 1995:92, January 1995:112, January 1996:116.

Service
Any activity or benefit that one party can offer to another that is essentially intangible and does not result in the ownership of anything.

can be called a product. In addition to tangible goods, products also include **services,** which are activities or benefits offered for sale that are essentially intangible and do not result in the ownership of anything. Examples include banking, airline, and home repair services.

Thus, broadly defined, products include such entities as *persons, places, organizations, activities,* and *ideas.* For example, by orchestrating several services and goods, companies can create, stage, and market experiences. Disneyland is an experience; so is a visit to Virgin Records or Indigo Books. In fact, as products and services increasingly become commodities, experiences have emerged for many firms as the next step in differentiating the company's offering. In recent years, for example, a rash of theme stores and restaurants have burst onto the scene offering much more than just merchandise or food:

> Stores such as Niketown, Michaels Arts and Crafts, and Hikers Haven draw consumers in by offering fun activities, fascinating displays, and promotional events, sometimes labelled "shoppertainment" or "entertailing". At theme restaurants such as the Hard Rock Cafe, the Rainfor-

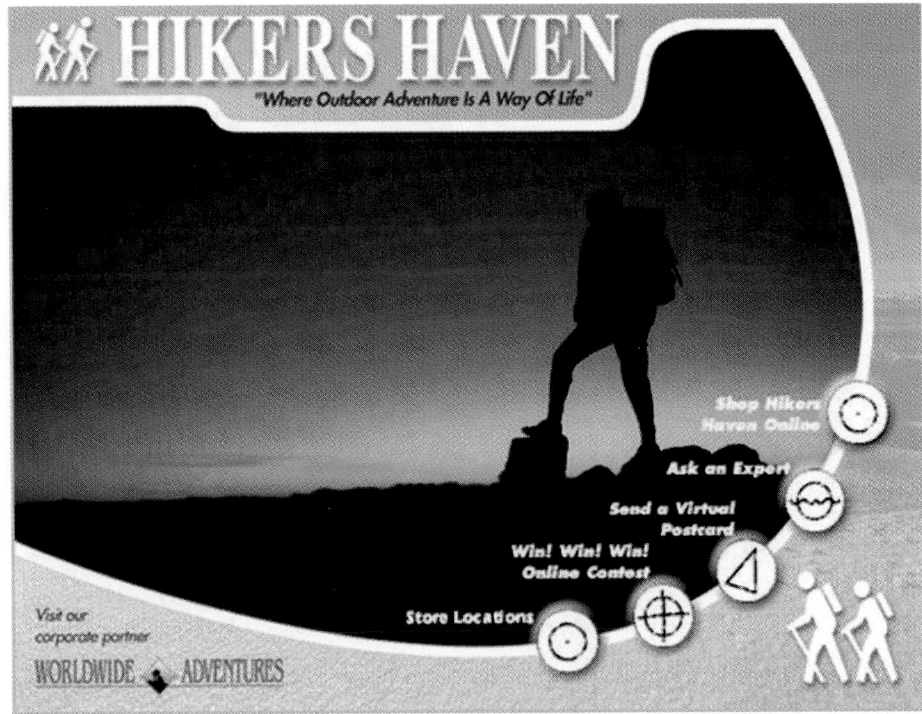

Hikers Haven works to create exciting customer experiences both on and off line.

est Cafe, or the House of Blues, the food is just a prop for what's known as "eatertainment." [One] entrepreneur in Israel has entered the experience economy with the opening of Cafe Ke'ilu, which roughly translates as "Cafe Make Believe." Manager Nir Caspi told a reporter that people come to cafes to be seen and to meet people, not for the food; Cafe Ke'ilu pursues that observation to its logical conclusion. The establishment serves its customers empty plates and mugs and charges guests $3 during the week and $6 on weekends for the social experience.[3]

Thus, the term "product" includes much more than just physical goods or services. Consumers decide which entertainers to watch on television, which places to visit on vacation, which organizations to support through contributions, and which ideas to adopt. To the consumer, these are all products.

Many sellers make the mistake of focusing more on the physical products they offer than on the benefits produced by these products. They see themselves as selling a product rather than providing a solution to a need. A manufacturer of drill bits may think that the customer needs a drill bit, but what the customer really needs is a hole. These sellers may suffer from "marketing myopia."[4] They forget that a physical product is only a tool to solve a consumer problem.

Value, Satisfaction, and Quality

Consumers usually face a broad array of products and services that might satisfy a given need. How do they choose among these many products and services? Consumers make buying choices based on their perceptions of the value that various products and services deliver.

Customer value The difference between the values the customer gains from owning and using a product and the costs of obtaining the product.

Customer value is the difference between the values the customer gains from owning and using a product and the costs of obtaining the product.[5] For example, Purolator customers gain a number of benefits. The most obvious are fast and reliable package delivery. However, when using Purolator, customers may also receive some status and image values. Using Purolator usually makes both the package sender and the receiver feel more important. When deciding whether to send a package via Purolator, customers will weigh these and other values against the money, effort, and psychic costs of using the service. Moreover, they will compare the value

Products do not have to be physical objects. Here the product is an idea: Smoking harms you and others.

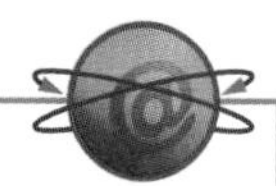

Purolator
www.purolator.com
Canada Post
www.mailposte.ca

of using Purolator against the value of using other shippers—UPS, Federal Express, Canada Post—and select the one that gives them the greatest delivered value.

Customers often do not judge product values and costs accurately or objectively. They act on *perceived* value. For example, does Purolator really provide faster, more reliable delivery? If so, is this better service worth the higher prices that Purolator charges? Canada Post argues that its express service is comparable and its prices are much lower. However, judging by the increasing number of people using courier services and fax machines, many consumers doubt these claims. The challenge faced by Canada Post, therefore, is to change these customer value perceptions.

Customer satisfaction
The extent to which a product's perceived performance matches a buyer's expectations.

Customer satisfaction depends on a product's perceived performance in delivering value relative to a buyer's expectations. If the product's performance falls short of the customer's expectations, the buyer is dissatisfied. If performance matches expectations, the buyer is satisfied. If performance exceeds expectations, the buyer is delighted. Outstanding marketing companies go out of their way to keep their customers satisfied. Satisfied customers make repeat purchases, and they tell others about their good experiences with the product. The key is to match customer expectations with company performance. Smart companies aim to *delight* customers by promising only what they can deliver, then delivering *more* than they promise.[6]

Often customer satisfaction is closely linked to quality. Thus many firms constantly strive to improve the quality of their offerings. Firms like Microsoft work diligently to uncover facets that drive buyers' perceptions of quality.

Exchange, Transactions, and Relationships

Exchange
The act of obtaining a desired object from someone by offering something in return.

Transaction
A trade between two parties that involves at least two things of value, agreed-upon conditions, a time of agreement, and a place of agreement.

Marketing occurs when people decide to satisfy needs and wants through exchange. **Exchange** is the act of obtaining a desired object from someone by offering something in return. Exchange is only one of many ways people can obtain a desired object. For example, hungry people can find food by hunting, fishing, or gathering fruit. They can beg for food or take food from someone else. Or they can offer money, another good, or a service in return for food. As a means of satisfying needs, exchange has much in its favour.

Whereas exchange is the core concept of marketing, a transaction is marketing's unit of measurement. A **transaction** consists of a trade of values between two parties. In a transaction, we must be able to say that one party gives *X* to another party and gets *Y* in return. For example, you pay Sears $350 for a television set.

Microsoft uses case studies from satisfied customers, like Clearwater Foods, to demonsrate how it creates value for its customers by developing cost-effective web businesses.

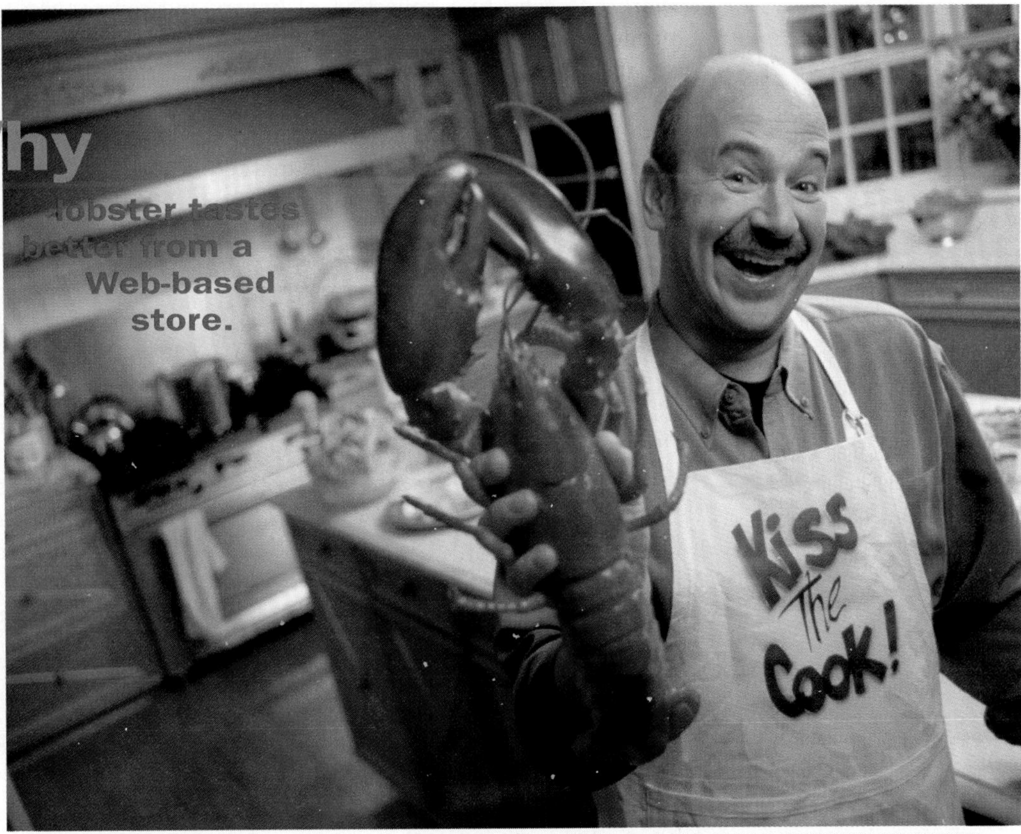

This is a classic *monetary transaction;* but not all transactions involve money. In a *barter transaction,* you might trade your old refrigerator for a neighbour's second-hand television set.

Relationship marketing The process of creating, maintaining, and enhancing strong, value-laden relationships with customers and other stakeholders.

Increasingly, marketing is shifting from trying to maximize the profit on each individual transaction to building mutually beneficial relationships with consumers, distributors, dealers, retailers, and suppliers. This is known as **relationship marketing.** Relationships consist of strong economic and social connections. They are fostered by mutual trust and commitment to the relationship as well as by the promise and consistent delivery of high-quality innovative products, good service, and fair prices.

Ultimately, a company wants to build a unique company asset called a *marketing network*. A marketing network consists of the company and all of its supporting stakeholders: customers, employees, suppliers, distributors, retailers, advertising agencies, and others with whom it has built mutually profitable business relationships. Increasingly, competition is not between companies but rather between whole networks, with the prize going to the company that has built the better network. The operating principle is simple: Build a good network of relationships with key stakeholders, and profits will follow.[7]

Markets

Market The set of all actual and potential buyers of a product or service.

The concept of exchange leads to the concept of a market. A **market** is the set of actual and potential buyers of a product. These buyers share a particular need or want that can be satisfied through exchange. The size of a market depends on the number of people who exhibit the need, have resources to engage in exchange, and are willing to offer these resources in exchange for what they want.

Originally, the term *market* stood for the place where buyers and sellers gathered to exchange their goods, such as a village square. Economists use the term *market* to refer to a collection of buyers and sellers who transact in a particular product class, as in the housing market or the grain market. Marketers, however, see the sellers as constituting an industry and the buyers as constituting a market. The relationship between the *industry* and the *market* is shown in Figure 1-2. Sellers and the buyers are connected by four flows. The sellers send products, services, and communications to the market; in return, they receive money and infor-

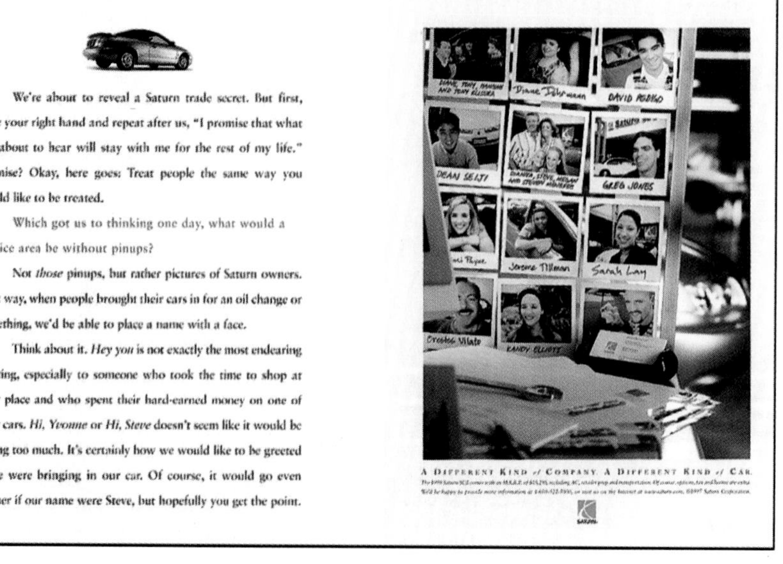

Saturn works continuously to build lasting relationships with its customers. Many dealers post "pinups" of their customers in service areas to help employees link people with their cars so service personnel can greet customers personally and knowledgeably.

FIGURE 1-2 A simple marketing system

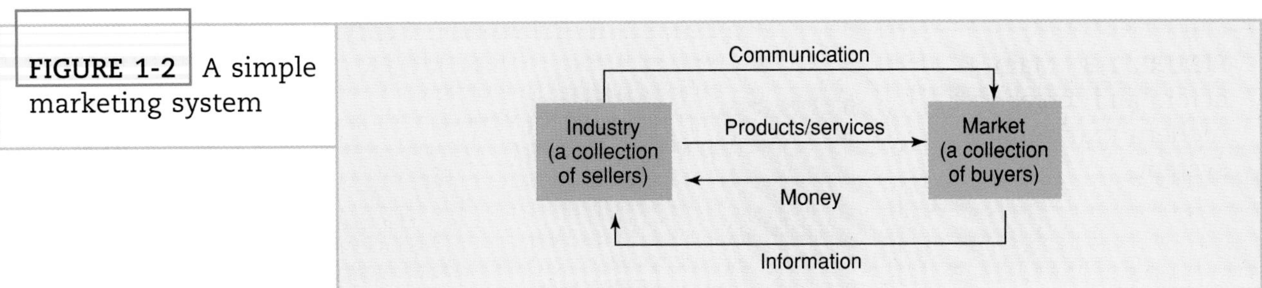

mation. The inner loop shows an exchange of money for goods; the outer loop shows an exchange of information.

Modern economies operate on the principle of division of labour, in which each person specializes in producing something, receives payment, and buys needed things with this money. Thus, modern economies abound in markets. Producers go to resource markets (raw material markets, labour markets, money markets), buy resources, turn them into goods and services, and sell them to intermediaries, who sell them to consumers. The consumers sell their labour, for which they receive income to pay for the goods and services they buy. The government is another market that plays several roles. It buys goods from resource, producer, and intermediary markets; it pays them; it taxes these markets (including consumer markets); and it returns needed public services. Thus, each nation's economy and the whole world's economy consist of complex interacting sets of markets that are linked through exchange processes.

Marketers are keenly interested in markets. Their goal is to understand the needs and wants of specific markets and to select the markets that they can serve best. In turn, they can develop products and services that will create value and satisfaction for customers in these markets, resulting in sales and profits for the company.

Marketing

The concept of markets brings us full circle to the concept of marketing. Marketing means managing markets to bring about exchanges for the purpose of satisfying human needs and wants. Thus, we return to our definition of marketing as a process by which individuals and groups obtain what they need and want by creating and exchanging products and value with others.

Exchange processes involve work. Sellers must search for buyers, identify their needs, design good products and services, set prices for them, promote them, and store and deliver them. Product development, research, communication, distribution, pricing, and service are core marketing activities. Although we normally think of marketing as being carried on by sellers, buyers also carry on marketing activities. Consumers do "marketing" when they search for the goods they need at prices they can afford. Company purchasing agents do "marketing" when they track down sellers and bargain for good terms.

Figure 1-3 shows the main elements in a modern marketing system. In the usual situation, marketing involves serving a market of end users in the face of competitors. The company and the competitors send their respective products and messages directly to consumers or through marketing intermediaries to the end users. All of the actors in the system are affected by major environmental forces—demographic, economic, physical, technological, political/legal, social/cultural.

Each party in the system adds value for the next level. Thus, a company's success depends not only on its own actions, but also on how well the entire value

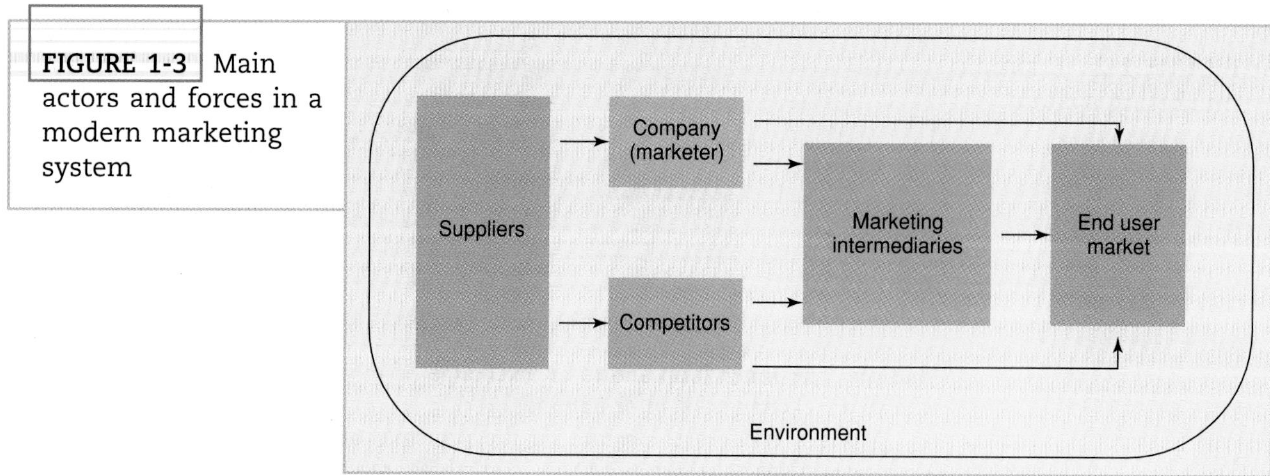

FIGURE 1-3 Main actors and forces in a modern marketing system

chain serves the needs of final consumers. Zellers cannot fulfill its promise "The lowest price is the law!" unless its suppliers provide merchandise at low costs. And Ford cannot deliver high quality to car buyers unless its dealers provide outstanding service.

Marketing Management

Marketing management
The analysis, planning, implementation, and control of programs designed to create, build, and maintain beneficial exchanges with target buyers for the purpose of achieving organizational objectives.

We define **marketing management** as the analysis, planning, implementation, and control of programs designed to create, build, and maintain beneficial exchanges with target buyers for the purpose of achieving organizational objectives. Thus, marketing management involves managing demand, which in turn involves managing customer relationships.

Demand Management

Most people think of marketing management as finding enough customers for the company's current output, but this is too limited a view. The organization has a desired level of demand for its products. At any point in time, there may be no demand, adequate demand, irregular demand, or too much demand, and marketing management must find ways to deal with these different demand states. Marketing management is concerned not only with finding and increasing demand, but also with changing or even reducing it.

Demarketing
Marketing to reduce demand temporarily or permanently—the aim is not to destroy demand, but only to reduce or shift it.

For example, Banff National Park is badly overcrowded in the summer. And power companies sometimes have trouble meeting demand during peak usage periods. In these and other cases of excess demand, **demarketing** is needed to reduce demand temporarily or permanently. The aim of demarketing is not to destroy demand, but only to reduce or shift it.[8] Thus, marketing management seeks to affect the level, timing, and nature of demand in a way that helps the organization achieve its objectives. Simply put, marketing management is *demand management.*

Building Profitable Customer Relationships

Managing demand means understanding and working with customers. A company's demand comes from two groups: new customers and repeat customers. Traditional marketing theory and practice have focused on attracting new customers and making the sale. Today, however, the emphasis is shifting. Beyond designing strategies to *attract* new customers and create *transactions* with them, companies now are striving to *retain* current customers and build lasting customer *relationships*.

Companies are realizing that losing a customer means more than losing a single sale—it means losing the entire stream of purchases that the customer would make over a lifetime of business. For example, the *customer lifetime value* of a Taco Bell customer exceeds $16 000. For General Motors or Ford, the customer lifetime value of a customer might well exceed $470 000. Thus, working to retain customers makes good economic sense.[9] The key to customer retention is superior customer value and satisfaction. With this in mind, many companies are going to extremes to keep their customers satisfied. (See Marketing Highlight 1-2.)

Marketing Management Practice

While all kinds of organizations use marketing, they practise it in widely varying ways, ranging from highly formalized procedures to very innovative processes. A recent book *Radical Marketing* praises such companies as Harley-Davidson, Virgin Atlantic Airways, and Boston Beer for succeeding by breaking many of the rules of marketing.[10] Instead of commissioning expensive marketing research, spending huge sums on mass advertising, and operating large marketing departments, these companies stretched their limited resources, lived close to their customers, and created more satisfying solutions to customer needs. They formed buyers' clubs, used creative public relations, and focused on delivering high product quality and winning long-term customer loyalty.

In fact, marketing practice often passes through three stages: entrepreneurial marketing, formulated marketing, and intrapreneurial marketing.

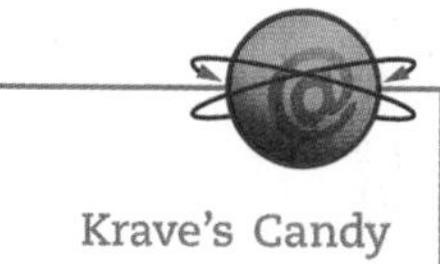

Krave's Candy
www.kraves.com

Entrepreneurial marketing: Most companies are started by individuals who live by their wits. They visualize an opportunity and knock on every door to gain attention. Two young entrepreneurs from Winnipeg using their grandmother's recipe for 'clodhoppers,' a chocolate and nut mixture, are working to found a major confectionery company called Krave's Candy. They have been going to trade shows and knocking on the doors of large retailers like Wal-Mart and Zellers to get their new product on store shelves. They have invested in eye-catching packaging to help move product off shelves. They have received awards as one of Canada's fastest growing companies and they have been featured on *Venture*. However, they are still experiencing growing pains and are scraping together every penny at their disposal to purchase supplies and market their product. Since they can't afford expensive advertising, they are hoping that the public relations coverage they have been receiving is helping to get their brand noticed. They are also going from store to store giving out samples to entice more consumers to try their product.

Formulated marketing: As small companies achieve success, they inevitably move toward more formulated marketing and begin to mimic the tactics used by their larger, more established rivals.

Take the case of the entrepreneurial company, Gap Adventure Tours:

Gap Adventure Tours
www.gap.ca

After 10 years of offering small group adventure holidays to less travelled places, Toronto-headquartered Gap Adventure Tours found itself at a crossroads. Although sales revenues had climbed to $70 million, it faced increased competition. It was also having trouble managing its supplier relationships and reservation system. To help overcome these problems, it hired its first professional marketer, Dave Bowen, who saw the challenge as bringing corporate discipline and a better market orientation to the small energetic firm. Dave first focused on market segmentation and better target marketing. Gap had to change the way it looked at customers and realize that it couldn't satisfy everybody. Dave also had a nose for inefficiencies. He worked to revamp the reservation system and added visual and verbal clarity to Gap's promotional brochures. Since demand had grown, functional stovepipes were producing more and more inefficiencies, so Dave worked to better link supply chain management with operations and marketing. Although there was some resistance to change, Gap is now trekking on toward smoother operations.[11]

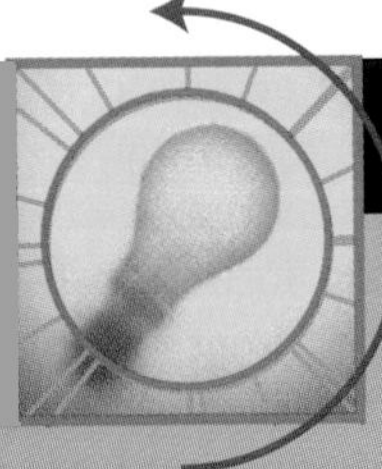

marketing highlight 1-2

Customer Relationships: Keeping Customers Satisfied

Some companies go to extremes to coddle their customers. Consider these examples:

- Although Speedy Muffler King Inc., a Toronto-based worldwide company, changes its advertisements depending on the country in which the outlet is located, it never changes its business philosophy, "Treat customers with respect, fix their cars fast, and do it properly." To build customer trust and demystify car repair, Speedy technicians carefully explain what needs fixing and what doesn't. Customers are welcome to watch the work being done. And so that individual owner-managers can effectively monitor both service demands and customer relationships, Speedy restricts its outlets to eight service bays, whereas competitors may have 20 or more. These practices have resulted in 90 percent of Speedy's customers being very satisfied with the service.
- Ted Abbott, president of James Ross Limited, a small manufacturing firm located in Brockville, Ontario that sells equipment to paper mills, personally calls customers if they have any complaints about his firm's products or services. He believes that customers want immediate and fair solutions if they experience problems. He notes that customers are frequently surprised that he is personally concerned about their complaints. This concern with customer satisfaction has helped this small firm take on a much larger global competitor both in Canada and worldwide.
- An American Express cardholder fails to pay more than $5000 of his September bill. He explains that during the summer he'd purchased expensive rugs in Turkey. When he got home, appraisals showed that the rugs were worth half of what he'd paid. Rather than asking suspicious questions or demanding payment, the American Express representative notes the dispute, asks for a letter summarizing the appraisers' estimates, and offers to help solve the problem. Until the conflict is resolved, American Express doesn't ask for payment.

From a dollars-and-cents point of view, these examples sound like a crazy way to do business. Yet studies show that going to such extremes to keep customers happy—though costly—goes hand in hand with good financial performance. Satisfied customers come back again and again. Thus, in today's highly competitive marketplace, companies can well afford to lose money on one transaction if it helps to cement a profitable long-term customer relationship.

Keeping customers satisfied involves more than simply opening a complaint department, smiling a lot, and being nice. Companies that do the best job of taking care of customers set high customer service standards and often make seemingly outlandish efforts to achieve them. At these companies, exceptional value and service are more than a set of policies or actions—they are a company-wide attitude, an important part of the overall company culture. Concern for the consumer becomes a matter of pride for everyone in the company. Four Seasons Hotels, long known for its outstanding service, tells its employees the story of Ron Dyment, a porter in Toronto who forgot to load a departing guest's briefcase in his taxi. Dyment called the guest, a lawyer in Washington, DC, and learned that he desperately needed the briefcase for a meeting the following morning. Without first asking for management approval, Dyment hopped on a plane and returned the briefcase. The company named Dyment Employee of the Year.

There's no simple formula for taking care of customers, but neither is it a mystery. For the companies that do it well, it's also very rewarding.

Sources: Bill Kelley, "Five companies that do it right—and make it pay," *Sales & Marketing Management,* April 1988:57–64; Timothy Pritchard, "Exhaustive management," *The Globe and Mail,* June 1994:B1, B5; Richard S. Teitelbaum, "Keeping promises," *Fortune,* special issue on "The Tough New Consumer," Autumn/Winter 1993:32-3; Patricia Sellers, "Companies that serve you best," *Fortune,* 31 May 1993:74–88; www.speedy.com.

Delighted customers come back again and again. American Express loves to tell stories about how its people have rescued customers from disasters ranging from civil wars to earthquakes, no matter what the cost.

Intrapreneurial marketing: Many large and mature companies get stuck in formulated marketing, poring over the latest Nielsen numbers, scanning market research reports, and trying to fine-tune dealer relations and advertising messages. These companies sometimes lose the marketing creativity and passion that they had at the start. They now need to re-establish within their companies the entrepreneurial spirit and actions that made them successful in the first place. They need to encourage more initiative and "intrapreneurship" at the local level. Their brand and product managers need to get out of the office, start living with their customers, and visualize new and creative ways to add value to their customers' lives. Kellogg Canada is in this stage of marketing and is working hard to re-energize its marketing.

The bottom line is that effective marketing can take many forms. There will be a constant tension between the formulated side of marketing and the creative side. It is easier to learn the formulated side of marketing, which will occupy most of our attention in this book. But we will also see how real marketing creativity and passion operate in many companies—whether small or large, new or mature—to build and retain marketplace success.

Marketing Management Philosophies

The role that marketing plays within a company varies with the overall strategy and philosophy of the firm. While some firms place a primary emphasis on tailoring their products and services to meet customers' needs, others focus on improving production efficiency of existing products. Some firms have mixed management philosophies, which can result in conflicts about the roles of the different functional areas (marketing, production, research and development, and so on) within the firm. There are five philosophies which determine the orientation firms take to marketing activities: the *production, product, selling, marketing,* and *societal marketing* philosophies.

The Production Concept

Production concept
The philosophy that consumers will favour products that are available and highly affordable and that management should, therefore, focus on improving production and distribution efficiency.

The **production concept** holds that consumers will favour products that are available and highly affordable. Therefore, management should focus on improving production and distribution efficiency. This concept is one of the oldest philosophies that guide sellers. The production concept is still a useful philosophy when the demand for a product exceeds the supply, and when the product's cost is too high and improved productivity is needed to bring it down. To its dismay, Ottawa's Corel Corporation found that a production orientation doesn't automatically lead to success. Corel believed that it could use efficient, low-cost production technologies to bring down prices in the office suites software market and take market share away from its giant rival, Microsoft. Corel announced its strategy with a huge advertising blitz, but Corel's strategy failed when its production capabilities could not meet the new levels of demand.[12]

Corel Corporation
www.corel.com

The Product Concept

Some managers define their business by the products they sell, rather than by the problem that the customer uses the product to solve.[13] But they are often rudely shocked. Buyers may well be looking for a better solution to a mouse problem, but not necessarily for a better mousetrap.

Product concept
The philosophy that consumers will favour products that offer the most quality, performance, and innovative features.

The **product concept** also can lead to "marketing myopia." For instance, many universities have assumed that high-school graduates want a liberal arts education and have thus overlooked the increasing challenge of vocational colleges, private training schools, and online education services.

The Selling Concept

Selling concept
The idea that consumers will not buy enough of the organization's products unless the organization undertakes a large-scale selling and promotion effort.

Many organizations follow the **selling concept,** which holds that consumers will not buy enough of the organization's products unless it undertakes a large-scale selling and promotion effort. Their aim is to sell what they make rather than make what the market wants. The concept is typically practised with *unsought goods*—those that buyers do not normally think of buying, such as encyclopedias or insurance—or when a firm has excess capacity.

Marketing based on hard selling carries high risks. It focuses on creating sales transactions rather than on building long-term, profitable relationships with customers. It assumes that customers who are coaxed into buying the product will like it. These are usually poor assumptions to make about buyers. Most studies show that dissatisfied customers do not buy again. Worse yet, while the average satisfied customer tells three others about good experiences, the average dissatisfied customer tells 10 others his or her bad experiences.[14]

The Marketing Concept

Marketing concept
The marketing management philosophy that holds that achieving organizational goals depends on determining the needs and wants of target markets and delivering the desired satisfactions more effectively and efficiently than competitors do.

The **marketing concept** holds that achieving organizational goals depends on determining the needs and wants of target markets and delivering the desired satisfactions more effectively and efficiently than competitors do. The marketing concept has been stated in such colourful ways as "We make it happen for you" (Marriott); "Reliability is our service" (CanPar); "To fly, to serve" (British Airways), and "We're not satisfied until you are" (GE).

The selling concept and the marketing concept are sometimes confused. Figure 1-4 compares the two concepts. The selling concept takes an *inside-out* perspective. It starts with the factory, focuses on the company's existing products, and calls for heavy selling and promotion to obtain profitable sales. It focuses heavily on customer conquest—getting short-term sales with little concern about who buys or why. In contrast, the marketing concept takes an *outside-in* perspective. It starts with a well-defined market, focuses on customer needs, coordinates all the marketing activities affecting customers, and makes profits by creating long-term customer relationships based on customer value and satisfaction. Thus, under the marketing concept, customer focus and value are the paths to sales and profits. In the words of one Ford executive, "If we're not customer driven, our cars won't be either."

Market orientation
The organization-wide generation of market intelligence pertaining to current and future customer needs, dissemination of the intelligence across departments, and the organization-wide responsiveness to it.

Firms that implement the marketing concept are said to have a **market orientation.** Authors like Kohli and Jaworski[15] translate the ideals implied by the marketing concept into specific activities that can be undertaken by firms. Firms with a market orientation focus on three things:

- *Intelligence generation.* This includes not just customer intelligence, but also analysis and interpretation of the forces that impinge on customer needs and preferences.

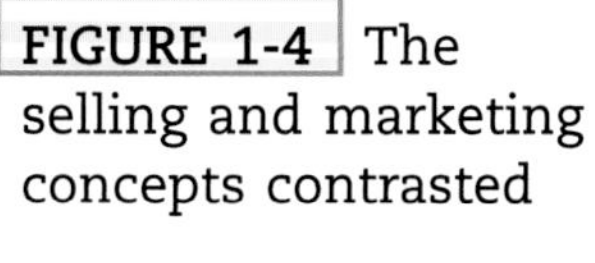

FIGURE 1-4 The selling and marketing concepts contrasted

- *Intelligence dissemination.* To affect firm performance, market intelligence must be communicated and disseminated throughout the firm.
- *Responsiveness.* They use market intelligence to respond to the evolving needs of selected target markets.

Thus, Kohli and Jaworski define market orientation as "the organization-wide generation of market intelligence pertaining to current and future customer needs, dissemination of the intelligence across departments, and organization-wide responsiveness to it."

Other authors, like Narver and Slater,[16] define market orientation as a culture leading to behaviours that result in the creation of superior value for customers. Three behaviours are key to the creation of a market orientation:

- *Customer orientation.* Firms are focused on building relationships with key customers and creating superior value for them.
- *Competitor orientation.* Firms scrutinize their competitors to ensure that they are keeping pace with industry trends and that they deliver more value to customers than their competitors.
- *Interfunctional coordination.* All functions within the firm, not just marketing, must be focused on building relationships and creating customer value.

Research has suggested that firms with a market orientation tend to be more profitable than their rivals. This may be especially true when firms combine innovativeness with the other components of market orientation.[17] Innovation may affect administrative processes, the technology platforms around which products are created, or production processes.

Many successful and well-known companies have adopted the marketing concept. Procter & Gamble, Disney, Corel, Bombardier, and Mountain Equipment Co-op follow it faithfully. L.L. Bean, the highly successful catalogue retailer of clothing and outdoor sporting equipment, dedicates itself to giving "perfect satisfaction in every way." For example, it recently revised its catalogues to make it easier for Canadian customers to place their orders. To inspire its employees to practise the marketing concept, L.L. Bean displays posters around its offices that proclaim the following:

People at L.L. Bean practise the marketing concept in everything they do every day.

> What is a customer? A customer is the most important person ever in this company—in person or by mail. A customer is not dependent on us, we are dependent on him [or her]. A customer is not an interruption of our work, he [or she] is the purpose of it. We are not doing a favor by serving him [or her], he [or she] is doing us a favor by giving us the opportunity to do so. A customer is not someone to argue or match wits with—nobody ever won an argument with a customer. A customer is a person who brings us his [or her] wants—it is our job to handle them profitably to him [or her] and to ourselves.

In contrast, many companies claim to practise the marketing concept but do not. They have the *forms* of marketing, such as a marketing vice-president, product managers, marketing plans, and marketing research, but this does not mean that they are *market-focused* and *customer-driven* companies. The question is whether they are finely tuned to changing customer needs and competitor strategies. Formerly great companies—General Motors, IBM, Sears, Zenith—all lost substantial market share because they failed to adjust their marketing strategies to the changing marketplace.

Implementing the marketing concept often means more than simply responding to customers' stated desires and obvious needs. *Customer-driven companies* research current customers to learn about their desires, gather new product and service ideas, and test proposed product improvements. Such customer-driven marketing usually works well when a clear need exists and when customers know what they want. In many cases, however, customers don't know what they want or even what is possible.

Such situations call for *customer-driving marketing*—understanding customer needs even better than customers do themselves and creating products and services that will meet existing and latent needs now and in the future.

Customers are notoriously lacking in foresight. Ten or 15 years ago, how many of us were asking for cellular telephones, fax machines and copiers at home, 24-hour discount brokerage accounts, DVD players, cars with on-board navigation systems, or hand-held global satellite positioning receivers? As Akio Morita, Sony's visionary leader puts it: "Our plan is to lead the public with new products rather than ask them what kinds of products they want. The public does not know what is possible, but we do. So instead of doing a lot of market research, we refine our thinking on a product and its use and try to create a market for it by educating and communicating with the public."[18]

Several years of hard work are needed to turn a sales-oriented company into a marketing-oriented company. The goal is to build customer satisfaction into the very fabric of the firm. Customer satisfaction is no longer a fad. It's become a way of life.[19]

The Societal Marketing Concept

Societal marketing concept The idea that the organization should determine the needs, wants, and interests of target markets and deliver the desired satisfactions more effectively and efficiently than competitors in a way that maintains or improves the consumer's and society's well-being.

The **societal marketing concept** holds that the organization should determine the needs, wants, and interests of target markets. It should then deliver superior value to customers in a way that maintains or improves the consumer's and the society's well-being. The societal marketing concept is the newest of the five marketing management philosophies. Companies embracing this concept include Canada's 900 credit unions and caisses populaires and such firms as the Upper Canada Brewing Company, which has saved $20 000 per year by following the "3Rs" philosophy of Reduce, Recycle, and Reuse. Imperial Oil is another company that firmly believes in "doing well by doing good." The firm has been one of Canada's leading corporate donors for over 80 years. It recently developed the Esso Kids Program, whereby the company supports over 200 activities, ranging from promoting childhood safety and injury prevention, to helping teenage parents raise their children, to funding post-secondary education, to supporting children's sporting activities such as swimming and hockey. Consumers have responded strongly to Imperial's efforts and the firm believes that giving consumers additional reasons to buy Esso products will help to build customer loyalty and relationships in an industry characterized by heavy brand-switching.[20]

The societal marketing concept questions whether the pure marketing concept is adequate in an age of environmental problems, resource shortages, rapid population growth, worldwide economic problems, and neglected social services. It asks if the firm that senses, serves, and satisfies individual wants is always doing what's best for consumers and society in the long run. According to the societal marketing concept, the pure marketing concept overlooks possible conflicts between consumer *short-run wants* and consumer *long-run welfare.*

Consider the fast-food industry. Most people view today's giant fast-food chains as offering tasty and convenient food at reasonable prices. Yet many consumer and environmental groups have voiced concerns. Critics point out that hamburgers, fried chicken, french fries, and most other fast foods sold are high in fat and salt. The convenient packaging leads to waste and pollution. Thus, in satisfying consumer wants, the highly successful fast-food chains may be harming consumer health and causing environmental problems.

Such concerns and conflicts led to the societal marketing concept. As Figure 1-5 shows, the societal marketing concept calls upon marketers to balance three considerations in setting their marketing policies: company profits, consumer wants, and society's interests. Originally, most companies based their marketing decisions largely on short-run company profit. Eventually, they began to recognize the long-run importance of satisfying consumer wants, and the marketing concept

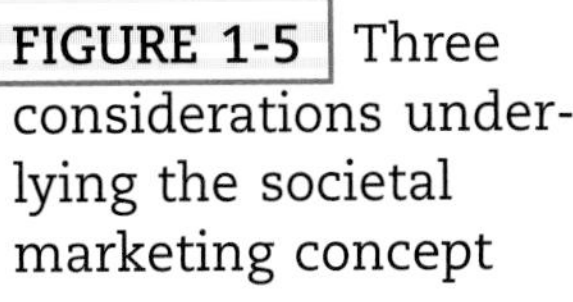

FIGURE 1-5 Three considerations underlying the societal marketing concept

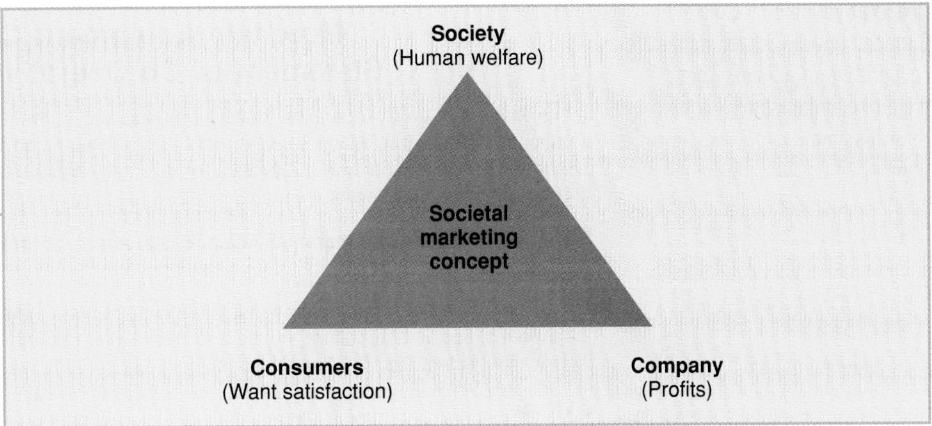

emerged. Now, many companies are beginning to consider society's interests when making their marketing decisions.

Marketing Challenges in the New "Connected" Millennium

As the world spins into the first decade of the twenty-first century, dramatic changes are occurring in the marketing arena. Richard Love of Hewlett-Packard observes: "The pace of change is so rapid that the ability to change has now become a competitive advantage." Technological advances, rapid globalization, and continuing social and economic shifts—all are causing profound changes in the marketplace. As the marketplace changes, so must those who serve it.

The major marketing developments today can be summed up in a single theme: *connectedness*. Now, more than ever before, we are all connected to each other and to things near and far in the world around us. Moreover, we are connecting in new and different ways. Where it once took months to travel across Canada, we can now travel around the globe in only hours. Where it once took weeks to receive news about important world events, we now see them "live" on satellite broadcasts. Where it once took days for a letter to reach its destination, it now takes only moments to correspond by e-mail.

In this section, we examine the major trends and forces that are changing the marketing landscape and challenging marketing strategy in this new, connected millennium. As shown in Figure 1-6 and discussed in the following pages, sweeping changes in connecting technologies are causing marketers to redefine how they connect with the marketplace—with their customers, with marketing partners inside and outside the company, and with the world around them. We first look at the dramatic changes that are occurring in the connecting technologies. Then, we examine how these changes are affecting marketing connections.

Technologies for Connecting

The major force behind the new connectedness is technology. Explosive advances in computer, telecommunications, information, transportation, and other connecting technologies have had a major impact on the way companies bring value to their customers. The technology boom has created exciting new ways to learn about and track customers, create products and services tailored to meet customer needs, distribute products more efficiently and effectively, and communicate with customers in large groups or one-to-one. For example, through video conferencing, marketing researchers at a company's headquarters in Vancouver can look in

Cooperatives like MEC and Canada's credit unions adhere to cooperative principles. These focus the organization on more than just profits.

Mountain Equipment Co-Op[21] Statement of Co-Operative Identity

The Statement on Co-operative Identity was adopted at the 1995 General Assembly of the International Co-operative Alliance (ICA), held in Manchester on the occasion of the Alliance's Centenary. The Statement was the product of a lengthy process of consultation involving thousands of co-operatives around the world.

The International Co-Operative Alliance Statement on the Co-Operative Identity

Definition

A co-operative is an autonomous association of persons united voluntarily to meet their common economic, social, and cultural needs and aspirations through a jointly-owned and democratically-controlled enterprise.

Values

Co-operatives are based on the values of self-help, self-responsibility, democracy, equality, equity, and solidarity. In the tradition of their founders, co-operative members believe in the ethical values of honesty, openness, social responsibility, and caring for others.

Principles

The co-operative principles are guidelines by which co-operatives put their values into practice.

1st Principle: Voluntary and Open Membership

Co-operatives are voluntary organizations, open to all persons able to use their services and willing to accept the responsibilities of membership, without gender, social, racial, political, or religious discrimination.

2nd Principle: Democratic Member Control

Co-operatives are democratic organizations controlled by their members, who actively participate in setting their policies and making decisions. Men and women serving as elected representatives are accountable to the membership. In primary co-operatives members have equal voting rights (one member, one vote) and co-operatives at other levels are organized in a democratic manner.

3rd Principle: Member Economic Participation

Members contribute equitably to, and democratically control, the capital of their co-operative. At least part of that capital is usually the common property of the co-operative. They usually receive limited compensation, if any, on capital subscribed as a condition of membership. Members allocate surpluses for any or all of the following purposes: developing the co-operative, possibly by setting up reserves, part of which at least would be indivisible; benefiting members in proportion to their transactions with the co-operative; and supporting other activities approved by the membership.

4th Principle: Autonomy and Independence

Co-operatives are autonomous, self-help organizations controlled by their members. If they enter into agreements with other organizations, including governments, or raise capital from external sources, they do so on terms that ensure democratic control by their members and maintain their co-operative autonomy.

5th Principle: Education, Training and Information

Co-operatives provide education and training for their members, elected representatives, managers, and employees so they can contribute effectively to the development of their co-operatives. They inform the general public—particularly young people and opinion leaders—about the nature and benefits of co-operation.

6th Principle: Co-operation among Co-operatives

Co-operatives serve their members most effectively and strengthen the co-operative movement by working together through local, national, regional, and international structures.

7th Principle: Concern for Community

While focusing on member needs, co-operatives work for the sustainable development of their communities through policies accepted by their members.

Adopted in Manchester (UK) 23 September 1995.

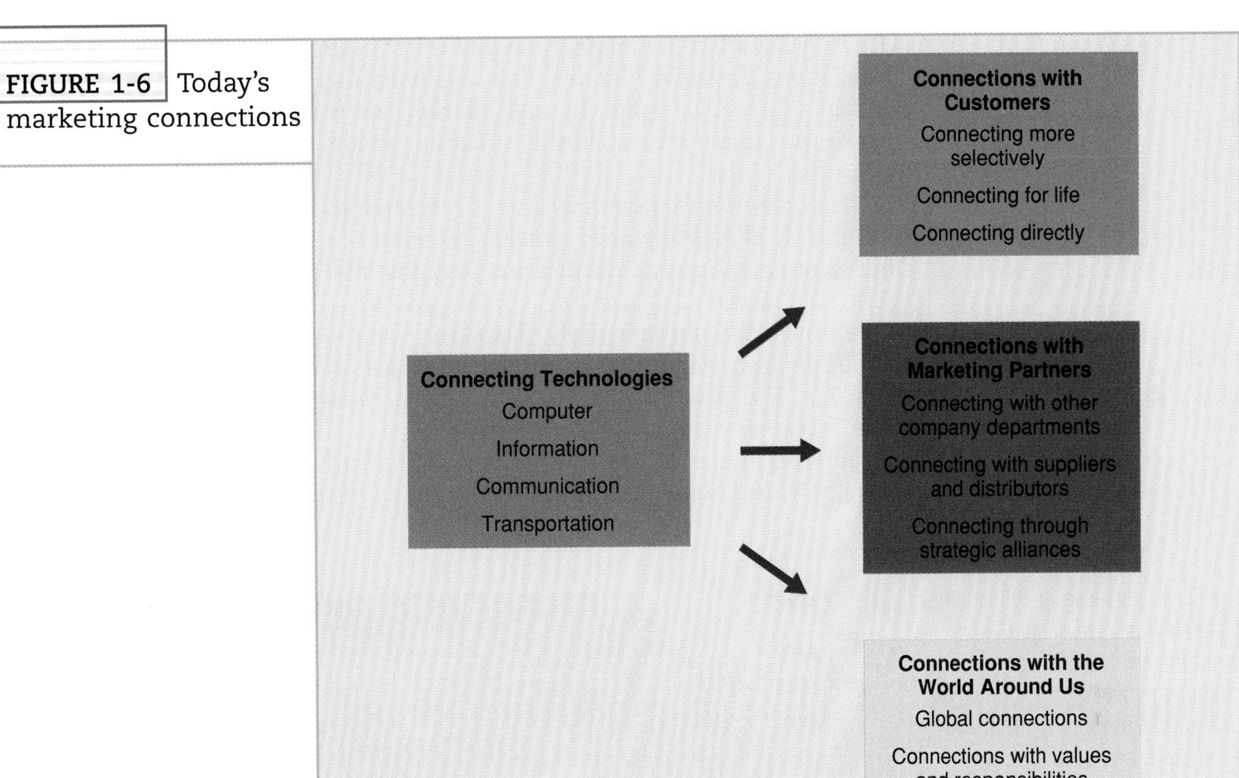

FIGURE 1-6 Today's marketing connections

on focus groups in Halifax or Paris without ever stepping onto a plane. With only a few clicks of a mouse button, a direct marketer can tap into online data services to learn anything from what car you drive to what you read to what flavour of ice cream you prefer.

Using today's powerful computers, marketers create detailed databases and use them to target individual customers with offers designed to meet their specific needs and buying patterns. With a new wave of communication and advertising tools—ranging from cell phones, fax machines, and CD-ROMs to interactive TV and video kiosks at airports and shopping malls—marketers can zero in on selected customers with carefully targeted messages. Through electronic commerce, customers can design, order, and pay for products and services without ever leaving home, and can receive their purchases in under 24 hours.

Rapid technology evolution is affecting every aspect of marketing. Consider the rapidly changing face of personal selling. Many companies now equip their salespeople with the latest sales automation tools, including the capacity to develop individualized multimedia presentations and customized market offerings and contracts. Many buyers now prefer to meet salespeople on their computer screens rather than in the office. An increasing amount of personal selling is occurring through video conferences or live Internet presentations, where buyers and sellers can interact across great distances without the time, costs, or delays of travel.

The Internet

Perhaps the most dramatic technology driving the connected age is the *Internet*. The Internet is a vast and burgeoning global web of computer networks with no central management or ownership. It was created during the late 1960s by the US

Department of Defense, initially to link government labs, contractors, and military installations. Today, the Internet links computer users of all types around the world. Anyone with a PC, a modem, and the right software—or an interactive TV—can browse the Internet to obtain information on almost any subject or can interact with other users.

The Internet has been hailed as the technology behind a new model for doing business. It allows anytime, anywhere connections to information, entertainment, and communication. Companies are using the Internet to build closer relationships with customers and marketing partners and to sell and distribute their products more efficiently and effectively. They are using intranets to connect with others within the firm, and extranets to make linkages with strategic marketing partners, suppliers, and dealers. Beyond competing in traditional marketplaces, they now have access to exciting new marketspaces.

Internet usage surged in the early 1990s with the development of the user-friendly World Wide Web. In North America alone, it is projected that 60 mil-

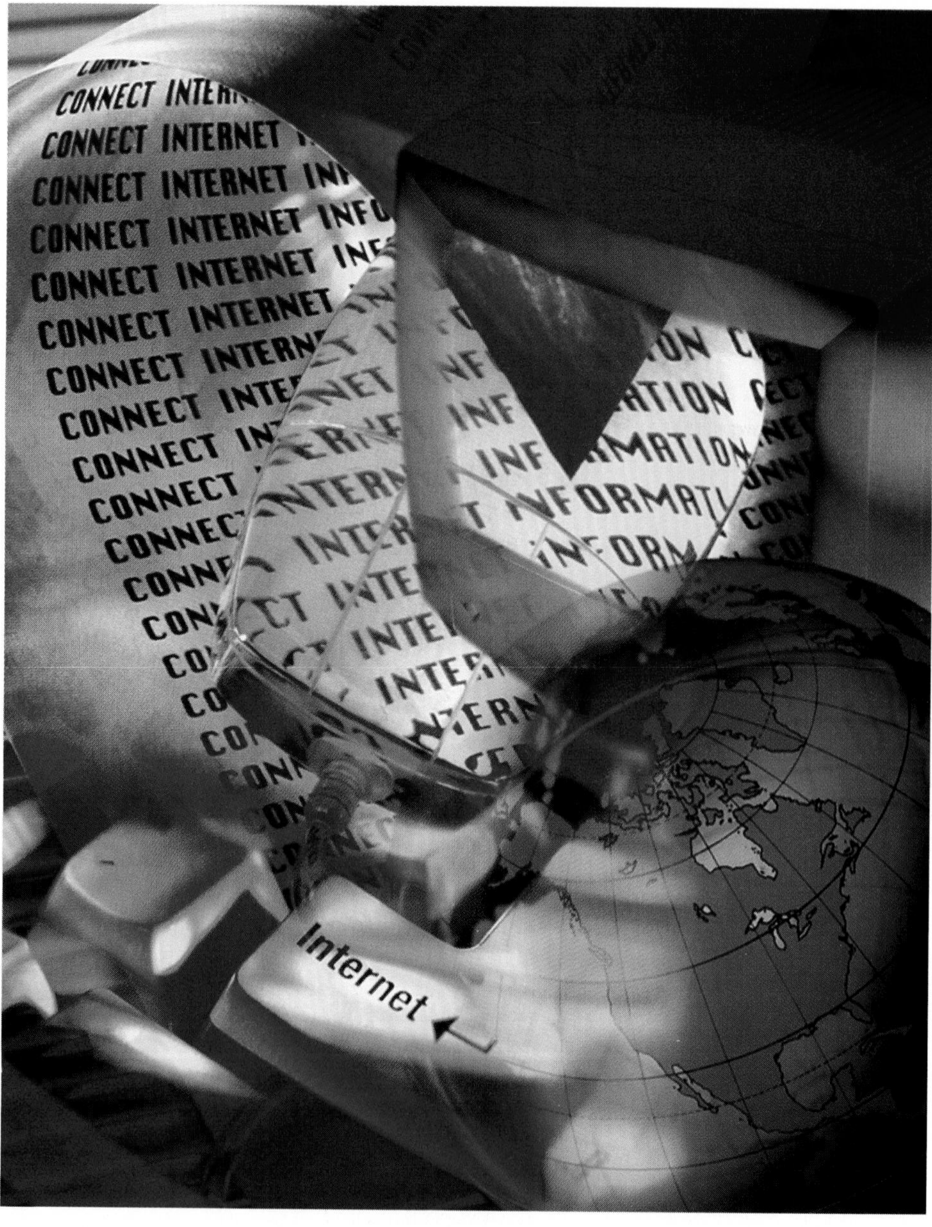

Explosive advances in connecting technologies have created exciting new ways to learn about customers and to create tailored products, distribute them more effectively, and communicate with customers in large groups or one-to-one.

lion households will be connected by the year 2003. Canada is one of the world's most connected countries. Its sophisticated telecommunications infrastructure, combined with government policy initiatives to ensure the protection of consumer privacy, has positioned Canada as the number two world player in e-commerce revenues, trailing only the US. The total value of customer orders received over the Internet was $4.4 billion in 1999. Of this total, $4.2 billion was generated by the private sector. This represents 0.2% of 1999 Canadian firms' operating revenues, according to the first-ever national snapshot of electronic commerce and the use of information and communications technologies conducted by Statistics Canada.[22]

The Internet is truly a worldwide phenomenon. Notes one analyst: "In just [a few short years], the Net has gone from a playground for nerds into a vast communications and trading center where. . . people swap information and do deals around the world. . . . More than 400 000 companies have hung **www.single.com** atop their digital doorways with the notion that being anywhere on the Net means selling virtually everywhere."[23] Companies of all types are now attempting to snare new customers on the Web. Many traditional "brick-and-mortar" companies have now ventured online in an effort to snare new customers and build stronger customer relationships. For example:

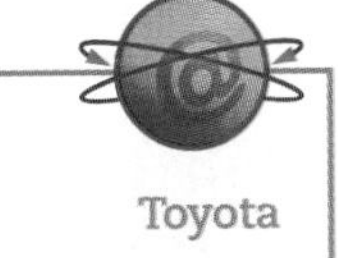

Toyota
www.toyota.com

Car makers such as Toyota use the Internet to develop relationships with owners as well as to sell cars. Toyota's site offers product information, dealer services and locations, leasing information, and much more. For example, visitors to the site can view any of seven lifestyle magazines—alt.Terrain, A Man's Life, Women's Web Weekly, Sportzine, Living Arts, Living Home, and Car Culture—designed to appeal to Toyota's well-educated, above-average-income target audience.

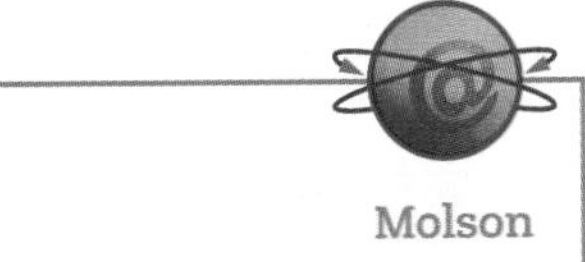

Molson
www.molson.com

Car-racing fans and music aficionados can cozy up with Molson by logging on to its Web site, where they can check out the latest line of beers, explore the company's history, or download information on Indy events or concerts given across Canada. They can also participate in chat rooms, join a fantasy hockey league, or get information on events at the Molson Centre. Although Molson has a mass-media presence, it can relate to customers in a more personal, one-to-one way through its Web page.

The Internet has also spawned an entirely new breed of companies—the so-called "dot-coms"—which operate only online. For example, justwhiteshirts.com operates a successful online men's clothing store.

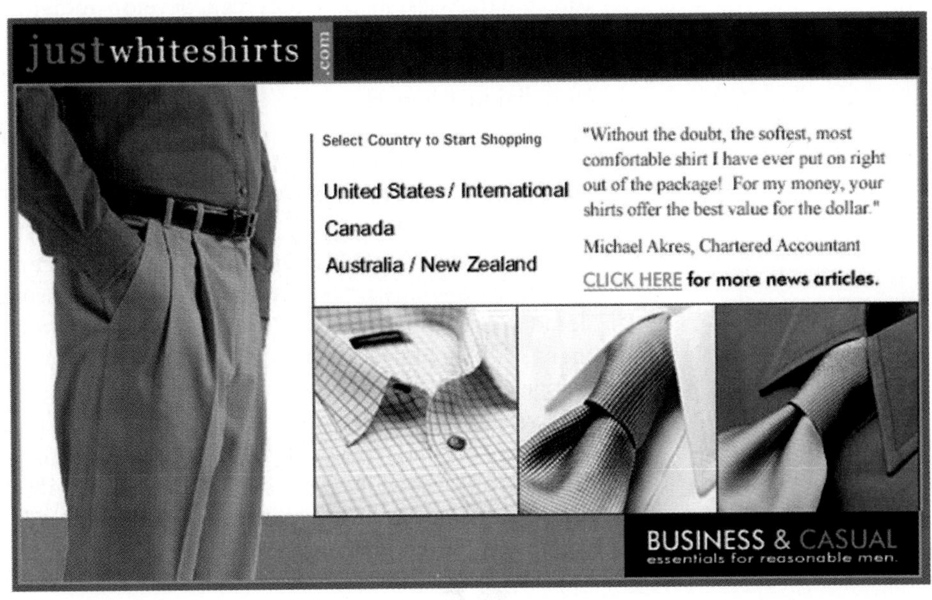

Companies of all types are now snaring new customers on the Web, including an entirely new breed of companies—the so-called "dot-coms," such as justwhiteshirts.com—which operate only online.

It seems that almost every business—from garage-based start-ups to established giants such as IBM, Nortel, CP Hotels, The Bay, and Air Canada—is setting up shop on the Internet. All are racing to explore and exploit the Web's marketing possibilities. However, for all its potential, the Internet does have drawbacks. Despite growing use of the Web for shopping, in a recent survey 54 percent of Web users said that they were not likely to use the Internet for online purchases ever in the future. Although the value of a Web site is difficult to measure, the actuality is that few companies have made much money from their Internet efforts.[24]

Thus, changes in connecting technologies are providing exciting new opportunities for marketers. We now look at the ways these changes are affecting how companies connect with their customers, marketing partners, and the world around us (see Figure 1-6 on page 23).

Connections with Customers

The most profound new developments in marketing involve the ways in which today's companies are connecting with their customers. Yesterday's companies focused on mass marketing to all comers at arm's length. Today's companies are selecting their customers more carefully and building more lasting and direct relationships with these carefully targeted customers.

Connecting with More Carefully Selected Customers

Few firms today still practise true *mass marketing*—selling in a standardized way to any customer who comes along. Most marketers realize that they don't want to connect with just any customers; instead, most are targeting fewer, potentially more profitable customers.

The world is a "salad bowl" of diverse ethnic, cultural, social, and locational groups. Although these groups have mixed together, they maintain diversity by keeping and valuing important differences. Moreover, customers themselves are connecting in new ways to form specific "consumer communities," in which buyers connect with each other by common interests, situations, and activities. Vancouver, Toronto, and Montreal are some of the world's most ethnically diverse cities.

Diversity has meant greater market fragmentation. In response, most firms have moved from mass marketing to segmented marketing, in which they target carefully chosen submarkets or even individual buyers. "One-to-one marketing" has become the order of the day for some marketers, who build extensive customer databases so that they can develop individual customer profiles based on preferences and past purchase behaviour. Then, they mine these databases to gain insights by which they can "mass-customize" their offerings to deliver greater value to individual buyers.

At the same time that companies are finding imaginative new ways to deliver more value to customers, they are also beginning to assess carefully the value of customers to the firm. They want to connect only with customers that they can serve profitably. Once they identify profitable customers, firms can create attractive offers and special handling to capture them and earn their loyalty. The financial services industry has led the way in assessing customer profitability. After decades of casting their nets to lure as many customers as possible, Canada's more than 3000 financial services companies are now mining their vast databases to compete more effectively by identifying winning customers and weeding out losing ones. The Royal Bank, for example, was highly successful in increasing its mortgage business when it sent targeted mailings to young adults who had an apartment number in their mailing address, using the insight that these individuals would soon be in the market for their first home. They not only offered these young people competitive mortgage rates, but also provided them with useful information on buying a first home.

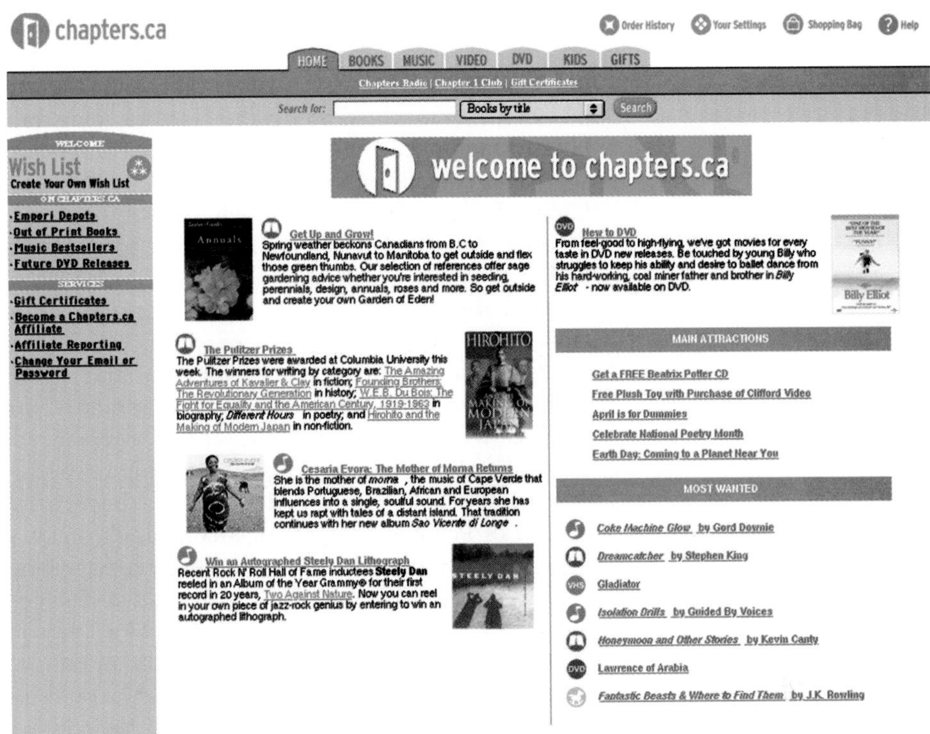

Chapters.ca began as an online bookseller to complement its bricks and mortar retail operation.

Connecting for a Customer's Lifetime

Companies are serving their carefully selected customers in a deeper, more lasting way. In the past, many companies focused on finding new customers for their products and closing sales with them. In recent years, this focus has shifted toward keeping current customers and building *lasting relationships* based on superior customer satisfaction and value. Increasingly, the goal is shifting from making a profit on each sale to making long-term profits by managing the lifetime value of a customer.

In turn, as businesses do a better and better job of keeping their customers, competitors find it increasingly difficult to acquire new customers by luring them away. As a result, marketers now spend less time figuring out how to increase "share of market" and more time trying to grow "share of customer." They offer greater variety to current customers and train employees to cross-sell and up-sell to market more products and services to existing customers. For example, Chapters.ca began as an online bookseller to complement its bricks and mortar retail operations. Now it also offers music, videos, and gifts. It has also acquired an online gardening site as a further means of increasing per-customer sales. In addition, based on each customer's purchase history, the company recommends related books, CDs, or videos that might be of interest. In this way, Chapters.ca captures a greater share of each customer's leisure and entertainment budget.

Connecting Directly

Beyond connecting more deeply, many companies are also taking advantage of new technologies that let them connect more *directly* with their customers. In fact, direct marketing is booming. Customers can now buy virtually all products without even stepping into a store—by telephone, mail-order catalogues, kiosks, and electronic commerce. Customers can surf the Internet and view pictures of almost any product, read the specs, shop among online vendors for the best prices and terms, speak with online vendors' shopping consultants, and even place and pay for their orders—all with only a few mouse clicks. Business-to-business purchasing over the Internet has increased even faster than online consumer buying. Business purchasing agents routinely shop on the Web for items ranging from standard office supplies to high-priced, high-tech computer equipment.

Some companies sell *only* via direct channels—firms such as Dell Computer, Lands' End, 1-800-Flowers, and Amazon.com, to name a few. Other companies use direct connections as a supplement to their other communications and distribution channels. For example, Procter & Gamble sells Pampers disposable diapers through retailers, supported by millions of dollars of mass-media advertising. However, P&G uses its www.pampers.com Web site to build relationships with young parents by providing information and advice on everything from diapering to baby care and child development. Similarly, you can't buy crayons from the Crayola Web site (www.crayola.com); however, you can find out how to remove crayon marks from your prized carpeting or freshly painted walls.

Direct marketing is redefining the buyer's role in connecting with sellers. Instead of being the targets of a company's one-way marketing efforts, customers are now active participants in shaping the marketing offer and process. Many companies now let customers design their own desired products online. For example, shoppers at the Lands' End site can build a "personal model" with their own hair colour, height, and shape. They then visit an online dressing room, where they can try clothes on the model to see how they would look in them. The site also gives buyers tips on how best to dress, given their individual body styles.

Lands' End Inc.
www.landsend.com

Some marketers have hailed direct marketing as the "marketing model of the next millennium." They envision a day when all buying and selling will involve direct connections between companies and their customers. Others, although agreeing that direct marketing will play a growing and important role, see it as just one more way to approach the marketplace. We will examine the exploding world of direct marketing in more detail in Chapter 8.

Connections with Marketing Partners

In these increasingly connected times, major changes are occurring in how marketers connect with important partners both inside and outside the company jointly to bring greater value to customers.

Connecting inside the Company

Traditionally, marketers played the role of intermediary, charged with understanding customer needs and representing the customer to different company departments, which then acted upon these needs. The old thinking was that marketing is done only by marketing, sales, and customer support people. However, in today's connected world, every functional area can interact with customers, especially electronically. In market oriented companies, marketing no longer has sole ownership of customer interactions. The new thinking is that every employee must be customer focused. David Packard, co-founder of Hewlett-Packard, wisely said: "Marketing is far too important to be left only to the marketing department."[25]

Today's forward-looking companies are reorganizing their operations to align them better with customer needs. Rather than letting each department pursue its own objectives, firms are linking all departments in the cause of creating customer value. Rather than assigning only sales and marketing people to customers, they are forming cross-functional customer teams. For example, Procter & Gamble assigns "customer development teams" to each of its major retailer accounts. These teams—consisting of sales and marketing people, operations and logistics specialists, market and financial analysts, and others—coordinate the efforts of many P&G departments toward serving the retailer and helping it to be more successful.

Connecting with Outside Partners

Rapid changes are also occurring in how marketers connect with their external partners—suppliers, channel partners, and even competitors. Most companies today are networked, relying heavily on partnerships with other firms.

Supply Chain Management. The supply chain encompasses all members of a chain of production, stretching from a firm's suppliers of raw materials and components to the retailers or the distribution point where the products are delivered to final buyers. For example, the supply chain for personal computers consists of suppliers of computer chips and other components, the computer manufacturer, and the distributors, retailers, and others who sell the computers to businesses and final customers. Each member of the supply chain creates and captures only a portion of the total value it generates.

The purpose of supply chain management is to strengthen connections among the partners all along the chain. Each member knows that their fortunes rest not only on how well they perform but also on how well their entire supply chain performs against competitors' supply chains. Rather than treating suppliers as vendors and distributors as customers, supply chain managers treat both as partners in delivering value to final consumers. For example, Wal-Mart works with such suppliers as Procter & Gamble, Rubbermaid, and Black & Decker to streamline logistics and reduce joint distribution costs, resulting in lower prices to consumers. Saturn works closely with carefully selected suppliers to improve quality and operations efficiency; it also works with its franchise dealers to provide top-grade sales and service support that will bring customers in the door and keep them coming back.

Strategic Alliances. Beyond managing the supply chain, today's companies are also discovering that they need strategic partners to be effective. In the new global environment, with greater competition from more and more products and choices, going it alone is going out of style. Strategic alliances are booming across the entire spectrum of industries and services. A recent study found that one in every four dollars earned by the top 1000 North American companies flows from alliances, double the rate in the early 1990s.[26] As Jim Kelly, CEO at UPS, puts it: "The old adage 'If you can't beat 'em, join 'em' is being replaced by 'Join 'em and you can't be beat.'" Or, as another analyst notes:

> [Think about] how Home Depot and other large retailers operate behind the scenes. They might sell do-it-yourself to consumers, but their own business proposition is do-it-together. Increasingly, enlightened companies are forming strategic alliances with customers, suppliers, and other venture partners. . . . They are replacing go-it-alone strategies with reliance on partnering. . . . Do-it-together means leveraging the strengths of a business partner to create more value and build more sales than either company could do alone. . . . Large companies often count on technological breakthroughs from tiny focused partners who, in turn, need large partners to reach international markets and build credibility. Every search for ways to build sales should include a search for partners who can help reach that goal faster.[27]

Many strategic alliances take the form of *marketing alliances*. These may be *product or service alliances,* in which one company licenses another to produce its product or two companies jointly market their complementary products. For instance, Apple Computer joined with Digital Vax to co-design, co-manufacture, and co-market a new product. Through *promotional alliances,* one company agrees to join in a promotion for another company's product or service. For example, McDonald's teamed up with Ty to offer Beanie Babies as a promotion for its value meals. Companies may form *logistics alliances* in which one company offers distribution services for another company's product. Abbott Laboratories warehouses and delivers all of 3M's medical and surgical products to hospitals across North America. Finally, one or more companies may join in special *pricing alliances,* as do hotel and rental car companies to offer mutual price discounts.

Companies need to give careful thought to finding partners who might complement their strengths and offset their weaknesses. Well-managed alliances can have a

Corning
www.corning.com

huge impact on sales and profits. Corning, the $5-billion-a-year glass and ceramics maker, is renowned for its partnerships and even defines itself as a "network of organizations." It derives half of its profits from joint ventures that apply its glass technology to various products in many countries. For example, Owens Corning Canada manufactures fibreglass insulation used in the construction of homes and buildings across North America. Corning's network also includes German and Korean electronics giants Siemens and Samsung and Mexico's biggest glass-maker, Vitro.

Connections with the World around Us

Beyond redefining their relationships with customers and partners, marketers are taking a fresh look at the ways in which they connect with the broader world around them. Here we look at trends toward increasing globalization, more concern for social environmental responsibility, and greater use of marketing by nonprofit and public sector organizations.

Global Connections

In a shrinking world, many marketers are now connected globally with their customers and marketing partners. The world economy has undergone radical change over the past two decades. Geographical and cultural distances have shrunk with the advent of jet planes, fax machines, global computer and telephone hookups, world television satellite broadcasts, and other technical advances. This has allowed companies to greatly expand their geographical market coverage, purchasing, and manufacturing. The result is a vastly more complex marketing environment for both companies and consumers.

Today, almost every company, large or small, is touched in some way by global competition—from the neighbourhood florist that buys its flowers from Mexican nurseries to the Vancouver electronics manufacturer that competes in its home markets with giant Japanese rivals. Fledgling Internet retailers that find themselves receiving orders from all over the world have to deal with the complexity of international laws and taxation systems that were once the domain only of large multinationals.

Both Canadian and American firms have been challenged in their home markets by the skillful marketing of European and Asian multinationals. Companies such as Toyota, Noika, Airbus, Siemens, Nestlé, Sony, and Samsung have often outperformed their North American rivals. However, Canadian companies in a wide range of industries have found new opportunities abroad. Nortel, SNC Lavalin, Labatt, BCE, Imperial Oil, Alcan, and Bombardier have developed truly global operations, making and selling their products worldwide. The North American Free Trade Agreement, signed in 1994, provided a boost to Canadian exporters, and even though the US is still our largest trading partner, Canadian firms market their products throughout the globe. Marketing Highlight 1-3 provides some examples of Canadian companies taking advantage of global marketing opportunities.

Today, companies are not only trying to sell more of their locally produced goods in international markets, but are also buying more components and supplies abroad. For example, Alfred Sung, one of Canada's top fashion designers, may choose cloth woven from Australian wool with designs printed in Italy. He will design a dress and fax the drawing to a Hong Kong agent, who will place the order with a Chinese factory. Finished dresses will be air-freighted to Montreal and New York, where they will be redistributed to department and specialty stores across North America.

Thus, managers in countries around the world are increasingly taking a global, not just local, view of the company's industry, competitors, and opportunities. They are asking: What is global marketing? How does it differ from domestic marketing? How do global competitors and forces affect our business? To what extent should we "go global"? Many companies are forming strategic alliances with foreign

marketing highlight 1-3

Going Global: Coca-Cola Dominates

The Coca-Cola Company is certainly no stranger to global marketing. Long the world's leading soft-drink maker, the company now sells its brands in more than 200 countries. In recent years, Coca-Cola has revved up every aspect of its global marketing. The result: world leadership in the soft-drink business.

The great "global cola wars" between Coca-Cola and rival Pepsi have become decidedly one-sided. To see how global they've become see the advertisements posted on the Web site (www.geog.okstate.edu/users/lightfoot/cola/cola133.htm). Coca-Cola now outsells Pepsi three to one overseas, and Coca-Cola boasts four of the world's five leading soft-drink brands: Coca-Cola, Diet Coke, Sprite, and Fanta. Coca-Cola has handed Pepsi a number of crushing international setbacks. As a result, Pepsi has recently experienced flat or declining international soft-drink sales. Coca-Cola has reported strong growth in Latin America, China, India, and the Philippines.

Pepsi is now retrenching its efforts abroad by focusing on emerging markets—China, India, and Indonesia—where Coke is growing, but where ample opportunities for growth still exist. Together, these three emerging markets boast 2.4 billion people, nearly half the world's population. With their young populations, exploding incomes, and underdeveloped soft-drink demand, they represent prime potential for Coca-Cola and Pepsi. For example, China's 1.2 billion consumers drink an average of only five servings of soft drinks per year, compared with 343 in North America, creating heady opportunities for growth. And Indonesia, with 200 million people, nearly all of them Muslims forbidden to consume alcohol, is what former Coca-Cola chairman and CEO Roberto Goizueta calls a "soft-drink paradise."

But even in these emerging markets, Pepsi will face a stiff challenge in Coca-Cola's international marketing savvy and heavy investment. For instance, by the end of the last century, Coca-Cola spent almost $2.8 billion building state-of-the-art Asian bottling plants and distribution systems. And Coca-Cola possesses proven marketing prowess. It carefully tailors its ads and other marketing efforts for each local market. For example, its Chinese New Year television ad featured a dragon in a holiday parade, adorned from head to tail with red Coke cans. The spot concluded: "For many centuries, the colour red has been the colour for good luck and prosperity. Who are we to argue with ancient wisdom?" In India, Coca-Cola aggressively cultivates a local image. It claimed official sponsorship for World Cup Cricket, a favourite national sport, and used Indian cricket fans rather than actors to promote Coke products. Coca-Cola markets effectively to both retailers and imbibers. Observes one Coke watcher: "The company hosts massive gatherings of up to 15 000 retailers to showcase everything from the latest coolers and refrigerators, which Coke has for loan, to advertising displays. And its salespeople go house-to-house in their quest for new customers. In New Delhi alone, workers handed out more than 100 000 free bottles of Coke and Fanta last year."

Nothing better illustrates Coca-Cola's surging global power than the explosive growth of Sprite. Sprite's advertising uniformly targets the world's young people with the tag line: "Image is nothing. Thirst is everything. Obey your thirst." The campaign taps into the rebellious side of teenagers, and into their need to form individual identities. According to Sprite's director of brand marketing: "The meaning of [Sprite] and what we stand for is exactly the same globally. Teens tell us it's incredibly relevant in nearly every market we go into." However, as always, Coca-Cola tailors its message to local consumers. In China, for example, the campaign has a softer edge. "You can't be irreverent in China, because it's not acceptable in that society. It's all about being relevant [to the specific audience]," notes the marketer. As a result of such smart targeting and powerful positioning, Sprite's worldwide sales have surged 35 percent in the past three years, making it the world's number-four soft-drink brand.

Coca-Cola's popularity is growing in China but it does not yet dominate Pepsi.

Coca-Cola's success as a global power has made it one of the most enduringly profitable companies in history. How profitable has Coca-Cola been over the decades? As of December 31, 2000, one share of Coca-Cola stock purchased at $40 in 1919 would be worth $6,282,154.

Sources: Quotations from Mark L. Clifford and Nicole Harris, "Coke pours into Asia," *Business Week*, 28 October 1996:72–7; and Mark Gleason, "Sprite is riding global ad effort to no. 4 status," *Advertising Age*, 18 November 1996:30. Also see Lori Bongiorno, "Fiddling with the formula at Pepsi," *Business Week*, 14 October 1996:42; and Patricia Sellers, "Why Pepsi needs to become more like Coke," *Fortune*, 3 March 1997:26–7; www.coca-cola.com; www.pepsi.com.

companies, even competitors, who serve as suppliers or marketing partners. Winning companies in the future may well be those that have built the best global networks.

Connections with Our Values and Social Responsibilities

Marketers are re-examining their connections with social values and responsibilities and with the very planet that sustains us. As the worldwide consumerism and environmentalism movements mature, today's marketers are being called upon to take greater responsibility for the social and environmental impact of their actions. Corporate ethics and social responsibility have become hot topics in almost every business arena, from the corporate boardroom to the business school classroom. And few companies can ignore the renewed and very demanding environmental movement.

The social responsibility and environmental movements will place even stricter demands on companies in the future. Some companies resist these movements, budging only when forced by legislation or consumer outcries. More forward-looking companies, however, readily accept their responsibilities to the world around them. They view socially responsible actions as an opportunity to do well by doing good—to profit by serving the best long-run interests of their customers and communities. Some companies—such as Mountain Equipment Co-op, the Royal Bank, Saturn, and The Body Shop—are practising "caring capitalism" and distinguishing themselves by being more civic-minded and caring. They are building social responsibility and action into their company value and mission statements. For example, Ben & Jerry's mission statement challenges all employees, from top management to ice cream scoopers in each store, to include concern for individual and community welfare in their day-to-day decisions.[28]

Broadening Connections

Increasingly, different kinds of organizations are using marketing to connect with customers and other important constituencies. In the past, marketing has been most widely applied in the for-profit business sector. In recent years, however, marketing also has become a major component in the strategies of many non-profit organizations.

According to the Canadian Centre for Philanthropy, Canada has over 80 000 registered charities and non-profit organizations. These range from small community-based organizations like the Brockville Volunteer Firefighters Association, to large national charities like the United Way and the Heart and Stroke Foundation. They also include churches, hospitals, museums, symphony orchestras, and universities. With cutbacks in government funding, competition for donors is intensifying and non-profit organizations are adapting more and more marketing practices. For example, some are building alliances. Witness the birth in 1998 of the Girl Child Network, a joint initiative funded by World Vision Canada, Foster Parents Plan of Canada, Christian Children's Fund of Canada, and Save the Children. The four organizations shared costs on a mass-market advertising campaign to address global issues that specifically affect young girls—child prostitution, child labour, and female genital mutilation.

The Arthritis Society, Care Canada, and other charities are turning to the data mining techniques and donor lifetime value analysis used by for-profit firms. Kelly Ducharme, database manager at Care Canada's Ottawa headquarters, notes that data mining is becoming a trend. It helps non-profits target their fundraising efforts while providing donors with more accountability. Care has been able to segment its 160 000-name donor base into a descending scale according to the period dur-

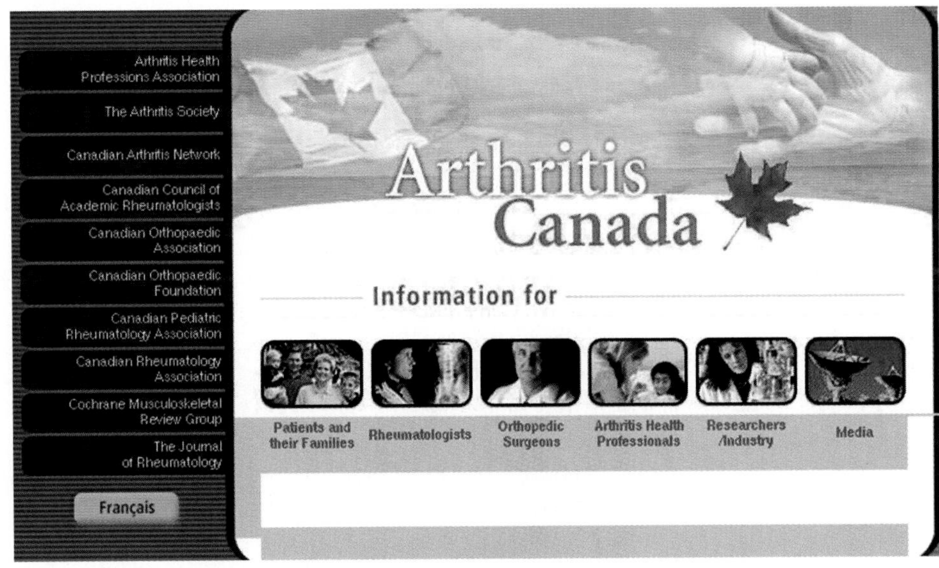

Many non-profits, like Arthritis Canada, are using data mining techniques to improve their fundraising and marketing efforts.

ing which the person made their last donation. They found that only 25 percent gave in the last 18 months, so rather than swallowing the massive mailing costs incurred with blanket mailings, Care targeted only those that passed the "recency" test. Response rates from its latest campaigns have been as high as nine percent compared to the four percent average for most non-profit campaigns. Keeping donors active is as important for non-profits as it is for firms to retain their customers. Experts note that it costs about $13 a name to acquire a new donor, so many non-profits are starting to realize that it's cheaper to get incremental revenue out of an existing donor than to try to find a new one.[29]

Even government agencies have shown an increased interest in marketing. The Canadian Army has a marketing plan to attract recruits; Transport Canada has a program to discourage drunk driving; and Health and Welfare Canada has long-standing social marketing campaigns to discourage smoking, excessive drinking, and drug use. Even once-stodgy Canada Post has developed innovative marketing programs to increase use of its priority mail services. Thus, it seems that every type of organization can connect through marketing. The continued growth of non-profit and public-sector marketing presents new and exciting challenges for marketing managers.

The New Connected World of Marketing

So, today, smart marketers of all kinds are taking advantage of new opportunities for connecting with their customers, their marketing partners, and the world around them. Table 1-2 compares the old marketing thinking to the new. The old marketing thinking saw marketing as little more than selling or advertising. It viewed marketing as customer acquisition rather than customer care. It emphasized trying to make a profit on each sale rather than trying to profit by managing customer lifetime value. It also concerned itself with trying to sell products rather than to understand, create, communicate, and deliver real value to customers.

Fortunately, this old marketing thinking is now giving way to newer ways of thinking. Today's smart marketing companies are improving their customer knowledge and customer connections. They are targeting profitable customers, then finding innovative ways to capture and keep these customers. They are forming more direct connections with customers and building lasting customer relationships.

TABLE 1-2 Marketing Connections in Transition

Old Marketing Thinking	New Marketing Thinking
Connections with customers	
Be sales and product centred	Be market and customer centred
Practise mass marketing	Target selected market segments or individuals
Focus on products and sales	Focus on customer satisfaction and value
Make sales to customers	Develop customer relationships
Get new customers	Retain customers
Grow share of market	Grow share of customer
Serve any customer	Serve profitable customers, "fire" losing ones
Communicate through mass media	Connect with customers directly
Make standardized products	Develop customized products
Connections with marketing partners	
Leave customer satisfaction and value to sales and marketing	Enlist all departments in the cause of customer satisfaction and value
Go it alone	Partner with other firms
Connections with the world around us	
Market locally	Market locally and globally
Assume profit responsibility	Assume social and environmental responsibility
Marketing only for corporations	Marketing for all organizations, including non-profits
Conduct commerce in market*places*	Conduct e-commerce in market*spaces*

They are using more targeted media and integrating their marketing communications to deliver meaningful and consistent messages through every customer contact. They are employing more technologies, such as video conferencing, sales automation software, and the Internet, intranets, and extranets. They see their suppliers and distributors as partners, not adversaries. In sum, they are forming new kinds of connections for delivering superior value to their customers.

We will explore all of these developments in more detail in later chapters. For now, we must recognize that marketing will continue to change dramatically as we move into the twenty-first century. The new millennium offers many exciting opportunities for forward-thinking marketers.

marketers speak out

Jeff Norton, Procter & Gamble

Jeff Norton graduated from Queen's University in 1997 from the Bachelor of Commerce program. He worked at Procter & Gamble Inc. in Toronto for two and a half years, marketing the Bounce fabric softener brand and leading the national introductions of Febreze and Dryel. In January 2000, Jeff accepted an opportunity to work at P&G's global headquarters in Cincinnati, Ohio. He is responsible for the strategic marketing of P&G's liquid dishwashing business.

P&G markets a vast array of consumer packaged goods that are known around the world for their high quality. The firm is also renowned as a founder of modern marketing practice. The company's insights about marketing have been on the leading edge of the discipline throughout its history.

When Jeff first began his full-time career with P&G, he appreciated the fact that the company offered a highly intensive training program—known as "brand college"—for new employees. During two intense weeks of interactive course sessions, P&G's new employees are taken through all phases of product marketing—from idea assessment to getting a product into consumers' hands through great advertising.

When Jeff first began as an assistant brand manager for Bounce, his days were filled with thinking about the executional details associated with marketing plans. Jeff's daily tasks swung between creative and analytic work. He worked to develop better promotions, always asking if there was a different place mentally or physically that Bounce should be positioned. This is quite a challenge since fabric softeners are low-involvement products. Next, Jeff reviewed vast amounts of data to try to identify hidden nuggets of information that could be leveraged into a big idea to help market the brand.

No matter what he is doing, Jeff tries to step back and think about how the detail-oriented work that fills his days relates to the big picture and to P&G's strategy. He focuses on where the brand fits in the category and into the overall business of the company. He reminds himself that nothing he does is in isolation from the overall objectives of P&G. "You can never just think that this is just a small product in global organization and that what you do doesn't really matter," Jeff stresses. It makes the ordinary, everyday things he does in his job seem more meaningful.

Jeff's first US assignment on P&G's North American Liquid Dish Businesses (Dawn, Ivory, Joy) was to develop marketing plans that would grow the $500 million portfolio of brands and defend their position against a major competitor that was trying to seize market leadership through new products, higher in-store spending in-store, and more advertising.

After analyzing the business from many angles, Jeff discovered that Dawn, the overall market share leader, had only a minimal presence in the sizeable and growing antibacterial (AB) sub-segment of the market. Dawn faced two serious issues. First, competition simply offered the consumer more variety in the antibacterial segment, and second, consumer awareness that Dawn even had an AB version was very low. Jeff's challenge, therefore, was to turn things around in this critical market segment.

Jeff's first task was to convince senior management on the strategic need for a new, antibacterial, version of Dawn. Then, after spending time in the "real world" with consumers, and working with a multi-functional team, "Dawn PowerPlus Antibacterial" dish detergent was born with a new formula, colour, perfume, and package.

Developing a new product to meet an unmet need was one challenge. Building a marketing plan that would drive consumer awareness of "Dawn PowerPlus Antibacterial" was another. After consulting with colleagues working on the Dish Detergent category elsewhere in the world, Jeff found an intriguing marketing concept from Spain. Spain's Fairy dish liquid brand worked with

Jeff Norton.

UNICEF (United National Children's Emergency Fund). When people purchased Fairy, P&G donated vaccines to the children of Senegal. Jeff believed a similar, improved program could also work in the US.

Jeff quickly won senior management support for the idea to link to sales of antibacterial dish detergent to a donation to UNICEF. He also had to elicit UNICEF's support. Instead of just licensing its logo, Jeff hoped to convince UNICEF to become an active partner in the promotion. UNICEF was soon onboard. Now all that remained was the development of a "cause related branding" strategy for Dawn and UNICEF.

It took a team of six people from UNICEF, P&G, and the advertising agency to bring the plan to life. Everyone was challenged to think of ways to make the program even bigger and give it greater impact. Instead of using only TV, print, and in-store advertising as was traditionally done, a truly holistic marketing plan was formed, which included such new elements as a public relations event, a partnership with other NGOs, and an Internet plan. The program ran from October 31 to December 31, 2000 and it was truly a win-win situation. Dawn raised US$240 000 for UNICEF and Dawn's antibacterial market share grew by over eight percent. This one program both helped a brand and a good cause.

Review of Concept Connections

Today's successful companies—whether large or small, for-profit or non-profit, domestic or global—share a strong customer focus and a heavy commitment to marketing. Many people think of marketing as only selling or advertising. But marketing combines many activities—marketing research, product development, distribution, pricing, advertising, personal selling, and others—designed to sense, serve, and satisfy consumer needs while meeting the organization's goals. Marketing seeks to attract new customers by promising superior value and to keep current customers by delivering satisfaction.

Marketing operates within a dynamic global environment. Rapid changes can quickly make yesterday's winning strategies obsolete. Marketers face many new challenges and opportunities. To be successful, companies will have to be strongly market focused.

1. **Define marketing and discuss its core concepts.**

   Marketing is a social and managerial process by which individuals and groups obtain what they need and want through creating and exchanging products and values with others. The core concepts of marketing are *needs, wants, and demands; products and services; value, satisfaction, and quality; exchange, transactions, and relationships;* and *markets. Wants* are the form assumed by human needs when shaped by culture and individual personality. When backed by buying power, wants become *demands.* People satisfy their needs, wants, and demands with products and services. A *product* is anything that can be offered to a market to satisfy a need, want, or demand. Products also include *services* and other entities such as *persons, places, organizations, activities,* and *ideas.*

2. **Explain the relationship between customer value, satisfaction, and quality.**

   In deciding which products and services to buy, consumers rely on their perception of relative value. *Customer value* is the difference between the values the customer gains from owning and using a product and the costs of obtaining and using the product. *Customer satisfaction* depends on a product's perceived performance in delivering value relative to a buyer's expectations. Customer satisfaction is closely linked with *quality.* Marketing occurs when people satisfy their needs, wants, and demands through exchange. Beyond creating short-term exchanges, marketers need to build long-term relationships with valued customers, distributors, dealers, and suppliers.

3. **Discuss marketing management and understand how marketers manage demand and build profitable customer relationships.**

   Marketing management is the analysis, planning, implementation, and control of programs designed to create, build, and maintain beneficial exchanges with target buyers for the purpose of achieving organizational objectives. It involves more than simply finding enough customers for the company's current output. At times, marketing is also concerned with changing or even reducing demand. Managing demand means understanding and working with customers. Beyond designing strategies to *attract* new customers and create *transactions* with them, today's companies are focusing on *retaining* current customers and building lasting *relationships* through offering superior customer value and satisfaction.

4. Compare the five marketing management philosophies.

Organizations can be guided by five different philosophies. The role that marketing plays within the firm depends on the corporate philosophy. The *production concept* holds that consumers favour products that are available and highly affordable; management's task is to improve production efficiency and bring down prices. The *product concept* holds that consumers favour products that offer the most quality, performance, and innovative features; thus, little promotional effort is required. The *selling concept* holds that consumers will not buy enough of the organization's products unless it undertakes a large-scale selling and promotion effort. The *marketing concept* holds that achieving organizational goals depends on determining the needs and wants of target markets and delivering the desired satisfactions more effectively and efficiently than competitors do. The *societal marketing concept* holds that the company should determine the needs, wants, and interests of target markets. Generating customer satisfaction and long-run societal well-being are the keys to achieving both the company's goals and its responsibilities.

5. Analyze the major challenges facing future marketers.

Dramatic changes in the marketplace are creating many marketing opportunities and challenges. Major marketing developments can be summed up in a single theme: connections. The explosive growth in connecting technologies—computer, telecommunications, information, and transportation technologies—has created exciting new ways for marketers to learn about and serve consumers, in large groups or one-to-one. Marketers are rapidly redefining how they connect with their customers, with their marketing partners, and with the world around them. They are choosing their customers more carefully and developing closer, more lasting, and more direct connections with them. Realizing that going it alone is going out of style, they are connecting more closely with other company departments and with other firms in an integrated effort to bring more value to customers. They are taking a fresh look at the ways in which they connect with the broader world, resulting in increased globalization, growing attention to social and environmental responsibilities, and greater use of marketing by non-profit and public-sector organizations. The new, connected millennium offers exciting possibilities for forward-thinking marketers.

Key Terms

Customer satisfaction *(p. 10)*
Customer value *(p. 9)*
Demands *(p. 7)*
Demarketing *(p. 14)*
Exchange *(p. 11)*
Market *(p. 12)*
Marketing *(p. 6)*
Market orientation *(p. 18)*
Marketing concept *(p. 18)*
Marketing management *(p. 14)*
Needs *(p. 6)*
Product *(p. 7)*
Product concept *(p. 17)*
Production concept *(p. 17)*
Relationship marketing *(p. 12)*
Selling concept *(p. 18)*
Service *(p. 8)*
Societal marketing concept *(p. 20)*
Transaction *(p. 11)*
Wants *(p. 6)*

Discussing the Issues

1. Answer the question "What is marketing?"
2. Discuss the concept of customer value and its importance to successful marketing. How are customer value and relationship marketing linked?
3. Marketing can be practised in many ways. Discuss the three stages through which marketing practice often passes. Identify each stage, describe the stage's characteristics, and provide an example of a company in that stage.

4. What is the single biggest difference between the marketing concept and the production, product, and selling concepts? Which concepts are easier to adopt in the short run? Which concept offers the best chances of long-run success? Why?

5. Select a company that makes a product that consumers want but which may run contrary to society's best interests (for example, tobacco, liquor, or environmentally harmful products). Considering the company's profit goals, discuss the ways in which it might resolve the conflicts that arise between satisfying individual wants and guarding societal welfare.

6. As we enter the new millennium, major marketing developments are summed up by a single theme: connectedness. List and discuss three important connections made possible by the connecting technologies (such as computer, information, and transportation technologies). Give examples of companies taking advantages of such connections.

7. Perhaps the most dramatic new technology driving the connected age is the Internet. Why is this true? Provide examples that demonstrate how marketers can use the Internet to (a) reach new customers, (b) form new distribution channels, and (c) meet or beat competition.

Marketing Applications

1. Companies can apply the marketing concept to their Web sites by including features that are important to customers and prospects. At the least, Web users want to know about product benefits and where they can buy products. However, sites that give users something beyond product descriptions create additional customer value and build long-term relationships. Many sites target specific customer segments by focusing on language, age, gender, or technical understanding. Finally, an important sign of customer orientation is having an e-mail address that is easy to remember, use, and communicate to the consumer. Evaluate the following Web site based on its apparent attention to the marketing concept: www.apple.com.
   a. What is the most important customer benefit stressed at this site?
   b. What new products did you find? Which one(s) did you find most interesting?
   c. To what extent does this site apply the marketing concept? Explain.
   d. Should anything be added to the site? Explain.
   e. How does Apple attempt to build relationships with Web site visitors? What "connections" is Apple attempting to make?

2. Few companies have done as much to apply the societal marketing concept as Mountain Equipment Co-op (MEC) (www.mec.ca). The company's founders made a strong and sincere commitment to a wide range of ecological and social causes.
   a. Visit the MEC Web site. What impresses you most? What marketing efforts are evident?
   b. What social and ecological causes does the company support?
   c. What values does the company communicate? Do these values appear to help or hinder its marketing efforts? What does it mean to MEC to operate as a non-profit?
   d. How does the company attempt to build relationships or "connections" with its members/customers?
   e. Many new competitors have entered the outdoor goods market. If you were a competitor seeking to expand market share, what vulnerabilities do you see at MEC that could be exploited? What can MEC do to overcome these vulnerabilities? Write a brief plan for doing this.

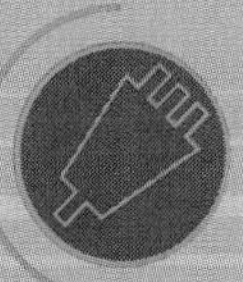

Internet Connections

The Marketing Concept

Web sites can demonstrate the marketing concept by exhibiting a company's special features to customers and prospects. Many sites target customer segments by language, gender, and age, providing slightly different content for each target. In general, Web users want to know about product benefits. However, sites that give surfers something of interest beyond product descriptions create additional value. The most attractive site advantages tend to be interactive. For example, e-mail and surveys allow for customer feedback; intelligent agents can find the right product to meet customers' needs; and retail locators tell customers where they can buy the product they need. Complete the following chart to indicate which benefits are supported on the Web sites of three athletic shoe companies. Then decide which firm is the most customer oriented.

For Discussion

1. Of the benefits listed in the chart, which three do you think are the most important? Why?
2. Overall, which site best embodies the marketing concept? Why?
3. Suggest one or more customer benefits not listed in the chart that the best site contains.
4. Based on your analysis of Nike's site, are they interested in relationship marketing? Support your answer.

Benefit	Nike www.nike.com	Reebok www.reebok.com	New Balance www.newbalance.com
Retail locator			
Nonproduct information			
Multiple languages			
Multiple targets: Gender			
Multiple targets: Age			
Multiple targets: Different sports			
Customer feedback			
Intelligent agents			
Fun to surf?			

Savvy Sites

Which are the best sites on the Web? Check out the following sites to see what the experts think:

- MediaMetrix (www.mediametrix.com) measures surfing behaviour in their panel of Internet users and releases listings of top sites ranked according to number of visitors.
- NetMarketing (www.netb2b.com) reviews and rates the top 200 Web sites in the business-to-business market.
- Webnet Web Ratings (www.webratings.net) is a non-profit organization that rates submitted Web sites on a 1-to-5 scale based on content, navigation of site, appearance, and ease of reading.

Notes

1. MEC corporate Web site (www.mec.ca); Eve Lazarus, "MEC facing marketing challenges," *Marketing Magazine,* 19 June 2000:2.
2. These are other definitions: "Marketing is the performance of business activities that direct the flow of goods and services from producer to consumer or user." "Marketing is getting the right goods to the right people at the right place at the right time at the right price with the right communication and promotion." "Marketing is the creation of a standard of living." The American Marketing Association offers this definition: "Marketing is the process of planning and executing the conception, pricing, promotion, and distributing of ideas, goods, and services to create exchanges that satisfy individual and organizational objectives."
3. See B. Joseph Pine II and James Gilmore, "Welcome to the experience economy," *Harvard Business Review,* July–August 1998:99. Also see Philip Kotler, *Marketing Management: Analysis, Planning, Implementation, and Control,* 10th ed., Upper Saddle River, NJ: Prentice Hall, 2000:3–5.
4. See Theodore Levitt's classic article, "Marketing myopia," *Harvard Business Review,* July–August 1960:45–56. For more recent discussions, see Dhananjayan Kashyap, "Marketing myopia revisited: A look through the 'colored glass of a client,'" *Marketing and Research Today,* August 1996: 197–201; Colin Grant, "Theodore Levitt's marketing myopia," *Journal of Business Ethics,* February 1999:397–406; and Jeffrey M. O'Brien, "Drums in the jungle," *MC Technology Marketing Intelligence,* March 1999:22–30.
5. For good discussions of defining and measuring customer value, see Howard E. Butz Jr. and Leonard D. Goodstein, "Measuring customer value: Gaining strategic advantage," *Organizational Dynamics,* Winter 1996:63–77; Robert B. Woodruff, "Customer value: The next source of competitive advantage," *Journal of the Academy of Marketing Science,* Spring 1997:139–53; James C. Anderson and James A. Narus, "Business marketing: Understand what customers value," *Harvard Business Review,* November–December 1998:53–61; and W. Chan Kim and Renee Mauborgne, "Creating new market space," *Harvard Business Review,* January–February 1999:83–93.
6. For more on customer satisfaction, see Jaclyn Fierman, "Americans can't get no satisfaction," *Fortune,* 11 December 1995:186; Richard A. Spreng, Scott B. MacKenzie, and Richard W. Olshavsky, "A reexamination of the determinants of customer satisfaction," *Journal of Marketing,* July 1996:15–32; Thomas A. Stewart, "A satisfied customer isn't enough," *Fortune,* 21 July 1997:112–3; and Subhash Sharma, Ronald W. Niedrich, and Greg Dobbins, "A framework for monitoring customer satisfaction," *Industrial Marketing Management,* May 1999:231–43.
7. See James C. Anderson, Hakan Hakansson and Jan Johanson, "Dyadic business relationships within a business network context," *Journal of Marketing,* 15 October 1994:1–15. For more discussion of relationship marketing, see Thomas W. Gruen, "Relationship marketing: The route to marketing efficiency and effectiveness," *Business Horizons,* November–December 1997:32–8; and John V. Petrof, "Relationship marketing: The emperor in used clothes," *Business Horizons,* March–April 1998:79–82.
8. For more discussion on demand states, see Kotler, *Marketing Management: Analysis, Planning, Implementation, and Control,* Chapter 1.
9. For more on assessing customer value, see Gordon A. Wyner, "Customer valuation: Linking behavior and economics," *Marketing Research,* Summer 1996:36–8; Gordon A. Wyner, "Which customers will be valuable in the future?" *Marketing Research,* Fall 1996:44–6; Bill Stoneman, "Banking on customers," *American Demographics,* February 1997:37–41; Paul D. Berger, "Customer lifetime value: Marketing models and applications," *Journal of Interactive Marketing,* Winter 1998:17–30; and Libby Estell, "This call center accelerates sales," *Sales & Marketing Management,* February 1999:72.
10. Sam Hill Glenn and Rifkin, *Radical Marketing,* New York: Harper Business, 1999.
11. "Mind the gap," *Venture,* November 7, 2000.
12. Patrick Brethour, "Corel launches attack on corporate market," *The Globe and Mail,* 24 September 1996:B4; Carolyn Leitch, "Corel warns loss may hit $4-million," *The Globe and Mail,* 26 September 1996:B1, B6.

13. Ralph Waldo Emerson offered this advice: "If a man . . . makes a better mousetrap . . . the world will beat a path to his door." Several companies, however, have built better mousetraps yet failed. One was a laser mousetrap costing $1500. Contrary to popular assumptions, people do not automatically learn about new products, believe product claims, or willingly pay higher prices.

14. Barry Farber and Joyce Wycoff, "Customer service: Evolution and revolution," *Sales & Marketing Management,* May 1991:47. Also see Jaclyn Fierman, "Americans can't get no satisfaction," *Fortune,* 11 December 1995:186–94.

15. John C. Narver and Stanley F. Slater (1990), "The effect of market orientation on business profitability," *Journal of Marketing,* 54 (October): 20–35.

16. Ajay K. Kohli and Bernard J. Jaworski (1990). "Market orientation: The construct, research propositions, and managerial implications," *Journal of Marketing,* 54(2): 1–18.

17. Jin K. Han, Namwoon Kim, and Rajendra K. Srivastava (1999). "Market orientation and organizational performance: Is innovation a missing link?" *Journal of Marketing,* 62 (October): 30–45.

18. Gary Hamel and C. K. Prahalad, "Seeing the future first," *Fortune,* 5 September 1994:64–70. Also see Philip Kotler, *Kotler on Marketing,* New York: Free Press, 1999:20–4.

19. Howard Schlossberg, "Customer satisfaction: Not a fad, but a way of life," *Marketing News,* 10 June 1991:18. Also see Bernard J. Jaworski and Ajay K. Kohli, "Market orientation: Antecedents and consequences," *Journal of Marketing,* July 1993:53–70; and E. K. Valentin, "The marketing concept and the conceptualization of market strategy," *Journal of Marketing Theory and Practice,* Fall 1996:16–27.

20. Speech by Barbara J. Hedjuk, President, Imperial Oil Charitable Foundation, Social Marketing for Business Conference, Toronto, 9 November 1995.

21. Co-operative Principles taken from the Mountain Equipment Co-op Web site, August 2000 (www. mec.ca).

22. Statistics Canada, "E-commerce and business use of the Internet," *The Daily,* 10 August 1999.

23. Robert D. Hof, "The 'click here' economy," *Business Week,* 22 June 1998:122–8.

24. Wallys W. Conhaim, "E-commerce," *Link-Up,* March–April 1998:8–10.

25. Philip Kotler, *Kotler on Marketing,* New York: Free Press, 1999:20.

26. Thor Valdmanis, "Alliances gain favor over risky mergers," *USA Today,* 4 February 1999:3B.

27. Rosabeth Moss Kanter, "Why collaborate?" *Executive Excellence,* April 1999:8.

28. See Ben & Jerry's full mission statement online at www.benjerry.com. For more reading on environmentalism, see William S. Stavropoulos, "Environmentalism's third wave," *Executive Speeches,* August–September 1996:28–30; Stuart L. Hart, "Beyond greening: Strategies for a sustainable world," *Harvard Business Review,* January–February 1997:67–76; and Michael Lounsbury, "From heresy to dogma: An institutional history of corporate environmentalism," *Administrative Science Quarterly,* March 1999:193–5. For more on marketing and social responsibility, see Daniel Kadlec, "The new world of giving," *Time,* 5 May 1997:62–4; Heather Salerno, "From selling cars to building playgrounds," *Washington Post,* 9 June 1997:F11; and "Can doing good be good for business?" *Fortune,* 2 February 1998:148G–J.

29. Mark De Wolf, "Non-profits take on private-sector marketing tactics," *Strategy: The Canadian Marketing Report,* 12 April 1999:D20. For other examples, and for a good review of nonprofit marketing, see Philip Kotler and Alan R. Andreasen, *Strategic Marketing for Nonprofit Organizations,* 5th ed., Upper Saddle River, NJ: Prentice Hall, 1996; Philip Kotler and Karen Fox, *Strategic Marketing for Educational Institutions,* Upper Saddle River, NJ: Prentice Hall, 1995; William P. Ryan, "The new landscape for nonprofits," *Harvard Business Review,* January–February 1999:127–36; Denise Nitterhouse, "Nonprofit and social marketing," *Nonprofit Management and Leadership,* Spring 1999:323–8.

Company Case 1

PRICELINE.COM: CHANGING BUSINESS IN THE NEW MILLENNIUM?

Creating value for customers means not only making better products and services but also helping consumers obtain those product and services easily. If you wanted a new shirt in the year 1701, you might have had it custom-made by your mother, grandmother, sister, or, if you had the money, a tailor. In 1801, you might have bought it at a draper's, a specialty store that sold clothes and a few other dry goods. By 1901, you could have purchased the shirt off the rack in one of the big new department stores, such as The Hudson Bay Company. In 1959, you'd have visited the new retailing institution of the day—the shopping centre. In 1979, it was the discount store; and in 1990, the warehouse store. In 2001, going full circle, consumers may well be ordering custom-made shirts again, this time over the Internet.

The industrial revolution created more goods less expensively, but it also required a new means of selling them. As product assortments swelled, retailers realized that the expanded assortments couldn't all be sold in limited-line shops. Thus developed the department store, where consumers could find many different types of goods under one roof. Shopping became easier through the aggregation of goods, and stores provided many services, such as credit and delivery of large goods. They carried merchandise across multiple price ranges with the best goods several floors above and real bargains in the basement. Social needs were accommodated with lunch and tea rooms, where weary shoppers could rest their feet and recuperate before continuing to shop.

As more and more goods poured into the market, no single store could accommodate them. Stores began to group together in central shopping districts or shopping centres to give consumers more choice. As competition for consumer dollars increased, some retailers began offering lower prices to attract shoppers away from department stores with their high overheads. Early discount stores reduced their services, even to the point of eliminating sales clerks, locating in low-rent locations, and operating in Spartan facilities. Eventually some of these discounters followed the department store idea of aggregating product assortments into larger stores such as warehouse stores.

Throughout this retailing evolution, aggregation and convenience seem to have been the guiding principles. Make it easier for consumers to shop by providing them with more goods in one location. Today, a prime example of these principles is the massive West Edmonton Mall, which features more than 800 retail, department, and specialty stores, an amusement park, dolphin pool, and skating rink—all under one roof. Even low-priced discounters have followed the aggregation principle. Category killers such as Office Depot or Home Depot offer deep assortments of goods in their product categories.

Aggregation and convenience also seem to be keywords for retailing in the beginning of the new millennium. Can you imagine a brick-and-mortar bookstore large enough to hold the entire inventory of Amazon.com? How about a flea market the size of eBay.com, or a shopping centre with as many vendors as America Online or Yahoo!? The Internet offers almost unlimited shopping possibilities, all from the comfort of your own home, whenever it's convenient for you, from anywhere on the globe.

From the department store to the Internet, the underlying business model is the same. A marketing intermediary, such as The Bay, Wal-Mart, and Chapters.ca, assembles an assortment of many items, often from far-flung and numerous sources, and makes them conveniently available to consumers in a single location. Consumers examine the merchandise, look at the price, and make a purchase decision. Sometimes, they can even have shopping assistants, or "bots" in the case of Internet shopping, do the search and comparison for them.

Some Internet merchants adjust this model a little. Online auction sites, such as those of eBay.com and Amazon.com, use dynamic pricing by allowing consumers to bid on items. However, most of the goods offered at auction are unique items, such as collectibles, rather than regular merchandise.

Priceline.com is building on the success of these online auction sites. At the Priceline Web site, consumers can bid on such non-unique items as airline tickets, mortgages, hotel rooms, autos, groceries, and even telephone time. Priceline lets consumers specify the goods they want and the price they are willing to pay, then determines whether one of its suppliers will accept that bid. Although much heralded as a new business model benefiting consumers, a closer examination suggests that Priceline's operation benefits sellers as much as or more than consumers.

In the airline industry, for example, where unsold seats are perishable, an airline always prefers to sell the seats, even at rock-bottom prices, than to leave them empty. So the airlines tell Priceline what prices they will accept for these seats and specify conditions. For example, if you want to fly from Toronto to Miami, you log on to Priceline, give dates, departure and destination cities, a price bid, and a credit card number. If your bid matches an airline price, Priceline completes the sale. However, you have no control over flight times or on which airline you fly, and frequently you may find yourself flying through smaller airports and making more plane changes. What's more, if the airline accepts your bid, you cannot refuse to buy the ticket. Thus, under the Priceline model, consumers trade price discounts for less convenience and choice—they are willing to fly whenever and on whatever routes the airlines select.

Similarly, selling space in hotels through Priceline is essentially a demand collection system. Consumers indicate where they want to go and what they want to pay, giving the hotels a picture of their daily demand. Consumers can specify the area of a city in which they wish to stay but not the specific hotel. The same holds true for mortgages and cars—consumers cannot specify the specific lender or dealer. Similarly, groceries purchased through Priceline must be picked up in a participating store. The consumer must still walk the aisles and when checking out must separate the bid items from those purchased at the regular price.

Even Priceline CEO Jay Walker admits that Priceline isn't going to help consumers find fantastic low rates. "We are not a discount ticket warehouse. We're the place to go when you can't find a published fare you can live with. The bottom line is that Priceline.com works best if you want to fly soon and face only the highest-price tickets, because you'll likely land the usual 21-day advance purchase fare." In such cases, it might well be worth giving up control over airlines, flight times, and routes.

Another Internet company, NexTag.com, follows a somewhat different model. Using NexTag, consumers can bid on computers, electronics, books, software, and movies. In each product category, would-be buyers get a list of sellers and their suggested prices. Once a consumer makes a bid, NexTag lets merchants compete for the business. The consumer gets to pick the merchant and even drive prices down. However, consumers need to do their homework before going online. To get a good deal, they need to check manufacturers' and retailers' regular prices and allow for some profit margin. Otherwise, there's no reason for the seller to accept their bid.

If they can't get rock-bottom prices on the Web, will people want to buy groceries and telephone time over the Internet? Even if they get a penny-per-minute reduction on a long-distance call, that's still a savings of only 60 cents an hour. Is it worth your time and effort to get a two-cent reduction on a can of peas? Two cents on fifty items amounts to only a $1 reduction at the store, and you must spend time making bids and waiting for acknowledgment of them. Thus, many analysts believe that low-priced items such as groceries and telephone calls are not suitable for Internet selling. For the time being, traditional sellers of low-priced items appear to be safe from Internet competition.

Further, the impact of dynamic pricing on the Internet may not be to lower prices significantly. Even with the lower prices offered by Internet sellers such as Amazon.com, price savings must be weighed against waiting for goods, the lack of personal assistance, and the want of an active shopping experience. Thus, the main benefit of such Internet shopping may simply be to make larger assortments of goods available than local retailers can.

Questions

1. How does the Internet illustrate the marketing concept in action?
2. Explain how department stores, shopping centres, discounters, and warehouse stores create value for consumers.
3. How do Internet sellers such as Priceline.com, NexTag.com, and Chapters.ca create value for consumers? Contrast this value creation with that of traditional retailers in question 2.
4. How does the Internet create value for goods and service producers?
5. Can a company like Priceline.com sell low-priced items such as groceries and telephone calls?
6. How does a firm like Priceline.com or Yahoo.ca exemplify the new model for connecting with customers as explained in the chapter?

Sources: "Going, going, gone," *Business Week,* 12 April 1999:30; "Let the buyer be in control," *Business Week,* 8 November 1999:100; "Priceline fills hotel demand niche," *Lodging Hospitality,* August 1999:69; Katherine T. Beddingfield, "Airfare roulette," *U.S. News & World Report,* 27 April 1998:75; Peter Elkind, "The hype is big, really big," *Fortune,* 6 September 1999:193; Louis Lavelle, "New Internet service allows savvy car buyers to name their price," *Knight-Ridder/Tribune Business News,* 14 July 1998; Nick Wingfield, "New battlefield for Priceline is diapers, tuna," *Wall Street Journal,* 24 September 1999:B1, B4.

video case 1

Going for Broke: The Looneyspoons Launch

The *Looneyspoons* cookbook was the creation of Janet and Greta Podleski, two sisters from Ottawa, Ontario, who believed that there was a market for a cookbook that took the mystery out of cooking low-fat food. As the name implies, the book does more than simply present recipes. Cartoons and jokes appear on every page, and even the recipe names, such as the Barbra Streisand-inspired "The Way We Stir," let readers know that the authors don't take themselves too seriously. However, the marketing efforts of this duo showed an incredible seriousness and dedication to their product. The book was launched into one of the most competitive book categories in the country. Since more than 2000 cookbooks are introduced in Canada a year (one every five hours), a strong marketing effort was required to get their product noticed.

Over an 18-month period, the Podleski sisters invested thousands of dollars and hours into product development for their book, typically testing five to six meals per day. Once the recipes were developed, they spent additional hours compiling the book. Both Janet and Greta had quit their jobs; after using all of their investments and RRSPs, they maximized their credit card debt and held desperation garage sales to finance the cookbook. Although they were convinced of the market viability of their product, publishers were harder to convince. After several publishers turned them down, Greta and Janet decided they needed a partner to help them publish the book themselves. They turned to David Chilton, the well-known financial advisor and author of *The Wealthy Barber*. Chilton was initially sceptical about the concept but, after speaking with the sisters at length and reviewing their marketing and book proposal, he became a one-third partner in their business, Granet Publishing.

Chilton convinced Janet and Greta that promotion was the critical factor that would lead to their success. He advised them to spend all of their available time making calls to the media to set up interviews and then to get on the road to promote the book. Chilton had spent 230 days a year on the road promoting his own book and knew first-hand the importance of an author being visible. The Podleski sisters set up promotional visits to retailers, book signings, and national radio and TV interviews, and often Chilton's association with the book opened retailer and media doors. At times, the partnership with Chilton was a double-edged sword, however. For example, in one half-hour radio interview scheduled with Janet and Chilton that was supposed to highlight *Looneyspoons,* the host of the show spent more than half of the time asking Chilton financial questions and only after 16 minutes asked Janet about the cookbook.

Distribution was another major concern. Unlike most products, books that are not sold by retailers can be returned to the publisher for a full refund for up to one year. This increased the pressure on the authors to continue to promote the book even after national retailers such as Chapters and Smithbooks had placed large orders. Shipping problems also complicated the distribution process. When the Podleskis arrived in Vancouver for a press tour, they discovered that no bookstores in the area had received books. This meant that the sisters had to call every bookstore in Vancouver to inform them that the book was available but was delayed due to shipping difficulties.

Tension in the Granet Publishing partnership developed when the Podleskis were unable to schedule the number of interviews that Chilton believed was necessary in important markets such as Vancouver. Chilton also wanted to focus efforts nationally while the Podleskis were thinking more on a local level. The difficulties in resolving these tensions were made worse by the physical distance between the partners. Chilton lives in the Kitchener-Waterloo area, while the Podleskis live in Ottawa. A meeting in the middle at a roadside motel cleared the air, refocused the efforts of the partnership, and allowed them to consider long-term plans such as the development of a second cookbook.

One month after the launch of *Looneyspoons,* 20 000 copies of the book had been sold, due in part to a national radio interview on CBC in which the recipes received a favourable review from Vicki Gabereau. Although this number of sales was almost as much as first-year sales of *The Wealthy Barber,* the partners, and especially Chilton, still had reservations. They ran out of books, which meant that another printing had to be done. And although several copies of the books had been sold, no money had been received from those orders yet, which meant that Chilton had to invest more money to cover the cost of the printing. On the positive side, book sales in Ottawa had reached a critical mass, which means that the books were being sold as a result of word of mouth alone. However, sales in other markets, such as Calgary, were spotty. Consequently, the Podleski sisters had to continue to try to keep *Looneyspoons* top of mind for both consumers and retailers.

Janet and Greta's tenaciousness paid off. *Looneyspoons: Low-Fat Food Made Fun!* was a runaway hit, spending 85 weeks on the Canadian national bestseller list. The sisters weren't content to stop there and were quick to cast their eye south of the border. Believing themselves to be performers as well as cooks, they worked to get bookings on talk shows like *The Today Show* and coverage in popular magazines such as *People*. To encourage bookings, the sisters promised to serve up a hefty helping of laughter along with low-fat cooking. They promised to reveal why D.I.E.T. is a four-letter word that really means "Deny Ingesting Everything Tasty." They targeted US palettes with dishes such as Miss American Thigh, Melrose Plates, Ross Perogies, and NYPD Blueberry Pancakes.

These public relations efforts certainly paid off. To date over 800 000 copies have been sold and the sisters have gone on to launch a new venture called "Crazy Plates." Visit them at www.crazyplates.com/cookbooks.html to see what they are cooking up now.

Questions

1. How would you characterize the marketing planning process followed by the publishing team so far?
2. Is a formal marketing planning process necessary or realistic in this kind of business situation?
3. What recommendations would you make for strengthening the marketing planning and implementation process for *Looneyspoons*?
4. Read the Marketers Speak Out profile of Jim Shenkman on page 81. What lessons could the sisters have learned from Jim?
5. Visit the two websites (www.looneyspoons.com and www.crazyplates.com/cookbooks.html). Be sure to click on the "Media Room" button. How are the sisters using the web to market themselves as well as their cookbooks and products?

Source: This case was prepared by Auleen Carson and is based on "Looneyspoons," *Venture* (22 December 1996).

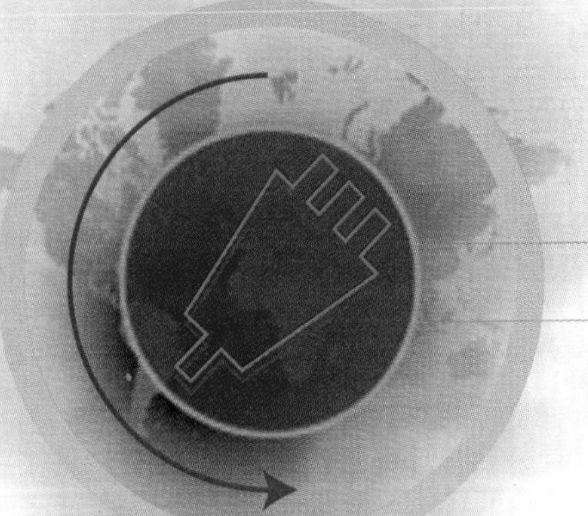

P A R T 1 2 3 4

Understanding Marketing and the Marketing Process

Concept Connections

After studying this chapter, you should be able to

1. Explain the importance of strategic planning and the different levels at which plans are formed.
2. Describe the strategies that businesses use to achieve competitive advantage in their marketplace.
3. Explain why many firms have moved toward a strategy of relationship marketing and describe the tools that they use to form relationships with their profitable customers.
4. Describe functional planning strategies and marketing's role in strategic planning.
5. Describe the marketing process and the forces that influence it.
6. List the marketing management functions, including the elements of a marketing plan.

chapter 2
Strategic Planning and the Marketing Process

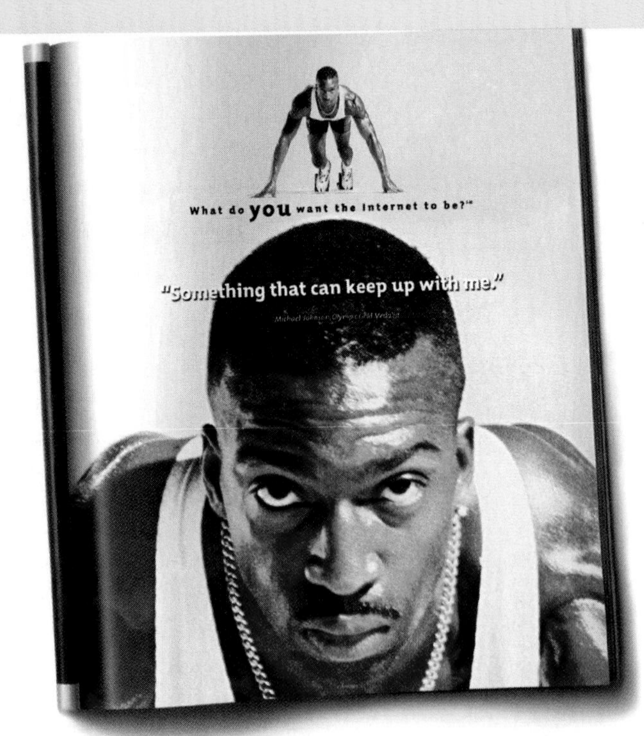

What do you want the Internet to be?™
"Something that can keep up with me."
Optical Internet
Keep up? Michael, we're building the new, high-performance Optical Internet. And it'll leave you looking like you're standing still. It's faster and more reliable than ever. Our Nortel Networks™OPTera™ Portfolio – which will carry Internet traffic, data and voice at 1.6 trillion bits per second on a single fiber strand – leads the industry in speed and capacity. Now we're introducing OPTera Packet Solutions. Finally, true convergence of optical and packet networking that enables service providers to carry all types of traffic on one network, economically. And creates new revenue-generating services. So come together, right now with Nortel Networks. And make the Internet whatever you want it to be. nortelnetworks.co
NORTEL NETWORKS
How the world shares ideas.

The great marketing stories in the high-tech industry today are all about foreseeing and driving change. According to *MC (Marketing Computers) Magazine,* no one has driven change inside a company as much as Bill Conner at Nortel Networks; as a result, it named him "Marketer of the Year 2000." Conner helped transform Nortel in fundamental ways. The road hasn't always been smooth, and change was deep—everything from a split from its former parent, BCE, to a name change (Nortel Networks was formerly Northern Telecom). It has also had to develop a new vision of itself and an understanding of emerging markets.

Nortel Networks, headquartered in Brampton, Ontario, was once regarded as a stodgy company manufacturing voice-telecommunications equipment. As 1999 closed, however, the company was ranked among the top dozen of the Internet economy by the likes of research company Giga Information Group of Cambridge, Massachusetts. One of the world's leading manufacturers of Internet gear, its vision is the creation of a high-performance Internet that is more reliable and faster than ever before.

Nortel Networks is one of Canada's dominant companies. In 1999 alone, the company's stock soared more than 300 percent; and in the first quarter of 2000, Nortel demonstrated revenue growth of 48 percent. This was no small feat, given that Nortel tackled US-based competitors like Cisco Systems Inc. of San Jose, California and Lucent Technologies of Murray Hill, New Jersey.

As you may now suspect, Nortel Networks is not only a Canadian giant, but also has long been a global leader. It operates in more than 100 countries and has offices and facilities in Canada, Europe, Asia-Pacific, Caribbean and Latin America, the Middle East, Africa, and the United States. It employs over 60 000 people worldwide. A British survey, the Templeton Global Performance Index, ranked Nortel as the best of the world's big multinationals in terms of actually making money overseas, putting it ahead of such other global heavyweights as Glaxo Wellcome PLC and Coca-Cola Co.

Nortel's stunning success results from strong strategic planning and its relentless dedication to a simple marketing strategy: Provide the most value and satisfaction to customers through product leadership and strong customer relationships. Some companies deliver superior value through convenience and low prices. In contrast, Nortel's strong connection with consumers rests on understanding their emerging needs, building relationships with them, and delivering superior value by creating a continuous stream of leading-edge products. Then, Nortel communicates its superior value directly to final buyers. The result is intense customer loyalty and preference. Bill Conner knows that technology alone is less important than how you shape it for customers. "It's about how you segment and deliver what they want and listen to them. That's the revolution going on here." For Bill, the ongoing question always is: "How do I create better customer value and better customer relationships?"

One analyst noted that Nortel "has a top-notch management team that really did see the future." Such an ability to envision the future doesn't just happen. It takes careful scanning of industry conditions, insight about competitors, and strong strategic planning to bring together the people and resources necessary to exploit opportunities. It also requires an integrated team with a clear sense of direction. Not an easy feat for a multinational firm that has been on an acquisition binge to better position itself for the new economy. In mid-1999, Milan Bekich, vice-president of corporate marketing, noted that the company wasn't unified the way it is now. "We were a lot of points of light doing a lot of things around the globe."

Marketing has played a significant role in Nortel's transformation. With its name change and the integration of its voice and data, wireline and wireless networks, Nortel launched a corporate branding campaign titled "Come Together." The campaign was so successful that unaided awareness of the firm jumped from single to double digits.

Nortel Networks
www.nortel.com

In September of 1999, Nortel entered the second phase of its corporate marketing campaign, using print and TV advertising. The campaign asked such celebrities as runner Michael Johnson and guitar player Carlos Santana, "What do you want the Internet to be?" Sprinter Johnson described his vision of the Net as "Someone that can keep up with me." The ad then goes on to explain how Nortel can meet Johnson's needs, because its optical networks are "light-speed fast." The ads then encouraged everyone to respond to the question on the Nortel Web site. The question tapped people's dreams and visions for the future. Nortel estimates that it got 2000 responses to the campaign and that its Web site traffic has since increased by 20 percent each month.

Nortel's strategy and marketing, however, don't depend just on traditional methods like TV spots or banner ads on the Web. You'll see some Nortel banner ads, but only a few, and they're carefully tracked for effectiveness. Nortel also builds its brand through a variety of tactics, from product placement on TV shows to sponsorship of car racing to ingredient marketing with its "Powered by Nortel Networks" logo. However, while the first phase of Web marketing was about creating awareness, the next phase of Internet marketing is about customer loyalty.

Part of the secret of having loyal customers is always offering them leading-edge products. Thus, Nortel invests heavily in research and development. It has a network in 17 different countries of research and development facilities, affiliated joint ventures, and other collaborations that foster innovative product development. Nortel Networks also operates world-class manufacturing plants in the United States, the United Kingdom, Canada, France, Mexico, Brazil, Turkey, and the Republic of Ireland.

Despite its market dominance and strong strategic planning, Nortel was unable to foresee the events that overtook it in 2001. A sharp downturn in the US, Asian and European economies caused many companies to delay previously planned capital expenditures. Stock analysts became increasingly sceptical about the soundness of investments in the technology sector of the stock market and John Roth, Nortel's CEO, suddenly announced his retirement. As a result, Nortel's sales plummeted, its earnings fell below earlier projections and workers were laid off. Its stock price took a roller-coaster ride that made both Canadian and global investors turn green. Yet, in the face of such turmoil, Nortel continued to unveil new high-performance networking solutions designed to help its customers maximize their profitability, reduce their network costs and increase their employee productivity. Can Nortel recover at Net speed? No one knows, but the strength of good strategy is being able to respond and remain flexible in the face of market adversity.[1]

All companies must look ahead and develop long-term strategies to meet the changing conditions in their industries. Each company must identify the game plan that makes the most sense, given its specific situation, opportunities, objectives, and resources. The difficult task of selecting an overall company strategy for long-run survival and growth is called strategic planning.

In this chapter, we look first at the organization's overall strategic planning. Next, we discuss marketing's role in the organization, as it is defined by the overall strategic plan. Finally, we explain the marketing management process—the process that marketers undertake to carry out their role in the organization.

Strategic Planning

Many companies operate without formal plans. In new companies, managers are sometimes so busy that they have no time for planning. In small companies, managers sometimes think that only large corporations need formal planning. In mature companies, many managers argue that they have done well without formal planning and that, therefore, it cannot be too important. They may resist taking the time to prepare a written plan. They may argue that the marketplace changes too quickly for a plan to be useful, that it would end up collecting dust.

Granted, planning is not much fun, and it takes time away from doing. Yet companies must plan. As Philip Kotler said, "If you fail to plan, you are planning to fail." Formal planning can yield many benefits for all types of companies, large and small, new and mature.

The process of planning may be as important as the plans that emerge. Planning encourages management to think systematically about what has happened, what is happening, and what might happen. It forces the company to sharpen its objectives and policies, leads to better coordination of company efforts, and provides clearer performance standards for control. The argument that planning is less useful in a fast-changing environment makes little sense. In fact, the opposite is true: Sound planning helps the company to anticipate and respond quickly to changes and to prepare better for sudden developments. Thus, planning turns out to be an essential part of good management.

Strategic planning
The process of developing and maintaining a strategic fit between the organization's goals and capabilities and its changing marketing opportunities.

Strategic business unit (SBU)
A unit of the company that has a separate mission and objectives and that can be planned independently from other company businesse.

We define **strategic planning** as the process of developing and maintaining a strategic fit between the organization's goals and capabilities and its changing marketing opportunities. There are various types of strategic plans that are developed to guide different levels of business. Since many firms are diversified and compete in multiple markets, they organize themselves into strategic business units. A **strategic business unit** (SBU) is an identifiable unit within a larger company with its own profit and loss responsibility. An SBU may have one or more divisions and product lines. For example, Bayer AG, the giant German chemical company, operates in six major sectors. In the health-related products sector, it has six SBUs: ethical products, self-medication, consumer products, diagnostic products, hospital products, and biotechnological products.

Given that Bayer operates a number of business units in six industry sectors, Bayer has a complex portfolio of businesses to manage. Thus, its strategic plan-

Corporate strategic planning
Setting the mission for the firm as a whole.

ning takes place at different levels of the organization.[2] It does **corporate strategic planning.** This plan sets the mission for the firm as a whole and addresses two major questions: What businesses should we be in? And how should these businesses be integrated?

Business unit strategy
Strategy that determines how the unit will compete in its business and how it will position itself among its competitors.

Strategies are also developed by each business unit. While the corporate strategy is the glue that holds the firm together, the **business unit strategy** determines how the unit will compete in its given business and how it will position itself among its competitors. The business unit strategy maps out resource allocation decisions among the different business functions as well as the best means of integrating the various functions. For example, it determines the proportion of resources going to such things as research and development, product design, operations, human resources, information technology, and marketing.

Functional strategy
Strategy that deals with questions of how the function can best support the business unit strategy.

Finally, each functional area (marketing, human resources, operations, and so on) within each business unit develops its own **functional strategy.** Functional strategies deal with questions of how the function can best support the business unit strategy. For example, if the business unit strategy sets an objective of gaining market share in its business arena, then the marketing strategy will outline the various action plans needed to help the business achieve its aim. It might describe how improvements in product quality, additional channels of delivery such as the Internet, and a new communication campaign will help the unit achieve its objective.

Figure 2-1 shows the steps in strategic planning and the relationship between the corporate, strategic business unit and marketing plans. Corporate strategic planning sets the stage for the rest of the firm's planning efforts. The corporate plan contains a clear statement of the company's mission. This mission then is turned into detailed supporting objectives that guide the whole company. Next, headquarters decides what portfolio of businesses and products is best for the company and how much support to give each. In turn, each business and product unit must develop detailed marketing and other departmental plans that support the company-wide plan. Thus, marketing planning occurs at the business unit, product, and market levels. It supports company strategic planning with more detailed planning for specific marketing opportunities.[3]

Strategic Planning and Small Business

Many discussions of strategic planning focus on large corporations with many divisions and products. However, small businesses also can benefit greatly from sound strategic planning. Whereas most small ventures start out with extensive business and marketing plans to attract potential investors, strategic planning often falls by the wayside once the business gets going. Entrepreneurs and presidents of small companies are more likely to spend their time "putting out fires" than planning. But what does a small firm do when it finds that it has taken on too much debt, when its growth is exceeding production capacity, or when it's losing market share to a competitor with lower prices? Strategic planning can help small business managers anticipate such situations and determine how to prevent or handle them. The King's Medical Company example and Marketing Highlight 2-1 illustrate how small companies have used very simple strategic planning tools to chart their course.

FIGURE 2-1 Steps in strategic planning

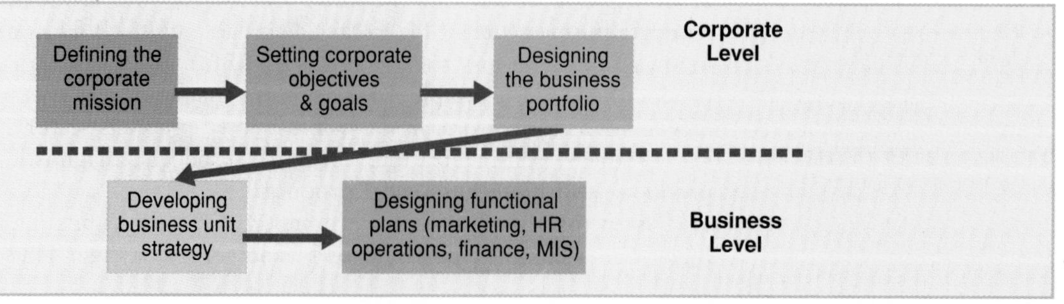

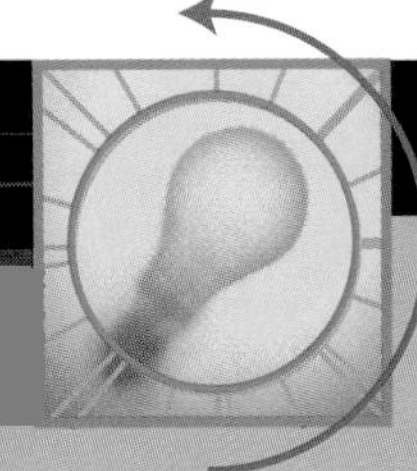

marketing highlight 2-1

Strategic Planning for Small Business Growth

Small businesses are responsible for much of the growth in the Canadian business sector. In recognition of this trend, the Canadian government has begun to focus more on helping entrepreneurs. *A Guide for Canadian Small Business* can be found on the Internet (www.rc.gc.ca). As a recent article on Canada's best-managed private companies noted, strategic planning is as important for small, private firms as it is for their much larger rivals. "We found that the winning companies all have a clear vision and a strategic direction . . . they were always focused. They recognize that they have a competitive advantage and are exploiting it." Two other factors—communicating corporate vision and enhancing employee morale—added to their success. The strategies of many small Canadian businesses are illustrated in the video cases that follow each chapter. Examples of other award-winning small Canadian businesses are given below.

Sabian Ltd.
Meductic, New Brunswick

Business: Musical cymbals

Employees: 100

Annual sales: $20 million

Forty percent of the cymbals sold around the world come from this small company located in New Brunswick. Its big-name clients include Big Sugar, Phil Collins, Elton John, Eric Clapton, and the Red Hot Chili Peppers. In fact, watch Big Sugar's video for the song "Diggin' a Hole," and you can see the Sabian brand name on the drummer's cymbal. The firm is highly focused and makes six different series of cymbals, which are exported to more than 95 countries. Knowing the market and the customer for this specialized product is at the heart of the company's strategy. The company must be highly customer focused since, according to company president Bill Jildjian, "Each musician decides which product is best suited to expressing him- or herself. In that respect it's more of a collaboration than a business deal."

Source: "Banging the drum in New Brunswick," *Financial Post*, 14 December 1996:42.

Cirque du Soleil
Montreal, Quebec

Business: Entertainment

Employees: 2100

Annual sales: $150 million

Through a series of five-year plans, Cirque du Soleil (www.cirquedusoleil.com), which was founded in 1984, transformed itself from a small group of street performers into a world renowned entertainment company. Cirque du Soleil began in 1984 by holding 50 performances viewed by 30 000 spectators. In 2000, that had grown to over 3000 performances, seen by more than six million. Since its beginnings, Cirque du Soleil has put on 15 000 performances, with a total audience in excess of 29 million.

The first years focused on issues of survival. Since there was no circus tradition in Canada, it had to build demand for its services from the ground up. Certainly, few Canadians thought of the circus as artistic, so the group had to carefully position the company in the minds of Canadians. Then, Cirque du Soleil began to develop five-year plans in 1989, only five years after its inception. The first plan outlined strategies for market expansion into Europe, Japan, and the United States. The second plan focused on the development of permanent venues for the circus, such as the ones now in place in Las Vegas and Disney World.

Source: "Balancing act finds its place in the sun," *Financial Post*, 14 December 1996:14; www.cirquedusoleil.com.

Mascoll Beauty Supply Ltd.
Toronto, Ontario

Business: Beauty products for African-Canadians

Employees: 25

Annual sales: Unknown

Beverley Mascoll established her business with $700, an idea, industry experience, and the trunk of her car. Beginning her firm with one product line—a hair relaxer she packaged at her kitchen table—she has developed her company into one that now sells over 3000 items. From the earliest days, she understood the power of niche marketing based on personal service. She offered a unique benefit in Canada. No other company was marketing beauty products designed specifically for individuals of African descent. Yet, Mascoll knew that black women spend six times more on hair care and cosmetics than do Caucasian women. Furthermore, they don't scrimp on these products, even when times are bad. Consequently, she discovered a recession-proof business. She also found a market where she could ride a growth wave.

When she started her business, fewer than 50 000 people of African descent lived in Canada. Since then, that number has grown ten-fold. Mascoll also understood that few beauticians knew how to treat "black hair." Thus, part of her strategy was to train her customers. She brought the hottest styles to Canada and invited people to their demonstrations,

thereby creating demand for her products. Today, Mascoll is not only successful, but also dedicated to giving back to her community. She has worked with Dalhousie University in Halifax to establish the first black history professorship chair in Canada and recently founded the Beverley Mascoll Community Foundation, a philanthropic organization that offers scholarships to deserving students, supports community work, and funds a summer camp for sick children.

Source: Margaret Cannon, "Looking good, doing good," *Report on Business*, December 1996:99–104.

Smart Technologies Inc.
Calgary, Alberta

Business: Interactive whiteboards

Employees: 100

Annual sales: $10 million

If your university is upgrading its classrooms to meet the needs of the electronic age, you will see Smart Technologies products becoming part of the classroom setting. Interactive electronic whiteboards allow users in classrooms or boardrooms to access and display information from the Internet, run video and CD-ROM presentations, or demonstrate spreadsheets in real time. They allow multiple sites to work from the same information display. In New Brunswick, students at 90 remote sites can participate in lectures. Nova Corporation of Alberta uses the technology to train its employees at 12 locations. Smart Technologies had great strategic insight about how a new market would evolve. With the costs of corporate travel rising rapidly, management believed that more and more meetings would be conducted without people flying to different locations to meet in person. Another key to the firm's strategy is forming partnerships with such firms as Intel and PictureTel Corporation, which have about half the global market for video-conferencing systems.

Source: "Magic moment in Vegas," *Financial Post*, 14 December 1996:46; smartdna.com.

The following steps summarize the process by which the small firms described above create their strategic plan, from which a number of department and individual employee plans follow. The process hinges on an assessment of the company, its place in the market, and its goals.

1. Identify the major elements of the business environment in which the organization has operated over the previous few years.
2. Describe the mission of the organization in terms of its nature and function for the next two years.
3. Explain the internal and external forces that will affect the mission of the organization.
4. Identify the basic driving force that will direct the organization in the future.
5. Develop a set of long-term objectives that will identify what the organization will become in the future.
6. Outline a general plan of action that defines the logistical, financial, and personnel factors needed to integrate the long-term objectives into the total organization.

Sources: Leslie Brokaw, "The secrets of great planning," *Inc.*, October 1992:152; Philip Kotler, *Marketing Management*, 10th ed., Upper Saddle River: Prentice Hall, 2000.

King's Medical Company provides an example of how one small company uses very simple strategic planning tools to chart its course every three years. King's Medical owns and manages magnetic resonance imaging (MRI) equipment—million-dollar-plus machines that produce X-ray-type pictures. Strategic planning has been the key to this small company's very rapid growth and high profit margins. As the company's owner claimed: "A lot of literature says there are three critical issues to a small company: cash flow, cash flow, cash flow. I agree those issues are critical, but so are three more: planning, planning, planning." King's Medical's planning process, which hinges on an assessment of the company, its place in the market, and its goals, includes the following steps:[4]

1. Identify the major elements of the business environment in which the organization has operated over the past few years.
2. Describe the mission of the organization in terms of its nature and function for the next two years.
3. Explain the internal and external forces that will have an impact on the mission of the organization.
4. Identify the basic driving force that will direct the organization in the future.
5. Develop a set of long-term objectives that will identify what the organization will become in the future.
6. Outline a general plan of action that defines the logistical, financial, and personnel factors needed to integrate the long-term objectives into the total organization.

Small, single-unit businesses will have only a corporate strategic plan and functional plans. Larger, multi-unit businesses will have a corporate plan, plans for each business unit, and plans for each functional unit. These different types of planning efforts are described in the next sections.

Corporate Strategic Planning

Defining the Company Mission

An organization exists to accomplish something. At first, it has a clear purpose or mission, but over time, its mission may become unclear as the organization grows and adds new products and markets or faces new conditions in the environment. When management senses that the organization is drifting, it must renew its search for purpose. It is time to ask: What is our business? Who is the customer? What do consumers value? What will our business be? What should our business be? These simple-sounding questions are among the most difficult the company will ever have to answer. Successful companies continuously raise these questions and answer them carefully and completely.

Mission statement
A statement of the organization's purpose—what it wants to accomplish in the larger environment.

Many organizations develop formal mission statements that answer these questions. A **mission statement** articulates the organization's purpose—what it wants to accomplish in the larger environment. A clear mission statement acts as an "invisible hand" that guides people in the organization so that they can work independently and yet collectively toward overall organizational goals. It also helps employees understand the values of the firm and sets ethical guidelines for both organizational and marketing behaviour. The public is increasingly demanding that companies adopt socially responsible behaviour. The ability of some firms, such as Loblaws, The Body Shop, and Mountain Equipment Co-op, to align ethical values with corporate missions has led them to be regarded with increased goodwill by many consumers.

Traditionally, companies have defined their businesses in product terms ("We manufacture furniture") or in technological terms ("We are a chemical-processing firm"). But mission statements should be *market-oriented* (see Marketing Highlight 2-2). Products and technologies eventually become outdated, but basic market needs

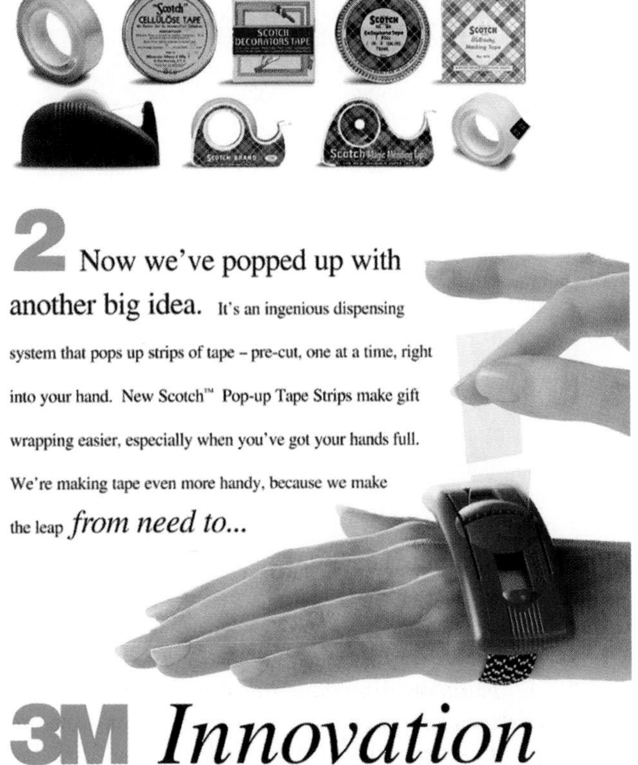

1 We've been on a roll for 67 years.
2 Now we've popped up with another big idea. It's an ingenious dispensing system that pops up strips of tape – pre-cut, one at a time, right into your hand. New Scotch™ Pop-up Tape Strips make gift wrapping easier, especially when you've got your hands full. We're making tape even more handy, because we make the leap from need to...
3M Innovation
© 3M 1997 78-6900-8329-6(1171)ii
For more information, call 1-800-3M-HELPS, or Internet: http://www.3M.com

Company mission: 3M does more than just make adhesives, scientific equipment, health care, and communications products. It solves people's problems by putting innovation to work for them.

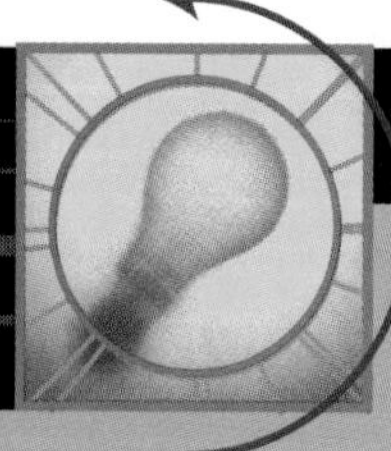

marketing highlight 2-2

IBM: Big Blue Dinosaur or E-Business Animal?

Only a decade ago, if you'd asked top managers at IBM what business they were in, they might well have answered, "We sell computer hardware and software." Labouring under a bad case of marketing myopia, a heavily product-focused IBM lost sight of its customers' needs. As a result, as customer needs changed, IBM didn't, and its fortunes slipped accordingly. By the early 1990s, "Big Blue's" market share and stock price were falling rapidly.

Since those sadly blue days, however, IBM has undergone a remarkable transformation. The turnaround started in 1993, when new CEO Lou Gerstner brought a renewed customer focus to IBM. As one of his first acts, Gerstner asked all top IBM managers to meet face-to-face with important customers—what he called "bear-hugging customers"—and report back concerning their problems and priorities. Gerstner and his managers learned that corporate computing is getting more and more confusing for customers. In this new high-tech, connected age, companies must master a dizzying array of information technologies to serve not only their customers but also their suppliers, distributors, and employees.

Gerstner realized that in this more complex computing world, customers are buying much more from IBM than just computer hardware and software. They are buying solutions to ever-more bewildering information technology (IT) problems. This realization led to a fundamental redefinition of IBM's business. Now, if you ask almost any IBM manager to define the business, they will tell you, "We deliver solutions to customers' information technology problems."

Most customers don't really care whose hardware or software they buy. As one customer noted, "I often don't know if I need hardware or software or services, and I don't care." What draws him to IBM is that Big Blue employs an unmatched breadth of products, people, and services to deliver an IT system that works. "I don't view IBM as a hardware vendor anymore," he says. "I think of them as an information technology [partner] that can help me in a number of different ways."

The new customer-solutions focus has greatly promoted the role of services relative to hardware and software in the IBM mix. The company now offers an expanded set of IT consulting, total systems management, strategic outsourcing, and e-business services that can help customers with everything from assessing, planning, designing, implementing, and running their IT systems to bringing them up to speed on e-commerce. Some companies, such as Eastman Kodak and Hertz, have outsourced their entire IT systems to IBM. In such deals, IBM runs the whole IT show—the customer's IT employees work for IBM, and IBM owns the customer's computers, which it then manages.

Services are now IBM's hottest growth area, accounting for almost 30 percent of the company's more than $120 billion in sales and 39 percent of its profits. Analysts predict that services will generate almost half of IBM's revenues by 2003. As one IBM watcher comments, "IBM—International Business Machines—is becoming IBS, where 'S' is for services, software, and solutions."

Still, few people realize that IBM is the world's largest supplier of IT services. To help change this perception, its Web site provides case studies outlining how IBM e-services have helped both firms and government find solutions to their problems. IBM also launched a $110 million global services ad campaign with the tag line "People Who Think. People Who Do. People Who Get It." To counter the out-of-date notion that IBM provides only computer hardware, the campaign profiles specific IBM people—the "strategists, problem solvers, implementers . . .

IBM
www.ibm.ca

may last forever. A market-oriented mission statement defines the business in terms of satisfying basic customer needs. Thus, Cantel is in the communications business, not the telephone business. 3M does more than just make adhesives, scientific equipment, and health-care products; it solves people's problems by putting innovation to work for them. Chapters Online Inc. sees itself not as a book company, but as a Canadian e-commerce company that serves as a *destination* for online shoppers. By building relationships with its customers, Chapters.ca can serve a variety of their online shopping needs—everything from books to gardening items in a secure, high-service environment. Table 2-1 provides several other examples of product-oriented versus market-oriented business definitions.

Management should avoid making its mission too narrow or too broad. A pencil manufacturer that says it is in the communication equipment business is stating its mission too broadly. Missions should be realistic—Singapore Airlines would be deluding itself if it adopted the mission to become the world's largest airline.

Missions should also be specific. Many mission statements are written for public relations purposes and lack specific, workable guidelines. The statement "We want to become the leading company in this industry by producing the highest-quality products with the best service at the lowest prices" sounds good, but it is full of general-who make sure that the solution you want is the solution you get." One ad showcases Nick Simicich, an IBM ethical hacker (unofficial title: "paid professional paranoid") who purposely invades customers' critical information systems to see if they're safe from more hostile hackers. According to an executive at IBM's advertising agency, the message is simple: "IBM has people who [can help you] excel in e-business and consulting, business recovery, and network systems management."

In this latest phase of its customer-solutions makeover, IBM is positioning itself as the "e-business solutions company." (It has coined e-business as a catch-all term for Internet, intranet, and e-commerce applications.) As more and more companies use the Internet as their primary connecting technology, e-business is growing explosively. IBM wants to be the company others turn to for e-business strategies and solutions.

In 1999, IBM introduced 20 new e-business services, including customer relationship management, business intelligence, supply chain management, and business process management services. Big Blue claims to have 10 000 e-business customers. For some, this means little more than having IBM host their Web sites on one of its servers. For others, it means having IBM create and implement a totally new business–customer connection. For example, the Canadian Intellectual Property Office selected IBM Global Services to help it move from a traditional paper-based process to one that is Web-enabled. Today, Canadians can access patent documents online. This not only reduces processing time, but it also gives the public better access to information it needs.

IBM defines its business as delivering solutions to customers' e-business problems. Nick Simicich, an IBM "ethical hacker" and "paid professional paranoid," helps protect customers' information systems against hackers.

E-business appears to be an ideal setting for IBM's soup-to-nuts menu of IT solutions. Over one-quarter of IBM's revenues now come from e-business products and services. Moreover, IBM appears to be capturing the minds of e-business customers as well as their purchases. As a result of both its e-business deeds and millions of dollars spent on worldwide advertising proclaiming its e-business prowess, IBM appears to own a major portion of the e-business position. In recent surveys, customers associated IBM with e-business seven times more than any of its competitors.

Thus, in a remarkably short time, IBM has transformed itself from a company that "sells computer hardware and software" to one that "delivers customer IT solutions." It's not the old IBM anymore, and the marketplace has responded strongly. Over the past four years, IBM has experienced steady sales growth, rapidly improving profits, and a five-fold increase in its stock price. By defining itself in terms of the customer needs it serves rather than the products it sells, IBM has been transformed "from a big blue dinosaur to an e-business animal."

Sources: Quotes from David Kirkpatrick, "IBM: From big blue dinosaur to e-business animal," *Fortune,* 26 April 1999:116–25; Laura Loro, "IBM touts position as No. 1 in IT services," *Advertising Age's Business Marketing,* April 1999:41. Also see www.ibm.ca; Bruce Caldwell, "IBM defines a concept while redefining itself," *Information Week,* 6 July 1998:74–5; Richard R. Rogoski, "Big Blue focuses initiative on improving e-commerce," *Triangle Business Journal,* 22 January 1999:31; Bradley Johnson, "IBM pushes the limits of business on the Internet," *Advertising Age,* 3 May 1999:S2, S10; and Ira Sager, "Big Blue at your service," *Business Week,* 21 June 1999:130–2.

ities and contradictions. Celestial Seasonings' mission statement is very specific: "Our mission is to grow and dominate the specialty tea market by exceeding consumer expectations with: The best-tasting, 100 percent natural hot and iced teas, packaged with Celestial art and philosophy, creating the most valued tea experience."[5]

Missions should fit the market environment. The organization should base its mission on its distinctive competencies. McDonald's could probably enter the solar energy business, but that would not take advantage of its core competence—providing low-cost food and fast service to large groups of customers.

Finally, mission statements should be motivating. A company's mission should not be stated as making more sales or profits—profits are only a reward for undertaking a useful activity. One recent study found that "visionary companies" set a purpose beyond making money. For example, the Walt Disney Company's aim is "making people happy." A company's employees need to feel that their work is significant and that it contributes to people's lives. Andyne Computing Limited, one of Canada's most successful software companies, captures its aspirations for the future in its mission statement: "Our mission is to be a world leader in providing information access and decision support for informed business decisions."[6]

TABLE 2-1 Market-Oriented Business Definitions

Company	Product-Oriented Definition	Market-Oriented Definition
M·A·C Cosmetics	We make cosmetics	We sell lifestyle and self-expression; tolerance of diversity, and a platform for the outrageous
Disney	We run theme parks and make films	We provide fantasies and entertainment
Zellers	We run discount stores	We offer products and services that deliver superior value to Canadians
Xerox	We make copying, fax, and other office machines	We make businesses more productive by helping them scan, store, retrieve, revise, distribute, print, and publish documents
Canadian Tire	We sell tools and home improvement items	We provide advice and solutions that transform ham-handed people into Mr. and Ms. Fixits

Designing the Business Portfolio

Business portfolio
The collection of businesses and products that comprise the company.

Guided by the company's mission statement and objectives, corporate strategic planners must plan its **business portfolio**—the collection of businesses and products that the company comprises. The best business portfolio is the one that best fits the company's strengths and weaknesses to opportunities in the environment. The company must analyze its current business portfolio and decide which businesses should receive more, less, or no investment, and develop growth strategies for adding new products or businesses to the portfolio.

Analyzing the Current Business Portfolio

Portfolio analysis
A tool that management uses to identify and evaluate the various businesses that make up the company.

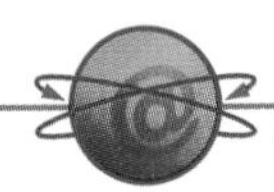

John Labatt Ltd.
www.labatt.ca

The major activity in strategic planning is business **portfolio analysis,** whereby management evaluates the businesses that make up the company. The company will want to put strong resources into its more profitable businesses and phase down or drop its weaker ones. For example, in recent years, John Labatt Ltd. has strengthened its portfolio by selling off its less attractive businesses, including food products (Ault Foods, Catelli-Primo Ltd., Johanna Dairies, and Everfresh Juice Co.) as well as its profitable Sports Network, to invest more heavily in products and technologies for its brewing business. Such tactics provided Labatt with the resources to develop its ice beer. The company benefited in two ways from this product launch: It was able to license the technology in foreign markets such as the United States, Europe, Japan, and Mexico, while also improving its market position in Canada.

The purpose of corporate strategic planning is to identify ways in which the company can best use its strengths to take advantage of attractive opportunities in the environment. Management's first step is to identify the key businesses—the strategic business units—making up the company. The next step is to evaluate each of the SBUs on two important dimensions—the attractiveness of the SBU's market or industry and the strength of the SBU's position in that market or industry. This analysis helps corporate planners decide how much support each deserves. In some companies, this is done informally. Other companies use formal portfolio-planning methods. One of the best-known portfolio-planning methods was developed by the Boston Consulting Group, a leading management consulting firm.

Growth–share matrix
A portfolio-planning method that evaluates a company's strategic business units in terms of their market growth rate and relative market share.

The Boston Consulting Group Approach

Using the Boston Consulting Group (BCG) approach, a company classifies all of its SBUs or products according to the **growth–share matrix** shown in Figure 2-2. On the vertical axis, market growth rate provides a measure of market attrac-

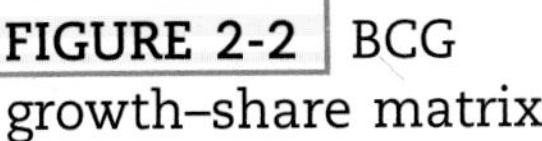

FIGURE 2-2 BCG growth–share matrix

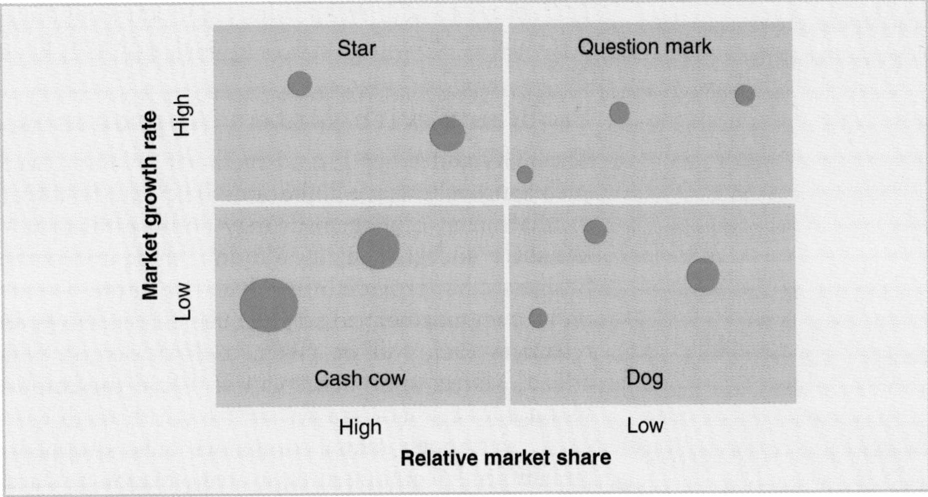

tiveness. On the horizontal axis, relative market share serves as a measure of company strength in the market. By dividing the growth–share matrix as indicated, four types of SBUs can be distinguished:

- **Stars.** Stars are high-growth, high-share businesses or products. They often need heavy investment to finance their rapid growth. Eventually their growth will slow down, and they will turn into cash cows.
- **Cash cows.** Cash cows are low-growth, high-share businesses or products. These established and successful SBUs need less investment to hold their market share. Thus, they produce a lot of cash that the company uses to pay its bills and to support other SBUs that need investment.
- **Question marks.** Question marks are low-share business units in high-growth markets. They require a lot of cash to hold their share, let alone increase it. Management has to think hard about which question marks it should try to build into stars and which should be phased out.
- **Dogs.** Dogs are low-growth, low-share businesses and products. They may generate enough cash to maintain themselves, but do not promise to be large sources of cash.

The 10 circles in the growth–share matrix represent a company's 10 current SBUs. The company has two stars, two cash cows, three question marks, and three dogs. The areas of the circles are proportional to the SBU's dollar sales. This company is in fair shape, although not in good shape. It wants to invest in the more promising question marks to make them stars, and to maintain the stars so that they will become cash cows as their markets mature. Fortunately, it has two good-sized cash cows whose income helps finance the company's question marks, stars, and dogs. The company should take decisive action concerning its dogs and its question marks. The picture would be worse if the company had no stars, if it had too many dogs, or if it had only one weak cash cow.

Once it has classified its SBUs, the company must determine what role each will play in the future. It can pursue one of four strategies for each SBU. The company can invest more in the business unit to build its share. It can invest just enough to hold the SBU's share at the current level. It can harvest the SBU, milking its short-term cash flow regardless of the long-term effect. Or it can divest the SBU by selling it or phasing it out and using the resources elsewhere.

As time passes, SBUs change their positions in the growth–share matrix. Each SBU has a life cycle. Many SBUs start out as question marks and move into the star category if they succeed. They later become cash cows, as market growth falls, then finally die off or turn into dogs toward the end of their life cycle. The company needs to add new products and units continuously so that some will become stars and, eventually, cash cows that will help finance other SBUs.

Problems with Matrix Approaches

The BCG and other formal methods revolutionized strategic planning. However, such approaches have limitations. They can be difficult, time consuming, and costly to implement. Management may find it difficult to define SBUs and measure market share and growth. In addition, these approaches focus on classifying current businesses but provide little advice for future planning. Management must still rely on its own judgment to set the business objectives for each SBU, to determine what resources each will be given, and to identify which new businesses should be added. Matrix approaches can also lead the company to place too much emphasis on market-share growth or growth through entry into attractive new markets.

Even though many companies have dropped formal matrix methods, they remain firmly committed to strategic planning. During the 1970s, many companies embraced high-level corporate strategy planning as a kind of magical path to growth and profits. By the 1980s, however, such strategic planning took a back seat to cost and efficiency concerns, as companies struggled to become more competitive through improved quality, restructuring, downsizing, and re-engineering. Recently, strategic planning has made a strong comeback. However, unlike former strategic-planning efforts, which rested mostly in the hands of senior managers, today's strategic planning has been decentralized. Companies are moving responsibility for strategic planning out of company headquarters and placing it in the hands of cross-functional teams of line and staff managers who are close to their markets. Some teams even include customers and suppliers in their strategic-planning processes.[7]

Developing Growth Strategies in the Age of Connectedness

Beyond evaluating current businesses, designing the business portfolio involves finding businesses and products that the company should consider in the future. Companies need growth if they are to compete more effectively, satisfy their stakeholders, and attract top talent. "Growth is pure oxygen," states one executive. "It creates a vital, enthusiastic corporation where people see genuine opportunity. . . . In that way, growth is more than our single most important financial driver; it's an essential part of our corporate culture." At the same time, a firm must be careful not to make growth itself an objective. The company's objective must be "profitable growth."

Marketing has the main responsibility for achieving profitable growth for the company. Marketing must identify, evaluate, and select market opportunities and lay down strategies for capturing them. One useful device for identifying growth opportunities is the *product–market expansion grid,*[8] shown in Figure 2-3. We apply it here to Tim Hortons, one of Canada's dominant food service retailers (see Marketing Highlight 2-3).

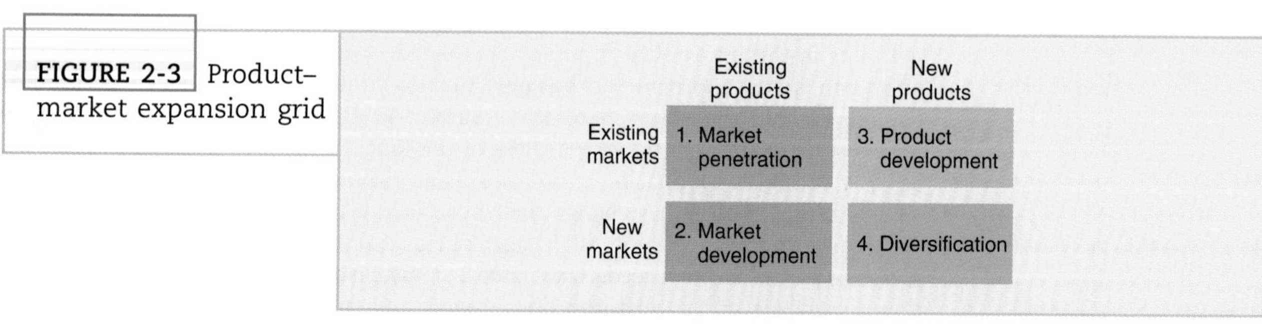

FIGURE 2-3 Product–market expansion grid

marketing highlight 2-3

Tim Hortons: Where Things Are Really Perking

Canadians, it appears, *always have time for Tim Hortons.* Generations of competitors have come and gone, but none have managed to defeat "Hortons," headquartered in Oakville, Ontario. In fact, it has become a Canadian icon. The doughnut chain's long-running "Roll up the Rim to Win" promotion has become a beloved part of Canadian slang, and scenes at the Hortons are shown weekly on comedy news show *Air Farce.* The dominance of the chain can be seen in these facts: One of every three cups of coffee sold in Canada comes from Tim Hortons, and each and every day Canadians dunk over three million doughnuts. It is one of Canada's largest employers, with over 42 000 people on the payroll. The firm has been remarkably successful over the last few years. Sales increased by 10.4 percent in 1998, on top of an eight percent increase a year earlier.

As impressive as these figures are, one has to wonder how Tim Hortons has achieved this success, offering such standard products as coffee and baked goods. Hortons' strategy is deceptively simple. First, it has followed one consistent product and positioning strategy throughout its history. Its promise of "Always Fresh" is never broken. Next, it builds outlets in focal areas until they reach a large enough critical mass to justify advertising. As Patti Jameson, director of corporate communications, notes, "Advertising is a lot more relevant to people when they actually see the stores on the street." Having the physical presence of a retail outlet made brand messages more relevant and meaningful.

Hortons spends about $3 million a year on advertising, and the tool has been an important weapon in its growth strategy. Throughout much of the 1990s, the chain's ads focused on its new products—bagels, sandwiches, and soup—to get consumers to see Tim Hortons as more than a doughnut shop. New products also increased revenues for both the corporation and its franchisees. Advertising also served to build the brand message that Hortons is "relaxed, caring, friendly and honest."

To further strengthen the equity of the brand, "feel-good advertising" followed the more traditional product advertising. The "True Stories" campaign (by Toronto agency Enterprise Advertising), which was launched in 1997, worked to build an emotional connection between Hortons and its customers. For example, musician Natalie MacMaster told viewers about her first cup of coffee—from Tim Hortons, of course. Another ad featured the crew of the *HMCS Toronto* and described how much they missed Tim's coffee while they were stationed in the Persian Gulf. Another ad even featured a four-legged customer, Sammi, a golden retriever, who picks up her owner's coffee from the drive-through.

Given Tim Hortons' track record, it's hard to imagine how it could expand any further (if your town is anything like mine). There seems to be an outlet on the corner of every major intersection. This is not surprising, given that the chain boasts over 1700 Canadian outlets. Yet even an institution needs to be willing to change and grow. And change is exactly what Hortons has done in recent years. In a bid to broaden its appeal and attract more women and young people, the chain has recently branched out into new product lines, such as iced cappuccino. It also retooled its lunchtime offerings last fall, offering Tim's Own brand of soups and sandwiches.

The firm isn't about to stop there. Tim Hortons plans to open between 170 and 175 new locations across Canada in the near future. It is also using the clout of its partner–owner, Wendy's, to tap into the US market. Since Hortons believes that the breakfast category is underdeveloped in the US and that Americans are poorly served by current "morning destinations," it sees tremendous opportunity south of the border. "In the U.S, they don't have high expectations for morning destinations. . . . People will grab a coffee from a gas station in the morning, [but] we're promising that consistent experience. No one else is really doing everyday morning coffee and baked goods very well." Two television spots and a series of radio ads each will portray Tim Hortons as the real reason morning people are so chipper. The tag line is: "Morning people. Where do they

Tim Hortons doesn't advertise until it has enough outlets in a region to justify the expense. It knows advertising has more impact when people can see its outlets in their daily travels.

come from?" While success in the highly competitive US market is far from guaranteed, if the history of professional hockey offers any indication, then Americans may also soon be claiming this Canadian institution as their own.

Sources: Natalie Bahadur, "Tim Hortons plans aggressive roll-out," *Strategy,* 29 March 1999:7; Lesley Daw, "More than just a doughnut shop," *Marketing Magazine On-line,* 20/27 December 1999; Scott Gardiner, "In praise of Saint Timmy," *Marketing Magazine On-line,* 21 August 2000; Laura Pratt, "Roll up the Rim major player for Tim Hortons," *Strategy,* 22 May 2000:22; Craig Saunders, "Tim Hortons issues wakeup call," *Strategy,* 14 February 2000:25; Sinclair Stewart, "Top client, retail–restaurants: Tim Hortons brews up fresh ideas," *Strategy,* 2 August 1999:7; Sinclair Stewart, "Tim Hortons brews new U.S. campaign," *Strategy,* 27 September 1999:3.

Market penetration
A strategy for company growth by increasing sales of current products to current market segments without changing the product in any way.

Tim Hortons' strategy is deceptively simple and has long been founded on **market penetration.** It works to open a critical mass of outlets in a pre-defined geographic region and then it supports them with advertising. Increased awareness and the building of strong brand equity in turn builds requests for new franchises—this is how Tim Hortons plans to continue expansion in both Quebec and western Canada. It also works to train people who come into Tim Hortons first thing in the morning for coffee and breakfast to return several times during the rest of the day. To that end, Hortons routinely upgrades and refurbishes its outlets, adding double drive-throughs and establishing satellite outlets in settings like hospitals and retail stores—bringing the restaurant to the consumer instead of the other way around. "Wherever you are," says one top manager, "there's a coffee and a donut waiting for you."

Product development
A strategy for company growth by offering modified or new products to current market segments.

Market development
A strategy for company growth by identifying and developing new market segments for current company products.

Diversification
A strategy for company growth by starting up or acquiring businesses outside the company's current products and markets.

Second, Tim Hortons' management focuses on **product development**—offering modified or new products to current markets. Hortons introduced bagels, sandwiches, and soup to get consumers to see it as more than a doughnut shop.

Third, the firm explores possibilities for **market development**—identifying and developing new markets for its current products. It has recently moved south of the border, opening 116 outlets in the northern United States.

Hortons could also consider **diversification.** It could start up or buy businesses outside of its current products and markets. For example, like Loblaws, it could begin offering financial services. It could leverage its strong brand name onto products like sportswear that fits with its friendly, relaxed image. However, it must take care: Companies that diversify too broadly into unfamiliar products or industries can lose their market focus.

Business Strategy

Corporations formulate business strategies to help them achieve their overall objectives as well as competitive advantage in their particular marketplaces. Monsanto, for example, operates in many businesses, including agriculture, pharmaceuticals, and food products. The corporation defines its mission as one of helping to feed the world's exploding population while also sustaining the environment. This mission leads to a hierarchy of business objectives to be achieved by its various units. Monsanto's overall objective is to create environmentally better products and get them to market faster at lower cost. For its part, the agricultural division's objective is to increase agricultural productivity and reduce chemical pollution by researching new pest- and disease-resistant crops that produce high yields without chemical spraying. But research is expensive and requires improved profits to plow back into research programs. So improving profits becomes another major business objective. Profits can be improved by increasing sales or reducing costs. Sales can be increased by improving the company's share of the domestic market, by entering new foreign markets, or both.

Topic: Working Together
CARING
ABOUT LIFE
IS ONE OF OUR
STRONGEST
INSTINCTS.
MONSANTO
Food • Health • Hope™

Monsanto defines its mission as one of "food, health, hope"—of helping to feed the world's exploding population while sustaining the environment. This mission leads to specific business and marketing objectives.

Competitive Position as a Determinant of Strategy and Profitability

The competitive strategy a business adopts and the success of that strategy depend on its position in an industry. Firms competing in a given industry or target market will, at any point in time, differ in their objectives and resources. Some firms will be large, others small. Some will strive for rapid market share growth, others for long-term profits. Some will have many resources, others will be strapped for funds. Some will be old and established, others new and fresh. Some firms will be acknowledged as leaders of their industry, while others will strive for this position. Others are content to follow the leader while the remainder work to carve out a protected market niche.

For market oriented firms, designing competitive business strategies often begins with a thorough competitor analysis. The company constantly compares the value and customer satisfaction delivered by its products, prices, channels, and promotion with that of its close competitors. In this way, it can discern areas of potential advantage and disadvantage. The company must formally or informally monitor the competitive environment to answer these and other important questions: Who are our competitors? What are their objectives and strategies? What are their strengths and weaknesses? And how will they react to different competitive strategies we might use? Competitive intelligence gathering will be discussed in Chapter 3.

A firm that dominates a market can adopt one or more of several market-leader strategies. Well-known leaders include Coca-Cola (soft drinks), McDonald's (fast food), Caterpillar (large construction equipment), Kodak (photographic film), Loblaws (grocery retailing), and Boeing (aircraft). Market challengers are runner-up companies that aggressively attack competitors to get more market share. For example, Pepsi challenges Coke, and Compaq challenges IBM. The challenger might attack the market leader, other firms of its size, or smaller local and regional competitors. Some runner-up firms will choose to follow rather than challenge the market leader. Firms using market-follower strategies seek stable market shares and profits by following competitors' product offers, prices, and marketing programs. Smaller firms in a market, or even larger firms that lack established positions, often adopt market-nicher strategies. These firms specialize in serving market niches that major competitors overlook or ignore (see Marketing Highlight 2-1). "Nichers" avoid direct confrontations with the majors by specializing along market, customer, product, or marketing-mix lines. Through smart niching, low-share firms in an industry can be as profitable as their larger competitors.

An SBU's position within the industry is another factor that influences its profitability. For example, the large firms that lead the industry have considerable buying power and clout with suppliers, so they can often negotiate the best prices for supplies and services. This superior buying power will improve their profitability. Market followers may not have to incur the costs of developing a market and educating consumers about the features and benefits of a new product, so they can sometimes have lower costs than leading edge firms.

Strategies for Strategic Business Units

Once an SBU thoroughly understands the implications of competitors' activities and its position in the marketplace, it must select a strategy that will help leverage its position. About two decades ago, Michael Porter suggested three winning strategies that businesses competing in a given industry could follow to achieve competitive advantage. Porter believed that SBU profitability was determined by both industry structure and by the strategies pursued by the different businesses in the industry.[9] The three winning strategies are:

Cost leadership
A volume-based strategy in which firms seek to exploit economies of scale to lower their costs. Having the lowest costs allows cost leadership firms to earn the highest margins at a given price for a good or service.

Differentiation
A strategy whereby firms leverage their skills in research, product development and marketing to offer distinctive products to the market at premium prices.

Focus
A strategy whereby a firm chooses to serve a small segment of the industry extremely well by focusing on either lower costs or differentiated products.

- **Overall cost leadership.** The SBU works hard to achieve the lowest costs of production and distribution so that it can price lower than its competitors and win a large market share. Texas Instruments and Wal-Mart are leading practitioners of this strategy.
- **Differentiation.** The company concentrates on creating a highly differentiated product line and marketing program so that it comes across as the class leader in the industry. Most customers would prefer to own this brand if its price is not too high. IBM and Caterpillar follow this strategy in computers and heavy construction equipment, respectively.
- **Focus.** The company focuses its effort on serving a few market segments well rather than going after the whole market. Thus, Mountain Equipment Co-op offers products only to outdoor enthusiasts who favour such non-motorized sports as rock climbing or kayaking rather than to a broader mix of people who enjoy such outdoor recreational activities as power boating or the use of all-terrain vehicles.

Companies that pursue a clear strategy—one of the above—are likely to perform well. The firm that carries out that strategy best will make the most profits. But firms that do not pursue a clear strategy—middle-of-the-roaders—do the worst. Sears, Chrysler, and International Harvester all encountered difficult times because they did not stand out as the lowest in cost, highest in perceived value, or best in serving some market segment. Middle-of-the-roaders try to be good on all strategic counts, but end up being not very good at anything.

More recently, marketing consultants Michael Treacy and Fred Wiersema offered a new classification of competitive marketing strategies.[10] They suggest that companies gain leadership positions by delivering superior value to their customers. Companies can pursue one of three strategies—called value disciplines—for delivering superior customer value:

Operational excellence The strategy of providing superior value by leading an industry in price and convenience.

- **Operational excellence:** The company provides superior value by leading its industry in price and convenience. It works to reduce costs and create a lean and efficient value delivery system. It serves customers who want reliable, good-quality products or services, but who want them inexpensively and easily. Examples include Dell Computer and Ikea.

Product leadership The strategy of providing superior value by offering a continuous stream of leading-edge products that make other products obsolete.

- **Product leadership:** The company provides superior value by offering a continuous stream of leading-edge products or services that make their own and competing products obsolete. It is open to new ideas, relentlessly pursues new solutions, and works to reduce cycle times so that it can get new products to market quickly. It serves customers who want state-of-the-art products and services, regardless of the costs in terms of price or inconvenience. Examples include Cognos and PeopleSoft.

Customer intimacy The strategy of providing superior value by precisely segmenting markets and then tailoring products to match exactly the needs of targeted customers.

- **Customer intimacy:** The company provides superior value by precisely segmenting its markets and then tailoring its products or services to match exactly the needs of targeted customers. It builds detailed customer databases for segmenting and targeting, and empowers its marketing people to respond quickly to customer needs. It serves customers who are willing to pay a premium to get precisely what they want, and it will do almost anything to build long-term customer loyalty and to capture customer lifetime value. Examples include Quarry Integrated Communications (located in Kitchener-Waterloo) and McKinsey Management Consultants.

Some companies successfully pursue more than one value discipline at the same time. For example, Federal Express excels at both operational excellence and customer intimacy. However, such companies are rare—few firms can be the best at more than one of these disciplines. By trying to be good at all of the value disciplines, a company usually ends up being best at none.

Treacy and Wiersema found that leading companies focus on and excel at a single value discipline, while meeting industry standards on the other two. They design their entire value delivery system to single-mindedly support the chosen discipline. For example, Wal-Mart knows that customer intimacy and product leadership are important. Compared with other discounters, it offers very good customer service and an excellent product assortment. Still, it offers less customer service and less depth in its product assortment than specialty and department stores that pursue customer intimacy or product leadership strategies. Instead, it focuses obsessively on operational excellence—on reducing costs and streamlining its order-to-delivery process to make it convenient for customers to buy just the right products at the lowest prices.

Classifying competitive strategies as value disciplines is appealing. It defines marketing strategy in terms of the single-minded pursuit of delivering value to customers. It recognizes that management must align every aspect of the company

Our produce manager, Saturday night.
We're fresh obsessed.

Dominion uses this ad to position itself as a product leader on the fresh food aisle.

with the chosen value discipline—from its culture, to its organization structure, to its operating and management systems and processes. This customer value focus has motivated firms to go one step further and form long-term relationships with their key customers.

Customer Relationship Marketing

Traditional marketing theory and practice have focused on attracting new customers rather than retaining existing ones. Today, however, although attracting new customers remains an important marketing task, the emphasis has shifted toward relationship marketing—creating, maintaining, and enhancing strong relationships with customers and other stakeholders. Beyond designing strategies to attract new customers and create transactions with them, companies are going all out to retain current customers and build profitable, long-term relationships with them.

Why the new emphasis on retaining and growing customers? In the past, many companies took their customers for granted. Facing an expanding economy and rapidly growing markets, companies could practise a "leaky bucket" approach to marketing. Growing markets meant a plentiful supply of new customers: Companies could keep filling the marketing bucket with new customers without worrying about losing old customers through holes in the bottom of the bucket.

However, companies today are facing new marketing realities. Changing demographics, more sophisticated competitors, and overcapacity in many industries—all of these factors mean that there are fewer customers to go around. Many companies are now fighting for shares of flat or fading markets. Thus, the costs of attracting new consumers are rising. In fact, it costs five times as much to attract a new customer as it does to keep a current customer satisfied.[11]

Companies are also realizing that losing a customer means losing more than a single sale: It means losing the entire stream of purchases that the customer would make over a lifetime of patronage. Here is a dramatic illustration of customer lifetime value: Stew Leonard, who operates a highly profitable single-store supermarket, says that he sees $75 000 flying out of his store every time he sees a sulking customer. Why? Because his average customer spends about $150 a week, shops 50 weeks a year, and remains in the area for about 10 years. If this cus-

Customer lifetime value: Stew Leonard's does all it can to keep customers satisfied.

tomer has an unhappy experience and switches to another supermarket, Stew Leonard has lost $75 000 in revenue. The loss can be much greater if the disappointed customer shares the bad experience with other customers and causes them to defect.

Similarly, the customer lifetime value of a Taco Bell customer exceeds $12 000. Lexus estimates that a single satisfied and loyal customer is worth $600 000 in lifetime sales.[12] Thus, working to retain and grow customers makes good economic sense. A company can lose money on a specific transaction but still benefit greatly from a long-term relationship.

Attracting, Retaining, and Growing Customers

The key to building lasting relationships is the creation of superior customer value and satisfaction. Satisfied customers are more likely to be loyal customers, and loyal customers are more likely to give the company a larger share of their business. We now look more closely at the concepts of customer value and satisfaction, loyalty and retention, and share of customer.

Relationship Building Blocks: Customer Value and Satisfaction

Attracting and retaining customers can be a difficult task. Today's customers face a vast array of product and brand choices, prices, and suppliers. The company must answer a key question: How do customers make their choices? The answer is that customers choose the marketing offer that they believe will give them the most value. They are satisfied with and continue to buy offers that consistently meet or exceed their value expectations. Let's look more closely at customer value and satisfaction.

Customer Value. Consumers buy from the firm that they believe offers the highest customer delivered value—the difference between total customer value and total customer cost (see Figure 2-4).[13] For example, suppose that a large construction firm wants to buy a bulldozer. It will buy the bulldozer from either

FIGURE 2-4
Customer delivered value

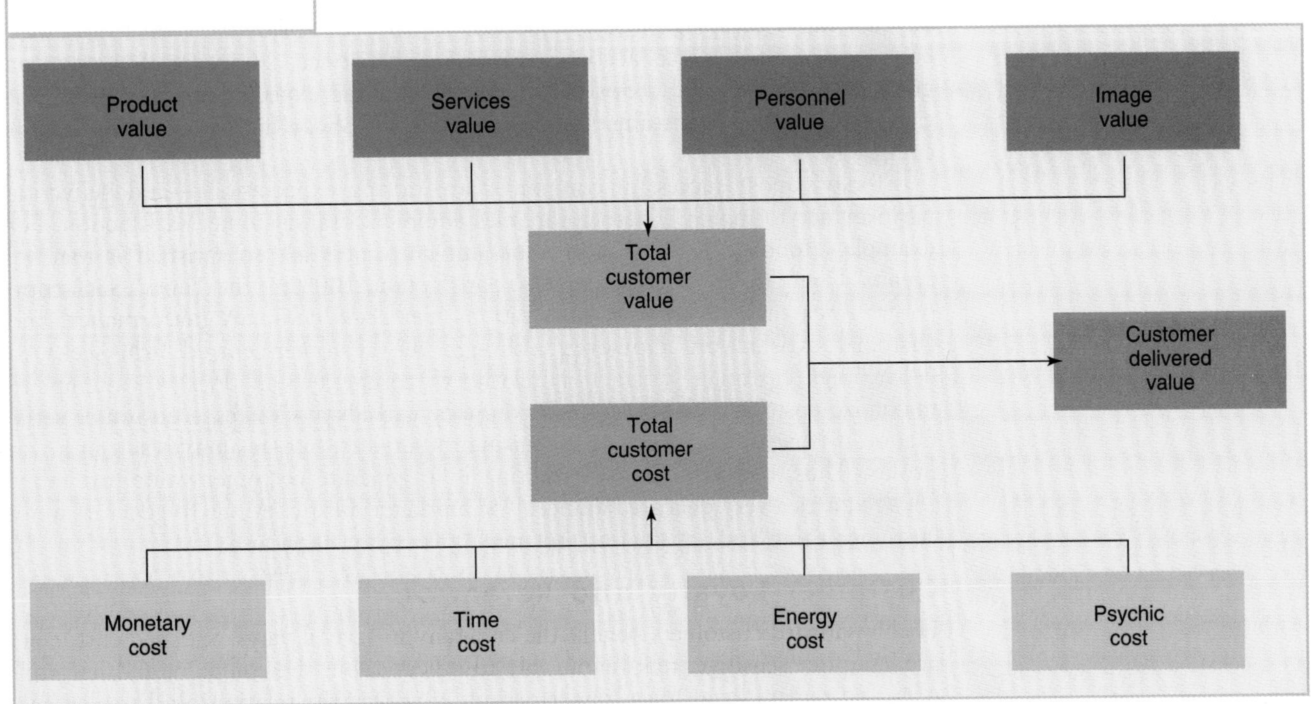

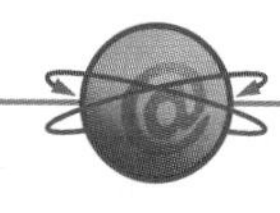

Caterpillar
www.caterpillar.com

Komatsu Ltd.
www.komatsu.com

Caterpillar or Komatsu. The salespeople for the two companies carefully describe their respective offers to the buyer. The construction firm evaluates the two competing bulldozer offers to assess which one delivers the greatest value. It adds all the values from four sources—product, services, personnel, and image. First, it judges that Caterpillar's bulldozer provides higher reliability, durability, and performance. It also decides that Caterpillar has better accompanying services—delivery, training, and maintenance. The customer views Caterpillar personnel as more knowledgeable and responsive. Finally, it places higher value on Caterpillar's reputation. Thus, the customer decides that Caterpillar offers more total customer value than does Komatsu.

Does the construction firm buy the Caterpillar bulldozer? Not necessarily. The firm will also examine the total customer cost of buying Caterpillar's bulldozer versus Komatsu's. The total customer cost is more than just monetary cost. As Adam Smith observed more than two centuries ago, "The real price of anything is the toil and trouble of acquiring it." Total customer cost includes the buyer's anticipated time, energy, and psychic costs. The construction firm evaluates these costs along with monetary costs to form a complete estimate of its costs. The buying firm now compares total customer value to total customer cost of each bulldozer. The firm then buys from the company that offers the highest delivered value.

Customer Satisfaction. As the Caterpillar example illustrates, buyers form expectations about the value of marketing offers and make buying decisions based on these expectations. Customer satisfaction with a purchase depends on the product's actual performance relative to a buyer's expectations. A customer might experience various degrees of satisfaction. If the product's performance falls short of expectations, the customer is dissatisfied. If performance matches expectations, the customer is satisfied. If performance exceeds expectations, the customer is highly satisfied or delighted.[14]

But how do buyers form their expectations? Expectations are based on the customer's past buying experiences, the opinions of friends and associates, and marketer and competitor information and promises. Marketers must be careful to set the right level of expectations. If they set expectations too low, they may satisfy those who buy but fail to attract enough buyers. In contrast, if they raise expectations too high, buyers are likely to be disappointed. For example, Holiday Inn ran a campaign a few years ago called "No Surprises," which promised consistently trouble-free accommodations and service. However, Holiday Inn guests still encountered a host of problems, and the expectations created by the campaign only made customers more dissatisfied. Holiday Inn had to withdraw the campaign.

Today's most successful companies are raising expectations—and delivering performance to match. These companies embrace total customer satisfaction. For example, Honda claims: "One reason our customers are so satisfied is that we aren't." Cigna Insurance vows "100% Satisfaction. 100% of the Time." Such companies track their customers' expectations, perceived company performance, and customer satisfaction. However, although the customer-centred firm seeks to deliver high customer satisfaction relative to competitors, it does not attempt to maximize customer satisfaction. A company can always increase customer satisfaction by lowering its price or increasing its services, but this may result in lower profits. Thus, the purpose of marketing is to generate customer value profitably. This requires a very delicate balance: The marketer must continue to generate more customer value and satisfaction but not "give away the house."

Customer Loyalty and Retention

Highly satisfied customers benefit the company in several ways. Satisfied customers are less price sensitive, talk favourably to others about the company and its products, and remain loyal for a longer period. However, the relationship between customer satisfaction and loyalty varies greatly across industries and competitive situations. Figure 2-5 shows the relationship between customer satisfaction and loyalty in five different markets.[15] In all cases, as satisfaction increases, so does loyalty. In highly competitive markets, such as those for automobiles and personal computers, there is surprisingly little difference between the loyalty of less satisfied customers and those who are merely satisfied. However, there is a tremendous difference between the loyalty of satisfied customers and completely satisfied customers.

Even a slight drop from complete satisfaction can create an enormous drop in loyalty. One study showed that completely satisfied customers are nearly 42 percent more likely to be loyal than merely satisfied customers. Two other studies, one by AT&T and the other by Xerox, suggested that just being satisfied isn't enough—customers must be highly satisfied, or the firm risks losing customers to competitors. Xerox found that its totally satisfied customers are six times more likely to repurchase Xerox products over the next 18 months than its satisfied customers.[16] Companies must aim high if they want to hold on to their customers. Customer delight creates an emotional affinity for a product or service, not just a rational preference, and this creates high customer loyalty.

At the same time, a high customer satisfaction rating doesn't guarantee customer loyalty. A major insurance firm learned this when comparing its performance to that of its competitor State Farm:

> A study comparing the competitor to State Farm showed only a 6.5 point spread between the percentage of respondents who were totally satisfied with the competitor and the percent totally satisfied with State Farm. So, how can we explain State Farm's consistently higher profitability over the years? The answer lies in customer loyalty. By using discounts and guarantees for long-term loyal customers and an agent compensation plan that encourages customer retention, State Farm has created strong customer loyalty. Although the study showed fairly minor differences in those totally satisfied, loyalty measures widened the gap between the companies. When customers were asked how strongly they preferred their life insurance company over others, there was an 11 percent spread between the competitor and State Farm. The gulf widened to a 15 percentage point State Farm lead on the statement, "I am very loyal to my company, it would take a lot to get me to switch." Twice as many respondents strongly agreed with the statement, "I would go out of my way to stay with my life insurance company," for State Farm than for the competitor.[17]

FIGURE 2-5 The relationship between customer satisfaction and customer loyalty

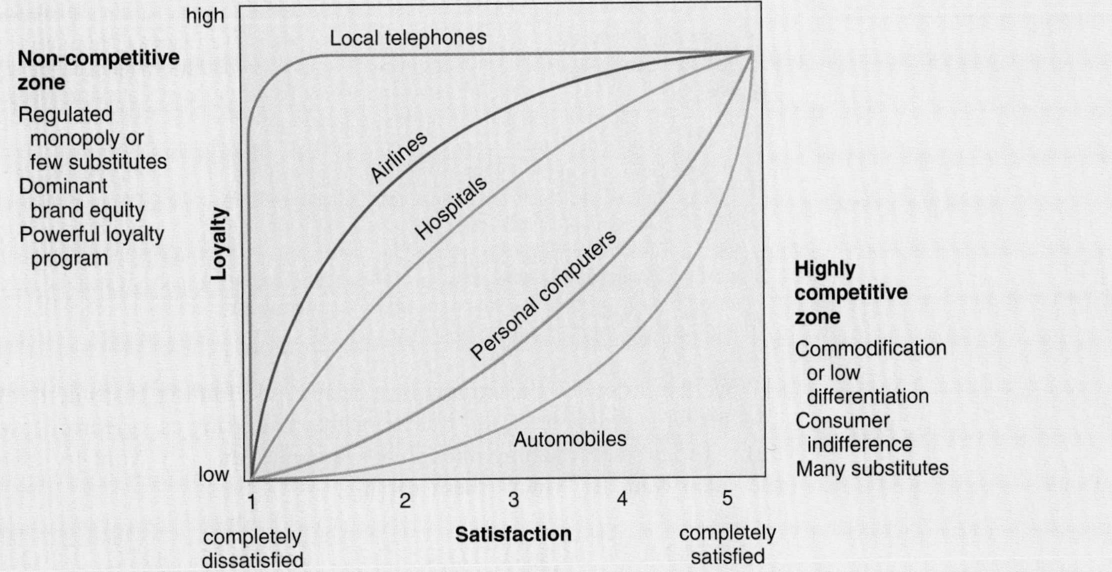

Source: Reprinted by permission of *Harvard Business Review*. From "Why Satisfied Customer Defect," by Thomas O. Jones and W. Earl Sasser, Jr., November–December 1995, pp. 91.

Thus, customer satisfaction remains an extremely important component in customer loyalty—a company will find it difficult to earn customer loyalty without first earning high levels of customer satisfaction. However, companies should also carefully examine customer loyalty itself, which often is a better indicator of customer attitudes and behaviour.

Growing "Share of Customer"

Beyond simple attracting and retaining good customers, marketers want to constantly increase their "share of customer." They want to capture a greater share of the customer's purchasing in their product categories, either by becoming the sole supplier of products the customer is currently buying or by persuading the customer to purchase additional company products. Thus, banks want a greater "share of wallet," supermarkets want to increase their "share of stomach," car companies want a greater "share of garage," and airlines want a greater "share of travel."

Today, the goal isn't to win some business from a lot of customers—it's to win all the business of current customers. Feverishly chasing market share is out; trying to maximize share of customers is in. Consider Gateway Computer's three-pronged strategy for attracting, retaining, and growing customers.[18]

> Gateway's strategy is built on a simple idea, writes *Business Week* analyst Steven Brull. "Grab customers early on and keep them generating incremental revenue through a variety of services. The relationship starts with the purchase of a PC. . . . Then Gateway [locks] in those customers through financing, Internet access, and a personalized portal that will steer them to Gateway's e-commerce sites." The first stage of Gateway's three-phase strategy centres on generating PC sales. Gateway attracts new buyers through media advertising, telemarketing, online selling, and its national network of almost 200 Gateway Country retail stores. It targets primarily first-time buyers and small businesses, customers who have not yet formed strong brand loyalties. Gateway's low prices, financing, and training classes make it easy for these new buyers to get started on a Gateway machine.
>
> The PC purchase is just the first stop on what Gateway hopes will be a lifelong journey with the customer. In phase two, the connection lengthens. To entice buyers online and to develop a more permanent relationship, Gateway offers a free one-year subscription to Gateway.net, the company's Internet access service. About 400 000 customers already subscribe to Gateway.net and the company is mounting a direct-marketing campaign to woo its five million customers who are not yet subscribers. It is also courting non-Gateway customers with sales pitches at its Gateway Country stores.
>
> In phase three, the relationship deepens. Beyond selling computers and linking customers to the Internet through Gateway.net, Gateway goes all out to earn a big share of customers' e-commerce business. "To keep customers coming back, Gateway offers each customer a customized home page created in partnership with portal Yahoo!" When completing a PC sale, Gateway reps collect information for tailoring home pages to individual preferences. When the PC is delivered, it comes complete with the personalized home page. Of course, the personalized Web page also puts customers within a mouse click of the company's SpotShop.com site. Once there, they can buy any of more than 30 000 items, including computer hardware, software, and accessories but also office and personal technology products, ranging from digital cameras and projectors to personal digital assistants. Thus, Gateway isn't just a PC company anymore—its interests in the customer go far beyond the initial sale. In fact, Gateway anticipates that, within the next two years or so, services such as training, consulting, and Internet access will account for more than a third of its sales and half its profits. More than any other PC company, Gateway has been focused on the ongoing relationship.

We can now see the importance of not just finding customers, but of keeping and growing them as well. Relationship marketing is oriented toward the long term. Today's smart companies, like Gateway, not only want to create customers, they also want to "own" them for life.

Customer Relationship Levels and Tools

Companies can build customer relationships at many levels—economic, social, technical, and legal—depending on the nature of the target market. At one extreme, a company with many low-margin customers may seek to develop basic

Gateway Computer uses a relationship-focused, three-pronged strategy for attracting, retaining, and growing customers.

relationships with them. For example, Procter & Gamble does not phone all of its Tide customers to get to know them personally and express its appreciation for their business. Instead, P&G creates relationships through brand-building advertising, sales promotions, a 1-800 customer response number, and its Tide ClothesLine Web site (www.tide.com). At the other extreme, in markets with few customers and high margins, sellers want to create full partnerships with key customers. For example, P&G customer teams work closely with Wal-Mart, Safeway, and other large retailers. Boeing works closely with American Airlines, Delta, and other airlines in designing its airplanes and ensuring that Boeing airplanes

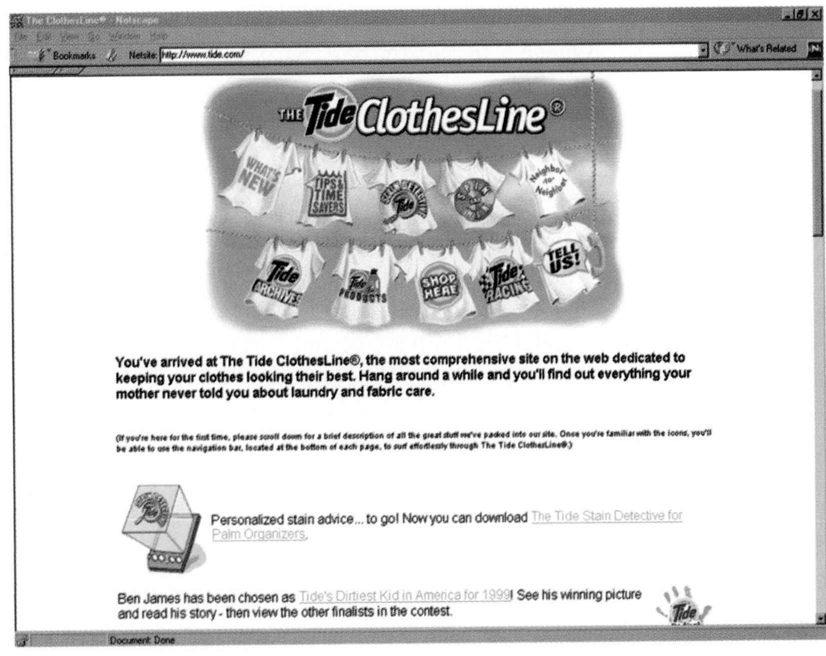

Procter & Gamble doesn't get to know Tide customers personally, but it does create close relationships through brand-building advertising, sales promotions, a toll-free customer response number, and its Tide ClothesLine Web site.

fully satisfy their requirements. In between these two extreme situations, other levels of relationship marketing are appropriate.

Today, more and more companies are developing customer loyalty and retention programs. Beyond offering consistently high value and satisfaction, marketers can use a number of marketing tools to develop stronger bonds with consumers.[19] First, a company might build value and satisfaction by adding financial benefits to the customer relationship. For example, many companies now offer frequency marketing programs, which reward customers who buy frequently or in large amounts. Air Canada offers frequent flier programs, Mariott Hotels give room upgrades to their frequent guests, and Zellers lets shoppers redeem Club Z points for gifts.

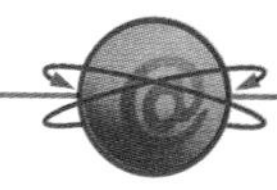

Harley-Davidson
www.harley-davidson.com

Other companies sponsor club marketing programs that offer members special discounts and other benefits. For example, Harley-Davidson sponsors the Harley Owners Group (HOG), which now numbers 330 000 members, about a third of all Harley owners. The first-time buyer of a Harley-Davidson motorcycle gets a free one-year membership with annual renewal costing $40. HOG benefits include a magazine (*Hog Tales*), a copy of the HOG Touring Handbook, a complete HOG World Atlas, an emergency pickup service, a specially designed insurance program, theft reward service, discount hotel rates, and a Fly & Ride program enabling members to rent Harleys while on vacation.[20]

A second approach is to add social benefits as well as financial benefits. Here, the company increases its social bonds with customers by learning individual customers' needs and wants and then personalizing its products and services. For example, to build better relationships with its customers, Saturn developed its now-famous "Drive-In Reunions." Beginning in 1994, Saturn invited Canadian owners and their families to drive-in movies to see Apollo 13. Thirty-nine thousand people responded to the invitation. Although the event was highly successful, Saturn marketing vice-president, Chuck Novak, asked himself, "How does this reflect our commitment to Saturn communities." This question led to Saturn's playground-building program. Saturn staff and interested community members have now constructed over 50 playgrounds across the country. Because many Saturn owners have families with young children, Saturn's efforts focus on things that enhance children's quality of life. Playgrounds aren't the only community need Saturn addresses, however. Its retailers are the eyes and ears of the company and when a community need arises, they let Saturn know. For example, Saturn helped plant trees in areas hard hit by the 1997 ice storm in eastern Ontario and Quebec; in North Bay, Saturn helped raise funds for a new heart-monitoring unit.[21]

A third approach to building customer relationships is to add structural ties as well as financial and social benefits. For example, a business marketer might supply customers with special equipment or computer linkages that help them manage their orders, payroll, or inventory. FedEx offers Web links to its customers to keep them from defecting to competitors such as UPS. Customers can use the Web site to link with FedEx's computers, arrange shipments, and check the status of their FedEx packages.

Relationship marketing means that marketers must focus on managing their customers as well as their products. At the same time, they don't want relationships with every customer. In fact, there are undesirable customers for every company. Ultimately, marketing involves attracting, keeping, and growing profitable customers. Thus, in addition to assessing the value that it delivers to customers, a firm should actively measure the value of individual customers to the firm. Once it has identified profitable customers, it can create attractive offers and special handling to bind these customers to the company for a lifetime. But what should the company do with unprofitable customers? If it can't turn them into profitable ones, it may even want to "fire" customers that are too unreasonable or that cost more to serve than they are worth.

Delivering Customer Value and Satisfaction

Marketers alone cannot deliver superior customer value and satisfaction. Although it plays a leading role, marketing can be only a partner in attracting, keeping, and growing customers. Relationship marketing requires that marketers work closely with other company departments to create customer value. Moreover, the company can be effective only to the extent that it works effectively with its marketing system partners (its suppliers and channel members) to form a competitively superior value-delivery network. Increasingly in today's marketplace, competition no longer takes place between individual competitors. Rather, it takes place between the entire value-delivery networks created by these competitors. Thus, Honda's performance against another automaker—say Toyota—depends on the quality of Honda's overall value-delivery network versus Toyota's. Companies no longer compete—their entire marketing networks do.

Planning Cross-Functional Strategies

Once the company has a corporate strategic plan that establishes what kinds of businesses it will operate and its objectives for each, and general plans for each business unit outlining how it will compete in its particular industry, then more detailed planning must take place. The major functional departments in each SBU—marketing, finance, accounting, purchasing, manufacturing, human resources, and others—must work together to accomplish strategic objectives.

Marketing strategies must be developed to support the objectives outlined in the business plan. For example, Monsanto's corporate objective may be to grow its market share. It will have SBUs operating in both domestic and new foreign markets, and since each each SBU faces different market circumstances, it will establish different plans depending on local conditions. The units operating overseas may cut prices and target the customers of large international firms. These are its broad strategies, however. Each broad strategy must then be defined in greater detail by each functional group. For example, one SBU may need to increase awareness of the product through promotion. This will require more salespeople and more advertising; thus, these requirements will have to be spelled out. In this way, the firm's mission is translated into a set of objectives for the current period. The objectives should be as specific as possible. The objective to "increase our market share" is not as useful as the objective to "increase our market share to 15 percent by the end of the second year."

Marketing's Role in Strategic Planning

There is much overlap between overall business unit strategy and marketing strategy. Marketing looks at consumer needs and the company's ability to satisfy them; these same factors guide the company mission and objectives as well as choices about industry and market selection. In many firms, marketing also provides a guiding philosophy—the marketing concept—which suggests that company strategy should revolve around serving the needs of important consumer groups. Next, marketing provides inputs to strategic planners by helping to identify attractive market opportunities and by assessing the firm's potential to take advantage of them. Finally, within individual business units, marketing designs strategies for reaching the unit's objectives. Once the unit's objectives are set, marketing's task is to carry them out profitably.

Marketing and the Other Business Functions

Marketers play an important role in delivering customer value and satisfaction. However, marketing cannot do this alone. Because consumer value and satisfaction are affected by the performance of other functions, all departments must work together to deliver superior value and satisfaction. Jack Welch, General Electric's highly regarded CEO, tells his employees: "Companies can't give job security. Only customers can!" He emphasizes that all General Electric people, regardless of their department, have an impact on customer satisfaction and retention. His message: "If you are not thinking customer, you are not thinking."[22]

Marketing plays an integrative role to help ensure that all departments work together toward this goal. Sometimes conflicts may occur between departments: operations may focus on suppliers and production, and finance on shareholders and sound investment. Yet marketers must get all departments to "think consumer" and to place the customer at the centre of company activity. Customer satisfaction requires a total company effort to deliver superior value to target customers.

> Creating value for buyers is much more than a "marketing function"; rather, [it's] analogous to a symphony orchestra in which the contribution of each subgroup is tailored and integrated by a conductor—with a synergistic effect. A seller must draw upon and integrate effectively . . . its entire human and other capital resources. . . . [Creating superior value for buyers] is the proper focus of the entire business and not merely of a single department in it.[23]

The DuPont "Adopt a Customer" program recognizes the importance of having people in all of its functions who are "close to the customer." For example, operators from DuPont's nylon-spinning mills visit customers' factories where DuPont nylon is transformed into swimsuits and other garments, talking to the operators about quality and other problems they encounter with the nylon. Then the DuPont operators represent their customers on the factory floor. If quality or delivery problems arise, the operators are more likely to see their adopted customers' perspective and to make decisions that will keep customers happy.[24]

The Marketing Process

The corporate strategic plan defines the company's overall mission and objectives. Within each business unit, marketing plays a role in helping to accomplish the overall strategic objectives. Marketing's role and activities in the organization are shown in Figure 2-6, which summarizes the entire **marketing process** and the forces influencing company marketing strategy.

Marketing process The process of (1) analyzing marketing opportunities; (2) selecting target markets; (3) developing the marketing mix; and (4) managing the marketing effort.

Marketing mix The set of controllable tactical marketing tools—product, price, place, and promotion—that the firm blends to produce the response it wants in the target market.

Target consumers stand in the centre. The company identifies the total market, divides it into smaller segments, selects the most promising segments, and focuses on serving and satisfying these segments. It designs a **marketing mix** composed of factors under its control—product, price, place, and promotion. To find the best marketing mix and put it into action, the company engages in marketing analysis, planning, implementation, and control. Through these activities, the company watches and adapts to the marketing environment. We will now look briefly at each element in the marketing process. In later chapters, we will discuss each element in more depth.

Connecting with Consumers

To succeed in today's competitive marketplace, companies must be customer centred—winning customers from competitors, then keeping and growing them by delivering greater value. But before it can satisfy consumers, a company must first understand their needs and wants. Thus, sound marketing requires a careful analysis of consumers.

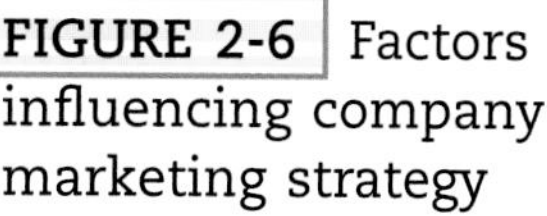

FIGURE 2-6 Factors influencing company marketing strategy

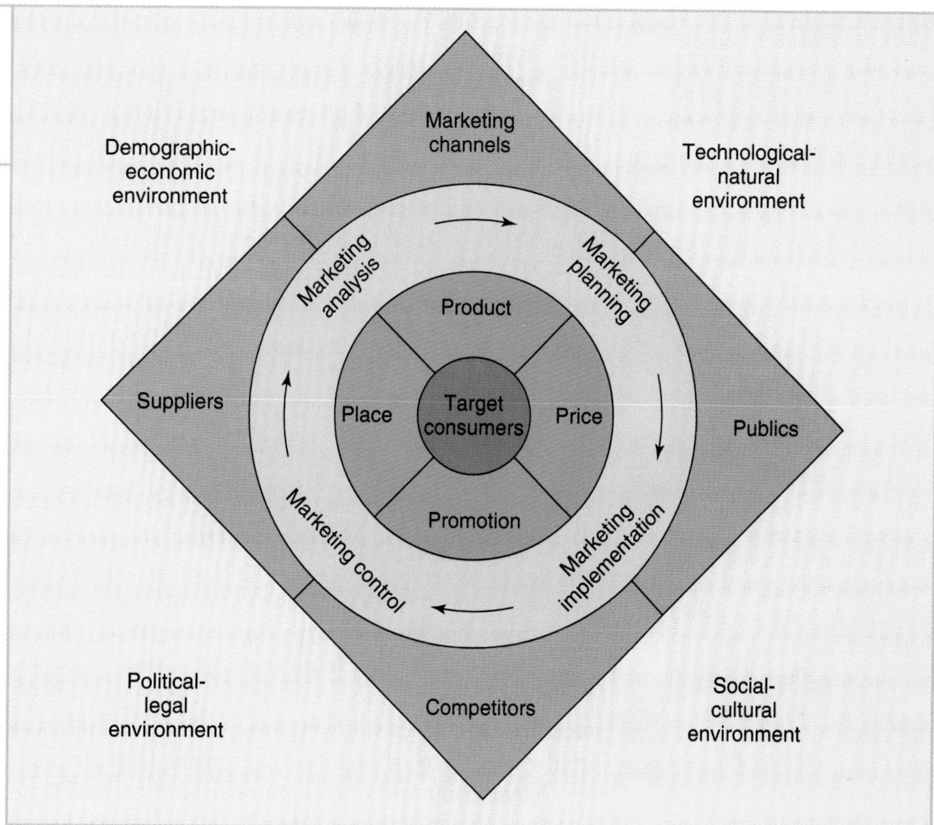

Terry Ortt, president of Canada's Journey's End Corp., understood the need for this type of information. Although conventional wisdom was that Journey's End customers were mainly businesspeople on two-day trips, after digging through 10 million guest registration cards, Ortt discovered that this was a myth. Instead of businesspeople, 45 percent of his guests were from rural areas. Understanding the value of this information, Ortt developed a sophisticated database to track guests' needs and wants—from the time they request wake-up calls to what they eat for breakfast. The power of a database lies in its ability to track customers' actual behaviour rather than their intentions or what they say they do. This information allows the firm to provide the unique services demanded by individual guests, reward them for repeat visits and multiple-night stays, and target promotional information on specials to each guest by name.[25]

Companies know that they cannot satisfy all consumers in a given market—at least not all consumers in the same way. There are too many different kinds of consumers with too many different kinds of needs. And some companies are in a better position to serve certain segments of the market. Thus, each company must divide up the total market, choose the best segments, and design strategies for profitably serving chosen segments better than its competitors do. This process involves three steps: market segmentation, market targeting, and market positioning.

Market Segmentation

The market consists of many types of customers, products, and needs, and the marketer has to determine which segments offer the best opportunity for achieving company objectives. Consumers can be grouped in various ways, based on geographic, psychographic, and behavioural factors. The process of dividing a market into distinct groups of buyers with different needs, characteristics, or behav-

Market segmentation
Dividing a market into distinct groups of buyers with different needs, characteristics, or behaviour, who might require separate products or marketing mixes.

iour, who might require separate products or marketing mixes, is called **market segmentation.**

Every market has market segments, but not all ways of segmenting a market are equally useful. For example, Tylenol would gain little by distinguishing between male and female users of pain relievers if both purchase the product to relieve headaches and respond to marketing efforts in the same way. A market segment consists of consumers who respond in a similar way to a given set of marketing efforts. In the car market, for example, consumers who choose the biggest, most comfortable car regardless of price compose one market segment. Another market segment comprises customers who care mainly about price and operating economy. It would be difficult to make one model of car that was the first choice of every consumer. Companies are wise to focus their efforts on meeting the distinct needs of one or more market segments.

Market Targeting

Market targeting
The process of evaluating each market segment's attractiveness and selecting one or more segments to enter.

After a company has defined market segments, it can enter one or many segments of a given market. **Market targeting** involves evaluating each market segment's attractiveness and selecting one or more segments to enter. A company should target segments in which it can generate the greatest customer value and sustain it over time. A company with limited resources might decide to serve only one or a few special segments. This strategy limits sales, but it can be very profitable. Or a company might choose to serve several related segments, perhaps those with different kinds of customers but with the same basic wants. Or a large company might decide to offer a complete range of products to serve all market segments.

Most companies enter a new market by serving a single segment; if this proves successful, they add segments. Large companies eventually seek full market coverage. They want to be the "General Motors" of their industry. GM says that it makes a car for every "person, purse, and personality." The leading company normally has different products designed to meet the special needs of each segment.

Market Positioning

After a company has decided which market segments to enter, it must decide what "positions" it wants to occupy in those segments. A product's position is the place the product occupies in consumers' minds relative to the competitors' products. To build preferences for their products, marketers must differentiate their brands from those of their competitors; otherwise, consumers would be indifferent about which brands they buy.

Market positioning
Arranging for a product to occupy a clear, distinctive, and desirable place relative to competing products in the minds of target consumers.

Market positioning is arranging for a product to occupy a clear, distinctive, and desirable place in the minds of target consumers relative to competing products. Thus, marketers plan positions that distinguish their products from competing brands and give them the greatest strategic advantage in their target markets. Chevy Blazer is "like a rock." Saturn is "a different kind of company, a different kind of car." Mazda has "a passion for the road," whereas Mercedes is "engineered like no other car in the world." Marketers of the upscale Bentley promise "18 handcrafted feet of shameless luxury." Such deceptively simple statements form the backbone of a product's marketing strategy.

In positioning its product, the company first identifies possible competitive advantages on which to build the position. For example, if the company has the capability of being the lowest-cost producer in an industry, it can position its products as offering the best value to consumers relative to all other competitors. There are many other ways to create a unique place in consumers' minds, however. Companies can position their products on the basis of superior quality, the image associated with a particular lifestyle relative to a particular competitor (for example, 7-Up "The Uncola"), or a unique feature or benefit. Cadbury's Canadian division recently launched a new chocolate bar, Time Out, using an integrated, multime-

ZEALOUS
The Bentley Arnage. 413 pound-feet of
relentless torque. 18 handcrafted feet of shameless luxury.
It's time to answer your id's impassioned plea.
1-877-300-8803 toll-free or www.bentleymotors.co.uk

Positioning: Bentley promises "18 handcrafted feet of shameless luxury." Such deceptively simple statements form the backbone of a product's marketing strategy.

dia campaign. Its positioning statement for the product could have been written as follows: For time-pressed adults (the target market) who need an energy boost (statement of need), Time Out (the brand) is a chocolate bar (product category), that is a perfect way to take a break (key benefit or reason to buy). Unlike rich, heavy chocolate bars (competitive offerings), our product is a light wafer snack with a chocolate wave (statement of differentiation). Once the company has chosen a desired position, it must take strong steps to deliver and communicate that position to target consumers. The company's entire marketing program should support the chosen positioning strategy.

Developing the Marketing Mix

Once the company has decided on its overall competitive marketing strategy, it is ready to begin planning the details of the marketing mix. The marketing mix is one of the major concepts in modern marketing. We define marketing mix as the set of controllable tactical marketing tools that the firm blends to produce the response it wants in the target market. The marketing mix consists of everything the firm can do to influence the demand for its product. The many possibilities can be collected into four groups of variables known as the "four Ps": product, price, place, and promotion.[26] Figure 2-7 shows the particular marketing tools under each P.

Product is the "goods-and-service" combination the company offers to the target market. Thus, a Ford Taurus "product" consists of nuts and bolts, spark plugs, pistons, headlights, and thousands of other parts. Ford offers several Taurus styles and dozens of optional features. The car comes fully serviced and with a comprehensive warranty that is as much a part of the product as the tailpipe.

Price is the amount of money customers have to pay to obtain the product. Ford calculates suggested retail prices that its dealers might charge for each Taurus. But Ford dealers rarely charge the full sticker price. Instead, they negotiate the price with each customer, offering discounts, trade-in allowances, and credit terms to adjust for the current competitive situation and to bring the price into line with the buyer's perception of the car's value.

Place includes company activities that make the product available to target consumers. Ford maintains a large body of independent dealerships that sell the

FIGURE 2-7 The four Ps of the marketing mix

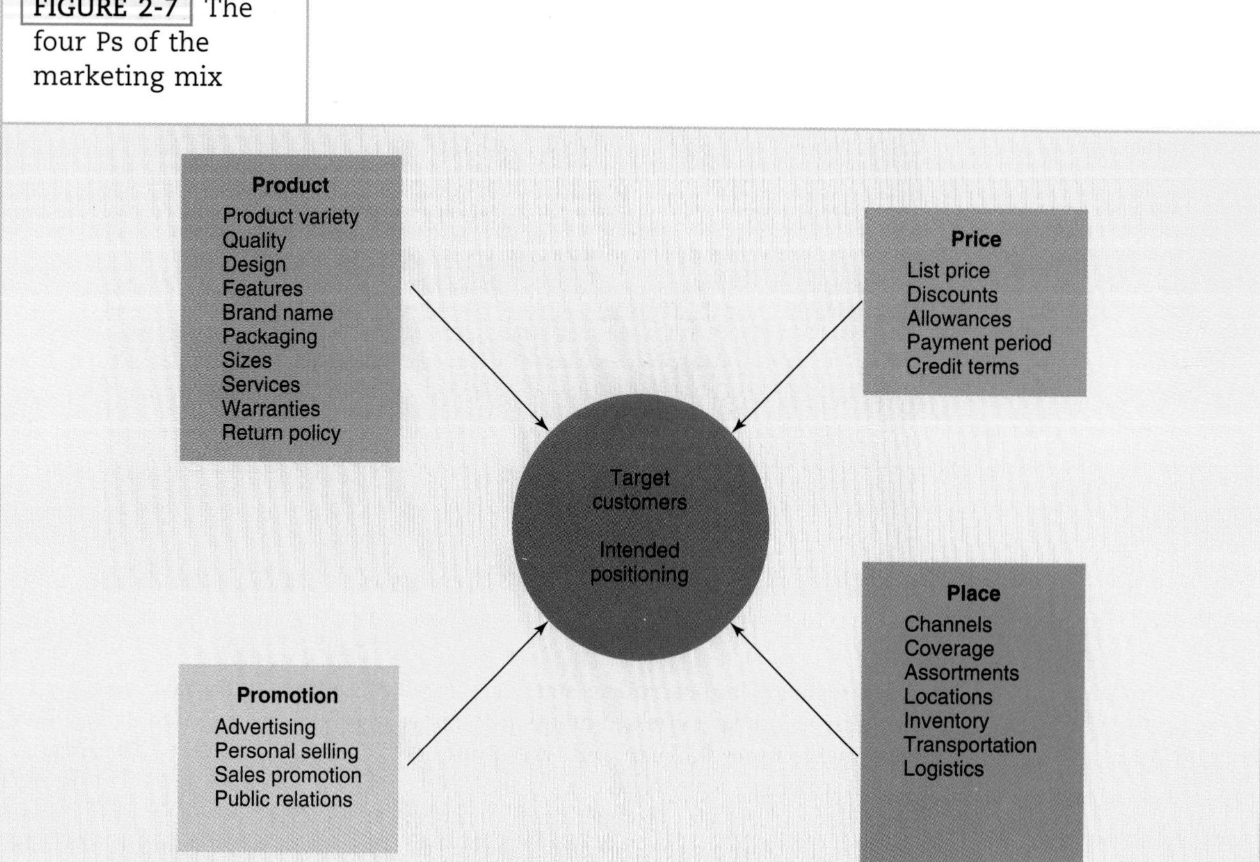

company's many different models. Ford selects its dealers carefully and supports them strongly. The dealers keep an inventory of Ford automobiles, demonstrate them to potential buyers, negotiate prices, close sales, and service the cars after the sale.

Promotion is the activities that communicate the merits of the product and persuade target customers to buy it. Ford spends more than $850 million worldwide each year on advertising to tell consumers about the company and its products. Dealership salespeople assist potential buyers and persuade them that Ford offers the best car for them. Ford and its dealers offer special promotions—sales, cash rebates, low financing rates—as added purchase incentives.

An effective marketing program blends all of the marketing mix elements into a coordinated program designed to achieve the company's marketing objectives by delivering value to consumers. The marketing mix constitutes the company's tactical tool kit for establishing strong positioning in target markets.

Some critics feel that the four Ps may omit or underemphasize certain important activities. For example, they ask, "Where are services? Just because they don't start with a P doesn't justify omitting them." The answer is that services, such as banking, airline, and retailing services, are products too. We might call them service products. "Where is packaging?" the critics might ask. Marketers would answer that they include packaging as just one of many product decisions. All said, as Figure 2-7 suggests, many marketing activities that might appear to be left out of the marketing mix are subsumed under one of the four Ps. The issue is not whether there should be four, six, or ten Ps so much as what framework is most helpful in designing marketing programs.

There is another concern, however, that is valid. It holds that the four Ps concept takes the seller's view of the market, not the buyer's view. From the buyer's viewpoint, in this age of connectedness, the four Ps might be better described as the four Cs:[27]

Four Ps	**Four Cs**
Product	Customer solution
Price	Customer cost
Place	Convenience
Promotion	Communication

Thus while marketers see themselves as selling a product, customers see themselves as buying value or a solution to their problem. Customers are interested in more than the price; they are interested in the total costs of obtaining, using, and disposing of a product. Customers want the product and service to be as conveniently available as possible. Finally, they want two-way communication. Marketers would do well to first think through the four Cs and then build the four Ps on that platform.

Managing the Marketing Effort

The company wants to design and put into action the marketing mix that will best achieve its objectives in its target markets. Figure 2-8 shows the relationship between the four marketing management functions—analysis, planning, implementation, and control. After careful analysis of its situation, the company develops overall strategic plans. These company-wide strategic plans are then translated into marketing and other plans for each division, product, and brand. Through implementation, the company turns the plans into actions. Control consists of measuring and evaluating the results of marketing activities and taking corrective action where needed. Finally, marketing analysis provides information and evaluations needed for all of the other marketing activities.

FIGURE 2-8 The relationship between analysis, planning, implementation, and control

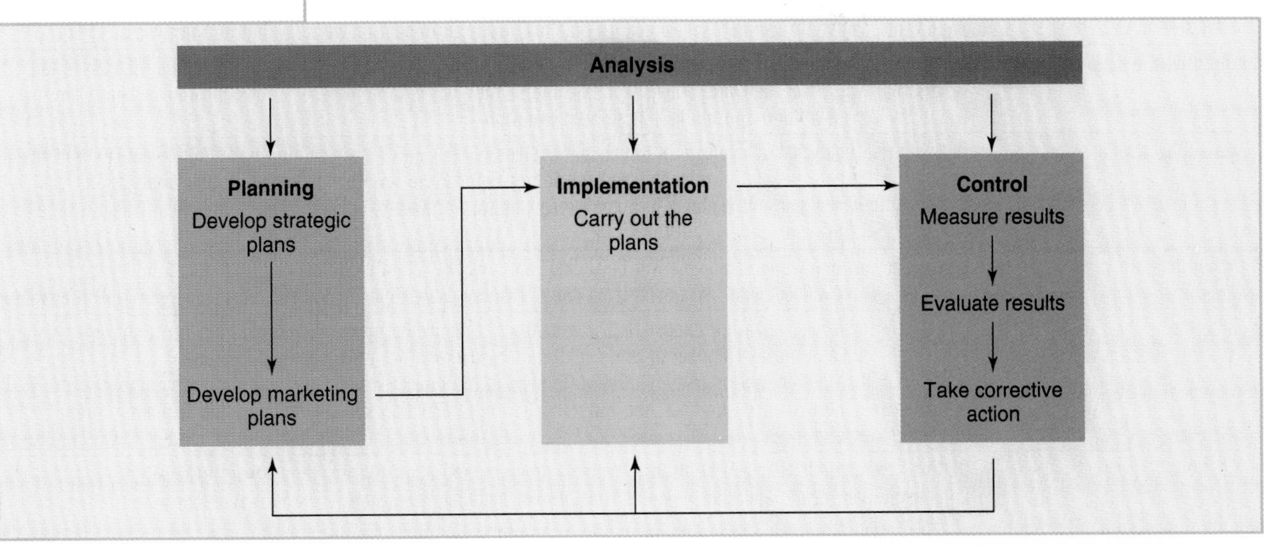

Marketing Analysis

Managing the marketing function begins with a complete analysis of the company's situation. The company must analyze its markets and marketing environment to identify attractive opportunities and avoid environmental threats. It must analyze company strengths and weaknesses, as well as current and possible marketing actions, to determine which opportunities it can best pursue. Marketing analysis feeds information and other inputs to each of the other marketing management functions. We discuss marketing analysis more fully in Chapter 4.

Marketing Planning

Through strategic planning, the company decides what it wants to do with each business unit. Marketing planning involves deciding on marketing strategies that will help the company attain its overall strategic objectives. A detailed marketing plan is needed for each business, product, or brand. What does a marketing plan look like? Our discussion focuses on product or brand plans.

Table 2-2 outlines the major sections of a typical product or brand plan. The plan begins with an executive summary that quickly overviews major assessments, goals, and recommendations. The main section of the plan presents a detailed

TABLE 2-2 Contents of a Marketing Plan

Section	Purpose
Executive summary	Presents a brief summary of the main goals and recommendations of the plan for management review, helping top management to find the plan's major points quickly. A table of contents should follow the executive summary.
Current marketing situation	Describes the target market and the company's position in it, including information about the market, product performance, competition, and distribution. This section includes: • A *market description* that defines the market and major segments, reviews customer needs, and outlines factors in the marketing environment, which may affect customer purchasing. • A *product review* that shows sales, prices, and gross margins of the major products in the product line. • A review of *competition* that identifies major competitors and assesses their market positions and strategies for product quality, pricing, distribution, and promotion. • A review of *distribution* that evaluates recent sales trends and other developments in major distribution channels.
Threat and opportunity analysis	Assesses major threats and opportunities that the product may face, helping management to anticipate important positive or negative developments that may have an impact on the firm and its strategies.
Objectives and issues	States the marketing objectives that the company would like to attain during the plan's term and discusses key issues that will affect their attainment. For example, if the goal is to achieve a 15 percent market share, this poses the key issue: How can market share be increased?
Marketing strategy	Outlines the broad marketing logic by which the business unit hopes to achieve its marketing objectives and the specifics of target markets, positioning, and marketing expenditure levels. It outlines specific strategies for each marketing mix element and explains how each responds to the threats, opportunities, and critical issues spelled out earlier in the plan.
Action program	Spells out how marketing strategies will be turned into specific action programs that answer the following questions: *What* will be done? *When* will it be done? *Who* is responsible for doing it? And *how much* will it cost?
Budgets	Details a supporting marketing budget that is essentially a projected profit-and-loss statement. It shows expected revenues (forecast number of units sold and the average net price) and expected costs (of production, distribution, and marketing). The difference is the projected profit. Once approved by higher management, the budget is the basis for materials buying, production scheduling, personnel planning, and marketing operations.
Controls	Outlines the controls that will be used to monitor progress and allow higher management to review implementation results and spot products that are not meeting their goals.

Marketers must continually plan their analysis, implementation, and control activities.

analysis of the current marketing situation and of potential threats and opportunities. It next states major objectives for the brand and outlines the specifics of a marketing strategy for achieving them.

A marketing strategy is the marketing logic by which the company hopes to achieve its marketing objectives. It consists of specific strategies for target markets, positioning, the marketing mix, and marketing expenditure levels. In this section, the planner explains how each strategy responds to threats, opportunities, and critical issues outlined earlier in the plan. Additional sections of the marketing plan lay out an action program for implementing the marketing strategy, along with the details of a supporting marketing budget. The last section outlines the controls that will be used to monitor progress and take corrective action.

Marketing Implementation

Planning good strategies is only a first step in successful marketing. A brilliant marketing strategy counts for little if the company fails to implement it properly. **Marketing implementation** is the process that turns marketing strategies and plans into marketing actions to accomplish strategic marketing objectives. Implementation involves day-to-day, month-to-month activities that effectively put the marketing plan to work. Whereas marketing planning addresses the what and why of marketing activities, implementation addresses the who, where, when, and how.

Marketing implementation
The process that turns marketing strategies and plans into marketing actions to accomplish strategic marketing objectives.

Many managers think that "doing things right"—implementation—is as important as, or even more important than, "doing the right things"—strategy. Yet both are critical to success. However, companies can gain competitive advantages through effective implementation. One firm can have essentially the same strategy as another, yet win in the marketplace through faster or better execution. Still, implementation is difficult: It is often easier to develop good marketing strategies than it is to execute them.

In an increasingly connected world, people at all levels of the marketing system must work together to implement marketing plans and strategies. At Black & Decker, for example, marketing implementation for the company's power tool products requires day-to-day decisions and actions by thousands of people both inside and outside the organization. Marketing managers make decisions about target segments, branding, packaging, pricing, promoting, and distributing. They connect with people elsewhere in the company to get support for their products and programs. They talk with engineering about product design, with manufacturing about production and inventory levels, and with finance about funding and cash flows. They also connect with outside people, such as advertising agencies to plan ad campaigns and the media to obtain publicity support. The sales force urges Home Depot, Wal-Mart, and other retailers to advertise Black & Decker products, provide ample shelf space, and use company displays.

Successful implementation depends on how well the company blends its people, organization structure, decision and reward systems, and company culture into a cohesive action program that supports its strategies. At all levels, the company must be staffed by people who have the needed skills, motivation, and personal characteristics. The company's formal organization structure plays an important role in implementing marketing strategy. So do its decision and reward systems. For example, if a company's compensation system rewards managers for short-run profit results, they will have little incentive to work toward long-run market-building objectives.

Finally, to be successfully implemented, the firm's marketing strategies must fit with its company culture, the system of values and beliefs shared by people in the organization. A study of North America's most successful companies found that these companies have almost cult-like cultures built around strong, market-oriented missions. At such companies as Wal-Mart, Microsoft, Nortel, Citicorp, Procter & Gamble, Walt Disney, and Hewlett-Packard, "employees share such a strong vision that they know in their hearts what's right for their company."[28]

Marketing Department Organization

The company must design a marketing department that can carry out marketing analysis, planning, implementation, and control. If the company is very small, one person might do all of the marketing work, including research, selling, advertising, and customer service. As the company expands, a marketing department organization emerges to plan and carry out marketing activities. In large companies, this department contains many specialists. Thus, General Mills has product managers, salespeople and sales managers, market researchers, advertising experts, and other specialists.

Modern marketing departments can be arranged in several ways. The most common form of marketing organization is functional, in which different marketing activities are headed by a functional specialist—a sales manager, advertising manager, marketing research manager, customer service manager, new product manager. A company that sells across the country or internationally often uses a geographic organization, in which its sales and marketing people are assigned to specific countries, regions, and districts: Geographic organization allows salespeople to settle into a territory, get to know their customers, and work with a minimum of travel time and cost.

Companies with many, very different products or brands often create a product management organization. Using this approach, a product manager develops and implements a complete strategy and marketing program for a specific product or brand. Procter & Gamble first used product management in 1929. A new company soap, Camay, was not doing well, and a young P&G executive was assigned to focus exclusively on developing and promoting this product. He was successful, and the company soon added other product managers.[29] Since then, many firms, especially in the food, soap, toiletries, and chemical industries, have set up product management organizations. Today, the product management system is firmly entrenched. However, recent dramatic changes in the marketing envi-

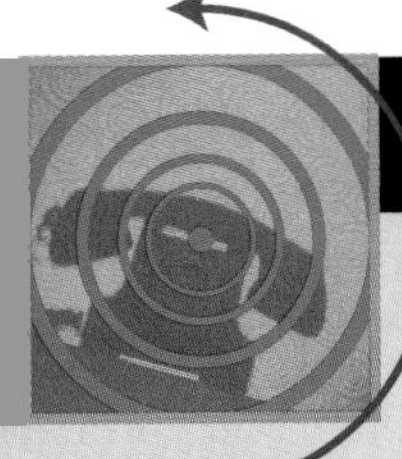

marketers speak out

Jim Shenkman, Entrepreneur

Jim Shenkman is good at coming up with new business ideas and turning them into reality. He took a small, family-owned, freight forwarding company and helped build it into the second-largest firm of its type in Canada. The firm was sold in the early 1980s when he realized that if you lacked the resources to operate on a world scale, like Federal Express, you could no longer play in the game.

He then turned his attention to getting an FM radio licence. Although his application was unsuccessful, he realized that there was an interesting hole in the Canadian communications market—there just wasn't enough trade information for broadcasters and producers. While there were many successful US publications covering different segments of this industry on a monthly, weekly, and even daily basis, most people he talked to didn't think even one publication combining all of these segments would succeed in Canada. In 1986, Jim formed Brunico Communications, Inc. and, without any previous experience in publishing or production, launched *Playback*. It wasn't long before sales were 2.5 times his original, most optimistic forecast. The biweekly paper positions itself as Canada's broadcast and production journal, serving the information needs and interests of those involved in Canadian TV broadcasting and in TV, film, and commercial production.

By 1989, with the success of *Playback* well established, Jim was getting restless again. There was a clear need for a publication that focused on strategies for marketers, rather than simply on the business of ad agencies and the media. Thus, *Strategy: The Canadian Marketing Report* was launched as a second, biweekly paper. The timing, however, was unfortunate. The economy was just heading into a long recession, resulting in cutbacks to the size and budgets of marketing departments, consolidations of companies, and a significant shift of marketing decision-making power to the United States. The new paper served a real need for marketers, however. *Strategy* survived and soon developed into the leading marketing publication in Canada.

With two successful publications under his belt, many would think that Jim would be content. Not likely! Soon he started to ask, "What next?" A chance conversation with a Canadian producer gave Jim the idea for an international magazine covering a niche sector in which Canada excelled: children's television. He attended a trade show in France and confirmed that the idea was a winner. Whereas the world already had 80 or more trade publications that covered the kids' market as part of their more general sector coverage, none offered an overall perspective. In January 1996, Brunico launched *KidScreen*, about reaching children through entertainment, and the title became a world leader in less than two years. *KidScreen*'s success has proven that a leading international magazine can be published out of Canada. It also resulted in the opening of a Brunico office in Los Angeles.

In 1997, *RealScreen* was born. This magazine is aimed at people who produce, broadcast, and market documentary, information magazine, and lifestyle programming. *RealScreen* became a hit from its very first issue and is the only publication of its kind in the world.

What next for Jim and his company? Well, Jim has realized that the real potential value of Brunico is based not simply on the paper publications he has launched, but on the brands that these titles represent. He sees the key to greater success as continued relationship building with his customers, catering to the information and marketing solutions they are seeking. The reputations of the publications and his organization can be leveraged into many ancillary products and services. Jim and his team are now launching innovative online services, conferences, award shows, newsletters, and directories, and are preparing to offer direct response marketing solutions.

Jim Shenkman.

Jim has learned a lot of lessons getting small, upstart ventures off the ground. First, no entrepreneur should ever underestimate the amount of financing that will be needed. There are only two times a businessperson should seek to raise funds, he believes. When your idea is just a dream you can get people excited enough to invest. And if you survive until the business is a proven success to the world at large, you can attract investment at a reasonable price. Getting start-up capital in Canada isn't as difficult as some people think, says Jim. If you have good ideas, the money to back them up is there. Often it is just as easy to raise a large sum of money as a small amount. And from personal experience, he says to always keep in mind the possibility of the next recession by having adequate financing and maintaining the flexibility to reduce costs quickly.

Jim has learned that being an expert in the field is not necessarily a prerequisite to success. Jim studied political science and urban studies before becoming a lawyer. He didn't know anything about the freight forwarding business, publishing, or film production when he started in these ventures. However, he is perceptive, willing to flout conventional wisdom, very organized, disciplined, and solution oriented. He attends conferences and trade shows to listen, look, and meet people, and reads related trade publications. Armed with the knowledge he acquires, he can quickly develop a business plan aimed at carving out a niche market for a product or service. He is a generalist with eyes wide open.

Ultimately, Jim aspires to be more than a successful entrepreneur. As exciting as it has been to identify good niche opportunities and offer better service and better products, he longs to be a true "agent of change." He marvels at those who have developed visions of serving markets in an entirely different manner. Examples that come to his mind include the pioneers behind Federal Express, CNN, Dell Computers, and 1-800-Flowers.

As you can see from the above paragraphs, Jim tries to follow his own advice. He's certainly been entrepreneurial and often among the first to identify trends and opportunities. Aside from new product ideas, Brunico was also one of the first in the world to use desktop publishing when the technology was just getting off the ground in the mid-1980s and among the first to offer full text searching of its Internet publications in the mid-1990s. Jim isn't sure just where the company's Internet products will take them, but he recognizes that this technology is revolutionizing the way people do business and marketing. By the time others have figured out its potential, you can bet Jim will already have moved on, always aspiring to be a visionary and, one day, a true agent of change.

Source: www.brunico.com

ronment have caused many companies to rethink the role of the product manager (see Marketing Highlight 2-4).

For companies that sell one product line to many different types of markets with different needs and preferences, a market management organization might be best. Many companies are organized along market lines. A market management organization is similar to the product management organization. Market managers are responsible for developing long-range and annual plans for the sales and profits in their markets. This system's main advantage is that the company is organized around the needs of specific customer segments.

Large companies that produce many different products flowing into many different geographic and customer markets use some combination of the functional, geographic, product, and market organization forms. This ensures that each function, product, and market receives its share of management attention. However, it can also add costly layers of management and reduce organizational flexibility. Still, the benefits of organizational specialization usually outweigh the drawbacks.[30]

Marketing Control

Marketing control
The process of measuring and evaluating the results of marketing strategies and plans, and taking corrective action to ensure that marketing objectives are attained.

Because many surprises occur during the implementation of marketing plans, the marketing department must practise constant marketing control. **Marketing control** involves evaluating the results of marketing strategies and plans and taking corrective action to ensure that objectives are attained. It involves the four steps shown in Figure 2-9. Management first sets specific marketing goals. It then measures its performance in the marketplace and evaluates the causes of any differences between expected and actual performance. Finally, management takes corrective action to close the gaps between its goals and its performance. This may require changing the action programs or even changing the goals.

Operating control involves checking ongoing performance against the annual plan and taking corrective action when necessary. Its purpose is to ensure that the company achieves the sales, profits, and other goals set out in its annual plan. It also involves determining the profitability of different products, territories, markets, and channels.

Marketing audit
A comprehensive, systematic, independent, and periodic examination of a company's environment, objectives, strategies, and activities to determine problem areas and opportunities and to recommend a plan of action to improve the company's marketing performance.

Strategic control involves considering whether the company's basic strategies are well matched to its opportunities. Marketing strategies and programs can quickly become outdated, and each company should periodically reassess its overall approach to the marketplace. A major tool for such strategic control is a **marketing audit.** This is a comprehensive, systematic, independent, and periodic examination of a company's environment, objectives, strategies, and activities to determine problem areas and opportunities. The audit provides good input for a plan of action to improve the company's marketing performance.[31]

marketing highlight 2-4

Brand Management or *Customer* Management?

Brand management has become a fixture in most consumer packaged-goods companies. Brand managers plan long-term brand strategy and watch over their brand's profits. Working closely with advertising agencies, they create national advertising campaigns to build market share and long-term consumer brand loyalty. The brand management system made sense in its earlier days, when the food companies were all-powerful, consumers were brand loyal, and national media could reach mass markets effectively. Recently, however, many companies have begun to question whether this system fits well with today's radically different marketing realities.

Two major environmental forces are causing companies to rethink brand management. First, consumers, markets, and marketing strategies have changed dramatically. Today's consumers face an ever-growing set of acceptable brands and are exposed to never-ending price promotions. Moreover, the rapid growth of the Internet and other communication technologies has given consumers more control over their information and buying environments. As a result, customers are more knowledgeable and less brand loyal. Second, larger, more powerful, and better-informed retailers are now demanding more trade promotions in exchange for scarce shelf space. The increase in spending for trade promotion leaves fewer dollars for national advertising, the brand manager's primary marketing tool. Retailers also want more customized "multi-brand" promotions that span many of the producer's brands and help retailers to compete better. Such promotions are beyond the scope of any single brand manager and must be designed at higher levels of the company.

These and other changes have significantly altered the way companies market their products, causing marketers to rethink the brand management system that has served them so well for many years. Although it is unlikely that brand managers will soon be extinct, many companies are now groping for alternative ways to manage their brands.

One alternative is to change the nature of the brand manager's job. For example, some companies are asking their brand managers to spend more time in the field working with salespeople, learning what is happening in stores and getting closer to the customer. Campbell Soup created "brand sales managers," a combination of product managers and salespeople charged with handling brands in the field, working with the trade, and designing more localized brand strategies.

As another alternative, Procter & Gamble, Colgate-Palmolive, Kraft-General Foods, RJR-Nabisco, and other companies have adopted category management systems. Under this system, brand managers report to a category manager who has total responsibility for an entire product line. For example, at Procter & Gamble, the brand manager for Dawn liquid dishwashing detergent reports to a manager who is responsible for Dawn, Ivory, Joy, and all other liquid detergents. The liquids manager, in turn, reports to a manager who is responsible for all of P&G's packaged soaps and detergents, including dishwashing detergents and liquid and dry laundry detergents.

Category management offers many advantages. First, rather than focusing on specific brands, category managers shape the company's entire category offering. This results in a more complete and coordinated category offer. Perhaps the most important benefit of category management is that it links up better with new retailer "category buying" systems, in which retailers have begun making their individual buyers responsible for working with all suppliers of a specific product category.

Some companies are combining category management with another concept: brand teams or category teams. For example, instead of having several cookie brand managers, Nabisco has three cookie category management teams—one each for adult rich cookies, nutritional cookies, and children's cookies. Headed by a category manager, each category team includes several marketing people—brand managers, a sales planning manager, and a marketing information specialist—who handle brand strategy, advertising, and sales promotion. Each team also includes specialists from finance, research and development, manufacturing, engineering, and distribution. Thus, category managers act as small businesspeople, with complete responsibility for an entire category and with a full complement of people to help them plan and implement category marketing strategies.

Thus, although brand managers are far from extinct, their jobs are changing. Such changes are much needed. The brand management system is product driven, not customer driven. Brand managers focus on pushing their brands out to anyone and everyone, and they often concentrate so heavily on a single brand that they lose sight of the marketplace. Even category management focuses on products, for example, "cookies" as opposed to "Oreos." But today, more than ever, companies must start not with brands, but with the needs of the consumers and retailers that these brands serve. Colgate recently took a step in this direction. It moved from brand management (Colgate brand toothpaste) to category management (all Colgate-Palmolive toothpaste brands) to customer-need management (customers' oral health needs). This last stage finally gets the organization to focus on customer needs.

Sources: See Robert Dewar and Don Schultz, "The product manager: An idea whose time has gone," *Marketing Communications,* May 1989:28–35; "Death of the brand manager," *The Economist,* 9 April 1994:67–8; and George S. Low and Ronald A. Fullerton, "Brands, brand management, and the brand manager system: A critical-historical evaluation," *Journal of Marketing Research,* May 1994:173–90.

FIGURE 2-9 The control process

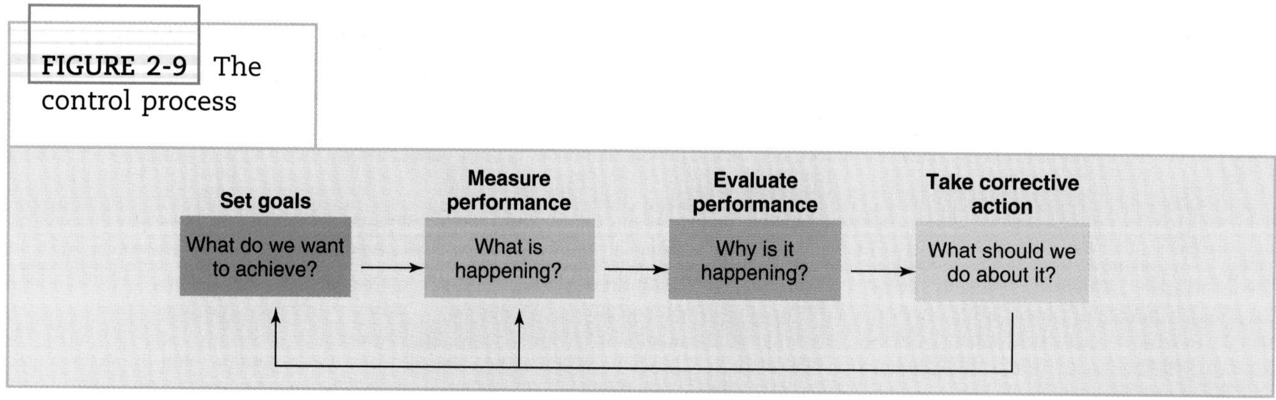

The marketing audit covers all major marketing areas of a business, not just a few trouble spots. It is normally conducted by an objective and experienced outside party who is independent of the marketing department. Table 2-3 shows the kinds of questions the marketing auditor might ask. The findings may come as a surprise—and sometimes as a shock—to management. Management then decides which actions make sense and how and when to implement them.

The Marketing Environment

Managing the marketing function would be hard enough if the marketer had to deal only with the controllable marketing mix variables. But the company operates in a complex marketing environment, consisting of uncontrollable forces to which the company must adapt. The environment produces both threats and opportunities. The company must carefully analyze its environment so that it can avoid the threats and take advantage of the opportunities.

The marketing environment includes forces close to the company that affect its ability to serve its consumers, such as other company departments, channel members, suppliers, competitors, and publics. It also includes broader demographic and economic forces, political and legal forces, technological and ecological forces, and social and cultural forces. The company must consider all of these forces when developing and positioning its offer to the target market. We discuss the marketing environment more fully in Chapter 3.

TABLE 2-3 Marketing Audit Questions

Marketing Environment Audit

1. The *macroenvironment:* What major demographic, economic, natural, technological, political, and cultural trends pose threats and opportunities for this company?
2. The *task environmnent:*
   - *Markets and customers:* What is happening to marketing size, growth, geographic distribution, and profits? What are the major market segments? How do customers make their buying decisions? How do they rate the company on product quality, value, and service?
   - *Other factors in the marketing system:* Who are the company's major competitors and what are their strategies, strengths, and weaknesses? How are the company's channels performing what trends are affecting suppliers? What key publics provide problems or opportunities?

Marketing strategy audit

1. *Business mission and marketing objectives:* Is the mission clearly defined and market-oriented? Has the company set clear objectives to guide marketing planning and performance?
2. *Marketing strategy:* Does the company have a strong marketing strategy for achieving its objectives?
3. *Budgets:* Has the company budgeted sufficient resources to segments, products, territories, and marketing mix elements?

Marketing organization audit

1. *Formal structure:* Are marketing activities optimally structured along functional, product, market, and territory lines?
2. *Functional efficiency:* Do marketing and sales communicate effectively? Is marketing staff well-trained, supervised, motivated, and evaluated?
3. *Cross-functional efficiency:* Do marketing people work well with people in operations, R&D, purchasing, human resources, information technology, and other non-marketing areas?

Marketing systems audit

1. *Marketing information system:* Is the marketing intelligence system providing accurate and timely information? Is the company using marketing research effectively?
2. *Marketing planning system:* Does the company prepare annual, long-term, and strategic plans? Are they used?
3. *Marketing control system:* Are annual plan objectives being achieved? Does management periodically analyze product, market, and channel sales and profitability?
4. *New product development:* Does the company have an effective new product development process? Has the company succeeded with new products?

Marketing productivity audit

1. *Profitability analysis:* How profitable are the company's different products, markets, territories, and channels? Should the company enter, expand, or withdraw from any business segments?
2. *Cost-effectiveness analysis:* Do any marketing activities have excessive costs? How can costs be reduced?

Marketing function audit

1. *Products:* What are the company's product line objectives? Should some current products be phased out or new products be added? Would some products benefit from changes in quality, features, or style?
2. *Price:* Are the company's pricing policies and procedures appropriate? Are prices in line with customers' perceived value?
3. *Place:* What are the company's distribution objectives and strategies? Should existing channels be changed or new ones added?
4. *Promotion:* Does the company have well-developed advertising, sales promotion, and public relations programs? Is the sales force large enough and well-trained, supervised, and motivated?

Review of Concept Connections

Strategic planning sets the stage for the rest of the company planning. Marketing contributes to strategic planning, and the overall plan defines marketing's role in the company. Although formal planning offers a variety of benefits to companies, not all companies use it or use it well. Many discussions of strategic planning focus on large corporations; however, small business also can benefit greatly from sound strategic planning.

1. **Explain the importance of strategic planning and the different levels at which plans are formed.**

   Strategic planning involves developing a strategy for long-run survival and growth. It sets the stage for the rest of the company planning and consists of five steps: defining the company's mission, setting objectives, designing a business portfolio, formulating strategies for the various business units, and developing functional plans. Defining a clear company mission begins with drafting a formal mission statement, which should be market oriented, realistic, motivating, and consistent with the market environment. The mission is then transformed into detailed supporting goals and objectives to guide the entire company. Based on those goals and objectives, the company headquarters designs a business portfolio, deciding which businesses and products should receive more or fewer resources. In turn, each business and product unit must develop detailed plans to support the corporation's overall objectives. To support the business unit's objectives, the functions within the unit each form plans. Marketing is one of the key functions. Comprehensive and sound marketing plans support business strategic planning by identifying specific opportunities.

2. **Describe the strategies that businesses use to achieve competitive advantage in their marketplace.**

   Once an SBU thoroughly understands the implications of competitors' activities and its position in the marketplace, it must select a strategy that will help it leverage its position. Michael Porter suggested three winning strategies that business competing within a given industry could follow to achieve competitive advantage: overall cost leadership, differentiation, and focus. More recently, marketing consultants Michael Treacy and Fred Wiersema offered a new classification of competitive marketing strategies, suggesting that companies gain leadership positions by delivering superior value to their customers. Companies can pursue any of three strategies, or value disciplines, for delivering superior customer value: operational excellence, product leadership, or customer intimacy. Classifying competitive strategies as value disciplines is appealing. It defines marketing strategy in terms of the single-minded pursuit of delivering value to customers. It recognizes that management must align every aspect of the company with the chosen value discipline—from its culture, to its organization structure, to its operating and management systems and processes. This customer value focus has motivated firms to go one step further and form long-term relationships with their key customers.

3. **Explain why many firms have moved toward a strategy of relationship marketing and describe the tools that they use to form relationships with their profitable customers.**

   Companies face tough competition. To survive, a company has to win customers and outperform competitors. Winning companies in today's marketplace have become adept at developing and implementing strategies for building customers, not merely building products. Thus, the focus is shifting toward customer relationship marketing. The new view is that marketing is the science and art of finding, retaining, and growing customers. The key to building lasting relationships is the creation of superior customer value and satisfaction, and companies need to understand the determinants of these important elements. Faced with a growing range of choices of products and services, consumers base their buying decisions on their perceptions of value. Customer delivered value is the difference between total customer value and total customer cost. Customers will usually choose the offer that maximizes their delivered value.

   Customer satisfaction results when a company's performance has fulfilled a buyer's expectations. Customers are dissatisfied if performance is below expectations, satisfied if performance equals expectations, and delighted if performance exceeds expectations. Satisfied customers buy more, are less price sensitive, talk favourably about the company, and remain loyal longer. Companies not only strive to gain customers but, perhaps more importantly, to retain and grow "share of customer." Companies must decide the level at which they want to build relationships with different market segments and individual customers, ranging from basic relationships to full partnerships. Which is best depends on a customer's lifetime value relative to the costs required to attract and keep that customer. Today's marketers use a number of specific marketing tools to develop stronger bonds with customers by adding financial and social benefits or structural ties.

To create customer value and satisfaction and to retain customers, companies must manage their value-delivery networks in a customer-orientated way. Each company department can be seen as a link in the firm's value chain. That is, each department carries out value-creating activities to design, produce, market, deliver, and support the firm's products. The firm's success depends on how well each department performs its work and on how well the activities of various departments are coordinated. In seeking a competitive advantage, a company must also look beyond its own value chain and into the customer value-delivery network, the system made up of the value chains of its suppliers, distributors, and, ultimately, customers. Today most companies are "partnering" with the other members of the supply chain to improve the performance of the customer value-delivery network.

4. Describe functional planning strategies and marketing's role in strategic planning.

Each of the company's functional departments provides inputs for strategic planning. Once strategic objectives have been identified, management within each business must prepare a set of functional plans that coordinates the activities of the marketing, finance, manufacturing, and other departments. A company's success depends on how well each department performs its customer value-adding activities and on how well the departments work together to serve the customer. Each department has a different idea about which objectives and activities are most important. The marketing department stresses the consumer's perspective, while the operations department may be more concerned with reducing production costs. To develop a system of plans that will best accomplish the firm's overall strategic objectives, marketing managers must work to understand other functional managers' perspectives.

Marketing plays an important role throughout the strategic planning process. It provides inputs to strategic planning concerning attractive market possibilities, and its customer focus serves as a guiding philosophy for planning. Marketers design strategies to help meet strategic objectives and prepare programs to carry them out profitably. Marketing also plays an integral role in helping ensure that departments work together harmoniously toward the goal of delivering superior customer value and satisfaction.

5. Describe the marketing process and the forces that influence it.

The marketing process matches consumer needs with the company's capabilities and objectives. Consumers are at the centre of the marketing process. The company divides the total market into smaller segments, selecting the segments it can best serve. It then designs a marketing mix to differentiate its marketing offer and position this offer in selected target segments. The marketing mix consists of product, price, place, and promotion decisions.

6. List the marketing management functions, including the elements of a marketing plan.

To find the best mix and put it into action, the company engages in marketing analysis, marketing planning, marketing implementations, and marketing control. The main components of a marketing plan are the executive summary, current marketing situation, threats and opportunities, objectives and issues, marketing strategies, action programs, budgets, and controls. To plan a good strategy is often easier than to carry it out. To be successful, a company must implement its strategy effectively. Implementation is the process that turns a marketing strategy into marketing actions.

Most of the responsibility for implementation goes to the company's marketing department. Modern marketing departments are organized in several ways. The most common form is the functional marketing organization, in which marketing functions are directed by separate managers who report to the marketing vice-president. The company might also use a geographic organization, in which its sales force or other functions specialize by geographic area. The company may also use the product management organization, in which products are assigned to product managers who work with functional specialists to develop and achieve their plans. Another form is the market management organization, in which major markets are assigned to market managers who work with functional specialists.

Marketing organizations carry out marketing control. Operating control involves monitoring current marketing results to ensure that the annual sales and profit goals will be achieved. Strategic control ensures that the company's marketing objectives, strategies, and systems fit with the current forecasted marketing environment. It uses the marketing audit to determine marketing opportunities and problems and to recommend short-run and long-run actions to improve overall marketing performance. Through these activities, the company watches and adapts to the marketing environment.

Key Terms

Business portfolio *(p. 56)*
Business unit strategy *(p. 50)*
Corporate strategic planning *(p. 50)*
Cost leadership *(p. 62)*
Customer intimacy *(p. 63)*
Differentiation *(p. 62)*
Diversification *(p. 60)*
Focus *(p. 62)*
Functional strategy *(p. 50)*
Growth–share matrix *(p. 56)*
Market development *(p. 60)*
Market penetration *(p. 60)*
Market positioning *(p. 74)*
Market segmentation *(p. 74)*
Market targeting *(p. 74)*
Marketing audit *(p. 82)*
Marketing control *(p. 82)*
Marketing implementation *(p. 79)*
Marketing mix *(p. 72)*
Marketing process *(p. 72)*
Mission statement *(p. 53)*
Operational excellence *(p. 63)*
Portfolio analysis *(p. 56)*
Product development *(p. 60)*
Product leadership *(p. 63)*
Strategic business unit (SBU) *(p. 49)*
Strategic planning *(p. 49)*

Discussing the Issues

1. Define *strategic planning*. List and briefly review the five steps in the strategic planning process.
2. In a series of job interviews, you ask three recruiters to describe the missions of their companies. One says, "To make profits." Another says, "To create customers." The third says, "To fight world hunger." Analyze and discuss what these mission statements tell you about each company.
3. An electronics manufacturer obtains the semiconductors it uses in production from a company-owned subsidiary that also sells to other manufacturers. The subsidiary is smaller and less profitable than are competing producers, and its growth rate has been below the industry average over the past five years. Define which cell of the BCG growth–share matrix this strategic business unit would fall into. What should the parent company do with this SBU?
4. As companies become more customer- and marketing-oriented, many departments find that they must change their traditional way of doing things. List several examples of ways that a company's finance, accounting, and engineering departments can help the company become more marketing-oriented.
5. Most universities and colleges seek strong relationships with their alumni. Considering the relationship-marketing approaches suggested in this text, formulate a plan that would keep you as a loyal alumnus of your university or college.
6. The competitive business strategy that is best for a company depends on its industry position. Which of the strategies described by Porter (cost leadership, differentiation, or focus) or the value disciplines developed by Treacy and Wiersema (operational excellence, product leadership, or customer intimacy) would be best for each of the following organizations? (a) The Toronto Raptors or the Vancouver Grizzlies, (b) General Electric's small appliances division, (c) The Canadian Cancer Society, (d) Chapters.ca.

Marketing Applications

1. E-commerce is experiencing explosive growth. Many experts predict that it is the marketing model of the future. Thus many people are now asking, "How does one get started in becoming a cyberpreneur?" Some examples of successful cyberpreneurs include www.violet.com, www.800Flowers.com, and www.hotwired.com (*Wired* magazine). Assume that you wish to start a business on the Internet.
   a. How would you look for a promising opportunity?
   b. Select a specific opportunity. What makes this opportunity distinctive and promising?

c. Describe your target market and how you would serve it differently than current businesses do.

d. What marketing mix would you use for your business?

e. Write a brief marketing plan (see Table 2-2) for this promising opportunity. After writing the plan, assess your chances for success in starting such a business.

2. Have you ever found yourself lost on some unknown and lonely road with no idea of how to get where you're trying to go? If so, you're just one of many consumers looking for a more certain and safer way to travel. Now, there's a solution. Auto navigation systems will not only plot your course, they'll help get you there on time and even book a room for you. Sound too good to be true? OnStar's on-board concierge system helps drivers answer all the irritating questions that plague most travellers. OnStar combines cutting-edge technology with attentive personal service to provide the travellers with safety, security, and convenience. Using global positioning satellites, OnStar can not only tell where you are, it can also help you get where you're going through personal directions delivered via an on-board telephone system. OnStar also provides remote diagnostics, remote door unlock, stolen vehicle tracking, roadside assistance, accident assistance, and many other services. In the future, the best friend a motorist may have is that friendly voice from OnStar that says "May I be of assistance?" (Visit www.onstar.com for more information.)

a. What customer value does OnStar deliver? How does it create customer satisfaction? How does it build relationships with customers?

b. What is OnStar's overall competitive strategy? What consumers should it target? What's the best way to reach this target market: through ads, via the Internet, via automobile dealers, or some other way? Explain.

c. How does OnStar use the marketing concept to enhance its business?

Internet Connections

Strategic Planning for Online Marketing

Online book selling is big business. The first successful online bookseller was Amazon.com, an exclusively online retailer. The company quickly established itself as the market leader. Attracted by the profit potential, Barnes & Noble, Borders, and others followed suit. Recently, Amazon has diversified into many other lines of business: music, video, electronics, toys, pharmaceuticals, and online auctions. Is this a good strategy for Amazon? To help you answer this question, conduct an analysis of the online toy industry. Complete the following table by first visiting www.bizrate.com to identify two of Amazon's toughest online toy store competitors. Review the BizRate comments and visit each competitor's site to complete the table. One online competitor, e-Toys, recently went bankrupt. Why do you think this occurred and what does it tell you about the nature of this industry?

For Discussion

Analyze Amazon's strategy by answering the following questions.

1. How does Amazon compare to its competition in the toy industry?
2. What is Amazon's mission statement? You can guess at this by reading about the company at www.amazon.com.
3. Does the toy business fit with Amazon's mission? Why, or why not?
4. Should Amazon be in the toy business? Justify your response.

5. Is there any synergy between Amazon's many product areas? If so, what is it?
6. Years ago, Sears advertised that "Sears has everything!" Is Amazon becoming the Sears of the Internet? If so, is this a good strategy?
7. Does Amazon pursue different product strategies in its UK and German operations?
8. Based on what you have learned, do you think Amazon is pursuing the correct strategy? Why, or why not?

Amazon	Other Competitor	Other Competitor
www.amazon.com		
Who rated site for BizRate?		
BizRate overall customer rating		
Products sold in addition to toys		
Market positioning*		
Competitive advantage*		
Competitive weakness*		

*infer from viewing site and ratings

Savvy Sites

- CNET (www.news.com) focuses on the latest news in the Internet and computer industries.
- Liszt (www.liszt.com) provides links to over 90 000 mailing lists. A subscriber can read and discuss trends in just about any industry.
- One way to evaluate the competition is to review financial analysts' comments at investment firms. Some firms that offer industry and individual firm analyses are Charles Schwab (www.schwab.com), Merrill Lynch (www.merrilllynch.com), and E*TRADE (www.etrade.com).
- Accenture (www.accenture.com) helps businesses understand their competitors and develop appropriate strategies.

Notes

1. Kathryn Dennis, "Bill Conner: Nortel Networks, Marketer of the Year 2000," *MC (Marketing Computers) Technology Marketing Intelligence*, February 2000 (www.marketingcomputers.com/issue/feb00/feature1/feature1a.asp); John Partridge, "Nortel tops U.K. survey of global firms," *Globe and Mail*, 27 April 2000; Andrew Whal, "Praying for John," *Canadian Business*, 21 August 2000; Andrea Zoe Aster, "Childers takes on Nortel brand," *Marketing Magazine*, 24 April 2000; "Nortel goes global with heroes ads," *Marketing Magazine*, 4 October 1999; www.nortelnetworks.com/corporate; Neil Murray, "Nortel Stock Saga Full of Lessons," *Canoe News*, February 26, 2001 (www.canoe.ca/moneymutualnews/feb26_nortellessons-sun.html); "Nortel Networks transforms enterprise voice and data networks with internet telephony and optical ethernet," Nortel News Release, May 9, 2001.
2. See Philip Kotler, *Kotler on Marketing*, New York: Free Press, 1999:165–6.
3. For a more detailed discussion of corporate- and business-level strategic planning as they apply to marketing, see Philip Kotler, *Marketing Management: Analysis, Planning, Implementation, and Control*, 10th ed., Upper Saddle River, NJ: Prentice Hall, 2000: Chapter 3.

4. Leslie Brokaw, "The secrets of great planning," *Inc.*, October 1992:152; and Kotler, *Marketing Management: Analysis, Planning, Implementation, and Control:* Chapter 3.
5. See Bradley Johnson, "Bill Gates' vision of Microsoft in every home," *Advertising Age,* 19 December 1994:14–5. For more on mission statements, see J. W. Graham and W. C. Havlick, *Mission Statements: A Guide to the Corporate and Nonprofit Sectors,* New York: Garland Publishing, 1994; P. Jones and L. Kahaner, *Say It and Live It: The 50 Corporate Mission Statements That Hit the Mark,* New York: Doubleday, 1995; Thomas A. Stewart, "A refreshing change: Vision statements that make sense," *Fortune,* 30 September 1996:195–6; and Christopher K. Bart, "Making mission statements count," *CA Magazine,* March 1999:37–8.
6. Andyne Computing Limited, *1996 Annual Report:2.*
7. See John A. Byrne, "Strategic planning," *Business Week,* 26 August 1996:46–51; Pete Bogda, "Fifteen years later, the return of 'strategy,'" *Brandweek,* February 1997:18; Diane Sanchez, "Now that's customer focus," *Sales & Marketing Management,* April 1998:24; Nryan W. Barry, "A beginner's guide to strategic planning," *The Futurist,* April 1998:33–6; and Ian Wilson, "Strategic planning for the millennium: Resolving the dilemma," *Long Range Planning,* August 1998:507–13.
8. H. Igor Ansoff, "Strategies for diversification," *Harvard Business Review,* September–October 1957:113–24.
9. Michael E. Porter, *Competitive Strategy: Techniques for Analyzing Industries and Competitors,* New York: Free Press, 1980: Chapter 2; and Porter, "What is strategy?" Also see James Surowiecki, "The return of Michael Porter," *Fortune,* 1 February 1999:135–8.
10. Michael Treacy and Fred Wiersema, "Customer intimacy and other value disciplines," *Harvard Business Review,* January–February 1993:84–93; Michael Treacy and Fred Wiersema, "How market leaders keep their edge," *Fortune,* 6 February 1995:88–98; Michael Treacy and Fred Wiersema, *The Discipline of Market Leaders: Choose Your Customers, Narrow Your Focus, Dominate Your Market,* Reading, MA: Addison-Wesley, 1997; and Fred Wiersema, *Customer Intimacy: Pick Your Partners, Shape Your Culture, Win Together,* Santa Monica, CA: Knowledge Exchange, 1998.
11. See Kevin J. Clancy and Robert S. Shulman, "Breaking the mold," *Sales & Marketing Management,* January 1994:82–4; Thomas O. Jones and W. Earl Sasser Jr., "Why satisfied customers defect," *Harvard Business Review,* November–December 1995:88–99; Susan Fournier, Susan Dobscha, and David Glen Mick, "Preventing the premature death of relationship marketing," *Harvard Business Review,* January–February 1998:42–50; and Erika Rasmusson, "Complaints can build relationships," *Sales & Marketing Management,* September 1999:89.
12. Libby Estell, "This call center accelerates sales," *Sales & Marketing Management,* February 1999:72.
13. For a thorough discussion on defining value, see Howard E. Butz Jr. and Leonard D. Goodstein, "Measuring customer value: gaining strategic advantage," *Organizational Dynamics,* Winter 1996:63–77; and Robert B. Woodruff, "Customer value: The next source of competitive advantage," *Journal of the Academy of Marketing Science,* Spring 1997:139–53.
14. For an excellent discussion of the determinants of customer satisfaction, see Richard A. Spreng, Scott B. MacKenzie, and Richard W. Olshavsky, "A reexamination of the determinants of customer satisfaction," *Journal of Marketing,* July 1996:15–32; and Ruth N. Bolton and Katherine N. Lemon, "A dynamic model of customers' usage of services: Usage as an antecedent and consequence of satisfaction," *Journal of Marketing,* May 1999:171–86.
15. Thomas O. Jones and W. Earl Sasser Jr., "Why satisfied customers defect." Also see Thomas A. Stewart, "A satisfied customer isn't enough," *Fortune,* 21 July 1997:112–3.
16. Thomas O. Jones and W. Earl Sasser Jr., "Why satisfied customers defect":91. For other examples, see Roger Sant, "Did he jump or was he pushed?" *Marketing News,* 12 May 1997:2,21.
17. Harry Seymour and Laura Rifkin, "Study shows satisfaction not the same as loyalty," *Marketing News,* 26 October 1998:40,42.
18. Quotes and other information from "Gateway ranks #1 in both client loyalty and U.S. consumer desktop shipments," press release accessed online at **www.gateway.com,** 15 June 1999; Steven V. Brull, "A net gain for Gateway," *Business Week,* 19 July 1999:77–8; Aaron Goldberg, "Going long," *MC Technology Marketing Intelligence,* May 1999:14; and Gary McWilliams, "Gateway managers to smooth out earnings and bull ahead in Internet-service business," *Wall Street Journal,* 12 July 1999:C2.
19. Leonard L. Berry and A. Parasuraman, *Marketing Services: Competing through Quality,* New York: Free Press, 1991:136–42.
20. See Louise O'Brien and Charles Jones, "Do rewards really create loyalty?" *Harvard Business Review,* May–June 1995:75–82; "Harley owners journey to meet their maker . . . again and again," *Colloquy* 5(4), 1997:13–4; Constance L. Hays, "What companies need to know is in the pizza dough," *New York Times,* 26 July 1998:3; and Richard G. Barlow, "Future looks bright for frequency marketing," *Marketing News,* 5 July 1999:14.
21. Chuck Novak, Saturn Canada brand manager, in an interview with Peggy Cunningham on 21 July 1999. David Bosworth, "GM attracts site seers," *Strategy,* 22 June 1998:D1; Sinclair Steward, "Putting the customer first," *Strategy,* 9 November 1998:21.
22. Philip Kotler, *Kotler on Marketing*:20–2.
23. John C. Narver and Stanley F. Slater, "The effect of a market orientation on business profitability," *Journal of Marketing,* October 1990:20–35.
24. See Brian Dumaine, "Creating a new company culture," *Fortune,* 15 January 1990:128; and Howard E. Butz Jr. and Leonard D. Goodstein, "Measuring customer value: Gaining strategic advantage," *Organizational Dynamics,* Winter 1996:63–77.
25. John Southerst, "Customer crunching," *Canadian Business,* September 1993:28–35.
26. The "four P" classification was first suggested by E. Jerome McCarthy, *Basic Marketing: A Managerial Approach,* Homewood, IL: Irwin, 1960. For more discussion of this classification scheme, see Walter van Waterschoot and Christophe Van den Bulte, "The 4P classification of the marketing mix revisited," *Journal of Marketing,* October 1992:83–93.
27. Robert Lauterborn, "New marketing litany: 4Ps passé; C-words take over," *Advertising Age,* 1 October 1990:26. Also see Kotler, *Marketing Management: Analysis, Planning, Implementation, and Control*:16.
28. Brian Dumaine, "Why great companies last," *Business Week,* 16 January 1995:129. See James C. Collins and Jerry I. Porras, *Built to Last: Successful Habits of Visionary Companies,* New York: HarperBusiness, 1995; Geoffrey Brewer, "Firing line: What separates visionary companies from all the rest?" *Performance,* June 1995:12–7; and Rob Goffee and Gareth Jones, *The Character of a Corporation: How Your Company's Culture Can Make or Break Your Business,* New York: HarperBusiness, 1998.
29. Joseph Winski, "One brand, one manager," *Advertising Age,* 20 August 1987:86. Also see Jack Neff, "P&G redefines the brand manager," *Advertising Age,* 13 October 1997:1,18; Alan J. Bergstrom, "Brand management poised for change," *Marketing News,* 7 July 1997:5; James Bell, "Brand management for the next

millennium," *The Journal of Business Strategy*, March–April 1998:7; and Jack Neff, "The new brand management," *Advertising Age*, 8 November 1999:S2,S18.

30. For more complete discussions of marketing organization approaches and issues, see Robert W. Ruekert, Orville C. Walker Jr., and Kenneth J. Roering, "The organization of marketing activities: A contingency theory of structure and performance," *Journal of Marketing*, Winter 1985:13–25; Ravi S. Achrol, "Evolution of the marketing organization: New forms for turbulent environments," *Journal of Marketing*, October 1991:77–93; and Geoffrey Brewer, "Love the ones you're with," *Sales & Marketing Management*, February 1997:38–45.

31. For details, see Kotler, *Marketing Management: Analysis, Planning, Implementation, and Control:* Chapter 20.

Company Case 2

Trap-Ease: The Big Cheese of Mousetraps

One April morning, Martha House, president of Trap-Ease, entered her office in Moncton, New Brunswick. She paused for a moment to contemplate the Ralph Waldo Emerson quotation that she had framed and hung near her desk: "If a man [can] . . . make a better mousetrap than his neighbor . . . the world will make a beaten path to his door." Perhaps, she mused, Emerson knew something that she didn't. She had the better mousetrap—Trap-Ease—but the world didn't seem all that excited about it.

Martha had just returned from the National Hardware Show in Toronto. Standing in the trade show display booth for long hours and answering the same questions hundreds of times had been tiring. Yet, this show had excited her. Each year, National Hardware Show officials held a contest to select the best new product introduced at the show. Of the more than 300 new products introduced at that year's show, her mousetrap had won first place. Such notoriety was not new for the Trap-Ease mousetrap. *Canadian Business* magazine had written an article about the mousetrap, and the television show *MarketPlace* and trade publications had featured it. Despite all of this attention, however, the expected demand for the trap had not materialized. Martha hoped that this award might stimulate increased interest and sales.

A group of investors who had obtained worldwide rights to market the innovative mousetrap had formed Trap-Ease in January. In return for marketing rights, the group agreed to pay the inventor and patent holder, a retired rancher, a royalty fee for each trap sold. The group then hired Martha to serve as president and to develop and manage the Trap-Ease organization.

The Trap-Ease, a simple yet clever device, is manufactured by a plastics firm under contract with Trap-Ease. It consists of a square, plastic tube measuring about 15 cm long and 4 cm square. The tube bends in the middle at a 30-degree angle, so that when the front part of the tube rests on a flat surface, the other end is elevated. The elevated ends holds a removable cap into which the user places bait (cheese, dog food, or some other tidbit). A hinged door is attached to the front end of the tube. When the trap is "open," this door rests on two narrow "stilts" attached to the two bottom corners of the door.

The trap works with simple efficiency. A mouse, smelling the bait, enters the tube through the open end. As it walks up the angled bottom toward the bait, its weight makes the elevated end of the trap drop downward. This elevates the open end, allowing the hinged door to swing closed, trapping the mouse. Small teeth on the ends of the stilts catch in a groove on the bottom of the trap, locking the door closed. The mouse can be disposed of live, or it can be left alone for a few hours to suffocate in the trap.

Martha believed that the trap had many advantages for the consumer when compared with traditional spring-loaded traps or poisons. It appeals to consumers who want a humane alternative to spring traps. Furthermore, with Trap-Ease, consumers can avoid the unpleasant mess they encounter with the violent spring-loaded traps—it creates no clean-up problem. Finally, the consumer can re-use the trap or simply throw it away.

Martha's early research suggested that women are the best target market for the Trap-Ease. Men, it seems, are more willing to buy and use the traditional, spring-loaded trap. The targeted women, however, do not like the traditional trap. They often stay at home and take care of their children. Thus, they want a means of dealing with the mouse problem that avoids the unpleasantness and risks that the standard trap creates in the home.

To reach this target market, Martha decided to distribute Trap-Ease through national grocery, hardware, and drug chains such as Safeway, Zellers, Canadian Tire, and Shoppers Drug Mart. She sold the trap directly to these large retailers, avoiding any wholesalers or other intermediaries.

The traps sold in packages of two, with a suggested retail price of $2.99. Although this price made the Trap-Ease about five times more expensive than smaller, standard traps, consumers appeared to offer little initial price resistance. The manufacturing cost for the Trap-Ease, including freight and packaging costs, was about 31 cents per unit. The company paid an additional 8.2 cents per unit in royalty fees. Martha priced the traps to retailers at $1.49 per unit and estimated that, after sales and volume discounts, Trap-Ease would realize net revenues from retailers of $1.29 per unit.

To promote the product, Martha had budgeted approximately $60 000 for the first year. She planned to use $50 000 of this amount for travel costs to visit trade shows and to make sales calls on retailers. She would use the remaining $10 000 for advertising. Because the mousetrap had generated so much publicity, however, she had not felt the need to do much advertising. Still, she had placed advertising in *Chatelaine* and in other "home and shelter" magazines. Martha was the company's only "salesperson," but she intended to hire more salespeople soon.

Martha had initially forecast Trap-Ease's first-year sales at 500 000 units. By the end of April, however, the company had sold only several thousand units. Martha wondered if most new products got off to such a slow start, or if she was doing something wrong. She had detected some problems, although none seemed overly serious. For one, there had not been enough repeat buying. For another, she had noted that many of the retailers kept their sample mousetraps on their desks as conversation pieces—she wanted the traps to be used and demonstrated. Martha wondered if consumers were also buying the traps as novelties rather than as solutions to their mouse problems.

Martha knew that the investor group believed that Trap-Ease had a "once-in-a-lifetime chance" with its innovative mousetrap. She sensed the group's impatience. She had budgeted approximately $150 000 in administrative and fixed costs for the first year (not including marketing costs). To keep the investors happy, the company needed to sell enough traps to cover those costs and make a reasonable profit.

In these first few months, Martha had learned that marketing a new product is not an easy task. For example, one national retailer had placed a large order with instructions that the order was to be delivered to the loading dock at one of its warehouses between 1:00 and 3:00 p.m. on a specified day. When the truck delivering the order had arrived late, the retailer had refused to accept the shipment. The retailer had told Martha it would be a year before she got another chance. Perhaps, Martha thought, she should send the retailer and other customers a copy of Emerson's famous quotation.

Questions

1. Martha and the Trap-Ease investors believe they face a "once-in-a-lifetime" opportunity. What information do they need to evaluate this opportunity? How do you think the group would write its mission statement? How would you write it?
2. Has Martha identified the best target market for Trap-Ease? What other market segments might the firm target?
3. How has the company positioned the Trap-Ease relative to the chosen target market? Could it position the product in other ways?
4. Describe the current marketing mix for Trap-Ease. Do you see any problems with this mix?
5. Who is Trap-Ease's competition?
6. How would you change Trap-Ease's marketing strategy? What kinds of control procedures would you establish for this strategy?
7. Develop a budget based on the numbers in the case. Is it realistic? Would you make changes?

video case 2

FIRING YOUR CUSTOMER!

With all the emphasis on developing strategies of customer intimacy and building better customer relationships, it seems unbelievable that some companies are actually trying to "fire" some customers. Nonetheless, a new trend is underway in companies' relations with their clients.

Businesses now have the technology to better analyze their databases in order to identify "deadbeat" customers—those that actually cost the company money instead of generating profits. How can a customer cost a company money, you might ask. The equation is simple. In some industries, such as telecommunications, the cost of acquiring new customers is high. Take the case of Clearnet. It and other competitors scrambled to get new customers for their services. They sold cell phones well below the cost of the phones just to get customers to sign up. However, while some customers remained loyal and turned out to be heavy users of the service, others switched from one provider to another and failed to generate the expected profits.

Keeping customers isn't cheap. Providing high quality service is costly. If a Clearnet customer ties up the help line frequently, but doesn't buy enough air time to offset the costs, the company loses out again. In other words, if customers don't generate enough revenue through their purchases to offset these costs and generate some profit, they actually cost the company money!

What has surprised many companies is the fact that unprofitable customers may constitute 25 to 30 percent of their clients. Armed with this knowledge, companies seem to have two alternatives. Firms like API Travel, a consultancy that serves top-end travellers, have chosen to fire some customers. Other companies are trying to lower the costs of serving less profitable customers.

This new thinking about customers is based on what has been labelled *customer relationship management or CRM,* technology-enabled marketing that merges the capabilities of the information technology department with the marketing department. The premise underlying CRM is that not all customers are alike, either in terms of their needs or in terms of the profits they will generate for the firm. The aim of a CRM program is the development and maintenance of mutually beneficial, long-term relationships with strategically significant customers. Who are these people? They are customers that the company believes have high lifetime value. In other words, they are the customers the company thinks it can serve well so that it can retain their loyalty over a lifetime of purchases, thus generating a stream of profits for the firm over the duration of the relationship.

CRM is more than technology, however. It is a way of organizing and thinking. For generations, companies have structured themselves around their key products or the key regions they serve. Thus, we have had product managers or country managers as job titles within firms. Today, this is changing as firms begin organizing around individual customers. Improved technology not only allows firms to build 'profiles' of these key customers so that they can serve them better, it also allows them to provide consistent service and products across multiple channels of distribution. For example, a bank that uses a CRM system can provide top quality service to its key customers no matter how the customer chooses to interact with the bank—in person at a branch, over the phone, by fax, by using an ATM or the Internet.

However, the strategy of managing customers is not without its risks. Social critics fear that people with low incomes may be blocked from receiving essential services. Others see a "customer class system" developing. While customers with high profit potential will get excellent service, other customers will be neglected. Furthermore, Canada is a relatively small marketplace and if enough customers are offended by being "fired," there may be a customer backlash. Of even greater concern is the fact that the high-cost customer of today may be tomorrow's profitable customer. Thus, firms are stepping lightly so as not to offend any of their customers.

Questions

1. What are the pros and cons of "firing" customers?
2. How could a company like Clearnet lower the costs of serving less profitable customers?
3. Do you agree that the use of CRM technologies will actually harm some members of society?

Sources: Peggy Cunningham prepared this case based on "Firing Your Customer," *Venture* (January 26, 1999). Also see Francis Buttle, "The S.C.O.P.E. of Customer Relationship Mangement," 2000, *CRM-Forum Resources* (www.crm-forum.com).

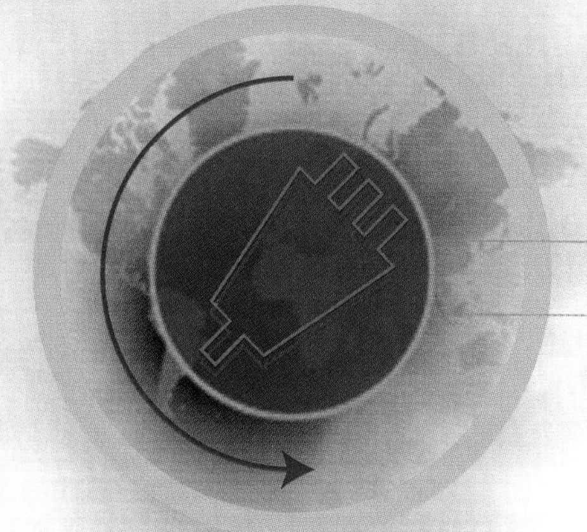

P A R T **1** 2 3 4

Understanding Marketing and the Marketing Process

Concept Connections

After studying this chapter, you should be able to

1. Describe the environmental forces that affect the company's ability to serve its customers.
2. Explain how changes in the demographic and economic environments affect marketing decisions.
3. Identify the major trends in the firm's natural and technological environments.
4. Explain the key changes in the political and cultural environments.
5. Discuss how companies can react to the marketing environment.

chapter 3

The Marketing Environment

As we hurtle into the new millennium, social experts are busy assessing the impact of numerous environmental forces on consumers and the marketers who serve them. Many people are excited but sometimes fearful about what the future may bring.

"Millennial fever" has hit the nation's baby boomers, the most commercially influential demographic group in history, especially hard. The oldest boomers, now in their fifties, are resisting the aging process with the vigour they once reserved for antiwar protests. Other factors are also at work. Today, people of all ages seem to feel a bit overworked, overstimulated, and overloaded. People "are overwhelmed . . . by the breathtaking onrush of the Information Age, with its high-speed modems, cell phones, and pagers. . . . While we hail the benefits of the wired '90s, at the same time we are buffeted by the rapid pace of change."

The result of this millennial fever is a yearning to turn back the clock, to return to simpler times. This yearning has in turn produced a massive nostalgia wave. "We are creating a new culture, and we don't know what's going to happen," explains a noted futurist. "So we need some warm fuzzies from our past." Marketers of all kinds have responded to these nostalgia pangs by recreating products and images that help take consumers back to "the good old days." Examples are plentiful: Kellogg has revived old Corn Flakes packaging, and car makers have created retro roadsters such as the Porsche Boxter. A Pepsi commercial rocks to the Rolling Stones' "Brown Sugar," James Brown's "I Feel Good" helps sell laxatives, and Janis Joplin's raspy voice crows, "Oh Lord, won't you buy me a Mercedes-Benz?" Disney developed an entire town—Celebration, Florida—to recreate the look and feel of 1940s neighbourhoods. Heinz reintroduced its classic glass ketchup bottle, supported by nostalgic "Heinz was there" ads showing two 1950s-era boys eating hot dogs at a ballpark. Master marketer Coca-Cola resurrected the old red button logo and its heritage contour bottle; its current ad theme, "Always Coca-Cola," encapsulates both the past and the future, according to a Coca-Cola marketing executive.

Perhaps no company has more riding on the nostalgia wave than Volkswagen. The original Volkswagen Beetle first sputtered into North America in 1949. With its simple, bug-like design, no-frills engineering, and economical operation, the Beetle was the antithesis of Detroit's chrome-laden gas guzzlers. Although most owners would readily admit that their Beetles were underpowered, noisy, cramped, and freezing in the winter, they saw these as endearing qualities. Overriding these minor inconveniences, the Beetle was cheap to buy and own, dependable, easy to fix, fun to drive, and anything but flashy.

During the 1960s, as young baby boomers by the thousands were buying their first cars, demand exploded, and the Beetle blossomed into an unlikely icon. Bursting with personality, the understated Bug came to personify an era of rebellion against convention. By the late 1970s, however, the boomers had moved on, Bug mania had faded, and Volkswagen had dropped Beetle production for the North American market. Still, more than 20 years later, the mere mention of these chugging oddities evokes smiles and strong emotions. Almost everyone over the age of 25, it seems, has a "feel-good" Beetle story to tell.

In an attempt to surf the nostalgia wave, Volkswagen recently introduced a New Beetle. Outwardly, the reborn Beetle resembles the original, tapping the strong emotions and memories of times gone by. Beneath the skin, however, the New Beetle is packed with modern features. According to an industry expert, "The Beetle comeback is . . . based on a combination of romance and reason—wrapping up modern conveniences in an old-style package. Built into the dashboard is a bud vase perfect for a daisy plucked straight from the 1960s. But right next to it is a high-tech, multispeaker stereo—and options like power windows, cruise control, and a power sunroof make it a very different car than the rattly old Bug. The new version . . . comes with all the modern features car buyers demand, such as four air bags and power outlets for cell phones. But that's not why VW expects folks to buy it. With a familiar bubble shape that still makes people smile as it skitters by, the new Beetle offers a pull that is purely emotional."

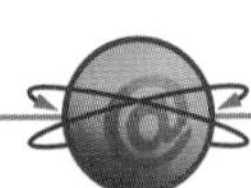

New Beetle
www.vw.com/newbeetle

Advertising for the New Beetle plays strongly on the nostalgia theme, while at the same time refreshing the old Beetle heritage. "If you sold your soul in the '80s," tweaks one ad, "here's your chance to buy it back." Other ads read, "Less flower, more power," and "Comes with wonderful new features. Like heat." Still another ad declares "0 to 60? Yes." The car's Web page summarized: "The New Beetle has what any Beetle always had. Originality. Honesty. A point of view. It's an exhaustive and zealous rejection of banality. Isn't the world ready for that kind of car again?"

Volkswagen invested $840 million to bring the New Beetle to market. However, this investment appears to be paying big dividends. Demand quickly outstripped supply. Even before the first cars reached VW showrooms, dealers across North America had long waiting lists of people who'd paid for the car without ever seeing it, let alone driving it. Volkswagen's initial first-year sales projections of 50 000 New Beetles in North America proved pessimistic. After only nine months, the company had sold more than 64 000 of the new Bugs in the United States and Canada. The smart little car also garnered numerous distinguished awards, including *Motor Trend*'s 1999 Import Car of the Year, *Time* magazine's The Best of 1998 Design, *Business Week*'s Best New Product, and 1999 North American Car of the Year, awarded by an independent panel of top journalists who cover the auto industry.

The New Beetle appears to be a cross-generational hit. Even kids too young to remember the original Bug appear to love this new one. "It's like you have a rock star here and everybody wants an autograph," states a VW sales manager. "I've never seen a car that had such a wide range of interest, from 16 year olds to 65 year olds." One wait-listed customer confirms the car's broad appeal. "In 1967, my Dad got me a VW. I loved it. I'm sure the new one will take me back," says the customer. "I'm getting the New Beetle as a surprise for my daughter, but I'm sure I'm going to be stealing it from her all the time."

Millennial fever results from the convergence of a wide range of forces in the marketing environment—from technological, economic, competitive, and demographic forces to cultural, social, and political ones. Most trend analysts believe that the nostalgia craze will only grow as the baby boomers continue to age. If so, the New Beetle, so full of the past, has a very bright future. "The Beetle is not just empty nostalgia," says Gerald Celente, publisher of *Trend Journal.* "It is a practical car that is also tied closely to the emotions of a generation." Says another trend analyst, the New Beetle "is our romantic past, reinvented for our hectic here-and-now. Different, yet deeply familiar—a car for the times."[1]

As Chapter 1 noted, marketers operate in an increasingly connected world. Today's marketers must connect effectively with customers, others in the company, and external partners in the face of major environmental forces that buffet all of these actors. A company's marketing environment comprises the actors and forces outside marketing that affect marketing management's ability to develop and maintain successful relationships with its target customers. The marketing environment offers both opportunities and threats. Successful companies know the vital importance of constantly watching and adapting to the changing environment.

As we enter the new millennium, both consumers and marketers wonder what the future will bring. The environment continues to change at a rapid pace. For example, think about how you buy groceries today. How will your grocery buying change over the next few decades? What challenges will these changes present for marketers? Here's what two leading futurists envision for the year 2025:[2]

> We won't be shopping in 21-aisle supermarkets in 2025, predicts Gary Wright, corporate demographer for Procter & Gamble. The growth of e-commerce and the rapid speed of the Internet will lead to online ordering of lower priced, nonperishable products—everything from peanut butter to coffee filters. Retailers will become "bundlers," combining these orders into large packages of goods for each household and delivering them efficiently to their doorsteps. As a result, we'll see mergers between retailing and home-delivery giants—think Wal-MartExpress, a powerful combo of Wal-Mart and Federal Express. Consumers won't waste precious time searching for the best-priced bundle. Online information agents will do it for them, comparing prices among competitors.
>
> Smart information agents also play a role in the world imagined by Ryan Mathews, futurist at First Matter LLC. By 2025, computers will essentially be as smart as humans, he contends, and consumers will use them to exchange information with on-screen electronic agents that ferret out the best deals online. Thanks to embedded-chip technology in the pantry, products on a CHR (continuous household replenishment) list—like paper towels and pet food—will sense when they're running low and reorder themselves automatically. If the information agent finds a comparable but cheaper substitute for a CHR product, the item will be switched instantly.

Some futurists predict that by 2020 most consumers will be ordering groceries online. Right now, however, Grocery Gateway is doing the shopping for some people living in Toronto.

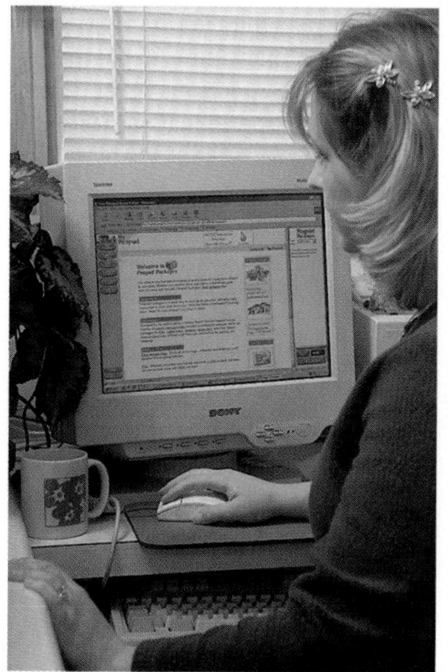

Such pictures of the future give marketers plenty to think about. A company's marketers take the major responsibility for identifying and predicting significant changes in the environment. More than any other group in the company, marketers must be the trend trackers and opportunity seekers. Although every manager in an organization needs to observe the outside environment, marketers have two special aptitudes. They have disciplined methods—marketing intelligence and marketing research—for collecting information about the marketing environment. They also spend more time in the customer and competitor environment. By conducting systematic environmental scanning, marketers are able to revise and adapt marketing strategies to meet new challenges and opportunities in the marketplace.

Marketing environment The factors and forces outside marketing's direct control that affect marketing management's ability to develop and maintain successful transactions with its target customers.

The **marketing environment** is composed of a *microenvironment* and a *macroenvironment*. The **microenvironment** consists of the forces close to the company that affect its ability to serve its customers—the company, suppliers, marketing channel firms, customer markets, competitors, and publics. The **macroenvironment** consists of the larger societal forces that affect the whole microenvironment—demographic, economic, natural, technological, political, and cultural forces. We look first at the company's microenvironment.

The Company's Microenvironment

Microenvironment The forces close to the company that affect its ability to serve its customers—the company, market channel firms, customer markets, competitors, and publics.

Macroenvironment The larger societal forces that affect the whole microenvironment—demographic, economic, natural, technological, political, and cultural forces.

Marketing management's job is to attract and build relationships with customers by creating customer value and satisfaction. However, marketing managers cannot accomplish this task alone. Their success depends on other actors in the company's microenvironment—other company departments, suppliers, and marketing intermediaries, which combine to make up the company's value delivery system, as well as customers, competitors, and various publics.

The Company

In designing marketing plans, marketing management takes other company groups into account—groups such as top management, finance, research and development (R&D), purchasing, manufacturing, and accounting. All these interrelated groups form the internal environment (see Figure 3-1). Top management sets the company's mission, objectives, broad strategies, and policies. Marketing managers must make decisions within the plans made by top management, and marketing plans must be approved by top management before they can be implemented.

Marketing managers also must work closely with other company departments. Finance is concerned with finding and using funds to carry out the marketing plan. R&D focuses on the problems of designing safe and attractive products. Purchasing worries about getting supplies and materials. Manufacturing is responsible for producing the desired quality and quantity of products. Accounting must measure revenues and costs to help marketing know how well it is achieving its objectives. Together, all of these departments have an impact on the marketing department's plans and actions. Under the marketing concept, all of these functions must "think consumer," and they should work in harmony to provide superior customer value and satisfaction.

FIGURE 3-1 The company's internal environment

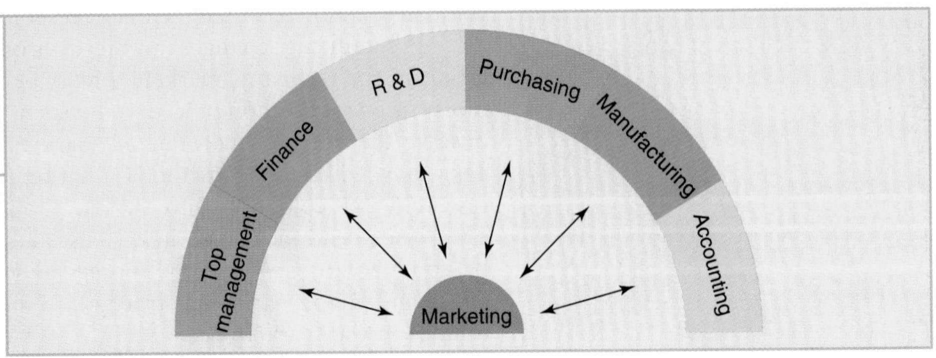

Suppliers

Suppliers are an important link in the company's overall customer "value delivery system." They provide the resources needed by the company to produce its goods and services. Supplier developments can seriously affect marketing. Marketing managers must be aware of supply availability—supply shortages or delays, labour strikes, and other events that can cost sales in the short run and damage customer satisfaction in the long run. Marketing managers also monitor the price trends of their key inputs. Rising supply costs may force price increases that can harm the company's sales volume.

Marketing Intermediaries

Marketing intermediaries
Firms that help the company promote, sell, and distribute its goods to final buyers; they include resellers, physical distribution firms, marketing service agencies, and financial intermediaries.

Marketing intermediaries help the company promote, sell, and distribute its goods to final buyers. They include *resellers, physical distribution firms, marketing services agencies,* and *financial intermediaries. Resellers* are distribution channel firms that help the company find customers or make sales to them. These include wholesalers and retailers who buy and resell merchandise. Selecting and working with resellers is not easy. No longer do manufacturers have many small, independent resellers from which to choose. They now face large and growing reseller organizations, which often have enough power to dictate terms or even shut the manufacturer out of large markets.

Physical distribution firms help the company stock and move goods from their points of origin to their destinations. Working with warehouse and transportation firms, a company must determine the best ways to store and ship goods, balancing such factors as cost, delivery, speed, and safety. *Marketing services agencies* are the marketing research firms, advertising agencies, media firms, and marketing consulting firms that help the company target and promote its products to the right markets. When the company decides to use one of these agencies, it must choose carefully, because these firms vary in creativity, quality, service, and price. *Financial intermediaries* include banks, credit companies, insurance companies, and other businesses that help finance transactions or insure against the risks associated with the buying and selling of goods. Most firms and customers depend on financial intermediaries to finance their transactions.

Like suppliers, marketing intermediaries form an important component of the company's overall value delivery system. In its quest to create satisfying customer relationships, the company must do more than just optimize its own performance. It must partner effectively with suppliers and marketing intermediaries to optimize the performance of the entire system.

Wendy's
www.wendys.com

Thus, today's marketers recognize the importance of working with their intermediaries as partners rather than simply as channels through which they sell their products. For example, Coca-Cola recently signed a 10-year deal with Wendy's that will make Coke the exclusive soft-drink provider to the fast-food chain, picking up more than 700 Wendy's franchises that were previously served by Pepsi. In the deal, Coca-Cola promised Wendy's much more than just its soft drinks. It pledged the powerful marketing support that comes along with an exclusive partnership with Coke.

> [Along with the soft drinks,] Wendy's gets a cross-functional team of 50 Coke employees from various regions across North America who are now dedicated to "understanding the nuances of Wendy's business," says [a Wendy's executive]. Wendy's also will benefit from Coke dollars in joint marketing campaigns. "There are significant, big-time marketing sponsorships that they can bring to Wendy's, as they have to other chains," [adds the executive]. "That's huge." Bigger still is the staggering amount of consumer research that Coca-Cola provides its partners. [Coke] provides both analysis of syndicated information and access to Coke's own internal research aimed at "trying to understand consumers as they eat out." Coke goes to great lengths to understand

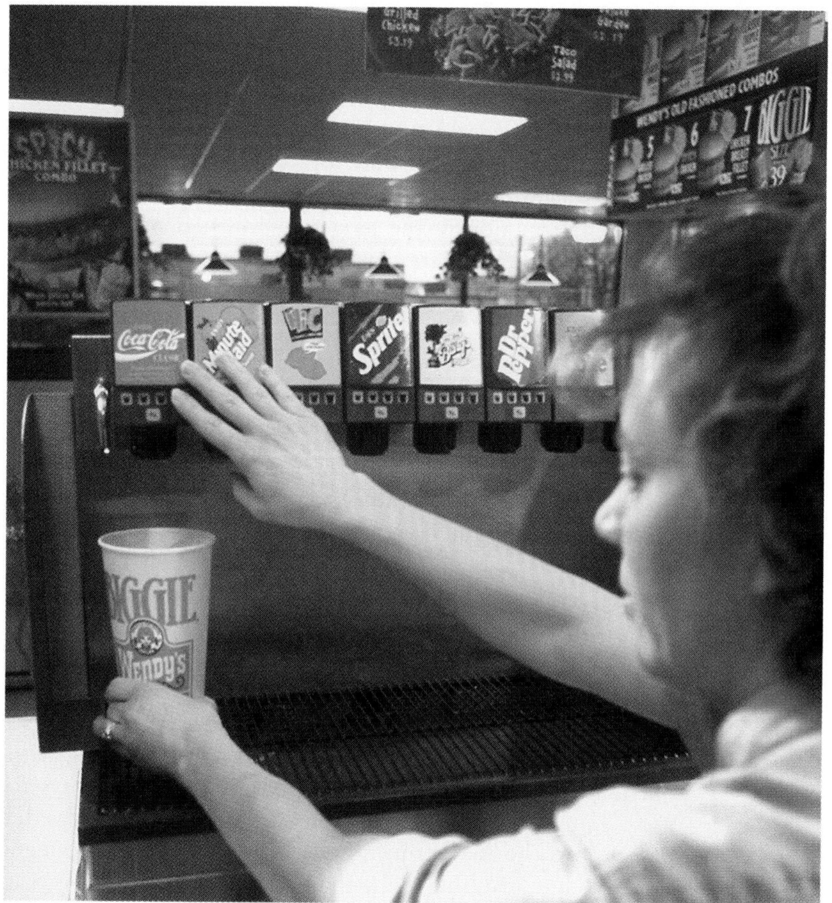

Working with intermediaries as partners: Wendy's deal with Coca-Cola brought it much more than just soft drinks. It brought the powerful marketing support that comes with an exclusive partnership with Coke.

beverage drinkers—and to make sure their partners can use those insights. . . . The company also has analyzed the demographics of consumers by region. Now franchise owners can determine which Coke brands are preferred by the clientele in their area. [Coca-Cola] also has been studying the design of drive-through menu boards to better understand which layouts, fonts, letter sizes, colors, and visuals induce consumers to order more food and drink. Coke even aids its partners with research on issues that are not related to soft drink sales, such as hiring and retaining workers while unemployment is low.[3]

Customers

The company needs to study its customer markets closely. Figure 3-2 shows five types of customer markets. *Consumer markets* consist of individuals and households that buy goods and services for personal consumption. *Business markets* buy goods and services for further processing or for use in their production process, whereas *reseller markets* buy goods and services to resell at a profit. *Government markets* are composed of government agencies that buy goods and services to produce public services or transfer the goods and services to others who need them. Finally, *international markets* consist of buyers in other countries, including consumers, producers, resellers, and governments. Each market type has special characteristics that call for careful study by the seller.

Competitors

Market oriented firms implementing the marketing concept know that, to be successful, they must provide greater customer value and satisfaction than their competitors. Thus, marketers must do more than just adapt to the needs of target con-

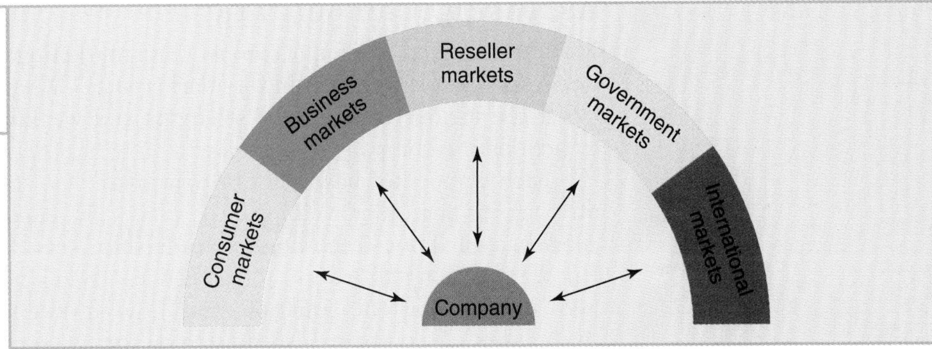

FIGURE 3-2 Types of customer markets

sumers. They also must gain strategic advantage by positioning their offerings strongly against those of competitors in the minds of consumers.

First, the company has to do a competitor analysis (see Figure 3-3)—identifying and assessing competitors and then selecting which competitors to attack or avoid.

Identifying Competitors

It seems like a simple task for a company to identify its competitors. At the narrowest, a company can define its competitors as other companies offering similar products and services to the same customers at similar prices. Thus, Coca-Cola might view Pepsi as a major competitor, but not Budweiser or Kool-Aid. Buick might see Ford as a major competitor, but not Mercedes or Hyundai.

But companies actually face a much wider range of competitors. The company may define competitors as all firms making the same product or class of products: Thus, Buick would see itself as competing against all other automobile makers. Even more broadly, competitors may include all companies making products that supply the same service: Here Buick would see itself competing not only against other automobile makers but also against companies that make trucks, motorcycles, or even bicycles. Finally, and still more broadly, competitors may include all companies that compete for the same consumer dollars: Here Buick would see itself competing with companies that sell major consumer durables, new homes, or vacations abroad.

Companies must avoid "competitor myopia." A company is more likely to be "buried" by its latent competitors than its current ones. For example, Canada's credit unions have long regarded the banks as their chief rivals. However, there is growing competition from non-traditional competitors. Companies like GM and Canadian Tire now offer their customers financial services. New partnerships are forming that also threaten to take business away from the credit unions. Loblaws now offers grocery shoppers the convenience of in-store banking through its partnership with CIBC. Similarly, Encyclopedia Britannica viewed itself as competing with other publishers of printed encyclopedias selling for as much as $2200 per set. However, it learned a hard lesson when *Microsoft Encarta*, an encyclopedia on CD-ROM, was introduced and sold for only $50. By the time Britannica introduced its own CD-ROM and online versions, its sales had plunged by more than 50 percent. Thus, Encyclopedia Britannica's real competitor was the computer.[4]

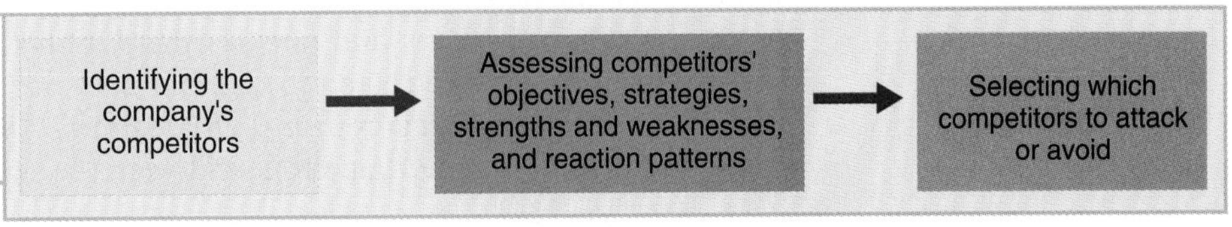

FIGURE 3-3 Steps in analyzing competitors

Identifying the company's competitors → Assessing competitors' objectives, strategies, strengths and weaknesses, and reaction patterns → Selecting which competitors to attack or avoid

Assessing Competitors

Having identified the main competitors, marketing management now asks: What does each competitor seek in the marketplace? What is each competitor's strategy? What are various competitors' strengths and weaknesses, and how will each react to actions the company might take?

Each competitor has a mix of objectives. The company wants to know the relative importance that a competitor places on current profitability, market share growth, cash flow, technological leadership, service leadership, and other goals. Knowing a competitor's mix of objectives reveals whether the competitor is satisfied with its current situation and how it might react to different competitive actions. A company also must monitor its competitors' objectives for various segments. If the company finds that a competitor has discovered a new segment, this may be an opportunity. If it finds that competitors plan new moves into segments now served by the company, it will be forewarned and, hopefully, forearmed.

The more one firm's strategy resembles that of another, the more the two firms compete. In most industries, the competitors can be sorted into groups that pursue different strategies. For example, in the major appliance industry, General Electric, Whirlpool, and Maytag all belong to the same strategic group. Each produces a full line of medium-price appliances supported by good service. Sub Zero and KitchenAid, on the other hand, belong to a different strategic group. They produce a narrower line of higher-quality appliances, offer a higher level of service, and charge a premium price.

Some important insights emerge from identifying strategic groups. For example, if a company enters one of the groups, the members of that group become its key competitors. Thus, the company needs to look at all of the dimensions that identify strategic groups in the industry. It needs to know each competitor's product quality, features, and mix; customer services; pricing policy; distribution coverage; sales force strategy; and advertising and sales promotion programs. It also must study the details of each competitor's R&D, manufacturing, purchasing, financial, and other strategies.

Marketers need to assess each competitor's strengths and weaknesses carefully to be able to answer the critical question: What can our competitors do? Companies normally learn about their competitors' strengths and weaknesses through secondary data, personal experience, and hearsay. They also can conduct primary marketing research with customers, suppliers, and dealers. Or they can benchmark themselves against other firms, comparing their company's products and processes with those of competitors or leading firms in other industries to find ways to improve quality and performance. Benchmarking has become a powerful tool for increasing a company's competitiveness.

Finally, the company wants to know: What will our competitors do? A competitor's objectives, strategies, and strengths and weaknesses go a long way toward explaining its likely actions, as well as its likely reactions to company moves such as price cuts, promotion increases, or new product introductions. In addition, each competitor has a philosophy of doing business, an internal culture, and guiding beliefs. Marketing managers need a deep understanding of a competitor's mentality if they want to anticipate how the competitor will act or react.

Each competitor reacts differently. Some do not react quickly or strongly to a competitor's move. They may feel their customers are loyal; they may be slow in noticing the move; they may lack the funds to react. Some competitors react only to certain types of moves and not to others. Other competitors react swiftly and strongly to any action. Procter & Gamble does not let a new detergent come easily into the market, so many firms avoid direct competition with P&G and look for easier prey, knowing that P&G will react fiercely if challenged.

In some industries, competitors live in relative harmony; in others, they fight constantly. Knowing how major competitors react gives the company clues on how best to attack competitors or how best to defend the company's current position.

Selecting Competitors to Attack and Avoid

A company largely selects its major competitors in making decisions on customer targets, distribution channels, and marketing mix strategy. These decisions define the strategic group to which the company belongs. Management now must decide which competitors to compete against most vigorously.

The company can focus on one of several classes of competitors. Most companies prefer to aim their shots at their weak competitors. This requires fewer resources and less time. But in the process, the firm may gain little. The argument could be made that the firm also should compete with strong competitors to sharpen its abilities. Furthermore, even strong competitors have some weaknesses, and succeeding against them often provides greater returns.

Most companies will compete with close competitors—those that resemble them most—rather than distant competitors. Thus, Chevrolet competes more against Ford than against Lexus. At the same time, the company may want to avoid trying to "destroy" a close competitor. In the late 1970s, Bausch & Lomb moved aggressively against other soft contact lens manufacturers with great success. However, this forced weak competitors to sell out to larger firms such as Schering-Plough and Johnson & Johnson. Faced with much larger competitors, Bausch & Lomb suffered the consequences. Johnson & Johnson acquired Vistakon, a small niche marketer with only $30 million in annual sales. Backed by Johnson & Johnson's deep pockets, however, the small but nimble Vistakon developed and introduced its innovative Acuvue disposable contact lenses. According to one analyst, "The speed of the [Acuvue] rollout and the novelty of [Johnson & Johnson's] big-budget ads left giant Bausch & Lomb . . . seeing stars." It wasn't long before Vistakon was number one in the fast-growing disposable segment capturing about 25 percent of the entire contact lens market.[5] In this case, success in hurting a close rival brought in tougher competitors.

A company really needs and strategically benefits from competitors. Competitors can help increase total demand. They can share the costs of market and product development and help to legitimize new technologies. They can serve less attractive segments or lead to more product differentiation. However, a company may not view all of its competitors as beneficial. An industry often contains "well-behaved" competitors and "disruptive" competitors.[6] Well-behaved competitors play by the rules of the industry. Disruptive competitors, in contrast, break the rules, and, in general, shake up the industry. For example, Air Canada finds many of its US competitors like American Airlines and Delta to be well-behaved competitors: They play by the rules and attempt to set their fares sensibly. But Air Canada finds West Jet and Royal Airlines disruptive competitors because they destabilize the airline industry through continual heavy price discounting and wild promotional schemes.

Publics

Public
Any group that has an actual or potential interest in or impact on an organization's ability to achieve its objectives.

The company's marketing environment also includes various publics. A **public** is any group that has an actual or potential interest in or impact on an organization's ability to achieve its objectives. Figure 3-4 shows seven types of publics.

- *Financial publics.* Financial publics influence the company's ability to obtain funds. Banks, investment houses, and shareholders are the major financial publics.

FIGURE 3-4 Types of publics

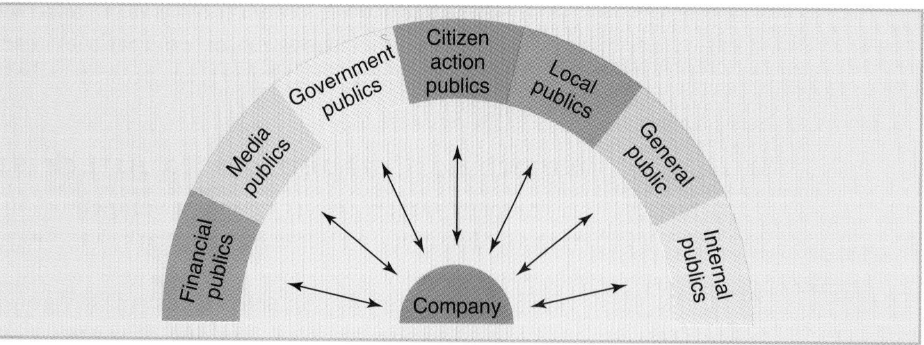

- *Media publics.* Media publics are those that carry news, features, and editorial opinion. They include newspapers, magazines, radio and television stations, and the World Wide Web.
- *Government publics.* Management must take into account government developments. Marketers must often consult the company's lawyers on issues of product safety, truth in advertising, and other matters.
- *Citizen-action publics.* A company's marketing decisions may be questioned by consumer organizations, environmental groups, minority groups, and others. Its public relations department can help it stay in touch with consumer and citizen groups.

Companies market to internal publics as well as to customers: Wal-Mart Canada Inc. includes employees as models in its advertising, making them feel good about working for the company.

- *Local publics.* Every company has local publics, such as neighbourhood residents and community organizations. Large companies usually appoint a community relations officer to deal with the community, attend meetings, answer questions, and contribute to worthwhile causes.
- *General public.* A company needs to be concerned with the general public's attitude toward its products and activities. The public's image of the company affects its buying.
- *Internal publics.* A company's internal publics include its workers, managers, volunteers, and the board of directors. Large companies use newsletters and other means to inform and motivate their internal publics. When employees feel good about their company, their positive attitude spills over into external publics.

A company can prepare marketing plans for these major publics as well as for its customer markets. Suppose the company wants a specific response from a particular public, such as goodwill, favourable word of mouth, or donations of time or money. The company would have to design an offer to this public that is attractive enough to produce the desired response.

The Company's Macroenvironment

The company and all of the other actors operate in a larger macroenvironment of forces that shape opportunities and pose threats to it. Figure 3-5 shows the six major forces in the company's macroenvironment. Marketers must track trends in the macroenvironment on both a national and international basis since business is becoming increasingly global. Since 80 percent of Canada's export trade is to the United States, keeping track of trends in the US marketplace is critical.[7] The continuing growth of the US economy has fuelled many Canadian businesses. While growth is forecast to continue, Canadian marketers must recognize that this growth may be slower than it has been previously. When the Hong Kong stock exchange tumbled in the fall of 1997, all North American marketers took note. Forecasts of sales that North American firms made in Asian markets had to be revised downward. In the remaining sections of this chapter, we examine these forces and show how they affect marketing plans.

Demographic Environment

Demography
The study of human populations in terms of size, density, location, age, sex, race, occupation, and other statistics.

Demography is the study of human populations in terms of size, density, location, age, sex, race, occupation, and other statistics. The demographic environment is of major interest to marketers because it involves people, and people make up markets. See Table 3.1.

FIGURE 3-5 Major forces in the company's macroenvironment

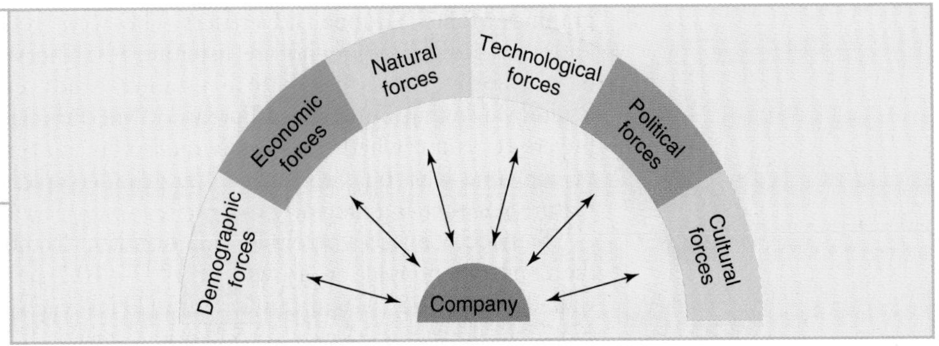

TABLE 3-1 Key Demographic and Economic Statistics from a Sample of APEC (Asia-Pacific Economic Cooperation Conference) Countries

Country	Population (in millions)	Rate Population Growth	Literacy Rate	GNP Per Capita ($ billions US)	Exports ($ billions US)	Imports ($ billions US)
Australia	18.1	1.2%	99%	$18 720	$53.1	$61.3
Canada	29.6	1.1%	98%	$19 380	$192.2	$168.4
China	1299.2	1.5%	73%	$620	$148.8	$132.1
Indonesia	193.3	1.8%	77%	$980	$45.4	$40.9
Hong Kong	6.2	2.1%	90%	$22 990	$173.9	$196.1
Japan	125.2	0.5%	99%	$39 640	$443.1	$336.0
Mexico	91.8	2.2%	87%	$3 320	$79.7	$72.9
South Korea	44.9	0.5%	99%	$9 700	$125.1	$135.1
United States	263.1	0.6%	97%	$26 980	$583.9	$771.3

Source: Asia Pacific Foundation of Canada, APEC Secretariat, adapted from the reprint in *Globe and Mail,* 19 November 1997:D4.

David Foot, an economist at the University of Toronto and author of the best-selling book *Boom, Bust & Echo: How to Profit from the Coming Demographic Shift,* believes that demographics explains about two-thirds of everything.[8] For example, how do you explain the rapid rise in the rates charged by babysitters? Easy, says Foot, when you realize that the huge pool of boomer parents relies on a relatively small pool of baby-bust teens. He has also shown that studying demographics helps to explain the growth of some leisure markets and the decline of others. Golf has experienced a 38 percent increase in popularity over the last 25 years, pushed by its popularity among baby-boomers.

People who study demographics assume that people do certain things and purchase certain things at certain ages. For example, people in their thirties tend to have begun their families and thus are the major purchasers of baby products. While demographic information can be useful when it comes to predicting macro trends and purchases within a product category, marketers should use the information with some caution. According to veteran Canadian pollster Allan Gregg, demographics "can be wildly simplistic."[9] Complex factors—everything from the marketing itself to an individual's values and attitudes—influence why a person buys a particular brand within a product category. Moreover, despite the best demographic predictions, people don't always follow predictable patterns. Given an aging North American population, many predicted that people would follow a healthier lifestyle and diet. But a recent report suggests that, "when it comes to food, Canadians are tired of worrying about what's good for them."[10] Unlike with many Europeans, vegetarianism isn't a lifestyle choice for many Canadians; in fact, only four percent of Canadians follow this type of diet.

New studies are being done to help overcome the shortcomings of using demographics alone. National advertisers who want to know more than just the age and sex of the people who are listening to radio will soon have access to plenty of qualitative data, thanks to a national study co-sponsored by the Canadian Radio Marketing Bureau and Bureau of Measurement. The study will allow media buyers to know whether an individual is an automotive purchaser, beer drinker, or someone who buys toothpaste, and understand the media habits and lifestyle features of that individual.[11]

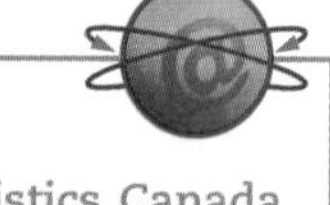

Statistics Canada
www.statcan.ca

Statistics Canada's report Recent Trends in Demography 1998–1999 shows that the country's population growth in 1997—10.7 per thousand—was the lowest in Canada since 1985. Total fertility rate (TFR) reached 1.55 children per woman in 1997, the lowest level ever recorded in Canada. If preliminary data for 1998 are confirmed, TFR could even be lower in 1998. Taken in conjunction with the decrease

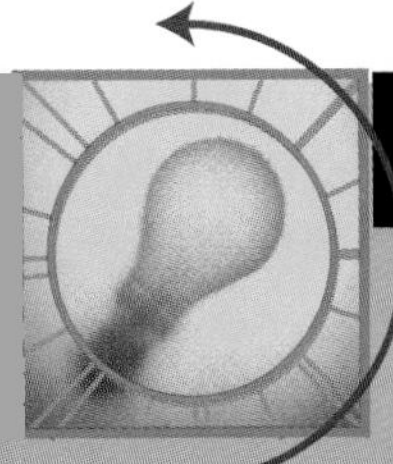

marketing highlight 3-1

If the World Were a Village

Canadian author Marshall McLuhan created the concept of the global village in the 1960s. With increasingly global communications, this concept is now becoming a reality. Think for a few minutes about the world and your place in it. If we reduced the world to a village of 1000 people who were representative of the world's population, this would be our reality:

- Our village would have 520 women and 480 men; 330 children and 60 people over age 65; 10 college graduates and 335 illiterate adults.
- We'd have 52 North Americans, 55 Russians, 84 Latin Americans, 95 Europeans, 124 Africans, and 584 Asians.
- Communication would be difficult: 165 of us would speak Mandarin, 86 English, 83 Hindu, 64 Spanish, 58 Russian, and 37 Arabic. The other half of us would speak one of more than 200 other languages.
- Among us, we'd have 329 Christians, 178 Moslems, 132 Hindus, 62 Buddhists, 3 Jews, 167 nonreligious, 45 atheists, and 84 others.
- About one-third of our people would have access to clean, safe drinking water. About half of our children would be immunized against infections.
- The woodlands in our village would be decreasing rapidly, and wasteland would be growing. Forty percent of the village's cropland, nourished by 83 percent of our fertilizer, would produce 72 percent of the food to feed its 270 well-fed owners. The remaining 60 percent of the land and 17 percent of the fertilizer would produce 28 percent of the food to feed the other 730 people. Five hundred people in the village would suffer from malnutrition.
- Of the 1000 people, 200 would control 75 percent of our village's wealth. Another 200 would receive only two percent of the wealth. Seventy people would own cars, one would have a computer, and that computer probably would not be connected to the Internet.

Source: The World Village Project Web site, May 1997, www.geocities.com/Athens/Forum/1910/wvp.html.

in immigration levels, this low fertility rate could accelerate the aging of the Canadian population if these trends continue. At the same time as the birth rate is falling, life expectancy continues to rise and gains recorded in 1997 were significant: 0.33 year for men and 0.18 year for women. The gap between life expectancy of men and women is decreasing but, as of now, it is still more than 5 years.

The world population is growing at an explosive rate. It now totals over 6.1 billion and will reach 7.9 billion by the year 2025.[12] This population explosion has been of major concern to governments and various groups around the world since the earth's finite resources can support a limited number of people, particularly at the living standards to which many countries aspire.

The explosive world population growth has major implications for business. A growing population means growing human needs to satisfy. Depending on purchasing power, it may also mean growing market opportunities. For example, to curb its skyrocketing population, the Chinese government passed regulations limiting families to one child each. As a result, Chinese children are spoiled and fussed over as never before. Known in China as "little emperors," Chinese children are being showered with everything from candy to computers as a result of what's known as the "six-pocket syndrome." As many as six adults—including parents, grandparents, great-grandparents, and aunts and uncles—may be indulging the whims of each child. This trend has encouraged toy companies such as Japan's Bandai Company (known for its Mighty Morphin Power Rangers), Denmark's Lego Group, and Mattel to enter the Chinese market.[13]

The world's large and highly diverse population poses both opportunities and challenges (see Marketing Highlight 3-1). Therefore, marketers must keep close track of demographic trends and developments in their markets, both at home and abroad—changing age and family structures, geographic population shifts, educational characteristics, and population diversity. Statistics Canada offers a wealth of information for marketers interested in demographic trends. Here, we discuss the most important demographic trends in Canada.

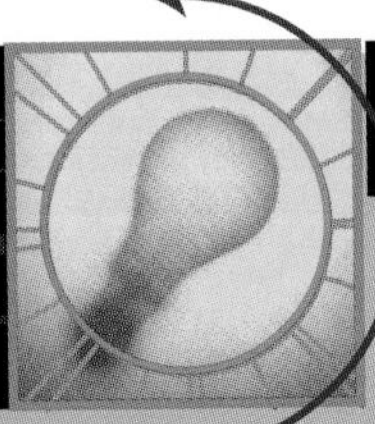

marketing highlight 3-2

The Baby Boomers, the Generation Xers, and the Sunshine Generation

Demographics involve people, and people make up markets. Thus, marketers track demographic trends and groups carefully. These are some of today's most important demographic groups:

The Baby Boomers

The postwar baby boom, which began in 1947 and ran through 1966, produced a population explosion. Since then, the baby boomers have become one of the largest forces shaping the marketing environment. The fact that Maureen Kempston Darkes, a 47-year-old lawyer, was recently named CEO of General Motors of Canada Ltd., is important not only because she is one of the few women to attain such a position, but also because it is an indication of the power that baby boomers, in general, are now wielding in Canadian business. The boomers have presented a moving target, creating new markets as they grew through infancy to pre-adolescent, teenage, young adult, and now middle age.

The baby boomers account for a third of the population but make up 40 percent of the workforce and earn over half of all personal income. Today, the aging boomers are moving to the suburbs, settling into home ownership, and raising families. Many people who are turning 45 are reaching a milestone many find unthinkable—becoming grandparents. However, they are determined to fight the stereotypes long associated with this life cycle stage. They are more active and look and feel younger than their predecessors did. Furthermore, they prefer not to be confronted with advertising or products that address their age or label them as being old; therefore, many products are being re-tooled to meet their needs in a more subtle way. This group is also responsible for the explosive growth of products such as seamless bifocals, large-print books, and Oil of Olay that helps combat wrinkles. Since 36 percent of the people going to the movies are over the age of 40, theatres have been aggressively refurbishing. It isn't enough just to show movies that appeal to older audiences; middle-aged people demand bigger screens, more comfortable seating, and better food.

Boomers are reaching their peak earning and spending years. They constitute a lucrative market for housing, furniture and appliances, children's products, low-calorie foods and beverages, physical fitness products, high-priced cars, convenience products, and financial services.

Baby boomers cut across all walks of life. But marketers have typically paid the most attention to the small upper crust of the boomer generation—its more educated, mobile, and wealthy segments. These segments have gone by many names. In the 1980s, they were called yuppies (young urban professionals); yummies (young upwardly mobile mommies), and dinks (dual-income, no-kids couples). In the 1990s, however, yuppies and dinks have given way to a new breed, with such names as dewks (dual earners with kids); mobys (mother older, baby younger); woofs (well-off older folks); or just plain grumpies (just what the name suggests).

The older boomers are now in their fifties; the youngest are in their thirties. Thus, the boomers are evolving from the "youthquake generation" to the "backache generation." They're slowing down, having children, and settling down. They're experiencing the pangs of midlife and rethinking the purpose and value of their work, responsibilities, and relationships. Community and family values have become more important, and staying home with the family has become their favourite way of spending an evening.

In examining the boomer market in Canada, it is significant that boomers are going from being net-borrowers to being net-savers. Many plan to retire early—almost one-third plan to stop working before they reach age 60. This has resulted in the recent phenomenal growth of Canadian mutual funds.

This increased wealth among boomers is also evident in the travel market. The generation who developed their wanderlust backpacking around Europe and Asia in their twenties now has the money to go beyond standard vacations. While boomers often seek vacations with an environmental focus or those that promise something exotic or thrilling, they also want to be coddled with a gourmet meal at the end of the day.

Even though some markets are benefiting, others are threatened as the boomers age. Once the prime consumers of Molson and Labatt beer, boomers are moving away from beer consumption, leaving these brewers with flat or declining markets.

The Generation Xers

Marketers' focus has shifted in recent years to a new group—those born between 1965 and 1976. Six million strong in Canada and representing $140 billion in disposable income, this group represents an extremely important market. Author Douglas Coupland calls them "Generation X." Others call them baby busters, the Nexus generation, twentysomethings, or yiffies—young, individualistic, freedom-minded, few.

Many who belong to the 25 to 36 age group hate the label "Generation X." In contrast to the boomers, who were an easy group to target, defining this younger generation is difficult. Companies that wish to market to them or recruit them as employees are turning to such firms as Toronto's d-Code Inc., a consulting company that helps compa-

Changing Age Structure of the Canadian Population

According to Statistics Canada the population of Canada is expected to exceed 31 million by 2001. The single most important demographic trend in Canada is the changing age structure of the population: The Canadian population is getting *older*. The median age of the Canadian population—the point at which half of the population is younger and half is older—is now 38. Just 30 years ago, the median age

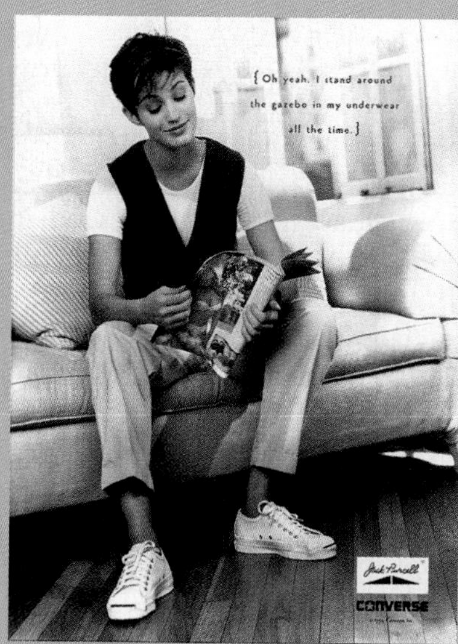
{ Oh yeah. I stand around
the gazebo in my underwear
all the time. }
CONVERSE

Converse targets Generation Xers with this black and white ad for Jack Purcell sneakers. The ad is "soft sell" and makes fun of a favourite Gen Xer target—advertising itself.

nies and governments appreciate what makes 18- to 34-year olds tick. This techno-savvy generation was raised on music, television, computers, and video games. They are satisfied, independent, and optimistic. Quality of life is more important than money to those entering the workforce; longer vacations and funky office space may be more important than the signing bonus. Lacking confidence in business and educational and government institutions, this group tends to be highly self-reliant. Their confidence is reflected in their number-one career choice—becoming an entrepreneur. However, this generation is also more likely to be unemployed or underemployed. They are more accepting of change than are baby boomers, and they delay getting married, having children, and buying a home longer than do their predecessors. Only 21 percent of members of this generation plan to buy a home in the next two years.

Marketers must remember that this generation is a highly diverse group and resent being clustered into a single market. They are also highly critical of advertising and are extremely savvy about its underlying purpose. As Eric Blais noted in *Marketing,* this is a generation "who no longer cares what McCain has done to their fries." Growing up on a diet of Saturday-morning cartoons and advertising promises that didn't deliver, they enjoy parodying advertising slogans, revelling in producing distorted advertising slogans such as "At Speedy, you're a nobody." However, Xers do share a set of influences. Increasing divorce rates and higher employment of mothers have made them the first generation of latchkey kids. Whereas the boomers created a sexual revolution, the Xers have lived in the age of AIDS.

The Xers buy lots of products, such as sweaters, boots, cosmetics, electronics, cars, fast food, beer, computers, and mountain bikes. However, their cynicism makes them savvy shoppers. Because they often did much of the family shopping when growing up, they are experienced shoppers. Their financial pressures make them value conscious, and they like lower prices and a more functional look.

Generation Xers share new cultural concerns. They care about the environment and respond favourably to companies such as The Body Shop and Ben & Jerry's, which have proven records of environmentally and socially responsible actions.

Generation Xers will have a big impact on the workplace and marketplace of the future. They are poised to displace the lifestyles, culture, and materialistic values of the baby boomers. By the year 2010, they will have overtaken the baby boomers as a primary market for almost every product category.

The Sunshine Generation

Also labelled the echo generation (the boomers' children) and the millennial (they will start to enter maturity after the year 2000), or Generation Y (building on the Generation X label), this generation was born between 1980 and 1995. While the oldest members are in their twenties, the youngest are still toddlers. This group is attracting increased attention from marketers because of its impact on certain product categories. Children's movies earn the biggest dollar at the box office, and they are a major market for fashion and consumer goods.

This group has been immersed in more technology than any previous generation. With greater access to information, they are more aware of global issues and have a sense of themselves as part of a larger world community. This awareness has a cost, however. They believe they have a calling to fix the problems created by the older generations—significant problems such as environmental degradation, war, crime, and poverty. The archetype of this generation is Craig Kielburger, the famous teenage Canadian activist who has developed a global campaign against child labour and founded the international youth movement Free the Children. How this generation will evolve remains a big question. They face a world full of questions and ambiguity about their roles as individuals, spouses, parents, workers, and consumers.

Sources: Howard Schlossberg, "Aging baby boomers give marketers a lot of changes to consider," *Advertising Age,* 12 April 1993:10; Campbell Gibson, "The four baby booms," *American Demographics,* November 1993:36–40; Cyndee Miller, "Xers know they're a target market, and they hate that," *Marketing News,* 6 December 1993:2,15; Jeff Giles, "Generalizations X," *Newsweek,* 6 June 1994:62–9; Nathan Cobb, "Agent X," *Boston Globe,* 28 September 1994:35,40; Nicholas Zill and John Robinson, "The Generation X difference," *American Demographics,* April 1995:24–39; Harvey Schacter, "Power shift," *Canadian Business,* August 1995:20–30; Eric Blais, "Generation X: Targeting a tough crowd that's not easily impressed," *Marketing,* 6 June 1994:13–5; Eric Beauchesne, "Generation X not the lost generation: Survey," *Kingston Whig Standard,* 15 June 1997:22; Christopher Harris, "Faith in Popcorn," *Globe and Mail,* 10 May 1997:C10; Deborah Jones, "Here comes the sunshine generation," *Globe and Mail,* 10 May 1997:D1,D2; Dorothy Lipovenko, "Growing old is a baby-booming business," *Globe and Mail,* 6 April 1996:A1,A4; Dorothy Lipovenko, "Rich boomers aiming to retire earlier than parents, poll says," *Globe and Mail,* 10 October 1996:B10; Gayle MacDonald, "The eyes and ears of a generation," *Globe and Mail,* 4 February 1997:B13; Leonard Zehr, "Gen-Xers heading home: Survey," *Globe and Mail,* 13 February 1997:B9; www.freethechildren.org.

Baby boom
The major increase in the annual birth rate following the Second World War and lasting until the early 1960s. The "baby boomers," now moving into middle age, are a prime target for marketers.

was 25.[14] Two reasons explain this trend. First, there is a long-term slowdown in the birth rate, so there are fewer young people to pull down the population's average age. Second, life expectancy is increasing, so there are more older people to pull up the average age.

During the **baby boom** that followed the Second World War and lasted until the early 1960s, the annual birth rate reached an all-time high. The baby boom created a huge "bulge" in age distribution—the nine million baby boomers now account for almost one-third of Canada's population. And as the baby-boom generation ages, the nation's average age increases. Because of its sheer size, many major demographic and socioeconomic changes in Canada and the United States are tied to the baby-boom generation (see Marketing Highlight 3-2).

Although there was a baby boom in both Canada and the US, Canadian marketers have to recognize that our baby boom was unique. It started later than the American version (1947 versus 1946) and lasted longer (the American boom ended in 1964; the Canadian boom continued until 1966). While the American baby boom resulted in 3.5 children per family, the Canadian boom produced four children. Furthermore, the baby boom was not a worldwide phenomenon. Only Australia and New Zealand among the other developed countries experienced the same expansion in the birth rate. In Europe, there was no baby boom, and in Japan, the birth rate declined during our baby boom years, which explains why these countries have a higher proportion of older people in their societies.[15]

The baby boom was followed by a "birth dearth," and by the mid-1970s the birth rate had fallen sharply. This decrease was caused by smaller family sizes, the result of the desire to improve personal living standards, the increasing number of women working outside the home, and improved birth control. Although family sizes are expected to remain smaller, the birth rate has climbed again as the baby boom generation moves through the child-bearing years and creates a second but smaller "baby boomlet." Following this boomlet, however, the birth rate will again decline as we move into the twenty-first century.[16]

Figure 3-6 shows the changing age distribution of the Canadian population through 2041. The differing growth rates for various age groups will strongly affect marketers' targeting strategies. For example, the upper end of the "tween" market, the 9- to 14-year-old offspring of the baby boom generation, is 2.5 million strong. They are grabbing marketers' attention not just because of the size of this "echo boom" market but also because of its spending power. New products are being developed just for them—GT Global Mutual Funds for Kids, Pillsbury's Pizza Pops, portable milkshakes called Milk Mania, L'Oreal Kids Shampoo and Conditioner, and Bonne Bell Lip Smackers. They're wired and media savvy, and marketers are rushing to build brand loyalty among them or create new brands

Toronto's Ch!ckaboom has been highly successful in targeting the large and growing tween girls' market.

ch!ckaboom
yorkdale

FIGURE 3-6 Age projection for Canada, provinces, and territories, 1993 to 2041

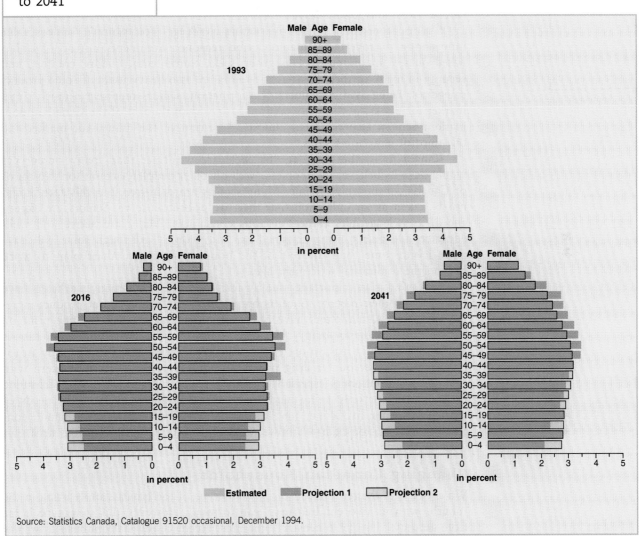

Source: Statistics Canada, Catalogue 91520 occasional, December 1994.

they might regard as "cool." One firm that illustrates how successful such a tactic can be is Toronto's Ch!ckaboom, a clothing retailer that specializes in serving girls 5 to 13 years of age.

- **Ch!ckaboom.** It is estimated that young girls alone have in excess of $700 million in disposable income. And they are twice as likely as boys the same age to spend it on clothes. Given this spending power, it isn't surprising that clothing retailers are rushing to entice them into stores. Le Chateau Junior Girl, GUESS?, and La Senza Girl's are just a few clothiers hoping to suit up this young crowd. What has Ch!ckaboom done that has made it stand out from its competition? "The best practice in retail is to respect my customer," says Ch!ckaboom owner, Nancy Dennis. She knows that the tween girl wants to have fun just as much as she wants to find the "in" clothes in her size. Thus, the stores offer events such as Spice Girl Days, birthday clubs, and Valentines and Halloween parties. An advocate of relationship marketing, Ch!ckaboom leverages its database to keep in contact with its diminutive customers. Ch!ckaboom hopes to expand across the country with the stores where tweens can drop in, meet friends, fiddle with accessories, and shop to their heart's content without having to deal with snobby salespeople breathing down their necks. You can bet there are many tweens hoping it does just that.[17]

At the other end of the spectrum, it is projected that almost 13 percent of Canadians will be over 65 by 2001, with the percentage increasing to 25 percent by 2031. As this group grows, so will the demand for retirement communities, quieter forms of recreation, single-portion food packaging, life-care and health-care services, and leisure travel.[18]

Seniors represent a unique marketing challenge. For example, seniors value information in advertising materials and reasoned arguments instead of claims based on sex and impulse. This group seeks convenience, quality, comfort, and security in many of their purchases. Seniors are also heavy users of some product categories. Being avid consumers of information, seniors represent a much larger market for books, newspapers, and magazines than the rest of the Canadian population. Seniors also represent almost 50 percent of the luxury car market and one-third of new home sales.

Canadians in the older age brackets are wealthier than many stereotypes would have us believe: "Whoopies" (well-off older people) account for two-thirds of Canada's disposable income. Many seniors are debt-free, but this fact should not be taken as an indication that they are price-insensitive. Seniors are experienced, knowledgeable, value-conscious consumers. Many are active and well-educated and resent being classified as "old people." Although some will have more leisure time than the rest of the population, many others plan to work beyond the traditional retirement age.

Packaging is an important issue for many seniors. While many marketers have responded to their dietary concerns by placing more details about product ingredients on labels, marketers have often forgotten that reading the fine print on packages is difficult for many older consumers. Wrestling with childproof caps is a source of constant frustration for individuals whose joints are inflamed by arthritis. Some over-the-counter drug producers have responded to this concern with easy-to-open containers especially designed for this market. Similarly, cleaning products are not only being made in smaller containers to meet the needs of seniors who often live alone, but they are also being made in easier-to-handle containers. Windex, for example, now comes in a bottle with an indented neck that is easier to grip.[19]

Changing Canadian Households

When one uses the term *household,* a stereotype of the typical family living in the suburbs with its two children may leap to mind. However, this stereotype is far from accurate. The 1996 census[20] (the most recent census data published by Statistics Canada) shows that common-law and lone-parent families together made up over one-quarter (26%) of all families in Canada, compared to one-fifth (20%) only a decade before.

Between 1991 and 1996, married-couple families increased by a mere 1.7 percent, while the number of lone-parent families increased by 19 percent and common-law families increased by 28 percent. In fact, in 1996, one couple in seven was living common law, compared to about one in nine in 1991. Almost half of the common-law-couple families included children, whether born to the current union or brought to the family from previous unions. Common-law families were by far most frequent in Quebec, which had 400 265, or 43 percent, of all such families in Canada. One couple in four (24%) in Quebec lived common law.

Overall, the total number of families in Canada increased by 6.6 percent to 7.8 million between 1991 and 1996, but the average family size is shrinking. In 1971, it was 3.7 people; in 1999, it was 3.1. Despite changes in families, married-couple families still constituted the large majority of families (74%); and the majority of families in Canada, about 65 percent, still had at least one child liv-

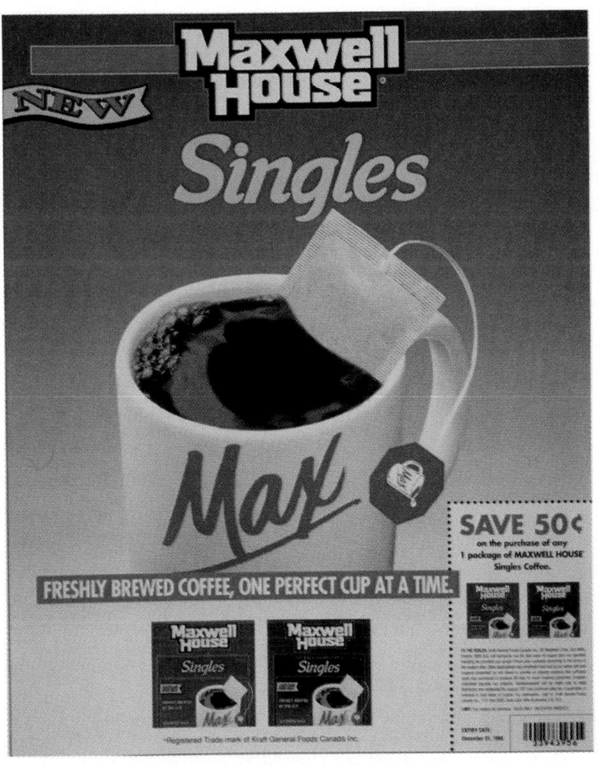

Maxwell House and other brands are targeting smaller households with single-serve portions.

ing at home. People in Canada are marrying later, however. The average age at which women now marry is 25, while it is 28 for men.

Responsibility for household tasks and the care of children is also changing. Fifty-five percent of all women aged 15 and over had jobs in 1999, up from 42 percent in 1976. As a result, women accounted for 46 percent of the workforce in 1999, up from 37 percent in 1976. The employment rate of women with children has grown particularly sharply in the past two decades, especially for those with pre-school-aged children. By 1999, 61 percent of women with children under age 3 were employed, more than double the figure in 1976.

Nonetheless, marriage appears to be a fragile bond for more and more individuals. At the time of the 1996 census, over 1.6 million people reported that they were divorced, a 28 percent increase from 1991. Women accounted for more than half of divorced individuals in 1996, since women do not remarry as often as men.

About 2.6 million people, 12 percent of the population aged 15 and over, lived alone in 1996, up slightly from 11 percent in 1991 and 10 percent in 1986. The aging of the population was largely responsible for this increase. Seniors accounted for more than a third of people living alone, and most of them (71%) were widows. As seniors get older, their likelihood of living alone increases significantly. While 22 percent of persons aged 65 to 74 lived by themselves in 1996, the proportion grew to 37 percent for those aged 75 to 84, and 48 percent for those aged 85 and over. Women aged 65 and over were more than twice as likely to live alone as men. In large part, this is explained by the fact that women often outlive their spouses and, when widowed, live on their own. Others living alone or in non-family households are young adults who leave home and move into apartments.

Population Growth and Shifts

The population of Canada increased by approximately 240 000 people in 1999, translating into an average growth rate of 0.20 percent. As Table 3-2 shows, however, growth rates across all provinces are not uniform: The populations of Newfoundland, Saskatchewan, and the Yukon decreased during the 1999–2000 period, while the populations of the other provinces either remained stable or grew.[21]

Canadians are a mobile people. For more than a century, Canadians have been moving from rural to urban areas. The urban areas show a faster pace of living, more commuting, higher incomes, and greater variety of goods and services than can be found in the small towns and rural areas that dot Canada. But Canada's cities are changing as well. Canadian cities are often surrounded by large suburban areas. Statistics Canada calls these combinations of urban and suburban populations "Census Metropolitan Areas" (CMAs). About 50 percent of Canada's population lives in the top 25 CMAs. These are listed in Table 3-3. Information about CMAs is useful for marketers trying to decide which geographical segments represent the most lucrative markets for their products and which areas are most critical in terms of buying media time. Marketers also track the relative growth of these markets to see which areas are expanding and which ones are contracting.

An estimated 277 000 people moved from one province to another in 1999, while about 900 000 moved from one CMA to another within their province. The Toronto CMA recorded a net inflow of 56 600 individuals, the largest net inflow of any CMA, at 12 people per 1000 living there. Vancouver recorded the second

TABLE 3-2 Canada's Population

	1 January 1999	1 April 1999	1 January 2000	1 April 2000	Variation in % 1999	Variation in % 2000
Canada	30 348 542	30 404 091	30 606 659	30 666 864	0.2	0.2
Newfoundland	543 164	541 631	541 559	540 159	−0.3	−0.3
Prince Edward Island	137 427	137 500	138 837	138 953	0.1	0.1
Nova Scotia	937 615	937 751	942 017	942 177	0.0	0.0
New Brunswick	753 816	754 103	756 625	756 990	0.0	0.0
Quebec	7 334 405	7 338 592	7 357 269	7 360 445	0.1	0.0
Ontario	11 431 503	11 463 544	11 575 079	11 612 101	0.3	0.3
Manitoba	1 139 567	1 141 484	1 145 900	1 147 583	0.2	0.1
Saskatchewan	1 027 865	1 027 850	1 027 172	1 026 214	0.0	−0.1
Alberta	2 935 753	2 948 070	2 978 804	2 989 999	0.4	0.4
British Columbia	4 008 775	4 014 730	4 043 658	4 052 434	0.1	0.2
Yukon	30 816	30 566	30 343	30 218	−0.8	−0.4
Northwest Territories	41 141	41 393	42 056	42 170	0.6	0.3
Nunavut	26 695	26 877	27 340	27 421	0.7	0.3

Source: Statistics Canada, "Demographic statistics, first quarter 2000 (preliminary)," *The Daily,* 20 June 2000, www.statcan.ca/.

largest net inflow of 21 610. Relative to the size of the population of the CMA, Calgary had a net inflow of 19 per 1000, the highest rate among CMAs. The Windsor CMA was a distant second, with a net inflow of 13 migrants per 1000.[22]

A Better-Educated and More White-Collar Population

Table 3-4[23] shows how the Canadian population is becoming better educated. Over the ten-year period from 1986 to 1996, the number of people without any degree or certificate dropped, while the numbers completing high school or a trade college increased. There was also a rise in the number of people completing a bachelor's degree. However, in the area of advanced degrees, the percentages remained constant over the 10-year period. The rising number of educated people will increase the demand for quality products, books, magazines, and travel. It suggests a decline in television viewing, because university-educated consumers watch less television than does the population at large. The workforce is also becoming more white collar. The 1997 census revealed that 28 percent of the workforce were classified as holding professional, managerial, and administrative positions, 26 percent worked in the fields of sales and service, and 12 percent worked in the areas of health care, education, or government services, compared to 26 percent of the workforce that worked as tradespeople, in manufacturing or primary industries.

Increasing Diversity

Countries vary in their ethnic and racial composition. At one extreme are homogeneous countries like Japan, where almost everyone is of Japanese descent. At the other are such countries as Canada and the United States whose populations are "salad bowls" of mixed races. Anyone who has walked the streets of Vancouver, Montreal, Calgary, or Toronto will immediately understand that visible minorities in Canada are a force to be reckoned with. The United Nations reported that Toronto is the world's most multicultural city, and the Canadian Advertising Foundation recently predicted that the combined purchasing power of ethnic markets will soon exceed $300 billion. Many ethnic markets are growing in size. For example, the Italian, German, and Chinese markets in Canada each have populations of over 400 000.

Nabisco is a firm that understands the power of ethnic marketing. Its product Magic Baking Powder was losing share in its traditional markets, but the firm

TABLE 3-3 Canada's Top 25 CMAs

Population Changes 1998–1999 and 1997–1998

	Population 1996	In	Out	Net	Net rate per 1000 population 1998–99	Net rate per 1000 population 1997–98
Calgary	815 985	50 650	33 812	16 838	18.6	28.0
Windsor	275 745	11 046	7 286	3 760	12.7	12.5
Toronto	4 232 905	151 377	94 770	56 607	12.3	15.8
Kitchener	379 345	19 019	14 368	4 651	11.4	11.2
Vancouver	1 813 935	74 298	52 686	21 612	10.8	13.3
Oshawa	266 585	14 864	11 780	3 084	10.7	13.4
Edmonton	854 230	38 345	30 182	8 163	8.9	12.7
Ottawa-Hull	1 000 940	38 714	29 890	8 824	8.4	7.8
Hamilton	617 815	24 852	19 783	5 069	7.7	9.4
Halifax	329 750	14 555	12 667	1 888	5.4	5.1
Montréal	3 287 645	78 791	64 385	14 406	4.2	3.1
London	393 905	16 947	15 519	1 428	3.4	5.1
St. Catharines-Niagara	367 795	10 198	9 213	985	2.5	5.5
Victoria	300 035	13 933	13 311	622	2.0	−0.3
Québec	663 885	17 452	16 858	594	0.9	−0.1
Saskatoon	216 445	10 868	10 700	168	0.7	3.7
Winnipeg	660 055	19 371	19 285	86	0.1	−3.0
Sherbrooke	144 575	6 393	6 438	−45	−0.3	3.1
Saint John	124 215	3 792	3 877	−85	−0.7	−6.5
Trois-Rivières	137 700	4 556	4 653	−97	−0.7	−2.5
Regina	191 485	7 911	8 068	−157	−0.8	−3.1
St. John's	172 095	5 762	5 947	−185	−1.1	−6.9
Chicoutimi-Jonquière	158 865	3 574	4 491	−917	−5.6	−3.4
Thunder Bay	124 325	3 861	4 635	−774	−6.1	−9.0
Sudbury	158 935	4 322	7 210	−2 888	−17.8	−13.5

Source: Statistics Canada, "Migration 1998/99," *The Daily,* 26 September 2000, www.statcan.ca/.

TABLE 3-4 Education Levels of the Canadian Population

Total	1986 19 634 100		1996 22 628 925	
No degree, certificate, or diploma	9 384 100	47%	8 331 615	37%
Secondary (high) school graduation certificate	3 985 820	20%	5 217 205	23%
Trades certificate or diploma	1 969 650	10%	2 372 000	11%
Other non-university certificate or diploma	2 034 465	10%	3 181 840	14%
University certificate or diploma below bachelor level	381 580	2%	525 560	2%
Bachelor's degree	1 254 250	6%	1 979 460	9%
University certificate or diploma above bachelor level	189 000	2%	310 820	2%
Medical degree	74 945	0.4%	105 050	0.5%
Master's degree	293 335	2%	501 505	2%
Earned doctorate	66 955	0.4%	103 855	0.5%

Source: Statistics Canada, *Statistical Profile of Canadian Communities,* www.statcan.ca/.

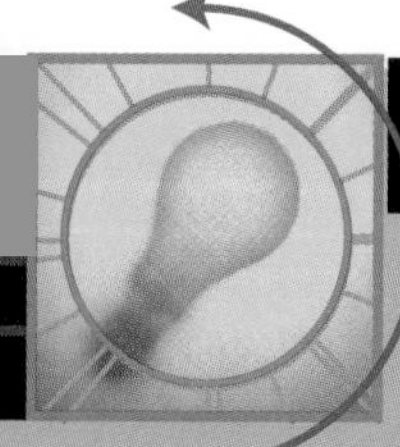

marketing highlight 3-3

Is Canada's Marketing Industry Racist?

This question was posed to 21 marketing specialists in 1997. While most respondents denied racism in Canadian marketing, they did stress that marketers should do more to reflect Canada's multicultural reality. Rather than being overtly racist, some members of the marketing community are racist by omission, claims Suzanne Keeler of the Canadian Advertising Foundation. These people just don't include people from different backgrounds on their management teams or in their advertisements. Instead of selecting people based on their individual characteristics, they make choices based on outdated stereotypes. While many respondents noted that more and more advertisers, especially those aiming products at young people, are using people from minority populations in their ads, others, such as Deanna Dolson, advertising director of *Aboriginal Voices* magazine, claim that many advertisers haven't "opened their eyes to what native culture is."

As the importance of global marketing grows, people from different ethnic and language groups will become increasingly valuable in the roles of marketing managers, advertising creative specialists, and account executives. Today, people in charge of new product development consider the opinions of ethnic groups when developing their product concepts. Some new product categories, such as ethnic foods, depend completely on understanding ethnic target populations. B.K. Sethi, publisher of *Ethnic Food Merchandiser,* doesn't believe any marketer can afford to be racist. Liz Torlée, chairperson of the Institute of Canadian Advertising, takes a similar stance. Advertising is "an all-embracing industry, and we have to be so much in tune with consumers that we are, I hope, constantly reflecting consumers' changing attitudes."

Source: Marketing, 3 March 1997.

revived its lacklustre performance when it targeted Chinese and Japanese restaurants with a sampling and promotion program for its product. Unlike baking powder's traditional market of consumers who were moving away from "scratch baking," this market valued quality baked goods. Sales in British Columbia alone increased by 14 percent as a result of this targeted sampling program.

Marketers must avoid negative stereotypes when it comes to serving ethnic markets. Seventeen percent of immigrants hold university degrees, compared with 11 percent of people born in Canada. Immigrants are also more likely to hold managerial or professional jobs and have more stable family lives than people born in Canada.

Targeting ethnic consumers involves far more than mere tokenism, many ethnic marketing specialists warn. Merely placing a person from a visible minority in an advertisement is not sufficient evidence that one is an ethnic marketer (see Marketing Highlight 3-3). Communicating in the consumer's native language is often mandatory, but marketers must also face the challenge of not alienating sophisticated second-generation individuals. The TD Bank recently demonstrated the power of providing information in potential customers' native language. The bank launched a Chinese Green Info Line to target potential Chinese investors. Over 300 callers per month take advantage of the service, which has generated considerable investments.

Marketers often have to place advertisements in media directed at the particular ethnic community they wish to serve. This task is becoming easier as more publications are being targeted to specific ethnic markets. Tele-Direct Publications has recently started distributing a Chinese edition of the *Yellow Pages,* and *Toronto Life* and *Maclean's* have recently launched Chinese editions. Ethnic television stations are offering programming in many cities. In terms of retailing, stores must be staffed with personnel who understand the language, customs, manners, and buying behaviour of the ethnic market.[24]

The diversity in the Canadian marketplace isn't restricted to ethnic markets. People's sexual orientation is another point of diversity, and there is growing tol-

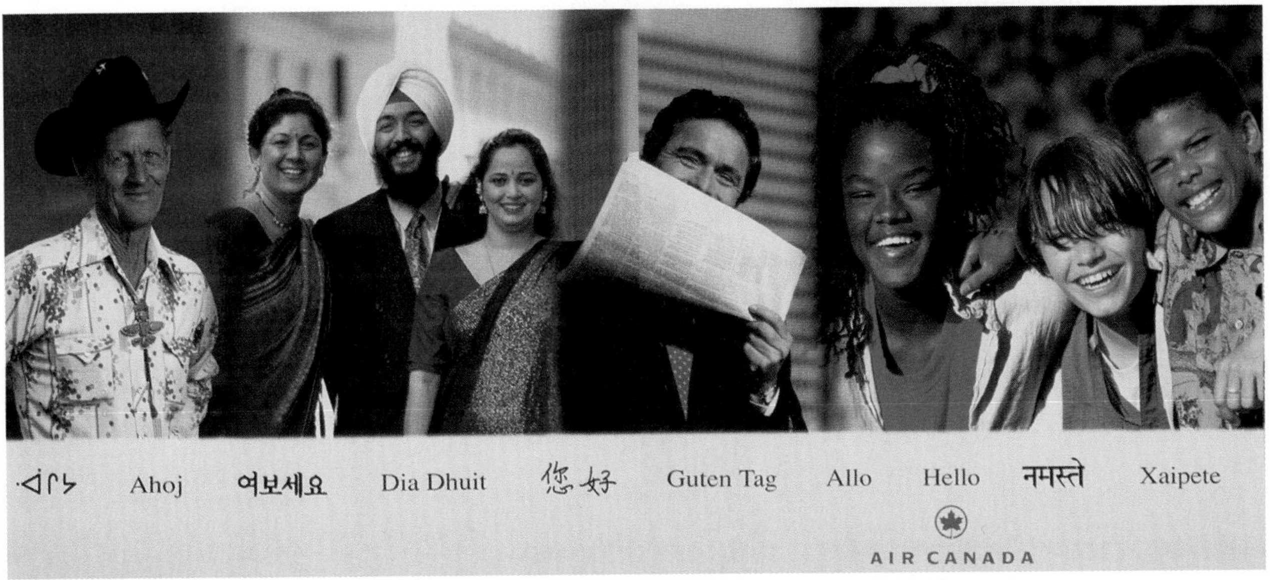

Many firms, such as Air Canada, are recognizing racial diversity in their advertising.

erance of alternative lifestyles in Canada. Over 600 000 people attended Lesbian and Gay Pride events in Toronto in 1997 alone. Since homosexual consumers tend to be cosmopolitan and have high incomes, they are desirable target markets for everything from health and beauty products, to travel, fashion, entertainment, and financial services. Nonetheless, until recently, few national advertisers, with the exception of the large breweries, created advertisements explicitly directed at this audience. One reason is the lack of research on this market; Statistics Canada, for example, doesn't even ask about sexual orientation in its surveys. Another reason is the dearth of middle-of-the-road media directed at these consumers. Finally, some marketers feared that advertising in gay media or at gay events would cause a backlash from heterosexual consumers.

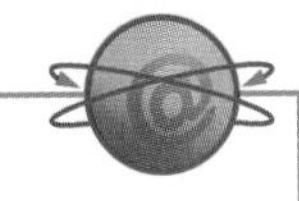

PrideNet
www.pridenet.com

These things are changing. Several research firms, including Environics, have started gathering information on the market. A growing body of media is directed at the gay community including electronic media, such as PrideNet. People who have experienced advertising to the gay community, such as Tom Blackmore, a partner in the Toronto-based advertising agency Robins Blackmore, says that clients who have used creative materials that are relevant to this audience have experienced remarkable successes from their campaigns. The one mistake that marketers can make with respect to this audience is doing nothing. "It is a market that people have ignored for way too long," he explains.[25]

Diversity goes beyond ethnicity or sexual preferences. For example, almost 18 percent of the Canadian population has some form of disability, and this group has considerable spending power as well as great need for tailored products and services. Not only do they value services that make daily life easier, like online grocery shopping from sites like GroceryGateway.com, but they are also a growing market for travel, sports, and other leisure-oriented products (see Marketing Highlight 3-4).

Economic Environment

Economic environment
Factors that affect consumer buying power and spending patterns.

Markets require buying power as well as people. The **economic environment** consists of factors that affect consumer purchasing power and spending patterns. Nations vary greatly in their levels and distribution of income. Some countries have *subsistence economies*—they consume most of their own agricultural and indus-

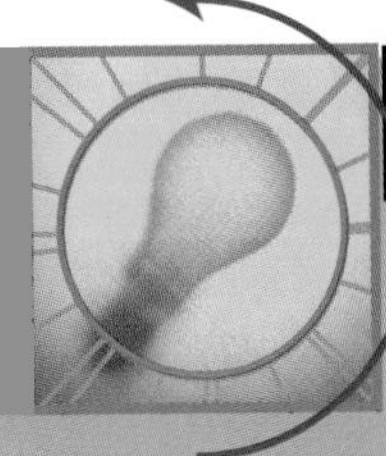

marketing highlight 3-4

Good Fun: Marketing Recreation to the Disabled

Julie Perez sees the difference when she goes to the Divi Hotels resort at Flamingo Beach on the Caribbean island of Bonaire. "It's famous for being totally accessible," she says. "The hotel brochures show the wheelchair access. The dive staff are trained and aware, and they really want to take disabled people diving. They're not afraid." Thirty-five-year-old Perez is an experienced scuba diver, a travel agent, and a quadriplegic. Before she had children, she made five trips a year to the Caribbean; these days, she gets there only once or twice a year.

People with disabilities constitute 17.7 percent of Canada's population. They are not only scuba diving, they are playing golf, riding horses, and white-water rafting. They surf the Internet, work in their gardens, and read. North American businesses are beginning to recognize the significance of this vast market of 52 million people who represent almost $1.2 trillion in spending power. This spending power is likely to increase even more in the years ahead, as the wealthier, freer-spending baby boomers enter the "age of disabilities." As a result, new stores, services, products, and publications pop up all the time to serve the disabled.

The non-profit Canadian Abilities Foundation provides a Web site (www.enablelink.org/main/main.htm) and magazine (*Abilities*) targeting people with disabilities. *Abilities* offers a wealth of information to its readers. If you search its online archives, you can find helpful information on accessible travel venues, everywhere from Niagara Falls to a cruise around Holland. Similarly, the American Association of People with Disabilities recently began publishing *Enable*. Both magazines hope to increase awareness among corporations that these people exist and need a wide range of products and services. They also hope to attract advertising from mainstream corporations.

Some firms have been formed just to serve the disabled market. Take the example of Tom Burns and Deborah Cappos of Nelson, British Columbia, who decided that parents of children with severe mobility restrictions shouldn't have to undertake a full-blown aerobic workout just to dress their kids. After two years of researching, designing, and testing, they launched a new line of clothing called "Mee Too." What makes the clothing so special? Not only does it look great

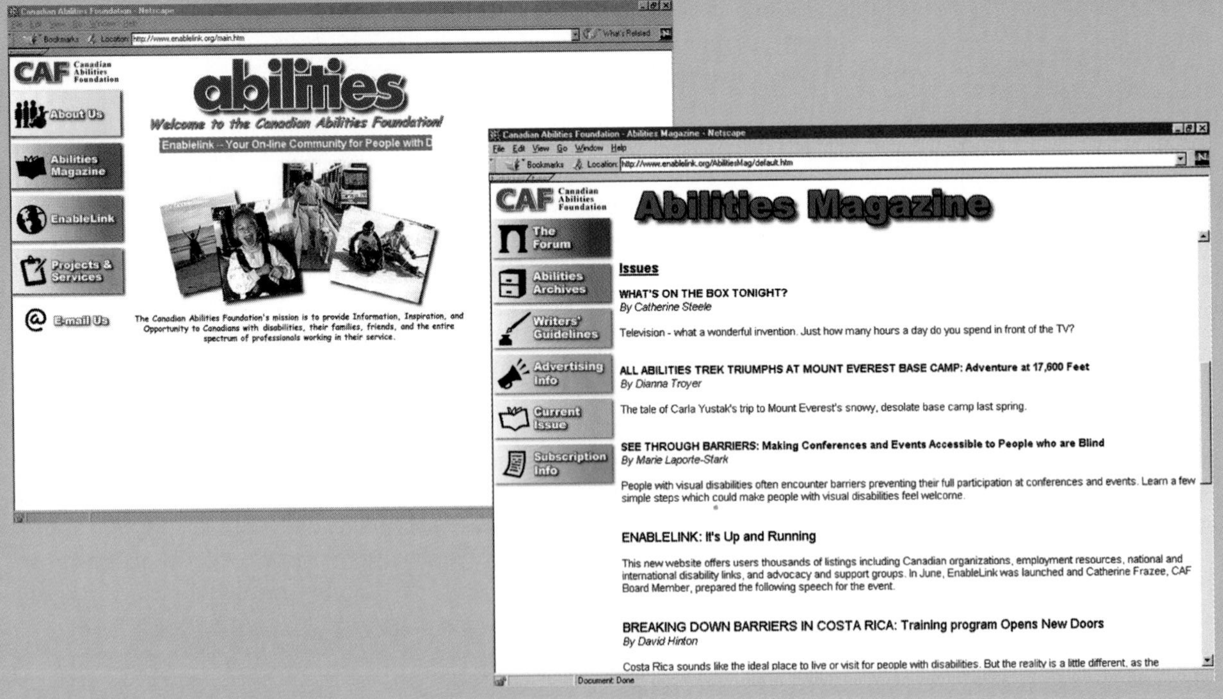

People with disabilities present a large and growing market. The Canadian Abilities Foundation provides a Web site (EnableLink) and magazine (*Abilities*) targeting this segment.

with its bright cheerful colours and contemporary styling, it's also tailored to meet the needs of this special market. Inconspicuously hidden beneath the surface of each piece of clothing are tons of cleverly hidden modifications that make the clothes very special. For example, all of the pants have a higher rise in the back to accommodate those who sit in wheelchairs. Tops have rugged wrist loops built into the inner seams to make lifting children easier. And the clothes have reinforcement in the appropriate wear zones, like on the back of the forearm for children in wheelchairs. All of the garments have snaps with Velcro under them so kids can learn to easily dress themselves. Given the range of disabilities that Canadian children face, the designers also offer custom tailoring. Founders Tom and Deborah note: "Our philosophy is to create clothes that really make life easier and more fun. We both just love kids! And it seems unacceptable that life for children who have disabilities and those who care for them should be any more difficult than it has to be!"

Other product and marketing efforts aimed at the disabled have been inspired by friends and relatives with disabilities. For example, Joe Montgomery, founder and president of Cannondale bicycles, has a son with cerebral palsy. The father saw a boy brimming with energy and determination and a love of horseback riding, swimming, skiing, and karate. But he also saw a child limited by wheelchairs he labelled "technological dinosaurs." A lightbulb went on, and Montgomery recognized that Cannondale could take the famous design of its high-end bicycles and make lightweight racing wheelchairs. "The market for lightweight wheelchairs is roughly $600 million per year," says company spokesman Bill Teel. "We're hoping to grab 10 percent of that in the next few years." Cannondale's strong brand name from bicycles should give the company a running start. "We've been getting calls nonstop since we made the first announcement," says Teel.

As Cannondale enters a market traditionally controlled by makers of conventional wheelchairs, the company plans to play by a different set of rules. Instead of selling the racing chairs at specialized medical equipment shops, Cannondale will sell them in bike shops. The company figures that kids in wheelchairs want to shop at the same stores as their ambulatory peers. "Younger kids in wheelchairs don't want to be Jim Knaub," Teel says, referring to a five-time wheelchair winner of the Boston Marathon. "They aspire to be Michael Jordan."

Catalogue shopping is convenient for everyone; those with mobility or other limitations are no exception. The adaptAbility Catalog from S&S Worldwide includes an extensive selection of "Leisure Time" products. These include large-face playing cards, automatic card shufflers, lightweight binoculars that double the size of television images, a pedal exerciser for use from a standard chair, and water dumbbells for low-impact water aerobics. Another S&S catalogue features people in wheelchairs using special bowling ramps and bowling ball pushers, taking shots on a mini-basketball set, and playing beanbag horseshoes.

People in the field, whether in business or as advocates for those with disabilities, have one simple piece of advice for those wanting to tap the disabled market: Make your product as accessible as possible. "Don't design for a disability," says ProMatura Group's Margaret Wylde. "Strive for universal design. A well-designed product is a benefit for lots and lots of people." Universal design means "products designed for the widest number of people," says Mary Lester, associate director of the Alliance for Technology Access, a group that works to make sure people with disabilities have access to the latest and greatest technology.

If a computer is made with built-in options for scanning or a more wrist-friendly keyboard, "it's a better product," Lester says. Anyone can benefit. "A company can, if it spends time on design from top to bottom, from the packaging to plugging it into the wall, enhance and enlarge its market," says Wylde. For instance, says former alliance director Fred Fiedler, people with disabilities led the move to "having the on–off button in front of the computer, instead of in the back where no one can reach." Vibrating pagers are another innovation, spurred by the hearing impaired but now popular with the general population. Oxo kitchen utensils have excellent grips, says Wylde, appealing not only to people with arthritis, but to anyone who prepares food. Its carrot peeler "looks neat, very stylish. Nothing about it says 'disability.'" She also praises Rubbermaid for adding a tab to the lip of its lids. "It's easier to use. Period."

By the same token, make advertising inclusive. "Ads that feature people with disabilities appeal to everyone," says the Packaged Facts report. "Able-bodied persons are not put off by seeing attractive people with disabilities in advertising." Advertisers should keep images positive. "People with disabilities are very sensitive to being portrayed as dependent, vulnerable, or as objects of pity," says Packaged Facts. "Already well aware of the difficulties they face, they like to see images of themselves overcoming these difficulties, transcending their limits, and living life as other people do."

Sources: Carol Taiji, "Hey, Mee Too!" *Abilities,* Winter 1992:61; Statistics Canada, "Population aged 15 and over with a disability, by nature of disability," *Canadian Statistics.* Also see Dan Frost, "The fun factor: Marketing recreation to the disabled," *American Demographics,* February 1998:54–8; Packaged Facts, *Marketing to Americans with Disabilities,* New York, 1997; and Michelle Wirth Fellman, "Selling IT goods to disabled end-users," *Marketing News,* 15 March 1999:1,17.

trial output. These countries offer few market opportunities. At the other extreme are *industrial economies,* which are rich markets for many different kinds of goods. Marketers must pay close attention to major economic trends and consumer spending patterns, both across and within their world markets.

Changes in Income

In the 1980s, the economy entered its longest peacetime boom. Consumers fell into a consumption frenzy, fuelled by income growth, federal tax reductions, rapid increases in housing values, and a boom in borrowing. They bought and bought, seemingly without caution, amassing record levels of debt. "It was fashionable to describe yourself as 'born to shop.' When the going gets tough, it was said, the tough go shopping. In the 1980s, many . . . became literally addicted to personal consumption."[26]

Free spending and high expectations were dashed by the recession in the early 1990s. Consumers have sobered up, pulled back, and adjusted to leaner times. Value marketing became the watchword for many marketers. They looked for ways to offer today's more financially cautious buyers greater value—just the right combination of product quality and good service at a fair price.

The late 1990s saw a turnaround in the economy.[27] During the last three years, unemployment rates in Canada fell to record lows. In 1997, the unemployment rate was 9.5 percent. By September 2000, it had fallen to 6.8 percent. The employment increase in September was split between full-time (+29 000) and part-time (+27 000) jobs. Two groups in particular have benefited from improved employment rates. Employment among youths posted a strong gain; however, much of the gain consisted of only part-time work. Moreover, the youth unemployment rate is still almost double the national average, standing at 12.7 percent. Employment among adult women has also improved, but in the case of this group, almost all of the gain consisted of full-time jobs. The baby boom generation is also now in its prime wage-earning period, and the number of small families headed by dual-career couples continues to increase. The median total income for both individuals and families began to increase. In 1998, median individual income was $20 100, an increase of 2.7 percent over 1997 levels after adjusting for inflation. People in Calgary had the largest rise in individual income at 4.3 percent, followed by Chicoutimi-Jonquière (+3.7%) and Saint John and Sherbrooke (+3.6%). The highest individual median total incomes were still recorded in Oshawa ($25 900) and Ottawa-Hull ($25 200). The rising median total income was largely due to an increase in employment income, increases in private pensions, and, to a lesser extent, higher provincial refundable tax credits and family benefits. The median family income also increased 2.1 percent from 1997 to 1998 to $47 300, after adjusting for inflation. Oshawa ($60 000) had the highest family income of all CMAs, followed by Windsor ($59 800). Table 3-5 shows how family income varies across the top 25 CMAs.

Paradoxes of the New Economy

For decades, many analysts predicted that advances in technology would create a leisure generation—people who worked less and had more time to enjoy life. While many people now have more time on their hands, few would consider themselves a leisure class. Many Canadians still rely on one, or multiple, part-time jobs. At the other end of the spectrum is a growing number of Canadians working more than 50 hours per week. Thus, while the average workweek remains at 40 hours, a growing number of people are working far less, and a growing number are working far more. This polarity in terms of hours worked is the paradox of the new economy.[28]

What are the reasons for these trends? Economic necessity is a prime culprit.

TABLE 3-5 1998 Median Family Income in Canada's Top 25 CMAs

	Family type		
	Husband–wife	Lone-parent	Total
Canada	52 500	22 700	47 300
Calgary	62 700	28 500	57 400
Chicoutimi	50 700	23 200	46 600
Edmonton	58 300	24 800	52 600
Halifax	56 200	20 400	50 100
Hamilton	62 000	25 000	56 400
Kitchener	61 400	25 500	56 300
London	59 200	23 600	53 200
Montréal	51 800	23 700	46 300
Oshawa	66 200	25 600	60 000
Ottawa-Hull	64 300	26 200	57 700
Québec	53 500	26 600	49 000
Regina	61 200	24 000	53 900
Saint John	50 600	17 300	44 100
Saskatoon	54 900	20 400	48 900
Sherbrooke	48 500	23 100	43 700
St. Catharines	55 400	23 600	50 200
St. John's	51 100	19 100	44 600
Sudbury	57 700	20 000	51 700
Thunder Bay	59 700	21 700	53 900
Toronto	57 800	26 800	51 800
Trois-Rivières	47 900	21 900	42 700
Vancouver	52 600	25 100	47 700
Victoria	57 300	25 700	51 900
Windsor	66 500	25 100	59 800
Winnipeg	55 000	24 000	49 600

Source: Statistics Canada, "Income of individuals 1998," *The Daily,* 10 August 2000, www.statcan.ca/.

In the 1950s and 1960s, a family could support itself on about 48 hours of employment. Today, family members must work 65 to 72 hours. This means that both spouses must work.[29]

Marketers must target their offerings to these two very different segments. While many who work part time will use their excess time to save money, others demand time-saving products. People at the time-pressed end of the continuum often don't even have time to eat or prepare meals. Kellogg's built an advertising campaign around this knowledge and positioned its breakfast bars as meals for people on the run. Grocery retailers are also taking notice. Since people aren't preparing meals at home the way they used to, grocers' market share is eroding. Today, about 38 percent of each food dollar is spent outside grocery stores in Canada; the average is 51 percent in the United States. Loblaws is experimenting with a strategy to win back harried consumers. The company has created *Take Me Marché:* kiosks in some stores, offering ready-to-eat meals and take-home food for people who want to eat at home but don't have time to cook.[30]

Marketers should pay attention to *income distribution* as well as average income. Income distribution in Canada is still very skewed. At the top are *upper-*

class consumers, whose spending patterns are not affected by current economic events and who are a major market for luxury goods. You might see some of these people frequenting the Second Cup coffee shop in upscale Rockcliffe Park, nestled close to the Ottawa River, where the average annual income is $74 000. There is also a comfortable *middle class,* which is somewhat careful about its spending but can still afford the good life some of the time. The *working class* must stick close to the basics of food, clothing, and shelter, and must try hard to save. Finally, the *underclass* (persons on welfare and many retirees) must count their pennies even when making the most basic purchases. People with Canada's lowest incomes are often found on native reserves. Of the 4400 communities ranked by income by Statistics Canada, the bottom 200 are almost all native. Education rates are low, unemployment is high, and individual incomes may be as low as $4000. One observer noted, "Reserves, especially in Western Canada, are somewhere between Mexico and Somalia in terms of standard of living. The disparity between the reserves and the rest of Canada is immense. It should be a major embarrassment."[31]

Walt Disney
www.disney.com

The growing income divide has sent marketers in opposite directions. On one hand, they have responded with a ceaseless array of pricey, upscale products aimed at satisfying the appetites of wealthy North Americans for "the very best": leather-lined SUVs as big as tanks, $2000 bed linen, restaurant-quality appliances, and vast cruise ships offering every form of luxurious coddling. On the other hand are companies that are now tailoring their marketing offers to two different markets—the affluent and the less affluent. For example, Walt Disney Company markets two distinct Winnie-the-Pooh bears:

> The original line-drawn figure appears on fine china, pewter spoons, and pricey kids' stationery found in upscale specialty and department stores, such as Nordstrom and Bloomingdale's. The plump, cartoon-like Pooh, clad in a red shirt and a goofy smile, adorns plastic key chains, polyester bed sheets, and animated videos. It sells in Wal-Mart stores and five-and-dime shops. Except at Disney's own stores, the two Poohs do not share the same retail shelf. [Thus, Disney offers both] upstairs and downstairs Poohs, hoping to land customers on both sides of the [income] divide.[32]

Changing Consumer Spending Patterns

Table 3-6 shows the proportion of total expenditures made by the average Canadian household in 1998 for major categories of goods and services.[33] Food, housing, and transportation use up most household income (48%). Consumer spending patterns have changed considerably in the last 50 years. In 1947, spending on the basics (food, clothing, housing, fuel) accounted for 69 cents out of every dollar. What expenditures account for the other 21 cents no longer spent on the basics? Canadians are spending more on two categories—what Statistics Canada refers to as personal goods and services; and recreation, entertainment, education, and cultural services. However, consumers at different income levels have different spending patterns. Some of these differences were noted over a century ago by Ernst Engel, who studied how people shifted their spending as their income rose. He found that as family income rises, the percentage spent on food declines, the percentage spent on housing remains constant (except for utilities such as gas, electricity, and public services, which decrease), and both the percentage spent on other categories and that devoted to savings increase. **Engel's laws** generally have been supported by later studies.

Engel's laws
Differences noted over a century ago by Ernst Engel in how people shift their spending across food, housing, transportation, health care, and other goods and services categories as family income rises.

Changes in such major economic variables as income, cost of living, interest rates, and savings and borrowing patterns have a large impact on the marketplace. Companies watch these variables by using economic forecasting. Businesses do not have to be wiped out by an economic downturn or caught short in a boom. With adequate warning, they can take advantage of changes in the economic environment.

TABLE 3-6 1998 Average Canadian Household Expenditures

Averages	
Household size	2.58
Expenditure detail	**Average expenditure per household $**
Food	5 880
Shelter	10 092
Household operation	2 362
Household furnishings and equipment	1 489
Clothing	2 201
Transportation	6 363
Health care	1 191
Personal care	693
Recreation	2 947
Reading materials and other printed matter	276
Education	679
Tobacco products and alcoholic beverages	1 214
Games of chance (net amount)	249
Miscellaneous	814
Total current consumption	**36 450**
Personal income taxes	10 965
Personal insurance payments and pension contributions	2 802
Gifts of money and contributions	1 144
Total expenditure	**51 362**

Source: Statistics Canada, "Average household expenditures, Canada, provinces and territories," *Canadian Statistics*, www.statcan.ca/.

Natural Environment

Natural environment
Natural resources that are needed as inputs by marketers or that are affected by marketing activities.

The **natural environment** is the natural resources that are needed as inputs by marketers or that are affected by marketing activities. Environmental concerns have grown steadily over the past two decades. Some trend analysts have labelled the 1990s as the "Earth Decade," claiming that the natural environment is the major worldwide issue facing business and the public. The Earth Day movement celebrated its thirtieth birthday in the year 2000; yet, in many cities around the world, air and water pollution have reached dangerous levels. World concern continues to mount over the depletion of the earth's ozone layer and the resulting "greenhouse effect," a dangerous warming of the earth. And many environmentalists fear that we soon will be buried in our own trash. Marketers should be aware of trends in the natural environment:

Growing shortages of raw materials. Air and water may seem to be infinite resources, but some groups see long-run dangers. Air pollution chokes many of the world's large cities. Remember how smoke from fires in Indonesia choked the air of whole nations? Great Lakes water levels are low, causing problems in many Canadian interior port cities, and water shortages are already a big problem in some parts of the United States and the world. Renewable resources, such as forests and food, also have to be used wisely. Non-renewable resources, such as oil, coal, and various minerals, pose a serious problem. Firms making products that require these scarce resources face large cost increases, even if the materials do remain available.

Increased pollution. Industry will almost always damage the quality of the natural environment. Consider the disposal of chemical and nuclear wastes; the dangerous mercury levels in the ocean; the quantity of chemical pollutants in the soil and food supply; and the littering of the environment with non-biodegradable bottles, plastics, and other packaging materials.

Increased government intervention in natural resource management. The governments of different countries vary in their concern and efforts to promote a clean environment. Some, like the German government, vigorously pursue environmental quality. Others, especially many poorer nations, do little about pollution, largely because they lack the needed funds or political will. The Canadian government passed the *Environmental Protection Act* in 1989. This Act established stringent pollution-control measures as well as the means for their enforcement, including fines as high as $1 million if regulations are violated. In the US, the Environmental Protection Agency (EPA) was created in 1970 to set and enforce pollution standards and to conduct pollution research. Thus, companies doing business in Canada and the US can expect strong controls from government and pressure groups. Instead of opposing regulation, marketers should help develop solutions to the material and energy problems facing the world.

Loblaw Companies Ltd.
www.loblaw.com

Concern for the natural environment has spawned the "green movement." Today, enlightened companies go beyond what government regulations dictate. They are developing *environmentally sustainable strategies* and practices in an effort to create a world economy that the planet can support indefinitely. They are responding to consumer demands with ecologically safer products, recyclable or biodegradable packaging, better pollution controls, and more energy-efficient operations. 3M's Pollution Prevention Pays program has led to a substantial reduction in pollution and costs. AT&T uses a special software package to choose the least harmful materials, cut hazardous waste, reduce energy use, and improve product recycling in its operations. McDonald's eliminated polystyrene cartons and now uses smaller, recyclable paper wrappings and napkins. Loblaws began its G.R.E.E.N. program in 1989; today, it is one of the most successful environmental businesses in the world. Over 100 new products have been launched since the program's inception, while manufacturing changes have helped make dozens of other products environmentally friendly. More and more, companies are recognizing the link between a healthy economy and a healthy ecology.[34]

Technological Environment

Technological environment
Forces that create new technologies, creating new product and market opportunities.

The **technological environment** is perhaps the most dramatic force now shaping our destiny. Technology has released such wonders as antibiotics, organ transplants, and notebook computers, and such horrors as nuclear missiles, nerve gas, and assault rifles.

The technological environment changes rapidly. Many of today's common products were not available even a hundred years ago. John A. Macdonald did not know about automobiles, airplanes, or the electric light. William Lyon Mackenzie King did not know about xerography, synthetic detergents, or earth satellites. And John Diefenbaker did not know about personal computers, compact disc players, or fax machines. Companies that do not keep up with technological change soon will find their products outdated. And they will miss new product and market opportunities. Marketers often face the difficult task of "envisioning" markets for products and services that didn't exist just a few years ago.

The costs of researching and developing new, complex technologies are rapidly increasing. The US leads the world in research and development (R&D) spending, but recent data suggest that it may lose its pre-eminent position to Japan and Scandinavia. Until recently, Canada hasn't had a sterling record when it comes to R&D expenditures. The Organization for Economic Cooperation and Development

(OECD) estimates that Canada was in tenth place on its innovation index in 1999. While Canada has been improving in this regard, other countries are racing ahead at a faster pace. Canada is working to turn things around. In 1994, it was ranked in twentieth spot in terms of competitiveness, took twelfth place in 1996, and held tenth position from 1997 to 1999. In 1999, the government invested $3.3 billion in research-related activities. It is investing heavily in education. Industry Canada and the National Research Council are funding new efforts to foster increased research. For example, Industry Canada supports partnering in such programs as the Canadian Network for the Advancement of Research, Industry and Education (CANARIE), and the Pre-Competitive Applied Research Network (PRECARN). Other government-backed initiatives are The Canada Foundation for Innovation, which awards funds to help post-secondary educational institutions, research hospitals and non-profit institutions modernize their research infrastructure and equip themselves for state of the art research. The 2000 federal budget allocated $900 million to the Foundation. Technology Partnerships Canada joins private and public sectors into partnerships to pursue high growth opportunities. These areas include environmental technologies, enabling technologies, and aerospace and defence industry technologies.[35]

It has long been believed that Canadian private sector R&D expenditures have been relatively low because many of the firms operating in Canada are branches of multinational firms that conduct R&D in their home markets. A recent study revealed that foreign-owned firms in Canada pursue research and development and innovation strategies more actively than do Canadian-owned firms.[36] The study challenges past conventional wisdom that has sometimes taken a jaundiced view of multinationals' role in Canada; it supports more recent views that multinationals decentralize activities from their home country to subsidiaries in Canada to exploit local competencies. It found that even though foreign subsidiaries have a privileged access to their parent company's research and development and technology, they perform research and development in Canada more often than do Canadian-owned firms that only serve the local economy. Not all Canadian-controlled firms lag multinationals operating in Canada. This study also compared foreign subsidiaries with Canadian corporations that have an international orientation. The analysis showed that the two groups are quite similar—both are about equally likely to conduct some form of research and development and to introduce innovations. The study concludes that it is as much the degree of a company's international orientation, or globalization, rather than the nationality of its ownership, that affects the level of innovation in the firm.

It is not surprising, therefore, that firms like IBM Canada, Bombardier (transportation equipment), Pratt & Whitney Canada (the aircraft engine manufacturer), CAE Inc. (a diversified maker of electronic products), or other international players like Merck Frosst Canada (pharmaceuticals), Bell Canada, and Alcan Aluminium are among Canada's top firms with regard to R&D expenditures.[37] Marketers in these and other firms need to understand the changing technological environment and the ways that new technologies can serve human needs. They need to work closely with R&D people to encourage more market-oriented research. They also must be alert to the possible negative aspects of any innovation that might harm users or arouse opposition.

Political Environment

Political environment
Laws, government agencies, and pressure groups that influence and limit various organizations and individuals in a given society.

Marketing decisions are strongly affected by developments in the political environment. The **political environment** consists of laws, government agencies, and lobby groups that influence and limit various organizations and individuals in a given society.

Marketers of new technologies engage in fierce battles to win over initial adopters. Two ads for new PCS digital communications services—one from Fido and the other from Clearnet—illustrate such a battle.

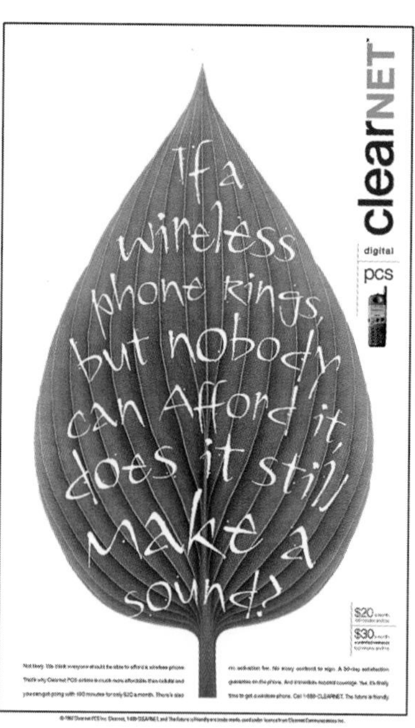

Legislation Regulating Business

Even the most liberal advocates of free-market economies agree that the system works best with at least some regulation. Well-conceived regulation can encourage competition and ensure fair markets for goods and services. Thus, governments develop *public policy* to guide commerce, by enacting laws and regulations that limit business for the good of society as a whole. Almost every marketing activity is subject to a wide range of laws and regulations.

Increasing Legislation

Legislation affecting business around the world has increased steadily over the years. Canada has many laws covering such issues as competition, fair trade practices, environmental protection, product safety, truth in advertising, packaging and labelling, pricing, and other important areas (see Table 3-7). The European commission has been active in establishing a new framework of laws covering competitive behaviour, product standards, product liability, and commercial transactions for the nations of the European Community. Some countries have especially strong consumerism legislation. For example, Norway bans several forms of sales promotion—trading stamps, contests, premiums—as being inappropriate or unfair ways of promoting products. Thailand requires food processors selling national brands to market low-price brands also, so that low-income consumers can find economy brands on the shelves. In India, food companies must obtain special approval to launch brands that duplicate those already existing on the market, such as additional soft drinks or new brands of rice.

Understanding the public-policy implications of a particular marketing activity is not a simple matter. For example, in Canada, many laws are created at the federal, provincial, and municipal levels, and these regulations often overlap. Moreover, regulations are constantly changing—what was allowed last year may now be prohibited, and what was prohibited may now be allowed. The North American Free Trade Agreement (NAFTA) replaced the Free Trade Agreement (FTA) in August 1992. It governs free trade between Canada, the United States, and Mexico. NAFTA is an historic document since it is the first trade agreement

TABLE 3-7 Major Federal Legislation Affecting Marketing

The Competition Act is a major legislative act affecting the marketing activities of companies in Canada. Specific sections and the relevant areas are:

- Section 34: Pricing—Forbids suppliers from charging different prices to competitors purchasing like quantities of goods (price discrimination). Forbids price-cutting that lessens competition (predatory pricing).
- Section 36: Pricing and Advertising—Forbids advertising prices that misrepresent the "usual" selling price (misleading price advertising).
- Section 38: Pricing—Forbids suppliers from requiring subsequent resellers to offer products at a stipulated price (resale price maintenance).
- Section 33: Mergers—Forbids mergers by which competition is, or is likely to be, lessened to the detriment of the interests of the public.

Other selected Acts that have an impact on marketing activities are:

- *National Trade Mark and True Labelling Act*—Established the term Canada Standard, or CS, as a national trademark; requires certain commodities to be properly labelled or described in advertising for the purpose of indicating material content or quality.
- *Consumer Packaging and Labelling Act*—Provides a set of rules to ensure that full information is disclosed by the manufacturer, packer, or distributor. Requires that all prepackaged products bear the quantity in French and English in metric as well as traditional Canadian standard units of weight, volume, or measure.
- *Motor Vehicle Safety Act*—Establishes mandatory safety standards for motor vehicles.
- *Food and Drug Act*—Prohibits the advertisement and sale of adulterated or misbranded foods, cosmetics, and drugs.
- *Personal Information Protection and Electronic Documents Act*—Establishes rules to govern the collection, use, and disclosure of personal information that recognize the right of privacy of individuals. The law recognizes the needs of organizations to collect, use, or disclose personal information for appropriate purposes. (For full details of the Act, see www.privcom.gc.ca/english/02_06_01_e.htm.)

between two developed nations and a developing country.[38] It is also the cornerstone for creating conditions that will help North American businesses compete worldwide. Access to low-cost inputs from the Mexican market helps US and Canadian firms respond to offshore price competition. These firms can better match strategies of Asian competitors such as the Japanese, who have access to low-cost inputs of material and labour in countries such as China. As trade between the three countries expands, the provisions of NAFTA will continue to be updated and amended. Marketers must work hard to keep up with changes in regulations and their interpretations.

Business legislation has been enacted for various reasons. The first is to *protect companies* from each other. Although business executives may praise competition, they sometimes try to neutralize it when it threatens them. So laws are passed to define and prevent unfair competition.

The second purpose of government regulation is to *protect consumers* from unfair business practices. Some firms, if left alone, would make shoddy products, tell lies in their advertising, and deceive consumers through their packaging and pricing. Various agencies have defined unfair business practices and enforce their regulation.

The third purpose of government regulation is to *protect the interests of society* against unrestrained business behaviour. Profitable business activity does not always create a better quality of life. Regulation arises to ensure that firms take responsibility for the social costs of their production or products.

Business executives must watch these developments of new laws and their enforcement when planning their products and marketing programs. Marketers need to know about the major laws protecting competition, consumers, and society, at the municipal, provincial, federal, and international levels.

Increased Emphasis on Ethics and Socially Responsible Actions. Written regulations cannot possibly cover all potential marketing abuses, and existing laws are often difficult to enforce. However, beyond written laws and regulations, business is also governed by social codes and rules of professional ethics. Enlightened companies encourage their managers to look beyond what the regulatory system allows and to simply "do the right thing." These socially responsible firms actively seek out ways to protect the long-run interests of their customers and the environment.

Business scandals and increased concerns about the environment have created fresh interest in ethics and social responsibility. Almost every aspect of marketing involves such issues. Unfortunately, because they usually involve conflicting interests, well-meaning people can disagree honestly about the right course of action in a particular situation. Thus, many industrial and professional trade associations have suggested codes of ethics, and many companies now are developing policies and guidelines to deal with complex social responsibility issues.

The boom in e-commerce and Internet marketing has created a new set of social and ethical issues. Issues as diverse as the online sale of prescription drugs, to fraudulent offers, to online gambling have troubled regulators and legitimate online marketers alike. No matter how troubling these issues appear, it is online information gathering, with and without consumers' knowledge, that has emerged as one of the most significant concerns. Not only do web-surfers knowingly provide information when they comply with online information requests, other information is gathered by sites that use cookies and web bugs—devices embedded in sites that track click stream data without the consumers' knowledge. While some governments, like the European Union and Canada, have recently passed legislation to better protect the privacy of web users, other countries, like the US, have little regulation in place to protect consumers' privacy and unauthorized use of their personal information.

Protecting children and other vulnerable groups from exposure to inappropriate material is another ethical concern that has arisen with online marketing. Protecting children from explicit sexual material and restricting access to "hate" sites or adult chat rooms is an ongoing challenge since all on-line marketers have great difficulty determining the demographic profile of users. Take the example of eBay.com, the online auction site. It recently found itself the victim of a 13-year-old boy who'd bid on and purchased on the site more than $3 million worth of rare art works and high-priced antiques, including a bed that once belonged to Canada's first prime minister. eBay has a strict policy against bidding by anyone under 18 but works largely on the honour system. Unfortunately, this honour system did little to prevent the teenager from taking a cyberspace joyride.[39]

Cyberspace has its own examples of more typical consumer abuses. For example, although America Online has been hugely successful and is a popular online service provider, it has lost millions of dollars due to consumer complaints about unethical marketing tactics:

> In 1998, America Online agreed to pay a $3.9 million penalty and revamp some of its business practices to settle deceptive-marketing complaints. In this instance, AOL failed to clearly notify consumers that the "50 free hours" in its online service's much-touted trial memberships must be used within a one-month period and that users would incur subscription fees after the first month. This was AOL's third settlement in less than two years. Previous settlements dealt with the company's data network congestion in early 1997 (due to a move to flat rate pricing that gave the company more subscriptions than it had equipment to handle) and efforts in late 1996 to switch customers to a higher-priced subscription plan. The three agreements not only cost the company $51 million in total, but created a barrage of negative publicity that AOL had to work hard to counter.[40]

Throughout this book, we present Marketing Highlight exhibits that summarize the main public policy and social responsibility issues surrounding major marketing decisions. These exhibits discuss the legal issues that marketers should understand and the common ethical and societal concerns that marketers face. In Chapter 18, we discuss a broad range of societal marketing issues in greater depth.

Cultural Environment

Cultural environment
Institutions and other forces that affect society's basic values, perceptions, preferences, and behaviours.

The **cultural environment** is composed of institutions and other forces that affect a society's basic values, perceptions, preferences, and behaviours. People grow up in a particular society that shapes their basic beliefs and values. They absorb a world view that defines their relationships with others. The following cultural characteristics can affect marketing decision making.

Persistence of Cultural Values

People in a society hold many beliefs and values. Their core beliefs and values have a high degree of persistence. For example, most Canadians believe in working, getting married, giving to charity, and being honest. While such values have been described as dull, reserved, and modest, Canadians view themselves as hard-working, generous, and sophisticated. These beliefs shape more specific attitudes and behaviours found in everyday life. *Core* beliefs and values are passed from parents to children and are reinforced by schools, churches, business, and government.

Secondary beliefs and values are more open to change. Believing in marriage is a core belief; believing that people should get married early in life is a secondary belief. Marketers have some chance of changing secondary values, but little chance of changing core values. For example, family-planning marketers could argue more effectively that people should get married later than that they should not get married at all.

Shifts in Secondary Cultural Values

Although core values are fairly persistent, cultural swings do occur. Consider the impact of popular music groups, movie personalities, and other celebrities on young people's hair styling, clothing, and sexual norms. Marketers want to predict cultural shifts to identify new opportunities or threats, so several firms offer "futures" forecasts. For example, the Environics marketing research firm tracks such regional values as "anti-bigness," "mysticism," "living for today," "away from possessions," and "sensuousness." Such information helps marketers cater to trends with appropriate products and communication appeals. (See Marketing Highlight 3-5 for a summary of today's cultural trends.)

The major cultural values of a society are expressed in people's views of themselves and others, as well as in their views of organizations, society, nature, and the universe.

People's Views of Themselves. People vary in their emphasis on serving themselves versus serving others. Some people seek personal pleasure, wanting fun, change, and escape. Others seek self-realization through religion, recreation, or the avid pursuit of careers or other life goals. People use products, brands, and services as a means of self-expression, and they buy products and services that match their views of themselves.

In the 1980s, personal ambition and materialism increased dramatically, with significant marketing implications: In a "me society," people buy their "dream cars" and take their "dream vacations." They tended to spend to the limit on self-indulgent goods and services. In contrast, people are now adopting more conservative behaviours and ambitions. They are more cautious in their spending patterns and more value driven in their purchases.

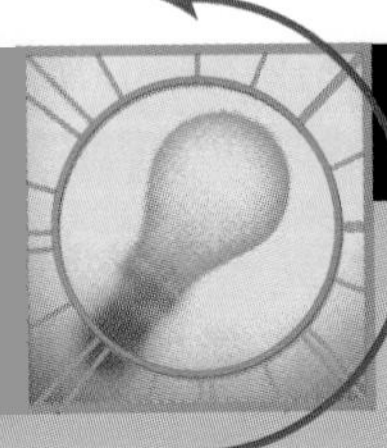

marketing highlight 3-5

Regional Differences in Culture Values and Product Usage

Canadian marketers must be sensitive to the regional differences that mark the country. Recent polls have shown that people in different parts of the nation have dramatically different values and beliefs. While it does not surprise most Canadians that Quebecers are fiercely independent, they might be surprised at the extent to which they live for today and place a high value on enjoying life. Seventy-one percent of Quebec residents agreed with the statement "We should eat, drink, and be merry, for tomorrow we may die," while people's agreement levels from other regions of Canada ranged from 17 to 43 percent. Quebecers are also more security conscious than other Canadians. They put greater importance on family and on the cultivation of friendships. Unlike the rest of Canada, they demonstrate a respect for authority. Picturing themselves as *au courant,* they stress fashion and being up to date on current events. Quebecers place less importance on earning a lot of money than do people from English Canada, and they pride themselves on being more emotional than English Canadians.

Regional differences are not just limited to those between French and English Canadians: Newfoundlanders think that they are the hardest-working segment of the Canadian population, while people from British Columbia express the greatest love of reading.

These regional values often translate into different patterns of product usage. Fredericton is the capital of white bread consumption. Montrealers eat more deep brown beans than other Canadians. Consumers in Halifax drink more Diet Coke per capita than other Canadians, and people from Manitoba and Saskatchewan have the highest per capita consumption of Kellogg's Corn Flakes. People from Quebec consume more than half of all tomato juice sold in Canada, but Quebecers are less likely to try new products, use no-name products, or make long-distance phone calls. While marketers are often at a loss when it comes to explaining how regional values translate into different product usage patterns, marketers must still be highly sensitive to these regional differences.

Sources: Rosemary Todd, "Food for thought," *Globe and Mail,* 12 March 1988:D2; Maclean's/CTV Poll, "A national mirror," *Maclean's,* 3 January 1994:12–5; "Portrait of the Quebec consumer," *Marketing,* 22 March 1993:14; "Quebec," advertising supplement to *Advertising Age,* 22 November 1993.

People's Views of Others. More recently, observers have noted a shift from a "me-society" to a "we-society" in which more people want to be with and serve others. Notes one trend tracker, "People want to get out, especially those 48 million people working out of their home and feeling a little cooped up [and] all those shut-ins who feel unfulfilled by the cyberstuff that was supposed to make them feel like never leaving home."[41] Moreover, materialism, flashy spending, and self-indulgence are being replaced by more sensible spending, saving, family concerns, and helping others. The aging baby boomers are limiting their spending to products and services that improve their lives instead of boosting their images. This suggests a bright future for products and services that serve basic needs rather than those relying on glitz and hype. It also suggests a greater demand for "social support" products and services that improve direct communication between people, such as health clubs and family vacations.

People's Views of Organizations. People have differing attitudes toward corporations, government agencies, trade unions, universities, and other organizations. By and large, people are willing to work for major organizations, and they expect them, in turn, to carry out society's work. In recent years, there has been

Farmers Co-operative Dairy Limited of Halifax believed Cape Breton fiddler Natalie MacMaster would have a strong appeal to Nova Scotians and featured her in a successful milk ad campaign.

a decline in organizational loyalty and a growing scepticism regarding business and political organizations and institutions. People are giving a little less to their organizations and are trusting them less.

This trend suggests that organizations need to find new ways to win consumer confidence. They need to review their advertising communications to ensure that their messages are honest. They also need to review their various activities to make sure that they are perceived to be "good corporate citizens." More companies are linking themselves to worthwhile causes, measuring their images with important publics, and using public relations to build more positive images (see Marketing Highlight 3-6).

People's Views of Society. People differ in their attitudes toward their society: Patriots defend it; reformers want to change it; malcontents want to leave it. People's orientation to their society influences their consumption patterns, levels of savings, and attitudes toward the marketplace.

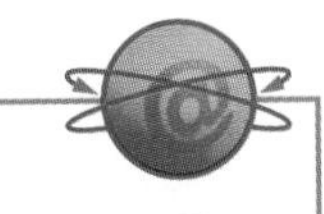

Clearly Canadian
www.clearly.ca
Upper Canada Brewing Company
www.uppercanada.com

The 1980s and 1990s saw an increase in consumer patriotism. Some companies such as Zellers responded with "made-in-Canada" themes and promotions. Others, such as Clearly Canadian and Upper Canada Brewing Company, made national identity part of their branding strategy. Canadians do not respond to in-your-face nationalistic appeals, but love the quirky humour of Labatt Blue's television campaign built around the insights about Canada's future by two early "voyageurs," or Molson Canadian's "I am Canadian" spots.

People's Views of Nature. People have differing attitudes toward the natural world: Some feel ruled by it, others feel in harmony with it, and still others seek to master it. A long-term trend has been people's growing mastery over nature through technology and the belief that nature is bountiful. More recently, however, people have recognized that nature is finite and fragile—that it can be destroyed or spoiled by human activities.

Love of nature is leading to more camping, hiking, boating, fishing, and other outdoor activities. Business has responded by offering more hiking gear, camping equipment, better insect repellents, and other products for nature enthusiasts. Tour operators are offering more tours to wilderness areas. Food producers have found growing markets for "natural" products such as natural cereal, natural ice cream, and health foods. Marketing communicators are using appealing natural backgrounds in advertising their products.

Tourism is the third largest industry in Canada. Positioning Canada as a pristine wilderness and spiritual refuge appeals to both Canadian and international consumers.

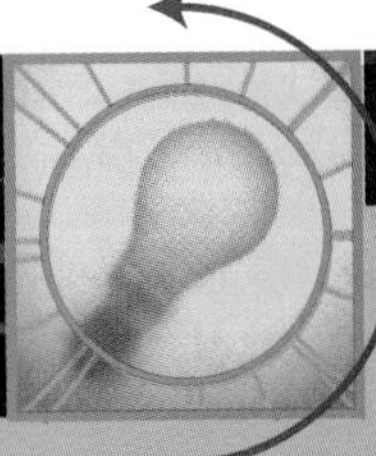

marketing highlight 3-6

Cause-Related Marketing: Doing Well by Doing Good

Cause-related marketing (CRM) involves the affiliation of corporate for-profit marketing activities with the fund-raising requirements of non-profit organizations. Growing in popularity, these programs have acted as marketing tools to target a vast array of market segments while also addressing a wide range of social issues. For example, Molson has linked its marketing of beer to building awareness among its target audience of 18- to 24-year-olds about sexually transmitted diseases while helping to fund AIDS research. Similarly, Chanel Canada has tied its marketing of high fashion to upscale consumers with support for the Mount Sinai hospital. Beatrice Foods sponsors "The Super Cities Walk" to raise funds for multiple sclerosis. Altamira, a mutual fund marketer, sponsors the opera as a way of attracting investment dollars from its target of business professionals.

CRM has become one of the hottest forms of corporate giving. It lets companies "do well by doing good" by linking purchases of the company's products or services with fund raising for worthwhile causes or charitable organizations. The term cause-related marketing was born in the early 1980s, when American Express offered to donate one cent for each use of its credit card to the restoration of the Statue of Liberty. American Express ended up contributing $1.7 million, but the cause-related campaign produced a 28 percent increase in card usage.

Companies now sponsor dozens of CRM campaigns each year. Many are backed by large budgets and a full complement of marketing activities. These are recent examples:

- Imperial Oil teamed with the Toronto Hospital for Sick Children to sponsor a CRM campaign to reduce preventable children's injuries, the leading killer of children. Imperial Oil founded Safe Kids Canada and has partnered with Zellers, Janssen Pharmaceutica, Ford Motor Company of Canada, and Bell Canada to educate the public about potential dangers in children's everyday activities, for example, in playing on unsafe playground equipment or in bicycling without a helmet. Labelling its program "strategic giving," the firm for the first time tied its philanthropic efforts to its marketing programs. Imperial decided to focus its giving on a single area where it believed it could make a difference—namely children's safety—rather than giving small sums to a wide range of charities. The program also involved Esso's franchised outlets.

The ads used in the campaign do not show Esso's products or services. Instead, they focus on children's safety issues, such as the use of car seats. The campaign was

Esso Kids Program
Esso
BECAUSE CANADA'S KIDS
ARE CANADA'S FUTURE
Each year in Canada, the Esso Kids Program supports hundreds of charities and organizations dedicated to the health and happiness of our greatest natural resource – the young people of our country.
Programs such as our founding sponsorship of Safe Kids Canada, support of the Smart Risk Foundation for the prevention of teen accidents and the Medals of Achievement program rewarding good sportsmanship and fairplay in youth hockey, all play a part in helping young Canadians reach their goals and dreams.
Imperial Oil
Esso

Esso promoted children's safety along with its corporate logo in its Safe Kids Canada campaign.

People's Views of the Universe. People vary in their beliefs about the origin of the universe and their place in it. Although many Canadians practise religion, religious conviction and practice have been dropping off gradually through the years. As people lose their religious orientation, they seek goods and experiences with more immediate satisfactions. During the 1980s, people increasingly measured success in terms of career achievement, wealth, and worldly possessions. Some futurists, however, have noted an emerging renewal of interest in religion, perhaps as part of a broader search for a new inner purpose. In the 1990s, people started moving away from materialism and "dog-eat-dog" ambition to seek more permanent values and a more certain grasp of right and wrong. As one trend tracker suggested: "The Nineties will see a marked change in the way society defines success, with achievements such as a happy family life and service to one's community replacing money as the measure of one's worth."[42] She continued, "The Nineties will be a far less cynical decade than the Eighties. Yes, we will still care what things cost. But we will seek to value only those things—family, community, earth, faith—that will endure."[43]

launched during the Stanley Cup playoffs and marks a watershed in Imperial's corporate giving efforts. In May 1995, Esso dealers donated one cent for every litre of gasoline sold. In addition to the donation, dealers handed out brochures to customers about children's safety issues. The campaign has been so successful that the Ontario Community Safety Council awarded its first Safety Promotion Award to Imperial Oil for helping people think about children's in-car safety.

- Procter & Gamble has sponsored many CRM campaigns. For a number of years, P&G has mailed out billions of coupons on behalf of the Special Olympics, helping make the event a household name. P&G supports its Special Olympics efforts with national advertising and public relations, and its salespeople work with local volunteers to encourage retailers to build point-of-purchase displays. Another of P&G's CRM efforts is its alignment of its Always line of feminine products with breast cancer research. The company established the Always Research Grant to support promising Canadian research in the field of breast cancer. P&G asked its employees to become involved by joining their October "Run for the Cure," and they donated the proceeds of sales of a lapel pin to the Breast Cancer Foundation.
- Education is a popular focal point for many CRM programs. Corporate funding for educational efforts is becoming increasingly important in many school districts where boards are facing shrinking budgets due to government funding cuts. For example, the Rocky View School District near Calgary is allowing the placement of advertisements on its 160 school buses. Pepsi-Cola Canada will give Toronto schools $1.14 million in return for exclusive rights to distribute their pop and juice in schools in the city over the next three years. The money resulting from the contract will help schools to fund services such as school lunch programs. Pepsi is also providing schools with a series of videos on topics ranging from substance abuse to staying in school.

CRM has stirred some controversy. Critics are concerned that it might eventually undercut traditional "no-strings" corporate giving, as more and more companies grow to expect marketing benefits from their contributions. Critics also worry that CRM will cause a shift in corporate charitable support toward more visible, popular, and low-risk charities—those with more certain and substantial marketing appeal. For example, MasterCard's "Choose to Make a Difference" campaign raises money for six charities, each selected in part because of its popularity in a consumer poll. Finally, critics worry that CRM is more a strategy for selling than a strategy for giving, and that "cause-related" marketing is really "cause-exploitative" marketing. Thus, companies using CRM might find themselves walking a fine line between increased sales and an improved image and charges of exploitation.

However, if handled well, cause-related marketing can greatly benefit both the company and the charitable organization. The company gains an effective marketing tool while building a more positive public image. The charitable organization gains greater visibility and important new sources of funding. This additional funding can be substantial. In total, such campaigns now contribute some $100 million annually to the coffers of charitable organizations, and surveys show that these cause-related contributions usually add to, rather than undercut, direct company contributions. Thus, when cause marketing works, everyone wins.

Sources: See Cyndee Miller, "Drug company begins its own children's crusade," *Marketing News*, 6 June 1988:1,2; "School kids snack for cash," *Advertising Age*, 2 February 1990:36; Melanie Rigney and Julie Steenhuysen, "Conscience raising," *Advertising Age*, 26 August 1991:19; Nancy Arnott, "Marketing with a passion," *Sales & Marketing Management*, January 1994:64–71; Geoffrey Smith, "Are good causes good marketing?" *Business Week*, 21 March 1994:64–5; Craig Smith, "The new corporate philanthropy," *Harvard Business Review*, May–June 1994:105–16; Naomi Klein, "Only Pepsi to be sold in schools," *Globe and Mail*, 15 January 1994:A15; James Pollock, "Educating the market," *Marketing*, 19 January 1995; Mark Stevenson, "What's in it for me?" *Canadian Business*, December 1993:54–60; and Imperial Oil, "A closer look at Safe Kids Canada," January 1995, www.imperialoil.ca.

Responding to the Marketing Environment

Someone once observed, "There are three kinds of companies: those who make things happen; those who watch things happen; and those who wonder what's happened."[44]

Many companies view the marketing environment as an "uncontrollable" element to which they must adapt. They passively accept the marketing environment and do not try to change it. They analyze the environmental forces and design strategies that will help the company avoid the threats and take advantage of the opportunities the environment provides.

Environmental management perspective A management perspective in which the firm takes aggressive actions to affect the publics and forces in its marketing environment rather than simply watching and reacting to them.

Other companies take an **environmental management perspective.**[45] Rather than simply watching and reacting, these firms take aggressive action to affect the publics and forces in their marketing environment. Such companies hire lobbyists to influence legislation affecting their industries and stage media events to gain favourable press coverage. They run advertorials—ads expressing editorial points

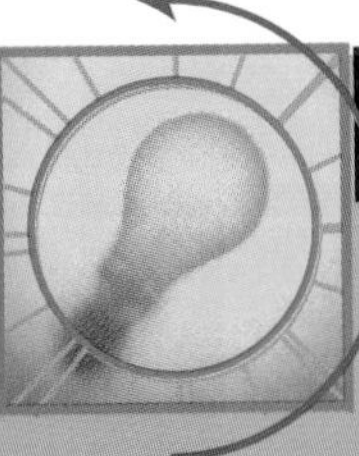

marketing highlight 3-7

Your Companysucks.com

Richard Hatch is one of the few people in this world with a passion for both Harley-Davidson motorcycles and collecting dolls and cute little toys. One day in 1997, the tattooed, 210-pound Hatch got into a shouting match with an employee in his local Wal-Mart and was banned from the store. Hatch claims that his actions didn't warrant his ousting. He says he'd complained to store managers for months that employees were snapping up the best Hot Wheels and NASCAR collectible toy cars before they hit the shelves.

Wal-Mart didn't budge, and the angry Hatch retaliated. He hired a Web designer and created the Wal-Mart Sucks Web site (www.walmartsucks.com). In just a few years, according to one account, the Web site "sprouted beyond Hatch's wildest dreams of revenge. More than 1500 customers have written in to attack rude store managers, complain about alleged insects in the aisles, offer shoplifting tips, and, from time to time, write romantic odes to cashiers." Hatch, who has amassed some 5000 Beanie Babies, also had a dispute with employees at his local Toys 'R' Us store about similar complaints. He was banished from there as well. His response? You guessed it: another sucks.com Web site.

An extreme event? Not anymore. As more and more well-intentioned grassroots organizations, consumer watchdog groups, or just plain angry consumers take their gripes to the Web, such "sucks.com" sites are becoming almost commonplace. A recent Yahoo! search for the words hate and sucks yielded 628 hits. The number of such sites isn't surprising given that anyone with a gripe against a company can potentially reach hundreds of thousands of people for about $150, the cost of registering a domain name for this type of "rogue" Web site. If you are wondering about businesses that are targets of a rogue site, just try typing in yourcompanynamesucks.com and see if anything comes up.

The sites target some highly-respected companies with some highly disrespectful labels: Microsucks; The I Hate Microsoft Page; Just Do Not Do It (Nike); America Offline; Untied Airlines: The Most Unfriendly Skies; The Unofficial BMW Lemon Site; and Allsnake: The Good Hands People?, to name a few. Some of these attack sites are little more than a nuisance. Others, however, can draw serious attention and create real headaches. "The same people who used to stand on [the] corner and rail against things to 20 people now can put up a Web site and rail in front of 2 million people," says William Comcowich, whose firm helps companies monitor what's said about them on the Internet. Rogue Web sites aren't illegal; they're protected under free

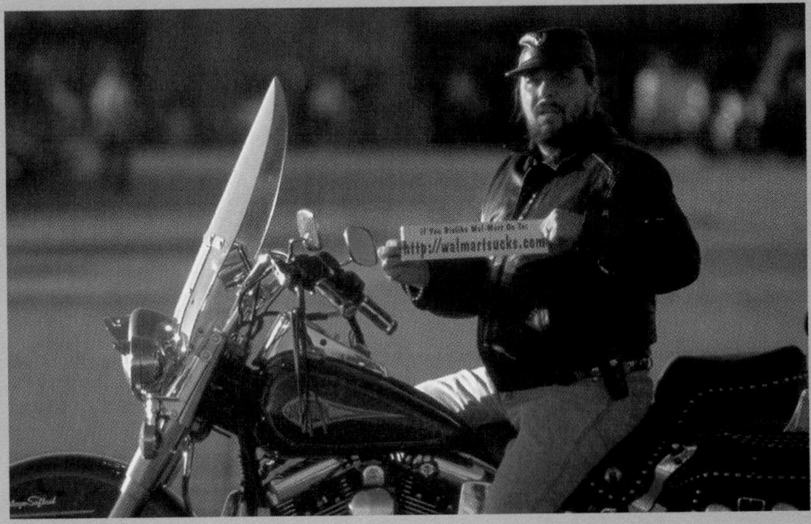

Environmental management: The best strategy for dealing with consumer hate sites is to address complaints directly. If a company solves my problems, why would I keep up the Web site?

of view—to shape public opinion. They press lawsuits and file complaints with regulators to keep competitors in line, and they form contractual agreements to better control their distribution channels.

Other companies find positive ways to overcome seemingly uncontrollable environmental constraints. Some forestry firms, including Noranda, have joined the Round Table on the Environment, a government-sponsored discussion group, to help all stakeholders affected by forestry policies better understand environmental concerns about forestry management. Cathay Pacific Airlines determined that many travellers were avoiding Hong Kong because of lengthy delays at immigration. Rather than assuming that this was a problem they could not solve, Cathay's senior staff asked the Hong Kong government how to avoid these immigra-

speech legislation. So the traditional corporate response has been litigation, citing trademark infringement. But legal action may bring more unwanted publicity than is worth the price.

The question remains, therefore: How should companies react to these attack sites? The real quandary for targeted companies is figuring out how far they can go to protect their image without fuelling the fire already raging at the sites. One point upon which all experts seem to agree: Don't try to retaliate in kind. "Avoid 'testosterosis'—or the urge to hit someone in the face because they are doing something you don't like," advises one consultant. "It's a free country, and the Web is completely unregulated. Don't get angry and think about doing foolish things."

Some companies have tried to silence the critics through lawsuits but few have succeeded. For example, Wal-Mart's attorneys threatened Hatch with legal action unless he shut down his Wal-Mart Sucks Web site. However, Hatch stood up to the giant retailer, and Wal-Mart eventually backed down. As it turns out, a company has legal recourse only when the unauthorized use of its trademarks, brand names, or other intellectual property is apt to be confusing to the public. No reasonable person is likely to be confused that Wal-Mart maintains and supports a site tagged walmartsucks.com. Beyond the finer legal points, Wal-Mart also feared that a lawsuit would only draw more attention to the consumer hate site. An industry analyst comments: "Those who operate hate sites adore posting cease-and-desist letters they receive from corporate attorneys. Such letters also validate their fight for the cause, whatever they perceive that to be, and they can use them to cast yet another negative spotlight on the company. They revel in the attention."

Given the difficulties of trying to sue consumer hate sites out of existence, some companies have tried other strategies. For example, most big companies now routinely buy up Web addresses for their firm names preceded by the words "Ihate" or followed by "sucks.com." In general, however, attempts to block, counterattack, or shut down consumer hate sites may be short-sighted. Such sites are often based on real consumer concerns. Hence, the best strategy might be to proactively monitor these sites and respond positively to the concerns they express.

Some targeted companies actively listen to concerns posted on hate sites and develop Web presentations to tell their own side of the story. For example, Nike is the target of at least eight different attack sites, mostly criticizing it for alleged unfair labour practices in Southeast Asia. In response, Nike commissioned an independent investigation of labour practices in its Indonesian factories and presented the results on its own Web site (www.Nikebiz.com). Monitoring consumer hate sites can yield additional benefits. For example, some sites can actually provide the targeted company with useful information. Walmartsucks.com posts customers' ratings of local stores for cleanliness, prices, and customer service, information that would be costly for Wal-Mart to develop on its own.

According to James Alexander, president of eWatch, an Internet monitoring service, the best strategy for dealing with consumer hate sites is to address their complaints directly. "If a company solves my problem," he says, "why would I keep up the Web site?" Take Dunkin' Donuts, for example. After a disgruntled customer established dunkindonuts.org, an attack site that appeared on many Internet search engines ahead of the company's own Web page, the company contacted about 25 people who had written in with complaints and offered them coupons for free doughnuts. "If this was where customers were going to post their comments, we thought it was important for us to go ahead and address them," says spokesperson Jennifer Rosenberg. Now, the company is in negotiations to buy the site from its founder, 25-year-old David Felton, who says he'll sell because "they have been taking complaints and responding." By proactively responding to a seemingly uncontrollable event in its environment, Dunkin' Donuts has been able to turn a negative into a positive. At Dunkin' Donuts, sucks.com is now allsmiles.com.

Sources: Quotes and excerpts from Leslie Goff, "YourCompanyNameHere sucks.com," *Computerworld*, 20 July 1998:57–8; and Mike France, "A site for soreheads," *Business Week*, 12 April 1999:86–90. Jane Langdon, "Web impacting corporate reputation: Companies want to know what's being said about them online—and by whom," *Strategy*, 10 April 2000:B8.

tion delays. After lengthy discussions, the airline agreed to make an annual grant-in-aid to the government to hire more immigration inspectors; but these reinforcements would service primarily the Cathay Pacific gates. The reduced waiting period increased customer value and thus strengthened Cathay's competitive advantage.[46]

Marketing management cannot always affect environmental forces. In many cases, it must settle for simply watching and reacting to the environment. For example, a company would have little success trying to influence geographic population shifts, the economic environment, or major cultural values. But whenever possible, smart marketing managers will take a *proactive* rather than a *reactive* approach to the marketing environment (see Marketing Highlight 3-7).

Review of Concept Connections

Companies must constantly watch and adapt to the *marketing environment* to seek opportunities and ward off threats. The marketing environment comprises all the actors and forces influencing the company's ability to transact business effectively with its target market.

1. **Describe the environmental forces that affect the company's ability to serve its customers.**

   The company's marketing environment has five microenvironmental and six macroenvironmental components. The microenvironment consists of other actors close to the company that combine to form the company's value delivery system or that affect its ability to serve its customers. The first microenvironmental component is the company's *internal environment*—its several departments and management levels—as it influences marketing decision making. The second component consists of the *marketing channel firms* that cooperate to create value—the suppliers and marketing intermediaries, including intermediaries, physical distribution firms, marketing services agencies, and financial intermediaries. The third component comprises the five types of customer *markets,* including consumer, producer, reseller, government, and international markets. The fourth component consists of *competitors,* and the fifth comprises the seven *publics* with an actual or potential interest in or impact on the company's ability to meet its objectives, including the financial, media, government, citizen action, and local, general, and internal publics.

   The *macroenvironment* consists of larger societal forces that affect the entire microenvironment—demographic, economic, natural, technological, political, and cultural forces. These six forces shape opportunities and pose threats to the company.

2. **Explain how changes in the demographic and economic environments affect marketing decisions.**

   Demography is the study of the characteristics of human populations. Today's demographic environment shows a changing age structure, shifting profiles of Canadian households, geographic population shifts, a more-educated and more white-collar population, and increasing diversity. The economic environment consists of factors that affect buying power and patterns. The economic environment is characterized by lower unemployment rates and shifting consumer spending patterns. Some "financially squeezed consumers" seek greater value—just the right combination of good quality and service at a fair price. The distribution of income also is shifting, leading to a two-tiered market. Many companies now tailor their marketing offers to two different markets—the affluent and the less affluent.

3. **Identify the major trends in the firm's natural and technological environments.**

   The natural environment shows four major trends: shortages of certain raw materials, increased costs of energy, higher pollution levels, and more government intervention in natural resource management. Environmental concerns create marketing opportunities for alert companies. The marketer should watch for four major trends in the technological environment: the rapid pace of technological change, high R&D budgets, the concentration by companies on minor product improvements, and increased government regulation. Companies that fail to keep up with technological change will miss out on new product and marketing opportunities.

4. **Explain the key changes in the political and cultural environments.**

   The political environment consists of laws, agencies, and groups that influence or limit marketing actions. The political environment has undergone three changes that affect marketing worldwide—increasing legislation regulating business, strong government agency enforcement, and greater emphasis on ethics and socially responsible actions. The cultural environment is made up of institutions and forces that affect a society's values, perceptions, preferences, and behaviours. The environment shows long-term trends toward a "we-society," a return to cautious trust of institutions, increasing patriotism, greater appreciation for nature, a new spiritualism, and search for more meaningful and enduring values.

5. **Discuss how companies can react to the marketing environment.**

   Companies can passively accept the marketing environment as an uncontrollable element to which they must adapt, avoiding threats and taking advantage of opportunities as they arise. Or they can take an environmental management perspective, proactively working to change the environment rather than simply reacting to it. Whenever possible, companies should try to be proactive rather than reactive.

Key Terms

Baby boom *(p. 111)*
Cultural environment *(p. 131)*
Demography *(p. 107)*
Economic environment *(p. 119)*
Engel's laws *(p. 124)*
Environmental management perspective *(p. 135)*
Macroenvironment *(p. 100)*
Marketing environment *(p. 100)*
Marketing intermediaries *(p. 101)*
Microenvironment *(p. 100)*
Natural environment *(p. 125)*
Political environment *(p. 127)*
Public *(p. 105)*
Technological environment *(p. 126)*

Discussing the Issues

1. McDonald's received a lot of adverse press and wasn't as successful in the late 1990s as it had been previously. What micro- and macroenvironment trends affected McDonald's throughout the 1990s? If you were in charge of marketing at McDonald's, what plans would you have made to deal with these trends?
2. Statistics Canada is posting tables on its Web site (**www.statcan.ca**) that outline some of its findings from the 1996 census. These include tables on population projects by age group and sex, the population of Census Metropolitan Areas (CMAs), and recent immigrants by last country of residence. Go to their Web site. Print one of these tables, analyze it, and describe how this information would help you design a marketing plan for a particular target audience.
3. Canada's ethnic populations are growing quickly. It is estimated that the six largest ethnic groups now encompass about 2.8 million people, almost 10 percent of the current population. What are the major challenges faced by marketers attempting to serve these populations?
4. What Canadian companies have successfully used the "green revolution" as leverage to market their products or services? Why have some of these efforts caused controversy among consumers and environmental groups? Do you think corporations should continue to pursue green marketing? Is it a fad or a long-term trend?
5. Businesses are feeling increasing pressure to be more ethically and socially responsible. The latest area of concern involves the Internet and e-commerce. What are the key issues regarding online ethics and social responsibilities? How should online businesses respond to these issues? Give an example of an online marketer that is not behaving responsibly. What would you propose to correct this situation?
6. Suppose that you have been assigned the task of explaining the core cultural values of people in Canada to a foreign marketer who wishes to sell a new line of men's and women's clothing in this country. Identify at least six core values that you think the foreign marketer would need to understand. Explain how the marketer might apply these values.
7. Assume that you are marketing manager for Air Canada and that your company has recently come under attack by Richard Hatch (see Marketing Highlight 3-7). Outline an action plan for proactively dealing with this situation.

Marketing Applications

1. Changes in the marketing environment mean that marketers must meet new consumer needs that may be very different from—even directly opposite to—those of the past. Mattel's Barbie dolls began as high-fashion playthings for young girls. In those days, Mattel assumed that most young girls would become homemakers and that high-fashion fantasy was an appropriate dream. Today, Mattel

seeks a very different role and relationship with young women. Visit Mattel's Barbie Web site at www.barbie.com. See if you can track changes in the marketing environment by looking at how Mattel has modified Barbie.

a. Make a list of the ways Barbie has changed to meet the evolving needs and expectations of young women. How do these modifications reflect female self-image, self-confidence, and life goals?

b. Apply your list to other gender-related Web sites, such as www.women.com and www.ivillage.com. Do you see any similarities with respect to trends reflected in these sites?

c. Using your list, construct a gender-sensitive marketing plan for a specific automobile brand that wishes to target young female drivers. How does your plan reflect what you have learned from the Barbie and other Web sites?

2. When Stanford University graduate students Jerry Yang and David Filo developed Yahoo!, they had little idea how far their revolutionary concept would go. Their original concept was to make "wasting time on the Internet" easier. Commercial applications came later. Today, more Internet users recognize the name Yahoo! than recognize Microsoft. One reason for Yahoo!'s popularity is its ability to focus on people's tastes rather than on just delivering information or access to every Web site possible. Yahoo! has become a full-blown package of information and services relating to health, real estate, finance, news, personalization, travel, and shopping. The major challenge now facing Yahoo! is how to convince corporate America that Yahoo! constitutes an effective advertising medium. Primary future challenges will come from America Online and Microsoft.

a. How will a portal site like Yahoo! affect a marketing company's technological environment?

b. Suppose you are marketing manager for a company that makes and sells consumer electronics products. After visiting Yahoo! at www.yahoo.com and competing sites, assess Yahoo! as an advertising medium for your product. What types of ads would you consider placing on such a site?

c. Given the rapid pace of change in the Internet environment, how do you think Yahoo! will fare in the future? Which environmental issues seem most critical to Yahoo!'s success? If you were the marketing manager of Yahoo!, what strategic alliances would you investigate?

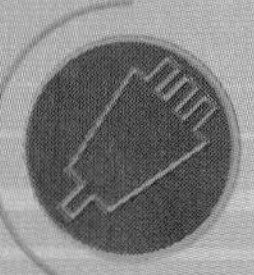

Internet Connections

Is "World Wide Web" a Misnomer?

In this chapter, you learned the importance of technology, demographics, and other macroenvironmental factors for a company's marketing efforts. The Internet's rapid growth creates opportunities for companies to reach consumers all over the globe. But is the Web truly global, or are some geographic markets better than others for online product offerings? In this exercise, you'll explore five countries to see which has the best potential for a firm wanting to sell music CDs online internationally. Locate information on Norway, Canada, India, Mexico, and Japan, and find as much information as possible to complete the table. Good sources for this exercise are listed in the Savvy Sites that follow, but you might also want to use a search engine to find information. Hint: The press releases at CyberAtlas are quite helpful.

For Discussion

1. Which country has the highest Internet penetration? The fastest growth rate?
2. Based on your research, what is the greatest barrier to Internet adoption outside Canada and the United States?
3. Which country has the best potential for selling music CDs online? Justify your selection.
4. What other key macroenvironmental factors would a firm have to consider before marketing to your selected country? Explain.
5. Based on your research, what advice do you have for a firm creating a Web site to sell CDs in your recommended country?

	Norway	Canada	India	Mexico	Japan
Total population					
Number online					
Percentage of population online					
Internet adoption growth rate					
Number who shop online					
Best demographic group for targeting					
Barriers to Internet adoption growth					

Savvy Sites

NUA Internet Surveys (www.nua.ie) contains lots of current statistics on Internet adoption in various countries.

- CyberAtlas (cyberatlas.internet.com) reprints published studies of Internet user demographics, geographics, and behaviour for many countries.
- The Department of Foreign Affairs and International Trade (DFAIT) (www.infoexport.gc.ca/) and Industry Canada (info.ic.gc.ca) maintain extensive databases that include statistics helpful to businesses, especially in the area of international trade.
- I-tools (www.iTools.com) helps you find "anything" on the Internet, including country population.

Notes

1. Quotes from James R. Rosenfield, "Millennial Fever," *American Demographics,* December 1997:47–51; Keith Naughton and Bill Vlasic, "The Nostalgia boom: Why the old is new again," *Business Week,* 23 March 1998:58–64; and "New Beetles: Drivers wanted," accessed online at www.vw.com/cars/newbeetle/main.html, 11 August 1998. Also see Greg Farrell, "Getting the Bugs out," *Brandweek,* 6 April 1998:30–40; "Beetle mania," *Adweek,* 13 July 1998:24; "Volkswagen's New Beetle selected 1999 North American Car of the Year," press release accessed online at www.vw.com, 4 January 1999; remarks by Jens Neumann at the 1999 North American International Auto Show, accessed online at www.vw.com, 4 January 1999; and Judann Pollack, "Heinz waxes nostalgic over revived glass bottle," *Advertising Age,* 3 May 1999:17.
2. Jennifer Lach, "Dateline America: May 1, 2025," *American Demographics,* May 1999:19–20.
3. Sarah Lorge, "The Coke advantage," *Sales & Marketing Management,* December 1998:17.
4. Philip B. Evans and Thomas S. Wurster, "Strategy and the new economics of information," *Harvard Business Review,* September–October 1997:70–83; Michael Krantz, "Click till you drop," Time, 20 July 1998:34–9; Ed Tallent, "Encyclopedia Britannica Online," *Library Journal,* 15 May 1999:138–9;

"Withering Britannica bets it all on the Web," *Fortune,* 22 November 1999:344. For more on identifying competitors, see Bruce H. Clark and David Montgomery, "Managerial identification of competitors," *Journal of Marketing,* July 1999:67–83.

5. See Michael Porter, *Competitive Advantage: Creating and Sustaining Superior Performance,* New York: Free Press, 1985:226–7; and Joseph Weber, "How J&J's foresight made contact lenses pay," *Business Week,* 4 May 1992:132.

6. See Porter, *Competitive Advantage:* Chapter 6.

7. Ian McGugan, "Cross-border quiz," *Canadian Business,* January 1996:31.

8. Jim McElgunn, "Foot puts the boot to current 'life-cycle' trends," *Marketing,* 15 June 1992:1; Daniel Stoffman, "Completely predictable people," *Report on Business,* November 1990:78–84; "Boomers slowing pace of leisure," *Toronto Star,* 20 June 1993:G3.

9. Elizabeth Church, "Birth bulge breeds its own industry," *Globe and Mail,* 24 September 1996:B12.

10. Jane Gadd, "Commitment to healthy diet declines," *Globe and Mail,* 11 November 1997:A10.

11. Patti Summerfield, "RMB rolls out national study," *Strategy,* 24 April 2000:18.

12. See the World Population clock, which gives daily estimates of the world population, at www.census.gov/cgibin/ipc/popclock. Many of the global statistical data in this chapter are drawn from the *World Almanac and Book of Facts,* 1993.

13. Sally D. Goll, "Marketing: China's (only) children get the royal treatment," *Wall Street Journal,* 8 February 1995:B1,B2.

14. John Kettle, "Kettle's future: Canada shows its age," *Globe and Mail,* 17 January 1997:B11.

15. Daniel Stoffman, "Completely predictable people," *Report on Business,* November 1990:78–84.

16. See Thomas Exter, "And baby makes 20 million," *American Demographics,* July 1991:55; Joseph Spiers, "The baby boomlet is for real," *Fortune,* 10 February 1992:101–4; Joe Schwartz, "Is the baby boomlet ending?" *American Demographics,* May 1992:9; and Christopher Farrell, "The baby boomlet may kick in a little growth," *Business Week,* 10 January 1994:66.

17. Mikala Folb, "Totally girl," *Marketing,* 4/11 January 1999:10–2; Shawna Steinberg, "Have allowance will transform economy," *Canadian Business,* 13 March 1998:59–71.

18. See Diane Crispell and William H. Frey, "American maturity," *American Demographics,* March 1993:31–42; Charles F. Longino, "Myths of an aging America," *American Demographics,* August 1994:36–43; Melissa Campanelli, "Selling to seniors: A waiting game," *Sales & Marketing Management,* June 1994:69.

19. Marina Strauss, "Seniors grasp for friendlier packaging," *Globe and Mail,* 7 October 1993:B4; *Today's Seniors,* October 1995:3–9; "The countdown to the 21st century," *Vision 2000,* The Royal Bank.

20. Statistics Canada, "1996 Census: Marital status, common-law unions and families," 14 October 1997; "Women in Canada," *The Daily,* 14 September 2000, www.statcan.ca/Daily/English/000914/d000914c.htm.

21. Statistics Canada, "Demographic statistics, first quarter 2000 (preliminary)," *The Daily,* 20 June 2000, www.statcan.ca/.

22. Statistics Canada, "Migration 1998/99," *The Daily,* 26 September 2000, www.statcan.ca/.

23. See the Statistics Canada *Statistical Profile of Canadian Communities,* which contains free information from the 1996 Census of Population, from approximately 6000 communities in Canada, www.statcan.ca/.

24. Jim McElgunn, "Wave of new ethnic media is announced," *Marketing,* 4 September 1995:3; Alanna Mitchell, "Study debunks immigrant myths," *Globe and Mail,* 13 July 1994:A1–2; Isabel Vincent, "Chasing after the ethnic consumer," *Globe and Mail,* 18 September 1995:A8; "Nailing the niche," *Marketing,* 18 September 1995:20.

25. Barbara Smith, "Special feature: Gay and lesbian marketing: Market becoming more accessible," *Strategy,* 18 September 1995:35.

26. James W. Hughes, "Understanding the squeezed consumer," *American Demographics,* July 1991:44–50. Also see Patricia Sellers, "Winning over the new consumer," *Fortune,* 29 July 1991:113–25; and Brian O'Reilly, "Preparing for leaner times," *Fortune,* 27 January 1992:40–7.

27. Statistics Canada, "Income of individuals 1998," *The Daily,* 10 August 2000; Statistics Canada, "Labour Force Survey," The Daily, 6 October 2000, www.statcan.ca/.

28. Margot Bigg-Clark, "Juggling jobs a '90s necessity," *Globe and Mail,* 28 July 1997:B1,B3; Harvey Schachter, "Slaves of the new economy," *Canadian Business,* April 1996:86–92.

29. Nancy DeHart, "Clocking in," *Kingston Whig-Standard,* 26 May 1997:15.

30. Zena Olijnyk, "Loblaw takes a run at time-starved diners," *Financial Post,* 11 November 1997:10.

31. Mark MacKinnon, "High-income neighbourhoods," *Globe and Mail,* 1 March 1999:B1; Mark MacKinnon, "The lowest incomes in Canada are found on native reserves," *Globe and Mail,* 1 March 1999:B2.

32. David Leonhardt, "Two-tier marketing," *Business Week,* 17 March 1997:82–90.

33. Statistics Canada, "Average household expenditures, Canada, provinces and territories," *Canadian Statistics,* www.statcan.ca/.

34. For more discussion, see the "Environmentalism" section in Chapter 18. Also see Patrick Carson and Julia Moulden, *Green Is Gold,* Toronto: Harper Business Press, 1991; Michael E. Porter and Claas van der Linde, "Green and competitive: Ending the stalemate," *Harvard Business Review,* September–October 1995:120–34; Stuart L. Hart, "Beyond greening: strategies for a sustainable world," *Harvard Business Review,* January–February 1997:67–76; Jacquelyn Ottman, "Environment winners show sustainable strategies," *Marketing News,* 27 April 1998:6; Lisa E. Phillips, "Green attitude," *American Demographics,* April 1999:46–7; and Forest L. Reinhardt, "Bringing the environment down to earth," *Harvard Business Review,* July–August 1999:149–57.

35. Bruce Little, "Canada ranks 10th in competitiveness study," *Globe and Mail,* 21 April 1999:B7. Also see the Industry Canada (**info.ic.gc.ca**) and NRC (**www.nrc.ca**) Web sites for descriptions of research initiatives.

36. Statistics Canada, "Multinational firms and the innovation process," *The Daily,* 27 June 2000, www.statcan.ca/.

37. "Top R&D companies," *Report on Business,* July 1995:91.

38. Canadian Government, *North American Free Trade Agreement: An Overview and Description,* August 1992.

39. "13-year-old bids over $3m for items in eBay auctions," *USA Today*, 30 April 1999:10B.

40. Rajiv Chandrasekaran, "AOL settles marketing complaints," *Washington Post*, 29 May 1998:F1.

41. See Cyndee Miller, "Trendspotters: 'Dark Ages' ending; so is cocooning," *Marketing News*, 3 February 1997:1,16.

42. Anne B. Fisher, "A brewing revolt against the rich," *Fortune*, 17 December 1990:89–94.

43. Anne B. Fisher, "What consumers want in the 1990s," *Fortune*, 21 January 1990:112. Also see Joseph M. Winski, "Who we are, how we live, what we think," *Advertising Age*, 20 January 1992:16–8; and John Huey, "Finding new heroes for a new era," *Fortune*, 25 January 1993:62–9.

44. Philip Kotler, *Kotler on Marketing*, New York: Free Press, 1999:3.

45. See Carl Zeithaml and Valerie A. Zeithaml, "Environmental Management: Revising the marketing perspective," *Journal of Marketing*, Spring 1984:46–53.

46. Howard E. Butz, Jr. and Leonard D. Goodstein, "Measuring customer value: Gaining the strategic advantage," *Organizational Dynamics*, Winter 1996:66–7.

Company Case 3

THE NEWEST AVON LADY—BARBIE!

SELLING TRADITION

"Ding-dong, Avon calling." With that simple advertising message over the past 115 years, Avon Products built a $6 billion worldwide beauty-products business. Founded in 1886, Avon deployed an army of women to sell its products. These "Avon ladies," 40 million of them over the company's history, met with friends and neighbours in their homes, showed products, took and delivered orders, and earned sales commissions. Through direct selling, Avon bypassed the battle for retail space and attention waged by its competitors in department stores, and later in discount drug stores and supermarkets. Direct selling also offered convenience for the customer, coupled with personal beauty-care advice from a friend.

Avon's plan worked well. Most members of its up to 65 000-member Canadian and 500 000-member US sales forces were homemakers who needed extra money, but did not want a full-time job outside the home. They developed client lists of friends and neighbours on whom they called from time to time. Customers could also call them between visits. Recruiting salespeople was easy, and a good salesperson could develop a loyal core of customers who made repeat purchases. Avon paid the salespeople a commission based on their sales, and a successful salesperson could earn an attractive income.

TIMES CHANGE

However, during the 1970s and 1980s, the environment changed. First, more women found that they needed to work outside the home. As a result, when Avon ladies rang the doorbell, often no one answered. Second, many Avon ladies decided that they needed more than part-time jobs, and Avon's annual sales force turnover rates soared to more than 200 percent. Third, because of high sales force turnover, many Avon customers wanting to see a salesperson could not find one. Fourth, more competitors, such as Amway, Mary Kay Cosmetics, and Tupperware, were competing for the pool of people interested in full- or part-time direct-selling jobs. Finally, in addition to all those factors, increasing mobility of the North American population meant that both customers and salespeople were moving. This made it difficult for salespeople to establish loyal, stable customer bases.

A NEW STRATEGY

To deal with these issues, in 1988, Avon Products tapped James E. Preston to serve as its chair and chief executive. Preston decided that Avon needed to overhaul its marketing strategy. First, he refocused the company on its core business—selling cosmetics, fragrances, and toiletries—and sold unrelated businesses. Next, he drastically cut prices on Avon products. Finally, he tried a new compensation program called "Leadership" that allowed sales representatives to earn up to 21 percent in bonuses based on the sales of new representatives they recruited. Such multilevel selling is common among direct-sales companies. However, by late 1991, Avon killed the program, arguing that it did not fit Avon's culture.

Preston believed that Avon had left as many as ten million former or potential customers stranded. These customers wanted to buy Avon products, but sales force turnover meant that they did not know how to find a salesperson or order products. Fourteen percent of women accounted for one-third of Avon's sales. Another

62 percent were fringe customers. These customers viewed Avon positively but did not buy regularly. Another 15 percent of women were potentially receptive to Avon, but were not necessarily interested in dealing with a traditional Avon sales representative.

Therefore, Preston decided to develop another program he called "Avon Select." The program featured a catalogue and toll-free telephone number that allowed direct-mail selling. Avon's research revealed that its median customer was 45 years old and had an average household income of under $45 000. The catalogue would reach younger, higher-income customers. Preston believed that, with a catalogue, the company could cut the median customer age to 38 and increase average household income to more than $45 000. Avon supported the catalogue program by kicking off a national advertising campaign that featured the slogan "Avon—The Smartest Shop in Town." To fund the advertising, the company cut sales commissions and incentives and laid off scores of executives.

As you might imagine, all these changes created a lot of turmoil at Avon. However, Preston vowed to keep pursuing changes. To keep customers, "change we did, change we must, and change we will," Preston asserted. To make good on his promise, he launched a $45 million ad campaign in 1994 with the theme, "Just Another Avon Lady." Market research showed that, despite all Avon's changes, consumers still thought of "Ding-dong" and the Avon lady when asked what they associated with the company. Observers wondered if the use of the term "lady" in the mid-1990s would cause negative reactions among many women. After all, even Avon had avoided using the term in advertising for 20 years.

In Canada, Montreal-based Avon went beyond increased advertising. The next time an Avon representative knocks on your door, she'll come bearing more than just cosmetics. The representative will carry a new glossy women's magazine called *Confidante*. Over 300 000 copies (60 000 are in French) are being distributed across Canada. Cost of the magazine is $2.99. "It's an image-builder for us, a way for us to talk to our customers," says Lucie Brodeur, product publicity manager for Avon Canada. While most of the magazine's ads are from Avon, the debut issues included non-competing advertisers, such as General Motors, Kellogg, Clairol, and Five Roses. In addition to the new magazine, the company is testing a new interactive kiosk called an "Interactive Makeup and Skin Care Centre" aimed at women who cringe at the thought of asking younger, more fashionable clerks for beauty advice. The kiosk, which is reminiscent of a photo booth, also serves as a mall poster medium. Once seated inside, visitors can view video clips and receive personalized beauty advice via a bilingual touch-screen multimedia program. At the end of the presentation, the visitor is offered a free Avon sample in exchange for her name and address.

Between 1992 and 1996, Avon's sales and profits rose slowly but steadily, driven primarily by sales in international markets. Then, in late 1997, Avon announced what might be its most radical change yet. It announced that it would soon test the idea of selling its products through retail stores. Although the company had been using retail stores in some foreign markets for years, this approach would be new to the North American market. Preston argued that no matter how great Avon's products were, many customers just weren't interested in buying from Avon ladies in a one-on-one situation. To pacify the company's sales reps, Avon said it would consider giving them a share of the new business either through franchising or referrals from the stores. It also announced that it would cut its product line by 30 percent to put its marketing resources behind fewer products, pursue the creation of global brands out of several of its skin-care and cosmetics products, and standardize its promotion efforts using the same promotions for its products around the world.

Global Reach

Avon has been working for a considerable time to transform itself into a global firm. The value of Avon's global reach and its 2.3 million sales representatives worldwide had not gone unnoticed by other firms wanting to crack international markets. Mattel, Inc. announced in 1997 that it would partner with Avon to allow its salespeople to begin selling its Barbie dolls. In a 1996 test, Avon sold $65 million worth of two versions of Barbie, including more than one million of one version in just two weeks. Andrea Jung, Avon's president of global marketing, noted that, "Our powerful distribution channel combined with their powerful brand is a huge opportunity."

Companies like Mattel are attracted to direct sales forces like Avon's for several reasons. In international markets, the companies do not have to wait for retailers to build stores if they use a direct sales force. Further, in many developing economies, being a direct sales rep may be the most attractive job for many women, thus making recruitment easy. However, there are problems. Turnover is often high, and many sales representatives are not really committed to the company. Further, many don't have formal business training or basic skills needed to perform their duties. Finally, in some countries, like China, the government can wrench a market away from a firm. Fearing that direct sales efforts took advantage of Chinese consumers and that sales meetings could be used as a venue to start secret societies and sell smuggled or fake goods, the government outlawed all direct sales. Avon and other direct sellers protested the move loudly. After considerable effort, Avon eventually convinced the Chinese government to let it restart its business. Avon agreed, however, to operate as a wholesaler, selling its products to retail stores.

Today, Avon is undergoing yet another facelift and is transforming itself under its new president and chief executive officer, Andrea Jung. After a long period of rationalization and cost-cutting so that it could compete as a "lean and mean" global firm, Avon is now moving to a "buy-side" mentality and is making more long-term marketing investments. It launched a new "Let's Talk" positioning campaign, the first global branding effort the company has ever done. Go to www.avon.ca to see one facet of the campaign. Avon has decided to expand the use of its Internet technology to strengthen its direct selling and invigorate the brand. While the Web site includes more product information, it won't be used to sell cosmetics directly to consumers. Avon still prefers to redirect consumers to their nearest Avon lady, showing a strong commitment to its 65 000 Canadian direct salesforce. Thus, the "Let's Talk" campaign is just the first leg in a race to make over the cosmetic giant and wipe out its image as grandma's brand.

The "Let's Talk" campaign was developed after Avon consulted with marketing departments in 13 key markets, including North America, Italy, Poland, Japan, the Philippines, and Taiwan. The aim of the research was to uncover women's commonalties as well as their differences. The $132-million campaign, which accounts for a 50 percent increase in ad spending for Avon, represents women and their relationships with other women and their beauty products. The campaign also heralds Avon's entry into such new categories as hair care products and even vitamins. Avon recently announced a strategic alliance with Roche Consumer Health to develop a line of vitamins and nutritional supplements. As Avon takes on the challenges of the twenty-first century, it is going to have more than just cosmetics to talk about.

Questions

1. Which actors in Avon's microenvironment and forces in the macroenvironment have been important in shaping its marketing strategies?
2. What microenvironmental and macroenvironmental factors should Avon consider as it works to expand its international marketing efforts?
3. Assess Avon's marketing strategy in North America. What marketing recommendations would you make to help Avon improve its marketing strategy on this continent?
4. Assess Avon's marketing strategy in international markets. What marketing recommendations would you make to help Avon improve its marketing strategy in international markets like China?

Sources: Astrid Van Den Broek, "Avon calling on global ad effort to change its image," *Marketing On-Line,* 26 June 2000; "Avon gets a green light to restart China business," *WWD,* 8 June 1998:27; "Avon kiosk doles out beauty advice," *Strategy,* 8 May 2000:7; William J. McDonald, "The ban in China: How direct marketing is affected," *Direct Marketing,* June 1998:16; Tara Parker-Pope, "Avon is calling with new way to make a sale," *Wall Street Journal,* 27 October 1997:B1; Tara Parker-Pope and Lisa Bannon, "Avon's new calling: Sell Barbie in China," *Wall Street Journal,* 1 May 1997:B1; Yumiko Ono, "Remember the Avon Lady? She's back," *Wall Street Journal,* 22 January 1995; Suein L. Hwang, "Updating Avon means respecting history without repeating it," *Wall Street Journal,* 4 April 1994:A1.

video case 3

Richard Branson: Global Entrepreneur

Richard Branson is an entrepreneur who is not afraid to face the challenges of the global business environment. Based in Britain, he has already had international success in such diverse businesses an entertainment, airlines, mutual funds, and cola. Take the success of Virgin Atlantic Air, for example. Founded in 1984, it carried just over 124 000 passengers. Today, its passenger load tops 3.5 million. In just 16 years, Virgin has grown to become the U.K.'s second largest airline. To ensure that its global growth continues, it recently merged with Singapore Airlines, a partnership seemingly made in heaven since both airlines are known for their award winning high quality service and innovative approach to airline travel.

Whether it's records or airline travel, Branson's vision for his company is to be a "total life company" by offering whatever consumers may want in lifestyle markets. While his Virgin brand name has been launched in several different geographic markets in Europe and the United States, Branson recently entered the Canadian market by opening a new Virgin music store in Vancouver.

Branson's first major business success was Virgin records, whose artists included such 1980s recording stars as Phil Collins and Boy George. He then used this expertise to expand into the music retail business. The Virgin megastores cater to all types of music tastes; the New York store, for example, has 1000 listening booths and boasts the largest selection of music of any music store in the world.

Branson has a reputation for being the small competitor who challenges the establishment. He constantly surveys the business environment to identify industries with large competitors that have become complacent. Virgin is especially adept at satisfying customers by beating competitors on price, quality, or service. For example, in the airline business Branson believed that there was room for a company that put the fun back in flying. His company, Virgin Atlantic Air, changed the experience of flying to one comparable to being in a nice restaurant or club. One of his current projects is to take on Levi Strauss, which he considers to be a good company but one that charges too much for jeans. His company will try to offer the same quality as the Levi's product at a reduced price.

The Virgin Group is Britain's largest private company. The sprawling empire includes 340 businesses and joint ventures and Branson contends that his biggest advantage is his all-embracing red-and-white brand that adorns everything from wedding dresses to vodka.

Thus, it is hard to think of Virgin as a small competitor. However, Virgin is not large in any one type of business and has no more than a 10 to 20 percent market share in any one industry. Branson has also tried to foster an entrepreneurial culture in his organization. The head office has only a small number of people who generate ideas for businesses and then pass them on to the companies that Branson controls. The people who manage these companies, managing directors, all have part ownership in the business and are given a lot of leeway in the management of the company. They are encouraged to be creative and are given the "freedom to make mistakes." In fact, Branson now regards his job as one of delegation and of empowering his employees to run the businesses.

Branson views his entrance into the Vancouver retail music business as only the first of many Canadian business ventures. Even though it only operates in Vancouver, you can visit the store online at www.virginmega.com. Today, Virgin drinks are distributed throughout Canada by Vancouver-based Leading Brands. In the west, the Virgin Megastore was used to create awareness of the beverages, but in the rest of Canada, Leading Brands had to use more unconventional promotions to market Virgin beverages. In Ontario and Quebec, for example, it runs contests for seven Fender Stratocaster guitars. Virgin Atlantic Air is now also operating routes between Canada and the U.K. and is lobbying to have the regulations that restrict its operations on domestic routes loosened so that it can rival Air Canada. Our national airline might be well advised to take note of Richard Branson's Canadian plans.

Given the entrepreneurial culture at Virgin, it is not surprising that the company is moving online. Branson's vision is to grow the Virgin Group's Web site, Virgin.com, to be one of the world's top 10 portals. Once established on the Web, he intends to sell consumers everything from cars and CDs to electricity, beginning in Britain and then rolling out worldwide. In fact, Branson is gearing up to launch two or three stand-alone Net businesses every three weeks.

Making Virgin an Internet powerhouse won't be easy. Branson faces formidable competition from global Net players such as Yahoo! Inc. and local rivals including Britain's No. 1 service provider, Freeserve PLC. One analyst believes that while Branson has strong products, his Web venture is weak on the kind of interesting content that draws traffic to most portals. However, Virgin also has its strengths. Millions of customers are already used to visiting Virgin Web sites to book tickets, buy phones, or manage their finances. It will be interesting to see if Branson can glide through cyberspace as readily as he has flown through other marketspaces.

Questions

1. Which factors in the Canadian marketing environment will affect Branson's success with the Virgin Megastores and Virgin Atlantic Air?
2. What environmental factors should Branson keep an eye on as he tries to build his online businesses?
3. How can global companies such as Branson's ensure that they have accurate tracking of the marketing environment in each country that they operate in?

Source: This case was prepared by Auleen Carson and is based on "Richard Branson," *Venture* (October 20, 1996); Astrid Van Den Broek, "Virgin Goes for the Unconventional," *Marketing On-line*, September 8, 2000; Kerry Capell, with Stanley Reed and Heidi Dawley in London, "Richard Branson Is No Techie, but He Loves the Web," *Business Week On-Line*, January 31, 2000.

P A R T 1 **2** 3 4

Developing Marketing Opportunities and Strategies

Concept Connections

After reading this chapter, you should be able to

1. Explain the importance of information to the company.
2. Define the marketing information system and discuss its parts.
3. Outline the four steps in the marketing research process.
4. Compare the advantages and disadvantages of various methods of collecting information.
5. Discuss the special issues some marketing researchers face, including public policy and ethics issues.

chapter 4

Marketing Research and Information Systems

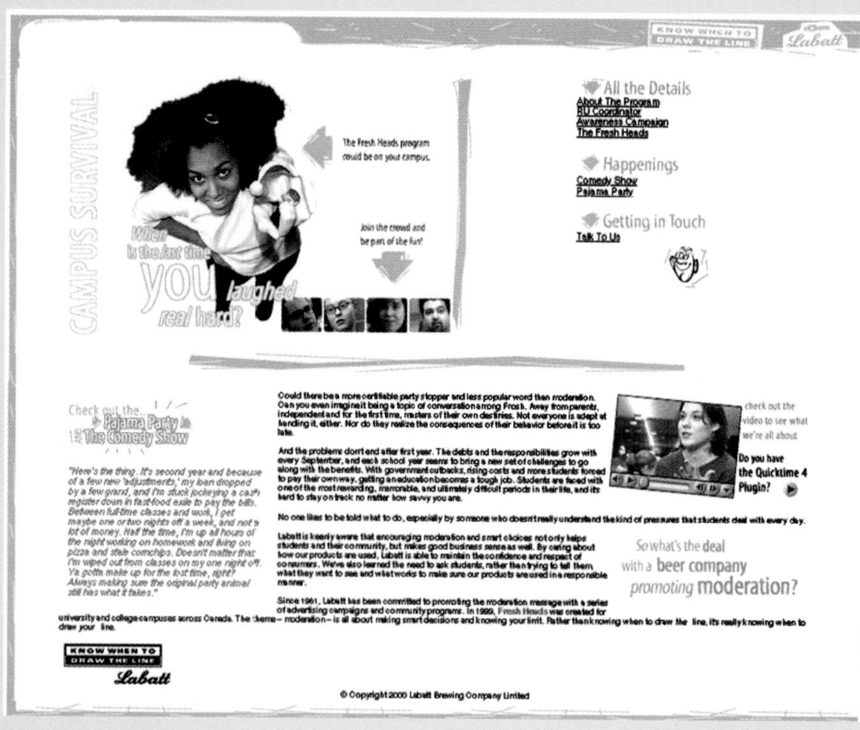

As Lara Mills of Canada's *Marketing Magazine* writes, "The story of Canada's big two brewers in the 1990s reads like a roller coaster corporate soap opera. . . . key executives and ad agencies came and went; breakthrough campaigns and products began with a bang and then fizzled; . . . battles were fought in court as well as the advertising arena; [and] millions of marketing dollars were spent."

Winning the battle for market supremacy is critical. The Canadian beer market represents $11 billion in sales. Each share point is worth $10 to $16 million in incremental revenue. Like sumo wrestlers, Canada's big two breweries—Molson and Labatt—and their big brands—Canadian and Blue—grapple each other for market dominance.

The beer market is a difficult one in which to compete. Demographics aren't on the side of these marketers. Baby boomers, once the prime target market, are now more health- and weight-conscious. Beer consumption has been dropping steadily in recent years. It had reached its peak in 1979, when the average Canadian consumed 85 litres of beer a year. Now, it is about 65 litres per capita. For brewers, Quebec is the only bright spot on the horizon: In that province, per capita consumption is 91 litres. Thus, beer marketers are fighting for share of a shrinking pie and can gain share only at the expense of their competitors. Along with a shrinking market, the giants have had to face increasing competition. Whereas only 15 years ago there were just eight beer companies in Canada, today there are 60. Microbreweries now account for approximately five percent of sales.

The battle for market share in the hearts and minds of those much-sought-after male beer drinkers aged 19 to 24 created some of the most memorable marketing initiatives ever seen in this country. There was Labatt's *Blade Runner*-ish TV spots for the launch of its new Ice Beer, starring Alexander Godunov with The Smiths' "How Soon Is Now" soundtrack in the early 1990s. Later came the "Out of the Blue" campaign, which transformed the image of Blue from the "beer my father drinks" to one of the hippest beverages on the market. Molson had its own breakthroughs, notably its award-winning "I Am" Canadian campaign for its flagship brand. The success of these campaigns didn't come by accident, however. They were built on a solid foundation of market research. Information and key insights were gleaned from focus groups, online surveys, old-fashioned polls, and new-age street teams.

In the beer industry, the company with the best information should win the marketing war. For this reason, the beer industry does some of the most sophisticated marketing research in the business world. Internal databases, government statistics, product codes, and scanner information from the points of sale allow beer-makers to "trace sales down to almost each and every case moving off the store shelf." But it is not enough to just have a rich database. Talented marketers must also glean insight from the information therein. Sometimes marketers hit the nail on the head. At other times, despite the best information, they miss the mark altogether. A case in point: Molson's Red Dog beer. Despite being lauded for its brilliant ad campaign, the product was withdrawn due to low sales after only six months. Similarly, Labatt Blue's two voyageurs—William and Jacques—made people feel good about Canadian icons, but failed to move beer off the shelves.

Interpretation of database information to glean consumer insights is especially important for beer markets for two reasons. First, decision making about beer is based on both emotional and rational responses, and distinct regional differences exist in the Canadian beer market. Unlike other packaged goods, where consumers make strictly rational choices based on the physical benefits of the product, beer is sold on image; blind taste tests have shown that little differentiates the taste of one brand from another. Second, beer drinkers tend to personally identify with the product—what they drink says a lot about their self-image. And self-images are often regionally based. Campaigns that work well in Atlantic Canada are often a flop in the west. Beer marketers target their national and regional brands, using values "consumers hold through life, rather than the passing fancies of youth."

However, insightful research has helped Labatt avoid "sensitive bullshit meters" so prevalent among the campus crowd. As Labatt attests: "If you want smart, skeptical university and college students to take your message seriously, then you'd better make sure it rings true to them." This was especially true when Labatt planned its "responsible use" program, known as "Fresh Heads." Labatt has been preaching moderation on Canadian campuses for more than a decade. Its efforts have been successful because the company has relied on insights gleaned from ongoing conversations with the target audience. Indeed, as Labatt's director of public affairs notes, its current on-campus campaign was essentially designed by students for students. "It's their program," she says "They've developed it. And it's their input, ownership and reaction that determines the program's success."

The Fresh Heads program, which features "dry" events and selected student coordinators to spread the moderation message, is now in its third year. Events include orientation week comedy shows that fit into the campus lifestyle and help get the point across to students in their own language. Fresh Heads also uses what Labatt calls a "guerrilla" advertising effort that weaves naturally into the fabric of everyday campus life. Stickers are plastered in pay phone booths, laundromats, and other locations, while specially designed coasters and rent cards pop up in cafeterias and residence halls, respectively. Since research has shown that the 19- to 24-year-old target audience is quick to tune out slick advertising, Labatt's "responsible use" creative looks like inexpensively-produced, student-originated materials. One bulletin board poster, for example, advertises a room available: "Hardwood floors, lots of lighting, furniture, spacious, etc. . . . Rent negotiable. Last roommate kicked out of school. No partyers." The only indication that this is, in fact, a corporate message is the presence of the Labatt "Know When to Draw the Line" slogan. As Labatt's agency confesses, "It's advertising, and we're writing it, but we're writing it after having heard [students] tell us what they're thinking about. I doubt we could have come up with this stuff without them."

During the conceptual stages of Fresh Heads, Labatt partnered with Toronto-based youth marketing consultancy d-Code, which conducted online research with Canadian students via chat rooms. Students were later brought in to assist with

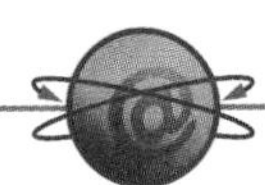

Labatt Breweries
www.labatt.com
Molson Breweries
www.molson.com

the development of the program and the brewery continues to consult with them in its efforts to improve Fresh Heads. Campus wellness centres and student unions have also proven invaluable in identifying areas of student concern. Labatt followed up with a Fresh Heads Web site (www.freshheads.labatt.com), initially designed to be purely informational. But with the help of students, the brewery planned to develop it into a "community- and content-oriented destination" for the target audience.[1]

To produce superior value and satisfaction for customers, companies need information at almost every turn. As the Labatt and Molson marketing story illustrates, good products and marketing programs begin with a thorough understanding of consumer needs and wants. Companies also need an abundance of information on competitors, resellers, and other actors and forces in the marketplace.

Increasingly, marketers are viewing information not just as an input for making better decisions but also as an important strategic asset and marketing tool. In today's marketing, a company's information may prove to be its chief competitive advantage. Competitors can copy each other's equipment, products, and procedures, but they cannot duplicate the company's information and intellectual capital. Several companies have recently recognized this by appointing vice-presidents of knowledge, learning, or intellectual capital.[2]

A century ago, most companies were small and knew their customers firsthand. Managers picked up marketing information by being around people, observing them, and asking questions. In more recent times, however, many factors have increased the need for more, better, and faster information. As companies become national or international in scope, they need more information on larger, more distant markets. As incomes increase and buyers become more selective, sellers need better information about how buyers respond to different products and appeals. As sellers use more complex marketing approaches and face more competition, they need information on the effectiveness of their marketing tools. Finally, in today's rapidly changing environments, managers need more up-to-date information to make timely decisions.

Fortunately, increasing information requirements have been met by an explosion of information technologies. The past 30 years have witnessed the emergence of small but powerful computers, fax machines, CD-ROM drives, videoconferencing, the Internet, and a host of other advances that have revolutionized information handling. Using improved information systems, companies can now acquire information in great quantities.

In fact, today's managers sometimes receive too much information. One study found that, with all the companies offering data and with all the information now available through supermarket scanners, a packaged-goods brand manager is bombarded with one million to one billion new numbers each week. Another study found that, on average, North American office workers spend 60 percent of their time processing documents; a typical manager reads about a million words a week. The typical business Internet user receives 25 e-mails a day; 15 percent of users receive between 50 and 100 e-mails per day. Thus, running out of information is not a problem, but seeing through the "data smog" is.[3]

Despite this glut of data, marketers frequently complain that they lack enough information of the right kind. A recent survey of managers found that, although half the respondents said they couldn't cope with the volume of information coming at them, two-thirds wanted even more. The researcher concluded that, "despite the volume, they're still not getting what they want."[4] Most marketing managers don't need more information; they need better information. Companies have greater capacity to provide managers with good information, but often have not made good use of it. Many companies are now studying their managers' information needs and designing information systems to meet those needs.

The Marketing Information System

Marketing information system (MIS)
People, equipment, and procedures to gather, sort, analyze, evaluate, and distribute needed, timely, and accurate information to marketing decision makers.

A **marketing information system** (MIS) consists of people, equipment, and procedures to gather, sort, analyze, evaluate, and distribute needed, timely, and accurate information to marketing decision makers. Figure 4-1 shows that the MIS begins and ends with marketing managers. First, it interacts with these managers to *assess information needs*. Next, it *develops needed information* from internal company records, marketing intelligence activities, and marketing research. *Information analysis* processes the information to make it more useful. Finally, the MIS *distributes information* to managers in the right form at the right time to help them make better marketing decisions.

Assessing Information Needs

A good marketing information system balances the information managers would *like* to have against what they really *need* and what is *feasible* to offer. The company begins by interviewing managers to find out what information they would like (see Table 4-1 for a useful set of questions). But managers do not always need all the information they ask for, and they may not ask for all they really need. Moreover, the MIS cannot always supply all the information managers request.

Some managers will ask for whatever information they can get without thinking carefully about what they really need. Too much information can be as harmful as too little. Other managers may omit things they ought to know, or may not know to ask for some types of information they should have. For example, managers might need to know that a competitor plans to introduce a new product in the coming year. Because they do not know about the new product, they do not think to ask about it. The MIS must watch the marketing environment to provide decision makers with information they need to make key marketing decisions.

FIGURE 4-1 The marketing information system

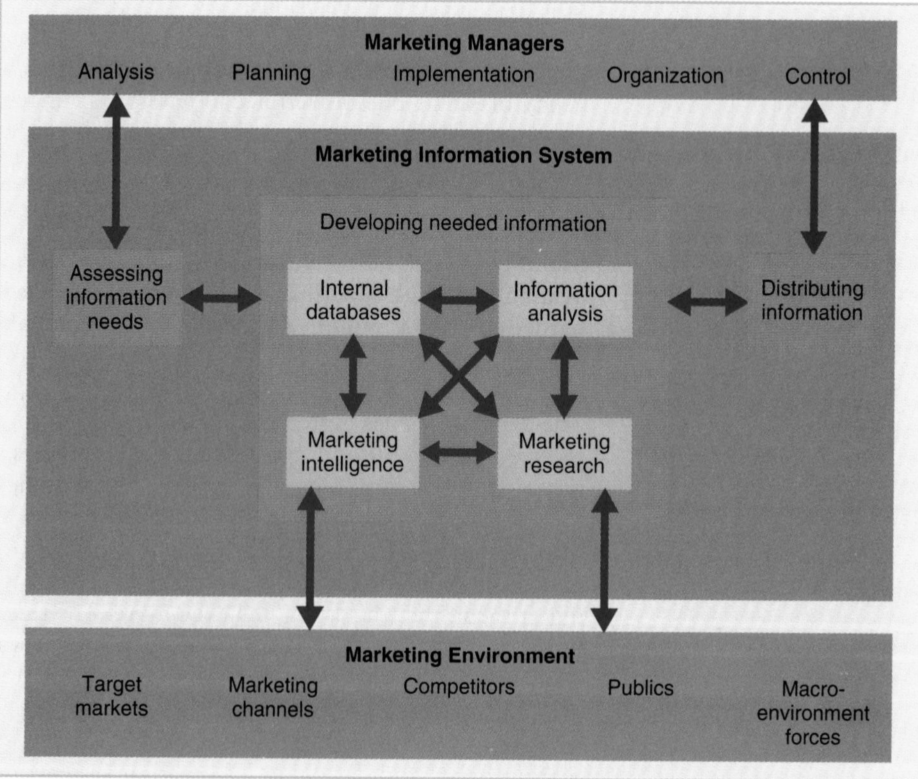

TABLE 4-1 Questions for Assessing Marketing Information Needs

1. What types of decisions do you make regularly?
2. What types of information do you need to make these decisions?
3. What types of useful information do you get regularly?
4. What types of information would you like to get that you are not getting now?
5. What types of information do you get now that you don't really need?
6. What information would you want daily? weekly? monthly? yearly?
7. What topics would you like to be kept informed about?
8. What databases would be useful to you?
9. What types of information analysis programs would you like to have?
10. What are the four most helpful improvements that could be made to the existing information system?

Sometimes the company cannot provide the needed information, either because it is not available or because of MIS limitations. For example, a brand manager might want to know how competitors will change their advertising budgets next year and how these changes will affect industry market shares. The information on planned budgets probably is not available. Even if it is, the company's MIS may not be advanced enough to forecast resulting changes in market shares.

Finally, the costs of obtaining, processing, storing, and delivering information can mount quickly. The company must decide whether the benefits of having an item of information are worth the costs of providing it, and both value and cost are often hard to assess. By itself, information has no worth; its value comes from its *use*. In many cases, additional information will do little to change or improve a manager's decision, or the costs of the information may exceed the returns from the improved decision. Marketers should not assume that additional information will always be worth obtaining. Rather, they should carefully weigh the costs of additional information against the benefits resulting from it.

Developing Information

The information needed by marketing managers can be obtained from *internal company records, marketing intelligence,* and *marketing research.* The information analysis system then processes this information to make it more useful for managers.

Internal Data

Internal databases
Information gathered from sources within the company that can be used to evaluate marketing performance and to detect marketing problems and opportunities.

Many companies build extensive **internal databases,** computerized collections of information obtained from data sources within the company. Marketing managers can readily access and work with information in the database to identify marketing opportunities and problems, plan programs, and evaluate performance.

Information in the database can come from many sources. The accounting department prepares financial statements and keeps detailed records of sales, costs, and cash flows. Manufacturing reports on production schedules, shipments, and inventories. The sales force reports on reseller reactions and competitor activities. The marketing department maintains a database of customer demographics, psychographics, and buying behaviour. The customer service department provides information on customer satisfaction or service problems. Research studies done for one department may provide useful information for several others. Managers can use information gathered from these and other sources in the company to evaluate performance, detect problems, and create new marketing opportunities.

These are examples of how companies use internal records information to make better marketing decisions:[5]

Canon Canada: Canon Canada recently introduced a 24-hour toll-free helpline to help the company better understand the home-office market. Since customer service and repair capabilities are key features of Canon's large-business marketing efforts, it uses this helpline to assess the effectiveness of these efforts for the relatively undeveloped home-office market.

Frito-Lay: Frito-Lay uses its sophisticated internal information system to analyze daily sales performance. Each day, Frito-Lay's salespeople report their day's efforts via hand-held computers to Frito-Lay headquarters. Twenty-four hours later, Frito-Lay's marketing managers have a complete analysis of the previous day's sales of Fritos, Doritos, and other brands. The system helps marketing managers make better decisions and makes the salespeople more effective. It greatly reduces the number of hours spent filling out reports, giving salespeople extra time for selling. Frito-Lay's sales are going up 10 to 12 percent a year without the addition of a single salesperson.

Internal databases can usually be accessed more quickly and less expensively than other information sources, but they also present some problems. Because internal information is collected for other purposes, it may be incomplete or in the wrong form for making marketing decisions—for example, sales and cost data used by the accounting department for preparing financial statements must be adapted for use in evaluating product, sales force, or channel performance. In addition, a large company produces great amounts of information, and keeping track of it is difficult. The database information must be well-integrated and readily accessible through user-friendly interfaces so that managers can find it easily and use it effectively. Increasingly, companies are creating data warehouses to house their customer data in a single, more accessible location. Then, using powerful data mining techniques, they search for meaningful patterns in the data and communicate them to managers (see Marketing Highlight 4-1).

Marketing Intelligence

Marketing intelligence is the systematic collection and analysis of publicly available information about competitors and developments in the marketing environment. A marketing intelligence system gathers, analyzes, and distributes information about the company's competitive, technological, customer, economic, social, and political and regulatory environments. Its goal is to improve strategic decision making by assessing and tracking competitors' actions, and by providing early warning of opportunities and threats. The marketing intelligence system determines what intelligence is needed, collects it by searching the environment, and delivers it to marketing managers.

Marketing intelligence
The systematic collection and analysis of publicly available information about competitors and development in the marketing environment.

Competitive intelligence is an aspect of market intelligence that has grown dramatically in recent years. Techniques range from quizzing the company's own employees, benchmarking competitors' products, researching the Internet, to having a presence at trade shows. More and more of Canada's large, leading edge firms such as CAE Electronics, BCE, Teleglobe Canada, Labatt, and Alcan have sophisticated CI systems in place. Here are two cases to help you understand the importance of competitive intelligence at two of Canada's leading companies:

High Performance Optical Component Solutions Group, Nortel Networks, Ottawa

Scott Hogan is a Strategic Market Analyst with the High Performance Optical Component Solutions group at Nortel Networks in Ottawa and one of the two Chapter Chairs for the Eastern Ontario chapter of the Society of Competitive Intelligence Professionals (www.scip.org). He takes his mantra from Frederick the Great, who said, "It is pardonable to be defeated, but never to be surprised." Professionals like Scott see competitive intelligence (CI) as a systematic and ethical program of gathering and analyzing information. They turn data into *actionable intelligence* that managers from sales, manufacturing, R&D, marketing, and product management can use in real time to make better decisions. Actionable intelligence is information that arrives at the desk of decision makers in time for them to act on it.

CI is also value-added information analysis. For example, Scott knows it isn't enough to report on the contents of a competitor's press release. His group must interpret what the press release means for the group's competitive strategy. Scott stresses that CI is not a crystal ball or a compilation of rumours flying around the Internet. Moreover, CI is *not* industrial espionage. Espionage is the use of illegal means to gather information. Scott emphasizes that Nortel follows strict ethic codes including its own Code of Business Conduct and the SCIP Code of Ethics.

CI is an early-warning tool to alter management to both threats and opportunities. For example, CI can help a company determine if it wants to continue its own product development if competitors have taken the lead. CI is an ongoing process used as a means of seeing outside the organization. CI is especially important in high-tech environments since product change is very short in comparison to some industries. The cycle time from product definition to product shipping is approximately 18 months and this cycle is constantly getting shorter. Furthermore, the optical landscape is comprised of a cloud of competitors that potentially lurk on every front—customers, suppliers and partners. Since some companies have customers in more than 100 countries, it has to be aware of competitors from diverse geographies.

If the scope of competition is so wide, CI may have to cover a wide market segment and the deployment of internal as well as external information resources. Scott agrees with another CI specialist, Leonard Fuld, who notes, "the golden intelligence nugget is likely to be close to home so examine all internally available data before going outside."

The Internet is one external resource Scott values. He uses both public and private sites such as Factiva (www.factiva.com), ISI (Institute for Scientific Information) (www.isinet.com/isi), Canada Institute for Scientific and Technical Information (NRC), and Thompson Financial.

As the above example shows, much intelligence can be collected from the company's own personnel—executives, engineers and scientists, purchasing agents, and the sales force. For example, a few years back, Xerox learned that listening to its own salespeople could pay off handsomely.

While talking with a Kodak copier salesperson, a Xerox technician learned that the Kodak salesperson was being trained to service Xerox products. The Xerox employee reported back to his boss, who in turn passed the news to Xerox's intelligence unit. Using such clues as a classified ad Kodak placed seeking new people with Xerox product experience, Xerox verified Kodak's plan—code-named Ulysses—to service Xerox copiers. To protect its profitable service business, Xerox designed a Total Satisfaction Guarantee, which allowed copier returns for any reason as long as Xerox did the servicing. By the time Kodak launched Ulysses, Xerox had been promoting its new program for three months.[7]

However, company people are often busy and fail to pass on important information. The company must sell its people on their importance as intelligence gatherers, train them to spot new developments, interact with them on an ongoing basis, and urge them to report intelligence back to the company.

The company can also get suppliers, resellers, and key customers to pass along important intelligence about competitors and their products. For example, before introducing its Good News disposable razor in the United States, Gillette told a large Canadian account about the planned US introduction date. The Canadian distributor promptly called Bic and told it about the impending product launch. By putting on a crash program, Bic was able to start selling its razor shortly after Gillette did.

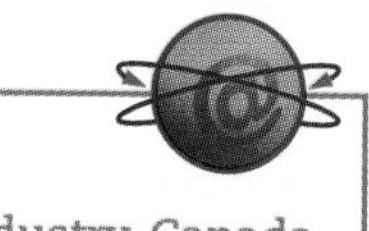

Industry Canada
http://strategis.ic.gc.ca

Government agencies are a good source of intelligence. For example, although a company can't legally photograph a competitor's plant from the air, publicly available aerial photos are often on file with the Canadian Geological Survey. Public records available from government offices on zoning and tax assessments can also provide clues about competitors' activities. Industry Canada's Web site posts a wealth of valuable information about Canadian businesses and industrial sectors.

Competitors themselves may reveal information through their annual reports, business publications, trade show exhibits, press releases, advertisements, and Web pages. The Internet is proving to be a vast new source of competitor-supplied information. Most companies now place volumes of information on their Web sites, providing details to attract customers, partners, suppliers, or franchisees, and that

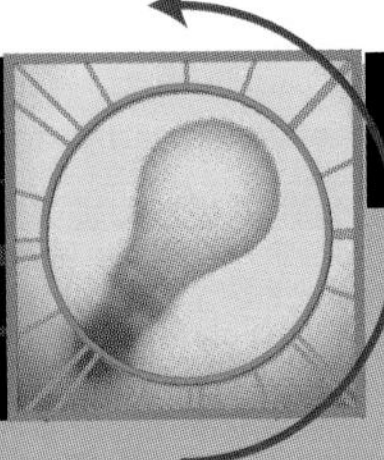

marketing highlight 4-1

Data Mining: There's Gold in Them Thar Databases

Most companies are awash in information about their customers. The trouble is that this information is widely scattered across the organization. It's buried deep in the separate databases, plans, and records of many different company functions and departments. To remedy this problem, many companies are developing data warehouses and using sophisticated data mining techniques to unearth data riches they didn't realize they had.

A data warehouse is a company-wide storehouse of customer information—a centralized database of detailed customer data that needs to be sifted through for gems. The purpose of a data warehouse is not to gather information—many companies have already amassed endless stores of information about their customers—but rather to allow managers to get at the information the company already has. Then, once the data warehouse brings the data together for analysis, the company uses high-powered data mining techniques to sift through the mounds of data and dig out interesting relationships and findings about customers.

Companies can gain many benefits from careful data warehousing and data mining. By understanding customers better, they can provide higher levels of customer service and develop deeper customer relationships. They can use the data to pinpoint high-value customers, target them more effectively, cross-sell the company's products, and create offers tailored to specific customer requirements.

For example, MCI Communications Corporation, the long-distance carrier, sifts through one trillion bytes of customer phoning data to craft new discount calling plans for different types of customers. Marriott's Vacation Club In-

This ad for SPSS data mining software targeted toward corporate researchers shows its many uses.

same information is available to competitors at the click of a mouse button. Press releases that never made it into the press are posted on Web sites, letting firms keep abreast of competitors' new products and organizational changes. Help wanted ads posted on the Web quickly reveal competitors' expansion priorities. For example, Allied Signal's Web site provides revenue goals and reveals the company's production-defect rate along with its plans to improve it.

Not only company-sponsored Web sites hold rich competitor intelligence ternational has managed to reduce its volume of mail offers while increasing its response rate by developing a model showing which customers in its database are most likely to respond to specific vacation offerings. VanCity and British Columbia's North Shore Credit Unions installed computerized "customer relationship management" systems that have allowed them to profile their members to improve the targeting of their services. Tesco, the British supermarket chain, notifies carefully selected groups, such as cheese buyers, when there will be a special sale of cheese. Lands' End can tell which of its two million customers should receive special mailings about specific clothing items that would fit their wardrobe needs.

These are some more detailed examples of companies that are benefiting from data warehousing and data mining:

> Shoppers Drug Mart wants you! And every other man and woman in Canada signed up in its new "Optimum" program. Shoppers plans to use Optimum to totally change the way it handles customers. "Ultimately, what we really want is a major commitment to customer relationship management (CRM) across the entire store," says Neil Everett, senior vice-president of marketing. "We've already got customers coming through the door," he says. "Our biggest challenge is, 'How do we do more business with those customers?' That's what CRM is about, whether you are a bank or a retailer." To do it, Shoppers needs to know its customers' purchasing habits so well that it can anticipate them and respond with direct marketing. Using information gathered as customers use their Optimum cards will allow Shoppers to do just that.

Calgary-based Royal Host Hotels and Resort's new loyalty program, RoomConnexx, will enable it to undertake true one-to-one marketing. Royal targets both business and leisure travellers through its 200 hotels located across Canada, including Travelodge, Holiday Inn, and Hilton. Their technology-enabled program will enable Royal to capture and sort relevant customer data in one place, across an entire business, no matter what location or chain the customer uses. Royal is taking a step-wise approach toward its one-to-one marketing goal. In Phase One, it will use a TV set-top box and keypad to offer entertainment options, such as movies, along with video-conferencing and high-speed Internet access. Next, using its expanded and integrated database will allow it to customize offerings directly to each guest. Finally, Royal Host will personalize each traveller's experience based on information collected and stored on a computer chip in each RoomConnexx "smart" card. As Dorothy Dowling, executive VP of sales and marketing, notes, "a person will enter their room and be personally greeted on the TV [and] their favourite TV programming will be available on demand."

Ping, the golf equipment manufacturer, has used data warehousing successfully for about two years. Its warehouse contains customer-specific data about every golf club it has manufactured and sold in the past 15 years. The database, which includes grip size and special assembly instructions, helps Ping design and build golf clubs specifically for each of its customers and allows for easy replacement. If a golfer needs a new nine iron, for example, he or she can call in the serial number and Ping will ship a duplicate of the club to him or her within two days of receiving the order—a process that used to take two to three weeks. This faster data processing has given Ping a competitive edge in a market saturated with new products. "We've been up; the golf market has been down," says Steve Bostwick, Ping's marketing manager. Bostwick estimates the golf market to be down about 15 percent, but he says Ping has experienced double-digit growth.

Most experts believe that a good data warehouse, by itself, can give a company a significant competitive advantage. It is no wonder that American Express has security guards watching over its 500 billion bytes of data on how its customers have used the company's 35 million green, gold, and platinum charge cards. Amex uses the database to include precisely targeted offers in its monthly mailing of customer bills.

Data warehousing and data mining benefits don't come without heavy cost, not only in collecting the original customer data but also in maintaining and mining it. But when it works, the benefits usually outweigh the costs. One study estimated that the average return on investment for a data warehouse over the course of three years is more than 400 percent. FedEx reports even more impressive returns, claiming that such techniques have helped it achieve an 8-to-1 return on its direct-marketing dollars.

Over the past few years, data warehousing and data mining have exploded onto the corporate research scene. According to one study, over 90 percent of Fortune 2000 firms either have a data warehouse or are in the process of developing one. "No question that companies are getting tremendous value out of this," says David Bramblett, owner of Data Warehouse Solutions. "Companies [are] looking for ways to bring disparate sources of customer information together, then get it to all the customer touch points." Adds another data warehousing consultant, these powerful new techniques can unearth "a wealth of information to target that customer, to hit their hot button."

Sources: Quotes and excerpts from Lesley Young, "The pick of the cards: Shoppers' new Optimum card is so customer-friendly the public is signing up in droves. And that's the kind of loyalty program you need to get one-to-one marketing right," *Marketing On-Line,* 16 October 2000; Sara Sellar, "Dust off that data," *Sales & Marketing Management,* May 1999:71–2; "What've you done for us lately?" *Business Week,* 14 September 1998:142–8; and Philip Kotler, *Kotler on Marketing,* New York: Free Press, 1999:29. Also see Stewart Deck, "Data mining," *Computerworld,* 29 March 1999:76; and Sunny Baker and Kim Baker, "The best little warehouse in business," *Journal of Business Strategy,* March–April 1999:32–7.

booty. Researchers can also glean valuable nuggets of information from trade association Web sites. For example, when he was controller of Stone Container's specialty packaging division, Gary Owen visited a trade association Web site and noticed that a rival had won an award for a new process using ultraviolet-resistant lacquers. The site revealed the machines' configuration and run rate, which Stone's engineers used to figure out how to replicate the process.[8]

Using Internet search engines such as Yahoo! or Infoseek, marketers can search specific competitor names, events, or trends and see what turns up. Intelligence seekers also pore through thousands of online databases, some of which are free. For example, AltaVista Canada and CanoeMoney partner to provide a huge stockpile of financial and other information on public companies. For a fee, companies can subscribe to any of more than 3000 online databases and information search services, such as Dialog, DataStar, Lexis-Nexis, Dow Jones News Retrieval, UMI ProQuest, and Dun & Bradstreet's Online Access. We discuss these and other online data services in more detail later in the chapter. Using such databases, companies can conduct complex information searches in a flash from the comfort of their offices. Companies with limited resources, or those that do not wish to devote the thousands of hours it takes to monitor the Web, can hire outside firms to undertake this task for them. For example, Company Sleuth provides users with a steady stream of intelligence data gleaned from the Internet. eWatch is another service used by hundreds of Canadian companies to monitor competitors' Web sites and relevant public discussion areas in cyberspace.[9]

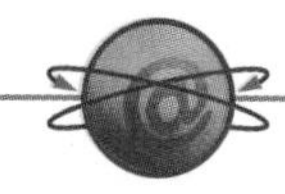

Company Sleuth
www.companysleuth.com

eWatch
www.ewatch.com

The growing use of marketing intelligence raises a number of ethical issues. Although most of the preceding techniques are legal, and some are considered to be shrewdly competitive, many involve questionable ethics. Clearly, companies should take advantage of publicly available information. However, they should not stoop to snoop. With all the legitimate intelligence sources now available, a company does not have to break the law or accepted codes of ethics to get good intelligence.[10]

Marketing Research

Managers cannot rely on only publicly available information; they often require formal studies of specific situations. Toshiba may need to know how many and what kinds of people or companies will buy its new super-fast laptop computer. Or Queen's University Executive Program needs to know what percentage of its target market has heard about it, how they heard, what they know, and how they feel. In such situations, the marketing intelligence system will not provide the detailed information needed. Managers will need marketing research.

Marketing research
The systematic design, collection, analysis, and reporting of data and findings relevant to a specific marketing situation facing an organization.

We define **marketing research** as the systematic design, collection, analysis, and reporting of data and findings relevant to a specific marketing situation facing an organization. Every marketer needs research. Marketing researchers engage in a wide variety of activities, ranging from market potential and market share studies, to assessments of customer satisfaction and purchase behaviour, to studies of pricing, product, place, and promotion activities.

The role of marketing researchers has been changing. In earlier periods, researchers were often consulted only to evaluate existing programs. Today, companies are investing in "success insurance." They are using research to help formulate new strategies. For example, the Co-operators Insurance Company of Guelph, Ontario conducted extensive research before launching its DirectProtect home and auto insurance. Research showed that consumers valued the convenience of buying insurance over the phone, but were hesitant to do so because of the impersonal nature of the transaction. To address this concern, DirectProtect supported the service launch with a television advertising campaign showing tiny insurance salespeople coming out of phones to assure potential customers that there really was a person at the end of the line.

Depending on its own research skills and resources, a company can conduct marketing research in its own research department or have some or all of it done by outside firms. Although most large companies have their own marketing research departments, they often use outside firms to do special research tasks or special studies.

Information Analysis

The information gathered by the company's marketing intelligence and marketing research systems requires analysis before marketing managers can use it in decision making. Advanced statistical analysis can reveal both the relationships within

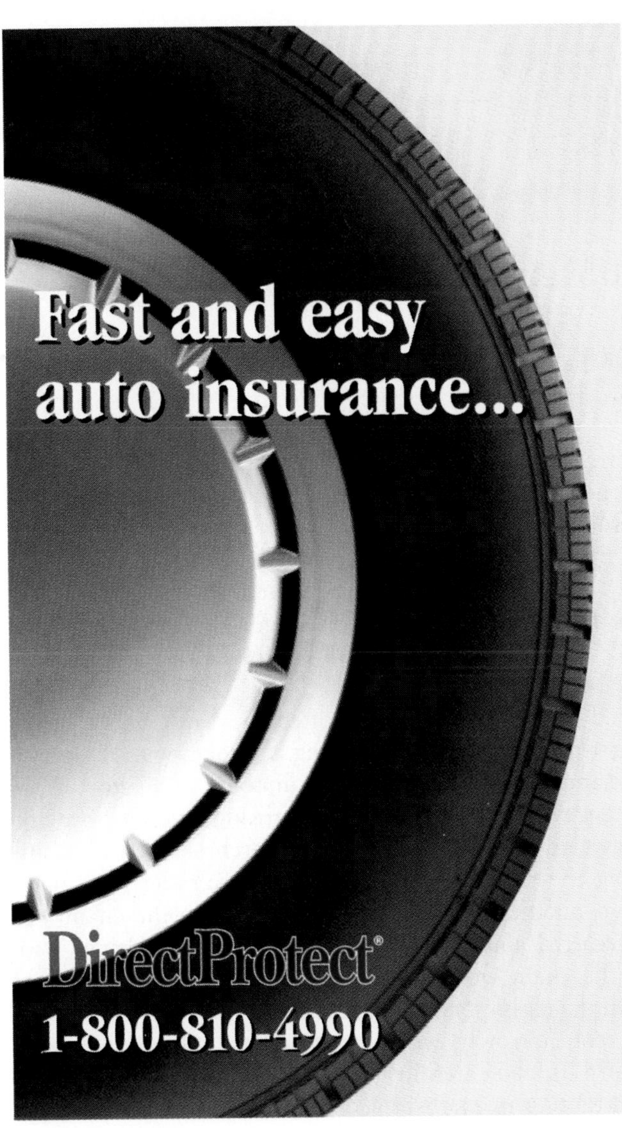

Research helped the Co-operators Insurance Company design its new DirectProtect home and auto insurance.

a set of data and their statistical reliability; such analysis allows managers to go beyond means and standard deviations in the data and to answer questions about markets, marketing activities, and outcomes.

Information analysis can also involve analytical models that will help marketers make better decisions. Each model represents some real system, process, or outcome. These models can help answer the questions of "what if" and "which is best." Over the past 20 years, marketing scientists have developed numerous models to help marketing managers make better marketing mix decisions, design sales territories and sales call plans, select sites for retail outlets, develop optimal advertising mixes, and forecast new product sales.[11]

Distributing Information

Marketing information has no value until managers use it to make better marketing decisions. The information gathered through marketing intelligence and marketing research must be distributed to the right marketing managers at the right time. Most companies have centralized marketing information systems that provide managers with regular performance reports, intelligence updates, and reports on the results of studies. Managers need these routine reports for making regular planning, implementation, and control decisions. But marketing managers also may need nonroutine information for special situations and on-the-spot decisions. For example, a sales manager having trouble with a large customer may want a summary of the account's sales and profitability over the past year. Or a retail store manager who has run out of a best-selling product may want to know the current inventory levels in the chain's other stores. In companies with only centralized information systems, these managers must request the information from the MIS staff and wait. Often, the information arrives too late to be useful.

Developments in information technology have caused a revolution in information distribution. With recent advances in computer hardware and software and telecommunications, most companies are decentralizing their marketing information systems. In many firms, marketing managers have direct access to the information network through personal computers and other means. From any location, they can obtain information from internal records or outside information services, analyze the information using statistical packages and models, prepare reports on a word processor or desktop publishing system, and communicate with others in the network through electronic communications. Such systems allow the managers to get the information they need directly and quickly and to tailor it to their own needs.

The Marketing Research Process

The marketing research process (see Figure 4-2) consists of four steps: *defining the problem and research objectives, developing the research plan, implementing the research plan,* and *interpreting and reporting the findings.*

FIGURE 4-2 The marketing research process

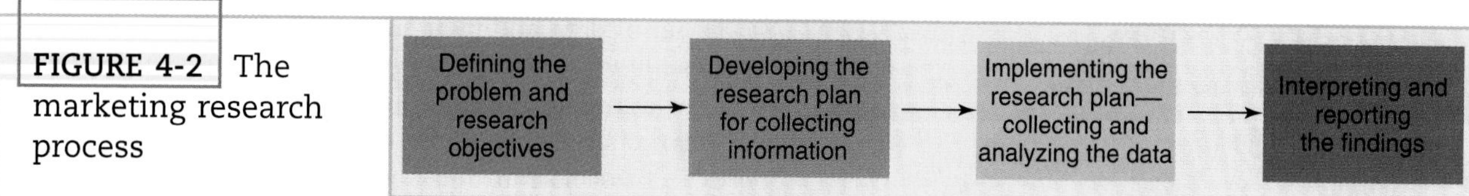

Defining the Problem and Research Objectives

The marketing manager and the researcher must work closely to define the problem carefully, and they must agree on the research objectives. The manager best understands the decision for which information is needed; the researcher best understands marketing research and how to obtain the information.

Managers must know enough about marketing research to help in planning and interpreting research results. If they know little about marketing research, they may obtain the wrong information, accept wrong conclusions, or ask for information that costs too much. Experienced marketing researchers who understand the manager's problem also should be involved at this stage. The researcher must be able to help the manager define the problem and suggest ways that research can help the manager make better decisions.

Defining the problem and research objectives is often the hardest step in the research process. The manager may know that something is wrong, without knowing the specific causes. For example, managers of a large discount retail store chain hastily decided that falling sales were caused by poor advertising, and they ordered research to test the company's advertising. When this research showed that current advertising was reaching the right people with the right message, the managers were puzzled. It turned out that the real problem was that the chain was not delivering the prices, products, and service promised in the advertising. With careful problem definition, the chain would have avoided the cost and delay of doing advertising research. In the classic New Coke case, the Coca-Cola Company defined its research problem too narrowly, with disastrous results.

After the problem has been defined carefully, the manager and researcher must set research objectives. A marketing research project can have one of three types of objectives. The objective of **exploratory research** is to gather preliminary information that will help define the problem and suggest hypotheses. The objective of **descriptive research** is to describe things such as the market potential for a product or the demographics and attitudes of consumers who buy the product. The objective of **causal research** is to test hypotheses about cause-and-effect relationships: For example, would a 10 percent decrease in tuition at a private school result in an enrolment increase sufficient to offset the reduced tuition? Managers often start with exploratory research and later follow with descriptive or causal research.

Exploratory research
Marketing research to gather preliminary information that will help to better define problems and suggest hypotheses.

Descriptive research
Marketing research to better describe marketing problems, situations, or markets, such as the market potential for a product or the demographics and attitudes of consumers.

Causal research
Marketing research to test hypotheses about cause-and-effect relationships.

The statement of the problem and research objectives guides the entire research process. The manager and researcher should put the statement in writing to ensure that they agree on the purpose and expected results of the research.

Developing the Research Plan

The second step of the marketing research process calls for determining the information needed, developing a plan for gathering it efficiently, and presenting the plan to marketing management. The plan outlines sources of existing data and spells out the specific research approaches, contact methods, sampling plans, and instruments that researchers will use to gather new data.

Determining Specific Information Needs

Research objectives must be translated into specific information needs. For example, suppose Campbell decides to research how consumers would react to the company replacing its familiar red and white soup cans with new bowl-shaped plastic containers that it has used successfully for some of its other products. The containers would cost more, but would allow consumers to heat the soup in a microwave oven and eat it without using dishes. This research might call for the following specific information:

- The demographic, economic, and lifestyle characteristics of current soup users. (Busy working couples might find the convenience of the new packaging worth the price; families with children might want to pay less and wash the pot and bowls.)
- Consumer-usage patterns for soup: how much soup they eat, where, and when. (The new packaging might be ideal for adults eating lunch on the go, but less convenient for parents feeding lunch to several children.)
- The number of microwave ovens in consumer and commercial markets. (The number of microwaves in homes and business lunchrooms will limit the demand for the new containers.)
- Retailer reactions to the new packaging. (Failure to get retailer support could hurt sales of the new package.)
- Consumer attitudes toward the new packaging. (The red and white Campbell soup can has become an institution. Will consumers accept the new packaging?)
- Forecasts of sales of both new and current packages. (Will the new packaging increase Campbell's profits?)

Campbell managers will need these and many other types of information to decide whether to introduce the new packaging.

Gathering Secondary Information

Secondary data
Information that already exists somewhere, having been collected for another purpose.

Primary data
Information collected for the specific purpose.

To meet the manager's information needs, the researcher can gather secondary data, primary data, or both. **Secondary data** consist of information that already exists somewhere, having been collected for another purpose. **Primary data** is information gathered during a research project to answer a specific research question.

Researchers usually start by gathering secondary data. The company's internal database is a good starting point; however, the company can also tap external information sources, ranging from company, public, and university libraries, to government and business publications. Table 4-2 describes a number of other important sources of secondary data, including commercial data services, online database services, and Internet data sources.

Commercial Data Sources. Companies can buy data reports from outside suppliers to suit a wide variety of marketing information needs. For example, two firms, Nielsen Marketing Research and Information Resources, Inc., sell data on brand shares, retail prices, percentages of stores stocking different brands, measures of trial and repeat purchasing, brand loyalty, and buyer demographics. Another firm, NPD Canada, maintains the country's longest running national diary panel, the *Consumer Panel of Canada*. It also has an *OnLine Panel* that companies can use to get insights about Canada's Web savvy population as well as compiling specialized reports such as the *Canadian Apparel Market Monitor,* and the *National Eating Trends,* which reports on in-home and out-of-home consumption behaviour.

Online databases
A compilation of marketing information that can be accessed online.

Online Databases and Internet Data Sources. Using commercial **online databases,** marketing researchers can conduct their own searches of secondary data sources. A recent survey of marketing researchers found that 81 percent use such

TABLE 4-2 Sources of Secondary Data

Government publications

Statistics Canada, Demography Division provides summary data on demographic, economic, social, and other aspects of the Canadian economy and society.

Periodicals and books

Canadian Markets, produced by the Financial Post Datagroup, provides annual demographic and retail data for over 700 Canadian urban and regional markets.

Scott's Directories lists, on an annual basis, manufacturers, their products, and their Standard Industrial Classification (SIC) codes, alphabetically as well as by city and region. The directory also provides the names and telephone and fax numbers of chief executives, as well as corporate information such as annual sales. Directories come in four volumes: Ontario, Quebec, Atlantic Canada, and Western Canada.

Canadian Trade Index and *Fraser's Canadian Trade Directory* provide information on manufacturers of different product categories, manufacturing equipment, and supplies.

Standard & Poor's Industry Surveys provide updated statistics and analyses of US industries.

Marketing journals include the *Canadian Journal of Marketing Research, Journal of Marketing, Journal of Marketing Research, Journal of Consumer Research,* and *Journal of the Academy of Marketing Science.*

Useful trade magazines include *Marketing, Advertising Age, Chain Store Age, Progressive Grocer, Sales & Marketing Management,* and *Stores.*

Useful general business magazines include *Canadian Business, The Globe and Mail Report on Business, Business Week, Fortune, Forbes,* and *Harvard Business Review.*

Commercial data services

These are a few of the dozens of commercial research houses selling data to subscribers:

ABI Inform (1983 to present) and *Business Abstracts* (1989 to present) are examples of CD-ROM databases available in most university libraries. They contain abstracts of articles on business appearing in academic journals and the business press.

(PMB) Print Measurement Bureau (Toronto) prepares product category reports that provide information about the users of over 1000 products and services. Compares the demographic profiles of users versus non-users, and heavy versus light users on dimensions such as age, education, marital status, income, occupation, employment status, region and city, household size, residence ownership, sex, and language. Data are also matched to location where main grocery shopping occurs and are usually gathered over a two-year period.

Canadian Grocer produces an annual *Directory of Chains* with information on head office locations, store locations, management names and functions, technologies used, buying policies, store sizes, private labels, and annual sales.

Card Reports provides annual information on Canadian media types, the gross rating points (GRP) associated with each, and the costs of placing advertisements in the various media.

A.C. Nielsen (a division of D&B Marketing Information Services) provides supermarket scanner data on sales, market share, and retail prices (ScanTrack), data on household purchasing (ScanTrack National Electronic Household Panel), data on television audiences (Nielsen National Television Index), and others.

Information Resources, Inc. provides supermarket scanner data for tracking grocery product movement (InfoScan) and single-source data collection (BehaviorScan).

The Arbitron Company provides local market radio audience and advertising expenditure information, along with other media and ad spending data.

MMRI (Simmons Market Research Bureau) provides annual reports covering television markets, sporting goods, and proprietary drugs, giving lifestyle and geodemographic data by sex, income, age, and brand preferences (selective markets and media reaching them).

NPD Canada offers the *Consumer Panel of Canada,* a national diary panel; the *Canadian Apparel Market Monitor;* the *National Eating Trends,* which reports on in-home and out-of-home consumption behaviour; and an *OnLine Panel.*

Equifax Canada is the country's largest information service, specializing in credit reports on both consumers and small businesses.

International data

These are a few of the many sources providing international information:

Euromonitor (www.euromonitor.com) sells a wide range of print and CD-ROM products including *European Marketing Data and Statistics, International Marketing Data and Statistics,* and *International Marketing Forecasts,* which can help marketers gain insights into international consumer markets.

TABLE 4-2 *continued*

United Nations publications include the *Statistical Yearbook,* a comprehensive source of international data for socioeconomic indicators; *Demographic Yearbook,* a collection of demographics data and vital statistics for 220 countries; and the *International Trade Statistics Yearbook,* which provides information on foreign trade for specific countries and commodities.

Europa Yearbook provides surveys on history, politics, population, economy, and natural resources for most countries of the world, along with information on major international organizations.

Other sources include *Political Risk Yearbook, Country Studies, OECD Economic Surveys, Economic Survey of Europe, Asian Economic Handbook,* and *International Financial Statistics.*

Internet data sources

Both large and small companies have developed Web sites as a means of communicating with their customers. Many company sites provide information about the history of the company, its products, and its financial information. Marketing research company sites provide some interesting insights into Canadian consumers; the Environics site, for example, lets users classify themselves on the 3SC Social Values Monitor. Governments also post information on the Web; for example, the Industry Canada site provides a wealth of information about various sectors of the economy. Marketers planning to enter the US market can glean background information from the US Census Bureau or from American Demographics. The US government's site is designed to help small businesspeople, and can be used by both Canadian and American marketers. At a number of online press services, such as Canoe, marketers can track the effectiveness of their own and other companies' public relations efforts. Ecola's 24-Hour Newsstand allows marketers to link with the Web sites of more than 2000 newspapers, journals, and computer publications. Publishers of marketing periodicals who post their material online can be a gold mine. Brunico Communications publishes *Strategy: The Canadian Marketing Report* online in addition to providing it in hard-copy format. Using keywords, marketers can search all editions for articles on a wide range of topics. Internet search engines such as Yahoo!, Excite, Lycos, or Infoseek also allow marketers to locate material on special topics. Publications such as the *Canadian Internet Directory* can facilitate the search for Canada's top Web sites.

Environics
www.environics.ca

Industry Canada
strategis.ic.gc.ca

US Census Bureau
www.census.gov

American Demographics
www.demographics.com

Canoe
www.canoe.ca

Ecola's 24-Hour Newsstand
www.ecola.com/news

Strategy: The Canadian Marketing Report
www.strategymag.com

online services.[12] A readily available online database exists to fill almost any marketing information need. General database services such as CompuServe, Dialog, and Lexis-Nexis put an incredible wealth of information at the keyboards of marketing decision makers. A company doing business in Germany, for example, can check out CompuServe's German Company Library of financial and product information on more than 48 000 German-owned firms. A Canadian auto parts manufacturer can punch up Dun & Bradstreet Financial Profiles and Company Reports to develop biographical sketches of key General Motors, Ford, and Chrysler executives. Just about any information a marketer might need—demographic data, today's news wire reports, or a list of active US trademarks—is available from online databases.[13]

The Internet offers a mind-boggling array of databases and other secondary information sources, many of which are free to the user. Beyond commercial Web sites offering information for a fee, almost every industry association, government agency, business publication, and news medium offers free information to those tenacious enough to find their sites. In fact, so many Web sites offer data that finding the right ones can almost become an overwhelming task.

Advantages and Disadvantages of Secondary Data. Secondary data can usually be obtained more quickly and at a lower cost than primary data. For example, an Internet or online database search might provide all the information that

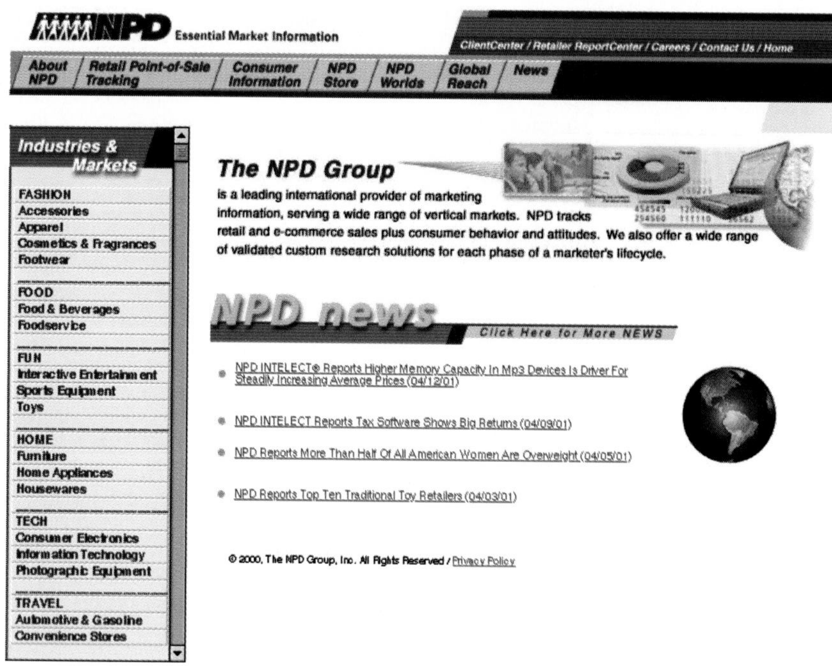

The NPD Group offers Canadian companies a wide range of research services to meet their information needs.

Campbell needs on microwave-oven usage, quickly and inexpensively. A study to collect primary information might take weeks or months to complete and cost thousands of dollars. Also, secondary sources sometimes can provide data that an individual company cannot collect on its own—information that either is not directly available or would be too expensive to collect. For example, it would be too expensive for Campbell to conduct a continuing retail store audit to find out about the market shares, prices, and displays of competitors' brands. But it can buy the InfoScan service from Information Resources, Inc.

Secondary data can also present problems. The needed information may not exist—researchers can rarely obtain all the data they need from secondary sources. For example, Campbell will not find existing information about consumer reactions to new packaging that it has not yet placed on the market. Even when data

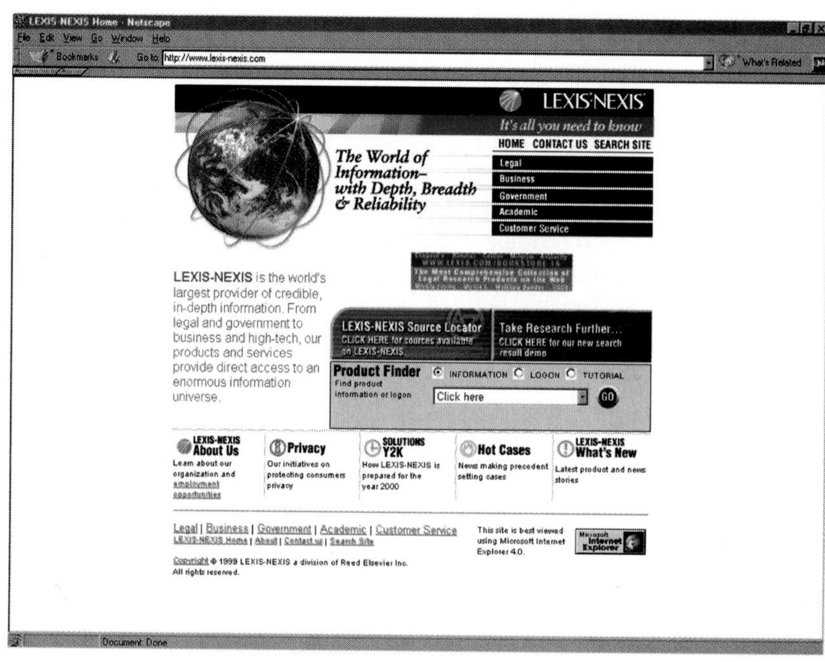

Online database services such as LEXIS-NEXIS put a wealth of information at the keyboards of marketing decision makers.

TABLE 4-3 Planning Primary Data Collection

Research Approaches	Contact Methods	Sampling Plan	Research Instruments
Observation	Mail	Sampling unit	Questionnaire
Survey	Telephone	Sample size	Mechanical instruments
Experiment	Personal	Sampling procedure	

can be found, they might not be very usable. The researcher must evaluate secondary information carefully to ensure that it is *relevant* (fits research project needs), *accurate* (reliably collected and reported), *current* (up-to-date enough for current decisions), and *impartial* (objectively collected and reported).

Secondary data provide a good starting point for research and often help to define problems and research objectives. In most cases, however, the company must also collect primary data.

Planning Primary Data Collection

Good decisions require good data. Just as researchers must carefully evaluate the quality of secondary information, they must also take care when collecting primary data to ensure that it will be relevant, accurate, current, and unbiased. Table 4-3 shows that designing a plan for primary data collection calls for a number of decisions on research approaches, contact methods, sampling plan, and research instruments.

Observational research
The gathering of primary data by observing relevant people, actions, and situations.

Research Approaches. **Observational research** is gathering primary data by observing relevant people, actions, and situations. For example, a maker of personal care products might pretest its ads by showing them to people and measuring eye movements, pulse rates, and other physical reactions. Or a bank might evaluate possible new branch locations by checking traffic patterns, neighbourhood conditions, and the location of competing branches. Steelcase used observation to help design new office furniture for use by work teams:

Observational research: Steelcase set up video cameras at various companies to study motions and behaviour patterns that customers themselves might not even notice. The result was the highly successful Personal Harbor modular office units.

To learn first-hand how teams actually operate, it set up video cameras at various companies and studied the tapes, looking for motions and behavior patterns that customers themselves might not even notice. It found that teams work best when they can do some work together and some privately. So Steelcase designed highly successful modular office units, called Personal Harbor. These units are "rather like telephone booths in size and shape." They can be arranged around a common space where a team works, letting people work together but also alone when necessary. Says a Steelcase executive, "Market data wouldn't necessarily have pointed us that way. It was more important to know how people actually work."[14]

Urban Outfitters, the fast-growing specialty clothing chain, prefers observation to other types of market research. "We're not after people's statements," notes the chain's president, "we're after their actions." The company develops customer profiles by videotaping and taking photographs of customers in its stores. This helps managers determine what people are actually wearing and allows them to make quick decisions about merchandise.[15]

Several companies sell information collected through *mechanical* observation. For example, Nielsen Media Research attaches *people meters* to television sets in selected homes to record who watches which programs. It then provides summaries of the size and demographic composition of audiences for different television programs. Television networks use these ratings to judge program popularity and to set fees for advertising time. Advertisers use the ratings when selecting programs for their commercials. *Checkout scanners* in retail stores record consumer purchases in detail. Consumer products companies and retailers use scanner information to assess and improve product sales and store performance. Some marketing research firms now offer **single-source data systems** that electronically monitor both consumers' purchases and their exposure to various marketing activities in an effort to better evaluate the link between the two (see Marketing Highlight 4-2).

Single-source data systems
Electronic monitoring systems that link consumers' exposure to television advertising and promotion (measured using television meters) with what they buy in stores (measured using store checkout scanners).

Observational research can be used to obtain information that people are unwilling or unable to provide: In some cases, observation may be the only way to obtain the needed information. In contrast, some things simply cannot be observed, such as feelings, attitudes and motives, or private behaviour. Long-term or infrequent behaviour is also difficult to observe. Because of these limitations, researchers often use observation along with other data collection methods.

Survey research is the approach best suited for gathering *descriptive* information. A company that wants to know about people's knowledge, attitudes, preferences, or buying behaviour often can find out by asking individuals directly.

Survey research
The gathering of primary data by asking people questions about their knowledge, attitudes, preferences, and buying behaviour.

Survey research is the most widely used method for primary data collection. The major advantage of survey research is its flexibility. It can be used to obtain many different kinds of information in many different situations. Depending on the survey design, it also may provide information more quickly and at lower cost than observational or experimental research.

However, survey research also presents some problems. Although many people believe constructing a good survey is a relatively easy matter, nothing could be further from the truth. Sometimes people are unable to answer survey questions because they cannot remember or have never thought about what they do and why. Or people may be unwilling to respond to unknown interviewers or talk about things they consider private. Respondents may answer survey questions even when they do not know the answer just to appear smarter or more informed. Or they may try to help the interviewer by giving pleasing answers. Finally, busy people may not take the time, or they might resent the intrusion into their privacy.

Experimental research
The gathering of primary data by selecting matched groups of subjects, giving them different treatments, controlling related factors, and checking for differences in group responses.

Whereas observation is best suited for exploratory research and surveys for descriptive research, **experimental research** is best suited for gathering *causal* information. Experiments involve selecting matched groups of subjects, giving them different treatments, controlling unrelated factors, and checking for differences in

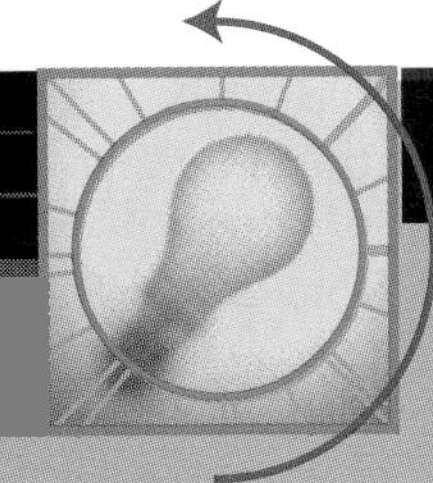

marketing highlight 4-2

Single-Source Data Systems: A Powerful Way to Measure Marketing Impact

Information Resources, Inc. (IRI), which operates in 26 countries, is a leader in providing innovative information and marketing software to companies engaged in the marketing, sales, and distribution of Canadian packaged and non-packaged goods. A major competitor of A.C. Nielsen, IRI knows all there is to know about the members of its panel households—what they eat for lunch; what they put in their coffee; and what they use to wash their hair, quench their thirsts, or make up their faces. The research company electronically monitors the television programs that these people watch and tracks the brands they buy, the coupons they use, where they shop, and what newspapers and magazines they read. These households are part of IRI's BehaviorScan service, a single-source data system that links consumers' exposure to television advertising, sales promotion, and other marketing efforts with their store purchases. BehaviorScan and other single-source data systems have revolutionized the way consumer products companies measure the impact of their marketing activities.

The basics of single-source research are straightforward, and the IRI BehaviorScan system provides a good example. IRI maintains a panel of households across Canada. The company meters each home's television set to track who watches what and when, and it quizzes family members to find out what they read. It carefully records important facts about each household, such as family income, age of children, lifestyle, and product and store buying history.

IRI also uses a panel of retail stores in each of its markets. For a fee, these stores agree to carry the new products that IRI wishes to test and they allow IRI to control such factors as shelf location, stocking, point-of-purchase displays, and pricing for these products.

Each BehaviorScan household receives an identification number. When household members shop for groceries in IRI panel stores, they give their identification number to the store checkout clerk. All the information about the family's purchases—brands bought, package sizes, prices paid—is recorded by the store's electronic scanner and immediately entered by computer into the family's purchase file. The system also records any other in-store factors that might affect purchase decisions, such as special competitor price promotions or shelf displays.

Thus, IRI builds a complete record of each household's demographic and psychographic makeup, purchasing behaviour, media habits, and the conditions surrounding purchase. But IRI takes the process a step further. Through cable television, IRI controls the advertisements being sent to each household. It can beam different ads and promotions to different panel households and then use the purchasing information obtained from scanners to assess which ads had more or less impact and how various promotions affected different kinds of consumers. In short, from a single source, companies can obtain information that links their marketing efforts directly with consumer buying behaviour.

BehaviorScan and other single-source systems have their drawbacks, and some researchers are sceptical. One hitch is that such systems produce truckloads of data—more than most companies can handle. Another problem is cost: single-source data can cost marketers hundreds of thousands of dollars a year per brand. Also, because such systems are set up in only a few market areas, usually small cities, the marketer often finds it difficult to generalize from the measures and results. Finally, although single-source systems provide important information for assessing the impact of promotion and advertising, they shed little light on the effects of other key marketing actions.

Despite these drawbacks, more and more companies are relying on single-source data systems to test new products and new marketing strategies. When properly used, such systems can provide marketers with fast and detailed information about how their products are selling, who is buying them, and what factors affect purchase.

Information Resources Inc. used this ad to announce its arrival in the Canadian marketplace.

Sources: See Joanne Lipman, "Single-source ad research heralds detailed look at household habits," *Wall Street Journal,* 16 February 1988:39; Joe Schwartz, "Back to the source," *American Demographics,* January 1989:22–6; Magid H. Abraham and Leonard M. Lodish, "Getting the most out of advertising and promotion," *Harvard Business Review,* May–June 1990:50–60; and Howard Schlossberg, "IRI, Nielsen slug it out in 'scanning wars,'" *Marketing News,* 2 September 1991:1,47.

group responses. Thus, experimental research tries to explain cause-and-effect relationships. Observation and surveys may be used to collect information in experimental research.

Before adding a new burger to the menu, researchers at McDonald's might use experiments to answer such questions as:

- How much will the new burger increase McDonald's sales?
- How will the new burger affect the sales of other menu items?
- Which advertising approach would have the greatest effect on sales of the burger?
- How would different prices affect the sales of the product?
- Should the new item be targeted toward adults, children, or both?

To test the effects of two different prices, McDonald's could set up the following simple experiment. It could introduce the new burger at one price in its restaurants in one city and at another price in restaurants in another city. If the cities are similar, and if all other marketing efforts for the burger are the same, then differences in sales in the two cities could be related to the price charged. More complex experiments could be designed to include other variables and other locations.

Contact Methods. Information can be collected by mail, telephone, or personal interview. Table 4-4 shows the strengths and weaknesses of each contact method.

Mail questionnaires can be used to collect large amounts of information at a low cost per respondent. Respondents may give more honest answers to more personal questions on a mail questionnaire than to an unknown interviewer in person or over the phone. Also, no interviewer is involved to bias the respondent's answers. However, mail questionnaires are not flexible—all respondents answer the same questions in a fixed order, and the researcher cannot adapt the questionnaire based on earlier answers. Mail surveys usually take longer to complete, and the response rate—the number of people returning completed questionnaires—is often very low. Finally, the researcher often has little control over the mail questionnaire sample. Even with a good mailing list, it is hard to control *who* at the mailing address fills out the questionnaire.

Telephone interviewing is the best method for gathering information quickly, and it provides greater flexibility than mail questionnaires. Interviewers can explain difficult questions, and they can skip some questions or probe on others, depending on the answers they receive. Response rates tend to be higher than with mail questionnaires, and telephone interviewing also allows greater sample control. Interviewers can ask to speak to respondents with the desired characteristics, or even by name.

However, with telephone interviewing, the cost per respondent is higher than with mail questionnaires. Also, people may not want to discuss personal questions

TABLE 4-4 Strengths and Weaknesses of the Three Contact Methods

	Mail	Telephone	Personal
1. Flexibility	Poor	Good	Excellent
2. Quantity of data that can be collected	Good	Fair	Excellent
3. Control of interviewer effect	Excellent	Fair	Poor
4. Control of sample	Fair	Excellent	Fair
5. Speed of data collection	Poor	Excellent	Good
6. Response rate	Poor	Good	Good
7. Cost	Good	Fair	Poor

Source: Adapted with permission of Macmillan Publishing Company from Donald S. Tull and Del I. Hawkins, *Marketing Research: Measurement and Method,* 6th ed., Macmillan Publishing Company, 1993.

with an interviewer. Using an interviewer also introduces interviewer bias—the way interviewers talk, how they ask questions, and other differences may affect respondents' answers. Finally, different interviewers may interpret and record responses differently and, under time pressures, some interviewers might even cheat by recording answers themselves without asking respondents questions.

Personal interviewing takes two forms—individual and group interviewing. *Individual interviewing* involves talking with people in their homes or offices, on the street, or in shopping malls. Such interviewing is flexible. Trained interviewers can hold a respondent's attention for a long time and can explain difficult questions. They can guide interviews, explore issues, and probe as the situation requires. They can show subjects actual products, advertisements, or packages and observe reactions and behaviour. In most cases, personal interviews can be conducted fairly quickly. However, individual personal interviews can cost three to four times as much as telephone interviews.

Focus group interviewing
Personal interviewing of a small group of people invited to gather for a few hours with a trained interviewer to discuss a product, service, or organization. The interviewer "focuses" the group discussion on important issues.

Group interviewing is used primarily in exploratory research. **Focus group interviewing** has become one of the major marketing research tools for gaining insight into consumer thoughts, attitudes, and feelings. A homogeneous group of about six to ten people selected from a population of interest is invited to gather for a few hours with a trained moderator to discuss a product, service, or organization. The participants typically are paid a small sum for attending. The meeting is held in a pleasant place, and refreshments are served to foster informality. The moderator encourages free and easy discussion, hoping that group interactions will bring out actual feelings, attitudes, and thoughts. At the same time, the moderator "focuses" the discussion—hence the name focus group interviewing. The comments are recorded in written notes or on videotapes that are studied later. Company representatives may observe the group through one-way mirrors. Although several focus groups may be conducted for one study (usually with different demographic groups), the small sample sizes and the sample selection procedure usually make it inappropriate to generalize from their findings.

Today, modern communications technology is changing the way that focus groups are conducted:

> In the old days, advertisers and agencies flew their staff to Halifax or Regina to watch focus groups from behind one-way mirrors. The staff usually spent more time in hotels and taxis than they did doing research. Today, they are staying home. Video-conferencing links, television monitors, remote-control cameras, and digital transmission are boosting the amount of focus group research done over long-distance lines. [In a typical video-conferencing system], two cameras focused on the group are controlled by clients who hold a remote keypad. Executives in a far-off boardroom can zoom in on faces and pan the focus group at will. . . . A two-way sound system connects remote viewers to the backroom, focus group room, and directly to the monitor's earpiece. [Recently], while testing new product names in one focus group, the [client's] creative director . . . had an idea and contacted the moderator, who tested the new name on the spot.[16]

In addition, with the development of the Internet, many companies are now conducting online focus groups:

> Janice Gjersten, director of marketing for WP-Studio, an online entertainment company, wanted to conduct traditional focus groups to gauge reaction to a new Web site. However, she found that an online focus group netted more honest answers. Gjersten contacted Cyber Dialogue, which provided focus group respondents drawn from its 10 000-person database. The focus group was held in an online chat room, which Gjersten "looked in on" from her office computer. Gjersten could interrupt the moderator at any time with flash e-mails unseen by the respondents. Although the online focus group lacked voice and body cues, Gjersten says she will never conduct a traditional focus group again. Not only were respondents more honest, but the cost for the online group was one-third that of a traditional focus group, and a full report came to her in one day, compared to four weeks.[17]

As this example suggests, the latest technology to hit marketing research is the fast-growing Internet. Increasingly, marketing researchers are collecting primary data through online (Internet) marketing research—Internet surveys and online focus groups. Although online research offers much promise, and some analysts predict that the Internet will soon be the primary marketing research tool, others

Video-conferencing allows executives in far-off boardrooms to "sit in" on focus group sessions.

are more cautious. Marketing Highlight 4-3 summarizes the advantages, drawbacks, and prospects for conducting marketing research on the Internet.

Which contact method is best depends on what information the researcher wants, as well as the number and types of respondents to be contacted. Advances in computers and communications have had a large impact on methods of obtaining information. Most research firms now do computer-assisted telephone interviewing (CATI). Professional interviewers call respondents around the country, often using phone numbers drawn at random. When the respondent answers, the interviewer reads a set of questions from a video screen and types the respondent's answers directly into the computer. YOUtv, a young Canadian company, believed that consumers would be more open and honest in their feedback to companies if they could use video booths that they could activate themselves. But just providing firms with this technology wasn't enough, explains Ian Chamandy, co-owner of YOUtv. The company's ability to transform the raw data into meaningful information was key when Cadbury Chocolate Canada decided to use YOUtv to search for a new couple to advertise Crispy Crunch chocolate bars.[18]

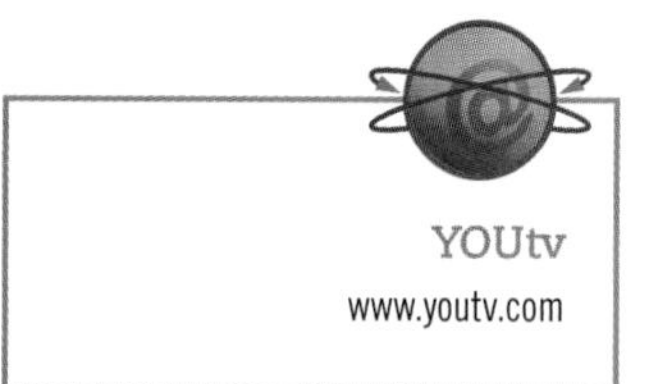

YOUtv developed a new research firm that provides interactive video booths to gather data and the ability to analyze them.

Other firms are using *computer interviewing*, in which respondents sit down at a computer, read questions from a screen, and type their own answers into the computer. Electronic focus groups, or electronic brainstorming, is becoming a powerful and efficient way for companies to gauge customer sentiments. Twelve people are invited to a lab where a researcher poses questions. Respondents enter their responses and can read other respondents' answers on a large screen. Some companies, such as Microsoft Canada, are conducting surveys using the Internet. The company received more than 55 000 responses in just over 24 hours to a survey it conducted asking about people's relationships with computers.[19]

The Royal Bank of Canada has mastered computer-assisted interviewing without making people actually use a computer. Under a large sign that asks customers to "tell us what you think," customers use a special pen to complete a questionnaire on an electronic board. The information can be downloaded directly into a database for later analysis.[20] Some US researchers use completely automated telephone surveys

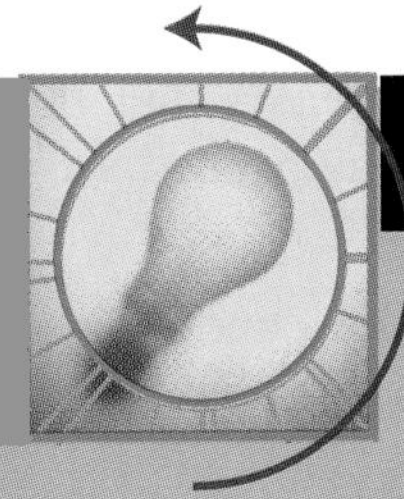

marketing highlight 4-3

Marketing Research on the Internet

Doing marketing research on the Internet is still in its infancy. But as the use of the World Wide Web and online services are becoming more habit than hype for consumers, online research has become a quick, easy, and inexpensive way to tap into their opinions. The potential of the Internet as a data collection tool is evident: Not only is it unlimited by geographic boundaries, it also offers almost instant responses. People can respond to questionnaires posted on Web sites in the privacy of their own homes at any time convenient to them. Currently, only a small proportion of Canadians use the Internet. However, online users tend to be better educated, more affluent, and younger than average consumers. A higher proportion are male. These are highly important consumers to companies offering products and services online. They are also some of the hardest consumers to reach when conducting a research study. Online surveys and chat sessions (or online focus groups) often prove effective in getting elusive teen, single, affluent, and well-educated audiences to participate.

"It's very solid for reaching hard-to-get segments," says one analyst. "Doctors, lawyers, professionals—people you might have difficulty reaching because they are not interested in taking part in surveys. It's also a good medium for reaching working mothers and others who lead busy lives. They can do it in their own space and at their own convenience."

Online research isn't right for every company or product. For example, mass marketers who need to survey a representative cross-section of the population will find online research methodologies less useful. "If the target for the product or service you're testing is inconsistent with the Internet user profile, then it's not the medium to use," Jacobson points out. "Is it the right medium to test Campbell's Chunky Soup? Probably not, but if you want to test how people feel about Campbell's Web site, yes."

When appropriate, online research offers marketers two distinct advantages over traditional surveys and focus groups: speed and cost-effectiveness. Online researchers routinely field quantitative studies and fill response quotas in a matter of days. Online focus groups require some advance scheduling, but results are virtually instantaneous. Notes an online researcher, "Online research is very fast, and time is what everybody wants now. Clients want the information yesterday."

Research on the Internet is also relatively inexpensive. Participants can dial in for a focus group from anywhere in the world, eliminating travel, lodging, and facility costs, making online chats less expensive than traditional focus groups. And for surveys, the Internet eliminates most of the postage, phone, labour, and printing costs associated with other survey approaches. Moreover, sample size has little influence on costs. "There's not a huge difference between ten and 10 000 on the Web," said Tod Johnson, head of NPD Group, a firm that conducts online research. "The cost [of research on the Web] can be anywhere from 10 percent to 80 percent less, especially when you talk about big samples."

However, using the Internet to conduct marketing research does have some drawbacks. One major problem is knowing who is in the sample. "If you can't see a person with whom you are communicating, how do you know who they really are?" asks Tom Greenbaum, president of Groups Plus. Moreover, trying to draw conclusions from a "self-selected" sample of online users, those who clicked through to a questionnaire or accidentally landed in a chat room, can be troublesome. "Using a convenient sample is a way to do research quickly, but when you're done, you kind of scratch your head and ask what it means."

To overcome such sample and response problems, NPD and many other firms that offer online services construct panels of qualified Web regulars to respond to surveys and participate in online focus groups. NPD's panel consists of 15 000 consumers recruited online and verified by telephone; Greenfield Online chooses users from its own database, then calls them periodically to verify that they are who they say they are. Another online research firm, Research Connections, recruits in advance by telephone, taking time to help new users connect to the Internet, if necessary.

Even when using qualified respondents, focus group responses can lose something in the translation. "You're missing all of the key things that make a focus group a viable method," says Greenbaum. "You may get people online to talk to each other and play off each other, but it's very different to watch people get excited about a concept." Eye contact and body language are lost in the online world. And while researchers can offer seasoned moderators, the Internet format greatly restricts respondent expressiveness. Similarly, technology limits researchers' capability to show visual cues to research subjects. But just as it hinders the two-way assessment of visual cues, Web research can actually permit some participants the anonymity necessary to elicit an unguarded response. "There are reduced social effects online," Jacobson says. "People are much more honest in this medium."

Some researchers are wildly optimistic about the prospects for marketing research on the Internet; others are more cautious. One expert predicts that in the next few years, 50 percent of all research will be done on the Internet. "Ten years from now, national telephone surveys will be the subject of research methodology folklore," he proclaims. "That's a little too soon," cautions another expert. "But in 20 years, yes."

Sources: Portions adapted from Ian P. Murphy, "Interactive research," *Marketing News,* 20 January 1997:1,17. Selected quotations from "NFO executive sees most research going to Internet," *Advertising Age,* 19 May 1997:50. Also see Brad Edmondson, "The wired bunch," *American Demographics,* June 1997:10–5; Charlie Hamlin, "Market research and the wired consumer," *Marketing News,* 9 June 1997:6; and Mariam Mesbah, "Special report: Research: Internet research holds potential," *Strategy,* 14 April 1997:40.

(CATS), which employ voice-response technology to conduct interviews, but the Canadian Radio-television and Telecommunication Commission has banned such devices in Canada.[21]

Sampling Plans. Marketing researchers usually draw conclusions about large groups of consumers by studying a small sample of the total consumer population. A **sample** is a segment of the population selected to represent the population as a whole. Ideally, the sample should be representative so that the researcher can make accurate estimates of the thoughts and behaviours of the larger population.

Sample
A segment of the population selected to represent the population as a whole.

Designing the sample requires three decisions. First, *who* is to be surveyed: What is the *sampling unit?* The answer to this question is not always obvious. For example, to study the decision-making process for a family automobile purchase, should the researcher interview the husband, wife, other family members, dealership salespeople, or all of these? The researcher must determine what information is needed and who is most likely to have it.

Second, *how many* people should be surveyed: What is the *sample size?* Large samples give more reliable results than small samples. However, it is not necessary to sample the entire target market or even a large portion to get reliable results. If well chosen, samples of less than one percent of a population can often give good reliability.

Third, *how* should the people in the sample be *chosen:* What is the *sampling procedure?* Table 4-5 describes different kinds of samples. Using *probability samples,* each member of the population has a known chance of being included in the sample, and researchers can calculate confidence limits for sampling error. But when probability sampling costs too much or takes too much time, marketing researchers often take *non-probability samples,* even though their sampling error cannot be measured. These varied ways of drawing samples have different costs and time limitations, as well as different accuracy and statistical properties. Which method is best depends on the needs of the research project.

Research Instruments. In collecting primary data, marketing researchers have a choice of two main research instruments—the questionnaire and mechanical devices. The questionnaire, by far the most common instrument, is very flexible: There are many ways to ask questions. Questionnaires must be developed carefully and tested before they can be used on a large scale. A carelessly prepared questionnaire usually contains several errors (see Table 4-6).

In preparing a questionnaire, the marketing researcher must first decide what

TABLE 4-5 Types of Samples

Probability Sample	
Simple random sample	Every member of the population has a known and equal chance of selection.
Stratified random sample	The population is divided into mutually exclusive groups (such as age groups), and random samples are drawn from each group.
	The population is divided into mutually exclusive groups (such as blocks), and the researcher draws a sample of the groups to interview.
Non-Probability Sample	
Convenience sample	The researcher selects the easiest population members from which to obtain information.
Judgment sample	The researcher uses his or her judgment to select population members who are good prospects for accurate information.
	The researcher finds and interviews a prescribed number of people in each of several categories.

TABLE 4-6 A Questionable Questionnaire

Suppose that a summer camp director had prepared the following questionnaire to use in interviewing the parents of prospective campers. How would you assess each question?

1. What is your income to the nearest hundred dollars?

   People don't usually know their income to the nearest hundred dollars, nor do they want to reveal their income that closely. Moreover, a researcher should never open a questionnaire with such a personal question.
2. Are you a strong or a weak supporter of overnight summer camping for your children?

   What do "strong" and "weak" mean?
3. Do your children behave themselves well at a summer camp? Yes ( ) No ( )

   "Behave" is a relative term. Furthermore, are "yes" and "no" the best response options for this question? Besides, will people want to answer this? Why ask the question in the first place?
4. How many camps mailed literature to you last April? this April?

   Who can remember this?
5. What are the most salient and determinant attributes in your evaluation of summer camps?

   What are "salient" and "determinant" attributes? Don't use big words on me!
6. Do you think it is right to deprive your child of the opportunity to grow into a mature person through the experience of summer camping?

   A loaded question. Given the bias, how can any parent answer "yes"?

questions to ask. Questionnaires frequently leave out questions that should be answered and include questions that cannot be answered, will not be answered, or need not be answered. Each question should be checked to see that it contributes to the research objectives.

The *form* of each question is also important. *Closed-end questions* include all the possible answers, and subjects make choices among them. Part A of Table 4-7 shows the most common forms of closed-end questions as they might appear in a survey of Air Canada's customers. *Open-end questions* allow respondents to answer in their own words. The most common forms are shown in Part B of Table 4-7. Open-end questions often reveal more than closed-end questions because respondents are not limited in their answers. Open-end questions are especially useful in exploratory research, when the researcher is trying to determine *what* people think but not measuring *how many* people think in a certain way. Closed-end questions, on the other hand, provide answers that are easier to interpret and tabulate.

Researchers should also use care in *wording* and *ordering* questions. They should use simple, direct, unbiased wording. Questions should be arranged in a logical order. The first question should create interest if possible, and difficult or personal questions should be asked last so that respondents do not become defensive.

Although questionnaires are the most common research instrument, *mechanical instruments* also are used. We discussed two mechanical instruments—people meters and supermarket scanners—earlier in the chapter. Another group of mechanical devices measures subjects' physical responses. For example, a galvanometer measures the strength of interest or emotions aroused by a subject's exposure to different stimuli, such as an ad or picture. The galvanometer detects the minute degree of sweating that accompanies emotional arousal. The tachistoscope flashes an ad to a subject at an exposure range from less than one-hundredth of a second to several seconds. After each exposure, respondents describe everything they recall. Eye cameras are used to study respondents' eye movements to determine at what points their eyes focus first and how long they linger on a given item.[22]

TABLE 4-7 Types of Questions

A. Closed-End Questions

Name	Description	Example
Dichotomous	A question offering two answer choices.	"In arranging this trip, did you personally phone Air Canada?" Yes ☐ No ☐
Multiple choice	A question offering three or more answer choices.	"With whom are you travelling on this fight?" No one ☐ Children only ☐ Spouse ☐ Business associates/friends/relatives ☐ Spouse and children ☐ An organized tour group ☐
Likert scale	A statement with which the respondent shows the amount of agreement or disagreement.	"Small airlines generally give better service than large ones." Strongly disagree 1 ☐ · Disagree 2 ☐ · Neither agree nor disagree 3 ☐ · Agree 4 ☐ · Strongly agree 5 ☐
Semantic differential	A scale is inscribed between two bipolar words, and the respondent selects the point that represents the direction and intensity of his or her feelings.	*Air Canada* Large _X_ : ___ : ___ : ___ : ___ : ___ : ___ : Small Experienced ___ : ___ : ___ : ___ : _X_ : ___ : Inexperienced Modern ___ : ___ : ___ : _X_ : ___ : ___ : Old-fashioned
Importance scale	A scale that rates the importance of some attribute from "not at all important" to "extremely important."	"Airline food service to me is" Exremely important 1 ___ · Very important 2 ___ · Somewhat important 3 ___ · Not very important 4 ___ · Not at all important 5 ___
Rating scale	A scale that rates some attribute from "poor" to "excellent."	"Air Canada's food service is" Excellent 1 ___ · Very good 2 ___ · Good 3 ___ · Fair 4 ___ · Poor 5 ___
Intention-to-buy scale	A scale that describes the respondent's intentions to buy.	"If in-flight telephone service were available on a long flight, I would" Definitely buy 1 ___ · Probably buy 2 ___ · Not certain 3 ___ · Probably not buy 4 ___ · Definitely not buy 5 ___

B. Open-End Questions

Name	Description	Example
Completely unstructured	A question that respondents can answer in an almost unlimited number of ways.	"What is your opinion of Air Canada?"
Word association	Words are presented, one at a time, and respondents mention the first word that comes to mind.	"What is the first word that comes to mind when you hear the following? Airline ________ Canada ________ Travel ________
Sentence completion	Incomplete sentences are presented, one at a time, and respondents complete the sentence.	"When I choose an airline, the most important consideration in my decision is ________
Story completion	An incomplete story is presented, and respondents are asked to complete it.	"I flew Air Canada a few days ago. I noticed that the exterior and interior of the plane had very soft colours. This aroused in me the following thoughts and feelings." *Now complete the story.*
Picture completion	A picture of two characters is presented, with one making a statement. Respondents are asked to identify with the other and fill in the empty balloon.	 Fill in the empty balloon.
Thematic Apperception Tests (TAT)	A picture is presented, and respondents are asked to make up a story about what they think is happening or may happen in the picture.	 Make up a story about what you see.

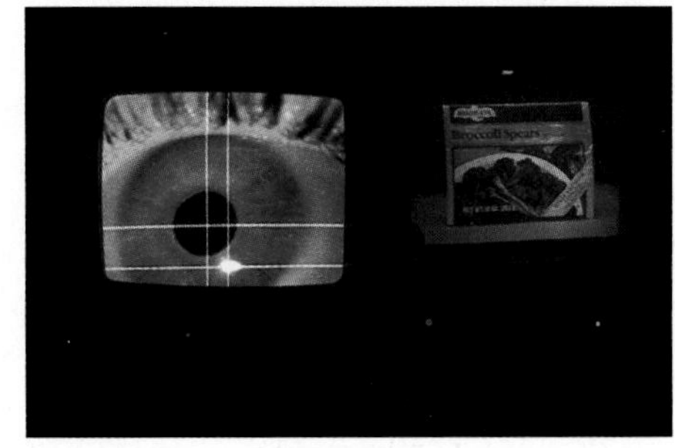

Mechanical research instruments: Eye cameras determine where eyes land and how long they linger on a given item.

Presenting the Research Plan

At this stage, the marketing researcher should summarize the plan in a *written proposal*. A written proposal is especially important when the research project is large and complex or when an outside firm carries it out. The proposal should cover the management problems addressed and the research objectives, the information to be obtained, the sources of secondary information or methods for collecting primary data, and the way the results will help management decision making. The proposal should also include research costs. A written research plan or proposal ensures that the marketing manager and researchers have considered all of the important aspects of the research and that they agree on why and how the research will be conducted.

Implementing the Research Plan

The researcher next puts the marketing research plan into action. This involves designing the research instrument and testing it, selecting the sample, and collecting, processing, and analyzing the information. Data collection can be carried out by the company's marketing research staff or by outside firms. The company keeps more control over the collection process and data quality by using its own staff; however, outside firms that specialize in data collection often can do the job more quickly and at lower cost.

The data collection phase of the marketing research process is generally the most expensive and the most subject to error. The researcher should watch fieldwork closely to ensure that the plan is implemented correctly and to guard against problems with contacting respondents, with respondents who refuse to cooperate or who give biased or dishonest answers, and with interviewers who make mistakes or take shortcuts.

Researchers must process and analyze the collected data to isolate important information and findings. They need to check data from questionnaires for accuracy and completeness and code it for computer analysis. The researchers then tabulate the results and compute averages and other statistical measures.

Interpreting and Reporting the Findings

The researcher must now interpret the findings, draw conclusions, and report them to management. The researcher should try not to overwhelm managers with numbers and fancy statistical techniques; rather, the researcher should present important findings that are useful in the major decisions faced by management.

Interpretation should not be left only to the researchers, however. They are often experts in research design and statistics, but the marketing manager knows more about the problem and the decisions that must be made. In many cases, findings can be interpreted in different ways, and discussions between researchers and managers will help identify the best interpretations. The manager will also want to check that the research project was conducted properly and that all the necessary analysis was completed. Or, after seeing the findings, the manager may have additional questions that can be answered through further sifting of the data. Finally, the manager is the one who ultimately must decide what action the research suggests. The researchers may even make the data directly available to marketing managers so that they can perform new analyses and test new relationships on their own.

Interpretation is an important phase of the marketing process. The best research is meaningless if the manager blindly accepts wrong interpretations from the researcher. Similarly, managers may have biased interpretations: They tend to accept research results that show what they expected and to reject those that they did not expect or hope for. Thus, managers and researchers must work closely when interpreting research results, and both must share responsibility for the research process and resulting decisions.[23]

Other Marketing Research Considerations

This section discusses marketing research in two special contexts: marketing research by small businesses and non-profit organizations, and international marketing research. Finally, we look at public policy and ethical issues in marketing research.

Marketing Research in Small Businesses and Non-Profit Organizations

Managers of small businesses and non-profit organizations often believe that marketing research can be done only by experts in large companies with big research budgets. But smaller organizations also can use many of the marketing research techniques discussed in this chapter in a less formal manner and at little or no expense.

Managers of small businesses and non-profit organizations can obtain good marketing information simply by *observing* things around them. For example, retailers can evaluate new locations by observing vehicle and pedestrian traffic. They can visit competing stores to check on facilities and prices. They can evaluate their customer mix by recording how many and what kinds of customers shop in the store at different times. They can monitor competitor advertising by collecting advertisements from local media.

Managers can conduct informal *surveys* using small convenience samples. The director of an art museum can learn what patrons think about new exhibits by conducting informal "focus groups," inviting small groups to lunch and having discussions on topics of interest. Retail salespeople can talk with customers visiting the store; hospital officials can interview patients. Restaurant managers can

Industry Canada's small business Web site lists articles full of advice to help small businesses.

make random phone calls during slack hours to interview consumers about where they eat out and what they think of various restaurants in the area.

Managers can also conduct their own simple *experiments*. For example, by changing the themes in regular fund-raising mailings and watching the results, a non-profit manager can determine much about which marketing strategies work best. By varying newspaper advertisements, a store manager can learn the effects of such things as ad size and position, price coupons, and media used.

Small organizations can obtain most of the secondary data available to large businesses. In addition, many associations, local media, chambers of commerce, and government agencies provide special help to small organizations. The Conference Board of Canada, federal government, and provincial governments offer dozens of free publications that give advice on topics ranging from preparing a business plan to ordering business signs. Local newspapers often provide information on local shoppers and their buying patterns. Many business schools will conduct marketing research for no charge as part of class projects.

In summary, secondary data collection, observation, surveys, and experiments can all be used effectively by small organizations with small budgets. Although these informal research methods are less complex and less costly, they must still be conducted carefully. And with surveys, managers must think carefully about the objectives of the research, formulate questions in advance, recognize the biases introduced by smaller samples and less skilled researchers, and conduct the research systematically.

International Marketing Research

The need for information about international markets is growing as increasing numbers of companies are operating on a multinational basis. Firms like the Angus Reid Group have begun to respond to this need; the company annually collects information on corporate and brand images, product usage and awareness, and values attitudes from 25 000 consumers living in 50 countries. A.C. Nielsen, the world's largest marketing research firm, has offices in more than 90 countries. "Assessment of global advertising campaigns, new product introductions, and customer satisfaction levels are key areas of concern."[24]

To meet their clients' needs, many Canadian research firms are forming partnerships and alliances with research firms throughout the world. Such partnerships allow Canadian firms to gather information in numerous markets since their partners speak the language and are familiar with the nuances of the local culture. It helps them to understand the sources of *secondary data* for that particular market and assess the reliability of that data. Millward Brown's Canadian unit, for example, achieved a global profile after conducting a 36-country brand development study for Levi Strauss. As Michael Adams, president of Toronto-based Environics, noted, "Multinational companies don't care if you're from Hamburg, Chicago or Toronto—they just want you to be able to deliver the goods."[25]

International marketing research can pose some unique challenges. For example, it may be difficult to develop good samples. Whereas North American researchers can use current telephone directories, census tract data, and several other sources of socioeconomic data to construct samples, such information is largely lacking in many countries.

Once the sample is drawn, the North American researcher can usually reach most respondents easily by telephone, by mail, or in person. Reaching respondents is often not as easy in other parts of the world. Researchers in Mexico cannot rely on telephone and mail data collection—most data collection is conducted door-to-door and concentrated in three or four of the largest cities. And most surveys in Mexico bypass the large segment of the population where native tribes speak languages other than Spanish. In some countries, few people have phones—there are only four phones per 1000 people in Egypt, six per 1000 in Turkey, and 32 per 1000 in Argentina. In other countries, the postal system is notoriously unreliable.

marketers speak out

Vanessa Vachon, Consumer & Market Knowledge, Procter & Gamble Canada

Vanessa Vachon is an Associate Manager in the Consumer & Market Knowlege department at Procter & Gamble Canada. Procter & Gamble is truly a global organization, with operations in 70 countries throughout the Americas, Africa, Asia, Europe, and the Middle East. It sells over 300 products to five billion consumers in 150 countries around the world.

P&G's aim is to improve the lives of the world's consumers. The company's success has been driven by two main factors: first, its ability to identify and understand consumers' needs all around the globe, and, second, to satisfy those needs currently and over time by using both creative and technical skills. P&G is recognized in the industry for being on the leading edge of consumer knowledge.

The Consumer & Market Knowledge department plays an important role in the company's success. The purpose of the department is to obtain a high level of consumer intelligence, insight, and innovation, as well as leverage research tools to effectively help initiatives progress from the idea generation stage, to successful marketplace introduction and sustained superior performance over time. The department is also instrumental in the development of new research techniques and analysis to enhance superior consumer understanding.

Vanessa graduated from Queen's University with a Bachelor in Commerce (Honours) in April of 2000. At school, she always had a broad range of interests in both her classes and extracurricular activities. For this reason, she did not specialize in a particular area and continued taking courses in marketing, finance, international business, industrial relations, accounting, and business policy. In addition, she also did extensive work with the Association of Collegiate Entrepreneurs, working on business ventures, and leading a conference for the club.

Although Vanessa hadn't planned to become a market researcher, her analysis of her skills and interests, which ranged from psychology to mathematics and advanced analysis, as well as her interest in international business and marketing led her to join the Consumer & Market Knowledge (market research) department at Procter & Gamble. She found a good fit, having a personality that is challenge-seeking, creative, motivated, enthusiastic, with a passion for winning.

Vanessa thinks Procter & Gamble is a great company that gives its employees the option to specialize in a discipline or develop broader skills across functions. It has excellent training programs and truly values every individual employee. It offers people many personal growth opportunities and challenges. P&G strongly believes that whenever you get too comfortable in a position, it's time to disturb the status quo.

As an Associate Manager in Consumer & Market Knowledge for Beauty Care (Olay and Cover Girl), Vanessa's primary role is to be the expert in consumer understanding for her business teams. In her role, she must assess the need to conduct research, and then design, field, and analyze research that will fill knowledge gaps and answer business questions. She provides perspective and recommendations on the viability and success potential of initiatives in the Canadian market. She identifies creative and more efficient ways to target con-

In Brazil, for instance, an estimated 30 percent of the mail is never delivered. In many developing countries, poor roads and transportation systems make certain areas hard to reach, making personal interviews difficult and expensive.[26]

Differences in culture from country to country, including language, cause additional problems for international researchers. For example, questionnaires must be prepared in one language and then translated into the languages of each country researched. Responses then must be translated back into the original language for analysis and interpretation. This adds to research costs and increases the risks of error. Translating a questionnaire from one language to another is anything but easy. Many idioms, phrases, and statements mean different things in different cultures. For example, a Danish executive noted: "Check this out by having a different translator put back into English what you've translated from English. You'll get the shock of your life. I remember [an example in which] 'out of sight, out of mind' had become 'invisible things are insane.' "[27]

Buying roles and consumer decision processes vary greatly between countries, further complicating international marketing research. Consumers in different countries also vary in their attitudes toward marketing research. People in one country may be very willing to respond; in other countries, non-response can be a major problem. For example, customs in some Islamic countries prohibit people from talking with strangers—a researcher simply may not be allowed to speak sumers. And, finally, she experiments with new research approaches and techniques.

Day-to-day, she participates in business team discussions and collaborates on a one-on-one basis with colleagues from other functions in both strategic and tactical discussions. She talks to her counterparts in different P&G sites around the world to share information on consumers. She collaborates with suppliers to design research that will best answer her teams' questions. Finally, she taps into the vast pool of data at P&G to broaden her understanding of Canadian consumers.

Vanessa's biggest hurdle when first joining P&G was learning to make timely decisions and recommendations with limited information. Unlike her experiences at school, she had no case studies with organized information to help her in her task. Vanessa found it challenging to clearly identify underlying issues and business questions and then translate those into appropriate objectives and research designs. In addition, when analyzing the research, it is sometimes difficult to read between the lines and truly capture what consumers are telling you. Moreover, she had to translate her insights into actionable recommendations to business teams. Accomplishing this task meant Vanessa had to tap all the knowledge she acquired in school and during on-the-job training.

Undaunted, Vanessa remains extremely motivated, positive, and enthusiastic. She can hardly believe all the skills she has learned, and all the projects she has worked on in only a short period of time with the company. Since day one, she has been given a large amount of responsibility and was treated as a full contributor by her business teams. She feels empowered by this amount of trust, and truly feels privileged to have the opportunity to work with a team of brilliant individuals, all working towards constantly improving the lives of the world's consumers.

Vanessa Vachon.

by phone with women about brand attitudes or buying behaviour. In some cultures, research questions often are considered too personal. In many Latin American countries, for example, people may feel embarrassed to talk with researchers about their choices of shampoo, deodorant, or other personal care products. Finally, even when respondents are *willing* to respond, they may not be *able* to because of high functional illiteracy rates.

Some of the insights and problems that arise when international marketing research is conducted and interpreted are evident when we examine American researchers' findings about Canadian consumers. The North American Free Trade Agreement has given many American firms the incentive to learn more about Canadians. Consider the validity of a recent study, conducted by the *Yankelovich Monitor,* designed to clarify the differences between American and Canadian consumers' responses to advertising.

The *Monitor* study suggests that Canadians are less homogeneous than Americans, less concerned with social conformity, and more open to pluralism. This pluralism has resulted in a lower sense of nationalism so that Canadian consumers do not respond to national symbols the way Americans do. The study concludes that a campaign like Chevrolet's "Heartbeat of America" would embarrass Canadians. The study suggests that Canadians are less imaginative than Americans and have less respect for age, experience, and government. The *Monitor* study also sug-

Some of the largest research services operate in many countries. Roper Starch Worldwide provides companies with information resources "from Brazil to Eastern Europe; from Cape Town to Beijing—if you are there, Roper Starch Worldwide is there."

gests that Canadians are rational consumers who are less susceptible to emotional, image-driven advertising appeals than their American counterparts. Canadians, the study notes, are practical and down to earth. They want advertising that tells them straightforward information: "How much does it cost?" "What will it do for me?" "What steps do I take to buy it or use it?" Furthermore, Canadians are less materialistic than Americans, less concerned with physical enhancement, but more concerned about the environment. Canadians are sometimes paradoxes. While they hanker for the outdoors, they are also more hedonistic than their counterparts south of the border. The study concludes, "I can see a typical Canadian tramping through the bush eating Haagen-Dazs ice cream!"[28]

Public Policy and Ethics in Marketing Research

Most marketing research benefits both the sponsoring company and its consumers. Through marketing research, companies learn more about consumers' needs, resulting in more satisfying products and services. A recent study conducted by the Canadian Survey Research Council found that 73 percent of Canadians liked being surveyed. Most consumers feel positively about marketing research and believe that it serves a useful purpose.[29] However, others strongly resent or even mistrust marketing research. A few consumers fear that researchers might use their findings to manipulate our buying. Others may have been taken in by previous "research surveys" that actually turned out to be attempts to sell them something. Most, however, simply resent the intrusion. They dislike mail or telephone surveys that are too long or too personal, or that interrupt them at inconvenient times. Increasing consumer resentment has become a major problem for the research industry, leading to lower survey response rates in recent years. The research industry is considering several possible responses. One is to expand its "Your Opinion Counts" program to educate consumers about the benefits of marketing research and to distinguish it from telephone selling and database building. Another is to provide a toll-free number that people can call to verify that a survey is legitimate.

To guard against inappropriate or harmful research practices in Canada, both the Canadian Marketing Association (www.cdma.org/main.html) and the Professional Marketing Research Society (PMRS) publish codes of ethics. You can read the full PMRS code on its Web site (www.pmrsaprm.com/About_Us/Conduct.html). A number of principles provide the foundation of the code. First is the importance of acting professionally and ensuring that methods used to address research questions are valid and reliable. Next are principles for dealing with research subjects. Subjects are not to be exposed to any risk or harm as a result of their participation in the research, their voluntary cooperation for participation in the research study must be sought, and their consent attained. Both organizations' codes deal with two major concerns—intrusions on consumer privacy and the misuse of research findings.

Intrusions on Consumer Privacy. While Canadians have long been concerned with protecting their privacy, the growth in numbers of people using the Internet has given more urgency to this issue. In a report released in August 1994, the Canadian privacy commissioner warned about the threat to privacy presented by the use of interactive computer technology and the ability of firms to merge databases from different businesses to cross-promote products and services. Canadian fears recently turned into a reality. When DoubleClick, a New York–based advertising firm, revealed plans to provide marketers with the names of anonymous Web surfers, there was a huge outcry on both sides of the border. David Jones, president of Electronic Frontier Canada in Kitchener, Ontario, says what made DoubleClick's practice especially dubious is that it went on without the consumer being aware of it. "There is not the usual knowledge and consent you should have when someone is collecting personal information."[30]

Canada is not alone in its concerns about privacy. In 1995, the European Union (EU) responded to this issue with its Directive on the Protection of Personal Data. The Directive establishes certain fundamentals: People must be aware that data about them are being collected; and consumers have fundamental rights, including the right of access to data, the right to know where data originated, the right to have inaccurate data rectified, and the right to withhold permission for certain uses of their personal information. Another critical aspect of the directive, from a North American perspective, was that it requires non-EU countries receiving EU data to ensure that the information is adequately protected.

The US and Canadian governments responded to the privacy issue differently. Quebec was the first government to establish regulations with regard to protecting privacy. While the US federal government opted to let business self-regulate with regard to privacy, the Canadian federal government passed the *Personal Information Protection and Electronic Documents Act*—Bill C6. Effective January 2001, the public sector and inter-provincial businesses now need consent to collect, use, or transfer information about an individual, or to use that information for purposes other than the original purpose for which it was collected. Moreover, every organization has to appoint a privacy officer to ensure compliance with the legislation and to field consumer inquiries and complaints. In three years, the legislation will extend to the entire private sector.[31] In addition to the new federal legislation, the Internet Advertising and Marketing Bureau of Canada (IAMBC) will scrutinize the practices of Internet marketers.

Misuse of Research Findings. Research studies can be powerful persuasion tools—companies often use study results as claims in their advertising and promotion. Today, however, many research studies appear to be little more than vehicles for pitching the sponsor's products. Few advertisers openly rig their research designs or blatantly misrepresent the findings—most abuses tend to be subtle "stretches." Consider these examples:[32]

A study by Chrysler contends that North Americans overwhelmingly prefer Chrysler to Toyota after test driving both. However, the study included only 100 people in each of two tests. More importantly, none of the people surveyed owned a foreign car, so they appear to be favourably predisposed to North American produced cars.

A poll sponsored by the disposable diaper industry asked: "It is estimated that disposable diapers account for less than two percent of the garbage in today's landfills. In contrast, beverage containers, third-class mail, and yard waste are estimated to account for about 21 percent of the garbage in landfills. Given this, in your opinion, would it be fair to ban disposable diapers?" Not surprisingly, 84 percent said "no."

Thus, subtle manipulations of the study's sample, or the choice or wording of questions, can greatly affect the conclusions reached. In other cases, so-called independent research studies are paid for by companies with an interest in the outcome. These are the kind of questionable practices the PMRS is on guard to prevent, since it firmly believes that such offences will undermine the credibility of the entire industry.

Review of Concept Connections

In today's complex and rapidly changing environment, marketing managers need more and better information to make effective and timely decisions. Fortunately, this greater need for information has been matched by the explosion of information technologies for supplying it. Using such technologies as small powerful computers, video-conferencing, and the Internet, companies can now handle great quantities of information—sometimes even too much. Yet marketers often complain that they lack enough of the right kind of information or have an excess of the wrong kind. In response, many companies are now studying their managers' information needs and designing information systems to satisfy those needs.

1. Explain the importance of information to the company.

Good products and marketing programs start with a thorough understanding of consumer needs and wants. Thus, the company needs sound information to produce superior value and satisfaction for customers. The company also requires information on competitors, resellers, and other actors and forces in the marketplace.

2. Define the marketing information system and discuss its parts.

The *marketing information system* (MIS) consists of people, equipment, and procedures to gather, sort, analyze, evaluate, and distribute needed, timely, and accurate information to marketing decision makers. A well-designed information system begins and ends with the user. The MIS first *assesses information needs* by interviewing marketing managers and surveying their decision environment to determine what information is desired, needed, and feasible to obtain. Next, the MIS *develops information* from internal databases, marketing intelligence activities, and marketing research. *Internal databases* provide information on the company's own sales, costs, inventories, cash flows, and accounts receivable and payable. Such data can be obtained quickly and cheaply but often need to be adapted for marketing decisions. *Marketing intelligence* activities supply marketing executives with everyday information about developments in the external marketing environment. Intelligence can be collected from company employees, customer, suppliers, and resellers, or by monitoring published reports, conferences, advertisements, competitor actions, and other activities in the environment. *Market research* consists of collecting information relevant to a specific marketing problem faced by the company. Finally, the MIS *distributes information* gathered from these many sources to the right managers in the right form and at the right time to help them make better marketing decisions.

3. **Outline the four steps in the marketing research process.**

The first step in the marketing research process is *defining the problem and setting the research objectives,* which may be exploratory, descriptive, or causal. The second step is *developing a research plan* for collecting data from primary and secondary sources. Secondary data collection involves tapping the company's internal database plus a wide range of external information sources, including libraries, commercial data services, online database services, Internet data sources, and government and business publications. Primary data collection involves choosing a research approach (observation, survey, experiment); selecting a contact method (mail, telephone, personal, computer, the Internet); designing a sampling plan (whom to survey, how many to survey, and how to choose them); and developing research instruments (questionnaire, mechanical). The third step is *implementing the marketing research plan* by gathering, processing, and analyzing the information. The fourth step is *interpreting and reporting the findings.* Additional information analysis helps marketing managers apply the information and provides them with sophisticated statistical procedures and models from which to develop more rigorous findings.

4. **Compare the advantages and disadvantages of various methods of collecting information.**

Both *internal* and *external* secondary data sources often provide information more quickly and at a lower cost than primary data sources, and they can sometimes yield information that a company cannot collect by itself. However, needed data might not exist in secondary sources, and, even if information can be found, it may be largely unusable. Researchers must also evaluate secondary information to ensure that it is *relevant, accurate, current,* and *impartial.* Primary research must also be evaluated for relevancy, accuracy, currency, and impartiality. Each primary data collection method has its own advantages and disadvantages. *Observational research* can obtain information that people are unwilling or unable to provide, yet some things cannot be observed. *Survey research* is flexible and well-suited for collecting *descriptive information,* but people may respond incorrectly or not at all for various reasons. *Experimental research* is best suited for collecting causal information but may be complex and difficult to control. Each of the various primary research contact methods—mail, telephone, personal interviews, or computer—also has advantages and drawbacks. For example, *mail questionnaires* can be used to collect large amounts of information inexpensively but tend to be inflexible, take a long time to complete, have a very low response rate, and permit little control over the sample. *Focus group interviewing* has become one of the major marketing research tools in *exploratory research* for gaining insight into consumer thoughts and feelings.

5. **Discuss the special issues some market researchers face, including public policy and ethics issues.**

Some marketers face special situations, such as in conducting marketing research for small businesses or non-profit organizations, or in international markets. Marketing research can be conducted effectively by small businesses and non-profit organizations with limited budgets. International marketing researchers follow the same steps as domestic researchers but often face more and different problems. All organizations need to respond responsibly to major public policy and ethical issues surrounding marketing research, including issues of intrusions on consumer privacy and misuse of research findings.

Key Terms

Causal research *(p. 160)*
Descriptive research *(p. 160)*
Experimental research *(p. 166)*
Exploratory research *(p. 160)*
Focus group interviewing *(p. 169)*
Internal databases *(p. 153)*
Marketing information system (MIS) *(p. 152)*
Marketing intelligence *(p. 154)*
Marketing research *(p. 158)*
Observational research (p. 165)
Online databases *(p. 161)*
Primary data *(p. 161)*
Sample *(p. 172)*
Secondary data *(p. 161)*
Single-source data systems *(p. 166)*
Survey research *(p. 166)*

Discussing the Issues

1. Marketing intelligence is an important aid to marketing managers for formulating strategy. What other benefits are derived from the marketing intelligence function? Assume that you have been hired as a consultant to a company that is developing a new digital camera. What types of intelligence tips would you offer the firm?
2. Using commercial online databases, marketing researchers can conduct their own searches of secondary data sources. A recent survey of marketing researchers confirmed that at least three-quarters of them use online services for conducting research. Go online, find a marketing research database, describe the database, and evaluate the services offered. Was the database free or fee-based?
3. Research objectives must be translated into specific information needs. Assume that you are the marketing research director for Apple Computer. What specific information might you need to pick two new colours for the popular iMac line of personal computers? List and briefly justify your choices.
4. Design a research program that would be appropriate in the following situations, and explain why:
   a. Kellogg wants to investigate the impact of young children on their parents' decisions to buy breakfast foods.
   b. Your university bookstore wants to get some insights into how students feel about the store's merchandise, prices, and service.
   c. Swiss Chalet is considering where to locate a new outlet in a fast-growing suburb.
5. Focus group interviewing is both a widely used and widely criticized research technique in marketing. List the advantages and disadvantages of focus groups. Suggest some kinds of questions that are suitable for exploration by using focus groups.
6. You have just finished a marketing research project for Bell Canada, testing different target segments' attitudes toward Bell's soon-to-be-launched advertising campaign. This morning, you received a call for research proposals from Sprint Canada. You are wondering how much of the knowledge you gained while doing the Bell study can be applied to the proposal for the new project. What would you recommend to the research director?
7. Conducting marketing research on the Internet is still in its infancy. Assume that your company is interested in developing a Web site to reach teenagers for the purpose of selling teen fashion clothing. How could you obtain information about your target market on the Internet? How could you learn more about their specific reactions to your proposed Web site? Could you get the information for free, or would there be a cost?
8. Increasing consumer concern and resentment has become a major problem for the research industry. Design a "Consumer Bill of Rights" that would guide the research industry and individual marketing researchers.

Marketing Applications

1. "Blind" taste tests often have surprising results. Demonstrate this by conducting a product test in your classroom.
   - Purchase three comparable brands of pop such as Coca-Cola, Pepsi, and a regional favourite or store brand of cola. Also buy three small paper cups for each student. Remove all identification from the bottles, including labels and caps, and use paper to cover any differences in bottle design. Label the brands with neutral terms such as Brand G, Brand H, and Brand I. Pour a small sample of each into labelled cups and distribute them.
   - Ask questions and tabulate the answers: (a) What brand do you normally prefer? (b) Which sample do you prefer? (c) What brand do you think each sample is?
   - Write students' preferences on the board, then reveal which brand was which sample. Are the results what you had expected? Why, or why not?
2. The Internet provides a unique means for targeting minority market segments and gathering information about their preferences. Statistics Canada publishes a number of reports that can help marketers learn more about ethnic markets. Go to www.statcan.ca/english/Pgdb/People/Population/

demo40a.htm, www.statcan.ca/english/Pgdb/, People/Population/demo25a.htm, or www.statcan.ca/Daily/English/971104/d971104.htm.

a. What seems to be the potential of marketing to minorities via the Internet?
b. What features of these sites might assist marketers wishing to reach minority markets?
c. Using the Statistics Canada Web site, determine the potential size of the Japanese-Canadian, Chinese-Canadian, and Black Canadian markets. What other information about these significant minorities can you find readily?
d. Using information from your research, develop a brief marketing plan for FUBU Clothing (www.fubu.com), an African-American clothing manufacturer that hopes to expand beyond the US market into Canada.

Internet Connections

Evaluating Online Research

Shopping for stuff on the Web? Have you tried using BizRate? BizRate is a shopping portal that scientifically surveys Web shoppers to get their ratings of online merchants. It surveys merchants' customers along ten dimensions to construct its ratings. The dimensions include ease of ordering, product selection, and price. The merchants voluntarily participate in this program, and the aggregate results are published on BizRate's Web site. Deja.com also surveys online consumers (tag line: "Deja.com before you buy"). Visit BizRate at www.bizrate.com and Deja at www.deja.com and complete this table:

For Discussion

1. Locate a copy of BizRate's point-of-sale survey on its site. What is the purpose of this survey?
2. Locate the follow-up survey. Define a research problem that an online company might have to warrant this particular survey research.
3. What incentive do merchants have to participate in BizRate's program?
4. Are BizRate and Deja competitors or complementary services? Explain.
5. Which site has a better privacy policy? Explain.
6. Which survey results do you find more reliable? Why?
7. Which survey results do you find more helpful? Why?

	BizRate	Deja
Collect data about merchants? (yes/no)		
Collect data about products? (yes/no)		
Use random sample? (yes/no)		
Who gets surveyed?		
Survey administered at time of purchase? (yes/no)		
What is the privacy policy?		

Savvy Sites

- The Yahoo Canada portal provides useful financial information on the performance of various Canadian stock exchanges and Canadian companies (ca.finance.yahoo.com). Many researchers use this site to find good secondary data.
- Ever wondered which search tool is best? The Search Engine Watch (www.searchenginewatch-com) provides ratings, features, and searching tips.
- NPD Group (www.npd.com) maintains panels of consumers around the world. Go to its site and learn how extensive these panels are.

Notes

1. Lara Mills, "As the beer world turns: Labatt Breweries and Molson," *Marketing On-Line,* 20/27 December 1999; Bernadette Johnson, "Labatt employs dry humour," *Strategy,* 8 May 2000:B4; David Menzies, "Molson muscle," *Marketing,* 21/28 August 1997:11; Louise Gagnon, "Aging Canadians are drinking less beer," *Marketing,* 21 July 1997:4; Kyle Stone, "Promotion commotion," *Report on Business,* December 1997:106; and Peter Boisseau, "The suds stud," *Canadian Business,* July 1997:41. Additional information on Molson and Labatt was found on their Web pages.
2. See Philip Kotler, *Kotler on Marketing,* New York: Free Press, 1999:73.
3. Joseph M. Winski, "Gentle rain turns into torrent," *Advertising Age,* 3 June 1991:34; David Shenk, *Data Smog: Surviving the Information Glut,* San Francisco: Harper San Francisco, 1997; Nancy Doucette, "Relieving information overload," *Rough Notes,* February 1998:26–7; and Diane Trommer, "Information overload—Study finds intranet users overwhelmed with data," *Electronic Buyers' News,* 20 April 1998:98.
4. Alice LaPlante, "Still drowning!" *Computer World,* 10 March 1997:69–70.
5. See Jeffrey Rotfeder and Jim Bartimo, "How software is making food sales a piece of cake," *Business Week,* 2 July 1990:54–5; and Terence P. Paré, "How to find out what they want," *Fortune* issue on "The tough new consumer," Autumn/Winter 1993: 39–41.
6. Material provided by Scott Hogan, High Performance Optical Component Solutions Group at Nortel Networks, Ottawa. The quote attributed to Frederick the Great, in John Nolan, *Confidential,* 1999. Also see Fuld & Co. (www.fuld.com), and the Society of Competitive Intelligence Professionals (www.scip.org).
7. See Suzie Amer, "Masters of intelligence," *Forbes,* 5 April 1999:18.
8. "Spy/Counterspy," *Context,* Summer 1998:20–1.
9. Danny Coggins, "Wired world: A way to eWatch what the competition is up to," *Marketing On-line,* 26 January 1998.
10. For more on marketing and competitive intelligence, see David B. Montgomery and Charles Weinberg, "Toward strategic intelligence systems," *Marketing Management,* Winter 1998:44–52; Morris C. Attaway Sr., "A review of issues related to gathering and assessing competitive intelligence," *American Business Review,* January 1998:25–35; and Larry Kanaher, *Competitive Intelligence: How to Gather, Analyze, and Use Information to Move Your Business to the Top,* Touchstone Books, 1998.
11. For a review of marketing models, see Gary Lilien, Philip Kotler, and Sridhar Moorthy, *Marketing Models,* Upper Saddle River, NJ: Prentice Hall, 1992; and Gary Lilien and Arvind Rangaswamy, *Marketing Engineering: Marketing Analysis and Planning in an Information Age,* Addison-Wesley Longman, 1998.
12. "Researching researchers," *Marketing Tools,* September 1996:35–6.
13. See Christel Beard and Betsy Wiesendanger, "The marketer's guide to online databases," *Sales & Marketing Management,* January 1993:36–41; and Susan Greco, "The online sleuth," *Inc.,* October 1996:88–9.
14. Justin Martin, "Ignore your customer," *Fortune,* 1 May 1995:121–6.
15. Justin Martin, "Ignore your customer":126.
16. Rebecca Piirto Heather, "Future focus groups," *American Demographics,* January 1994:6. For more on focus groups, see Thomas L. Greenbaum, "Focus group by video next trend of the '90s," *Marketing News,* 29 July 1996:4; Howard Furmansky, "Debunking the myths about focus groups," *Marketing News,* 23 June 1997:2; and Judith Langer, "15 myths of qualitative research: It's conventional, but is it wisdom?" *Marketing News,* 1 March 1999:13.
17. Sarah Schafer, "Communications: Getting a line on customers," *Inc. Technology,* 1996:102. Also see "Online or off target?" *American Demographics,* November 1998:20–1; Langer, "15 myths of qualitative research: It's conventional, but is it wisdom?":13–4; and James Heckman, "Turning the focus online," *Marketing News,* 28 February 2000:15.
18. Janet McFarland, "YOUtv captures customer feedback," *Globe and Mail,* 19 November 1996:B15.
19. Lesley Daw, "Customer polling takes to the Net," *Marketing,* 27 January 1997:3.
20. Gail El Baroudi, "Bank survey is a hit," *Globe and Mail,* 7 October 1997:C5.
21. Diane Crispell, "People talk, computers listen," *American Demographics,* October 1989:8; and Peter J. DePaulo and Rick Weitzer, "Interactive phones technology delivers survey data quickly," *Marketing News,* 6 June 1994:33–4.

22. For more on mechanical measures, see Michael J. McCarthy, "Mind probe," *Wall Street Journal,* 22 March 1991:B3.

23. For a discussion of the importance of the relationship between market researchers and research users, see Christine Moorman, Gerald Zaltman, and Rohit Deshpande, "Relationships between providers and users of market research: The dynamics of trust within and between organizations," *Journal of Marketing Research,* August 1992:314–28; Christine Moorman, Rohit Deshpande, and Gerald Zaltman, "Factors affecting trust in market research relationships," *Journal of Marketing,* January 1993:81–101; and Arlene Farber Sirkin, "Maximizing the client–researcher partnership," *Marketing News,* 13 September 1994:38.

24. David Bosworth, "Special report: Research: Canadian market research going global," *Strategy,* 1 September 1997:27.

25. Bosworth, "Special report: Research: Canadian market research going global":27.

26. Many of the examples in this section are found in Subhash C. Jain, *International Marketing Management,* 3rd ed., Boston: PWS-Kent Publishing Company, 1990:334–9. Also see Vern Terpstra and Ravi Sarathy, *International Marketing,* Chicago: The Dryden Press, 1991:208–13; and Jack Honomichl, "Research cultures are different in Mexico, Canada," *Marketing News,* 5 May 1993:12–3.

27. Subhash C. Jain, *International Marketing Management*:338.

28. Denis Bruce, "So what's the difference, eh?" *Marketing,* 26 September 1994:16–9.

29. David Chilton, "Canadians don't mind being surveyed," *Strategy,* 1 April 1996:5.

30. David Eggleston, "Canadians condemn DoubleClick profiling plans," *Strategy,* 13 March 2000:2.

31. Susan Vogt, "Online privacy laws all over the map," *Strategy,* 11 September 2000:12.

32. Cynthia Crossen, "Studies galore support products and positions, but are they reliable?" *Wall Street Journal,* 14 November 1991:A1,A9.

Company Case 4

Enterprise Rent-A-Car: Measuring Service Quality

Kevin Kirkman wheeled his shiny, blue BMW coupe into his driveway, parked the car, and stepped out to check his mailbox as he did every day when he arrived home. As he flipped through all the catalogues and credit-card offers, he noticed a letter from Enterprise Rent-A-Car.

The Wreck

Earlier that month, he'd been involved in a car accident: As he was driving to work one rainy morning, another car had been unable to stop on the slick pavement and had plowed into his car as he waited at a stoplight. Thankfully, neither Kevin nor the other driver had been hurt, but both cars had sustained considerable damage. In fact, Kevin had been unable to drive his car.

Kevin had used his cellular phone to call the police; and while waiting for the officers to arrive at the accident scene, he had called his auto insurance agent. The agent had assured Kevin that his policy included coverage to pay for a rental car while he was having his car repaired. He had advised Kevin to have the car towed to a nearby auto repair shop and had given him the telephone number for the Enterprise Rent-A-Car office that served his area. The agent had noted that his company recommended using Enterprise for replacement rentals and that Kevin's policy would cover up to $25 per day of the rental fee.

Once Kevin had checked his car in at the body shop and made the necessary arrangements, he had called the Enterprise office. Within 10 minutes, an Enterprise employee had arrived at the repair shop to pick him up. They had returned to the Enterprise office where Kevin had completed the paperwork to rent a Chevy Lumina. He had driven the rental car for 12 days before the repair shop had completed work on his car.

"Don't know why Enterprise would be writing me now," Kevin thought. "The insurance company paid the $25 per day, and I paid the extra because the Lumina cost a little more than that. Wonder what the problem could be?"

Tracking Customer Satisfaction

When Kevin opened the envelope, he discovered that it contained a survey to determine how satisfied he was with his rental experience. The survey was accompanied by a cover letter that thanked him for using Enterprise and asked him to complete the survey so that the company could continue to improve its service. The survey

FIGURE 4-3 Service quality survey

Please mark the box that best reflects your response to each question.

	Completely Satisfied	Somewhat Satisfied	Neither Satisfied Nor Dissatisfied	Somewhat Dissatisfied	Completely Dissatisfied
1. Overall, how satisfied were you with your recent car rental from Enterprise on January 1, 2000?	☐	☐	☐	☐	☐

2. What, if anything, could Enterprise have done better? *(Please be specific)* ____________________

____

____

3a. Did you experience any problems during the rental process? Yes ☐ No ☐

3b. If you mentioned any problems to Enterprise, did they resolve them to your satisfaction? Yes ☐ No ☐ Did not mention ☐

	Excellent	Good	Fair	Poor	N/A
4. If you personally called Enterprise to reserve a vehicle, how would you rate the telephone reservation process?	☐	☐	☐	☐	☐

	Both at start and end of rental	Just at start of rental	Just at end of rental	Neither time
5. Did you go to the Enterprise office	☐	☐	☐	☐
6. Did an Enterprise employee give you a ride to help with your transportation needs	☐	☐	☐	☐

7. After you arrived at the Enterprise office, how long did it take you to:	Less than 5 minutes	5–10 minutes	11–15 minutes	16–20 minutes	21–30 minutes	More than 30 minutes	N/A
♦ pick up your rental car?	☐	☐	☐	☐	☐	☐	☐
♦ return your rental car?	☐	☐	☐	☐	☐	☐	☐

8. How would you rate the ...	Excellent	Good	Fair	Poor	N/A
♦ timeliness with which you were either picked up at the start of the rental or dropped off afterwards?	☐	☐	☐	☐	☐
♦ timeliness with which the rental car was either brought to your location and left with you or picked up from your location afterwards?	☐	☐	☐	☐	☐
♦ Enterprise employee who handled your paperwork ...					
♦ at the START of the rental?	☐	☐	☐	☐	☐
♦ at the END of the rental?	☐	☐	☐	☐	☐
♦ mechanical condition of the car?	☐	☐	☐	☐	☐
♦ cleanliness of the car interior/exterior?	☐	☐	☐	☐	☐

	Yes	No	N/A
9. If you asked for a specific type or size of vehicle, was Enterprise able to meet your needs?	☐	☐	☐

	Car repairs due to accident	All other car repairs/ maintenance	Car was stolen	Business	Leisure/ vacation	Some other reason
10. For what reason did you rent this car?	☐	☐	☐	☐	☐	☐

	Definitely will call	Probably will call	Might or might not call	Probably will not call	Definitely will not call
11. The next time you need to pick up a rental car in the city or area in which you live, how likely are you to call Enterprise?	☐	☐	☐	☐	☐

	Once—this was first time	2 times	3–5 times	6–10 times	11 or more times
12. Approximately how many times in total have you rented from Enterprise (including this rental)?	☐	☐	☐	☐	☐

	0 times	1 time	2 times	3–5 times	6–10 times	11 or more times
13. Considering <u>all rental companies</u>, approximately how many times <u>within the past year</u> have you rented a car in the city or area in which you live (including this rental)?	☐	☐	☐	☐	☐	☐

itself was just one page with 13 questions (see Figure 4-3).

Enterprise executives believe that the company has become the largest car rental company in North America (in terms of revenue, number of cars in service, and number of rental locations) because of its laser-like focus on customer satisfaction, and because of its concentration on serving the home-city replacement market. Enterprise aims to serve customers like Kevin who are involved in car accidents and who suddenly find themselves without a car. While the better-known companies such as Hertz and Avis battled for business in the cut-throat airport market, Enterprise quietly built its business by cultivating insurance agents and body-shop managers as referral agents, so that when one of their clients or customers needed a replacement vehicle, the agents would recommend Enterprise. Although such replacement rentals account for about 80 percent of Enterprise's business, the company also serves the discretionary market (leisure/vacation rentals) and business market (renting cars to businesses for their short-term needs).

Throughout its history, Enterprise has followed the advice of its founder, Jack Taylor, who believed that if the company took care of its customers first and its employees second, profits would follow. As a result, the company tracks customer satisfaction carefully.

About one in 20 customers receive a letter like Kevin's. The letters are mailed to customers selected at random about seven days following completion of a rental. On average, about 30 percent of the surveyed customers will return the completed survey in the enclosed postage-paid envelope. They mail the surveys to an outside service firm, which compiles the results and provides the company with monthly reports that employees in the branches can use to review their performance.

Continuous Improvement

Enterprise has been using the survey form for several years. However, its managers wonder how they could improve the survey. Should the survey ask additional questions? How could the company improve the response rate? Is the mail questionnaire the best way to collect customer satisfaction data? Are there any sampling issues or response biases in its system?

Kevin glanced through his living-room window at his BMW sitting in the driveway. "That's amazing," he thought. "You could never tell it had been in a wreck. The repair shop did a great job, and I'm satisfied with Enterprise also. Guess I should complete this survey to let the company know."

Questions

1. Analyze Enterprise's service quality survey. What information is it trying to gather? What are its research objectives?
2. What decisions has Enterprise made with regard to primary data collection—research approach, contact methods, sampling plan, and research instruments?
3. In addition to or instead of the mail survey, how else could Enterprise gather information about its customers (besides satisfaction) and competitors?
4. What recommendations would you make to Enterprise about its survey process and data-collection strategy?

Source: Officials at Enterprise Rent-A-Car contributed to and supported development of this case.

video case 4

Qualitative Research: Burrowing Deeply into the Minds of Customers

Much of the material in Chapter 4 centres on a discussion of quantitative research methods. Quantitative research uses large representative samples, asks structured questions and codes responses into numerical form that can be statistically analyzed. However, many researchers today are beginning to realize the value of *qualitative research* (research that relies on information collected from small samples that cannot be readily quantified). The data must be interpreted by the research analyst. Some research firms, like ABM Research Ltd. of Toronto, do more qualitative than quantitative studies. At ABM, qualitative work comprises 70 percent of the business.

Whether researchers use quantitative or qualitative methods depends on their theoretical orientation. Some researchers are grounded in *cognitive theory*, which, stated simply, suggests that people in general say *what they mean* and *mean what they say*. Thus, researchers who adhere to this theoretical framework use surveys or ask direct verbal questions and apply literal interpretations to the responses. Others believe that *conative theory* better explains humans' abilities to understand their own actions. This theory is based on the premise that individuals cannot *fully* explain themselves or the meanings of their actions. Therefore, to gain an understanding of what motivates purchase decisions or brand associations, researchers use projective techniques and creative research approaches to delve beyond the spoken (or written) word. They might ask respondents to describe a brand as a person, to do word association tasks, make projective drawings, or develop collages around a specific theme.

Qualitative and quantitative research approaches are often seen as complementary. Qualitative research may be conducted in the early stages of a project to gain a deep understanding of what motivates some people's behaviour. However, if the marketer wants to ensure that the findings gleaned from the qualitative studies are generalizable to larger populations she will also do quantitative research.

Focus group interviews are one form of qualitative research. Typically, a focus group moderator will spend two or three hours talking to 8 to 12 participants, while other researchers and clients watch from behind a two-way mirror. As the group members interact, rich information can be elicited since each member can build on the thoughts of other participants. Researchers watching the group can also learn about the emotional components of issues by observing participants' body language.

Even though focus groups are widely used, they aren't without their challenges. Handled badly, focus groups can lead a marketer to completely misread consumer attitudes with disastrous results. Professor Lindsay Meredith of Simon Fraser University compares focus groups to chainsaws. "A focus group is a tremendous help if you know what you're doing with it. If you don't, you're going to lose a leg," says Meredith.

One common problem with focus group research is that the group may not be representative of the target market. That's what happened to Enbridge Home Services, formerly Consumers Gas, a company that used focus group research to help it develop a television ad for gas fireplaces. The focus group that was used to test the ad (which showed two middle-aged people in a passionate embrace in front of a store's fireplace display) was comprised of young people who found the concept amusing. But when the ad was broadcast, complaints poured in from older consumers. Says Steve Letwin, President of Enbridge Home Services, "The focus groups that we used probably didn't get that kind of sample in there."

Because of this and other challenges, the people who run focus groups today say that they are being forced to come up with new ways to extract information from consumers. Behaviour is becoming much tougher to understand using traditional focus group methods. As Alison Findlay of In-Sync Research in Toronto notes, consumers "are often quite unconscious of how they feel, [and] they are unconscious about why they do the things they do."

To help overcome this challenge, research companies are turning to other qualitative methods to better help them understand consumers. David Rink, Vice President of Vancouver's Marktrend Research, experiments with games to draw out attitudes people may not know they have. In a recent project for Happy Planet, an organic juice company, Rink had focus group participants go shopping, after giving them specific themes for the products they were to buy. Participants were also asked to draw pictures of what they imagined typical Happy Planet juice buyers would look like.

Other firms, like In-Sync Research, are experimenting with a technique that sounds like something from the Monty Python comedy. They 'plant' a person in the group to argue with other participants so researchers can better understand how people see the relative merits of a product.

Still other research agencies are hiring cultural anthropologists who use ethnographic methods to gain insight into human behaviour. They observe behaviours as they happen, often participating in activities of interest in natural settings. Ethnography can help marketers understand how products and brands fit into consumer lifestyles. It can show how consumers actually use products, the triggers that prompt product or brand usage or those that act as barriers to usage. Ethnography can help researchers better understand the emotions, beliefs and values consumers attach to products, brands and experiences as well as the language used by consumers to talk about their products, brands and experiences.

If researchers don't have the time or resources to embed themselves deeply into the consumer's culture, they may use other more time efficient techniques. For example, David Rink, of Marktrend, needed to better understand snowboarders. He sent a group of them out with disposable cameras, asking them to document their lives. The snowboarders returned with predictable pictures of parties and good times, but also surprising signals that snowboarders have mainstream attitudes about success. Mixed in with the pictures of beer and wild times were images of expensive sports cars and stereo equipment. The client, the manufacturer of Option snowboards, designed a new ad campaign based on the research. As you can see, researchers are being highly creative in the methods they use to see into the minds of consumers.

Questions

1. Why are qualitative methods becoming more popular with market researchers?
2. Describe some of the limitations of focus group interviews.
3. What are qualitative researchers doing to overcome these challenges?
4. Why are many marketing researchers focusing less on the question: "Which is the most appropriate research methodology?" and starting to ask instead, "Which is the most appropriate combination of research methods?"

Source: This case was written by Peggy Cunningham and is based on "Focus Groups," *Venture* (September 5, 2000) and material supplied by Stephanie Zablocki, ABM Research Ltd., Toronto. For more information on qualitative research and focus group interviews, also see Liza Finlay, "Seeing Clearly: You get the most from market research when you know what you're looking for: Three case studies of how companies honed their marketing strategies with tightly focused research," *Marketing On-Line,* May 22, 2000; Marion Plunkett, "Checking in early with consumers: Upfront qualitative research provides a strong foundation for building creative ideas," *Marketing On-Line,* February 22, 1999; Lesley Young, "Focus group results rule changes," *Marketing On-Line,* March 5, 2001.

P A R T 1 **2** 3 4

Developing Marketing Opportunities and Strategies

Concept Connections

When you finish this chapter, you should be able to

1. Define the consumer market and construct a simple model of consumer buyer behaviour.
2. Name the four major factors that influence consumer buyer behaviour.
3. List and understand the stages in the buyer decision process.
4. Describe the adoption and diffusion process for new products.

chapter 5

Consumer Markets and Consumer Buyer Behaviour

Few brands engender such intense loyalty as that found in the hearts of Harley-Davidson owners. "The Harley audience is granitelike" in its devotion, laments the vice-president of sales for competitor Yamaha. As one quote on the Harley Web site notes, "You don't see people tattooing Yamaha on their bodies." Each year, in early March, more than 400 000 Harley bikers rumble through the streets of Daytona Beach, Florida, to attend Harley-Davidson's Bike Week celebration. Bikers from across North America lounge on their low-slung Harleys, swap biker tales, and sport T-shirts proclaiming "I'd rather push a Harley than drive a Honda."

Riding such intense emotions, Harley-Davidson has rumbled its way to the top of the fast-growing heavyweight motorcycle market. Both the segment and Harley's sales are growing rapidly. In fact, for several consecutive years, sales have far outstripped supply, with customer waiting lists of up to three years for popular models and street prices running well above suggested list prices. "We've seen people buy a new Harley and then sell it in the parking lot for $4000 to $5000 more," says one dealer.

Harley-Davidson's marketers spend a great deal of time thinking about customers and their buying behaviour. They want to know who their customers are, what they think and how they feel, and why they buy a Harley rather than a Yamaha, or a Suzuki, or a big Honda American Classic. Why are Harley buyers so fiercely loyal? These are difficult questions—even Harley owners themselves don't know exactly what motivates their buying. But Harley management puts top priority on understanding customers and what makes them tick.

Who rides a Harley? You might be surprised. It's no longer the Hell's Angels crowd—the burly, black-leather-jacketed rebels and "biker chicks" that once composed Harley's core clientele. New motorcycles are attracting a new breed of riders—older, more affluent, and better educated. Harley now appeals more to "rubbies" (rich urban bikers) than to rebels. While the average Harley customer is a 43-year-old husband with a median household income of $94 000, women are an increasingly important target market. While they currently account for only 15 percent of Harley-Davidson's market, the number of female riders is growing fast.

Female riders are in their thirties and from moderate- to high-income groups. To reach this growing audience, the Canadian division of Harley-Davidson recently commissioned female-specific advertising that built on the themes of independence, strength, and freedom, using the headline, "You never took a back seat before." The ads feature five professional Canadian women who own Harleys, including a pilot, a computer training specialist, and a bank manager. The ads ran in *Chatelaine* and *Modern Woman* magazines.[1]

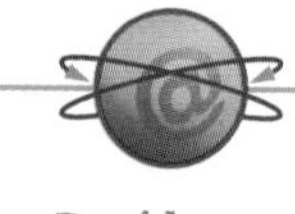

Harley-Davidson
www.harley-davidson.com/

Harley-Davidson makes good bikes, and, to keep up with its shifting market, the company has upgraded its showrooms and sales approaches. But Harley customers are buying a lot more than just a quality bike and a smooth sales pitch. To gain a better understanding of customers' deeper motivations, Harley-Davidson conducted focus groups in which it invited bikers to make cut-and-paste collages of pictures that expressed their feelings about Harley-Davidsons. (Can't you just see a bunch of hard-core bikers doing this!) The company then mailed out 16 000 surveys containing a typical battery of psychological, sociological, and demographic questions, as well as subjective questions such as: "Is Harley more typified by a brown bear or a lion?" The research revealed seven core customer types: adventure-loving traditionalists; sensitive pragmatists; stylish status seekers; laid-back campers; classy capitalists; cool-headed loners; and cocky misfits. However, all owners appreciated their Harleys for the same basic reasons. "It didn't matter if you were the guy who swept the floors of the factory or if you were the CEO at that factory, the attraction to Harley was very similar," explains a Harley executive. "Independence, freedom, and power were the universal Harley appeals."

These studies confirm that Harley customers are doing more than just buying motorcycles. They're making a lifestyle statement and displaying an attitude. As one analyst suggests: "Never mind that [you're] a dentist or an accountant. You [feel] wicked astride all that power." Your Harley renews your spirits and announces your independence. The classic look, the throaty sound, the very idea of a Harley—all contribute to its mystique. Owning this "North American legend" makes you a part of something bigger—a member of the Harley family. The fact that you have to wait to get a Harley makes it all that much more satisfying to have one. In fact, the company deliberately restricts its output. "Our goal is to eventually run production at a level that's always one motorcycle short of demand," says Harley-Davidson's chief executive.

Thus, understanding buyers is an essential but difficult task for Harley-Davidson—buyers are moved by a complex set of deep and subtle emotions. Buyer behaviour springs from deeply held values and attitudes, from buyers' views of the world and their place in it, from what they think of themselves and what they think of others, from common sense, and from whimsy and impulse.

Such strong emotions and motivations are captured in a recent Harley-Davidson advertisement. It shows a close-up of an arm, the biceps adorned with a Harley-Davidson tattoo. The headline asks, "When was the last time you felt this strongly about anything?" The ad copy outlines the problem and suggests a solution:

> Wake up in the morning and life picks up where it left off. You do what has to be done. Use what it takes to get there. And what once seemed exciting has now become part of the numbing routine. It all begins to feel the same. Except when you've got a Harley-Davidson. Something strikes a nerve. The heartfelt thunder rises up, refusing to become part of the background. Suddenly things are different. Clearer. More real. As they should have been all along. The feeling is personal. For some, owning a Harley is a statement of individuality. To the uninitiated, a Harley-Davidson motorcycle is associated with a certain look, a certain sound. Anyone who owns one will tell you it's much more than that. Riding a Harley changes you from within. The effect is permanent. Maybe it's time you started feeling this strongly. Things are different on a Harley.[2]

The Harley-Davidson example shows that many factors affect consumer buying behaviour. Buying behaviour is never simple, yet understanding it is the essential task of marketing management.

Consumer buying behaviour
The buying behaviour of final consumers—individuals and households who buy goods and services for personal consumption.

Consumer market
All the individuals and households who buy or acquire goods and services for personal consumption.

This chapter explores the dynamics of consumer behaviour and the consumer market. **Consumer buying behaviour** refers to the buying behaviour of final consumers—individuals and households who buy goods and services for personal consumption. All of these final consumers together form the **consumer market.** The Canadian consumer market consists of about 29 million people who consume many billions of dollars worth of goods and services each year, making it one of the most attractive consumer markets in the world. The world consumer market consists of more than six billion people; at present growth rates, the world population will reach eight billion people by 2025.[3]

Consumers around the world vary tremendously in age, income, education level, and tastes. They also buy an incredible variety of goods and services. How these diverse consumers connect with each other and with other elements of the world around them has an impact on their choices among various products, services, and companies. Here we examine the fascinating array of factors that affect consumer behaviour.

Model of Consumer Behaviour

Consumers make many buying decisions every day. Most large companies research consumer buying decisions in great detail to answer questions about what consumers buy, where they buy, how and how much they buy, when they buy, and why they buy. Marketers can study actual consumer purchases to find out the what, where, and how much; but learning about the why of consumer buying behaviour is not so easy—the answers are often locked deep in the consumer's head.

The central question for marketers is: How do consumers respond to various marketing efforts the company might use? The company that really understands how consumers will respond to different product features, prices, and advertising appeals has a great advantage over its competitors. The starting point is the stimulus–response model of buyer behaviour shown in Figure 5-1. This figure shows that marketing and other stimuli enter the consumer's "black box" and produce certain responses. Marketers must determine what is in the buyer's black box.[4]

Marketing stimuli consist of the four Ps: product, price, place, and promotion. Other stimuli include major forces and events in the buyer's environment: economic, technological, political, and cultural. All of these inputs enter the buyer's black box, where they are turned into a set of observable buyer responses: product choice, brand choice, dealer choice, purchase timing, and purchase amount.

The marketer wants to understand how the stimuli are changed into responses inside the consumer's black box, which has two parts. First, buyers' characteristics influence how they perceive and react to the stimuli. Second, the buyers' decision processes affect their behaviour. This chapter looks first at buyer characteristics as they affect buying behaviour, and then discusses the buyer decision process.

FIGURE 5-1 Model of buyer behaviour

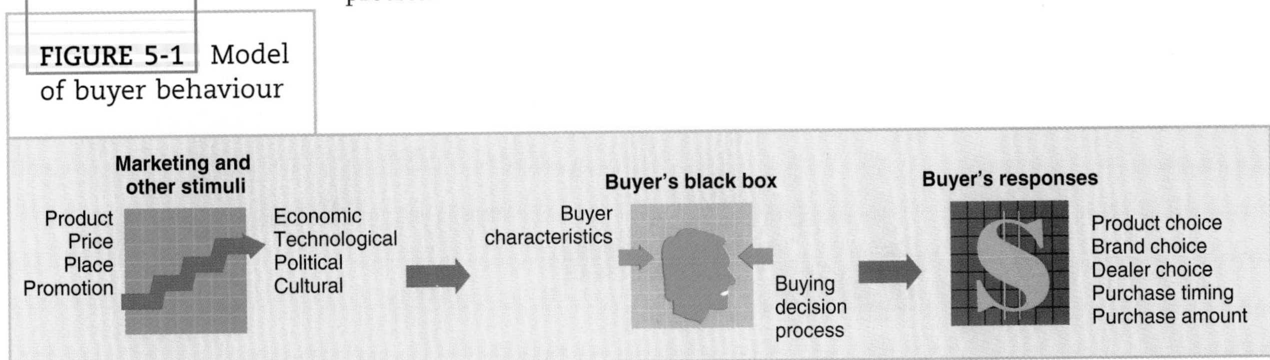

Characteristics Affecting Consumer Behaviour

Consumer purchases are influenced strongly by cultural, social, personal, and psychological characteristics, shown in Figure 5-2. For the most part, marketers cannot control such factors, but they must take them into account. To help you understand these concepts, we apply them to the case of a hypothetical consumer—Jennifer Wong, a 26-year-old brand manager working for a multinational packaged-goods company in Toronto. Jennifer was born in Vancouver, but her grandparents came from Hong Kong. She's been in a relationship for two years, but isn't married. She has decided that she wants to buy a vehicle but isn't sure she can afford a car. She rode a motor scooter while attending university and is now considering buying a motorcycle—maybe even a Harley.

Cultural Factors

Cultural factors exert the broadest and deepest influence on consumer behaviour. The marketer needs to understand the role played by the buyer's *culture, subculture,* and *social class.*

Culture

Culture
The set of basic values, perceptions, wants, and behaviours learned by a member of society from family and other important institutions.

Culture is the most basic determinant of a person's wants and behaviour. Human behaviour is largely learned. Growing up in a society, a child learns basic values, perceptions, wants, and behaviours from the family and other important institutions. The 1999 and 2000 *Maclean's* annual polls of Canadian values and attitudes revealed that over 90 percent of Canadians believe that our country has a distinct culture and values. Almost 80 percent of Canadians believe that our identity is based on a strong sense of our own history, rather than simply a desire not to be Americans. The majority of Canadians noted that our flag, the achievements of prominent Canadians such as artists and scientists, our climate and geography, our social safety net, our international role, and our multicultural and multiracial make-up are symbols of our uniqueness. Canadians want the government to take a tough stand on law and order and see rebuilding our social institutions as a government priority. They strongly favoured investments in the CBC and our health care and education systems over tax cuts in the 2000 poll. Furthermore, we are becoming an increasingly confident and optimistic people who no longer see ourselves as boring or sexually repressed.[5] Another recent study outlined some other basic values shared by Canadians:

FIGURE 5-2 Factors influencing consumer behaviour

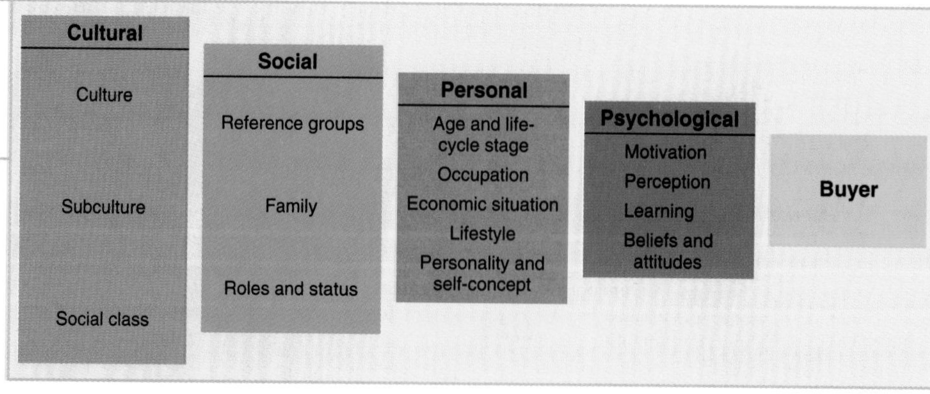

> Canada is a country that believes in freedom, dignity, respect, equality and fair treatment, and opportunity to participate. It is a country that cares for the disadvantaged at home and elsewhere, a country that prefers peaceful solutions to disputes. Canada is a country that, for all its diversity, has shared values.[6]

Canadians still see government as the leader in the fight to protect unique Canadian values from the inroads of American influence. There is a long tradition behind this belief. In 1877, Sir Wilfrid Laurier said that the only way to defend one's ideas and principles was to make them known. The federal government still follows this agenda. The Department of Foreign Affairs and International Trade (DFAIT) sees a large part of its role as actively promoting and defending, on the international scene, the interests and values that Canadians hold dear. It lists these core values as our belief in respect for human rights, in democracy as a means of promoting stability and prosperity, in an international system ruled by law not power, in sustainable development, and in culture and education as routes to success.[7]

Respect for diversity has also long been part of our heritage. Canada had two founding nations. The most recent census data available (1996) show that people reporting English origins (anglophones) account for nearly 60 percent of Canada's population. However, the proportion of the population whose mother tongue was French (francophones) declined gradually between 1971 and 1996 to less than 24 percent. Nonetheless, English-French bilingualism has gained ground across the country. Over four million Canadians report that they can speak both English and French. The proportion of francophones who are bilingual is almost five times that of anglophones. Not surprisingly, Quebec has the largest number of bilingual Canadians (35 percent). New Brunswick is the second most bilingual province.[8]

Canada is becoming more multicultural and multilingual, largely as a result of increased immigration. In 1996, there were 4.7 million people who reported a mother tongue other than English or French, a 15.1 percent increase from 1991: This increase was two and a half times faster than the overall growth rate of the Canadian population (5.7 percent). Canadian advertisers have been quick to recognize this fact. In its award winning ad "The Rant," Molson's Joe yells his belief in "diversity, not assimilation!" touching a theme close to the fabric of our national identity.

Cultural values are constantly shifting. The traditional self-image of Canada as a kinder country, less individualistic, less obsessed with wealth, believing in government as a force for good, remains; but these beliefs are no longer unchallenged. Canada still sees itself as the guardian of fairness, and people remain intolerant of frantic consumerism and overly hectic lifestyles. But the 1999 annual *Maclean's* poll of Canadians' values noted that many issues that had once split the country were no longer news. For example, in the 1980s, debate about the desirability of the Free Trade Agreement with the United States threatened to polarize the country, but today it is merely a blip on our emotional radar screen. In fact, while 23 percent of Canadians still think that free trade is responsible for making us more like Americans, another 34 percent finger the Internet. Still others attribute the inroads made by American values as a result of the pervasiveness of American media (48 percent), and US investment in our economy (35 percent).[9]

Canadians expect all their institutions, including business, to honour the Canadian core values. Thus, marketers are expected to treat customers fairly and equally. They are to market products safely and honestly. Marketers who ignore the differences between Canada's regions do so at their peril. In addressing these differences, however, marketers are expected to be inclusive in their marketing policies and not to unfairly discriminate across segments. Marketers are required to reflect the diversity of Canadian society in their advertising. Finally, they are expected to deal with all groups of Canadians respectfully and not to promote negative stereotypes.

Every group or society has a culture, and cultural influences on buying behaviour may vary greatly between countries. Failure to adjust to these differences can result in ineffective marketing or embarrassing mistakes. For example, business representatives of a US community seeking more business from Taiwan discovered this the hard way. They arrived in Taiwan bearing gifts of green baseball caps. The visitors later learned that, according to Taiwan culture, a man wears green to signify that his wife has been unfaithful. The head of the community delegation later noted: "I don't know whatever happened to those green hats, but the trip gave us an understanding of the extreme differences in our cultures."[10] International marketers must understand the culture in each international market and adapt their marketing strategies accordingly.

Marketers are always trying to identify *cultural shifts* to discover new products that might be wanted. For example, the cultural shift toward greater concern about health and fitness has created a huge industry for exercise equipment and clothing, lower-fat and more natural foods, and health and fitness services. And the increased desire for leisure time has resulted in more demand for convenience products and services, such as microwave ovens, fast food, and catalogue shopping.

Subculture

Subculture
A group of people with shared value systems based on common life experiences and situations.

Each culture contains smaller **subcultures**, or groups of people with shared value systems based on common life experiences and situations. Subcultures include nationalities, religions, racial groups, and geographic regions. Many subcultures make up important market segments, and marketers often design products and marketing programs tailored to their needs. These are examples of three such important subculture groups:

Native Canadians. Native Canadians are making their voices heard both in the political arena and in the marketplace. There are 416 000 status Indians in Canada. When Métis, non-status natives, and Inuit are added to this group, the number swells to 712 000. Not only do these Native Canadians have distinct cultures which influence their values and purchasing behaviour, but they also have profoundly influenced the rest of Canada through their art, love of nature, and concern for the environment. Banks have been particularly responsive to the unique needs of Aboriginal Canadians.[11] Scotiabank, for example, has maintained its relationship with First Nations people through its three on-reserve branches and 24 Aboriginal banking centres. It also uses a lot of grassroots marketing and public relations efforts, including its sponsorship of the Aboriginal Achievement Awards and ten annual scholarships of $2500 for young Aboriginal entrepreneurs. CIBC found that cultural symbols can better link a firm with its native customers. On its Web site at www.cibc.com/aboriginal, CIBC features a medicine wheel to symbolize CIBC's holistic and integrated approach to achieving "balance and harmony in (its) relationship with Aboriginal people." The symbol was selected as an indication of CIBC's respect for the cultural integrity and diversity of Aboriginal people in Canada.

Canada's ethnic consumers. Consumers from ethnic groups represent some of the fastest-growing markets in Canada. In Toronto, for example, close to 42 percent of the population consists of visible minorities, and its four major ethnic population groups—Chinese, Italian, Portuguese, and South Asian—account for $13 billion in consumer spending. Marketing to ethnic communities isn't just an issue for marketers working in Vancouver, Toronto, and Montreal. Even smaller centres, such as Ottawa, Edmonton, and Calgary, have growing ethnic populations. The Canadian Advertising Foundation projected that visible minorities will have as much as $300 billion in purchasing power nationwide by the year 2001.[12]

CIBC uses the symbol of the medicine wheel on its Web site to show its respect for the cultural integrity and diversity of Aboriginal people in Canada.

Specialized media have been springing up across Canada to serve these communities. Besides newspapers targeting these communities, there is a growing number of local multi-ethnic broadcasters, like Toronto-based CFMT International. Such stations don't just attract ads from small local businesses; a number of national clients such as Royal Bank of Canada, mbanx, Canadian Tire, and General Motors of Canada are coming on board. There are also several national television services aimed at specific cultural groups. Fairchild Television targets Chinese-Canadians, Telelatino Network focuses on Italians and Latin Americans, and the Asian Television Network seeks to serve South Asians. Black Entertainment Television is another national specialty channel in addition to Vision TV, which targets a number of cultural and faith groups. Viewers receive these services via cable or direct-to-home satellite TV.[13]

Some marketers have seen the wisdom of targeting religious communities as well as visible minorities. For example, 351 705 people across Canada in 2000 identified themselves as being of Jewish ethnic origin. Hallmark Canada saw a growing opportunity to serve this market. While it has offered cards for Jewish holidays for many years, it now also offers such products as Star of David cookie cutters, wooden dreidel toys, themed wrapping paper, and paper party items sub-branded under its Tree of Life brand to give them a unique identity. Ontario's LCBO also decided to improve its service to the Jewish community by expanding its wine selection. It increased the range of kosher products on its shelves from 15 to over 80. Kosher means that the foods and other products adhere to Jewish dietary laws and are processed to meet the requirements of a rabbi or a rabbinical organization. While the LCBO has carried some kosher wines for many years, availability was often limited to key Jewish holidays such as Passover and

NEW
KOSHER
WINES
Traditionally sweet or dry and contemporary: check out the options this Passover.

Ontario's liquor board is targeting the Jewish community with ads in its in-store magazine, *Food & Drink.*

Hanukkah. Today, LCBO outlets feature "kosher kiosks," or outlets within LCBO stores located in Toronto, Hamilton, Kingston, London, Peterborough, Windsor, Kitchener-Waterloo, and Ottawa.[14]

Marketers must track evolving trends in various ethnic communities. Consider Chinese-Canadians, for example. In the past, most members of this ethnic group came from Hong Kong. Today they are arriving from Taiwan and mainland China. Why should marketers be concerned where Chinese immigrants come from? Primarily for language reasons. While the Chinese who come from Hong Kong speak Cantonese, people from Taiwan and mainland China often speak Mandarin. Marketers must also be aware of the differences between new immigrants and those who are "integrated immigrants"—people who are second-, third-, fourth-, fifth-, and even sixth-generation Chinese-Canadians. Although marketing information often must be translated into the language of new immigrants, integrated immigrants communicate mainly in English. While Chinese-Canadians are influenced by many of the values of their adopted country, they may also share some values rooted in their ethnic history. Since they come from families who have experienced great political and social turmoil, Chinese-Canadians cling to "life-raft" values: trust family, work hard, be thrifty, save, and have liquid and tangible goods. Air Canada used its knowledge of these values in a campaign that linked Chinese-Canadians' need for security and the desire to keep connected to their homeland with Air Canada's services.[15]

Many ethnic groups believe that they have been neglected or misrepresented by marketers. A Canadian Advertising Foundation study revealed that 80 percent of people belonging to visible minorities believed that advertising has been targeted almost exclusively at "white" people. Yet 46 percent of this group stated that they would be more likely to buy a product if its advertising featured models from visible minority populations.

Let's consider our hypothetical consumer. How will Jennifer Wong's cultural background influence her decision about whether to buy a motorcycle? Jennifer's parents certainly won't approve of her choice. Tied strongly to the values of thrift and conservatism, they believe that she should continue taking the subway instead of purchasing a vehicle. However, Jennifer identifies with her Canadian friends and colleagues as much as she does with her family. She views herself as a modern woman in a society that accepts women in a wide range of roles, both conventional and unconventional. She has female friends who play hockey and rugby. And women riding motorcycles are becoming a more common sight in Toronto.

Internet users. People who "surf the Net" also have a culture that marketers ignore at their peril. Internet users have their own language, norms, values, and etiquette or "netiquette." One recent *Globe and Mail* headline claimed, "Internet has transformed life!"[16] While this may be hyperbole, it has certainly revolutionized the way we shop, communicate, and learn. One 16-year-old Ottawa teenager, for example, claimed, "I spend a lot of time on the computer talking to people. My life sort of revolves around it."

About 56 percent of Canadians used the Internet between November 1999 and January 2000, compared to 59 percent of Americans. The first Canadian Internet audience information and usage data from Nielsen/NetRatings indicate that, in one month, Canadian Web surfers spent nearly 30 more minutes online than

Air Canada linked itself to the Chinese community merging two symbols: Canadian maple leaves (the airline's brand symbol) and Chinese embroidery.

US Internet users, averaging more sessions and page views. Table 5-1 outlines the findings from the Nielsen study.[17]

Canada is number two in the world in terms of the proliferation of home computers and Internet access, trailing the US. It is not surprising that marketers are working hard to target Canadian Internet users. They must remember, however, that hard-sell marketing is definitely unacceptable on the Web, and marketers who violate this norm may be "flamed" or "mail bombed" by irate Web users.

Today's Internet users are not the stereotypical 14-year-old computer nerd, pounding away on a computer in the basement. One reason that retailers are so interested in using the Internet as a marketing channel is the compelling demographic characteristics of Internet users. First, they are above-average spenders. Internet users tend to be highly educated people in white-collar jobs who earn high incomes. In Canada, the largest group of Internet users (29 percent) fall in the 35 to 44 age group. People 25 to 35 years of age make up the next largest group (27 percent), followed by the youth market, those 18 to 24, who represent 21 percent of the Internet population This market is highly attractive, given its technological sophistication and willingness to make Internet purchases. People aged 45 to 54 make up 15 percent of Internet users, while those over 55 constitute only eight percent of the Internet usage group.

Historically, male Internet users have outnumbered female Internet users. Recent surveys, however, have shown that users are now 60 percent men and 40 percent women. As consumer acceptance of the Internet grows, it is expected that the Internet population will more closely resemble that of the general public.[18]

Unlike any group of consumers before them, Internet users are powerful and in control. The consumer is the one who chooses to access a Web site, and mar-

TABLE 5-1 Activity for the Average Internet User at Home in Canada versus the US in May 2000

	Canada	United States
Number of sessions per month	20	18
Number of unique sites visited	18	10
Page views per month	726	662
Page views per surfing session	37	36
Time spent per month	9:34:60	9:05:24
Time spent during surfing session	0:29:16	0:29:50
Duration of a page viewed	0:00:47	0:00:50
Average click rate for top banners	0.37	0.49
Active Internet universe (had access and actually surfed)	8.1 million	82.7 million
Current Internet universe estimate (had access but did not necessarily go online)	13.1 million	134.2 million

keters must adjust to the idea that the Internet is a means of two-way communication between a customer and a vendor, not the one-way street that media advertising represents. In other words, "They're not just listening to what the corporation wants to tell them, they're choosing the information that appeals to them." And Internet users value information.

Several articles have claimed that the Internet hasn't lived up to its promise as a marketing tool. Those who make this claim base their argument on the fact that few users actually make purchases over the Internet (even though Canadians are expected to spend $21 million for online purchases annually). However, before marketers deny the value of the Internet, they must understand how and why people use the technology. Most people who use the Internet do so for communication purposes, primarily e-mail. Another third use it for information and reference. Ten percent use it to access online magazines.[19] The fact that many Internet users use the technology as a source of information is important for marketers, especially those selling goods and services that require extensive information searches. Auto or real estate purchases fall into this category. Purchasers of mutual funds are renowned "information hounds," who conduct extensive comparisons among competing products.

While many consumers use the Internet in the information search stage of the purchase process, few use it in the final step in the transaction process for several reasons. People are worried about providing their credit card numbers when making an Internet purchase. Since consumers can't see or touch a product offered for sale over the Internet, they fear they will have little recourse if the product they order isn't the right one, isn't delivered, or arrives broken. Consumers also have privacy concerns: They are concerned that the information they provide when making a purchase or requesting information may be sold or given to another organization without their permission. The Internet allows people to purchase from companies located anywhere in the world; however, consumers may not know anything about these companies. Thus, corporate credibility and reputation are especially important for people using the Internet. The Canadian Institute of Chartered Accountants (CICA) worked jointly with the American Institute of Certified Public Accountants (AICPA) to develop criteria and a Webtrust logo that would be placed on the sites of reliable companies. The seal provides assurance for consumers and businesses that vendors' Web sites meet high standards of business practice with regard to disclosure of consumer information, transaction integrity, and information protection. You can find more information about this program on the CICA Web site (www.cica.ca/cica/cicawebsite.nsf/public/SPWTe_generalfaqs).[20]

How does being part of the Internet generation affect Jennifer Wong and her purchase decision? Jennifer is highly computer literate. She uses a computer daily at

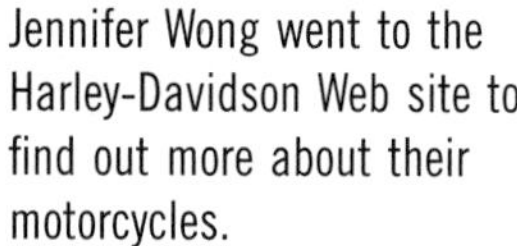

Jennifer Wong went to the Harley-Davidson Web site to find out more about their motorcycles.

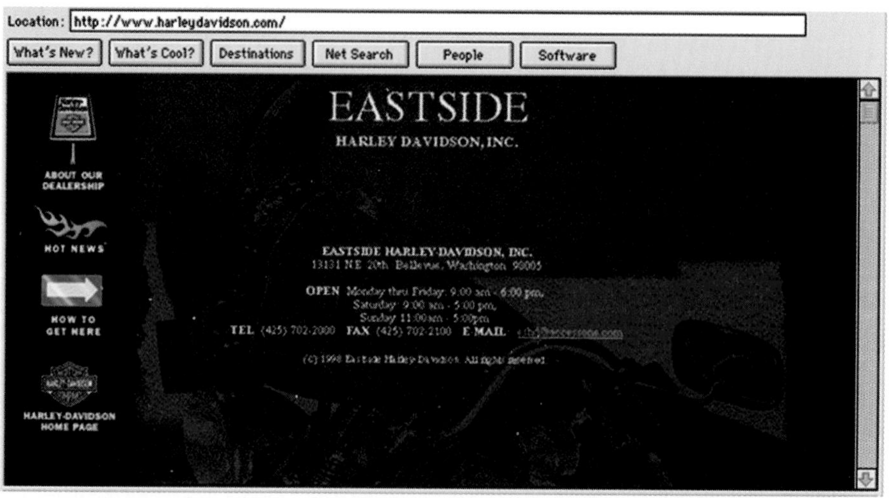

work, carries a laptop when attending meetings outside Toronto, and has a computer in her apartment. One of the first things she did when considering a motorcycle purchase was to log on to the Internet. She learned a great deal simply by browsing the sites of such manufacturers as Honda, Yamaha, and Harley-Davidson. She especially liked the Harley site and the annual events listed for Harley owners. She was concerned that most of these events took place in the United States, however. Using their response button, she requested information on dealers in her area and information about specific models. Jennifer also found several chat groups and posted questions to members of these groups, especially women riders.

Social Class

Social classes
Relatively permanent and ordered divisions in a society whose members share similar values, interests, and behaviours.

Almost every society has some form of social class structure. **Social classes** are society's relatively permanent and ordered divisions whose members share similar values, interests, and behaviours. Social class is determined by a combination of occupation, income, education, wealth, and other variables. In some social systems, members of different classes are reared for certain roles and cannot change their social positions. In Canada, however, the lines between social classes are not fixed and rigid: People can move to a higher social class or drop into a lower one. Marketers are interested in social class because people within a given social class tend to exhibit similar buying behaviour, showing distinct product and brand preferences in areas such as clothing, home furnishings, leisure activity, and automobiles.

In 2000, Compusearch Micromarketing and Data Systems conducted a study that allowed them to develop profiles of the top five percent of the Canadian population.[21] They grouped households based on such factors as average household income, education, and house value. The resulting 12 distinct profiles allow marketers to gain insights about groups' lifestyles, geographic locations, and media habits.

Compusearch labelled one group the "Canadian Establishment," comprising 0.17 percent of Canadian households. People in this group live in the most affluent neighbourhoods in expensive, older dwellings often purchased with inherited money. They are typically business owners and professionals who drink scotch, read the *National Post,* attend the opera, and fly first class. Another group is identified as "Asian Heights" (0.71 percent), primarily people of Chinese origin. They have large families, live in heavily mortgaged homes, attend fashion shows, enjoy eating exotic foods, and love to buy home entertainment equipment. Many are two-income families who balance the stress of commuting with the stress of their managerial and white-collar jobs. A third group, comprising 1.79 percent of Canada's households, is described as "Young Urban Professionals," or "Yuppies." These young singles drink specialty coffee and premium beer, read *Wired,* watch MTV, and live in rented older homes and apartments in the downtown areas of large cities. Most of Canada's affluent population lives in Toronto (37 percent). Vancouver has the next highest concentration (16 percent), followed by Montreal (11 percent) and Calgary (6 percent). Jennifer Wong's social class may affect her motorcycle decision. As a member of the Asian Heights group, Jennifer finds herself frequently buying brand-name products that are fashionable and popular with her friends and extended family.

Social Factors

A consumer's behaviour also is influenced by social factors, such as membership in *small groups* and *family,* and *social roles and status.*

Groups

Group
Two or more people who interact to accomplish individual or mutual goals.

A person's behaviour is influenced by many small **groups.** Groups that have a direct influence and to which a person belongs are called *membership groups.* Some are *primary groups* with which a person has regular but informal interaction—such as family, friends, neighbours, and co-workers. A person also has less regular interaction with the more formal *secondary groups*—organizations such as religious groups, professional associations, and trade unions.

Reference groups serve as direct (face-to-face) or indirect points of comparison or reference in forming a person's attitudes or behaviour. People often are influenced by reference groups to which they do not belong. For example, an *aspirational group* is one to which the individual wishes to belong. For example, a teenage hockey player hopes to play someday for the Montreal Canadiens: He identifies with this group, although there is no face-to-face contact between him and the team. Marketers try to identify the reference groups of their target markets. Reference groups expose a person to new behaviours and lifestyles, influence the person's attitudes and self-concept, and create pressures to conform that may affect the person's product and brand choices.

The importance of group influence varies across products and brands. It tends to be strongest when the product is visible to others whom the buyer respects. Purchases of products that are bought and used privately are not much affected by group influences because neither the product nor the brand will be noticed by others. Manufacturers of products and brands subjected to strong group influence must figure out how to reach **opinion leaders,** people within a reference group who, because of special skills, knowledge, personality, or other characteristics, exert influence on others.

Opinion leaders
People within a reference group who, because of special skills, knowledge, personality, or other characteristics, exert influence on others.

Many marketers try to identify opinion leaders for their products, so that they can direct marketing efforts toward them. In other cases, they create advertisements to simulate opinion leadership, thereby reducing the need for consumers to seek advice from others. For example, the hottest trends in teenage music, language, and fashion often start in Canada in major cities, then quickly spread to more mainstream youth in the suburbs. Thus, clothing companies who hope to appeal to these fickle and fashion-conscious youth often make a concerted effort to monitor urban opinion leaders' style and behaviour. Levi-Strauss is a good example:

> In recent years, Levi-Strauss has been squeezed by the competition as teens and youth flock to designer labels and more "cool" brands. To revitalize sales for its Silver Tab line of clothing, the company's ad agency sent out employees to build a network of contacts familiar with the urban scene, including club-hoppers, stylists, photographers, and disk jockeys. The agency kept a scrapbook of people and looks and separated them into "tribes" defined by the music they like, including electronica, hip-hop and rap, and retro soul music. Its illustrated ads appealing to hip-hop and rap culture featured the statement "It's bangin', son," which means "cool," and teenagers clad in Silver Tab clothing—baggy pants, hip huggers, tiny tops—and wearing accessories such as nose rings, beepers, and chunky gold jewelry.[22]

If Jennifer Wong buys a motorcycle, both the product and the brand will be visible to others she respects. Therefore, her decision to buy the motorcycle and her brand choice may be influenced strongly by some of her groups, such as friends who belong to a weekend motorcycle club. Jennifer often feels left out when these friends leave for weekend road trips.

Family

Marketers have extensively researched the family, the most important consumer buying organization in society. Since family members can have a strong influence on buyer behaviour, marketers are interested in the roles and influence of the husband, wife, and children on the purchase of different products and services.

Husband–wife involvement depends on product category and on stage in the buying process. Buying roles change with evolving consumer lifestyles. In Canada and the US, the wife has traditionally been the main purchasing agent for the family, especially for food, household products, and clothing. But with 70 percent of women holding jobs outside the home and the willingness of husbands to do more of the family's purchasing, this is changing. For example, women buy about 45 percent of all cars and men account for about 40 percent of food-shopping dollars.[23] Many teenagers are now responsible for doing the grocery shopping. Because these roles depend on ethnicity and social classes, as always, marketers must research specific patterns in their target markets.

Changes in family buying behaviour suggest that marketers who've typically sold their products to only women or only men are now courting the opposite sex. For example, consider the hardware business:

> Women now account for nearly half of all hardware-store purchases. Home improvement retailer Builders Square identified this trend early and has capitalized on it by turning what had been an intimidating warehouse into a user-friendly retail outlet. The new Builders Square II outlets feature decorator design centres at the front of the store. To attract more women to these stores, Builders Square runs ads targeting women in *Home, House Beautiful, Woman's Day,* and *Better Homes and Gardens.* The retailer even offers bridal registries. Says a marketing director at Builders Square, "It's more meaningful to them to have a great patio set or gas grill than to have fine china."[24]

Children can also have a strong influence on family buying decisions. Chevrolet recognizes these influences in marketing its Chevy Venture minivan:

> In an issue of *Sports Illustrated for Kids,* which attracts mostly 8- to 14-year-old boys, the inside cover featured a brightly coloured two-page spread for the Chevy Venture to woo [what it calls] "back-seat consumers." [GM] is sending the minivan into malls and showing previews of Disney's Hercules on a VCR inside. "We're kidding ourselves when we think kids aren't aware of brands," says [Venture's brand manager], adding that even she was surprised at how often parents told her that kids played a tie-breaking role in deciding which car to buy.[25]

In the case of expensive products and services, husbands and wives more often make joint decisions. Although Jennifer isn't married, her boyfriend will influence her choice. He purchased a motorcycle last year and really loves it. Since he rarely lets Jennifer drive it, she really relates to the slogan on the new Harley-Davidson ads proclaiming, "You never took a back seat before!"

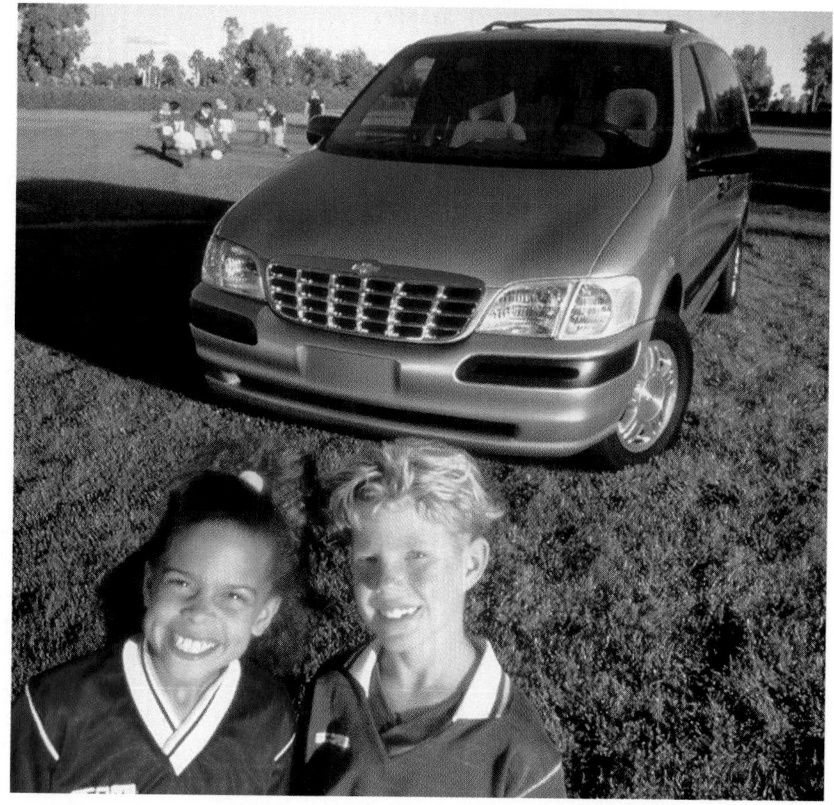

Family buying influences: Children can exert a strong influence on family buying decisions. Chevrolet actively woos these "back-seat consumers" in its marketing for the Chevy Venture minivan.

Roles and Status

A person belongs to many groups—family, clubs, organizations. The person's position in each group can be defined in terms of both role and status. A *role* consists of the activities that others expect from the person. Each role carries a *status* reflecting the general esteem society gives it. People often choose products that show their status in society. Jennifer occupies many roles simultaneously. In her role as a daughter, she has lower status than her parents and grandparents, so she often acquiesces to their opinions with respect to family matters. In her role as a brand manager, Jennifer has high status and assumes a leadership role in her brand group. Jennifer also wants to be a leader in her social activities and often organizes group activities. Her desire to be a leader causes her to identify with leading status brands such as Harley-Davidson.

Personal Factors

A buyer's decisions are also influenced by such personal characteristics as *age and life cycle stage, occupation, economic situation, lifestyle,* and *personality and self-concept.*

Age and Life Cycle Stage

People change in the kinds of goods and services they buy over their lifetimes. Tastes in food, clothes, furniture, and recreation are often related to age. Buying is also shaped by the stage of the *family life cycle*—the stages through which families might pass as they mature. Table 5-2 lists the stages of the family life cycle. Marketers often define their target markets in terms of life cycle stage and develop appropriate products and marketing plans for each stage. Traditional family life cycle stages include young singles and married couples with children. Today's marketers are increasingly catering to a growing number of alternative, non-traditional stages such as unmarried couples, couples marrying later in life, childless couples, single parents, extended parents (those with young adult children returning home), and same-sex couples.

Occupation

People's occupations may determine the goods and services that they buy. Outside workers buy warm clothing and heavy boots; hospital workers wear pastel clothing; and workers in some service industries wear uniforms. Marketers try to iden-

TABLE 5-2 Life Cycle Stages

Young	Middle-Aged	Older
Single	Single	Older married
Single with children	Same-sex couples	Older unmarried
Married without children	Same-sex couples with children	Older with children again
Married with children	Married without children	
Divorced with children	Married with children	
	Married without dependent children	
	Divorced without children	
	Divorced with children	
	Divorced without dependent children	

Source: Adapted from Patrick E. Murphy and William A. Staples, "A modernized family life cycle," *Journal of Consumer Research,* June 1979:16; © Journal of Consumer Research, Inc., 1979. Also see Leon G. Schiffman and Leslie Lazar Kanuk, *Consumer Behavior,* Englewood Cliffs, NJ: Prentice Hall, 1994:361–70.

tify the occupational groups that have an above-average interest in their products and services. A company can even specialize in making products needed by an occupational group. Thus, computer software companies design different products for brand managers, accountants, engineers, lawyers, and doctors.

Economic Situation

A person's economic situation affects product choice. Marketers of income-sensitive goods watch trends in personal income, savings, and interest rates. If economic indicators point to a recession, marketers can take steps to redesign, reposition, and reprice their products.

Lifestyle

Lifestyle
A person's pattern of living as expressed in his or her activities, interests, and opinions.

Psychographics
The technique of measuring lifestyles and developing lifestyle classifications; it involves measuring the major AIO dimensions (activities, interests, opinions).

People coming from the same subculture, social class, and occupation may have quite different lifestyles. **Lifestyle** is a person's pattern of living as expressed in his or her **psychographics.** It involves measuring consumers' major *AIO dimensions—activities* (work, hobbies, shopping, sports, social events), *interests* (food, fashion, family, recreation), and *opinions* (about themselves, social issues, business, products). Lifestyle captures something more than the person's social class or personality; it profiles a person's whole pattern of acting and interacting in the world.

Several research firms have developed lifestyle classifications. The most widely used is the SRI *Values and Lifestyles (VALS)* typology. VALS2 classifies people according to how they spend their time and money. It divides consumers into eight groups based on two major dimensions: self-orientation and resources (see Figure 5-3). Self-orientation groups include *principle-oriented* consumers who buy based on their views of the world; *status-oriented* buyers who base their purchases on the actions and opinions of others; and *action-oriented* buyers who are driven by their desire for activity, variety, and risk taking. Consumers within each orientation are further classified into those with *abundant resources* and those with *minimal resources*. Consumers with either very high or very low levels of resources are classified without regard to their self-orientation (actualizers, strugglers).

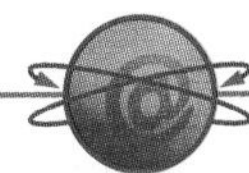

iVALS-Internet VALS
future.sri.com/vals/iVALS.index.html

SRI has recently developed a new lifestyle classification system for Internet users. By logging on to SRI's site, you can complete a questionnaire and determine which Internet user group you belong to and compare yourself with people in other categories.

Forrester Inc. examines people's desire and ability to invest in technology. See Marketing Highlight 5-1 for new insights on how to segment these markets.

These lifestyle classifications are by no means universal—they can vary significantly between countries. For example, McCann-Erickson London found the following British lifestyles: Avant Guardians (interested in change); Pontificators (traditionalists, very British); Chameleons (follow the crowd); and Sleepwalkers (contented underachievers).[26] Michael Adams, president of Environics Research Group Ltd., wrote *Sex in the Snow: Canadian Social Values at the End of the Millennium* to capture significant psychographic changes in the Canadian marketplace. He believes that psychographic changes eclipse demographic factors among Canadians. While his classification system begins with demographic factors, he divides the Canadian population along age-based lines into three groups: those over 50, baby boomers, and Generation Xers. Furthermore, he asserts that 12 value-based "tribes" exist within these broader groups. Table 5-3 provides descriptions of these groups.

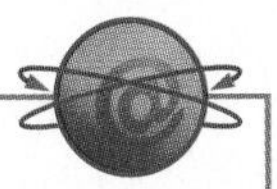

Environics 3SC Survey
www.environics.net/erg/survey/3cs/index.shtml

When used carefully, the lifestyle concept can help the marketer understand changing consumer values and how they affect buying behaviour. For example, lifestyle information has helped marketers of cellular phones target consumers. While early users of the products were often corporate executives and salespeople

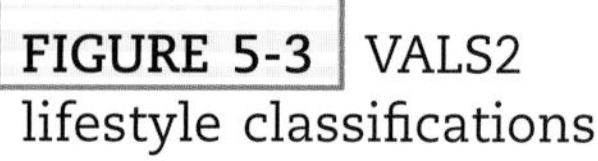

FIGURE 5-3 VALS2 lifestyle classifications

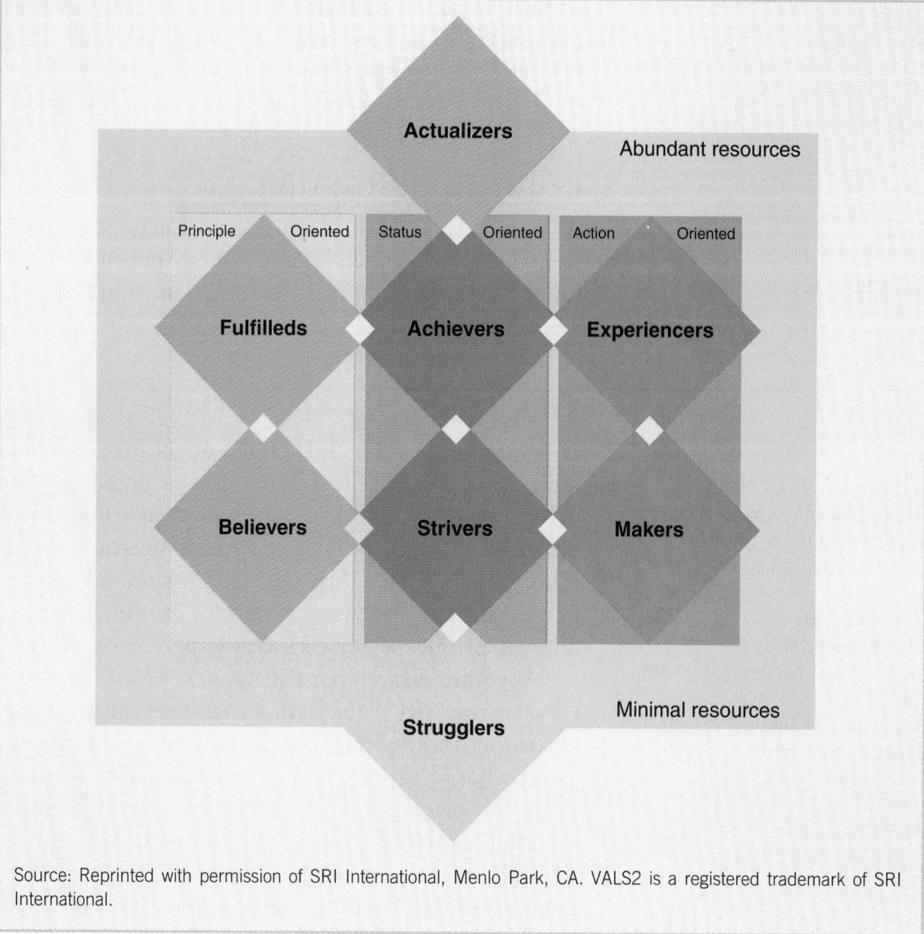

Source: Reprinted with permission of SRI International, Menlo Park, CA. VALS2 is a registered trademark of SRI International.

By using this advertisement, Pontiac targeted an audience living a specific lifestyle.

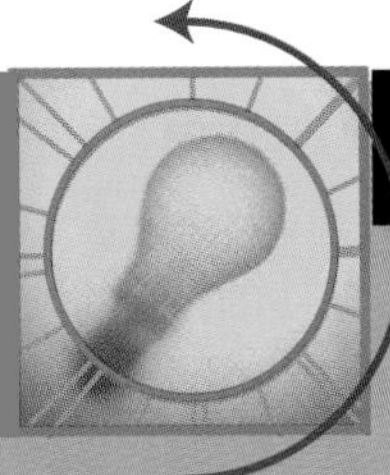

marketing highlight 5-1

Mouse Potatoes and Techno-Strivers: What Makes Technology Buyers Click?

Traditional market research may tell you who buys household computers. It may even tell you the kind of lifestyles they live. However, it won't tell you who in the household is using the computer and why. For example, it won't tell you that the wife is using the PC to take a distance-learning course, that the son is using it to download computer games from various Web sites, that the daughter is using it to log on to about a dozen chat groups, or that the husband, a confirmed technophobe, only logs on once in a blue moon to get stock quotes. A marketer who promotes the newest online gizmo to the husband will surely miss the mark.

Several new market research tools have emerged to help marketers of technology products get a better read on the buying habits of technology buyers and users. These new tools segment consumers based on technology types. Two of the most prominent approaches under development are Forrester Inc.'s "Technographics," which segments consumers according to motivation, desire, and ability to invest in technology, and SRI Consulting's iVALS, which focuses on attitudes, preferences, and behaviour of online service and Internet users. Forrester Research developed its Technographics scheme by hiring NPD, a polling and research firm, to survey 131 000 consumers. The framework splits people into 10 categories, including:

Fast Forwards are the biggest spenders on computer technology. Fast Forwards are early adopters of new technology for home, office, and personal use.

New Age Nurturers are also big spenders but focused on technology for home uses, such as a family PC.

Mouse Potatoes are consumers who are dedicated to interactive entertainment and willing to spend for the latest in "technotainment."

Techno-Strivers are consumers who use technology primarily to gain a career edge.

Handshakers are older consumers, typically managers, who don't touch computers at work, leaving them to younger assistants.

SRI's iVALS also divides consumers into 10 segments, but the focus is on Internet use. Some of the iVALS segments are:

Wizards are the most skilled and active Internet users for whom mastery of technology figures prominently in their identities.

Immigrants are recent arrivals to cyberspace who usually are familiar with only very specific parts of the Internet and are drawn online because they have to be for work or school.

Socialites are users who are strongly oriented toward social aspects of the Internet and who are prominent participants in online discussions. They are iVALS's youngest segment, mostly under 30 years of age.

Both Technographics and iVALS reinforce the idea of a dual-tier society, but

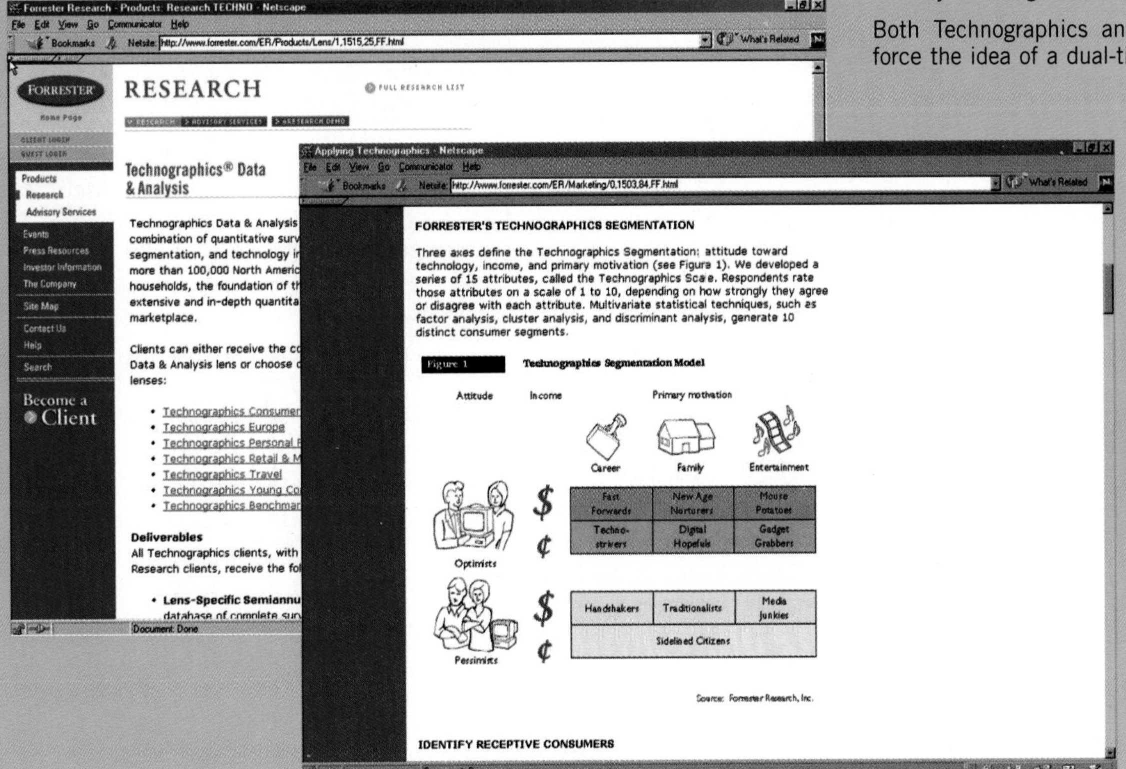

Technology buyer lifestyles: Forrester's "Technographics" approach segments consumers according to their motivation, desire, and ability to invest in technology.

one that is based on knowledge, not income. For instance, people who are more computer savvy are perfect targets for an electronic banking product that allows them to pay bills, switch money between accounts, and check balances on the computer. Those who are not computer literate will still write cheques by hand, send payments through "snail mail," and stand in line for a bank teller.

Yet the new market research tools reveal many shades in the spectrum between "the knows" and "the know nots." For instance, Delta Airlines wants to use Technographics to better target online ticket sales. It is creating marketing campaigns for time-strapped "Fast Forwards" and "New Age Nurturers," and eliminating the "technology pessimists" from its list of targets. "Traditional market research gives you a picture of the universe," says Paula Lai, manager of Delta's marketing research. But what good is that picture today, she adds, if it doesn't tell you who will book tickets online?

Sources: Andy Hines, "Do you know your technology type?" *The Futurist,* September-October 1997:10–1; Paul C. Judge, "Are tech buyers different?" *Business Week,* 26 January 1998:64–5,68; Josh Bernoff, Shelley Morrisette, and Kenneth Clemmer, "The Forrester Report," Forrester Research, Inc., 1998; future.sri.com, March 2000; www.forrester.com, February 2000.

who used their cars as their offices, later users often bought cellular phones for quite different reasons.[27] For example, while 46 percent of Bell Mobility's customers still cite business reasons as their primary motivation for purchasing a cellular phone, 34 percent now say they bought them for safety reasons. Another 19 percent of users purchased mobile phones just for convenience.

TABLE 5-3 The Social Value "Tribes" of Canada

Groups	% Pop. & Size	Motivators	Values	Exemplar
The Elders:				
Rational Traditionalists	15% 3.5M	Financial independence, stability, and security.	Value safety, reason, tradition, and authority. Religious.	Winston Churchill
Extroverted Traditionalists	7% 1.7M	Traditional communities and institutions. Social status.	Value tradition, duty, family, and institutions. Religious.	Jean Chrétien
Cosmopolitan Modernists	6% 1.4M	Traditional institutions. Nomadic, experience seeking.	Education, affluence, innovation, progress, self-confidence, world perspective.	Pierre Trudeau
The Boomers:				
Disengaged Darwinists	18% 4.3M	Financial independence, stability, and security.	Self-preservation, nostalgia for the past.	Mike Harris
Autonomous Rebels	10% 2.4M	Personal autonomy, self-fulfillment, and new experiences.	Egalitarian, abhor corruption, personal fulfillment, education. Suspicion of authority and big government.	John Lennon
Anxious Communitarians	9% 2.1M	Traditional communities, big government, and social status.	Family, community, generosity, duty. Needs self-respect. Fearful.	Martha Stewart
The Gen-Xers:				
Aimless Dependents	8% 1.9M	Financial independence, stability, security. Fearful.	Desire for independence. Disengagement.	Courtney Love
Thrill-Seeking Materialists	7% 1.7M	Traditional communities, social status, experience-seeking.	Money, material possessions. recognition, living dangerously	Calvin Klein
Autonomous Postmaterialists	6% 1.4M	Personal autonomy and self-fulfillment.	Freedom, human rights, egalitarian, quality of life.	Bart Simpson
Social Hedonists	4$ .9M	Experience seeking, new communities.	Esthetics, hedonism, sexual freedom, instant gratification.	Janet Jackson
New Aquarians	4% .9M	Experience seeking, new communities.	Ecologism, hedonism.	Tori Amos

Source: Adapted from Michael Adams, "The demise of demography," *Globe and Mail,* 8 January 1997:D5; and Ann Walmsley, "Canadian specific," *Report on Business,* March 1997:15–6.

Personality
A person's distinguishing psychological characteristics that lead to relatively consistent and lasting responses to his or her own environment.

Personality and Self-Concept

Each person's distinct personality influences his or her buying behaviour. **Personality** refers to the unique psychological characteristics that lead to relatively consistent and lasting responses to one's own environment. Personality is usually described in terms of traits, such as self-confidence, dominance, sociability, autonomy, defensiveness, adaptability, and aggressiveness. Personality can be useful in analyzing consumer behaviour for certain product or brand choices. For example, coffee makers have discovered that heavy coffee drinkers tend to be high on sociability. Thus, Maxwell House ads show people relaxing and socializing over a cup of steaming coffee.

Many marketers use a concept related to personality—a person's *self-concept,* or *self-image,* based on the idea that people's possessions contribute to and reflect their identities; that is, "we are what we have." Therefore, to understand consumer behaviour, marketers must first understand the relationship between consumer self-concept and possessions. For example, the founder and chief executive of Barnes & Noble, one of the largest booksellers in the United States, notes that people buy books to support their self-images:

> People have the mistaken notion that the thing you do with books is read them. Wrong. . . . People buy books for what the purchase says about them—their taste, their cultivation, their trendiness. Their aim . . . is to connect themselves, or those to whom they give the books as gifts, with all the other refined owners of Edgar Allen Poe collections or sensitive owners of Virginia Woolf collections. . . . [The result is that] you can sell books as consumer products, with seductive displays, flashy posters, an emphasis on the glamour of the book, and the fashionableness of the bestseller and the trendy author.[28]

Jennifer Wong falls into Michael Adams's psychographic category of thrill-seeking materialists. Since she values material possessions, recognition, and the idea of living dangerously, owning a motorcycle instead of a traditional car appeals to her. Since her personality is outgoing, daring, and active, she will favour a mode of transportation that projects the same qualities.

Psychological Factors

A person's buying choices are further influenced by four major psychological factors: *motivation, perception, learning,* and *beliefs and attitudes.*

Motivation

We know that Jennifer Wong became interested in buying a motorcycle. Why? What is she *really* seeking? What *needs* is she trying to satisfy?

A person has many needs at any one time. Some are *biological,* arising from states of tension such as hunger, thirst, or discomfort. Others are *psychological,* arising from the need for recognition, esteem, or belonging. Most of these needs will not be strong enough to motivate the person to act at any given time. A need becomes a *motive* when it is aroused to a sufficient level of intensity. A **motive,** or *drive,* is a need that is sufficiently pressing to direct the person to seek satisfaction. Psychologists have developed theories of human motivation. Two of the most popular—the theories of Sigmund Freud and Abraham Maslow—have quite different meanings for consumer analysis and marketing.

Motive (drive)
A need that is sufficiently pressing to drive the person to seek satisfaction of the need.

Freud's Theory of Motivation. Freud assumed that people are largely unconscious of the real psychological forces shaping their behaviour. He saw the person as growing up and repressing many urges. These urges are never eliminated or under perfect control; they emerge in dreams, in slips of the tongue, in neurotic and obsessive behaviour, or ultimately in psychoses.

Thus, Freud suggested that a person does not fully understand his or her motivation. Jennifer Wong, for example, may claim that her motive for buying a motorcycle is to satisfy her need for more convenient transportation. At a deeper level, however, she may be purchasing the motorcycle to impress others with her daring, and her desire to be a free spirit who doesn't follow convention.

Motivation researchers collect in-depth information from small samples of consumers to uncover the deeper motives for their product choices. They use nondirective depth interviews and various projective techniques—such as word association, sentence completion, picture interpretation, and role-playing—to throw the ego off-guard. Motivation researchers have reached some interesting and sometimes odd conclusions about what may be in the buyer's mind regarding certain purchases. For example, one classic study concluded that consumers resist prunes because they are wrinkled and remind people of sickness and old age. Despite its sometimes unusual conclusions, motivation research remains a useful tool for marketers seeking a deeper understanding of consumer behaviour (see Marketing Highlight 5-2).[29]

Maslow's Theory of Motivation. Abraham Maslow sought to explain why people are driven by particular needs at particular times.[30] Why does one person spend much time and energy on personal safety and another on gaining the esteem of others? Maslow's answer is that human needs are arranged in a hierarchy, from the most pressing to the least pressing. Maslow's hierarchy of needs, shown in Figure 5-4, contains *physiological* needs, *safety* needs, *social* needs, *esteem* needs, and *self-actualization* needs, in order of importance. A person tries to satisfy the most important need first. When that need is satisfied, it will stop being a motivator and the person will then try to satisfy the next most important need. For example, starving people (physiological needs) will not take an interest in the latest happenings in the art world (self-actualization needs), nor in how they are perceived or esteemed by others (social or esteem needs), nor even in whether they are breathing clean air (safety needs). But as each important need is satisfied, the next most important need will come into play.

What light does Maslow's theory throw on Jennifer Wong's interest in buying a motorcycle? We can guess that Jennifer has satisfied her physiological, safety, and social needs; they do not motivate her interest in motorcycles. Her interest may come from a strong need for more esteem from others. Or it may come from a need for self-actualization—she may want to be a daring person and express herself through product ownership.

Perception

A motivated person is ready to act. How the person acts is influenced by his or her perception of the situation. Two people with the same motivation and in the same situation may act quite differently because they perceive the situation differently. When Jennifer Wong and her boyfriend visited a motorcycle dealership to look at bikes, the salesperson directed most of his comments to Jennifer's boyfriend even though Jennifer's boyfriend kept reminding him that the bike was for Jennifer. Jennifer was furious at being ignored. Even though she liked one of the bikes in the showroom, she vowed not to buy from that company.

Why do people perceive the same situation differently? All of us learn by the flow of information through our five senses: sight, hearing, smell, touch, and taste. However, each of us receives, organizes, and interprets this sensory information in an individual way. **Perception** is the process by which people select, organize, and interpret information to form a meaningful picture of the world.

Perception
The process by which people select, organize, and interpret information to form a meaningful picture of the world.

People form different perceptions of the same stimulus due to three perceptual processes: selective attention, selective distortion, and selective retention. People are exposed to a great number of stimuli every day. For example, the average person may be exposed to more than 1500 ads in a single day. It is impossible for a person to pay attention to all these stimuli. *Selective attention*—the tendency for

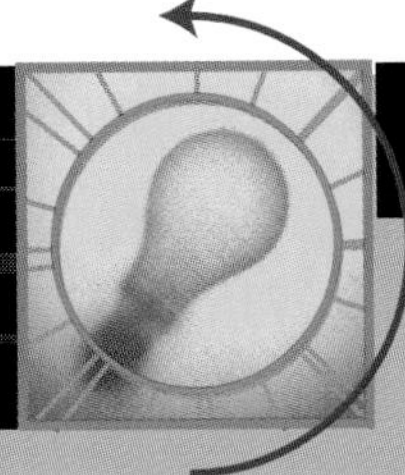

marketing highlight 5-2

"Touchy-Feely" Research into Consumer Motivations

The term "motivation research" refers to qualitative research designed to probe consumers' hidden, subconscious motivations. Because consumers often don't know or can't describe just why they act as they do, motivation researchers use a variety of non-directive and projective techniques to uncover underlying emotions and attitudes toward brands and buying situations. The techniques range from sentence completion, word association, and inkblot or cartoon interpretation tests, to having consumers describe typical brand users or form daydreams and fantasies about brands or buying situations. Some of these techniques verge on the bizarre. One writer offers the following tongue-in-cheek summary of a motivation research session:

> Good morning, ladies and gentlemen. We've called you here today for a little consumer research. Now, lie down on the couch, toss your inhibitions out the window, and let's try a little free association. First, think about brands as if they were your *friends.* Imagine you could talk to your TV dinner. What would he say? And what would you say to him? . . . Now, think of your shampoo as an animal. Go on, don't be shy. Would it be a panda or a lion? A snake or a wooly worm? For our final exercise, let's all sit up and pull out our magic markers. Draw a picture of a typical cake-mix user. Would she wear an apron or a negligee? A business suit or a cancan dress?

Such projective techniques seem pretty goofy. But more and more, marketers are turning to these touchy-feely approaches to probe consumer psyches and develop better marketing strategies.

Many advertising agencies employ teams of psychologists, anthropologists, and other social scientists to carry out motivation research. One agency routinely conducts one-on-one, therapy-like interviews to delve into the inner workings of consumers. Another agency asks consumers to describe their favourite brands as animals or cars (say, Cadillacs versus Chevrolets) to assess the prestige associated with various brands.

Still another agency asks consumers to draw figures of typical brand users:

> In one instance, the agency asked 50 interviewees to sketch likely buyers of two different brands of cake mixes. Consistently, the group portrayed Pillsbury customers as apron-clad, grandmotherly types, while they pictured Duncan Hines purchasers as svelte, contemporary women.

In a similar study, American Express had people sketch likely users of its gold card and of its green card. Respondents depicted gold card holders as active, broad-shouldered men; green card holders were perceived as "couch potatoes" lounging in front of television sets. Based on these results, the company positioned its gold card as a symbol of responsibility for people capable of controlling their lives and finances.

Some motivation research studies use more basic techniques, such as mingling with or watching consumers to find out what makes them tick. British-based advertising agency Saatchi & Saatchi hired an anthropologist to spend time in Texas sidling up to Wrangler blue jeans wearers at rodeos and barbecues. His findings showed what the jeans company suspected: Wrangler buyers identify with cowboys. The company responded by running ads with plenty of Western touches.

In an effort to understand the teenage consumer market better, ad agency BSB Worldwide videotaped teenagers' rooms in 25 countries. It found surprising similarities across countries and cultures:

> From the steamy playgrounds of Los Angeles to the stately boulevards of Singapore, kids show amazing similarities in taste, language, and attitude. . . . From the gear and posters on display, it's hard to tell whether the rooms are in Los Angeles, Mexico City, or Tokyo. Basketballs sit alongside soccer balls. Closets overflow with staples from an international, unisex uniform: baggy Levi or Diesel jeans, NBA jackets, and rugged shoes from Timberland or Doc Martens.

Similarly, researchers at Sega of America's ad agency have learned a lot about videogame buying behaviour by hanging around with 150 kids in their bedrooms and by shopping with them in malls. Above all else, they learned, do everything fast. As a result, in Sega's most recent 15-second commercials, some images fly by so quickly that adults cannot recall seeing them, even after repeated showings. The kids, weaned on MTV, recollect them keenly.

Some marketers dismiss such motivation research as mumbo-jumbo. And these approaches do present some problems: The samples are small, and researcher interpretations of results are often highly subjective, sometimes leading to rather exotic explanations of otherwise ordinary buying behaviour. However, others believe strongly that these approaches can provide interesting nuggets of insight into the relationships between consumers and the brands they buy. To marketers who use them, motivation research techniques provide a flexible and varied means of gaining insights into deeply held and often mysterious motivations behind consumer buying behaviour.

Motivation research: When asked to sketch figures of typical cake-mix users, subjects portrayed Pillsbury customers as grandmotherly types and Duncan Hines buyers as svelte and contemporary.

Sources: Excerpts from Annetta Miller and Dody Tsiantar, "Psyching out consumers," *Newsweek,* 27 February 1989:46–7; and Shawn Tully, "Teens: The most global market of all," *Fortune,* 6 May 1994:90–7. Also see Rebecca Piirto, "Words that sell," *American Demographics,* January 1992:6; and "They understand your kids," *Fortune,* special issue, Autumn/Winter 1993:29–30.

FIGURE 5-4 Maslow's hierarchy of needs

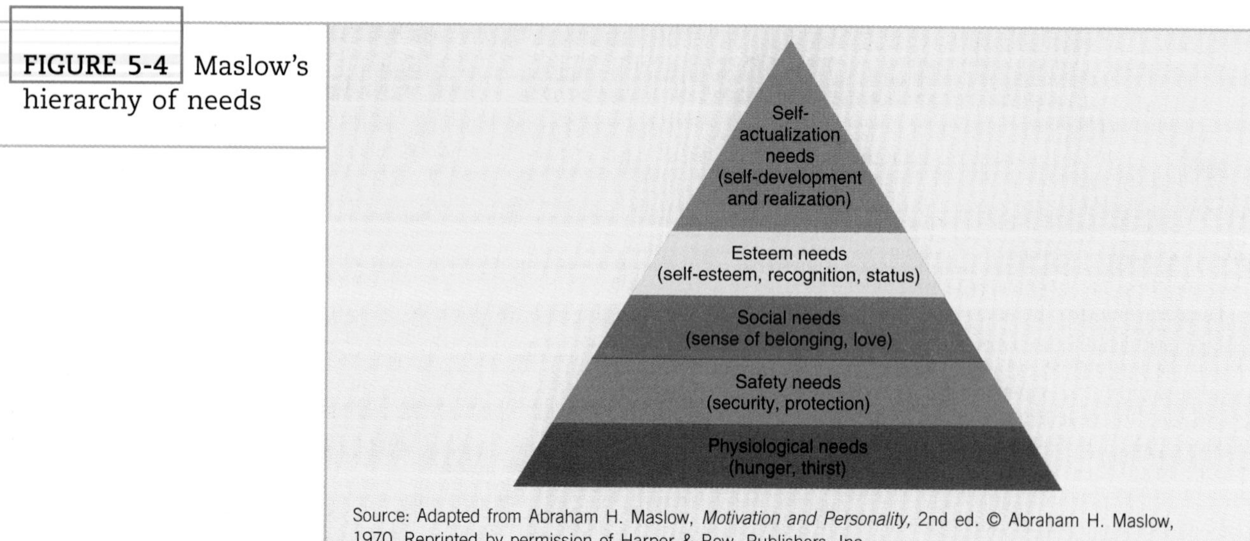

Source: Adapted from Abraham H. Maslow, *Motivation and Personality,* 2nd ed. © Abraham H. Maslow, 1970. Reprinted by permission of Harper & Row, Publishers, Inc.

people to screen out most of the information to which they are exposed—means that marketers must work especially hard to attract the consumer's attention. Their message will be lost on most people who are not in the market for the product. Moreover, even people who are in the market may not notice the message unless it stands out from the surrounding sea of other ads.

Even noted stimuli do not always come across in the intended way. Each person fits incoming information into an existing mind-set. *Selective distortion* is the tendency of people to interpret information in a way that will support what they already believe. Jennifer Wong may hear the salesperson mention some good and bad points about a competing motorcycle; but because she already has a strong leaning toward Harley, she is likely to distort those points to conclude that Harley is the better motorcycle. Selective distortion means that marketers must try to understand consumers' perspectives and how these will affect interpretations of advertising and sales information.

People also forget much that they learn. They tend to retain information that supports their attitudes and beliefs. Because of *selective retention,* advertisers try to frame messages in ways that are consistent with people's existing beliefs. Jennifer is likely to remember good points made about the Harley and to forget good points made about competing motorcycles.

Interestingly, although most marketers worry about whether their offers will be perceived at all, some consumers worry that they will be affected by marketing messages without even knowing it—through subliminal advertising. In 1957, a researcher announced that he had flashed the phrases "Eat popcorn" and "Drink Coca-Cola" on a screen in a New Jersey movie theater every five seconds for 1/300th of a second. He reported that although viewers did not consciously recognize these messages, they absorbed them subconsciously and bought 58 percent more popcorn and 18 percent more Coke. Suddenly advertisers and consumer-protection groups became intensely interested in subliminal perception. People voiced fears of being brainwashed, and Canada declared the practice illegal. Although the researcher later admitted to making up the data, the issue has not died. Some consumers still fear that they are being manipulated by subliminal messages.

Numerous studies by psychologists and consumer researchers have found no link between subliminal messages and consumer behaviour. It appears that subliminal advertising simply doesn't have the power attributed to it by its critics. Most advertisers scoff at the notion of an industry conspiracy to manipulate consumers through "invisible" messages. As one advertising agency executive put it, "We have enough trouble persuading consumers using a series of up-front 30-second ads—how could we do it in 1/300th of a second?"

Learning

Learning
Changes in an individual's behaviour arising from experience.

When people act, they learn. **Learning** describes changes in an individual's behaviour arising from experience. Learning theorists say that most human behaviour is learned. Learning occurs through the interplay of *drives, stimuli, cues, responses,* and *reinforcement.*

We saw that Jennifer Wong has a drive for self-actualization. A *drive* is a strong internal stimulus that calls for action. Her drive becomes a motive when it is directed toward a particular *stimulus object,* in this case a motorcycle. Jennifer's response to the idea of buying a motorcycle is conditioned by the surrounding cues. *Cues* are minor stimuli that determine when, where, and how the person responds. Seeing motorcycles roaring along the Toronto streets, hearing about Harley's 75th anniversary special edition cycle, and receiving her boyfriend's support for buying her own motorcycle are all *cues* that can influence Jennifer's *response* to her interest in buying a motorcycle.

Suppose Jennifer buys a Harley. If she attends the company's weekend events, makes new friends, and simply enjoys riding the bike around Toronto, her decision will be reinforced. If she decides to upgrade from her first bike to a more upscale model, the probability is greater that she will buy another Harley.

The practical significance of learning theory for marketers is that they can build up demand for a product by associating it with strong drives, using motivating cues, and providing positive reinforcement.

Beliefs and Attitudes

Belief
A descriptive thought that a person holds about something.

Through doing and learning, people acquire beliefs and attitudes. These, in turn, influence their buying behaviour. A **belief** is a descriptive thought that a person has about something. Jennifer Wong may believe that a Harley-Davidson is a classic bike, that it has more power than its rivals, and that it stands up well to urban driving conditions. These beliefs may be based on real knowledge, opinion, or faith, and may or may not carry an emotional charge.

Marketers are interested in the beliefs that people formulate about specific products and services, because these beliefs compose product and brand images that affect buying behaviour. If some of the beliefs are wrong and prevent purchase, the marketer will want to launch a campaign to correct them.

Attitude
A person's consistently favourable or unfavourable evaluations, feelings, and tendencies toward an object or idea.

People have attitudes about religion, politics, clothes, music, food, and almost everything else. An **attitude** describes a person's relatively consistent evaluations, feelings, and tendencies toward an object or idea. Attitudes put people into a frame of mind of liking or disliking things, of moving toward or away from them. Thus, Jennifer may hold such attitudes as "Buy the best."

Attitudes are difficult to change. A person's attitudes fit into a pattern, and to change one attitude may require difficult adjustments in many others. Thus, a company should usually try to fit its products into existing attitudes rather than attempt to change attitudes. However, there are exceptions in which the great cost of trying to change attitudes may pay off.

An unspoken rule in food marketing is to avoid using newspaper ads. "Given the general standard of newsprint reproduction, that tempting plate of pasta is likely to wind up with all the appetite appeal of a used muffler." But breaking the rules helped the Quebec Milk Producers

What your
inner child
is thirsting for.
milk

The Quebec Milk Producers' newspaper campaign not only won awards, but also changed adults' attitudes toward milk.

(La Fédération des Producteurs de Lait du Quebec) change the attitude of adults over 30 and get them back into the habit of drinking milk. And non-traditional, newspaper advertising proved to be the best way to reach this older target audience on a daily basis. In contrast to other newspaper advertising that tends to be visually clamorous and overloaded with information, the Quebec Milk Producers kept their ads relatively clean and uncluttered, and, thus, they gave themselves a better shot at standing out. Since adults already knew the health benefits of milk, creators of the campaign decided to take a different tack and decided to play upon the consumer's emotional connection with the product. Each ad showed milk in a simple, highly recognized receptacle—a glass, jug, carton, plastic container, and a baby bottle—on a white background. Each photo was overlaid by a catchy phrase. It was these headlines—"What your inner child is thirsting for," "Remember, you used to cry for it," "The mother of all beverages"—that made an emotional connection between these adult consumers and the product. Was the campaign a success? Not only did it win five Coq d'Or awards, it was "the first time in 25 years of working in advertising that I've ever gotten so many calls and letters from people saying they love our campaign," says Nicole Dubé, director of advertising and promotions for the milk marketers at La Fédération des Producteurs de Lait du Québec.[31]

Like the Quebec adults who changed their attitudes about drinking more milk after seeing a great ad campaign, Jennifer Wong responded to the ad shown at the beginning of this chapter. The headline grabbed her attention. Like the women shown in the ad photo, Jennifer "never took a back seat before." She was more inclined than ever to go and buy a Harley.

We can now appreciate the many forces acting on consumer behaviour. The consumer's choice is a result of the complex interplay of cultural, social, personal, and psychological factors. Although many of these factors cannot be influenced by the marketer, they can be useful in identifying interested buyers and in shaping products and appeals to serve consumer needs better.

We have examined the influences that affect buyers and are now ready to look at how consumers make buying decisions—consumer buying roles, types of buying decision behaviour, and the buyer decision process.

Consumer Buying Roles

The marketer needs to know what people are involved in the buying decision and what role each person plays. For many products, it is fairly easy to identify the decision maker. For example, men typically choose their own shaving equipment and women choose their own clothes. However, consider the purchase of a family car. The oldest child might suggest buying a new car. A friend might advise the family on what kind of car to buy. The husband might choose the brand. The wife might select the price range. The husband and wife might then make the final decision jointly, and the wife might use the car more than her husband.

People can play any of several roles in a buying decision:

- *Initiator* is the person who first suggests or thinks of the idea of buying a particular product or service
- *Influencer* is a person whose views or advice influences the buying decision
- *Decider* is the person who ultimately makes a buying decision or any part of it—whether to buy, what to buy, how to buy, or where to buy
- *Buyer* is the person who makes an actual purchase
- *User* is the person who consumes or uses a product or service

Knowing the main buying participants and the roles they play helps the marketer fine-tune the marketing program.

Types of Buying Decision Behaviour

Buying behaviour depends on the product, whether a tube of toothpaste, tennis racket, expensive camera, or new car. More complex decisions usually involve more buying participants and more buyer deliberation. Figure 5-5 shows types of consumer buying behaviour based on the degree of buyer involvement and the degree of differences between brands.[32]

Complex Buying Behaviour

Complex buying behaviour
Consumer buying behaviour in situations characterized by high consumer involvement in a purchase and significant perceived differences between brands.

Consumers undertake **complex buying behaviour** when they are highly involved in a purchase and perceive significant differences between brands. Consumers may be highly involved when the product is expensive, risky, purchased infrequently, and highly self-expressive. Typically, the consumer has much to learn about the product category. For example, a personal computer buyer may not know what attributes to consider. Many product features carry no real meaning: a "Pentium III chip," "32-bit Soundblaster," or "64 megs of RAM."

This buyer will pass through a learning process, first developing beliefs about the product, then attitudes, and then making a thoughtful purchase choice. Marketers of high-involvement products must understand the information-gathering and evaluation behaviour of high-involvement consumers. They need to help buyers learn about product-class attributes and their relative importance, and about what the company's brand offers on the important attributes. Marketers need to differentiate their brand's features, perhaps by describing the brand's benefits using print media with long copy. They must motivate store salespeople and the buyer's acquaintances to influence the final brand choice.

Dissonance-Reducing Buying Behaviour

Dissonance-reducing buying behaviour
Consumer buying behaviour in situations characterized by high involvement but few perceived differences between brands.

Dissonance-reducing buying behaviour occurs when consumers are highly involved with an expensive, infrequent, or risky purchase, but see little difference between brands. For example, consumers buying carpeting may face a high-involvement decision because carpeting is expensive and self-expressive. Yet buyers may consider most carpet brands in a given price range to be the same. In this case, because perceived brand differences are not large, buyers may shop around to learn what is available, but buy relatively quickly. They may respond primarily to a good price or for convenience.

After the purchase, consumers might experience *postpurchase dissonance,* or after-sale discomfort, when they notice certain disadvantages of the purchased carpet brand or hear favourable things about brands not purchased. To counter such

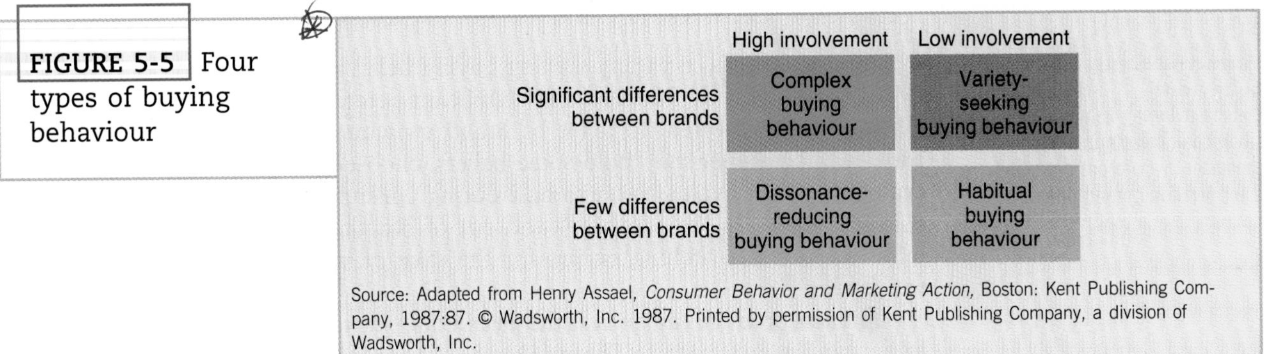

FIGURE 5-5 Four types of buying behaviour

Source: Adapted from Henry Assael, *Consumer Behavior and Marketing Action,* Boston: Kent Publishing Company, 1987:87. © Wadsworth, Inc. 1987. Printed by permission of Kent Publishing Company, a division of Wadsworth, Inc.

dissonance, the marketer's after-sale communications should provide evidence and support to help consumers feel good about their brand choices.

Habitual Buying Behaviour

Habitual buying behaviour
Consumer buying behaviour in situations characterized by low consumer involvement and few significant perceived brand differences.

Habitual buying behaviour occurs under conditions of low consumer involvement and little significant brand difference. Consider salt, for example. Consumers have little involvement in this product category—they simply go to the store and reach for a brand. If they keep reaching for the same brand, it is out of habit rather than strong brand loyalty. Consumers appear to have low involvement with most low-cost, frequently purchased products.

In such cases, consumer behaviour does not pass through the usual belief-attitude-behaviour sequence. Consumers do not search extensively for information about the brand, evaluate brand characteristics, and make weighty decisions about which brand to buy. Instead, they passively receive information as they watch television or read magazines. Ad repetition creates *brand familiarity* rather than *brand conviction*. Consumers do not form strong attitudes toward a brand; they select the brand because it is familiar. Because they are not highly involved with the product, consumers may not evaluate the choice even after purchase. Thus, the buying process involves brand beliefs formed by passive learning, followed by purchase behaviour, which may or may not be followed by evaluation.

Because buyers are not highly committed to any brands, marketers of low-involvement products with few brand differences often use price and sales promotions to stimulate product trial. In advertising for a low-involvement product, ad copy should stress a few key points. Visual symbols and imagery are important because they can be remembered easily and associated with the brand. Ad campaigns should include high repetition of short-duration messages. Television is usually more effective than print media because it is a low-involvement medium suitable for passive learning. Advertising planning should be based on classical conditioning theory, in which buyers learn to identify a certain product by a symbol repeatedly attached to it.

Marketers can try to convert low-involvement products into higher-involvement ones by linking them to some involving issue. Procter & Gamble does this when it links Crest toothpaste to avoiding cavities. Or the product can be linked to some involving personal situation. Nestlé did this in a series of ads for Taster's Choice coffee, each consisting of a new soap-opera-like episode featuring the evolving romantic relationship between two neighbours. At best, these strategies can raise consumer involvement from a low to a moderate level. However, they are not likely to propel the consumer into highly involved buying behaviour.

Variety-Seeking Buying Behaviour

Variety-seeking buying behaviour
Consumer buying behaviour in situations characterized by low consumer involvement but significant perceived brand differences.

Consumers undertake **variety-seeking buying behaviour** in situations characterized by low consumer involvement, but significant perceived brand differences. In such cases, consumers often do a lot of brand switching. For example, when buying cookies, a consumer may hold some beliefs, choose a cookie brand without much evaluation, then evaluate that brand during consumption. But the next time, the consumer may choose another brand out of boredom or simply to try something different. Brand switching occurs for the sake of variety rather than due to dissatisfaction.

In such product categories, the marketing strategy may differ for the market leader and minor brands. The market leader will try to encourage habitual buying behaviour by dominating shelf space, keeping shelves fully stocked, and run-

FIGURE 5-6 Buyer decision process

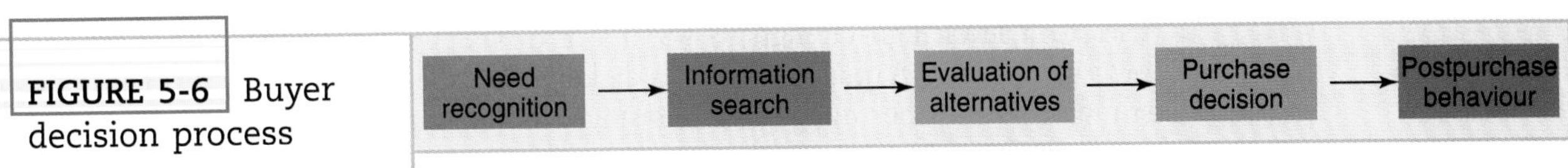

ning frequent reminder advertising. Challenger firms will encourage variety seeking by offering lower prices, special deals, coupons, free samples, and advertising that presents reasons for trying something new.

The Buyer Decision Process

We shall now examine the stages that buyers pass through to reach a buying decision. Figure 5-6 shows how the consumer passes through five stages: *need recognition, information search, evaluation of alternatives, purchase decision,* and *postpurchase behaviour.* Clearly, the buying process starts long before the actual purchase and continues long after. Marketers need to focus on the entire buying process rather than just on the purchase decision.

The figure implies that consumers pass through all five stages with every purchase. But in more routine purchases, consumers often skip or reverse some of these stages. A woman buying her regular brand of toothpaste would recognize the need and go right to the purchase decision, skipping information search and evaluation. However, we use this model because it shows all the considerations that arise when a consumer faces a new and complex purchase situation. To illustrate this model, we will again follow Jennifer Wong and try to understand how she became interested in buying a motorcycle, and the stages she went through to make her final choice.

Need recognition
The first stage of the buyer decision process in which the consumer recognizes a problem or need.

Need Recognition

The buying process starts with **need recognition.** The buyer senses a difference between his or her *actual* state and some *desired* state. The need can be triggered by *internal stimuli* when one of the person's normal needs—hunger, thirst, sex—

Need recognition can be triggered by advertising. This ad asks an arresting question that alerts parents to the need for a high-quality bike helmet.

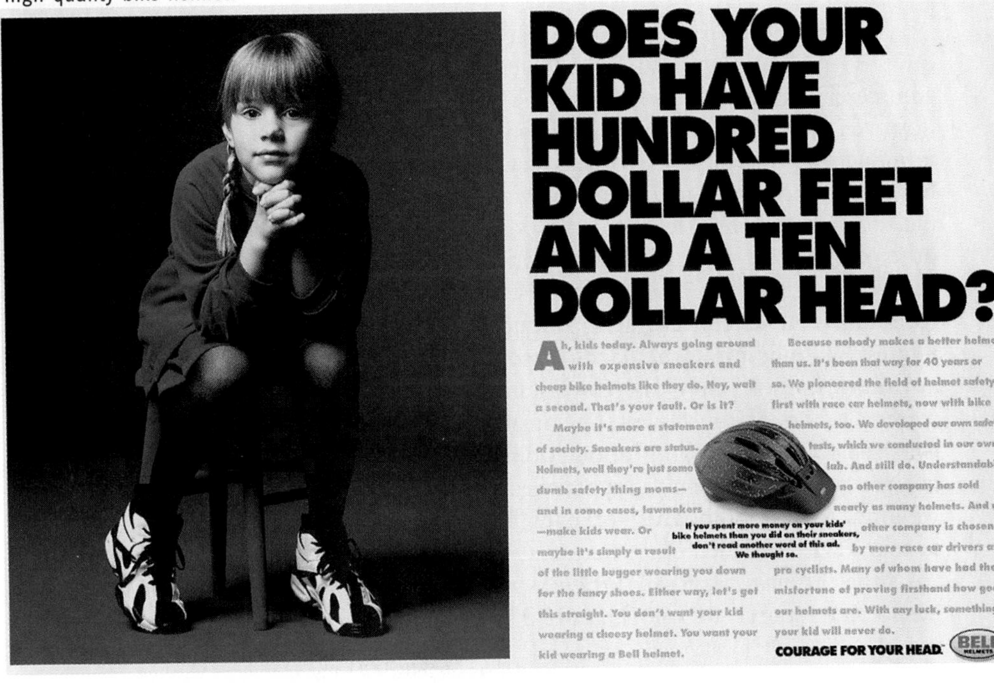

rises to a level high enough to become a drive. A need can also be triggered by *external stimuli.* A person passes a bakery and the smell of freshly baked bread stimulates his or her hunger. At this stage, the marketer should research consumers to determine what kinds of needs or problems arise, what brought them about, and how they led the consumer to this particular product.

Jennifer Wong might answer that she felt the need for more convenience when it came to transportation. Her office recently relocated and is no longer near a subway station. She first considered buying a car, but soon realized that parking in downtown Toronto would pose a problem. The rising cost of gas also concerned her. Thus, her focus turned to another option—a motorcycle. By gathering such information, the marketer can identify the factors that most often trigger interest in the product and can develop marketing programs that involve these factors.

Information Search

An aroused consumer may or may not search for more information. If the consumer's drive is strong and a satisfying product is near at hand, the consumer is likely to buy it. If not, the consumer may store the need in memory or undertake an **information search** related to the need.

Information search
The stage of the buyer decision process in which the consumer is aroused to search for more information; the consumer may simply have heightened attention or may go into active information search.

At one level, the consumer may simply enter *heightened attention.* Jennifer Wong becomes more receptive to information about motorcycles. She pays attention to motorcycle ads, bikes used by friends, and conversations about motorcycles. Or Jennifer may go into *active information search,* in which she looks for reading material, surfs the Internet, phones friends, and gathers information in other ways. The amount of searching she does depends on the strength of her drive, the amount of information she starts with, the ease of obtaining more information, the value she places on additional information, and the satisfaction she gets from searching.

The consumer can obtain information from several sources:

- *Personal sources:* family, friends, neighbours, acquaintances
- *Commercial sources:* advertising, salespeople, dealers, packaging, displays
- *Public sources:* mass media, consumer-rating organizations
- *Experiential sources:* handling, examining, using the product

The influence of these information sources depends on the product and the buyer. Generally, the consumer receives the most information about a product from commercial sources—those controlled by the marketer. The most effective sources, however, tend to be personal. Personal sources appear to be even more important in influencing the purchase of services.[33] Commercial sources normally *inform* the buyer, but personal sources *legitimize* or *evaluate* products for the buyer. For example, doctors typically learn of new drugs from commercial sources, but turn to other doctors for evaluative information.

People often ask others—friends, relatives, acquaintances, professionals—for recommendations concerning a product or service. Thus, companies have a strong interest in building such *word-of-mouth* sources. These sources have two chief advantages. First, they are convincing: Word of mouth is the only promotion method that is of consumers, by consumers, and for consumers. Having loyal, satisfied customers that brag about doing business with you is the dream of every business owner. Not only are satisfied customers repeat buyers, but they are also walking, talking billboards for your business. Second, the costs are low. Keeping in touch with satisfied customers and turning them into word-of-mouth advocates costs the business relatively little. As more and more consumers turn to the Internet, a new source of information is emerging. Often called electronic word of

marketers speak out

Lindsey Davis, Product Assistant, Kraft Canada

Lindsey Davis is a new product assistant in children's cereals at Kraft Canada. She works on Post Cereal kids brands, including Honeycomb, Sugar Crisp, Alpha-Bits, and Fruity Pebbles. Her target audience is children between 4 and 13, with "gatekeeper moms" as a secondary target market to consider (as mom makes most of the purchase decisions in Canadian households).

Kraft Canada Inc. is a wholly owned subsidiary of Kraft Foods Inc. of Chicago, Illinois. Today, Kraft Canada is one of the largest consumer packaged food companies in the country. Kraft manufactures four of the top 10 grocery store items in Canada: Kraft Dinner Pasta Dinner, Maxwell House Instant Coffee, Kraft Thin Singles Process Cheese Slices, and Cheez Whiz Process Cheese Spread. Over the past five years, Kraft Canada has donated more than 3.6 million kilograms of food to food banks across Canada.

Lindsey works at Kraft's head office in Don Mills, Ontario, but she works closely with team members from manufacturing and sales in offices and plants across the country.

As an undergraduate, Lindsey at first didn't consider marketing. She wasn't sure exactly what marketers did, and coming from Victoria, British Columbia, she didn't have any role models in the field. (Corporations had many sales offices in her area, but few had large marketing departments.) However, she knew that she was interested in business. When she took her first marketing course, she realized she was especially interested in the consumer side of commerce. Unlike MIS or finance, fields that focus on technology and monetary exchanges, Lindsey found that she was drawn to marketing because it "has a personality." It offered her a chance to draw people together from other functional areas and distant locations so that they share the same goals and understand the strategic direction of the brand.

Lindsey's first project at Kraft was developing a line extension for Alpha-Bits cereal. "I was responsible for doing everything," Lindsey says excitedly. She worked on a new package design, communicated the benefits to the sales organization, worked with the advertising agency to promote the brand extension, and helped the manufacturing plant to develop prototypes and explain product research. Since this was her first major project, Lindsey was thorough in her approach. She had to clearly state her objectives for the project and keep her focus on the overall brand strategy. She had to know from the beginning what she wanted the new package to convey to consumers and what information she wanted to jump off the shelf.

Lindsey believes that more and more packaged goods companies are realizing the value of extending key brands. Rather than constantly introducing new products, firms are beginning to concentrate on core brands and leveraging their value. Consumers already know what the brand stands for, and research to guide decisions is already in place. However, it is important to keep core brands fresh, Lindsey stresses. Developing line extensions allows marketers to communicate new information to consumers and excite the sales force about brand innovations.

What Lindsey especially likes about her job at Kraft is the opportunity to learn by doing. "You dive right in," Lindsey says. "From the first day, you don't watch, you do!" This also means that Lindsey had to be willing to accept responsibility and make her own decisions. In fact, she has had to work for some time without direct supervision from a product manager. While this has meant that the learning curve is steep, it is also exciting to be able to gain new skills quickly. She has worked feverishly to understand the equities of her brand—learning everything from why certain colours matter in packaging to what the brand means to consumers in the target group.

Another thing about Kraft that Lindsey values is its great new training program. New hires at Kraft work on various brands for one to six months and then begin a training program that they attend one or two days each week for 15 weeks. They learn everything from how the budgeting system works to how the sales force is organized to the commercialization process at Kraft. Lindsey gained insights about how to motivate teams and how to develop critical paths for project management. This training, along with the opportunity to work with a product manager who was interested in Lindsey's personal development, has helped her to acquire the skills she will need as she moves to higher levels of the organization.

Technology is posing a new set of challenges for Lindsey. Kraft sees the Internet as a "wide open sky" in terms of marketing opportunities. It is an exciting medium that allows brand managers to give their products dimension and bring brand personalities alive. However, there are a lot of copyright and legal issues to be considered, especially when marketing to young children. While the Internet can be a valuable medium for gathering information about consumers, privacy issues must be considered and consumer information must be protected from unauthorized use. Using an Internet site for national advertising is also problematic, since in Quebec advertising to children isn't allowed. While Lindsey wants to have her brands on the leading edge of communication technology, she knows that she has to wrestle with these issues.

Finally, working with a large multinational firm can have both pluses and

Lindsey Davis.

minuses, Lindsey believes. As part of Kraft North America, Lindsey can quickly adopt innovative ideas developed for the US marketplace and implement strategies that have a track record of success there. However, Lindsey knows that there are differences between Canadian and American consumers and she has to know what they are. For example, people in the children's cereals brand group in Canada have worked to keep their products wholesome. While many of the cereals are sweetened, Kraft Canada doesn't want to cross the line of making them appear more like candy. Adding marshmallows and frosting is appealing to US consumers, but people at Kraft Canada constantly have to make the case that Canadian consumers value more nutritious, healthy products.

Lindsey is happy she accepted the job at Kraft Canada. Like anyone looking for a first job, Lindsey felt some uncertainty about whether she had made the right choice. That uncertainty has vanished. Lindsey believes that if you are the type of person who thrives on challenge, who has the energy and drive to make things happen, who is interested in consumers and the way they think, then working for a large packaged-goods company is the right place for you. Lindsey believes that the skills she has learned in taking on project leadership roles have broadened her horizons and are an important part of the lifelong learning that will translate into all parts of her life.

mouth, consumers are increasingly sharing information about products and services online. Take the case of online dating:[34]

> Today, with 7.1 million single adults in Canada, an 18.8 percent increase over 1990, online dating services aren't just places for lonely sociopaths. In fact, online dating is quietly becoming the norm for many people. Witness the enormous success of Interactive Media Group's (Canada) Webpersonals. It alone boasts a lonely hearts club of more than one million North Americans who exchange a staggering five million messages a month. While people browse listings for free, they pay for blocks of time in the chatrooms. The service generates over $85 million a year in revenue in Canada and the US and it even offers services for the gay community. But it is only one of the many wired lonely hearts clubs. There are small players as well as the giants. For example, London, Ontario-based QualitySoulmates.com operates with only four employees, but has over 17 000 member profiles online. How do people find out about these sites? Largely due to word-of-mouth referrals. As one operator noted, "More than one-quarter of [our] members have stated that friends recommended them to the service."

As more information is obtained, the consumer's awareness and knowledge of the available brands and features increase. In her information search, Jennifer Wong learned about the many available brands of motorcycles. The information also helped her drop certain brands from consideration. A company must design its marketing mix to make prospects aware of and knowledgeable about its brand. It should carefully identify consumers' sources of information and the importance of each source. Consumers should be asked how they first heard about the brand, what information they received, and what importance they placed on different information sources.

Evaluation of Alternatives

Alternative evaluation
The stage of the buyer decision process in which the consumer uses information to evaluate alternative brands in the choice set.

We have seen how the consumer uses information to arrive at a set of final brand choices. How does the consumer choose between the alternative brands? The marketer needs to know about **alternative evaluation**—that is, how the consumer processes information to arrive at brand choices. Unfortunately, consumers do not use a simple and single evaluation process in all buying situations. Instead, several evaluation processes are at work.

How consumers evaluate purchase alternatives depends on the individual consumer and the specific buying situation. In some cases, consumers use careful calculations and logical thinking. At other times, the same consumers do little or no evaluating, instead buying on impulse and relying on intuition. Sometimes consumers make buying decisions on their own; sometimes they turn to friends, consumer guides, or salespeople for buying advice.

Suppose Jennifer has narrowed her choices to four motorcycles. And suppose that she is primarily interested in four attributes—quality, ease of handling, ergonomic design, and price. Jennifer has formed beliefs about how each brand rates on each attribute. The marketer wishes to predict which motorcycle Jennifer will buy.

Clearly, if one motorcycle rated best on all the attributes, we could predict that Jennifer would choose it. But the brands vary in appeal. Some buyers will base their buying decision on only one attribute, and their choices are easy to predict. If Jennifer wants ease of handling above everything, she will buy the motorcycle that rates highest on this attribute. But most buyers consider several attributes, each with different importance. If we knew the importance weights that Jennifer assigns to each of the four attributes, we could predict her motorcycle choice more reliably.

Marketers should study buyers to determine how they actually evaluate brand alternatives. If they know what evaluative processes go on, marketers can take steps to influence the buyer's decision. Motorcycle manufacturers that want to appeal directly to women riders can design products to appeal specifically to them. Models such as Harley's Sportster 883 Hugger are lighter in weight than some of their traditional models, with higher seats and easier handling. The company has also moved away from traditional motorcycle colours to power colours such as red. At the same time, the firm has retained traditional features such as Harley's unique engine, so "the streets never sound the same."

Purchase Decision

Purchase decision
The stage of the buyer decision process in which the consumer actually buys the product.

In the evaluation stage, the consumer ranks brands and forms purchase intentions. Generally, the consumer's **purchase decision** will be to buy the most preferred brand, but two factors can come between the purchase *intention* and the purchase *decision*. The first factor is the *attitudes of others*. If Jennifer's friends ride Honda motorcycles, chances of her buying a Harley will be reduced.

The second factor is *unexpected situational factors*. The consumer may form a purchase intention based on such factors as expected income, expected price, and expected product benefits. However, unexpected events can change the purchase intention. Jennifer may lose her job, some other purchase may become more urgent, or a close competitor may drop its price. Thus, preferences and even purchase intentions do not always result in actual purchase choice.

Postpurchase Behaviour

Postpurchase behaviour
The stage of the buyer decision process in which consumers take further action after purchase based on their satisfaction or dissatisfaction.

The marketer's job does not end when the product is bought. After purchasing the product, the consumer will be satisfied or dissatisfied and will engage in **postpurchase behaviour** of interest to the marketer. What determines whether the buyer is satisfied or dissatisfied with a purchase? The answer lies in the relationship between the *consumer's expectations* and the product's *perceived performance*. If the product falls short of expectations, the consumer is disappointed; if it meets expectations, the consumer is satisfied; if it exceeds expectations, the consumer is delighted.

Consumers base their expectations on information they receive from sellers, friends, and other sources. If the seller exaggerates the product's performance, consumer expectations will not be met, and dissatisfaction will result. The larger the gap between expectations and performance, the greater the consumer's dissatisfaction. This suggests that sellers should make product claims that accurately represent the product's performance, so that buyers are satisfied. Marketing Highlight 5-3 shows how good marketers handle their dissatisfied customers.

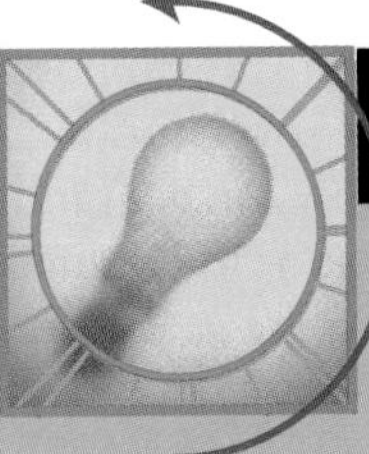

marketing highlight 5-3

Got a Problem? Just Phone, Fax, E-Mail, or "Teleweb" Us!

What should companies do with dissatisfied customers? Everything they can! Unhappy customers not only stop buying but also can quickly damage the company's image; Studies show that customers tell many more other people about bad experiences than about good ones. However, dealing effectively with gripes can actually boost customer loyalty and the company's image. Enlightened companies don't try to hide from dissatisfied customers; they go out of their way to encourage customers to complain, then bend over backward to make disgruntled buyers happy again.

The first opportunity to handle gripes often comes at the point of purchase. Many firms teach their customer contact people how to resolve problems and defuse customer anger. However, most companies have also set up call centres and Web sites to coax out and deal with consumer problems and questions.

Today, over two-thirds of all North American manufacturers offer toll-free numbers to handle complaints, inquiries, and orders. For example, in its first ten years, the Gerber help line (1-800-GERBER) received more than 4 million calls. Help line staffers, most of them mothers or grandmothers themselves, handle customer concerns and provide baby care advice 24 hours a day, 365 days a year, to more than 2400 callers a day. The help line is staffed by English-, French-, and Spanish-speaking operators, and interpreters are available for most other languages. Callers include new parents, day care providers, and even health professionals. One in five of all calls to the help line comes from men. Callers ask a wide variety of questions, from when to feed a baby specific foods to how to babyproof a home. "It used to be that mom or grandmom was right around the corner to answer your baby questions," notes the manager of the Gerber help line. "But more and more, that's not the case. For new or expectant parents, it's nice to know that they can pick up the phone any time of the day and talk to someone that understands and can help."

General Electric's Answer Center may be one of the most extensive 800-number systems. It handles more than 3 million calls a year, only five percent of them complaints. At the heart of the system is a giant database that provides the centre's service reps with instant access to more than a million answers about 8500 models in 120 product lines. The centre receives some unusual calls, as when a submarine off the Connecticut coast requested help fixing a motor. Still, according to GE, its people resolve 90 percent of complaints or inquiries on the first call, and complainers often become even more loyal customers. Although the company spends an average of $5.00 per call, it reaps two to three times that much in new sales and warranty savings. GE has also set up the GE Online Answer Center (www.ge.com/oac) to help customers obtain information about its products and services, locate dealers, and get answers to frequently requested topics.

As Susan Leigh, marketing and communications manager for Bell Canada's Contact Centre Solutions Team notes, call centres themselves have evolved dramatically. Instead of just being a bank of phones staffed by people who receive complaints, they've become high-tech and high-touch operations that help companies to keep customers from defecting, lure customers from the competition, target the most profitable customers, and increase repeat customer purchases. Traditional call centres have grown into sophisticated technology-driven *contact centres* that are the hub of the enterprise and the focal point for managing customer relationships.

Today, enabled by computer-telephony integration, companies use their contact centres to leverage existing customer information to enhance, maintain, and manage customer relationships throughout their life cycles. Today's multi-media contact centres can be accessed through the Internet and a host of other vehicles—interactive video kiosks, telephone, e-mail, and fax. The idea is to make customers' interactions with companies seamless and uniform, no matter which form of communication they choose.

Integrate the telephone—long a medium for developing customer rela-

Keeping customers happy: The Gerber help line has fielded more than 4 million calls providing baby care advice 24 hours a day, 365 days a year, to more than 2400 callers a day.

tionships—with Web technology and you have a "teleweb" connection, a powerful means of handling customer questions and concerns. This technology lets a customer browse a Web site on a PC at the same time that a customer service agent browses the site. The two can talk over a separate telephone line or an Internet connection to discuss problems or compare products. Operators can synchronize the Web screens viewed by a company's agents and their customers as they talk. The technology even lets either party draw circles around words or pictures for both to see. This may not seem like a big deal, but in discussions about a complex technological device, it helps if customer and agent are viewing a common diagram.

Bell helps its clients develop and improve their customer contact centres. Experience has shown that building a contact centre can spearhead enormous changes in the way a firm delivers its services and relates to its customers. With Bell's help, a firm's contact centre can anticipate and respond to shifts in customer needs and preferences while reducing costs and increasing revenues. Leigh notes that contact centres have become critical to customer-focused business strategies and are often the differentiating factor that allows a company to gain a significant competitive advantage. "For instance, a sudden spike in calls to a customer service number often suggests breakdowns elsewhere in the organization, perhaps in quality control, marketing, or shipping," Leigh suggests. "If companies don't bother to find out why their customer service agents are suddenly swamped, they may never address the root of the problem."

The best way to keep customers happy is to provide good products and services in the first place. Short of that, however, a company must develop a good system for ferreting out problems and connecting with customers. Such a system is much more than just a necessary evil—customer happiness usually shows up on the company's bottom line. One recent study found that dollars invested in complaint-handling and customer contact systems yield an average return of between 100 and 200 percent. Maryanne Rasmussen, vice-president of worldwide quality at American Express, offers this formula: "Better complaint handling equals higher customer satisfaction equals higher brand loyalty equals higher performance."

Today's business-to-business marketers, like Bell, go out of their way to give customers every opportunity for contact. For example, Indus International, a maker of enterprise asset management software, launched CareNet, a Web site designed to boost retention by simplifying customer contact. The site lets clients access product information, pose questions to service reps, and find solutions to specific problems. Customers are also encouraged to give feedback on the Web and post solutions to production problems. So far, Indus's clients are impressed. CareNet had 30 users in its first month, but this number jumped to 600 just 10 months later.

Sources: Quotes from Susan Leigh, "Customer contact centres a tool for growth," *Strategy,* 7 June 1999:D14; Ziff Communications, "On Mother's Day, advice goes a long way," *PR Newswire,* 2 May 1995; Alessandra Bianchi, "Lines of fire," *Inc. Technology,* 1988:36–48; and Matt Hamblen, "Call centers and Web sites cozy up," *Computerworld,* 2 March 1998:1. Also see Roland T. Rust, Bala Subramanian, and Mark Wells, "Making complaints a management tool," *Marketing Management,* Fall 1992:41–5; Tibbett L. Speer, "They complain because they care," *American Demographics,* May 1996:13–4; John F. Yarbrough, "Dialing for dollars," *Sales & Marketing Management,* January 1997:60–7; Geoffrey Brewer, "The customer stops here," *Sales & Marketing Management,* March 1998:31–6; and Marcia Stepanek, "You'll wanna hold their hands," *Business Week,* 22 March 1999:EB30–1.

The Buyer Decision Process for New Products

We have looked at the stages buyers go through in trying to satisfy a need. Buyers may pass quickly or slowly through these stages, and some of the stages may even be reversed. Much depends on the nature of the buyer, the product, and the buying situation.

New product
A good, service, or idea that is perceived by some potential customers as new.

Adoption process
The mental process through which an individual passes from first hearing about an innovation to final adoption.

We now look at how buyers approach the purchase of new products. A **new product** is a good, service, or idea that is perceived by some potential customers as new. It may have been around for a while, but our interest is in how consumers learn about products for the first time and make decisions on whether to adopt them. We define the **adoption process** as "the mental process through which an individual passes from first learning about an innovation to final adoption,"[35] and *adoption* as the decision by an individual to become a regular user of the product.

Stages in the Adoption Process

Consumers pass through five stages in the process of adopting a new product:

- *Awareness.* The consumer becomes aware of the new product, but lacks information about it.
- *Interest.* The consumer seeks information about the new product.

- *Evaluation.* The consumer considers whether trying the new product makes sense.
- *Trial.* The consumer tries the new product on a small scale to improve his or her estimate of its value.
- *Adoption.* The consumer decides to make full and regular use of the new product.

This model suggests that the new product marketer should consider how to help consumers move through these stages. A manufacturer of large-screen televisions may discover that many consumers in the interest stage do not move to the trial stage because of uncertainty and the large investment. If these same consumers would be willing to use a large-screen television on a trial basis for a small fee, the manufacturer should consider offering a trial-use plan with an option to buy.

Individual Differences in Innovativeness

People differ greatly in their readiness to try new products. In each product area, there are "consumption pioneers" and early adopters. Other individuals adopt new products much later. People can be classified into the adopter categories shown in Figure 5-7. After a slow start, an increasing number of people adopt the new product. The number of adopters reaches a peak and then drops off as fewer non-adopters remain. Innovators are defined as the first 2.5 percent of the buyers to adopt a new idea (those beyond two standard deviations from mean adoption time); the early adopters are the next 13.5 percent (between one and two standard deviations); and so forth.

The five adopter groups have differing values. *Innovators* are venturesome—they try new ideas at some risk. *Early adopters* are guided by respect—they are opinion leaders in their communities and adopt new ideas early but carefully. The *early majority* are deliberate—although they rarely are leaders, they adopt new ideas before the average person. The *late majority* are sceptical—they adopt an innovation only after most people have tried it. Finally, *laggards* are tradition bound—they are suspicious of changes and adopt the innovation only when it has become something of a tradition itself.

This adopter classification suggests that an innovating firm should research the characteristics of innovators and early adopters and should direct marketing efforts at them. In general, innovators tend to be relatively younger, better educated, and higher in income than later adopters and non-adopters. They are more receptive to unfamiliar things, rely more on their own values and judgment, and are more

FIGURE 5-7 Adopter categorization on the basis of relative time of adoption of innovations

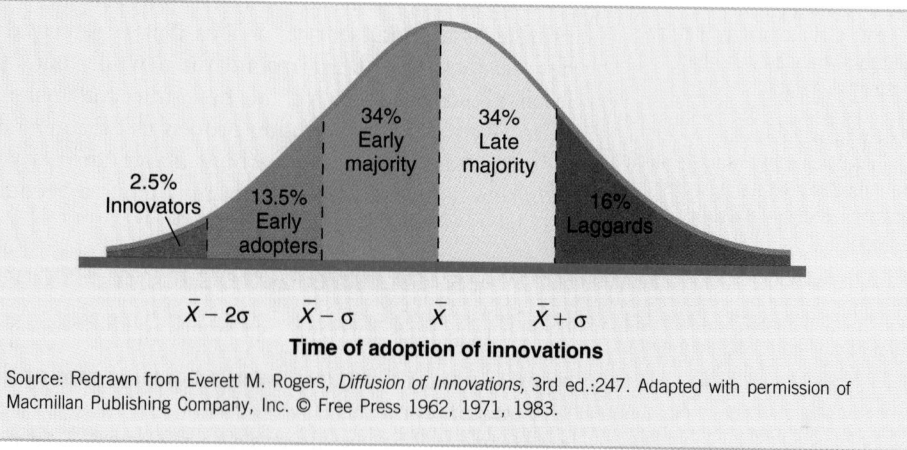

Source: Redrawn from Everett M. Rogers, *Diffusion of Innovations,* 3rd ed.:247. Adapted with permission of Macmillan Publishing Company, Inc. © Free Press 1962, 1971, 1983.

willing to take risks. They are less brand loyal and more likely to take advantage of special promotions such as discounts, coupons, and samples.

Influence of Product Characteristics on Rate of Adoption

The characteristics of the new product affect its rate of adoption. Some products catch on almost overnight (Frisbees), whereas others take a long time to gain acceptance (personal computers). Five characteristics are especially important in influencing an innovation's rate of adoption. For example, consider the characteristics of large-screen televisions in relation to the rate of adoption:

- *Relative advantage* is the degree to which the innovation appears superior to existing products. The greater the perceived relative advantage of using a large-screen TV—say, in picture quality and ease of viewing—the sooner such TVs will be adopted.
- *Compatibility* is the degree to which the innovation fits the values and experiences of potential consumers. Large-screen TVs, for example, are highly compatible with the lifestyles found in upper-middle-class homes.
- *Complexity* is the degree to which the innovation is difficult to understand or use. Large-screen TVs are not very complex and will, therefore, take less time to penetrate homes than more complex innovations.
- *Divisibility* is the degree to which the innovation may be tried on a limited basis. Large-screen TVs are expensive. To the extent that people can lease them with an option to buy, their rate of adoption will increase.
- *Communicability* is the degree to which the results of using the innovation can be observed or described to others. Because large-screen TVs lend themselves to demonstration and description, their use will spread faster among consumers.

Some other characteristics that influence the rate of adoption are initial and ongoing costs, risk and uncertainty, and social approval. The new product marketer must research all these factors when developing the new product and its marketing program.

Consumer Behaviour across International Borders

Understanding consumer behaviour is difficult enough for companies marketing within the borders of a single country. For companies operating in many countries, however, understanding and serving the needs of consumers can be daunting. Although consumers in different countries may have some things in common, their values, attitudes, and behaviours often vary greatly. International marketers must understand such differences and adjust their products and marketing programs accordingly.

Sometimes the differences are obvious. For example, in Canada and the United States, where most people eat cereal regularly for breakfast, Kellogg focuses its marketing on persuading consumers to select a Kellogg brand rather than a competitor's brand. In France, however, where most people prefer croissants and coffee or no breakfast at all, Kellogg advertising simply attempts to convince people that they should eat cereal for breakfast. Its packaging includes step-by-step instructions on how to prepare cereal.

Often differences across international markets are more subtle. They may result from physical differences in consumers and their environments. For example, Remington makes smaller electric shavers to fit the smaller hands of Japanese consumers and battery-powered shavers for the British market where few bathrooms have electrical outlets. Other differences result from varying customs. Consider the following examples:

- Shaking your head from side to side means "no" in most countries but "yes" in Bulgaria and Sri Lanka.
- In South America, Southern Europe, and many Arab countries, touching another person is a sign of warmth and friendship. In Asia, it is considered an invasion of privacy.
- In Norway or Malaysia, it's rude to leave something on your plate when eating; in Egypt, it's rude *not* to leave something on your plate.[36]

Failing to understand such differences in customs and behaviours between countries can mean disaster for a marketer's international products and programs.

Marketers must decide on the degree to which they will adapt their products and marketing programs to meet the unique cultures and needs of consumers in various markets. On the one hand, they want to standardize their offerings to simplify operations and take advantage of cost economies. On the other hand, adapting marketing efforts within each country results in products and programs that better satisfy the needs of local consumers. The question of whether to adapt or standardize the marketing mix across international markets has created a lively debate in recent years.

Review of Concept Connections

The Canadian consumer market consists of about 29 million people who consume many billions of dollars worth of goods and services each year, making it one of the most attractive consumer markets in the world. The world consumer market consists of more than six billion people. Consumers around the world vary greatly in age, income, education level, and tastes. Understanding how these differences affect consumer *buying behaviour* is one of the biggest challenges marketers face.

1. Define the consumer market and construct a simple model of consumer buyer behaviour.

The *consumer market* consists of all the individuals and households who buy or acquire goods and services for personal consumption. The simplest model of consumer buyer behaviour is the stimulus–response model. According to this model, marketing stimuli (the four Ps) and other major forces (economic, technological, political, cultural) enter the consumer's "black box," and produce certain responses. Once in the black box, these inputs produce observable buyer responses, such as product choice, brand choice, purchase timing, and purchase amount.

2. Name the four major factors that influence consumer buyer behaviour.

Consumer buyer behaviour is influenced by four key sets of buyer characteristics: cultural, social, personal, and psychological. Although many of these factors cannot be influenced by the marketer, they can be useful in identifying interested buyers and in shaping products and appeals to serve consumer needs better. *Culture* is the most basic determinant of a person's wants and behaviour. It includes the basic values, perceptions, preferences, and behaviours that a person learns from family and other important institutions. *Subcultures* are "cultures within cultures" that have distinct values and lifestyles, and can be based on anything from age to ethnicity. People with different cultural and subcultural characteristics have different product and brand preferences. As a result, marketers may want to focus their marketing programs on the special needs of certain groups.

Social factors also influence a buyer's behaviour. A person's *reference groups*—family, friends, social organizations, professional associations–-strongly affect product and brand choices. The buyer's age, life-cycle stage, occupation, economic circumstances, lifestyle, personality, and other *personal characteristics* influence his or her buying decisions. Consumer *lifestyles*—the whole pattern of acting and interacting in the world—are also an important influence on purchase decisions. Finally, consumer buying behaviour is influenced by four major *psychological factors*—motivation, perception, learning, and beliefs and attitudes. Each of these factors provides a different perspective for understanding the workings of the buyer's black box.

3. **List and understand the stages in the buyer decision process.**

When making a purchase, the buyer goes through a decision process consisting of *need recognition, information search, evaluation of alternatives, purchase decision,* and *postpurchase behaviour.* The marketer's job is to understand the buyer's behaviour at each stage and the influences that are operating. During *need recognition,* the consumer recognizes a problem or need that could be satisfied by a product or service in the market. Once the need is recognized, the consumer is aroused to seek more information and moves into the *information search* stage. With information in hand, the consumer proceeds to *alternative evaluation,* when the information is used to evaluate brands in the choice set. From there, the consumer makes a *purchase decision* and actually buys the product. In the final stage of the buyer decision process, *postpurchase behaviour,* the consumer takes action based on satisfaction or dissatisfaction.

4. **Describe the adoption and diffusion process for new products.**

The product adoption process is composed of five stages: awareness, interest, evaluation, trial, and adoption. Initially, the consumer must become aware of the new product. *Awareness* leads to *interest,* and the consumer seeks information about the new product. Once information has been gathered, the consumer enters the *evaluation* stage and considers buying the new product. Next, in the *trial* stage, the consumer tries the product on a small scale to improve his or her estimate of its value. If the consumer is satisfied with the product, he or she enters the *adoption* stage, deciding to use the new product fully and regularly.

With respect to the diffusion of new products, consumers respond at different rates, depending on both the consumer's and the product's characteristics. Consumers may be innovators, early adopters, early majority, late majority, or laggards. *Innovators* are willing to try risky new ideas; *early adopters*—often community opinion leaders—accept new ideas early but carefully; the *early majority*—rarely leaders—decide deliberately to try new ideas, doing so before the average person does; the *late majority* try an innovation only after most people have adopted it; whereas *laggards* adopt an innovation only after it has become a tradition itself. Manufacturers try to bring their new products to the attention of potential early adopters, especially those who are opinion leaders.

Key Terms

Adoption process *(p. 225)*
Alternative evaluation *(p. 222)*
Attitude *(p. 215)*
Belief *(p. 215)*
Complex buying behaviour *(p. 217)*
Consumer buying behaviour *(p. 195)*
Consumer market *(p. 195)*
Culture *(p. 196)*
Dissonance-reducing buying behaviour *(p. 217)*
Group *(p. 203)*
Habitual buying behaviour *(p. 218)*
Information search *(p. 220)*
Learning *(p. 215)*
Lifestyle *(p. 207)*
Motive (or drive) *(p. 211)*
Need recognition *(p. 219)*
New product *(p. 225)*
Opinion leaders *(p. 204)*
Perception *(p. 212)*
Personality *(p. 211)*
Postpurchase behaviour *(p. 223)*
Psychographics *(p. 207)*
Purchase decision *(p. 223)*
Social classes *(p. 203)*
Subculture *(p. 198)*
Variety-seeking buying behaviour *(p. 218)*

Discussing the Issues

1. List several factors that you could add to the model in Figure 5-1 to make it a more complete description of consumer behaviour.
2. Assume that you are the marketing manager for Zellers. Your objective is to compete more effectively against Wal-Mart by serving important

subculture segments better. To assist your marketing team in preparing a marketing strategy to meet this objective, construct a profile of each of the following subcultures: (a) Aboriginal consumers, (b) Asian-Canadians, and (c) Jewish consumers.

3. In designing the advertising for a soft drink, which would you find more helpful: information about consumer demographics or consumer lifestyles? Give examples of how you would use each type of information.
4. The basic self-concept premise is that people's possessions contribute to and reflect their identities. How do advertisers on MuchMusic use the idea of self-concept to market their products? Give specific illustrations (visit www.muchmusic.com for additional information). Assess MuchMusic's approach to advertising.
5. Abraham Maslow sought to explain why people are driven by particular needs at particular times. Which level of Maslow's hierarchy applies best to the following situations: (a) purchasing the newest, fastest personal computer; (b) purchasing food at lunch time; (c) adjusting your clothing choices to reflect the latest trends; (d) serving on the United Way fund-raising board; and (e) purchasing a smoke detector for your home? Explain your choices.
6. Think about a very good or very bad experience you have had with a product. Discuss how this experience shaped your beliefs about this product. How long will these beliefs last?
7. Consumers play many different roles in the buying process: initiator, influencer, decider, buyer, and user. Describe purchases in which you've played these different roles.
8. For many people, changing to a healthier lifestyle would be an innovation. This might require changes in diet, exercise, smoking, and drinking. Discuss this innovation in terms of its relative advantage, compatibility, complexity, divisibility, and communicability. Is a healthy lifestyle likely to be adopted quickly by most Canadians?

Marketing Applications

1. SRI has categorized Internet users according to iVALS segments, a VALS typology designed for Net users. Companies that market on the Web can use this information to develop their appeals, strategies, and promotions. The concept is that consumers' purchases are shaped by the interplay of their psychological, physical, demographic, and material resources. Visit SRI at www.future.sri.com and follow the links to the iVALS questionnaire. Complete the survey to determine your iVals type. Answer these questions:
   a. What is your iVALS type? Do you agree with the assessment? Why or why not?
   b. How do iVALS segments differ from the VALS segments discussed in this chapter?
   c. How can marketers use iVALS information to serve consumers better? Name five types of products or services for which iVALS information would be particularly useful. Explain.
   d. How could advertisers use iVALS or VALS information to communicate better with consumers? Find three advertising examples from Web sites or current magazines that might be designed around iVALS or VALS segments. Explain your reasoning.
   e. After reading Marketing Highlight 5-1, compare the iVALS approach to the Technographics scheme. Which do you prefer? Why?
2. What's holding up high-definition television (HDTV)? A year after its introduction, what was projected to be one of the greatest electronic viewing innovations since colour, HDTV was struggling with low penetration, limited reception, scarce content, and heavy controversy. Why? Some blame poor marketing; others point to technical snafus. Whatever the reasons, digitalization of television pictures has been slow to develop and few consumers have been willing to plunk down $5000 to watch the new and improved picture. (For more information on HDTV, see Sony at www.sony.com, Toshiba at www.toshiba.com, or Panasonic at www.panasonic.com.)
   a. Based on the information provided in the chapter, why is adoption of HDTV so slow to develop?
   b. Profile the characteristics of likely early adopters.

As marketing manager for a large electronics superstore that carries HDTVs, devise a strategy to get early adopters into your store to see and preview this new form of television.

c. When customers visit your store to see the new HDTVs, they are bound to have concerns that must be overcome before sales can occur. What might these concerns be? Considering the consumer behaviour model presented in the chapter, design a strategy for overcoming these concerns.

d. What do you think will be the future of HDTV? What other products and industries will HDTV affect?

Internet Connections

Psychographic Classification of Consumers

SRI Consulting, through the Business Intelligence Center online, features the Values and Lifestyles Program (VALS). Many marketers who wish to understand the psychographics of both existing and potential customers use this market segmentation program. Companies and advertisers on the Web can use this information to develop their sites. Visit SRI at sri.com and follow links to the VALS questionnaire. Take the survey to determine your type and then read all about your type. Use this information for the discussion questions below the table. Also of interest to marketers in the global economy are the psychographic differences between cultures. SRI recently created two new segmentation programs: Geo-VALS and Japan-VALS. Complete the following table about the nine Japan-VALS segments and characteristics as they are presented on the site.

For Discussion

1. What is your VALS type? Does it describe you well? Why or why not?
2. What four products have high indexes for your type? Do you buy these products?
3. How do the US-based VALS segments differ from Japan-VALS segments? What does this say about consumer differences between the two cultures?
4. Why do you think SRI designed a separate typology for Japanese consumers?
5. Other than product design, how can marketers use information from Japan-VALS?

Japan-VALS Type	% of Population	Characteristics

Savvy Sites

- GeoCities (geocities.yahoo.com) offers free home pages to anyone who wants to be located in one of its "neighbourhoods." These home page clusters are divided into 41 topics, from art to women. This is an interesting example of psychographic segmentation by self-selection.
- DoubleClick (www.doubleclick.com) serves ads from clients to users as they log on to various sites. Ads are targeted by psychographics and geographic location of user.
- Ad-Up (www.ad-up.com) provides psychographic and "affinity" targeting for advertisers looking for markets among Web users.

Notes

1. Mariam Mesbah, "Harley mag ad targets women: *Advertising in Chatelaine, Modern Woman,*" *Strategy,* 28 April 1997:1.
2. Quotes from Richard A. Melcher, "Tune-up time for Harley," *Business Week,* 8 April 1997:90–4; Ian P. Murphy, "Aided by research, Harley goes whole hog," *Marketing News,* 2 December 1996:16,17; and Dyan Machan, "Is the hog going soft," *Forbes,* 10 March 1997:114–9. Also see "Hot stuff," *Money,* April 1997:174.
3. See Philip Cateora, *International Marketing,* 8th ed., Homewood, IL.: Irwin, 1993:74–5.
4. Marketing scholars have developed several models of the consumer buying process. The most prominent models come from John A. Howard and Jagdish N. Sheth, *The Theory of Buyer Behavior,* New York: John Wiley, 1969; Francesco M. Nicosia, *Consumer Decision Processes,* Englewood Cliffs, NJ: Prentice Hall, 1966; James F. Engel, Roger D. Blackwell, and Paul W. Miniard, *Consumer Behavior,* 5th ed., New York: Holt, Rinehart & Winston, 1986; and James R. Bettman, *An Information Processing Theory of Consumer Choice,* Reading, MA: Addison-Wesley, 1979. For a summary, see Leon G. Schiffman and Leslie Lazar Kanuk, *Consumer Behavior,* 5th ed., Englewood Cliffs, NJ: Prentice Hall, 1994:644–56.
5. Allan R. Gregg, "Coming of age: After a rough ride, Canada's mood has returned to the confident outlook found in 1984's first year-end poll," Bruce Wallace, "What makes a Canadian? We're certain we're unique, but we don't seem to know precisely what sets us apart from others," *Maclean's,* 20 December 1999: Cover Story; Robert Sheppard, "We Are Canadian," *Maclean's,* 25 December 2000: Cover; www.macleans.ca/2000/12/25/cover/45320.shtml.
6. Ministry of Supply and Services Canada, *Shared Values: The Canadian Identity,* 1991:1; Craig McKie and Keith Thompson, *Canadian Social Trends,* Toronto: Thompson Educational Publishing, Inc.
7. Department of Foreign Affairs and International Trade, "Canada in the world," 1999, www.dfait-maeci.gc.ca/english/foreignp/cnd-world/chap5.htm.
8. Statistics Canada, "1996 Census: Mother tongue, home language and knowledge of languages," *The Daily,* 2 December 1997.
9. Allan R. Gregg, "Coming of age: After a rough ride, Canada's mood has returned to the confident outlook found in 1984's first year-end poll," and Bruce Wallace, "What makes a Canadian? We're certain we're unique, but we don't seem to know precisely what sets us apart from others," *Maclean's.*
10. For this and other examples of the effects of culture in international marketing, see Cateora, *International Marketing,* Chapter 4.
11. Carey Toane, "Veering off from the mainstream: Marketers are finding divergent ways beyond traditional advertising to reach ethnic consumers," *Marketing On-Line,* 5 June 2000; Patrick Lejtenyi, "Underlying differences: Market researchers must be diligent about identifying subcultures within ethnic groups," *Marketing On-Line,* 5 June 2000.
12. Sinclair Stewart, "Special report: Multicultural marketing: A long and winding road: While the numbers suggest Canada's ethnic communities are well worth wooing, national advertisers are still reluctant to embark on a multicultural mission," *Strategy,* 17 August 1998:20.
13. Paul Nayyar, "Multicultural marketing: Plethora of media vehicles target ethnic groups, But lack of research data still creating obstacles for national advertisers," *Strategy,* 15 February 1999:29.
14. Carey Toane, "Veering off from the mainstream: Marketers are finding divergent ways beyond traditional advertising to reach ethnic consumers," *Marketing On-Line,* 5 June 2000.
15. Jennifer Lynn, "Approaching diversity," *Marketing,* 30 July 1995:15; David Menzies, "TD Bank opens a branch in cyberspace," *Marketing,* 19 June 1995:11; James Pollock, "Opening doors of opportunity," *Marketing,* 18 September 1995; Isabel Vincent, "Chasing after the ethnic consumer," *The Globe and Mail,* 18 September 1995; Craig McKie and Keith Thompson, *Canadian Social Trends.*
16. Keith McArthur, "Internet has transformed life," *Globe and Mail,* 22 March 2000:B11.
17. Nielsen/NetRatings, "Canadian Internet users spend more time online than U.S. Web surfers," *Reports on Internet Usage in Canada,* 26 June 2000.
18. Industry Canada, "Internet usage statistics and user characteristics: Demographic characteristics of Internet users," Canadian Internet Retailing Report, 23 October 1998:Chapter 3.1, strategis.ic.gc.ca/SSG/ir01621e.html.
19. Steve Ferley, "PMB '97 reveals that Canadian Internet usage patterns fall along both language and demographic lines," 1997:16.

20. Randy Carr, "The five big hurdles on the road of electronic commerce," *Digital Marketing in Marketing,* 5 May 1997:16; John Southerst, "Accountants design 'deal of approval' for Web trade," *The Globe and Mail,* 2 December 1997:B15.

21. "Lifestyles of the rich," *National Post,* 22 April 2000:E11.

22. Courteny Kane, "Advertising: TBWA/Chiat Day brings 'street culture' to a campaign for Levi-Strauss Silver Tab clothing," *New York Times,* 14 August 1998:D8.

23. Debra Goldman, "Spotlight men," *Adweek,* 13 August 1990:M1–M6; Dennis Rodkin, "A manly sport: Building loyalty," *Advertising Age,* 15 April 1991:S1,S12; Nancy Ten Kate, "Who buys the pants in the family?" *American Demographics,* January 1992:12; and Laura Zinn, "Real men buy paper towels, too," *Business Week,* 9 November 1992:75–6.

24. Jeffery Zbar, "Hardware builds awareness among women," *Advertising Age,* 11 July 1994:18.

25. David Leonhardt, "Hey kids, buy this," *Business Week,* 30 June 1997:62–7. Also see Kay M. Palan and Robert E. Wilkes, "Adolescent–parent interaction in family decisions," *Journal of Consumer Research,* September 1997:159–69.

26. "Ad agency finds five global segments," *Marketing News,* 8 January 1990:9, 17.

27. Salem Alaton, "Look who's going cellular," *Globe and Mail,* 5 December 1995:C1.

28. Myron Magnet, "Let's go for growth," *Fortune,* 7 March 1994:70.

29. See Annetta Miller and Dody Tsiantar, "Psyching out consumers," *Newsweek,* 27 February 1989:46–7; and Rebecca Piirto, "Words that sell," *American Demographics,* January 1992:6.

30. Abraham H. Maslow, *Motivation and Personality,* 2nd ed., New York: Harper & Row, 1970:80–106. Also see Rudy Schrocer, "Maslow's hierarchy of needs as a framework for identifying emotional triggers," *Marketing Review,* February 1991:26, 28.

31. David Todd, "Quebec Milk Producers play on emotional ties," *Strategy,* 1 March 1999:31; Stephanie Whittaker, "Milk grows up," *Marketing On-Line,* 9 August 1999.

32. See Henry Assael, *Consumer Behavior and Marketing Action,* Boston: Kent Publishing, 1987:Chapter 4. An earlier classification of three types of consumer buying behaviour—routine response behaviour, limited problem solving, and extensive problem solving—can be found in John A. Howard and Jagdish Sheth, *The Theory of Consumer Behavior,* New York: John Wiley, 1969:27–28. Also see John A. Howard, *Consumer Behavior in Marketing Strategy,* Englewood Cliffs, NJ: Prentice Hall, 1989.

33. For these and other examples, see William J. Stanton, Michael J. Etzel, and Bruce J. Walker, *Fundamentals of Marketing,* New York: McGraw-Hill, Inc., 1991:536.

34. Andrea Zoe Aster, "Caught in love's web," *Marketing On-Line,* 25 September 2000. For more on word-of-mouth sources, see Philip Kotler and Peggy Cunningham, *Marketing Management: Analysis, Planning, Implementation, and Control,* 10th ed., Toronto: Prentice Hall, 2000:560.

35. The discussion draws heavily on Everett M. Rogers, *Diffusion of Innovations,* 3rd ed., New York: Free Press, 1983. Also see Hubert Gatignon and Thomas S. Robertson, "A propositional inventory for new diffusion research," *Journal of Consumer Research,* March 1985:849–67.

36. For these and other examples, see William J. Stanton, Michael J. Etzel, and Bruce J. Walker, *Fundamentals of Marketing,* New York: McGraw-Hill, Inc., 1991:536.

Company Case 5

The Looney School of Tennis

Craig Smith, president of the Looney School of Tennis, had some difficult decisions to make. The Looney School of Tennis, incorporated for nine months, had two "arms": school tennis programs and summer club management. During the school year, the Looney School of Tennis focused on running low-cost tennis programs in local private and public elementary schools. Although this was not the most profitable arm of the company, it was extremely important as it served to provide a broad base of customers for the second more profitable arm of the company, summer club management. While Craig was generally pleased with the level of success his company had reached in such a short period, two problem areas needed his immediate attention. First, to attract new elementary schools, Craig had initiated a free promotion to interested schools. This involved providing a demonstration lesson to every gym class in the school, which took, on average, two full days of instruction. While this promotion had proved very successful in attracting new customers, it was also very costly and Craig was unsure if he could continue with it. Second, Craig also had to resolve the dissatisfaction level of his tennis director, Justin Mondoux, who was unhappy with his current level of compensation.

Craig was hoping to reach some decisions and to implement "solutions" to these problem areas in time for the upcoming 1996 season.

Background

In 1991, Craig Smith was thinking about tennis. As a competitive player and high-performance tennis coach for over 11 years, he was concerned about the overall decline in participation in the sport. In the 1970s, the tennis industry went through a dramatic growth period, but by the 1990s, the industry was hurting. The sport was simply not capturing the imagination of youngsters, and this resulted in a decline in tennis club membership and interest in competitive tennis events.

As a result of his increasing concern over this industry "recession," Craig decided to volunteer his time to local private and public schools to run tennis programs to introduce children to the sport of tennis and hopefully increase awareness and interest in the sport. This volunteer program met with overwhelming success. Feedback from both parents and teachers was excellent, and membership in local tennis clubs increased. In 1995, Craig decided to incorporate the Looney School of Tennis, an innovative grassroots company aimed at promoting the sport of tennis by offering low-cost, quality tennis lessons throughout the Ottawa-Carleton area.

The Company

The Looney School of Tennis has one product: tennis lessons. It tailors the product to meet the needs of purchasers by offering lessons at various times and locations. The company emphasizes the fun aspect of the sport through grassroots school programming and by offering an innovative promotion strategy. The objective is to sell a high volume of top-quality, yet reasonably priced tennis lessons to both children and adults. Although children are the main target of Looney School lessons, adult programs are also offered in the summer club programs.

During the school year, Craig focuses his attention on running tennis programs through the private and public schools in the Ottawa-Carleton region. These programs introduce groups of about 20 children, at $3 per child per lesson, to the fun, athletic and positive dimensions of the sport. Lessons are held in the school gymnasium or, weather permitting, in the school yard (see Appendix 1).

Once the school year is over, the company shifts its focus to community tennis club management. More specifically, summer clubs, particularly those concerned with low membership levels, hire the Looney School of Tennis to completely design and oversee their summer programs. This involves the recruitment, supervision, and compensation of certified tennis professionals as well as the complete design, promotion, and implementation of all club programs, leagues, children's camps, and private lessons.

The two arms of the company complement each other. A large percentage of children or their parents are interested in having the students continue on with the sport after the introduction in the school. Parents traditionally contact the Looney School for information on tennis programs or camps offered nearby. The Looney School can then direct the children to the nearest community club managed by the company. The school programming offered by the Looney School is therefore an excellent platform to direct interest sparked by the school programs to the second focus of the company, summer club management.

The company was started with a low capital investment. Other than the computer purchased after incorporation, the yearly liability insurance fee, and the business telephone expense, the only expenses are variable costs of office supplies, photocopying, and the hourly wages paid to the instructors.

Specialized Wilson Sporting Equipment was provided under a sponsorship arrangement to the Looney School after incorporation. Such equipment as mini-tennis racquets and tennis nets are provided to all students for their use, free of charge, during Looney School lessons. This specialized equipment is easier for the children to handle and provides them with better control in playing the sport. This, in turn, results in higher success and self-confidence while taking part in the lessons.

Since the Looney School's goal is high-volume sales, the need for a large part-time staff is critical. Through his coaching activities, Craig Smith has personal contact with many high-performance, provincially ranked tennis players who are interested in teaching to gain experience and to work toward their coaching certification. They are dynamic, energetic, and very good with children, and are placed in the Looney School "hierarchy" according to their age, experience, and interpersonal skills. From bottom to top, the hierarchy is:

- Looney trainees: 15 hours of volunteer lessons
- Looney assistants: $6 per hour (uncertified) or $8 per hour (certified)
- Looney pros: $10 per hour (certified only)
- Tennis director: $12 per hour—Justin Mondoux
- President: Craig Smith

Looney assistants are generally promoted to Looney pros after one full year. During the summer months, Looney pros become community club head pros. This is flexible and subject to change, depending on the assessment of their progress. Craig Smith continually trains and supervises all staff.

The satisfaction level from the schools and parents alike has been very high. Feedback has indicated that the schools are very impressed with the high quality of the lessons and particularly shocked at their low cost. In fact, the company captured the interest of local television station CJOH TV, which hosted two segments on the company, aired during the six o'clock news. This directly increased school bookings and resulted in increased awareness of the company.

The main challenge for the Looney School is to capture the interest of children, the main users of the Looney School product, who currently find the sport dull and "uncool." Fortunately for the Looney School, the massive promotional efforts launched by tennis sporting good manufacturers such as Wilson, Nike, Head, and Prince appear to be paying off, as industry reports forecast an improvement in participation rates and racquet sales. Although the children are the principal users of the lessons and hence the prime initiator in the decision-making process, it is critical that the Looney School be successful in reaching the schools. The Looney School must convince the Ottawa-Carleton school boards that Looney lessons will be of value to the students, parents, and teachers. School boards are looking for convenient low-cost services that provide diversity in school programming, interest in students, and satisfaction of parents. After-school programs are particularly appealing to parents who prefer to have their children participate in a healthy, low-cost, after-school activity rather than straight supervision.

The main problem facing the Looney School concerns the two-day free promotions offered to interested Ottawa-Carleton schools. As many of the schools are initially unsure of the success of running tennis programs in a gymnasium, the Looney School of Tennis decided to offer demonstrations to every gym class in the school, free of charge. This promotion appealed greatly to the schools and resulted, on average, in the booking of three schools for every 10 demonstrations provided. Most schools would book three sessions of tennis programs, with each program offering five lessons to a particular class.

Although the promotions were in great demand, the related expenses were high. For each demonstration the Looney School provided, it incurred a salary expense of about \$120 (or 6 hours × 2 days × \$10) as well as a photocopying expense for flyers of about \$35 (350 flyers × \$0.10). This resulted in a total promotion expense of \$155 per demo, with no guarantee of a future sale. Craig felt this situation required further attention. Before deciding whether it was worthwhile to change the current set-up, Craig considered two options.

The first option was to request a voluntary contribution of one or two loonies from the students. In this scenario, a flyer would be sent home with the children before the demonstration, requesting that a contribution be provided to defray the costs to the company. On average, 350 students attend each two-day demonstration. Craig felt that it would not be unreasonable to expect that half of the people would make some sort of contribution.

Craig decided to approach four schools, booked for upcoming demonstrations, to obtain feedback on this option. None of these schools objected to soliciting a voluntary contribution from the student. Therefore, Craig decided to go ahead with a trial run on these schools to assess the reaction of the parents. Results from this trial are provided in Appendix 2.

Craig's second option was to charge each child a flat fee for the demonstration. However, he had not yet approached the schools about this option as he was unsure what their reaction would be.

The second problem that required Craig's attention was the compensation package for his tennis director, Justin Mondoux. Justin had been complaining about working only one or two hours at a time, at his hourly wage, and was looking for an improvement in his compensation package. Therefore, Craig was seriously considering changing Justin's compensation from an hourly wage to a commission. In this scenario, Justin would be responsible for making contact and visiting with all the schools and booking and conducting all free demonstrations on his own time. In return, he would receive 35 percent of the profits for each school booked for follow-on lessons. This way, the company would be incurring a "salary expense" only upon a sale. Not only would this address the concern of the costly demonstrations, but it would also serve to resolve the staffing problem and free up valuable time for Craig Smith, who very much needed to devote time to other areas of the business. On the other hand, Craig was concerned he would lose personal contact with the schools if he implemented this option.

Craig needed to give serious thought to the various alternatives before deciding what changes, if any, he should make and the likely effect these changes would have on the satisfaction level of his customers and staff.

Appendix 1

The Product—School Programming

After School/Lunch-time Lessons: Programs are offered in packages of five lessons at \$3 per lesson per child and lessons are offered either during lunch hour or as an after-school program. The lessons are given in the school gym or, weather permitting, in the school yard.

End of School Tennis Fair: Toward the end of the school year, the Looney School offers to local private and public Ottawa-Carleton schools the option to book an "end of school tennis fair." This allows the children to finish their school year "with an ace." Children from a local primary school are bused to a nearby tennis club managed by the Looney School of Tennis. Here the children experience playing on a "real" tennis court. The fair demonstrates to the children how accessible tennis can be and how it can be played in their own neighbourhood. Children who participate in the Tennis Fair receive a certificate that he or she is a "100% tennis fanatic." The certificate also provides a phone number for more information on how to get involved in summer Looney lessons and camps at a nearby club.

Appendix 2

TRIAL DEMONSTRATIONS

School A The first school visited is in an upper-middle-class suburb of Ottawa, where the average home is valued at about $205 000 and municipal taxes average $3200. This area consists exclusively of single-family homes, where about 80 percent of the occupants in the district own their own home. The majority of families are dual-income professionals in their mid-forties. There are no public courts within a one-kilometre radius of the community.

Of the 239 students in this school who attended the demonstrations, 177 provided a contribution, averaging $1.67. The average age of the children was 10, with only 15 percent having ever played the sport previously.

School B The second school that received a free demonstration is in a working-class area of the city, with the average home valued at about $123 000 and municipal taxes running at about $1700. About 40 percent of the predominantly single-income families own their own homes. The dwellings are a mixture of semi-detached houses, townhouses, and apartment complexes. There are two public courts within a one-kilometre radius of the community.

Of the 305 students who attended the demonstrations, 189 contributed with an average contribution of $0.41. The average age of the children was 12, with only eight percent having ever played the sport before.

School C The third school is also in a working-class district not far from the second school. The area consists mostly of garden homes, valued at about $112 000 and municipal taxes at $1500. Only 35 percent of the families own their own homes. These households consisted mainly of blue-collar workers in their mid-thirties. There are no public courts within walking distance of the community.

Of the 347 students in this school, 208 returned with an average contribution of $0.38. The average age of the children was 8, with 12 percent having ever played the sport.

School D The last school is in a middle-class district, with the average home valued at about $175 000 and municipal taxes of about $2500. Most families in this area are dual-income young professionals, with about 75 percent owning their own home. There is one public court within walking distance of the community.

Of the 198 students who attended the demonstration, 127 contributed an average of $1.42. The average age of the children was 10, with only five percent having ever been exposed to the sport.

District	A Upper-middle Class	B Working Class	C Working Class	D Middle Class
Home value	$205 000	$123 000	$112 000	$175 000
Taxes	$3200	$1700	$1500	$2500
Percentage of homes owned	80	40	35	75
Number of public courts	0	2	0	1
Number of students	239	305	347	198
Total contribution	177	189	208	127
Average contribution	$1.67	$0.41	$0.38	$1.42
Average age	10	12	8	10
Percentage played before	15	8	12	5

QUESTIONS

1. What is Craig Smith selling?
2. What are the strengths and weaknesses of his company and its marketing plan?
3. What threats does Craig face?
4. What opportunities might he exploit?
5. Why must Craig have a thorough understanding of consumer behaviour? Why is tennis not viewed as a "cool" sport?
6. What market segments has Craig been serving? Can he present the same marketing program to each segment?
7. What alternatives can you suggest to Craig to help him solve his problems? How would you compare these alternatives?
8. What final recommendations would you make to Craig?

video case 5

TEENAGE TARGETS

Teens are the hot demographic. They have the money and the numbers. Canadian teens alone spend an estimated $10 billion a year on goods and services. Thus, it's not surprising that a lot of companies want to tap into this lucrative market. In music, fashion, TV, movies and everything else it's all Teen, Teen, Teen. But teens are a challenging market to reach and media clutter has become the rule rather than the exception.

A recent international report released by Euro RSCG Worldwide labelled this demographic "screenagers" since they are the product of the computer age. Screenagers have accumulated more technological know-how, more images, more information, and more music than any previous generation. Their world has always included VCRs, pagers, mobile phones, TV remotes, video games and CD-ROM libraries. For much of their lives, the Internet has been up and running.

Classifying teens into segments for the purpose of target marketing is becoming increasingly difficult. Teens are a fickle bunch. As the offspring of our rapidly-changing society, teens have adopted a multi-faceted lifestyle. They can morph from one identity to the next as frequently and effortlessly as they change TV channels. In other words, teens are paradoxical. While teens might buy their jeans at the local Goodwill store, they might also own a Bang & Olufsen stereo.

Determining what media to use to reach teens is a thorny question. Some favour teen-targeted magazines like *Watch* and *Bang*. Others claim using the Internet is the solution. There's no doubt teens are spending more time on the Net. But whether they're doing so at the expense of their TV viewing is a matter of hot debate. Nielsen, the media rating firm, says TV viewing among teens has remained fairly constant since 1996 and teens continue to view approximately 16 hours a week.

Rather than seeing the two media as rivals, some analysts believe that television and the Internet complement one another nicely. David Chung, president of MaxxMedia, notes, "If teens are using the Net more, it presents an opportunity. It doesn't mean that TV is no longer an effective medium for reaching that group. It's just another medium or channel for us to reach our client's customers." Teens, in fact, may be using different media simultaneously since research shows they are the masters of multi-tasking. What teenager can't talk on the phone, listen to the radio, watching TV, surf the Net and do homework all at the same time?

Not surprisingly, there are almost as many approaches to marketing to teens are there are teen lifestyles. Some marketers use models spouting hip language, funky clothes and gross-out antics. Others, like Wal-Mart, put real kids in their advertising. "There's nothing more appealing than honesty," says Andrew Pelletier, director of public affairs at Wal-Mart in Mississauga, Ontario. Other firms have turned to piggybacking or cross promotions, using one brand (or icon) to promote another. For example, Tommy Hilfiger sponsors Britney Spears.

MuchMusic, Canada's king of youth marketing, links music and sports to help sponsors connect with teens. Take its *SnowJob* live music event held recently at the Sun Peaks Resort near Kamloops, B.C. Anyone with a ski pass could travel up the mountain to watch the music and other activities over the six days of the event. The event was filmed and produced enough footage to fill hours of TV time. Sponsors of the event included Nike, Pantene, Sprite, Beer.com and Ford Motor Company of Canada, who hoped that the "attitude" epitomized by the event would rub off on them and better help them position their products in the minds of young people.

Questions

1. What differentiates the teen market from any group that has preceded it?
2. How do teens view marketing? How do these attitudes affect marketers' abilities to reach this group?
3. Procter and Gamble aims its Cover Girl cosmetics at teenage girls. Playland aims to get more 15-year-old boys into its entertainment complex. If you were a marketing manager at either firm, how would you communicate effectively with teens?

Sources: This case was written by Peggy Cunningham based on *Undercurrents,* "Brands and Bands," and *Liz Adams,* "Doing what comes naturally," *Strategy,* July 17, 2000, p. D5; Claudine Dupont, "Unrebellious Youth: Old assumptions about marketing to the young don't work with the screenagers," *Marketing On-Line,* January 3/10, 2000; Michael Gillings, "Edgy SnowJob helps sponsors reach youth," *Strategy,* March 12, 2001, p. B8; Bernadette Johnson, "Teen study raises debate: Everyone agrees Net usage is rising—but is it at TV's expense? *Strategy*, June 5, 2000, p. 3; Sarah Smith, "Warts and All: More marketers are choosing real kids over polished actors in an effort to connect with their target," *Marketing On-Line,* March 1/8, 2001.

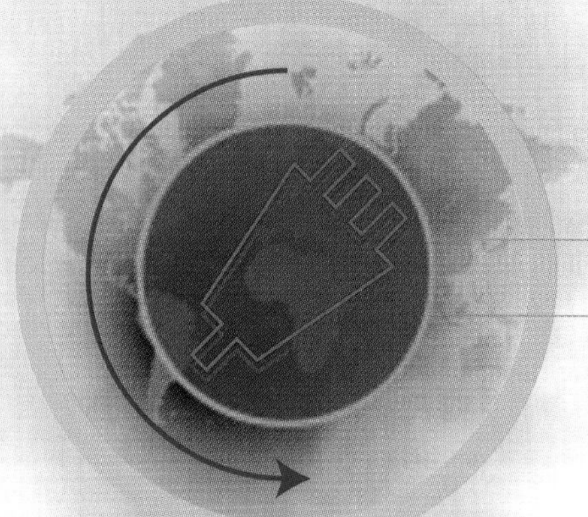

Concept Connections

When you finish this chapter, you should be able to

1. Define the business market and explain how business markets differ from consumer markets.
2. Identify the major factors that influence business buyer behaviour.
3. List and define the steps in the business buying decision process.
4. Compare the institutional and government markets and explain how they make their buying decisions.

chapter 6

Business Markets and Business Buyer Behaviour

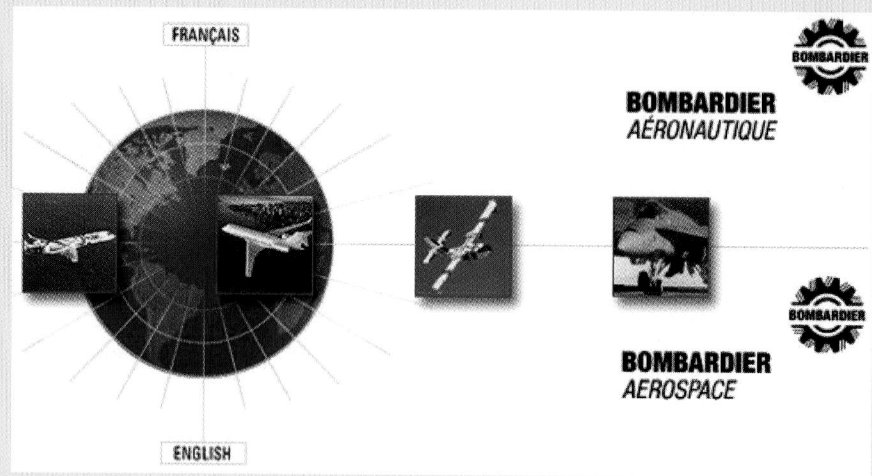

If anyone knows how to market to business and government clients, it is Bombardier, a company that has twice been voted the most respected company in Canada. While Bombardier may not be a household word, it is well known across the country as the maker of snowmobiles and Sea-Doo® watercrafts. In addition to these well known recreational products, however, it also designs and markets transit systems ranging from high speed rail and rapid transit systems to commuter rail, light rail, monorail and automated people mover systems to government buyers from countries as diverse as Turkey, Malaysia, the United States, and Canada. Bombardier is also a world leader in the aerospace industry. Here the firm markets business and regional aircraft to both private businesses as well as government buyers.

Bombardier's mission is to be the leader in all the markets in which it operates. The firm is known for its strategic thinking and heavy investment in new product development. In fact, Bombardier has invested more than any other manufacturer in introducing new products. Each year over the past twelve years, Bombardier has certified and launched one new airplane aimed at a key niche market.

Bombardier's strategy was founded on insights gained through years of studying the aircraft market. When Bombardier first observed that large airlines were moving to a hub and spoke strategy, it forecast that a host of new small airlines would be needed to fly passengers to the system hubs. Bombardier knew that these airlines, in both North America and Europe, would need small, efficient airplanes to fly these routes. Focus on this market would have the additional advantage of helping the firm avoid head-to-head competition with the likes of Boeing and Airbus in the large passenger-plane market. Knowledge of the needs of regional airlines helped Bombardier develop their highly successful Dash 8 Regional turboprop aircraft, one of the most successful regional planes in the world. Bombardier also foresaw the explosive growth in international business and positioned itself to provide aircraft to CEOs who had to travel around the world to visit their far-flung operations. This insight led to the birth of the Global Express Aircraft—known as the "Lamborghini of the sky"—which is purchased by CEOs, heads of state, and sheiks, who must part with $48 million to enjoy its gold-plated luxury.

In 2001, from its headquarters in Montreal, Bombardier racked up revenues of $16.1 billion dollars. Today, it is the world's third

largest aircraft-maker, trailing only Boeing and Airbus Industrie. Bombardier has also leaped to the top of the passenger railcar industry with its acquisition of DaimlerChrysler's rail unit, Adtranz. Bombardier employs 79 000 people, including 24 000 Canadians, in 24 countries. Earning more than 90 percent of its revenues from markets outside Canada, it sells aircraft to corporate and government customers in 60 countries.

Bombardier
www.bombardier.com/

In March 2000, Bombardier received its largest aircraft order yet, a $2.9 billion contract to build regional aircraft for two subsidiaries of Delta Airlines. Bombardier's list of clients is long and includes such private international firms as American Airlines, Deutsche Lufthansa AG, Paris-based TAG Aeronautics, Scandinavian Airlines, and a Japanese firm that wants to market Bombardier's amphibious fire-fighting aircraft in earthquake-prone Japan. The firm has entered completely new markets. To break new ground, Bombardier has also entered into strategic alliances with several international aerospace leaders. For example, it is partnering with Swiss-based Global Aviation Ltd. to make an onslaught on the Chinese market.

Bombardier also serves government clients. Through its affiliation with Canadair, Bombardier has more than 50 years of experience serving the military in both Canada and the US. It helps these countries' armed forces maintain, repair, and overhaul their aircraft. Since government clients are very cost sensitive, Bombardier locates facilities near its clients' operations. This not only increases responsiveness and flexibility, it also ensures cost-effective service delivery and tight security requirements.

Exploring exciting new products and new markets isn't all that is involved in marketing aircraft, however. To market its new executive aircraft, Bombardier must recognize the importance of rational motives and objective factors in buyers' decisions. Customers justify the expense of a corporate jet on utilitarian grounds, such as security, flexibility, responsiveness to customers, and efficient time use. A company buying a jet will evaluate Bombardier's aircraft on quality and performance, prices, operating costs, and service. At times, these "objective factors" may appear to be the only things that drive the buying decision. But having a superior product isn't enough to land the sale: Bombardier also must consider the more subtle human factors that affect the choice of a jet.

The purchase process may be initiated in a company by the chief executive officer (CEO), a board member wishing to increase efficiency or security, the company's chief pilot, or through Bombardier's efforts, such as advertising or a sales visit. The CEO will be central in deciding whether to buy the jet, but will be heavily influenced by the company's pilot, financial officer, and members of top management. The involvement of so many people in the purchase decision creates a group dynamic that Bombardier must factor into its sales planning. Who composes the buying group? How will the parties interact? Who will dominate and who will submit? What priorities do the individuals have?

Each party in the buying process has subtle roles and needs. For example, the salesperson who tries to impress both the CEO with depreciation schedules and the chief pilot with minimum runway statistics will almost certainly not sell a plane if he or she overlooks the psychological and emotional components of the buying decision. The chief pilot, as an equipment expert, often has veto power over purchase decisions and may be able to stop the purchase of a certain brand of jet by simply expressing a negative opinion about, say, the plane's bad-weather capabilities. In this sense, the pilot not only influences the decision but also serves as an information "gatekeeper" by advising management on which equipment to select. The users of the jet—middle and upper management of the buying company, important customers, and others—may have at least an indirect role in choosing the equipment. Although the corporate legal staff will handle the purchase agreement and the purchasing department will acquire the jet, these parties may have little to say about whether or how the plane will be obtained and which type will be selected.

According to one salesperson, in dealing with the CEO the biggest factor is not the plane's hefty price tag but its image. You need the numbers for support, but if you can't excite the kid inside the CEO with the raw beauty of the new plane, you'll never sell the equipment. If you sell the excitement, you sell the jet.

Making the sale is only half of the job, however. Both Bombardier's government and business clients require after-sales service and support. To improve this facet of its operations, Bombardier announced the launch of a customer-focused e-business initiative in October 2000. "Our objective is simple: to offer Bombardier Aerospace customers better service, faster response, more information and more productive use of their business aircraft assets by making information and other resources available for their use on the World Wide Web," stated Rob Gillespie, president, Bombardier Aerospace, Business Aircraft. The site will also make sophisticated aircraft management software tools available to customers. Authorized users will be welcomed by a personalized Web page, and access to information and services will be individually tailored to customers' specific needs. Bombardier sees its new e-business program as another reflection of the company's commitment to enhancing customer relationships.

As the Bombardier example shows, selling corporate jets to business buyers has some similarities to selling cars and kitchen appliances to families. Bombardier asks the same questions as consumer marketers: Who are the buyers and what are their needs? How do buyers make their buying decisions and what factors influence these decisions? What marketing program will be most effective? What after-sales services are needed? But the answers to these questions are more complex for the business marketer. One of Bombardier's chief assets is its superior knowledge of its business and government clients' needs. It is this knowledge that keeps Bombardier Aerospace flying high.[1]

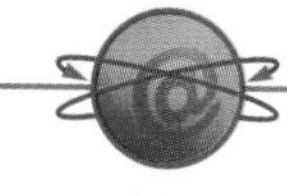

Kraft Canada
www.kraftcanada.com/

In one way or another, most large companies sell to other organizations. Many companies, such as Alcan Aluminium, NOVA Corp., Laidlaw, 3M Canada, and Nortel Networks, sell *most* of their products to other businesses. Even large consumer products companies, which make products used by final consumers, must first sell their products to other businesses. For example, Kraft Canada makes many familiar consumer products—Post cereals, Kraft Dinner, Jell-O, Kraft peanut butter, and others. But to sell these products to consumers, Kraft Canada must first sell them to the wholesalers and retailers that serve the consumer market.

Business market All of the organizations that buy goods and services to use in the production of other products and services or for the purpose of reselling or renting them to others at a profit.

The **business market** consists of all the organizations that buy goods and services to use in the production of other products and services that are sold, rented, or supplied to others. The majority of the players in this marketplace are small businesses, not large firms. In fact, of the 2.5 million businesses in Canada, 60 percent or 1.5 million of them are described as small office/home office (SOHO) firms, that is, businesses having fewer than 50 employees. Furthermore, this classification of firms is projected to grow. In 2000, some 17 percent of adults described themselves as self-employed versus 14 percent in 1997. While we may have a mental image of the typical entrepreneur as being a young person running a dot-com enterprise, a recent study revealed that 43 percent of SOHO owners are over 50. The number of women small business owners also grew in the early 1990s, but the percentage has dropped to 29 percent in 2000, from 37 percent in 1997.[2]

Business buying process The decision-making process by which business buyers establish the need for purchased products and services and identify, evaluate, and choose among alternative brands and suppliers.

The **business buying process** describes how business buyers determine their needs and identify, evaluate and choose among alternative brands and suppliers.[3] Like marketers of consumer goods, companies that sell to other businesses must do their best to understand their customers' buying processes. For example, a number of firms are realizing the potential of serving the small business market and are working to

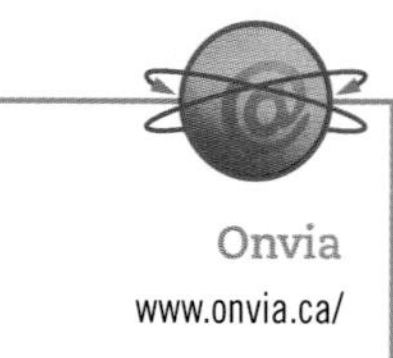

Onvia
www.onvia.ca/

understanding its unique needs. Take the case of Vancouver-based Onvia, which is now a leading, online business-to-business marketplace for small business buyers and sellers. Founder Glenn Ballman's vision was to provide small businesses with the tools they needed to build their businesses and manage day-to-day operations. So he developed a comprehensive site where owners of small businesses can find everything they need in just one place—everything from office supplies, business machines, phone systems and furniture to services such as payroll, telecommunications and technical support.[4]

Business Markets

The business market is *huge:* Consider the buying power of just one industry, the Canadian computer equipment industry, for example. It is the eighth-largest in the world: Over 300 companies are involved in the industry, generating $5.8 billion in revenues and employing 14 000 people.[5] Add to this the thousands of other firms operating in Canada and you quickly realize that business markets involve far more dollars and items than do consumer markets. For example, consider the large number of business transactions involved in producing and selling a single set of Goodyear tires. Various suppliers sell Goodyear the rubber, steel, equipment, and other goods that it needs to produce the tires. Goodyear then sells the finished tires to retailers, who in turn sell them to consumers. Thus, many sets of *business* purchases were made for only one set of *consumer* purchases. In addition, Goodyear sells tires as original equipment to manufacturers who install them on new vehicles, and as replacement tires to companies that maintain their own fleets of company cars, trucks, buses, or other vehicles.

Characteristics of Business Markets

In some ways, business markets are similar to consumer markets: Both involve people who assume buying roles and make purchase decisions to satisfy needs. However, business markets differ in many ways from consumer markets.[6] The main differences, shown in Table 6-1 and discussed below, are in *market structure and demand,* the *nature of the buying unit,* and the *types of decisions and the decision process* involved.

Market Structure and Demand

The business marketer typically deals with *far fewer but far larger buyers* than the consumer marketer does. For example, when Goodyear sells replacement tires to final consumers, its potential market includes the owners of the millions of cars currently in use in Canada and the United States. But Goodyear's fate in the business market depends on getting orders from one of only a few large auto makers. Even in large business markets, a few buyers typically account for most of the purchasing.

Business markets are also more *geographically concentrated.* Over 70 percent of the manufacturers in Canada are located in Ontario and Quebec, and most of these are found along the narrow corridor between Windsor and Quebec City.[7] Further, business demand is **derived demand**—it ultimately derives from the demand for consumer goods. General Motors Canada buys steel because consumers buy cars. If consumer demand for cars drops, so will the demand for steel and all the other products used to make cars. Therefore, business marketers sometimes promote their products directly to final consumers to increase business demand. For example, Intel's long-running "Intel Inside" advertising campaign sells personal computer buyers on the virtue of Intel microprocessors. The

Derived demand
Business demand that ultimately comes from (derives from) the demand for consumer goods.

TABLE 6-1 Characteristics of Business Markets

Marketing Structures and Demand

- Business markets contain *fewer but larger buyers.*
- Business customers are more *geographically concentrated.*
- Business buyer demand *derives* from final consumer demand.
- Demand in many business markets is *more inelastic*—not affected as much in the short run by price changes.
- Demand in business markets *fluctuates more,* and more quickly.

Nature of the Buying Unit

- Business purchases involve *more buyers.*
- Business buying involves a *more professional purchasing effort.*

Types of Decisions and the Decision Process

- Business buyers usually face more *complex buying decisions.*
- The business buying process is *more formalized.*
- Business buyers and sellers work more closely together and build close long-term *relationships.*

Other Characteristics

- Business buyers often *buy directly* from producers, rather than through retailers or wholesalers.
- Business buyers often practise *reciprocity,* buying from suppliers who also buy from them.
- Business buyers more often *lease* equipment rather than buying it outright.

increased demand for Intel chips boosts demand for the PCs containing them, and both Intel and its business partners win.

Many business markets have *inelastic demand;* that is, total demand for many business products is not affected much by price changes, especially in the short run. A drop in the price of leather will not cause shoe manufacturers to buy much more leather unless it results in lower shoe prices that, in turn, will increase consumer demand for shoes.

Finally, business markets have more *fluctuating demand.* The demand for many business goods and services tends to change more—and more quickly—than the demand for consumer goods and services does. A small percentage increase in consumer demand can cause large increases in business demand. Sometimes a rise of only 10 percent in consumer demand can cause as much as a 200 percent rise in business demand during the next period.

With smart card security, nobody will mess with it.
The new Acer TravelMate 350 can only be started by inserting a personal smart card. Thanks to its PlatinumPAS™ security system. And there's more. A magnesium-alloy protective casing makes it lighter, yet 15x stronger. Built-in 802.11b and infrared connectivity opens you to a wireless world. With quick-access keys, comfortably curved keyboard, Intel® Pentium® III processor, and 10GB HDD with Disk Anti-Shock Protection. Looking for the most secure notebook in the world? We hear you.
www.acer.ca 1-800-565-ACER
Acer PCs use genuine Microsoft® Windows®.
www.microsoft.com/piracy/howtotell
2 Business Hour Warranty Service
in the Greater Toronto Area
acer
we hear you

Intel's long-running "Intel Inside" logo has worked to boost *derived demand* for both Intel chips and computers, like Acer, that use them.

Nature of the Buying Unit

Compared with consumer purchases, a business purchase usually involves *more buyers* and a *more professional purchasing effort.* Often, business buying is done by trained purchasing agents who spend their working lives learning how to buy better. The more complex the purchase, the more likely that several people will participate in the decision-making process. Buying committees composed of technical experts and top management are common in the buying of major goods. As one observer notes, "It's a scary thought: Your customers may know more about your company and products than you do. . . . Companies are putting their best and brightest people on procurement patrol."[8] Therefore, business marketers must have well-trained salespeople to deal with well-trained buyers.

Types of Decisions and the Decision Process

Business buyers usually face *more complex* buying decisions than do consumer buyers. Purchases often involve large sums of money, complex technical and economic considerations, and interactions among many people at many levels of the buyer's organization. Because the purchases are more complex, business buyers may take longer to make their decisions. For example, the purchase of a large computer system might take many months or more than a year to complete and could involve millions of dollars, thousands of technical details, and dozens of people ranging from top management to lower-level users.

The business buying process tends to be *more formalized* than the consumer buying process. Large business purchases usually call for detailed product specifications, written purchase orders, careful supplier searches, and formal approval. The buying firm might even prepare policy manuals that outline the purchase process.

Finally, in the business buying process, buyer and seller are often much *more dependent* on each other. Consumer marketers are usually at a distance from their customers. In contrast, business marketers may roll up their sleeves and work closely with their customers during all stages of the buying process—from helping customers define problems, to finding solutions, to supporting after-sale operation. They often customize their offerings to individual customer needs. In the short run, sales go to suppliers who meet buyers' immediate product and service needs. However, business marketers also must build close long-term partnerships with customers. In recent years, relationships between customers and suppliers have been changing from downright adversarial to close and chummy:

Motoman, a leading supplier of industry robotic systems, and Stillwater Technologies, a contract tooling and machinery company and a key supplier to Motoman, are tightly integrated. Not only do they occupy office and manufacturing space in the same facility, they also link their telephone and computer systems and share a common lobby, conference room, and employee cafeteria. Philip Morrison, chairman and CEO of Motoman, says it's like "a joint venture without the

Business marketers often work closely with their customers throughout the buying and consuming process. In this award-winning business ad, Fujitsu promises more than just high-tech products: "Our technology helps keep you moving upward. And our people won't let you down."

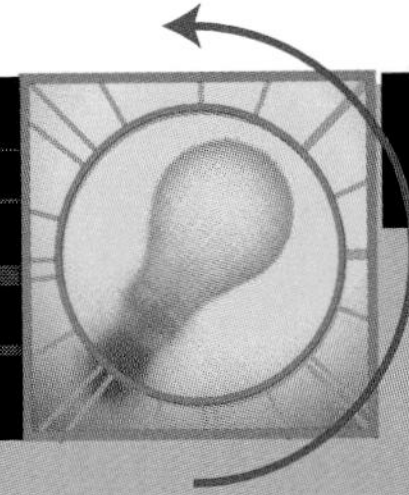

marketing highlight 6-1

Business Marketers Sell Customer Success

In the late 1980s, the Dow chemical company realigned its dozen or so widely varied plastics businesses into a single business unit called Dow Plastics. One of the first things Dow had to do was to decide how to position its new division competitively. Initial research with Dow's and competitors' customers showed that Dow Plastics rated a distant third in customer preference behind industry leaders, DuPont and GE Plastics. The research also revealed, however, that customers were unhappy with the poor service that they received from all three suppliers. "Vendors peddled resins as a commodity," says the head of Dow Plastics' research and advertising agency. "They competed on price and delivered on time, but gave no service."

These findings led to a positioning strategy that went far beyond simply selling good products and delivering them on time. Dow Plastics set out to build deeper relationships with customers. The company was selling not just products and services, but customer success. Says the agency executive, "Whether they're using Dow's plastics to make bags for Safeway or for complex aerospace applications, we have to help them succeed in their markets." This new thinking was summed up in the positioning statement: "We don't succeed unless you do."

The new positioning helped Dow Plastics to become a customer-oriented company. It got Dow out of selling plastics and into selling customer success. The slogan and underlying philosophy created a unifying identity for the business—one based on building relationships with customers and helping them to succeed with their own businesses. Customer problems became more than just engineering challenges. Dow's customers sell to somebody else, so the company now faced new challenges of marketing to and helping satisfy customers' customers.

As a result of its new customer-relationship orientation, Dow Plastics has now become a leader in the plastics industry. The customer success philosophy permeates everything the business does. Whenever company people encounter a new product or market, the first question they always ask is, "How does this fit with 'We don't succeed unless you do'?"

Sources: Portions adapted from Nancy Arnott, "Getting the picture: The grand design—We don't succeed unless you do," *Sales & Marketing Management,* June 1994:74–6; www.dow.com/cgi-bin/frameup.cgi?/plastics.

Dow Plastics tells customers, "We don't succeed unless you do." Building deeper customer relationships helped Dow move from number three to become a leader in its market.

paperwork." Short delivery distances are just one benefit of the unusual partnership. Also key is the fact that employees of both companies have ready access to each other and can share ideas on improving quality and reducing costs. This close relationship has also opened the door to new opportunities. Both companies had been doing work for Honda Motor Company, and Honda suggested that the two work together on systems projects. The symbiotic relationship makes the two bigger and better than they could be individually.[9]

In the long run, business marketers keep a customer's sales by meeting current needs *and* by working with customers to help them succeed with their own customers (see Marketing Highlight 6-1).[10]

FIGURE 6-1 A model of business buyer behaviour

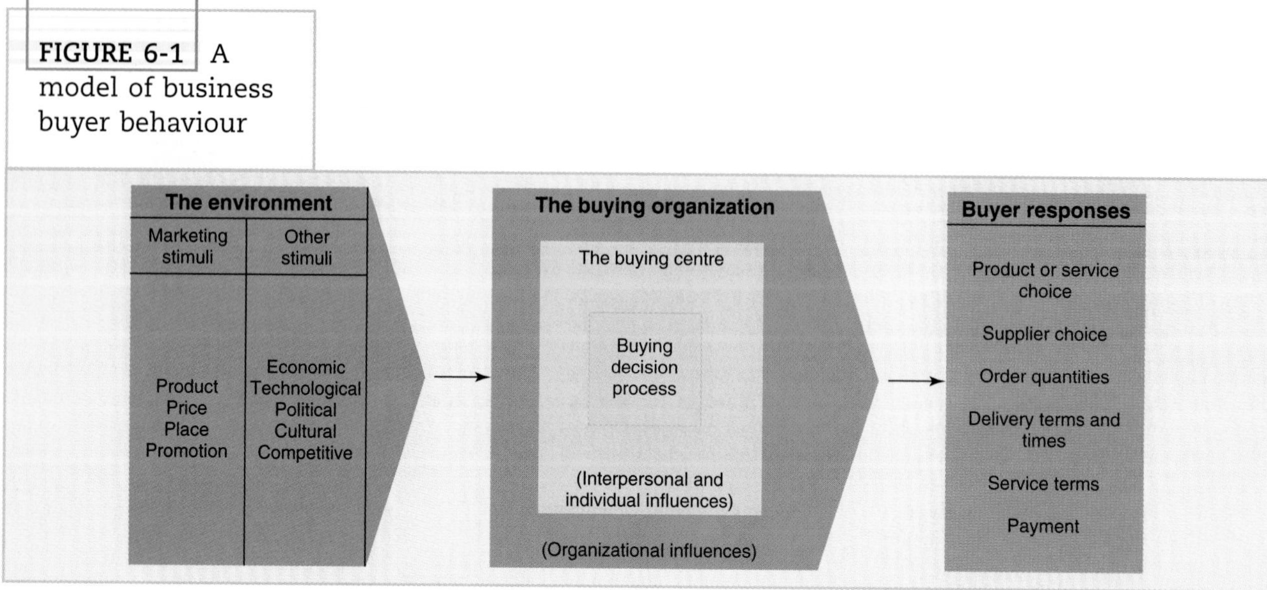

A Model of Business Buyer Behaviour

At the most basic level, marketers want to know how business buyers will respond to various marketing stimuli. Figure 6-1, a model of business buyer behaviour, shows how marketing and other stimuli affect the buying organization and produce certain buyer responses. As with consumer buying, the marketing stimuli for business buying consist of the four Ps: product, price, place, and promotion. Other stimuli include major forces in the environment: economic, technological, political, cultural, and competitive. These stimuli enter the organization and are turned into buyer responses: product or service choice; supplier choice; order quantities; and delivery, service, and payment terms. To design a good marketing mix, the marketer must understand what happens within the organization to turn stimuli into purchase responses.

Within the organization, buying activity consists of two major parts: the buying centre, comprising all the people involved in the buying decision, and the buying decision process. The model shows that the buying centre and the buying decision process are influenced by internal organizational, interpersonal, and individual factors as well as by external environmental factors.

Business Buyer Behaviour

The model in Figure 6-1 suggests four questions about business buyer behaviour: What buying decisions do business buyers make? Who participates in the buying process? What are the major influences on buyers? How do business buyers make their buying decisions?

Major Types of Buying Situations

There are three major types of buying situations.[11] At one extreme is the *straight rebuy,* which is a fairly routine decision. At the other extreme is the *new task,* which may call for thorough research. In the middle is the *modified rebuy,* which requires some research.

Straight rebuy
A business buying situation in which the buyer routinely reorders something without any modifications.

In a **straight rebuy,** the buyer reorders something without any modifications. It is usually handled on a routine basis by the purchasing department. Based on past buying satisfaction, the buyer simply chooses from the various suppliers on its list. "In" suppliers try to maintain product and service quality. They often propose automatic reordering systems so that the purchasing agent will save reordering time. "Out" suppliers try to offer something new or exploit dissatisfaction so that the buyer will consider them. They try to get their foot in the door with a small order and then enlarge their purchase share over time.

Modified rebuy
A business buying situation in which the buyer wants to modify product specifications, prices, terms, or suppliers.

In a **modified rebuy,** the buyer wants to modify product specifications, prices, terms, or suppliers. The modified rebuy usually involves more decision participants than the straight rebuy. "In" suppliers may become nervous and feel pressured to put their best foot forward to protect an account. "Out" suppliers may view the modified rebuy situation as an opportunity to make a better offer and gain new business.

New task
A business buying situation in which the buyer purchases a product or service for the first time.

A company buying a product or service for the first time faces a **new task** situation. In such cases, the greater the cost or risk, the larger the number of decision participants and the greater their efforts to collect information will be. The new task situation is the marketer's greatest opportunity and challenge. The marketer not only tries to reach as many key buying influences as possible, but also provides help and information.

The buyer makes the fewest decisions in the straight rebuy and the most in the new task decision. In the latter, the buyer must decide on product specifications, suppliers, price limits, payment terms, order quantities, delivery times, and service terms. The order of these decisions varies with the situation, and different decision participants influence each choice.

Systems buying
Buying a packaged solution to a problem, without all the separate decisions involved.

Many business buyers prefer to buy a packaged solution to a problem from a single seller. Called **systems buying,** this practice began with government buying of major weapons and communication systems. Instead of buying and putting together all the components, the government asked for bids from suppliers that would supply the components *and* assemble the package or system.

Sellers have recognized that buyers like this method and have adopted systems selling as a marketing tool.[12] Systems selling is a two-step process. First, the supplier sells a group of interlocking products. For example, the supplier sells not only glue, but also applicators and dryers. Second, the supplier sells a system of production, inventory control, distribution, and other services to meet the buyer's need for a smooth-running operation.

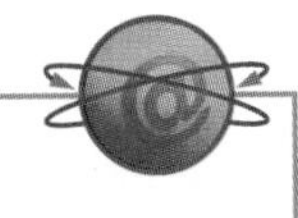

Enron Corp.
www.enron.com/

Systems selling is a key business marketing strategy for winning and holding accounts. The contract often goes to the firm that provides the most complete solution to customers' problems. For example, Enron, the world's leading energy company, is best known for providing the natural gas and electricity that its customers use to power their buildings. Enron discovered that companies actually spend far more on the other elements of their energy systems, including energy equipment inside their facilities and the employees who maintain it, than on paying for the energy itself. To help customers meet their complete power management needs, it started Enron Energy Services (EES), a division that offers entire energy management solutions. Now customers, such as Canada-based Quebecor World Inc., the world's largest commercial printer, can turn over all of their energy management needs to Enron. Enron will not only supply or manage electricity and natural gas at more than 60 Quebecor World facilities, it will also identify, analyze, design and implement energy infrastructure improvements. Enron's vision is that if it has to do with managing buildings, keeping them lit and warm in the winter and cool in the summer, it should be its domain. Such systems selling has produced stunning results for Enron: In only three years, EES's sales grew seven-fold.[13] This is true systems selling.

Participants in the Business Buying Process

Buying centre
All the individuals and units that participate in the business buying decision process.

Who does the buying of the trillions of dollars worth of goods and services needed by business organizations? The decision-making unit of a buying organization is called its **buying centre,** defined as all of the individuals and units that participate in the business decision-making process.[14]

Users
Members of the organization who will use the product or service; users often initiate the buying proposal and help define product specifications.

Influencers
People in an organization's buying centre who affect the buying decision; they often help define specifications and provide information for evaluating alternatives.

Buyers
People who make the actual purchase.

Deciders
People in the organization's buying centre who have formal or informal power to select or approve the final suppliers.

Gatekeepers
People in the organization's buying centre who control the flow of information to others.

The buying centre includes all members of the organization who play any of five roles in the purchase decision process:[15]

- **Users** are members of the organization who will use the product or service. In many cases, users initiate the buying proposal and help define product specifications.
- **Influencers** affect the buying decision. They often help define specifications and provide information for evaluating alternatives. Technical personnel are particularly important influencers.
- **Buyers** have formal authority to select the supplier and arrange terms of purchase. Buyers may help shape product specifications, but they play their major role in selecting vendors and in negotiating. In more complex purchases, buyers may include high-level officers participating in the negotiations.
- **Deciders** have formal or informal power to select or approve the final suppliers. In routine buying, the buyers are often the deciders, or at least the approvers.
- **Gatekeepers** control the flow of information to others. For example, purchasing agents often have authority to prevent salespersons from seeing users or deciders. Other gatekeepers include technical personnel and even personal secretaries.

The buying centre is not a fixed and formally identified unit within the buying organization. It is a set of buying roles assumed by different people for different purchases. The size and composition of the buying centre varies for different products and for different buying situations. For some routine purchases, one person—such as a purchasing agent—may assume all the buying centre roles and serve as the only person involved in the buying decision. For more complex purchases, the buying centre may include 20 or 30 people from different levels and departments in the organization. According to one survey, the average number of people involved in a buying decision ranges from about three (for services and items used in day-to-day operations) to almost five (for such high-ticket purchases as construction work and machinery). Another survey detected a trend toward team-based buying—87 percent of surveyed purchasing executives at Fortune 1000 companies in the year 2000 expected teams of people from different functions to be making buying decisions.[16]

Business marketers working in global markets may face even greater levels of buying-centre influence. A study comparing the buying decision processes in the United States, Sweden, France, and Southeast Asia found that US buyers may be loners compared with their counterparts in some other countries. Sweden had the highest team buying effort while the US had the lowest, even though firms in both countries had similar demographics. In making purchasing decisions, Swedish firms depended on technical staff, both their own and suppliers', much more than the firms in other countries.[17]

A buying centre may be composed of people from more than one firm. Organizations often form alliances when developing new global products, and representatives from each organization entering the alliance may be part of the buying centre. Bombardier uses this strategy. Since the costs and risks of developing new aircraft are so high, Bombardier partners with its suppliers at the design stage. Together they determine the new plane's specifications and the components that will go into it.[18]

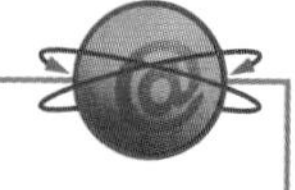

Baxter International
www.baxter.com/

The buying centre concept presents a major marketing challenge. The business marketer must learn who participates in the decision, each participant's relative influence, and what evaluation criteria each decision participant uses. For example, Baxter International, the large health-care products and services company, sells

Nokia portrays its products in the context of its key customers' lives.

disposable surgical gowns to hospitals. It tries to identify the hospital personnel involved in this buying decision. These personnel are the vice-president of purchasing, the operating room administrator, and the surgeons. Each participant plays a different role. The vice-president of purchasing analyzes whether the hospital should buy disposable gowns or reusable gowns. If analysis favours disposable gowns, then the operating room administrator compares competing products and prices and makes a choice. This administrator considers the gown's absorbency, antiseptic quality, design, and cost, and typically buys the brand that meets requirements at the lowest cost. Finally, surgeons affect the decision later by reporting their satisfaction or dissatisfaction with the brand.

The buying centre usually includes some obvious participants who are involved formally in the buying decision. It may also involve less obvious, informal participants, some of whom may actually make or strongly affect the buying decision. Sometimes, even the people in the buying centre are unaware of all the buying participants. As the Bombardier example shows, numerous stakeholders are involved in the decision. Their buying motives may vary from practical, mundane reasoning to subtle, hard-to-uncover psychological wants and fears.

Major Influences on Business Buyers

Business buyers are subject to many influences when they make their buying decisions. Some marketers assume that the major influences are economic. They think buyers will favour the supplier who offers the lowest price, or the best product, or the most service. They concentrate on offering strong economic benefits to buyers. However, business buyers actually respond to both economic and personal factors. Far from being cold, calculating, and impersonal, business buyers are human and social as well. They react to both reason and emotion.

Business-to-business marketers recognize that business buyers use not only rational decision making when making purchases, but also emotion. You might expect that an advertisement promoting large trucks to corporate truck fleet buyers would stress objective technical, performance, and economic factors such as fuel usage. However, a recent ad for Volvo heavy-duty trucks shows two drivers arm wrestling and claims, "It solves all your fleet problems. Except who gets to drive." Volvo's insight was that in an era of industry-wide driver shortages, the type of truck a fleet provides can help a firm attract qualified drivers. Thus, the Volvo ad stresses the raw beauty of the truck and its comfort and roominess, features that make it more appealing to drivers. The ad concludes that Volvo trucks are "built to make fleets more profitable and drivers a lot more possessive."

When suppliers' offers are similar, business buyers have little basis for strictly rational choice. Because they can meet organizational goals with any supplier, buyers can allow personal factors to play a larger role in their decisions. However,

Volvo uses both rational and emotional claims to appeal to business buyers.

when competing products differ greatly, business buyers are more accountable for their choice and tend to pay more attention to economic factors.

Figure 6-2 shows various groups of influences on business buyers—environmental, organizational, interpersonal, and individual.[19]

Environmental Factors

Business buyers are influenced heavily by factors in the current and expected *economic environment,* such as the level of primary demand, the economic outlook, and the cost of money. As economic uncertainty rises, business buyers cut back on new investments and attempt to reduce their inventories.

An increasingly important environmental factor is shortages in key materials. Many companies now are more willing to buy and hold larger inventories of scarce materials to ensure adequate supply. Business buyers are also affected by technological, political, and competitive developments in the environment. Culture and customs can strongly influence business buyer reactions to the marketer's behaviour and strategies, especially in the international marketing environment (see Marketing Highlight 6-2). The business marketer must consider these factors, determine how they will affect the buyer, and try to turn these challenges into opportunities.

FIGURE 6-2 Major influences on business buying behaviour

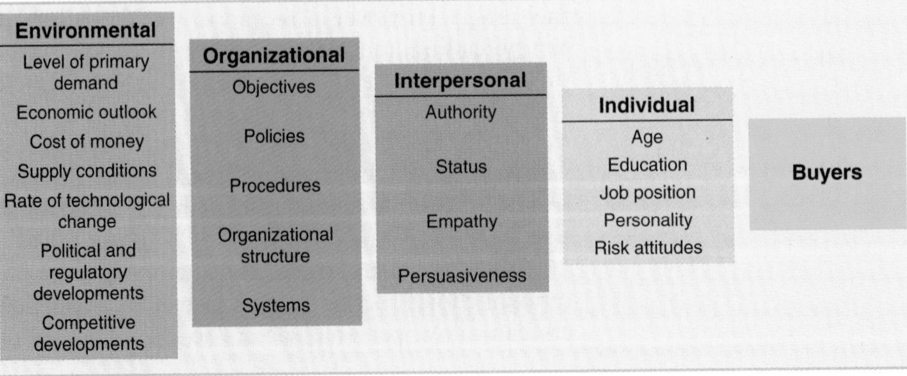

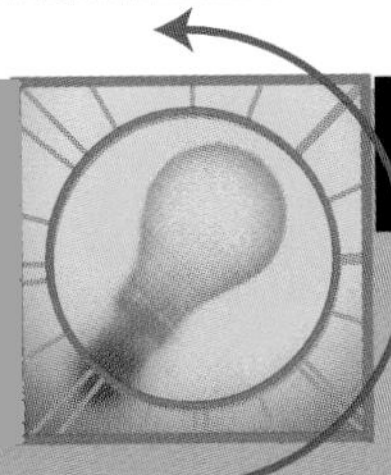

marketing highlight 6-2

International Marketing Manners: When in Rome, Do as the Romans Do

Picture this: Consolidated Amalgamation, Inc. thinks it's time that the rest of the world enjoyed the same fine products it has offered Canadian consumers for two generations. It dispatches vice-president Harry E. Slicksmile to Europe to explore the territory. Harry stops first in London, where he makes short work of some bankers—he phones them. He handles Parisians with similar ease. After securing a table at La Tour d'Argent, he greets his luncheon guest, the director of an industrial engineering firm, with the words, "Just call me Harry, Jacques."

In Germany, Harry is a powerhouse. Whisking through a lavish, state-of-the-art marketing presentation, complete with flip charts and audiovisuals, he shows 'em that this prairie boy *knows* how to make a buck. Heading on to Milan, Harry strikes up a conversation with the Japanese businessman sitting next to him on the plane. He flips his card onto his neighbour's tray and, when the two say good-bye, shakes hands warmly and clasps the man's right arm. Later, for his appointment with the owner of an Italian packaging-design firm, our hero wears his comfy corduroy sport coat, khaki pants, and deck shoes. Everybody knows Italians are zany and laid back, right?

Wrong. Six months later, Consolidated Amalgamation has nothing to show for the trip but a pile of bills. In Europe, they weren't wild about Harry.

This hypothetical case has been exaggerated for emphasis. Businesspeople are seldom such dolts. But experts say success in international business has much to do with knowing the territory and its people. By learning English and extending themselves in other ways, the world's business leaders have met North Americans more than halfway. In contrast, North Americans too often do little except assume that others will march to their music. "We want things to be just like they are at home when we travel. Fast. Convenient. Easy. So we demand that others change," says one world trade expert. "I think more business would be done if we tried harder."

Poor Harry tried, all right, but in all the wrong ways. The English do not, as a rule, make deals over the phone as much as North Americans do. It's not so much a "cultural" difference as a difference in approach. The French neither like instant familiarity—questions about family, church, or alma mater—nor refer to strangers by their first names. "That poor fellow, Jacques, probably wouldn't show anything, but he'd recoil. He'd *not* be pleased," explains an expert on French business practices. "It's considered poor taste," he continues. "Even after months of business dealings, I'd wait for him or her to make the invitation [to use first names. . . . You are always right, in Europe, to say 'Mister or 'Madam.' Calling secretaries by their first names would also be considered rude: "They have a right to be called by the surname. You'd certainly ask—and get—permission first."

Harry's flashy presentation would likely have been a flop with the Germans, who dislike overstatement and ostentation. According to one German expert, however, German businesspeople have become accustomed to dealing with North Americans. Although differences in body language and customs remain, the past 20 years have softened them.

When Harry Slicksmile grabbed his new Japanese acquaintance by the arm, the executive probably considered him disrespectful and presumptuous. Harry made matters worse by tossing his business card. The Japanese revere the business card as an extension of self and as an indicator of rank. They do not *hand* it to people, they *present* it—with both hands. In addition, the Japanese are sticklers about rank. Unlike North Americans, they don't heap praise on subordinates in a room; they will praise only the highest-ranking official present.

Hapless Harry's last gaffe was assuming that Italians are like Hollywood's stereotypes of them. The flair for design and style that has characterized Italian culture for centuries is embodied in the businesspeople of Milan and Rome. They dress beautifully and admire flair, but they blanch at garishness or impropriety in others' attire.

To compete successfully in global markets, or even to deal effectively with international firms in their home markets, North American companies must help their managers to understand the needs, customs, and cultures of international business buyers. These are additional

To succeed in global markets, North American companies must help their managers understand the needs, customs, and cultures of international business buyers.

examples of a few rules of social and business etiquette that North American managers should understand when doing business abroad:

- **France:** Dress conservatively, except in the south where more casual clothes are worn. Do not refer to people by their first names—the French are formal with strangers. It should be noted that Europeans who speak French are more formal than their North American counterparts. Thus, North American should not rush to "tutoyer."
- **Germany:** Be especially punctual. A businessperson invited to someone's home should present flowers, preferably unwrapped, to the hostess. Don't give red roses, flowers that are only for lovers. During introductions, greet women first and wait until they extend their hands before extending yours.
- **Italy:** Whether you dress conservatively or go native in a Giorgio Armani suit, keep in mind that Italian businesspeople are style-conscious. Make appointments well in advance. Prepare for and be patient with Italian bureaucracies.
- **United Kingdom:** Toasts are often given at formal dinners. If the host honours you with a toast, be prepared to reciprocate. Business entertaining is done more often at lunch than at dinner.
- **Saudi Arabia:** Although men will kiss each other in greeting, they will never kiss a woman in public. A businesswoman should wait for a man to extend his hand before offering hers. If a Saudi offers refreshment, accept—it is an insult to decline it.
- **India:** Although businesspeople here speak English, Canadians cannot assume that doing business will be smooth sailing. India is a conservative society marked by contrasts—a peasant culture on one hand, and European-educated professionals on the other. Business deals take a long time to close and may be impossible without the assistance of an Indian agent to help firms understand India's impenetrable bureaucracy.
- **Japan:** Don't imitate Japanese bowing customs unless you understand them thoroughly—who bows to whom, how many times, and when. It's a complicated ritual. Presenting business cards is another ritual. Carry many cards, present them with both hands so your name can be easily read, and hand them to others in order of descending rank. Expect Japanese business executives to take time making decisions and to work through all of the details before making a commitment.

Sources: Adapted from Susan Harte, "When in Rome, you should learn to do what the Romans do," *Atlanta Journal-Constitution,* 22 January 1990:D1,D6. Also see Lufthansa's *Business Travel Guide/Europe;* Sergey Frank, "Global negotiating," *Sales & Marketing Management,* May 1992:64–9; and Brian Banks, "English too," *Canadian Business,* January 1995:20–35.

Organizational Factors

Each buying organization has its own objectives, policies, procedures, structure, and systems, which the business marketer must understand. Questions such as these arise: How many people are involved in the buying decision? Who are they? What are their evaluative criteria? What are the company's policies and limits on its buyers?

Wal-Mart, for example, believes that the conduct of its supplier can be transferred to Wal-Mart and can affect its reputation. Therefore, Wal-Mart not only has very strict standards and buying procedures, it encourages its partners to follow the same principles as those that guide its own business. These principles include providing value and service to customers by offering quality merchandise at low prices every day; a dedication to partnership among key stakeholders—associates, management, and vendors; and a commitment to the communities in which stores and distribution centres are located. To aid its 'vendor partners,' Wal-Mart's supplier development department posts a complete set of supplier guidelines on its Web site.

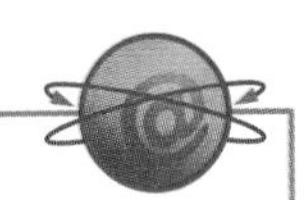

Wal-Mart Supplier Information
www.walmartstores.com/supplier/

Interpersonal Factors

The buying centre usually includes many participants who influence each other. The business marketer often finds it difficult to determine what kinds of *interpersonal factors* and group dynamics enter into the buying process. As one writer notes, "Managers do not wear tags that say 'decision maker' or 'unimportant person.' The powerful are often invisible, at least to vendor representatives."[20] Nor does the buying centre participant with the highest rank always have the most influence. Participants may have influence in the buying decision because they control rewards and punishments, are well liked, have special expertise, or have a special relationship with other important participants. Interpersonal factors are often very subtle. When-

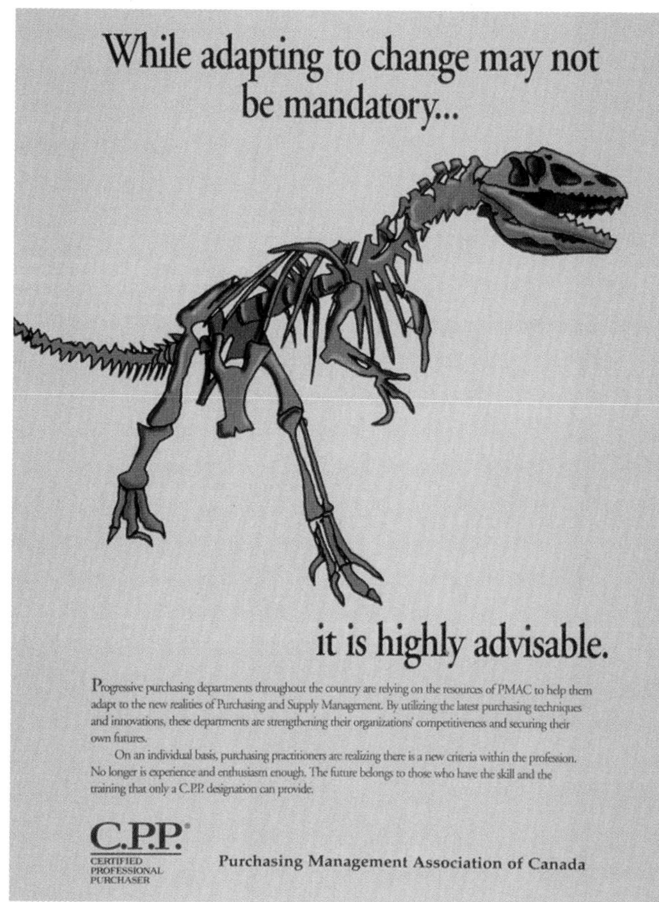

While adapting to change may not be mandatory...
it is highly advisable.
Progressive purchasing departments throughout the country are relying on the resources of PMAC to help them adapt to the new realities of Purchasing and Supply Management. By utilizing the latest purchasing techniques and innovations, these departments are strengthening their organizations' competitiveness and securing their own futures.
On an individual basis, purchasing practitioners are realizing there is a new criteria within the profession. No longer is experience and enthusiasm enough. The future belongs to those who have the skill and the training that only a C.P.P. designation can provide.
C.P.P.
CERTIFIED PROFESSIONAL PURCHASER
Purchasing Management Association of Canada

Professional purchasers are tough-minded negotiators bent on improving the profitability of their firms. Dealing with them requires highly trained sales personnel.

ever possible, business marketers must try to understand these factors and design strategies that take them into account.

Individual Factors

Each participant in the business buying decision process brings in personal motives, perceptions, and preferences. These individual factors are affected by such personal characteristics as age, income, education, professional identification, personality, and attitudes toward risk. Also, buyers have different buying styles. Some may be technical types who make in-depth analyses of competitive proposals before choosing a supplier. Other buyers may be intuitive negotiators who are adept at pitting sellers against one another for the best deal.

The Business Buying Process

Table 6-2 lists the eight stages of the business buying process.[21] Buyers who face a new task buying situation usually go through all stages of the buying process. Buyers making modified or straight rebuys may skip some stages. We shall examine these steps for the typical new task buying situation.

Problem Recognition

The buying process begins when someone in the company recognizes a problem or need that can be met by acquiring a specific good or service. **Problem recognition** can result from internal or external stimuli. Internally, the company may decide to launch a new product that requires new production equipment and materials. Or

Problem recognition
The first stage of the business buying process in which someone in the company recognizes a problem or need that can be met by acquiring a good or a service.

TABLE 6-2 Major Stages of the Business Buying Process in Relation to Major Buying Situations

	Buying Situations		
Stages of the Buying Process	**New Task**	**Modified Rebuy**	**Straight Rebuy**
1. Problem recognition	Yes	Maybe	No
2. General need description	Yes	Maybe	No
3. Product specification	Yes	Yes	Yes
4. Supplier search	Yes	Maybe	No
5. Proposal solicitation	Yes	Maybe	No
6. Supplier selection	Yes	Maybe	No
7. Order-routine specification	Yes	Maybe	No
8. Performance review	Yes	Yes	Yes

Source: Adapted from Patrick J. Robinson, Charles W. Faris, and Yoram Wind, *Industrial Buying and Creative Marketing,* Boston: Allyn & Bacon, 1967:14.

As this UUNET Canada ad shows, business marketers often use advertising to alert customers to potential problems and then show how their products and services can provide solutions.

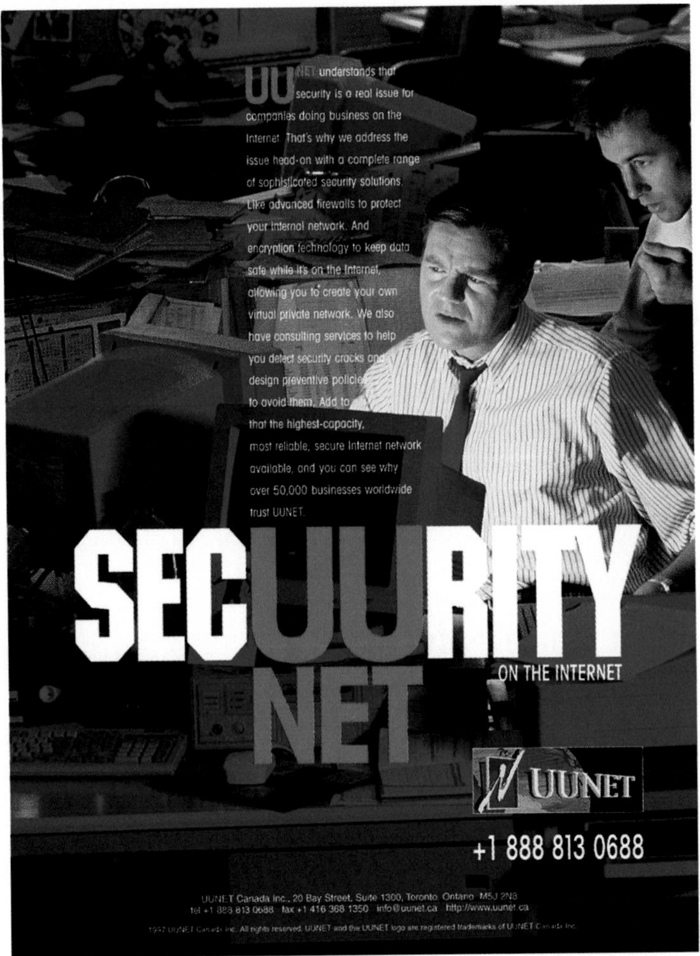

a machine may break down and need new parts. Perhaps a purchasing manager is unhappy with a current supplier's product quality, service, or prices. Externally, the buyer may get some new ideas at a trade show, see an ad, or receive a call from a salesperson who offers a product that is better or less expensive. In fact, in their advertising, business marketers often alert customers to potential problems, and then show how their products provide solutions.

General Need Description

General need description The stage in the business buying process in which the company describes the general characteristics and quantity of a needed item.

Product specification The stage of the business buying process in which the buying organization decides on and specifies the best technical product characteristics for a needed item.

Value analysis An approach to cost reduction in which components are studied carefully to determine if they can be redesigned, standardized, or made by less costly methods of production.

Having recognized a need, the buyer next prepares a **general need description** that describes the characteristics and quantity of the needed item. For standard items, this process presents few problems. For complex items, however, the buyer may have to work with others—engineers, users, consultants—to define the item. The team may want to rank the importance of reliability, durability, price, and other attributes desired in the item. In this phase, the alert business marketer can help the buyers define their needs and provide information about the value of different product characteristics.

Product Specification

The buying organization then develops the item's technical **product specifications,** often with the help of a value analysis engineering team. In a **value analysis** approach to cost reduction, the team carefully studies components to determine if they can be redesigned, standardized, or made by less costly methods of production. Thus, they determine the best product characteristics and specify them accordingly. Sellers, too, can use value analysis as a tool to help secure a new account. By showing buyers a better way to make an object, outside sellers can turn straight rebuy situations into new task situations that give them a chance to obtain new business.

Nortel Networks
www.nortelnetworks.com/

Many firms, such as Nortel Networks, are becoming increasingly concerned about whether the materials they use in the design of new products are environmentally sensitive. In addition, the ability to completely recycle their products is an issue. Vendors who can offer materials to aid Nortel with this goal have considerable advantages in making sales to this firm.

Supplier Search

Supplier search The stage of the business buying process in which the buyer tries to find the best vendors.

The buyer now conducts a **supplier search** to find the best vendors. The buyer can compile a small list of qualified suppliers by reviewing trade directories, doing a computer search, or phoning other companies for recommendations. Today, companies are turning to the Internet to find suppliers. For marketers, this has helped level the playing field—smaller suppliers can be listed in the same online catalogues for a nominal fee:

> Worldwide Internet Solutions Network, better known as WIZnet (**www.wiznet.net**), has built a global interactive virtual library of business-to-business catalogues. At last report, its database included complete specifications for more than 10 million products and services from 45 000 manufacturers, distributors, and industrial service providers. For purchasing managers, who routinely receive a foot-high stack of mail each day—much of it catalogues—this kind of one-stop shopping is an incredible time saver and price saver, because it allows easier comparison shopping. More than just electronic *Yellow Pages,* WIZnet includes all specifications for the products right in the system and offers secure e-mail to communicate directly with vendors to ask for requests for bids or to place an order. More than 10 000 product specs are added to WIZnet each week, and its database includes catalogues from many countries including Germany, Taiwan, and the Czech Republic.[22]

The newer the buying task and the more complex and costly the item, the more time the buyer will spend searching for suppliers. The supplier's task is to get listed in major directories and build a good reputation in the marketplace. Salespeople should watch for companies in the process of searching for suppliers and ensure that their firm is considered.

Many business buyers go to extremes in searching for and qualifying suppliers. Consider the hurdles that Xerox has set up in qualifying suppliers:

> Xerox qualifies only suppliers who meet ISO 9000 international quality standards (see Chapter 18). But to win the company's award—certification status—a supplier must first complete the Xerox Multinational Supplier Quality Survey. The survey requires the supplier to issue a quality assurance manual, adhere to continuous improvement principles, and demonstrate effective systems implementation. Once a supplier has been qualified, it must participate in Xerox's continuous supplier involvement process, in which the two companies work together to create specifications for quality, cost, delivery times, and process capability. The final step toward certification requires a supplier to undergo additional quality training and evaluation. Not surprisingly, only 176 suppliers worldwide have achieved the 95 percent rating required for certification as a Xerox supplier.[23]

Proposal Solicitation

Proposal solicitation The stage of the business buying process in which the buyer invites qualified suppliers to submit proposals.

In the **proposal solicitation** stage of the business buying process, the buyer invites qualified suppliers to submit proposals. In response, some suppliers will send only a catalogue or a salesperson. However, when the item is complex or expensive, the buyer will usually require detailed written proposals or formal presentations from each potential supplier. Business marketers must be skilled in researching, writing, and presenting proposals in response to buyer proposal solicitations. Proposals should be marketing documents, not just technical documents. Presentations should inspire confidence and should make the marketer's company stand out from the competition.

Supplier Selection

Supplier selection
The stage of the business buying process in which the buyer reviews proposals and selects a supplier or suppliers.

The members of the buying centre now review the proposals and select a supplier or suppliers. During **supplier selection,** the buying centre often draws up a list of the desired supplier attributes and their relative importance. In one survey, purchasing executives listed the following attributes as most important in influencing the relationship between supplier and customer: quality products and services, on-time delivery, ethical corporate behaviour, honest communication, and competitive prices.[24] Other important factors include repair and servicing capabilities, technical aid and advice, geographic location, performance history, and reputation. The members of the buying centre will rate suppliers against these attributes and identify the best suppliers.

As part of the buyer selection process, buying centres must decide how many suppliers to use. In the past, many companies preferred a large supplier base to ensure adequate supplies and to obtain price concessions. These companies would insist on annual negotiations for contract renewal and would often shift the amount of business they gave to each supplier from year to year. Increasingly, however, companies are reducing the number of suppliers. Such companies as Ford, Motorola, and Allied Signal have cut the number of suppliers by 20 to 80 percent. These companies expect their preferred suppliers to work closely with them during product development and they value their suppliers' suggestions.

There is even a trend toward single sourcing, using one supplier. Using a single supplier can improve inventory control and can translate into more consistent product performance. Many companies, however, are still reluctant to use single sourcing. They fear that they may become too dependent on the single supplier or that the single-source supplier may become too comfortable in the relationship and lose its competitive edge. Some marketers have developed programs that address these concerns. For example, GC Electronics has a "one source lowest price guarantee program," which promotes the reduced transaction and purchasing costs of using it as a single source. However, if after being with the program for a while, distributors can show that they could have gotten a better deal elsewhere, GC offers them a six percent rebate.[25]

Order-Routine Specification

Order-routine specification
The stage of the business buying process in which the buyer writes the final order with the chosen supplier(s), listing the technical specifications, quantity needed, expected time of delivery, return policies, and warranties.

The buyer now prepares an **order-routine specification.** It includes the final order with the chosen supplier or suppliers and lists items such as technical specifications, quantity needed, expected time of delivery, return policies, and warranties. In the case of maintenance, repair, and operating items, buyers may use *blanket contracts* rather than periodic purchase orders. A blanket contract creates a long-term relationship in which the supplier promises to resupply the buyer as needed at agreed prices for a set period. The seller holds the stock and the buyer's computer automatically prints out an order to the seller when stock is needed. A blanket order eliminates the expensive process of renegotiating a purchase each time stock is required. It also allows buyers to write more but smaller purchase orders, resulting in lower inventory levels and carrying costs.

Blanket contracting leads to more single-source buying and to buying more items from that source. This practice locks the supplier in tighter with the buyer and makes it difficult for other suppliers to break in unless the buyer becomes dissatisfied with prices or service.

Performance Review

Performance review
The stage of the business buying process in which the buyer rates its satisfaction with suppliers, deciding whether to continue, modify, or drop them.

In this stage, the buyer reviews supplier performance. The buyer may contact users and ask them to rate their satisfaction. The **performance review** may lead the buyer to continue, modify, or end the arrangement. The seller's job is to monitor the same factors used by the buyer to ensure that it is giving the expected satisfaction.

The eight-stage model provides a simple view of the business buying decision process. The actual process is usually much more complex. In the modified rebuy or straight rebuy situation, some of these stages would be compressed or bypassed. Each organization buys in its own way, and each buying situation has unique requirements. Different buying centre participants may be involved at different stages of the process. Although certain buying process steps usually do occur, buyers do not always follow them in the same order, and they may add other steps. Often, buyers will repeat certain stages of the process.

Business Buying on the Internet

During the past few years, incredible advances in information technology have changed the face of the business-to-business marketing process. Increasingly, business buyers are purchasing many kinds of products and services electronically, either through electronic data interchange (EDI) links or on the Internet. Such "cyberpurchasing" gives buyers access to new suppliers, lowers purchasing costs, and hastens order processing and delivery. In turn, business marketers are connecting with customers online to share marketing information, sell products and services, provide customer support services, and maintain ongoing customer relationships. In addition to their own Web pages on the Internet, they are establishing extranets that link their company's communications and data with its regular suppliers and distributors.

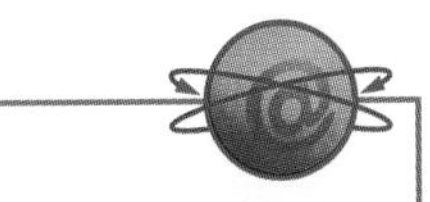

Business Depot/Staples
www.staples.ca/

So far, most of the products bought by businesses through Internet and extranet connections are maintenance, repair, and operations (MRO) materials. To take advantage of this, Business Depot, which operates Staples and Bureau en Gros stores across Canada, is using the Net in a bid to become a one-stop online shop for the growing small business market in Canada. The new site carries the retailer's entire catalogue of supplies, over 5000 products plus an extended line of technology products and computer equipment. It also offers a variety of time-saving options and personalization features designed to cater primarily to business customers with fewer than four employees. The site has already exceeded the sales goals set for it three-fold, indicating that Canadian small business customers are definitely ready to shop online. "The one thing that amazed us the most when we launched was just how quickly people started getting on the site, without us doing any advertising," says the site manager. But that's not the only surprise. The current users are skewed toward rural areas, and roughly 20 percent of Business Depot's online customers are from Quebec. To promote the site, Business Depot has set up strategic alliances with other companies and sites like CIBC that cater to small business customers. Along with its US parent, Business Depot is aiming for $1 billion in online sales and one million online customers by the end of 2003 for its North American business.[26]

The actual dollar amount spent on these MRO materials pales in comparison to the amount spent for items like airplane parts, computer systems, and steel tubing. Yet, MRO materials make up 80 percent of all business orders, and the transaction costs for order processing are high. Thus, companies have much to gain by streamlining the MRO buying process on the Web.

General Electric, one of the world's biggest purchasers, plans to be buying all of its general operating and industrial supplies online within the next two years. Five years ago, GE set up its Trading Process Network, a central Web site through which all GE business units could make their purchases. The site was so successful that GE has now opened it up to other companies, creating a vast electronic cyberbuying clearinghouse (see Marketing Highlight 6-3).

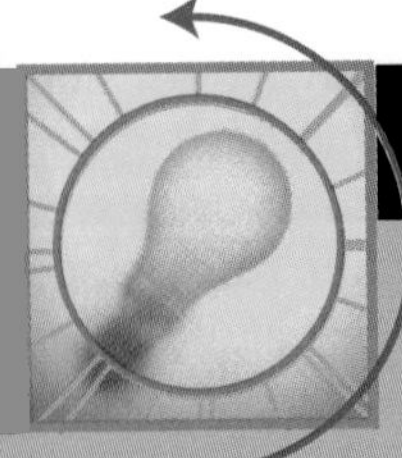

marketing highlight 6-3

General Electric's Business-to-Business Cyberbazaar

To most consumers, all the buzz about Internet buying has focused on Web sites selling computers, software, clothing, books, flowers, or other retail goods. However, consumer goods sales via the Web are dwarfed by the Internet sales of business goods. In fact, business-to-business cyberbuying now accounts for about 78 percent of the dollar value of all e-commerce transactions.

General Electric is among the pioneers in Internet purchasing. In early 1995, GE's information services division (GEIS) launched a Web site that allowed buyers in GE's many divisions to purchase industrial products electronically. This Web site let GE buyers snap out requests for bids to thousands of suppliers, who could then respond over the Internet. Such electronic purchasing has saved GE's many divisions money, time, and piles of paperwork. According to a *Forbes* account, here's how it works:

> Last month the machinery at a GE Lighting factory broke down. GE Lighting needed custom replacement parts, fast. In the past GE would have asked for bids from just four North American suppliers. There was just too much hassle getting the paperwork and production-line blueprints together and sent out to [a long list of] suppliers. But this time it posted the specifications and "requests for quotes" on GE's Web site—and drew seven other bidders. The winner was a Hungarian [vendor] . . . that would not [even] have been contacted in the days of paper purchasing forms. The Hungarian firm's replacement parts arrived quicker, and GE Lighting paid just $480 000, a 20 percent savings.

Within little more than a year, GEIS's Internet purchasing system had logged more than $525 million worth of purchases by GE divisions, at a 10 to 15 percent savings in costs and a five-day reduction in average order time. In 1997, GE purchased $1.5 billion worth of materials via the Internet and by the end of 2000 expected to be buying $7.5 billion worth, a 20 percent savings over the old way.

Based on its own success, GE opened its online procurement services to other companies in the form of the trading process network (TPN) (www.tpn.geis.com). TPN is an online purchasing service that lets member buyers prepare bids, select suppliers, and post orders to its Web site. Users can select items they wish to buy and use a purchasing card for payment. Once the order is placed, TPN sends a purchase order to a selected supplier or asks for bids from several qualified suppliers. Users of the TPN service have experienced up to a 50 percent reduction in order cycle times, 30 percent reduction in procurement costs, and 20 percent reduction in material costs.

Despite likely competition from such e-business giants as IBM and Microsoft, GEIS has developed a formidable head start in providing Internet purchasing services. According to Orville Bailey, manager of the TPN project, the toughest part of setting up such a system is just getting it started. Buyers don't want to sign on until plenty of suppliers are already on board. "It's the classic chicken-or-the-egg problem," says Bailey. Here, however, GE's tremendous size gives it a crucial advantage. Its various divisions spend more than $45 billion a year buying goods and services from other companies. So when GE announced that it would be looking for bids over the Web, suppliers scurried to sign up. Now, with its own network of industrial goods suppliers already in place, GEIS has little difficulty reselling the Internet purchasing system to other companies that want to take advantage of what GE has built.

GEIS charges buyers an initial fee of $115 000 for access to its TPN site, plus an annual fee based on buying volume. Suppliers can sign on for free. The first outside buying firm to sign on with TPN was Textron Automotive, a subsidiary of the $14 billion Textron, Inc. According to *Forbes*, "Like GE, Textron Automotive buys a lot of raw materials and components: resin, ashtrays, metal clips, and other parts used in auto dashboards and paneling. By year end, Textron Automotive hopes to place all its orders—more than $750 million a year—over the GE Information Services Web site." Such big users, along with thousands of smaller ones, have put GEIS well on its way to creating a vast cyberbazaar.

Thus, the Internet promises to greatly change the face of business buying and hence the face of business-to-business marketing. As one expert suggests, "Internet presence is becoming as common as business cards and faxes." To stay in the game, business-to-business marketers will need a well-conceived Internet marketing strategy to support their other business marketing efforts. General Electric envisions a near future in which hundreds of thousands of firms exchange trillions of dollars worth of industrial goods in cyberspace—with GEIS running the show, of course.

Sources: Extracts from Scott Woolley, "Double click for resin," *Forbes,* 10 March 1997:132. Also see Dana Blankenhorn, "GE's e-commerce network opens up to other marketers," *Advertising Age's Business Marketing,* May 1997:M4,M11; "Consolidated Edison of New York selects GE's Trading Process Network to facilitate internet sourcing," press release, www.tpn.geis.com, 10 February 1998; Robert D. Hof, "The 'click here' economy," *Business Week,* 22 June 1998:122–8; John Evan Frook, "Buying behemoth—By shifting $5B in spending to extranets, GE could ignite a development frenzy," *Internetweek,* 17 August 1998:1; Richard Waugh and Scott Elliff, "Using the Internet to achieve purchasing improvements at General Electric," *Hospital Materiel Management Quarterly,* November 1998:81–3; and James Carbone, "Internet buying on the rise," *Purchasing,* 25 March 1999:51–6.

The rapid growth of business-to-business cyberbuying promises many benefits. It will:[27]

- *Shave transaction costs for both buyers and suppliers.* A Web-powered purchasing program eliminates the paperwork associated with traditional requisition and ordering procedures. At National Semiconductor, the $110 to $375 cost of processing each paper-based requisition has been cut to just $4.50 per electronic order.
- *Reduce time between order and delivery.* Time savings are particularly dramatic for companies with many overseas suppliers. Adaptec, a leading supplier of computer storage, used an extranet to tie all of its Taiwanese chip suppliers together in a kind of virtual family. Now messages from Adaptec flow in seconds from its headquarters to its Asian partners, and Adaptec has reduced the time between the order and delivery of its chips from as long as 16 weeks to just 55 days, the same turnaround time for companies that build their own chips.
- *Create more efficient purchasing systems.* One key motivation for GE's massive move to online purchasing has been a desire to get rid of overlapping purchasing systems across its many divisions. "We have too many purchasing systems to count," said Randy Rowe, manager of GE's corporate initiatives group. "We're looking to enable each division to manage its purchasing on extranets with financial data [concentrated in] a centralized platform."
- *Forge more intimate relationships between partners and buyers.* Robert Mondavi Corporation puts satellite images of its vineyards out over its extranet so that its independent growers can pinpoint potential vineyard problems and improve the grapes Mondavi purchases from them.
- *Level the playing field between large and small suppliers.* By using Internet technology to establish secure, standing information links between companies, extranets have helped firms do business with smaller suppliers. Currently most large manufacturers use EDI to order supplies, because it provides a secure means of coding and exchanging standardized business forms. However, EDI is an expensive system; it can cost as much as $75 000 to add a single trading partner to an EDI network, compared to $1500 for a company to join GE's Trading Process Network. Moving business-to-business commerce onto the Web also levels the playing field between local and foreign suppliers, because purchasers can source materials from suppliers all over the globe for no additional transaction cost.

The rapidly expanding use of cybersourcing, however, also presents some problems. On the downside, it will:

- *Cut purchasing jobs for millions of clerks and order processors.* All these savings and efficiencies derived from cyberbuying don't come without a price. National Semiconductor reduced its purchasing staff by more than half when it took its purchasing activities online. On the other hand, for many purchasing professionals, going online means reducing drudgery and paperwork and spending more time managing inventory and working creatively with suppliers.
- *Erode supplier–buyer loyalty.* At the same time that the Web makes it possible for suppliers and customers to share business data and even collaborate on product design, it can also erode decades-old customer–supplier relationships. Many firms are using the Web to search for better suppliers. Japan Airlines (JAL) has used the Internet to post orders for in-flight materials such as plastic cups. On its Web site, it posts drawings and specifications that will attract proposals from any firm that comes across the site, rather than from just the usual Japanese suppliers.
- *Create potential security disasters.* Over 80 percent of companies say security is the leading barrier to expanding electronic links with customers and partners. Although e-mail and home banking transactions can be protected through basic en-

cryption, the secure environment that businesses need to carry out confidential interactions is still lacking. However, security is of such high priority that companies are spending millions of research dollars on it. Companies are creating their own defensive strategies for keeping hackers at bay. Cisco Systems, for example, specifies the types of routers, firewalls, and security procedures that its partners must use to safeguard extranet connections. In fact, the company goes even further: It sends its own security engineers to examine a partner's defences and holds the partner liable for any security breach that originates from its computer.

Institutional and Government Markets

So far, our discussion of organizational buying has focused largely on the buying behaviour of business buyers. Much of this discussion also applies to the buying practices of institutional and government organizations. However, these two non-business markets have additional characteristics and needs, which we now address.

Institutional Markets

Institutional market
Schools, hospitals, nursing homes, prisons, and other institutions that provide goods and services to people in their care.

The **institutional market** consists of schools, hospitals, nursing homes, prisons, and other institutions that provide goods and services to people in their care.

Many institutional markets are characterized by low budgets and captive patrons. For example, hospital patients have little choice but to eat whatever food the hospital supplies. A hospital purchasing agent must decide on the quality of food to buy for patients. Because the food is provided as part of a total service package, the buying objective is not profit. Nor is strict cost minimization the goal—patients receiving poor-quality food will complain to others and damage the hospital's reputation. Thus, the hospital purchasing agent must search for institutional food vendors whose quality meets or exceeds a certain minimum standard and whose prices are low.

Many marketers set up separate divisions to meet the special characteristics and needs of institutional buyers. For example, Heinz produces, packages, and prices its ketchup and other products differently to better serve the requirements of hospitals, universities, and other institutional markets.

Government Markets

Government market
Governmental units—federal, provincial, and municipal—that purchase or rent goods and services for carrying out the main functions of government.

The **government market** offers large opportunities for many companies. Federal, provincial, and municipal governments contain buying units. And various levels of government in countries around the world offer vast selling opportunities. Government buying and business buying are similar in many ways. But there are also differences that must be understood by companies that wish to sell products and services to governments. To succeed in the government market, sellers must locate key decision makers, identify the factors that affect buyer behaviour, and understand the buying decision process.

The Department of Public Works and Government Services Canada helps to centralize the buying of commonly used items in the civilian section (for example, office furniture and equipment, vehicles, fuels) and in standardizing buying procedures for the other agencies. Federal military buying is carried out by the Department of National Defence.

Government organizations typically require suppliers to submit bids, and normally they award the contract to the lowest bidder. In some cases, the government unit will make allowance for the supplier's superior quality or reputation for completing contracts on time. Governments will also buy on a negotiated contract basis, primarily in the case of complex projects involving major R&D costs and risks, and in cases where little competition exists.

Government organizations tend to favour domestic over foreign suppliers. A major complaint of multinationals operating in Europe is that each country shows

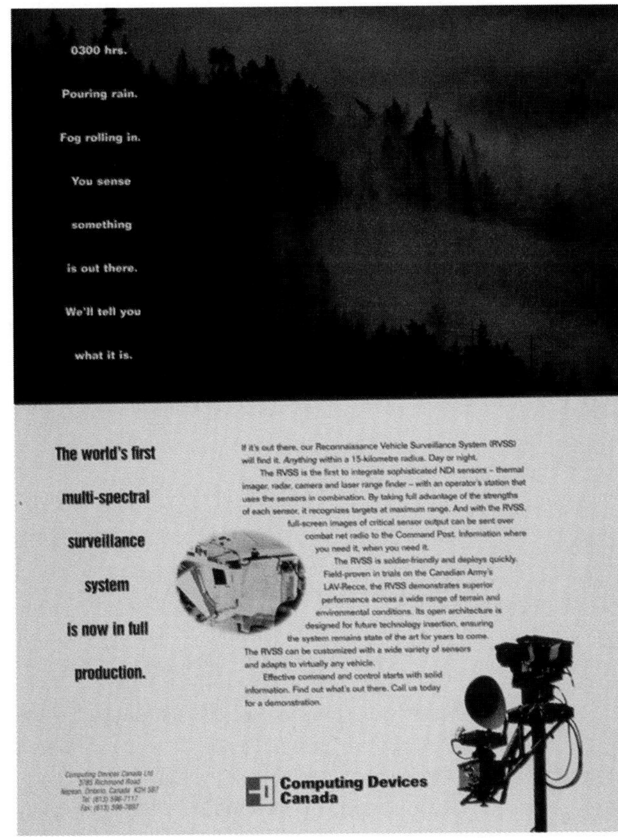

The government market offers many opportunities for companies.

favouritism toward its nationals, despite superior offers made by foreign firms. The European Economic Commission is gradually removing this bias. In an effort to improve the competitiveness of Canadian businesses, products purchased by the government are evaluated for the potential to be marketed worldwide. In its infancy, Bombardier was given a boost as a supplier of military vehicles. Rations developed by Magic Pan for the Canadian military are marketed to global institutions.

Like consumer and business buyers, government buyers are affected by environmental, organizational, interpersonal, and individual factors. One unique aspect of government buying is that it is carefully watched by outside publics, from Parliament to various private groups interested in how the government spends taxpayers' money. Because their spending decisions are subject to public review, government organizations require considerable paperwork from suppliers, who often complain about excessive paperwork, bureaucracy, regulations, decision-making delays, and frequent shifts in procurement personnel.

Most governments provide would-be suppliers with detailed guides describing how to sell to the government. The federal government issues a weekly bulletin, *Government Business Opportunities,* to alert prospective suppliers to the government's plans to purchase products or services. Both federal and provincial governments offer guides to help business firms understand their purchasing policies.[28]

Contracts Canada
contractscanada.gc.ca/

Federal, provincial, and municipal governments are now posting information online to help businesses better understand their purchasing processes and supplier selection criteria. On the federal government Web site Contracts Canada, for example, you can find a wealth of information with only a click of the mouse on the "How we buy" or "What we buy" buttons. You can also access information about how to become a registered government supplier, as well as a list of current contract opportunities. The Canadian Business Service Centre is another site the government established to help Canadian businesses. This site is a gold mine of information on a variety of topics such as training, importing, and taxation. It features online workshops for small businesses as well as a comprehensive database of government services and programs.

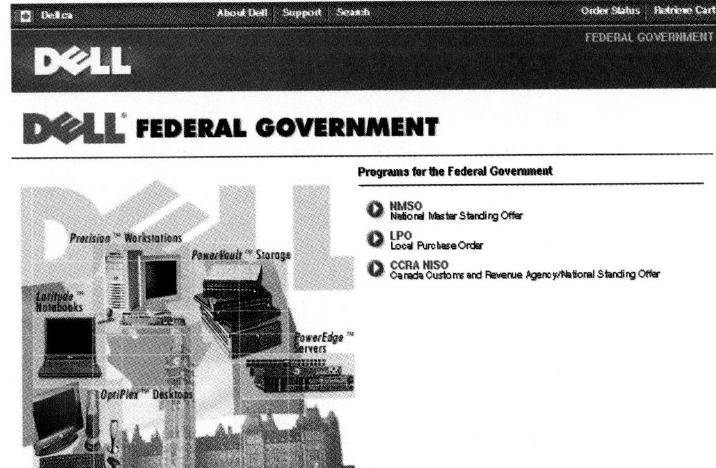

Dell Computer provides special Web sites for government buyers.

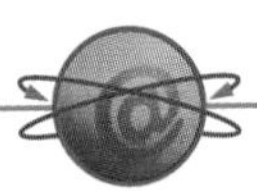

Canadian Business Service Centre
www.cbsc.org/

Many companies that sell to the government have not been marketing-oriented for a number of reasons. Total government spending is determined by elected officials rather than by any marketing effort to develop this market. Government buying has emphasized price, making suppliers invest their effort in technology to bring down costs. When the product's characteristics are specified carefully, product differentiation is not a marketing factor. Nor do advertising or personal selling matter much in winning bids on an open-bid basis.

As provincial governments downsize and move toward privatization, there are growing opportunities. Firms ranging from professional engineering firms to cleaning contractors are bidding to take over functions that government employees formerly performed. Many companies, such as Bombardier, SNC Lavalin, Eastman Kodak, Goodyear, and Computing Devices Canada (CDC), have people who specialize in marketing to governments both nationally and internationally.

Review of Concept Connections

Business markets and consumer markets are alike in some key ways. For example, both include people in buying roles who make purchase decisions to satisfy needs. But business markets also differ in many ways from consumer markets. For one thing, the business market is *enormous,* far larger than the consumer market. Within Canada alone, the business market includes more than one million organizations that annually purchase billions of dollars worth of goods and services.

1. Define the business market and explain how business markets differ from consumer markets.

The *business market* consists of all organizations that buy goods and services to use in the production of other products and services or to resell or rent to others at a profit. Compared with consumer markets, business markets usually have fewer, larger buyers who are more geographically concentrated. Business demand is *derived,* largely *inelastic,* and more *fluctuating*. More buyers are usually involved in the business buying decision, and business buyers are better trained and more professional than are consumer buyers. In general, business purchasing decisions are more complex, and the buying process is more formal than consumer buying.

2. Identify the major factors that influence business buyer behaviour.

Business buyers make decisions that vary with the three types of buying situations: *straight rebuys, modified rebuys,* and *new tasks.* These tasks are handled by the buying centre, the decision-making unit of a buying organization, which can consist of many different persons playing many different roles. The business marketer needs to know the following: Who are the major participants? In what decisions do they exercise influence? What is their relative degree of influence? What evaluation criteria do each decision participant use? The business marketer also needs to understand the major environmental, interpersonal, and individual influences on the buying process.

3. List and define the steps in the business buying decision process.

The business buying decision process itself can be quite involved, with eight basic stages: (1) *problem recognition*—someone in the company recognizes a problem or need that can be met by acquiring a product or a service; (2) *general need description*—the company determines the general characteristics and quantity of the needed item; (3) *product specification*—the buying organization decides on and specifies the best technical product characteristics for the needed item; (4) *supplier search*—the buyer seeks the best vendors; (5) *proposal solicitation*—the buyer invites qualified suppliers to submit proposals; (6) *supplier selection*—the buyer reviews proposals and selects a supplier or suppliers; (7) *order-routine specification*—the buyer writes the final order with the chosen supplier(s), listing the technical specifications, quantity needed, expected time of delivery, return policies, and warranties; (8) *performance review*—the buyer rates its satisfaction with suppliers, deciding whether to continue, modify, or cancel the relationship.

4. Compare the institutional and government markets and explain how they make their buying decisions.

The *institutional market* consists of schools, hospitals, prisons, and other institutions that provide goods and services to people in their care. These markets are characterized by low budgets and captive patrons. The vast *government market* consists of government units—federal, provincial, and municipal—that purchase or rent goods and services for carrying out the main functions of government. Government buyers purchase products and services for defence, education, public welfare, and other public needs. Government buying practices are highly specialized and specified, with open bidding or negotiated contracts characterizing most of the buying. Government buyers operate under the watchful eye of Parliament and many private watchdog groups. Therefore, they tend to require more forms and signatures, and to respond more slowly and deliberately when placing orders.

Key Terms

Business buying process *(p. 243)*
Business market *(p. 243)*
Buyers *(p. 250)*
Buying centre *(p. 249)*
Deciders *(p. 250)*
Derived demand *(p. 244)*
Gatekeepers *(p. 250)*
General need description *(p. 256)*
Government market *(p. 262)*
Influencers *(p. 250)*
Institutional market *(p. 262)*
Modified rebuy *(p. 249)*
New task *(p. 249)*
Order-routine specification *(p. 258)*
Performance review *(p. 258)*
Problem recognition *(p. 255)*
Product specification *(p. 256)*
Proposal solicitation *(p. 257)*
Straight rebuy *(p. 248)*
Supplier search *(p. 257)*
Supplier selection *(p. 258)*
Systems buying *(p. 249)*
Users *(p. 250)*
Value analysis *(p. 256)*

Discussing the Issues

1. Although business markets are similar in many ways to consumers markets, significant differences exist. What similarities and difference might Staples (www.staples.com) or Office Depot (www.office-depot.com) encounter in selling to the business market versus the consumer market the following products: (a) a personal computer, (b) paper for a printer or photocopier, (c) a desk chair, and (d) paper clips?
2. Using the auto industry as an example, demonstrate the concept of derived demand. How might derived demand affect the industry in the following product categories: (a) steel, (b) CD players, (c) safety air bags, (d) On Star roadside assistance service, and (e) customized chrome wheels? What consumer trends would affect these products and their demand by the auto industry?
3. Compare Figure 5-1 (in the previous chapter) with Figure 6-1. What similarities and differences do you find in inputs and outputs of these two buying models? What additions would you recommend for either or both models? Explain.
4. Identify which of the major types of buying situations are represented by the following: (a) Chrysler's purchase of computers that go in cars and adjust engine performance to changing driving conditions, (b) Volkswagen's purchase of spark plugs for its line of vans, and (c) Honda's purchase of light bulbs for a new Acura model.
5. Illustrate how the concept of systems buying might work if your university or college decided to purchase a new master computer system that would integrate all administrative, faculty, and student information requirements into a single system. The system could be accessed by users on or off campus. What would be the component parts of such a system? How would you go about selling such a system to the college or university?
6. Assume you are selling cars to a company for use as fleet by the company's sales force. The salespeople would like bigger, more comfortable cars, which would be more profitable for you. However, the company's fleet buyer prefers smaller, more economical cars. Who might be in the buying centre for this purchase? How could you meet the different needs of these participants?
7. Many business buyers are now purchasing prod-

ucts and services electronically, either through electronic data interchange (EDI) links or on the Internet. What are the benefits of such "cyberpurchasing"? What are the negatives? What is the future of this growing field of commerce? Illustrate your view with an example.

Marketing Applications

1. Many companies use outside suppliers to produce raw materials or parts instead of producing these components themselves. In the extreme, companies like Dell Computer own no production facilities and have suppliers make everything to order. This type of company has been nicknamed a "virtual corporation."
   a. Do you think that buyers and suppliers are likely to be more cooperative or more adversarial in this type of corporate structure?
   b. List the advantages and disadvantages of this sort of supplier relationship for both the buyer and the supplier.
   c. Explain how the supplier search process might work in the Dell "virtual corporation" example.
   d. Go to the Dell Web site at www.dell.com and review the information on the company. What can you determine about the "outside" parts that are contained in a Dell computer—for example, the processor, monitor, or CPU itself? Do buyers know which components are original Dell parts and which are not? Would this be of concern to potential buyers?
   e. In such a situation, what would be the most important considerations in supplier selections?
2. Performance review is one of the most critical stages in a business buying process. Perhaps nowhere is this more important than in the highly competitive aircraft manufacturing business. No matter what the size of the airplane, once the purchase is made, the buyer is tied to the manufacturer for a long time because of service and parts requirements. "Air wars" are currently being fought between Europe's Airbus Industrie, Canada's Bombardier, and Brazil's Embraer. To a lesser extent the same competitive conflict exists in the smaller personal aircraft market between Cessna and Lear Jet. Who will eventually win these dramatic competitive struggles is still up in the air. (For additional information on these companies, see www.airbus.com, www.boeing.com, www.bombardier.com, www.embraer.com, www.cessna.textron.com, and www.learjet.com.)
   a. Apply Figure 6-1 to either of the preceding competitive situations and discuss the critical factors that might be found in such a business buying situation.
   b. How would performance review be conducted in either of these situations? Who might be responsible for such a performance review?
   c. Refer to Figure 6-2. Which specific components might be involved in a performance review of aircraft safety?
   d. Find a recent example of "air war" competitiveness and bring the example to class for discussion. How does your example relate to business-to-business marketing and business buying?

Internet Connections

Online Databases

Many business-to-business (B2B) marketers use the services of firms that provide information on other companies through their databases. Dun & Bradstreet is popular and has a fine reputation for both its paper and online company profiles. The Yellow Book, founded in 1930, also provides information for businesses seeking suppliers or other contacts. Finally, AskAlex Directory serves a niche market for businesses wanting a particular type of information. In this exercise, you will visit all three online firms, check out their services, and evaluate their appropriateness for various business situations. Start by completing the table.

Discussion Questions

1. If your firm were looking for an office supply company in Manhattan to replace its current supplier, which of the three databases would you use? Explain.
2. If you wanted to quickly find the phone number of an office supply firm in Tampa, Florida, which database would you use? Why?
3. Which database offers the broadest range of services? Explain.
4. Under what circumstances would the AskAlex business database be useful to a company?
5. If you were a salesperson for IBM and prospecting for new business customers, which database would you use? Why?
6. Overall, which database company is the best in your opinion? Explain.
7. If you were going to start an online database firm to serve the B2B market, what would you do differently from these three firms?

	Dun & Bradstreet **www.dnb.com**	Yellow Book **www.yellowbook.com**	AskAlex Directory **askalex.co.uk**
Database size			
Geographic coverage			
Cost for using the database			
Specific company profile information in database			
Three important services			
Useful for a supplier search?			
Useful for a supplier selection?			
Useful for finding prospective business customers?			
Database includes government market?			
Competitive edge			

Savvy Sites

- EDS (www.eds.com), located in Toronto and Dallas, "develops solutions for complex business issues" including management and solutions consulting, information solutions, and business process management.
- Ad-Up (www.ad-up.com) and Click-Through, Inc. (www.clickthrough.com) are online full-service advertising agencies that help business clients find appropriate sites for their banner advertisements. For a list of similar services, visit Advertising World at the University of Texas (advweb.cocomm.utexas.edu/world/).
- Intel (www.intel.com) provides a lot of information on its Web site for such business clients as software and hardware developers, business computing, and channel members. It is especially helpful for e-business managers.

Notes

1. Casey Mahood, "Bombardier lands huge jet order," *Globe and Mail,* 30 March 2000:B1,B15; Hélèna Katz, "Hot wheels! To get good traction in the expanding all-terrain market, newcomer Bombardier must build its brand," *Marketing On-line,* www.aerospace.bombardier.com; Bombardier news release, "Bombardier Aerospace launches e-business customer service initiative," 10 October 2000; Ann Gibbon, "Bombardier lands 24-plane deal, *Globe and Mail,* 23 January 1996:B1. Portions adapted from Thomas V. Bonoma, "Major sales: Who really does the buying," *Harvard Business Review,* May–June 1982, © President and Fellows of Harvard College 1982, all rights reserved.
2. Bernadette Johnson, "Profile of Canada's SOHO market is evolving: OgilvyOne study," *Strategy,* 17 July 2000:D14.
3. This definition was adapted from Frederick E. Webster, Jr. and Yoram Wind, *Organizational Buying Behavior,* Englewood Cliffs, NJ: Prentice Hall, 1972:2.
4. "SiteLines," *Strategy,* 22 May 2000:D4.
5. Industry Canada, *Sector Competitiveness Framework Series: Computer Equipment,* 12 May 1997, strategis.ic.gc.ca.
6. For discussions of similarities and differences in consumer and business marketing, see Edward F. Fern and James R. Brown, "The industrial/consumer marketing dichotomy: A case of insufficient justification," *Journal of Marketing,* Fall 1984:68–77; and Ron J. Kornakovich, "Consumer methods work for business marketing: Yes; no," *Marketing News,* 21 November 1988: 4,13–4.
7. "Canadian markets 1988/89," *Financial Post,* Toronto: Maclean Hunter, 1989.
8. Sarah Lorge, "Purchasing power," *Sales & Marketing Management,* June 1998:43–6.
9. John H. Sheridan, "An alliance built on trust," *Industry Week,* 17 March 1997:66–70.
10. See James C. Anderson and James A. Narus, "Value-based segmentation, targeting, and relationship-building in business markets," ISBM Report #12–1989, University Park, PA: The Institute for the Study of Business Markets, Pennsylvania State University, 1989; Lawrence A. Crosby, Kenneth R. Evans, and Deborah Cowles, "Relationship quality and services selling: An interpersonal influence perspective," *Journal of Marketing,* July 1990:68–81; Barry J. Farber and Joyce Wycoff, "Relationships: Six steps to success," *Sales & Marketing Management,* April 1992:50–8; and Minda Zetlin, "It's all the same to me," *Sales & Marketing Management,* February 1994:71–5.
11. Patrick J. Robinson, Charles W. Faris, and Yoram Wind, *Industrial Buying Behavior and Creative Marketing,* Boston: Allyn & Bacon, 1967. Also see Erin Anderson, Weyien Chu, and Barton Weitz, "Industrial purchasing: An empirical exploration of the buyclass framework," *Journal of Marketing,* July 1987: 71–86.
12. For more on systems selling, see Robert R. Reeder, Edward G. Brierty, and Betty H. Reeder, *Industrial Marketing: Analysis, Planning, and Control,* Englewood Cliffs, NJ: Prentice Hall, 1991:264–7.
13. Sarah Lorge, "Enron," *Sales & Marketing Management,* July 1999:48–52; "Enron Energy Services, Canadian-based printer ink $1B energy management deal," *American City Business Journals Inc.,* 31 May 2000, www.bizjournals.com/houston/stories/2000/05/29/daily4.html.
14. Webster and Wind, *Organizational Buying Behavior:*6. For more reading on buying centres, see Bonoma, "Major sales: Who really does the buying"; and Donald W. Jackson, Jr., Janet E. Keith, and Richard K. Burdick, "Purchasing agents' perceptions of industrial buying center influence: A situational approach," *Journal of Marketing,* Fall 1984:75–83.
15. Webster and Wind, *Organizational Buying Behavior:*78–80.
16. For results of both surveys, see "I think you have a great product, but it's not my decision," *American Salesman,* April 1994: 11–3. For more on influence strategies within buying centres, see R. Venkatesh, Ajay K. Kohli, and Gerald Zaltman, "Influence strategies in buying centers," *Journal of Marketing,* October 1995:71–82.
17. Melvin R. Matson and Esmail Salshi-Sangari, "Decision making in purchases of equipment and materials: A four-country comparison," *International Journal of Physical Distribution & Logistics Management,* 1993, 23(8):16–30.
18. Bruce Livesey, "Ceiling unlimited," *Report on Business,* April 1997:42.
19. Webster and Wind, *Organizational Buying Behavior:*33–7.
20. Bonoma, "Major sales":114. Also see Ajay Kohli, "Determinants of influence in organizational buying: A contingency approach," *Journal of Marketing,* July 1989:50–65.
21. Robinson, Faris, and Wind, *Industrial Buying Behavior:*14.
22. John H. Sheridan, "Buying globally made easier," *Industry Week,* 2 February 1998:63–4; and information accessed online at www.wiznet.net, September 1999.
23. See "Xerox Multinational Supplier Quality Survey," *Purchasing,* January 1995:112.
24. See "What buyers really want," *Sales & Marketing Management,* October 1989:30.
25. See Kitty Vineyard, "Trends . . . in single sourcing," *Electrical Apparatus,* November 1996:12; and Anne Millen Porter, "Supply alliances pose new ethical threats," *Purchasing,* 20 May 1999:20–6.
26. Bernadette Johnson, "Business Depot targets SOHO sector," *Strategy,* 19 June 2000:D1.
27. See Robert Yoegel, "The evolution of B-to-B selling on the Net," *Target Marketing,* August 1998:34; Andy Reinhardt in San Mateo, "Extranets: Log on, link up, save big," *Business Week,* 22 June 1998:134; "To byte the hand that feeds," *The Economist,* 17 January 1998:61–2; John Evan Frook, "Buying behemoth—By shifting $5B in spending to extranets, GE could ignite a development frenzy," *Internetweek,* 17 August 1998:1; John Jesitus, "Procuring an edge," *Industry Week,* 23 June 1997:56–62; Ken Brack, "Source of the future," *Industrial Distribution,* October 1998:76–80; and James Carbone, "Internet buying on the rise," Purchasing, 25 March 1999:51–6.
28. See Ottawa: Supply and Services, *Government Business Opportunities,* and *Selling to Government: A Guide to Government Procurement in Canada.*

Company Case 6

Biofoam: Not Just Peanuts!

Like diamonds, polystyrene peanuts are forever. The stash of them is growing at a rate of at least 110 million kilograms annually. Since their introduction in 1970, they have become one of the most popular forms of packaging material. They are lightweight, inexpensive, and resilient. They conform to any shape, protect superbly, resist shifting in transit, and leave no dusty residue on the goods they protect. And, of course, they are indestructible. In fact, that's the problem. Nearly every one of those peanuts used since 1970 is still with us—blowing in the wind or taking up space in a landfill. Worse yet, they will be with us for another 500 years. They're wonderful, but they're just not environmentally sound.

A small firm, Biofoam, believes that it has solved this problem. It sells peanuts made from grain sorghum, which are also known as Biofoam. To make these sorghum peanuts, the company strips the grain of its nutritional value, presses it into pellets, and conveys it through a giant popper. The process creates a product that looks like tan cheese doodles, which is not surprising considering that the inventors originally started out to make a snack food. But since no one wanted to eat these tan cheese doodles, the inventors had to find other uses for them. According to Ed Alfke, Biofoam's CEO, the sorghum peanuts do as good a job as the best foam peanuts but don't cost any more. Moreover, they hold no electrostatic charge, so they won't cling to nylons or other synthetic fibres (like your carpet or clothes). Better yet, they are "absolutely, frighteningly natural," says Tom Schmiegel, a veteran of the plastics industry.

To dispose of a Biofoam peanut, you can throw it in the garbage, toss it on your front lawn; dump it in your compost bin; put it in your dog's or cat's bowl; set it out with salsa at your next party; or simply wash it down your drain. The peanut dissolves in water and has some—although limited—nutritional value. Alfke bought into the company because of its environmentally positive stance. He is convinced that green companies will profit from a global regulatory climate that's increasingly hostile to polluters. "The writing is on the wall for companies that are not environmentally friendly," he says.

Biofoam initially targeted retailers who wanted to send an environmentally friendly message to their customers, and included a Biofoam pamphlet explaining the advantages of the Biofoam peanut. The company targeted the heaviest users of Styrofoam peanuts—organizations like the Home Shopping Network, which consumes 10 to 20 truckloads of loose fill each day at peak volume. To date, Biofoam has signed two major accounts—the Fuller Brush Company and computer reseller MicroAge.

Eventually, Biofoam will have to expand beyond environmentally sensitive firms into a broader market. To convince potential users to use Biofoam peanuts, Alfke has developed a seemingly flawless option: to be environmentally responsible without paying more or sacrificing convenience. He is willing to install machines on the customer's premises to produce peanuts in-house, an arrangement that would give Biofoam rent-free production sites across North America. He'll even provide an employee to operate the machinery. Although this strategy might sound unusual, it has been used by other companies such as Haloid (now Xerox) to sell copies and by Tetra-Pak to sell juice boxes and milk cartons.

The in-house arrangement benefits both the customer and Biofoam. Users receive immediate, reliable, just-in-time delivery combined with on-site service and a five-year price guarantee with no intermediaries involved. With Biofoam on-site, users never run out of packaging and avoid the expense of stockpiling materials. And lower production costs make Biofoam price competitive with that polystyrene. For Biofoam, the arrangement provides a rent-free network of regional manufacturing facilities and an intimacy with each customer. Because the host company will consume only about one-third of the output, Biofoam plans to sell the excess to smaller firms in the host's area.

However, this in-house production arrangement is not without disadvantages. From the host's perspective, the machinery takes up 1500 square feet of space that could be used to produce something else. Furthermore, some of the output of that 1500 square feet goes to other firms, benefiting Biofoam but doing nothing for the host. And the host has a non-employee working in its plant. In addition, the peanut-making machinery is intrusive. It consists of three machines—an extruder, a conditioning chamber, and a de-duster—joined by ducts and conveyor belts. The machines make a lot of noise (like a giant air conditioner), making conversation in the vicinity impossible. The process creates a smell roughly akin to that of the inside of an old barn, and the machines produce heat, which is a potentially troubling problem. Thus, on closer inspection, the in-house arrangement is not entirely desirable. Without this arrangement, however, costs rise considerably. If it had to ship the peanuts to users, Biofoam would have to raise prices by 10 to 18 percent.

The polystyrene loose-fill industry is a dense, fragmented patchwork of diverse companies. It includes oil companies, chemicals producers, fill manufacturers, and regional distributors—all of which would suffer from Biofoam's success. The industry is much more rough-and-tumble than Alfke had expected. So far, Biofoam has a microscopic market share. The company's 1995 sales totalled only $3.6 million—not much in an industry with potential sales of $215 to $750 million a year. But the $3.6 million represented a five-fold increase over the previous year, before Alfke hit the scene. Alfke projects sales of $115 million by the year 2000, yielding 30 percent pre-tax profits. These projections include sales of products other than sorghum peanuts. Alfke plans to add injectable Biofoam and stiff Biofoam packaging materials. Other promising applications have been suggested, such as using Biofoam to absorb oil spills or in medicinal applications, but Alfke doesn't want to discuss those. For now, "It's important that we try to stay focused," he claims.

Can Alfke reach his ambitious goals? Many industry observers say no. Environmental claims, say these observers, don't have the same impact that they used to have. "That was something we worried about three years ago," says one purchasing agent. Even Biofoam's sales representatives are finding the market less environmentally concerned. Others, however, are more optimistic. For example, although she agrees that the newness of environmentally responsible packaging has worn off, Nancy Pfund, general partner of Hambrecht and Quist's Environmental Technology Fund, believes that many firms are still interested in environmentally friendly packaging. She notes that companies have "internalized a lot of environmental procedures without making a lot of noise about it. You also have younger people who grew up learning about the environment in school now entering the consumer market. That's a very strong trend." Such consumers will demand more responsible packaging.

Are companies that use Biofoam pleased with it? Well, some yes, some no. On the positive side is MicroAge Computer. According to Mark Iaquinto, facilities manager, MicroAge had been searching for an acceptable alternative to polystyrene. Now that it's found Biofoam, he believes that it can stop searching. On the negative side, Norbert Schneider, president of Fuller Brush Company, has concerns about the way the product crumbles in boxes filled with sharp-pointed brushes. Alfke says that Biofoam is working on a solution, but if it doesn't find one soon, Fuller Brush may change packaging suppliers.

Other firms such as Enviromold and American Excelsior have entered the market with biodegradable, water-soluble foams. Made from corn-starch-based thermoplastics, the products can be rinsed down the drain after use. They can be used in loose-fill packaging applications or be moulded in place into shaped packaging. They compare favourably with traditional packaging materials in terms of cost and performance.

Consequently, facing a stiffly competitive industry, new competitors, and a softening of environmental concerns, Biofoam faces challenges going forward. But none of this dents Alfke's enthusiasm. "I've seen a lot of deals," he claims, "and I've never, ever seen a deal as good as this one." As the successful founder and developer of Rent-A-Wreck, Alfke was a multimillionaire before age 40. After selling his interest in Rent-A-Wreck, seeking another firm to buy into, he sank millions of his own money into Biofoam. As an experienced businessman, no doubt he has seen a lot of deals. He really believes in this one, but is he right?

QUESTIONS

1. Outline Biofoam's current marketing strategy. Which elements of the marketing mix are most important for Biofoam to focus on?
2. What is the nature of demand in the loose-fill packaging industry? What factors shape that demand?
3. If you were a buyer of packaging materials, would you agree to Biofoam's offer of machines inside your plant? If not, how could Biofoam overcome your objections?
4. What environmental and organizational factors are likely to affect the loose-fill packaging industry? How will these factors affect Biofoam?
5. Is Alfke right? Is this a good deal? Would you have bought into the firm? Why or why not?

Sources: "The latest trends in . . . protective packaging," *Modern Materials Handling,* October 1996:P8–P12; "What the experts say," *Inc.,* October 1996:54–5; Robert D. Leaversuch, "Water-soluble foams offer cost-effective protection," *Modern Plastics,* April 1997:32–5; David Whitford, "The snack food that's packing America," *Inc.,* October 1996:51–5.

video case 6

INFLUENCING BUSINESS BUYING: TRADE MAGAZINES IN CANADA

The Canadian trade magazine industry is in the business of serving business. Over 900 trade magazine titles in Canada provide information to businesspeople in all types of industries—from housewares and fashion to mining and plastics. Although many businesspeople rely on Canadian trade publications to assist them in their purchasing decisions, these magazines may be threatened by a World Trade Organization decision that will remove existing trade barriers and allow US publishers to distribute their trade publications in Canada.

As businesspeople who are readers contend, trade magazines provide a comprehensive and ongoing guide to doing business in a particular industry. The publications typically include detailed information on suppliers and their products and services, identify notable trends in the industry, and discuss general business tools and how they apply to a specific industry. One reader described one trade magazine as an "index of how to get in touch with anything you need to" in a particular industry.

Unlike most consumer publications, trade magazines are usually provided to their readers free of charge. Trade magazine publishers rely almost exclusively on advertising dollars to support their publications. In total, trade magazines in Canada collect about $150 million in advertising every year from suppliers who hope to influence business decision making with their advertisements.

Ownership in the trade magazine industry is also different from the consumer magazine sector. While two giants, Maclean Hunter and Southam, own about 70 percent of consumer magazines, together they own only 10 percent of the trade magazines. Small publishers—such as Laurie O'Halloran, publisher of *Home Style,* and Pat Maclean, who publishes *Canadian Jeweller and Style*—tend to dominate the trade magazine business. This fragmented pattern of ownership may make the demise of Canadian trade magazines even more likely if US competitors enter, since small publishers may not have the resources to fight the bigger competitors.

O'Halloran targets the annual $5 billion housewares industry with her *Home Style* magazine, which she publishes from her home office. While O'Halloran has some concern that large US publications may try to enter her business, she is confident that they would not be able to serve the needs of the Canadian housewares industry the way she can. She cites cultural differences in the way Canadians live and buy as barriers to US publishers hoping to provide a trade magazine aimed at the Canadian housewares industry. She claims that these competitors would simply not be able to provide the accurate, high-quality information that she can provide to her readers.

Not everyone shares O'Halloran's confidence, however. The Canadian government is concerned about the future of the trade magazine industry and other cultural industries affected by the World Trade Organization decision and may appeal it. Meanwhile, for now, the Canadian trade magazine industry continues to influence the purchase behaviour of businesses in a variety of business markets.

Questions

1. What characteristics of business markets make the use of trade magazines so popular among buyers in these markets?
2. How do trade magazines fit in the buying behaviour process of decision makers in business markets? What types of buying situations would lend themselves to the use of trade magazines?
3. Do you agree with O'Halloran that Canadian trade magazines, compared to American publications, can offer something unique to Canadian business people?

Source: This case was prepared by Auleen Carson and is based on "Trade Magazines," *Venture* (February 9, 1997).

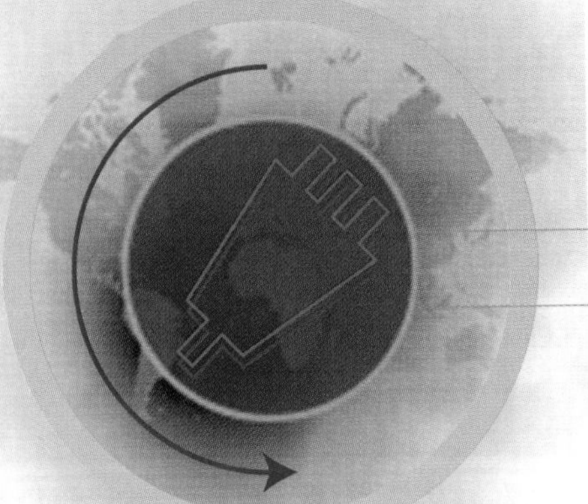

P A R T 1 **2** 3 4

Developing Marketing Opportunities and Strategies

Concept Connections

When you finish this chapter, you should be able to

1. Define the three steps of target marketing: market segmentation, market targeting, and market positioning.
2. List and discuss the major levels of market segmentation and bases for segmenting consumer and business markets.
3. Explain how companies identify attractive market segments and choose a market coverage strategy.
4. Explain how companies can position their products for maximum competitive advantage in the marketplace.

chapter 7 Market Segmentation, Targeting, and Positioning for Competitive Advantage

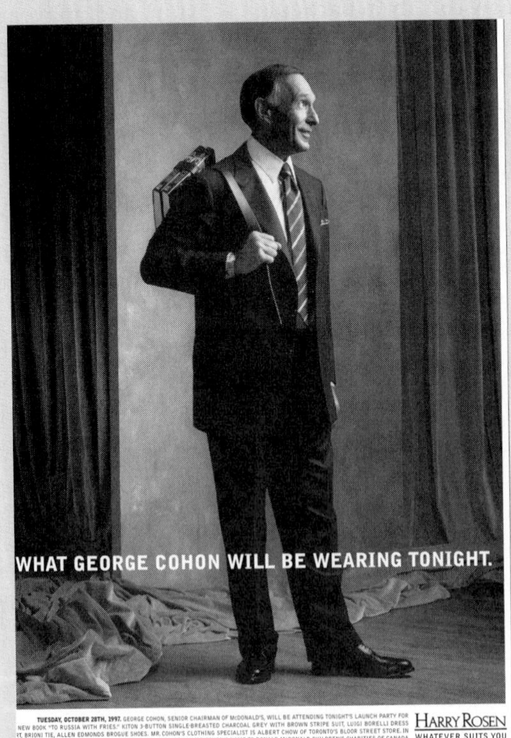

WHAT GEORGE COHON WILL BE WEARING TONIGHT.
TUESDAY, OCTOBER 28TH, 1997. GEORGE COHON, SENIOR CHAIRMAN OF McDONALD'S, WILL BE ATTENDING TONIGHT'S LAUNCH PARTY FOR
NEW BOOK "TO RUSSIA WITH FRIES." KITON 3-BUTTON SINGLE-BREASTED CHARCOAL GREY WITH BROWN STRIPE SUIT, LUIGI BORELLI DRESS
RT, BRIONI TIE, ALLEN EDMONDS BROGUE SHOES. MR. COHON'S CLOTHING SPECIALIST IS ALBERT CHOW OF TORONTO'S BLOOR STREET STORE. IN
RECIATION FOR APPEARING HERE, A DONATION WILL BE MADE IN MR. COHON'S NAME TO RONALD McDONALD CHILDREN'S CHARITIES OF CANADA.
HARRY ROSEN
WHATEVER SUITS YOU
NTREAL · OTTAWA · TORONTO · LONDON · WINNIPEG · CALGARY · EDMONTON · VANCOUVER · BUFFALO
1-800-917-6736

Harry Rosen, an icon of Canadian retailing, has built his business around solving problems for his customers. And one of the main problems for men is that they are not "born shoppers." In fact, Harry Rosen has built his business around a single premise: "When it comes to clothes, most men don't have a clue." Rather than planning their purchases, they shop on impulse. Instead of developing an integrated wardrobe that works for many occasions, they typically have a mishmash of clothes that may be wrong for all occasions. Harry doesn't mince words on the subject: "Some of my private clients have a closet full of clothes, and nothing to wear."

After a short stint working for Tip Top Tailors, Harry Rosen and his brother opened their first store in Toronto in 1954 using $500 from their personal savings to launch the business. Forty-six years later, Rosen has 17 stores located in major cities across Canada as well as one in Buffalo, New York. Rosen has built his business around the cult of his personality, his willingness to move with the times, and his ability to get to know his customers. Even today, at age 69, Harry spends his Saturdays on the floor of his flagship store in Toronto. Across Canada, his stores are known for fashion, a professional sales approach, and personal service.

Harry Rosen stores don't try to meet the needs of all consumers. Instead, they focus on the high-end niche of the men's-wear market. Rosen's $150 million in annual sales represent 28 percent of the sales in that market. Rosen targets businessmen and locates his stores close to the heart of the business district in each city in which he operates. He knows the importance of keeping up with the times in the fashion business. Therefore, he is revamping his stores once again so that they appeal more to younger men, with whom he is currently building relationships. Rosen confesses that it took him awhile to learn to serve men who wear earrings, even though he knows that many are career-oriented MBAs. In the process, however, Harry knows that he must not lose touch with his older, highly profitable clientele of established business professionals.

Harry Rosen also understands that today's consumers differ from their predecessors in important ways. They are more sophisticated and less caught up in the pursuit of the novel. They are much

more hard-nosed about value, and quality—rather than price—is their primary concern. This group of consumers want shopping made easier, they demand service, and they resent being treated as a homogeneous group. They want their clothes to say individual things about them. This has made one-to-one marketing an imperative. To accomplish this strategy, retailers such as Harry Rosen must listen to customers at every opportunity and track them on an ongoing basis.

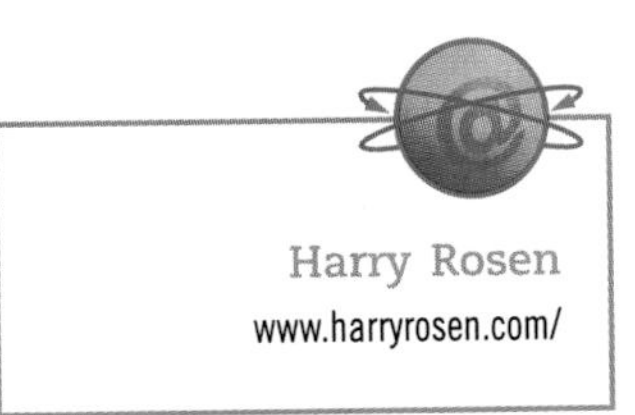

Although Harry Rosen has always practised some form of relationship marketing, today his efforts are more high-tech. The company maintains a computerized database that records information captured at the point of sale. The system tracks the client's size, style, and manufacturer preferences. It records each item that the client has purchased. Since men often don't shop on a regular basis, sales associates use the information to notify clients when shipments from their favoured manufacturers arrive or when specials are offered on that line of clothing. Contacting clients directly leads to about 35 percent of Harry Rosen's sales.

Recognizing that their target market of business professionals are extremely pressed for time, the database also allows Harry Rosen's sales associates to encourage clients to make appointments to visit the store. The sales associate stands ready with pre-selected merchandise that precisely meets the client's needs. This information not only helps clients to shop more efficiently, but it also assists potential gift buyers. By checking the database, a sales associate can ensure them they are not duplicating an item that a client already has and that the gift they purchase will complement the individual's wardrobe. The database also allows the company to precisely target its direct mailings of the company's semi-annual men's fashion magazine, *harry*, to its more than 250 000 clients.

Harry Rosen's advertising supports his highly targeted, relationship-building strategy. He advertises almost exclusively in the business section of newspapers. His ads, created for over 35 years by Reid Bell, helped the firm tell its story, acquaint customers with its stores and staff members, and build its image. In a recent speech honouring the company with the Newspaper Marketing Bureau's special award for creative excellence in Canadian daily newspaper advertising, it was noted that ads for Harry Rosen stores always assumed an intelligent consumer who enjoys provocative advertising. When Reid Bell retired in 1996, Harry Rosen turned to avant-garde agency Roche Macaulay and Partners to continue the tradition. For the first time, ads for Harry Rosen stores featured well-known Canadians such as George Cohon, senior chair of McDonald's Restaurants of Canada, dressed impeccably in a $4195 Rosen suit, shirt, and tie. The campaign is tied together with the tag line, "What [so-and-so] will be wearing today."

Harry Rosen's fashion savvy and ability to build lifelong relationships with customers have given the company an edge over other top-end men's-wear specialty stores such as Studio 67 and Holt Renfrew as well as department store boutiques such as Tommy Hilfiger or Hugo Boss. Competition for men's fashion is getting tougher in Canada, however. Hollywood fashion favourite Giorgio Armani just reopened Emporio Armani in Harry's backyard. It is three times the size of the old outlet. Armani is no small competitor. Offering both women's and men's fashion, Armani has a worldwide empire of 2000 stores that generate over $2 billion in sales. Harry isn't standing still, however. He also has plans for expansion and is heading south of the border to test his mettle against retail legends such as Nordstrom and Saks Fifth Avenue.[1]

Markets

Organizations that sell to consumer and business markets recognize that they cannot appeal to all buyers in those markets, or at least not to all buyers in the same way. Buyers are too numerous, too widely scattered, and too varied in their needs and buying practices. In an era of fierce global competition, companies vary widely in their abilities to serve different segments of the market. Rather than try to compete in an entire market, sometimes against superior competitors, each company must identify the parts of the market that it can serve best.

Market segmentation Dividing a market into distinct groups of buyers with different needs, characteristics, or behaviour who might require separate products or marketing mixes.

Market targeting The process of evaluating each market segment's attractiveness and selecting one or more segments to serve.

Market positioning Arranging for a product to occupy a clear, distinctive, and desirable place relative to competing products in the minds of target consumers.

Most companies are moving away from mass marketing to *target marketing*—identifying market segments, selecting one or more of them, and developing products and marketing mixes tailored to each. In this way, sellers can develop the right product for each target market and adjust their prices, distribution channels, and advertising to reach the target market efficiently. Instead of scattering their marketing efforts—the "shotgun" approach, they can focus on the buyers who have greater purchase interest—the "rifle" approach.

Figure 7-1 shows the three major steps in target marketing. The first is **market segmentation**—dividing a market into distinct groups of buyers with different needs, characteristics, or behaviour who might require separate products or marketing mixes. The company identifies different ways to segment the market and develops profiles of the resulting market segments. The second step is **market targeting**—evaluating each market segment's attractiveness and selecting one or more of the market segments to enter. The third step is **market positioning**—setting the competitive positioning for the product and creating a detailed marketing mix.

Market Segmentation

Markets consist of buyers, who differ in one or more ways—in their wants, resources, locations, buying attitudes, and buying practices. Through market segmentation, companies divide large, heterogeneous markets into smaller segments that can be reached more efficiently with products and services that match their unique needs. In this section, we discuss five important segmentation topics: levels of market segmentation, segmenting consumer markets, segmenting business markets, segmenting international markets, and requirements for effective segmentation.

Levels of Market Segmentation

Because buyers have unique needs and wants, each buyer is potentially a separate market. Ideally, a seller would design a separate marketing program for each buyer. However, although some companies attempt to serve buyers individually, many others cannot afford such a fine-grained approach and do not find complete segmen-

FIGURE 7-1 Steps in market segmentation, targeting, and positioning

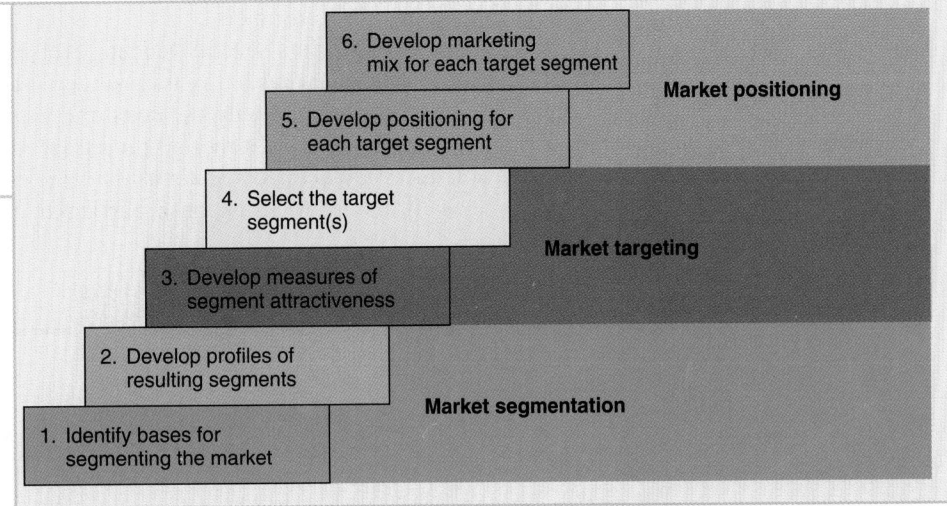

tation worthwhile. Instead, they look for broader classes of buyers who differ in their product needs or buying responses. Thus, market segmentation can be carried out at many different levels. Companies can practise no segmentation (mass marketing), complete segmentation (micromarketing), or something in between (segment marketing or niche marketing). See Figure 7-2.

Mass Marketing

Companies have not always practised target marketing. For most of the twentieth century, major consumer product companies held fast to *mass marketing*—mass producing, mass distributing, and mass promoting the same product in the same way to all consumers. Henry Ford epitomized this marketing strategy when he offered the Model-T Ford to all buyers, with the reassurance that they could have the car "in any colour as long as it is black." Similarly, Coca-Cola at one time produced only one drink for the whole market, hoping it would appeal to everyone.

The traditional argument for mass marketing is that it creates the largest potential market, which leads to the lowest costs, which translates into either lower prices or higher margins. However, many factors now make mass marketing more difficult. For example, the world's mass markets have slowly splintered into a profusion of smaller segments—the baby boomers here, the Gen-Xers there; here the Chinese market, there the French-Canadian market; here working women, there single parents; here Eastern Canada, there the West. Today, marketers find it difficult to create a single product or program that appeals to all of these diverse groups. The proliferation of advertising media and distribution channels has also made it difficult to practise "one-size-fits-all" marketing:

> [Consumers] . . . have more ways to shop: at giant malls, specialty shops, and superstores; through mail-order catalogues, home shopping networks, and virtual stores on the Internet. And they are bombarded with messages pitched through a growing number of channels: broadcast and narrow-cast television, radio, online computer networks, the Internet, telephone services such as fax and telemarketing, and niche magazines and other print media.[2]

No wonder some have claimed that mass marketing is dying. Not surprisingly, many companies are retreating from mass marketing and turning to segment marketing.

Segment Marketing

Segment marketing Marketing that recognizes that buyers differ in their needs, perceptions, and buying behaviours.

A company that practises **segment marketing** recognizes that buyers differ in their needs, perceptions, and buying behaviours. The company tries to isolate broad segments that compose a market and adapts its offers to more closely match the needs of one or more segments. Thus, GM has designed specific models for different income and age groups. In fact, it sells models for segments with varied *combinations* of age and income. For instance, GM designed its Buick Park Avenue for older, higher-income consumers.

Segment marketing offers several benefits over mass marketing. The company can market more efficiently, targeting its products or services, channels, and communications programs toward only the consumers it can serve best. The company can also market more effectively by fine-tuning its products, prices, and programs to the needs of carefully defined segments. And the company may face fewer competitors if fewer firms are focusing on a particular market segment.

FIGURE 7-2 Levels of marketing segmentation

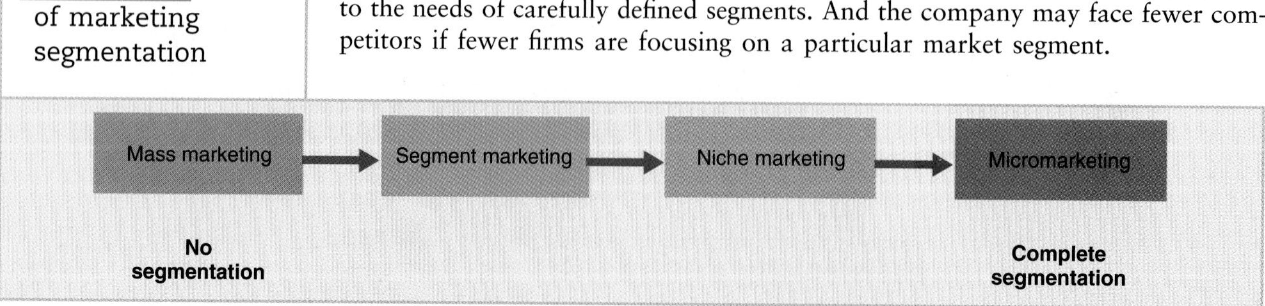

Niche Marketing

Niche marketing
Marketing that focuses on subgroups within the large identifiable groups in a market.

Market segments are normally large identifiable groups within a market—for example, luxury car buyers, performance car buyers, utility car buyers, and economy car buyers. **Niche marketing** focuses on subgroups within these segments. A *niche* is a more narrowly defined group, usually identified by dividing a segment into subsegments or by defining a group with a distinctive set of traits who may seek a special combination of benefits. For example, the utility vehicles segment might include light-duty pick-up trucks and sport utility vehicles (SUVs). And the SUV sub-segment might be further divided into standard SUV (as served by Ford and Chevrolet) and luxury SUV (as served by Lexus) niches.

Whereas segments are fairly large and typically attract several competitors, niches are smaller and usually attract only one or a few competitors. Niche marketers presumably understand their niche's needs so well that their customers willingly pay a price premium. For example, Ferrari receives a high price for its cars because its loyal buyers feel that no other automobile comes close to offering the product-service-membership benefits that Ferrari does.

Niche marketing offers smaller companies an opportunity to compete by focusing their limited resources on serving niches that larger competitors may consider unimportant or simply overlook. For example, T&T Supermarkets, a small Vancouver-area grocery retailer, has grown rapidly by catering to the burgeoning Asian market that makes up 25 percent of the Lower Mainland population.[3] However, large companies also practise niche marketing. For example, American Express offers not only its traditional green cards but also gold cards, corporate cards, and even platinum cards aimed at a niche consisting of the top-spending one percent of its 36 million cardholders.[4] And Nike makes athletic gear for not only basketball, running, and soccer, but also for smaller niches such as biking, rugby, and street hockey.

Marriott markets to a variety of segments with packages adapted to their varying needs. To business travellers, it offers a "king-sized desk, an ergonomic chair, and outlets and dataports at eye level." To family travellers, it offers "Together time from Marriott: Kids eat and stay free."

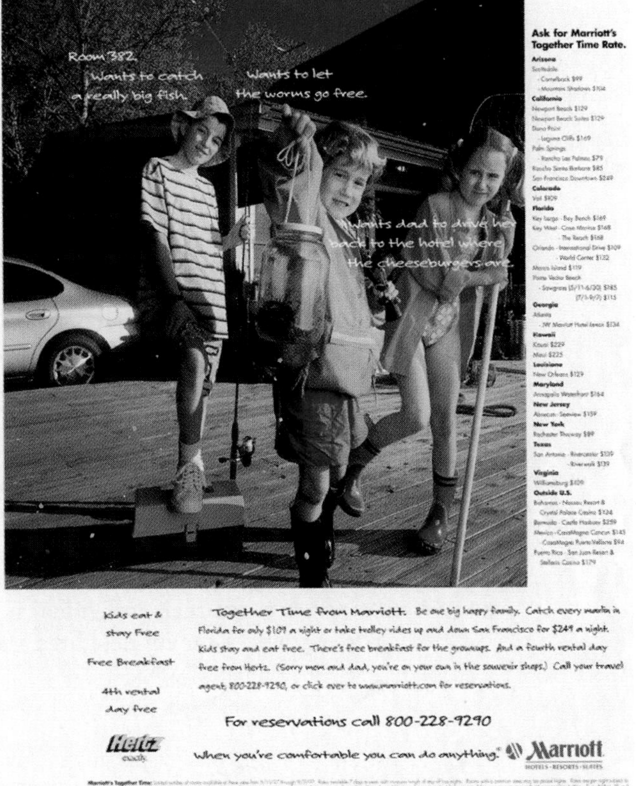

Niches are the norm in many markets. As an advertising agency executive observed: "There will be no market for products that everybody likes a little, only for products that somebody likes a lot."[5] Other experts assert that companies will have to "niche or be niched."[6]

Micromarketing

Segment and niche marketers tailor their offerings and marketing programs to meet the needs of various market segments. At the same time, however, they do not customize their offerings to individual customers. Thus, segment marketing and niche marketing fall between the extremes of mass marketing and micromarketing. **Micromarketing** is the practice of tailoring products and marketing programs to suit the tastes of specific individuals or locations. Micromarketing includes *local marketing* and *individual marketing*.

Micromarketing
The practice of tailoring products and marketing programs to suit the tastes of specific individuals or locations.

Local marketing
The practice of tailoring brands and promotions to the needs and wants of local customer groups.

Local Marketing. **Local marketing** involves tailoring brands and promotions to the needs and wants of local customer groups—cities, neighbourhoods, and even specific stores. Thus, retailers such as Sears and Wal-Mart routinely customize each store's merchandise and promotions to match its specific clientele and neighbourhood demographics. Kraft helps supermarket chains identify the specific cheese assortments and shelf positioning that will optimize cheese sales in low-income, middle-income, and high-income stores, and ethnic communities.

Local marketing has some drawbacks. It can drive up manufacturing and marketing costs by reducing economies of scale. It can also create logistical problems as companies try to meet the varied requirements of different regional and local markets. And a brand's overall image might be diluted if the product and message vary in different locations. Still, as companies face increasingly fragmented markets, and as new supporting technologies develop, the advantages of local marketing often outweigh the drawbacks. Local marketing helps a company to market more effectively in the face of pronounced regional and local differences in community demographics and lifestyles. It also meets the needs of the company's "first-line customers," retailers, who prefer more fine-tuned product assortments for their neighbourhoods.

Individual marketing
The practice of tailoring products and marketing programs to the needs and preferences of individual customers.

Individual Marketing. In the extreme, micromarketing becomes **individual marketing**—tailoring products and marketing programs to the needs and preferences of individual customers. Individual marketing has also been labelled "markets-of-one marketing," "customized marketing," and "one-to-one marketing".[7] One-to-one marketing isn't new. For centuries consumers were served as individuals: The tailor custom-made the suit, the cobbler designed shoes for the individual, the cabinet maker crafted furniture to order. Today, however, new technologies are permitting many companies to return to customized marketing. More powerful computers, detailed databases, robotic production, and immediate and interactive communication media such as e-mail, fax, and the Internet—all have combined to foster "mass customization."[8] *Mass customization* is the ability to prepare on a mass basis individually designed products and services tailor-made to individual needs (see Marketing Highlight 7-1).

Consumer marketers are now providing custom-made products. For example, Dell Computer can deliver computers to individual customers loaded with customer-specified hardware and software. Grocery Gateway, the online grocery shopping and delivery service, lets customers create the virtual supermarket that best fits their individual needs. Ritz-Carlton Hotels creates custom-designed experiences for its delighted guests:

> Check into any Ritz-Carlton hotel around the world, and you'll be amazed at how well the hotel's employees anticipate your slightest need. Without ever asking, they seem to know that you want a nonsmoking room with a king-size bed, a non-allergenic pillow, and breakfast with decaffeinated coffee in your room. How does Ritz-Carlton work this magic? The hotel employs a system that combines information technology and flexible operations to customize the hotel expe-

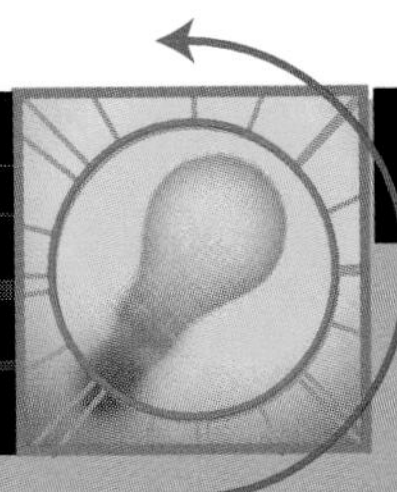

marketing highlight 7-1

Markets of One: Anything You Can Digitize, You Can Customize

Imagine walking into a booth that bathes your body in patterns of white light and, in a matter of seconds, captures your exact three-dimensional form. The resulting digitized data are imprinted on a credit card, which you then use to order customized clothing. No, this isn't a scene from the next *Star Wars* sequel; it's a peek ahead at how you will be able to buy clothing in the not-so-distant future. A consortium of over 100 apparel companies has banded together to develop body scanning technology in the hope of making mass customization the norm.

Although body scanning technology and smart cards carrying customer measurements are still in development, many companies are now using existing technologies to tailor their products to individual customers. These are just a few examples:

> Reflect.com is a 100 percent direct-to-consumer Web site that not only allows a consumer to customize a cosmetic product's formula, scent, and packaging, but also create an experience that reflects her needs and desires. The cyberbrand is a spin-off business founded by Procter & Gamble and represents its first online effort at one-to-one marketing. Critical Mass, which has been winning international clients because of its ability to personalize sites, scored the $1.49 million account to build an e-commerce beauty destination when Reflect.com first launched its initial site two years ago. Creative and web development have now been brought inhouse. Reflect.com continues to be a leader in customized beauty care, having recently created its one millionth customized product.

The Canadian Imperial Bank of Commerce uses its sophisticated database to improve customer retention. The database contains up to 150 pieces of information on each CIBC client. By looking at specific variables, the bank can differentiate between clients who intend to remain with the bank and those who are likely to switch to another provider. The bank develops scores for individual customers based on such behavioural information as whether they pay credit card bills on time and whether they transfer funds to buy registered retirement savings plans with another institution. When clients are identified as people who are likely to switch to another bank, they become the target of a new communications campaign that involves direct-mail pieces, personal calls from a bank representative, a newsletter about the benefits of one of the CIBC financial services they use, and offers of special rates on loans and mortgages.

Mattel: Since 1998, girls have been able to log on to www.barbie.com and design their own Special Friend Barbie doll. They choose the doll's skin tone, eye colour, hairdo and hair colour, clothes, accessories, and name. They even fill out a questionnaire detailing their doll's likes and dislikes. When Barbie's Special Friend arrives in the mail, the girls find the doll's name on the packaging along with a computer-generated paragraph about her personality.

CDuctive lets customers cut their own CDs online. A customer who likes acid jazz can click on the category, see 30 titles, and sample a 45-second snatch of each. With a few keystrokes, the customer can then order a $21 CD with all the tunes he or she has selected.

Paris Miki: At this Tokyo eyeglass store, special software allows technicians to design lenses and frames that conform to the shape of the customer's face. Using a monitor, various styles are superimposed on a scanned image of the person's face. The customer then chooses a style, the glasses are made up, and the person walks out with a pair of glasses designed and fitted for him or her alone.

Consumer goods marketers aren't the only ones going one-to-one. Business-to-business marketers are also providing customers with tailor-made goods, often less expensively and more quickly than it used to take to make standardized ones. Particularly for small companies, mass customization provides a way to stand out against larger competitors:

Telus, Canada's second-largest telecommunications company, sees one-to-one marketing as a core strategy for targeting small to medium-sized businesses. Telus knows that other Canadian telephone companies can offer products and services to these businesses. To

Reflect.com offers customized, one-of-a-kind cosmetics, and skin, hair and fragrance products for online shoppers.

make itself stand out from the crowd, Telus focuses on customer service and tailors solutions to meet small firms' unique communication needs.

Telus began targeting the small and medium-sized business market with the belief that customers wanted them to be "data-centric," but feedback made it clear that small businesses wanted more than just data services. What they wanted was a full-service provider. Telus uses behavioural segmentation and its database to develop predictive models so that it spends its marketing resources on targeting and retaining top customers. As one Telus manager notes, "It will really allow us to decide if this is a customer who we can afford to market to, and to what degree." These techniques enabled Telus to launch a personalized direct mail campaign to small business in British Columbia. This campaign was followed by telemarketing blitz. Telus was delighted that these joint efforts generated 21 percent more sales per contact than with an untargeted list. To drive home the point that Telus is clearly positioned as a full solutions provider for small and medium-sized business, the company also created three TV spots in which business people talk about what Telus is doing for them.

Two trends are behind the growth in one-to-one marketing. One is the increasing emphasis on customer value and satisfaction. Today's consumers have very high expectations and expect products and services that meet their individual needs. Yet, it would be prohibitively expensive or downright impossible to meet these individual demands if it weren't for rapid advances in new technologies. Data warehouses allow companies to store trillions of bytes of customer information. Computer-controlled factory equipment and industrial robots can now quickly readjust assembly lines. Bar code scanners make it possible to track parts and products. Most important of all, the Internet ties it all together and makes it easy for a company to interact with customers, learn about their preferences, and respond.

Indeed, the Internet appears to be the ultimate one-to-one medium. The notion of personal service on the Internet might seem like an oxymoron, but it's rapidly becoming a reality. Consider the following example:

Soon after Jeri Capozzi logged on to the online nursery Garden Escape last winter, she was hooked. It wasn't just because the World Wide Web site offered unusual plants, such as hyacinth beans, firecracker, and dog's tooth violet. It's because Garden Escape created a personal store just for her. Greeted by name on her personal Web page when she visits, Capozzi can take notes on a private online notepad, tinker with garden plans using the site's interactive design program, and get answers from the Garden Doctor. So far, [she] has spent $900 at Garden Escape and has no plans to shop at any other nursery. With service that personal, she says, "I probably will never leave."

Thus, just as mass production was the marketing principle of the last century, mass customization is becoming the marketing principle for the twenty-first century. The world appears to be coming full circle—from the good old days when customers were treated as individuals, to mass marketing when nobody knew your name, and back again. As Joseph Pine, author of *Mass Customization,* concludes, "Anything you can digitize, you can customize."

Sources: See Fawzia Sheikh, "Calgary agency Critical Mass hits the big time . . . twice," *Marketing On-Line,* 25 October 1999; Eve Lazarus, "The Telus target," *Marketing On-Line,* 22 May 2000; Gordon Arnaut, "Getting to know you; getting to know all about you," *Globe and Mail,* 15 February 1994:B27; Erick Schonfeld, "The customized, digitized, have-it-your-way economy," *Fortune,* 28 September 1998:115–24; Marc Ballon, "Sale of modern music keyed to customization," *Inc.,* May 1998:23,25; Robert D. Hof, "Now it's your Web," *Business Week,* 5 October 1998:164–76; Don Peppers, Martha Rogers, and Bob Dorf, "Is your company ready for one-to-one marketing?" *Harvard Business Review,* January–February 1999:151–60; and Otis Port, "Customers move into the driver's seat," *Business Week,* 4 October 1999:103–6.

rience. At the heart of the system is a huge customer database, which contains information about guests gathered through the observations of hotel employees. Each day, hotel staffers—from those at the front desk to those in maintenance and housekeeping—discreetly record the unique habits, likes, and dislikes of each guest on small "guest preference pads." These observations are then transferred to a corporate-wide "guest history database." Every morning, a "guest historian" at each hotel reviews the files of all new arrivals who have previously stayed at a Ritz-Carlton and prepares a list of suggested extra touches that might delight each guest. Guests have responded strongly to such markets-of-one service. Since inaugurating the guest-history system in 1992, Ritz-Carlton has boosted guest retention by 23 percent. An amazing 95 percent of departing guests report that their stay has been a truly memorable experience.

Business-to-business marketers are also finding new ways to customize their offerings. For example, Motorola salespeople now use hand-held computers to custom-design pagers following a business customer's wishes. The design data are transmitted to the Motorola factory, and production starts within 17 minutes. The customized pagers are ready for shipment within two hours.

The move toward individual marketing mirrors the trend in consumer *self-marketing*. Increasingly, customers are taking more responsibility in determining which products and brands to buy. Consider two purchasing agents with two different purchasing styles. The first sees several salespeople, each trying to persuade the agent to buy his or her product. The second sees no salespeople but rather logs on to the Internet; searches for information and evaluations of available products; interacts electronically with various suppliers, users, and product analysts; and then identifies the best offer. The second purchasing agent has taken more responsibility for the buying process, and the marketer has had less influence over her buying decision.

As the trend toward more interactive dialogue and less advertising monologue continues, self-marketing will grow in importance. As more buyers look up consumer reports, join Internet product discussion forums, and place orders via phone or online, marketers will have to influence the buying process in new ways. They will need to involve customers more in all phases of the product development and buying process, increasing opportunities for buyers to practise self-marketing. We will examine the trends toward one-to-one marketing and self-marketing further in Chapter 17.

Segmenting Consumer Markets

There is no single way to segment a market. A marketer has to try different segmentation variables, alone and in combination, to find the best way to view the market structure. Table 7-1 outlines the major variables that might be used in segmenting consumer markets. Here we look at the major *geographic, demographic, psychographic,* and *behavioural variables.*

Geographic Segmentation

Geographic segmentation Dividing a market into different geographical units such as nations, provinces, regions, counties, cities, or neighbourhoods.

Geographic segmentation calls for dividing the market into different geographical units such as nations, regions, provinces, counties, cities, or neighbourhoods. A company may decide to operate in one or a few geographical areas, or to operate in all areas but pay attention to geographical differences in needs and wants.

Many companies are "regionalizing" their marketing programs—localizing their products, advertising, promotion, and sales efforts to fit the needs of individual regions, cities, and even neighbourhoods. For example, Absolut, the makers of vodka, launched a regional advertising campaign aimed at East Coast consumers.[9]

Marketers at Absolut Vodka realize Canadians have strong regional ties. This first regional ad used by Absolut appeared in *Atlantic Progress,* an East Coast business magazine.

TABLE 7-1 Major Segmentation Variables for Consumer Markets

Variable	Typical Breakdown
	Geographic
Region	Maritimes, Quebec, Ontario, Prairies, British Columbia, Northern Territories
City size	Under 5000; 5000–20 000; 20 000–50 000; 50 000–100 000; 100 000–250 000; 250 000–500 000; 500 000–1 000 000; 1 000 000–4 000 000; 4 000 000 and over
Density	Urban, suburban, rural
Climate	Northern, Southern, Coastal, Prairie, Mountain
	Demographic
Age	Under 6, 6–11, 12–19, 20–34, 35–49, 50–64, 65+
Gender	Male, female
Family size	1–2, 3–4, 5+
Family life cycle	Young, single; young, married, no children; young, married, youngest child under 6; young, married, youngest child 6 or over; older, married, with children; older, married, no children under 18; older, single; same-sex partners; unmarried partners, no children; unmarried partners, with children; other
Income	Under $10 000; $10 000–15 000; $15 000–20 000; $20 000–30 000; $30 000–50 000; $50 000–75 000; $75 000 and over
Occupation	Professional and technical; managers, officials, and proprietors; clerical, sales; craftspeople, foremen; operatives; farmers; retired; students; homemakers; unemployed
Education	Grade school or less; some high school; high school graduate; college; some university; university graduate; post-graduate
Religion	Catholic, Protestant, Jewish, Muslim, other
Ethnic origin	African-Canadian, Asian, British, French, German, Scandinavian, Italian, Latin American, Native Canadian, Middle Eastern, Japanese
	Psychographic
Lifestyle	Achievers, believers, strivers
Personality	Compulsive, gregarious, authoritarian, ambitious
	Behavioural
Purchase occasion	Regular occasion, special occasion
Benefits	Sought quality, service, economy
User status	Non-user, ex-user, potential user, first-time user, regular user
Usage rate	Light user, medium user, heavy user
Loyalty status	None, medium, strong, absolute
Readiness state	Unaware, aware, informed, interested, desirous, intending to buy
Attitude toward product	Enthusiastic, positive, negative, hostile

Demographic Segmentation

Demographic segmentation
Dividing the market into groups based on such demographic variables as age, sex, family size, family life cycle, income, occupation, education, religion, race, and nationality.

Demographic segmentation means dividing the market into groups based on such demographic variables as age, gender, family size, family life cycle, income, occupation, education, religion, race, and nationality. Demographic factors are the most popular bases for segmenting customer groups. One reason is that consumer needs, wants, and usage rates often vary closely with demographic variables. Another is that demographic variables are easier to measure than most other types of variables. Even when marketers first define market segments using other bases, such as personality or behaviour, they must know their demographic characteristics to assess the size of the target market and to reach it efficiently.

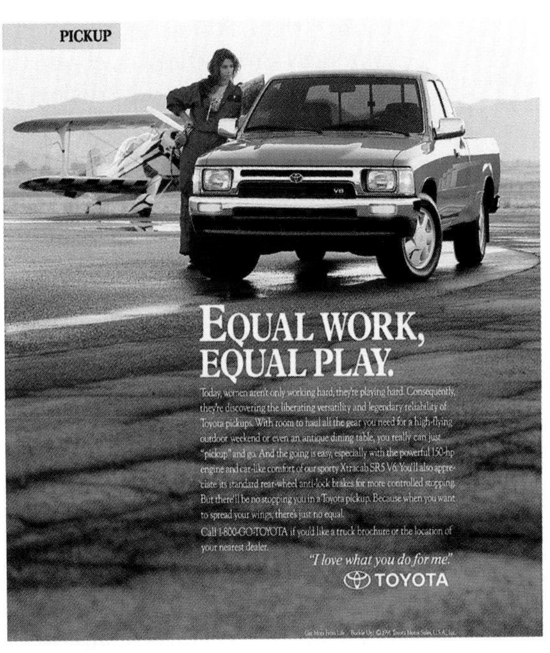

Demographic segmentation: Johnson & Johnson targets children with Band-Aid Sesame Street Bandages—Big Bird and Cookie Monster "help turn little people's tears into great big smiles." Toyota is marketing to women who "aren't only working hard, they're playing hard."

Age and Life Cycle Stage. Consumer needs and wants change with age. Some companies use **age and life cycle segmentation,** offering different products or using different marketing approaches for different age and life cycle groups. One of the largest challenges for today's marketers has been trying to determine what makes the youth market—those aged 18 to 25—tick, even though, as Edward Caffyn of Toronto-based advertising agency MacLaren McCann notes, "We've labelled them, prodded them, followed them, partied with them."[10] First, many young adults just don't like advertisers, don't want to be sold to, and don't want to be related to. Second, they defy the generalizations that marketers tend to make.

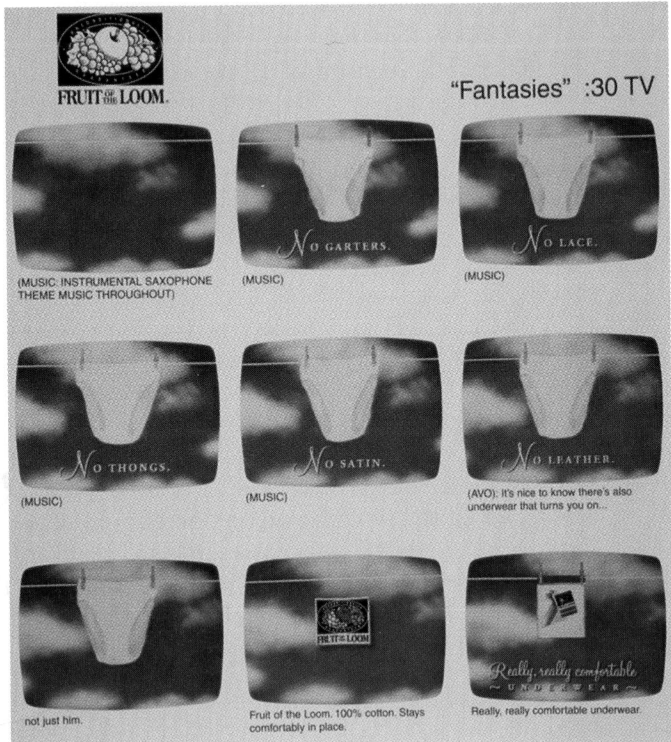

The award-winning Fruit of the Loom campaign illustrates effective gender-based segmentation.

Age and life cycle segmentation
Dividing a market into different age and life cycle groups.

Rather than falling into a well-defined, age-based segment, young adults are extremely diverse, and celebrate their differences rather than their similarities. Even though they disdain advertising, they enjoy watching ads, and advertising is often a topic of conversation. But since an ad intrudes on their viewing, it must provide something to compensate for the interruption. It must amuse and entertain. It can't make the mistake of telling them what is cool or implying that if you use the advertised product, you will be cool. The youth market is too savvy and cynical to accept that kind of pitch. Young adults want ads that tell them about the company and the product, and then leave it up to the viewer to decide whether they like you and your products. Ads that work share this common trait. Diesel Jeans creates a quirky world of its own; Molson Canadian's "I Am" campaign lays out the essence of a brand and asks the viewer to accept it or not; and Calvin Klein ads deal with people more than they do with clothes and imply, "Be who you gotta be and everything will be cool."[11]

Marketers must be careful to guard against stereotypes when using age and life cycle segmentation. Although you might find some 70-year-olds in wheelchairs, you will find others on yachts. Becel, Canada's leading margarine, used this insight to develop its award-winning TV campaign. Similarly, whereas some 40-year-old couples are sending their children off to university, others are just beginning new families. Thus, age is often a poor predictor of a person's life cycle, health, work or family status, needs, and buying power.

Gender segmentation
Dividing a market into different groups based on sex.

Gender. **Gender segmentation** has long been used in clothing, cosmetics, and magazines. For example, although early deodorants were used by both sexes, many producers are now featuring brands for one sex only. Procter & Gamble was among the first with Secret, a brand specially formulated for a woman's chemistry, packaged and advertised to reinforce the female image.

Many marketers use segmentation based on gender.[12] Merrill Lynch, for example, offers a *Financial Handbook for Women Investors* who want to "shape up their finances." Owens-Corning consciously aimed a major advertising campaign for home insulation at women after its study on women's role in home improvement showed that two-thirds were involved in materials installation, with 13 percent doing it themselves. Half the women surveyed compared themselves with Bob Vila rather than Martha Stewart.

The automobile industry knows women buy nearly half of all new cars sold and influence 80 percent of all new car purchasing decisions. Thus, women have become a valued target market for the auto companies. "Selling to women should be no different than selling to men," notes one analyst. "But there are subtleties that make a difference."[13] Women have different frames and greater safety concerns. To address these issues, automakers are designing cars with hoods and trunks that are easier to open, seats that are easier to adjust, and seat belts that fit women better. They've also increased their safety focus, emphasizing such features as air bags and remote door locks.

Gender is also important when it comes to understanding consumer behaviour at the grocery checkout counter. Men compose 37 percent of Canada's principal grocery shoppers. These men are younger than the average grocery shopper, ranging in age from 25 to 34. They are also more likely to be professionals, business owners, or senior managers who live in Quebec or British Columbia. The factors that drive male grocery shoppers differ from those that concern women. Men are not as likely to clip coupons or buy no-name products. They seem to care little about products with environmental claims. They are less concerned about nutrition than their female counterparts, showing lower preferences for reduced-calorie or "light" products. Finally, men want convenience and are willing to pay higher prices for it.[14]

Income segmentation
Dividing a market into different income groups.

Income. **Income segmentation** has long been used by the marketers of such products and services as automobiles, boats, clothing, cosmetics, and travel. Many

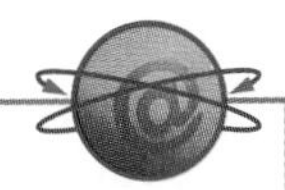

Neiman Marcus
www.neimanmarcus.com/

companies target affluent consumers with luxury goods and convenience services. Stores such as Neiman Marcus, which mail their Christmas catalogues to wealthy Canadian consumers, pitch everything from expensive jewellery, fine fashions, and exotic furs to glazed Australian apricots priced at $20 a pound.

At the other end of the spectrum are those with restricted income. Marketers must be aware that many low-income people are quite different from traditional stereotypes. Instead of being poorly educated, many fall into "the young and the jobless" class. The unemployment rate for people aged 15 to 24 is about 16 percent. Many of those who are employed can find only part-time work; others who have university educations are trying to repay the loans that allowed them to pursue a degree. They are often forced to return home and live with their parents. These living arrangements free them from the burden of paying rent and buying groceries, which allows them to make more eclectic purchases with their limited income, often on entertainment-related products and services such as music, movies, and video games, as well as clothing.[15]

Psychographic Segmentation

Psychographic segmentation
Dividing a market into different groups based on lifestyle or personality characteristics.

Psychographic segmentation divides buyers into groups based on lifestyle or personality characteristics. People in the same demographic group can have very different psychographic makeups.

Lifestyle. People's interest in various goods is affected by their lifestyles, and the goods they buy express those lifestyles. Marketers are increasingly segmenting their markets by consumer lifestyles, which can yield big payoffs:[16]

> Toronto-based Modrobes Saldebus Lounge Clothing Inc. was born to target the casual student lifestyle. Their comfortable, easy-care clothing has been a hit. The firm began with a single product—something every student needed—exam pants! As founder, Steve "Sal" Debus, exclaimed, "I had the idea to design these pants for student life. . . . You could eat, sleep, drink, party, get up the next day and go to class in them and still look good." With little money for distribution, he went from campus to campus selling Exam Pants. His sales pitch soon had the clothing flying off the folding tables he used to display his wares. Sal promised prospective buyers that if his pants weren't the most comfortable piece of clothing they had ever owned, he would refund their money. Who could resist such an offer? Today, Modrobes sells its clothing line through 350 stores, including Athletes World as well as their own Toronto retail store. Creative new products, consumer insight, and carefully crafted advertising help Modrobes target consumers whose lifestyles match that of the founder. Not a bad model for success.

Personality. Marketers also have used personality variables to segment markets, giving their products personalities that correspond to consumer personalities. Successful market segmentation strategies based on personality have been used for such products as cosmetics, cigarettes, insurance, and liquor.[17]

Nokia differentiated itself by creating cellular phones in a range of colours that allowed people to express themselves through a functional product. Lillian Tepera, Nokia's marketing manager, says cellular phones are like watches: "They're there to serve a purpose, but people want something more than a grey or black rectangular box. People are looking for an expression of who they are, not just something to call their stockbroker with."[18]

Behavioural Segmentation

Behavioural segmentation
Dividing a market into groups based on consumer knowledge, attitude, use, or response to a product.

Behavioural segmentation divides buyers into groups based on their knowledge, attitudes, uses, or responses to a product. Many marketers believe that behaviour variables are the best starting point for building market segments.

Occasion segmentation
Dividing a market into groups according to occasions when buyers get the idea to buy, actually make their purchase, or use the purchased item.

Occasions. Buyers can be grouped according to occasions when they get the idea to buy, actually make their purchase, or use the purchased item. **Occasion segmentation** can help firms build up product usage. For example, orange juice is most often consumed at breakfast, but orange growers have promoted drinking orange juice as a cool and refreshing drink at other times of the day. Some holidays, such as Mother's Day, Father's Day, and Halloween were originally promoted partly to increase the sale of candy, flowers, cards, and other gifts.

Many marketers prepare special offers and ads for holiday occasions. For example, Beatrice Foods runs special Thanksgiving and Christmas ads for Reddi-wip in the US during October and December, months that account for 30 percent of all whipped cream sales. Electronics retailer RadioShack Canada, based in Barrie, Ontario, launched a new E-Gift program in its stores for the 2000 holiday season. The E-Gifts are electronic gift certificates in denominations of $25, $50 and $100 in the form of plastic cards with magnetic strips.[19]

Benefit segmentation
Dividing a market into groups according to the different benefits that consumers seek from the product.

Benefits Sought. A powerful form of segmentation is to group buyers according to the *benefits* they seek from the product. **Benefit segmentation** requires finding the major benefits people look for in the product class, the kinds of people who look for each benefit, and the major brands that deliver each benefit. One of the best examples of benefit segmentation was conducted in the toothpaste market (see Table 7-2). Research found four benefit segments: economic, medicinal, cosmetic, and taste. Each benefit group had special demographic, behavioural, and psychographic characteristics. For example, the people seeking to prevent decay tended to have large families, were heavy toothpaste users, and were conservative. Each segment also favoured certain brands. Most current brands appeal to one of these segments. For example, Crest toothpaste stresses protection and appeals to the family segment, whereas Aim looks and tastes good and appeals to children.

Companies can use benefit segmentation to clarify the benefit segment to which they are appealing, its characteristics, and the major competing brands. They also can search for new benefits and launch brands that deliver them.

Beatrice Foods practises occasion segmentation in running special US Thanksgiving and Christmas Reddi-wip ads in November and December.

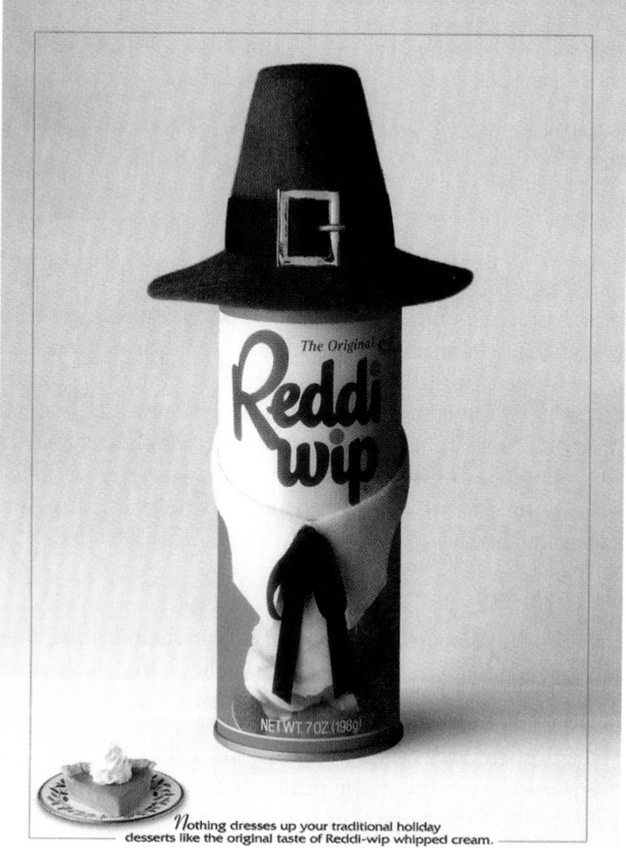

The Original
Reddi wip
NET WT. 7 OZ. (198g)
Nothing dresses up your traditional holiday desserts like the original taste of Reddi-wip whipped cream.

User Status. Markets can be segmented into groups of non-users, ex-users, potential users, first-time users, and regular users of a product. Potential users and regular users may require different kinds of marketing appeals. For example, one study found that blood donors are motivated by need—understanding the need for blood and blood products within the community, and with the potential of their own need for blood in the future. Blood donors were also found to be very receptive to being telerecruited to make additional blood donations; most target markets are not receptive to telerecruiters. This suggests that social agencies should use different marketing approaches for keeping current donors and attracting new ones. A company's market position will also influence its focus. Market share leaders will focus on attracting potential users, whereas smaller firms will focus on attracting current users away from the market leader.

Usage Rate. Markets can also be segmented into light-, medium-, and heavy-user groups. Heavy users are often a small percentage of the market, but account for a high percentage of total consumption. Marketers usually prefer to attract one heavy user to their product or service rather than several light users. A study of branded ice cream buyers showed that heavy users make up only 18 percent of all buyers but consume 55 percent of all the ice cream sold; on average, these heavy users pack away 52 litres of ice cream a year versus only 10 litres for light users. Despite the importance of heavy users, light users can also represent important targets:[20]

TABLE 7-2 Benefit Segmentation of the Toothpaste Market

Benefit Segments	Demographics	Behaviour	Psychographics	Favoured Brands
Economy (low price)	Men	Heavy users	High autonomy, value oriented	Brands on sale
Medicinal (decay prevention)	Large families	Heavy users	Hypochondriac, conservative	Crest
Cosmetic (bright teeth)	Teens, young adults	Smokers	High sociability, active	Aqua-Fresh, Ultra Brite
Taste (good tasting)	Children	Spearmint lovers	High self-involvement, hedonistic	Colgate, Aim

Source: Adapted from Russell J. Haley, "Benefit segmentation: A decision-oriented research tool," *Journal of Marketing,* July 1968: 30–5. Also see Haley, "Benefit segmentation: Backwards and forwards," *Journal of Advertising Research,* February–March 1984: 19–25; and Haley, "Benefit segmentation—20 years later," *Journal of Consumer Marketing,* 1, 1984: 5–14.

Makers of Lea & Perrins® Worcestershire Sauce, Danone International Brands Canada Inc., knew that most people were light users of their product. People used Lea & Perrins only occasionally, typically for Bloody Caesars. Few consumers were aware of the product's versatility, thereby limiting the brand's sales growth. While the firm could have tried to attract new users to the category, it believed a better route was to target the current light users with exciting ideas on how to use the product to enliven everyday meals. Given consumers' hectic lives, dishes had to be easy to remember and simple to prepare. Since print is best at communicating food's appeal, a variety of general interest and women's service magazines were selected. The ads couldn't just be "recipe ads," because they wouldn't stand out from the clutter of other food ads in the magazines. Thus, the advertising needed to communicate Lea & Perrins Worcestershire Sauce premium point-of-difference. Exotic ingredients are what set Lea & Perrins apart from competitive brands, so the advertising had to communicate this differentiating feature. Not only did the program significantly increase sales, it opened up additional channels of communication between the firm and its customers once they started calling Lea & Perrins' toll-free number to request advertised recipe books featuring new uses for the product.

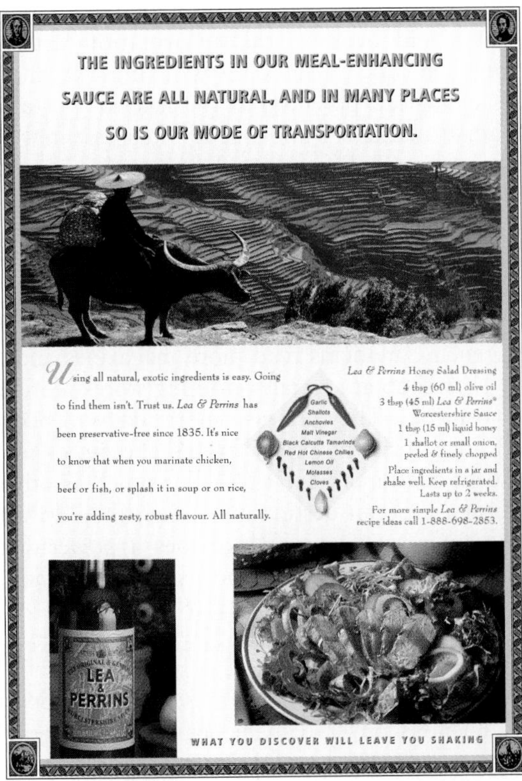

Lea & Perrins' award-winning campaign targeted light users with ideas to enliven everyday meals while also promoting the brand's high-quality ingredients.

Loyalty Status. A market can also be segmented by consumer loyalty. Consumers can be loyal to brands (Tide), stores (The Bay), and companies (Ford). Buyers can be divided into groups according to their degree of loyalty. Some consumers are completely loyal—they buy one brand all the time. Others are somewhat loyal—they are loyal to two or three brands of a given product or favour one brand while sometimes buying others. Still other buyers show no loyalty to any brand. They either want something different each time they buy or they buy whatever is on sale.

A company can learn a lot by analyzing loyalty patterns in its market. It should start by studying its own loyal customers. Colgate finds that its loyal buyers are more middle class, have larger families, and are more health conscious. These characteristics identify the target market for Colgate. By studying its less loyal buyers, the company can identify which brands are most competitive with its own. If many Colgate buyers also buy Crest, Colgate can attempt to improve its positioning against Crest, possibly by using direct-comparison advertising. By looking at customers who are shifting away from its brand, the company can learn about its marketing weaknesses. As for non-loyals, the company may attract them by putting its brand on sale.

Companies need to be careful when using brand loyalty in their segmentation strategies. What appear to be brand-loyal purchase patterns may reflect little more than *habit, indifference,* a *low price,* or *unavailability* of other brands. Thus, frequent or regular purchasing may not be the same as brand loyalty, and marketers must examine the motivations behind observed purchase patterns.

Using Multiple Segmentation Bases

Marketers rarely limit their segmentation analysis to one or a few variables. Rather, they use multiple segmentation bases in an effort to identify smaller, better defined target groups. Thus, a bank may not only identify a group of wealthy retired adults, but within that group distinguish several segments depending on their current income, assets, savings and risk preferences, and lifestyles. In other cases, companies may begin by using one segmentation base, then expand by using other bases.

One of the most promising developments in multivariable segmentation is "geodemographic" segmentation. IRI Canada, a market information company, offers results from its retail-purchase checkout tracking systems to Canadian marketers. The data allow marketers to follow the purchase patterns of each store's trading area and overlays this information with geodemographic census data. Firms can then link census data with lifestyle and purchase patterns to develop estimates of market potential at the level of postal codes or neighbourhoods.

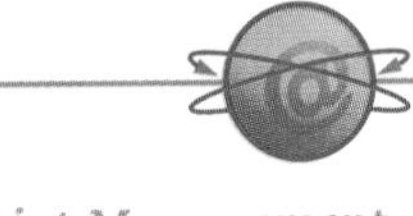

Print Measurement Bureau
www.pmb.ca/

Canadian marketers know it is often essential to combine income with information on regional differences. A Print Measurement Bureau study revealed that regional differences act as powerful determinants of Canadians' behaviour and choices. When one looks at the narrow segment of affluent consumers, one finds not only that the concentration of this group varies by region, but also by buying and lifestyle habits. Affluent consumers living in Quebec, for example, have significantly different preferences from affluent consumers living in other provinces. High-income French Canadians read more magazines and live in more moderately priced housing. They shop at specialty clothing stores more often and spend more on clothing and cosmetics. They are also more likely to bike, golf, swim, or ski than other affluent Canadians, who prefer to jog, garden, or visit health clubs. Although Quebec's affluent consumers don't travel as much as other high-income Canadians, they prefer Latin American destinations when they do travel. Thus, it can be seen that geodemographic segmentation provides a powerful tool for refining demand estimates, selecting target markets, and shaping promotion messages.

Segmenting Business Markets

Consumer and business marketers use many of the same variables to segment their markets. Business buyers can be segmented geographically or by benefits sought, user status, usage rate, and loyalty status. Yet, business marketers use some additional variables. As Table 7-3 shows, these include business customer *demographics* (industry, company size); *operating characteristics; purchasing approaches; situational factors;* and *personal characteristics.*[21]

The table lists questions that business marketers should ask to determine which customers they want to serve. By pursuing segments instead of the whole market, companies have a much better opportunity to deliver value to consumers and to receive maximum rewards for close attention to consumer needs. Thus, Hewlett-Packard's Computer Systems Division targets specific industries that promise the best growth prospects, such as telecommunications and financial services. Its "red team" sales force specializes in developing and serving these major customers, while its "blue team" telemarkets to smaller accounts and to those that don't fit neatly into the industries that H-P strategically targets.[22]

A company can also set up separate systems for dealing with larger or multiple-location customers. Steelcase, a major producer of office furniture, for example, segments customers into 10 industries, including banking, insurance, and electronics. Company salespeople work with independent Steelcase dealers to handle smaller, local, or regional customers in each segment. But since many national multiple-location customers, such as Exxon or IBM, have special needs that may

TABLE 7-3 Major Segmentation Variables for Business Markets

Demographics
Industry: Which industries that buy this product should we focus on?
Company size: What size companies should we focus on?
Location: What geographical areas should we focus on?
Operating Variables
Technology: What customer technologies should we focus on?
User/non-user status: Should we focus on heavy, medium, or light users or non-users?
Customer capabilities: Should we focus on customers needing many services or few services?
Purchasing Approaches
Purchasing function organization: Should we focus on companies with highly centralized or decentralized purchasing organizations?
Power structure: Should we focus on companies that are engineering dominated, finance dominated, or marketing dominated?
Nature of existing relationships: Should we focus on companies with which we already have strong relationships or go after the most desirable companies?
General purchase policies: Should we focus on companies that prefer leasing? Service contracts? Systems purchases? Sealed bidding?
Purchasing criteria: Should we focus on companies that are seeking quality? Service? Price?
Situational Factors
Urgency: Should we focus on companies that need quick delivery or service?
Specific application: Should we focus on certain applications of our product rather than all applications?
Size of order: Should we focus on large or small orders?
Personal Characteristics
Buyer–seller similarity: Should we focus on companies whose people and values are similar to ours?
Attitudes toward risk: Should we focus on risk-taking or risk-avoiding customers?
Loyalty: Should we focus on companies that show high loyalty to their suppliers?

Source: Adapted from Thomas V. Bonoma and Benson P. Shapiro, *Segmenting the Industrial Market,* Lexington, MA: Lexington Books, 1983. Also see John Berrigan and Carl Finkbeiner, *Segmentation Marketing: New Methods for Capturing Business,* New York: Harper-Business, 1992.

Steelcase segments its markets based on the industries its customers operate in—in this case, B.C. Tel.

go beyond the scope of individual dealers, Steelcase uses national accounts managers to help its dealer networks handle these accounts.

Within a target industry and customer size, the company can segment by purchase approaches and criteria. As in consumer segmentation, many marketers believe that buying behaviour and benefits provide the best basis for segmenting business markets.[23]

Segmenting International Markets

Few companies have either the resources or the will to operate in all, or even most, countries. Although some large companies, such as Coca-Cola or Sony, sell products in as many as 200 countries, most international firms focus on a smaller set. Operating in many countries presents new challenges: Even countries that are close together can differ dramatically in their economic, cultural, and political composition. Thus, just as they do within their domestic markets, international firms need to group their world markets into segments with distinct buying needs and behaviours.

Companies can segment international markets using one or a combination of variables. They can segment by *geographic location,* grouping countries by regions such as Western Europe, the Pacific Rim, the Middle East, or Africa. In fact, countries in many regions already have organized geographically into market groups or "free trade zones," such as the European Union and the North American Free Trade Association. These associations reduce trade barriers between member countries, creating larger and more homogeneous markets.

Geographic segmentation assumes that nations close to one another will have many common traits and behaviours. Although this is often the case, there are many exceptions. For example, although the United States and Canada have much in common, overlooking differences between the two countries can be dangerous. Furthermore, both differ culturally and economically from Mexico. Even within a region, consumers can differ widely. For example, many marketers think that all Central and South American countries, with their 400 million inhabitants, are the same. However, the Dominican Republic is no more like Brazil than Italy is like Sweden. Many Latin Americans don't speak Spanish, including 140 million Portuguese-speaking Brazilians and the millions in other countries who speak various Indian dialects.[24]

World markets can be segmented on the basis of *economic factors*. For example, countries can be grouped by population income levels or by their overall level of economic development. Some countries, such as the so-called Group of Seven—the United States, Britain, France, Germany, Japan, Canada, Italy, and Russia—have established, highly industrialized economies. Other countries have newly industrialized or developing economies (Singapore, Taiwan, Korea, Brazil, Mexico). Still others are less developed (China, India). A company's economic structure shapes its population's product and service needs and, thus, the marketing opportunities it offers.

Countries can be segmented by *political and legal factors,* such as the type and stability of government, receptivity to foreign firms, monetary regulations, and the amount of bureaucracy. Such factors can play a crucial role in a company's choice of which countries to enter and how. *Cultural factors* also can be used, grouping markets according to common languages, religions, values and attitudes, customs, and behavioural patterns.

Segmenting international markets on the basis of geographic, economic, political, cultural, and other factors assumes that segments should consist of clusters of countries. However, many companies use a different approach, called

Intermarket segmentation Forming segments of consumers who have similar needs and buying behaviour even though they are located in different countries.

intermarket segmentation. Using this approach, they form segments of consumers who have similar needs and buying behaviour, even though they are located in different countries. For example, Mercedes-Benz targets the world's well-to-do, regardless of their country. MTV targets the world's teenagers. One study of more than 6500 teenagers from 26 countries showed that teens around the world live surprisingly parallel lives. As one expert notes, "From Rio to Rochester, teens can be found enmeshed in much the same regimen: . . . drinking Coke, . . . dining on Big Macs, and surfin' the Net on their computers." Teens around the world study, shop, and sleep. They are exposed to many of the same major issues: love, crime, homelessness, ecology, and working parents. In many ways, they have more in common with each other than with their parents. MTV bridges the gap between cultures, appealing to what teens around the world have in common.[25]

Requirements for Effective Segmentation

Clearly, there are many ways to segment a market, but not all segmentations are effective. For example, buyers of table salt could be divided into blond and brunette customers, but hair colour is not known to affect one's purchase of salt. Furthermore, if all salt buyers bought the same amount of salt each month, believed all salt is the same, and wanted to pay the same price, the company would not benefit from segmenting this market.

To be useful, market segments must have the following characteristics:

- *Measurability*. The size, purchasing power, and profiles of the segments can be measured. Certain segmentation variables are difficult to measure. For example, there are around four million left-handed people in Canada—which is 15 percent of the population. Yet few products are targeted toward this left-handed segment. The major problem may be that the segment is hard to identify and measure. There are no data on the demographics of lefties, and Statistics Canada does not keep track of left-handedness in its surveys. Private data companies keep reams of statistics on other demographic segments, but not on left-handers.[26]
- *Accessibility*. The market segments can be effectively reached and served. Suppose a food company finds that heavy users of its brands are new Canadians. Unless there are media in the language spoken by these individuals, they will be difficult to reach.
- *Substantiality*. The market segments are large or profitable enough to serve. A segment should be the largest possible homogeneous group worth pursuing with a tailored marketing program. It would not pay, for example, for an automobile manufacturer to develop cars for people who are under four feet tall.

Teens show surprising similarity no matter where in the world they live. Therefore, many companies target teenagers with worldwide marketing campaigns.

- *Actionability.* Effective programs can be designed for attracting and serving the segments. For example, although one small airline identified seven market segments, its staff was too small to develop separate marketing programs for each one.

Market Targeting

Once marketing segmentation has revealed its market segment opportunities, the firm must evaluate the segments and decide how many and which ones to target.

Evaluating Market Segments

In evaluating different market segments, a firm must look at three factors: segment size and growth, segment structural attractiveness, and company objectives and resources.

Segment Size and Growth

The company must first collect and analyze data on current segment sales, growth rates, and expected profitability for various segments. It will be interested in segments that have the right size and growth characteristics. But "right size and growth" is a relative matter. Some companies will want to target segments with large current sales, a high growth rate, and a high profit margin. However, the largest, fastest-growing segments are not always the most attractive ones for every company. Smaller companies may find that they lack the skills and resources needed to serve the larger segments, or that these segments have too many competitors vying for market share. Such companies may select segments that are smaller and less attractive, in an absolute sense, but that are potentially more profitable for them.

Segment Structural Attractiveness

A segment may have desirable size and growth and still not offer attractive profits. The company must examine several major structural factors that affect long-run segment attractiveness.[27] For example, a segment is less attractive if it already contains many strong and aggressive *competitors*. The existence of many actual or potential *substitute products* may limit prices and the profits that can be earned in a segment. The relative *power of buyers* also affects segment attractiveness. If the buyers in a segment possess strong bargaining power relative to sellers, they will try to force prices down, demand more quality or services, and set competitors against one another, all at the expense of seller profitability. Finally, a segment may be less attractive if it contains *powerful suppliers* who can control prices or reduce the quality or quantity of ordered goods and services. Suppliers tend to be powerful when they are large and concentrated, when few substitutes exist, or when the supplied product is an important input.

Company Objectives and Resources

Even if a segment has the right size and growth and is structurally attractive, the company must consider its own objectives and resources in relation to that segment. Some attractive segments could be dismissed quickly because they do not mesh with the company's long-run objectives. Although such segments may be tempting in themselves, they may divert the company's attention and energies away from its main goals. Or they may be a poor choice from an environmental, political, or social responsibility viewpoint. For example, in recent years, several companies and industries have been criticized for unfairly targeting vulnerable segments—children, the aged, low-income earners, and others—with questionable products or tactics (see Marketing Highlight 7-2).

marketing highlight 7-2

Socially Responsible Market Targeting

Market segmentation and targeting form the core of modern marketing strategy. Smart targeting helps companies to be more efficient and effective by focusing on the segments that they can satisfy best. Targeting also benefits consumers—companies reach specific groups of consumers with offers carefully tailored to satisfy their needs. However, market targeting sometimes generates controversy and concern. Issues usually involve the targeting of vulnerable or disadvantaged consumers with controversial or potentially harmful products.

For example, over the years the cereal industry has been heavily criticized for its marketing efforts directed toward children. Critics worry that sophisticated advertising, in which high-powered appeals are presented through the mouths of lovable animated characters, will overwhelm children's defences. They claim that toys and other premiums offered with cereals will distract children and make them want a particular cereai for the wrong reasons. All of this, critics fear, will entice children to gobble too much sugared cereal or to eat poorly balanced breakfasts. The marketers of toys and other children's products have been similarly battered, often with justification. Some critics have even called for a complete ban on advertising to children. Children cannot understand the selling intent of the advertiser, critics reason, so any advertising targeted toward children is inherently unfair.

For these reasons, in 1980, the Quebec government banned all advertising to children under age 13. The other provinces follow the Code of Advertising to Children developed by a partnership between the Canadian Association of Broadcasters and the Advertising Standards Council. The code includes the stipulation that advertisements cannot directly urge children to pressure their parents to buy products. If products, such as cereals, use premiums as part of their promotion program, then the advertising must give at least as much time to the product description as it does to the premium. The code forbids the use of well-known puppets, persons, or characters (including cartoon characters) as product endorsers.

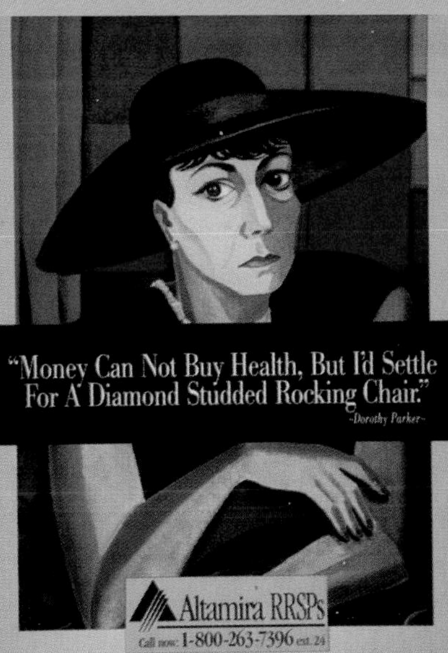

"Money Can Not Buy Health, But I'd Settle For A Diamond Studded Rocking Chair."
-Dorothy Parker-
Altamira RRSPs
Call now: 1-800-263-7396

Financial firms are recognizing the special needs of women as they target their products.

While the code has improved children's advertising on those television and radio stations licensed by the Canadian Radio-television and Telecommunications Commission (CRTC), it has not stopped the spillover advertising from the United States, where 75 percent of the advertisements seen by Canadian children originate. While many of these ads are adapted to meet Canadian standards, others shown on American cable channels do not adhere to Canadian standards. For example, voice-overs are often added to children's commercials run in Canada giving information such as "batteries not included" or "some assembly required" since this is a Canadian, not an American, requirement.

Cigarette, beer, and fast-food marketers also have generated much controversy in recent years by their attempts to target vulnerable segments. For example, McDonald's and other chains have drawn criticism for pitching their high-fat, salt-laden fare to low-income consumers who are much more likely to be heavy consumers. R.J. Reynolds took heavy flak in 1990 when it announced plans to market Uptown, a menthol cigarette targeted toward low-income blacks. It quickly dropped the brand in the face of a loud public outcry and heavy pressure from African-American leaders.

Labatt Breweries of Canada was criticized for marketing its new ice beer to young male consumers. While young males have traditionally been the main target of many brands of beer, Labatt drew criticism because of the product's higher alcohol levels, especially in the brand extension, Maximum Ice.

Women have long been concerned that they pay more for certain products and services than their male counterparts. For example, women are protesting when they are charged more than men for dry cleaning the same type of clothing. They object to paying three to four times more than men for a haircut. Research that sent white males, African-Americans, and women to bargain for new cars at 100 dealerships revealed that white men were offered better deals when they purchased cars than were women or ethnic consumers.

While some marketers are criticized for the segments they target and for the marketing programs directed at those segments, other firms are reproached for not targeting certain groups of consumers. For example, many critics charge that the poor, who are four times less likely to buy or own a computer, have been totally left off the information highway. Many firms have also been reluctant to target the gay or lesbian markets. Hiram Walker is one of the first mainstream marketers to specifically target lesbian women. Their ads for Tuaca liqueur clearly suggest that the female characters are more interested in cultivating relationships with other women, using a headline from the personal ads, "Cool girl seeks sociable silent type to share 'la dolce vita.'"

Not all attempts to target children, minorities, or other special segments draw such criticism. In fact, most provide benefits to targeted consumers. For example, recent statistics reveal that women compose around 42 percent of Canada's 4.5 million RRSP contributors. While many financial institutions believe that you should reach women with your general marketing efforts, others, such as Trimark Investment Management and

Altamira, are running programs with women as their specific target. Altamira broke through the rush of RRSP advertising by using pithy quotations from notable women. These firms note that women want information, not sales pitches. Furthermore, they value financial information presented at convenient times that fit into the busy schedules inherent in two-income families, such as lunch-time financial seminars. They want advice presented in a friendly, easy-to-understand format. Whereas many male customers will not admit when they do not know something, women will ask questions about financial matters but do not want to be made to feel stupid for asking.

Colgate-Palmolive's Colgate Junior toothpaste is another product targeted in a socially responsible manner. It has special features designed to get children to brush longer and more often—it's less foamy, has a milder taste, and contains sparkles, and it comes out of the tube in a star-shaped column. And some cosmetics companies have responded to the special needs of minority segments by adding products specifically designed for black, Hispanic, or Asian women. For example, M·A·C Cosmetics offers a wide range of colours that appeal to various ethnic groups.

Thus, in market targeting, the issue is not really *who* is targeted but rather *how* and for *what*. Controversies arise when marketers attempt to profit at the expense of targeted segments—when they unfairly target vulnerable segments or target them with questionable products or tactics. Socially responsible marketing calls for segmentation and targeting that serve not just the interests of the company, but also the interests of those targeted.

Sources: Excerpts from "PowerMaster," *Fortune,* 13 January 1992:82. Also see "Selling sin to blacks," *Fortune,* 21 October 1991:100; Dorothy J. Gaiter, "Black-owned firms are catching an Afrocentric wave," *Wall Street Journal,* 8 January 1992:B2; Cyndee Miller, "Cosmetics firms finally discover the ethnic market," *Marketing News,* 30 August 1993:2; Michael Wilke, "Toy companies take up diversity banner," *Advertising Age,* 27 February 1995:1,8; Bruce Little, "Poor left behind in computer revolution," *Globe and Mail,* 15 January 1996:B11; Jim McElgunn, "Money, marketing and gender," *Marketing,* 30 January 1995:11–3; Cyndee Miller, "The ultimate taboo," *Marketing News,* 29(17):1,18; Marina Strauss, "Labatt targeted youth, consultant says," *Globe and Mail,* 21 July 1995:B3; Keith J. Tuckwell, *Canadian Marketing in Action,* 3d ed., Scarborough: Prentice-Hall Canada Inc., 1996:27; Chris Cobb, "Toying with children's minds," *Kingston Whig-Standard,* 18 December 1993:2; "Are auto dealers biased? *Business Week,* 14 August 1995:26.

If a segment fits the company's objectives, the company then must decide whether it possesses the skills and resources needed to succeed in that segment. If the company lacks the strengths needed to compete successfully in a segment and cannot readily obtain them, it should not enter the segment. Even if the company possesses the *required* strengths, it needs to employ skills and resources *superior* to those of the competition to win in a market segment. The company should enter only segments where it can offer superior value and gain advantages over competitors.

Selecting Market Segments

Target market
A set of buyers sharing common needs or characteristics that the company decides to serve.

After evaluating different segments, the company must decide which and how many segments to serve. This is the problem of *target market selection.* A **target market** consists of a set of buyers who share common needs or characteristics that the company decides to serve. Figure 7-3 shows that the firm can adopt one of three market coverage strategies: *undifferentiated marketing, differentiated marketing,* and *concentrated marketing.*

Undifferentiated Marketing

Undifferentiated marketing
A market coverage strategy in which a firm ignores market segment differences and pursues the whole market with one offer.

Using an **undifferentiated marketing** strategy, a firm ignores market segment differences and pursues the whole market with one offer. The offer focuses on what is *common* in the needs of consumers rather than on what is *different.* The company designs a product and a marketing program that will appeal to the largest number of buyers. It relies on mass distribution and mass advertising, and it aims to give the product a superior image in people's minds. As noted earlier in this chapter, most modern marketers, however, have strong doubts about this strategy. Difficulties arise in developing a product or brand that will satisfy all consumers. Moreover, mass marketers often have trouble competing with more focused firms that do a better job of satisfying the needs of specific segments and niches.

FIGURE 7-3 Three market coverage strategies

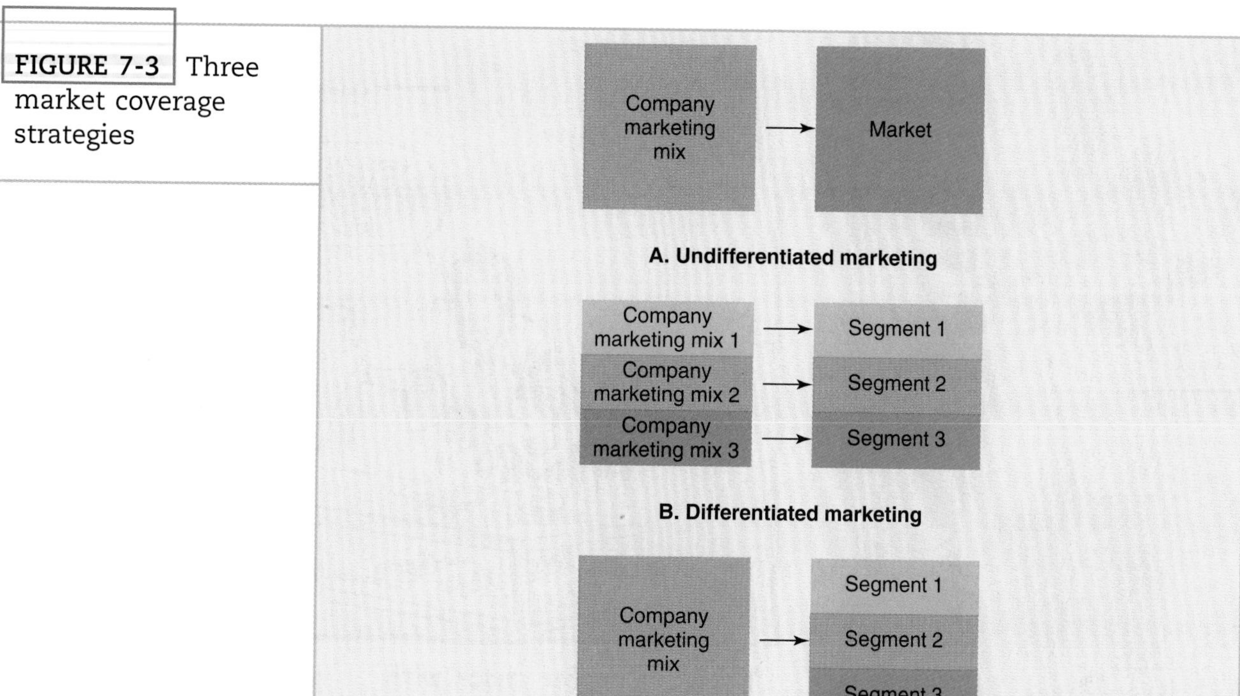

Differentiated Marketing

Differentiated marketing A market coverage strategy in which a firm targets several market segments and designs separate offers for each.

Using a **differentiated marketing** strategy, a firm targets several market segments and designs separate offers for each. General Motors tries to produce a car for every "purse, purpose, and personality." Nike offers athletic shoes for a dozen or more sports. And Weston Foods appeals to the needs of different shopper segments with its No Frills discount stores, Loblaws SuperCentres, and Price Club Warehouse stores. Cadbury Chocolate Canada changed the way chocolate bars were marketed by targeting its Mr. Big candy bars to teenagers, its Crispy Crunch bars to young adults, and its most recent offering, Time Out, to harried businesspeople. Cadbury identified a segment of the market that no other candy manufacturer was serving. By offering product and marketing variations, these companies hope for higher sales and a stronger position within each market segment. They hope that a stronger position in several segments will strengthen consumers' overall identification of the company with the product category. They also hope for more loyal purchasing, because the firm's offer better matches each segment's desires.

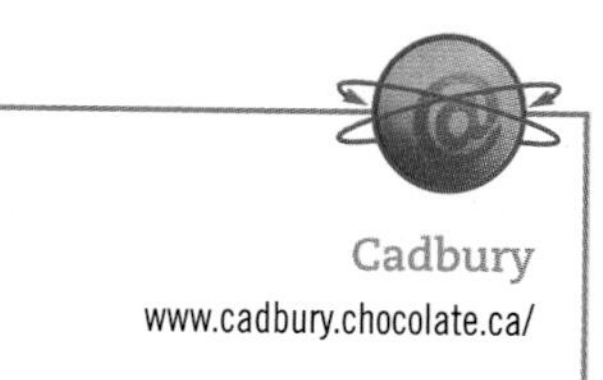

Cadbury
www.cadbury.chocolate.ca/

Differentiated marketing typically creates more total sales than does undifferentiated marketing, and a growing number of firms have adopted this strategy. Procter & Gamble gets a higher total market share with 11 brands of laundry detergent than it could with only one. But differentiated marketing also increases the costs of doing business. Modifying a product to meet different market segment needs usually involves extra research and development, engineering, or special tooling costs. A firm usually finds it more expensive to produce, say, 10 units of 10 different products than 100 units of one product. Developing separate marketing plans for the separate segments requires extra marketing research, forecasting, sales analysis, promotion planning, and channel management. And trying to reach different market segments with different advertising increases promotion costs. Thus, the company must weigh increased sales against increased costs when deciding on a differentiated marketing strategy.

Cadbury Canada, makers of Mr. Big and Time Out chocolate bars, uses a differentiated marketing strategy in creating distinct marketing mixes for different market segments.

Concentrated marketing
A market coverage strategy in which a firm goes after a large share of one or a few submarkets.

Concentrated Marketing

The third market coverage strategy, **concentrated marketing,** is especially appealing to companies with limited resources. Instead of pursuing a small share of a large market, the firm pursues a large share of one or a few submarkets. For example, Oshkosh Truck is the world's largest producer of airport rescue trucks and front-loading concrete mixers. Recycled Paper Products concentrates on the market for alternative greeting cards. And Clearly Canadian concentrates on a narrow segment of the soft-drink market.

Today, the low cost of setting up shop on the Internet makes it even more profitable to serve seemingly minuscule niches. Small businesses, in particular, are realizing riches from serving small niches on the Web. Here's one "Webpreneur" who achieved astonishing results:[28]

> *Ostrichesonline.com.* Whereas Internet giants like music retailer CDnow and bookseller Amazon.com have yet to even realize a profit, Steve Warrington is earning a six-figure income online selling ostriches and every product derived from them (www.ostrichesonline.com). Launched for next to nothing on the Web, Warrington's business generated $6 million in sales in 1999. The site tells visitors everything they ever wanted to know about ostriches and much, much more—it supplies ostrich facts, ostrich pictures, an ostrich farm index, and a huge ostrich database and reference index. Visitors to the site can buy ostrich meat, feathers, leather jackets, videos, eggshells, and skin care products derived from ostrich body oil.

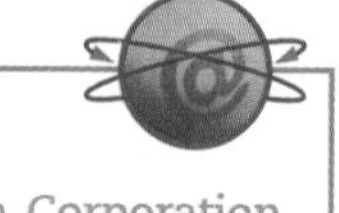

Gennum Corporation
www.gennum.com/

Concentrated marketing provides an excellent way for new small businesses to get a foothold against larger, more resourceful competitors. No firm knows this better than Gennum, an integrated chip manufacturer located in Burlington, Ontario. The firm has built a formidable presence in niche markets ignored by its large multinational rivals.[29] This marketing-driven company began unobtrusively by supplying the world market with integrated circuits for hearing aids. Its technologies have had a substantial influence on the miniaturization of hearing aids around the world. Ninety percent of the company's revenues come from its export markets and it has been surprisingly successful in selling chips to the Japanese, who are renowned as masters of the art.

Through concentrated marketing, the firm achieves a strong market position in the segments (or niches) it serves because of its greater knowledge of the segments' needs and the special reputation it acquires. It also enjoys many operating economies because of specialization in production, distribution, and promotion. If the segment is well chosen, the firm can earn a high rate of return on its investment.

At the same time, concentrated marketing involves risks. The particular market segment can turn sour. Or larger competitors may decide to enter the same segment. For example, while many niche marketers, such as Jill McDonough, a 27-year-old Calgary entrepreneur who founded Schwartzie's Bagel Noshery, have been highly successful, they always fear that this success will attract big players, like Tim Hortons, into their marketplace. If small niche players like McDonough do not have the marketing resources to compete, they are often forced to sell out to their larger competitors. For these reasons, many companies prefer to diversify in several market segments.

Choosing a Market Coverage Strategy

Companies need to consider many factors when choosing a market coverage strategy. Which strategy is best depends on *company resources:* When the firm's resources are limited, concentrated marketing makes the most sense. The best strategy also depends on the degree of *product variability:* Undifferentiated marketing is more suited for uniform products such as grapefruit or steel; differentiation or concentration are more suited to products that can vary in design, such as cameras and cars. The *product's stage in the life cycle* also must be considered: When a firm introduces a new product, it is practical to launch only one version, and undifferentiated marketing or concentrated marketing makes the most sense; in the mature stage of the product life cycle, differentiated marketing begins to make more sense. Another factor is *market variability:* If most buyers have the same tastes, buy the same amounts, and react the same way to marketing efforts, undifferentiated marketing is appropriate. Finally, *competitors' marketing strategies* are important: When competitors use segmentation, undifferentiated marketing can be suicidal; when competitors use undifferentiated marketing, a firm can gain an advantage by using differentiated or concentrated marketing.

Positioning for Competitive Advantage

Product position
The way the product is defined by consumers on important attributes—the place the product occupies in consumers' minds relative to competing products.

Once a company has decided which segments of the market it will enter, it must decide what "positions" it wants to occupy in those segments. A **product's position** is the way the product is *defined by consumers* on important attributes—the place the product occupies in consumers' minds relative to competing products. Thus, Tide is positioned as a powerful, all-purpose family detergent; Solo is positioned as a liquid detergent with fabric softener; Cheer is positioned as the detergent for all temperatures. In the automobile market, Toyota Tercel and Subaru are positioned on economy, Mercedes and Cadillac on luxury, and Porsche and BMW on performance. Volvo positions powerfully on safety.

Consumers are overloaded with information about products and services. They cannot re-evaluate products every time they make a buying decision. To simplify the buying process, consumers organize products into categories—they "position" products, services, and companies in their minds. A product's position is the com-

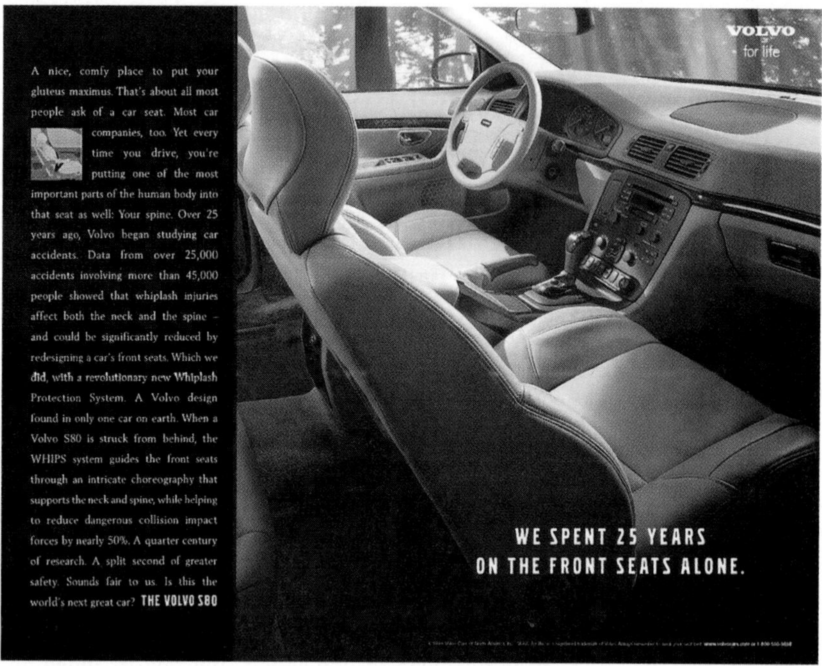

Volvo positions powerfully on its competitive advantage—safety. All most people want from a car seat is "a nice, comfy place to put your gluteus maximus." However, when a Volvo is struck from behind, a sophisticated system "guides the front seats through an intricate choreography that supports the neck and spine, while helping to reduce dangerous collision impact forces."

plex set of perceptions, impressions, and feelings that consumers hold for the product compared with competing products. Consumers position products with or without the help of marketers. But marketers do not want to leave their products' positions to chance. They must *plan* positions that will give their products the greatest advantage in selected target markets, and they must design marketing mixes to create these planned positions. Mark Smith, a Canadian positioning consultant, provides companies with a set of tools to help them improve their position strategies. See Marketing Highlight 7–3.

Positioning Alternatives

Marketers have numerous alternatives for positioning their products and services. They can position their products on specific product *attributes,* such as low price or taste. They can make claims based on the *benefits* provided, such as Crest reduces cavities. Usage occasions are also used to create positions—Hallmark has long claimed their cards are for occasions when you "want the very best," while FedEx has made the promise "when you absolutely, positively need the package there." Another approach is to position the product or service for a certain class of users—marketers of SUVs, therefore, appeal to urban dwellers who dream of the great outdoors. Products and services can also be positioned directly against a competitor. For example, Labatt Blue Light distinguishes itself from other light beers with the slogan, "Tastes like a beer, not water." Finally, products and services can be positioned for different product classes. For example, Camay hand soap is positioned with bath oils rather than with soap.

The Brick
www.thebrick.com/

Even though firms work hard to maintain a consistent and focused long-term positioning strategy, the time may come when they need to create a new position. Edmonton-based home furnishings retailer The Brick faced this challenge when it decided it was time to target a younger, more quality-conscious adult. Using the theme "The right stuff, the right price," it launched a new TV and newspaper ad that promised such additional services as delivery, installation, and repairs in addition to its sales events.[30]

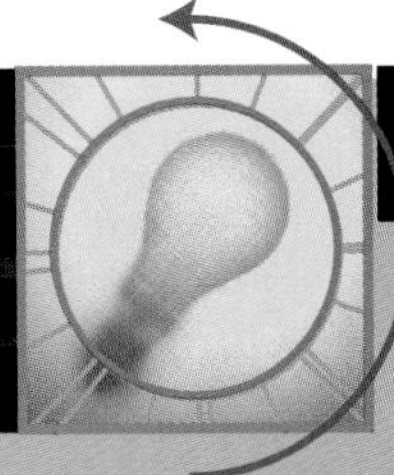

marketing highlight 7-3

Hourglass 1998 Positioning Method

What Is Positioning?

Concepts. Positioning is a battle of concepts. The objective is to find and attach a brand representing a product to a high-ranking concept in the consumer's mind. In today's crowded and confusing marketplace, absolutely nothing is better than owning a word in the consumer's mind.

Positioning concepts for toothpaste include: cavity fighter = *Crest;* tarter and gum disease = *Colgate;* fresh breath = *CloseUp;* white teeth = *Pearl Drop.* Companies battle over the best concepts on which to position their products. However, there are rules to the positioning game and many pitfalls. Mistakes at this level directly affect market share and new product development. Successful strategic positioning requires a clear understanding of all 3Cs of marketing—company, consumer and competition. Basically, positioning is a strategy game of "capture the concept."

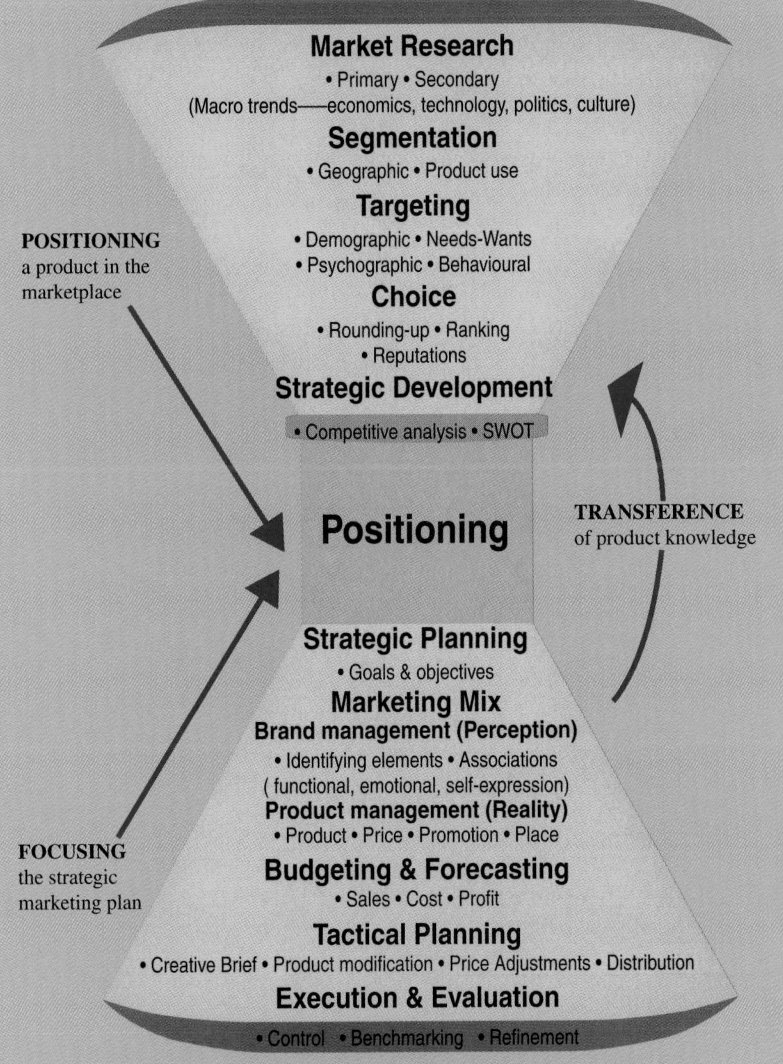

Exhibit A

The Problem

Confusion. Today's consumers are bombarded with choice—25 181 new products in 1998; supermarkets with 40 000 SKUs; 150 TV channels; 1000+ ads viewed per day. How do you break though the clutter?

Hourglass1998™ Positioning Chart

Strategy Tool. The Hourglass1998 Positioning Chart is a strategic planning tool that helps marketers clearly visualize all 3Cs of marketing. It pinches the traditional marketing process, creating a focal point for all marketing activities (Exhibit A). A perfect hourglass shape is formed when the entire marketing mix mirrors the target market's expectations. Ideally, a brand image transfers into the consumer's mind, becoming the brand's reputation. The method was developed and refined over several years by Mark E. Smith as he assisted hundreds of companies in defining their positioning strategy. In 1998, the detailed charting system (not shown) was able to accurately plot over 100 checkpoints and combine over 52 marketing theories, all on a one-page template.

What Is the Main Benefit?

Simplicity. The Hourglass1998 Positioning Chart is a simple tool that helps strategists define, refine, align, and differentiate their products' positioning strategy. It helps marketers visualize and convey important marketing principles such as positioning, focus, differentiation, niche marketing, segmentation, targeting, gap analysis, relativity, repositioning, flanking, opposites, polarity, category killers, brand management, control, ranking, force, division, product management, USP, 4Ps, depth, brand equity, sacrifice, fragmentation, leadership, choice modelling, consistency, knowledge networks, family branding, 4Ds, alignment, mirroring, bait-and-switch, line-extensions, transference, brand building, and conversion. It is a quick, simple and effective way to understand the perceptual battlefield. Every strategist needs a map.

Exhibit B

1. Alignment & repositioning:

Marketing executives can accurately test the alignment of the brand or product mix. *Eatons'* brand *image* became severely misaligned with its "conservative" *reputation* when it tried to reposition itself as a "hip" fashion store for young people.

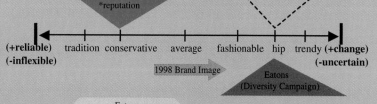

Up-Scale Department Stores

Older Conservative Target (Market Size) *reputation

Young Modern Target (Market Size)

(+reliable) (-inflexible) tradition conservative average fashionable hip trendy (+change) (-uncertain)

1998 Brand Image

Eatons (Diversity Campaign)

Eatons (Product Lines)

2. Brand building & comparison:

Marketing executives can compare the components of each brand mix in competing products. As the brand identities of the two coffee shops fill out, the differences are very apparent. *Tim Hortons* dominates by being *consistently* fast, fresh and friendly.

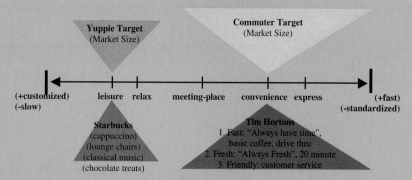

Coffee Shops

Yuppie Target (Market Size)

Commuter Target (Market Size)

(+customized) (-slow) leisure relax meeting-place convenience express (+fast) (-standardized)

Starbucks (cappuccino) (lounge chairs) (classical music) (chocolate treats)

Tim Hortons
1. Fast: "Always have time", basic coffee, drive thru
2. Fresh: "Always Fresh", 20 minute
3. Friendly: customer service

3. Focus: Category killer

Marketing executives can clearly plan category killers. *Home Depot, Future Shop, Chapters* and *Toys 'R' Us* are using *"concentration of force"* to rip out a category from the generalist department stores; the *strong* (deep and narrow) versus the *weak* (broad and shallow).

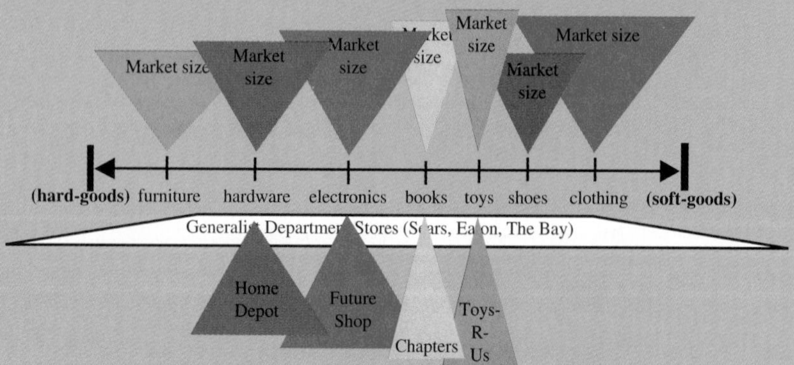

Different from Other Methods?

Big Picture. The Hourglass1998 Positioning Method is unique because it puts a position into context relative to the customer, company and competition. Seeing the "big picture" makes strategic planning easier.

Exact Formulas

Focus. The precise formula for exact positioning can be derived. An example would be, "What is the common denominator between Harvard, Rolex, Rolls-Royce, Glen Abby Golf Course, and Rosedale?" Prestige is the main positioning attribute. It is a formula made up of three sub-attributes: Prestige = Quality + Price + Exclusivity.

Description of the Method

The chart starts with a line on which product attributes are ranked and plotted according to the laws and principles of marketing. The upper half of the hourglass represents the uncontrollable target markets. The bottom half represents various controllable competing products. Each product strives to be first to build a reputation on a high-ranking attribute. Exhibit B shows a few of the many positioning strategies and manoeuvres that can be illustrated using the chart.

Source: Mark E. Smith, positioning consultant and professor specializing in positioning theory in post-graduate marketing management & international marketing at Humber College, Toronto; www.hourglass1998.com.

Choosing a Positioning Strategy

Some firms find it easy to choose their positioning strategy. For example, a firm well known for quality in certain segments will go for this position in a new segment if there are enough buyers seeking quality. But in many cases, two or more firms will go after the same position. Then, each will have to find other ways to set itself apart, such as promising "high quality for a lower cost" or "high quality with more technical service." Each firm must differentiate its offer by building a unique bundle of competitive advantages that appeal to a substantial group within the segment.

The positioning task consists of three steps: identifying a set of possible competitive advantages on which to build a position, selecting the right competitive advantages, and effectively communicating and delivering the chosen position to the market.

Identifying Possible Competitive Advantages

Consumers typically choose products and services that give them the greatest value. Thus, the key to winning and keeping customers is to understand their needs and buying processes better than competitors do and to deliver more value. To the extent that a company can position itself as providing superior value to selected target markets, either by offering lower prices than competitors do or by providing more benefits to justify higher prices, it gains **competitive advantage.** But solid positions cannot be built on empty promises. If a company positions its product as *offering* the best quality and service, it must then *deliver* the promised quality and service. Thus, positioning begins with actually *differentiating* the company's marketing offer so it will give consumers more value than competitors' offers do.

Competitive advantage
An advantage over competitors gained by offering consumers greater value, either through lower prices or by providing more benefits that justify higher prices.

To find points of differentiation, marketers must think through the customer's entire experience with the company's product or service. An alert company can find ways to differentiate itself at every point where it comes in contact with customers.[31] In what specific ways can a company differentiate its offer from those of competitors? A company or market offer can be differentiated along the lines of *product, service, personnel,* or *image.*

Product Differentiation. Differentiation of physical products takes place along a continuum. At one extreme there are highly standardized products that allow little variation: chicken, steel, aspirin. Yet even here, meaningful differentiation is possible. For example, Scott Paper and P&G have successfully differentiated paper towels—creating demand for higher-quality products.

At the other extreme are products that are highly differentiated, such as automobiles, commercial buildings, and furniture. Here the company faces an abundance of design parameters. It can offer a variety of standard or optional *features* not provided by competitors. Thus, Volvo provides new and better safety features; Air Canada's fleet of Airbus 340 jets offers passengers wider seating. Companies also can differentiate their products on *performance.* Whirlpool designs its dishwasher to run more quietly; Procter & Gamble formulates Liquid Tide to get clothes cleaner. *Style* and *design* also can be important differentiating factors. Thus, many car buyers pay a premium for Jaguars because of their extraordinary look, even though Jaguar has sometimes had a poor reliability record. Similarly, companies can differentiate their products on such attributes as *consistency, durability, reliability,* or *repairability.*

Service Differentiation. In addition to differentiating its physical product, a firm can differentiate itself by the amount and quality of service it offers customers. For example, Chapters.ca won over many Canadians who were ordering books from Amazon.com by providing faster and less expensive book delivery.

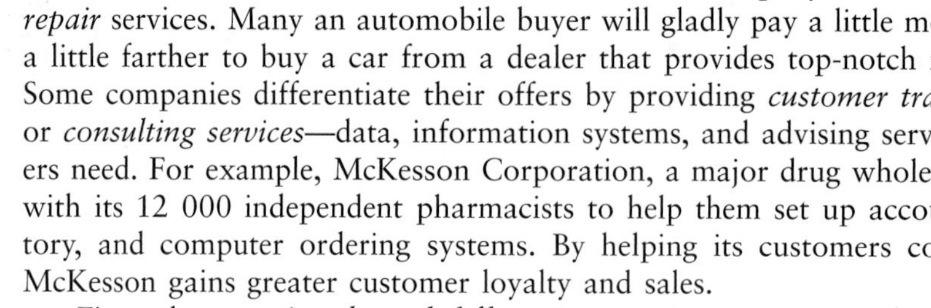

Installation services can also differentiate one company from another, as can *repair* services. Many an automobile buyer will gladly pay a little more and travel a little farther to buy a car from a dealer that provides top-notch repair service. Some companies differentiate their offers by providing *customer training* services or *consulting services*—data, information systems, and advising services that buyers need. For example, McKesson Corporation, a major drug wholesaler, consults with its 12 000 independent pharmacists to help them set up accounting, inventory, and computer ordering systems. By helping its customers compete better, McKesson gains greater customer loyalty and sales.

ING Direct
www.ingdirect.ca/

Firms that practise *channel differentiation* gain competitive advantage through the way they design their channel's coverage, expertise, and performance. The entry of virtual bank ING Direct shook up Canada's financial services industry with its online channel strategy and promises of higher interest rates on savings and more convenient banking. Dell Computer and Avon distinguish themselves by their high-quality direct channels. Science Diet pet food achieves success by going against tradition, distributing its products only through veterinarians and pet stores.

Personnel Differentiation. Companies can gain a strong competitive advantage through people differentiation—hiring and training better people than their competitors do. Toronto's Four Seasons Hotel is famous for its people and the service it provides to the business travellers it has targeted since the early 1970s. For years, it has set the standard for business travellers by offering state-of-the art amenities. But it is not just the hotel facilities that bring in repeat customers; it is the hotel's world-class service. For example, when a Chicago-based executive was stranded without his luggage due to a flight cancellation, the hotel sent a toiletries kit to his room so he could freshen up while hotel staff went out to purchase shirts and underwear for him. And Four Seasons employees consider it all in a day's work to fly to New York to return luggage or business papers left behind by distracted business travellers. The hotel concierge, Nancy Shulman, does everything in her power to make guests feel welcome and comfortable, including renting a chartered plane to get a first-time father home for a premature delivery or sodding a balcony to make a guest's dog feel more at home.[32]

Image Differentiation. Even when competing offers look the same, buyers may perceive a difference based on company or brand image differentiation. A company or brand image should convey the product's distinctive benefits and positioning. Developing a strong and distinctive image calls for creativity and hard work. A company cannot implant an image in the public's mind overnight using only a few advertisements. If "Motorola" means "quality," this image must be supported by everything the company says and does.

Symbols can provide strong company or brand recognition and image differentiation. Companies design signs and logos that provide instant recognition. They associate themselves with objects or characters that symbolize quality or other attributes, such as the McDonald's golden arches, the Prudential rock, or the Pillsbury doughboy. The company might build a brand around some famous person, as Nike did with its Air Jordan basketball shoes. Some companies even become associated with colours, such as IBM (blue) or Campbell (red and white).

The chosen symbols must be communicated through advertising that conveys the company or brand personality. The ads attempt to establish a storyline, a mood, a performance level—something distinctive about the company or brand. The atmosphere of the physical space in which the organization produces or delivers its products and services can be another powerful image generator. Hyatt hotels have become known for their atrium lobbies and Swiss Chalet restaurants for their chalet-look. Thus, a bank that wants to distinguish itself as the "friendly bank" must choose the right building and interior design, layout, colours, materials, and furnishings to reflect these qualities.

"With Larry as our business consultant, no way we're going down the same old road."
Ken Kotowich, President and CEO
Unicity Integrated Logistics Inc.
Larry Scarth, CMA
The courage to innovate.
The skill to execute.
The vision that sees beyond a narrow understanding of the possible, and recognizes that limits are there only as signposts along the way.
To find out how Larry Scarth and over 40,000 CMAs across Canada are changing the way companies like Unicity Integrated Logistics Inc. look for business solutions, call or visit our website.
CMA CANADA
Certified Management Accountant
Shaping the Future
1 877 CMA-6622
www.cma-canada.org
MANAGEMENT WITHOUT LIMITS

Both firms and professional organizations like CMA Canada often use their great people to differentiate themselves.

A company can create an image through the types of events it sponsors: Imperial Oil and IBM have identified themselves closely with cultural events, such as symphony performances and art exhibits. Other organizations support popular causes: Heinz gives money to hospitals and Quaker gives food to the homeless.

Selecting the Right Competitive Advantages

Suppose a company is fortunate enough to discover several potential competitive advantages. It must choose the ones on which to build its positioning strategy. It must decide *how many* differences to promote and *which ones*.

How Many Differences to Promote? Many marketers think that companies should aggressively promote only one benefit to the target market. Ad man Rosser Reeves said a company should develop a *unique selling proposition* (USP) for each brand and stick to it. Each brand should choose an attribute and tout itself as "number one" on that attribute. Buyers tend to remember "number one" better, especially in an overcommunicated society. Thus, Crest toothpaste consistently promotes its anti-cavity protection, and Volvo promotes safety. What are some of the "number one" positions to promote? The major ones are "best quality," "best service," "lowest price," "best value," and "most-advanced technology."

Other marketers think that companies should position themselves on more than one differentiating factor. This may be necessary if two or more firms are claiming to be best on the same attribute. Steelcase, an office furniture systems company, differentiates itself from competitors on two benefits: best on-time delivery and best installation support.

As the mass market is fragmenting into many small segments, companies are trying to broaden their positioning strategies to appeal to more segments. For example, Unilever introduced the first "3-in-1" bar soap—Lever 2000—offering cleansing, deodorizing, *and* moisturizing benefits. Clearly, many buyers want all three benefits, and the challenge was to convince them that one brand can deliver all three. Judging from Lever 2000's outstanding success, Unilever easily met the challenge.

However, as companies increase the number of claims for their brands, they risk disbelief and a loss of clear positioning. In general, a company needs to avoid three major positioning errors. The first is *underpositioning*—failing to position the company at all. Some companies discover that buyers have only a vague idea of the company or that they do not know anything special about it. The second error is *overpositioning*—giving buyers too narrow a picture of the company. Thus, a consumer might think that the Steuben glass company makes only fine art glass costing $1400 and up, when in fact it makes affordable fine glass starting at around $70. Finally, companies must avoid *confused positioning*—leaving buyers with a confused image of a company.

Zellers
www.hbc.com/zellers/

Zellers faced an identity crisis as it struggled to ward off arch-rival Wal-Mart. Zellers went from positioning itself as the store where the "Lowest Price is the Law," to suggesting Zellers was the place "where young families shop." Next, it went to brand-building advertisements for its Martha Stewart and Gloria Vanderbilt house brands. Then there was another about-face with Zellers ads suggesting that the retailer was the place for "Everyday home fashions." It finally went back to its roots and is again stressing value with more price-promotional advertising and its Club Z loyalty program.[33]

Which Differences to Promote? Not all brand differences are meaningful or worthwhile. Not every difference makes a good differentiator. Each difference has the potential to create company costs as well as customer benefits. Therefore, the company must carefully select the ways in which it will distinguish itself from com-

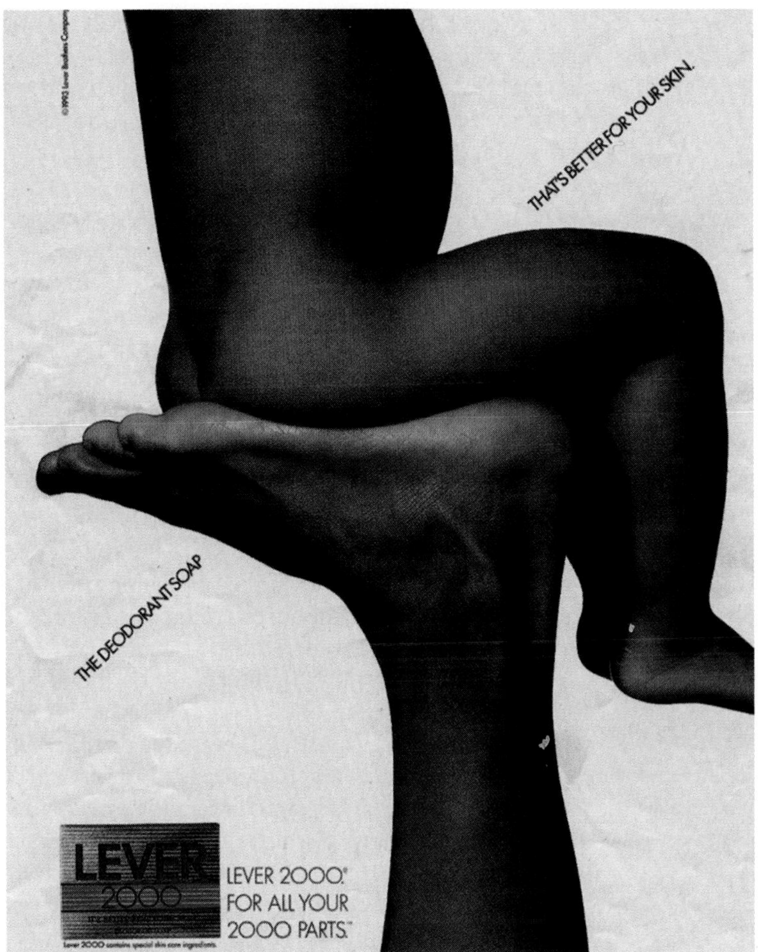

Unilever positioned its best-selling Lever 2000 soap on three benefits in one: cleansing, deodorizing, and moisturizing. It's good "for all your 2000 parts."

petitors. A difference is worth establishing to the extent that it satisfies the following criteria:

- *Important:* The difference delivers a highly valued benefit to target buyers.
- *Distinctive:* Competitors do not offer the difference, or the company can offer it in a more distinctive way.
- *Superior:* The difference is superior to other ways that customers might obtain the same benefit.
- *Communicable:* The difference is communicable and visible to buyers.
- *Pre-emptive:* Competitors cannot easily copy the difference.
- *Affordable:* Buyers can afford to pay for the difference.
- *Profitable:* The company can introduce the difference profitably.

Many companies have introduced differentiations that failed one or more of these tests. The Westin Stamford hotel in Singapore advertised that it was the world's tallest hotel, a distinction that was not important to many tourists—in fact, it turned many off. Polaroid's Polarvision, which produced instantly developed home movies, bombed too. Although Polarvision was distinctive and even pre-emptive, it was inferior to another way of capturing motion, namely, camcorders.

Selecting an Overall Positioning Strategy

Consumers typically choose products and services that give them the greatest value. Therefore, marketers want to position their brands on the key benefits that they

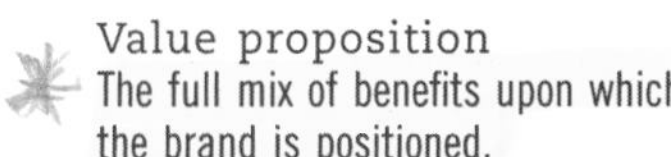

Value proposition The full mix of benefits upon which the brand is positioned.

offer relative to competing brands. The full positioning of a brand is called the brand's **value proposition**—the full mix of benefits upon which the brand is positioned. It is the answer to the customer's question "Why should I buy your brand?" Volvo's value proposition hinges on safety but also includes reliability, roominess, and styling, all for a price that is higher than average but seems fair for this mix of benefits.

Figure 7-4 shows possible value propositions upon which a company might position its products. In the figure, the five green cells represent winning value propositions—positioning that gives the company competitive advantage. The orange cells, however, represent losing value propositions, and the centre cell represents at best a marginal proposition. In the following sections, we discuss the five winning value propositions companies can use to position their products: more for more, more for the same, the same for less, less for much less, and more for less.[34]

More for More. "More for more" positioning involves providing the most upscale product or service and charging a higher price to cover the higher costs. Rolex watches, Mont Blanc writing instruments, Mercedes-Benz automobiles—each claims superior quality, craftsmanship, durability, performance, or style, and charges a price to match. Not only is the marketing offer high in quality, it also offers prestige to the buyer. It symbolizes status and a lofty lifestyle. Often, the price difference exceeds the actual increment in quality.

Sellers offering "only the best" can be found in every product and service category, from hotels, restaurants, food, and fashion to cars and kitchen appliances. Consumers are sometimes surprised, even delighted, when a new competitor enters a category with an unusually high-priced brand. Starbucks coffee entered as a very expensive brand in a largely commodity category; Haagen-Dazs came in as a premium ice cream brand at a price never before charged. In general, companies should be on the lookout for opportunities to introduce a "much more for much more" brand in any underdeveloped product or service category. Yet "more for more" brands can be vulnerable. They often invite imitators who claim the same quality but at a lower price. Luxury goods that sell well during good times may be at risk during economic downturns when buyers become more cautious in their spending.

Lexus Canada
www.lexuscanada.com/

More for the Same. Companies can attack a competitor's "more for more" positioning by introducing a brand offering comparable quality but at a lower price. For example, Toyota introduced its Lexus line with a "more for the same" value proposition. Its headline read: "Perhaps the first time in history that trading a $100,000 car for a $54,000 car could be considered trading up." It communicated the high quality of its new Lexus through rave reviews in car magazines,

FIGURE 7-4 Possible value propositions

Benefits \ Price	More	The same	Less
More	More for more	More for the same	More for less
The same			The same for less
Less			Less for much less

through a widely distributed videotape showing side-by-side comparisons of Lexus and Mercedes-Benz automobiles, and through surveys showing that Lexus dealers were providing customers with better sales and service experiences than were Mercedes dealerships. Many Mercedes-Benz owners switched to Lexus, and the Lexus repurchase rate has been 60 percent, twice the industry average.

The Same for Less. Offering "the same for less" can be a powerful value proposition—everyone likes a good deal. For example, Chapters.ca sells the same book titles as its brick-and-mortar competitors but at lower prices, and Dell Computer offers equivalent quality at a better "price for performance." Discounts stores such as Wal-Mart and "category killers" such as Winners, Business Depot, Costco, and Sportmart also use this positioning. They don't claim to offer different or better products. Instead, they offer many of the same brands as department stores and specialty stores but at deep discounts based on superior purchasing power and lower-cost operations.

Other companies develop imitative but lower-priced brands in an effort to lure customers away from the market leader. For example, Advanced Micro Devices (AMD) and Cyrix make less expensive versions of Intel's market-leading microprocessor chips. Many personal computer companies make "IBM clones" and claim to offer the same performance at lower prices.

Less for Much Less. A market almost always exists for products that offer less and therefore cost less. Few people need, want, or can afford "the very best" in everything they buy. In many cases, consumers will gladly settle for less than optimal performance or give up some of the bells and whistles in exchange for a lower price. For example, many travellers seeking lodgings prefer not to pay for what they consider unnecessary extras, such as a pool, cable television, attached restaurant, or mints on the pillow. Motel chains such as Holiday Inn Express suspend some of these amenities and charge less accordingly. Calgary-based WestJet is another firm that understands the power of appealing to price-sensitive passengers:[35]

> Since its founding in 1996, WestJet has pursued a "bums in seats," no-frills marketing strategy that emphasizes routes and fares. It charges incredibly low prices by not serving food, not assigning seats, and not using travel agents. Today, it is shifting its marketing strategy as it moves away from its concentration on serving people in its western home, to becoming a national carrier capable of taking on giant rival, Air Canada. As evidence of the power of its "less for much less" strategy, the airline is growing and has now increased its fleet from three to 23 planes. While the airline continues to emphasize value and price, it is also working on image building. However, the public shouldn't expect splashy, multimillion-dollar campaigns. "WestJet has always emphasized good value, and we believe people want to see that philosophy reflected in our corporate marketing and advertising," says the company's marketing director.

"Less for much less" positioning involves meeting consumers' lower performance or quality requirements at a much lower price. For example, Family Dollar and Dollar General stores offer more affordable goods at very low prices. Costco warehouse stores offer less merchandise selection and consistency, and much lower levels of service; as a result, they charge rock-bottom prices.

More for Less. Of course, the winning value proposition would be to offer "more for less." Many companies claim to do this. Dell Computer claims to have better products and lower prices for a given level of performance. Procter & Gamble claims that its laundry detergents provide the best cleaning and everyday low prices. In the short run, some companies can actually achieve such lofty positions. For example, when it first opened for business, Home Depot had arguably the best product selection and service and at the lowest prices compared to local hardware stores and other home improvement chains. Yet in the long run, companies will find it very difficult to sustain such best-of-both positioning. Offering more usually costs more, making it difficult to deliver on the "for less" promise. Companies that try to deliver both may lose out to more focused competitors.

All said, each brand must adopt a positioning strategy designed to serve the needs and wants of its target markets. "More for more" will draw one target market, "less for much less" will draw another. Thus, in any market, there is usually room for many different companies, each successfully occupying different positions.

The important thing is that each company develop its own winning positioning strategy, one that makes it special to its target consumers. Offering only "the same for the same" provides no competitive advantage, leaving the firm in the middle of the pack. Companies offering one of the three losing value propositions—"the same for more," "less for more," and "less for the same"—will inevitably fail. Here, customers soon realize that they've been underserved, tell others, and abandon the brand.

Communicating and Delivering the Chosen Position

Once it has chosen a position, the company must take steps to deliver and communicate the desired position to target consumers. Positioning the company calls for concrete action, not just talk. If the company decides to build a position on better quality and service, it must first *deliver* that position. Designing the marketing mix—product, price, place, and promotion—essentially involves working out the tactical details of the positioning strategy. Thus, a firm that seizes on a "high-quality position" knows that it must produce high-quality products, charge a high price, distribute through high-quality dealers, and advertise in high-quality media. It must hire and train more service people, find retailers who have a good reputation for service, and develop sales and advertising messages that broadcast its superior service. This is the only way to build a consistent and believable high-quality, high-service position.

Companies often find it easier to develop a good positioning strategy than to implement it. Establishing a position or changing one usually takes a long time. Ottawa Transit, for example, faced the task of repositioning its bus service. It had a totally new product, its Transitway system—a series of roadways dedicated solely to express buses. However, its real challenge lay in creating a new image for the service. Not only did Ottawa Transit have to convince its riders that this wasn't a regular bus line, but it also had to completely redesign its image with its own employees, including its drivers, as well as other such important stakeholder groups as the media. It began with an outdoor campaign to develop its new identity of buses as a system of rapid transit instead of cumbersome, slow, inconvenient vehicles. It sent information kits on the service to households in Ottawa. It circulated new maps of the system, designed to look more like subway routes than bus lines to reinforce the image of speed and convenience. Television and radio ads were run to further disseminate the new image. It remains to be seen if consumers quickly grasp the concept.[36]

The Ottawa Rapid Transit Project
mhgc.net/oats/

In contrast, positions that have taken years to build can quickly be lost. Once a company has built the desired position, it must take care to maintain the position through consistent performance and communication. It must closely monitor and adapt the position over time to match changes in consumer needs and competitors' strategies. However, the company should avoid abrupt changes that might confuse consumers. Instead, a product's position should evolve gradually as it adapts to the ever-changing marketing environment.

Review of Concept Connections

Organizations that sell to consumer and business markets recognize that they cannot appeal to all buyers in those markets, or at least not to all buyers in the same way. Buyers are too numerous, too widely scattered, and too varied in their needs and buying practices. Therefore, most companies are moving away from mass marketing and practising *target marketing*—identifying market segments, selecting one or more of them, and developing products and marketing mixes tailored to each. In this way, sellers can develop the right product for each target market and adjust their prices, distribution channels, and advertising to reach the target market efficiently.

1. Define the three steps of target marketing: market segmentation, market targeting, and market positioning.

The three steps of target marketing are market segmentation, market targeting, and market positioning. *Market segmentation* is the act of dividing a market into distinct groups of buyers with different needs, characteristics, or behaviour, who might require separate products or marketing mixes. Once the groups have been identified, *market targeting* evaluates each market segment's attractiveness and suggests one or more segments to enter. *Market positioning* consists of setting the competitive positioning for the product and creating a detailed marketing plan.

2. List and discuss the major levels of market segmentation and bases for segmenting consumer and business markets.

Market segmentation can be carried out at many different levels, including no segmentation (mass marketing), complete segmentation (micromarketing), or something in between (segment marketing or niche marketing). *Mass marketing* involves mass producing, mass distributing, and mass promoting about the same product in about the same way to all consumers. Using *segmented marketing,* the company isolates broad segments that make up a market and adapts its offerings to more closely match the needs of one or more segments. *Niche marketing* focuses on more narrowly defined subgroups within these segments, groups with distinctive sets of traits that may seek a special combination of benefits. *Micromarketing* is the practice of tailoring products and marketing programs to suit the tastes of specific individuals and locations. Micromarketing includes *local marketing* and *individual marketing*.

There is no single way to segment a market. The marketer tries different variables to see which give the best segmentation opportunities. For consumer marketing, the major segmentation variables are geographic, demographic, psychographic, and behavioural. In *geographic segmentation,* the market is divided into different geographical units such as nations, provinces, regions, counties, cities, or neighbourhoods. In *demographic segmentation,* the market is divided into groups based on demographic variables, including age, sex, family size, family life cycle, income, occupation, education, religion, race, and nationality. In *psychographic segmentation,* the market is divided into different groups based on lifestyle or personality characteristics. In *behavioural segmentation,* the market is divided into groups based on consumers' knowledge, attitudes, uses, or responses to a product.

Business marketers use many of the same variables to segment their markets. But business markets can also be segmented by business consumer *demographics* (industry, company size), *operating characteristics, purchasing approaches,* and *personal characteristics.* The effectiveness of segmentation analysis depends on finding segments that are *measurable, accessible, substantial,* and *actionable.*

3. Explain how companies identify attractive market segments and choose a market coverage strategy.

To target the best market segments, the company first evaluates each segment's size and growth characteristics, structural attractiveness, and compatibility with company resources and objectives. It then chooses one of three market coverage strategies: ignoring segment differences (*undifferentiated marketing*), developing different market offers for several segments (*differentiated marketing*), or going after one or a few market segments (*concentrated marketing*). Much depends on company resources, product variability, product life-cycle stage, and competitive marketing strategies.

4. Explain how companies can position their products for maximum competitive advantage in the marketplace.

Once a company has decided which segments to enter, it must decide on its *market positioning* strategy, which positions to occupy in its chosen segments. The positioning task consists of three steps: identifying a set of possible competitive advantages upon which to build a position, choosing the right competitive advantages, and selecting an overall positioning strategy. The brand's full positioning is called its value proposition—the full mix of benefits upon which the brand is positioned. In general, companies can choose from one of five winning value propositions upon which to position their products: more for more, more for the same, the same for less, less for much less, or more for less. They must then effectively communicate and deliver the chosen position to the market.

Key Terms

Age and life cycle segmentation *(p. 283)*
Behavioural segmentation *(p. 285)*
Benefit segmentation *(p. 286)*
Competitive advantage *(p. 301)*
Concentrated marketing *(p. 296)*
Demographic segmentation *(p. 282)*
Differentiated marketing *(p. 295)*
Gender segmentation *(p. 284)*
Geographic segmentation *(p. 281)*
Income segmentation *(p. 284)*
Individual marketing *(p. 278)*
Intermarket segmentation *(p. 291)*
Local marketing *(p. 278)*
Market positioning *(p. 275)*
Market segmentation *(p. 275)*
Market targeting *(p. 275)*
Micromarketing *(p. 278)*
Niche marketing *(p. 277)*
Occasion segmentation *(p. 285)*
Product position *(p. 297)*
Psychographic segmentation *(p. 285)*
Segment marketing *(p. 276)*
Target market *(p. 294)*
Undifferentiated marketing *(p. 294)*
Value proposition *(p. 306)*

Discussing the Issues

1. Describe how the Ford Motor Company has moved from mass marketing to segment marketing. Do you think the company will be able to move toward niche marketing or micromarketing? If so, how? How is the company using its Web site (www.ford. com) to change its market segmentation approach?
2. How can a company devise a marketing strategy that will have a mass appeal yet recognize individual differences? One solution is to construct a strategy based on gender segmentation. Construct a brief gender-based strategy for a company attempting to market the following items: (a) a new blade razor, (b) a denim overshirt, (c) a Mazda Miata sports car, (d) life insurance, or (e) Oakley sunglasses.
3. Using Table 7-2 as a model, along with information found in the chapter opening vignette, construct a benefit segmentation table for men's clothing. Identify the major benefit segments, their characteristics, and their favoured brands. Explain how you constructed your table and the potential benefits of your approach.
4. There are many ways to segment a market. However, not all segmentations are effective. Apply the five attributes listed in the text for effective segmentation to assess the usefulness of each of the following segments: (a) Internet users, (b) pager owners, (c) voters, and (d) adult students who return to college to get an undergraduate degree.
5. In 1994, Netscape appeared to be just another Silicon Valley start-up headed down the road to ruin. This was before the World Wide Web exploded to become the centre of a generation's universe and Netscape's position in the marketplace changed dramatically. Choose one of the three market coverage strategies described in the chapter and design a marketing strategy for Netscape for the next five years. Consider the market coverage strategy of archrival Microsoft and other important competitors. Explain why your market coverage strategy is best for the company. (See www.netscape.com for additional information.)
6. Social responsibility will be an important factor affecting the targeting marketing strategies of most firms in the new millennium. Provide an example of an organization that you believe takes a socially responsible approach to targeting markets. Explain your reasoning.

7. Apply the three steps for choosing and implementing a positioning strategy to assess in depth the positioning of one of the following products: (a) Dodge trucks, (b) President's Choice Financial, (c) Chapters.ca, or (d) American Express blue card. Explain your reasoning.

Marketing Applications

1. "Tweens"—youths aged 8 to 14—face pressures to grow up quickly. They surround themselves with computers, electronic gadgets, music, clothing, magazines, and other gear that expresses their lifestyle. How do marketers reach this important group? Firms like Nike, Gap, Sony, Pepsi, and Cover Girl have managed to strike the right notes. Primary influences on the tweens and their $18 billion in annual spending include friends, television and movies, and entertainment and sports idols. Such spending has commanded the attention of both traditional and Internet marketers. Research shows that the tweens are among the most targeted youth groups by today's marketers. To learn more about marketing to tweens, visit the following Web sites: Gap—www.gap.com, Tommy Hilfiger—www.tommy.com, Delia's—www.delias.com, the Limited Too—www.limitedtoo.com, and Nintendo—www.nintendo.com.
   a. Using these and other data sources, profile the tweens market segment.
   b. How do companies appear to be marketing to this segment?
   c. What strategies seem most popular with the Web sites mentioned above?
   d. Choose a company that currently markets to older youths and young adults. Explain how this company might attract tweens to its products.
   e. What types of social responsibility issues might be encountered by a company targeting this group?
2. Is it time to trade in your highlighter for something more reliable? How many times during class or while studying do you underline a word, topic, or key phrase? Too many, right? Siemens (www.siemens.com) is betting that it has found a better way to process and store information. The Siemens Pocket Reader is a new portable digital highlighter. This small handheld scanner is easy to operate—you simply drag the battery-powered "pen" across the text you want to scan. The device stores up to 40 000 characters (about 20 pages) that you can then transfer to your PC for later processing and study. At $150, this new-age "highlighter" might well be worth the price.
   a. What market segments might be interested in this new product?
   b. What form of segmentation should Siemens use?
   c. What market coverage strategy makes the most sense?
   d. How should Siemens position the product?
   e. Outline the appeals that might be used in an advertising campaign for the product. What headline would be appropriate for an advertisement in your university or college newspaper?

Internet Connections

Online Target Marketing

As the Internet matures, Web sites will focus to serve very specific target markets. University students are often surprised to learn that one of the most active groups online is older adults. ThirdAge is a Web site dedicated to this market segment. Visit www.thirdage.com and check out its media kit. Analyze how it characterizes the demographic and psychographic profiles of its users. Now visit www.snowball.com (at the other end of the age spectrum) and complete the table for its users. You may also find useful information on these two market segments at Statistics Canada (www.statcan.ca) and American Demographics (www.demographics.com).

For Discussion

1. Who are some of the sponsors of the ThirdAge Web site? Of Snowball?
2. Browse through the sites. What types of products seem to appeal to ThirdAge users? To Snowball users?
3. Look at the lists of the sites' sponsors. Do any of the companies on the ThirdAge site also target the Snowball demographic? Give some examples.
4. In general, how do the articles differ in content for each market?
5. Based on questions 1 to 4, write a one-sentence positioning statement for each site.
6. What segmentation variable(s) is ThirdAge using for defining its target market?
7. How are the sites designed to appeal to their target audiences?

	Statistic Profile of a ThirdAge User	Profile of a Snowball User
Age		
Income		
Online purchase behaviour		
Online investing		
Time spent online		
Online activities		
Psychographic characteristics		

Savvy Sites

- At TicketMaster's site (www.ticketmaster.com), one can locate *events* by *geographic location:* two important segmentation variables.
- The Yahoo! search engine (ca.yahoo.com) has a feature that allows users to receive a personalized Yahoo! page. This service, "My Yahoo," is a good example of micromarketing.
- Martha Stewart's site (www.marthastewart.com) targets a particular psychodemographic—women who want to spend time beautifying their home or menus. Reading about her various media outlets is like reading a textbook study in market segmentation.

Notes

1. Showwei Chu, "The customer is always wrong," *Canadian Business,* 28 November 1997:35–7; Leanne Delap, "Armani's worldwide concerns," *Globe and Mail,* 22 November 1997:C29; David Olive, "A brown study," *Report on Business Magazine,* November 1997:12; Laura Pratt, "Special report: Reaching the new consumer: Understanding changing expectations," *Strategy,* 11 November 1996:38; Barbara Smith, "Treating consumers as individuals," *Strategy,* 24 August 1992:12,16,18; "Special feature: Excellence in retailing awards," *Strategy,* 24 June 1996:21; www.harryrosen.com.

2. Regis McKenna, "Real-time marketing," *Harvard Business Review,* July–August 1995:87.
3. Eve Lazarus, "Supermarket chain caters to Asian shoppers," *Marketing,* 24 February 1997:2.
4. Edward Baig, "Platinum cards: Move over AmEx," *Business Week,* 19 August 1996:84.
5. Laurel Cutler, quoted in "Stars of the 1980s cast their light," *Fortune,* 3 July 1989:76.
6. Robert E. Linneman and John L.Stanton, Jr., *Making Niche Marketing Work: How to Grow Bigger by Acting Smaller,* New York: McGraw-Hill, 1991.
7. See Don Peppers and Martha Rogers, *The One-to-One Future: Building Relationships One Customer at a Time,* New York: Currency/Doubleday, 1993.
8. See B. Joseph Pine II, *Mass Customization,* Boston: Harvard Business School Press, 1993; B. Joseph Pine II, Don Peppers, and Martha Rogers, "Do you want to keep your customers forever?" *Harvard Business Review,* March–April 1995:103–14; Christopher W. Hart, "Made to order," *Marketing Management,* Summer 1996:11–22; and James H. Gilmore and B. Joseph Pine II, "The four faces of customization," *Harvard Business Review,* January–February 1997:91–101.
9. "Absolut East," *Marketing,* 18 September 1995:2.
10. Edward Caffyn, "Just try to sell me," *Marketing,* 4 August 1997:13–4.
11. Gregory Skinner, "Youth marketing: Calvin's the dude who rocks the nation," *Strategy,* 20 January 1997:13.
12. Jill Vardy, "Rogers set to launch portal for women," *Financial Post,* 12 May 2000:C9; Alice Z. Cuneo, "Advertisers target women, but market remains elusive," *Advertising Age,* 10 November 1997:1,24.
13. "Automakers learn better roads to women's market," *Marketing News,* 12 October 1992:2. Also see Betsy Sharkey, "The many faces of Eve," *Adweek,* 25 June 1990:44–9; Tim Triplett, "Automakers recognizing value of women's market," *Marketing News,* 11 April 1994:1,2; and Leah Rickard, "Subaru, GMC top push to win over women," *Advertising Age,* 3 April 1995:524.
14. Raymond Serafin, "I am woman, hear me roar . . . in my car," *Advertising Age,* 7 November 1994:1,8.
15. Deborah Read, "The young and the jobless," *Report on Business,* April 1996:117–8.
16. Astrid Van Den Broek, "Targeting yourself," *Marketing,* 2 August 1999:9.
17. For a detailed discussion of personality and buyer behaviour, see Leon G. Schiffman and Leslie Lazar Kanuk, *Consumer Behavior,* 5th ed., Englewood Cliffs, NJ: Prentice Hall, 1994: Chapter 5.
18. Bobbi Bulmer, "Nokia aims 'fashionable' phones at women," *Marketing,* 22 September 1997:3.
19. "RadioShack giving E-Gifts this holiday season," *Adnews On-Line Daily,* 13 November 2000, www.adnews.com.
20. Helena Lazar, "Creating new habits: Well-targeted ads encourage light users to pour on the sauce," *Marketing On-line,* 20 September 1999; Warren Thayer, "Target heavy buyers!" *Frozen Food Age,* March 1998:22–4.
21. See Thomas V. Bonoma and Benson P. Shapiro, *Segmenting the Industrial Market,* Lexington, MA: Lexington Books, 1983. For examples of segmenting business markets, see Kate Bertrand, "Market segmentation: Divide and conquer," *Business Marketing,* October 1989:48–4.
22. Daniel S. Levine, "Justice served," *Sales & Marketing Management,* May 1995:63–71.
23. For more on segmenting business markets, see John Berrigan and Carl Finkbeiner, *Segmentation Marketing: New Methods for Capturing Business,* New York: HarperBusiness, 1992; Rodney L. Griffith and Louis G. Pol, "Segmenting industrial markets," *Industrial Marketing Management,* 23, 1994:39–46; Stavros P. Kalafatis and Vicki Cheston, "Normative models and practical applications of segmentation in business markets," *Industrial Marketing Management,* November 1997:519–30; and James C. Anderson and James A. Narus, *Business Market Management,* Upper Saddle River, NJ: Prentice Hall, 1999: 44–7.
24. Marlene L. Rossman, "Understanding five nations of Latin America," *Marketing News,* 11 October 1985:10; as quoted in Subhash C. Jain, *International Marketing Management,* 3rd ed., Boston: PWS-Kent Publishing Company, 1990:366.
25. Cyndee Miller, "Teens seen as the first truly global consumer," *Advertising Age,* 27 March 1995:9; Shawn Tully, "Teens: The most global market of all," *Fortune,* 16 May 1994:90–7. Also see Matthew Klein, "Teen green," *American Demographics,* February 1998:39.
26. See Joe Schwartz, "Southpaw strategy," *American Demographics,* June 1988:61; and "Few companies tailor products for lefties," *Wall Street Journal,* 2 August 1989:2.
27. See Michael Porter, *Competitive Advantage,* New York: Free Press, 1985:4–8, 234–236.
28. Paul Davidson"Entrepreneurs reap riches from net niches," *USA Today,* 20 April 1998:B3; and information accessed online from www.ostrichesonline.com, February 2000.
29. "Raking in the chips," *Report on Business,* April 1992:39–40.
30. "The Brick rebrands itself in new campaign," *AdNews On-Line Daily,* 8 November 2000.
31. For an interesting discussion of finding ways to differentiate marketing offers, see Ian C. MacMillan and Rita Gunther McGrath, "Discovering new points of differentiation," *Harvard Business Review,* July–August 1997:133–45.
32. Anne Dimon, "The concierge can turn out to be your friend in need," *Globe and Mail Report on Business Travel,* 13 February 1996:C9; Jeremy Ferguson, "Where rescue operations are routine," *Globe and Mail Report on Business Travel,* 13 February 1996:C9.
33. Marina Strauss, "Zellers returns to pitching prices," *The Globe and Mail,* 13 March 2000:B1,B3; Fawzia Sheikh, "Zellers plans to expand its brands," *Marketing On-line,* 17 May 1999.
34. See Philip Kotler, *Kotler on Marketing,* Upper Saddle River, NJ: Prentice Hall, 1999:59–63.
35. Norma Ramage, "West Jet flies with a new strategy," *Marketing On-Line,* 25 October 1999; Keith McArthur, "West Jet market flies by Air Canada's," *Globe and Mail,* 5 April 2001:B1.
36. Sean Eckford, "Ottawa transit effort reworks image of the bus," *Marketing,* 16 October 1995:3.

Company Case 7

Enterprise Rent-A-Car: Selling the Dream in the Fast Lane

On a bright January 1998 morning, Deanna Pittman, Enterprise Rent-A-Car's area rental manager for Ottawa, got out of her Dodge Intrepid at Enterprise's new office. She admired the line of clean cars and the new office with its green and white Enterprise sign. To Deanna, it seemed that dreams really did come true.

In 1991, Deanna had graduated with a degree in industrial relations from Queen's University in Kingston. When she'd first scheduled a job interview with Enterprise, Deanna had been sceptical. Although she didn't know much about the company, she wasn't certain that she'd like renting cars for a living or working a retail job that included washing cars. But she'd seen the potential to advance quickly, develop strong management skills, and learn about running a business.

Once hired, Deanna had been promoted quickly to management assistant, then to branch manager at Enterprise's new office in Rockcliffe Park, an Ottawa subdivision. In five years, she became area manager, giving her responsibility for the Ottawa area—supervising three branch offices with 22 employees, 495 cars, and annual revenues of more than $4.5 million. Deanna felt as though she were running her own business. Enterprise gave its managers considerable autonomy and paid them based on a percentage of their branches' profits. Deanna's starting salary had been in line with those of her classmates, but within three years, her pay had doubled. There couldn't be many other companies, Deanna thought, in which a person of her age could have so much responsibility, so much fun, and such high earnings.

Company Background

Deanna's good fortune mirrored that of Enterprise itself. The company's founder, Jack Taylor, started Enterprise in 1962 with a single location and 17 cars in St. Louis, Missouri. Since then, Enterprise has grown dramatically to become the largest rental car company in North America. Enterprise Rent-A-Car has nearly 4000 offices located throughout the United States, Canada, the United Kingdom, Ireland, and Germany. Known as the non-airport rental car company, Enterprise has recently expanded into airports to extend their low-rate, high-service approach to travellers as well as local renters. In fact, Enterprise had grown at a compound annual rate of 25 percent for the past 11 years. By 1997, the company had more than 325 000 cars, $4.5 billion in sales, $7.5 billion in assets, and over 30 000 employees.

A Winning Strategy

Analysts attribute Enterprise's success to several factors. First, cars have become a more important part in people's lives: They just can't do without their cars, even for a day or two. And, as more families have both adults working or are single-parent families, there is often no one else in the family who can pick up people when they have car problems. Tied in to this, the courts ruled in the 1970s that insurance companies had to offer coverage so that insured motorists could rent a replacement car if they lost the use of their car. As a result, those insurance companies began to offer rental replacement coverage in their policies.

Beyond these environmental factors, the company's success resulted from its focus on one segment of the rental car market. Instead of following Hertz, Avis, and other rental car companies by setting up branches at airports to serve national travellers, Enterprise built an extensive network of neighbourhood locations serving the "home-city" market—people who needed rental cars as replacements when their cars were wrecked, stolen, or in the shop. Because these customers were often stranded at a body shop or garage and had no easy way to get to a rental office, Enterprise offered to pick them up.

However, Enterprise's first customer in the replacement market is often the referral source—the insurance agent or auto body shop employee who recommends Enterprise to the stranded customer. So, employees visit the referral sources frequently, often taking them doughnuts or pizza as a way of thanking them for their business. They call on referral sources who may not be doing business with Enterprise, and they keep insurance agents apprised of a car's repair status.

Auto Rental News, an industry trade publication, estimates that the replacement market is growing by 10 to 15 percent per year (see Exhibit 1). The entire rental car market, including airport rentals and the travel segment, is about $21 billion.

Enterprise's rental rates in the replacement market tend to be lower than those for comparable rentals at airport-based companies—some analysts estimate up to 30 percent lower. The company tends to locate its offices

Exhibit 1 The Replacement Car Rental Market

Competitors, revenue estimates, and other market data[1].

I. Competitor	1996 Revenue	Percent Replacement[2]	Cars in Service
1. Enterprise Rent-A-Car	$2.61 billion[3]	78	315 000
2. Ford and Chrysler Systems	$490 million	92	82 250
3. Snappy Car Rental	$100 million	100	15 500
4. U-Save Auto Rental	$115 million	60	13 500
5. Rent-A-Wreck	$85 million	35	10 942
6. Premier Car Rental	$66 million	100	9 500
7. Advantage Rent-A-Car	$76 million	33	9 000
8. Spirit Rent-A-Car	$50 million	100	7 500
9. Super Star Rent-A-Car	$43 million	100	5 250
10. Many independent companies	$750 million	53	
11. Airport-based companies: Hertz, Avis, Budget, Dollar, National, Thrifty, Alamo[4]	$360 million	100	

II. Industry average pricing

Estimated industry average price per day for replacement rentals, not including additional insurance coverages or other rentals, such as cellular phones: Industry average daily rental is $23. Industry average rental period for replacement rentals is 12 days. Additional insurance coverages produce about five percent of revenue, with other rental options producing about two percent of revenue. Per-day rental rates are often established through rational contracts with insurance companies or automobile manufacturers' or dealers' warranty reimbursement programs. There are about 160 major North American rental markets. Airport-based rental rates vary widely depending on competition. Airport rental companies also negotiate corporate rates with individual companies.

III. Overall rent-a-car market

Overall 1996 market estimated at $14.62 billion broken down as follows:

Business rentals—40 percent, Leisure/Discretionary rentals—33 percent, Replacement rentals—27 percent.

IV. Advertising

Advertising Age estimated that car rental companies spent $384.4 million in measured advertising in 1994, about 2.8 percent of revenue. It estimated that Enterprise spent $22 million in 1994, up from $13 million in 1993. Enterprise's 1994 spending compared with $47 million spent by Hertz, $31 million by Alamo, and $24 million by Avis (27 September 1995).

Notes:

1. Estimates provided by *Auto Rental News.* Data is for case discussion purposes only. Use in case does not imply certification of estimates by Enterprise.
2. Replacement market includes insurance replacement, rentals, mechanical repair rentals, dealer loaner rentals, and warranty rentals.
3. *Auto Rental News* estimate of rental revenue excluding leasing, seven percent of revenue is from airport/traveller rentals, and 93 percent is from local market rentals. Local market includes replacement, business, and leisure rentals, with business and leisure about equal for Enterprise.
4. Includes the portion of airport-based companies' revenue from local market operations that target the replacement market, including Hertz $130 000; Budget $126 000; National $135 000; Dollar $63 500; and Thrifty $34 000.

Source: *Auto Rental News*

in city areas where the rent is much lower than at the airport. It also keeps its cars a little longer than the typical airport rental company. These two factors and a focus on efficient operations helped it keep rates lower.

A second segment of the home-city market that Enterprise has begun to serve is the "discretionary" or "leisure/vacation" segment. Friends or relatives may visit and need a car, or the family may decide to take a vacation and feel that the family car is not as dependable or comfortable as they would like. Many people rent just to keep the extra kilometres off the family car.

Finally, Enterprise is also experiencing growth in the local corporate market. Many small businesses and some large ones have found that it's easier and less expensive for them to rent their fleets from Enterprise than to try to maintain their own fleets. Colleges and universities have realized that it's less expensive to rent a 15-passenger van when the soccer team travels than to keep a van full time for only occasional use.

Enterprise's success in the home-city market has attracted competition. Although Enterprise had the largest share of that market, a handful of major regional competitors, such as Spirit and Snappy, when combined, captured a large market share. The airport rental companies, such as Hertz, Avis, and Alamo, got only a small portion of the home-city business. Hertz is just starting a small operation that focuses on the home-city replacement market. Local "mom-and-pop" firms that often have just one office and a few cars serve the remainder of the market.

Enterprise has grown very quietly, depending on its referral sources and word-of-mouth promotion. It wasn't until 1989 that the company did its first national advertising. At that time, marketing research demonstrated that if you showed people a list of company names and asked them to identify the rental car companies, only about 20 percent knew Enterprise. The company started advertising nationally but kept its ads low key. By 1997, it had more than quadrupled its annual advertising and promotion spending, using the theme "Pick Enterprise. We'll pick you up." However, although the company's research shows that Enterprise's overall awareness is up substantially, only about one-third of those surveyed are aware of the company's pick-up service, and only about one-third are aware that it has branches nearby.

The Importance of Culture

The company's strategy, driven by Jack Taylor's philosophy, worked well. Taylor believed that the employees' and the company's first job was to serve the customer. Taylor urged his employees to do whatever they had to do to make the customer happy. Sometimes it meant waiving charges. Other times, it meant stopping everything and running out to pick up a stranded customer.

Further, Taylor believed that after customers came employees. He believed that to satisfy customers, a company had to have satisfied, challenged employees who worked as a team. All of Enterprise's branch employees, from assistant manager on up, earn a substantial portion of their pay based on branch profitability. In addition, the company has a profit-sharing plan for all employees. Enterprise hired primarily university graduates and promoted from within. Ninety-nine percent of its managers started as management trainees at the branch level, so they understand the customer-oriented culture. As important, they understand their local markets and the needs of customers in those markets. Thus, Enterprise is really a collection of small, independent businesses, with the corporation providing capital and logistical support.

Finally, Taylor believed that if the company took care of its customers and employees, profits would follow. Sure enough, Enterprise has consistently been profitable in an industry where many firms have not.

What's Next?

How can Enterprise continue to grow and prosper in the face of growing competition? The company believes it can double its revenues by the year 2001, but to do so, it must wrestle with a number of growth-related issues.

First, it must continue to attract and retain university graduates. The company needed to hire over 5000 management trainees in 1999 alone, and that number will increase. Yet many grads, like Deanna Pittman, may know very little about Enterprise and may not want to work for a rental car company. How can Enterprise do a better job of recruiting university graduates?

Second, Enterprise must examine its marketing strategy. Which markets should it target? How should it position itself there? Are there new services it could offer that would make sense given its current strategy? How can it do a better job of increasing Enterprise's awareness among targeted customers? How should it respond as new competitors, including the airport-based firms such as Hertz, attack the home-city market?

Perhaps the most important question is how can Enterprise continue to grow without losing its focus and without losing the corporate culture that has been so important in helping it and its employees, like Deanna Pittman, realize their dreams?

Questions

1. How are the buyer decision processes different for someone renting a replacement car because of a wreck, for someone renting a car for leisure/vacation purposes, for a business renting a car, and for a college graduate looking for a job?
2. Why should the rental car market be segmented?
3. What marketing recommendations would you make to Enterprise to help it improve its recruiting?
4. What marketing recommendations would you make to Enterprise to improve its marketing strategy?
5. Will Enterprise's strategy continue to work in international markets?

Source: Enterprise Rent-A-Car supported development of this case. *Auto Rental News* also provided information. This case is adapted from a longer case with the same title authored by Lew Brown, Gary Armstrong, and Philip Kotler, available from Enterprise.

video case 7

Modrobes: From University Case Competition to the Real World Firm

Some people have entrepreneur written all over them. One of those people is Steve "Sal" Debus, or Saldebus, a young man who describes himself as an artist, not just a clothing designer and merchandiser. He began his career at age 10 designing shoes for his favourite brand name firms—Nike, Brooks and Converse. Although he never actually received a royalty for his "new and funky" shoe pictures, he kept the vision alive and was determined to create his own style.

His first winning idea came about as the result of the sore butt he got while writing four-hour political science exams while attending Brock University. It was then that "Exam Pants"—lightweight, extremely comfortable utility pants—were born. Similar to those worn by operating room physicians, the main stylistic difference was the quilted foam padding sewn into the seat of the pants, easy access side pockets, a widened leg and a secret pocket. "Hey, they were so damn comfortable I wore them every day for a month," exclaimed Sal. However, the pants had one limitation. Since Sal wasn't too enthused with his new nickname, "Fat Ass," he went on to make a slightly different style.

With little money for distribution, Sal went from campus to campus selling Exam Pants off folding tables, where his sales pitch grabbed a lot of attention. He promised prospective buyers that if his pants weren't the most comfortable piece of clothing they had ever owned, he would refund their money. Who could resist such an offer? His first year sales were $70 000.

Today he's the president of his own company, Toronto-based Modrobes Saldebus Lounge Clothing Inc., a firm he established in 1995. His line of comfortable, easy-care, casual clothing has been a hit with young people. Using eyebrow-raising slogans like "I want you in my pants" and unconventional advertising like stickers customers can paste on their snowboards has led to sales topping $2 million. Speaking in the voice of his customers has made everyone, from customers to suppliers to distribution partners, sit up and listen.

Sal could leave the selling to someone else—his pants are available in over 350 stores—but he still hits the road in order to keep in touch with the ever changing youth market. In the summer of 1999, for example, he and his team went off to Rome, NY, to the Woodstock music festival, his first foray into the US market.

Keeping in touch is important because Sal has lofty dreams for the young company. He hopes his firm will generate $60 million in sales in the next five years as a result of his new online venture (www.modrobes.com) and sales to the US. He sees it as a rival for the big players like Levi Strauss. He thinks he can make inroads against the jeans companies since denim is not a good fit for modern style. People aren't working in factories but behind computers, where they need clothing that's more comfortable and lighter weight, Sal believes. Before reaching this lofty goal, however, there are some significant hurdles in his path. None of these seem to worry Sal, who has his own style in taking on these challenges.

Questions

1. How has market segmentation helped Sal Debus market his products effectively?
2. Sal does a lot of marketing at events. How can events help him expand his business into new target markets?
3. Visit the Modrobes website. What is Modrobes doing to make the site interesting and valuable for different market segments?

Sources: This case was written by Peggy Cunningham based on *Venture* #724; Hilary Davidson, "Built for Comfort and Chic," *National Post*, June 24, 2000; Astrid Van Den Broek, "Targeting Yourself," *Marketing*, August 2, 1999, p. 9; www.modrobes.com.

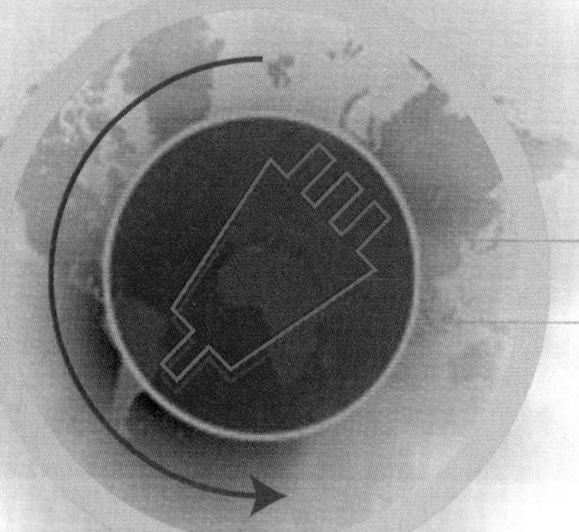

PART 1 2 **3** 4

Developing the Marketing Mix

Concept Connections

When you finish this chapter, you should be able to

1. Define product and the major classifications of products and services.
2. Describe the roles of product and service branding, packaging, labelling, and product support services.
3. Explain the decisions that companies make when developing product lines and mixes.
4. Identify the four characteristics that affect the marketing of a service.
5. Discuss the additional marketing considerations that services require.

chapter 8

Product and Services Strategies

Some companies don't sell products, they sell experiences. Such is the case with Intrawest, a firm that defines its mission as creating "memories for our guests and staff as the best mountain, beach and resort experience . . . again and again." To achieve this mission, Intrawest has to rely on its employees to deliver superior service to its guests. Thus, its employees are not just highly motivated, they are also passionate about their work. They have a sense of excitement and commitment that is so visible, it is a tangible asset to the company. This excitement is transferred to every guest. Intrawest's employees have mastered the art of integrating their product and service.[1]

Intrawest, headquartered in Vancouver, is North America's leading developer and operator of mountain "destination" resorts. The company owns and operates magnificent, award-winning ski areas: Whistler, Blackcomb, and Panorama in British Columbia; Tremblant and Mont Ste. Marie in Quebec; Blue Mountain in Ontario; Stratton in Vermont; Copper in Colorado; Mammoth in California; and Snowshoe in West Virginia. In the 1999–2000 season, Intrawest hosted 6.2 million skiers and snowboarders at its resorts. The company builds, markets, and sells resort accommodation and real estate, mainly condominiums, at the base of each hill. But its success has as much to do with the company's focus on the customer and the experiences it creates as it does with the physical facilities. According to company officials, "What drives the mountain resort business is the quality of the experience our guests and owners come away with."[2]

However, some people, including demographer David Foot, don't believe that investing in active sports facilities is a wise decision as the population ages. Statistics seem to support Foot's analysis. The number of skiers and snowboarders in Canada has declined from a high of 21.5 million ski visits to 16 million. So why is Intrawest investing in more ski hills? The company cites two reasons for its decision. First, Intrawest knows that there is a growing vacation industry in which people come to mountain resorts not only to ski but also to participate in various activities throughout the summer and winter. Second, Intrawest believes that demographics are on their side. Their research reveals that the average age of a person purchasing a recreational property is 50. These purchasers have sufficient disposable income to afford

this type of luxury item. Since the leading edge of the baby boom group is entering their fifties, Intrawest believes that it is well positioned to take advantage of a growth market. The company also believes that this group wants recreational activities where they can bring along younger family members so they can all enjoy an activity such as skiing. Developing a love of mountains and outdoor sports in the young represents a future marketing opportunity for Intrawest.

Selling a recreational property isn't the end goal for Intrawest, however. The company stresses that selling a mountain home or renting a time-share is just the beginning, not the end of its task. It is the long-term stream of revenue received from people returning again and again to its resorts that makes the company profitable over the long term. Rather than relying on skiing alone, Intrawest is investing money in its properties: It is building mountain-top theatres, water parks, children's play areas, entertainment centres, and outdoor educational facilities. In other words, it is creating year-round recreational experiences that appeal to people from around the world who are interested in "destination" vacations.

Thus, Intrawest's strategic edge lies in its ability to integrate three sectors of the leisure industry: resort operations (skiing, golfing, hiking, mountain biking, retail, food and beverage), resort real estate development, and its vacation club (or time-share) business. Intrawest also has a network of operations from which the company achieves economies of scale: They market together, purchase together, and learn from each other.

Marketing is an important part of the company's strategy. It is investing to build equity in the brand name Intrawest. It wants the name to be synonymous worldwide with unique resort experiences in breathtaking places. Building brand equity is a costly exercise, so developing an effective and efficient marketing program is important. To accomplish its goals, Intrawest has turned to database marketing. It began to build its database with lists of season pass holders. It added

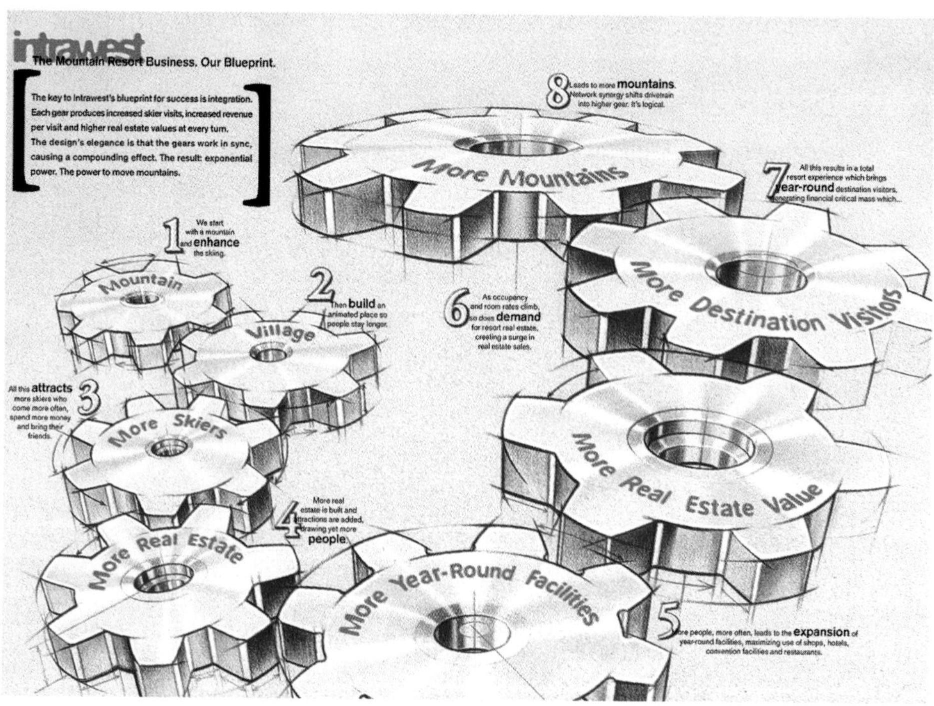

This graphic shows how the parts of Intrawest's business strategy are linked.

the names of resort visitors, leads from consumer shows, and replies generated from cards in its advertisements. Intrawest enters lifestyle information into its database so that it can develop profiles of people who will generate the most long-term value for the firm. It can then target its marketing efforts directly at these individuals.

While Intrawest markets its products and services primarily to baby boomers, it also understands the importance of other age groups. The company is starting to target younger people—those aged 18 to 35—who compose the largest single segment of customers for mountain resorts. These people are high-frequency guests who have more flexibility in choosing the time for their vacation than do people with school-age children. Intrawest also recognizes the importance of teenagers, who significantly influence the choice of family vacations. Teenagers have also driven the interest in extreme sports and represent an important group of buyers for sports gear. To appeal to these groups, Intrawest uses humour in its breakthrough advertising directed at its target audience of affluent North American, European, and Japanese consumers. Its ads also include the company's toll-free telephone number and its Web site address.

Understanding the company's target market is important. Intrawest competes not only for these customers with other mountain resorts in Canada, the United States, Europe, and Japan, but also for market share with all other leisure companies, from cruise ships to amusement parks. For this reason, Intrawest wants to offer such a variety of vacation choices within the Intrawest network that guests will return again and again.

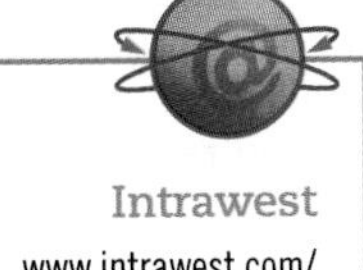

Intrawest
www.intrawest.com/

Go to their Web site and click on the button "Our Success Formula" to see Intrawest's strategy spelled out. It has helped them generate over $1.2 billion in revenues. Having the strategic vision to integrate product and service strategies can be a powerful and profitable endeavour.[3]

Clearly, Intrawest is marketing more than just a place to ski. The company is selling experiences, and, while these may be based on such physical features as magnificent mountain peaks, people keep coming back as much for the service as they do for the product. Thus, this chapter begins with a deceptively simple question: *What is a product?* Companies create offerings that may be *product dominated* or *service dominated.* We suggest that the package of benefits offered to customers by many firms is a subtle mix of product and service benefits. We go on to describe ways to classify products sold to consumer and business markets. Next, we describe links between the way the product is classified and suitable marketing strategies for products in that particular classification. For product-dominated offerings, many decisions have to be made not only about product design, but also about *branding, packaging, labelling,* and *product support services.* Marketing managers must also develop product lines and product mixes. The last section of the chapter deals with the challenges associated with marketing *service-dominated* products. Services present special marketing challenges since they are *simultaneously produced and consumed,* and are *intangible, perishable,* and *variable.*

What Is a Product?

Product
A cluster of benefits that can be offered to a market for attention, acquisition, use, or consumption that might satisfy a want or need. It includes physical objects, services, persons, places, organizations, and ideas.

A Sony CD player, a Supercuts haircut, a Celine Dion concert, a Jasper vacation, a GMC truck, H&R Block tax preparation services, and advice from an attorney are all products. We define a **product** as a cluster of benefits that can be offered to a market for attention, acquisition, use, or consumption and that might satisfy a want or need. Products include more than just tangible goods. Broadly defined, products include physical objects, services, persons, places, organizations, ideas, or mixes of these entities. Thus, throughout this text, we use the term product broadly to include any or all of these entities.

Service
Any activity or benefit that one party can offer to another that is essentially intangible and does not result in the ownership of anything tangible.

Because of their importance in the world economy, we give special attention to **services.** Services are a form of product that consist of activities, benefits, or satisfactions offered for sale that are essentially intangible and do not result in the ownership of anything. Examples are banking, hotel accommodation, tax preparation, and home repair services. We shall look at services more closely at the end of this chapter.

Products, Services, and Experiences

A company's offer to the marketplace often combines both tangible goods and intangible services. Each component can be a minor or a major part of the total offer. At one extreme, the offer may be product dominated and consist of a *pure tangible good,* such as soap, toothpaste, or salt—no services accompany the product. At the other extreme are service-dominated offerings—an intangible benefit is created for the customer but no physical product is exchanged. Examples include a doctor's exam, a university lecture, or financial services. Between these two pure extremes, however, many goods and services combinations are possible.

A company's offer may consist of a *tangible good with accompanying services.* For example, Ford offers more than just automobiles. Its offer also includes repair and maintenance services, warranty fulfillment, showrooms and waiting areas, and a host of other support services. A *hybrid offer* consists of equal parts of goods and services. For instance, people patronize restaurants both for their food and their service. A *service with accompanying goods* consists of a major service along with supporting goods. For example, Air Canada passengers primarily buy transportation service, but the trip also includes some tangibles, such as food, drinks, and an airline magazine. The service also requires a capital-intensive good—an airplane—for its delivery, but the primary offer is a service.

As products and services become more commodity-like, many companies are moving to a new level in creating value for their customers. To differentiate their offers, they are developing and delivering total customer experiences. Whereas products are tangible and services are intangible, experiences are memorable. Whereas products and services are external, experiences are personal and take place in the minds of individual consumers. Companies like Intrawest that market experiences realize that customers are really buying much more than just products and services. They are buying what those offers will do for them—the experiences they gain in purchasing and consuming these products and services (see Marketing Highlight 8-1).

Levels of Product

Core product
The problem-solving services or core benefits that consumers are really buying when they obtain a product.

Product planners need to consider the product on three levels. The most basic level is the **core product,** which addresses the question: *What is the buyer really buying?* As Figure 8-1 illustrates, the core product stands at the centre of the total product. It consists of the problem-solving services or core benefits that consumers seek when they buy a product. A woman buying lipstick buys more than lip colour. Charles Revlon of Revlon recognized this early: "In the factory, we make cosmetics; in the store, we sell hope." Theodore Levitt has pointed out that buyers "do not buy quarter-inch drills; they buy quarter-inch holes." Thus, when designing products, marketers must first define the core *benefits* the product will provide to consumers.

Actual product
A product's parts, quality level, features, design, brand name, packaging, and other attributes that combine to deliver core product benefits.

The product planner must next build an **actual product** around the core product. Actual products can have up to five characteristics: a *quality level, features, design,* a *brand name,* and *packaging.* For example, Sony's PlayStation is an actual product. Its brand name, software, styling, features, packaging, and other attributes have all been combined carefully to deliver the core benefit—exciting entertainment.

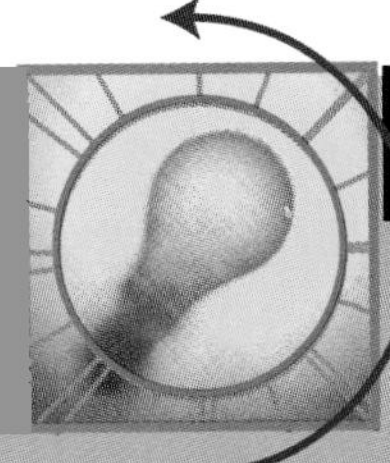

marketing highlight 8-1

Beyond Products and Services: Welcome to the Experience Economy

In their book *The Experience Economy,* Joseph Pine and James Gilmore argue that, as products and services become less differentiated, companies are moving to a new level in creating value for customers. As the next step in differentiating their offers, beyond simply making products and delivering services, companies are staging, marketing, and delivering memorable experiences. Consider the evolution of the birthday cake:

> [In an] agrarian economy, mothers made birthday cakes from scratch, mixing farm commodities (flour, sugar, butter, and eggs) that together cost mere dimes. As the goods-based industrial economy advanced, moms paid a dollar or two to Betty Crocker for premixed ingredients. Later, when the service economy took hold, busy parents ordered cakes from the bakery or grocery store, which, at $10 or $15, cost ten times as much as the packaged ingredients. Now, . . . time-starved parents neither make the birthday cake nor even throw the party. Instead, they spend $100 or more to "outsource" the entire event to McDonald's, the Discovery Zone, the Rainforest Cafe, or some other business that stages a memorable event for the kids—and often throws in the cake for free. Welcome to the emerging experience economy. . . . From now on, leading-edge companies—whether they sell to consumers or businesses—will find that the next competitive battleground lies in staging experiences.

Experiences are sometimes confused with services, but experiences are as distinct from services as services are distinct from goods. Whereas products and services are external, experiences exist only in the mind of the individual. They are rich with emotional, physical, intellectual, or spiritual sensations created within the consumer. According to Pine and Gilmore:

> An experience occurs when a company intentionally uses services as the stage, and goods as props, to engage individual customers in a way that creates a memorable event. . . . To appreciate the difference between services and experiences, recall the episode of the old television show *Taxi* in which Iggy, a usually atrocious (but fun-loving) cab driver, decided to become the best taxi driver in the world. He served sandwiches and drinks, conducted tours of the city, and even sang Frank Sinatra tunes. By engaging passengers in a way that turned an ordinary cab ride into a memorable event, Iggy created something else entirely—a distinct economic offering. The experience of riding in his cab was more valuable to his customers than the service of being transported by the cab—and in the TV show, at least, Iggy's customers happily responded by giving bigger tips. By asking to go around the block again, one patron even paid more for poorer service just to prolong his enjoyment. The service Iggy provided—taxi transportation—was simply the stage for the experience that he was really selling.

Experiences have always been important in the entertainment industry—Disney has long manufactured memories through its movies and theme parks. Today, however, all kinds of firms are recasting their traditional goods and services to create experiences. For example, restaurants create value well beyond the food they serve. Starbucks patrons are paying for more than just coffee. "Customers at Starbucks are paying for staged experiences," comments one analyst. "The company treats patrons to poetry on its wallpaper and tabletops, jaunty apron-clad performers behind the espresso machine, and an interior ambience that's both cozy and slick, marked by earth tones, brushed steel, and retro music (also for sale). Few people leave without feeling a little more affluent, sophisticated, or jazzed."

Many retailers also stage experiences. Niketown stores create "shoppertainment" by offering interactive displays, engaging activities, and promotional events in a stimulating shopping environment. At Sharper Image, "people play with the gadgets, listen to miniaturized stereo equipment, sit in massage chairs, and then leave without paying for what they valued, namely, the experience." Newer Loblaws stores have the visual appeal of small town markets. In their upstairs cafés, shoppers can enjoy a cup of coffee while listening to a live string quartet one day, a country and western band the next.

Toronto-based Playdium Entertainment's 29 Canadian locations bill themselves as "entertainment centres." While some might call them hyped up video arcades, Playdium's goal is to make game playing a rich and engaging experience, not just an addictive pastime. Much of the distinction between arcade and "entertainment centre" comes down to the way in which the experience is packaged, according to Playdium's design consultants: "We wanted to create an immersive environment." Walking into a Playdium centre is a visual experience. Graphic displays serve to heighten the energy and excitement of the place while working to guide visitors from one zone—for example, Speed, Sports, Music, Kids—to the next. "The fun of the game should start long before people start playing," the design team notes.

In San Francisco, Sony of America developed Metreon, an "interactive entertainment experience," where visitors can shop, eat, drink, play, or simply soak up the experiences (check it out at www.metreon.com). The huge Metreon complex features 15 theatres, including a Sony-IMAX theatre, eight theme restaurants, and several interactive attractions. Visitors can also experience any of nine interactive stores, including the flagship Discovery Channel Store. In all, Metreon offers a dazzling experience that far transcends the goods and services assortment it contains. Sony sums up the experience this way:

> Use your eyes, ears, hands, and brain . . . sensory overload to a phenomenal degree. . . . Four floors and 350 000 square feet jam-packed with ways to entertain and escape into a whole new reality. Dazzle a date. Bring wonder to your kids. Shop in amazement. Have fun with your friends. Whenever you want real entertainment, head to Metreon.

The experience economy goes beyond the entertainment and retailing businesses. All companies stage experiences whenever they engage customers in a personal, memorable way:

In the travel business, former British Airways chairman Sir Colin Marshall has noted that the "commodity mind-set" is to "think that a business is merely performing a function—in our case, transporting people from point A to point B

Sony's Metreon markets an "interactive entertainment experience."

on time and at the lowest possible price." What British Airways does, according to Sir Colin, is "to go beyond the function and compete on the basis of providing an experience." The company uses its base service (the travel itself) as the stage for a distinctive en route experience—one that attempts to transform air travel into a respite from the traveller's normally frenetic life.

Business-to-business marketers also stage experiences for their customers. For example, one computer installation and repair company has found a way to turn its otherwise humdrum service into a memorable encounter. Calling itself the Geek Squad, it sends "special agents" dressed in white shirts with thin black ties and pocket protectors, carrying badges, and driving old cars. Toronto's iPIX offers virtual real estate tours to real estate agents. These tours allow agents and their clients to tour residential, rental, or even commercial properties and see multiple rooms, view interiors and exteriors, and make informed choices easily, all from the comfort of home or office, 24 hours a day, seven days a week. You can take a sample tour yourself by visiting their Web site (www.ipix.com).

Thus, as we move into the new millennium, marketers seeking new ways to bring value to customers must look beyond the goods and services they make and sell. They must find ways to turn their offers into total customer experiences. As the experience economy grows, Pine and Gilmore caution, it "threatens to render irrelevant those who relegate themselves to the diminishing world of goods and services."

Sources: Excerpts and quotes from B. Joseph Pine II and James Gilmore, "Welcome to the experience economy," *Harvard Business Review*, July–August 1998:97–105; Wendy Cuthbert, "Playdium creates order from chaos," *Strategy*, 13 March 2000:24; Wade Roush, "Now playing: Your business," *Technology Review*, May–June 1999:96; www.metreon.com September 1999; and www.ipix.com. Also see B. Joseph Pine and James H. Gilmore, *The Experience Economy*, New York: Free Press, 1999.

Augmented product Additional consumer services and benefits built around the core and actual products.

Finally, the product planner must build an **augmented product** around the core and actual products by offering additional consumer services and benefits. Sony must offer more than just a video game player. It must provide consumers with a complete solution to their entertainment needs. Thus, when consumers buy a Sony PlayStation, Sony and its dealers also might give buyers a warranty on parts and workmanship, free tips on how to maximize their game-playing experiences, quick repair services when needed, a toll-free telephone number to call if they have prob-

FIGURE 8-1 Three levels of product

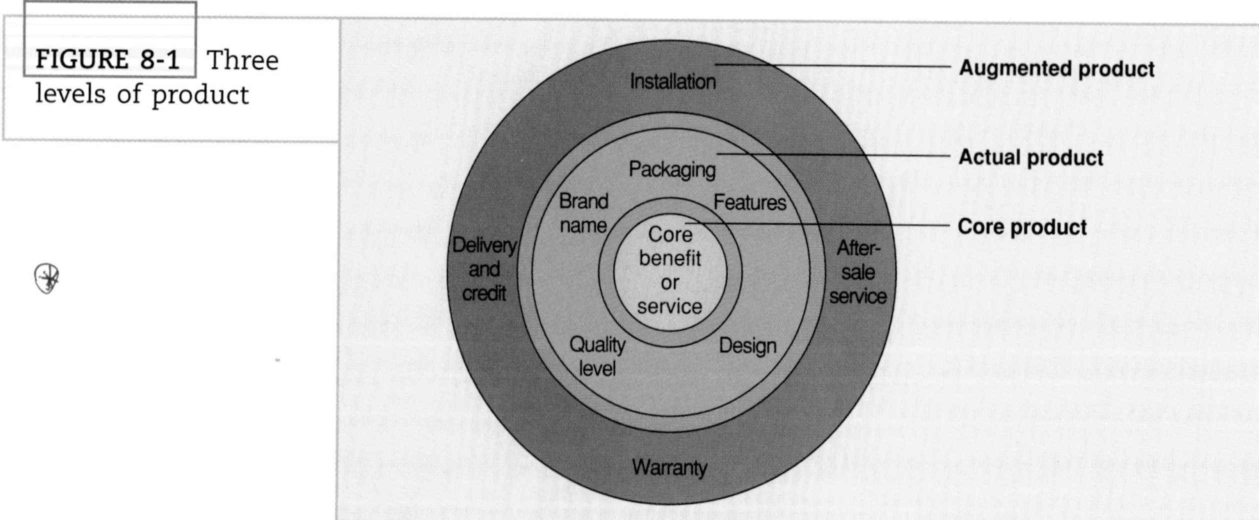

Now you can get everything from news to games on your Clearnet phone. You can even do Internet banking and shopping. To see how simple it is to get on the wireless Web, visit www.myclearnet.com
The future is friendly.
Unlimited wireless surfing starting at $10 a month*

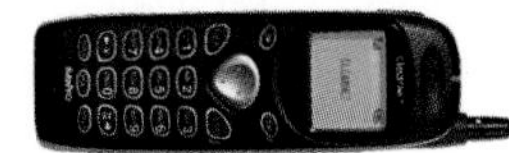

Have it delivered to your phone.

NATIONAL POST
PM IGNORED BRAIN DRAIN WARNING
College suspends, fines psychiatrist
Women bigger Net users than men: study
© 2000 Clearnet PCS Inc. *Must be a Clearnet PCS voice client.
clearNET
pcs

PLAYDIUM.

NATIONAL POST
Yellow Pages
Indigo
Books Music & more
www.indigo.ca
Bloomberg.com
canada.com
More content is being added all the time. To find out what's new, visit us at www.myclearnet.com

Clearnet's pcs is a complex bundle of intangible features that deliver one core benefit—allowing consumers to connect anywhere, anytime.

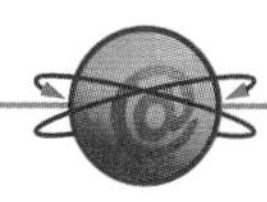

The Station
www.station.sony.com/

lems or questions, and a Web site that not only allows them to try new games, but makes them part of the PlayStation community. To the consumer, all of these augmentations become an important part of the total product.

Therefore, a product is more than a simple set of tangible features. Consumers tend to see products as complex bundles of benefits that satisfy their needs. When developing products, marketers first must identify the *core* consumer needs the product will satisfy. They must then design the *actual* product and find ways to *augment* it to create the bundle of benefits that will best satisfy consumers.

Product Classifications

Products and services fall into two broad classes based on the types of people that use them—*consumer products* and *industrial products*. Broadly defined, products also include other marketable entities such as organizations, persons, places, and ideas.

Consumer Products

Consumer products
Products bought by final consumers for personal consumption.

Consumer products are those bought by final consumers for personal consumption. Marketers usually classify these goods further based on *how consumers go about buying them*. Consumer products include *convenience products, shopping products, specialty products,* and *unsought products*. Since these products differ in the ways consumers buy them, they differ in how they are marketed (see Table 8-1).

Convenience products
Consumer products and services that the customer usually buys frequently, immediately, and with a minimum of comparison and buying effort.

Convenience products are consumer products and services that the customer usually buys frequently, immediately, and with a minimum of comparison and buying effort. They are usually low priced and are found in many types of retail outlets so they are available when customers need them. Convenience products can be divided into *staples, impulse products,* and *emergency products*. *Staples* are products that consumers buy on a regular basis, such as milk, toothpaste, and electric power. *Impulse products* are purchased with little planning or search effort. These products are normally widely available. Thus, chocolate bars and magazines are placed next to checkout counters in many stores because shoppers may not otherwise think of buying them. Customers buy *emergency products* when their need is urgent—umbrellas during a rainstorm, travel insurance at an airport, or boots and shovels during the year's first snowstorm.

TABLE 8-1 Marketing Considerations for Consumer Products

Marketing Considerations	Type of Consumer Product			
	Convenience	Shopping	Specialty	Unsought
Customer buying behaviour	Frequent purchase, little planning, little comparison or shopping effort, low customer involvement	Less frequent purchase, much planning and shopping effort, comparison of brands on price, quality, style	Strong brand preference and loyalty, special purchase effort, little comparison of brands, low price sensitivity	Little product awareness, knowledge (or if aware, little or even negative interest)
Price	Low	Higher	High	Varies
Place	Widespread in convenient locations	Selective in fewer outlets	Exclusive in only one or a few outlets per market area	Varies
Promotion	Mass promotion by the producer	Advertising and personal selling by both producer and resellers	More carefully targeted promotion by both producer and resellers	Aggressive advertising and personal selling by producer and resellers
Examples	Toothpaste, magazines, laundry detergent	Major appliances, televisions, furniture, clothing	Luxury goods, such as Rolex watches or fine crystal	Life insurance, dental services

Shopping products
Consumer goods and services that the customer, in the process of selection and purchase, characteristically compares on such bases as suitability, quality, price, and style.

Shopping products are less-frequently purchased consumer products and services that customers compare carefully on suitability, quality, price, and design. When buying shopping products and services, consumers spend much time and effort in gathering information and making comparisons. Examples include furniture, clothing, vacations, and restaurant meals. Shopping products and services are offered through fewer outlets than convenience goods and services, but marketers provide more sales support to aid consumers in their comparisons.

Specialty products
Consumer products and services with unique characteristics or brand identification for which a significant group of buyers is willing to make a special purchase effort.

Specialty products are consumer products and services with unique characteristics or brand identification for which a significant group of buyers is willing to make a special purchase effort. Examples include specific brands and types of cars, high-priced photographic equipment, and investment services. A Rolls-Royce, for example, is a specialty product because buyers are usually willing to travel great distances to buy one. Buyers normally do not compare specialty products. They invest only the time needed to reach dealers carrying the wanted products. Although these dealers do not need convenient locations, they still must let buyers know where to find them.

Unsought products
Consumer products and services that the consumer either does not know about or knows about but does not normally think of buying.

Unsought products are consumer products and services that the consumer either does not know about or knows about but does not normally think of buying. Most major innovations are unsought until the consumer becomes aware of them through advertising. Classic examples of known but unsought products are life insurance, funeral plans, and blood donations. By their very nature, unsought products require a lot of advertising, personal selling, and other marketing efforts.

Industrial Products

Industrial products
Products and services bought by individuals and organizations for further processing or for use in conducting a business.

Industrial products are those products and services purchased for further processing or for use in conducting a business. Thus, the distinction between a consumer product and an industrial product is based on the *purpose* for which the product is bought. If a consumer buys a lawn mower for use around home, the lawn mower is a consumer product. If the same consumer buys the same lawn mower for use in a landscaping business, the lawn mower is an industrial product.

There are three groups of industrial products: *materials and parts, capital items,* and *supplies and services.*

Materials and parts
Industrial products that enter the manufacturer's product completely, including raw materials and manufactured materials and parts.

Materials and parts are industrial products that become part of the buyer's product through further processing or as components. They include raw materials and manufactured materials and parts. *Raw materials* include farm products (wheat, cotton, livestock, fruits, vegetables) and natural products (fish, lumber, crude petroleum, iron ore). Farm products are supplied by many small producers who turn them over to marketing intermediaries that process and sell them. *Manufactured materials and parts* include component materials (iron, yarn, cement, wires) and component parts (small motors, tires, castings). Component materials usually are processed further—for example, pig iron is made into steel, and yarn is woven into cloth. Most manufactured materials and parts are sold directly to industrial users. Price and service are the major marketing factors; branding and advertising tend to be less important.

Capital items
Industrial products that partly enter the finished product, including installations and accessory equipment.

Capital items are industrial products that aid in the buyer's production or operations. They include installations and accessory equipment. *Installations* include buildings (factories, offices) and fixed equipment (generators, drill presses, large computers, elevators). Because installations are major purchases, they are usually bought directly from the producer after a long decision period. *Accessory equipment* includes portable factory equipment and tools (hand tools, lift trucks) and office equipment (fax machines, desks). They have a shorter life than installations and simply aid in the production process. Most sellers of accessory equipment use intermediaries because the market is spread out geographically, the buyers are numerous, and the orders are small.

Supplies and services
Industrial products that do not enter the finished product at all.

Supplies and services are industrial products that include operating supplies (lubricants, coal, computer paper, pencils) and repair and maintenance items (paint, nails, brooms). Supplies are the convenience products of the industrial field because they usually are purchased with a minimum of effort or comparison. *Business services* include maintenance and repair services (window cleaning, computer repair) and business advisory services (legal, management consulting, advertising). These services are usually supplied under contract. The factors associated with the successful marketing of professional services to industrial buyers were analyzed by de Brentani and Ragot of Concordia University.[4]

Organizations, Persons, Places, and Ideas

Marketers have broadened the concept of a product from tangible products and services to include other "marketable entities"—organizations, persons, places, and ideas.

Organizations often carry out activities to "sell" the organization itself. *Organization marketing* consists of activities undertaken to create, maintain, or change the attitudes and behaviour of target consumers toward an organization. Both for-profit and non-profit organizations practise organization marketing. Business firms sponsor public relations or corporate advertising campaigns to polish their images. Non-profit organizations, such as churches, universities, charities, museums, and performing arts groups, market their organizations to raise funds and attract members or patrons. *Image advertising* is a major tool that companies use to market themselves to various publics.

All kinds of people and organizations practise *person marketing*—activities undertaken to create, maintain, or change attitudes or behaviour toward particular people. Prime ministers and provincial premiers skillfully market themselves, their parties, and their platforms to get needed votes and program support. Entertainers and sports figures such as Celine Dion and Tiger Woods use marketing to promote their careers and improve their impact and incomes. Professionals such as dentists, lawyers, accountants, and architects market themselves to build their reputations and increase business. Business leaders use person marketing as a strategic tool to develop their companies' fortunes as well as their own. Businesses, charities, sports teams, fine arts groups, religious groups, and other organizations also use person marketing. Creating or associating with well-known personalities often helps these organizations achieve their goals better.

Place marketing involves activities undertaken to create, maintain, or change attitudes or behaviour toward particular places. Examples include business site marketing and tourism marketing. *Business site marketing* involves developing, selling, or renting business sites for factories, stores, offices, warehouses, and conventions. Both provinces and municipalities try to sell companies on the advantages of locating new plants in their areas. Even entire nations, such as Indonesia, Ireland, Greece, Mexico, and Turkey have marketed themselves as good locations for business investment. *Tourism marketing* involves attracting vacationers to spas, resorts, cities, provinces, and nations. The effort is carried out by travel agents, airlines, motor clubs, oil companies, hotels, motels, and government agencies. Today almost every city, province, and country markets its tourist attractions. The government of Canada uses its Web site to inform residents and tourists about attractions and events. Saskatchewan markets itself as "clean, green, and welcoming." New Brunswick announces, "There's Fishing . . . and then there's New Brunswick's world-famous trophy fishing!"

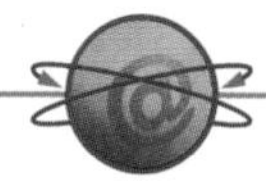

Attractions Canada
www.attractionscanada.com/

Ideas also can be marketed. In one sense, all marketing is the marketing of an idea, whether it be the general idea of brushing your teeth or the specific idea that Crest provides the most effective decay prevention. Here, however, we narrow our focus to the marketing of *social ideas,* such as public health campaigns to reduce smoking, alcoholism, drug abuse, and overeating; environmental campaigns to promote wilderness protection, clean air, and conservation; and other campaigns such as family planning, human rights, and racial equality. This area has been called **social marketing,** and it includes the creation and implementation of programs seeking to increase the acceptability of a social idea, cause, or practice within targeted groups. For example, YWCAs across Canada promote a "week without violence," a Calgary group called Street Teams advertises to stop child prostitution, and the United Way runs ads to show how they help people in their local communities. But social marketing involves much more than just advertising. Many public marketing campaigns fail because they assign advertising the primary role and fail to develop and use all the marketing mix tools.[5]

Social marketing
The creation and implementation of programs seeking to increase the acceptability of a social idea, cause, or practice within targeted groups.

Individual Product Decisions

Figure 8-2 shows the important decisions in the development and marketing of products. We shall focus on decisions about *product attributes, branding, packaging, labelling,* and *product support services.*

Product quality
The ability of a product to perform its functions; it includes the product's overall durability, reliability, precision, ease of operation and repair, and other valued attributes.

Product Attributes

Developing a product or service involves defining the benefits that the product will offer. These benefits are communicated and delivered by such product attributes as *quality, features,* and *design.*

This Street Teams advertisement is designed to stop child prostitution.

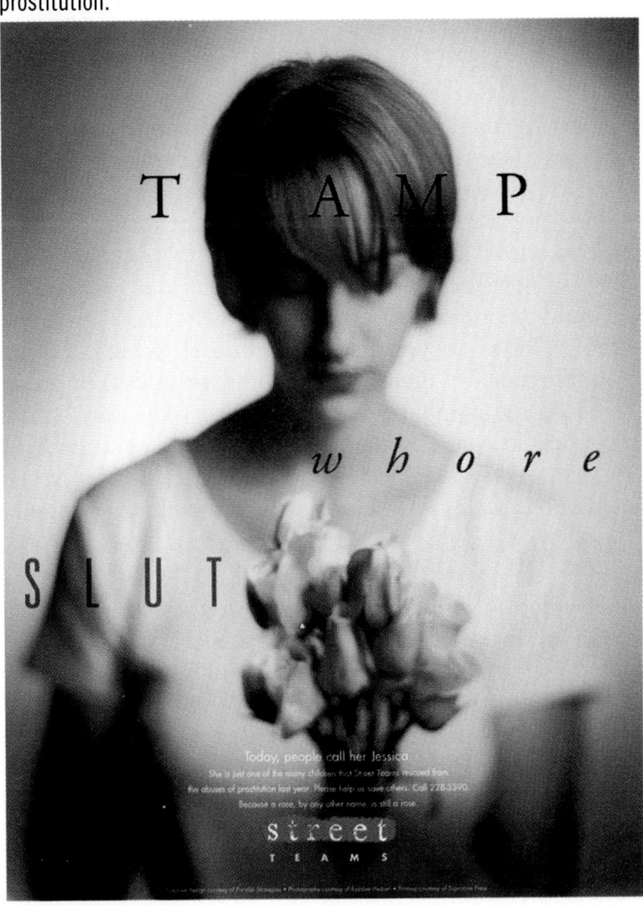

Product Quality

Quality is one of the marketer's major positioning tools. **Product quality** has two dimensions—level and consistency. In developing a product, the marketer must first choose a quality level that will support the product's position in the target market. Here, product quality means *performance quality*—the level at which a product performs its functions. For example, a Rolls-Royce provides higher performance quality than a Chevrolet: it has a smoother ride, is made from more luxurious materials, handles better, and lasts longer. Companies rarely try to offer the highest possible performance quality level—few customers want or can afford the high levels of quality offered in products such as a Rolex watch. Instead, companies choose a quality level that matches target market needs and the quality levels of competing products.

Beyond quality level, high quality can also mean the *consistency* with which the quality is delivered. Here, product quality means *conformance quality*—freedom from defects and *consistency* or reliability—in delivering a targeted level of performance. All companies should strive for high levels of conformance quality. In this sense, a Chevrolet can have just as much quality as a Rolls-Royce. Although a Chevy doesn't perform as well as a Rolls, it can consistently deliver the quality that customers pay for and expect.

During the past two decades, a renewed emphasis on quality has spawned a global quality move-

FIGURE 8-2
Individual product decisions

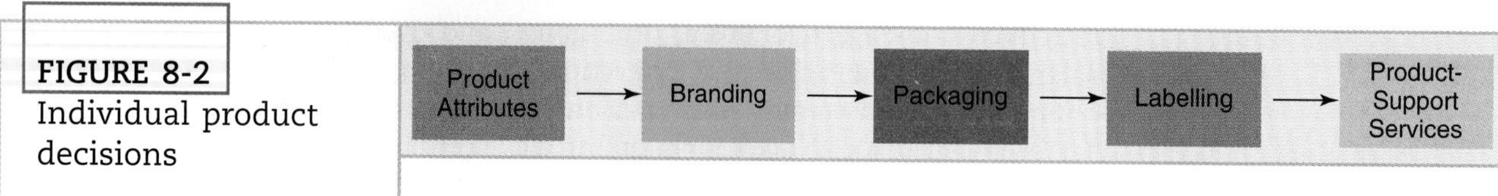

ment. Most firms implemented total quality management (TQM) programs, efforts to constantly improve product and process quality in every phase of their operations. Recently, however, the TQM movement has drawn criticism. Too many companies viewed TQM as a magic cure-all and created token total quality programs that applied quality principles only superficially. Today, companies are taking a "return on quality" approach, viewing quality as an investment and ensuring that quality improvements are tied to bottom-line results.[6]

Beyond reducing product defects, the ultimate goal of total quality is to improve customer value. For example, when Motorola first began its TQM program in the early 1980s, its goal was to greatly reduce manufacturing defects. Later, however, Motorola's quality concept evolved into one of customer-defined quality and total customer satisfaction. "Quality," noted Motorola's vice-president of quality, "has to do something for the customer. . . . Our definition of a defect is 'if the customer doesn't like it, it's a defect.'" Similarly, Siemans defines quality this way: "Quality is when our customers come back and our products don't."[7] As more companies have moved toward such customer-driven definitions of quality, their TQM programs are evolving into customer satisfaction and customer retention programs.

Thus, many companies today have turned customer-driven quality into a potent strategic weapon. They create customer satisfaction and value by consistently and profitably meeting customers' needs and preferences for quality. In fact, quality has now become a competitive necessity—in the twenty-first century, only companies with the best quality will thrive.

Product Features

A product can be offered with varying features. A "stripped-down" model, one without any extras, is the starting point. The company can create higher-level models by adding more features. Features are a competitive tool for differentiating the company's product from competitors' products. Being the first producer to introduce a needed and valued new feature is one of the most effective ways to compete.

How can a company identify new features and decide which ones to add to its product? The company should periodically survey buyers who have used the product and ask these questions: How do you like the product? Which specific features of the product do you like most? Which features could we add to improve the product? The answers provide the company with a rich list of feature ideas. The company can then assess each feature's *value* to customers versus its *cost* to the company. Features that customers value little in relation to costs should be dropped; those that customers value highly in relation to costs should be added.

Product Style and Design

Product design
The process of designing a product's style and function: creating a product that is attractive; easy, safe, and inexpensive to use and service; and simple and economical to produce and distribute.

Another way to add customer value is through distinctive **product design.** Some companies have reputations for outstanding design, such as Black & Decker in cordless appliances and tools, Steelcase in office furniture and systems, Bose in audio equipment, and Ciba Corning in medical equipment. Design can be one of the most powerful competitive weapons in a company's marketing arsenal.[8]

Design is a larger concept than style. *Style* simply describes the appearance of a product. Styles can be eye-catching or yawn-inspiring. A sensational style may grab attention, but it does not necessarily make the product *perform* better. Unlike style, *design* is more than skin deep—it goes to the very heart of a product. Good design contributes to a product's usefulness as well as to its looks.

Good style and design can attract attention, improve product performance, cut production costs, and give the product a strong competitive advantage in the target market. For example, consider Apple's iMac personal computer:

> Who said that computers have to be beige and boxy? Apple's iMac is anything but. The iMac features a sleek, egg-shaped monitor and hard drive, all in one unit, in a futuristic translucent turquoise casing. There's no clunky tower or desktop hard drive to clutter up your office area. There's also no floppy drive—with more and more software being distributed via CDs or the Internet, Apple thinks the floppy is on the verge of extinction. Featuring one-button Internet access, this is a machine designed specifically for cruising the Internet (that's what the "i" in "iMac" stands for). The dramatic iMac won raves for design and lured buyers in droves. Only one month after the iMac hit the stores in the summer of 1998, it was the number-two best-selling computer. By mid-1999, it had sold more than a million units, marking Apple's re-emergence as a legitimate contender in the personal computer industry.[9]

Branding

Brand
A name, term, sign, symbol, or design, or a combination of these, intended to identify the goods or services of one seller or group of sellers and to differentiate them from those of competitors.

Perhaps the most distinctive skill of professional marketers is their ability to create, maintain, protect, and enhance brands for their products and services. A **brand** is a name, term, sign, symbol, or design, or a combination of these, that identifies the maker or seller of a product or service. Canada's *Report on Business* magazine conducted an international poll in 2000 to determine what were the greatest logos of all time. Want to guess the winners? The Michelin Man took the number one spot, and the London underground logo followed as number two. In third place was a non-profit logo, the Red Cross. The Nike swoosh, a symbol designed to convey speed and movement, grabbed fourth place while the Volkswagen logo, the icon for the "people's car," drove into fifth spot. Canadian brand logos were among the top 50. The Esso logo was given 28th place and CN's logo took 38th spot.[10]

Consumers view a brand as an important part of a product: It gives products and services a personality that consumers can relate to and can add value to a product. For example, most consumers would perceive a bottle of White Diamonds perfume as a high-quality, expensive product. But the same perfume in an unmarked bottle would likely be viewed as lower in quality, even if the fragrance were identical.

Branding has become so important that today hardly anything goes unbranded. Salt is packaged in branded containers; automobile parts—spark plugs, tires, filters—bear brand names; and even fruits and vegetables are branded—Sunkist oranges, Dole pineapples, and Chiquita bananas.

Nowhere is the battle of the brands heating up more than on the Internet. Bell Canada–backed Sympatico-Lycos, Microsoft-funded MSN.ca, and Yahoo.ca are each spending heavily to build their brands. Microsoft is dropping millions dur-

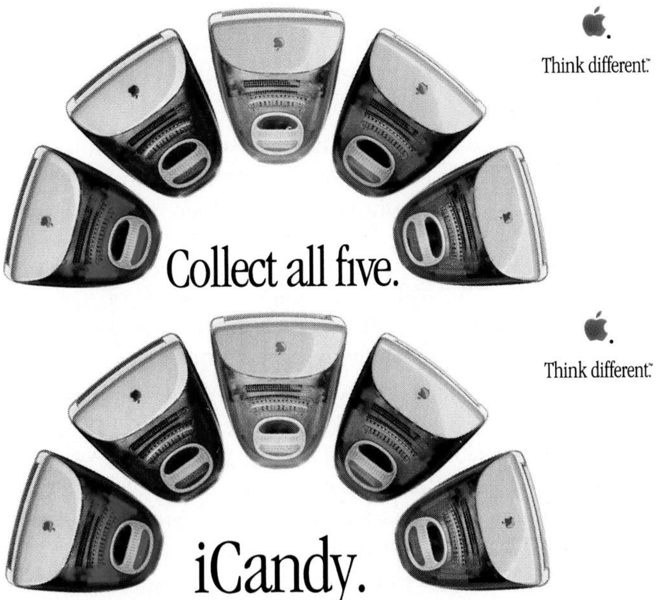

Apple Canada discovered that breakthrough design can revolutionize a market and attract buyers in droves.

ing its "Make It Your Home" campaign designed to build the brand and highlight MSN.ca's Internet services and content. Yahoo is working to build its personality as being "fun and interactive." Rogers Communications's Excite Canada is using its "Driven to Shop" contest to increase brand awareness and attract new users. AOL Canada's goal is to make itself one of the "top 10 consumer brands" in Canada, says CEO Stephen Bartkiw; while its parent, America Online commands one of the top spots in American consumers' minds, it is hardly a blip in Canadian surfers' screens. Branding efforts aren't restricted to business-to-consumer (B2C) online companies, however. The business-to-business (B2B) sector is also branding heavily. Firms that offer their clients software and custom solutions to solve their e-commerce problems and manage their supply chains, such as Ariba, Commerce One, and Broadvision, are also working to give their brands a makeover. As one Toronto-based consultant noted, "New Economy brands seem to be rewarded for agile repositioning and reinvented [brand] imagery."[11]

Branding helps buyers in many ways. Brand names help consumers identify products that might benefit them. Brands also tell the buyer something about product quality. Buyers who always buy the same brand know that they will get the same features, benefits, and quality each time they buy. Branding also gives the seller several advantages. The brand name becomes the basis on which a whole story can be built about a product's special qualities. The seller's brand name and trademark provide legal protection for unique product features that otherwise might be copied by competitors. And branding helps the seller to segment markets. For example, General Mills can offer Cheerios, Wheaties, Total, Lucky Charms, and many other cereal brands, not just one general product for all consumers.

A brand is a seller's promise to consistently deliver a specific set of features, benefits, and services to buyers. The best brands convey a warranty of quality. According to one marketing executive, a brand can deliver up to four levels of meaning:

- *Attributes.* A brand first brings to mind certain product attributes. For example, the Mercedes brand suggests such attributes as "well engineered," "well built," "durable," "high prestige," "fast," "expensive," and "high resale value."
- *Benefits.* Customers do not buy attributes; they buy benefits. Therefore, attributes must be translated into functional and emotional benefits. Michelin's famous slogan, "You've got a lot riding on your tires," along with its famous baby-centred advertising, gave parents peace of mind and made them feel as if they were the parents of the year by just buying a tire. It is not surprising that the Michelin Man won the *Report on Business* contest in 2000 as the world's best-known logo, given the power of this brand.[12]
- *Values.* A brand also says something about the buyer's values. CP, for example, assures its business customers that it "loves stuff" just as much as its clients love their possessions, and therefore, takes the same care of the goods it transports as the owner would.
- *Personality.* A brand also projects a personality. Motivation researchers sometimes ask, "If this brand were a person, what kind of person would it be?" The brand will attract people whose actual or desired self-images match the brand's image.

Brand Equity

Brand equity
The value of a brand, based on its brand loyalty, name awareness, perceived quality, strong brand associations, and other assets such as patents, trademarks, and channel relationships.

Brands vary in the amount of power and value they have in the marketplace. A powerful brand has high **brand equity,** a function of high brand loyalty, name awareness, perceived quality, strong brand associations, and other assets such as patents, trademarks, and channel relationships.

A brand with strong brand equity is a valuable asset. Measuring the actual equity of a brand name is difficult. However, according to one estimate, the brand equity of Coca-Cola is $126 billion, Microsoft is $85 billion, and IBM is $66 billion.[13] The world's top brands include Harlequin, Campbell, Sony, Mercedes-Benz, and McDonald's (see Marketing Highlight 8-2).

Moving the stuff you love

At Canadian Pacific Railway we love stuff too. This year we'll carry 217,929 remote-controlled toys, 902,947 alkaline batteries, 900,000 cases of paper cups, 13,182,000 kilos of ice cream, 46,358 packages of carpet stain remover, and 97,000 pairs of earplugs.

All as if they were ours.

CANADIAN PACIFIC RAILWAY

www.cpr.ca

Canadian Pacific Railway uses an intergrated advertising program consisting of outdoor, print and television to communicate the relevance of the CPR in the lives of Canadians.

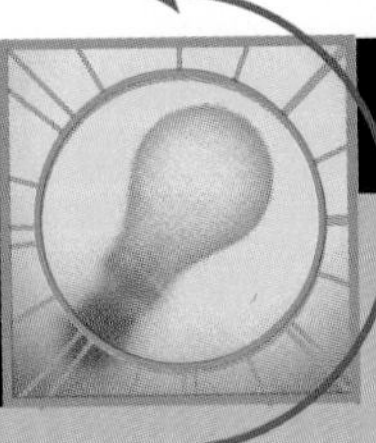

marketing highlight 8-2

Harlequin: One of the World's Most Powerful Brand Names

If you were asked to name the world's most powerful brand names, Coca-Cola, Toyota, McDonald's, Sony, Disney, Kodak, or BMW would probably spring to mind. But it may surprise you to learn that one of the leading world brands is a home-grown Canadian product—Harlequin romance novels. With annual revenues in excess of $470 million, Harlequin contributes over 45 percent of the operating revenues of its parent, Torstar Corp., publisher of the *Toronto Star,* and it remains phenomenally profitable. It makes 15 percent on every book it sells (three to four times the industry average), and it sells about 180 million books a year worldwide.

The firm had humble beginnings. Founded in Winnipeg in 1949 by Richard Bonnycastle, Harlequin began by reprinting books sold in the United Kingdom or the United States. Harlequin's advance is another story of a woman being the power behind the throne. Bonnycastle's wife, Mary, first noticed how popular romances were with readers, and she suggested that the firm specialize in the genre. This, combined with another marketing insight, led to much of Harlequin's success. Rather than distributing its products in bookstores, Harlequin placed them where women shopped, in supermarkets and drugstores. The rest is history. The firm enjoyed growth rates in excess of 25 percent throughout the 1970s. However, many analysts thought that the women's movement of the 1980s would spell disaster for the company. How wrong they were! Harlequin has been labelled a company with products written for women, by women.

While many people have made fun of the romance genre, Harlequin attributes much of its success to having a high-quality marketing program. Quality begins with the product. The product, its books, are much higher quality than most literary critics care to admit, Harlequin believes. They are written according to well-researched, carefully designed plot lines by over 1500 authors. Product quality is followed up with superb production capabilities and topped off by top-notch advertising.

Harlequin conducts meticulous market research to understand the demographics and attitudes of the market. Its North American readers are mainly women whose average age is 39. They are well educated, with over half having some university education. They are employed and have household incomes of about $35 000. Story setting is important to them. While Texas is the most popular location for romance, readers do not like stories set in Washington, DC or other circus venues. Most of all, readers want happy endings. High-quality research has enabled Harlequin to target the segment of heavy users. While most Canadians buy only six books a year, Harlequin's romance readers spend $30 a month on books.

You might not consider packaging to be an important aspect of marketing when it comes to selling paperbacks, but it is another of Harlequin's secrets of success. In Harlequin's case, the package is the book's cover. Careful research is again conducted to help Harlequin's 100 to 125-plus illustrators create the right cover to attract readers who may be searching through stores that carry hundreds of titles.

Another key to Harlequin's success is high repeat sales rates. This is where strong brand equity helps. Readers know what to expect from Harlequin. This consumer confidence has made acceptance of the 72 new titles Harlequin introduces every month almost a certainty. Brand equity also lowers Harlequin's costs of advertising and promotion since its loyal readers are highly familiar with the brand and all that it stands for.

Harlequin's success is not confined to the North American market. It sells books in over 100 markets in 23 languages. It keeps costs low by following its standardized marketing strategy. Harlequin also attributes its success to formulating alliances with overseas partners that help the firm establish a distribution system, gain access to the television and print media essential to build demand, and handle the repatriation of book royalties (that is, ensure that Harlequin receives the profits generated by overseas book sales).

In its continual quest to find new ways to serve the romance novel reader, Harlequin Enterprises was one of the first

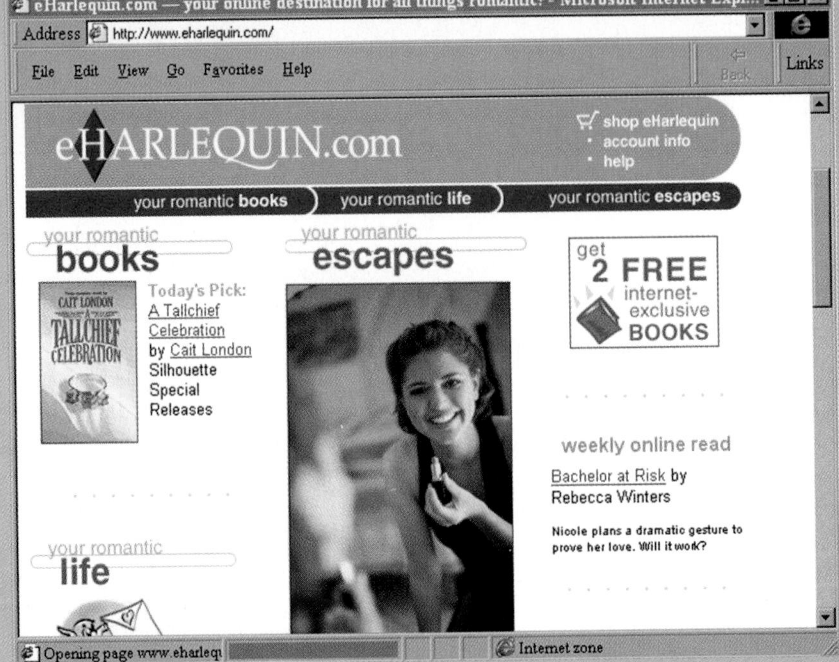

Harlequin uses its strong brand equity to effectively market its products on the Web.

movers when it came to marketing online. It launched www.romance.net in 1996. In 2000, the firm launched eHarlequin.com, a site whose mission is to provide "romance lovers with a safe and engaging place to escape the day-to-day pressures of a busy lifestyle. On the site, visitors can interact with like-minded romance readers in addition to purchasing romance novels with ease and comfort." Not an organization to avoid hyperbole, eHarlequin calls itself "the *ultimate* destination for romantic escape on the Internet."

So the next time you think about powerful brands, think about Harlequin, a firm that has found success through branding and superior product management in an industry plagued by high failure rates.

Sources: Kevin Brown, "The top 200 mega-brands," *Advertising Age*, 2 May 1994:33; Gina Mallet, "The greatest romance on earth," *Canadian Business,* August 1993:19–23. See also Paul Grescoe, *The Merchants of Venus*, Raincoast Books, 1997; www.romance.net.

High brand equity provides a company with many competitive advantages. A powerful brand enjoys a high level of consumer brand awareness and loyalty. Because consumers expect stores to carry the brand, the company has more leverage in bargaining with resellers. Because the brand name carries high credibility, the company can more easily launch line and brand extensions; thus, Coca-Cola leveraged its well-known brand to introduce Diet Coke and Procter & Gamble introduced Ivory dishwashing detergent. Above all, a powerful brand offers the company some defence against fierce price competition.

Some analysts view brands as *the* major enduring asset of a company, outlasting the company's specific products and facilities. Yet every powerful brand really represents a set of loyal customers. Therefore, the fundamental asset underlying brand equity is *customer equity*. This suggests that the proper focus of marketing planning is that of extending loyal *customer lifetime value*, with brand management serving as a major marketing tool.

Branding poses challenging decisions to the marketer. Figure 8-3 shows the key branding decisions.

Brand Name Selection

A good name can add greatly to a product's success. However, finding the best brand name is a difficult task. It begins with a careful review of the product and its benefits, the target market, and proposed marketing strategies. What are desirable qualities for a brand name?

- It should suggest something about the product's benefits and qualities. Examples: Beautyrest, Craftsman, Sunkist, Spic and Span, Snuggles.
- It should be easy to pronounce, recognize, and remember. Short names help. Examples: Tide, Aim, Puffs. But longer ones are sometimes effective. Examples: "Love My Carpet" carpet cleaner, "I Can't Believe It's Not Butter" margarine, President's Choice "Too Good To Be True" products.
- It should be distinctive. Examples: Taurus, Kodak, Esso.
- It should translate easily into foreign languages. Before spending $100 million to change its name to Exxon, Standard Oil of New Jersey tested the name in 54 languages in more than 150 foreign markets. It found that another choice—Enco—referred to a stalled engine when pronounced in Japanese.

FIGURE 8-3 Major branding decisions

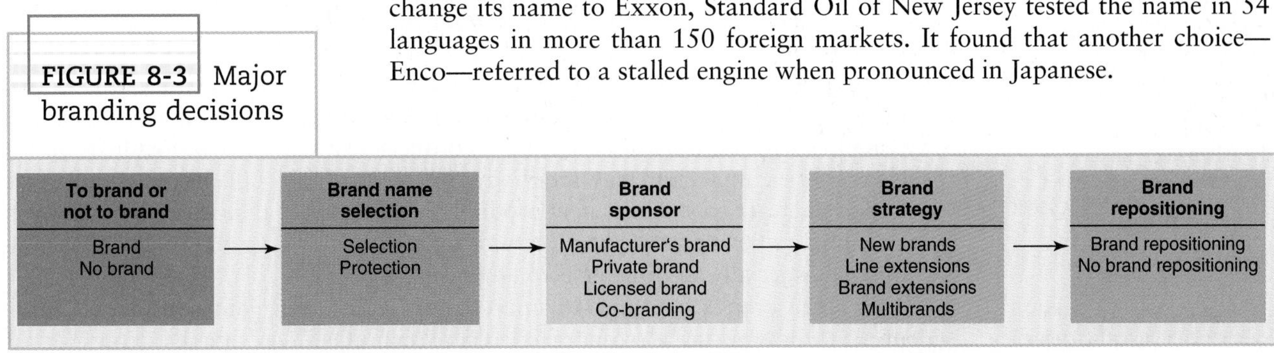

YOU CAN'T RUN FROM YOUR PROBLEMS.
YOU CAN, HOWEVER, CLIMB FROM THEM.

The best way to deal with life's problems is to, well, deal with them. We just think you should do it someplace incredible. Outward Bound is an exhilarating wilderness journey of self-discovery. A journey that provides you with challenges, skills training, and adventure that can help you deal with whatever life can throw at you. You'll spend your days hiking, climbing or canoeing, and your evenings reflecting and getting reacquainted with someone truly special. You. We provide all the equipment. All you need is an open mind. Because we believe that when you're 300 feet off the ground, chances are, your problems are going to look really small.
Call 1 800 268-7329 for a copy of our course brochure.

Service-dominated organizations, such as Outward Bound, also have to build brand recognition to market their products.

- It should be capable of registration and legal protection. A brand name cannot be registered if it infringes on existing brand names. Also, brand names that are merely descriptive or suggestive may be unprotectable. For example, Labatt registered the name Ice for its new beer and invested millions in establishing the name with consumers. But the courts later ruled that the term Ice is generic and that Labatt could not use the Ice name exclusively.

Once chosen, the brand name must be protected. Many firms try to build a brand name that will eventually become identified with the product category. Brand names such as Frigidaire, Kleenex, Levi's, Jell-O, Scotch Tape, Formica, and Fiberglas have succeeded in this way. However, their very success may threaten the company's rights to the name. Many originally protected brand names, including cellophane, aspirin, nylon, kerosene, linoleum, yo-yo, trampoline, escalator, thermos, and shredded wheat, are now names that any seller can use.

Brand Sponsor

A manufacturer has four sponsorship options. The product may be launched as a **manufacturer's brand** (or **national brand**): Kellogg and IBM, for example, sell their output under their own brand names. Or the manufacturer may sell to resellers who give it a **private brand** (also called **store brand** or **distributor brand**). Although most manufacturers create their own brands, others market *licensed brands*. Finally, two companies can *co-brand* a product, such as General Mills and Hershey Foods combining brands to create Reese's Peanut Butter Puffs cereal.

Manufacturers' Brands versus Private Brands. Manufacturers' brands have long dominated the retail scene. However, an increasing number of department and discount stores, supermarkets, gas stations, clothiers, drugstores, and appliance dealers have their own brands. For example, Sears created several names—Kenmore appliances, Diehard batteries, Craftsman tools, Weatherbeater paints—that buyers look for and demand. Canadian Tire's private-label tires are as well known as the manufacturers' brands of Goodyear and Bridgestone. Wal-Mart introduced its price-driven Great Value brand, which may eventually include more than 1000 items across most major food categories.[14]

Although private brands are often hard to establish, they can yield higher profit margins for the intermediary. They also give intermediaries exclusive products that cannot be bought from competitors, resulting in greater store traffic and loyalty.

The competition between manufacturers' and private brands is called the *battle of the brands*. In this battle, retailers have many advantages. They control what products they stock, where they go on the shelf, and which ones they will feature in local circulars. They charge manufacturers **slotting fees**—payments demanded by retailers before they will accept new products and find "slots" for them on the shelves. For example, Safeway required a payment of $25 000 from a small pizza roll manufacturer to stock its new product. Retailers price their store brands lower than comparable manufacturers' brands, thereby appealing to budget-conscious shoppers, especially in difficult economic times.

As store brands continue to improve in quality and gain consumers' confidence, they are posing a strong challenge to manufacturers' brands. Consider the

Manufacturer's brand (national brand)
A brand created and owned by the producer of a product or service.

Private brand (distributor or store brand)
A brand created and owned by a reseller of a product or service.

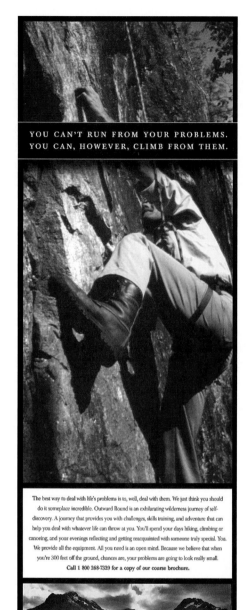

Slotting fees
Payments demanded by retailers from producers before they will accept new products and find "slots" for them on the shelves.

case of Loblaws. Its private-label brands, President's Choice and No Name, account for about one-third of all weekly spending by the company's estimated 12 million customers. Its President's Choice Decadent Chocolate Chip Cookies are now the leading cookie brand in Canada. Loblaws' President's Choice cola racks up 50 percent of Loblaws' canned cola sales. Based on this success, the private-label powerhouse has expanded into a wide range of food categories. It now offers more than 2500 items under the President's Choice label, ranging from cookies, paper, and frozen desserts to prepared foods and boxed meats. In a partnership with CIBC, Loblaws extended its brand into financial services under the brand name President's Choice Financial. The President's Choice brand has become so popular that Loblaws now licenses it to retailers across the United States and eight other countries where Loblaws has no stores of its own. Here Decadent Chocolate Chip Cookies have won out again and are beating out Nabisco's Chips Ahoy brand in many markets.[15]

Food retailing is very concentrated in Canada. The big five retailers control more than 80 percent of sales. Thus, it is not surprising that store brands represent a powerful force in this country. Many store brands are high quality and command a significant share in their product category.

Every Canadian household buys at least some store brands. One study revealed that the average Canadian consumer buys 4.6 store-branded products on each shopping trip. Some store brands appeal to value-conscious consumers who note that these brands cost 10 to 40 percent less than nationally branded products.[16]

The market share for private brands is expected to grow as more retailers launch and extend their lines of store brands. IGA and Food City, members of the Oshawa Group Ltd., launched 125 products under their store brand name, Our Compliments. Dominion uses the name Master Choice to identify its high-end store brands, while Safeway Canada uses Stonehenge Farms to denote its store brands. Even regional retailers have entered the fray. Selection Zel is used by Provigo of Quebec and Sobeys Select is used by the Nova Scotia–based retailer. Zellers, motivated by the success that supermarkets have enjoyed with private-label food and paper products, launched its own private-label line of health and beauty aids, household cleaning products, and fashion items under such names as Truly Beauty, Truly Clean, and Truly Casual. The retailer hopes the line of Truly products will generate $200 million in sales a year. Zellers is using its Canadian heritage as the foundation for its brand-building efforts.[17]

In US supermarkets, private-label products account for 20 percent of US supermarket sales. Private labels are even more prominent in Europe, accounting for as much as 36 percent of supermarket sales in Britain and 24 percent in France. French retail giant Carrefour sells more than 3000 in-house brands, ranging from cooking oil to car batteries.[18] Some marketing analysts predict that private brands eventually will knock out all but the strongest manufacturers' brands.

We cannot assume, however, that national brands are doomed. Take the case of the "cola wars," in which Coke and Pepsi made a significant counter-attack against the private-label upstart Cott. To fend off private brands, leading brand marketers have to invest in R&D to bring out new brands, new features, and continuous quality improvements. They must design strong advertising programs to maintain high awareness and preference. And they must find ways to "partner" with major distributors in a search for distribution economies and improved joint performance.

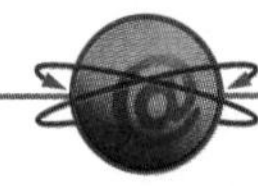

Jones Soda Co.
www.jonessoda.com/

A recent trend in branding is the move toward the creation of personal brands.[19] While personal brands have been around for some time—consider personalized licence plates, for example—people are increasingly able to create brands uniquely their own. Canada Post is offering a service allowing people to put a photo of their choice on postage stamps. Vancouver-based Urban Juice and Soda Company, bottlers of Jones Soda, has a program on its Web site to allow consumers to have the

Loblaws President's Choice store brands are so powerful that they not only dominate some categories, they are also sold under licence in nine other countries, including the US, where Loblaws has no stores.

labels of their soda customized with photos of their choice. People can even have cosmetics and personal hygiene products custom made and packaged by going to the Reflect.com site.

Licensing. Most manufacturers take years and spend millions to create their own brand names. However, some companies license names or symbols created by other manufacturers, names of well-known celebrities, and characters from popular movies and books. For a fee, any of these can provide an instant and proven brand name. Apparel and accessories sellers pay large royalties to adorn their products—from blouses to ties, and linens to luggage—with the names or initials of such fashion innovators as Alfred Sung, Calvin Klein, Pierre Cardin, Gucci, and Halston. Sellers of children's products attach an almost endless list of character names to clothing, toys, school supplies, linens, dolls, lunch boxes, cereals, and other items. The character names range from such classics as Disney, Peanuts, Winnie the Pooh, Muppets, Scooby Doo, and Dr. Seuss characters to the more recent Teletubbies, Pokemon, Powerpuff Girls, Rugrats, and Blue's Clues characters. Almost half of all retail toy sales come from products based on television shows and movies such as *The Rugrats, The Grinch,* or *Star Wars.*

Name and character licensing has grown rapidly in recent years. Annual retail sales of licensed products in the United States and Canada grew from $6 billion in 1977 to $82 billion in 1987 and more than $107 billion today. The fastest-growing licensing category is corporate brand licensing, as more for-profit and non-profit organizations license their names to generate additional revenues and brand recognition (see Marketing Highlight 8-3). Even the Vatican engages in licensing: Heavenly images from its art collection, architecture, frescoes, and manuscripts are now imprinted on such earthly objects as T-shirts, ties, glassware, candles, and ornaments.

Many companies have mastered the art of peddling their established brands and characters. For example, through savvy marketing, Warner Brothers has turned Bugs Bunny, Daffy Duck, and its more than 100 other Looney Tunes characters into the

marketing highlight 8-3

From Harley-Davidson Armchairs to Coca-Cola Fishing Lures: The Rise of Corporate Branding

When BMW bought the Rolls-Royce name—nothing else, just the name—for $90 million, it confirmed what savvy investors have always known: A strong brand name is one of the most valuable assets a company has. Now companies are realizing that they shouldn't confine such assets to their showrooms, stationery, business cards, or the company's core product. A growing number of companies from the Fortune 500 to the non-profit sector are licensing their names to generate additional brand recognition and revenues. That's why we're suddenly seeing products like Pillsbury Doughboy potholders, Coca-Cola Picnic Barbie, Crayola house paints, Jeep bicycles, Royal Doulton perfume, and Harley-Davidson armchairs and baby clothes.

In 1999, retail sales of all licensed products totalled more than $200 billion worldwide. Corporate brand licensing, the fastest-growing category, claimed 22 percent of that total, the same amount earned from entertainment property licensing. One of the most sought-after properties is the Olympic symbol, one of the world's most recognized brands. Since it has international reach, and touches everyone—young and old, male and female—many corporations wanted to associate themselves with the 2000 Sydney games. However, the Canadian Olympics Association is very careful when selecting companies to be associated with the brand. Kim Smither, managing director of Toronto-based International Licensing & Marketing, the exclusive marketing agency for the Canadian Olympic Association, notes, "We have to make sure that the companies who do associate with it are in keeping with the brand—that they are what we would consider top-of-class, just as the Olympics is. . . . We choose particular licensees not just because they can produce certain products, but because of the type of brand they have. Take Roots, for example—it's a very high-end brand, and they do a wonderful job with us."

When it comes to corporate brand licensing, few companies can equal Coca-Cola, whose extraordinary success has inspired hundreds of companies to follow suit. Yet few people know that Coca-Cola's entry into licensing was purely defensive. In the early 1980s, lawyers advised the company that if it didn't enter the Coca-Cola T-shirt market, others legally could. Coca-Cola responded by setting up a licensing program, which started modestly but now consists of a large department overseeing some 320 licensees in 57 countries producing more than 10 000 products, ranging from baby clothes and boxer shorts to earrings, a Coca-Cola Barbie doll, and even a fishing lure shaped like a tiny Coke can. Last year alone, licensees sold 50 million licensed Coca-Cola products.

Although most companies have long sold promotional merchandise bearing their names and logos to dealers and distributors, there is a real shift to full-scale retail merchandising. And companies are making this shift both to capitalize on brand awareness in current markets and to extend their brands into new markets. For example, Caterpillar and John Deere, both companies with narrow markets, are now licensing a wide range of products aimed at generating additional sales among those already hooked on their brands. Visitors to the online John Deere Mall (mall.deere.com) discover an array of licensed products that includes everything from logo hats, shirts, jackets, mugs, and watches to John Deere versions of Canon calculators, Victorinox penknives, Mini Mag-Lite flashlights, and hand-rubbed rosewood pens.

Sometimes companies get into licensing as a way to extend the brand to a new target market. Although a Harley-Davidson armchair seems like an unlikely product, it's the motorcycle company's way of reaching out to women, who make up only nine percent of its market. Harley also licenses toys, including a Barbie dressed in a "very feminine outfit" to appeal to future generations of Harley purchasers. The ultimate goal is to sell more bikes to buyers who are not part of the core market.

At the same time that corporate brand licensing lets companies reap some of the value they've built up in their brands, it also provides an additional tool for building even more brand value. For example, Unilever has invested heavily in advertising to create positioning and personality for its Snuggle fabric softener brand and for the cute little Snuggle Bear that appears on the label. Now, licensing the Snuggle Bear for use on other carefully selected products, says a Unilever brand manager, "will be another way to . . . help Snuggle leave lasting impressions long after our 30-second commercial is over."

What's in corporate licensing for the licensees, the manufacturers who pay large sums for the right to use corporate brand names or trademarks on their products? Compared to celebrity and entertainment names, corporate brands are much less risky. For example, what happens to a product brandishing a sports celebrity's name when that celebrity is busted for drugs? Or what can a manufacturer do with all its Godzilla backpacks after the *Godzilla* movie flops (as it did)? Corporate brands are much safer bets. Many have been around for decades and have a proven, surprisingly strong appeal for customers. There are powerful forces behind the impulse to buy a Coke beach

Coca-Cola partners with some 320 licensees to produce over 10 000 products ranging from Coca-Cola Barbie to fashion apparel.

towel, a Good Humor die-cast truck, Harley-Davidson boots, or Doulton perfume. Says Seth Siegel, co-chairman of the Beanstalk Group, which manages licensing for Coca-Cola and Harley-Davidson, "We live in a . . . society [where] people still love to surround themselves with icons that move them."

Sources: Quotes and other information from "Let the Games begin: Olympics applies stringent sponsorship guidelines to safeguard its brand," *Strategy,* 17 July 2000:20; Constance L. Hays, "Licensing of names adds to image and profit," *New York Times,* 12 June 1998:D1; Carl Quintanilla, "Advertising: Caterpillar, Deere break ground in consumer-product territory," *Wall Street Journal,* 20 June 1996:B2; Robert Oas, "Licensed merchandise sales decrease, but corporate merchandise is on the rise," *Potentials,* April 1999:8; Laura Petrecca, "'Corporate brands' put licensing in the spotlight," *Advertising Age,* 14 June 1999:1; and "Licensing industry sets trends for the future at L!CENSING 99," International, *International Licensing Industry Merchandisers' Association,* press release, accessed online at www.licensing.org, 8 June 1999.

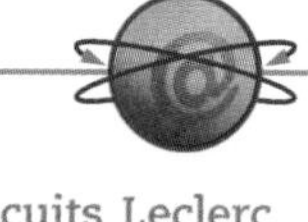

Biscuits Leclerc
www.leclerc.ca/

world's favourite cartoon brands. The Looney Tunes licence, arguably the most sought-after non-sports licence in the industry, generates $6 billion in annual retail sales. Warner Brothers has yet to tap the full potential of many of its secondary characters. The Tasmanian Devil, for example, initially appeared in only five cartoons. But through cross-licensing agreements with such organizations as Harley-Davidson and the NFL, Taz has become something of a pop icon. In a real marketing coup, Quebec City–based Biscuits Leclerc licensed the whirling cartoon dervish for its Le P'tit Bonjour (Sweet Mornings) cereal. Biscuits Leclerc, an independent packaged goods manufacturer largely unknown outside of the Quebec market, knew from the outset that if Le P'tit Bonjour were to stand any chance against the powerhouse brands of Kellogg, General Mills, or Post, it needed instant notoriety and it was the Taz who accomplished this task. While a number of private-label cereal brands have appeared on supermarket shelves in recent years, Biscuits Leclerc is the first independent Canadian manufacturer to launch a brand of its own into this country's $862 million breakfast cereal market since 1934, when Canadian consumers were introduced to Weetabix.[20]

Co-branding
The practice of using the established brand names of two different companies on the same product.

Co-Branding. Although companies have been **co-branding** products for many years, there has been a recent resurgence in co-branded products. Co-branding is the practice of using two established brand names of different companies on the same product. In most co-branding situations, one company licenses another company's well-known brand to use with its own. At other times, companies co-brand to share the costs of advertising or increase the credibility of a service. For example, in its advertising IBM Canada features companies and organizations it has helped become e-businesses. Canada Post runs an ad that features Intrawest's CEO to reinforce its claims about the power of using direct marketing (see page 516). Co-branding has also become an important tool as Internet marketers work to increase the credibility of their sites. Many online marketers partner with such well-known brands as Visa, MasterCard and E-Trust to give on-line consumers a greater sense of trust in their offerings.[21]

Co-branding offers many advantages. Because each brand dominates in a different category, the combined brands create broader consumer appeal and greater brand equity. Co-branding also allows companies to enter new markets with minimal risk or investment. For example, by licensing its Healthy Choice brand to Kellogg, ConAgra entered the breakfast segment with a solid product that was backed by Kellogg's substantial marketing support. In return, Kellogg could leverage the brand awareness of the Healthy Choice name in cereal.

Co-branding also has its limitations. Such relationships usually involve complex legal contracts and licences. Co-branding partners must carefully coordinate their advertising, sales promotion, and other marketing efforts. Finally, when co-branding, each partner must trust the other will take good care of its brand. As one Nabisco manager puts it, "Giving away your brand is a lot like giving away your child—you want to make sure everything is perfect."[22]

FIGURE 8-4 Four brand strategies

		Product Category: Existing	Product Category: New
Brand Name	Existing	Line extension	Brand extension
	New	Multibrands	New brands

Brand Strategy

A company has four choices of brand strategy (see Figure 8-4). It can introduce *line extensions*—existing brand names extended to new forms, sizes, and flavours of an existing product category; *brand extensions*—existing brand names extended to new product categories; *multibrands*—new brand names introduced in the same product category; or *new brands*—new brand names in new product categories.

Line extension
Using a successful brand name to introduce additional items in a given product category under the same brand name, such as new flavours, forms, colours, added ingredients, or package sizes.

Line Extensions. A **line extension** is an introduction of an additional item in a given product category under the same brand name, such as a new flavour, form, colour, ingredient, or package size. Dannon recently introduced several line extensions, including seven new yogurt flavours. The vast majority of new product activity consists of line extensions.

A company might introduce line extensions as a low-cost, low-risk way to introduce new products to meet consumer desires for variety, to use excess capacity, or simply to command more shelf space from resellers. Line extensions involve some risks, however. An overextended brand name can lose its specific meaning or its unique selling proposition. As brand names are extended, they may be associated with products that do not possess the core qualities of the original branded offering. Line extensions will not sell enough to cover their development listing and promotion costs. Or, even when they sell enough, the sales may come at the expense of other items in the line. A line extension works best when it takes sales away from competing brands, not when it "cannibalizes" the company's other items.[23]

Brand extension
Using a successful brand name to launch a new or modified product in a new category.

Brand Extensions. A **brand extension** involves the use of a successful brand name to launch new or modified products in a new category. Fruit of the Loom launched new lines of socks, men's fashion underwear, women's underwear, and athletic apparel. Swiss Army Brand Sunglasses, Disney Cruise Lines, and Snackwell's Snackbar are all brand extensions.

There are many advantages to a brand extension strategy. A brand extension

Too many line extensions can confuse or frustrate consumers. A shopper at the local supermarket may be confronted by 30 different brands, flavours, and sizes of oat cereal alone.

gives a new product instant recognition and faster acceptance. It also saves the high advertising costs usually required to build a new brand name. At the same time, a brand extension strategy involves some risk. Such brand extensions as Bic pantyhose, Heinz pet food, LifeSavers gum, and Clorox laundry detergent met early deaths. The extension may dilute the image of the main brand. In June 2000, Canadian business press headlines proclaimed, "The beaver has landed!" in recognition of one of the most unusual brand extensions ever announced. Fashion icon Roots Canada announced that it was going to partner with Skyservice Airlines to launch Roots Air, a new airline aimed at the business traveller. Using spokesperson Dan Aykroyd, the new venture created quite a stir. While many forecast that the venture would experience a rapid descent, others believed that Roots was making a savvy move and would appeal to younger business travellers who wanted a more fun and hip way to fly.[24]

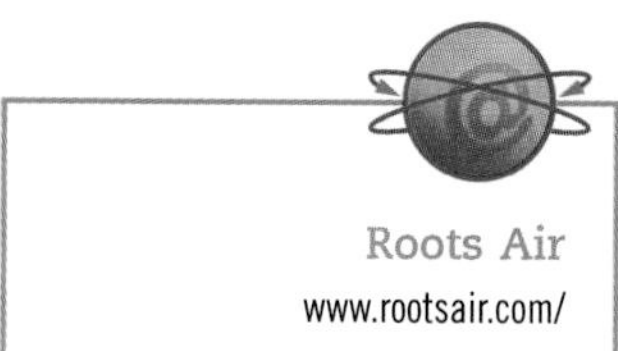

Roots Air
www.rootsair.com/

If a brand extension fails, it may harm consumer attitudes toward the other products carrying the same brand name. Further, a brand name may not be appropriate to a particular new product, even if it is well made and satisfying—would you consider buying Texaco milk or Alpo chili? And a brand name may lose its special positioning in the consumer's mind through overuse. Companies that are tempted to transfer a brand name must research how well the brand's associations fit the new product.[25]

Multibranding
A strategy under which a seller develops two or more brands in the same product category.

Multibrands. Companies often introduce additional brands in the same category. **Multibranding** offers a way to establish different features and appeal to different buying motives. Thus, Procter & Gamble markets 11 brands of laundry detergent. Multibranding also allows a company to lock up more reseller "shelf space." Or the company may want to protect its major brand by setting up *flanker* or *fighter brands*. For example, Seiko uses different brand names for its higher-priced watches (Seiko Lasalle) and lower-priced watches (Pulsar) to protect the flanks of its mainstream Seiko brand. Companies may also develop separate brand names for different regions or countries, perhaps to suit different cultures or languages. For example, P&G dominates the North American laundry detergent market with Tide, which in all its forms captures more than a 40 percent market share. In Europe, however, P&G leads with its Ariel detergent brand, whose annual sales of $2.1 billion make it Europe's number-two packaged-goods brand.

A major drawback of multibranding is that each brand may obtain only a small market share, and none may be very profitable. The company may end up spreading its resources over many brands instead of building a few brands to a highly profitable level. In this case, the company should reduce the number of brands it sells in a given category and set up tighter screening procedures for new brands.

New Brands. A company may create a new brand name when it enters a new product category for which none of the company's current brand names are appropriate. For example, Japan's Matsushita uses separate names for its different families of products: Technics, Panasonic, National, and Quasar. Or, the company may believe that the power of its existing brand name is waning and a new brand name is needed. Finally, the company may obtain new brands in new categories through acquisitions. For example, S.C. Johnson & Son, marketer of Pledge furniture polish, Glade air freshener, Raid insect spray, Edge shaving gel, and many other well-known brands, added several new powerhouse brands through its acquisition of Drackett Company, including Windex, Drano, and Vanish toilet bowl cleaner.

As with multibranding, offering many new brands can result in a company spreading its resources too thin. And in some industries, such as consumer packaged goods, consumers and retailers have become concerned that there are already too many brands with too few differences between them. Thus, Procter & Gamble, Frito-Lay, and other large consumer product marketers are now pursuing *megabrand* strategies—weeding out weaker brands and focusing their marketing

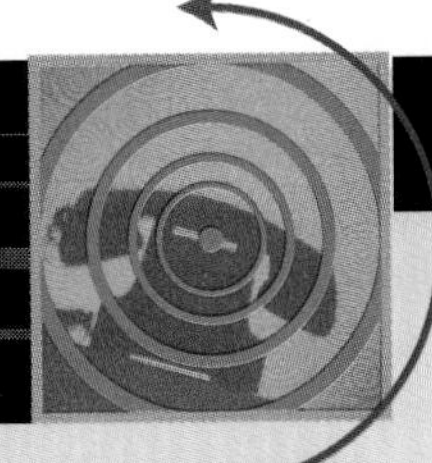

marketers speak out

Anne Lavack, Consumer Evaluation of Brand Extensions and Core Brands

Anne Lavack, a professor and researcher at the University of Winnipeg, is very interested in brand-related issues and has recently been studying brand extensions. She has agreed to share her insights with us . . .

Brand extensions involve the application of an established brand name to new products in order to capitalize on the equity of the original brand name to capture new market segments. The use of the established core brand name on the new brand extension product signals the consumer about some of the qualities or characteristics of that new product. Although brand extensions aid in generating consumer acceptance for a new product by linking the old with the new product, they also risk decreasing or harming the equity that has been built up within the company name or core brand name. An inappropriate brand extension can create damaging associations, which may be very difficult for a company to overcome.

Brand extensions come in two primary forms: horizontal and vertical. A horizontal brand extension involves the application of an existing brand name to a new product introduction, either in a similar product class or in a completely new product category. An example would be Ivory soap introducing brand extensions, such as Ivory detergent or Ivory dishwashing liquid. A vertical extension involves introducing a similar brand in the same product category, but usually at a different price or quality point. For example, vertical brand extensions are a familiar strategy in the automobile market, where a variety of models are introduced at different price and quality levels (e.g., Toyota's Tercel, Corolla, and Camry).

The direction of a vertical brand extension may be characterized as either a step up or a step down from the core brand. An example of a step-up vertical brand extension is Purina O.N.E., an upscale brand extension of Purina's regular cat and dog foods. The Courtyard Inn by Marriott is an example of a step-down extension of the Marriott Hotel chain. Previous research has indicated that introducing a vertical brand extension may have a negative impact on the core brand evaluation. Therefore, distancing techniques are used in an attempt to reduce the dilution of the core brand that occurs when a vertical brand extension is introduced.

Professor Lavack and her colleagues conducted research to explore the effectiveness of these distancing techniques. Results of two experiments made her believe that the introduction of a vertical brand extension has a negative impact on the consumer evaluation of the core brand regardless of whether the new brand extension was a step-up or step-down version. Thus, it isn't surprising that it has become a common practice for car manufacturers who introduce a new upscale automobile to give it a completely new brand name, rather than treat it as an extension of an existing brand. This has certainly been the case in the upscale new car introductions of Acura, Infiniti, and Lexus (from the makers of Honda, Nissan, and Toyota, respectively). New luxury brands are not tainted by the lower quality of the existing brand.

The experimental results also show that distancing techniques are also useful means to reduce the dilution of the core brand image. Putting greater distance between the core brand and the brand extension results in less harm to the core brand. This may imply that the prestige-oriented brands can effectively use distancing to lessen the negative impact on the core brand image. However, greater distancing leads to a significantly less favourable evaluation of the brand extension in the step-down extension.

The results of Lavack's studies suggest that there is a tradeoff in the case of step-down extensions. While greater distancing is beneficial for the core brand, it is detrimental for the step-down brand extension. Thus, the use of distancing should be related to the strategic goals of the company (i.e., whether to focus resources on maintaining the core brand or whether to concentrate on the newly introduced step-down brand extension). If maintaining the core brand image is most important, distancing techniques should be used when introducing a vertical brand extension. However, if the potential for capturing new segments with the step-down brand extension is deemed to be a more profitable strategy in the long run, the step-down extension should be closely tied to the core brand and distancing techniques should not be used.

Anne Lavack.

Sources: Material for this highlight was drawn from Chung K. Kim, Anne M. Lavack, and Margo Smith, *Journal of Business Research,* 47, 2000. Also see Kevin Lane Keller and David A. Aaker, "The Effects of Sequential Introduction of Brand Extensions," *Journal of Marketing Research,* 29 (February 1992):35–50; Mary W. Sullivan (1990), "Measuring Spillovers in Umbrella Branded Products," *Journal of Business,* 63(3):309–329; Peter Dacin and Daniel C. Smith (1994), "The Effect of Brand Portfolio Characteristics on Consumer Evaluations of Brand Extensions," *Journal of Marketing Research,* 31(2):229–242; Barbara Loken and Deborah Roedder John (1993), "Diluting Brand Beliefs: When Do Brand Extensions Have a Negative Impact?" *Journal of Marketing,* 57(3):71–84; Srinivas K Reddy, Susan L. Holak, and Subodh Bhat (1994), "To Extend or Not to Extend: Success Determinants of Line Extensions," *Journal of Marketing Research,* 31(2):243–262.

dollars on brands that can achieve the first or second market share positions in their categories.[26]

Packaging

Packaging
The activities of designing and producing the container or wrapper for a product.

Packaging involves designing and producing the container or wrapper for a product. Some marketers have called packaging a fifth P, to go alongside price, product, place, and promotion. The package may include the product's primary container—

the tube holding Colgate toothpaste; a secondary package that is thrown away when the product is about to be used—the cardboard box containing the toothpaste; and the shipping package necessary to store, identify, and ship the product—a corrugated box carrying six dozen tubes of Colgate toothpaste. Labelling is also part of packaging and consists of printed information appearing on or with the package.

The primary function of the package used to be to contain and protect the product. However, numerous factors have made packaging an important marketing tool. Increased competition and clutter on retail store shelves means that packages must perform many sales tasks—from attracting attention, to describing the product, to making the sale. Companies are realizing the power of good packaging to create instant consumer recognition of the company or brand. For example, in an average supermarket that stocks 15 000 to 17 000 items, the typical shopper passes by some 300 items per minute, and 53 percent of all purchases are made on impulse. In this highly competitive environment, the package may be the seller's last chance to influence buyers. It becomes a "five-second commercial." The Campbell Soup Company estimates that the average shopper sees its familiar red and white can 76 times a year, creating the equivalent of $36 million worth of advertising.[27]

The package can also reinforce the product's positioning. Coca-Cola's familiar contour bottle speaks volumes about the product inside. "Even in a shadow, people know it's a Coke," observes a packaging expert. "It's a beautiful definition of how a package can influence the way a consumer perceives a product. People taste Coke differently from a contour bottle versus a generic package."[28]

Innovative packaging can give a company an advantage over competitors. Liquid Tide quickly attained a 10 percent share of the heavy-duty detergent market, partly because of the popularity of its container's innovative drip-proof spout and cap. In contrast, poorly designed packages can cause headaches for consumers and lost sales for the company (see Marketing Highlight 8-4). For example, Planters LifeSavers Company recently attempted to use innovative packaging to create an association between fresh-roasted peanuts and fresh-roasted coffee. It packaged its Fresh Roast Salted Peanuts in vacuum-packed "Brik-Pacs," similar to those used for ground coffee. Unfortunately, the coffee-like packaging worked too well: Consumers mistook the peanuts for a new brand of flavoured coffee and ran them through supermarket coffee-grinding machines, creating a gooey mess, disappointed customers, and lots of irate store managers.[29]

Packaging concept
What the package should be or do for the product.

A marketer must make many decisions in developing a good package for a new product. The first task is to establish the **packaging concept,** which states what the package should *be* or *do* for the product. Should the main functions of the package be to offer product protection, introduce a new dispensing method, suggest certain qualities about the product or the company, or something else? Decisions then must be made on specific elements of the package, such as size, shape, materials, colour, text, and brand mark. These elements must work together to support the product's position and marketing strategy. The package must be consistent with the product's advertising, pricing, and distribution.

Product safety is a major packaging concern. We have all learned to deal with hard-to-open "childproof" packages. After the product tampering scares in the 1980s, most drug producers and food makers are now putting their products in tamper-resistant packages. In making packaging decisions, the company must also heed growing environmental concerns and make decisions that serve society's interests as well as immediate customer and company objectives. Shortages of paper, aluminum, and other materials suggest that marketers should try to reduce packaging. Many packages end up as broken bottles and crumpled cans littering the streets and countryside. All of this packaging creates a major problem in solid waste disposal, requiring huge amounts of labour and energy.

Fortunately, many companies have gone "green." S.C. Johnson repackaged

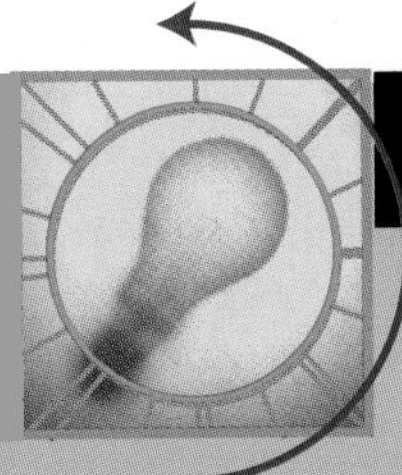

marketing highlight 8-4

Those Frustrating, Not-So-Easy-to-Open Packages

Some things, it seems, will never change. This classic letter from an angry consumer to Robert D. Stuart, then chairman of Quaker Oats, beautifully expresses the utter frustration all of us have experienced in dealing with so-called easy-to-open packages.

Dear Mr. Stuart:

I am an 86-year-old widow in fairly good health. (You may think of this as advanced age, but for me, that description pertains to the years ahead. Nevertheless, if you decide to reply to this letter I wouldn't dawdle, actuarial tables being what they are.)

As I said, my health is fairly good. Feeble and elderly, as one understands these terms, I am not. My two Doberman pinschers and I take a brisk three-mile walk every day. They are two strong and energetic animals, and it takes a bit of doing to keep "brisk" closer to a stroll than a mad dash. But I manage because as yet I don't lack the strength. You will shortly see why this fact is relevant.

I am writing to call your attention to the cruel, deceptive, and utterly [false] copy on your Aunt Jemima buttermilk complete pancake and waffle mix. The words on your package read, "to open—press here and pull back."

Mr. Stuart, though I push and press and groan and strive and writhe and curse and sweat and jab and push, poke and ram . . . whew!—I have never once been able to do what the package instructs—to "press here and pull back" the [blankety-blank]. It can't be done! Talk about failing strength! Have you ever tried and succeeded?

My late husband was a gun collector who among other lethal weapons kept a Thompson machine gun in a locked cabinet. It was a good thing that the cabinet was locked. Oh, the number of times I was tempted to give your package a few short bursts.

The lock and a sense of ladylike delicacy kept me from pursuing that vengeful fantasy. Instead, I keep a small cleaver in my pantry for those occasions when I need to open a package of your delicious Aunt Jemima pancakes.

For many years, that whacking away with my cleaver served a dual purpose. Not only to open the [blankety-blank] package but also to vent my fury at your sadists who willfully and maliciously did design that torture apparatus that passes for a package.

Sometimes just for the [blank] of it I let myself get carried away. I don't stop after I've lopped off the top. I whack away until the package is utterly destroyed in an outburst of rage, frustration, and vindictiveness. I wind up with a floorful of your delicious Aunt Jemima pancake mix. But that's a small price to pay for blessed release. (Anyway, the pinschers lap up the mess.)

So many ingenious, considerate (even compassionate) innovations in package closures have been designed since Aunt Jemima first donned her red bandana. Wouldn't you consider the introduction of a more humane package to replace the example of marketing malevolence to which you resolutely cling? Don't you care, Mr. Stuart?

I'm really writing this to be helpful and in that spirit I am sending a copy to Mr. Tucker, president of Container Corp. I'm sure their clever young designers could be of immeasurable help to you in this matter. At least I feel it's worth a try.

Really, Mr. Stuart, I hope you will not regard me as just another cranky old biddy. I am The Public, the source of your fortunes.

Ms. Roberta Pavloff
Malvern, PA

Source: This letter was reprinted in "Some designs should just be torn asunder," *Advertising Age*, 17 January 1983:M54.

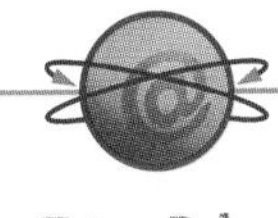

Tetra Pak
www.tetrapak.com/

Agree Plus shampoo in a stand-up pouch using 80 percent less plastic; and P&G eliminated outer cartons from its Secret and Sure deodorants, saving 3.4 million pounds of paperboard per year. Tetra Pak, a major Swedish multinational company, provides an example of the power of innovative packaging that takes environmental concerns into account.

Tetra Pak invented an "aseptic" package that enables milk, fruit juice, and other perishable liquid foods to be distributed without refrigeration or preservatives. Not only is this packaging more environmentally responsible, it also provides economic and distribution advantages. Aseptic packaging allows companies to distribute beverages over a wider area without investing in refrigerated trucks and warehouses. Supermarkets can carry Tetra Pak packaged products on ordinary shelves, allowing them to save expensive refrigerator space. Tetra's motto is "a package should save more than it cost." Tetra Pak promotes the benefits of its packaging to consumers directly and even initiates recycling programs to save the environment.

Tetra Pak advertises the benefits of its environmentally responsible packaging directly to consumers and initiates recycling programs. As this ad to producers suggests, it's "more than the package."

Labelling

Labels range from simple tags attached to products to complex graphics that are part of the package. They perform several functions, and the seller must decide which ones to use. At the very least, the label *identifies* the product or brand, such as the name Sunkist stamped on oranges. The label can *describe* several things about the product—who made it, where it was made, when it was made, its contents, how it is to be used, and how to use it safely. Finally, the label may *promote* the product with attractive graphics.

There has been a long history of legal and ethical concerns about labels. Labels have the potential to mislead customers, fail to describe important ingredients, and fail to include needed safety warnings. Labelling regulations depend on the type of product being sold. The *Consumer Packaging and Labelling Act,* which covers many non-food products, was passed to protect consumers from labelling or packaging that is false or misleading. The *Weights and Measures Act* deals with the units of measurement on labels. The Government of Canada Web site's "Consumer Packaging and Labelling" page details the requirements for the principal display panel of prepackaged, non-food consumer products.

Government of Canada
strategis.ic.gc.ca/

Consumer advocates have long lobbied for additional legislation that would require such things as open dating so that consumers can ascertain product freshness, unit pricing so that consumers can compare products in standard measurement units, and percentage labelling to reveal the percentage of ingredients such as sugar and fat. In response to these concerns, Health Canada initiated a review of its policies on nutrition labelling in 1998. The review resulted in new proposals with regard to nutrition labelling. By the end of 2001, it will be mandatory on all packaged foods. Labels will be in an easy-to-read, standardized format. They will provide an expanded list of ingredients including calories, fats, sodium, carbohydrate, fibre, sugar, protein, vitamin A, vitamin C, calcium, and iron. Serving size information will have to be more consistent. To see an example of the new nutrition facts panel for food products, go to www.hc-sc.gc.ca/hppb/nutrition/labels/e_before.html.

Product Support Services

Product support services
Services that augment actual products.

Customer service is another element of product strategy. A company's offer to the marketplace usually includes some services, which can be a minor or a major part of the total offer. Later in the chapter we discuss services as products in themselves. Here, we discuss **product support services**—services that augment actual products. More and more companies are using product support services as a major tool in gaining competitive advantage.

A company should design its product and support services to meet the needs of target customers profitably. The first step is to survey customers periodically to assess the value of current services and to obtain ideas for new ones. For example, Cadillac holds regular focus group interviews with owners and watches complaints that come into its dealerships. From this careful monitoring, Cadillac learned that buyers are very upset by repairs that are not done correctly the first time.

Once the company has assessed the value of various support services to customers, it must assess the costs of providing these services. It can then develop a package of services that will both delight customers and yield profits to the company. Based on its consumer interviews, Cadillac set up a system directly linking each dealership with a group of 10 engineers who can help mechanics with difficult repairs. Such actions helped Cadillac jump, in one year, from fourteenth to seventh in independent rankings of service.[30]

Many companies use the Internet to provide support services that were not possible before. For example, Pratt & Whitney Canada, the world's leading producer of engines for corporate jets, commuter aircraft, and helicopters, uses its Web site to provide information on engine maintenance. Air Canada provides a support Web site for its frequent flyer members: Members can book tickets, check the status of their frequent flyer accounts, and take advantage of special member fares.

Product Decisions and Social Responsibility

Product decisions can attract public attention. Therefore, marketers should carefully consider public policy issues and regulations concerning acquiring or dropping products, patent protection, product quality and safety, and product warranties.

Canadian manufacturers must navigate a complex web of government departments and legislation when considering their product policies. Agriculture Canada, the Canadian Food Inspection Agency, and the Consumer Products Division of Health Canada, for example, govern food and product safety. The Competition Bureau regulates many aspects of the marketing of products. The *Competition Act*'s provisions cover pricing and advertising, not just the maintenance of a competitive marketplace. When considering a merger that would give a firm access to new products, a company has to be aware that the government may invoke the *Competition Act* if it thinks the merger would lessen competition. Companies dropping products must be aware that they have legal obligations, written or implied, to their suppliers, dealers, and customers who have a stake in the discontinued product. Companies must also must obey patent laws when developing new products. A company cannot make its product illegally similar to another company's established product. Firms may also have to be aware of legislation controlled by Environment Canada and the Department of Transport.

Federal statutes cover product safety (except electrical equipment), competition, labelling, and weights and measures. The *Hazardous Products Act,* for example, controls the marketing of dangerous or potentially dangerous consumer and industrial products; the *Food and Drug Act* covers safety of cosmetics as well as food and drugs. Both acts can be found on the Canadian Department of Justice Web site. Provincial statutes deal with such matters as conditions of sale, guarantees, and licensing, as well as unfair business practices.

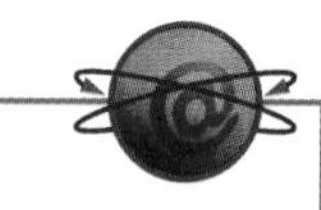

Canadian Department of Justice
canada.justice.gc.ca/

Consumers who have been injured by a defectively designed product can sue the manufacturer or dealer. The number of product liability suits have been increasing, and settlements often run to millions of dollars. This, in turn, has resulted in huge increases in the cost of product liability insurance premiums. Some companies pass these higher rates along to consumers by raising prices. Others are forced to discontinue high-risk product lines.

Product Line Decisions

Product line
A group of products that are closely related because they function in a similar manner, are sold to the same customer groups, are marketed through the same types of outlets, or fall within given price ranges.

We have looked at product strategy decisions—branding, packaging, labelling, and services—for individual products. But product strategy also calls for building a product line. A **product line** is a group of products that are closely related because they function in a similar manner, are sold to the same customer groups, are marketed through the same types of outlets, or fall within given price ranges. For example, General Motors produces several lines of cars, Nike produces several lines of athletic shoes, and Nortel produces several lines of telecommunications products. In developing product line strategies, marketers face a number of tough decisions.

The major product line decision is *line length.* The line is too short if the manager can increase profits by adding items; the line is too long if the manager can increase profits by dropping items. Product line length is influenced by company objectives. Companies that want to be positioned as full-line companies or that are seeking high market share and growth usually carry longer lines. Companies that are keen on high short-term profitability generally carry shorter lines consisting of selected items.

Product lines tend to lengthen over time. The sales force and distributors may pressure the manager for a more complete product line to satisfy their customers. Or, the product line manager may want to add items to the line to increase sales and profits. However, as the manager adds items, costs rise for design and engineering, inventory, manufacturing changeover, order processing, transportation, and promotion to introduce new items. Eventually top management calls a halt to the mushrooming product line. Unnecessary or unprofitable items or services are pruned from the line to increase overall profitability. This pattern of uncontrolled product line growth followed by heavy pruning is typical and may repeat itself many times.

The company must, therefore, extend its product lines carefully. It can systematically increase the length of its product line in two ways: by *stretching* it or *filling* it. Every company's product line covers a certain range of the products offered by the industry as a whole. For example, BMW automobiles are located in the medium-high price range of the automobile market. Toyota focuses on the low-to-medium price range. *Product line stretching* occurs when a company lengthens its product line beyond its current range. Figure 8-5 shows that the company can stretch its line downward, upward, or both ways.

Stretching Downward

Many companies initially locate at the upper end of the market and later stretch their lines downward. A company may stretch downward to plug a market hole that otherwise would attract a new competitor or to respond to a competitor's

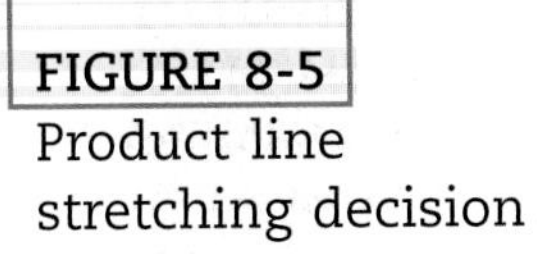

FIGURE 8-5
Product line stretching decision

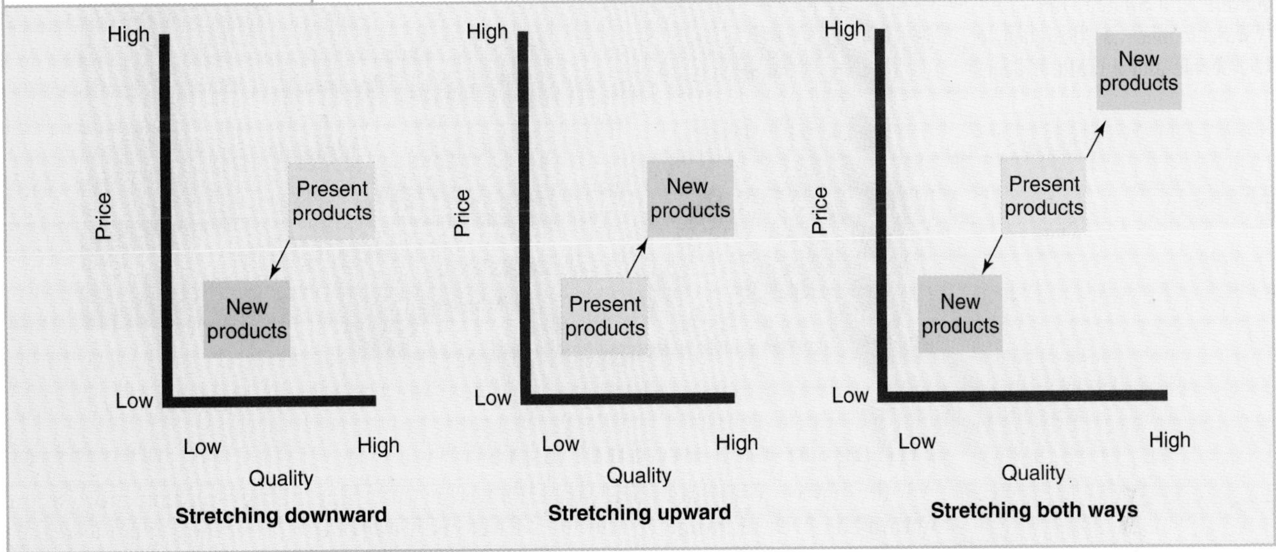

attack on the upper end. Or it may add low-end products because it finds faster growth taking place in the low-end segments. Mercedes stretched downward for all these reasons. Facing a slow-growth luxury car market and attacks by Japanese auto makers on its high-end positioning, Mercedes introduced several smaller, lower-priced models. These included the sporty SLK hard-top convertible (priced at a modest \$56 000) and the A-Class line (\$28 000). And in a joint venture with Switzerland's Swatch watchmaker, Mercedes launched the \$14 000 Smart micro-compact car, an environmentally correct second car.[31]

Stretching Upward

Companies at the lower end of the market may want to stretch their product lines upward. They may be attracted by a faster growth rate or higher margins at the higher end, or they may simply want to position themselves as full-line manufacturers or add prestige to their current products. For example, General Electric added its Monogram line of high-quality built-in kitchen appliances targeted at the select few households earning more than \$140 000 a year and living in homes valued at over \$550 000.

Stretching Both Ways

Companies in the middle range of the market may decide to stretch their lines in both directions. Marriott did this with its hotel product line. Along with regular Marriott hotels, it added the Marriott Marquis line to serve the upper end of the market, and the Courtyard and Fairfield Inn lines to serve the lower end. Each branded hotel line is aimed at a different target market. Marriott Marquis aims to attract and please top executives; Marriotts, middle managers; Courtyards, salespeople; and Fairfield Inns, vacationers and others on a low travel budget. The major risk with this strategy is that some travellers will trade down after finding that the lower-price hotels in the Marriott chain give them pretty much everything they want. However, Marriott would rather capture its customers who move downward than lose them to competitors.

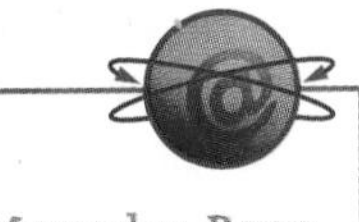

Mercedes-Benz
www.mercedes-benz.com/
Marriott
www.marriott.com/

Mercedes stretched its product line in introducing several smaller, lower-priced models, including the Smart microcompact car in a joint venture with Swatch. The "Swatchmobile" is "designed for two people and a crate of beer."

Filling in the Product Line

An alternative to product line stretching is product line filling—adding more items within the present range of the line. Reasons for *product line filling* include reaching for extra profits, trying to satisfy dealers, trying to use excess capacity, trying to be the leading full-line company, and trying to plug holes to keep out competitors. Thus, Sony filled its Walkman line by adding solar-powered and waterproof Walkmans and an ultralight model that attaches to a sweatband for joggers, bicyclers, tennis players, and other exercisers. However, line filling is overdone if it results in cannibalization and customer confusion. The company must ensure that new items are noticeably different from existing ones.

Product Mix Decisions

Product mix (or product assortment)
The set of all product lines and items that a particular seller offers for sale to buyers.

An organization with several product lines has a product mix. A **product mix** (or **product assortment**) is the set of all product lines and items that a particular seller offers for sale. Avon's product mix consists of four major product lines: cosmetics, jewellery, fashions, and household items. Each product line consists of several sublines. For example, cosmetics breaks down into lipstick, blush, powder, and so on. Each line and subline has many individual items. Altogether, Avon's product mix includes 1300 items. In contrast, a large supermarket handles as many as 17 000 items; a typical Zellers stocks 15 000 items; and General Electric manufactures about 250 000 items.

A company's product mix has four important dimensions: width, length, depth, and consistency. Table 8-2 illustrates these concepts with selected Procter & Gamble consumer products. The *width* of P&G's product mix refers to the number of different product lines the company carries. The table shows a product mix width of six lines. (In fact, P&G produces many more lines, including mouthwashes, paper products, disposable diapers, health care products, and cosmetics.) The *length* of P&G's product mix refers to the total number of items the company carries. While P&G has over 300 brands, the table shows only 60 of these. We can also compute the average length of a line at P&G by dividing the total length (here 60) by the number of lines (here 6). In the table, the average P&G product line consists of 10 brands.

The *depth* of P&G's product mix refers to the number of versions offered of each product in the line. Thus, if Tide comes in three forms (powder, liquid, and tablets) and three formulations (regular, with bleach, scented), Tide has a depth

TABLE 8-2 Product Mix Width and Product Line Length Shown for Selected Procter & Gamble Products

← Product Mix Width →

Product Line Length (↕)

Fabric Care	Household Care	Deodorants	Personal Cleansing	Prestige Fragrances	Hair Care
Tide Original Powder	Mr. Clean	Old Spice Deodorant	Camay	Hugo Boss	Head & Shoulders
Ultra Tide Powder	Mr. Clean Top Job	Old Spice Red Zone	Ivory	Giorgio	Pantene Shampoo
Liquid Tide	Mr. Clean Wipe-Ups	Secret	Ivory Moisture Care	Helmet Lang	Pantene Conditioner
Deep Clean Liquid Tide	Febreze	Sure	Safeguard	Herve Leger	Pantene Hair Spray
Liquid Tide Mountain Spring	Cascade		Zest		Pert Plus
Tide Rapid Action Tablets	Cascade Rinse Aid		Olay Beauty Bar		Physique
Powder Ultra Tide with Bleach	Fit Fruit & Vegetable Wash		Olay Cleanser		Vidal Sassoon Shampoo
Gain Fresh Scent	Dawn Dishwashing Liquid		Olay Moisturizing Body Wash		Vidal Sassoon Conditioner
Febreze Clean Wash	Ivory Dishwashing Liquid		Coast		Vidal Sassoon Styling Gel
Bold	Joy Dishwashing Liquid				
Bold 3	Comet				
Cheer	Spic & Span				
Ivory Snow	Swiffer				
Bounce					
Bounce Fresh Scent					
Bounce Gentle Breeze					
Bounce Free					
Downy					
Downy Premium Care					
Dryel					
Oxydol					

of nine. By counting the number of versions within each brand, we can calculate the average depth of P&G's product mix.

The *consistency* of the product mix refers to how closely related the various product lines are in end use, production requirements, distribution channels, or in some other way. P&G's product lines are consistent insofar as they are consumer products. The lines are less consistent insofar as they perform different functions for buyers, and go through different distribution channels.

These product mix dimensions provide the handles for defining the company's product strategy. The company can increase its business in four ways. It can add new product lines, thus widening its product mix: In this way, its new lines build on the company's reputation in its other lines. The company can lengthen its existing product lines to become a more full-line company. Or it can add more product versions of each product and thus deepen its product mix. Finally, the company can pursue more product line consistency—or less—depending on whether it wants to have a strong reputation in a single field or in several fields.

Services Marketing

A major world trend in recent years has been the dramatic growth of services. In 1997, world trade in commercial services, measured on a balance of payments basis, accounted for about one-fifth of total global exports. In fact, a variety of service industries—from banking, insurance, and communications to transporta-

The convenience industry offers services that save you time—for a price.

tion, travel, and entertainment—now account for well over 60 percent of the economy in developed countries around the world. As a result of rising affluence, more leisure time, and the growing complexity of products that require servicing, North America has become the world's first service economy. Service industries account for over two-thirds of Canada's GDP, almost three-quarters of employment in the country, and nearly 90 percent of new job creation. Moreover, the service sector continues to grow faster than other sectors of the economy.[32]

Service industries vary greatly. *Governments* offer services through courts, employment services, hospitals, loan agencies, military services, police and fire departments, postal service, regulatory agencies, and schools. *Private non-profit organizations* offer services through museums, charities, churches, colleges, foundations, and hospitals. A large number of *business organizations* offer services—airlines, banks, hotels, insurance companies, consulting firms, medical and law practices, entertainment companies, real estate firms, advertising and research agencies, and retailers.

Some North American service businesses are very large, with total sales and assets in the millions of dollars. There are also tens of thousands of smaller service providers. Selling services presents some special problems that call for special marketing solutions.

Nature and Characteristics of a Service

Service
Any activity or benefit that one party can offer to another that is essentially intangible and does not result in the ownership of anything.

A **service** is any activity or benefit that one party can offer to another that is essentially intangible and does not result in the ownership of anything. Its production may or may not be tied to a physical product. Such activities as renting a hotel room, depositing money in a bank, travelling on an airplane, visiting a psychiatrist, getting a haircut, having a car repaired, watching a professional sport, seeing a movie, having clothes cleaned at a dry cleaner, and getting advice from a lawyer all involve buying a service.

Service intangibility
A major characteristic of services—they cannot be seen, tasted, felt, heard, or smelled before they are bought.

A company must consider four special characteristics of services when designing marketing programs: *intangibility, inseparability, variability,* and *perishability.* These characteristics are summarized in Figure 8-6 and discussed below.

Service intangibility means that services cannot be seen, tasted, felt, heard, or smelled before they are bought. For example, people undergoing cosmetic surgery

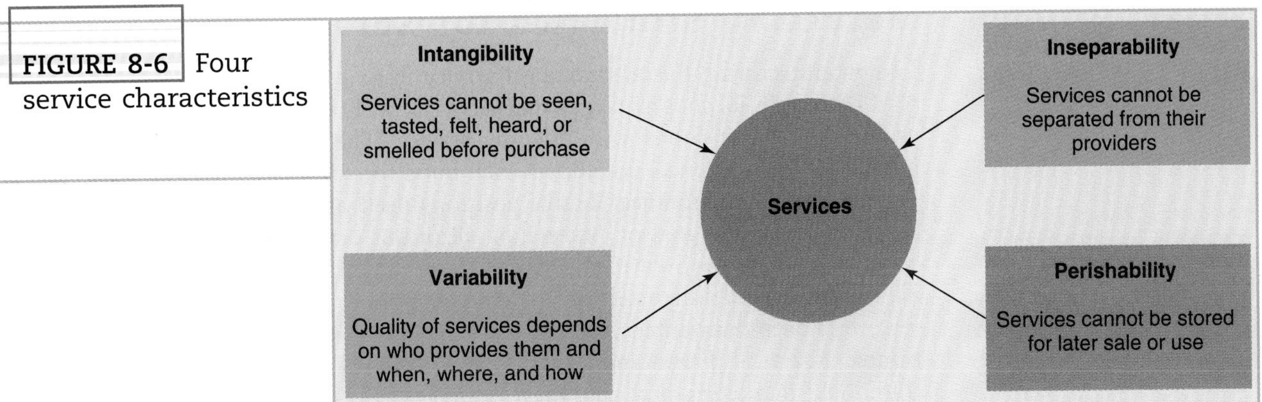

FIGURE 8-6 Four service characteristics

cannot see the result before the purchase, and airline passengers have nothing but a ticket and the promise of safe delivery to their destinations.

To reduce uncertainty, buyers look for "signals" of service quality. They draw conclusions about quality from the place, people, price, equipment, and communication material that they can see. Therefore, the service provider's task is to make the service tangible in one or more ways. Whereas product marketers try to add intangibles to their tangible offers, service marketers try to add tangibles to their intangible offers.

Physical goods are produced, then stored, later sold, and still later consumed. In contrast, services are first sold, then produced and consumed at the same time. **Service inseparability** means that services cannot be separated from their providers, whether the providers are people or machines. If a service employee provides the employee service, then the employee is a part of the service. Because the customer is also present as the service is produced, *provider–customer interaction* is a special feature of services marketing. Both the provider and the customer affect the service outcome. Gerry Moore, director of the CN customer support centre, explains, "We're counting on our customers to help us move forward together. . . . They work with us to provide accurate, timely information, such as bills of lading and short-term production forecasts."[33]

Service inseparability
A major characteristic of services—they are produced and consumed at the same time and cannot be separated from their providers, whether the providers are people or machines.

Service variability means that the quality of services depends on who provides them as well as when, where, and how they are provided. For example, some hotels, such as the Westin or Marriott, have reputations for providing better services than others. But within a given Marriott hotel, one registration desk employee may be cheerful and efficient, whereas another standing just a few feet away may be unpleasant and slower. Even the quality of each employee's service varies according to his or her energy and frame of mind at the time of each customer encounter. Service firms can take several steps to help manage service variability. They can select and carefully train their personnel to give good service. They can provide employee incentives that emphasize quality, such as employee-of-the-month awards or bonuses based on customer feedback.

Service variability
A major characteristic of services—their quality may vary greatly, depending on who provides them and when, where, and how they are provided.

Service perishability means that services cannot be stored for later sale or use. Some dentists charge patients for missed appointments because the service value existed only at that point and disappeared when the patient did not show up. The perishability of services is not a problem when demand is steady. However, when demand fluctuates, service firms often have problems. For example, public transport corporations have to own much more equipment than they would if demand were even throughout the day. Thus, service firms often design strategies for producing a better match between demand and supply. For instance, hotels and resorts charge lower prices in the off-season to attract more guests. And restaurants hire part-time employees to serve during peak periods.

Service perishability
A major characteristic of services—they cannot be stored for later sale or use.

Marketing Strategies for Service Firms

Like manufacturing businesses, good service firms use marketing to position themselves strongly in chosen target markets. A&W Foods of Canada positions itself as combining fast foods with friendly service. The Westin Hotel chain positions itself to offer excellence, yet allows each hotel to retain its individual personality—for example, the Winnipeg Westin positions itself as "the finest hotel in our marketplace," with the goal of "exceeding all of our customers' expectations by delivering exceptional and caring service." WestJet positions itself to compete against Air Canada. Modelling itself on the American innovator Southwest Airlines, WestJet offers deep-discounted fares combined with no-frills service: no meals and no printed tickets.[34] These and other service firms establish their positions through traditional marketing mix activities.

However, because services differ from tangible products, they often require additional marketing approaches. In a product business, products are fairly standardized and can sit on shelves waiting for customers. But in a service business, the customer and frontline service employee *interact* to create the service. Thus, service providers must work to interact effectively with customers to create superior value during service encounters. Effective interaction, in turn, depends on the skills of front-line service employees, and on the service production and support processes backing these employees.

The Service-Profit Chain

Successful service companies focus their attention on both their employees and customers. They understand the *service-profit chain,* which links service firm profits with employee and customer satisfaction. This chain consists of five links.[35]

- *Healthy service profits and growth*—superior service firm performance, which results from . . .
- *Satisfied and loyal customers*—satisfied customers who remain loyal, repeat purchase, and refer other customers, which results from . . .
- *Greater service value*—more effective and efficient customer value creation and service delivery, which results from . . .
- *Satisfied and productive service employees*—more satisfied, loyal, and hardworking employees, which results from . . .
- *Internal service quality*—superior employee selection and training, a quality work environment, and strong support for those dealing with customers.

Therefore, reaching service profits and growth goals begins with taking care of those who take care of customers.

This suggests that service marketing requires more than just traditional external marketing using the four Ps. Figure 8-7 shows that service marketing also

FIGURE 8-7 Three types of marketing in service industries

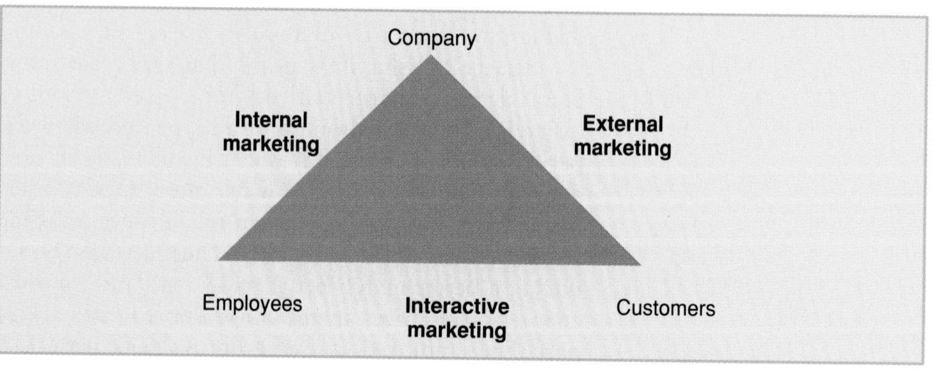

Internal marketing
Marketing by a service firm to train and effectively motivate its customer-contact employees and all the supporting service people to work as a team to provide customer satisfaction.

Interactive marketing
A type of marketing where the perceived service quality depends heavily on the quality of the buyer-seller interaction during the service encounter.

requires both *internal marketing* and *interactive marketing*. **Internal marketing** means that the service firm must effectively train and motivate its customer-contact employees and all the supporting service people to work as a *team* to provide customer satisfaction. For the firm to deliver consistently high service quality, marketers must get everyone to practise customer orientation. In fact, internal marketing must *precede* external marketing.

Interactive marketing means that perceived service quality depends heavily on the quality of the buyer-seller interaction during the service encounter. In product marketing, product quality often depends little on how the product is obtained. But in services marketing, service quality depends on both the service deliverer and the quality of the delivery. Thus, service marketers cannot assume that they will satisfy the customer simply by providing good technical service. They must also master interactive marketing skills. Thus, Ritz-Carlton orients its employees carefully, instills in them a sense of pride, and motivates them by recognizing and rewarding outstanding service deeds (see Marketing Highlight 8-5).

As competition and costs increase and as productivity and quality decrease, more marketing sophistication is needed. Service companies face three major marketing tasks: They want to increase their *competitive differentiation, service quality*, and *productivity*.

Managing Service Differentiation

In these days of intense price competition, service marketers often complain about the difficulty of differentiating their services from those of competitors. To the extent that customers view the services of different providers as similar, they care less about the provider than the price.

The solution to price competition is to develop a differentiated offer, delivery, and image. The *offer* can include *innovative features* that set one company's offer apart from competitors' offers. For example, airlines introduced such innovations as in-flight movies, advance seating, air-to-ground telephone service, and frequent-flyer award programs to differentiate their offers. British Airways even offers international travellers a sleeping compartment, hot showers, and cooked-to-order breakfasts.

Service companies can differentiate their service *delivery* by having more able and reliable customer-contact people, by developing a superior physical environment in which the service product is delivered, or by designing a superior delivery process. For example, a bank can offer its customers electronic home banking as a better way to deliver banking services than having to drive, park, and wait in line.

Finally, service companies can differentiate their images through symbols and branding. Service marketers often find themselves challenged to find an intangible symbol of an intangible benefit. For example, Royal Bank's stylized "Leo the Lion" (although you have to look hard to see it) symbolizes strength and power—desirable qualities of a large bank. Some credit unions in British Columbia have tried to differentiate themselves from the larger banks by showing humorous versions of the larger banks. B.C. Central Credit union chose to symbolize its virtues through peaceful wilderness settings, punctuated by the angry cry of bank customers who "can't take it anymore."

Managing Service Quality

One of the major ways a service firm can differentiate itself is by delivering consistently higher quality than its competitors do. Many companies are finding that outstanding service quality can give them a potent competitive advantage that leads to superior sales, profit performance, and customer retention.[36] A service firm's ability to hang on to its customers depends on how consistently it delivers value to them. The key is to exceed the customers' service-quality *expectations*. As the chief executive at American Express puts it, "Promise only what you can deliver and deliver *more* than you promise!"[37] These expectations are based on past expe-

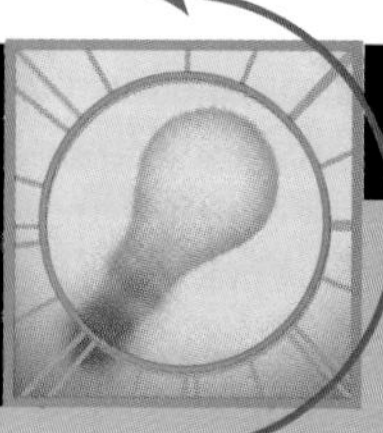

marketing highlight 8-5

Ritz-Carlton: Taking Care of Those Who Take Care of Customers

Ritz-Carlton, a chain of luxury hotels renowned for outstanding service, caters to the top five percent of corporate and leisure travellers. The company's credo sets lofty customer service goals: "The Ritz-Carlton Hotel is a place where the genuine care and comfort of our guests is our highest mission. We pledge to provide the finest personal service and facilities for our guests who will always enjoy a warm, relaxed yet refined ambience. The Ritz-Carlton experience enlivens the senses, instills well-being, and fulfills even the unexpressed wishes and needs of our guests." The company's Web page concludes: "Here a calm settles over you. The world, so recently at your door, is now at your feet."

The credo is more than just words on paper—Ritz-Carlton delivers on its promises. In surveys of departing guests, some 95 percent report that they've had a truly memorable experience. In fact, at Ritz-Carlton, exceptional service encounters have become almost commonplace. Take the experiences of Nancy and Harvey Heffner, who stayed at the Ritz-Carlton Naples, in Naples, Florida (recently rated the best hotel in the United States, and fourth best in the world, by *Travel & Leisure* magazine):

> "The hotel is elegant and beautiful," Mrs. Heffner said, "but more important is the beauty expressed by the staff. They can't do enough to please you." When the couple's son became sick last year in Naples, the hotel staff brought him hot tea with honey at all hours of the night, she said. When Mr. Heffner had to fly home on business for a day and his return flight was delayed, a driver for the hotel waited in the lobby most of the night.

Such personal, high-quality service has also made the Ritz-Carlton a favourite among conventioneers. Comments one convention planner, "They not only treat us like kings when we hold our top-level meetings in their hotels, but we just never get any complaints."

In 1992, Ritz-Carlton became the first hotel company to win the Malcolm Baldrige National Quality Award. Since its incorporation in 1983, the company has received virtually every major award that the hospitality industry bestows. More importantly, service quality has resulted in high customer retention: Over 90 percent of Ritz-Carlton customers return. Despite its hefty room rates, the chain enjoys a 70 percent occupancy rate, almost nine points above the industry average.

Most of the responsibility for keeping guests satisfied falls to Ritz-Carlton's customer-contact employees. Thus, the hotel chain takes great care in selecting its personnel. "We want only people who care about people," notes Patrick Mene, the company's vice-president of quality. Once selected, employees are given intensive training in the art of coddling customers. New employees attend a two-day orientation, in which top management drums into them the "20 Ritz-Carlton Basics." Basic number one: "The Credo will be known, owned, and energized by all employees."

Employees are taught to do everything they can so they never lose a guest. "There's no negotiating at Ritz-Carlton when it comes to solving customer problems," says Mene. Staff learn that anyone who receives a customer complaint owns that complaint until it's resolved (Ritz-Carlton Basic number eight). They are trained to drop whatever they're doing to help a customer—no matter what they're doing or what their department. Ritz-Carlton employees are empowered to handle problems on the spot, without consulting higher-ups. Each employee can spend up to $3000 to redress a guest grievance, and each is allowed to break from his or her routine for as long as needed to make a guest happy. "We master customer satisfaction at the individual level," adds Mene. "This is our most sensitive listening post . . . our early warning system." Thus, while competitors are still reading guest comment cards to learn about customer problems, Ritz-Carlton has already resolved them.

Ritz-Carlton instills a sense of pride in its employees. "You serve," they are told, "but you are not servants." The company motto states, "We are ladies and gentlemen serving ladies and gentlemen." Employees understand their role in Ritz-Carlton's success. "We might not be able to afford a hotel like this," says employee Tammy Patton, "but we can make it so people who can afford it will want to keep coming here."

And so they do. When it comes to customer satisfaction, no detail is too small. Customer-contact people are taught to greet guests warmly and sincerely, using guest names when possible. They learn to use the proper language with guests—phrases such as good morning, certainly, I'll be happy to, welcome back, and my pleasure; never Hi or How's it going? The Ritz-Carlton Basics urge employees to escort guests to another area of the hotel rather than pointing out directions, to answer the phone within three rings and with a "smile," and to take pride and care in their personal appearance. As Jorge Gonzalez, general manager of the Ritz-Carlton Naples, puts it, "When you invite guests to your house, you want everything to be perfect."

Ritz-Carlton recognizes and rewards

THE RITZ-CARLTON®

CREDO

The Ritz-Carlton Hotel is a place where the genuine care and comfort of our guests is our highest mission.

We pledge to provide the finest personal service and facilities for our guests who will always enjoy a warm, relaxed yet refined ambience.

The Ritz-Carlton experience enlivens the senses, instills well-being, and fulfills even the unexpressed wishes and needs of our guests.

THREE STEPS OF SERVICE

1
A warm and sincere greeting. Use the guest name, if and when possible.

2
Anticipation and compliance with guest needs.

3
Fond farewell. Give them a warm good-bye and use their name, if and when possible.

THE EMPLOYEE PROMISE

At The Ritz-Carlton, our Ladies and Gentlemen are the most important resource in our service commitment to our guests.

By applying the principles of trust, honesty, respect, integrity and commitment, we nurture and maximize talent to the benefit of each individual and the company.

The Ritz-Carlton fosters a work environment where diversity is valued, quality of life is enhanced, individual aspirations are fulfilled, and The Ritz-Carlton mystique is strengthened.

"We Are Ladies and Gentlemen Serving Ladies and Gentlemen"

The credo and employee promise: Ritz-Carlton knows that to take care of customers, you must first take care of those who take care of customers.

employees who perform feats of outstanding service. Under its 5-Star Awards program, outstanding performers are nominated by peers and managers, and winners receive plaques at dinners celebrating their achievements. For on-the-spot recognition, managers award Gold Standard Coupons, redeemable for items in the gift shop and free weekend stays at the hotel. Ritz-Carlton further rewards and motivates its employees with such events as Super Sports Day, an employee talent show, luncheons celebrating employee anniversaries, a family picnic, and special themes in employee dining rooms. As a result, Ritz-Carlton's employees appear to be just as satisfied as its customers. Employee turnover is less than 30 percent a year, compared with 45 percent at other luxury hotels.

Ritz-Carlton's success is based on a simple philosophy: To take care of customers, you must first take care of those who take care of customers. Satisfied employees deliver high service value, which then creates satisfied customers. Satisfied customers, in turn, create sales and profits for the company.

Sources: Quotes from Edwin McDowell, "Ritz-Carlton's keys to good service," *New York Times,* 31 March 1993:D1; Howard Schlossberg, "Measuring customer satisfaction is easy to do—Until you try," *Marketing News,* 26 April 1993:5,8; Ginger Conlon, "True romance," *Sales & Marketing Management,* May 1996:85–90; and the Ritz-Carlton Hotel Company, LLC at www.ritzcarlton.com. Also see Don Peppers, "Digitizing desire," *Forbes,* 10 April 1995:76; and "Ritz-Carlton Hotels reign in three categories of Travel & Leisure's 'World Best Awards' list," accessed online.

riences, word of mouth, and service firm advertising. If *perceived service* of a given firm exceeds *expected service,* customers are apt to use the provider again.

Unfortunately, service quality is harder to define and judge than product quality. It is harder to get agreement on the quality of a haircut than on the quality of a hair dryer, for instance. People judge the quality of a service on five dimen-

Service companies differentiate their images through symbols and branding. Note the familiar "Allstate: You're in good hands" brand and symbol at the bottom of this ad.

GOOD HANDS.
IMAGINE 25,000 ROLLING BILLBOARDS AGAINST
DRUNK DRIVING. THAT'S THE NUMBER OF MADD
RED RIBBONS AGENT AMY DeNUCCI HANDED OUT

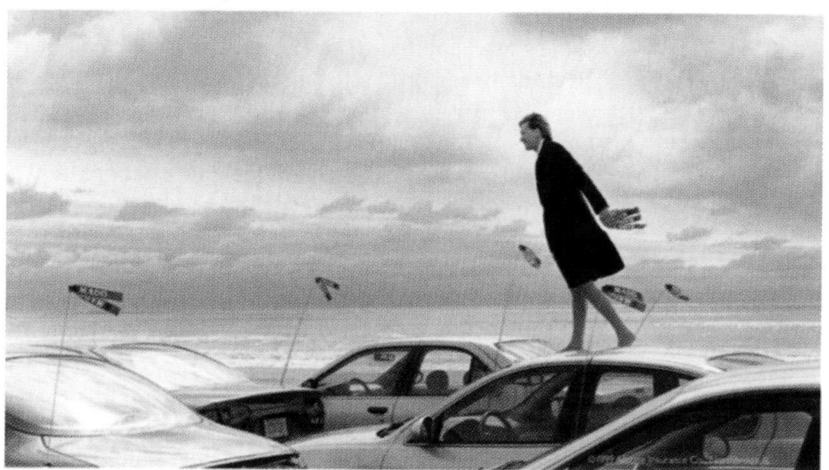

IN ONE YEAR. INSTEAD OF JUST TAKING CARE OF
CUSTOMERS AFTER AN ACCIDENT, SHE PREFERS
PREVENTING THEM.
AT WORK.

Allstate

sions. They assess the *credibility* of the service. Strong brand names and guarantees increase consumers' perceptions of service credibility. They also want service providers to be *empathetic* and understand their needs and problems. Services must also be *reliable*. People expect that the service is delivered with consistent quality. People expect services to be *responsive* and to deal with them as individuals. Finally, people judge service quality using the *tangible cues* that surround service provision. Marketers carefully design the physical setting, or servicescape, where the customer receives the service to create particular perceptions. For example, in a store where the lighting is soft, the colour scheme is black, gold, and silver, and background classical music is played, people may perceive that they are receiving high-quality, prestigious service. Conversely, when they enter a store and see bare cement walls, tile floors, and smell popcorn, shoppers are likely to expect discount prices and limited service. Whatever the level of service provided, it is important that the service provider clearly define and communicate that level so that its employees know what they must deliver and customers know what they will get.

Many service companies have invested heavily to develop streamlined and efficient service-delivery systems. They want to ensure that customers will receive consistently high-quality service in every service encounter. Unlike product manufacturers who can adjust their machinery and inputs until everything is perfect, service quality always will vary since quality depends on the interactions between employees and customers. As hard as they try, even the best companies will have an occasional late delivery, burned steak, or grumpy employee. However, although a company cannot always prevent service problems, it can learn to recover from them. And good *service recovery* programs can turn angry customers into loyal ones. In fact, good recovery can win more customer purchasing and loyalty than if things had gone well in the first place.[38]

The first step is to *empower* front-line service employees—to give them the authority, responsibility, and incentives they need to recognize, care about, and tend to customer needs. At Marriott, for example, employees at all levels are given the authority to do whatever it takes to solve guests' problems on the spot while ferreting out the cause of those problems. At the CN customer support centre, representatives are expected to take total ownership for their customers' requests: everything from daily car orders to billing issues. The centre combines high-tech with a human element. Toll-free numbers allow customers to access the centre. As soon as a call comes in, the customer's profile appears on the service representative's computer screen. Customers deal with the same service rep each time they call, providing a sense of continuity. The state-of-the-art communication lets customers save money by giving them information on empty rail cars available throughout the system.[39]

Studies of well-managed service companies show that they share a number of common virtues regarding service quality. They are *"customer obsessed"* and have a history of *top management commitment to quality*. For instance, the Canadian Imperial Bank of Commerce responds to customer telephone messages by the next business day, and each branch has a quality representative assigned to train and monitor quality standards.

The best service providers also set high service quality standards. Swissair, for example, aims to have 96 percent or more of its passengers rate its service as good or superior; otherwise, it takes action. A 98 percent accuracy standard may sound good, but using this standard, 64 000 Federal Express packages would be lost each day. Top service companies do not settle merely for "good" service, they aim for 100-percent defect-free service.[40]

The top service firms *watch service performance closely*—both their own and that of competitors. They use such methods as comparison shopping, customer surveys, and suggestion and complaint forms. For example, General Electric sends out 700 000 response cards each year to households who rate their service people's performance.

Good service companies also communicate their concerns about service quality to employees and provide performance feedback. At Federal Express, quality measurements are everywhere. When employees walk in the door in the morning, they see the previous week's on-time percentages. Then, the company's in-house television station gives them detailed breakdowns of what happened yesterday and any potential problems for the day ahead.[41]

High service quality is especially important when people go cybershopping. While recent studies suggest that Canadians are techno-enthusiasts who are quicker than citizens of other countries to pick up on services like online banking and high-speed Internet access, they are also equally quick to reject companies that fail to provide them with dependable, high-quality service. Many Canadians have had bad online shopping experiences: About 25 percent of these disgruntled consumers state they would never shop online again; another 25 percent noted they would never shop on that problematic site again; and six percent went as far as swearing never to shop at the bricks-and-mortar version of the online retailer again.[42]

Managing Productivity

With their costs rising rapidly, service firms are under great pressure to increase service productivity. They can do so in several ways. The service providers can train current employees better, or they can hire new ones who will work harder or more skillfully for the same pay. Or the service providers can increase the quantity of their service by giving up some quality. Doctors have moved toward handling more patients and giving less time to each. The provider can "industrialize the service" by adding equipment and standardizing production, as in McDonald's assembly-line approach to fast-food retailing. However, companies must avoid pushing productivity so hard that doing so reduces perceived quality. Attempts to industrialize a service or to cut costs can make a service company more efficient in the short run but reduce its longer-run ability to innovate, maintain service quality, or respond to consumer needs and desires.

Leading service providers have found that they can harness the power of technology to improve service quality while reducing costs. For example, many companies have used the Internet to improve customer access to information about their services. Skiers can visit the Whistler Mountain Web site, for instance, and

Whistler Mountain improves its customer service through use of its Web page.

find the answers to a wide range of questions that many skiers ask. Not only can they find out the hours of operation and current snow conditions, but they can also learn when it makes more sense to buy a season pass than individual day tickets. Provision of information online not only reduces the service provider's costs, but also provides customers with more complete, readily accessible answers to their queries.

International Product and Services Marketing

International product and service marketers face special challenges. They must figure out what products and services to introduce and in which countries. Then, they must decide how much to standardize or adapt their products and services for world markets. On the one hand, companies would like to standardize their offerings. Standardization helps to develop a consistent worldwide image, as well as lower manufacturing costs and eliminate duplication of research and development, advertising, and design efforts. On the other hand, consumers around the world differ in their cultures, attitudes, and buying behaviours. And markets vary in their economic conditions, competition, legal requirements, and physical environments. Companies usually must respond to these differences by adapting their product and service offerings. Something as simple as an electrical outlet can create big product problems:

> Those who have travelled across Europe know the frustration of electrical plugs, different voltages, and other annoyances of international travel. . . . Philips, the electrical appliance manufacturer, has to produce 12 kinds of irons to serve just its European market. The problem is that Europe does not have a universal [electrical] standard. The ends of irons bristle with different plugs for different countries. Some have three prongs, others two; prongs protrude straight or angled, round or rectangular, fat, thin, and sometimes sheathed. There are circular plug faces, squares, pentagons, and hexagons. Some are perforated and some are notched. One French plug has a niche like a keyhole; British plugs carry fuses.[43]

Packaging also presents challenges for international marketers. Packaging issues can be subtle. For example, names, labels, and colours may not translate easily from one country to another. Packaging may also have to be tailored to meet the physical characteristics of consumers in various parts of the world. For instance, soft drinks are sold in smaller cans in Japan to better fit the smaller Japanese hand. Thus, although product and package standardization can produce benefits, companies usually must adapt their offerings to the unique needs of specific international markets.

Service marketers also face special challenges when going global. Some service industries have a long history of international operations. For example, banks had to provide global services to meet the foreign exchange and credit needs of their home-country clients wanting to sell overseas. In recent years, many banks have become truly global operations; Germany's Deutsche Bank, for example, has branches in over 40 countries.

The travel industry also moved naturally into international operations. North American hotel chains have expanded internationally. Air Canada has formed alliances with other world carriers so they can fly tourists and business travellers around the world. The early worldwide dominance of American Express has now been matched by Visa and MasterCard.

Professional and business services industries—accounting, engineering, management consulting, and advertising—have globalized. The international growth of these firms followed the globalization of the manufacturing companies they serve. For example, as their client companies began to use global marketing and advertising strategies, advertising agencies and other marketing services firms responded by globalizing their own operations.

Retailers are among the latest service businesses to go global. As their home markets become saturated with stores, retailers such as Wal-Mart, Toys 'R' Us, Office Depot, Saks Fifth Avenue, and Disney are expanding into faster-growing

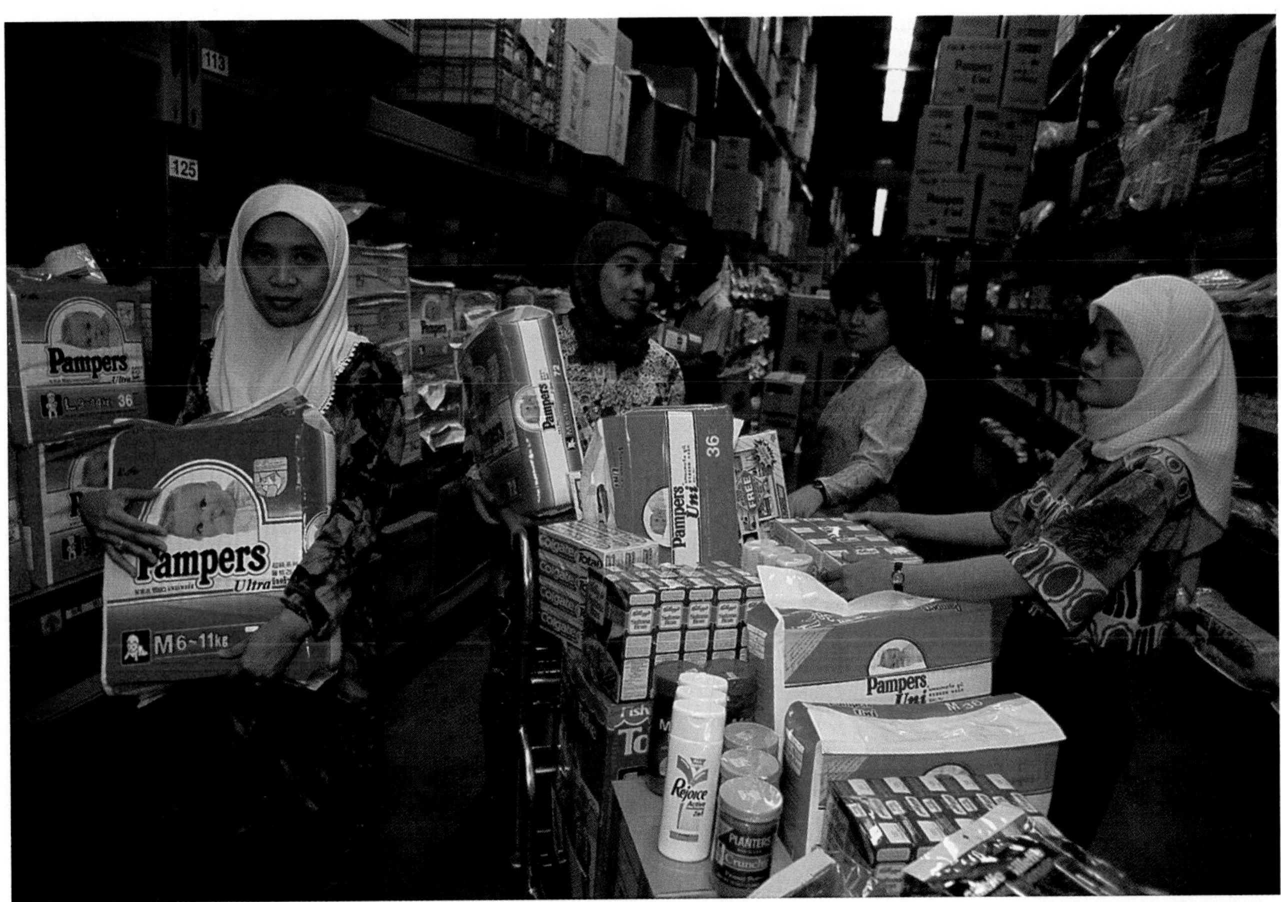

Retailers are among the latest service businesses to go global. Here Malaysian shoppers buy North American products in Dutch-owned Makro store in Kuala Lumpur.

markets abroad. Japanese retailer Yaohan now operates the largest shopping centre in Asia, the 21-storey Nextage Shanghai Tower in China, and Carrefour of France is the leading retailer in Brazil and Argentina. Asian shoppers now buy North American products in Dutch-owned Makro stores, now Southeast Asia's biggest store group with sales in that region of more than $2.8 billion.[44]

Service companies wanting to operate in other countries are not always welcomed with open arms. Whereas manufacturers usually face straightforward tariff, quota, or currency restrictions when attempting to sell their products in another country, service providers are likely to face more subtle barriers. In some cases, rules and regulations affecting international service firms reflect the host country's traditions. In others, they appear to protect the country's own fledgling service industries from large global competitors with greater resources. In still other cases, however, the restrictions seem to have little purpose other than to make entry difficult for foreign service firms.

A Turkish law, for example, forbids international accounting firms from bringing capital into the country to set up offices and requires them to use the names of local partners in their marketing rather than their own internationally known company names. In Buenos Aires, an accountant must have the equivalent of a high-school education in Argentinean geography and history. In New Delhi, India, international insurance companies are not allowed to sell property and casualty policies to the country's fast-growing business community or life insurance to its huge middle class.[45]

Despite these difficulties, the trend toward growth of global service companies continues, especially in banking, airlines, telecommunications, and professional services. Service firms are no longer simply following their manufacturing customers; they are taking the lead in international expansion.

Review of Concept Connections

A product is more than a set of tangible features. In fact, many marketing offers consist of combinations of both tangible goods and service. Offerings range from *pure tangible goods* at one extreme to *pure services* at the other. Each product or service offered to customers can be viewed on three levels. The *core product* consists of the core, problem-solving benefits that consumers seek when they buy a product. The *actual product* exists around the core and includes the quality level, features, design, brand name, and packaging. The *augmented product* is the actual product plus the various services and benefits offered with it, such as warranty, free delivery, installation, and maintenance.

1. Define product and the major classifications of products and services.

Products encompass more than simply tangible goods. Broadly defined, a *product* is anything that can be offered to a market for attention, acquisition, use, or consumption that might satisfy a want or need. Products include physical objects, services, persons, places, organizations, ideas, or mixes of these entities. Services are products that consist of activities, benefits, or satisfactions offered for sale that are essentially intangible, such as banking, hotel accommodation, tax preparation, and home repair services.

Products and services fall into two broad classes based on the types of consumers that use them. *Consumer products,* those bought by final consumers, are usually classified according to consumer shopping habits—convenience products, shopping products, specialty products, and unsought products. *Industrial products,* purchased for further processing or use in conducting a business, are classified according to their cost and the way they enter the production process—materials and parts, capital items, and supplies and services. Other marketable entities, such as organizations, persons, places, and ideas, can also be thought of as products.

2. Describe the roles of product and service branding, packaging, labelling, and product support services.

Companies develop strategies for items in their product lines by making decisions about product attributes, branding, packaging, labelling, and product support services. *Product attribute* decisions involve the quality, features, and design the company will offer. *Branding* decisions include selecting a brand name, garnering brand sponsorship, and developing a brand strategy. *Packaging* provides many key benefits, such as protection, economy, convenience, and promotion. Package decisions often include designing *labels,* which identify, describe, and possibly promote the product. Companies also develop *product support services,* which enhance customer service and satisfaction and safeguard against competitors.

3. Explain the decisions that companies make when developing product lines and mixes.

Most companies produce a product line rather than a single product. A *product line* is a group of products that are related in function, customer purchase needs, or distribution channels. In developing a product line strategy, marketers face a number of decisions. *Line stretching* involves extending a line downward, upward, or in both directions to occupy a gap that might otherwise be filled by a competitor. In contrast, *line filling* involves adding items within the present range of the line. The set of product lines and items offered to customers by a particular seller compose the *product mix*. The mix can be described by four dimensions—width, length, depth, and consistency—which are the tools for developing the company's product strategy.

4. Identify the four characteristics that affect the marketing of a service.

As we move toward a *world service economy,* marketers need to know more about marketing services. *Services* are characterized by four key characteristics. First, services are *intangible*—they cannot be seen, tasted, felt, heard, or smelled. Services are also *inseparable* from their service providers. Services are *variable* because their quality depends on the service provider as well as the environment surrounding the service delivery. Finally, services are *perishable,* so they cannot be inventoried, built up, or back ordered. Each characteristic poses problems and marketing requirements. Marketers work to find ways to make the service more tangible, to increase the productivity of providers who are inseparable from their products, to standardize the quality in the face of variability, and to improve demand movements and supply capacities in the face of service perishability.

5. Discuss the additional marketing considerations that services require.

Good service companies focus attention on *both* customers and employees. They understand the *service-profit chain* that links service firm profits with employee and customer satisfaction. Services marketing strategy calls for not only external marketing but also *internal marketing* to motivate employees and *interactive marketing* to create service delivery skills among service providers. To succeed, service marketers must create *competitive differentiation*, offer high *service quality*, and find ways to increase *service productivity*.

Key Terms

Actual product *(p. 322)*
Augmented product *(p. 324)*
Brand *(p. 331)*
Brand equity *(p. 332)*
Brand extension *(p. 341)*
Capital items *(p. 327)*
Co-branding *(p. 340)*
Consumer products *(p. 326)*
Convenience products *(p. 326)*
Core product *(p. 322)*
Industrial products *(p. 327)*
Interactive marketing *(p. 355)*
Internal marketing *(p. 355)*
Line extension *(p. 341)*
Manufacturer's brand (or national brand) *(p. 336)*
Materials and parts *(p. 327)*
Multibranding *(p. 342)*
Packaging *(p. 343)*
Packaging concept *(p. 344)*
Private brand (or store brand) *(p. 336)*
Product *(p. 321)*
Product design *(p. 330)*
Product line *(p. 348)*
Product mix (or product assortment) *(p. 350)*
Product quality *(p. 329)*
Product support services *(p. 347)*
Service *(p. 322)*
Service inseparability *(p. 353)*
Service intangibility *(p. 352)*
Service perishability *(p. 353)*
Service variability *(p. 353)*
Shopping products *(p. 327)*
Slotting fees *(p. 336)*
Social marketing *(p. 329)*
Specialty products *(p. 327)*
Supplies and services *(p. 328)*
Unsought products *(p. 327)*

Discussing the Issues

1. What is Intrawest's core, tangible product? How has it augmented this product? What service offerings does it combine with its core product? Has this combination of physical products and services created a competitive advantage for the firm relative to its competitors? Would you buy Intrawest stock, given the prediction by David Foot that participation in active sports such as skiing will decline? Are demographics alone sufficient to explain buyer behaviour?
2. Explain the primary differences between products and services. Give illustrations of marketing offers that highlight these differences. Provide an example of a "hybrid offer."
3. List and explain the core, actual, and augmented products of the educational experience that universities offer. How are these different, if at all, from the product offered by community colleges?
4. Because the classes of consumer products differ in the ways that consumers buy them, they also differ in how they are marketed. (a) Select what might typically be considered an unsought product and suggest how a marketer might convert this product into a specialty, shopping, or convenience product. (b) Explain how some personal computer manufacturers have been able to convert their specialty products into broader-based shopping products.
5. People can be thought of as products. (a) Using the federal election of 2000, indicate how the leading candidates for prime minister marketed themselves to the public. Think carefully about the tactics used, the advertising themes presented, and the images that were transmitted. (b) Construct a marketing profile of each of the major candidates. (c) From this analysis, what can you conclude about person marketing?
6. Brand name and symbol licensing has become a multibillion-dollar worldwide business. Using information from Marketing Highlight 8-2 and elsewhere in the chapter, devise a plan for licensing your school's logo, mascot, and other brand symbols. Your objective is to create toys, sportswear, gifts, and logo items that will have national appeal. Could co-branding also be an option? Explain.
7. For many years, there was one type of Coca-Cola and one type of Tide. Now we find Coke Classic,

Diet Coke, Cherry Coke, and several other versions of this popular soft drink. Tide detergent comes in Ultra, Liquid, Unscented, and several other formulations. It seems that almost every major brand has been greatly extended, some even past the breaking point. List the issues such brand extensions raise for manufacturers, retailers, and consumers.

8. What are internal and interactive marketing? Give an example of how a specific firm or organization might use these concepts to increase the effectiveness of its services marketing. How might these concepts be linked to services differentiation?

Marketing Applications

1. The core product in the automobile industry is transportation. The major problem-solving benefit is getting from one place to another quickly and safely. However, most automobile manufacturers differentiate their products with additional service benefits. The service approaches are almost as varied as are the automobile manufacturers themselves. Examine the Web sites for Ford (www.ford.ca), General Motors (www.gmcanada.com), Chrysler (www. daimler-chrysler.ca), Honda (www.honda.ca), Lexus (www.lexuscanada.com), Mercedes-Benz (www. mercedes-benz.ca), and Toyota (www.toyota.ca). Look beyond the automobiles themselves and closely examine the manufacturers' services and service options.
   a. What primary services do the various automobile manufacturers offer? Prepare a grid that compares each company with the others.
   b. What services do the different companies appear to offer in common? What services do they use to differentiate themselves from one another?
   c. Do any of the sites suggest that a company understands the service-profit chain? Explain.
   d. Do any of the auto companies use interactive marketing with respect to the service component? Explain.
   e. Visit the Saturn Web site at www.saturncanada. com. Does anything make this company different from those you have already visited? What seems to be the company's focus and differential advantage? Suggest ways in which Saturn could use its service component to compete more effectively against its competitors.
   f. What role does the Internet play in the product/ service strategies of the companies in question 1?

2. To expand beyond its core software business, Microsoft has created kiosks (boutiques) inside Tandy Corp.'s Radio Shack stores. Microsoft believes that if consumers receive information about the Web from sources other than just the Internet itself, they will more quickly accept the Internet as essential in their daily lives. It plans to construct 7000 "stores within stores" to demonstrate Microsoft products and services. The kiosks will explain to consumers the choices for connecting to the Web, including computers, hand-held devices, and MSN's WebTV. See www.microsoft.com and www.radioshack.com for details.
   a. What benefits will this new retailing venture produce for Microsoft and Radio Shack? What difficulties?
   b. Describe the core, actual, or augmented products associated with this new partnership.
   c. Has a service-profit chain been created? Explain.
   d. Given recent court rulings against Microsoft, how might this new partnership be viewed under the *Competition Act*?
   e. How should Radio Shack's and Microsoft's competitors respond to this new retailing approach?

Internet Connections

Service Strategies

The core service in the airline industry is transportation. The problem-solving benefit for the customer is travel from one place to another. To differentiate their services, airlines provide many additional benefits. To visit Europe, you might consider KLM Royal Dutch

Airlines, British Airways, or Lufthansa. Review the Web sites of these airlines and complete the table to evaluate their services.

For Discussion

1. How would you classify airlines using consumer product categories: convenience, shopping, specialty, or unsought products?
2. Which airline brand name best conveys a quality image to you?
3. How does each airline differentiate itself from the others: KLM? British Airways? Lufthansa?
4. If Lufthansa expanded by developing a tourist hotel, would you recommend a brand extension or a new brand? Justify your choice.
5. Which airline would you choose for your European travel? Why?

	KLM Royal Dutch Airlines www.klm.com	British Airways www.british-airways.com	Lufthansa www.lufthansa.com
Many destinations?			
Attractive frequent flyer program?			
Other service features			
Evidence of service quality			
Evidence of competitive positioning strategy			
Ways customers can give feedback to company at site			

Savvy Sites

- Network solutions (www.networksolutions.com) manages many of the domain names on the Internet. To use its brand name as a domain name in its Web address, each company in this exercise had to register at this site.
- The Gap site (www.gap.com) contains lots of information about its product mix. It even allows you to dress a male or female figure in your favorite Gap clothes.
- E*TRADE (www.etrade.com) is one of the first to offer investors online stock trading at a low price. Visit this site and see how it differentiates itself through a variety of services.

Notes

1. Intrawest, 1997 Annual Report, Vancouver, BC.
2. Intrawest, 1997 Annual Report, Vancouver, BC.
3. Ann Gibbon, "Big seen as best for ski resorts," *Globe and Mail,* 17 September 1996:B1,B4; Patti Summerfield, "Special report: Top database marketers: Top in hotels and tourism: Intrawest delivers multi-resort message," *Strategy,* 21 July 1997:DR12; Steve Threndyle, "Turning the corner: Canada's ski industry grows for the future," *Supplement to the Financial Post Magazine,* October 1996:1–8; Konrad Yarabuski, "Intrawest plans peak success," *Globe and Mail,* 29 September 1997:B1,B11; Erica Zlomislic, "Whistler targets American skiers," *Strategy,* 18 August 1997:8.

4. Ulrike de Brentani Emmanuel Ragot, "Developing new business-to-business professional services: What factors impact performance?" *Industrial Marketing Management*, November 1996: 517–30.

5. See V. Rangan Kasturi, Sohel Karim, and Sheryl K. Sandberg, "Do better at doing good," *Harvard Business Review*, May–June 1996:42–54; Alan R. Andreasen, *Marketing Social Change: Changing Behavior to Promote Health, Social Development, and the Environment*, San Francisco: Jossey-Bass, 1995; Alan R. Andreasen, Rob Gould, and Karen Gutierrez, "Social marketing has a new champion," *Advertising Age*, 7 February 2000:38; www.adcouncil.org, February 2000.

6. See Roland T. Rust, Anthony J. Zahorik, and Timothy L. Keiningham, "Return on quality (ROQ): Making service quality financially accountable," *Journal of Marketing*, April 1995:58–70; Valerie A. Zeithamel, Leonard L. Berry, and A. Parasuraman, "The behavioral consequences of service quality," *Journal of Marketing*, April 1996:31–46; and Otis Port, "The Baldrige's other reward," *Business Week*, 10 March 1997:75.

7. Philip Kotler, *Kotler on Marketing*, New York: Free Press, 1999:17.

8. Joseph Weber, "A better grip on hawking tools," *Business Week*, 5 June 1995:99. For more on product design, see Peter H. Bloch, "Seeking the ideal form: Product design and consumer response," *Journal of Marketing*, July 1995:16–29.

9. See "Hot RIP: The floppy disk," *Rolling Stone*, 20 August 1998:86; Owen Edwards, "Beauty and the box," *Forbes*, 5 October 1998:131; Bob Woods, "iMac drives Apple's Q2 results," *Computer Dealer News*, 30 April 1999:39; and Eleftheria Parpis, "Show toppers," *Adweek*, 10 May 1999:31–2.

10. Alice Rawsthorn, "The world's top 50 logos," *Report on Business Magazine*, November 2000:84–100.

11. Quote from Will Novosedlik, "Successful branding key to tomorrow's Internet leaders," *Globe and Mail*, 14 May 2000:B16. Bernadette Johnson, "Internet portals put on branding push: Control of e-commerce gateway at stake," *Strategy*, 6 November 2000:1.

12. Rawsthorn, "The world's top 50 logos."

13. Emily DeNitto, "They aren't private labels anymore—They're brands," *Advertising Age*, 13 September 1993:8; Warren Thayer, "Loblaws exec predicts: Private labels to surge," *Frozen Food Age*, May 1996:1.

14. Jennifer Lawrence, "Brands beware, Wal-Mart adds giant house label," *Advertising Age*, 5 April 1993:1,45.

15. Emily DeNitto, "They aren't private labels anymore—They're brands," *Advertising Age*, 13 September 1993:8; Warren Thayer, "Loblaws exec predicts: Private labels to surge," *Frozen Food Age*, May 1996:1; "Marketscan," *Canadian Grocer*, February 2000; "President's Choice continues brisk pace," *Frozen Food Age*, March 1998:17–8; David Dunne and Chakravarthi Narasimhan, "The new appeal of private labels," *Harvard Business Review*, May–June 1999:41–52; Marina Strauss, "Oshawa Group plans to fire up private-label war," *Globe and Mail*, 3 June 1994:B1–B2.

16. Strauss, "Oshawa Group plans to fire up private-label war."

17. Fawzia Sheikh, "Zellers aims for $200M in Truly sales," *Marketing On-line*, 8 March 1999; Bud Jorgensen, "Cott cashes in, makes enemies," *Globe and Mail*, 8 January 1994:B1,B6.

18. See Patrick Oster, "The Eurosion of brand loyalty," *Business Week*, 19 July 1993:22; Marcia Mogelonsky, "When stores become brands," *American Demographics*, February 1995:32–8; John A. Quelch and David Harding, "Brands versus private labels: Fighting to win," *Harvard Business Review*, January–February 1996:99–109; Stephanie Thompson, "Private label marketers getting savvier to consumption trends," *Brandweek*, 24 November 1997:9; and David Dunne and Chakravarthi Narasimham, "The new appeal of private labels," *Harvard Business Review*, May–June 1999:41–52.

19. Jan Wong, "Putting your own stamp on snail mail," *Globe and Mail*, 2 May 2000:A1,A6; Wendy Stueck, "Thirsty? Get your personalized pop on line," *Globe and Mail*, 16 March 2000: B1,B4.

20. See Wendy Cuthbert, "Biscuits Leclerc scores major licensing coup: Signs deal with Warner Bros. for right to use Looney Tunes characters," *Strategy*, 5 July 1999:25; Terry Lefton, "Warner Brothers' not very looney path to licensing gold," *Brandweek*, 14 February 1994:36–7; Robert Scally, "Warner builds brand presence, strengthens 'Tunes' franchise," *Discount Store News*, 6 April 1998:33; and Adrienne Mand, "Comet cursors bring WB characters to Web," *Adweek*, 19 April 1999:113. Silvia Sansoni, "Gucci, Armani, and . . . John Paul II?" *Business Week*, 13 May 1996:61; Bart A. Lazar, "Licensing gives known brands new life," *Advertising Age*, 16 February 1998:8; Robert Oas, "Licensed merchandise sales decrease, but corporate merchandise is on the rise," *Potentials*, April 1999:8; and Laura Petrecca, "'Corporate Brands' put licensing in the spotlight," *Advertising Age*, 14 June 1999:1.

21. David Eggleston, "Patriot flexes muscles for Barbie: Canadian computer firm joins with Mattel to market licensed PCs," *Strategy*, 16 August 1999:1; Jean Gaudreau, "The principles of online branding," *Strategy*, 13 September 1999:29.

22. Phil Carpenter, "Some cobranding caveats to obey," *Marketing News*, 7 November 1994:4; Karen Benezra, "Coke, Mattel ink pact for collectable Barbie," *Brandweek*, 14 October 1996:5; Tobi Elkin, "Brand builders," *Brandweek*, 2 February 1998:16–8; Stephanie Thompson, "Brand buddies," *Brandweek*, 23 February 1998:22–30; Gabrielle Solomon, "Co-branding alliances: Arranged marriages made by marketers," *Fortune*, 12 October 1998:188.

23. For more on line extensions, see Kevin Lane Keller and David A. Aaker, "The effects of sequential introduction of line extensions," *Journal of Marketing Research*, February 1992:35–50; and Srinivas K. Reddy, Susan L. Holak, and Subodh Bhat, "To extend or not to extend: Success determinants of line extensions," *Journal of Marketing Research*, May 1994:243–62; James Pollock, "Between the lines," *Marketing*, 17 April 1995:14.

24. Lisa Wright, "Rooting for a beaver with wings," *Toronto Star*, 8 June 2000:A1,A34.

25. Robert M. McMath, "Chock full of (pea)nuts," *American Demographics*, April 1997:60.

26. See Ira Teinowitz, "Brand proliferation attacked," *Advertising Age*, 10 May 1993:1,49; and Jennifer Lawrence, "P&G strategy: Build on brands," *Advertising Age*, 23 August 1993:3,31.

27. See Bill Abrams, "Marketing," *Wall Street Journal*, 20 May 1982:33; and Bernice Kanner, "Package deals," *New York*, 22 August 1988:267–8.

28. See Joan Holleran, "Packaging speaks volumes," *Beverage Industry*, February 1998:30.

29. Wallace Immen, "How to judge a food by its cover," *Globe and Mail*, 31 May 1994:A16.

30. See Ronald Henkoff, "Service is everybody's business," *Fortune*,

27 June 1994:48–60; Adrian Palmer and Catherine Cole, *Services Marketing: Principles and Practice,* Englewood Cliffs, NJ: Prentice Hall, 1995:56–60; and Fanglan Du, Paula Mergenhagen, and Marlene Lee, "The future of services," *American Demographics,* November 1995:30–47.

31. John Templeman, "A Mercedes in every driveway?" *Business Week,* 26 August 1996:38–40; and Sam Pickens and Dagmar Mussey, "Swatch taps Zurich shop to develop Euro car ads," *Advertising Age,* 19 May 1997:32.
32. See Industry Canada's Web site and Henkoff, "Service is everybody's business."
33. CN promotional brochure.
34. Terry Bullick, "No-frills airline takes flight in Western Canada," *Marketing,* 19 February 1996:2.
35. See James L. Heskett, Thomas O. Jones, Gary W. Loveman, W. Earl Sasser, Jr., and Leonard A. Schlesinger, "Putting the service-profit chain to work," *Harvard Business Review,* March–April 1994:164–74.
36. For excellent discussion on defining and measuring service quality, see A. Parasuraman, Valerie A. Zeithaml, and Leonard L. Berry, "A conceptual model of service quality and its implications for future research," *Journal of Marketing,* Fall 1985:41–50; Zeithaml, Parasuraman, and Berry, *Delivering Service Quality: Balancing Customer Perceptions and Expectations,* New York: The Free Press, 1990; J. Joseph Cronin, Jr. and Steven A. Taylor, "Measuring service quality: A reexamination and extension," *Journal of Marketing,* July 1992:55–68; and Parasuraman, Zeithaml, and Berry, "Reassessment of expectations as a comparison standard in measuring service quality: Implications for further research," *Journal of Marketing,* January 1994:111–24.
37. John Paul Newport, "American Express: Service that sells," *Fortune,* 20 November 1989. Also see Frank Rose, "Now quality means service too," *Fortune,* 22 April 1991:97–108.
38. Christopher W. L. Hart, James L. Heskett, and W. Earl Sasser, Jr., "The profitable art of service recovery," *Harvard Business Review,* July–August 1990:148–56.
39. CN promotional brochure.
40. See James L. Heskett, W. Earl Sasser, Jr., and Christopher W. L. Hart, *Service Breakthroughs,* New York: Free Press, 1990.
41. Barry Farber and Joyce Wycoff, "Customer service: Evolution and revolution," *Sales & Marketing Management,* May 1991:44–51.
42. David Atkin, "Online shoppers hate bad service," *Financial Post,* 8 March 2000:C5.
43. Philip Cateora, *International Marketing,* 8th ed., Homewood, IL, Irwin, 1993:270.
44. Carla Rapoport, "Retailers go global," *Fortune,* 20 February 1995:102–8.
45. Lee Smith, "What's at stake in the trade talks," *Fortune,* 27 August 1990:76–7.

Company Case 8

The Skisailer

Early in 1987, David Varilek was given the bad news about the worldwide sales of his invention, the Skisailer. The management at Mistral, the company that had invested in David's innovation, informed him that the first-year sales of Skisailer had failed to match the target and that the future of the product was in doubt. Only 708 Skisailers had been sold in the first season the product was on sale. Mistral, which manufactured and marketed the product worldwide, had already invested more than half a million dollars in the project. The management was seriously considering dropping the product from its line the next year.

Realizing that such an initial setback could jeopardize the future of his four-year-old invention, in March 1987, David asked a group of MBA students at a leading international school of management in Switzerland to study the market potential for Skisailer and recommend what needed to be done to revive sales. The students completed the first phase of the project and presented David with their findings, which the 23-year-old inventor reviewed.

The Invention

Skisailer was based on a concept that combined downhill skiing and windsurfing in a new sport: skisailing. As a Swiss native, David Varilek considered himself "born on skis." However, he had always been frustrated by not being able to ski on the flat snow fields that surrounded his home in the winter season.

In 1983, in his own garage, David invented a connection bar that could be fixed onto regular skis while still allowing them to be directed with great flexibility. A windsurfing rig, consisting of a connecting bar and a sail, could then be installed on the connection bar and, with enough wind, flat snow surfaces could become great fun for skiing. The idea was subsequently patented under the Swiss law. A major feature of the invention was that the Skisailer's design also allowed "windskiers" to use regular downhill skis and almost any type of windsurfing rig, an innovation that limited the buyer's expense. The connection bar and the sail were easy to install. Lateral clamps used for attaching the connection bar to the skis did not damage them in any way except for small grooves on the side of each ski. Only five centimetres of the ski's length were held rigid, and the rest retained normal flexibility. Safety had been an important consideration in developing the Skisailer; three self-releasing safety mechanisms were installed on the product.

The Skisailer could be used on either smooth slopes or flat surfaces. The ideal surface for skisailing had the kind of hard-packed snow usually found on groomed ski slopes, but the Skisailer could also be used on ice, where it could achieve speeds of up to 100 kilometres an hour. Skisailing in deep snow or slightly uphill required stronger wind. For use at high speeds, a safety helmet was recommended.

According to David Varilek, skisailing was as much fun as windsurfing even though it had to be done in cold weather. "For identical sensations, skisailing is easier to learn and handle than windsurfing," David claimed. "You can get on and get off the Skisailer easily, and you are always on your feet. Another great thing with the Skisailer is that you can take advantage of the terrain to perform the same kind of loopings as on sea waves. The Skisailer is a great vehicle for discovering variety in the surroundings."

Mistral Windsurfing AG

In 1987, Mistral Windsurfing AG was a company affiliated with the ADIA Group, a $1 billion conglomerate headquartered in Lausanne, Switzerland, which had its activities centered around ADIA Interim, a company providing temporary personnel to companies around the world.

ADIA had acquired Mistral in 1980 as part of its diversification strategy. The acquisition was seen as an opportunity to enter a rapidly growing industry. Consistency in marketing and product policy over the previous 10 years had made Mistral a leader in the worldwide windsurfing industry. This success was grounded in technological competence, permanent innovation, high quality standards, a selective international distribution policy, and strong financial backing. Thus, in a fiercely competitive market for windsurfing equipment, characterized by the rise and fall of brands and manufacturers, Mistral was occupying a leading position. To Martin Pestalozzi, the president of ADIA, the Skisailer represented a good opportunity to extend Mistral's product line at a time when Mistral management was increasingly concerned about the future of the windsurfer market.

Mistral and the Windsurfer Market

The fathers of the modern windsurfer were Californians Hoyle Schweitzer and James Drake, who had developed the concept and registered the Windsurfer brand. They had applied for and received a patent in 1970 for their device, which was a cross between a surfboard and a sailboat.

In the early 1970s, Schweitzer bought out Drake and developed his firm, Windsurfing International, from a living-room operation into a multimillion-dollar corporation with branches in six countries. Due to its North American patents, Windsurfing International was able to hold a virtual monopoly in the United States and Canada until 1979 when a number of other firms entered the market.

Meanwhile, competition in the European windsurfing equipment market was years ahead of North America. First introduced to the European market by Ten Cate, a Dutch firm, windsurfing enjoyed an unprecedented growth, particularly in France and Germany. Even as the industry matured in the mid-1980s, it maintained growth in terms of dollar volume, though not in units. Interest in windsurfing had grown from a small pool of enthusiasts to a large and growing population, an estimated two to three million people internationally.

Established in 1976 in Bassersdorf near Zurich, Switzerland, Mistral rapidly won an international reputation among windsurfers. Its success was enhanced by two promotional strategies. First, from the start, Mistral had signed up Robby Naish, a young Californian who had won all the major distinctions and titles in this sport. Using Mistral equipment, Robby Naish had become the 1977 World Champion at age 12 and had dominated this sport ever since. In 1986, he won the world title for the tenth time in a row. Second, Mistral had promoted its brand by supplying several hundred windsurfs free of charge to such leisure organizations as Club Méditerranée that gave the brand visibility around the world.

Mistral also enjoyed an advantage over other windsurf manufacturers by concentrating on the upper price and quality range of the market. Worldwide, Mistral's equipment was considered the best. Robby Naish's name and the high quality and reliability of Mistral's products had helped build an extensive network of distributors in 30 countries. In 1980, the company had its own subsidiary in the US, where it generated about one-third of its global sales and market share. Mistral was also directly represented in a number of European countries, including France, Germany, and the Benelux. For the rest of the world, Mistral used exclusive agents who were responsible for selling Mistral products in specific regions.

Recent Market Developments in Windsurfing

A number of factors had recently combined to dampen the sales of windsurfs in the US market. Patent infringement fights had led to the forced withdrawal of Bic and Tiga, both French manufacturers, from the market. With a total sales of 16 000 units, the two companies were among the major brands in the US. Meanwhile, a number of European manufacturers had gone bankrupt, thus reducing even further the supply of and marketing expenditures on windsurfing equipment. Market saturation had also contributed to the decline of sales from 73 000 units in 1985 to 62 000 in 1986.

In Europe, where windsurfing had grown at spectacular rates over the years, the market was showing signs of a slowdown. According to the French market research group ENERGY, windsurfing equipment sales in France had risen from less than 600 units in 1974 to more than 115 000 units in early 1980s. However, cool weather conditions as well as general market saturation had reduced French sales to 65 000 units in 1986. In Germany, the second-largest market after France, sales had also declined to below 60 000 units from the high levels of the early 1980s. Sales had levelled off in Italy at around 35 000 units, in Holland at 45 000 units, and in Switzerland at 15 000 units.

European sales were dominated by European brands. In France, for example, Bic and Tiga together accounted for 45 000 sales; Mistral was the top imported brand. In Germany, Klepper was the leading local brand; Mistral was a distant fourth in market share. In 1986, the distribution of Mistral's global sales of 45 620 units was the United States, 25 percent; Europe, 30 percent; and the rest of the world, 45 percent. Windsurfing equipment accounted for 60 percent of the company's $52 million sales, while the rest was divided between sportswear (20%) and spare parts and accessories (20%).

The Skisailer and Mistral's Diversification Policy

Mistral Windsurfing AG had contacted David Varilek at the beginning of 1984 after ADIA management learned about the Skisailer from a four-page article in a major Swiss magazine. David was interested in establishing a relationship with Mistral because the company was the world leader in windsurfing equipment.

The Skisailer seemed an appropriate product diversification for Mistral. The Skisailer could also fit in with the new line of winter sportswear and other ski-related products that Mistral's management was planning to develop. Mistral had full support from ADIA to launch the project.

In the spring of 1984, a contract for development, manufacturing, and distribution of the Skisailer was formally signed between David Varilek and Mistral. For the duration of the agreement, all Skisailer patent and trademark rights would be transferred to Mistral, but David would serve as technical adviser to the company and would receive in return a two percent royalty on sales. It was also agreed that David would demonstrate the Skisailer in competitions and exhibitions where Mistral was participating. Should total sales fall short of 5000 units by the end of 1986, either party could terminate the agreement, with trademarks and patents reverting back to David Varilek. Mistral could also counter any competitive offer made to David, a "first right of refusal."

Introducing the Skisailer

During the summer of 1984, two prototypes of the Skisailer were developed at Mistral for presentation in November at ISPO, the largest European sports exhibition held annually in Munich, Germany. Between May and November 1984, the engineers developed several innovations that were added to the Skisailer. For example, the connecting bar and mounting blocks were strengthened to resist shocks and low temperatures. The equipment was also modified to accommodate the Mistral windsurf sailing rig.

At ISPO, the Skisailer was widely acclaimed as a truly innovative product that would certainly win public enthusiasm. However, at this early stage of development, the product still lacked promotional support. No pamphlet, video, or pictures had been developed to present the product and educate potential users. David thought that the pictures used to introduce the product to Mistral's distributors were not attractive enough to trigger interest and buying. Nevertheless, some distributors liked the product and placed immediate orders.

The formal launch of Skisailer got under way in 1986. Mistral produced 2000 Skisailers, consisting of a mast foot, sail (available from its standard windsurf line), and the connecting bar. They were to be distributed worldwide through the company's network of wholesalers and independent sports shops in large and medium-sized cities. For example, in Lausanne, a city of 250 000 inhabitants with 30 skishops and three windsurf equipment stores, Skisailer was sold in three locations. Of the three stores, two specialized in ski equipment and the third sold windsurfing products.

Skisailer was priced at $410 retail; the price included the bar connection and its mounting blocks, but excluded the sail and mast, which cost an additional $590. Retail margins on the Skisailer and its rig were set at 35 percent. The wholesale margins were also 35 percent. Skisailer cost Mistral $85 per unit to produce and ship to distributors; the cost for the sailing rig was around $200.

It seemed to David that the 1986 promotional budget of $15 000 set for Skisailer was too low. Mistral management had already turned down a $35 000 proposal from David to produce a promotional video showing Skisailer in action. Nevertheless, David decided to arrange for the shooting of such a video on his own at Mammoth Lake, California. Mistral later refunded David the $10 000 that the video had cost him.

As of early 1987, Mistral had invested more than $500 000 in Skisailer:

Engineering and tooling	$214 000
Other costs	74 000
Development costs	**288 000**
Inventory: Assembled and spares	
At central warehouse	180 000
At distributors	68 000
Total	**$536 000**

Market Research Findings

Because of his concern about the future of the Skisailer, David had commissioned the group of MBA students to study the global market for Skisailer and report on their findings. By early fall, the students had completed the first phase of their study, which dealt with estimating the market potential for Skisailer, competing products, ski market developments, and a survey of buyers, retailers, and wholesalers. A summary of the findings follows.

Potential Market

Based on interviews with buyers of the Skisailer, the team had learned that the potential customers were likely to be those who did both skiing and windsurfing. Building on industry reports suggesting a total worldwide population of 2 million windsurfers and 30 million skiers, the team estimated that a maximum of 60 percent of windsurfers, or a total of 1.2 million individuals, were also skiers. The "realizable market" for the Skisailer, according to the MBA students, was far below this maximum, however. They identified at least four "filters," which together reduced the realizable market potential to a fraction of the maximum:

Filter 1: Customer type. As a relatively new sport, Skisailer appealed to a group of enthusiasts whom the MBA students referred to as "innovators." Their study suggested that these buyers were in the 15 to 25 age bracket, liked sports but, for the most part, could not afford the price tag of the Skisailer. The next most likely group of buyers, called "early adopters," were older, less sporty, and more image conscious. The team believed that sufficient penetration of the first segment was necessary before the second group would show any interest in the new product.

Filter 2: Location. Users of the Skisailer reported that ideal skisailing conditions, such as flat ice- or snow-covered fields, were not always accessible. This location factor, the team believed, reduced the potential for the product.

Filter 3: Climate. The Skisailer required not only suitable snow or ice, but also a good wind. The minimum required wind speed was around 20 kilometres an hour. The study identified a number of regions as meeting both the needed snow and wind conditions: Scandinavia and central Europe, certain parts of North America, and parts of Southern Australia.

Filter 4: Competing products. Four similar products were identified but, according to the student report, all lacked brand image, wide distribution, and product sophistication. Although information on competing products was scanty, the students had assembled the information in Exhibit 1 from different sources.

Exhibit 1 Competing Products

Brand (origin)	Retail Price	Total Units Sold	Main Sales Area
Winterboard (Finland)	$395	4000	Finland, United States
Ski Sailer (Australia)	$90	3500	Australia, United States
ArticSail (Canada)	$285	3000	Canada, United States
Ski Sailer (United States)	$220	300	United States

Based on their initial estimate of the maximum size of the potential market, as well as the limiting effects of the four filters, the students arrived at an estimate of 20 000 units as the total realizable market for Skisailer (see Exhibit 2). This volume, they believed, could grow by as much as 10 percent a year.

Exhibit 2 Skisailer Market Potential

Market	Size	%	Filters
Potential market	1.2 million	100	Customer type
Available market	800 000	66	Location, climate
Qualified market	80 000	7	Indirect competition (monoski, skates, etc.)
Served market	40 000	3.5	Direct competition (Winterboard, ArticSail, etc.)
Realizable market	20 000	1.7	Customer type

Exhibit 3 Skisailer Achievable Sales Estimate

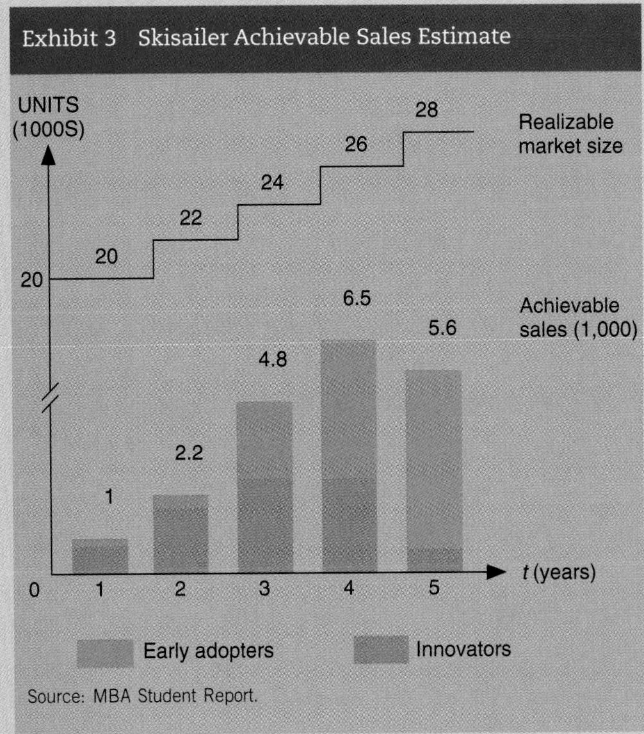

Source: MBA Student Report.

Competing Products

Winterboard

Winterboard, a light windsurfing board with skis, had been invented in Finland. It could be used on both ice and snow, and its performance was said to be impressive. Some rated the Winterboard as the best-performing windski after the Skisailer. In terms of sales, Winterboard had been the most successful windski product. Over the previous five years, 4000 units have been sold, mainly in Scandinavia and the United States, in regular sports shops. Winterboard was being sold at a retail price of $395, excluding the sailing rig. Retail margins were 40 percent. The skis were already integrated into the board and did not need to be purchased as an extra.

According to the research team, Winterboard's management believed that prices, retail margins, and advertising expenditures were relatively unimportant in their marketing strategy. The key to success was organizing events, because people wanted sportive social gathering on weekends in the winter. When they had to go out snowsailing in the cold by themselves, they quickly lost interest.

Australian-made Ski Sailer

This product was essentially a simple bar with a mastfoot on it that could be attached to normal ski boots and used with either conventional skis or roller skates. The Ski Sailer had an equalizing slide and joint mechanism, so such manoeuvres as parallel turns, jump turns, and snowplowing were possible. Any sailing rig could be fitted to the Ski Sailer's mast post.

The US distributor for this product reported cumulative sales of about 3000 units—30 percent through ski shops, 70 percent through surf shops—at a retail price of $90 each. But he admitted that he had lost interest in the product when he realized that only customers who were tough and resistant to the cold enjoyed windsurfing in the wintertime. This meant a much smaller customer base than for his other leisure and sportswear products.

ArticSail Board

This product was essentially a W-shaped surfboard for use on snow, ice, or water. It was distributed by Plastiques L.P.A. Ltd. in Mansonville, Quebec, about 70 kilometres from the US border. The ArticSail was especially designed for snow and ice, but could also be used on water, in which case the rear filler plates would be replaced by two ailerons, also supplied with the board. Adjustable footstraps, included with the board, also had to be repositioned for use on water. The product was made of a special plastic, usable at both normal and very low temperatures. The producer warned users to watch for objects that could damage the underside of the sled.

The company reported a cumulative sales of about 3000 units (600 estimated for the winter of 1987–1988), mostly in Canada, at a retail price of $285 (including a 38 percent retail margin). Promotion expenses were about 15 percent on Canadian and US sales, mainly spent on a two-person team demonstrating at skisailing resorts.

American-made Ski Sailer

Yet another Ski Sailer had been invented by a young Californian, Carl Meinberg. The American Ski Sailer also used a small board mounted on skis and was similar to the product developed by David Varilek. On his own, the inventor had sold about 50 Ski Sailers retailing at $220 each. During the winter season, Carl Meinberg toured a number of ski resorts, demonstrating the

Ski Sailer; he spent the rest of the year selling his invention.

Recent Developments in the World Ski Market

As background to their study, the research team also obtained information on the ski market. The 1986 sales of downhill (also called alpine) and cross-country skis are given in Exhibit 4.

Exhibit 4 World Market of Alpine and Cross-Country Skis: 1985–1986 Season

Ski Sales	Pairs Sold
Apline	
Austria, Switzerland, Germany	1 450 000
Rest of Europe	1 550 000
United States and Canada	1 600 000
Japan	1 100 000
Other	300 000
Total	6 000 000
Cross-Country	
Austria, Switzerland, Germany	700 000
Scandinavia	800 000
Rest of Europe	400 000
United States and Canada	750 000
Other countries	150 000
Total	2 800 000

The total world alpine skiing population was estimated at 30 million people in 1987. Competition in the ski market was intensive, and production capacity exceeded demand by an estimated 25 to 30 percent in 1987. Prices for skis were under pressure, and retailers used discounts to build traffic. Retail profits were highest on sales of accessories and skiwear.

In distribution, specialty shops were losing market share to the large chains. Production was concentrated, with seven manufacturers controlling 80 percent of the market. The falling exchange rate for the US dollar had put the large European producers such as Fischer and Kneissel at a disadvantage in the US market.

Marketing skis depended heavily on successes in world championships and the image associated with the winning skis. In the mid-1980s, customers in the United States appeared to be losing interest in skiing, but these signs had not been observed in Europe and Japan, where the sport remained popular at a stable level.

A new innovation in skiing was the snowboard, a product with increasing popularity among younger customers. A snowboard was essentially a single large ski with two ski bindings positioned in a similar way as the footstraps on a windsurfer. The board had been available in the US for many years, but had only recently been introduced in Europe. Snowboard's worldwide sales had doubled every year, reaching an estimated 40 000 in the 1986 season. One US manufacturer Burton accounted for 50 percent of the market. Many manufacturers of winter products had taken advantage of the opportunity and had started producing their own versions of the snowboard. The product was very popular in the European distribution channels, and expectations for further growth were high.

Buyers' Survey

The research team had interviewed a small number of Skisailer customers in Germany, Austria, the Benelux countries, the US, and Canada. Highlights of their comments on the advantages and disadvantages of the Skisailer follow:

Advantages of the Product

- Sure, skisurfing in winter is great; it's a lot of fun.
- You can do quick manoeuvres, nice turns, beautiful power turns, and fast changes of the grips. It (the Skisailer) gives a good opportunity to train for windsurfing, as you have to drive the way you surf—with the pressure on the inner ski.
- I did not have any problem with turns.
- It is not difficult to learn if you have some feeling for sailing.
- It simulates surfing in your backyard.
- It is the right device if you want to do something on Sunday afternoon (with no time to drive somewhere in your car).
- Fun, different, new, good.
- It is the only thing with a mountain touch that you can use on the plain.
- It turns. That makes it much more fun than the other products on the market. You can do jives, curve jives, jumps. . . . It is close to sailing a shore boat . . . it's a lot of fun.
- If the conditions are ideal, it's a lot of fun.

Disadvantages of the Product

- The feet get twisted; sailing on the wind requires exceptional twisting of the legs and knees.
- Both of the white caps at the end of the bar came off and it was virtually impossible to get spare parts.
- Difficult in heavy snow.
- Difficult to find the perfect conditions.

- You use it three or four times a season. For this, the price is too high.
- It is uncomfortable to use. You have to loosen up your boots; otherwise, the rim of the shoe cuts into your twisted leg.
- If the snow is too deep, you cannot use it. What you want is strong wind.
- The price is too high.
- My problem is that there is hardly any wind in winter.
- In the beginning, I was getting stiff in the unnatural position and my knees hurt, but later I got more relaxed and with time you have a lot of fun.
- In mid-winter, it is too cold to use it; spring is ideal.
- In my environment, there is no space to do it, no lakes, no fields.
- For a backyard product, the price is too high. Even Mistral's good image doesn't help. Maybe this will change if the product is better known.
- Customers watched the video with enthusiasm, but when they learned the price, enthusiasm was nil. We are offering our last piece now at a discount of 40 percent.
- If you ski and windsurf, your hobbies cost you a lot of money. Often the early user is the sportive freak with a low income. How will you convince him about the product?

Retailers' Opinions of the Mistral Skisailer

A dozen retailers of the Skisailer—in Germany, Canada, Austria, and France—were also surveyed. Highlights of their comments follow:

Advantages of the Product

- You could sell a lot of them in the first year, but I do not see it as the absolute "barnstormer."
- It is a first-year novelty.
- It is a lot of fun in the snow . . . and for people with a lot of money. It is a new gimmick.
- It combines two favourite sports . . . skiing and windsurfing.
- It is better than all self-built products . . . you have full movability.
- Easy to use. It is an original idea.
- You can use your ski, it is flexible and easy to store.
- Very thoroughly constructed, very stable.

Disadvantages of the Product

- Unhappy with product. Usable only under specific weather conditions.
- It is only a fad.
- You just don't drive with your ski to a lake and try it on the ice.
- Maybe it sells better in a winter shop.
- Your position on the skis is abnormal—the snowboard is a better alternative.
- We do not think that it will be a fast-turning product. . . .
- Impossible to sell—nobody tried it.

Distributors' Comments

The research team interviewed Mistral distributors in 10 different countries in Europe and North America. Highlights of comments from five distributors follow:

Europe

- We first learned about the Skisailer at ISPO in Munich and ordered some.
- From Mistral we got some folders and the video. If you see it on the video, you want to use the Skisailer right away.
- We did not support the retailers very much because we felt that the Skisailer's marketing was not done professionally from the beginning. For instance, Skisailer deliveries were late.
- The product would have potential if the price were lower and the promotion were done professionally all the way through.
- We bought the Skisailer, which is good for use in our winter climate, after Mistral contacted us in 1985.
- The product is expensive and not really functional.
- Promotion was not good at all, only a few folders and a video, which was not free of charge. When there were product breakdowns, spare parts were not available.
- A Finnish competitor now has captured the market with a product that looks like a surfboard with two skis fitted into it. We have the right places for skisailing here!
- We used all our contracts and spent approximately $7500 in mid-1987 to promote this product on television.
- The retail price is too high for a product to be used only a few weekends in the winter.

- The snowboard, especially made for surfing on ski slopes, is much more fashionable.
- Surf and ski shops make higher margins on clothing and accessories that are sold in larger quantities.
- You don't create a product first and then look for the market; this is the wrong way around. The Skisailer is more a product for Scandinavia and similar regions in America or Canada.
- We didn't know the product but found the demonstration film to be convincing. Therefore, we organized ski resort demonstrations in the French Alps at racing events where there are many spectators. We also pushed about 40 Skisailers in several retail shops.
- For this product, finding suitable locations where you can have a training session with wind and snow is necessary.
- We estimate that the retailers have sold about half their inventory, but we do not want to get more involved and have the rest sent back to us. Retailers are looking for customer demand, which is lacking.

North America

- I cannot see further sales of the Skisailer without more product support. At low temperatures the rubber joints failed, but when we asked for replacements, there was no reply from Mistral. In the end, we had to strip other Skisailers to get the spare parts.
- We have good skisailing conditions (in southern Ontario/Quebec) and a group of interested enthusiasts here. The product has been promoted to thousands of people! The folder and video are very good.
- On a trade show in Toronto, the product was well received except for the price, which is a problem.

UNIT SALES			
Country	To Distributors	To Retailers	To End Users
United States and Canada	233	98	45
Germany	250	50	10
Switzerland	42	30	1
France	56	40	20
Benelux	60	0	0
Others	67	12	4
Total shipped	708	230	80

Conclusion

In reviewing the research team's report, David was searching for clues that could explain the Skisailer's poor performance in its first selling season. Was it the product design that needed further refinement? Or the Skisailer's price, which was perceived by some as being high? Was the absence of high promotional support, which he always suspected to be a problem, a key factor? Or maybe Mistral's selective distribution was the core issue? What else could explain why his invention had failed to match everybody's expectations?

An additional piece of information had heightened the need for immediate action. David had just received the final sales and inventory figures for the Skisailer from Mistral; while 708 units had been sold to the trade, only 80 units had been bought at retail.

David knew that Mistral management was about to review the future of the Skisailer. He feared that without a convincing analysis and action plan from him, the Skisailer would be dropped from Mistral's line. He was, therefore, impatiently waiting for the MBA research team's recommendations based on the data already collected.

Questions

1. What type of product is the Skisailer? To whom does it appeal? Has the company properly identified the target market?
2. Define the main elements of the marketing program for the Skisailer. What are the program's strengths and weaknesses? What obstacles have limited the product's success?
3. Evaluate the research done by the MBA team. Do you agree with their methods and the conclusions arising from their study? How confident are you in the estimates of the product's market potential?
4. What are David's options? What criteria would you use to assess the various options? What should David do? Why have you made this recommendation?

Source: This case was written by Professors Dominique Turpin and Kamran Kashani as a basis for class discussion rather than to illustrate either effective or ineffective handling of an administrative situation.

video case 8

PORTELLO: REPOSITIONING FOR GROWTH

In an industry dominated by such large companies as Coca-Cola and Pepsi, is there still room for small players in the soft-drink industry? Raj Rajerdiani believes so. He obtained the Canadian rights to a British soft drink called Portello, a beverage that has been sold around the world for more than 100 years in places such as the United Kingdom, India, Guyana, and Somalia. With just $30 000 as his start-up capital and an office in his basement, Raj started Bay Hill Impex, the company that would sell Portello in Canada. Within a short time the business became a family venture, employing his daughter, Natasha, his son, Neil, and his son-in-law, Amar.

Initially, Raj defined his target market as new immigrants to Canada since he believed that newcomers to Canada are often interested in finding some of the products they enjoyed in their homelands. Consequently, Raj established distribution agreements with small, ethnic grocery stores in the Toronto area whose clientele was consistent with his target market. This strategy was moderately successful: annual sales reached $750 000. But Raj believed that this market was limited and that true growth for his company would only be achieved by capturing larger markets. To broaden the target market and make the product available in mainstream distribution channels, he initiated discussions with some supermarkets, hoping to secure distribution arrangements.

In another attempt to reach additional target markets, Natasha and Neil tried to distribute Portello in nightclubs. They devised a cross-promotion strategy with a dance-format radio station that put the station's logo on the label of every bottle of Portello. In return, Portello received free advertising on the station. The promotion was ideal from Bay Hill's perspective since it didn't involve any additional costs. However, the idea of targeting nightclub patrons ended up being a risky strategy. Some nightclubs couldn't pay for the products as a result of unreliable club management and there seemed to be a poor match between the product and the consumers who frequented the clubs.

A year after abandoning the nightclub strategy, Portello is being repositioned to capture a broader target market. Armed with a strategic study conducted by three business students from the University of Western Ontario Business School, the management ream at Bay Hill has significantly changed its marketing strategy in preparation for targeting a larger, mainstream market. For example, instead of carrying out discussions with one supermarket at a time, the company has signed an agreement with a food distributor who will sell the product to large supermarkets for a percentage of sales. They have also decided to increase the price of Portello slightly, a move that they believe consumers will not notice but that will help to pay for changes such as the purchase of a new labelling machine. Packaging changes will also be made with the objective of marketing the product more visible on competitive supermarket shelves.

The management team at Bay Hill is also looking forward to geographic expansion. While current business is centered in Ontario, they are now moving into the rest of Canada. A trade show in Vancouver offered the company an opportunity to talk to distributors in Western Canada and assess competition. The next challenge will be entering the US market. Now that Raj has obtained the US rights to Portello, he will be preparing a marketing strategy to enter that market, building on the lesson she has learned in Canada.

Questions

1. Do you think that the Portello brand name is an asset? Why or why not?
2. The packaging for Portello is going to be changed to target more of a mainstream market. What packaging changes would you recommend?
3. What changes, if any, should Raj and the Bay Hill Impex management team make to their current marketing strategy before introducing Portello in the United States?

Source: The case was prepared by Auleen Carson and is based on "Portello Repeat and Update," *Venture* (March 30, 1997).

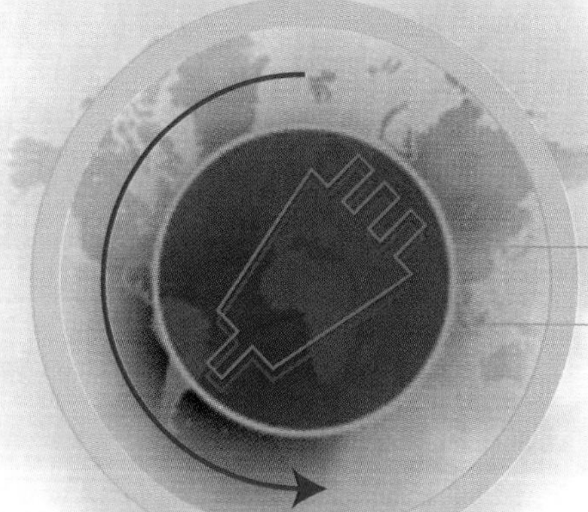

PART 1 2 **3** 4

Developing the Marketing Mix

Concept Connections

When you finish this chapter, you should be able to

1. Explain how companies find and develop new product ideas.
2. List and define the steps in the new-product development process.
3. Describe the stages of the product life cycle.
4. Describe how marketing strategies change over the product's life cycle.

chapter 9

New-Product Development and Life-Cycle Strategies

"New products!" declares Gillette's chairman and CEO, Alfred M. Zeien, "That's the name of the game." Since Gillette's foundingin 1901, its heavy commitment to innovation has kept the company razor sharp. Gillette is best known for its absolute dominance of the razor-and-blades market. However, all of its divisions—Duracell batteries, Gillette toiletries and cosmetics (Right Guard, Soft & Dri), stationery products (Parker, Paper Mate, and Waterman pens), Oral-B toothbrushes, and Braun electrical appliances—share common traits: Each is profitable, fast-growing, number one worldwide in its markets, and anchored by a steady flow of innovative new product offerings. In 1998, 40 percent of Gillette's sales came from products that didn't exist five years before. "Gillette is a new product machine," said one Wall Street analyst.

New products don't just happen at Gillette. New-product success starts with a company-wide culture that supports innovation. Whereas many companies try to protect their successful existing products, Gillette encourages innovations that will cannibalize its established product hits. "They know that if they don't bring out a new zinger, someone else will," observed an industry consultant. Gillette also accepts blunders and dead ends as a normal part of creativity and innovation. It knows that it must generate dozens of new product ideas to get just one success in the marketplace. The company scorns what CEO Zeien calls "putting blue dots in the soap powder"—attaching superficial frills to existing products and labelling them innovations. However, Gillette strongly encourages its people to take creative risks in applying cutting-edge technologies to find substantial improvements that make life easier for customers.

New-product development is complex and expensive, but Gillette's mastery of the process has put the company in a class of its own. For example, Gillette spent $275 million on designing and developing its Sensor family of razors, garnering 29 patents along the way. It spent an incredible $1.5 billion on the development of Sensor's successor, the triple-bladed Mach3, and applied for 35 more patents. Competing brands Bic and Wilkinson have managed to claim significant shares of the disposable-razor market, and Schick, Norelco, and Remington compete effectively in electric razors with Gillette's Braun unit. But Gillette, with its stunning technological superiority, operates with virtually no competition worldwide in the burgeoning cartridge-razor sector. Backed by Gillette's biggest new

product launch ever, the Mach3 strengthened the company's stranglehold on this market. Within only a few months of its introduction, the new razor and blades were number-one sellers.

At Gillette, it seems that almost everyone gets involved in one way or another with new-product development. Even people who don't participate directly in the product design and development are likely to be pressed into service testing prototypes. Every working day at Gillette, 200 volunteers from various departments come to work unshaven, troop to the second floor of the company's gritty South Boston manufacturing and research plant, and enter small booths with a sink and mirror. There they take instructions from technicians on the other side of a small window as to which razor, shaving cream, or aftershave to use. The volunteers evaluate razors for sharpness of blade, smoothness of glide, and ease of handling. When finished, they enter their judgments into a computer. In a nearby shower room, women perform the same ritual on their legs and underarms. "We bleed so you'll get a good shave at home," says one Gillette employee.

This type of research supported Gillette's launch of its shaving gel Satin Care into the Canadian marketplace. Aimed at women, the gel is similar to Gillette's shaving gel for men, but with a few key differences: It has distinct packaging, a scent that women find more appealing, and extra moisturizers. Although 80 percent of women shave their legs regularly, the women's market is underdeveloped. Many women still use their partner's shaving products, a trend that Gillette hopes to reverse.

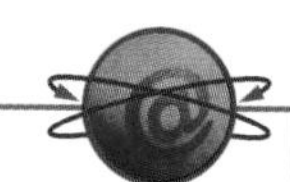

The Gillette Company
www.gillette.com/

Gillette also excels at bringing new products to market. The company understands that, once introduced, fledgling products need generous manufacturing and marketing support to thrive in the hotly competitive consumer products marketplace. To deliver the required support, Gillette has devised a formula that calls for R&D, capital investment, and advertising expenditures—which it refers to collectively as "growth drivers."

Gillette's Cavalcade of Sports, a made-in-Canada promotional campaign that has run annually in the August-September period since its inception in 1971, has long acted as one of these drivers. Gillette uses it as an umbrella program that unites all of its premium brands. Different brands may be played up in the promotion from year to year. Several years ago, Gillette's SensorExcel shaving system was spotlighted. In the year 2000–2001, attention will focus on the Mach3 system and the Duracell Ultra line of batteries. While the essential components of the Cavalcade have remained consistent from year to year, Gail MacDonald, director of promotion, sponsorship and event marketing, knows that the secret to success for a long-running promotion is to refresh it constantly. "We have to be innovative," she says. "That's one of the reasons the Cavalcade has such great staying power." At "Sports Celebration 2000," winners were invited to an interactive sporting event at Toronto's SkyDome and received their choice of six fantasy sports trips anywhere in North America plus $25 000 in spending money. MacDonald says the company tries to offer prizes with appeal to a wide audience—not just sports enthusiasts. Gillette's retail partners such as Shoppers Drug Mart love the promotion because it brings business into their outlets. Getting retailers involved early in the effort is another key to the Cavalcade's success. Gillette invited its retail partners to a special event at SkyDome six months in advance of the campaign roll-out to showcase the promotion and encourage retailers to buy in. It's a win–win situation, MacDonald says: The $2-million annual promotion drives sales for Gillette, and creates in-store activity for the participating retailers.

Thus, over the decades, superior new products combined with innovative marketing programs have been the cornerstone of Gillette's amazing success. The company commands the loyalty of more than 700 million shavers in 200 countries around the globe. These customers have purchased hundreds of millions of Gillette razors and billions of blades, giving Gillette more than 70 percent of the wet-shave market in North America and 72 percent of the $10.5-billion worldwide market. It's not surprising that in 1999, Gillette was named by the American Marketing Association as its New Product Marketer of the Year.[1]

As with Gillette, new products have been the life blood of many firms, and Canadians have had a long history as inventors in this process. McIntosh apples, Pablum, frozen fish, and instant mashed potatoes are food products that all originated in Canada. Canadians are responsible for developing such sports and leisure activities as basketball, five-pin bowling, table hockey, and Trivial Pursuit. Many of these inventions spawned entire industries. The modern communications industry was born with the invention of the telephone (Alexander Graham Bell). Reginald Fessenden, born near Sherbrooke, Quebec, was known as the father of radio after he invented amplitude modulation (AM) radio and transmitted his first broadcast in 1900. Another Canadian, Charles Fenerty, with his ability to make paper from wood pulp, founded that industry. Modern air travel was made possible by another Canadian, Wallace Rupert Turnbull, who developed the variable-pitch propeller.

Dr. Cluny McPherson, of St. John's, Newfoundland, invented the gas mask used to save the lives of many allied soldiers in the First World War. A quintessentially Canadian tool, the snowblower was invented in 1925 by Quebec resident Arthur Sicard. Olivia Poole invented the Jolly Jumper, the internationally popular baby seat, in the 1950s, and Steve Pacjack of Vancouver invented the beer case with a tuck-in handle that helps you lug your beer home. Three Canadian Olympic sailors—Bruce Kirby, Hans Fogh, and Ian Bruce—designed the world-class Laser sailboat in 1970. Wendy Murphy, a medical research technician, developed the Weevac 6—so named because it can carry six wee babies. Her idea was born when she realized, during the devastation of the 1985 Mexico City earthquake, that no apparatus existed to evacuate young children. Dr. Dennis Colonello designed the Abdomenizer in 1986 while practising as a chiropractor in northern Ontario. Before you laugh, note that he has rung up more than $100 million in sales. Dr. Frank Gunston, of Brandon, Manitoba, may have been one of the most philanthropic inventors. After developing and building a total knee-joint replacement, he decided not to patent his invention. This made it freely available to manufacturers and allowed patients needing the joint to benefit quickly from the technology and walk without pain. He received the prestigious Manning Principal Award in 1989 for his efforts.[2] To learn more about Canadian inventions and inventors, explore the About.com inventors' Web site.

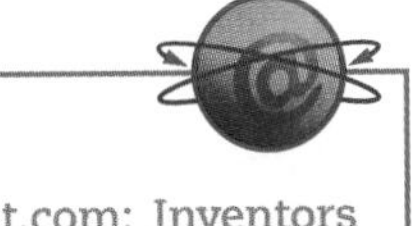

About.com: Inventors
inventors.about.com/science/inventors/library/weekly/

Canada is the birthplace of many inventors: James Gosling invented Java.

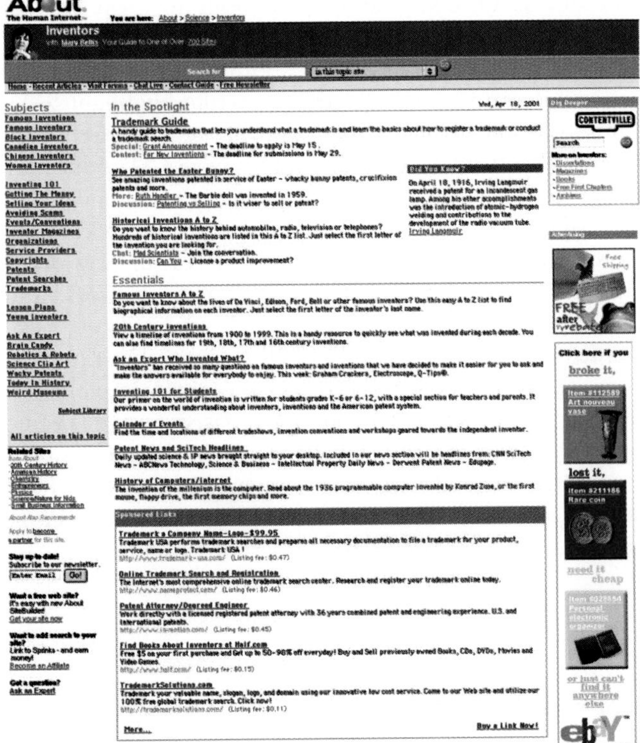

A company has to be good at developing and managing new products. Every product seems to go through a life cycle—it is born, goes through several phases, and eventually dies, as newer products come along that better serve consumer needs. This product life cycle presents two major challenges. First, because all products eventually decline, the firm must be good at developing new products to replace aging ones (the problem of *new-product development*). Second, the firm must be good at adapting its marketing strategies in the face of changing tastes, technologies, and competition, as products pass through life cycle stages (the problem of *product life cycle strategies*). We first look at the problem of finding and developing new products and then at the problem of managing them successfully over their life cycles.

New-Product Development Strategy

New-product development
The development of original products, product improvements, product modifications, and new brands through the firm's own R&D efforts.

Given the rapid changes in consumer tastes, technology, and competition, companies must develop a steady stream of new products and services. A firm can obtain new products in two ways. One is through *acquisition*—by buying a whole company, a patent, or a licence to produce someone else's product. The other is through **new-product development** in the company's own research and development department. By *new products,* we mean original products, product improvements, product modifications, and new brands that the firm develops through its own R&D efforts. In this chapter, we concentrate on new-product development.

Innovation can be very risky. Ford lost $485 million on its Edsel automobile; RCA lost $800 million on its SelectaVision videodisc player; and Texas Instruments lost a staggering $920 million before withdrawing from the home computer business. Other costly product failures from sophisticated companies include New Coke (Coca-Cola Company), Vim Micro Liquid (Unilever), Zap Mail electronic mail (Federal Express), Polarvision instant movies (Polaroid), Crystal Pepsi (PepsiCo), Clorox detergent (Clorox Company), and McLean Burgers (McDonald's).

New products continue to fail at a disturbing rate. One study estimated that new consumer packaged goods (consisting mostly of line extensions) fail at a rate of 80 percent. Another study suggested that of the staggering 25 000 new consumer food, beverage, beauty, and health care products to hit the market each year, only 40 percent will be around five years later. Moreover, failure rates for new industrial products may be as high as 30 percent.[3] Why do so many new products fail? There are several reasons. Although an idea may be good, the market size may have been overestimated. Perhaps the actual product was not designed as well as it should have been. Or maybe it was incorrectly positioned in the market, priced too high, or advertised poorly. A high-level executive might push a favourite idea despite poor marketing research findings. Sometimes the costs of product development are higher than expected, and sometimes competitors fight back harder than expected.

Because so many new products fail, companies are anxious to learn how to improve their odds of new product success. One way is to identify successful new products and determine what they have in common. Another is to study new-product failures to see what lessons can be learned (see Marketing Highlight 9–1). One study found that the number one success factor is a *unique superior product,* one with higher quality, new features, and higher value in use. Another key success factor is a *well-defined product concept* prior to development, in which the company carefully defines and assesses the target market, the product requirements, and the benefits before proceeding.[4] In all, to create successful new products, a company must understand its consumers, markets, and competitors, and develop products that deliver superior value to customers.

So companies face a problem—they must develop new-products, but the odds weigh heavily against success. The solution lies in strong new-product planning. It must set specific criteria for new-product idea acceptance, based on the specific *strategic role* the product is expected to play. The product's role may be to help the company remain an innovator, to defend its market share, or to get a foothold in a new market. The company also requires a systematic *new-product development process* for finding and growing new products.

The New-Product Development Process

The *new-product development process* for finding and growing new products consists of eight major steps (see Figure 9-1).

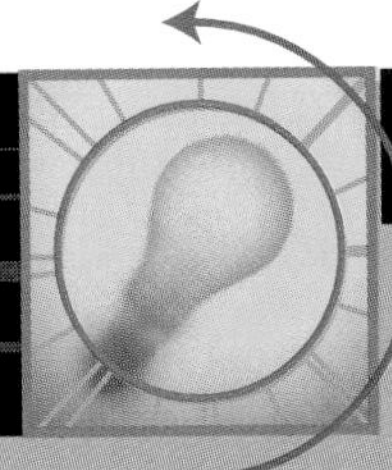

marketing highlight 9-1

Mr. Failure's Lessons for Sweet Success

Strolling the aisles at Robert McMath's New Product Showcase and Learning Center is like finding yourself in some nightmare version of a supermarket. There's Gerber food for adults (puréed sweet-and-sour pork and chicken Madeira), Hot Scoop microwaveable ice cream sundaes, Ben-Gay aspirin, Premier smokeless cigarettes, and Miller Clear Beer. How about Richard Simmons Dijon Vinaigrette Salad Spray, Look of Buttermilk shampoo, or garlic cake in a jar, parsnip chips, and aerosol mustard? Most of the 80 000 products on display were abject flops. Behind each of them are squandered dollars and hopes, but McMath, the genial curator of this product graveyard, believes that even failure—or perhaps especially failure—offers valuable lessons.

The New Product Showcase and Learning Center is a place where product developers pay hundreds of dollars an hour to visit and learn from others' mistakes. McMath's unusual showcase represents $6 billion in product investment. From it, he has distilled dozens of lessons for an industry that, by its own admission, has a very short memory. McMath "draws large audiences and commands a hefty speaking fee by decrying the convoluted thought processes of marketers, package designers, and consumer-opinion pundits who brought these and thousands of other duds-in-the-making to market," comments one analyst. "He gets laughs when he asks, 'What were they thinking?'" For those who can't make the trip to the centre or pay a steep consulting fee, McMath has now put his unique insights into a book by that same name, *What Were They Thinking?* Here are a few of the marketing lessons McMath offers:

- *Offer real value:* Many classic flops failed to deliver what customers really wanted. New Coke flopped when Coca-Cola failed to see the real value of the Coke brand to customers—tradition as well as taste. Ford pitched its Edsel as revolutionary; consumers saw it as merely revolting. Consumers quickly snuffed out R.J. Reynolds's Premier smokeless cigarettes. It seemed like a good idea at the time—who could argue against a healthier, nonpolluting cigarette? But Premier didn't deliver what smokers really wanted—smoke.
- *Cherish thy brand!* The value of a brand is its good name, which it earns over time. People become loyal to it. They trust it to deliver a consistent set of attributes. Don't squander this trust by attaching your good name to something totally out of character. Louis Sherry No Sugar Added Gorgonzola Cheese Dressing was everything that Louis Sherry, known for its rich candies and ice cream, shouldn't be: sugarless, cheese, and salad dressing. Similarly, when you hear the name Ben-Gay, you immediately think of the way that Ben-Gay cream sears and stimulates your skin. Can you imagine swallowing Ben-Gay aspirin? Or how would you feel about quaffing a can of Exxon fruit punch or Kodak quencher? Cracker Jack cereal, Smucker's premium ketchup, and Fruit of the Loom laundry detergent were other misbegotten attempts to stretch a good name. What were they thinking?
- *Be different:* Me-too marketing is the number one killer of new products. Most such attempts fail. The ones that succeed usually require resources and persistence beyond the capabilities of most marketers. Pepsi-Cola led a very precarious existence for decades before establishing itself as the major competitor to Coca-Cola. More to the point, though, Pepsi is one of the few survivors among dozens of other brands that have challenged Coke for more than a century. Ever hear of Toca-Cola? Coco-Cola? Yum-Yum cola? French Wine of Cola? How about King-Cola, "the royal drink"? More recently, Afri Cola failed to attract African American soda drinkers and Cajun Cola pretty well flopped in the land of gumbo. All things being equal, an established product has a distinct advantage over any new product that is not notably different.
- *But don't be too different:* Some products are notably different from the products, services, or experiences that consumers normally purchase. Too different. They fail because consumers don't relate to them. You can tell that some innovative products are doomed as soon as you hear their names: Toaster Eggs; Cucumber antiperspirant spray; Health-Sea sea sausage; Look of Buttermilk shampoo. Other innovative ideas have been victims of a brand's past success. For example, Nabisco's Oreo Little Fudgies, a confectionery product with a chocolate coating meant to compete with candy, sounds like a natural. But for many years

The New Product Showcase and Learning Center is a nightmare version of a supermarket. Its shelves are stacked with failures, representing squandered dollars and hopes.

Nabisco has encouraged people to pull apart Oreo cookies and lick out the filling. And it's very messy to open an Oreo with a chocolate coating. What was Nabisco thinking?

- *Accentuate the positive:* Don't be fooled by the success of all the *Dummy's Guide to . . .* books. People usually don't buy products that remind them of their shortcomings. Gillette's For Oily Hair Only shampoo wavered because people did not want to confess that they had greasy hair. People will use products that discreetly say "for oily hair" or "for sensitive skin" in small print on containers that are otherwise identical to the regular product. But they don't want to be hit over the head with reminders that they are overweight, have bad breath, sweat too much, or are elderly. Nor do they wish to advertise their faults and foibles to other people by carrying such products in their grocery carts. Really, what were they thinking?

Sources: See Paul Lukas, "The ghastliest product launches," *Fortune,* 16 March 1996:44; Jan Alexander, "Failure Inc.," *Worldbusiness,* May–June 1996:46; and Ted Anthony, "Where's Farrah Shampoo? Next to the Salsa Ketchup," *Marketing News,* 6 May 1996:13. Quotes from Gary Slack, "Innovations and idiocies," *Beverage World,* 15 November 1998; and Cliff Edwards, "Where have all the Edsels gone?" *Greensboro News Record,* 24 May 1999:B6. Bulleted points based on information in Robert M. McMath and Thom Forbes, *What Were They Thinking? Money-Saving, Time-Saving, Face-Saving Marketing Lessons You Can Learn from Products That Flopped,* New York: Times Business, 1999.

Idea Generation

Idea generation
The systematic search for new product ideas.

New-product development starts with **idea generation**—the systematic search for new product ideas. A company usually has to generate many ideas to find a few good ones. At Gillette, of every 45 carefully developed new product ideas, three make it into the development stage, and only one eventually reaches the marketplace. DuPont found that it can take as many as 3000 raw ideas to produce just two winning commercial products. And pharmaceutical companies may require 6000 to 8000 starting ideas for every successful commercial new product.[5]

New product ideas come from internal sources, customers, competitors, distributors and suppliers, and others. Using *internal sources,* the company can find new ideas through formal research and development. It can pick the brains of its scientists, engineers, manufacturing personnel, and salespeople. Some companies have developed successful "intrapreneurial" programs that encourage employees to think up and develop new product ideas. For example, 3M's well-known "15 percent rule" allows employees to spend 15 percent of their time "bootlegging"—working on projects of personal interest whether or not those projects directly benefit the company. The spectacularly successful Post-it notes evolved out of this program. Similarly, Texas Instruments' IDEA program provides funds for employees who pursue their own ideas. Among the successful new products to come out of the IDEA program was TI's Speak 'n' Spell, the first children's toy to contain a

FIGURE 9-1 Major stages in new product development

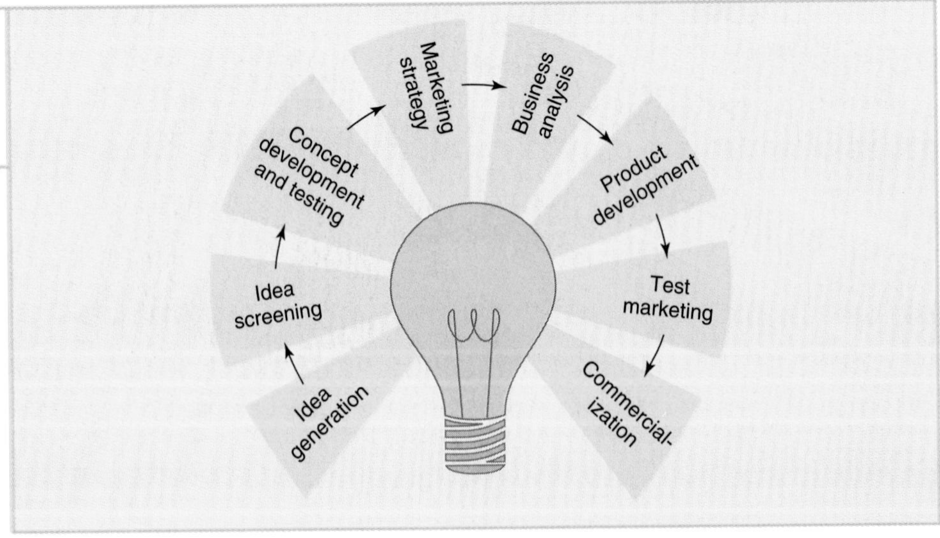

microchip. Many other speaking toys followed, ultimately generating several hundred million dollars for TI.[6]

Good new-product ideas result from watching and listening to *customers*. The company can conduct surveys or focus groups to learn about consumer needs and wants. It can analyze customer questions and complaints to find new products that better solve consumer problems. Company engineers or salespeople can meet with customers to get suggestions. Kellogg Canada sought some consumer insights with the launch of its Jacks Pack initiative in 2000. In a bid to forge better connections with the youth market, Kellogg turned the future of its Apple Jacks cereal brand over to a panel of 21 youngsters aged 15 and under. The Jacks Pack "brand management team" will influence all key marketing decisions for the cereal, including new package designs and advertising campaigns. The program is part of an effort to re-establish Apple Jacks in the Canadian market. Although the brand has been intermittently marketed since 1989, it has suffered from low demand. It was relaunched in February 2000. Mark Childs, vice-president of marketing for Kellogg, says, "When you think about it, it's such a simple idea—to have a kids' brand managed by kids, as opposed to a bunch of suits." Too much kid-targeted marketing these days amounts to one-way communication. "What this idea does is bring back the concept of two-way communication and feedback," Childs says.[7]

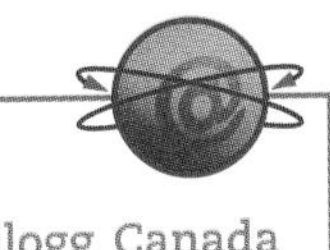

Kellogg Canada
www.kelloggs.ca/

Competitors are another good source of new product ideas. A company can watch competitors' ads and other communications for clues about their new products. Or it can buy competing new products, take them apart to see how they work, analyze their sales, and decide whether it should introduce a new product of its own.

Distributors and suppliers can pass along information about consumer problems and new product possibilities. Suppliers can tell the company about new concepts, techniques, and materials that can be used to develop new products. Other idea sources include trade magazines, shows, and seminars; government agencies; new-product consultants; advertising agencies; marketing research firms; university and commercial laboratories; and inventors. Kraft Canada got the idea for its line of herb dressings, which it launched in the summer of 1995, from a variety of sources. It observed that consumers were using herbs as a means of avoiding salt in their diets. It noted that sales of fresh herbs had risen dramatically in grocery stores. The company monitored food trends in restaurants and cooking shows and noted the addition of fresh herbs to many dishes. Finally, Kraft Canada worked with their own people in the Kraft Kitchens to determine what varieties of herbs would work best in their pourable dressings.

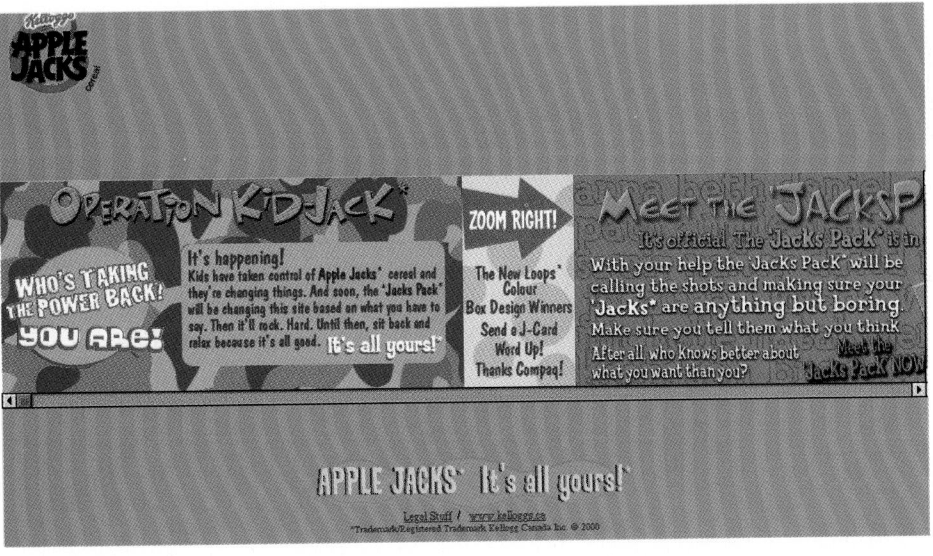

Kellogg Canada's Jacks Pack team is helping the firm understand the youth market. Meet them at www.jackspack.kelloggs.ca/main.cfm.

Finally, many new-product ideas come from *entrepreneurs* who may found new companies around their innovations. Take the case of three young women from northern Ontario who decided to take the mystery out of football. Their CD-ROM, *Football Made EZ,* scored when it snagged a seal of approval from the NHL. Their idea gave birth to their company, Angel Lake Multimedia Inc., located in Elliot Lake, a small Northern Ontario mining community.[8]

The search for new-product ideas should be systematic rather than haphazard. Otherwise, few new ideas will surface, and many good ideas will sputter in and die. Top management can avoid these problems by installing an idea management system that directs the flow of new ideas to a central point where they can be collected, reviewed, and evaluated. In setting up such a system, the company can do any or all of the following:[9]

- Appoint a respected senior person to be the company's idea manager.
- Create a multidisciplinary idea management committee of people from R&D, engineering, purchasing, operations, finance, and sales and marketing to meet regularly and evaluate proposed new product and service ideas.
- Set up a toll-free number for anyone who wants to send a new idea to the idea manager.
- Encourage all company stakeholders—employees, suppliers, distributors, dealers—to send their ideas to the idea manager.
- Set up formal recognition programs to reward those who contribute the best new ideas.

The idea-manager approach yields two favourable outcomes. First, it helps create an innovation-oriented company culture. It shows that top management supports, encourages, and rewards innovation. Second, it yields a larger number of ideas, among which will be found some especially good ones. As the system matures, ideas will flow more freely. No longer will good ideas wither for the lack of a sounding board or a senior product advocate.

Idea Screening

Idea screening
Screening new product ideas to identify good ideas and drop poor ones as soon as possible.

The purpose of idea generation is to create a large number of ideas. The purpose of the succeeding stages is to *reduce* that number. The first idea-reducing stage is **idea screening.** The purpose of screening is to identify good ideas and drop poor ones as soon as possible. Product development costs rise greatly in later stages. The company wants to proceed only with the product ideas that will turn into profitable products. As one marketing executive suggests, "Three executives sitting in a room can get 40 good ideas richocheting off the wall in minutes. The challenge is getting a steady stream of good ideas out of the labs and creativity campfires, through marketing and manufacturing and all the way to consumers."[10]

Many companies require their executives to write up new-product ideas on a standard form that can be reviewed by a new-product committee. The write-up describes the product, the target market, and the competition. It makes some rough estimates of market size, product price, development time and costs, manufacturing costs, and rate of return. The committee then evaluates the idea against a set of general criteria. At Kao Company, the large Japanese consumer products company, the committee asks such questions as: Is the product truly useful to consumers and society? Is it good for our particular company? Does it mesh well with the company's objectives and strategies? Do we have the people, skills, and resources to make it succeed? Does it deliver more value to customers than competing products? Is it easy to advertise and distribute?

Surviving ideas can be screened further using a simple rating process such as the one shown in Table 9-1. The first column lists factors required for the successful launching of the product in the marketplace. In the next column, manage-

TABLE 9-1 Product Idea Rating Process

	(A)					(B)							(A × B)
						Fit between Product Idea and Company Capabilities							
New-Product Success Factors	Relative Importance	.0	.1	.2	.3	.4	.5	.6	.7	.8	.9	.10	Idea Rating
Company strategy and objectives	.20									X			.160
Marketing skills and experience	.20										X		.180
Financial resources	.15								X				.105
Channels of distribution	.15									X			.120
Production capabilities	.15									X			.120
Research and development	.10								X				.070
Purchasing and supplies	.05						X						.025
Total	1.00												.780*

*Rating scale: .00–.40, poor; .50–.75, fair; 76–1.00, good. Minimum acceptance level: .70

ment rates these factors on their relative importance. Thus, management believes that marketing skills and experience are very important (.20), and purchasing and supplies competence is of minor importance (.05). Next, on a scale of .0 to 1.0, management rates how well the new product idea fits the company's profile on each factor. Here, management feels that the product idea fits very well with the company's marketing skills and experience (.9), but not too well with its purchasing and supplies capabilities (.5). Finally, management multiplies the importance of each success factor by the rating of fit to obtain an overall rating of the company's ability to launch the product successfully. Thus, if marketing is an important success factor, and if this product fits the company's marketing skills, this will increase the overall rating of the product idea. In the example, the product idea scored .74, which places it at the high end of the "fair idea" level. The checklist promotes a more systematic product idea evaluation and basis for discussion; however, it is not designed to make the decision for management.

Concept Development and Testing

Product concept
A detailed version of the new product idea stated in meaningful consumer terms.

An attractive idea must be developed into a **product concept.** It is important to distinguish between a *product idea*, a *product concept*, and a *product image*. A product idea is an idea for a possible product that the company can see itself offering to the market. A product concept is a detailed version of the idea stated in meaningful consumer terms. A product image is the way consumers perceive an actual or potential product.

Concept Development

Concept development
Expanding the new product idea into various alternative forms.

During the concept development stage, the firm develops a detailed outline of the new product idea, stated in meaningful consumer terms. DaimlerChrysler is getting ready to commercialize its experimental fuel-cell-powered electric car. This car's low-polluting fuel-cell system runs directly off liquid hydrogen. It is highly fuel efficient (75 percent more efficient than gasoline engines) and gives the new car an environmental advantage over standard internal combustion engine cars. DaimlerChrysler is road testing its NECAR 4 (New Electric Car) subcompact prototype and plans to deliver the first fuel-cell cars to customers in 2004. Based on the tiny Mercedes A-Class, the car accelerates quickly, reaches speeds of 144 kilometres per hour, and has a 448-kilometre driving range, giving it a huge edge over battery-powered electric cars that travel only about 128 kilometres before needing 3 to 12 hours of recharging.[11]

DaimlerChrysler's task is to develop its fuel-cell-powered car into alternative product concepts, find out how attractive each concept is to customers, and choose the best one.

DaimlerChrysler's task is to develop this new product into alternative product concepts, find out how attractive each concept is to customers, and choose the best one. It might create the following product concepts for the fuel cell electric car:

- *Concept 1* A moderately priced subcompact designed as a second family car to be used around town. The car is ideal for running errands and visiting friends.
- *Concept 2* A medium-cost sporty compact appealing to young people.
- *Concept 3* An inexpensive subcompact "green" car appealing to environmentally conscious people who want practical transportation and low pollution.

Concept Testing

Concept testing Testing new product concepts with a group of target consumers to find out if the concepts have strong consumer appeal.

Concept testing calls for testing new product concepts with groups of target consumers. The concepts may be presented to consumers symbolically or physically. Here, in words, is Concept 3:

> An efficient, fun-to-drive, fuel-cell-powered subcompact car that seats four. This high-tech wonder runs on hydrogen created from methanol fuel, providing practical and reliable transportation with almost no pollution. It goes up to 130 km per hour and, unlike battery-powered electric cars, never needs recharging. It's priced, fully equipped, at $30 000.

For some concept tests, a word or picture description might be sufficient. However, a more concrete and physical presentation of the concept will increase the reliability of the concept test. Today, some marketers are finding innovative ways to make product concepts more real to concept test subjects. For example, some are using virtual reality to test product concepts. Virtual reality programs use computers and sensory devices (such as gloves or goggles) to simulate reality. For example, a designer of kitchen cabinets can use a virtual reality program to help a customer "see" how his or her kitchen would look and work if remodelled with the company's products. Although virtual reality is still in its infancy, its applications are increasing daily.[12]

After being exposed to the concept, consumers may be asked to react to it by answering the questions in Table 9-2. The answers will help the company decide which concept has the strongest appeal. For example, the last question asks about the consumer's intention to buy. Suppose 10 percent of the consumers said they "definitely" would buy and another five percent said "probably." The company could project these figures to the full population in this target group to estimate sales volume. Even then, the estimate is uncertain because people do not always carry out their stated intentions.

TABLE 9-2 Questions for Electric Car Concept Test

1. Do you understand the concept of an electric car?
2. Do you believe the claims about the electric car's performance?
3. What are the major benefits of the electric car compared with a conventional car?
4. What improvements in the car's features would you suggest?
5. For what uses would you prefer an electric car to a conventional car?
6. What would be a reasonable price to charge for the electric car?
7. Who would be involved in your decision to buy such a car? Who would drive it?
8. Would you buy such a car? (Definitely, probably, probably not, definitely not)

Many firms routinely test new product concepts with consumers before attempting to turn them into actual new products. Every month, Richard Saunders Inc.'s Acu-POLL research system tests 35 new product concepts in person on 100 nationally representative grocery-store shoppers. The poll rates participants' interest in buying a given new product, their perceptions of how new and different the product idea is, and their judgment of the product's value compared with its price. In one poll, Nabisco's Oreo Chocolate Cones concept received a rare A+ rating, meaning that consumers think it is an outstanding concept that they would try and buy. Other product concepts didn't fare so well. Nubrush anti-bacterial toothbrush spray disinfectant, from Applied Microdontics, received an F: Consumers found Nubrush to be overpriced, and most don't think they have a problem with "infected" toothbrushes.[13]

Marketing Strategy Development

Marketing strategy development
Designing an initial marketing strategy for a new product based on the product concept.

Suppose DiamlerChrysler finds that Concept 3 for the fuel-cell-powered car tests best. The next step is **marketing strategy development**—designing an initial marketing strategy for introducing this car to the market.

The *marketing strategy statement* consists of three parts. The first part describes the target market; the planned product positioning; and the sales, market share, and profit goals for the first few years. Thus:

> The target market is younger, well-educated, moderate-to-high income individuals, couples, or small families seeking practical, environmentally responsible transportation. The car will be positioned as more economical to operate, more fun to drive, less expensive than today's internal combustion engine cars, and less restricting than battery-powered electric cars that must be recharged regularly. The company will aim to sell 100 000 cars in the first year, at a loss of not more than $20 million. In the second year, the company will aim for sales of 120 000 cars and a profit of $36 million.

The second part of the marketing strategy statement outlines the product's planned price, distribution, and marketing budget for the first year:

> The fuel-cell-powered electric car will be offered in three colours and will have optional air-conditioning and power-drive features. It will sell at a retail price of $30 000—with 15 percent off the list price to dealers. Dealers who sell more than 10 cars per month will receive an additional discount of five percent on each car sold that month. An advertising budget of $29 million will be divided equally between national and local advertising. Advertising will emphasize the car's fun and low emissions. During the first year, $140 000 will be spent on marketing research to find out who is buying the car and their satisfaction levels.

The third part of the marketing strategy statement describes the planned long-run sales, profit goals, and marketing mix strategy:

> DaimlerChrysler intends to capture a three percent long-run share of the total auto market and realize an after-tax return on investment of 15 percent. To achieve this, product quality will start high and improve over time. Price will be raised in the second and third years if competition

permits. The total advertising budget will be raised each year by about 10 percent. Marketing research will be reduced to $86 000 per year after the first year.

Business Analysis

Business analysis
A review of the sales, costs, and profit projections for a new product to determine whether these factors satisfy the company's objectives.

Once management has decided on its product concept and marketing strategy, it can evaluate the business attractiveness of the proposal. **Business analysis** involves reviewing the sales, costs, and profit projections for a new product to determine whether they satisfy the company's objectives. If they do, the product can move to the product development stage.

To estimate sales, the company should examine the sales history of similar products and survey market opinion. It should estimate minimum and maximum sales to assess the range of risk. After preparing the sales forecast, management can estimate the expected product costs and profits, including marketing, R&D, manufacturing, accounting, and finance costs. The company then uses the sales and costs figures to analyze the new product's financial attractiveness.

Product Development

Product development
Developing the product concept into a physical product to ensure that the product idea can be turned into a workable product.

So far, the product may have existed only as a word description, a drawing, or perhaps a crude mock-up. If the product concept passes the business test, it moves into **product development.** Here, R&D or engineering develops the product concept into a physical product. The product development step, however, now calls for a large jump in investment. It will show whether the product idea can be turned into a workable product.

The R&D department will develop one or more physical versions of the product concept, with the aim of designing a prototype that will satisfy and excite consumers and that can be produced quickly and at budgeted costs. Developing a successful prototype can take days, weeks, months, or even years. Often, products undergo rigorous functional tests to ensure that they perform safely and effectively. These are examples of such functional tests:[14]

Mattel, Inc.
www.mattel.com/

A scuba-diving Barbie doll must swim and kick for 15 straight hours to satisfy Mattel that she will last at least one year. But because Barbie may find her feet in small owners' mouths rather than in the bathtub, Mattel has devised another, more tortuous test: Barbie's feet are clamped by two steel jaws to make sure that her skin doesn't crack—and choke—potential owners.

At Shaw Industries, temps are paid $5 an hour to pace up and down five long rows of sample carpets for up to eight hours a day, logging an average of 22 kilometres each. One regular reads three mysteries a week while pacing and shed 20 kilograms in two years. Shaw Industries counts walkers' steps and figures that 20 000 steps equal several years of average carpet wear.

Heinz Canada's Toddler Peach Cobbler took four years to develop.

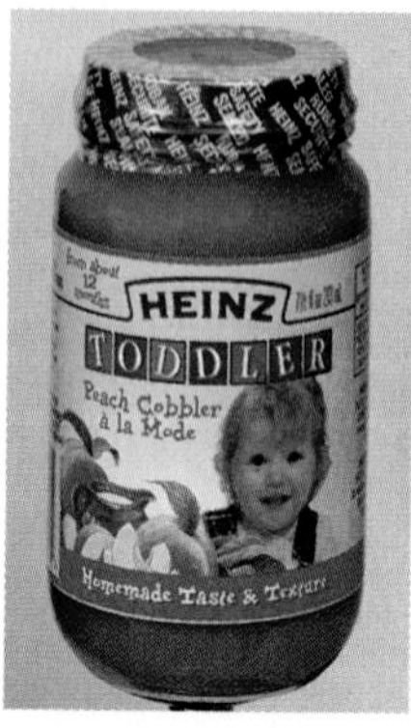

Diana Yanik, coordinator of product development at the Heinz Company of Canada, sits tensely watching eight specially trained testers enter partitioned booths where they taste three small bowls with variations of Heinz's new product, Toddler Peach Cobbler. Reaching this point took four years and involved hundreds of decisions for Yanik, including finding a new type of peach that would withstand various processing methods. Careful testing is essential for Canada's "most health-conscious and finicky consumers"—small children who can barely hold a fork or spoon. The process began when Heinz's research revealed that mothers wanted a food to challenge children who were just beginning to develop teeth. Consequently, the product concept was born: a baby food with pieces that were large enough for a child to chew, but that did not pose a choking hazard. Prototypes were tested on 900 mothers and their children. Following dozens of recipe changes, $400 000 of specialized equipment, and weeks of rigid safety testing, the product was finally ready for supermarket shelves, where it soon became a hit.

The prototype must have the required functional features and also convey the intended psychological characteristics. The fuel-cell-powered car, for example, should strike consumers as being well built and safe. Management must learn what makes consumers decide that a car is well built. For some, this means having "solid-sounding" doors when they are slammed. For others, it is the result of independent crash tests.

Test Marketing

Test marketing
The stage of new product development in which the product and marketing program are tested in more realistic market settings.

If the product passes functional and consumer tests, the next step is **test marketing,** the stage at which the product and marketing program are introduced into more realistic market settings. Test marketing gives the marketer experience with marketing the product before going to the expense of full introduction. It lets the company test the product and its marketing program—positioning strategy, advertising, distribution, pricing, branding and packaging, and budget levels.

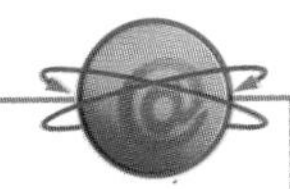

Pillsbury
www.pillsbury.com/
Swiffer
www.swiffer.com/

The amount of test marketing needed varies with each new product. Test marketing costs can be enormous, and test marketing takes time that may allow competitors to gain advantages. When the costs of developing and introducing the product are low, or when management is already confident about the new product, the company may do little or no test marketing. Companies often do not test market simple line extensions or copies of successful competitor products. For example, Procter & Gamble introduced its Folger's decaffeinated coffee crystals without test marketing, and Pillsbury rolled out Chewy granola bars and chocolate-covered Granola Dipps with no standard test market. However, when introducing a new product requires a big investment, or when management is not sure of the product or marketing program, a company may do a lot of test marketing. Lever, for instance, spent two years testing its highly successful Lever 2000 bar soap before introducing it internationally.

An interesting test market idea was Labatt Breweries' "Copper Vote '95." During a 17-day period, Labatt pitted two beers, identified only as Labatt X and Labatt Y, against each other. Consumers voted on their favourite. However, despite participation by 117 000 consumers, the product later failed.

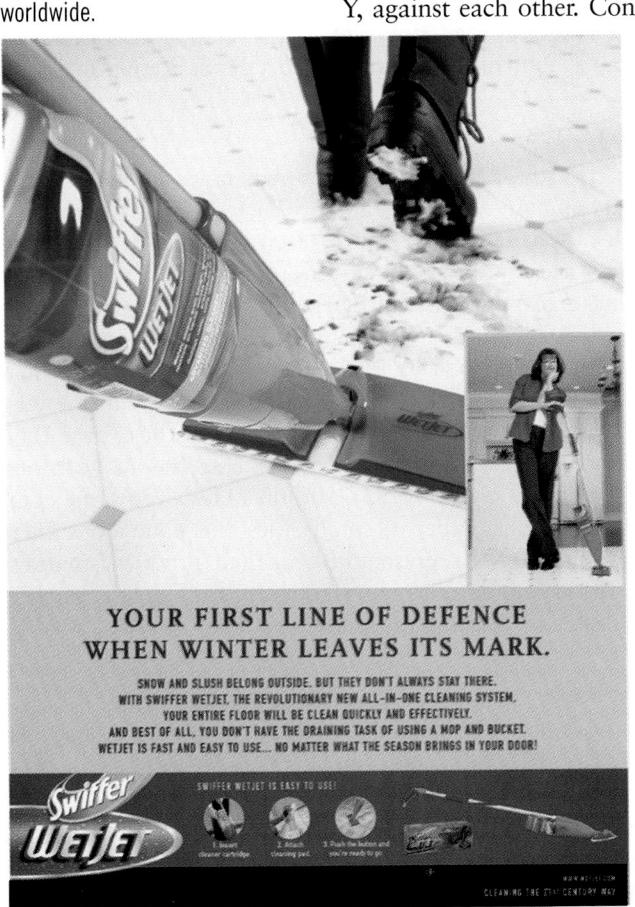

Procter & Gamble is test marketing the Swiffer WetJet in Canada and Belgium before launching the product worldwide.

The costs of test marketing can be high, but they are often small compared with the costs of making a major mistake. For this reason, Procter & Gamble is using Canada as a test market for its new battery-operated floor cleaning appliance, the Swiffer WetJet, a "wet cousin" of the popular Swiffer Sweeper.[15] According to P&G's market research director, Canada was selected as a test market because of Canadian consumers' enthusiastic response to the Swiffer Sweeper when it was introduced. Test marketing for the new product will include both television and print advertisements, in-store demonstrations, and other "exciting marketing tactics developed specifically for the WetJet." P&G also launched the WetJet in Belgium a few weeks after its Canadian launch, and will assess results from the two test markets before it undertakes a worldwide rollout.

Test marketing can also be used to determine not only a product's overall viability but also everything from the appropriate advertising spending levels to final packaging and shelf placement. Janet Finlay, manager of market research for Toronto-based Cadbury Chocolate Canada, says that the objectives of test marketing can include, but are not limited to:[16]

- determining the target market profile;
- assessing consumer acceptability, trial, repeat purchase rate and cycle;

- evaluating trade reception and distribution penetration;
- determining the most effective media spend and promotions;
- gauging customer satisfaction;
- determining improvements that will be made before a national launch.

When using test marketing, consumer products companies usually choose one of three approaches—standard test markets, controlled test markets, or simulated test markets.

Standard Test Markets

Using standard test markets, the company finds a small number of representative test cities, conducts a full marketing campaign in these cities, and uses store audits, consumer and distributor surveys, and other measures to gauge product performance. The results are used to forecast national sales and profits, discover potential product problems, and fine-tune the marketing program.

Standard test markets have some drawbacks. They may be very costly—the average standard test market costs over $4 million, and they take a long time—some last as long as three years. Competitors often do whatever they can to make test market results hard to read. They cut their prices in test cities, increase their promotion, or even buy up the product being tested. Finally, standard test markets give competitors a look at the company's new product well before it is introduced nationally. Thus, competitors may have time to develop defensive strategies, and may even beat the company's product to the market. For example, while Clorox was still test marketing its new detergent with bleach in selected markets, P&G launched Tide with Bleach nationally. Tide with Bleach quickly became the segment leader; Clorox later withdrew its detergent.

Despite these disadvantages, standard test markets are still the most widely used approach for major market testing. However, many companies today are shifting to quicker and cheaper controlled and simulated test marketing methods.

Controlled Test Markets

Several research firms keep controlled panels of stores that have agreed to carry new products for a fee. The company with the new product specifies the number of stores and geographical locations it wants. The research firm delivers the product to the participating stores and controls shelf location, amount of shelf space, displays and point-of-purchase promotions, and pricing according to specified plans. Sales results are tracked to determine the impact of these factors on demand.

Controlled test marketing systems such as Nielsen's ScanTrack and Information Resources Inc.'s (IRI) BehaviorScan track individual behaviour from the television set to the checkout counter.[17] Controlled test markets take less time than standard test markets (six months to a year) and usually cost less (a year-long BehaviorScan test might cost from $275 000 to $2 750 000). However, some companies are concerned that the limited number of small cities and panel consumers used by the research services may not be representative of their products' markets or target consumers. And, as in standard test markets, controlled test markets allow competitors to get a look at the company's new product.

ACNielsen Canada
www.acnielsen.ca/

Simulated Test Markets

Companies can also test new products in a simulated shopping environment. The company or research firm shows ads and promotions for various products, including the new product being tested, to a sample of consumers. It gives consumers a small amount of money and invites them to a real or laboratory store where they may keep the money or use it to buy items. The researchers note how many consumers buy the new product and competing brands. This simulation provides a measure of the trial and the commercial's effectiveness against competing commercials. The researchers then ask consumers the reasons for their purchase or nonpurchase. Some weeks later, they interview the consumers by phone to determine product attitudes, usage, satisfaction, and repurchase intentions. Using sophisticated computer models, the researchers then project national sales from results of the simulated test market. Recently, some marketers have begun to use new high-tech approaches to simulate test market research, such as virtual reality and the Internet (see Marketing Highlight 9-2).

Simulated test markets overcome some of the disadvantages of standard and controlled test markets. They usually cost much less, can be run in eight weeks, and keep the new product out of competitors' view. Yet, because of their small samples and simulated shopping environments, many marketers do not consider simulated test markets to be as accurate or reliable as larger, real-world tests. Still, simulated test markets are used widely, often as "pre-test" markets. Because they are fast and inexpensive, one or more simulated tests can be run to quickly assess a new product or its marketing program. If the pre-test results are strongly positive, the product may be introduced without further testing. If the results are very poor, the product may be dropped or substantially redesigned and retested. If the results are promising but indefinite, the product and marketing program may be tested further in controlled or standard test markets.

Commercialization

Commercialization
Introducing a new product into the market.

Test marketing gives management the information needed to make a final decision about whether to launch the new product. If the company goes ahead with **commercialization**—introducing the new product into the market—it will face high costs. The company may have to build or rent a manufacturing facility. And it may have to spend, in the case of a new consumer packaged good, between $14 million and $140 million for advertising and sales promotion in the first year.

The company launching a new product must first decide on introduction *timing*. If DaimlerChrysler's new fuel-cell electric car will eat into the sales of the company's other cars, its introduction may be delayed. If the electric car can be improved further, or if the economy is down, the company may wait until the following year to launch it.

Next, the company must decide *where* to launch the new product—a single location, a region, the national market, or the international market. Few companies have the confidence, capital, and capacity to launch new products into full national or international distribution. They will develop a planned *market rollout* over time. In particular, small companies may enter attractive cities or regions one at a time. Larger companies, however, may quickly introduce new models into several regions or into the full national market.

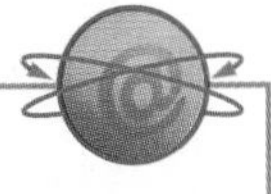

Colgate-Palmolive
www.colgate.com/

Companies with international distribution systems may introduce new products through global rollouts. Colgate-Palmolive uses a "lead-country" strategy. For example, it launched its Palmolive Optims shampoo and conditioner first in Australia, the Philippines, Hong Kong, and Mexico, then rapidly rolled it out into Europe, Asia, Latin America, and Africa.

Speeding up New Product Development

Sequential product development
A new product development approach in which one company department works individually to complete its stage of the process before passing the new product along to the next department and stage.

Many companies organize their new product development process into an orderly sequence of steps, starting with idea generation and ending with commercialization. Under this **sequential product development** approach, one company department works individually to complete its stage of the process before passing the new product along to the next department and stage. This orderly, step-by-step process can help bring control to complex and risky projects. But it also can be

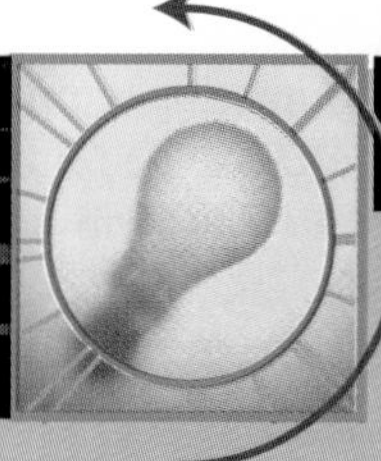

marketing highlight 9-2

Virtual Reality Test Marketing: The Future Is Now

It's a steamy summer Saturday afternoon. Imagine that you're stopping off at the local supermarket to pick up some icy bottles of your favourite sports drink before heading to the tennis courts. You park the car, cross the parking lot, and walk through the store's automatic doors. You head for aisle five, passing several displays along the way, and locate your usual brand of sports drink. You pick it up, check the price, and take it to the check-out counter. Sounds like a pretty typical shopping experience, doesn't it? But in this case, the entire experience took place on your computer screen, not at the supermarket.

You've just experienced virtual reality—the wave of the future for test marketing and concept-testing research. Firms like Canada Market Research and Gadd International Research have developed CD-ROM tools—Visionary Shopper and Simul-Shop—that recreate shopping situations in which researchers can test consumers' reactions to such factors as product positioning, store layouts, and package designs. For example, suppose a cereal marketer wants to test reactions to a new package design and store-shelf positioning. Using Visionary Shopper or Simul-Shop on a standard desktop PC, test shoppers begin their shopping spree with a screen showing the outside of a grocery store. They click to enter the virtual store and are guided to the appropriate store section. Once there, they can scan the shelf, pick up various cereal packages, rotate them, study the labels—even look around to see what is on the shelf behind them. Using the touch screen, they can "purchase" the product or return it to the shelf. About the only thing they can't do is open the box and taste the cereal. The virtual shopping trip includes full sound and video, along with a guide who directs users through the experience and answers their questions.

Virtual reality testing can take any of several forms. Alternative Realities Corporation (ARC) has created a virtual reality amphitheatre called the VisionDome. The Dome offers 360 by 160 degrees of film projection, allowing as many as 40 people to participate simultaneously in a virtual reality experience. The VisionDome is like an IMAX theatre, but with one big difference—it's interactive. "When you use a computer to generate an image . . . you have the advantage of making that image interactive," comments an ARC executive. When conducting research on a car, he suggests, "we can go into a VisionDome, see that car in three dimensions, look at it from every angle, take it out for a test drive, and allow the customer to configure that car exactly the way he wants it." Caterpillar foresees enormous potential for the Dome. "We can put one of our tractors in a VisionDome and actually have a customer sit in it and test it under whatever conditions they would use it for," says a Caterpillar design engineer. "The ability to immerse people in the product makes it a phenomenal [research and sales] tool."

Virtual reality as a research tool offers

Gadd's Simul-Shop creates realistic on-screen shopping situations in which researchers can test consumers' reactions to such factors as product positioning, store layouts, and package designs. But not taste.

dangerously slow. In fast-changing, highly competitive markets, such slow-but-sure product development can result in product failures, lost sales and profits, and crumbling market positions. "Speed to market" and reducing new-product-development "cycle time" have become pressing concerns to companies in all industries.

To get their new products to market more quickly, many companies are adopt-

several advantages. For one, it's relatively inexpensive. A firm can conduct a virtual store study for only about $36 000, including initial programming and the actual research on 75 to 100 people. This makes virtual reality research accessible to firms that can't afford full market testing campaigns or the expense of creating actual mock-ups for each different product colour, shape, or size. Another advantage is flexibility. A virtual reality store can display an almost infinite variety of products, sizes, styles, and flavours in response to consumers' desires and needs. Research can be conducted in almost any simulated surrounding, ranging from food store interiors and new car showrooms to farm fields or the open road. The technique also offers great interactivity, allowing marketers and consumers to work together via computer on designs of new products and marketing programs.

Finally, virtual reality has great potential for international research, which has often been difficult for marketers to conduct. With virtual reality, researchers can use a single standardized approach to evaluate products and programs worldwide. Consider this example:

One multinational company has begun to conduct virtual shopping studies in North and South America, Europe, Asia, and Australia. Researchers create virtual stores in each country and region using the appropriate local products, shelf layouts, and currencies. Once the stores are online, a product concept can be quickly tested across locations. When the studies are completed, the results are communicated to headquarters electronically. The analysis reveals which markets offer the greatest opportunity for a successful launch.

Virtual reality research also has its limitations. The biggest problem: Simulated shopping situations never quite match the real thing. Observes one expert, "Just because it's technically [feasible], that doesn't mean that when you put [people] behind a computer you're going to get true responses. Any time you simulate an experience you're not getting the experience itself. It's still a simulation."

So what's ahead for virtual reality in marketing? Some pioneers are extremely enthusiastic about the technology—not just as a research tool, but as a place where even real buying and selling can occur. They predict that the virtual store may become a major channel for personal and direct interactions with consumers—interactions that encompass not only research but also sales and service. They see great potential for conducting this type of research over the Internet, and virtual stores have become a reality on the Web. As one observer notes, "This is what I read about in science-fiction books when I was growing up. It's the thing of the future." For many marketers, that future is already a virtual reality.

Sources: Quotations and extracts from Raymond R. Burke, "Virtual shopping: Breakthrough in marketing research," *Harvard Business Review,* March–April 1996:120–31; Tom Dellacave, Jr., "Curing market research headaches," *Sales & Marketing Management,* July 1996:85; Brian Silverman, "Get 'em while they're hot," *Sales & Marketing Management,* February 1997:47–8,52; and Jo Marney, "Design testing goes digital," *Marketing,* 24 March 1997, www.marketingmag.com.

Simultaneous (or team-based) product development
An approach to developing new products in which various company departments work closely together, overlapping the steps in the product development process to save time and increase effectiveness.

ing a faster, team-oriented approach called **simultaneous (or team-based) product development.** Under this approach, company departments work closely together, overlapping the steps in the product development process to save time and increase effectiveness. Instead of passing the new product from department to department, the company assembles a team of people from various departments, which stays with the new product from start to finish. Such teams usually include people from the marketing, finance, design, manufacturing, and legal departments, and even supplier and customer companies.

Top management gives the product development team general strategic direction, but no clear-cut product idea or work plan. It challenges the team with stiff and seemingly contradictory goals—"turn out carefully planned and superior new products, but do it quickly"—and then gives the team whatever freedom and resources it needs to meet the challenge. In the sequential process, a bottleneck at one phase can seriously slow the entire project. In the simultaneous approach, if one functional area hits snags, it works to resolve them while the team moves on.

Black & Decker
www.blackanddecker.com

Black & Decker used the simultaneous approach—what it calls "concurrent engineering"—to develop its Quantum line of tools targeted to serious do-it-yourselfers. B&D assigned a "fusion team," called Team Quantum and consisting of 85 Black & Decker employees from around the world, to get the right product line to customers as quickly as possible. The team included engineers, finance people, marketers, designers, and others from the United States, Britain, Germany, Italy, and Switzerland. From idea to launch, including three months of consumer research, the team developed the highly acclaimed Quantum line in only 12 months.

The simultaneous approach has some limitations. Super-fast product development can be riskier and more costly than the slower, more orderly sequential approach. Moreover, it often creates increased organizational tension and confusion. And the company must take care that rushing a product to market doesn't adversely affect its quality—the objective is not just to create products faster, but to create them better and faster. Despite these drawbacks, in rapidly changing industries facing increasingly shorter product life cycles, the rewards of fast and flexible product development far exceed the risks. Companies that get new and improved products to the market faster than competitors often gain a dramatic competitive edge. They can respond more quickly to emerging consumer tastes and charge higher prices for more advanced designs. As one auto industry executive states, "What we want to do is get the new car approved, built, and in the consumer's hands in the shortest time possible. . . . Whoever gets there first gets all the marbles."[18]

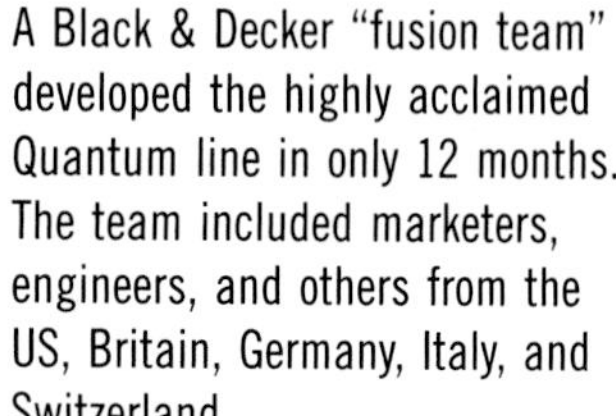

A Black & Decker "fusion team" developed the highly acclaimed Quantum line in only 12 months. The team included marketers, engineers, and others from the US, Britain, Germany, Italy, and Switzerland.

Product Life-Cycle Strategies

Product life cycle (PLC) The course of a product's sales and profits over its lifetime. It involves five distinct stages: product development, introduction, growth, maturity, and decline.

After launching the new product, management wants it to enjoy a long and happy life. Although it does not expect the product to sell forever, management wants to earn a decent profit to cover all the effort and risk that went into launching it. Management is aware that each product will have a life cycle, although it cannot know the exact shape and length in advance.

Figure 9-2 shows a typical **product life cycle (PLC)**, the course that a product's sales and profits take over its lifetime. The product life cycle has five stages:

1. *Product development* begins when the company finds and develops a new product idea. During product development, sales are zero and the company's investment costs mount.
2. *Introduction* is a period of slow sales growth as the product is being introduced in the market. Profits are non-existent in this stage because of the heavy expenses of product introduction.
3. *Growth* is a period of rapid market acceptance and increasing profits.
4. *Maturity* is a period of slowdown in sales growth because the product has achieved acceptance by most potential buyers. Profits level off or decline because of increased marketing outlays to defend the product against competition.
5. *Decline* is the period when sales fall off and profits drop.

Not all products follow this S-shaped product life cycle. Some products are introduced and die quickly; others stay in the mature stage for a long, long time. Some enter the decline stage and are then cycled back into the growth stage through strong promotion or repositioning.

The PLC concept can describe a *product class* (gasoline-powered automobiles), a *product form* (minivans), or a *brand* (the Ford Taurus). The PLC concept is different for each case. Product classes have the longest life cycles—the sales of many product classes stay in the mature stage for a long time. Product forms, in contrast, tend to have the standard PLC shape. Product forms such as "cream deodorants," the "rotary telephone," and "phonograph records" passed through a regular history of introduction, rapid growth, maturity, and decline. A specific brand's life cycle can change quickly because of changing competitive attacks and responses. For example, although teeth-cleaning products (product class) and toothpastes (product form) have enjoyed fairly long life cycles, the life cycles of individual brands are much shorter.

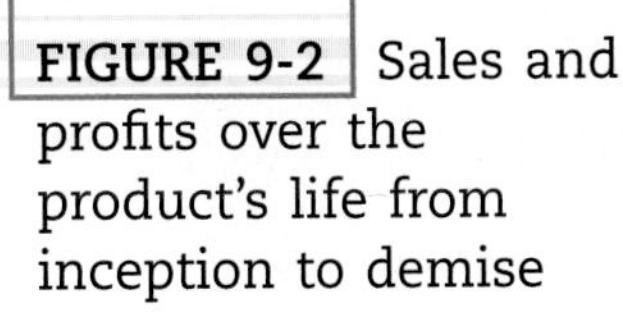

FIGURE 9-2 Sales and profits over the product's life from inception to demise

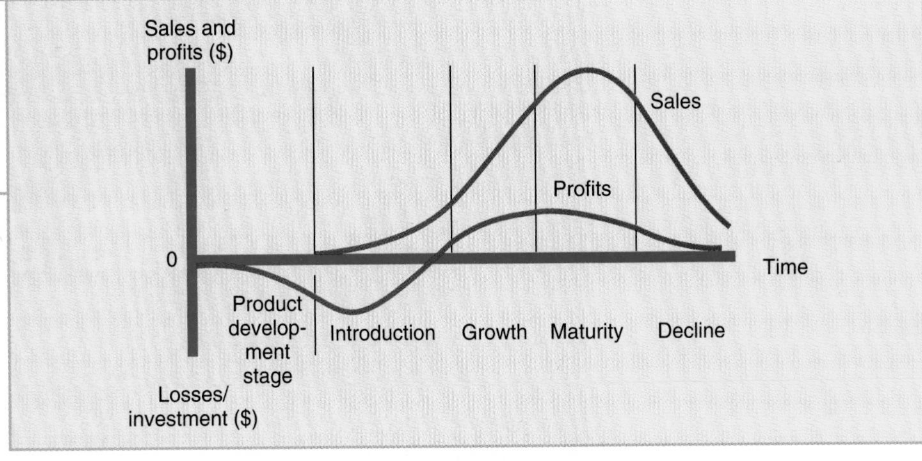

FIGURE 9-3 Life cycles of styles, fashions, and fads

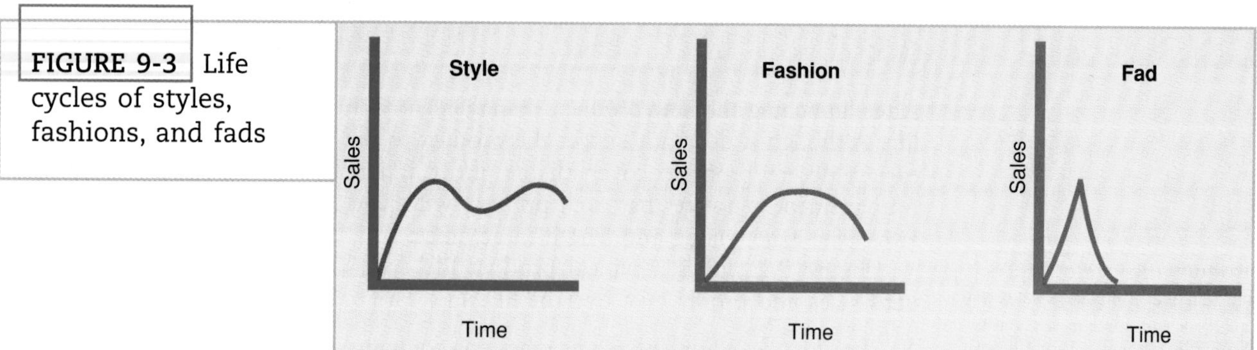

Style
A basic and distinctive mode of expression.

Fashion
A currently accepted or popular style in a given field

The PLC concept can also be applied to what are known as styles, fashions, and fads. Their special life cycles are shown in Figure 9-3. A **style** is a basic and distinctive mode of expression. For example, styles appear in homes (Victorian, ranch, modern); clothing (formal, casual); and art (realistic, surrealistic, abstract). Once a style is invented, it may last for generations, coming in and out of vogue. A style has a cycle showing several periods of renewed interest. A **fashion** is a currently accepted or popular style in a given field. For example, the "preppie look" in the clothing of the late 1970s gave way to the "loose and layered look" of the

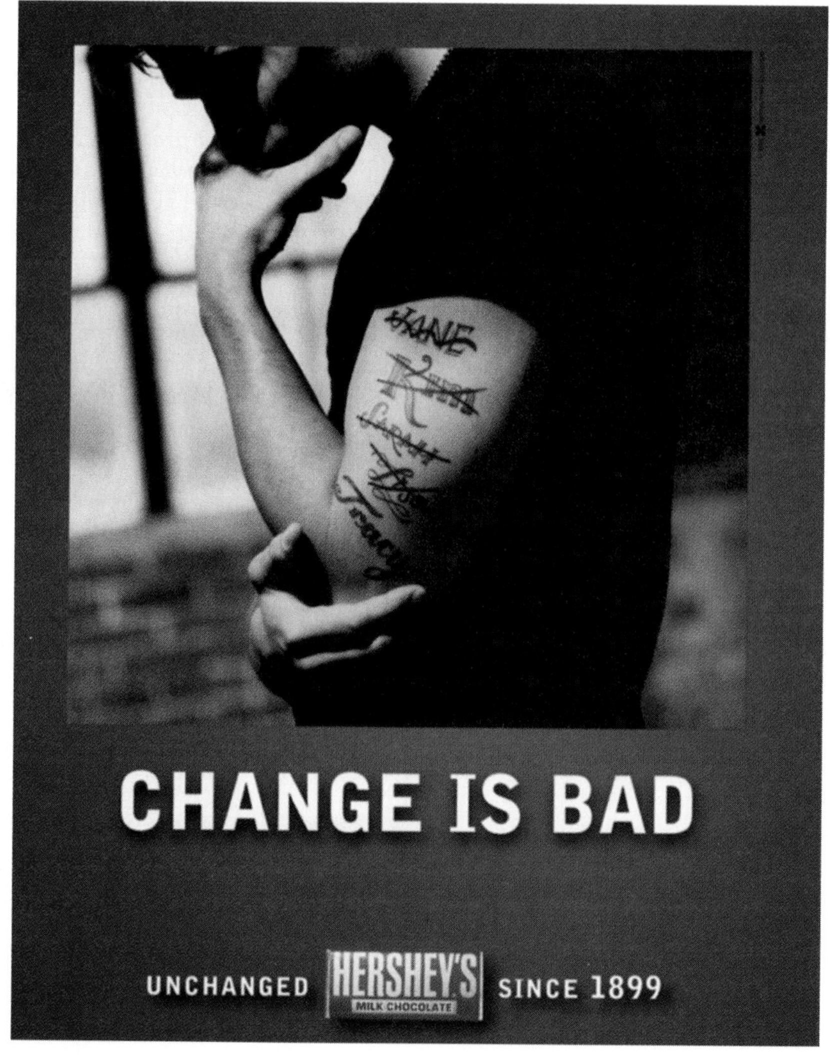

Companies want their products to enjoy long and happy life cycles. Hershey's chocolate bars have been "unchanged since 1899."

1980s, which in turn yielded to the less conservative but more tailored look of the 1990s. Fashions tend to grow slowly, remain popular for a while, then decline slowly. **Fads** are fashions that enter quickly, are adopted with great zeal, peak early, and decline very fast. They last only a short time and tend to attract only a limited following. Fads of the 1990s included Buzz Lightyear action figures, Jurassic Park Dinosaurs, Furbys, and Britney Spears dolls. Fads do not survive for long because they normally do not satisfy a strong need or satisfy it well.

Fads
Fashions that enter quickly, are adopted with great zeal, peak early, and decline very fast.

Marketers can use the PLC concept as a framework for describing how products and markets work. But using the PLC concept for forecasting product performance or for developing marketing strategies presents some practical problems.[19] For example, managers may have trouble identifying which stage of the PLC the product is in, identifying when the product moves into the next stage, and determining the factors that affect the product's movement through the stages. In practice, it is difficult to forecast the sales level at each PLC stage, the length of each stage, and the shape of the PLC curve.

Using the PLC concept to develop marketing strategy can also be difficult because strategy is both a cause and a result of the product's life cycle. The product's current PLC position suggests the best marketing strategies, and the resulting marketing strategies affect product performance in later life cycle stages. Yet, when used carefully, the PLC concept can help in developing good marketing strategies for different stages of the product life cycle.

We looked at the product development stage of the product life cycle in the first part of the chapter. We now look at strategies for each of the other life cycle stages.

Introduction Stage

Introduction stage
The product life cycle stage when the new product is first distributed and made available for purchase.

The **introduction stage** starts when the new product is first launched. Introduction takes time, and sales growth is apt to be slow. Such well-known products as instant coffee, frozen orange juice, and powdered coffee creamers lingered for many years before they entered a stage of rapid growth.

In this stage, profits are negative or low because of the low sales and high distribution and promotion expenses. Much money is needed to attract distributors and build their inventories. Promotion spending is relatively high to inform consumers of the new product and get them to try it. Because the market is not generally ready for product refinements at this stage, the company and its few competitors produce basic versions of the product. These firms focus their selling on buyers who are most ready to buy.

A company, especially the *market pioneer,* must choose a launch strategy that is consistent with its intended product positioning: The initial strategy is just the first step in a grander marketing plan for the product's entire life cycle. If the pioneer chooses its launch strategy to make a "killing," it will be sacrificing long-run revenue for the sake of short-run gain. As the pioneer moves through later stages of the life cycle, it will have to continuously formulate new pricing, promotion, and other marketing strategies. It has the best chance of building and retaining market leadership if it plays its cards correctly from the start.

Growth Stage

Growth stage
The product life cycle stage in which a product's sales start climbing quickly.

If the new product satisfies the market, it will enter a **growth stage,** in which sales will start climbing quickly. The early adopters will continue to buy, and later buyers will start following their lead, especially if they hear favourable word of mouth. Attracted by the opportunities for profit, new competitors will enter the market. They will introduce new product features, and the market will expand. The increase in competitors leads to an increase in the number of distribution outlets, and sales jump just to build reseller inventories. Prices remain where they are or fall only slightly. Companies keep their promotion spending at the same or a slightly higher level. Educating the market remains a goal, but now the company must also meet the competition.

Profits increase during the growth stage, as promotion costs are spread over a large volume and as unit manufacturing costs fall. The firm uses several strategies to sustain rapid market growth as long as possible. It improves product quality and adds new product features and models. It enters new market segments and new distribution channels. It shifts some advertising from building product awareness to building product conviction and purchase, and it lowers prices at the right time to attract more buyers.

In the growth stage, the firm faces a trade-off between high market share and high current profit. By spending a lot of money on product improvement, promotion, and distribution, the company can capture a dominant position. In doing so, however, it gives up maximum current profit, which it hopes to make up in the next stage.

Discreet Logic
www.discreet.com/

Discreet Logic Inc. of Montreal faces this quandary. It produces software that allows film-makers to generate special effects such as the huge break in the highway that confronts the racing bus in *Speed*. As the result of exploding demand, Discreet has experienced remarkable growth. Its owners, however, realize that it has to avoid "hitting the wall"—being unable to sustain the cash flow essential to support their growth.

Maturity Stage

Maturity stage
The product life cycle stage where sales growth slows or levels off.

At some point, a product's sales growth will slow down, and the product will enter a **maturity stage.** This maturity stage normally lasts longer than the previous stages, and it poses strong challenges to marketing management. Most products are in the maturity stage of the life cycle, and therefore most of marketing management deals with the mature product.

The slowdown in sales growth results in many producers with many products to sell. In turn, this overcapacity leads to greater competition. Competitors begin marking down prices, increasing their advertising and sales promotions, and increasing their R&D budgets to find better versions of the product. These steps lead to a drop in profit. Some of the weaker competitors start dropping out, and the industry eventually contains only well-established competitors.

Although many products in the mature stage appear to remain unchanged for long periods, most successful ones are actually evolving to meet changing consumer needs (see Marketing Highlight 9-3). Product managers should do more than simply ride along with or defend their mature products—a good offence is

Discreet Logic faces the challenge of managing the growth phase of the product life cycle.

marketing highlight 9-3

Age-Defying Products or Just Skillful PLC Management?

Some products are born and die quickly. Others, however, seem to defy the product life cycle, enduring for decades or even generations with little or no apparent change in their makeup or marketing. Look deeper, however, and you'll find that such products are far from unchanging. Rather, skillful product life cycle management keeps them fresh, relevant, and appealing to customers. Here are examples of three products that might have been only fads but instead were turned into long-term market winners with plenty of staying power.

Kraft Dinner

The Barenaked Ladies sing about it, and university students, adults, and children across Canada wolf down an incredible 246 000 boxes of KD a day. Nine out of ten Canadian households buy the product. Kraft Dinner is not only Kraft Canada's biggest business from a volume standpoint, but is also the country's number-one-selling grocery item holding a 75 percent share of the market. Not bad for basic food that has been close to the hearts of Canadians since 1937. In fact, per capita, Canadians eat three times more Kraft dinner than their American counterparts.

Despite its Canadian success, senior brand manager Gannon Jones confesses that "it's a business that's been suffering over the last while." In an ever changing market, "You can't sit back and simply expect the brand to continue to be popular without trying to keep it relevant with consumers." The very popularity of the product presents its own challenges. How, you might ask, can you get Canadians to eat even more of the stuff? The biggest danger in trying to revitalize the brand is making changes that will alienate KD's core customers, just like Coke did when it introduced New Coke.

For a period, managers of the product had become too reliant on price to drive the KD business. Today that is history. Kraft has put a lot of its market research muscle, new product development skills, and advertising savvy behind revitalizing the brand. Rather than just talking to kids, as had become its habit, Kraft Canada decided it needed to reconnect with adults. So, Kraft and its agency, J. Walter Thompson, asked cultural anthropologist Grant McCracken to study the brand to uncover consumer insights about KD.

This research, along with 15 000 videos of Canadians talking about why they love Kraft Dinner, revealed that everyone has their own "KD truths." Such truths could be any of those special moments we all remember about eating KD at university since it was all we could afford on our tight budgets, to eating it with our culinary-challenged dad while mom was away. The first TV spot based on these research insights was a hit. Dubbed "Laundry Night," it was targeted to young adults as well as moms. It featured a group of university-age guys filing into a laundromat, where

The Kraft Dinner website helps consumers experience the brand with its comic book pages packed with outrageous fun.

one of them uses a washing machine to prepare KD. When another patron gives him a look, he shrugs and says, "My night to cook."

Kraft has also been busy on other fronts. The famous blue and yellow box was given a face lift, giving the lettering a 3-D look. New product versions were developed. These include Easy Mac Macaroni & Cheese, a microwaveable, snack-size extension. Kraft called the launch of this product its biggest in Canada in a decade. The TV campaign used to launch the product, titled "Dog Gone Girl," won praise among viewers and critics alike. It shows a young man returning home, finding nothing in his apartment but his dog. Although not overly concerned about being abandoned by his girlfriend, he is hungry and manages to make Easy Mac in the dog's dish.

The born-again brand has even managed to score in cyberspace. As *Marketing Magazine*'s digital critic notes, "I love this site. I have always thought of Kraft Dinner more as entertainment than food and that is the approach taken with this Web site. No fuzzy lifestyle shots of happy families or time-pressed yuppies, just lurid comic book pages of outrageous fun." You can visit the Internet's cheesiest site at www.kraftdinner.com.

Beanie Babies

When Ty Inc. unleashed Beanie Babies on the market in 1993, most experts saw them as just a passing fad. Priced under $5, the tiny bean-filled creatures were designed by company founder Ty Warner as a back-to-basics toy that kids could buy with their own allowance money. Soon, however, adults began compulsively collecting the floppy little animals, and the company couldn't get them onto store shelves fast enough.

Yet Ty quickly realized that scarcity would be the key to keeping the Beanie Babies craze going—and going and going. The company became adept at maintaining consumer demand by limiting distribution to small gift and specialty stores. Each store is limited to 36 toys of each style per month. Ty also adds to the hype by regularly retiring old characters and replacing them with many new ones. There are just over 200 styles of Beanie Babies, with about 150 of them retired. Retired models fetch as much as $1000 from hard-core collectors. When new models or retirements are announced, visits to the company's Web site skyrocket. By mid-1999, the site had received almost 3 billion visits.

Thus, long after the experts would have predicted the demise of these cute little critters, avid collectors are still lining up to get their hands on new styles. In a typical scenario, Penny Madsen, who manages the gift shop in the Adventureland amusement park, says that she receives 15 or 20 calls a day asking whether the store has certain Beanies in stock. Even though Adventureland doesn't advertise its Beanie Babies, when new styles are expected, "People will be standing outside our gate at 6 in the morning, waiting until we open at 10," says Madsen. Even more impressive, they willingly pay the $20 gate admission just to get into the gift shop.

Crayola Crayons

Over the past century, Binney & Smith's Crayola crayons have become a household staple in more than 60 countries around the world. Few people can forget their first pack of "64s"—64 beauties neatly arranged in the familiar green and yellow flip-top box with a sharpener on the back. The aroma of a freshly opened Crayola box still drives kids into a frenzy and takes members of the older generation back to some of their fondest childhood memories.

In some ways, Crayola crayons haven't changed much since 1903, when they were sold in an eight-pack for a nickel. But a closer look reveals that Binney & Smith has made many adjustments to keep the brand out of decline. The company has added a steady stream of new colours, shapes, sizes, and packages. It has gradually increased the number of colours from the original eight in 1903 (red, orange, yellow, green, blue, black, brown, and violet) to 96 in 1999. In 1962, as a result of the civil rights movement, it changed its crayon colour "flesh" to "peach"; and in 1992, it added multicultural skin tones by which "children are able to build a positive sense of self and respect for cultural diversity." Binney & Smith has also extended the Crayola brand to new markets—Crayola markers, watercolour paints, themed stamps and stickers, and stencils. The company has licensed the Crayola brand for use on everything from lunch boxes and children's apparel to house paints. Finally, the company has added several programs and services to help strengthen its relationships with Crayola customers. For example, its *Crayola Kids* magazine and Crayola Web site offer features for the children along with expert advice to parents on helping develop reading skills and creativity.

Not all of Binney & Smith's life cycle adjustments have been greeted favourably by consumers. For example, in 1990, to make room for more modern colours, it retired eight colours from the time-honoured box of 64—raw umber, lemon yellow, maize, blue grey, orange yellow, orange red, green blue, and violet blue—into the Crayola Hall of Fame. The move unleashed a groundswell of protest from loyal Crayola users, who formed such organizations as the RUMPS—the Raw Umber and Maize Preservation Society—and the National Committee to Save Lemon Yellow. Company executives were flabbergasted—"We were aware of the loyalty and nostalgia surrounding Crayola crayons," a spokesperson says, "but we didn't know we [would] hit such a nerve." The company reissued the old standards in a special collector's tin—it sold all of the 2.5 million tins made.

Thus, Crayola continues its long and colourful life cycle. Through smart product life cycle management, Binney & Smith, now a subsidiary of Hallmark, has dominated the crayon market for almost a century. Sixty-five percent of all American children between the ages of two and seven pick up a crayon at least once a day and colour for an average of 28 minutes. Nearly 80 percent of the time, they pick up a Crayola crayon.

Sources: See John Heinzl, "Kraft Dinner serves up a new look," *Globe and Mail*, 13 January 1999:B30; Lara Mills, "Kraft builds ads around 'KD truths,'" *Marketing On-Line*, 26 April 1999; "Easy Mac simplifies Kraft Dinner," *Marketing On-Line*, 6 September 1999; Michael Cavanaugh, "The digital eye," *Marketing On-Line*, 13 March 2000; Kathleen Deslauriers, "Easy Mac stirs up awareness," *Strategy*, 13 March 2000:18; Gary Samuels, "Mystique marketing," *Forbes*, 21 October 1996:276; Carole Schmidt and Lynn Kaladjian, "Ty connects hot-property dots," *Brandweek*, 16 June 1997:26; Joyce Cohen, "Fans still lining up to haul in Beanie Babies," *Amusement Business*, 18 January 1999:4; www.ty.com, February 2000; "Hue and cry over Crayola may revive old colors," *Wall Street Journal*, 14 June 1991:B1; Margaret O. Kirk, "Coloring our children's world since '03," *Chicago Tribune*, 29 October 1986: 5:1; Becky Ebenkamp, "Crayola heritage tack continues with $6–7M," *Brandweek*, 1 February 1999:5; www.crayola.com, February 2000; Gene Del Vecchio, "Keeping it timeless, trendy," *Advertising Age*, 23 March 1998:24.

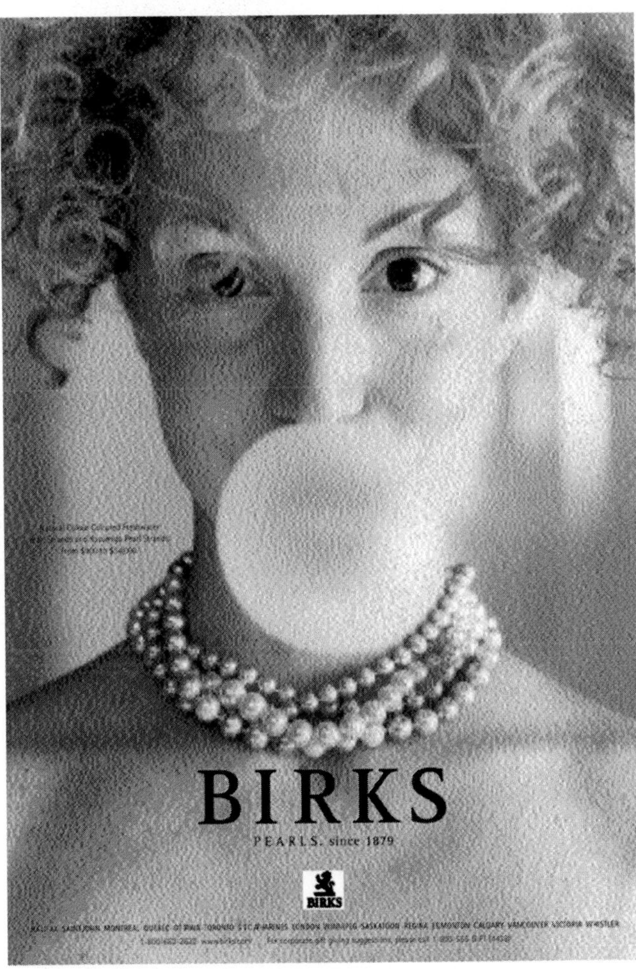

In its maturity stage, Birks, one of Canada's oldest companies, is aiming advertising at a younger audience to broaden its appeal.

the best defence. They should consider modifying the market, product, and marketing mix.

In *modifying the market,* the company tries to increase the consumption of the current product. It looks for new users and market segments. Johnson & Johnson targeted the adult market with its baby powder and shampoo; AirWair Canada Ltd., the company that markets Doc Martens footwear, began targeting consumers aged 25 to 50 years, with its message of quality and durability.[20] The manager also looks for ways to increase usage among present customers. Campbell does this by offering recipes and convincing consumers that "soup is good food." Or the company may want to reposition the brand to appeal to a larger or faster-growing segment. Arrow introduced its new line of casual shirts and announced, "We're loosening our collars."

The company can also try *modifying the product*—changing such product characteristics as quality, features, or style to attract new users and to inspire more usage. It can improve the product's quality and performance—its durability, reliability, speed, taste. Or it can add new features that expand the product's usefulness, safety, or convenience. Sony keeps adding new styles and features to its Walkman and Discman lines, and Volvo adds new safety features to its cars. Finally, the company can improve the product's styling and attractiveness. Thus, car manufacturers restyle their cars to attract buyers who want a new look. The makers of consumer food and household products introduce new flavours, colours, ingredients, or packages to revitalize consumer buying.

Finally, the company may decide to *modify the marketing mix*. Marketers also can try to improve sales by changing one or more marketing mix elements. They can cut prices to attract new users and competitors' customers. They can launch a better advertising campaign or use aggressive sales promotions—trade deals, cents-off, premiums, and contests. Montreal-based jeweller Henry Birks & Sons recently decided to use television advertising for the first time ever. The campaign broke just before the 2000 Christmas shopping season and used the Birks blue box and the tag line "Think inside the box." Birks hopes to reach a younger audience with this alteration to its marketing mix.[21] The company can also move into larger market channels, using mass merchandisers, if these channels are growing. Finally, the company can offer new or improved services to buyers.

Decline Stage

The sales of most product forms and brands eventually dip. The decline may be slow, as in the case of oatmeal cereal; or rapid, as in the case of phonograph records. Sales may plunge to zero, or they may drop to a low level where they continue for many years. This is the **decline stage.**

Decline stage
The product life cycle stage in which a product's sales decline.

Sales decline for many reasons, including technological advances, shifts in consumer tastes, and increased competition. As sales and profits decline, some firms withdraw from the market. Those remaining may prune their product offerings. They may drop smaller market segments and marginal trade channels, or they may cut the promotion budget and reduce their prices further.

Carrying a weak product can be very costly to a firm, and not just in profits. There are many hidden costs. A weak product may take up too much of management's time. It often requires frequent price and inventory adjustments. It requires advertising and sales force attention that might be better used to make "healthy" products more profitable. A product's failing reputation can cause customer concerns about the company and its other products. The biggest cost may well lie in the future. Keeping weak products delays the search for replacements, creates a lopsided product mix, hurts current profits, and weakens the company's foothold on the future.

For these reasons, companies need to pay more attention to their aging products. The firm's first task is to identify those products in the decline stage by regularly reviewing sales, market shares, costs, and profit trends. Then, management must decide whether to maintain, harvest, or drop each of these declining products.

Management may decide to *maintain* its brand without change in the hope that competitors will leave the industry. For example, Procter & Gamble made good profits by remaining in the declining liquid-soap business as others withdrew. Or management may decide to reposition the brand in hopes of moving it back into the growth stage of the product life cycle. Facing a slumping market, Vlasic reinvented the sliced pickle: [22]

Vlasic Foods International
www.vlasic.com/

Pickle consumption has been declining about two percent a year since the 1980s, but following successful new product introductions, sales generally get a prolonged boost. Vlasic began its quest for a blockbuster pickle in the mid-1990s after focus groups revealed that people hate it when pickle slices slither out the sides of hamburgers and sandwiches. At first the company decided to slice its average pickles horizontally into strips and marketed them as "Sandwich Stackers." The only problem was that the strips usually contained the soft seedy part of the cucumber, not the crunchy part. The company then embarked on "Project Frisbee," an effort to create a giant pickle chip. In 1998, after years of research and development, Vlasic created a cucumber ten times larger than the traditional pickle cucumber. The pickle slice, or "chip," is large enough to cover the entire surface of a hamburger and is stacked a dozen high in jars. The Sandwich Stackers line now accounts for about 20 percent of Vlasic's pickle sales.

Management may decide to *harvest* the product, which means reducing various costs (plant and equipment, maintenance, R&D, advertising, sales force) and hoping that sales hold up. If successful, harvesting will increase the company's profits in the short run. Or management may decide to *drop* the product from the line. It can sell it to another firm or simply liquidate it at salvage value. If the company plans to find a buyer, it will not want to run down the product through harvesting.

Table 9-3 summarizes the key characteristics of each stage of the product life cycle. The table also lists the marketing objectives and strategies for each stage.[23]

TABLE 9-3 Summary of Product Life Cycle Characteristics, Objectives, and Strategies

	Introduction	Growth	Maturity	Decline
Characteristics				
Sales	Low	Rapidly rising	Peak	Declining
Costs	High per customer	Average per customer	Low per customer	Low per customer
Profits	Negative	Rising	High	Declining
Customers	Innovators	Early adopters	Middle majority	Laggards
Competitors	Few	Growing number	Stable number beginning to decline	Declining number
Marketing Objectives				
	Create product awareness and trial	Maximize market share	Maximize profit while defending market share	Reduce expenditure and milk the brand
Strategies				
Product	Offer a basic product	Offer product extensions, service, warranty	Diversify brand and models	Phase out weak items
Price	Use cost-plus	Price to penetrate market	Price to match or best competitors	Cut price
Distribution	Build selective	Build intensive	Build more intensive	Go selective: phase out unprofitable outlets
Advertising	Build product awareness among early adopters and dealers	Build awareness and interest in the mass market	Stress brand differences and benefits	Reduce to level needed to retain hard-core loyals
Sales Promotion	Use heavy sales promotion to entice trial	Reduce to take advantage of heavy consumer demand	Increase to encourage brand switching	Reduce to minimal level

Source: Philip Kotler, *Marketing Management: Analysis, Planning, Implementation, and Control,* 8th ed., Englewood Cliffs, NJ: Prentice Hall, 1994:365.

Review of Concept Connections

Organizations must develop effective new product and service strategies. Their current products face limited life spans and must be replaced by newer products. But new products can fail—the risks of innovation are as great as the rewards. The key to successful innovation lies in a total company effort, strong planning, and a systematic *new-product development* process.

1. **Explain how companies find and develop new product ideas.**

   Companies find and develop new product ideas from various sources. Many new product ideas stem from *internal sources*. Companies conduct formal research and development, "pick the brains" of their employees, and brainstorm at executive meetings. *Customers* are also a rich source of new product ideas. By conducting surveys and focus groups and analyzing customer questions and complaints, companies can generate new product ideas that will meet specific consumer needs. *Competitors* are another source of new product ideas. Companies track competitors' offerings and inspect new products, dismantling them, analyzing their performance, and deciding whether to introduce a similar or improved product. Finally, *distributors and suppliers* may offer new product ideas. Resellers are close to the market and can pass along information about consumer problems and new product possibilities. Suppliers can tell the company about new concepts, techniques, and materials that can be used in new product development.

2. **List and define the steps in the new-product development process.**

   The new product development process consists of eight sequential stages. A process starts with *idea generation*, which may draw inspiration from internal sources, customers, competitors, suppliers, and others. *Idea screening* reduces the number of ideas based on the company's own criteria. Ideas that pass the screening stage continue through *product concept development,* in which a detailed version of the new product idea is stated in meaningful consumer terms. In the next stage, *concept testing,* new product concepts are tested with a group of target consumers to determine whether the concepts have strong consumer appeal. Strong concepts proceed to *marketing strategy development,* in which an initial marketing strategy for the new product is developed from the product concept. In the *business analysis stage,* a review of the sales, costs, and profit projections for a new product is conducted to determine whether the new product is likely to satisfy the company's objectives. With positive results here, the ideas become more concrete through *test marketing* and finally are launched during *commercialization.*

3. **Describe the stages of the product life cycle.**

Each product has a *life cycle* marked by a changing set of problems and opportunities. The sales of the typical product follow an S-shaped curve composed of five stages. The cycle begins with the *product development stage* when the company finds and develops a new product idea. The *introduction stage* is marked by slow growth and low profits as the product is distributed to the market. If successful, the product enters a *growth stage,* which offers rapid sales growth and increasing profits. During this stage, the company tries to improve the product, enter new market segments and distribution channels, and reduce its prices slightly. Next is a *maturity stage* when sales growth slows down and profits stabilize. The company seeks strategies to renew sales growth, including market, product, and marketing mix modification. Finally, the product enters a *decline stage* in which sales and profits dwindle. The company's task during this stage is to recognize the decline, and to decide whether it should maintain, harvest, or drop the product. If the product is discontinued, it may be sold to another firm or liquidated for salvage value.

4. **Describe how marketing strategies change over the product's life cycle.**

In the *introduction stage,* the company must choose a launch strategy consistent with its intended product positioning. Much money is needed to attract distributors and build their inventories, and to inform consumers of the new product and achieve trial. In the *growth stage,* companies continue to educate potential consumers and distributors. In addition, the company works to stay ahead of the competition and sustain rapid market growth by improving product quality; adding new product features and models; entering new market segments and distribution channels; shifting some advertising from building product awareness to building product conviction and purchase; and lowering prices at the right time to attract new buyers. In the *maturity stage,* companies continue to invest in maturing products and consider modifying the market, the product, and the marketing mix. When *modifying the market,* the company attempts to increase the consumption of the current product. When *modifying the product,* the company changes some of the product's characteristics—such as quality, features, or style—to attract new users or inspire more usage. When *modifying the market mix,* the company works to improve sales by changing one or more of the marketing mix elements. Once the company recognizes that a product has entered the *decline stage,* management must decide whether to *maintain* the brand without change, hoping that competitors will drop out of the market; *harvest* the product, reducing costs and trying to maintain sales; or *drop* the product, selling it to another firm or liquidating it at salvage value.

Key Terms

Business analysis *(p. 388)*
Commercialization *(p. 391)*
Concept development *(p. 385)*
Concept testing *(p. 386)*
Decline stage *(p. 401)*
Fads *(p. 397)*
Fashion *(p. 396)*
Growth stage *(p. 397)*
Idea generation *(p. 382)*
Idea screening *(p. 384)*
Introduction stage *(p. 397)*
Marketing strategy development *(p. 387)*
Maturity stage *(p. 398)*
New-product development *(p. 380)*
Product concept *(p. 385)*
Product development *(p. 388)*
Product life cycle (PLC) *(p. 395)*
Sequential product development *(p. 391)*
Simultaneous product development *(p. 393)*
Style *(p. 396)*
Test marketing *(p. 389)*

Discussing the Issues

1. Assume that you are an idea manager responsible for generating new product ideas in a company. How would you structure the new product development process? What sources of new ideas would be most valuable?
2. Less than one-third of new product ideas come from customers. Does this low percentage suggest that few companies employ the marketing concept philosophy of "find a need and fill it"? Why or why not?
3. Assume that you have been hired by General Motors to develop three alternative product concepts for a voice-activated, verbal Internet link it plans to make available in its luxury cars. This system would allow an automobile's occupants to access the Internet, e-mail, and e-shopping sites while driving or riding around. In developing the three concepts, think carefully about who would use such a system and when, where, and how. Which of your three concepts do you think has the greatest potential?
4. Discuss the advantages and disadvantages of the three approaches to test marketing. If you were the marketing research director for Frito-Lay, which of the three approaches would you use to test market a new brand of snack chips made from dried bananas? Explain.
5. Discuss the differences between a style, a fashion, and a fad. Then visit the Sharper Image Web site (www.sharperimage.com) and find examples of products that fit each category. Explain your choices.
6. Pick a soft drink, car, fashion, food product, or electronic appliance and trace the product's life cycle. Explain how you separated the stages of the product's evolution. Project where this life cycle will go from here.
7. What strategic options are open to the marketers of products in the mature stage of the product life cycle? Select a specific product (other than those mentioned in the chapter) that illustrates each of the strategic options that you have identified.
8. Which product life cycle stage, if any, is the most important? Which stage is the riskiest? Which stage appears to hold the greatest profit potential? Which stage needs the greatest amount of "hands-on" management? Be certain to explain the thinking behind each of your answers.

Marketing Applications

1. In NASCAR driver Richard Petty's heyday, the Plymouth Road Runner was the "baddest boy" on the block. Recently, however, DaimlerChrysler announced that it would eliminate the Plymouth brand and transition Plymouth products into the Chrysler line. Many loyal customers are asking, "Why is this happening?" The short answer is that as Plymouth traded its muscle-car mystique for the more staid image that goes with affordable cars and minivans, it lost its positioning in the marketplace. Sales of Plymouth's major models—Breeze, Neon, and the Voyager minivan—have fallen off steadily in recent years.
   a. Go to the Plymouth Web site at www.plymouthcars.com and examine DaimlerChrysler's comments about the demise of the Plymouth brand. Summarize these comments.
   b. Examine the strategies presented in the chapter for a mature or declining product. Which of these did DaimlerChrysler try with Plymouth? What decline-phase strategies are now being used? What, if anything, might Daimler Chrysler have done differently with the Plymouth brand?
   c. If you were given the task of turning the Plymouth brand around, what actions would you take?
   d. If you were given the task of merging the Plymouth brand with the popular Chrysler brand, what actions would you take?
2. "Danger, Will Robinson! Danger!" might be one of the most memorable phrases ever uttered by a robot. However, today, the phrase would more likely be "Buy Me! Take Me Home!" Who will offer the first practical, affordable home robot? NASA? Intel? Sony? Lego? Did you say Lego? Yes, the same little company that developed those great plastic building

blocks has now developed several models of home robots (such as the R2-D2 model from Star Wars) that sell for as little as $220. These Lego model kits contain Lego pieces, light and touch sensors, gears, and a minicomputer brick that forms the core of the system. The small, efficient robots already perform many hard-to-believe tasks (without complaining), and Lego is making daily upgrades. Copycat competitors have already begun a modification frenzy that will one day produce an awesome personal assistant. See www.lego.com, www.legomindstorms.com, www.lugnet.com, and www.crynwr.com/lego-robotics for more information.

a. Who might the first customers be for a Lego robot? Explain.
b. Project the product life cycle for this new product. Explain your thinking.
c. Outline a strategy for positioning this product away from the toy category and into the "personal device" category.
d. What tag line would you select for a first Lego robot ad appearing in the *National Post?* In *Canadian Business?*
e. Design a quick test market study for the Lego robot that would be administered at the annual computer and software convention (COMDEX) in Las Vegas.

Internet Connections

New Service Opportunity

One new service development on the Internet involves providing core business operations for other businesses. The business receiving the service is said to be outsourcing a portion of its operations. Businesses may outsource anything from order processing to shipping. In fact, it is possible to outsource nearly all core operations. The outsourcing trend is particularly prevalent among online storefronts. Outsourcing makes a lot of sense since most online storefronts need virtually the same functionality. Why reinvent the wheel? Online storefronts need ways to find, support, bill, and collect payments from customers. Storefronts also need to build inventories, keep them in warehouses, and ship them when customers place orders. Finally, the technology to conduct electronic transactions and keep track of the data is especially important for Internet selling. Two companies rushing to provide these services are Digital River and Pandesic. Visit these companies online and complete the following table to indicate which services they provide, using the marketing mix categories as a guideline. Hint: Refer to other chapters in this book to see which services might be appropriate in each of the four Ps.

For Discussion

1. In which marketing mix strategies do these firms specialize?
2. What are the advantages of outsourcing key business operations?
3. What are the disadvantages of outsourcing key business operations?
4. Are outsourcing services better for start-up corporations or for existing businesses?
5. Are outsourcing services better for large businesses or small businesses?
6. If you were designing a new service firm to compete with these companies, what services would you offer?
7. Which firm would you use if you wanted to start a new company to sell products online?

	Pandesic www.pandesic.com	Digital River www.digitalriver.com
Product (e.g., sales analysis)		
Price (e.g., online pricing)		
Distribution place (e.g., warehousing)		
Promotion (e.g., attracting customers)		

Savvy Sites

- The NPD Group (www.npd.com) provides custom research for every product life cycle (PLC) stage. Of special interest is its Home Testing Institute (HTI) consumer panel composed of 350 000 households
- IBM (www.ibm.com) maintains an archive of US Patent & Trademark Office (USPTO) patent descriptions (and some images) from 1971 to date. To access this patent server, search for "patent" at the site.
- BUY.com (www.buy.com) is the "Internet Superstore," offering products at or near cost and selling advertising to build revenue.

Notes

1. Quotes from Wendy Cuthbert, "Gillette scores with Cavalcade of Sports," *Strategy,* 22 May 2000:21; Lawrence Ingrassia, "Taming the monster: How big companies can change," *Wall Street Journal,* 10 December 1992:A1,A6; William H. Miller, "Gillette's secret to sharpness," *Industry Week,* 3 January 1994: 24–30; Linda Grant, "Gillette knows shaving—And how to turn out hot new products," *Fortune,* 14 October 1996:207–10; and Dana Canedy, "Gillette's strengths in razors undone by troubles abroad," *New York Times,* 19 June 1999:3. Also see William C. Symonds, "Would you spend $1.50 for a razor blade?" *Business Week,* 27 April 1998:46; James Heckman, "Razor sharp: Adding value, making noise with Mach3 intro," *Marketing News,* 29 March 1999:E4,E13; and William C. Symonds, "The big trim at Gillette," Business Week, 8 November 1999:42.
2. "Bright ideas," *Royal Bank Reporter,* Fall 1992:6–15.
3. Kevin J. Clancy and Robert S. Shulman, *The Marketing Revolution: A Radical Manifesto for Dominating the Marketplace,* New York: Harper Business, 1991:6; Robert G. Cooper, "New product success in industrial firms," *Industrial Marketing Management,* 1992:215–23. Also see Gary Strauss, "Building on brand names: Companies freshen old product lines," *USA Today,* 20 March 1992:B1,B2.
4. Robert G. Cooper and Elko J. Kleinschmidt, *New Product: The Key Factors in Success,* Chicago: American Marketing Association, 1990.
5. Jon Berry and Edward F. Ogiba, "It's your boss: Why new products fail," *Brandweek,* 19 October 1992:16; Linda Grant, "Gillette knows shaving—And how to turn out hot new products"; Rosabeth Moss Kanter, "Don't wait to innovate," *Sales & Marketing Management,* February 1997:22–4; Greg A. Stevens and James Burley, "3,000 raw ideas equals 1 commercial success!" *Research-Technology Management,* May/June 1997:16–27.
6. See Tim Stevens, "Idea dollars," *Industry Week,* 16 February 1998:47–9.
7. Peter Vamos, "Kellogg asks kids: Cereal maker launches Jacks Pack initiative with panel of young advisors under 15," *Strategy,* 14 August 2000:1.
8. Elizabeth Church, "Are you ready for some football?" *Globe and Mail,* 21 January 1999:B13; Mark Stevenson, "The idiots guide to football," *National Post,* 23 January 1999:A20.
9. Philip Kotler, *Kotler on Marketing,* New York: Free Press, 1999: 43–4.
10. Brian O'Reilly, "New ideas, new products," *Fortune,* 3 March 1997:61–4.
11. See "DaimlerChrysler plans '04 launch of fuel cell car," *Ward's Auto World,* April 1999:25; and William J. Cook, "A Mercedes for the future," *U.S. News & World Report,* 29 March 1999:62.
12. See Raymond R. Burke, "Virtual reality shopping: breakthrough in marketing research," *Harvard Business Review,* March–April 1996:120–31; and Brian Silverman, "Get 'em while they're hot," *Sales & Marketing Management,* February 1997:47–52.

13. Adrienne Ward Fawcett, "Oreo cones make top grade in poll," *Advertising Age,* 14 June 1993:30. Also see Linda Fitzpatrick, "Qualitative concept testing tells us what we don't know," *Marketing News,* 23 September 1996:11.

14. See Faye Rice, "Secrets of product testing," *Fortune,* 28 November 1994:172–4; Simone Collier, "The littlest gourmet," *Report on Business,* April 1997:68–74.

15. Chris Powell, "Sink or swim? Test markets allow a company to evaluate whether a new product will float before taking the plunge into a national rollout," *Marketing On-Line,* 30 October 2000.

16. Powell, "Sink or swim?"

17. See Howard Schlossberg, "IRI, Nielsen slug it out in "Scanning Wars," *Marketing News,* 2 September 1991:1,47.

18. See Hirotaka Takeuchi and Ikujiro Nonaka, "The new new-product development game," *Harvard Business Review,* January–February 1986:137–46; Craig A. Chambers, "Transforming new product development," *Research-Technology Management,* November–December 1996:323–8; and Srikant Datar, C. Clark Jordan, Sunder Kekre, Surendra Rajiv, and Kannan Srinivasan, "Advantages of time-based new product development in a fast-cycle industry," *Journal of Marketing Research,* February 1997: 36–49. For a good review of research on new product development, see Shona L. Brown and Kathleen M. Eisenhardt, "Product development: past research, present findings, and future directions," *Academy of Management Review,* April 1995:343; and Jerry Wind and Vijay Mahajan, "Issue and opportunities in new product development," *Journal of Marketing Research,* February 1997:1–12.

19. See George S. Day, "The product life cycle: Analysis and applications issues," *Journal of Marketing,* Fall 1981:60–7; John E. Swan and David R. Rink, "Fitting marketing strategy to varying life cycles," *Business Horizons,* January–February 1982:72–6; and Sak Onkvisit and John J. Shaw, "Competition and product management: Can the product life cycle help?" *Business Horizons,* July–August 1986:51–62.

20. Lara Mills, "Doc Martens stepping out to reach an older market," *Marketing,* 23 October 1995:2.

21. "Birks on-air for first time in new campaign," *Adnews On-Line Daily,* 30 November 2000.

22. Vanessa O'Connell, "Food: After years of trial and error, a pickle slice that stays put," *Wall Street Journal,* 6 October 1998:B1; "Vlasic's hamburger-size pickles," *Wall Street Journal,* 5 October 1998:A26; and "Vlasic Foods International FY2000 new products," www.vlasic.com, July 1999.

23. For a more comprehensive discussion of marketing strategies over the course of the product life cycle, see Philip Kotler, *Marketing Management,* 8th ed., Englewood Cliffs, NJ: Prentice Hall, 1994:Chapter 14.

Company Case 9

LifeSource Nutrition: Succeeding Where Campbell Soup Failed

Mmm! Smart Food

How would you feel about eating a steady diet of frozen foods to improve your health? Well, that's what Campbell Soup wanted you to do when it cooked up a line of mostly frozen meals designed to reduce certain health risks such as heart disease and diabetes. Campbell introduced the product line, calling it Intelligent Quisine (IQ), in a test market in January 1997.

How IQ made it to the test market is an interesting story. In 1991, Campbell realized the soup market was mature and offered very little growth potential. As a result, the company began to beef up its research and development efforts, devoting about one percent of sales to R&D. A senior vice-president noted that the company's R&D efforts were guided by two objectives: "stay with the customer" and "focus on big opportunities."

While exploring diversification ideas related to its core business, CEO David W. Johnson stumbled onto the idea of "introducing the first and only meal program clinically proven to help people reduce cholesterol, blood pressure, and blood sugar." Johnson saw an explosive market potential for "functional food"—food that tasted good, was good for you, and was as effective therapeutically as a drug. Observers dubbed this type of food "nutraceuticals." Campbell thought it could offer a convenient meal program to a target market of 60 million people who suffered from a wide range of health problems like high cholesterol, high blood pressure, and hypertension. That number actually grew to 100 million when people who were at risk of getting these problems were factored in. In addition, research showed that 52 percent of the population believed food products could help reduce cancer and disease.

The company then spent two years gathering a medical advisory board that included specialists in heart disease, nutrition, and diabetes. The board also included representatives from such organizations as the American Heart Association. Campbell worked with the advisory board and conducted clinical research on 800 patients to help design the IQ products.

By 1997, Campbell had spent $55 million to develop the product line. It consisted of 41 meals, mostly frozen, that included breakfasts such as French toast or egg sandwiches, lunches such as chili or stew, and dinners such as pasta or chicken. It also included snacks such as pretzels and cookies.

During the 15-month test market, participants purchased 21 IQ meals each week for a price of about $120 per week. The participants had to agree to stick with the program for four to ten weeks. With a discount, the recommended 10-week program actually cost about $1050. Consumers had to commit to eating only IQ meals and to changing other habits. With each weekly order, Campbell included printed materials that offered advice on diet, exercise, and behavioural change. Participants could also use prepaid phone cards to talk with dietitians.

Campbell decided to distribute the meals directly to consumers using UPS to make weekly deliveries of the frozen meals. The company selected direct distribution because it believed that retailers would not be able to keep the complete line of 41 meals in stock.

Campbell used television, radio, and print ads to promote the program and a toll-free number for consumers to call to place an order. The ads touted IQ's ability to reverse certain medical conditions such as high blood pressure and high blood sugar. "I ate cheesecake and my cholesterol went down 15 points," one ad proclaimed. In addition, the company had its sales representatives call on doctors and other health professionals, much as sales representatives for drug companies did.

At first glance, the test market seemed to be successful. In just 10 weeks, one consumer reported that she had lost 10 pounds and seen her cholesterol drop from 240 to 200. Another consumer had her blood sugar drop from 300 to between 110 and 135. She was even able to stop taking a prescription medication.

Overall, however, Campbell considered the test market a failure. Although the company had a sales target of 40 000 orders, fewer than 2500 people ordered just over six weeks of meals. Despite the homework that went into the project, it failed to meet Campbell's expectations. In early 1998, the company announced that it was pulling the plug on IQ. One analyst noted, "We are all waiting for the boom in nutraceuticals, but thus far there haven't been many opportunities to make money at it." Another analyst observed that it was never clear there would be a market for the product. "It never struck me as something that was very promising."

Jumping into the Soup

Just as Campbell announced its decision, LifeSource Nutrition Solutions, an Emeryville, California-based company, announced it would tackle the problem of offering nutritionally balanced meals. LifeSource is a spinoff of Age Wave, a consulting company started in 1986 by Ken Dychtwald. Age Wave specialized in advising firms on how to market to people over 50. Once Age Wave reached $15 million in revenue, Dychtwald stopped consulting and started a business incubator to create businesses that would serve the mushrooming population of people over 50. Dychtwald commented that, "The food industry has typically catered to the needs and time pressures of young adults while often neglecting the taste and nutrient needs of mature women and men."

LifeSource, which is also funded by Monsanto, operates in San Francisco and Los Angeles. In its current markets, it runs two central production kitchens where culinarians and nutritionists prepare nutraceutical foods and beverages that meet or exceed the dietary requirements of the American Heart Association, National Institutes of Health, and American Diabetes Association. Each of its 24 nutrient-rich meals, which include soups and smoothie beverages, address such common conditions as congestive heart failure, coronary artery disease, and diabetes. The company also offers free nutritional counselling and nutrition materials.

Unlike Campbell Soup, however, LifeSource conducted no clinical research to help in developing its products. The company did, however, assemble a science advisory board to make sure it understood the link between diet and health.

LifeSource's meals target customers over 50 who have risk factors for diabetes and heart disease. These people either can't or don't want to cook for themselves, or they don't have the energy or the means to get to the grocery store. Of the $1400 billion annual North American food market, only about $140 billion represents nutraceutical foods, and only about $14 billion of that amount is fortified foods (as opposed to natural fruits and vegetables). Moreover, there is a growing trend to "home meal replacements"—fully prepared foods that consumers purchase either to take home or for home delivery.

Once the company prepares the meals, it flash-freezes them in its own cold-storage facilities. Then, the company has its own fleet of vans and drivers deliver the meals. It decided on direct distribution to avoid problems with the freeze-thaw cycle. Controlling the food's temperature after production is critical to maintaining quality.

The company has not forgotten taste. Whereas a Meals-on-Wheels dinner of roast beef with red potatoes may not excite your taste buds, LifeSource's Creole cod, rice, and red chili beans, and an orange mango smoothie makes for a flashier, tastier offering. Moreover, nothing on a Meals-on-Wheels menu is fortified.

However, the average cost of a Meals-on-Wheels dinner is $7.961, with the client paying only $1.87 (welfare programs cover the balance of the cost for needy consumers). LifeSource, on the other hand, prices its dinners at $8.70 per entrée, its lunches from $4.80 to $6.30, its soups at $3.75, and its smoothies and desserts at $1.65 to $2.20. There is no delivery charge with a minimum eight-item order. People over 50, the company notes, represent only 27 percent of the population but control 70 percent of the total net worth of North American households.

LifeSource promotes its products through direct mail, direct-response advertising, and public relations. It also has a Web site, **www.lifesourcenutrition.com**, where consumers can place orders and get other valuable information about health and nutrition.

Perhaps the most important difference between IQ and the LifeSource plan is that the company has positioned its plan as giving consumers free choice. Campbell's tied its meal program to a physician network. A LifeSource spokesperson noted, "There's a customization of diets to reach individuals' health goals, and if they want to substitute 15, 20, or 50 percent of their diet, it's up to them. It's not based on clinical research—it's voluntary compliance."

A Success or Another Failure?

Will LifeSource succeed where Campbell failed? LifeSource reports that after experiencing a 50 percent reorder rate in its California markets, it is cautiously optimistic about its new products. In late 1999, it planned to expand to Seattle, Phoenix, and Salt Lake City; and, if all goes well, it plans a national rollout over the next four to seven years. Observers believe there is an opportunity for nutraceuticals and that Campbell's failure doesn't mean others will fail. However, a food industry analyst notes that, "It certainly is a niche that is extremely complex."

Questions

1. Outline Campbell Soup's marketing strategy for Intelligent Quisine and describe its new product development process. Why do you believe IQ failed?
2. Outline LifeSource Nutrition's marketing strategy for its products and describe its new-product development process. How are its strategy and its new-product development process alike or different from Campbell's?
3. Do you believe there is a market for nutraceuticals? Why or why not?
4. What marketing recommendations would you make to LifeSource Nutrition to help it be successful in this market?

Sources: "Takeout meals for specialized diets," *Food Management,* June 1999:10; Rick Desloge, "Monsanto puts $10 million in baby boomers' nutrition," *St. Louis Business Journal,* 4 January 1999:6; Kitty Kevin, "A golden age for meal solutions," *Food Processing,* October 1998:37; Jake Holden, "High-tech take-out," *American Demographics,* October 1998; Claudia D. O'Donnell, "Campbell's R&D cozies up to the consumer," *Prepared Foods,* September 1997:26; Vanessa O'Connell, "Campbell decides its IQ health meals may be ahead of the curve for foods," *Wall Street Journal,* 27 April 1998:B8; Stephanie Thompson, "Eyeing an aging America, food giants broaden inroads into nutraceuticals," *Brandweek,* 6 January 1997:8; www.lifesourcenutrition.com.

video case 9

PROFITING FROM THE NET

Matt Harrop dropped out of high school in the mid-1990s to start his own business, Interlog, an Internet service provider (ISP) in Toronto. Although he knew his business, like the Internet itself, could grow fast, he had no idea how fast. For most of its first year of operation, Interlog experienced growth of 15 percent a month. While this kind of growth is the envy of most business owners, managing that growth effectively turned out to be Matt's biggest business challenge.

Matt started Interlog in response to his own dissatisfaction as an ISP customer. ISPs are companies that provide a gateway to the Internet for computer users. They generally have several phone lines and computer modems that allow easy access to the Internet for their customers. As a customer, Matt thought that existing ISPs were not doing a very good job and that he could do better. With a small bank loan, virtually no business plan, and one phone line, Matt started Interlog.

There were only three other ISPs in business in Toronto when Matt started, so competition was minimal. But demand was exploding as more businesses and consumers began to want access to the Internet. The resulting growth of Interlog was overwhelming. In one year, the company went from one phone line to 300 to service an end-of-the-year customer base of 6000 users. The company had to move twice during this time to keep up with the increased amount of hardware necessary to run the business and the increasing numbers of staff that were being hired to keep up with customer demand. During this first year, Matt recognized that he needed help with the management of the business. His strength was technical expertise, not management. He needed someone to help him effectively cope with the rate of growth that the company was experiencing. Matt's 26-year-old brother, Lorian, a lawyer, was brought into the business as president to provide management leadership.

One problem caused by the rapid growth in the ISP industry was Interlog's inability to grow fast enough. An area that suffered was customer service. Interlog simply could not hire people fast enough to provide enough customer support. Matt and Lorian soon realized that service counts in the ISP business. Customers were demanding more and better service from all ISP service providers. If their phone connection was interrupted or if their software was not working properly while on the Internet, customers wanted to be able to talk to someone at their ISP who could solve the problem. Increasing competition in the industry fuelled customer demands. At the end of Interlog's first year in business, there were 80 ISP companies in business, and customers were becoming more choosy. Interlog hired more employees to handle customer support: By the end of the first year of operation, it had 20 employees, most in jobs related to customer technical support.

Financing the growth of Interlog has been another challenge. Despite their success, Matt and Lorian have had difficulty getting outside financing to help pay for the company's growth. Interlog is a profitable company in an otherwise unprofitable industry so getting investors has proven almost impossible. As a result the brothers have relied on bank lines of credit and leasing to see them through periods of growth.

The second year of business saw continuing rapid growth for Interlog, about 10 percent a month. The company was forced during this second year to become a larger, more formalized organization. At the end of year two of business, its 75 employees were servicing 30 000 customers. Since the systems in place for running the company were not developed for such a large organization, several changes were required. A new marketing department was created and the accounting and billing operation was completely revised to handle larger numbers of customers. The company offices had moved to the heart of the financial district in Toronto and now also included a storefront operation.

As Matt begins his third year of business, he has not become complacent. He is well aware that the key to his success is the ability to change. Since the industry changes almost daily, both he and his organization have to be adaptable and creative. As Matt says, "If I can't think of something new and different, then I may as well not be in this business."

Questions

1. What do you think the shape of the product life cycle for the ISP industry will look like?
2. What stage of the product life cycle is the ISP industry in right now? What implications does this have for the management of Interlog both now and in the future?

Source: This case was prepared by Auleen Carson and is based on "Internet Geeks," *Venture* (March 30, 1997).

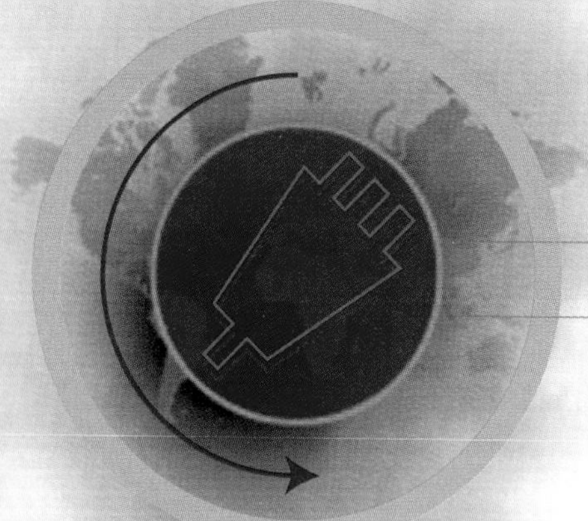

P A R T 1 2 3 4

Developing the Marketing Mix

Concept Connections

When you finish this chapter, you should be able to

1. Identify and define the internal factors affecting a firm's pricing decisions.
2. Identify and define the external factors affecting pricing decisions, including the impact of consumer perceptions of price and value.
3. Contrast the three general approaches to setting prices.
4. Describe the major strategies for pricing new products and product lines.
5. Discuss the key issues related to initiating and responding to price changes.

chapter 10

Pricing Strategies

For over eight decades, Kellogg has been hanging out with Canadians in the morning. Until recently, investment analysts saw the company as a virtual money machine. Over the 1990s, annual returns to Kellogg's shareholders averaged 19 percent, with gross margins running as high as 55 percent. Over the previous 30 years, Kellogg's sales had grown at one and a half times the industry growth rate and its share of the North American cereal market had consistently exceeded 40 percent. By 2000, Kellogg had about 43 percent of the Canadian ready-to-eat cereal market by physical volume, or $550 million in terms of 1999 dollar sales. It was followed by Kraft's Post Cereals, products that held 18 percent of the market, General Mills with 17 percent market share, private label with 12 percent of the market, and Quaker Oats with 8 percent. Kellogg also holds about 42 percent of the worldwide market, with a 48 percent share in Asia and Europe and 69 percent of the Latin America marketplace. Things, it seemed, could only get better for Kellogg.

These dazzling numbers, however, hid the fact that Kellogg's cereal empire had begun to lose its lustre. Much of its recent success, especially in the US, had come at the expense of cereal customers. Kellogg's recent gains—and those of major competitors General Mills, Post, and Quaker—had come not from innovative new products, creative marketing programs, and operational improvements that added value for customers, but rather almost entirely from price increases that padded the sales and profits of the cereal makers.

Throughout most of the 1980s and early 1990s, Kellogg had boosted profit margins by steadily raising prices on its Rice Krispies, Special K, Raisin Bran, and Frosted Flakes—often twice a year. For example, by early 1996, a 14-ounce box of Raisin Bran that sold for US$2.39 in 1985 was going for as much as US$4.00 to $5.00, but with little or no change in the costs of the materials making up the cereal or its packaging. Since World War II, no food category had had more price increases than cereal. The price increases were very profitable for Kellogg and the other cereal companies. On average, the cereal makers were reaping more than twice the operating margins of the food industry as a whole. However, the relentless price increases became increasingly difficult for customers to swallow.

Not surprisingly, in 1994, the cereal industry's pricing policies began to backfire as frustrated consumers retaliated with a quiet fury. Cereal buyers began shifting away from branded cereals toward less expensive private-label brands; by 1995, private labels were devouring 10 percent of the North American cereal market, up from a little more than five percent only five years earlier. Worse, many people switched to less expensive, more portable hand-held breakfast foods, such as bagels, muffins, and breakfast bars. As a result, total North American cereal sales began falling off by three to four percent a year. Kellogg's sales and profits sagged, and its North American market share dropped to 36 percent. By early 1996, after what most industry analysts viewed as years of outrageous and self-serving pricing policies, Kellogg and the other cereal makers faced a full-blown crisis.

Belated research showed that exorbitant pricing was indeed the cause of the industry's problems. "Every statistic, every survey we took only showed that our customers were becoming more and more dissatisfied." Customers were "walking down cereal aisles, clutching fistfuls of coupons and looking all over the shelves, trying to match them with a specific brand." Post Cereals was the first to boost its soggy sales by slashing an average of 20 percent off prices on its 22 cereal brands, a surprise move that rocked the industry.

Quaker Oats Canada
www.quakeroats.ca/

At first, Kellogg, General Mills, and Quaker held stubbornly to their premium prices. However, cereal buyers began switching in droves to Post's lower-priced brands, and Post quickly stole four points from Kellogg's market share alone. Kellogg and the others had little choice but to follow Post's lead. Kellogg announced price cuts averaging 19 percent on two-thirds of all brands sold in the US, marking the start of what would become a long and costly industry price war. In recanting their previous pricing excesses, the cereal makers swung wildly in the opposite direction, caught up in layoffs, plant closings, and other cost-cutting measures and fresh rounds of price cutting. "It reminds me of one of those World War I battles where there's all this firing but when the smoke clears you can't tell who won," noted an industry analyst. In fact, it appears that nobody won, as the fortunes of all competitors suffered.

Kellogg was perhaps the hardest hit of the major competitors. Post Cereal's parent company, consumer goods powerhouse Philip Morris, owner of Kraft, derived about two percent of its sales and profits from cereals and could easily offset the losses elsewhere. However, Kellogg, which counted on domestic cereal sales for 42 percent of its revenues and 43 percent of its operating profits, suffered enormously. Its operating margins were halved, and even after lowering its prices, Kellogg's revenues and profits continued to decline.

Kellogg finally looked to Canada to understand how to rebuild the category. Cereal marketers in Canada and the US had reacted very differently when faced with the price pressure presented by private-label brands. As one Canadian marketer noted, "What [the price cuts] served to do was to take money out of the category that's designed to fund new products, build advertising behind a brand-building program, and really generate news and excitement and variety within the category." Mark Childs, vice-president of marketing for Kellogg Canada, based in Etobicoke, Ontario, took a different approach from his American counterparts. He began with a re-evaluation of the competitive arena. Mark recognized that Kellogg's rivals included not only other packaged goods firms, but also quick-service restaurants like Tim Hortons and McDonald's. He also quickly realized that price discounting wasn't the answer. Instead, he placed a renewed emphasis on understanding his customers and what types of products held relevance and appeal for them. To maintain its leadership position, Mark believed that Kellogg Canada had to keep the pipeline full of fresh and innovative ideas. Vector, a "meal replacement in a flaked format," developed in Canada, was the offspring of this thinking. Launched in April 1999, Vector earned both Canadian and international awards for product innovation.

It wasn't long before the US marketers began following Canada's lead. Recently, Kellogg and the other cereal titans quietly began pushing ahead with modest price increases to fund the product innovation and marketing support necessary to stimulate growth in the stagnant cereal category. Today, despite its problems, Kellogg remains the industry leader. The Kellogg brand name is still one of the world's best known and most respected. Kellogg's recent initiatives to cut costs, get reacquainted with its customers, and develop innovative new products and marketing programs—all of which promise to add value for customers rather than simply cutting prices—has investors cautiously optimistic about Kellogg's future. But events of the past five years teach an important lesson. When setting prices, as when making any other marketing decisions, a company can't afford to focus just on its own costs and profits. Instead, it must focus on customers' needs and the value they receive from the company's total marketing offer. If a company doesn't give customers full value for the price they're paying, they'll go elsewhere. In this case, Kellogg stole profits by steadily raising prices without also increasing customer value. Customers paid the price in the short run—but Kellogg is paying the price in the long run.[1]

All for-profit organizations and many non-profit organizations must set prices on their products or services. Price goes by many names:[2]

> Price is all around us. You pay *rent* for your apartment, *tuition* for your education, and a *fee* to your . . . dentist. The airline, railway, taxi, and bus companies charge you a *fare;* the local utilities call their price a *rate;* and the local bank charges you *interest* for the money you borrow. The price for driving your car on [the Rainbow Bridge] is a *toll,* and the company that insures your car charges you a *premium*. The guest lecturer charges an *honorarium* to tell you about a government official who took a *bribe* to help a shady character steal *dues* collected by a trade association. Clubs or societies to which you belong may make a special *assessment* to pay unusual expenses. Your regular lawyer may ask for a *retainer* to cover her services. The "price" of an executive is a *salary,* the price of a salesperson may be a *commission,* and the price of a worker is a *wage*. Finally, although economists would disagree, many of us feel that *income taxes* are the price we pay for the privilege of making money.

Price
The amount of money charged for a product or service, or the sum of the values that consumers exchange for the benefits of having or using the product or service.

In the narrowest sense, **price** is the amount of money charged for a product or service. More broadly, price is the sum of all the values that consumers exchange for the benefits of having or using the product or service. Historically, price has been the major factor affecting buyer choice. This is still true in poorer nations, among poorer groups, and with commodity products. However, non-price factors have become more important in buyer choice behaviour in recent decades.

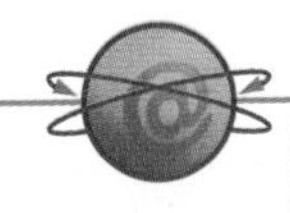

MSN eShop
www.eshop.com/

PriceSCAN
pricescan.com/

Throughout most of history, prices were set by negotiation between buyers and sellers. *Fixed price* policies—setting one price for all buyers—is a relatively modern idea that arose with the development of large-scale retailing at the end of the nineteenth century. Now, a hundred years later, the Internet promises to reverse the fixed pricing trend and take us back to an era of *dynamic pricing*—charging different prices depending on individual customers and situations (see Marketing Highlight 10-1). The Internet, corporate networks, and wireless set-ups are connecting sellers and buyers as never before. Such Web sites as MSN eShop and PriceSCAN.com allow buyers to quickly and easily compare products and prices. Online auction sites like eBay.com and Amazon.com make it easy for buyers and sellers to negotiate prices on thousands of items—from refurbished computers to antique tin trains. At the same time, new technologies allow sellers to collect detailed data about customers' buying habits, preferences—even spending limits—so they can tailor their products and prices.[3]

Price is the only element in the marketing mix that produces revenue; all other

marketing highlight 10-1

Back to the Future: Dynamic Pricing on the Web

The Internet is more than a new "marketspace"—it's actually changing the rules of commerce. Take pricing, for example. From the mostly fixed pricing policies of the nineteenth century, the Web now seems to be taking us back—into a new age of fluid pricing. "Potentially, [the Internet] could push aside sticker prices and usher in an era of dynamic pricing," says *Business Week* writer Robert Hof, "in which a wide range of goods would be priced according to what the market will bear—instantly, constantly." Here's how the Internet is changing the rules of pricing for both sellers and buyers.

Sellers can:

- *Charge lower prices, reap higher margins.* Web buying and selling can result in drastically lower costs, allowing online merchants to charge lower prices and still make higher margins. "The vastly lower cost of selling online provides plenty of riches to go around," observes Hof. "Thanks to their Internet connections, buyers and sellers around the world can connect at almost no cost—making instant bargaining [economically feasible]." Reduced inventory and distribution costs add to the savings. For example, by selling online and making its computers to order, Dell Computer greatly reduces inventory costs and eliminates retail markups. It shares the savings with buyers in the form of the "lowest price per performance."
- *Monitor customer behaviour and tailor offers to individuals.* With the help of new technologies, Web merchants can now target special prices to specific customers. For example, Personify Inc. has software that allows Internet sellers such as Amazon.com or Virtual Vineyards to assess each visitor's "clickstream," the way the person navigates the Web site, then instantaneously tailor products and prices to that shopper's specific behaviour. A visitor who behaves like a price-sensitive shopper may be offered a lower price. The Internet also lets sellers give certain customers special access to special prices. CDnow, the online music vendor, for example, e-mails a special Web site address with lower prices to certain buyers—say, new buyers whom it wants to encourage or heavy users whom it wants to reward. If you don't know the secret address, you pay full price.
- *Change prices on the fly according to changes in demand or costs.* Just ask such online catalogue retailers as Lands' End, Spiegel, or Fingerhut. With printed catalogues, a price is a price, at least until the next catalogue is printed. Online sellers, however, can change prices for specific items on a day-by-day or even hour-by-hour basis. Such flexible pricing lets sellers adjust quickly to changing costs, drop prices and offer promotions to boost sales for slow-moving items, and nudge prices upward to improve margins on hot-selling goods. Many business marketers use their extranets—the private networks that link them with suppliers and customers—to get a precise handle on inventory, costs, and demand at any given moment and adjust prices instantly.

Both sellers and buyers can:

- *Negotiate prices in online auctions and exchanges.* Want to sell that antique pickle jar that's been collecting dust for generations? Post it on www.eBay.com, the world's biggest online flea market. Want to purchase vintage baseball cards at a bargain price? Go to Boekhout's Collectibles Mall at www.azww.com. Want to dump that excess inventory? Try adding an auction feature to your own Web site—Sharper Image claims it's getting 40 percent of retail for excess goods sold via its online auction site, compared with only 20 percent from liquidators.

Suddenly the age-old art of haggling is back in vogue. Experts predict that in the year 2002, more than $193 billion worth of goods and services will be sold through Internet auctions, up from only $5.7 billion in 1998. Of the thousands of Internet auction sites, Onsale, eBay, and Amazon.com Auctions are the largest. More than 12 million bids have been placed at Onsale since it opened for business in 1995. At eBay, which began when its owner used the Web to find a market for his girlfriend's vintage Pez dispenser collection, about a million registered users have bid on 700 000 items in more than 1000 categories.

Buyers like auctions because, quite simply, they like the bargains they find. Sellers like auctions because, over the Internet, the cost per transaction drops dramatically. Thus, it becomes practical—even profitable—to auction an item for mere dollars rather than thousands of dollars. For example, the seller can program its computers to accept the 3000 best bids higher than $2.10 for 3000 pieces of costume jewellery. Business marketers, whose transactions account for 68 percent of online auction sales, also use auctions to offer time-sensitive deals and gauge interest on possible price points for new products.

Buyers can:

- *Get instant price comparisons from thousands of vendors.* The Internet gives consumers access to reams of data about products and prices. According to Hof, "In the physical world, buyers face all kinds of obstacles to getting the best deal—far-flung suppliers, limited time to do research, middlemen who keep a tight lid on information. . . . On the Web, shopping's a snap. Buyers can quickly compare information about products and vendors almost anywhere." New online comparison guides—such as

elements represent costs. Price is also one of the most flexible elements of the marketing mix. Unlike product features and channel commitments, price can be changed quickly. At the same time, pricing and price competition is the number one problem facing many marketing executives. Yet, many companies do not handle pricing well. Paul Hunt, director of the Strategic Pricing Division at The Advantage Group in Toronto, notes that the average company can increase its prof-

The Internet is ushering in an era of fluid pricing. MySimon is an independent site that provides product comparisons and guides and searches all merchant sites for the best prices.

CompareNet and PriceSCAN—spring up daily, giving product and price comparisons at the click of a mouse. CompareNet, for instance, lets consumers compare prices on more than 100 000 consumer products. Other sites offer intelligent shopping agents—such as MySimon, Junglee, and Jango—that seek out products, prices, and reviews. MySimon (www.mySimon.com), for instance, takes a buyer's criteria for a PC, camcorder, or collectible Barbie, then roots through top sellers' sites to find the best match at the best price.

- *Find and negotiate lower prices.* With market information and access come buyer power. In addition to finding the vendor with the best price, both consumers and industrial buyers armed with price information can often negotiate lower prices.

In search of the best possible deal on a Palm Pilot organizer, Stephen Manes first checked PriceSCAN.com, an online price comparison site, where he learned that buysoware.com had the high-tech gadget for only $537. Buysoware, however, was "out of stock," as was the second lowest-priced vendor, mcglen.com. Undaunted, Stephen skipped to the other end of the list where he found that PC Zone was offering the device for $673, and it was in stock. "Time to haggle," said Stephen. "I picked up the phone. In seconds, an eager salesperson quoted me the official price. 'I saw it at buy.com for $537,' I said, omitting mention of the word[s 'out of stock']. 'I don't know if I can match buy.com,' came the response. 'But we can do it for $562.'" Stephen snapped up the offer, saving himself a bundle off the store price.

Business buying on the Internet dwarfs consumer buying, so it's no wonder that business buyers have also learned the price advantages of shopping the Web. For example, hoping to save some money, United Technologies Corporation tried something new in 1999. Instead of the usual haggling with dozens of individual vendors to secure printed circuit boards for various subsidiaries worldwide, UTC put the contract out on FreeMarkets, an online marketplace for industrial goods. To the company's delight, bids poured in from 39 suppliers, saving UTC a cool $15 million off its initial $36 million estimate. Says a UTC executive, "The technology drives the lowest price in a hurry."

Will dynamic pricing sweep the marketing world? "Not entirely," says Hof. "It takes a lot of work to haggle—which is why fixed prices happened in the first place." However, he continues, "Pandora's e-box is now open, and pricing will never be the same. For many . . . products, millions of buyers figure a little haggling is a small price to pay for a sweet deal."

Sources: Quotes and extracts from Robert D. Hof, "Going, going, gone," *Business Week,* 12 April 1999:30–2; Robert D. Hof, "The buyer always wins," *Business Week,* 22 March 1999:EB26–8; and Stephen Manes, "Off-Web dickering," *Forbes,* 5 April 1999:134. Also see Amy E. Cortese, "Good-bye to fixed pricing?" *Business Week,* 4 May 1998:71–84; Scott Woolley, "I got it cheaper than you," *Forbes,* 2 November 1998:82–4; Scott Woolley, "Price war!" *Forbes,* 14 December 1998:182–4; and Michael Krauss, "Web offers biggest prize in product pricing game," *Marketing News,* 6 July 1998:8.

itability by a whopping 25 to 60 percent just by improving its pricing processes. He stresses, however, that effective pricing does not mean nickel-and-diming customers; it means practising value-based pricing. When customers perceive that they are receiving superior value, they'll be willing to pay the price to get it. Hunt's research suggests that companies with successful pricing policies follow five "best practices" with regard to their pricing strategy.

- *They develop a one percent pricing mindset:* Since a one percent difference in price can have a dramatic impact on profit, everyone in the company must understand the importance of maintaining prices and think carefully about how even short-term discounts can affect their profitability.
- *They consistently deliver more value:* Since the most successful organizations consistently deliver more value to their customers, they are able to increase margins as a result. To deliver value, companies need insight into how their offering uniquely satisfies the customer's needs. Thus, getting close to their customers is the most critical factor in value-based pricing, since satisfied customers are profitable customers.
- *They price strategically, not opportunistically:* Paul Hunt stresses that firms should pursue price-conscious customers only if they represent the firm's core market. This is a viable strategy only for firms like Wal-Mart with a low cost structure that enables them to compete consistently on a price platform. Otherwise, the more an organization caters to price-conscious customers to boost volume, the more it puts its core business at risk by pursuing customers who don't value the product or service more than the price.
- *They know their competitors:* Their pricing strategy is driven by knowledge rather than fear.
- *They make pricing a process:* Pricing should be treated as a continual process rather than a one-time event that erodes into ad hoc or "gut-feel" pricing.[4]

In addition to not following these five guidelines, other common mistakes are pricing that is too cost oriented; prices that are not revised often enough to reflect market changes; pricing that does not take the rest of the marketing mix into account; and prices that are not varied enough for different products, market segments, and purchase occasions.

In this chapter, we focus on how to set prices—the factors that marketers must consider when setting prices, general pricing approaches, pricing strategies for new product pricing, product mix pricing, price changes, and price adjustments for buyer and situational factors.

Factors to Consider When Setting Prices

A company's pricing decisions are affected by both internal company and external environmental factors (see Figure 10-1).[5]

Internal Factors Affecting Pricing Decisions

Internal factors affecting pricing include the company's marketing objectives, marketing mix strategy, costs, and organization.

Marketing Objectives

Before setting price, the company must decide on its strategy for the product. If the company has selected its target market and positioning carefully, then its marketing mix strategy, including price, will be fairly straightforward. If General Motors decides to produce a new sports car to compete with European sports cars in the high-income segment, this suggests charging a high price. First Canada Inns, Best Value Inns, and Days Inn have positioned themselves as motels that provide economical rooms for budget-minded travellers; this position requires charging a low price. Thus, pricing strategy is largely determined by decisions on market positioning. And the clearer a firm is about its objectives, the easier it is to set price.

First Canada Inns
www.first-canada-inns.com/

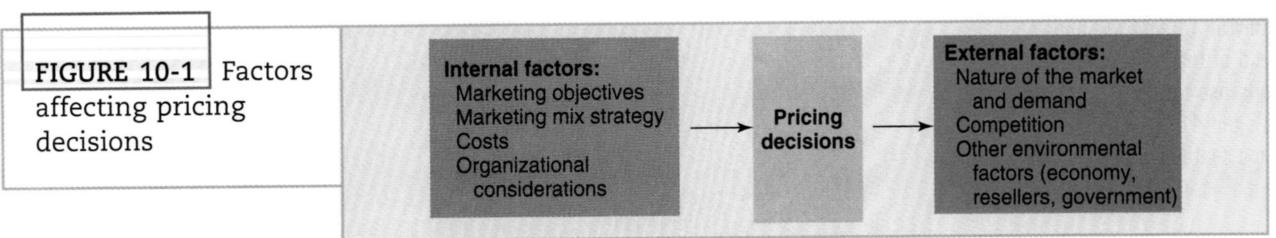

FIGURE 10-1 Factors affecting pricing decisions

Examples of common objectives are *survival, current profit maximization, market share leadership,* and *product quality leadership.*

Companies set *survival* as their major objective if they are troubled by too much capacity, heavy competition, or changing consumer wants. To keep a plant going, a company may set a low price, hoping to increase demand. In this case, profits are less important than survival. As long as their prices cover variable costs and some fixed costs, they can stay in business. However, survival is only a short-term objective. In the long run, the firm must learn how to add value or face extinction.

Many companies use *current profit maximization* as their pricing goal. They estimate what demand and costs will be at different prices and choose the price that will produce the maximum current profit, cash flow, or return on investment. In all cases, the company wants current financial results rather than long-run performance. Other companies want to obtain *market share leadership.* They believe that the company with the largest market share will enjoy the lowest costs and highest long-run profit. To become the market share leader, these firms set prices as low as possible. A variation of this objective is to pursue a specific market share gain. Suppose the company wants to increase its market share from 10 to 15 percent in one year; it will search for the price and marketing program that will achieve this goal.

A company may decide that it wants to achieve *product quality leadership.* This normally calls for charging a high price to cover such quality and the high cost of R&D. Hewlett-Packard focuses on the high-quality, high-price end of the hand-held calculator market. Gillette's product superiority lets it price its Mach3 razor cartridges at a 50 percent premium over its own SensorExcel and competitors' cartridges. Maytag has long built high-quality washing machines and priced them higher. Its ads use the long-running Maytag slogan, "Built to last longer," and feature the Maytag repairman, who's lonely because no one ever calls him for service. The ads point out that washers are custodians of what is often a $450 to $600 load of clothes, making them worth the higher price tag. For instance, at $1648, Maytag's Neptune, a front-loading washer without an agitator, sells for double what most other washers cost because the company's marketers claim that it uses less water and electricity and prolongs the life of clothing by being less abrasive.[6]

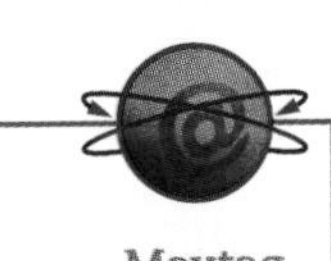

Maytag
www.maytag.com/

A company also can use price to attain other more specific objectives. It can set prices low to prevent competition from entering the market or set prices at competitors' levels to stabilize the market. It can set prices to keep the loyalty and support of resellers or to avoid government intervention. It can reduce prices temporarily to create excitement for a product or to draw more customers into a retail store. It can price one product to help the sales of other products in the company's line. Thus, pricing may play an important role in helping to accomplish the company's objectives at many levels.

Non-profit and public organizations may adopt a number of other pricing objectives. A university aims for *partial cost recovery,* knowing that it must rely on private gifts and government grants to cover the remaining costs. A non-profit theatre company may price its productions to fill the maximum number of theatre seats. A social service agency may set a *social price* geared to the varying income situations of different clients.

Maytag targets the high-quality end of the appliance market. Its ads use the long-running Maytag slogan, "Built to last longer," and feature the lonely Maytag repairman.

Marketing Mix Strategy

Price is only one of the marketing mix tools that a company uses to achieve its marketing objectives. Price decisions must be coordinated with product design, distribution, and promotion decisions to form a consistent and effective marketing program. Decisions made for other marketing mix variables can affect pricing decisions. For example, producers using many resellers who are expected to support and promote their products may have to build larger reseller margins into their prices. The decision to position the product on high performance quality means that the seller must charge a higher price to cover higher costs.

Companies often make their pricing decisions first and then base other marketing mix decisions on the prices they want to charge. Here, price is a crucial product positioning factor that defines the product's market, competition, and design. Many firms support such price positioning strategies with a technique called *target costing,* a potent strategic weapon. Target costing reverses the usual process of first designing a new product, determining its cost, and then asking "Can we sell it for that?" Instead, it starts with an ideal selling price and targets, or controls costs, to ensure that the price is met.

The original Swatch watch provides a good example of target costing. Rather than starting with its own costs, Swatch surveyed the market and identified an unserved segment of watch buyers who wanted "a low-cost fashion accessory that also keeps time." Armed with this information about market needs, Swatch set out to give consumers the watch they wanted at a price they were willing to pay, and it managed the new product's costs accordingly. Like most watch buyers, targeted consumers were concerned about precision, reliability, and durability. However, they were also concerned about fashion and affordability. To keep costs down, Swatch designed fashionable simpler watches that contained fewer parts and that were constructed from high-tech but less expensive materials. It then developed a revolutionary automated process for mass producing the new watches and exercised strict cost controls throughout the manufacturing process. By managing costs carefully, Swatch was able to create a watch that offered just the right blend of fashion and function at a price consumers were willing to pay. As a result of its initial major success, consumers have placed increasing value on Swatch products, allowing the company to introduce successively higher-priced designs.[7]

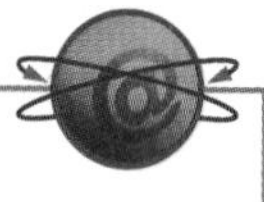

Swatch
www.swatch.com/

Other companies de-emphasize price and use other marketing mix tools to create *non-price* positions. Often, the best strategy is not to charge the lowest price, but rather to differentiate the marketing offer to make it worth a higher price. For years, Johnson Controls, a producer of climate-control systems for office buildings, used initial price as its primary competitive tool. However, research showed that customers were more concerned about the total cost of installing and maintaining a system than about its initial price. Repairing broken systems was expensive, time consuming, and risky. Customers had to shut down the heat or air conditioning in the whole building, disconnect a lot of wires, and face the danger of electrocution. Johnson decided to change its strategy. It designed an entirely new system called Metasys. To repair the new system, customers need only pull out an old plastic module and slip in a new one—no tools required. Metasys costs more to make than the old system, and customers pay a higher initial price, but it costs less to install and maintain. Despite its higher asking price, the new Metasys system brought in $700 million in revenues in its first year.[8]

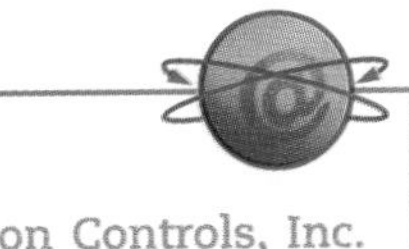

Johnson Controls, Inc.
www.jci.com/

Thus, the marketer must consider the total marketing mix when setting prices. If the product is positioned on non-price factors, then decisions about quality, promotion, and distribution will strongly affect price. If price is a crucial positioning factor, then price will strongly affect decisions made about the other marketing mix elements. However, even when featuring price, marketers need to remember that customers rarely buy on price alone. Instead, they seek products that give them the best value in terms of benefits received for the price paid. Therefore, the company must consider price along with all the other marketing mix elements when developing the marketing program.

Costs

Costs set the floor for the price that the company can charge for its product. The company wants to charge a price that both covers all its costs for producing, distributing, and selling the product and delivers a fair rate of return for its effort and risk. A company's costs may be an important element in its pricing strategy. Many companies work to become the "low-cost producers" in their industries. Companies with lower costs can set lower prices that result in greater sales and profits.

Fixed costs
Costs that do not vary with production or sales level.

Types of Costs. A company's costs take two forms—fixed and variable. **Fixed costs** (also known as overhead) are costs that do not vary with production or sales level. For example, a company must pay each month's bills for rent, heat, interest, and executive salaries, whatever the company's output.

Variable costs
Costs that vary directly with the level of production.

Variable costs depend directly on the level of production. Each personal computer produced by Compaq involves a cost of computer chips, wires, plastic, packaging, and other inputs. These costs tend to be the same for each unit produced. They are called *variable* because their total varies with the number of units produced.

Total costs
The sum of the fixed and variable costs for any given level of production.

Total costs are the sum of the fixed and variable costs for any given level of production. Management wants to charge a price that will at least cover the total production costs. The company must watch its costs carefully: If it costs the company more than competitors to produce and sell a similar product, the company will have to charge a higher price or make less profit, putting it at a competitive disadvantage.

Costs at Different Levels of Production. To price wisely, management needs to know how its costs vary with different levels of production. For example, suppose Texas Instruments (TI) has built a plant to produce 1000 hand-held calculators per day. Figure 10-2A shows the typical short-run average cost (SRAC) curve. It shows that the cost per calculator is high if TI's factory produces only a few per day. But as production moves up to 1000 calculators per day, average cost falls. This is because fixed costs are spread over more units, with each one bearing a smaller fixed cost. TI can try to produce more than 1000 calculators per day, but average costs will increase because the plant becomes inefficient. Workers have

FIGURE 10-2 Cost per unit at different levels of production per period

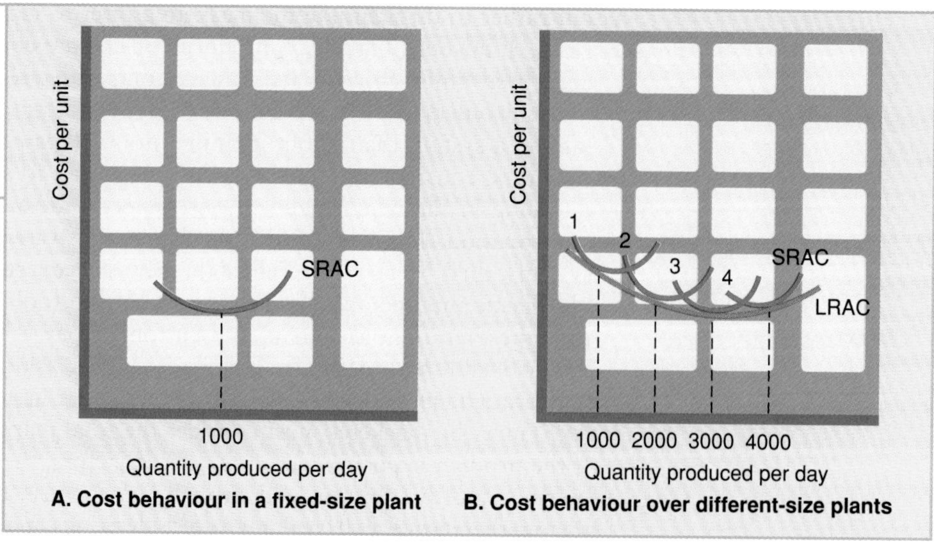

to wait for machines, the machines break down more often, and workers get in each other's way.

If TI believed it could sell 2000 calculators a day, it should consider building a larger plant. The plant would use more efficient machinery and work arrangements. Also, the unit cost of producing 2000 calculators per day would be lower than the unit cost of producing 1000 calculators per day, as shown in the long-run average cost (LRAC) curve (Figure 10-2B). In fact, a 3000-capacity plant would be even more efficient, according to Figure 10-2B. But a 4000 daily production plant would be less efficient because of increasing diseconomies of scale—too many workers to manage, paperwork slows things down, and so on. Figure 10-2B shows that a 3000 daily production plant is the best size to build if demand is strong enough to support this level of production.

Costs as a Function of Production Experience. Suppose TI runs a plant that produces 3000 calculators per day. As TI gains experience in producing hand-held calculators, it learns how to do it better. Workers learn shortcuts and become more familiar with their equipment. With practice, the work becomes better organized, and TI finds better equipment and production processes. With higher volume, TI becomes more efficient and gains economies of scale. As a result, average cost tends to fall with accumulated production experience. This is shown in Figure 10-3.[9] Thus, the average cost of producing the first 100 000 calculators is $10 per calculator. When the company has produced the first 200 000 calculators, the average cost has fallen to $9. After its accumulated production experience doubles again to 400 000, the average cost is $7. This drop in the average cost with accumulated production experience is called the **experience curve** (or the **learning curve**).

Experience curve (learning curve)
The drop in the average per-unit production cost that comes with accumulated production experience.

If a downward-sloping experience curve exists, this is highly significant for the company. Not only will the company's unit production cost fall, but it will also fall faster if the company makes and sells more during a given period. But the market must stand ready to buy the higher output. And to take advantage of the experience curve, TI must get a large market share early in the product's life cycle. This suggests the following pricing strategy. TI should price its calculators low; its sales will then increase, and its costs will decrease through gaining more experience, and then it can lower its prices further.

Some companies have built successful strategies around the experience curve. During the 1980s, Bausch & Lomb solidified its position in the soft contact lens market by using computerized lens design and steadily expanding its one Soflens

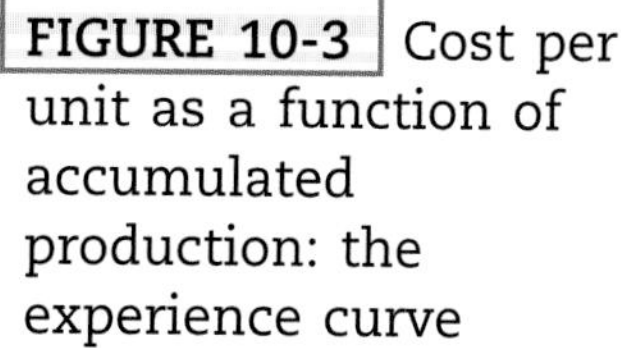

FIGURE 10-3 Cost per unit as a function of accumulated production: the experience curve

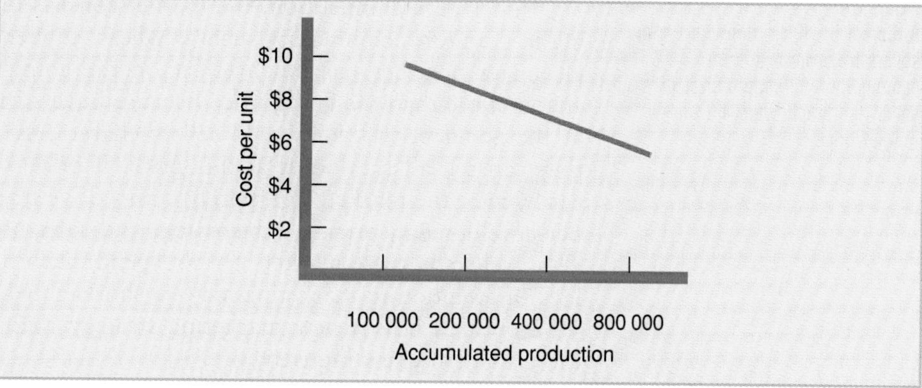

plant. As a result, its market share climbed steadily to 65 percent. However, a single-minded focus on reducing costs and exploiting the experience curve will not always work. Experience curves became somewhat of a fad during the 1970s, and like many fads, the strategy was sometimes misused. Experience curve pricing carries some major risks. The aggressive pricing might give the product a cheap image. The strategy also assumes that competitors are weak and not willing to fight it out by meeting the company's price cuts. Finally, while the company is building volume under one technology, a competitor may find a lower-cost technology that lets it start at lower prices than the market leader, who still operates on the old experience curve.

Organizational Considerations

Management must decide who within the organization should set prices. In small companies, prices often are set by top management rather than by the marketing or sales departments. In large companies, pricing typically is handled by divisional or product line managers. In industrial markets, salespeople may be allowed to negotiate with customers within certain price ranges. Even so, top management sets the pricing objectives and policies, and it often approves the prices proposed by lower-level management or salespeople. In industries in which pricing is a key factor, such as aerospace, railway, and oil, companies often have a pricing department to set the best prices or help others in setting them. This department reports to the marketing department or top management. Others who have an influence on pricing include sales managers, production managers, finance managers, and accountants.

External Factors Affecting Pricing Decisions

External factors that affect pricing decisions include the nature of the market and demand, competition, and other environmental elements.

The Market and Demand

Whereas costs set the lower limit of prices, the market and demand set the upper limit. Both consumer and industrial buyers balance the price of a product or service against the benefits of owning it. Therefore, before setting prices, the marketer must understand the relationship between price and demand for its product. In this section, we explain how the price–demand relationship varies for different types of markets and how buyer perceptions of price affect the pricing decision. We then discuss methods for measuring the price–demand relationship.

Pricing in Different Types of Markets. The seller's pricing freedom depends on the type of market the company operates in. Economists recognize four types of markets, each presenting a different pricing challenge.

Pure competition
A market in which many buyers and sellers trade in a uniform commodity—no single buyer or seller has much effect on the going market price.

Under **pure competition,** the market consists of many buyers and sellers trading in a uniform commodity such as wheat, copper, or financial securities. No single buyer or seller has much effect on the going market price. A seller cannot charge more than the going price because buyers can obtain as much as they need at the going price. Nor would sellers charge less than the market price because they can sell all they want at this price. If price and profits rise, new sellers can easily enter the market. In a purely competitive market, marketing research, product development, pricing, advertising, and sales promotion play little or no role. Thus, sellers in these markets do not spend much time on marketing strategy. This lack of attention to marketing may be shortsighted, however. Marketing Highlight 10-2 outlines how a new marketing strategy changed the base of competition in the Canadian dairy industry.

Monopolistic competition
A market in which many buyers and sellers trade over a range of prices rather than a single market price.

Under **monopolistic competition,** the market consists of many buyers and sellers who trade over a range of prices rather than a single market price. A range of prices occurs because sellers can differentiate their offers to buyers. Either the physical product can be varied in quality, features, or style, or the accompanying services can be varied. Buyers see differences in sellers' products and will pay different prices for them. Sellers try to develop differentiated offers for different customer segments and, in addition to price, freely use branding, advertising, and personal selling to set their offers apart. H.J. Heinz, Vlasic, Bick's, and several other national brands of pickles compete with dozens of regional and local brands, all differentiated by price and non-price factors. Because there are many competitors, each firm is less affected by competitors' marketing strategies than in oligopolistic markets.

Oligopolistic competition
A market in which there are a few sellers who are highly sensitive to each other's pricing and marketing strategies.

Under **oligopolistic competition,** the market consists of a few sellers who are highly sensitive to each other's pricing and marketing strategies. The product can be uniform (steel, aluminum) or non-uniform (cars, computers). There are few sellers because it is difficult for new sellers to enter the market. Each seller is alert to competitors' strategies and moves. If a steel company slashes its price by 10 percent, buyers will quickly switch to this supplier. The other steelmakers must respond by lowering their prices or increasing their services. An oligopolist is never sure that it will gain anything permanent through a price cut. In contrast, if an oligopolist raises its price, its competitors might not follow this lead. The oligopolist then would have to retract its price increase or risk losing customers to competitors.

Pure monopoly
A market in which there is a single seller—it may be a government monopoly, a private regulated monopoly, or a private non-regulated monopoly.

In a **pure monopoly,** the market consists of one seller. The seller may be a government monopoly (Canada Post), a private regulated monopoly (Trans Alta Utilities), or a private non-regulated monopoly (DuPont when it introduced nylon). Pricing is handled differently in each case. A government monopoly can pursue a variety of pricing objectives. It may set a price below cost because the product is important to buyers who cannot afford to pay full cost. Or it may set the price

Canadian pickle marketer Bick's sets its pickles apart from dozens of other brands using both price and non-price factors.

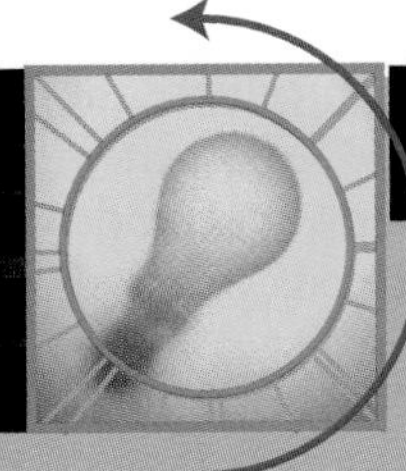

marketing highlight 10-2

Reinventing Milk: Shaking up Competition

Companies selling commodities in industries long regarded as purely competitive struggle to free themselves from price-based competition. Consider the shake-up of the $2.5-billion dairy industry caused by Toronto-based Ault Foods Limited. Demand for milk has fallen in recent years as aging consumers switch to bottled waters and juices. And for years, grocery stores have used milk as a loss leader to generate customer traffic. Ault Foods' introduction of Lactantia PürFiltre milk can be viewed as a strategy to differentiate its product and escape the limitations of pure price competition. The company hoped that its claims of fresher taste and longer shelf life would enable it to charge a premium price for its product. Ault Foods planned to charge 10 to 15 cents per litre more for its new product.

Developing a new form of milk wasn't an easy endeavour. It took Ault Foods four years to research the opportunity among consumers and to then develop the technology to meet consumer tastes. The company ran up bills of more than $8 million in the process. Ault was originally attempting to develop a cholesterol-free product, but realized that this technology was still years away. It decided, instead, to concentrate on the microfiltration process that eliminated the bacteria left behind by pasteurization.

Lactantia escaped price-based competition with its introduction of PürFiltre milk.

The January 1995 launch caused considerable excitement in the staid dairy industry. Mike Pierce, director of product promotions at the Ontario Milk Marketing Board, enthusiastically stated, "This move de-commodifies milk. Instead of just being the loss leader at grocery stores, milk could be brand-marketed and the processor could gain more margin."

Quebec producers didn't take long to recognize the power of the strategy. Natrel, the province's largest dairy company, launched Ultra'milk, a premium milk with extended shelf life. Premium milk has been popular in Quebec for some time, controlling 10 percent of the market. But launching such a new product is not inexpensive. Natrel accompanied the launch with a $1.3-million ad campaign.

Competitive reaction to Ault's introduction of Lactantia PürFiltre was swift. Fearing that Ault's claims of a new, pure milk would turn away consumers from regular milk, other firms readied for battle. Cries of misleading advertising were heard throughout the marketplace. Beatrice Foods Ltd. led the attacks. First, it ran newspaper ads showing a mother nursing an infant with the headline: "With one exception, there's no milk more pure, more fresh, or more nutritious than Beatrice." It also conducted a series of taste tests that showed that consumers couldn't distinguish between PürFiltre and Beatrice's milk and sought a court injunction to stop Ault from making its taste-based advertising claims. The courts, however, sided with Ault, viewing Beatrice's efforts as a rival's attempt to thwart competition.

Ault Foods had hoped to gain 15 percent of the market with its new product. However, its sales have been far from this target, reaching only 4.6 percent of the market in Ontario and 13 percent in Quebec. Ault Foods' efforts to gain share have been stymied by its inability to gain intensive distribution for the product in Ontario. One of the main problems was its inability to get shelf space in the Loblaw chain. Loblaw is owned by George Weston Ltd., a firm that also owns the dairy firm Neilson, a long-time competitor of Ault Foods. In August 1995, Neilson launched its own product, Trufiltre, which used microfiltering as well as an enrichment technique that gives its low-fat milk a rich taste. Trufiltre does not offer longer shelf life, however. The product has proven to be popular with Loblaw shoppers and now accounts for 20 percent of Neilson's carton milk sales.

Sources: Laura Medcalf, "Cash cow," *Marketing,* 30 October 1995:10; "Natrel launches premium milk in Quebec," *Marketing,* 23 October 1995:1; Laura Medcalf, "Trufiltre joins high-tech milk battle," *Marketing,* 11 September 1995:4; James Pollock, "Ault whips up the dairy industry with PürFiltre," *Marketing,* 13 March 1995:2; Marina Strauss, "Industry cries over premium milk," *Globe and Mail,* 15 January 1995:B1,B14.

to either cover costs or produce good revenue. It may even set the price quite high to decrease consumption. Until recently, this is how the Canadian government sought to decrease tobacco sales. In a regulated monopoly, the government permits the company to set rates that will yield a "fair return"—one that will let the company maintain and expand its operations as needed. Non-regulated monopolies are free to price at what the market will bear. However, they do not always charge the full price for a number of reasons: a desire not to attract competition, a desire to penetrate the market faster with a low price, or a fear of government regulation.

Consumer Perceptions of Price and Value. In the end, the consumer will decide whether a product's price is right. Pricing decisions, like other marketing mix decisions, must be buyer-oriented. When consumers buy a product, they exchange something of value—the price—to get something of value—the benefits of having or using the product. Effective, buyer-oriented pricing involves understanding how much value consumers place on the benefits they receive from the product and setting a price that fits this value.

Companies often find it hard to measure the values that customers will attach to their products. How do you value the way people feel when they wear brand-name or designer clothes, for example? But consumers do use these values to evaluate a product's price. If the perceived price is greater than the product's value, consumers will not buy the product. If the perceived price is below the product's value, they will buy it, but the seller loses profit opportunities. Marketers, therefore, must understand the consumer's reasons for buying the product and set price according to consumer perceptions of the product's value.

Demand curve
A curve that shows the number of units the market will buy at different possible prices in a given time period.

Analyzing the Price–Demand Relationship. Each price the company might charge will lead to a different level of demand. The relation between the price charged and the resulting demand level is shown in the **demand curve** in Figure 10-4. The demand curve shows the number of units the market will buy in a given time period, at different prices that might be charged. In the usual case, demand and price are inversely related: The higher the price, the lower the demand. Consumers with limited budgets probably will buy less of something if its price is too high. And the company will sell less if it raises its price from P_1 to P_2.

In the case of prestige goods, the demand curve sometimes slopes upward. For example, Gibson Guitar Corporation recently toyed with the idea of lowering its prices to compete more effectively with Japanese rivals like Yamaha and Ibanez. To its surprise, Gibson found that its instruments didn't sell as well at lower prices. "We had an inverse [price–demand relationship]," noted Gibson's chief executive officer. "The more we charged, the more product we sold." Gibson's slogan promises: "The world's finest musical instruments." It turns out that low prices simply aren't consistent with "Gibson's century old tradition of creating investment-quality instruments that represent the highest standards of imaginative design and masterful craftsmanship."[10] However, if the company charges too high a price, the level of demand will be lower.

Most companies try to measure their demand curves by estimating demand at different prices. The type of market makes a difference. In a monopoly, the demand curve shows the total market demand resulting from different prices. If the company faces competition, its demand at different prices depends on whether competitors' prices stay constant or change with the company's own prices.

In measuring the price–demand relationship, the market researcher must not

FIGURE 10-4 Demand curves

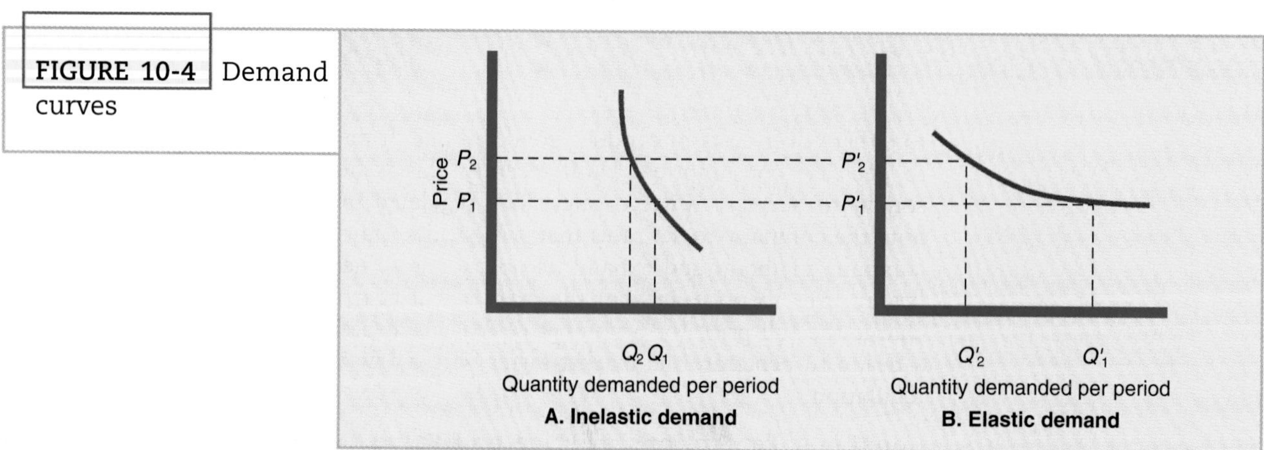

Gibson was surprised to learn that the demand curve sometimes slopes upward, when its high-quality instruments didn't sell well at lower prices.

allow other factors affecting demand to vary. For example, if Sony increases its advertising at the same time as it lowers its television prices, it would not know how much of the increased demand was due to the lower prices and how much was due to the increased advertising. The same problem arises if the lower price is set over a holiday weekend—more gift giving over the holidays causes people to buy more televisions. Economists show the impact of non-price factors on demand through shifts in the demand curve rather than movements along it.

Price elasticity
A measure of the sensitivity of demand to changes in price.

Price Elasticity of Demand. Marketers also need to know **price elasticity**—how responsive demand will be to a change in price. Consider the two demand curves in Figure 10-4. In Figure 10-4A, a price increase from P_1 to P_2 leads to a relatively small drop in demand from Q_1 to Q_2. In Figure 10-4B, however, the same price increase leads to a large drop in demand from Q'_1 to Q'_2. If demand hardly changes with a small change in price, we say the demand is *inelastic*. If demand changes greatly, we say the demand is *elastic*. The price elasticity of demand is given by this formula:

Price elasticity of demand = % change in quantity demanded/% change in price

Suppose demand falls by 10 percent when a seller raises its price by two percent. Price elasticity of demand is therefore −5 (the minus sign confirms the inverse relation between price and demand) and demand is elastic. If demand falls by two percent with a two percent increase in price, then elasticity is −1. In this case, the seller's total revenue stays the same: The seller sells fewer items but at a higher price that preserves the same total revenue. If demand falls by one percent when price is increased by two percent, then elasticity is −1/2 and demand is inelastic. The less elastic the demand, the more it pays for the seller to raise the price.

What determines the price elasticity of demand? Buyers are less price sensitive when the product they are buying is unique or when it is high in quality, prestige, or exclusiveness. They are also less price sensitive when substitute products are hard to find or when they cannot easily compare the quality of substitutes. Finally, buyers are less price sensitive when the total expenditure for a product is low relative to their income or when the cost is shared by another party.[11]

If demand is elastic rather than inelastic, sellers should consider lowering their price. A lower price produces more total revenue. This practice makes sense as long as the extra costs of producing and selling more do not exceed the extra revenue. At the same time, most firms want to avoid pricing that turns their products into commodities. In recent years, deregulation and the instant price comparisons afforded by the Internet and other technologies have increased consumer price sensitivity, turning products ranging from telephones and computers to new automobiles into commodities in consumers' eyes. Seven Toyota dealers in southern Manitoba responded to this pressure with new pricing and sales tactics designed primarily to address the concerns of the 60 percent of car buyers who surf the Web before kicking the tires. Toyota's "product advisors" point potential customers to the Access Toyota Web site and explain that the price shown is the "drive-away" price for the vehicle selected—not the manufacturer's suggested retail price (MSRP), but a price that provides a reasonable profit for the dealer and a fair cost for the customer who buys or leases. In other words . . . no haggling.[12]

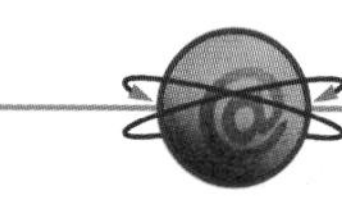

Access Toyota
www.access.toyota.ca/

Marketers need to work harder than ever to differentiate their offerings when a dozen competitors are selling virtually the same product at a comparable or lower price. More than ever, companies need to understand the price sensitivity of their customers and prospects and the trade-offs people are willing to make between price and product characteristics. In the words of marketing consultant Kevin Clancy, those who target only the price sensitive are "leaving money on the table."[13]

Competitors' Costs, Prices, and Offers

Another external factor affecting the company's pricing decisions is competitors' costs and prices and possible competitor reactions to the company's own pricing moves. A consumer who is considering the purchase of a Canon camera will evaluate Canon's price and value against the prices and values of comparable products made by Nikon, Minolta, Pentax, and others. In addition, the company's pricing strategy may affect the nature of the competition it faces. If Canon follows a high-price, high-margin strategy, it may attract competition. A low-price, low-margin strategy, however, may stop competitors or drive them out of the market.

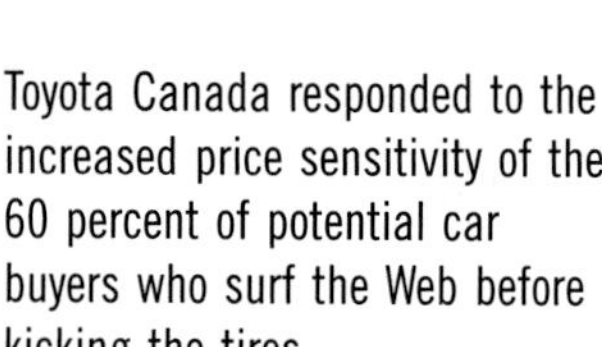

Toyota Canada responded to the increased price sensitivity of the 60 percent of potential car buyers who surf the Web before kicking the tires.

Canon needs to benchmark its costs against its competitors' costs to learn whether it is operating at a cost advantage or disadvantage. It also needs to learn the price and quality of each competitor's offer. Once Canon is aware of competitors' prices and offers, it can use them as a starting point for its own pricing. If Canon's cameras are similar to Nikon's, it will have to price close to Nikon or lose sales. If Canon's cameras are not as good as Nikon's, the firm will not be able to charge as much. If Canon's products are better than Nikon's, it can charge more. Basically, Canon will use price to position its offer relative to the competition.

Other External Factors

When setting prices, the company also must consider other factors in its external environment. *Economic conditions* can have a strong impact on the firm's pricing strategies. Such economic factors as boom or recession, inflation, and interest rates influence pricing decisions because they affect both the costs of producing a product and consumer perceptions of the product's price and value. The company must also consider what impact its prices will have on other parties in its environment. How will *resellers* react to various prices? The company should set prices that give resellers a fair profit, encourage their support, and help them to sell the product effectively. The *government* is another important external influence on pricing decisions. Finally, *social concerns* may have to be considered. In setting prices, a company's short-term sales, market share, profit goals, as well as the ability of the vulnerable to afford them may have to be tempered by broader societal considerations.

General Pricing Approaches

The price the company charges will be somewhere between one that is too low to produce a profit and one that is too high to produce any demand. Figure 10-5 summarizes the major considerations in setting price. Product costs set a floor to the price; consumer perceptions of the product's value set the ceiling. The company must consider competitors' prices and other external and internal factors to find the best price between these two extremes.

Companies set prices by selecting one or more of these three general pricing approaches: the *cost-based approach* (cost-plus pricing, break-even analysis, and target profit pricing); the *buyer-based approach* (perceived-value pricing); and the *competition-based approach* (going-rate and sealed-bid pricing).

Cost-Based Pricing

Cost-Plus Pricing

Cost-plus pricing
Adding a standard markup to the cost of the product.

The simplest pricing method is **cost-plus pricing**—adding a standard markup to the cost of the product. Construction companies, for example, submit job bids by estimating the total project cost and adding a standard markup for profit. Lawyers, accountants, and other professionals typically price by adding a standard markup

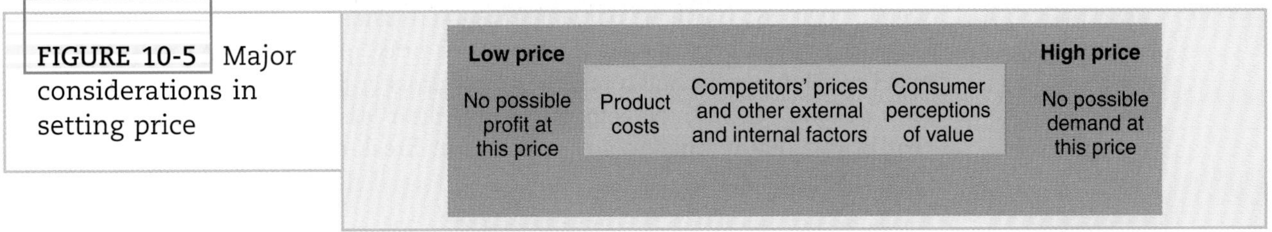

FIGURE 10-5 Major considerations in setting price

to their costs. Some sellers tell their customers they charge cost plus a specified markup; for example, aerospace companies price this way to the government.

To illustrate markup pricing, suppose a toaster manufacturer had the following costs and expected sales:

Variable cost	\$10
Fixed cost	\$300 000
Expected unit sales	50 000

Then the manufacturer's cost per toaster is given by:

Unit cost = Variable cost + Fixed costs/Unit sales = \$10 + \$300 000/50 000 = \$16

Now suppose the manufacturer wants to earn a 20 percent markup on sales. The manufacturer's markup price is given by:[14]

Markup price = Unit cost/(1 − Desired return on sales) = \$16/1 − .2 = \$20

The manufacturer will charge dealers \$20 a toaster and make a profit of \$4 per unit. The dealers, in turn, will mark up the toaster. If the dealers want to earn 50 percent on sales price, they will mark up the toaster to \$40 (\$20 + 50% of \$40). This number is equivalent to a *markup on cost* of 100 percent (\$20/\$20).

Does using standard markups to set prices make sense? Generally, no. Any pricing method that ignores demand and competitors' prices is not likely to lead to the best price. Suppose the toaster manufacturer charged \$20 but only sold 30 000 toasters instead of 50 000. Then the unit cost would have been higher since the fixed costs are spread over fewer units, and the realized percentage markup on sales would have been lower. Markup pricing only works if that price actually brings in the expected level of sales.

Still, markup pricing remains popular for many reasons. First, sellers are more certain about costs than about demand. By tying the price to cost, sellers simplify pricing—they do not have to make frequent adjustments as demand changes. Second, when all firms in the industry use this pricing method, prices tend to be similar and price competition is thus minimized. Third, many people believe that cost-plus pricing is fairer to both buyers and sellers. Sellers earn a fair return on their investment but do not take advantage of buyers when buyers' demand becomes great.

Break-Even Analysis and Target Profit Pricing

Break-even pricing (target profit pricing)
Setting price to break even on the costs of making and marketing a product; or setting price to make a target profit.

Another cost-oriented pricing approach is **break-even pricing,** or a variation called **target profit pricing.** The firm tries to determine the price at which it will break even or make the target profit it is seeking. Target pricing is used by General Motors, which prices its automobiles to achieve a 15 to 20 percent profit on its investment. This pricing method is also used by public utilities, which must make a fair return on their investment.

Target pricing uses the *break-even chart,* which shows the total cost and total revenue expected at different sales volume levels. Figure 10-6 shows a break-even chart for our toaster manufacturer. Fixed costs are \$300 000 regardless of sales volume. Variable costs are added to fixed costs to form total costs, which rise with volume. The total revenue curve starts at zero and rises with each unit sold. The slope of the total revenue curve reflects the price of \$20 per unit.

The total revenue and total cost curves cross at 30 000 units. This is the *break-even volume.* At \$20, the company must sell at least 30 000 units to break even; that is, for total revenue to cover total cost. Break-even volume can be calculated with this formula:

Break-even volume = Fixed cost/Price − Variable cost = \$300 000/\$20 − \$10 = 30 000

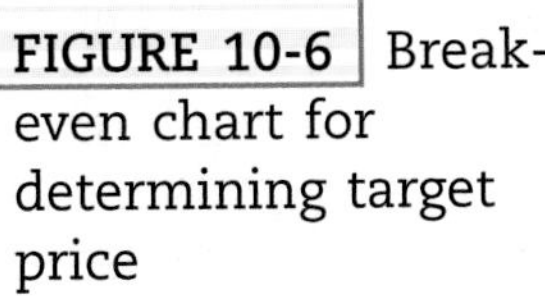

FIGURE 10-6 Break-even chart for determining target price

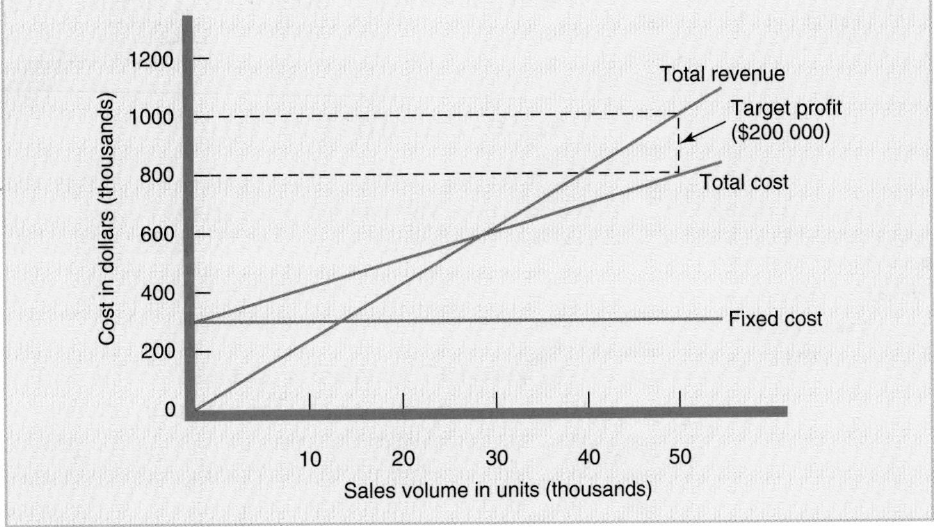

If the company wants to make a target profit, it must sell more than 30 000 units at $20 each. Suppose the toaster manufacturer has invested $1 000 000 in the business and wants to set price to earn a 20 percent return, or $200 000. In that case, it must sell at least 50 000 units at $20 each. If the company charges a higher price, it will not need to sell as many toasters to achieve its target return; but the market may not buy even this lower volume at the higher price. Much depends on the price elasticity and competitors' prices.

The manufacturer should consider different prices and estimate break-even volumes, probable demand, and profits for each. Table 10-1 shows that as price increases, break-even volume drops (column 2). But as price increases, demand for the toasters also falls off (column 3). At the $14 price, because the manufacturer clears only $4 per toaster ($14 less $10 in variable costs), it must sell a very high volume to break even. Even though the low price attracts many buyers, demand still falls below the high break-even point, and the manufacturer loses money. At the other extreme, with a $22 price the manufacturer clears $12 per toaster and must sell only 25 000 units to break even. But at this high price, consumers buy too few toasters, and profits are negative. The table shows that a price of $18 yields the highest profits. Note that none of the prices produce the manufacturer's target profit of $200 000. To achieve this target return, the manufacturer will have

TABLE 10-1 Break-Even Volume and Profits at Different Prices

(1) Price	(2) Unit Demand Needed to Break Even	(3) Expected Unit Demand at Given Price	(4) Total Revenues (1) × (3)	(5) Total Costs*	(6) Profit (4) – (5)
$14	75 000	71 000	$ 994 000	$1 100 000	–$ 32 000
16	50 000	67 000	1 072 000	970 000	102 000
18	37 500	60 000	1 080 000	900 000	180 000
20	30 000	42 000	840 000	720 000	120 000
22	25 000	23 000	506 000	530 000	–24 000

*Assumed fixed costs of $300 000 and constant unit variable costs of $10.

to search for ways to lower fixed or variable costs, thus lowering the break-even volume.

Value-Based Pricing

Value-based pricing Setting price based on buyers' perceptions of value rather than on the seller's cost.

An increasing number of companies are basing their prices on the product's perceived value. **Value-based pricing** uses buyers' perceptions of value, not the seller's cost, as the key to pricing. Value-based pricing means that the marketer cannot design a product and marketing program and then set the price. Price is considered along with the other marketing mix variables *before* the marketing program is set.

Figure 10-7 compares cost-based pricing with value-based pricing. Cost-based pricing is product driven. The company designs what it considers to be a good product, determines the costs of making the product, and sets a price that covers costs plus a target profit. Marketing must then convince buyers that the product's value at that price justifies its purchase. If the price turns out to be too high, the company must settle for lower markups or lower sales, both resulting in disappointing profits.

Value-based pricing reverses this process. The company sets its target price based on customer perceptions of the product value. The targeted value and price then drive decisions about product design and what costs can be incurred. As a result, pricing begins with analyzing consumer needs and value perceptions, and the price is set to match consumers' perceived value.

A company using value-based pricing must find out what value buyers assign to different competitive offers. Measuring perceived value, however, can be difficult. Sometimes consumers are asked how much they would pay for a basic product and for each benefit added to the offer. Or a company may conduct experiments to test the perceived value of different product offers. If the seller charges more than the buyers' perceived value, the company's sales will suffer. Many companies overprice their products, which then sell poorly. Other companies underprice products, which sell very well but produce less revenue than they would if prices were raised to the perceived value level.

In the 1990s, marketers noted a fundamental shift in consumer attitudes toward price and quality. Many companies changed their pricing approaches to bring them into line with changing economic conditions and consumer price per-

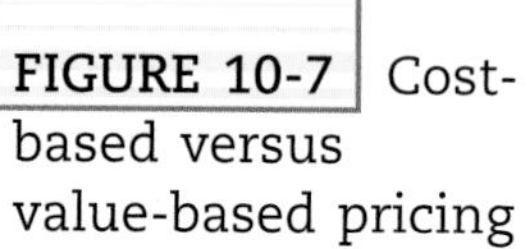

FIGURE 10-7 Cost-based versus value-based pricing

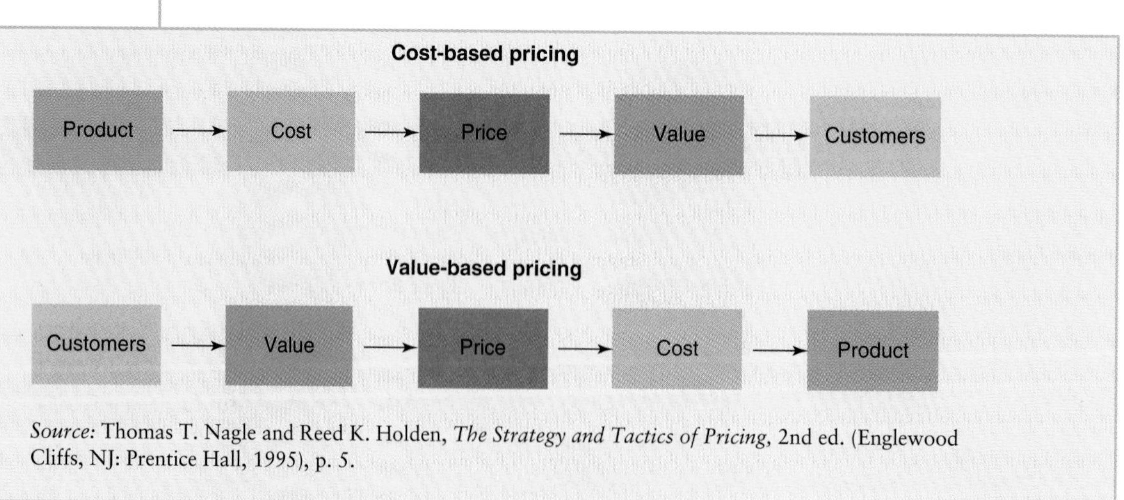

Source: Thomas T. Nagle and Reed K. Holden, *The Strategy and Tactics of Pricing*, 2nd ed. (Englewood Cliffs, NJ: Prentice Hall, 1995), p. 5.

ceptions. According to Jack Welch, CEO of General Electric, "The value decade is upon us. If you can't sell a top-quality product at the world's best price, you're going to be out of the game. . . . The best way to hold your customers is to constantly figure out how to give them more for less."[15]

Value pricing
Setting price based on the right combination of quality and good service at a fair price.

Therefore, marketers are adopting **value pricing** strategies—offering just the right combination of quality and good service at a fair price. In many cases, this has involved the introduction of less expensive versions of established, brand-name products. Campbell introduced its Great Starts Budget frozen-food line, Holiday Inn opened several Holiday Express budget hotels, Revlon's Charles of the Ritz created the Express Bar collection of affordable cosmetics, and fast-food restaurants such as Taco Bell and McDonald's offered "value menus." In other cases, value pricing has involved redesigning existing brands to offer more quality for a given price or the same quality for less.

In many business-to-business marketing situations, the pricing challenge is to find ways to adjust the value of the company's marketing offer to escape price competition and to justify higher prices and margins. This is especially true for suppliers of commodity products, which are characterized by little differentiation and intense price competition. In such cases, many companies adopt *value-added* strategies. Rather than cutting prices to match competitors, they attach value-added services to differentiate their offers and thus support higher margins (see Marketing Highlight 10-3).

An important type of value pricing at the retail level is *everyday low pricing (EDLP)*. EDLP involves charging a constant, everyday low price with few or no temporary price discounts. In contrast, *high-low pricing* involves charging higher prices on an everyday basis, but running frequent promotions to temporarily lower prices on selected items below the EDLP level.[16]

In recent years, high-low pricing has given way to EDLP in retail settings ranging from General Motors and Chrysler car dealerships to grocery stores like Quebec's Metro chain. Retailers adopt EDLP for many reasons, the most important of which is that constant sales and promotions are costly and have eroded consumer confidence in the credibility of everyday shelf prices. Consumers also have less time and patience for such time-honoured traditions as watching for supermarket specials and clipping coupons.

The leader of EDLP is Wal-Mart, which practically defined the concept. Except for a few sale items every month, Wal-Mart promises everyday low prices on everything it sells. In contrast, Sears' attempts at EDLP failed. To offer everyday low prices, a company must first have everyday low costs. Wal-Mart's EDLP strategy works well because its expenses are only 15 percent of sales. When Wal-Mart first entered Canada, Zellers began a price war with the American giant in an attempt to defend its well-known slogan, "Where the lowest price is the law!" However, Zellers soon learned that to win such a battle, lowest costs must also be the law! Since Zellers' operating costs were higher than Wal-Mart's, its profits were squeezed and the company had to abandon the fight.

Competition-Based Pricing

Consumers base their judgments of a product's value on the prices that competitors charge for similar products.

Going-rate pricing
Setting price based largely on following competitors' prices rather than on company costs or demand.

One form of *competition-based pricing* is **going-rate pricing,** in which a firm bases its price largely on competitors' prices, with less attention paid to its own costs or to demand. The firm can charge the same, more, or less than its major competitors. In oligopolistic industries that sell a commodity such as steel, paper,

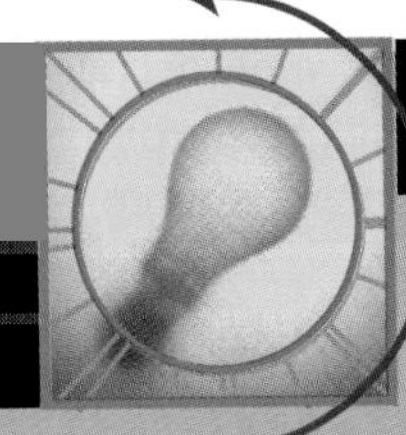

marketing highlight 10-3

The Value of Value-Added

When a company finds its major competitors offering a similar product at a lower price, the natural tendency is to try to match or beat that price. While the idea of undercutting competitors' prices and watching customers flock to you is tempting, dangers are associated with this approach. Successive rounds of price cutting can lead to price wars that erode the profit margins of all competitors in an industry. And price wars are numerous and bloody. For example, Molson and Labatt matched each other's price reductions in the summer of 1997 and finally called the battle a draw. McDonald's slashed its prices on Big Macs in an attempt to regain share from Wendy's and Burger King. Ultramar Ltée triggered one of Quebec's most dramatic gasoline price wars in the summer of 1996: Although it claims to have built awareness and increased traffic, Quebec's independent gas retailers claimed foul and asked the Federal Bureau of Competition to investigate Ultramar's price policy. A year-long price war waged between Sobeys and Superstore Atlantic not only squeezed the margins of the two combatants, but it also drove Wade Enterprises, a 78-year-old company, out of business. Thus, while numerous companies enter price wars with the intention of burying their competitors, such wars can easily backfire. Discounting a product can erode brand equity and cheapen it in the minds of customers. "It ends up being a losing battle," notes one marketing executive. "You focus away from quality, service, prestige—the things brands are all about." Another expert stresses that "pricing strategy requires the skilful manoeuvring of a diplomat, not the heavy, bloodied hand of a general. Unfortunately, all too many managers . . . know more about winning pricing battles than about preventing those that are not worth fighting."

Roughly the number of people who've switched back to Bell in the last month.

Bell

Rather than fighting an unprofitable price war, Bell stressed its service quality and reliability to win back customers.

or fertilizer, firms normally charge the same price. The smaller firms follow the leader: They change their prices when the market leader's prices change, rather than when their own demand or costs change. Some firms may charge a bit more or less, but they hold the amount of difference constant. Thus, minor gasoline retailers usually charge a few cents less than the major oil companies, without letting the difference increase or decrease. Going-rate pricing is quite popular. When demand elasticity is hard to measure, firms feel that the going price represents the collective wisdom of the industry concerning the price that will yield a fair return. They also feel that holding to the going price will prevent harmful price wars.

Sealed-bid pricing Setting price based on how the firm thinks competitors will price rather than on its own costs or demand—used when a company bids for jobs.

Competition-based pricing is also used when firms bid for jobs. Using **sealed-bid pricing**, a firm bases its price on how it thinks competitors will price rather than on its own costs or on the demand. The firm wants to win a contract, and winning the contract requires pricing less than other firms. Yet the firm cannot set

So, what can a company do when a competitor undercuts its price? This was the question that Bell Canada asked itself when the $8-billion-a-year long-distance market was deregulated in 1994. Bell refused to enter a price war believing that, as the industry incumbent, it had the most to lose. While new competitors such as Sprint Canada offered promotions such as "15¢ a minute, anywhere, anytime!" Bell focused instead on winning back customers by emphasizing the service, support, and reliability that it could offer. Bell believes that focusing on price alone won't allow its competitors to forge ties with their customers. As one consultant noted, "If you tell consumers *price, price, price* all the time, that's what they'll think is important . . . and you will be rewarded with disloyalty as soon as your price isn't the lowest on the block."

Another strategy is to price above competitors and convince customers that the product is worth it. In this way, the company differentiates its offer and shifts the focus from price to value. But what if the company is operating as a supplier in a "commodity" business, where the products of all competitors seem similar? In such cases, the company must find ways to "decommodify" its products. It can do this by developing value-added services that differentiate its offer and justify higher prices and margins.

Increasingly, today's winning suppliers are those that provide value-added services for their customers. These are examples of how suppliers, both small and large, are using value-added services to give them a competitive edge:

- *Jefferson Smurfit Corp.* When General Electric expanded a no-frost refrigerator line in 1990, it needed more shipping boxes, and fast. Jefferson Smurfit, a $6.4-billion packaging supplier, assigned a coordinator to juggle production from three of its plants—and sometimes even divert product intended for other customers—to keep GE's plant humming. This kind of value-added hustling helped Jefferson Smurfit win the GE appliance unit's "Distinguished Supplier Award." It has also sheltered Smurfit from the bruising struggle of competing only on price. "Today, it's not just getting the best price but getting the best value—and there are a lot of pieces to value," says a vice-president for procurement at Emerson Electric Company, a major Smurfit customer that has cut its supplier count by 65 percent.
- *Microsystems Engineering Company.* "The way we sell on value is by differentiating ourselves," says Mark Beckman, director of sales for Microsystems, a software company. "My product is twice as much as my nearest competitor, but we sell as much as—if not more than—our competition." Rather than getting into price wars, Microsystems adds value to its products by adding new components and services. "[Customers] get more for their money," says Beckman. "We get the price because we understand what people want." When customers see the extra value, price becomes secondary. Ultimately, Beckman asserts, "Let the customer decide whether the price you're charging is worth all the things they're getting." What if the answer is no? Beckman would suggest that dropping price is the last thing you want to do. Instead, look to the value of value-added.

Sources: Jim Morgan, "Value added: From cliché to the real thing," *Purchasing,* 3 April 1997:59–61; Richard A. Melcher, "The middlemen stay on the march," *Business Week,* 9 January 1995:87; James E. Ellis, "There's even a science to selling boxes," *Business Week,* 3 August 1992:51–2; Erika Rasmusson, "The pitfalls of price cutting," *Sales & Marketing Management,* May 1997:17; David R. Henderson, "What are price wars good for? Absolutely nothing," *Fortune,* 12 May 1997:156; Gail Chiasson, "Ultramar shakes up Quebec gas retailing," *Marketing,* 12 August 1996, marketingmag.com/search; Donalee Moulton, "Atlantic Canada food fight claims first casualty," *Marketing,* 15 July 1996, marketingmag.com/search; Gayle MacDonald, "High stakes in burger bargains," *Globe and Mail,* 28 February 1997:B11; Sean Silcoff, "The price is (rarely) right," *Canadian Business,* February 1997:62–6; www.bell.ca/; www.smurfit.ie/; www.sprintcanada.ca/.

its price below a certain level. It cannot price below cost without harming its position. In contrast, the higher the company sets its price above its costs, the lower its chance of getting the contract.

Companies bringing out a new product face the challenge of setting prices for the first time. They can choose between two strategies: *market skimming pricing* and *market penetration pricing*.

Market Skimming Pricing

Market skimming pricing Setting a high price for a new product to skim maximum revenues layer by layer from the segments willing to pay the high price; the company makes fewer but more profitable sales.

Many companies that invent new products initially set high prices to "skim" revenues layer by layer from the market. Intel is a prime user of this strategy, called **market skimming pricing.** When Intel introduces a new computer chip, it charges the highest price it can, given the benefits of the new chip over competing chips.

It sets a price that makes it *just* worthwhile for some segments of the market to adopt computers containing the chip. As initial sales slow down, and as competitors threaten to introduce similar chips, Intel lowers the price to draw in the next price-sensitive layer of customers.

When Intel first introduced its Pentium chips, it priced them at about $1400 each. As a result, computer producers priced their first Pentium PCs at $4800 or more, attracting as customers only serious computer users and business buyers. However, after introduction, Intel cut Pentium prices by 30 percent per year, eventually allowing the price of Pentium PCs to drop into the typical price range of home buyers. In this way, Intel skimmed a maximum amount of revenue from the various segments of the market.[17]

Market skimming makes sense only under certain conditions. First, the product's quality and image must support its higher price, and enough buyers must want the product at that price. Second, the costs of producing a smaller volume cannot be so high that they cancel the advantage of charging more. Finally, competitors should not be able to enter the market easily and undercut the high price.

Market Penetration Pricing

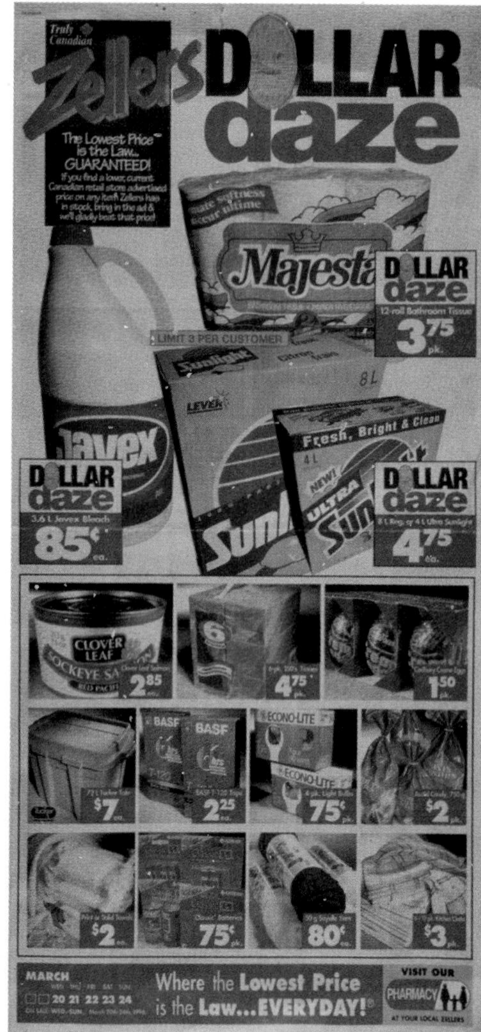

Zellers practises market-penetration pricing. It stresses value and savings in its advertising, stating, "Where the Lowest Price is the Law . . . Everyday!"

Market penetration pricing Setting a low price for a new product to attract a large number of buyers and a large market share.

Rather than setting a high initial price to *skim* off small but profitable market segments, some companies use **market penetration pricing.** They set a low initial price to *penetrate* the market quickly and deeply—to attract a large number of buyers quickly and win a large market share. The high sales volume results in falling costs, allowing the company to cut its price even further. For example, Dell and Gateway used penetration pricing to sell high-quality computer products through lower-cost mail-order channels. Their sales soared when IBM, Compaq, Apple, and other competitors selling through retail stores could not match their prices. Home Depot, Zellers, and other discount retailers also use penetration pricing. They charge low prices to attract high volume. The high volume results in lower costs that, in turn, let the discounters keep prices low.

Several conditions favour setting a low price. First, the market must be highly price sensitive so that a low price produces more market growth. Second, production and distribution costs must fall as sales volume increases. Finally, the low price must help keep out the competition—otherwise the price advantage may be only temporary. Or the new low-price competitor must have a low-cost structure that existing competitors cannot, or will not, match.

Product Mix Pricing Strategies

If the product is part of a product mix, the firm looks for a set of prices that maximizes the profits on the total product mix. Pricing is difficult because the various products have related demand and costs and face different degrees of competition. *Product line pricing, captive product pricing,* and *product bundle pricing* are three product mix pricing situations managers may face when making pricing decisions.

Product Line Pricing

Companies usually develop product lines rather than single products. Toro, for example, makes many different lawn mowers, ranging from simple walk-behind versions priced at $259.95, $299.95, and $399.95, to elaborate riding mowers priced at $1000 or more. Each successive lawn mower in the line offers more features. Kodak offers not just one type of film, but an assortment including regular Kodak film, higher-priced Kodak Royal Gold film for special occasions, and still higher-priced Advantix APS film for Advanced Photo System cameras. It offers each of these brands in a variety of sizes and film speeds. In **product line pricing,** management must decide on the price steps to set between the various products in a line.

Product line pricing
Setting the price steps between various products in a product line based on cost differences between the products, customer evaluations of different features, and competitors' prices.

The price steps must take into account cost differences between the products in the line, customer evaluations of their different features, and competitors' prices. If the price difference between two successive products is small, buyers will usually buy the more advanced product. This will increase company profits if the cost difference is smaller than the price difference. If the price difference is large, however, customers will generally buy the less advanced products.

In many industries, sellers use well-established *price points* for the products in their line. Thus, men's clothing stores may carry men's suits at three price levels: $185, $285, and $385. The customer probably will associate low-, average-, and high-quality suits with the three price points. Even if the three prices are raised a little, men typically will still buy suits at their own preferred price points. The seller's task is to establish perceived quality differences that support the price differences.

Captive Product Pricing

Captive product pricing
Setting a price for products that must be used along with a main product, such as blades for a razor and film for a camera.

Companies that make products that must be used along with a main product use **captive product pricing.** Examples of captive products are razor blades, camera film, and computer software. Producers of the main products (razors, cameras, and computers) often price them low and set high markups on the supplies. Thus, Polaroid prices its cameras low because it makes its money on the film it sells. And Gillette sells low-priced razors but makes money on the replacement blades.

Kodak practises product line pricing in offering different types of film priced at different levels.

Product Bundle Pricing

Product bundle pricing
Combining several products and offering the bundle at a reduced price.

Using **product bundle pricing,** sellers combine several of their products and offer the bundle at a reduced price. Thus, theatres and sports teams sell season tickets at less than the cost of single tickets; hotels sell specially priced packages that include room, meals, and entertainment; computer makers include attractive software packages with their personal computers. Price bundling can promote the sale of products that consumers might not otherwise buy, but the combined price must be low enough to get them to buy the bundle.[18]

Marketers must be cautious and avoid overbundling services. When new products are bundled with previous offers and consumers are given no choice but to buy the new bundle of products or services, adverse consumer reaction may result. This was the situation faced by Rogers Cablesystems Ltd., Canada's largest cable television provider, in early 1995. Rogers bundled its new specialty TV channels with existing cable television packages and demanded an increased payment of $2 to $4 per month for the added services. The company used a technique called negative-option marketing, automatically providing services unless consumers notify the company that they do not want them. Consumer complaints caused Rogers to revise its marketing plan, but not before provincial legislators in British Columbia, Ontario, Nova Scotia, and Manitoba promised to investigate the negative-option practice.[19]

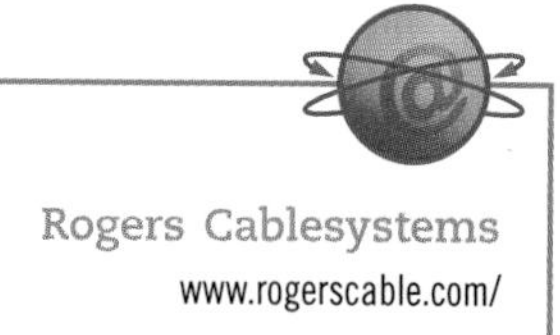

Rogers Cablesystems
www.rogerscable.com/

Price-Adjustment Strategies

Companies usually adjust their basic prices to account for various customer differences and changing situations.

Discount and Allowance Pricing

Cash discount
A price reduction to buyers who pay their bills promptly.

Quantity discount
A price reduction to buyers who buy large volumes.

Allowances
Promotional money paid by manufacturers to retailers in return for an agreement to feature the manufacturer's products in some way.

Most companies adjust their basic price to reward customers for certain responses, such as early payment of bills, volume purchases, and off-season buying. These price adjustments—called discounts and allowances—can take many forms. For example, a **cash discount** is a price reduction to buyers who pay their bills promptly. A typical example is "2/10, net 30," which means that, although payment is due within 30 days, the buyer can deduct two percent if the bill is paid within 10 days. The discount must be granted to all buyers meeting these terms. Such discounts are customary in many industries and help to improve the sellers' cash situation and reduce bad debts and credit collection costs.

A **quantity discount** is a price reduction to buyers who buy large volumes. A typical example is "$10 per unit for less than 100 units, $9 per unit for 100 or more units." Under the provisions of the *Competition Act,* quantity discounts must be offered equally to all customers and must not exceed the seller's cost savings associated with selling large quantities. These savings include lower selling, inventory, and transportation expenses. Discounts provide an incentive to the customer to buy more from one given seller, rather than from many different sources.

Allowances are another type of reduction from the list price. *Trade-in allowances* are price reductions given for turning in an old item when buying a new one. They are most common in the automobile industry, but are also given for other durable goods. *Promotional allowances* are payments or price reductions to reward dealers for participating in advertising and sales-support programs.

Segmented Pricing

Segmented pricing
Selling a product or service at two or more prices, where the difference in prices is not based on differences in costs.

Companies often adjust their basic prices to allow for differences in customers, products, and locations. In **segmented pricing,** the company sells a product or service at two or more prices, even though the difference in prices is not based on differences in costs. Segmented pricing takes several forms:

Ramada uses customer segment pricing, time pricing, and other incentives to attract family travellers during the summer season. This summer, "four adults can stay in the same room for the cost of just one, and kids always stay free."

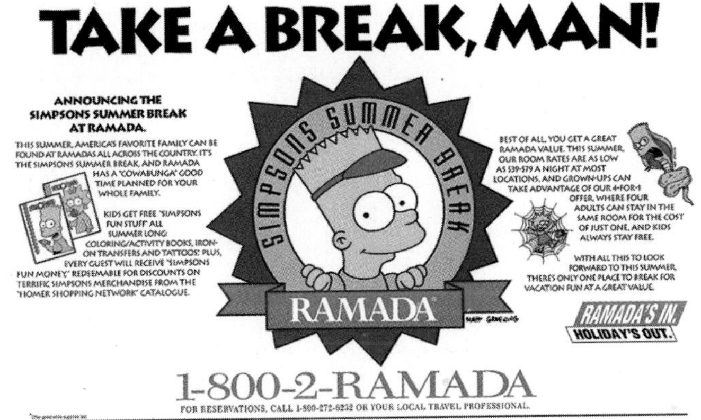

- *Customer segment pricing*. Different customers pay different prices for the same product or service. Museums, for example, will charge a lower admission for students and senior citizens.
- *Product form pricing*. Different versions of the product are priced differently, but not according to differences in their costs. For instance, Black & Decker prices its most expensive iron at $54.98, which is $10 more than the price of its next most expensive iron. The top model has a self-cleaning feature, yet this extra feature costs only a few more dollars to make.
- *Location pricing*. Different locations are priced differently, even though the cost of offering each location is the same. For instance, theatres vary their seat prices because of audience preferences for certain locations, and universities charge higher tuition for overseas students.
- *Time pricing*. Prices vary by the season, the month, the day, and even the hour. Public utilities vary their prices to commercial users based on the time of day and weekend versus weekday. The telephone company offers lower "off-peak" charges, and resorts give seasonal discounts.

For segmented pricing to be an effective strategy, certain conditions must exist. The market must be segmentable, and the segments must show different degrees of demand. Members of the segment paying the lower price should not be able to turn around and resell the product to the segment paying the higher price. Competitors should not be able to undersell the firm in the segment being charged the higher price. Nor should the costs of segmenting and watching the market exceed the extra revenue obtained from the price difference. The practice should not lead to customer resentment and ill will. The segmented pricing must be legal and ethical, and segmented prices should reflect real differences in customers' perceived value (see Marketing Highlight 10-4).

Psychological Pricing

Price says something about the product. For example, many consumers use price to judge quality. A $100 bottle of perfume may contain only $3 worth of scent, but some people are willing to pay $100 because this price indicates something special.

Psychological pricing
A pricing approach that considers the psychology of prices and not simply the economics; the price is used to say something about the product.

In using **psychological pricing,** sellers consider the psychology of prices and not simply the economics. One study of the relationship between price and quality perceptions of cars found that consumers perceive higher-priced cars as having higher quality.[20] By the same token, higher-quality cars are perceived to be even higher priced than they actually are. When consumers can judge the quality of a product by examining it or by calling on past experience with it, they use price less to judge quality. When consumers cannot judge quality because they lack the information or skill, price becomes an important quality signal.

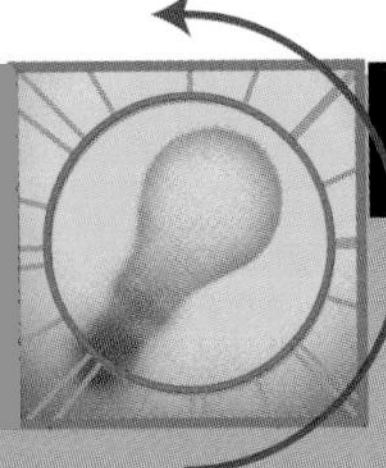

marketing highlight 10-4

Weblining—Segmented Pricing or Discrimination?

Concern about segmented pricing is growing as companies increasingly use their databases to build profiles of consumers. The oceans of information available on the Internet, combined with fast computers to process the data, allow companies to maintain the equivalent of profit-and-loss statements on every customer. While some customers benefit, others are forced to pay more for products and services or, even worse, may no longer be served at all.

Some banks colour code customers according to the level of profitability they represent for the bank. While customer reps are trained to treat everyone politely, the level of service customers receive and the fees they pay for that service or product depends on the coloured square that appears on the rep's computer screen when the customer's account number is entered. Greens, for example, might get better interest rates on their credit card balances. Reds may pay higher fees for such basic services.

A new term has been coined to describe this practice—Weblining—the information age version of that nasty old practice of redlining, in which lenders, insurance companies, and other businesses marked whole neighbourhoods off-limits because of the perceived risk the residents represent, their low incomes, or their racial background. Redlining was damned because it was based on geographic stereotypes, not concrete evidence that specific individuals were poor credit risks. Webliners claim to have more evidence against the people they refuse to serve. Nonetheless, refusal to provide services or products to groups of customers, especially those who are disadvantaged, has given rise to accusations of discrimination. Firms, therefore, have to ensure that their classifications are fair and accurate. They can't be based on irrelevant, outdated, or inaccurate profiling data. Moreover, information must not be compiled without the user's knowledge.

Using clickstream data and transaction histories, companies can sort people into categories and, in some cases, predict how they will behave. Forrester Research says some 23 percent of companies are beginning to use the Net to "micro-segment" customers. By 2002, the number could swell to 60 percent.

Weblining has added fuel to the fire for those concerned about personal privacy when they surf the Net. Montreal's Zero-Knowledge, which markets a software program called *Freedom,* has responded to people's concerns. The program enables surfers to "anonymize" themselves on the Internet by creating a pseudonym that masks their true identities when they go online, thus making their travels on the Web untraceable.

Sources: Marcia Stepanek, "Weblining: Companies are using your personal data to limit your choices—And force you to pay more for products," *Businessweek Online,* 3 April 2000; Edward Robinson, "As the privacy debate rages on, a handful of entrepreneurs is gambling on business models built around your online identity," *Business 2.0,* 12 September 2000, www.business2.com/content/magazine/indepth/2000/08/22/17926.

Montreal's Zero-Knowledge markets software to help people protect their online privacy.

Reference prices
Prices that buyers carry in their minds and refer to when they look at a given product.

Another aspect of psychological pricing is **reference prices**—prices that buyers carry in their minds and refer to when looking at a given product. They may form the reference price by noting current prices, remembering past prices, or assessing the buying situation. Sellers can influence or use these consumers' reference prices when setting price. For example, a company could display its product next to more expensive ones to imply that it belongs in the same class. Department stores often sell women's clothing in separate departments differentiated by price: Clothing found in the more expensive department is assumed to be of better quality. Companies also can influence consumers' reference prices by stating high manufacturer's suggested prices, by indicating that the product was originally priced much higher, or by pointing to a competitor's higher price.

Promotional Pricing

Promotional pricing
Temporarily pricing products below the list price, and sometimes even below cost, to increase short-run sales.

With **promotional pricing,** companies temporarily price their products below list price and sometimes even below cost. Promotional pricing takes several forms. Supermarkets and department stores will price a few products as *loss leaders* to attract customers to the store in the hope that they will buy other items at normal markups. Sellers also use *special event pricing* in certain seasons to draw more customers. Thus, linens are promotionally priced every January to attract weary Christmas shoppers back into stores. Manufacturers sometimes offer *cash rebates* to consumers who buy the product from dealers within a specified time; the manufacturer sends the rebate directly to the customer. Rebates have recently been popular with automakers and producers of durable goods and small appliances. Some manufacturers offer *low-interest financing, longer warranties,* or *free maintenance* to reduce the consumer's "price." This practice has recently become a favourite of the auto industry. Or, the seller may simply offer *discounts* from normal prices to increase sales and reduce inventories.

Promotional pricing, however, can have adverse effects. Used too frequently and copied by competitors, price promotions can create "deal-prone" customers who wait until brands go on sale before buying them. Or, constantly reduced prices can erode a brand's value in the eyes of customers. Marketers sometimes use price promotions as a quick fix instead of sweating through the difficult process of developing effective longer-term strategies for building their brands. In fact, one observer notes that price promotions can be downright addictive to both the company and the customer: "Price promotions are the brand equivalent of heroin: easy to get into but hard to get out of. Once the brand and its customers are addicted to the short-term high of a price cut it is hard to wean them away to real brand building. . . . But continue and the brand dies by 1,000 cuts."[21]

Geographical Pricing

A company also must decide how to price its products to customers located in different parts of the country or world. Should the company risk losing the business of more distant customers by charging them higher prices to cover the higher shipping costs? Or should the company charge all customers the same prices regardless of location?

f.o.b. origin pricing
A geographic pricing strategy in which goods are placed free on board a carrier; the customer pays the freight from the factory to the destination.

Uniform delivered pricing
A geographic pricing strategy in which the company charges the same price plus freight to all customers, regardless of their location.

Zone pricing
A geographic pricing strategy in which the company sets up two or more zones. All customers within a zone pay the same total price; the more distant the zone, the higher the price.

As the first question implies, one option is to ask each customer to pay for shipping from the supplier's factory. This is called **f.o.b. origin pricing,** which means that the goods are placed free on board (f.o.b.) a carrier. At that point, the title and responsibility pass to the customer, who pays the freight from the factory to the destination. While many believe this is the fairest way to assess freight charges, it means that more distant customers pay higher prices making the firm vulnerable to competitors in the customers' local area. A second option is **uniform delivered pricing.** Here, the company charges the same price to all customers, regardless of their location. It includes the average freight cost in its calculation of prices and then passes these charges along to all customers. This may make a firm's goods more expensive in its local market, but gives the firm a better chance of winning over distant customers. Other advantages of uniform delivered pricing are that it is fairly easy to administer and it lets the firm advertise its price nationally. **Zone pricing** is a third option that represents a compromise between f.o.b. origin pricing and uniform delivered pricing. The company sets up two or more zones. All customers within a given zone pay a single total price; the more distant the zone, the higher the price.

International Pricing

Companies that market their products internationally must decide what prices to charge in the different countries in which they operate. In some cases, a company can set a uniform worldwide price. For example, Canadair sells its jetliners at about the same price everywhere, whether in the United States, Europe, or a Third World country. However, most companies adjust their prices to reflect local market conditions and cost considerations.

The price that a company should charge in a specific country depends on many factors, including economic conditions, competitive situations, laws and regulations, and development of the wholesaling and retailing system. Consumer perceptions and preferences also may vary among countries, calling for different

Companies that market their products internationally must decide what prices to charge in the different countries.

prices. Or the company may have different marketing objectives in various world markets, which require changes in pricing strategy. For example, Sony may introduce a new product into mature markets in highly developed countries with the goal of quickly gaining mass-market share—this would call for a penetration pricing strategy. In contrast, it may enter a less developed market by targeting smaller, less price-sensitive segments—in this case, market skimming pricing makes sense.

Costs play an important role in setting international prices. Travellers abroad are often surprised to find that goods that are relatively inexpensive at home carry outrageously higher price tags in other countries. A pair of Levis selling for $42 in Canada goes for about $87 in Tokyo and $122 in Paris. A McDonald's Big Mac selling for a modest $2.25 here costs $7.99 in Moscow. In some cases, such *price escalation* results from differences in selling strategies or market conditions. In most instances, however, it is simply a result of the higher costs of selling in foreign markets—the additional costs of modifying the product, higher shipping and insurance costs, import tariffs and taxes, costs associated with exchange rate fluctuations, and higher channel and physical distribution costs.

Thus, international pricing presents some special problems and complexities. We discuss international pricing issues in more detail in Chapter 17.

Price Changes

After developing their initial pricing, companies often must initiate price changes due to changes in market conditions or to respond to price changes by competitors. Companies may find it desirable to initiate price cuts or price increases. In either case, they must anticipate possible buyer and competitor reactions.

Excess capacity, falling market shares, or strong price competition may lead a firm to consider cutting its price. But as the airline, construction equipment, and other industries have learned in recent years, cutting prices in an industry loaded with excess capacity may lead to price wars and declines in profitability as competitors try to hold on to market share. A company also may cut prices in a drive to dominate the market through lower costs. Either the company starts with lower costs than its competitors or it cuts prices in the hope of gaining market share that will further cut costs through larger volume. President's Choice, for example, used a low-cost, low-price strategy to introduce its private-label beer.

In contrast, many companies have had to raise prices in recent years, often as the result of rising costs. Trucking firms in Canada, for example, have recently been forced to raise prices in the face of rising fuel costs. Another factor leading to price increases is overdemand: When a company cannot supply all its customers' needs, it can raise its prices, ration products to customers, or both.

Price increases can not only cover rising costs, they can significantly improve a firm's profitability. For example, if the company's profit margin is three percent of sales, a one percent price increase will increase profits by 33 percent if sales volume is unaffected. Price increases, however, may be resented by customers, dealers, and even their own sales force.

Whether the price is raised or lowered, the action will affect buyers, competitors, distributors, and suppliers and may interest government as well. In passing on price increases to customers, the company must avoid the image of price gouging: The price increases should be supported with a company communication program telling customers why prices are being increased.

A firm considering a price change also has to worry about the reactions of its competitors. How can the firm determine the likely reactions of its competitors? The problem is complex because, like the customer, the competitor can interpret a company price cut in many ways. It may think the company is trying to grab a larger market share, that it is doing poorly and trying to boost its sales, or that it wants the whole industry to cut prices to increase total demand. When there are several competitors, the company must guess each competitor's likely reaction. If all competitors behave alike, this amounts to analyzing only a typical competitor. In contrast, if the competitors do not behave alike—perhaps because of differences in size, market shares, or policies—then separate analyses are necessary. However, if some competitors will match the price change, there is good reason to expect that the rest also will match it.

Responding to Price Changes

In addition to thinking about how competitors will react to its price changes, a firm has to determine how it should respond to a price change initiated by a competitor. It needs to consider several issues: Why did the competitor change the price? Is the price change temporary or permanent? What will happen to the company's market share and profits if it does not respond? Are other companies going to respond? And what are the competitor's and other firms' responses to each possible reaction likely to be?

As well, the company must make a broader analysis. It must consider its own product's stage in the life cycle, the product's importance in the company's product mix, the intentions and resources of the competitor, and the possible consumer reactions to price changes. Since a competitor's price changes may come as a surprise to the firm, it must constantly plan ahead and consider contingencies and possible responses to competitive moves.

Figure 10-8 shows the ways a company can assess and respond to a competitor's price cut. It may simply decide to hold its current price and profit margin if it believes that it will not lose too much market share, or if cutting its own price would cause it to lose too much profit. It may decide that it should wait and respond when it has more information on the effects of the competitor's price change. If the company decides that effective action can and should be taken, it can respond in four ways. First, if the market is price sensitive or the company is in danger of losing significant market share, it could reduce its price to match the competitor's price. Alternatively, the company could maintain its price but raise the perceived quality of its offer by improving its communications, stressing the relative quality of its product over that of the lower-price competitor. Or, the company could improve quality and increase price, moving its brand into a higher price position. Finally, the company could launch a low-price "fighting brand." This is necessary if the particular market segment being lost is price sensitive and will not respond to arguments of higher quality.

FIGURE 10-8
Assessing and responding to a competitor's price change

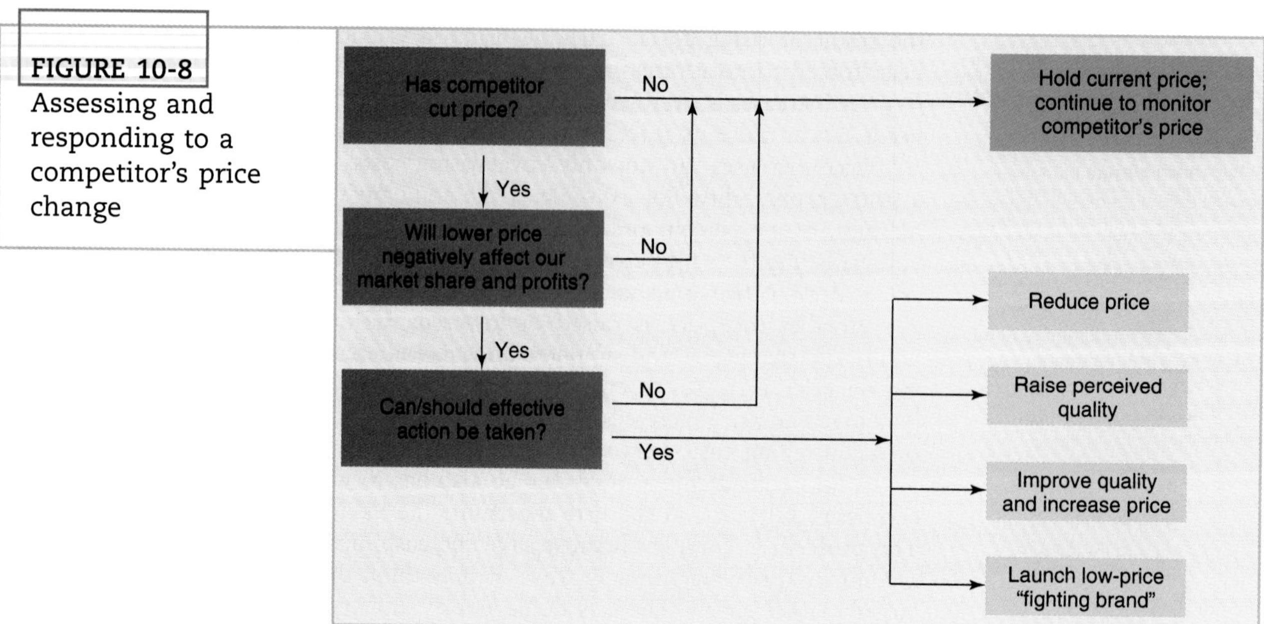

Pricing strategies and tactics form an important element of a company's marketing mix. In setting prices, companies must carefully consider a great many internal and external factors before choosing a price that will give them the greatest competitive advantage in selected target markets. However, companies are not usually free to charge whatever prices they wish. Several laws restrict pricing practices, and a number of ethical considerations affect pricing decisions. Marketing Highlight 10-5 discusses the many public policy and ethical issues surrounding pricing.

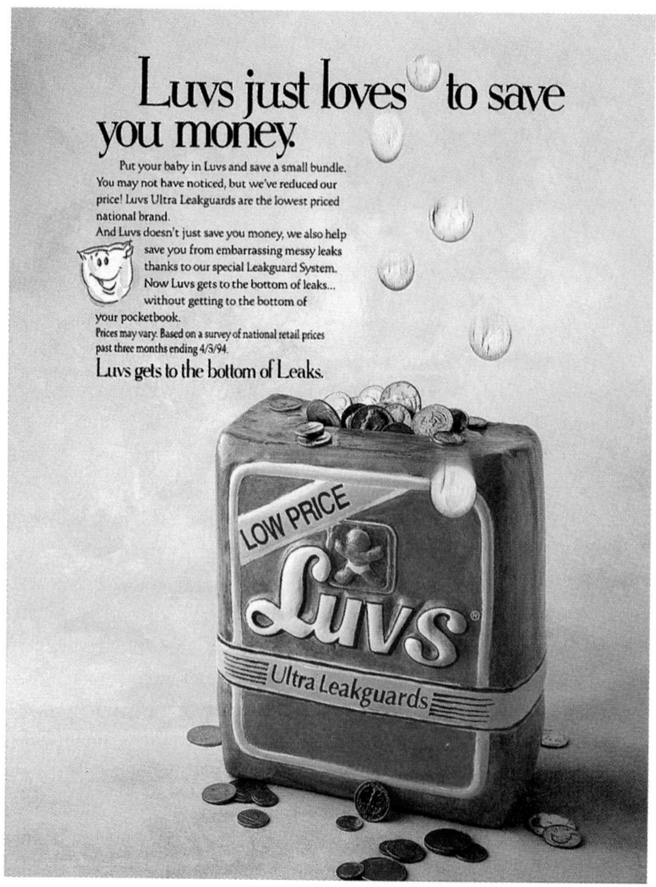

When challenged on price by store brands and other low-priced entrants, Procter & Gamble turned Luvs disposable diapers into a fighting brand.

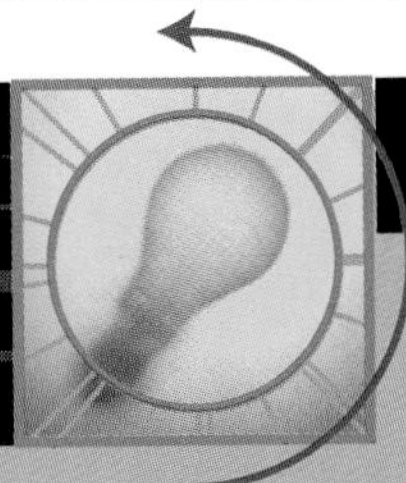

marketing highlight 10-5

Public Policy and Pricing

When Russia lifted controls on bread prices as part of its dramatic move toward a free-market economy, Moscow bakers phoned around each morning to agree on regular rounds of price increases. This caused the *Wall Street Journal* to comment: "They still don't get it!" Those who have grown up under a well-regulated, free-market economy understand that such price fixing is clearly against the rules of fair competition. Setting prices is an important element of a competitive marketplace.

Legal issues surrounding pricing are outlined in Sections 34, 36, and 38 of the *Competition Act.* Canadian pricing legislation was designed with two goals in mind: to foster a competitive environment and to protect consumers. Although pricing decisions made by firms do not generally require regulatory approval, Canadian marketers should be aware of three areas of concern: price fixing, price discrimination, and deceptive pricing (also called misleading price advertising).

Price Fixing

Federal legislation on price fixing states that sellers must set prices without talking to competitors. Otherwise, price collusion is suspected. Price fixing is illegal per se—that is, the government does not accept any excuses for price fixing. Even a simple conversation between competitors can have serious consequences. The legal charge under the *Competition Act* for offences of this nature is conspiracy. Six Ottawa hotels were each fined from $60 000 to $80 000 after they were convicted of colluding to fix prices offered to government employees. Bid rigging is another indictable offence under the clauses pertaining to price fixing. A number of cases in the construction industry have resulted in heavy fines being levied when competitors have been found guilty of rigging the prices of their bids. These cases have made most executives very reluctant to discuss prices in any way with competitors. In obtaining information on competitors' pricing, they rely only on openly published materials, such as trade association surveys and competitors' catalogues.

Price Discrimination. Section 34 of the *Competition Act* seeks to ensure that sellers offer the same price terms to a given level of trade. For example, every retailer is entitled to the same price terms whether the retailer is Sears or the local bicycle shop. However, price discrimination is allowed if the seller can prove that its costs are different when selling to different retailers—for example, that it costs less per unit to sell a large volume of bicycles to Sears than to sell a few bicycles to a local dealer. In other words, quantity or volume discounts are not prohibited. However, discriminatory promotional allowances (those not offered on proportional terms to all other competing customers) are illegal. Thus, large competitors cannot negotiate special discounts, rebates, and price concessions that are not made proportionally available to smaller competitors. For example, a small customer purchasing one-third as much as a larger competitor must receive a promotional allowance equal to one-third of what the large competitor was offered.

Although functional discounts (offering a larger discount to wholesalers than to retailers) are legal in the United States, they are illegal in Canada. In Canada, retailers and wholesalers are considered competing customers who must receive proportionally equal promotional allowances. Often Canadian marketers, who work for multinational firms, must explain the differences in the law to their US counterparts. Canadian marketers must also keep in mind that it is illegal for a buyer to knowingly benefit from any form of price discrimination. Price differentials may be used to "match competition" in "good faith," provided the firm is trying to meet competitors at its own level of competition and the price discrimination is temporary, localized, and defensive rather than offensive.

Canadian marketers are allowed to offer price breaks for one-shot deals such as store-opening specials, anniversary specials, and stock clearance sales. However, regional price differentials that limit competition are illegal. Canadian firms cannot price products unreasonably low in one part of the country with the intent of driving out the competition. Finally, resale price maintenance is also illegal. Canadian manufacturers can only suggest prices; it is illegal to require retailers to sell at a stipulated manufacturer's price.

Deceptive Pricing

Section 36 of the *Competition Act* covers areas where pricing and advertising practices converge. For example, firms cannot advertise a product at a low price, carry very limited stock, and then tell consumers they are out of the product so that they can entice them to switch to a higher-priced item. This "bait and switch" advertising is illegal in Canada. Firms must offer their customers "rain cheques" to avoid legal sanctions if advertised items are not stocked in sufficient quantities to cover expected demand.

Deceptive pricing occurs when a seller states prices or price savings that are not actually available to consumers. Some deceptions are difficult for consumers to discern, such as when an airline advertises a low one-way fare that is available only with the purchase of a round-trip ticket, or when a retailer sets artificially high "regular" prices, then announces "sale" prices close to its previous everyday prices.

Ethical Issues

Compliance with the law is considered the minimum standard when judging whether pricing practices are ethical. For example, although charging inordinately high prices is not illegal, such a practice may lead to ethical concerns. Ethical criticisms have been levied when higher prices are charged for groceries in poor areas where consumers have limited access to transportation and have few choices in terms of retail outlets.

Other ethical questions centre on whether consumers can understand prices and realistically compare them. For example, consumer advocates have condemned many car leasing contracts since the legal language used in the contracts prevents consumers from fully understanding the price they are paying for the car.

Ethical concerns about pricing also arise when consumers must negotiate prices. Often those who can least afford to pay a higher price (such as the poor, very young, elderly, or disabled) have the least ability to negotiate prices. These concerns arise when prices are not fixed. This is the case when people purchase cars, houses, professional services, or attend street markets. Many consumers are unaware that even when prices appear fixed, they may be subject to negotiation. For example, many consumers don't know that they can negotiate with their bank for more favourable terms on a consumer loan.

Sources: See the *Competition Act*, Sections 34–38, and N. Craig Smith and John A. Quelch, *Ethics in Marketing*, Boston: Irwin, 1993:389–404.

Review of Concept Connections

Price can be defined narrowly as the amount of money charged for a product or service, or more broadly as the sum of the values that consumers exchange for the benefits of having and using the product or service. Despite the increased role of non-price factors in the modern marketing process, price remains an important element in the marketing mix. It is the only element in the marketing mix that produces revenue; all other elements represent costs. Price is also one of the most flexible elements of the marketing mix. Unlike product features and channel commitments, price can be raised or lowered quickly. Even so, many companies are not good at handling pricing. Pricing decisions are subject to an incredibly complex array of environmental and competitive forces. Pricing problems often arise because prices are too cost-oriented, not revised frequently enough to reflect market changes, not consistent with the rest of the marketing mix, or not varied enough for differing products, market segments, and purchase occasions. A company sets not a single price, but rather a pricing structure that covers different items in its line. This pricing structure changes over time as products move through their life cycles. The company adjusts product prices to reflect changes in costs and demand and to account for variations in buyers and situations. As the competitive environment changes, the company considers when to initiate price changes and when to respond to them.

1. **Identify and define the internal factors affecting a firm's pricing decisions.**

   Many internal factors influence the company's pricing decisions, including the firm's marketing objectives, marketing mix strategy, costs, and organization for pricing. The pricing strategy is largely determined by the company's target market and positioning objectives. Pricing decisions affect and are affected by product design, distribution, and promotion decisions. Therefore, pricing strategies must be carefully coordinated with the other marketing mix variables when designing the marketing program.

   Costs set the floor for the company's price—the price must cover all the costs of making and selling the product, plus a fair rate of return. Common pricing objectives include survival, current profit maximization, market share leadership, and product quality leadership.

   To coordinate pricing goals and decisions, management must decide who within the organization is responsible for setting price. In large companies, some pricing authority may be delegated to lower-level managers and salespeople, but top management usually sets pricing policies and approves proposed prices. Production, finance, and accounting managers also influence pricing decisions.

2. **Identify and define the external factors affecting pricing decisions, including the impact of consumer perceptions of price and value.**

   External factors that influence pricing decisions include the nature of the *market and demand; competitors' prices and offers;* and factors such as the *economy, reseller needs*, and *government actions*. The seller's pricing freedom varies with different types of markets. Pricing is especially challenging in markets characterized by monopolistic competition or oligopoly.

   The more inelastic the demand, the higher the company can set its price. Ultimately, the consumer determines demand and decides whether the company has set the right price. The consumer weighs the price against the perceived values of acquiring and using the product. Consumers differ in the values they assign to different product features, and marketers often vary their pricing strategies for different price segments. Consumers also compare a product's price to the prices of competitors' products. As a result, a company must learn the price and quality of competitors' offers and use them as a starting point for its own pricing. When assessing the market and demand, the company estimates the demand curve, which shows the probable quantity purchased per period at alternative price levels.

3. Contrast the three general approaches to setting prices.

A company can select one or a combination of three general pricing approaches: the *cost-based approach* (cost-plus pricing, break-even analysis, and target profit pricing); the *value-based approach;* and the *competition-based approach.* Cost-based pricing sets prices based on the seller's cost structure while value-based pricing relies on consumer perceptions of value to drive pricing decisions. Competition-based pricing has two major variations. In *going-rate pricing,* the firm sets prices based on what competitors are charging. *Sealed-bid pricing* forces the company to set prices based on what they think the competition will charge.

4. Describe the major strategies for pricing new products and product lines.

Companies design a pricing structure that covers all their products. Pricing is a dynamic process, and pricing strategies usually change as a product passes through its life cycle. In pricing innovative new products, it can follow a skimming policy by initially setting high prices to "skim" the maximum amount of revenue from various segments of the market. Or it can use penetration pricing by setting a low initial price to penetrate the market deeply and win a large market share.

When the product is part of a product mix, the firm searches for a set of prices that will maximize the profits from the total mix. In product line pricing, the company decides on price steps for the entire set of products it offers. In addition, the company must set prices for captive products (products that are required for use of the main product) and product bundles (combinations of products at a reduced price).

5. Discuss the key issues related to initiating and responding to price changes.

Companies apply a variety of price adjustment strategies to account for differences in consumer segments and situations. One is discount and allowance pricing, whereby the company establishes *cash or quantity discounts,* or varying types of *allowances.* A second strategy is *segmented pricing,* whereby the company sells a product at two or more prices to accommodate different customers, product forms, locations, or times. Sometimes companies consider more than economics in their pricing decisions, using *psychological pricing* to better communicate a product's intended position. In *promotional pricing,* a company offers discounts or temporarily sells a product below list price as a special event, sometimes even selling below cost as a loss leader. Another approach is geographical pricing, whereby the company decides how to price to distant customers, choosing from such alternatives as *f.o.b. pricing, uniform delivered pricing,* or *zone pricing.* Finally, *international pricing* means that the company adjusts its price to meet different conditions and expectations in different world markets.

When a firm considers initiating a price change, it must consider customers' and competitors' reactions. There are different implications to initiating price cuts and initiating price increases. Buyer reactions to price changes are influenced by the meaning that customers see in the price change. Competitors' reactions flow from a set reaction policy or a fresh analysis of each situation.

A company must consider many factors in responding to a competitor's price changes. It must try to understand the competitor's intent as well as the likely duration and impact of the change. If a swift reaction is desirable, the firm should preplan its reactions to different possible price actions by competitors. When facing a competitor's price change, the company can sit tight, reduce its own price, raise perceived quality, improve quality and raise price, or launch a fighting brand.

Key Terms

Allowances *(p. 438)*
Break-even pricing (target profit pricing) *(p. 430)*
Captive product pricing *(p. 437)*
Cash discount *(p. 438)*
Cost-plus pricing *(p. 429)*
Demand curve *(p. 426)*
Experience curve (learning curve) *(p. 422)*
Fixed costs *(p. 421)*
f.o.b. origin pricing *(p. 441)*
Going-rate pricing *(p. 433)*
Market penetration pricing *(p. 436)*
Market skimming pricing *(p. 435)*
Monopolistic competition *(p. 424)*
Oligopolistic competition *(p. 424)*
Price *(p. 415)*
Price elasticity *(p. 427)*

Product bundle pricing *(p. 438)*
Product line pricing *(p. 437)*
Promotional pricing *(p. 440)*
Psychological pricing *(p. 439)*
Pure competition *(p. 424)*
Pure monopoly *(p. 424)*
Quantity discount *(p. 438)*
Reference prices *(p. 440)*
Sealed-bid pricing *(p. 434)*
Segmented pricing *(p. 438)*
Total costs *(p. 421)*
Uniform delivered pricing *(p. 441)*
Value-based pricing *(p. 432)*
Value pricing *(p. 433)*
Variable costs *(p. 421)*
Zone pricing *(p. 441)*

Discussing the Issues

1. Assume you are the vice-president for financial affairs at your university or college. Like many Canadian institutions, your school has suffered from government cutbacks over the last three years. Therefore, you are under tremendous pressure to increase revenue. Raising tuition fees is one option that would help accomplish your aim. However, you suspect that raising tuition will anger students and lead to declining enrollments. What internal and external pricing factors should you consider before you make your decision? Explain.
2. A seller's pricing freedom depends on the type of market. Economists generally recognize four types of markets, each presenting a different pricing challenge. Identify each of these market forms and discuss the pricing challenges facing each one.
3. Genentech, a high-tech pharmaceutical company, has developed a clot-dissolving drug called TPA. This drug can halt a heart attack in progress. It has been proven that TPA saves lives, minimizes hospital stays, and reduces damage to the heart itself. It was initially priced at $2200 per dose. What pricing approach does Genentech appear to be using? Is this approach justified? Is demand for this drug likely to be price elastic?
4. A US federal judge ruled that Microsoft is acting like a monopolist with regard to tying (or bundling) the sales of its popular Windows 95, 98, and 2000 operating systems software to its Web browser product. What pricing strategy does Microsoft seem to be using? Take a side in the monopoly debate and state how you would resolve this ongoing problem.
5. Which pricing strategy—market skimming or market penetration—does each of the following companies use? (a) McDonald's, (b) Harry Rosen (men's clothing), (c) Bic Corporation (disposable pens, lighters, razors, and related products), and (d) IBM (personal computers). Are these the right strategies for each company? Explain.
6. A clothing store sells men's suits at three price levels: $180, $250, and $340. If shoppers use these price points as reference prices when comparing different suits, what would be the effect of adding a new line of suits priced to sell at $280? Would you expect sales of the $250 suits to increase, decrease, or stay the same? Why? What would be the effect of adding a line of suits priced at $450?
7. Companies often adjust their basic prices to allow for differences in customers, products, and locations. List and briefly describe the different forms of segmented pricing. Provide an example (other than those provided in the text) of each of these forms. Which forms might be used in pricing products on the Internet? Explain.
8. Some analysts see predatory pricing by a strong, competitive marketer as extremely damaging to competition and a well-functioning economy. Others view it simply as good, healthy competition. Take a stand on this issue and discuss your view. Consider questions of ethics, long-term survival, the competitive environment, consumer benefits and welfare, and shareholder profit.

Marketing Applications

1. As Marketing Highlight 10-1 indicates, the Internet is having an impact on pricing. Consider the effect of the Internet and its associated technology on pricing in the music business. Music is sold in retail stores such as HMV (www.HMV.com) and Chapters (www.chapters.ca), in discount outlets such as

Sam the Record Man (www.SamtheRecordMan.com) or Circuit City (www.circuitcity.com), and via the Internet on such sites as Movie Madness (shop.store.yahoo.com/movie-madness-ca), Columbia House Canada (www.columbiahousecanada.com), and CD Plus (www.cd-plus.com). All of these sellers price music differently. However, MP3 technology (www.mp3.com) has drastically altered the music retailing business. Using this technology, any music enthusiast with a computer and CD writeable capability can download music via the Internet directly from the source and copy it to a CD, cutting out retailers and other intermediaries. Projections are that this same technology will eventually have an impact on the videotape and movie businesses in much the same way. The recording and entertainment industry may never be the same.

a. Visit the Web sites mentioned above. What can you tell about their pricing policies? What strategies seem to be in place?
b. How will MP3 technology affect the pricing strategies of traditional distributors?
c. The music industry is concerned that MP3 technology, while having substantial promise for legitimate distribution, may result in a dramatic increase in music piracy and bootlegging. What ethical issues are associated with this technology and its use on the Internet?
d. Considering the demand for music, design a pricing strategy that could be used by a music retailer to compete with a music producer using MP3 technology to sell directly to consumers.

2. If you want the best airfare deals, look to the Internet—many others do. Experts say that the key to getting the best fares is to avoid locking yourself into a single approach, whether it's using a reservation call centre, a flesh-and-blood travel agent, an online agent, or an airline's Web site. Smart consumers do their homework, paying attention to full-fare prices, markdown rates, restrictions, and competitive booking options. Currently, the top airline sites for domestic travel are Air Canada (www.aircanada.ca), Canada 3000 (www.Canada3000.com), and WestJet (www.westjet.com). Non-airline sites include AOL Travel (www.aol.com), Travelocity (www.travelocity.com), Expedia (www.expedia.com), Lowestfare (www.lowestfare.com), and Cheaptickets (www.cheaptickets.com).

   a. Investigate a sampling of these Web sites. What can you determine about the ticket pricing policies of airlines? Do they apply any of the pricing strategies discussed in the chapter?
   b. Design a trip and use several of the sites to explore the cost of tickets. Critique your experience. How much does pricing have to do with your choice of a booking procedure and airline? What other factors are important?
   c. Which of the sites for obtaining airline tickets seems the best?
   d. How should travel agencies deal with the increasing use of online ticket purchasing?
   e. What is the future of online booking and the travel agency industry. What impact will this have on airline pricing?

Internet Connections

Product Mix Pricing Strategies

In the automotive industry, slightly altered versions of the same vehicle are sometimes marketed under different brand names. For example, the Ford Explorer and the Mercury Mountaineer are essentially the same vehicle. The Mountaineer is shipped with a greater number of standard features and a higher price tag. It was designed to appeal to women and contains many safety features important to this target group. Visit the Edmunds car buying service at www.edmunds.com. Look under new trucks for the Ford Explorer and the Mercury Mountaineer. Find the least expensive base model for each vehicle and complete the chart below. For each feature on which you compare the vehicles, list that feature by name. Then indicate which of the models is equipped with the feature.

For Discussion

1. What new product pricing strategy do you think Mercury used when it introduced the Mountaineer?
2. Do you think the extra features listed above cost the manufacturer the difference in price charged?

3. Is the manufacturer using psychological pricing as well? How?
4. Why do you think Ford introduced its "Explorer look-alike" under the Mercury brand rather than extending the Explorer line and using product form pricing?
5. Visit the Automobile Protection Association Web site (www.apa.ca/apa_eng/home_en.htm). How does this organization help consumers get the best price for the car of their choice?

Item	Ford Explorer	Mercury Mountaineer
Price (MSRP)		
Feature (specify)		
Feature (specify)		
Feature (specify)		
Feature (specify)		

Savvy Sites

- Want to find the cheapest place online to purchase your textbooks? Try the shopping agent MySimon (www.mysimon.com).
- The *Competition Act* and Competition Bureau are concerned with price discrimination. The Canada-wide Law Pages (www.wwlia.org/ca-comp1.htm) maintains a posting on this area.
- Online auctions are huge business and demonstrate the Internet's ability to allow different prices for different surfers. See eBay (www.ebay.com) to compare prices on various auctions for one product.
- At Priceline (www.priceline.com) customers can name their own prices for airline tickets, hotel rooms, cars, and more.

Notes

1. See Lara Mills, "Cereal sales buck soggy U.S. trend," *Marketing On-Line,* 18 January 1999; Peter Vamos, "Top client, food & beverage: Kellogg keeping its cereal fresh," *Strategy,* 31 July 2000:B11; John Greenwald, "Cereal showdown," *Time,* 29 April 1996:60; "Cereal thriller," *Economist,* 15 June 1996:59; Gretchen Morgenson, "Denial in Battle Creek," *Forbes,* 7 October 1996:44; Judann Pollack, "Post's price play rocked category, but did it work?" *Advertising Age,* 1 December 1997:24; Carleen Hawn, "General Mills tests limits," *Forbes,* 6 April 1998:48; Judann Pollack, "Price cuts unsettling to cereal business," *Advertising Age,* 28 September 1998:S10; Rekha Balu, "Kellogg increases prices on majority of cereal brands," *Wall Street Journal,* 15 December 1998:B23; Susan Pulliam, "Kellogg, long treated as stale by Wall Street, shows signs of putting some snap in its walk," *Wall Street Journal,* 16 February 1999:C2,C3; Terril Yue Jones, "Outside the box," *Forbes,* 14 June 1999:52–3; and Amy Kover, "Why the cereal business is soggy," *Fortune,* 6 March 2000.
2. See David J. Schwartz, Marketing Today: *A Basic Approach,* 3rd ed., New York: Harcourt Brace Jovanovich, 1981:270–3.
3. See Amy E. Cortese, "Good-bye to fixed pricing?" *Business Week,* 4 May 1998:71–84; Robert D. Hof, "The buyer always wins," *Business Week,* 22 March 1999:EB26–8; and Robert D. Hof, "Going, going, gone," *Business Week,* 12 April 1999:30–2.
4. Paul Hunt, "Pricing for profit," *Marketing On-Line,* 26 April 1999.
5. For an excellent discussion of factors affecting pricing decisions, see Thomas T. Nagle and Reed K. Holden, *The Strategy and Tactics of Pricing,* 2nd ed., Englewood Cliffs, NJ: Prentice Hall, Inc., 1995:Chapter 1.
6. See Steve Gelsi, "Spin-cycle doctor," *Brandweek,* 10 March

1997:38–40; Tim Stevens, "From reliable to 'Wow,'" *Industry Week*, 22 June 1998:22–6; and William C. Symonds, "'Build a better mousetrap' is no claptrap," *Business Week*, 1 February 1999:47.

7. Timothy M. Laseter, "Supply chain management: The ins and outs of target costing," *Purchasing*, 12 March 1998:22–5; www.swatch.com.
8. Brian Dumaine, "Closing the innovation gap," *Fortune*, 2 December 1991:56–62.
9. Accumulated production is drawn on a semi-log scale so that equal distances represent the same percentage increase in output.
10. Joshua Rosenbaum, "Guitar maker looks for a new key," *Wall Street Journal*, 11 February 1998:B1; and information obtained from www.gibson.com, February 2000.
11. See Nagle and Holden, *The Strategy and Tactics of Pricing*: Chapter 4.
12. Judy Waytiuk, "No haggle, no hassle," *Marketing On-Line*, 28 August 2000.
13. Kevin J. Clancy, "At what profit price?" *Brandweek*, 23 June 1997:24–8.
14. The arithmetic of markups and margins is discussed in Appendix 2, "Marketing Arithmetic," found on the companion Website for this text.
15. See Philip Kotler, *Kotler on Marketing*, New York: Free Press, 1999:54.
16. See Stephen J. Hoch, Xavier Drèze, and Mary E. Purk, "EDLP, hi-lo, and margin arithmetic," *Journal of Marketing*, October 1994:16–27.
17. Andy Reinhardt, "Pentium: The next generation," *Business Week*, 12 May 1997:42–3.
18. See Nagle and Holden, *The Strategy and Tactics of Pricing*:225–8; and Manjit S. Yadav and Kent B. Monroe, "How buyers perceive savings in a bundle price: An examination of a bundle's transaction value," *Journal of Marketing Research*, August 1993: 350–8.
19. Ross Howard, "Rogers caves in on cable channels," *Globe and Mail*, 6 January 1995:A1; Ross Howard, "Rogers says new channels in jeopardy," *Globe and Mail*, 7 January 1995:A1,A4.
20. Mary W. Sullivan, "How brand names affect the demand for twin automobiles," *Journal of Marketing Research*, May 1998:154–65.
21. Tim Ambler, "Kicking price promotion habit is like getting off heroin—hard," *Marketing*, 27 May 1999:24.

Company Case 10

PeoplePC: Is There a Free Lunch?

What's Going On?

Economists tell us that there is no such thing as a free lunch. Well, perhaps. But it certainly seems that many personal computer and Internet companies are trying to come up with one. The 22 December 1999 issue of the *Wall Street Journal* carried a full-page ad with the words "100% Off" in bold letters centred on the page. The ad from Juno Online Services went on to advise, "Starting now, Juno is offering full Internet access for free. From free Web access to premium dial-up and broadband services, everybody's getting it."

But perhaps not everyone is getting it. How can a company give away a service for which millions of people have been paying about $20 per month? What's going on? How can Juno and other companies make these offers? And what about Egreetings Network, Inc.? In 1998, when this Internet company began offering e-mail birthday cards for $.75 to $4.50 each, only 300 000 people signed up for the service. Then, the company decided to ditch its pricing strategy and give its cards away for free. By mid-1999, it had 7 000 000 registered users. Egreetings' CEO Gordon Tucker admits, "Charging for cards was a small idea. Giving them away is a really big idea."

Giving Things Away

Is this some form of cyber-suicide? You might argue that a company giving away an electronic greeting card is not really giving away very much. But how do you explain the offer by Free-PC? The price of personal computers was already plummeting. In fact, computers priced below $1000 were accounting for the majority of sales—some were as inexpensive as $750. Then, along came Free-PC. In February 1999, the company announced that it would give away 10 000 personal computers. All that interested consumers had to do was to register at its Web site (www.freepc.com) and provide detailed demographic information about themselves and their families including name, address, sex, age, e-mail address, marital status, makes and models of family cars, and lifestyle information from a list of 26 categories.

The company indicated it would review the applications it received and implied that it would select them to create a pool of users who would be attractive to advertisers. The company also announced that it planned to charge 200 advertisers $15 000 each for a 90-day period, a time during which Free-PC would direct their ads to the lucky 10 000. Free-PC guaranteed the advertisers one million impressions during the period. It argued that it provided real targeting using the 60 pieces of demographic data it tracked, along with response data on each variable. Moreover, advertisers could deliver media-rich ads and test different ad messages to see which got the best responses.

When Free-PC opened its Web site, over 1.2 million people logged on and applied for the 10 000 free PCs. Applicants the company selected received a full-featured Compaq Presario Internet PC with pre-installed software and unlimited access to the Internet, which included e-mail service and technical support.

Consumers had to agree to log on to the Internet at least 10 hours per month. If customers did not live up to this commitment, FreePC would ask them to return their PCs. Whenever they surfed the Internet, consumers' monitor screens contained a bar down the right side and across the bottom, occupying about 40 percent of the screen in total, that displayed ads and other marketing messages. The company called the Free-PC network the first permission-based, one-to-one targeted marketing network. Free-PC's Web site explained that, by having so much information, "you will help us to make sure that the ads and services that appear in the small frame around the screen are relevant to you. And, just like you don't want to waste your time with meaningless ads, advertisers don't want to waste money displaying ads to people who aren't interested in their products."

Jumping on the Bandwagon

More than a dozen companies quickly jumped on the Free-PC bandwagon, with some adding new twists. Enchilada (www.enchilada.com) threw in Internet access along with the computer to offer "the whole enchilada" for $599. The offer includes the computer and three years of Internet access. However, you have to pay extra for a monitor, warranty, and extended technical support.

InterSquid (www.intersquid.com) offered a PC and Internet access for $45.95 per month with a 30-month commitment: Applicants had to commit to a costly credit check, or pay the total amount, about $1350, up front. MyFreePC.com (www.myfreepc.com) provided a low-end computer and Internet access for $40.18 per month; however, people had to commit to 19 months of service and, to avoid an interest-bearing loan, pay up front.

PeoplePC

In late 1999, Nicholas Grouf, a 31-year-old Harvard MBA, launched PeoplePC and added the latest twist. PeoplePC offers a brand-name PC, such as Compaq or Toshiba, including a monitor and free Internet service through MCI Worldcom's UUNet. In addition to the computer and Internet access, PeoplePC subscribers get around-the-clock technical support and even in-home computer repair service if required. The cost is $37.43 per month for three years.

After the three-year period, PeoplePC will give you a new computer if you want to sign up again. The company planned to sign up 400 000 people in its first wave.

PeoplePC's plan differs in several ways from Free-PC's plan. PeoplePC's program requires only a minimum amount of personal information as a part of the registration process. Second, PeoplePC will not use an ad-supported business model. That is, it will not require that buyers devote some of their screen space to ads, or pledge to be online for a certain number of hours per month. Rather, PeoplePC sees itself as a membership-based model in which it will use its members' buying power to get them good deals on products and services. In a sense, the company serves as an Internet shopping club. It will earn money by getting a fee from the product or service provider whenever a PeoplePC member buys something. For example, at the PeoplePC home page, a member can click on a button marked, "Special Offers for PeoplePC Members." Offers include five percent off at wine.com, 10 percent off at chipshot.com, 15 percent off at Ashford.com, and a $150 sign-up bonus from E*TRADE.

PeoplePC will earn between $75 and $150 for each member who signs up with E*TRADE. That's much less than the average $600 most online brokers must spend to acquire a new customer. Moreover, the company lets each e-tailer decide how much to pay PeoplePC. Although this might seem to encourage e-tailers to take advantage of the company, Nicholas Grouf argues that the more a company pays, the harder PeoplePC will work for it. "Every company knows just how much it pays in customer acquisition costs. If it costs $1000 to get a customer, and we get just 10 percent of that for doing the same work, it's still a lucrative business." PeoplePC will also have three-year commitments from customers, allowing it to sell that receivable to a bank and get its money quickly.

To attract members, PeoplePC kicked off a $40 million multimedia promotion campaign in late 1999, starting with spots during game three of the World Series. Additional television, newspaper, and online ads that followed those spots used the tag line: "It's for people." In November 1999, the company reported that phone calls were coming in at four times the predicted rate, and it had increased the number of representatives answering phones from 100 to 500.

A Free-for-All

One observer noted, "Time and again, do-it-for-free companies are coming in and spoiling an industry for everyone else. But it's a fact on the Internet: People expect a lot of things for free. And if you don't give it away, some other start-up will." Internet companies rush to sign up large numbers of people and earn money either by selling advertising or earning fees from online vendors. One wonders what consumers expect for free. Moreover, are there enough advertising revenues or indirect fees to support all these Web sites? With MP3.com giving away music, e-Fax.com giving away fax service, and Juno.com giving away Internet access, we may soon find out how much a free lunch really costs.

Questions

1. What internal and external factors affect e-commerce pricing decisions?
2. What marketing objectives and pricing approaches are PeoplePC and Free-PC pursuing?
3. What is the nature of costs for a company like PeoplePC? Which costs are fixed and which are variable? What are the implications of this cost structure?
4. How can companies like PeoplePC make offers that appear to be free or almost free? What are the true costs to the consumer?
5. What marketing recommendations would you make to PeoplePC?

Sources: "PeoplePC energizes personal computer shopping this holiday season," *PR Newswire,* 14 December 1999:1460; Nikhil Hutheesing, "Matchmaker," *Forbes,* 15 November 1999:222; "PeoplePC to unveil investors' backing totaling $65 million," *Wall Street Journal,* 1 November 1999:B13; Tobi Elkin, "Newcomer PeoplePC rolls $40 mil campaign: Online discounts and ecard offer form backbone of trouble-free PC-buying pitch," *Advertising Age,* 11 October 1999:85; Cade Metz, "Nearly free PCs," *PC Magazine,* 1 September 1999:177; George Anders, "Eager to boost traffic, more internet firms give away services," *Wall Street Journal,* 28 July 1999:A1; Makoto Ushida, "Cyberslice: Free-PC wave hits Japanese shore," *Asahi Shimbun/Asahi Evening News,* 26 July 1999:ASAH6396762. Also see www.freepc.com, www.peoplepc.com, and homepeoplepc.com.

video case 10

WEDDING BILLS

Companies can choose from a variety of methods when setting their prices. These range from adding a fixed amount to the cost of a product to taking into account the psychological value that consumers attach to the product. One of the best examples of the latter, and one that many of you will face someday, is the price charged for the products and services used in wedding celebrations.

When it comes to spending money for their wedding, many cautious consumers lay out far more than is rationally justified. The reason for this is that the wedding industry uses a series of techniques, some of which are unethical and others of which are illegal, to sell to this market. Salespeople work on "pushing the right buttons" to get the happy couple to spend more than required. One method they use is to sell the feeling. They talk to the couple about the fact that it is their special day and that everything should be storybook perfect. They tell the couple they should settle for nothing less than the best. This approach works best if the salesperson develops a strong rapport with the couple, and especially the bride, during the sales presentation. The bride is the most important party in this event because she has the greatest say in the products and services purchased.

The gown is one area where wedding planners and bridal shops have developed a number of methods to get brides to spend more than necessary. One illegal method they use is to remove the manufacturer's labels from the gowns: This makes it impossible for the bride to do any comparison shopping because she does not know who made the gown. Another method is to have the bride order a gown one to two sizes larger than necessary. Brides are told that wedding dresses are often cut small and to get one that fits correctly requires ordering a larger size. The real purpose is to force the bride to pay for alterations. This can drive up the cost of a gown by an additional $200. Accessories for the gown such as veils, trains, and headdresses are aggressively sold. Why? They offer higher profit margins than the gown.

Premium prices are not limited to the gown. Caterers, halls, hotels, and printers that specialize in weddings have their own premium pricing methods. This includes everything from charging $50 for four litres of fruit punch that cost $3 in the grocery store to charging $14 for a coin, purported to bring good luck, which is only worth 10 cents. The bride and groom may also encounter service fees from the caterer. These fees reflect the royalty the caterer pays the reception hall to be listed as a recommended supplier. The florist industry has its own special method of setting prices for weddings. Consultants in the United States have nicknamed the practice the "Mercedes Syndrome." It involves the florist watching to see the brand of car the bride arrives in and setting the prices based on this observation. The more expensive the car, the higher the prices charged.

Questions

1. How would you describe the pricing strategy used by the wedding industry?
2. What are some examples of optional product pricing in the case?
3. Do you think the wedding industry is engaging in psychological pricing? Why or why not?
4. In your opinion, do you think the pricing method used by the wedding industry is ethical? Why or why not?

Source: This case was prepared by Robert Warren and is based on "Wedding Bills," *MarketPlace* (April 2, 1996).

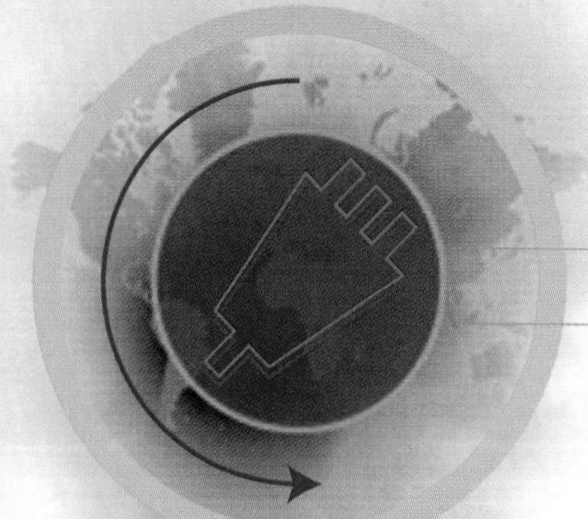

PART 1 2 3 4

Developing the Marketing Mix

Concept Connections

When you finish this chapter, you should be able to

1. Explain why companies use distribution channels and the functions that these channels perform.
2. Discuss how channel members interact and organize to perform the work of the channel.
3. Identify the major channel alternatives open to a company.
4. Discuss the nature and importance of physical distribution.
5. Analyze integrated logistics, including how it may be achieved and its benefits to the company.

chapter 11

Distribution Channels and Logistics Management

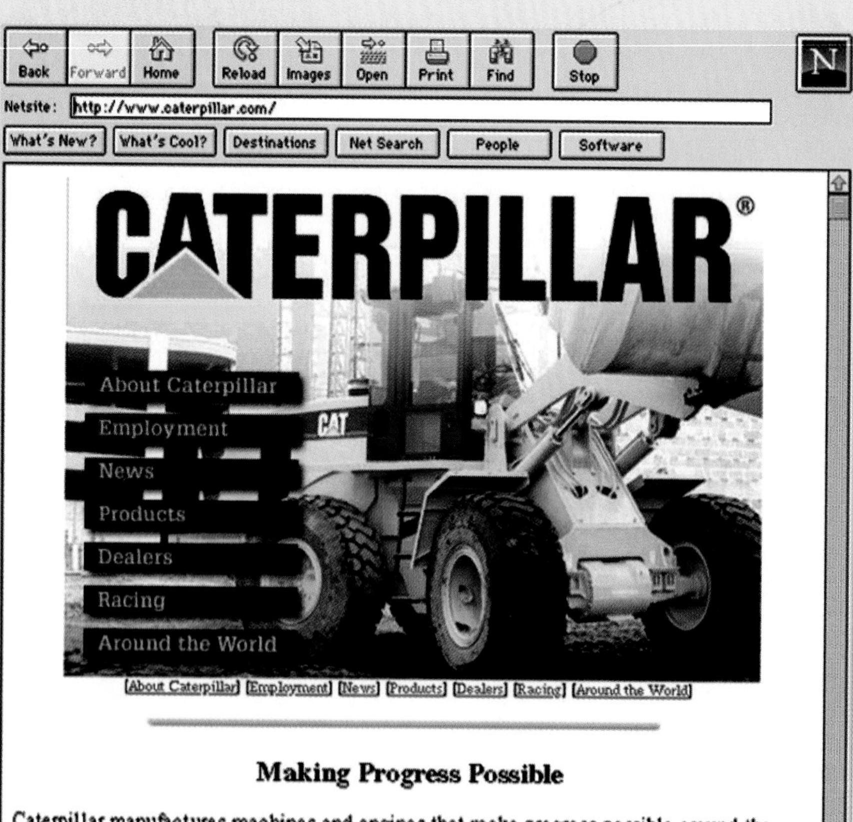

For more than 50 years, Caterpillar has dominated the world's markets for heavy construction and mining equipment. Despite market swings and major competitive challenges, the big Cat keeps on purring. Its Web site brags, "Caterpillar manufactures machines and engines that make progress possible around the world. Its familiar yellow tractors, crawlers, loaders, and trucks are a common sight at construction sites in nearly 200 countries. With sales of $31 billion, Caterpillar is half again as large as its nearest competitor. It now captures more than a 40 percent share of the world's heavy construction equipment market, selling more than 300 products in nearly 200 countries. Caterpillar has posed six straight record years of record sales."

Many factors contribute to Caterpillar's enduring success—high-quality products, flexible and efficient manufacturing, a steady stream of innovative new products, and a lean organization that is responsive to customer needs. Although Caterpillar charges premium prices for its equipment, its high-quality and trouble-free operation provides greater long-term value. Yet these are not the most important reasons for Caterpillar's dominance. Instead, Caterpillar chairman and CEO, Glen Barton, credits the company's focus on customers and its worldwide distribution system, which does a superb job of taking care of every customer need. Former CEO Donald Fites agrees: "The biggest reason for Caterpillar's success has been our system of distribution and product support and the close customer relationships it fosters. . . . The backbone of that system is our 192 dealers around the world who sell and service our [equipment]."

Caterpillar's dealers provide a wide range of important services to customers. Fites summarizes:

> After the product leaves our door, the dealers take over. They are the ones on the front line. They're the ones who live with the product for its lifetime. They're the ones customers see. Although we offer financing and insurance, they arrange those deals for customers. They're out there making sure that when a machine is delivered, it's in the condition it's supposed to be in. They're out there training a customer's operators. They service a product frequently throughout its life, carefully monitoring a machine's health and scheduling repairs to prevent costly downtime. The customer . . . knows that there is a $31 billion-plus company called Caterpillar. But the dealers create the image of a company that doesn't just stand *behind* its products but *with* its products, anywhere in the world. Our dealers are the reason that our motto—Buy the Iron, Get the Company—is not an empty slogan.

Caterpillar's dealers build strong customer relationships in their communities. "Our independent dealer in Novi, Michigan or in Bangkok, Thailand knows so much more about the requirements of customers in those locations than a huge corporation like Caterpillar could," says Fites. Competitors often bypass their dealers and sell directly to big customers to cut costs or make more profits for themselves. However, Caterpillar wouldn't think of going around its dealers. "The knowledge of the local market and the close relations with customers that our dealers provide are worth every penny," Fites asserts. "We'd rather cut off our right arm than sell directly to customers and bypass our dealers."

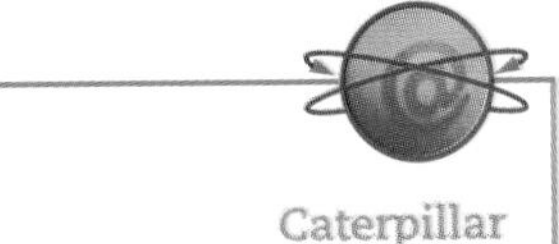

Caterpillar
www.caterpillar.com/

Caterpillar and its dealers work in close harmony to find better ways to bring value to customers. Says Fites, "We genuinely treat our system and theirs as one." The entire system is linked by one worldwide computer network. For example, working at his desk computer, Fites can check to see how many Caterpillar machines in the world are waiting for parts. Closely linked dealers play a vital role in almost every aspect of Caterpillar's operations, from product design and delivery, to product service and support financing and insurance, to market intelligence and customer feedback.

In the heavy-equipment industry, where equipment downtime can mean big losses, Caterpillar's exceptional service gives it a huge advantage in winning and keeping customers. For example, consider Freeport-McMoRan, a Caterpillar customer that operates one of the world's largest copper and gold mines, 24 hours a day, 365 days a year. Located high in the mountains of Indonesia, the mine is accessible only by aerial cableway or helicopter. Freeport-McMoRan relies on more than 500 pieces of Caterpillar mining and construction equipment—worth several hundred million dollars—including loaders, tractors, and mammoth 24-ton, 2000-plus horsepower trucks. Many of these machines cost more than $1 million apiece. When equipment breaks down, Freeport-McMoRan loses money fast. Therefore, it gladly pays a premium price for machines and service it can count on. And it knows that it can count on Caterpillar and its outstanding distribution network for superb support.

The close working relationship between Caterpillar and its dealers comes down to more than just formal contracts and business agreements. According to Fites, the powerful partnership rests on a handful of basic principles and practices:

- *Dealer profitability.* Caterpillar's rule: "Share the gain as well as the pain." When times are good, Caterpillar shares the bounty with its dealers rather than trying to grab all the riches for itself. When times are bad, Caterpillar protects its dealers. For example, in the mid-1980s, facing a depressed global construction equipment market and cut-throat competition, Caterpillar sheltered its dealers by absorbing much of the economic damage. The company lost almost $1 billion in just three years but didn't lose a single dealer. In contrast, competitors' dealers struggled and many failed. As a result, Caterpillar emerged with its distribution system intact and a stronger competitive position than ever.
- *Extraordinary dealer support.* Nowhere is this support more apparent than in the company's parts delivery system—the fastest and most reliable in the industry. Caterpillar maintains 22 parts facilities around the world, which stock 320 000 different parts and ship 84 000 items per day, about one per second every day of the year. In turn, dealers have made huge investments in inventory, warehouses, fleets of trucks, service bays, diagnostic and service equipment, and information technology. Together, Caterpillar and its dealers guarantee parts delivery within 48 hours anywhere in the world. The company ships 80 percent of parts orders immediately, and 99 percent on the same day the order is received. In contrast, it's not unusual for competitors' customers to wait four or five days for a part.

- *Communications.* Caterpillar communicates with its dealers—fully, frequently, and honestly. According to Fites, "There are no secrets between us and our dealers. We have the financial statements and key operating data of every dealer in the world. . . . In addition, virtually all Caterpillar and dealer employees have real-time access to continually updated databases of service information, sales trends and forecasts, customer satisfaction surveys, and other critical data. . . . [Moreover,] virtually everyone from the youngest design engineer to the CEO now has direct contact with somebody in our dealer organizations."
- *Dealer performance.* Caterpillar does all it can to ensure that its dealerships are run well. It closely monitors each dealership's sales, market position, service capability, financial situation, and other performance measures. It genuinely wants each dealer to succeed, and when it identifies a problem it jumps in to help. As a result, Caterpillar dealerships, many of which are family businesses, tend to be stable and profitable. The average Caterpillar dealership has remained in the hands of the same family for more than 50 years. Some actually predate the 1925 merger that created Caterpillar.
- *Personal relationships.* In addition to more formal business ties, Caterpillar forms close personal ties with its dealers in a kind of family relationship. Fites relates the following example: "When I see Chappy Chapman, a retired executive vice-president, . . . out on the golf course, he always asks about particular dealers or about their children, who may be running the business now. And every time I see those dealers, they inquire, 'How's Chappy?' That's the sort of relationship we have. . . . I consider the majority of dealers [to be] personal friends."

Thus, Caterpillar's superb distribution system serves as a major source of competitive advantage. The system is built on a firm foundation of mutual trust and shared dreams. Caterpillar and its dealers feel a deep pride in what they are accomplishing together. As Fites puts it, "There's a camaraderie among our dealers around the world that really makes it more than just a financial arrangement. They feel what they're doing is good for the world because they are part of an organization that makes, sells, and tends to the machines that make the world work."[1]

Marketing channel decisions are among the most important decisions that management faces. A company's channel decisions directly affect every other marketing decision. The company's pricing depends on whether it uses mass merchandisers or high-quality specialty stores. The firm's sales force and advertising decisions depend on how much persuasion, training, and motivation the dealers need. Whether a company develops or acquires certain new products may depend on how well those products fit the abilities of its channel members.

Some companies pay too little attention to their distribution channels, sometimes with damaging results. Other companies use imaginative distribution systems to *gain* a competitive advantage. Federal Express's creative and imposing distribution system made it the leader in the small-package delivery industry. General Electric gained a strong advantage in selling its major appliances by supporting its dealers with a sophisticated computerized order-processing and delivery system. And Dell Computer revolutionized its industry by selling direct rather than through retail stores. Charles Schwab & Company pioneered the delivery of financial services via the Internet.

Distribution channel decisions often involve long-term commitments to other firms. Ford, IBM, or Pizza Hut, for example, can easily change their advertising, pricing, or promotion programs. They can scrap old products and introduce new ones as market tastes demand. But when they set up distribution channels through contracts with franchisees, independent dealers, or large retailers, they cannot readily replace these channels with company-owned stores if conditions change. Therefore, management must design its channels carefully, with an eye on tomorrow's likely selling environment as well as today's.

This chapter examines four major questions about distribution channels: What is the nature of distribution channels? How do channel firms interact and organize to do the work of the channel? What problems do companies face in designing and managing their channels? and What role does physical distribution play in attracting and satisfying customers? In Chapter 12, we shall look at distribution channel issues from the perspective of retailers and wholesalers.

The Nature of Distribution Channels

Distribution channel (marketing channel)
A set of interdependent organizations involved in the process of making a product or service available for use or consumption by the consumer or business user.

Most producers use intermediaries to bring their products to market. They try to forge a **distribution channel,** a set of interdependent organizations involved in the process of making a product or service available for use or consumption by the consumer or business user.[2]

Why Are Marketing Intermediaries Used?

Why do producers give some of the selling job to intermediaries? After all, doing so means giving up some control over how and to whom the products are sold. However, intermediaries create greater efficiency in making goods available to target markets. Through their contacts, experience, specialization, and scale of operation, intermediaries usually offer the firm more than it can achieve on its own.

Figure 11-1 shows how using intermediaries can provide economies. Part A shows three manufacturers, each using direct marketing to reach three customers. This system requires nine different contacts. Part B shows the three manufacturers working through one distributor, who contacts the three customers. This system requires only six contacts. In this way, intermediaries reduce the amount of work that must be done by both producers and consumers.

From the economic system's point of view, the role of marketing intermediaries is to transform the assortments of products made by producers into the assortments wanted by consumers. Producers make narrow assortments of products in large quantities, but consumers want broad assortments of products in small quantities. In the distribution channels, intermediaries buy the large quantities of many producers and break them down into the smaller quantities and

FIGURE 11-1 How a marketing intermediary reduces the number of channel transactions

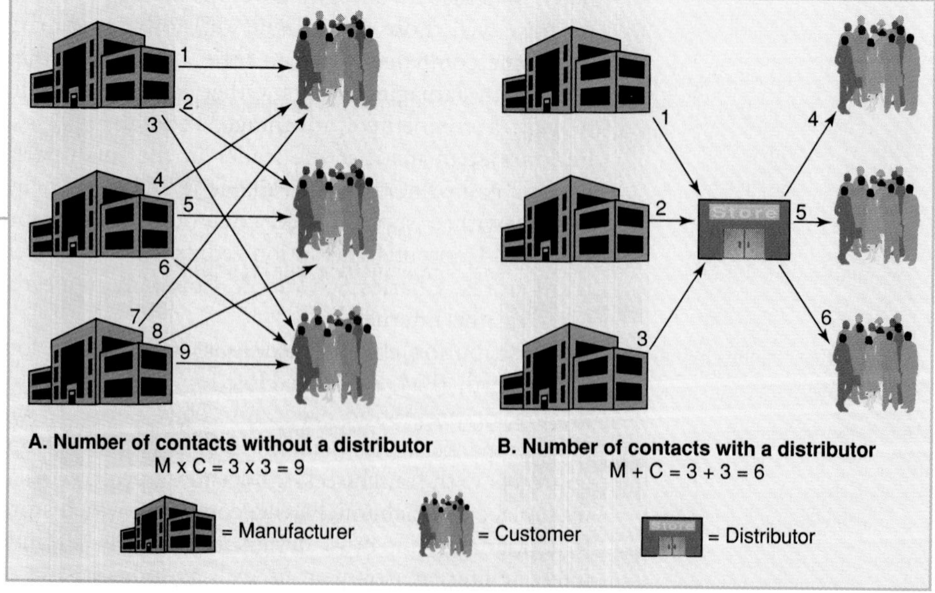

broader assortments wanted by consumers. Thus, intermediaries play an important role in matching supply and demand.

The concept of distribution channels is not limited to the distribution of tangible products. Producers of services and ideas also face the problem of making their output *available* to target populations. In the private sector, retail stores, hotels, banks, and other service providers take great care to make their services conveniently available to target customers. In the public sector, service organizations and agencies develop "educational distribution systems" and "health-care delivery systems" for reaching sometimes widely spread populations. Hospitals must be located to serve various patient populations, and schools must be located close to the children who need to be taught. Communities must locate their fire stations to provide rapid coverage of fires, and polling stations must be placed where people can vote conveniently.

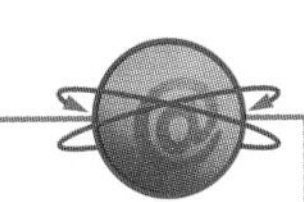

University of Calgary
www.ucalgary.ca/

Queen's University
www.queensu.ca/

Innovative universities are finding that they have to go to students if students are unable to come to them. For example, the University of Calgary forecasts that in just a few years, many of its students will be older, working, and taking classes off-campus. The university has joined a consortium of international universities that use computers to share professors, students, and ideas.[3] The term "distance education" has been coined to describe these programs. Queen's University has one of the most advanced systems of distance education. It was the first university to develop a national MBA program. Students work in study groups and are linked to professors through interactive video-conferencing facilities in 16 cities across Canada from Victoria to St. John's. Other universities, such as the University of Western Ontario, have been quick to follow suit.

Distribution Channel Functions

A distribution channel moves goods from producers to consumers. It overcomes the major time, place, and possession gaps that separate goods and services from those who would use them. Members of the marketing channel perform many key functions. Some help to complete transactions:

- *Information:* gathering and distributing marketing research and intelligence information about actors and forces in the marketing environment needed for planning and aiding exchange.
- *Promotion:* developing and spreading persuasive communications about an offer.
- *Contact:* finding and communicating with prospective buyers.
- *Matching:* shaping and fitting the offer to the buyer's needs, including such activities as manufacturing, grading, assembling, and packaging.
- *Negotiation:* reaching an agreement on price and other terms of the offer so that ownership or possession can be transferred.

Others help to fulfill the completed transactions:

- *Physical distribution:* transporting and storing goods.
- *Financing:* acquiring and using funds to cover the costs of the channel work.
- *Risk taking:* assuming the risks of carrying out the channel work.

The question is not *whether* these functions need to be performed—they must be—but rather *who* is to perform them. All the functions have three things in common: They use up scarce resources, they often can be performed better through specialization, and they can be shifted between channel members. To the extent that the manufacturer performs these functions, its costs go up and its prices have to be higher. At the same time, when some of these functions are shifted to intermediaries, the producer's costs and prices may be lower, but the intermediaries must charge more to cover the costs of their work. In dividing the work of the channel, the various functions should be assigned to the channel members who can perform them most efficiently and effectively to provide satisfactory assortments of goods to target consumers.

Channel level
A layer of intermediaries that performs some work in bringing the product and its ownership closer to the final buyer.

Direct marketing channel
A marketing channel that has no intermediary levels.

Number of Channel Levels

Distribution channels can be described by the number of channel levels involved. Each layer of marketing intermediaries that performs some work in bringing the product and its ownership closer to the final buyer is a **channel level.** Because the producer and the final consumer both perform some work, they are part of every channel. We use the number of intermediary levels to indicate the length of a channel. Figure 11-2A shows several consumer distribution channels of different lengths.

Channel 1, called a **direct marketing channel,** has no intermediary levels. It consists of a company selling directly to consumers. Avon, Amway, and Tupperware sell their products door to door or through home and office sales parties. Mountain Equipment Co-op sells clothing directly through mail order and by telephone, as well as through its own stores. Tilley Endurables Inc., makers of the famous Tilley hat sported by sailors, was among the award winners at the 12th Annual Catalogue Conference. The Tilley catalogue was praised because it uses no phony layout tricks, and staff members and customers of Tilley Endurables are used to model its clothing. The catalogue helps to differentiate the company since the owner's personality comes through every product description. Though Tilley's

Tilley Endurables Inc.
www.tilley.com/

FIGURE 11-2
Consumer and business marketing channels

Channel 1: Manufacturer → Consumer
Channel 2: Manufacturer → Retailer → Consumer
Channel 3: Manufacturer → Wholesaler → Retailer → Consumer
Channel 4: Manufacturer → Wholesaler → Jobber → Retailer → Consumer

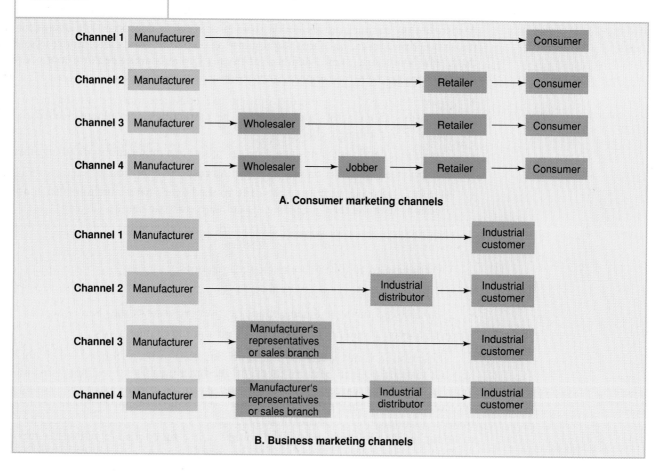

A. Consumer marketing channels

Channel 1: Manufacturer → Industrial customer
Channel 2: Manufacturer → Industrial distributor → Industrial customer
Channel 3: Manufacturer → Manufacturer's representatives or sales branch → Industrial customer
Channel 4: Manufacturer → Manufacturer's representatives or sales branch → Industrial distributor → Industrial customer

B. Business marketing channels

What other hat comes with a 4-page Owner's Manual?

Clearly, the Tilley is no ordinary Hat. Worn by peace-keepers and travellers alike, the Tilley is the happy result of one man's headstrong search for perfection. That man is Alex Tilley, who started out trying to design an impossible hat and ended up creating a Canadian legend. Now available in six distinct models, they float, tie on, repel water, and protect you rain or shine. Trends come and go, but a Tilley Hat is yours for life. Guaranteed for life by its persnickety inventor, AlexTilley maker, of the finest travel and adventure clothing in the world

Tilley Endurables

Call 1-800-ENDURES (1-800-363-8737) for Mail Order or the Tilley dealer nearest you.
Toronto: 900 Don Mills Rd. • Queen's Quay Terminal – 207 Queen's Quay W.
Montreal: 1050 Laurier Ave. W. • Vancouver: 2401 Granville St. • www.tilley.com

In a direct marketing channel, Tilley Endurables sells to Canadians and other customers around the world through its Web site and catalogue.

recent catalogues use professional models, the pages are full of real and, at times, amusing customer testimonials along with personal comments from Alex Tilley and his world-travelled daughter, Alison.

Indirect marketing channels
Channels containing one or more intermediary levels.

The remaining channels in Figure 11-2A are **indirect marketing channels.** Channel 2 contains one intermediary level. In consumer markets, this level is typically a retailer. The makers of televisions, cameras, tires, furniture, major appliances, and many other products sell their goods directly to large retailers such as Leon's and Sears, which then sell the goods to final consumers. Channel 3 contains two intermediary levels, a wholesaler and a retailer. This channel often is used by small manufacturers of food, drugs, hardware, and other products. Channel 4 contains three intermediary levels. In the meat-packing industry, for example, jobbers usually come between wholesalers and retailers. The jobber buys from wholesalers and sells to smaller retailers who generally are not served by larger wholesalers. Distribution channels with even more levels are sometimes found, but less often. From the producer's point of view, a greater number of levels means less control and greater channel complexity.

Figure 11-2B shows some common business distribution channels. The business marketer can use its own sales force to sell directly to business customers. It also can sell to industrial distributors, who in turn sell to business customers. It can sell through manufacturer's representatives or its own sales branches to business customers, or it can use these representatives and branches to sell through industrial distributors. Thus, business markets commonly include multi-level distribution channels.

All of the institutions in the channel are connected by several types of *flows.* These include the *physical flow* of products, the *flow of ownership,* the *payment flow,* the *information flow,* and the *promotion flow.* These flows can make even channels with only one or a few levels very complex.

Channel Behaviour and Organization

Distribution channels are more than simple collections of firms tied together by various flows. They are complex behavioural systems in which people and companies interact to accomplish individual, company, and channel goals. Some channel systems consist only of informal interactions among loosely organized firms; others consist of formal interactions guided by strong organizational structures. Moreover, channel systems do not stand still—new types of intermediaries surface, and whole new channel systems evolve. Here we look at channel behaviour and at how members organize to do the work of the channel.

Channel Behaviour

A distribution channel consists of firms that have banded together for their common good. Each channel member depends on the others. For example, a Ford dealer depends on the Ford Motor Company to design cars that meet consumer needs. In turn, Ford depends on the dealer to attract consumers, persuade them to buy Ford cars, and service cars after the sale. The Ford dealer also depends on other dealers to provide good sales and service that will uphold the reputation of Ford and its dealer body. In fact, the success of individual Ford dealers depends on how well the entire Ford distribution channel competes with the channels of other auto manufacturers.

Each channel member plays a role in the channel and specializes in performing one or more functions. For example, IBM's role is to produce personal computers that consumers will like and to create demand through national advertising. Future Shop's role is to display these IBM computers in convenient locations, to answer buyers' questions, to close sales, and to provide service. The channel is most effective when each member is assigned the tasks it can do best.

Because the success of individual channel members depends on overall channel success, all channel firms should work together smoothly. They should understand and accept their roles, coordinate their goals and activities, and cooperate to attain overall channel goals. By cooperating, they can more effectively sense, serve, and satisfy the target market.

However, individual channel members rarely take such a broad view. They are usually more concerned with their own short-run goals and their dealings with those firms closest to them in the channel. Cooperating to achieve overall channel goals sometimes means giving up individual company goals. Although channel members depend on one another, they often act alone in their own short-run best interests. They often disagree on the roles each should play—on who should do what and for what rewards. Such disagreements over goals and roles generate **channel conflict.**

Channel conflict
Disagreement between marketing channel members on goals and roles—who should do what and for what rewards.

Horizontal conflict occurs between firms at the same level of the channel. For instance, some Ford dealers complained about other dealers in their city who stole sales from them by being too aggressive in their pricing and advertising or by selling outside their assigned territories. Some Pizza Inn franchisees complained about other Pizza Inn franchisees cheating on ingredients, giving poor service, and hurting the overall Pizza Inn image.

Vertical conflict, which is more common, is that between different levels of the same channel. A recent instance took place when dealerships decided to wage war on Ford Canada:[4]

> Car dealerships are among Canada's largest small businesses. Their dilemma: They depend on a single supplier for their inventory, and minor disputes are frequent. However, in an unprecedented letter written in March 2000 sent to all Ford dealers in Canada, the president of the Canadian Automobile Dealers Association lashed out at Ford Canada for its "unilateral, autocratic and confrontational" actions that pose a "threat to the Canadian dealer network." The letter was written as a result of dealer complaints that arose as a result of Ford Canada's new retail strategy called Ford Retail Networks (FRN). Ford wants to limit dealer autonomy and institute more customer-friendly sales tactics such as single-price selling. To accomplish this, Ford Canada hopes to become a 40 percent shareholder in the dealers' operations. Dealers believe they are being forced to sell out to Ford as a result of "punitive performance contracts," and as a result, dialogue between Ford and its retailers has broken down.

Some conflict in the channel takes the form of healthy competition. Such competition can be good for the channel—without it, the channel could become passive and non-innovative. But sometimes conflict can damage the channel. For the channel as a whole to perform well, each channel member's role must be specified and channel conflict must be managed. Cooperation, role assignment, and conflict management in the channel are attained through strong channel leadership. The channel will perform better if it includes a firm, agency, or mechanism that has the power to assign roles and manage conflict.

Vertical Marketing Systems

Historically, distribution channels have been loose collections of independent companies, each showing little concern for overall channel performance. These *conventional distribution channels* have lacked strong leadership and have been troubled by damaging conflict and poor performance. An important recent channel development is the *vertical marketing systems* that have emerged to challenge conventional marketing channels. Figure 11-3 contrasts the two types of channel arrangements.

Conventional distribution channel
A channel consisting of one or more independent producers, wholesalers, and retailers, each a separate business seeking to maximize its own profits even at the expense of profits for the system as a whole.

Vertical marketing system (VMS)
A distribution channel structure in which producers, wholesalers, and retailers act as a unified system. One channel member owns the others, has contracts with them, or has so much power that they all cooperate.

A **conventional distribution channel** consists of one or more independent producers, wholesalers, and retailers. Each is a separate business seeking to maximize its own profits, even at the expense of profits for the system as a whole. No channel member has much control over the other members, and no formal means exists for assigning roles and resolving channel conflict. In contrast, a **vertical marketing system (VMS)**, which consists of the same players—producers, wholesalers, and retailers—acts as a unified system since one channel member owns the others, has contracts with them, or wields so much power that all members of the system cooperate. The VMS can be dominated by the producer, wholesaler, or retailer. Vertical marketing systems came into being to control channel behaviour and manage channel conflict. They achieve economies through size, bargaining power, and elimination of duplicated services. The three major types of VMSs are corporate, contractual, and administered. Each type uses a different means for setting up leadership and power in the channel.

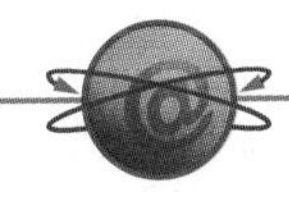

Goodyear Tire & Rubber Co.
www.goodyear.com/

Corporate VMS

Corporate VMS
A vertical marketing system that combines successive stages of production and distribution under single ownership—channel leadership is established through common ownership.

A **corporate VMS** combines successive stages of production and distribution under single ownership. In a corporate VMS, cooperation and conflict management are handled through regular organizational channels. For example, Sears obtains more than 50 percent of its goods from companies that it partly or wholly owns. Bell markets telephones and related equipment through its own chain of Bell World stores. George Weston Inc., owner of Loblaw, operates a soft-drink bottling operation, an ice-cream-making plant, and a bakery that supplies stores with everything from bagels to birthday cakes.

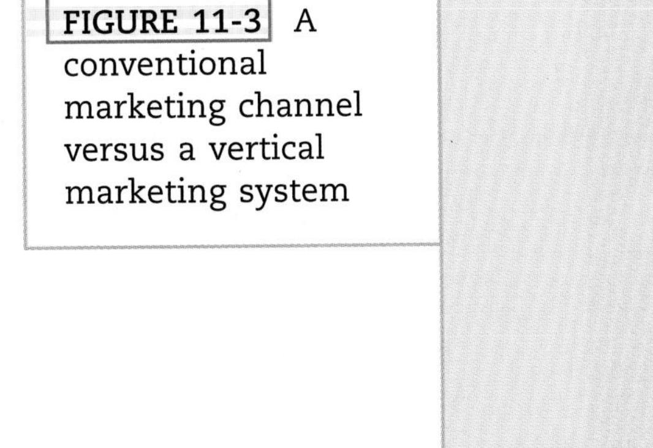

FIGURE 11-3 A conventional marketing channel versus a vertical marketing system

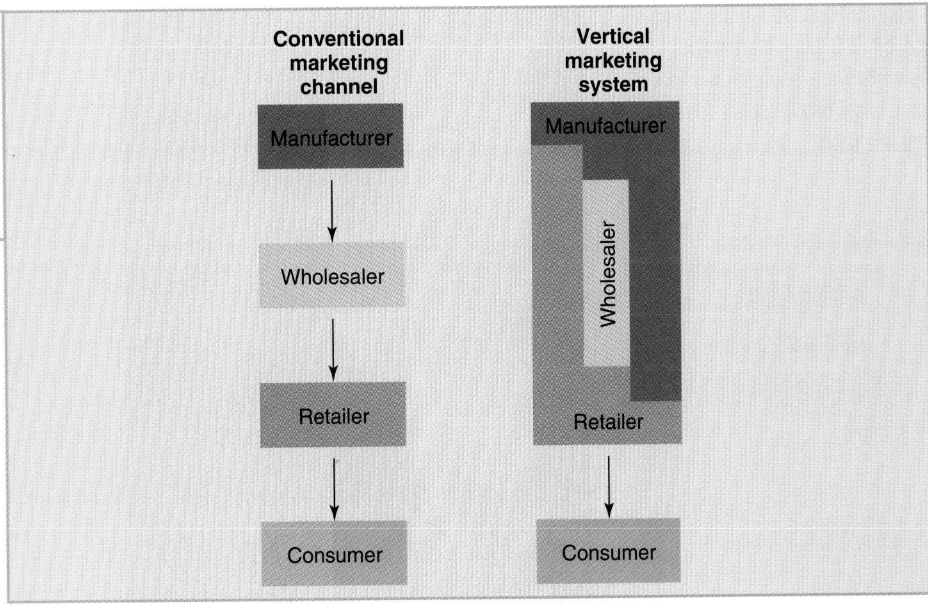

Gallo, the world's largest winemaker, does much more than simply turn grapes into wine. It owns the trucking firm that transports the wines, the bottling company that makes the containers, and even a firm that makes the bottle caps. Whereas most wineries concentrate on production while neglecting marketing, Gallo participates in every aspect of selling "short of whispering in the ear of each imbiber."[5]

Contractual VMS

Contractual VMS
A vertical marketing system in which independent firms at different levels of production and distribution join together through contracts to obtain more economies or sales impact than they could achieve alone.

Wholesaler-sponsored voluntary chains
Contractual vertical marketing systems in which wholesalers organize voluntary chains of independent retailers to help them compete with large corporate chain organizations.

Retailer cooperatives
Contractual vertical marketing systems in which retailers organize a new, jointly owned business to carry on wholesaling and possibly production.

A **contractual VMS** consists of independent firms at different levels of production and distribution that join together through contracts to obtain more economies or sales impact than each could achieve alone. Contractual VMSs have expanded rapidly in recent years. There are three types of contractual VMSs: wholesaler-sponsored voluntary chains, retailer cooperatives, and franchise organizations.

Wholesaler-sponsored voluntary chains are systems in which wholesalers organize voluntary chains of independent retailers to help them compete with large chain organizations. The wholesaler develops a program in which independent retailers standardize their selling practices and achieve buying economies that let the group compete effectively with chain organizations. Examples include the Independent Grocers Alliance (IGA) and Western Auto.

Retailer cooperatives are systems in which retailers organize a new, jointly owned business to carry on wholesaling and possibly production. Members buy most of their goods through the retailer co-op and plan their advertising jointly. Profits are passed back to members in proportion to their purchases. Nonmember retailers also may buy through the co-op but do not share in the profits. Cooperatives, which have a long history in Canada, are used to market services as well as products. In fact, thanks to the efforts of Alphonse and Dorimène Desjardins, founders of the first caisse populaire, le Mouvement Desjardins of Quebec recently celebrated its 100th anniversary. Today over 10 million Canadians (that's one in three) take advantage of retail banking services provided by Canada's more than 2000 credit unions. These financial institutions offer many of the same services as banks. However, they are member owned and devoted to cooperative principles and community service. In addition, through the services offered by Credit Union Central, they cooperate to offer such unique products as Ethical Mutual Funds.

Toronto's HEPCOE Credit Union, led by CEO Alan Marentette, benefits from being a member of a large retail cooperative organization.

Franchise organization
A contractual vertical marketing system in which a channel member, called a franchiser, links several stages in the production–distribution process.

In **franchise organizations,** a channel member called a *franchiser* links several stages in the production–distribution process. Franchising has been the fastest-growing retailing form in recent years. Canada has more than 65 000 franchise operations (four times more per capita than the United States) that ring up over $90 billion in sales. In fact, 40 percent of every dollar spent on retail items is spent at a franchise.[6] Almost every kind of business has been franchised—from motels and fast-food restaurants to dental centres and dating services, from wedding consultants and maid services to funeral homes and fitness centres. Although the basic idea is an old one, some forms of franchising are quite new.

The three forms of franchise systems are:

- *Manufacturer-sponsored retailer franchise system:* Found in the automobile industry. Ford, for example, licenses dealers to sell its cars; the dealers are independent businesspeople who agree to meet various conditions of sales and service.
- *Manufacturer-sponsored wholesaler franchise system:* Found in the soft-drink industry. Coca-Cola, for example, licenses bottlers (wholesalers) in various markets who buy Coca-Cola syrup concentrate and then carbonate, bottle, and sell the finished product to retailers in local markets.
- *Service-firm-sponsored retailer franchise system:* A service firm licenses a system of retailers to bring its service to consumers. Examples are found in the auto-rental business (Hertz, Avis); the fast-food service business (Tim Hortons); and the motel business (Holiday Inn, Ramada Inn).

The fact that most consumers cannot tell the difference between contractual and corporate VMSs shows how successfully the contractual organizations compete with corporate chains. Chapter 12 discusses the various contractual VMSs.

Administered VMS

Administered VMS
A vertical marketing system that coordinates successive stages of production and distribution, not through common ownership or contractual ties but through the size and power of one of the parties.

An **administered VMS** coordinates successive stages of production and distribution—not through common ownership or contractual ties but through the size and power of one of the parties. Manufacturers of a top brand can obtain strong trade cooperation and support from resellers. General Electric, Procter & Gamble, Kraft, and Campbell, for example, can command unusual cooperation from resellers regarding displays, shelf space, promotions, and price policies. And large retailers like The Bay and Toys 'R' Us can exert strong influence on the manufacturers that supply the products they sell.

Horizontal Marketing Systems

Horizontal marketing systems
A channel arrangement in which two or more companies at one level join together to follow a new marketing opportunity.

Another channel development is the **horizontal marketing system,** in which two or more companies at one level join together to follow a new marketing opportunity. By working together, companies can combine their capital, production capabilities, or marketing resources to accomplish more than any one company could alone. Companies can join forces with competitors or non-competitors.[7] They may work with each other on a temporary or permanent basis, or they may create a separate company. The operations of the system may be confined to the domestic market, or they may span the globe.

- Canada's two largest wineries, T.G. Bright & Co. Ltd. and Cartier & Inniskillin Vintners Inc., once major competitors, have merged. Together they have sales in excess of $130 million, placing them in the top 10 of North American wine marketers. Given the strength and size of large American vintners (such as Gallo, described earlier), the two formed an alliance so that they could have the economies of scale and resources necessary to export into the US market.

- Forming successful horizontal marketing systems is essential in an era of global business and global travel. Air Canada is part of the Star Alliance, whose partners include United Airlines, Lufthansa, SAS, and Thai Airways International. It battles other alliances such as the one formed by American Airlines, British Airways, Japan Airlines, and Qantas. This partnership allows Air Canada to offer flights to 642 US cities. It can also link the routes that the different partners fly so that passengers can have seamless travel around the world. Air Canada benefits from the marketing efforts of its partners in their home countries and bookings they make for travellers coming to Canada. These alliances improve customer satisfaction since they ensure passengers have shorter layovers, more convenient connections, and less hassle transferring their baggage.[8]

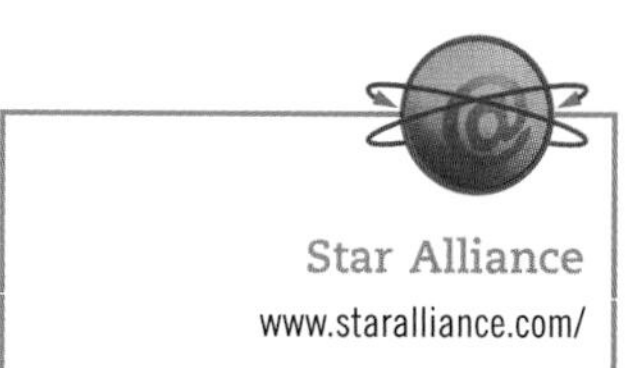

The number of horizontal marketing systems has increased dramatically in recent years, and the end is nowhere in sight.

Hybrid Marketing Systems

Hybrid marketing channels Multichannel distribution systems in which a single firm sets up two or more marketing channels to reach one or more customer segments.

In the past, many companies used a single channel to sell to a single market or market segment. Today, with the proliferation of customer segments and channel possibilities, many companies have adopted *multichannel distribution systems*—often called **hybrid marketing channels**—setting up two or more marketing channels to reach one or more customer segments. The use of hybrid channel systems has increased dramatically in recent years.

Membership in a horizontal marketing system helps Air Canada market its services efficiently worldwide.

FIGURE 11-4 Hybrid marketing channel

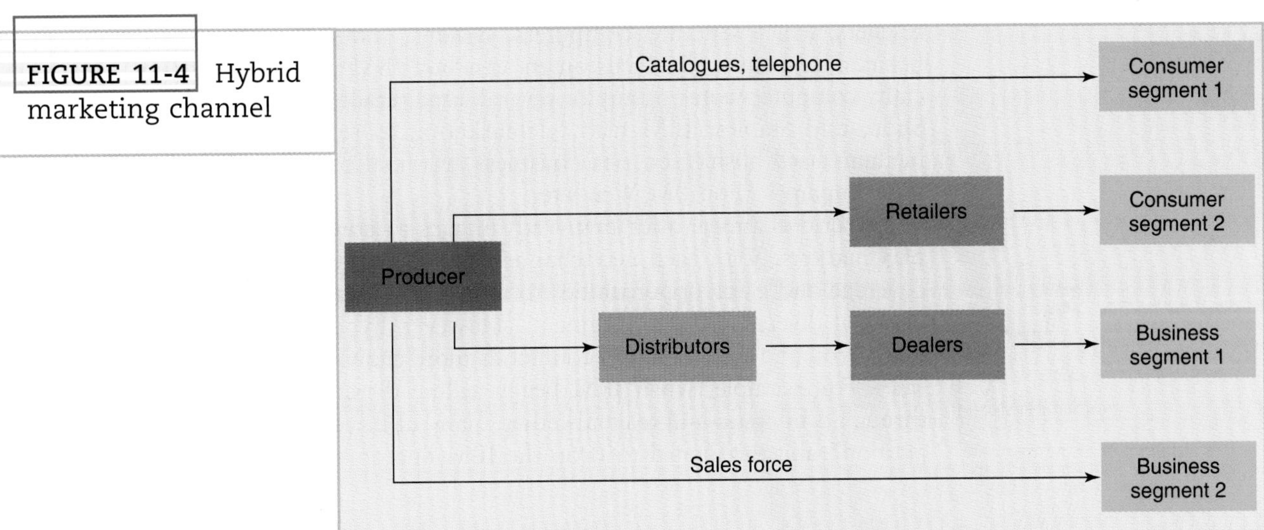

Figure 11-4 shows a hybrid channel. In the figure, the producer sells directly to consumer segment 1 using direct-mail catalogues and telemarketing, and reaches consumer segment 2 through retailers. It sells indirectly to business segment 1 through distributors and dealers, and to business segment 2 through its own sales force.

IBM uses such a hybrid channel effectively. For years, IBM sold computers only through its own sales force, which sold its large systems to business customers. However, the market for computers and information technology exploded into a profusion of products and services for dozens of segments and niches, ranging from large corporate buyers to small businesses to home and home office buyers. As a result, IBM had to dramatically rethink the way it goes to market. To serve the diverse needs of these many segments, IBM added 18 new channels in less than 10 years. In addition to selling through the vaunted IBM sales force, IBM also sells through a comprehensive network of distributors and value-added

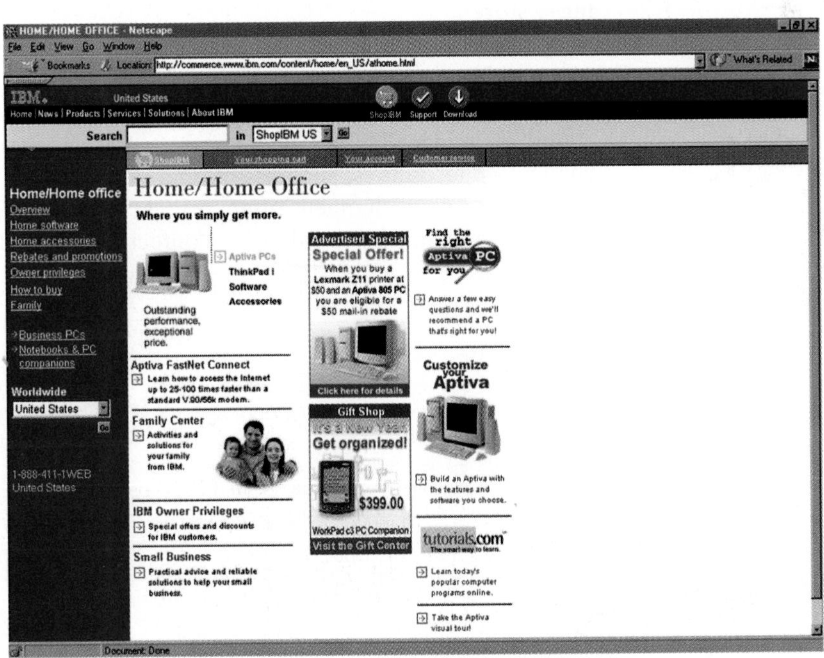

IBM uses a hybrid channel effectively, selling through its own sales force, distributors and value-added resellers, specialty computer stores and large retailers, and its ShopIBM Web site.

resellers, which sell IBM computers, systems, and services to a variety of special business segments. Final customers can buy IBM personal computers from specialty computer stores or any of several large retailers, including Wal-Mart, Future Shop, and Staples. IBM uses telemarketing to service the needs of small and medium-sized businesses. Both business and final consumers can buy online from the company's ShopIBM Web site.[9]

Hybrid channels offer many advantages to companies facing large and complex markets. With each new channel, the company expands its sales and market coverage and gains opportunities to tailor its products and services to the specific needs of diverse customer segments. However, hybrid channel systems are harder to control, and they generate conflict as more channels compete for customers and sales. For example, when IBM began selling directly to customers at low prices through catalogues and telemarketing, many of its retail dealers cried "unfair competition" and threatened to drop the IBM line or to give it less emphasis.

Changing Channel Organization

Changes in technology and the rapid growth of direct and online marketing are having a profound impact on the nature and design of marketing channels. One major trend is **disintermediation**—a big term with a clear message and important consequences. Disintermediation means that more and more, product and service producers are bypassing intermediaries and going directly to final buyers, or that radically new types of channel intermediaries are emerging to displace traditional ones.

Disintermediation
Removing traditional intermediaries to sell directly to final buyers.

Thus, in many industries, traditional intermediaries are dropping by the wayside. Companies like Dell Computer are selling directly to final buyers, eliminating retailers from their marketing channels. E-commerce merchants are growing rapidly in number and size, displacing some traditional bricks-and-mortar retailers. Consumers can buy flowers from 1-800-Flowers.com; books, videos, CDs, toys, and other goods from Chapters.ca or Indigo.ca; household products from Wal-Mart; groceries from GroceryGateway.com; clothes from Danier Leather or Roots; and consumer electronics from buy.com, all without ever visiting a store.

Disintermediation presents problems and opportunities for both producers and intermediaries (see Marketing Highlight 11-1). To avoid being swept aside, traditional intermediaries must find new ways to add value in the supply chain. To remain competitive, product and service producers must develop new channel opportunities, such as Internet and other direct channels. However, developing these new channels often brings them into direct competition with their established channels, resulting in conflict. To ease this problem, companies often look for ways to make going direct a plus for both the company and its channel partners:

> Going direct is rarely an all-or-nothing proposition. To trim costs and add business, Hewlett-Packard opened three direct-sales Web sites—Shopping Village (for consumers), HP Commerce Center (for businesses buying from authorized resellers), and Electronic Solutions Now (for existing contract customers). However, to avoid conflicts with its established reseller channels, HP forwards all its Web orders to resellers, who complete the orders, ship the products, and get the commissions. In this way, HP gains the advantages of direct selling but also boosts business for resellers. Unfortunately, although this compromise system reduces conflicts, it also creates inefficiencies. "That all sounds great and everyone's happy," says a distribution consultant, "but kicking the customer over to the reseller . . . is a lot more expensive than letting customers order directly from the manufacturer. HP is spending a fair chunk of change to set this up, plus the business partner still wants eight percent margins for getting the product to the customer." To be truly efficient in the long run, HP eventually will have to find ways for its resellers to add value or drop them from the direct channel.[10]

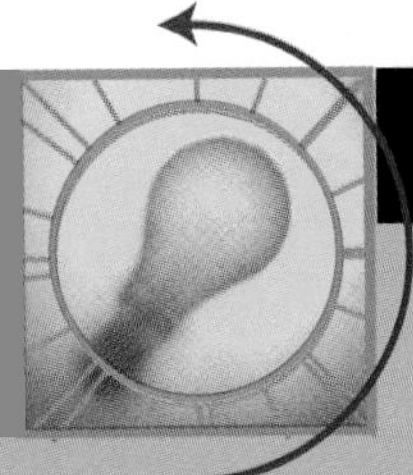

marketing highlight 11-1

Disintermediation: A Fancy Word but a Clear Message

Bayridge Travel in Kingston, Ontario typifies the kind of business most threatened by the advent of new marketing channels, particularly the surge in Internet selling. They fear travellers like Canada's Internet guru, Jim Carroll, who notes that, "In the last two years, I've bought some $75 000 worth of airline tickets on the Internet. . . . By doing so directly through the Web sites of various airlines, I've cut travel agents out of several thousand dollars worth of commissions."

Thus, like other traditional travel agencies, Bayridge faces some scary new competitors: giant online travel supersites such as Expedia or Travelocity, which let consumers surf the Web for rock-bottom ticket prices. To make matters worse, the airlines themselves are opening Web sites to sell seats, not only their own but competitors' as well. For example, visitors to the United Airlines Web site can purchase tickets on more than 500 other airlines. These new channels give consumers more choices, but they threaten the very existence of Bayridge Travel and other traditional travel agents.

Resellers in dozens of industries face similar situations as new channel forms threaten to make them obsolete. There's even a fancy 17-letter word to describe this phenomenon: *disintermediation*. Bob Westrope, director of the electronic markets group with KPMG in Toronto, believes it represents "a shift in the structure of our economy not seen since the dawning of the industrial age." Strictly speaking, disintermediation means the elimination of a layer of intermediaries from a marketing channel. For example, for years personal computer makers assumed that customers needed hands-on buying experience, with lots of point-of-sale inventory and hand-holding sales assistance from retailers. Then, along came Dell Computer with a new distribution formula: Bypass retailers and sell made-to-order computers directly to consumers. By eliminating retailers, Dell eliminated many costs and inefficiencies from the traditional computer supply chain.

More broadly, disintermediation includes not just the elimination of channel levels through direct marketing but also the displacement of traditional resellers by radically new types of intermediaries. For example, the publishing industry had for decades assumed that book buyers wanted to purchase their books from small, intimate neighbourhood bookshops. Then, along came the book superstores—Barnes & Noble and Chapters—with their huge inventories and low prices. Disintermediation occurred as the new intermediaries rapidly displaced traditional independent booksellers. Then, most recently, online booksellers like Amazon.com and Indigo.ca emerged to threaten the category killers. Amazon.com doesn't eliminate the retail channel—it's actually a new type of retailer that increases consumers' channel choices rather than reducing them. Still, disintermediation has occurred as Amazon.com and the superstores' own Web sites are displacing traditional bricks-and-mortar retailers.

Disintermediation is often associated with the surge in e-commerce and online selling. In fact, the Internet is a major disintermediating force. By facilitating direct contact between buyers and sellers, the Internet is displacing channels in industries ranging from books, apparel, toys, drugs, and consumer electronics to travel, stock brokerage, and real estate services. However, disintermediation can involve almost any new form of channel competition. For example, Dell bypassed retailers through telephone and mail-order selling long before it took to the Internet.

Disintermediation works only when a new channel form succeeds in bringing greater value to consumers. Thus, if Amazon.com weren't giving buyers greater convenience, selection, and value, it wouldn't be able to lure customers away from traditional retailers. If Dell's direct channel weren't more efficient and effective in serving the needs of computer buyers, traditional retail channels would have little to fear. However, the huge success of these new channels suggests that they are bringing greater value to significant segments of consumers.

From a producer's viewpoint, although eliminating unneeded intermediaries makes sense, disintermediation can be very difficult. One analyst summarizes this way:

> You thought electronic commerce would bring nothing but good news. Here at last, you reasoned, is a way to add customers, boost market share, and cut sales costs. All manufacturers have to do is set up an electronic conduit between themselves and their customers and voilà, instant sales channel. There's just one little hitch. Those same thoughts terrify the retailers, distributors, and resellers that account for up to 90 percent of manufacturers' revenues. They fear that their role between company and customer will be rendered obsolete by the virtual marketplace. And that puts manufacturers in a bind. Either they surrender to the seductions of e-commerce and risk a mutiny from those valuable partners, or they do nothing and risk the wrath of [successful e-commerce competitors].

Thus, Dell had the advantage of starting from scratch in designing its direct channel—it didn't have to jump from one channel model to another. However, for Compaq, IBM, and other computer producers that are already locked into traditional retail channels, disintermediation presents real problems. To compete more effectively with Dell, both Compaq and IBM have now developed their own direct sales operations. For instance, Compaq has shifted its ratio of traditional channel sales to direct sales from 98 to 2 only a year ago to about 80 to 20 today. However, although the direct channel helps Compaq to compete better with Dell, it worries and displeases the established retail partners that Compaq counts on for the bulk of its sales.

Still, most producers know that when more effective channels come along, they have no choice but to change. There is a Dell at work or in waiting in every industry, and traditional producers can't afford to wait very long to get inefficiencies out of their distribution channels. For example, many of Canada's banks and credit unions are moving rapidly away from their bricks-and-mortar branches to electronic banking as they face new competitors, like ING Direct. Thus, despite the risks, most companies are more afraid of being late to

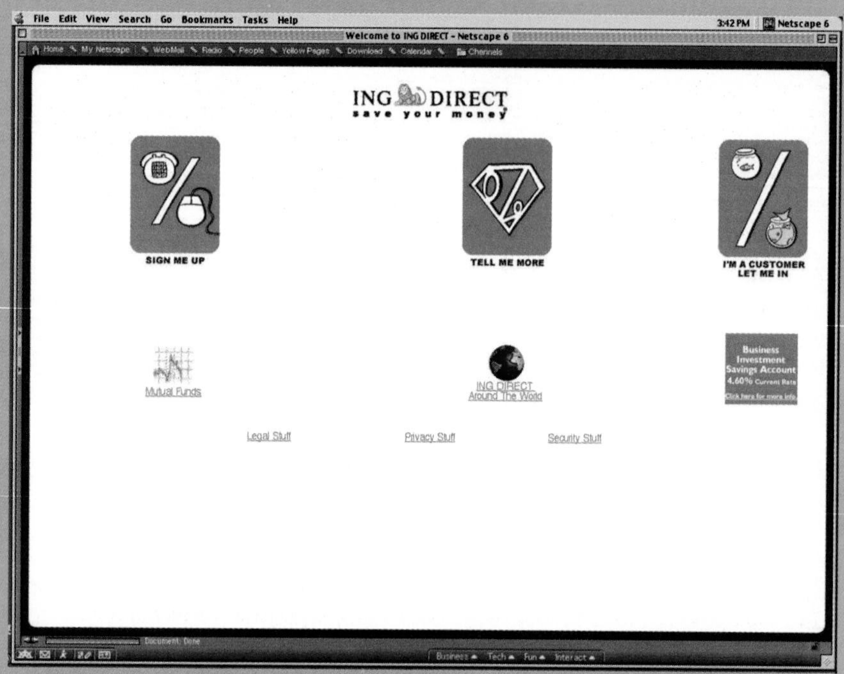

Electronic marketer ING Direct is forcing banks and credit unions to change their distribution strategies.

stead of becoming just another no-frills Internet trading operation, Schwab has done competitors one better. It plies customers with a wealth of financial and company information, helping them to research and manage their accounts and assuming the role of investment adviser. Schwab is even teaching courses on Web trading at some of its 300 branches. Thus, rather than dragging its feet or fighting the change, Schwab embraced the new channel as a competitive opportunity. The gamble paid off handsomely. Schwab remains North America's largest discount stockbroker and ranks number one online with a 28 percent share of the online market, twice the share of nearest competitor E*Trade.

Disintermediation is a big word, but the meaning is clear. Those who continually seek new ways to add real value for customers have little to fear. However, those who fall behind in adding value risk being swept aside by their customers and channel partners.

the party than of angering their channel partners. For many businesses, the major question often is not whether to move to a new, high-growth channel but how quickly and what to do with the established channel.

What about traditional resellers? How can they avoid being "Amazoned"? The answer lies in continually looking for new ways to create real customer value. Many companies threatened by Internet competitors have themselves learned to leverage the Web to serve customers better. For example, Bayridge Travel now de-emphasizes airline ticket sales and specializes in a market niche—cruises. The owner plans to do what computers can't: She will get to know her customers so well that she can provide personal advice on the cruises she books. Still, she'll use a Web site to launch this newly reformulated travel business.

Discount brokerage Charles Schwab & Company also proves the value point. Facing a horde of price-cutting e-commerce competitors who got there first—including E*Trade—Schwab jumped into the Internet with both feet. However, in-

Sources: Quotes from Jim Carroll, "Futures: When old partners become new competitors," *Marketing On-Line,* 22 November 1999; Rochelle Garner, "Mad as hell," *Sales & Marketing Management,* June 1999:55–61; and Maricris G. Briones, "What technology wrought: Distribution channel in flux," *Marketing News,* 1 February 1999:3,15. Also see "Special report: Technology and communications tools for marketers: Disintermediation: No more middleman," *Strategy,* 1 March 1999–21; Evan I. Schwartz, "How middlemen can come out on top," *Business Week,* 9 February 1998:ENT4-7; James Champy, "How to fire your dealers," *Forbes,* 14 June 1999:141; Stewart Alsop, "Is there an Amazon.com for every industry?" *Fortune,* 11 January 1999:159–60; and Daniel Roth, "E*Trade's plan for world domination," *Fortune,* 2 August 1999:95–8.

Channel Design Decisions

We shall now look at several channel decisions facing manufacturers. In designing marketing channels, manufacturers struggle between what is ideal and what is practical. A new firm usually starts by selling in a limited market area. Because it has limited capital, it typically uses only a few existing intermediaries in each market—a few manufacturers' sales agents, a few wholesalers, some existing retailers, a few trucking companies, and a few warehouses. Deciding on the *best* channels might not be a problem: The problem might simply be how to convince one or a few good intermediaries to handle the line.

If the new firm is successful, it may branch out to new markets. In smaller markets, the firm may sell directly to retailers; in larger markets, it may sell through distributors. In one part of the country, it may grant exclusive franchises because that is the way merchants normally work; in another, it may sell through all outlets willing to handle the merchandise. In this way, channel systems often evolve to meet market opportunities and conditions. However, for maximum effectiveness, channel analysis and decision making should be more purposeful. Designing a channel system calls for analyzing consumer service needs, setting the channel objectives and constraints, identifying the major channel alternatives, and evaluating them.

Analyzing Consumer Service Needs

Marketing channels can be thought of as *customer value delivery systems* in which each channel member adds value for the customer. Thus, designing the distribution channel starts with determining what values consumers in various target segments want from the channel.[11] Do consumers want to buy from nearby locations or are they willing to travel to more distant centralized locations? Would they rather buy over the phone or through the mail? Do they want immediate delivery or are they willing to wait? Do consumers value breadth of assortment or do they prefer specialization? Do consumers want many add-on services (delivery, credit, repairs, installation) or will they obtain these elsewhere? The more decentralized the channel, the faster the delivery; the greater the assortment provided, and the more add-on services supplied, the greater the channel's service level.

But providing the fastest delivery, greatest assortment, and most services may not be possible or practical. The company and its channel members may not have the resources or skills needed to provide all the desired services. Also, providing higher levels of service results in higher costs for the channel and higher prices for consumers. The company must balance consumer service needs not only against the feasibility and costs of meeting these needs but also against customer price preferences. The success of off-price and discount retailing shows that consumers are often willing to accept lower service levels if this means lower prices.

Setting the Channel Objectives and Constraints

In the first phase of creating channels, the company states its channel objectives in terms of the desired service level of target consumers; usually, several segments want different levels of channel service. It then decides which segments to serve and the best channels to use in each case. In each segment, the company wants to minimize the total channel cost of meeting customer service requirements.

The company's channel objectives are influenced by its nature, products, marketing intermediaries, competitors, and the environment. For example, the company's size and financial situation determine which marketing functions it can handle itself and which it must give to intermediaries. Companies selling perishable products may require more direct marketing to avoid delays and too much handling. In some cases, a company may want to compete in or near the same outlets that carry competitors' products. In other cases, producers may avoid the channels used by competitors. Avon, for example, set up a profitable door-to-door selling operation rather than going head-to-head with other cosmetics makers for scarce positions in retail stores. Finally, environmental factors such as economic conditions and legal constraints can affect channel objectives and design. For example, in a depressed economy, producers want to distribute their goods in the most economical way, using shorter channels and dropping unneeded services that add to the final price of the goods.

Identifying Major Alternatives

Once it has defined its channel objectives, the company identifies its major channel alternatives in terms of *types* of intermediaries, *number* of intermediaries, and the *responsibilities* of each channel member.

Product characteristics affect channel decisions: Fresh flowers must be delivered quickly with minimum handling.

Types of Intermediaries

A firm should identify the types of channel members available to carry out its channel work. For example, suppose a manufacturer of test equipment has developed an audio device that detects poor mechanical connections in any machine with moving parts. Company executives think this product would have a market in all industries where electric, combustion, or steam engines are made or used. This market includes such industries as aviation, automobile, railway, food canning, construction, and oil. The company's current sales force is small, and the problem is how best to reach these different industries. The following channel alternatives may emerge from management discussion:

- *Company sales force.* Expand the company's direct sales force. Assign salespeople to territories and have them contact all prospects in the area or develop separate company sales forces for different industries.
- *Manufacturer's agency.* Hire manufacturer's agents—independent firms whose sales forces handle related products from many companies—in different regions or industries to sell the new test equipment.
- *Industrial distributors.* Find distributors in the different regions or industries who will buy and carry the new line. Give them exclusive distribution, good margins, product training, and promotional support.

Sometimes it is too difficult or expensive to use a preferred channel and the company must develop another one. Sometimes new forms of distribution evolve for old products. The pharmacy industry in Canada has been challenged by a new type of intermediary—the emerging drugs-by-mail companies. Although less than one percent of prescriptions are filled by mail in Canada, the concept is catching on. When two Canadian entrepreneurs found that they couldn't buy goods from their favourite American online retailers because they either refused to ship to Canada or they required the payment of exorbitant shipping fees, they founded ShipToCanada.com Inc. They are betting that American businesses will find it quicker and easier to use their turnkey service rather than setting up their own shipping departments to handle Canadian orders.[12]

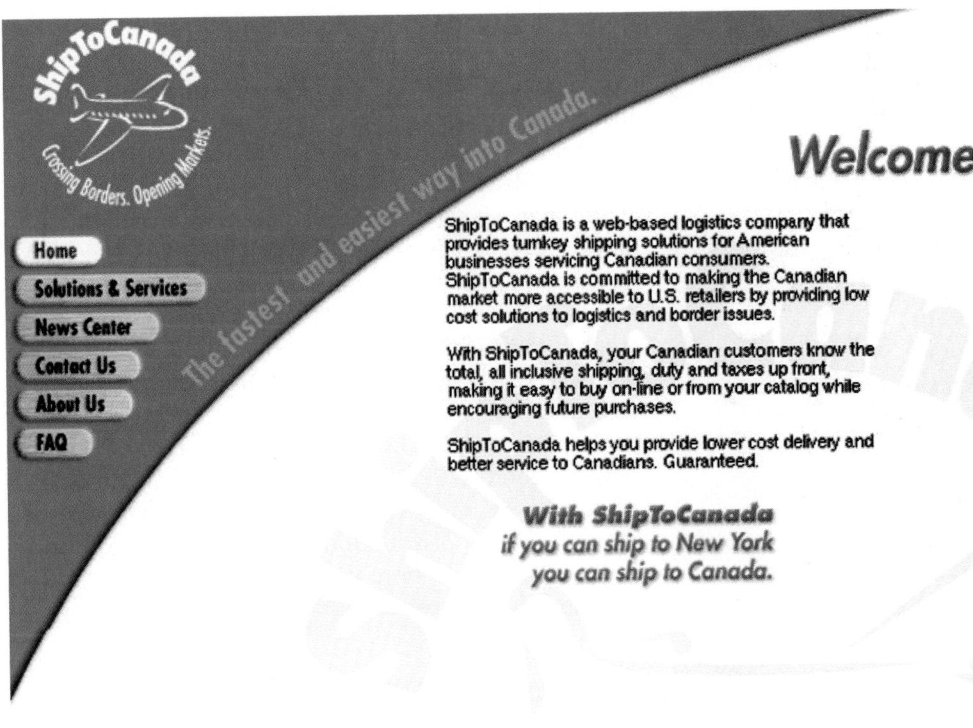

New logistics businesses, like ShipToCanada.com, have been founded to serve the needs of Internet marketers.

Number of Marketing Intermediaries

A company also must determine the number of channel members to use at each level. Three strategies are available: intensive distribution, exclusive distribution, and selective distribution.

Intensive distribution
Stocking the product in as many outlets as possible.

Producers of convenience products and common raw materials typically seek **intensive distribution**—a strategy in which they stock their products in as many outlets as possible. These goods must be available where and when consumers want them. For example, toothpaste, candy, and other similar items are sold in millions of outlets to provide maximum brand exposure and consumer convenience. Warner Lambert, Campbell, Coca-Cola, and other consumer goods companies distribute their products in this way.

Exclusive distribution
Giving a limited number of dealers the exclusive right to distribute the company's products in their territories.

By contrast, some producers deliberately limit the number of intermediaries handling their products. The extreme form of this practice is **exclusive distribution,** in which the producer gives only a limited number of dealers the exclusive right to distribute its products in their territories. New automobiles and prestige women's clothing often enjoy exclusive distribution. For example, Rolls-Royce dealers are few and far between—even large cities may have only one or two dealers. By granting exclusive distribution, Rolls-Royce gains stronger distrib-

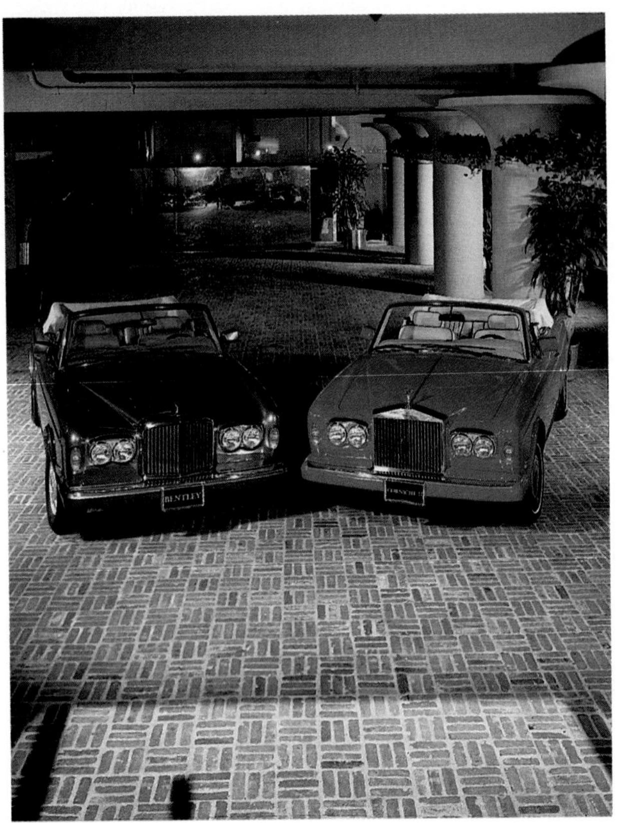

Rolls-Royce sells exclusively through a limited number of dealerships. Such exclusive distribution enhances the car's image and generates stronger dealer support.

utor selling support and more control over dealer prices, promotion, credit, and services. Exclusive distribution also enhances the car's image and allows for higher markups.

Between intensive and exclusive distribution lies **selective distribution**—the use of more than one but fewer than all of the intermediaries who are willing to carry a company's products. Most television, furniture, and small appliance brands are distributed in this manner. For example, Maytag, Whirlpool, and General Electric sell their major appliances through dealer networks and selected large retailers. By using selective distribution, they do not have to spread their efforts over many outlets, including many marginal ones. They can develop good working relationships with selected channel members and expect a better-than-average selling effort. Selective distribution gives producers good market coverage with more control and less cost than does intensive distribution.

Selective distribution
The use of more than one but fewer than all of the intermediaries who are willing to carry the company's products.

Responsibilities of Channel Members

The producer and intermediaries must agree on the terms and responsibilities of each channel member. They must agree on price policies, conditions of sale, territorial rights, and specific services to be performed by each party. The producer should establish a list price and a fair set of discounts for intermediaries. It must define each channel member's territory, and it should be careful about where it places new resellers. Mutual services and duties need to be spelled out carefully, especially in franchise and exclusive distribution channels. For example, Tim Hortons provides franchisees with promotional support, a record-keeping system, training, and general management assistance. In turn, franchisees must meet company standards for physical facilities, cooperate with new promotion programs, provide requested information, and buy specified food products.

Evaluating the Major Alternatives

Suppose a company has identified several channel alternatives and wants to select the one that will best satisfy its long-run objectives. The firm must evaluate each alternative against economic, control, and adaptive criteria.

Using *economic criteria,* a company compares the likely profitability of the channel alternatives. It estimates the sales that each channel would produce and the costs of selling different volumes through each channel. The company must also consider *control issues.* Using intermediaries usually means giving them some control over the marketing of the product, and some intermediaries take more control than others. Other things being equal, the company prefers to retain as much control as possible. Finally, the company must apply *adaptive criteria.* Channels often involve long-term commitments to other firms, making it difficult to adapt the channel to the changing marketing environment. The company wants to keep the channel as flexible as possible. Thus, to be considered, a channel involving long-term commitment should be greatly superior on economic and control grounds.

Designing International Distribution Channels

International marketers face many additional complexities in designing their channels. Each country has its own unique distribution system that has evolved over time and changes very slowly. These channel systems can vary widely from country to country. Thus, global marketers usually must adapt their channel strategies to the existing structures within each country. In some markets, the distribution system is complex and hard to penetrate, consisting of many layers and large numbers of intermediaries. Consider Japan:[13]

> The Japanese distribution system stems from the early seventeenth century when cottage industries and a [quickly growing] urban population spawned a merchant class. . . . Despite Japan's economic achievements, the distribution system has remained remarkably faithful to its antique pattern. . . . [It] encompasses a wide range of wholesalers and other agents, brokers, and retailers, differing more in number than in function from their [North] American counterparts. There are myriad tiny retail shops. An even greater number of wholesalers supplies goods to them, layered tier upon tier, many more than most [North American] executives would think necessary. For example, soap may move through three wholesalers plus a sales company after it leaves the manufacturer before it ever reaches the retail outlet. A steak goes from rancher to consumers in a process that often involves a dozen middle agents. . . . The distribution network . . . reflects the traditionally close ties among many Japanese companies . . . [and places] much greater emphasis on personal relationships with users. . . . Although [these channels appear] inefficient and cumbersome, they seem to serve the Japanese customer well. . . . Lacking much storage space in their small homes, most Japanese homemakers shop several times a week and prefer convenient [and more personal] neighbourhood shops.

Many Western firms have had great difficulty breaking into the closely knit, tradition-bound Japanese distribution network.

At the other extreme, distribution systems in developing countries may be scattered and inefficient, or altogether lacking. China and India are huge markets, each containing hundreds of millions of people. In reality, however, these markets are much smaller than the population numbers suggest. Because of inadequate distribution systems in both countries, most companies can profitably access only a small portion of the population located in each country's most affluent cities.[14]

The Japanese distribution system is remarkably traditional: A profusion of tiny retail shops is supplied by an even greater number of small wholesalers.

Thus, international marketers face a wide range of channel alternatives. Designing efficient and effective channel systems between and within various country markets poses a difficult challenge. We discuss international distribution decisions further in Chapter 18.

Channel Management Decisions

Once the company has reviewed its channel alternatives and decided on the best channel design, it must implement and manage the chosen channel. Channel management calls for selecting and motivating individual channel members and evaluating their performance over time.

Selecting Channel Members

Producers vary in their ability to attract qualified marketing intermediaries. Some producers have no trouble signing up channel members. For example, Toyota had no trouble attracting new dealers for its Lexus line. In fact, it had to turn down many would-be resellers. In some cases, the promise of exclusive or selective distribution for a desirable product will draw plenty of applicants.

At the other extreme are producers who have to work hard to line up enough qualified intermediaries. For example, in 1986 when distributors were approached about an unknown, new game called Nintendo, many refused to carry the product: They had recently been burned by the failure of Atari. But two Canadian distributors, Larry Wasser and Morey Chaplick, owners of Beamscope, accepted the product. Not a bad move considering that within one year after that decision, their sales went from next to nothing to $24 million![15]

Nintendo
www.nintendo.com/

When selecting intermediaries, the company should determine what characteristics distinguish the better ones. It will want to evaluate the channel member's years in business, other lines carried, growth and profit record, cooperativeness, and reputation. If the intermediaries are sales agents, the company will want to evaluate the number and character of other lines carried, and the size and quality of the sales force. If the intermediary is a retail store that wants exclusive or selective distribution, the company will want to evaluate the store's customers, location, and future growth potential.

Motivating Channel Members

Selected channel members must be continuously motivated to do their best. The company must sell not only *through* the intermediaries but also *to* them. Most producers see the problem as finding ways to gain intermediary cooperation. They use the carrot-and-stick approach. At times they offer such *positive* motivators as higher margins, special deals, premiums, cooperative advertising allowances, display allowances, and sales contests. At other times they use such *negative* motivators as threatening to reduce margins, slow down delivery, or end the relationship altogether. A producer using this approach usually has not done a good job of studying the needs, problems, strengths, and weaknesses of its distributors.

More advanced companies try to forge long-term partnerships with their distributors. This involves building a planned, professionally managed, vertical marketing system that meets the needs of both the manufacturer *and* the distributors.[16] Procter & Gamble and Wal-Mart work together to create superior value for final consumers. They jointly plan merchandising goals and strategies, inventory levels, and advertising and promotion plans. Similarly, General Electric works closely with its smaller independent dealers to help them be successful in selling the company's products (see Marketing Highlight 11-2). In managing its channels, a company must convince distributors that they can make their money by being part of an advanced vertical marketing system.

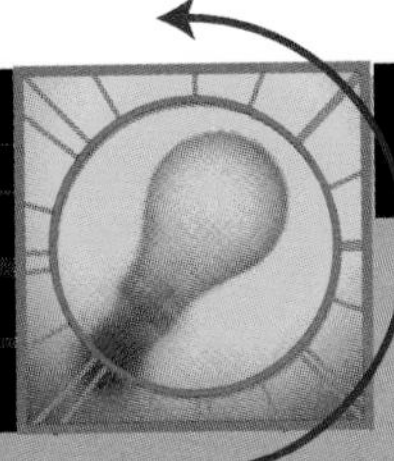

marketing highlight 11-2

General Electric Adopts a "Virtual Inventory" System to Support Its Dealers

Before the late 1980s, General Electric worked at selling through its dealers rather than to them or with them. GE operated a traditional system of trying to load up the channel with GE appliances, on the premise that "loaded dealers are loyal dealers." Loaded dealers would have less space to feature other brands and would recommend GE appliances to reduce their high inventories. To load its dealers, GE would offer the lowest price when the dealer ordered a full-truck load of its appliances.

GE eventually realized that this approach created many problems, especially for smaller independent appliance dealers who could not afford to carry a large stock. These dealers were hard-pressed to meet price competition from larger multibrand dealers. Rethinking its strategy from the point of view of creating dealer satisfaction and profitability, GE created an alternative distribution model called the Direct Connect system. Under this system, GE dealers carry only display models. They rely on a "virtual inventory" to fill orders. Dealers can access GE's order-processing system 24 hours a day, check on model availability, and place orders for next-day delivery. Using the Direct Connect system, dealers also can get GE's best price, financing from GE Credit, and no interest charges for the first 90 days.

Dealers benefit by having much lower inventory costs while still having a large virtual inventory available to satisfy their customers' needs. In exchange for this benefit, dealers must commit to selling nine major GE product categories, generating 50 percent of their sales from GE products, opening their books to GE for review, and paying GE every month through electronic funds transfer.

As a result of Direct Connect, dealer profit margins have skyrocketed. GE also has benefited. Its dealers now are more committed and dependent on GE, and the new order-entry system has saved GE substantial clerical costs. GE now knows the actual sales of its goods at the retail level, which helps it to schedule its production more accurately. It now can produce in response to demand rather than to meet inventory replenishment rules. And GE has been able to simplify its warehouse locations so as to be able to deliver appliances to 90 percent of its customers within 24 hours. Thus, by forging a partnership, GE has helped both its dealers and itself.

Source: See Michael Treacy and Fred Wiersema, "Customer intimacy and other discipline values," *Harvard Business Review,* January–February 1993:84–93.

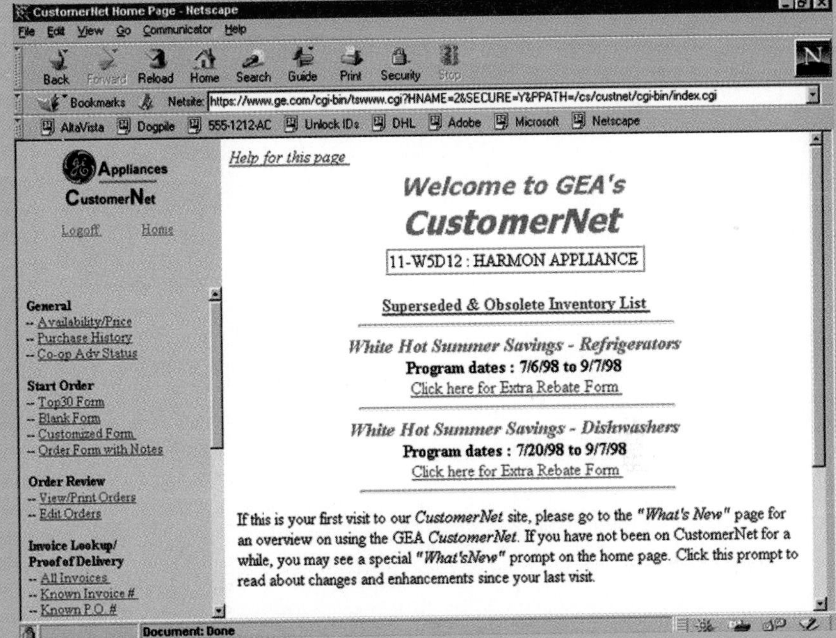

GE creates dealer satisfaction and profitability with its Customer Net system, benefiting both dealers and GE.

Evaluating Channel Members

The producer must regularly check each channel member's performance against such standards as sales quotas, average inventory levels, customer delivery time, treatment of damaged and lost goods, cooperation in company promotion and training programs, and services to the customer. The company should recognize and reward intermediaries who are performing well. Those who are performing poorly should be helped or, as a last resort, replaced.

Finally, manufacturers need to be sensitive to their dealers. Those who treat their dealers lightly risk not only losing their support but also causing some legal problems. Marketing Highlight 11-3 describes the rights and duties of manufacturers and their channel members.

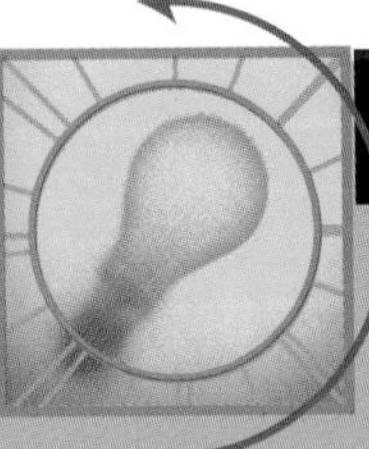

marketing highlight 11-3

Public Policy and Distribution Ethics

Supply chain management, logistics, and distribution present managers with countless ethical dilemmas, concerning what types of suppliers a company should use to the types and uses of power that are appropriate to ensure channel members comply with channel policies. The American Marketing Association (AMA) code of ethics (under which Canadian marketers also operate) focuses on issues of market power in the section dealing with distribution. Ethical marketers are advised to not manipulate product availability for purposes of exploitation and to not use coercion in the marketing channel. This code puts into question practices around these issues:

Exclusive Dealing

Many producers and wholesalers like to develop exclusive channels for their products. When the seller allows only certain outlets to carry its products, this strategy is called *exclusive distribution.* When the seller requires that these dealers not handle competitors' products, its strategy is called *exclusive dealing.* Both parties benefit from exclusive arrangements: The seller obtains more loyal and dependable outlets, and the dealers obtain a steady source of supply and stronger seller support. But exclusive arrangements exclude other producers from selling to these dealers. They are legal as long as they do not substantially lessen competition or tend to create a monopoly and as long as both parties enter into the agreement voluntarily.

Exclusive Territories

Exclusive dealing often includes exclusive territorial agreements. The producer may agree to not sell to other dealers in a given area, or the buyer may agree to sell only in its own territory. The first practice is normal under franchise systems as a way to increase dealer enthusiasm and commitment. It is also perfectly legal—a seller has no legal obligation to sell through more outlets than it wishes. The second practice, whereby the producer tries to keep a dealer from selling outside its territory, has become a major legal issue.

Tying Agreements

Producers of a strong brand sometimes sell it to dealers only if the dealers will take some or all of the rest of the line—*full-line forcing.* Even though the practice isn't illegal, it causes considerable channel conflict.

Dealers' Rights

Producers are free to select their dealers, but their right to terminate dealers is somewhat restricted. In general, sellers can drop dealers "for cause." But they cannot drop dealers if, for example, the dealers refuse to cooperate in a doubtful legal arrangement, such as exclusive dealing or tying agreements.

Sources of Supply

As price competition increases in many industries, many firms look to overseas suppliers who can provide them with low-cost inputs. A number of ethical concerns have arisen as a result of this practice, including the loss of jobs in Canada's manufacturing sector and the use of overseas suppliers that follow questionable practices. For example, in the sporting goods market, firms have been criticized for using suppliers that pay low wages (wages far below what they pay celebrities to endorse their products) to suppliers that are reported to produce goods in *sweatshops* that use child or prison labour. Few Canadians want to think that the high-fashion apparel they wear or the sports equipment they use is made by children forced to labour instead of going to school.

Another group of firms has come under scrutiny because of the countries within which they operate. Profits from Talisman Energy's operations in Sudan, for example, are believed by some to support the Sudanese government's civil war and the violation of the human rights of some of its citizens. Similarly, De Beers, the famous diamond miner, has been requested to ensure that it does not market "conflict diamonds," stones sold by governments that use the revenue to fund wars. While Talisman has been resistant to changing its practices, De Beers took a more proactive stance. It is working with a number of organizations, including the United Nations, to provide documentation certifying the origin of all stones and banning those coming from questionable sources from international diamond exchanges.

Purchasing and Shelving Policies

Coming up with winning products is a major challenge—getting goods into stores where consumers can see and purchase them is often even a bigger hurdle. Retailing in Canada is becoming increasingly concentrated, and some manufacturers believe it helps to pay a bribe to the store's representatives, or buyers, to facilitate the process. In the garment industry, these payments are known as

Physical Distribution and Logistics Management

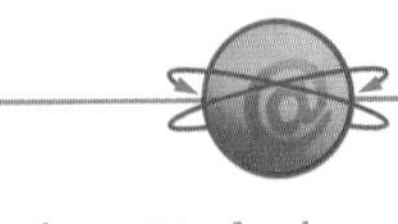

American Marketing Association
www.ama.org/

In today's global marketplace, selling a product is sometimes easier than getting it to customers. Companies must decide on the best way to store, handle, and move their products and services so that they are available to customers in the right assortments, at the right time, and in the right place. Logistics effectiveness has a major impact on both customer satisfaction and company costs. A poor distribution system can destroy an otherwise good marketing effort. We shall consider the *nature and importance of marketing logistics, goals of the logistics system, major logistics functions,* and the need for *integrated logistics management.*

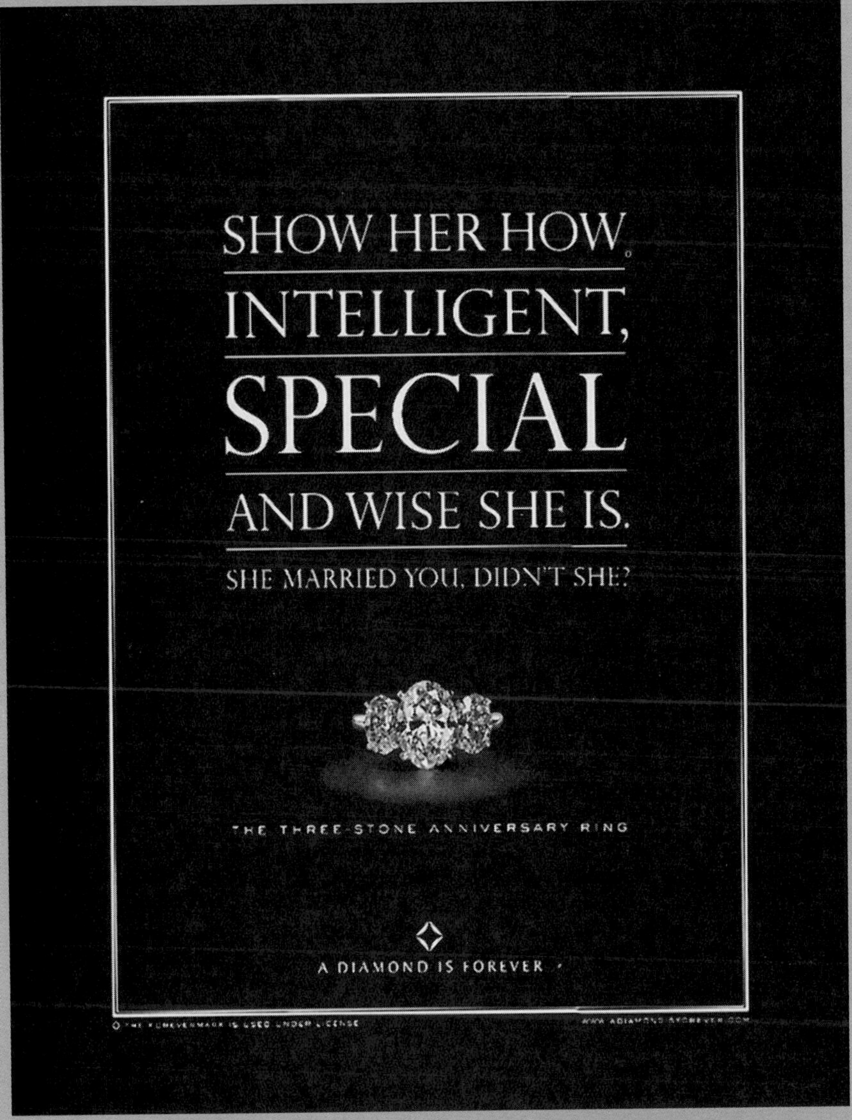

SHOW HER HOW
INTELLIGENT,
SPECIAL
AND WISE SHE IS.
SHE MARRIED YOU, DIDN'T SHE?
THE THREE-STONE ANNIVERSARY RING
A DIAMOND IS FOREVER

De Beers has been proactive in its efforts to avoid buying or selling "conflict diamonds."

kickbacks, payola, or shmeer. Salespeople have long worked to woo buyers with everything from lavish dinners to tickets to sporting events. However, the line has been stretched, and some buyers are treated to golf trips in Palm Beach or even cash payments. Wal-Mart Canada recently fired one of its buyers and worked with the RCMP to press charges against another who allegedly demanded money from suppliers who wanted Wal-Mart to stock their goods. To counter the practice, firms are developing strict codes of conduct for both purchasing agents and salespeople. Many codes ban giving or accepting any gifts.

Another issue related to the acquisition of shelf space that is hotly debated is the use of *slotting allowances* or *fees.* Manufacturers pay these fees to stock, display, and support new products. One study suggests that these fees represent about 16 percent of all new product introduction costs. Often negotiated in secret, they have sparked considerable controversy. Many manufacturers believe they are being held to ransom by retailers. Others contend that only large firms can afford to pay these hefty sums, thereby restricting the entry of small, entrepreneurial firms from the marketplace. Retailers, on the other hand, claim that they are just fair compensation of the 2000 to 3000 new items they are asked to stock each year. Since many of these product will fail, the fees are compensation for taking on this risk as well as covering the costs of listing, stocking, and managing the shelf space for these products. No matter what side of the issue you sit on, you cannot deny that these fees lead to higher retail prices for consumers.

Sources: Marina Strauss, "Wal-Mart supplier was asked for kickbacks," *Globe and Mail,* 2 February 2000; P.N. Bloom, G.T. Gundlach, and J.P. Cannon, "Slotting allowances and fees: Schools of thought and the views of practicing managers," *Journal of Marketing,* April 2000:92–108; Andrew Stodart, "Fight for your rights: Marketers are being far too passive about the growing concentration of retail power in this country," *Marketing On-Line,* 31 May 1999; United Church of Canada news release, "Talisman Energy Inc. rejects shareholder proposal," 8 March 1999, www.uccan.org/news/990308a.htm.

Nature and Importance of Physical Distribution and Marketing Logistics

Physical distribution (marketing logistics)
The tasks involved in planning, implementing, and controlling the physical flow of materials, final goods, and related information from points of origin to points of consumption to meet customer requirements at a profit.

To some managers, physical distribution means only trucks and warehouses. But modern logistics is much more than this. **Physical distribution—or marketing logistics**—involves planning, implementing, and controlling the physical flow of materials, final goods, and related information from points of origin to points of consumption to meet customer requirements at a profit. In short, it involves getting the right product to the right customer in the right place at the right time.

Traditional physical distribution typically starts with products at the plant and

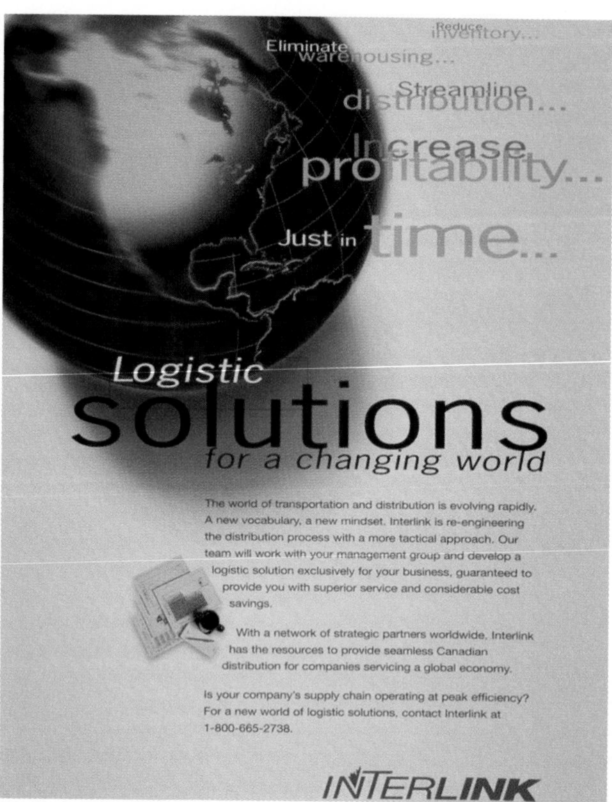

Interlink's advertisement stresses the need to think of total solutions as a way of approaching logistics problems.

low-cost solutions to get them to customers. Today's marketers, however, prefer *market logistics* thinking, which starts with the marketplace and works backwards to the factory. Logistics addresses not only the problem of outbound distribution (moving products from the factory to customers), but also the problem of inbound distribution (moving products and materials from suppliers to the factory). It involves the management of entire *supply chains*, value-added flows from suppliers to final users, as shown in Figure 11-5. Thus, the logistics manager's task is to coordinate the whole channel physical distribution system—the activities of suppliers, purchasing agents, marketers, channel members, and customers. These activities include forecasting, information systems, purchasing, production planning, order processing, inventory, warehousing, and transportation planning.

Companies are placing greater emphasis on logistics for several reasons. First, customer service and satisfaction have become the cornerstones of marketing strategy in many businesses, and distribution is an important customer service element. Effective logistics is becoming a key to winning and keeping customers. Companies are finding that they can attract more customers by giving better service or lower prices through better physical distribution. On the other hand, companies may lose customers when they fail to supply the right products on time.

Second, logistics is a major cost element for most companies. In one study, 10.5 percent the gross domestic product of many countries is accounted for by such functions as wrapping, bundling, loading, unloading, sorting, reloading, and transporting goods."[17] About 15 percent of an average product's price is accounted for by shipping and transport alone. Poor physical distribution decisions result in high costs. Even large companies sometimes make too little use of modern decision tools for coordinating inventory levels; transportation modes; and plant, warehouse, and store locations. Improvements in physical distribution efficiency can yield tremendous cost savings for both the company and its customers.

Third, the explosion in product variety has created a need for improved logistics management. In 1911, the typical A&P grocery store carried only 270 items. The shopkeeper could keep track of this inventory on about 10 pages of notebook paper. Today, the average A&P carries a bewildering stock of more than 16 700 items, over 60 times the number in 1911.[18] Ordering, shipping, stocking, and controlling such a variety of products presents a sizeable logistics challenge.

Finally, improvements in information technology have created opportunities for major gains in distribution efficiency. The increased use of computers, point-of-sale scanners, uniform product codes, satellite tracking, electronic data interchange (EDI), and electronic funds transfer (EFT) has allowed companies to create advanced systems for order processing, inventory control and handling, and transportation routing and scheduling.

Goals of the Logistics System

Some companies state their logistics objective as providing maximum customer service at the least cost. Unfortunately, no logistics system can both maximize customer service and minimize distribution costs. Maximum customer service implies rapid delivery, large inventories, flexible assortments, liberal returns policies, and

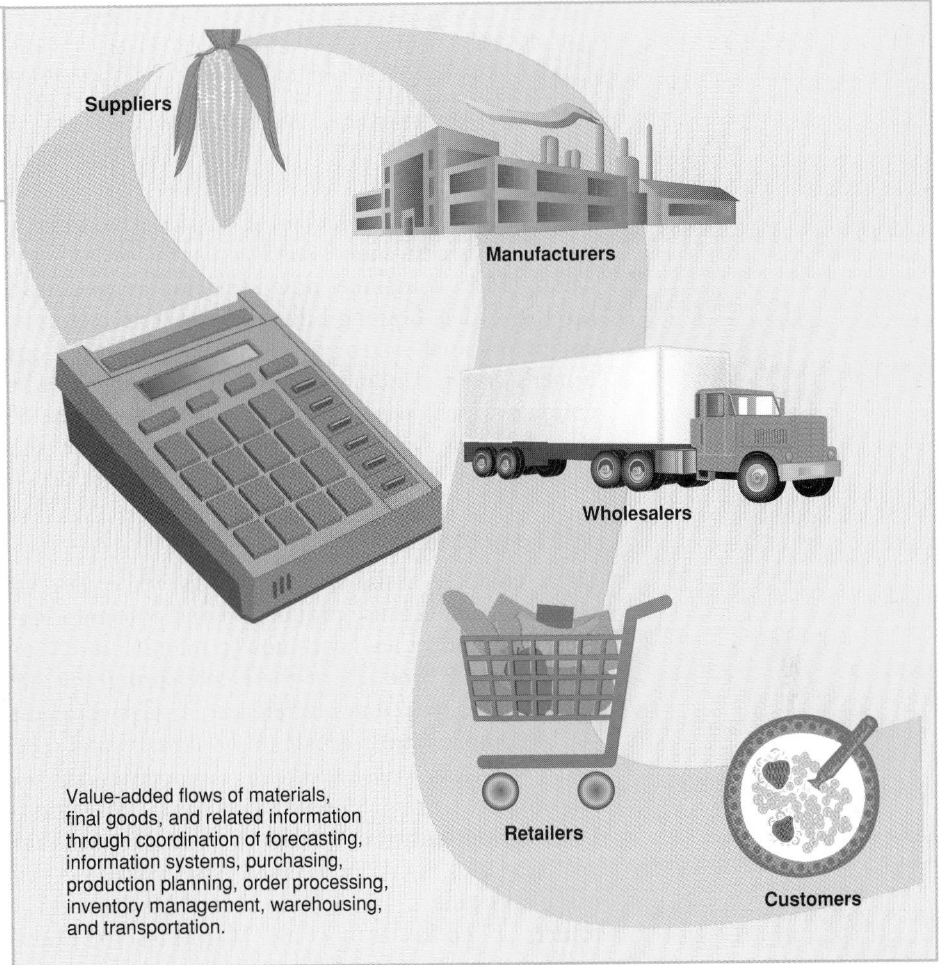
Suppliers
Manufacturers
Wholesalers
Retailers
Customers
Value-added flows of materials, final goods, and related information through coordination of forecasting, information systems, purchasing, production planning, order processing, inventory management, warehousing, and transportation.

FIGURE 11-5
Managing supply chains through marketing logistics

other services—all of which raise distribution costs. In contrast, minimum distribution costs imply slower delivery, smaller inventories, and larger shipping lots—which represent a lower level of overall customer service.

The goal of the marketing logistics system should be to provide a targeted level of customer service at the least cost. A company must first research the importance of various distribution services to its customers and then set desired service levels for each segment. The company typically will want to offer at least the same level of service as its competitors. But the objective is to maximize *profits*, not sales. Therefore, the company must weigh the benefits of providing higher levels of service against the costs. Some companies offer less service than their competitors and charge a lower price. Other companies offer more service and charge higher prices to cover higher costs.

Major Logistics Functions

Once it has set its logistics objectives, the company is ready to design a logistics system that will minimize the cost of attaining them. The major logistics functions include *order processing, warehousing, inventory management,* and *transportation.*

Order Processing

Orders can be submitted in many ways—by mail or telephone, through salespeople, or via computer and electronic data interchange (EDI). In some cases, the suppliers might actually generate orders for their customers:[19]

> One Kmart quick response program calls for selected suppliers to manage the retailer's inventory replenishment for their products. Kmart transmits daily records of product sales to the vendor, who analyzes the sales information, comes up with an order, and sends it back to Kmart through EDI. Once in Kmart's system, the order is treated as though Kmart itself created it. Says a Kmart executive, "We don't modify the order, and we don't question it. . . . Our relationship with those vendors is such that we trust them to create the type of order that will best meet our inventory needs."

Once received, orders must be processed quickly and accurately. Both the company and its customers benefit when the order-processing steps are carried out efficiently. Most companies now use computerized order-processing systems that speed up the order-shipping-billing cycle. For example, General Electric operates a computer-based system that, upon receipt of a customer's order, checks the customer's credit standing as well as whether and where the items are in stock. The computer then issues an order to ship, bills the customer, updates the inventory records, sends a production order for new stock, and relays the message back to the salesperson that the customer's order is on its way—all in less than 15 seconds.

Warehousing

Every company must store its goods while they wait to be sold. A storage function is needed because production and consumption cycles rarely match. For example, Toro and other lawn-mower manufacturers must produce all year long and store up their product for the heavy spring and summer buying season. The storage function overcomes differences in needed quantities and timing.

A company must decide on *how many* and *what types* of warehouses it needs, and *where* they will be located. Companies can use either *storage warehouses* or *distribution centres*. Storage warehouses store goods for moderate to long periods. **Distribution centres** are designed to move goods rather than just store them. They are large and highly automated warehouses designed to receive goods from various plants and suppliers, take orders, fill them efficiently, and deliver goods to customers as quickly as possible. Wal-Mart, for example, operates huge distribution centres. One centre, which serves the daily needs of 165 Wal-Mart stores, contains some 28 acres of space under a single roof. Laser scanners route as many as 190 000 cases of goods per day along 18 kilometres of conveyer belts, and the centre's 1000 workers load or unload 310 trucks daily.[20]

Distribution centre
A large, highly automated warehouse designed to receive goods from various plants and suppliers, take orders, fill them efficiently, and deliver goods to customers as quickly as possible.

Warehousing facilities and equipment technology have improved greatly in recent years. Older, multi-storey warehouses with slow elevators and outdated materials-handling methods are facing competition from newer, single-storey *automated warehouses* with advanced materials-handling systems under the control of a central computer. In these warehouses, only a few employees are necessary. Computers read orders and direct lift trucks, electric hoists, or robots to gather goods, move them to loading docks, and issue invoices. These warehouses have reduced worker injuries, labour costs, theft, and breakage and have improved inventory control.

Inventory Management

Inventory levels affect customer satisfaction. The major problem is maintaining the delicate balance between carrying too much inventory and carrying too little. Carrying too much inventory results in higher-than-necessary inventory carrying costs and stock obsolescence. Carrying too little may result in stock-outs, costly emergency shipments or production, and customer dissatisfaction. In making inventory decisions, management must balance the costs of carrying larger inventories against resulting sales and profits.

Inventory decisions involve knowing both *when* and *how much* to order. In deciding when to order, the company balances the risks of running out of stock against the costs of carrying too much. In deciding how much to order, the com-

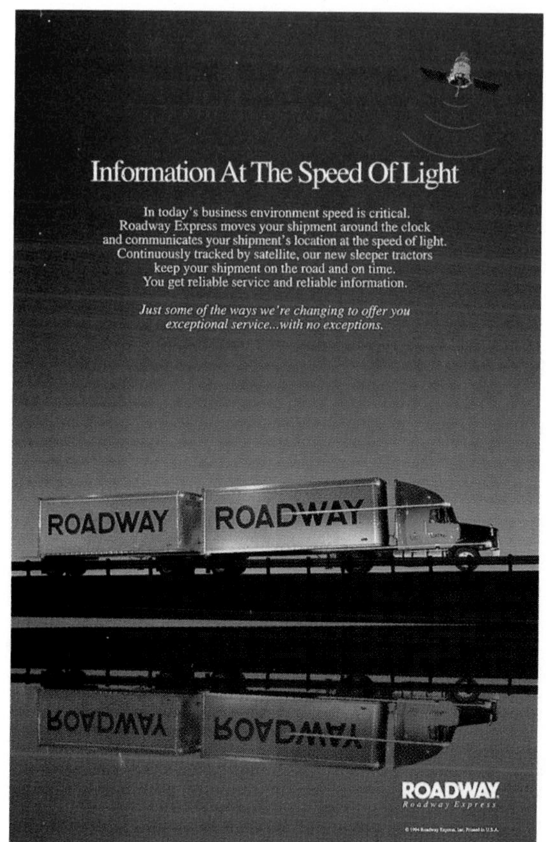

Information At The Speed Of Light
In today's business environment speed is critical. Roadway Express moves your shipment around the clock and communicates your shipment's location at the speed of light. Continuously tracked by satellite, our new sleeper tractors keep your shipment on the road and on time. You get reliable service and reliable information.
Just some of the ways we're changing to offer you exceptional service...with no exceptions.
ROADWAY
ROADWAY
ROADWAY

Roadway and other trucking firms have added many services in recent years, such as satellite tracking of shipments and sleeper tractors that keep freight moving around the clock.

pany needs to balance order-processing costs against inventory carrying costs. Larger average-order size results in fewer orders and lower order-processing costs, but it also means larger inventory carrying costs.

During the past decade, many companies have greatly reduced their inventories and related costs through *just-in-time* logistics systems. Through such systems, producers and retailers carry only small inventories of parts or merchandise, often only enough for a few days of operations. New stock arrives exactly when needed, rather than being stored in inventory until being used. Just-in-time systems require accurate forecasting along with fast, frequent, and flexible delivery, so that new supplies will be available when needed. However, these systems result in substantial savings in inventory carrying and handling costs.

Transportation

Marketers need to take an interest in their company's *transportation* decisions. The choice of transportation carriers affects the pricing of products, delivery performance, and condition of the goods when they arrive—all of which affect customer satisfaction. In shipping goods to its warehouses, dealers, and customers, the company can choose between five transportation modes: rail, truck, water, pipeline, and air.

Rail. Because most of Canada's population is contained in a belt that is only 300 km wide but 6400 km long, rail still carries most of the country's freight. Railways are one of the most cost-effective modes for shipping large amounts of bulk products—coal, sand, minerals, farm and forest products—over long distances. In addition, railways recently have begun to increase their customer services. Both CN and CP have designed new equipment to handle special categories of goods, provided flatcars for carrying truck trailers by rail (piggyback), and provided in-transit services such as the diversion of shipped goods to other destinations en route and the processing of goods en route. Thus, after decades of losing out to truckers, railways appear ready for a comeback.[21]

Roadway Express
www.roadway.com/

Truck. Trucks have increased their share of transportation steadily and now account for 25 percent of total cargo. They account for the largest portion of transportation *within* cities rather than *between* cities. Trucks are highly flexible in their routing and time schedules. They can move goods door to door, saving shippers the need to transfer goods from truck to rail and back again at a loss of time and risk of theft or damage. Trucks are efficient for short hauls of high-value merchandise. In many cases, their rates are competitive with railway rates, and trucks can usually offer faster service. Trucking firms have added many services in recent years. For example, Roadway Express now offers satellite tracking of shipments and sleeper tractors that move freight around the clock.

Water. A lot of goods are moved by ships and barges on coastal and inland waterways. On the one hand, the cost of water transportation is very low for shipping bulky, low-value, non-perishable products such as sand, coal, grain, oil, and metallic ores. On the other hand, water transportation is the slowest transportation mode and is sometimes affected by the weather. Thus although many goods are shipped across the Great Lakes and through the St. Lawrence Seaway in the warmer months, these routes are impassable in the winter.

Pipeline. Pipelines are used for shipping petroleum, natural gas, and chemicals from sources to markets. Pipeline shipment of petroleum products costs less than rail shipment but more than water shipment. Most pipelines are used by their owners to ship their own products.

Air. Although air carriers transport under one percent of the nation's goods, they are becoming more important as a transportation mode. Air-freight rates are much higher than rail or truck rates, but air freight is ideal when speed is needed or distant markets have to be reached. Among the most frequently air-freighted products are perishables (fresh fish, cut flowers) and high-value, low-bulk items (technical instruments, jewellery). Companies find that air freight also reduces inventory levels, packaging costs, and the number of warehouses needed.

Increasingly, shippers are using intermodal transportation—combining two or more modes of transportation. *Piggyback* describes the use of rail and trucks; *fishyback,* water and trucks; *trainship,* water and rail; and *airtruck,* air and trucks. Combining modes provides advantages that no single mode can deliver. Each combination offers advantages to the shipper. For example, not only is piggyback cheaper than trucking alone but it also provides flexibility and convenience.

In choosing a transportation mode for a product, shippers must balance many considerations: speed, dependability, availability, cost, and others. Thus, if a shipper needs speed, air and truck are the prime choices. If the goal is low cost, then water or pipeline might be best.

Integrated Logistics Management

Integrated logistics management
The logistics concept that emphasizes teamwork, both inside the company and between all the marketing channel organizations, to maximize the performance of the entire distribution system.

Many companies are now adopting **integrated logistics management.** They recognize that providing better customer service and trimming distribution costs requires *teamwork,* both inside the company and among all the marketing channel organizations. Inside the company, the functional departments must work closely together to maximize the company's own logistics performance. The company must also integrate its logistics system with those of its suppliers and customers to maximize the performance of the entire distribution system.

Cross-Functional Teamwork inside the Company

In most companies, responsibility for logistics activities is assigned to different functional units—marketing, sales, finance, manufacturing, purchasing. Too often, each function tries to optimize its own logistics performance without regard for the activities of the other functions. However, transportation, inventory, warehousing, and order processing activities interact, often in an inverse way. For example, lower inventory levels reduce inventory carrying costs. But they may also reduce customer service and increase costs from stockouts, back orders, special production runs, and costly fast-freight shipments. Because distribution activities involve strong trade-offs, decisions by different functions must be coordinated to achieve superior overall logistics performance.

Thus, the goal of integrated logistics management is to harmonize all of the company's distribution decisions. Close working relationships between functions can be achieved in several ways. Some companies have created permanent logistics committees comprising managers responsible for different physical distribution activities and transportation engineers. These committees meet often to set policies for improving overall logistics performance. Companies can also create management positions that link the logistics activities of functional areas. For example, Procter & Gamble has created *supply managers,* who manage all of the supply chain activities for each of its product categories.[22] Many companies have a vice-president of logistics with cross-functional authority. The location of the logistics functions within the company is a secondary concern. The important thing is that the company coordinate its logistics and marketing activities to create high market satisfaction at a reasonable cost.

Building Channel Partnerships

The members of a distribution channel are linked closely in delivering customer satisfaction and value. One company's distribution system is another company's supply system. The success of each channel member depends on the performance of the entire supply chain. For example, Zellers can charge the lowest prices at retail only if its entire supply chain—thousands of merchandise suppliers, transport companies, warehouses, and service providers—operates at maximum efficiency.

Companies must do more than improve their own logistics. They must also work with other channel members to improve whole-channel distribution. Smart companies coordinate their logistics strategies and building strong partnerships with suppliers and customers to improve customer service and reduce channel costs.

These channel partnerships can take many forms. Many companies have created *cross-functional, cross-company teams.* Procter & Gamble has a team of about 100 people in Bentonville, Arkansas, home of Wal-Mart. They work with their counterparts at Wal-Mart to jointly find ways to squeeze costs out of their distribution system. Working together benefits not only P&G and Wal-Mart, but also their final consumers.[23]

Other companies partner through *shared projects.* For example, many larger retailers are working closely with suppliers on in-store programs. Western Publishing Group, publisher of Little Golden Books for children, formed a partnership with Toys 'R' Us. Western and the giant toy retailer coordinated their marketing strategies to create mini-bookstore sections—called Books 'R' Us—within each Toys 'R' Us store. Toys 'R' Us provides the locations, space, and customers; Western serves as distributor, consolidator, and servicer for the Books 'R' Us program. Clearly, both the supplier and customer benefit from such partnerships.[24]

Channel partnerships can also take the form of *information sharing* and *continuous inventory replenishment* systems. Suppliers link up with customers to share information and coordinate their logistics decisions:[25]

> Bailey Controls, a manufacturer of control systems for big factories, from steel and paper mills to chemical and pharmaceutical plants, . . . treats some of its suppliers almost like departments of its own plants. Bailey has plugged two of its main electronics suppliers into itself. Future Electronics is hooked in through an electronic data interchange system. Every week, Bailey electronically sends Future its latest forecasts of what materials it will need for the next six months so that Future can stock up in time. Bailey itself stocks only enough inventory for a few days of operation, as opposed to the three or four months' worth it used to carry. Whenever a bin of parts falls below a designated level, a Bailey employee passes a laser scanner over the bin's bar code, instantly alerting Future to send the parts at once. Arrow Electronics . . . is plugged in even more closely: It has a warehouse in Bailey's factory, stocked according to Bailey's twice-a-month forecasts. Bailey provides the space, Arrow the warehouseman and the $750 000 of inventory.

As a result of such partnerships, many companies have switched from *anticipatory-based distribution systems* to *response-based distribution systems.*[26] In anticipatory distribution, the company produces the amount of goods called for by a sales forecast. It builds and holds stock at various supply points such as the plant, distribution centres, and retail outlets. A response-based distribution system, in contrast, is *customer triggered.* The producer continuously builds and replaces stock as orders arrive. It produces what is currently selling. For example, Japanese car makers take orders for cars, then produce and ship them within four days. Some large appliance manufacturers, such as Whirlpool and GE, are moving to this system. Benetton, the Italian fashion house, uses a *quick-response system,* dyeing its sweaters in the colours that are currently selling instead of trying to guess long in advance which colours people will want. Producing for order rather than for forecast substantially cuts down inventory costs and risks.

Third-party logistics provider
An integrated logistics company that performs any or all of the functions required to get their clients' products to market.

Third-Party Logistics

While most businesses perform their own logistics functions, a growing number of firms now outsource this function to **third-party logistics providers** such as Ryder Systems, UPS Worldwide Logistics, FedEx Logistics, Roadway Logistics Services,

Western Publishing Group partners with Toys 'R' Us to create mini-bookstore sections within each store: Toys 'R' Us provides the locations, space, and customers; Western serves as distributor, consolidator, and servicer for the Books 'R' Us program.

or Emory Global Logistics. Such integrated logistics companies perform any or all of the functions required to get their clients' product to market. For example, Emory's Global Logistics unit provides clients with coordinated, single-source logistics services including supply chain management, customized information technology, inventory control, warehousing, transportation management, customer service and fulfillment, and freight auditing and control.

Companies use third-party logistics providers for several reasons. First, because getting the product to market is their main focus, these providers can often do it more efficiently and at lower cost than clients whose strengths lie elsewhere. According to a recent study, outsourcing warehousing alone typically results in 10 to 15 percent cost savings.[27] Second, outsourcing logistics frees a company to focus more intensely on its core business. Finally, integrated logistics companies understand the increasingly complex logistics environment. This can be especially helpful to companies attempting to expand their global market coverage. For example, companies distributing their products across Europe face a bewildering array of environmental restrictions that affect logistics, including packaging standards, truck size and weight limits, and noise and emissions pollution controls. By outsourcing its logistics, a company can gain a complete cross-European distribution system without incurring the costs, delays, and risks associated with setting up its own system.[28]

Review of Concept Connections

Marketing channel decisions are among the most important decisions that management faces. A company's channel decisions directly affect every other marketing decision. Each channel system creates a different level of revenues and costs and reaches a different segment of target consumers. Management must make channel decisions carefully, incorporating today's needs with tomorrow's likely selling environment. While some companies pay too little attention to their distribution channels, others have used imaginative distribution systems to gain competitive advantage.

1. **Explain why companies use distribution channels and the functions that these channels perform.**

   Most producers use intermediaries to bring their products to market. They try to forge a *distribution channel*—a set of interdependent organizations involved in the process of making a product or service available for use or consumption by the consumer or business user. Through their contacts, experience, specialization, and scale of operation, intermediaries usually offer the firm more than it can achieve on its own. Distribution channels perform many key functions. Some help *complete* transactions by gathering and distributing *information* needed for planning and aiding exchange; by *developing* and spreading persuasive communications about an offer; by performing *contact* work—finding and communicating with prospective buyers; by *matching*—shaping and fitting the offer to the buyer's needs; and by entering into *negotiation* to reach an agreement on price and other terms of the offer so that ownership can be transferred. Other functions help to *fulfill* the completed transactions by offering *physical distribution*—transporting and storing goods; *financing*—acquiring and using funds to cover the costs of the channel work; and *risk taking*—assuming the risks of carrying out the channel work.

2. **Discuss how channel members interact and organize to perform the work of the channel.**

   The channel is most effective when each member is assigned the tasks it can do best. Because the success of individual channel members depends on overall channel success, all channel firms should work together smoothly. They should understand and accept their roles, coordinate their goals and activities, and cooperate to attain overall channel goals. By cooperating, they can more effectively sense, serve, and satisfy the target market.

   In a large company, the formal organization structure assigns roles and provides needed leadership. But in a distribution channel composed of independent firms, leadership and power are not formally set. Traditionally, distribution channels have lacked the leadership needed to assign roles and manage conflict; however, new types of channel organizations have recently appeared that provide stronger leadership and improved performance.

3. **Identify the major channel alternatives open to a company.**

   Each firm identifies alternative ways to reach its market. Available means vary from direct selling to using one, two, three, or more intermediary *channel levels*. Marketing channels face continuous and sometimes dramatic change. Three of the most important trends are the growth of *vertical, horizontal,* and *hybrid marketing systems*. These trends affect channel cooperation, conflict, and competition. *Channel design* begins with assessing customer channel-service needs and company channel objective and constraints. The company then identifies the major channel alternatives in terms of the *types* of intermediaries, the *number* of intermediaries, and the *channel responsibilities* of each. Each channel alternative must be evaluated according to economic, control, and adaptive criteria. Channel management calls for selecting qualified intermediaries and motivating them. Individual channel members must be evaluated regularly.

4. **Discuss the nature and importance of physical distribution.**

   Just as the marketing concept is receiving increased recognition, more business firms are paying attention to the *physical distribution*, or *marketing logistics*. Logistics is an area of potentially high cost savings and improved customer satisfaction. Marketing logistics involves coordinating the activities of the entire *supply chain* to deliver maximum value to customers. No logistics system can both maximize customer service and minimize distribution costs. Instead, the goal of logistics management is to provide a *targeted* level of service at the least cost. The major logistics functions include *order processing, warehousing, inventory management,* and *transportation*.

5. **Analyze integrated logistics, including how it may be achieved and its benefits to the company.**

The *integrated logistics concept* recognizes that improved logistics requires teamwork—in the form of close working relationships across functional areas inside the company and across various organizations in the supply chain. Companies can achieve logistics harmony among functions by creating cross-functional logistics teams, integrative supply manager positions, and senior-level logistics executives with cross-functional authority. Channel partnerships can take the form of cross-company teams, shared projects, and information-sharing systems. Through such partnerships, many companies have switched from *anticipatory-based distribution systems* to customer-triggered *response-based distribution systems*. Today, some companies are outsourcing their logistics functions to third-party logistics providers to save costs, increase efficiency, and gain faster and more effective access to global markets.

Key Terms

Administered VMS *(p. 467)*
Channel conflict *(p. 464)*
Channel level *(p. 462)*
Contractual VMS *(p. 466)*
Conventional distribution channel *(p. 465)*
Corporate VMS *(p. 465)*
Direct marketing channel *(p. 462)*
Disintermediation *(p. 470)*
Distribution centre *(p. 484)*
Distribution channel (marketing channel) *(p. 460)*
Exclusive distribution *(p. 475)*
Franchise organization *(p. 467)*
Horizontal marketing systems *(p. 467)*
Hybrid marketing channels *(p. 468)*
Indirect marketing channel *(p. 463)*
Integrated logistics management *(p. 486)*
Intensive distribution *(p. 475)*
Physical distribution (marketing logistics) *(p. 481)*
Retailer cooperatives *(p. 466)*
Selective distribution *(p. 476)*
Third-party logistics provider *(p. 487)*
Vertical marketing system (VMS) *(p. 465)*
Wholesaler-sponsored voluntary chains *(p. 466)*

Discussing the Issues

1. The Book-of-the-Month Club (BOMC) has been successfully marketing books by mail for over 50 years. Discuss why so few publishers sell books directly by mail. How will competition from new companies like Amazon.com affect BOMC?
2. Analyze why franchising is such a fast-growing form of retail organization. Why do you think franchising is a more popular way of doing business in Canada than it is in the United States?
3. Describe the kinds of horizontal and vertical channel conflict that might occur in one of the following: (a) the personal computer industry, (b) the automobile industry, (c) the music industry, or (d) the clothing industry. How would you remedy the problems you have just described?
4. Give your own example of each of the three major forms of vertical marketing system described in the chapter. What advantages do such systems have over traditional channel organizations?
5. What is disintermediation? Give an example other than those discussed in the chapter. What opportunities and problems does disintermediation present for traditional retailers? Explain.
6. Which distribution strategy—intensive, selective, or exclusive—is used for each of the following products and why? (a) Piaget watches, (b) Acura automobiles, and (c) Crispy Crunch candy bars.
7. The chapter discusses four basic logistics functions. Which of these functions is most important for: (a) Quicken's QuickTax income tax preparation software; (b) Faith Hill's newest country music release; (c) a Toyota Camry; and (d) an issue of *Wired* magazine (www.wired.com).
8. Regarding outsourcing: (a) Why would a company choose to outsource its distribution function? (b) What major factors contribute to a successful outsourcing relationship? What are the potential dangers of such a relationship? (c) Give an example of a company that could benefit from outsourcing its logistics, and suggest some practical outsourcing alternatives for the company. (For more information on outsourcing, see the Outsourcing Institute's Web site at www.outsourcing.com.)

Marketing Applications

1. Internet giant Amazon.com has thrown open its doors not only to its customers but also to its competitors. Recent expansions by this "Wal-Mart of the Web" include zShops, where any other retailer can set up shop on Amazon.com's site; an All Product Search feature that helps shoppers find any product for sale on the Web no matter where it is sold; the addition of toy, consumer electronics, and home improvement items to the Amazon site; the addition of a live auction to the site; and investment in and links to numerous "dot-com" retailers, including a sports site Gear.com (www.gear.com), Pets.com (www.pets.com), HomeGrocer.com (www.homegrocer.com), and Drugstore.com (www.drugstore.com). Amazon is betting that these moves will make it more like a mall on the Internet. Its ambitious goal is to sell everything to everyone on the Internet. Despite many potential hurdles, Amazon.com has become a force with which even Wal-Mart must reckon.
   a. Review Amazon.com's expansion strategy. What are the benefits and challenges of each expansion move?
   b. How is Amazon.com using distribution to its advantage?
   c. Review the Amazon.com Web site at www.amazon.com. What other changes or expansion would you recommend? Why?
   d. How is Amazon.com affecting traditional retail distribution channels? How should Wal-Mart react to Amazon.com?
2. You know about the Internet, but have you ever heard of an extranet? An extranet is the result of a company opening part of its own internal network (or intranet) to trusted suppliers, distributors, and other selected external business partners. Via such extranets, a company can communicate quickly and efficiently with its partners, complete transactions, and share data. A supplier might analyze the customer's inventory needs. (Boeing booked $150 million in parts orders from airline customers in one year.) Partners might swap customer lists for interrelated products and services or share purchasing systems to gain savings through more efficient purchasing. (General Electric claims that $750 million of purchasing costs can be saved using an extranet.) Imagine the strategic advantages created when virtual partners communicate in seconds about shifting supply and demand situations, customer requests and opportunities, and just-in-time inventory needs. Purchase processing times can be reduced from weeks to minutes at enormous cost savings, which can then be passed along to consumers.
   a. What role will extranets play in distribution decisions for retailers, wholesalers, and manufacturers?
   b. Discuss the potential dangers and benefits of an extranet system.
   c. How might Home Depot employ an extranet in its dealings with suppliers? What types of activities and information might be shared on this extranet? How might this save time and costs?
   d. How does the extranet concept fit with outsourcing (if at all)?

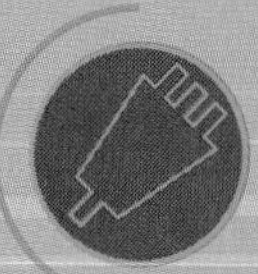

Internet Connections

Hybrid Marketing Channels

Many companies have adopted multichannel distribution systems, or hybrid marketing channels. This allows them to reach different customer segments simultaneously. One segment that publishers would like to reach is university students. Traditionally, students have been reached through the campus bookstore, which is probably where you bought this book. But what if the bookstore were out of stock and you needed the text right away? You have alternatives. For example, you can purchase the book directly from Pearson Education Canada by phone, or you can order it online from a Web bookstore. Visit Pearson Education at www.pearsoned.ca to explore these options. Get price quotes from at least three of the online retailers listed.

For Discussion

1. Which distribution channel offers the lowest prices (don't forget to include shipping charges)?
2. Is the shipping time for the off-campus channels substantial enough to present a hardship for the university and college student segment?
3. Are there advantages to the campus bookstore that the off-campus channels cannot provide?
4. What are the advantages to the publisher for maintaining a multichannel distribution system? Disadvantages?
5. Why doesn't Pearson Education display the text on its site and simply charge users for using and printing it?

	Shipping **Retailer Price**	Shipping **Charge Time**
Campus bookstore		
Pearson Education by phone		
Amazon www.amazon.com		
Chapters (online) www.chapters.ca		
Indigo (online) www.indigo.ca		
Bookstore at another university (if online, specify)		

Savvy Sites

- Bertelsmann (www.bertelsmann.de) is one of the largest multimedia giants, owning sites such as www.bugjuice.com for alternative music and other hot Web properties all over the globe.
- *The Globe and Mail* (www.globeandmail.ca), *Financial Post* (www.nationalpost.com), and *Wall Street Journal* (www.wsj.com) all deliver their news products online. Marketers can search *Strategy* magazine's Web site (www.strategymag.com/search.asp) for free; but to use the complete *Marketing On-Line* site (www.marketingmag.ca), they must buy an annual subscription to the magazine first.
- Want to get global news before online media get it? Search Reuters (www.reuters.com), a premier news service. Their archives are helpful for research projects.

Notes

1. Quotes from Donald V. Fites, "Make your dealers your partners," *Harvard Business Review,* March–April 1996:84–95; and De Ann Weimer, "A new Cat on the hot seat," *Business Week,* March 1998:56–62. Also see Peter Elstrom, "This Cat keeps on purring," *Business Week,* 20 January 1997:82–4; "Caterpillar CEO optimistic about company's future," press release accessed online at www.cat.com, April 14, 1999; and "Best sales forces: Caterpillar," *Sales & Marketing Management,* July 1999:64.
2. Louis Stern and Adel I. El-Ansary, *Marketing Channels,* 4th. ed., Englewood Cliffs, NJ: Prentice Hall, 1992:3.
3. Alanna Mitchell, "U of C won't go by book," *Globe and Mail,* 13 December 1995:A1,A14.
4. Ian Jack, "Dealers declare war on Ford Canada," *Financial Post,* 31 March 2000:C1,C5; Greg Keenan, "Ford targets bigger stake in dealerships," *Globe and Mail,* 18 November 1998:B1,B16.
5. Jaclyn Fierman, "How Gallo crushes the competition," *Fortune,* 1 September 1986:27.
6. See Richard C. Hoffman and John F. Preble, "Franchising into the twenty-first century," *Business Horizons,* November–December 1993:35–43; "Canada's largest franchise-only show returns," advertising supplement, *Globe and Mail,* 24 September 1997:1; and Industry Canada's franchising Web site strategis.ic.gc.ca/SSG/dm01179e.html.
7. This has been called "symbiotic marketing." For more reading, see Lee Adler, "Symbiotic marketing," *Harvard Business Review,* November–December 1966:59–71; P. Varadarajan and Daniel Rajaratnam, "Symbiotic marketing revisited," *Journal of Marketing,* January 1986:7–17; and Gary Hamel, Yves L. Doz, and C. D. Prahalad, "Collaborate with your competitors—and win," *Harvard Business Review,* January–February 1989:133–9.
8. Peter Fitzpatrick, "Airlines of the world—unite," *Financial Post,* 22 November 1997:8.
9. See Rowland T. Moriarity and Ursula Moran, "Managing hybrid marketing systems," *Harvard Business Review,* November–December 1990:146–55; Frank V. Cespedes and E. Raymond Corey, "Managing multiple channels," *Business Horizons,* July–August 1990:67–77; Geoffrey Brewer, "Lou Gerstner has his hands full," *Sales & Marketing Management,* May 1998:36–41; and www.direct.ibm.com.
10. Rochelle Garner, "Mad as hell," *Sales & Marketing Management,* June 1999:55–9.
11. See Louis W. Stern and Frederick D. Sturdivant, "Customer-driven distribution systems," *Harvard Business Review,* July–August 1987:34–5.
12. David Akin, "Passage to the north," *Financial Post,* 23 May 2000:C7; Angela Kryhul, "Prescription for savings," *Marketing,* 6 December 1993:11.
13. Subhash C. Jain, *International Marketing Management,* 3rd ed., Boston: PWS-Kent Publishing, 1990:489–91. Also see Emily Thronton, "Revolution in Japanese retailing," *Fortune,* 7 February 1994:143–7.
14. See Philip Cateora, *International Marketing,* 7th ed., Homewood, IL: Irwin, 1990:570–1.
15. Jennifer Wells, "We can get it for you wholesale," *Report on Business,* March 1995:52–62.
16. See James A. Narus and James C. Anderson, "Turn your industrial distributors into partners," *Harvard Business Review,* March–April 1986:66–71; and Marty Jacknis and Steve Kratz, "The channel empowerment solution," *Sales & Marketing Management,* March 1993:44–9.
17. Ronald Henkoff, "Delivering the goods," *Fortune,* 18 November 1994:64–78. Also see Shlomo Maital, "The last frontier of cost reduction," *Across the Board,* February 1994:51–52.
18. Maital, "The last frontier of cost reduction":52.
19. "Linking with vendors for just-in-time service," *Chain Store Age Executive,* June 1993:22A–24A; Joseph Weber, "Just get it to the stores on time," *Business Week,* 6 March 1995:66–7.
20. John Huey, "Wal-Mart: Will it take over the world?" *Fortune,* 30 January 1989:52–64.
21. Shawn Tully, "Comeback ahead for railroads," *Fortune,* 17 June 1991:107–13.
22. "Managing logistics in the 1990s," *Logistics Perspectives,* Cleveland: Anderson Consulting, July 1990:1–6.
23. Sandra J. Skrovan, "Partnering with vendors: The ties that bind," *Chain Store Age Executive,* January 1994:6MH–9MH.
24. Skrovan, "Partnering with vendors":6MH; Susan Caminiti, "After you win, the fun begins," *Fortune,* 2 May 1994:76.
25. Myron Magnet, "The new golden rule of business," *Fortune,* 21 February 1994:60–4. For a related example, see Justin Martin, "Are you as good as you think you are?" *Fortune,* September 1996:145–6.
26. Based on an address by Professor Donald J. Bowersox at Michigan State University on 5 August 1992.
27. Gail DeGeorge, "Ryder sees the logic of logistics," *Business Week,* 5 August 1996:56.
28. See Stern El-Ansary, and Coughlan, *Marketing Channels:*160; Patrick Byrne, "A new roadmap for contract logistics," *Transportation & Distribution,* April 1993:58–62; Ronald Henkoff, "Delivering the goods," *Fortune,* 18 November 1994:64–77; and Scott Wooley, "Replacing inventory with information," *Forbes,* 24 March 1997:54–8.

Company Case 11

Icon Acoustics: Bypassing Tradition

The Dream

Like most entrepreneurs, Dave Fokos dreams a lot. He imagines customers eagerly phoning Icon Acoustics in Ottawa to order his latest, custom-made stereo speakers. He sees sales climbing, cash flowing, and hundreds of happy workers striving to produce top-quality products that delight Icon's customers.

Like most entrepreneurs, Dave has taken a long time to develop his dream. While majoring in electrical engineering at Queen's University, Dave discovered that he had a strong interest in audio engineering. Following graduation, Dave landed a job as a speaker designer with Conrad-Johnson, a high-end audio-equipment manufacturer. Within four years, Dave had designed 13 speaker models and decided to start his own company.

Dave identified a market niche that he felt other speaker firms had overlooked. The niche consisted of "audio addicts"—people who love to listen to music and appreciate first-rate stereo equipment. These affluent, well-educated customers are genuinely obsessed with their stereo equipment. "They'd rather buy a new set of speakers than eat," Dave observes.

Dave faced one major problem—how to distribute Icon's products. He had learned from experience at Conrad-Johnson that most manufacturers distribute their equipment primarily through stereo dealers. Dave did not hold a high opinion of most such dealers; he felt that they too often played hardball with manufacturers, forcing them to accept thin margins. Furthermore, the dealers concentrated on only a handful of well-known producers who provided mass-produced models. This kept those firms that offered more customized products from gaining access to the market. Perhaps most disturbing, Dave felt that the established dealers often sold not what was best for customers, but whatever they had in inventory that month.

Dave dreamed of offering high-end stereo loudspeakers directly to the audio-obsessed, bypassing the established dealer network. By going directly to the customers, Dave could avoid the dealer markups and offer top-quality products and service at reasonable prices.

The Plan

At age 28, Dave set out to turn his dreams into reality. Some customers who had come to know Dave's work became enthusiastic supporters of his dream and invested $189 000 in Icon. With their money and $10 000 of his own, Dave started Icon in a rented facility in an industrial park.

The Market. About 335 stereo-speaker makers compete for a $3 billion annual North American market for audio components. About 100 of these manufacturers sell to the low- and mid-range segments of the market, which account for 90 percent of the market's unit volume and about 50 percent of its value. In addition to competing with each other, US manufacturers also compete with Japanese firms that offer products at affordable prices. The remaining 235 or so manufacturers compete for the remaining 10 percent of the market's unit volume and 50 percent of the value—the high end—where Dave hopes to find his customers.

Icon's Marketing Strategy. To serve the audio addicts segment, Dave offers only the highest-quality speakers. He has developed two models: the Lumen and the Parsec. The Lumen stands 45 cm high, weighs 11 kg, and is designed for stand mounting. The floor-standing Parsec is 1.2 m high and weighs 43 kg. Both models feature custom-made cabinets that come in natural or black oak and walnut. Dave can build and ship two pairs of the Lumen speakers or one pair of the Parsec speakers per day by himself. To have an adequate parts inventory, he had to spend $50 000 of his capital on the expensive components.

Dave set the price of the Lumen and Parsec at $795 and $1795 per pair, respectively. He selected these prices to provide a 50 percent gross margin. He believes that traditional dealers would sell equivalent speakers at retail at twice those prices. Customers can call Icon on a toll-free number to order speakers or to get advice directly from Dave. Icon pays for shipping and any return freight via Federal Express—round-trip freight for a pair of Parsecs costs $486.

Dave offers to pay for the return freight because a key part of his promotional strategy is a 30-day, in-home, no-obligation trial. In his ads, Dave calls this "The 43200 Minute, No Pressure Audition." This trial period allows customers to listen to the speakers in their actual listening environment. In a dealer's showroom, the customer must listen in an artificial environment and often feels pressure to make a quick decision.

Dave believes that typical high-end customers may

buy speakers for "non-rational" reasons: They want a quality product and good sound, but they also want an image. Therefore, Dave has tried to create a unique image through the appearance of his speakers and to reflect that image in all of the company's marketing. He spent over $40 000 on distinctive stationery, business cards, a brochure, and a single display ad. He also designed a laminated label he places just above the gold-plated input jack on each speaker. The label reads: "This loudspeaker was handcrafted by [the technician's name who assembled the speaker goes here in his/her own handwriting]. Made in Canada by Icon Acoustics, Inc.

To get the word out, Dave concentrates on product reviews in trade magazines and on trade shows, such as the High End Hi-Fi show in New York. Attendees at the show cast ballots to select "The Best Sound at the Show." In the balloting, among 200 brands, Icon's Parsec speakers finished fifteenth. Among the top 10 brands, the least expensive was a pair priced at $2400, and six of the systems were priced from $8000 to $18 000. A reviewer in an issue of *Stereophile* magazine evaluated Icon's speakers and noted: "The overall sound was robust and dynamic, with a particularly potent low end. Parts and construction quality appeared to be first rate. Definitely a company to watch."

Dave made plans to invest in a slick, four-colour display ad in *Stereo Review,* the consumer stereo magazine with the highest circulation (600 000). He also expected another favourable review in *Stereophile* magazine.

The Reality

Dressed in jeans and a hooded sweatshirt, Dave pauses in the middle of assembling a cardboard shipping carton, pulls up a chair, and leans against the concrete-block wall of his manufacturing area. Reflecting on his experiences during his first year in business, Dave realizes he's learned a lot in jumping all the hurdles the typical entrepreneur faces. Dave experienced quality problems with the first cabinet supplier. Then, he ran short of a key component after a mix-up with a second supplier. Despite his desire to avoid debt, he had to borrow $50 000 from a bank. Prices for his cabinets and some components had risen, and product returns had been higher than expected (19 percent for the past six months). These price and cost increases put pressure on his margins, forcing Dave to raise his prices (to those quoted earlier). Despite the price increases, his margins remained below his 50 percent target.

Still, Dave feels good about his progress. The price increase does not seem to have affected demand. The

Exhibit 1 Icon Acoustics' Pro-Forma Financials ($ in thousands)

			Year		
	1	2	3	4	5
Pairs of speakers sold	224	435	802	1256	1830
Total sales revenue	$303	$654	$1299	$2153	$3338
Cost of Sales					
Materials and packaging	$130	$281	$561	$931	$1445
Shipping	$43	$83	$157	$226	$322
Total cost of sales	$173	$364	$718	$1157	$1767
Gross profit	$130	$290	$581	$996	$1571
Gross margin	43%	44%	45%	46%	47%
Expenses					
New property and equipment	$3	$6	$12	$15	$18
Marketing	$13	$66	$70	$109	$135
General and administrative	$51	$110	$197	$308	$378
Loan repayment	$31	$31	$0	$0	$0
Outstanding payables	$30	$0	$0	$0	$0
Total expenses	$128	$213	$279	$432	$531
Pretax profit	$2	$77	$302	$564	$1040
Pretax margin	1%	12%	23%	26%	31%

few ads and word-of-mouth advertising appear to be working. Dave receives about five phone calls per day, with one in seven calls leading to a sale. Dave also feels the stress of the long hours and the low pay, however. He is not able to pay himself a high salary—just $9500 this year.

Dave reaches over and picks up his most recent financial projections from a workbench (see Exhibit 1). He believes that this will be a break-even year—then he'll have it made. As Dave sets the projections back on the workbench, his mind drifts to his plans to introduce two exciting new speakers—the Micron ($2495 per pair) and the Millennium ($7995 per pair). He also wonders if there is a foreign market for his speakers. Should he use his same direct marketing strategy for foreign markets, or should he consider distributors? The dream continues.

QUESTIONS

1. What functions do traditional stereo dealers perform?
2. Why has Dave Fokos decided to establish a direct channel? What objectives and constraints have shaped his decision?
3. What consumer service needs do Dave's customers have?
4. What problems will Dave face as a result of his channel decisions? What changes would you recommend in Dave's distribution strategy, if any? Will his strategy work in foreign markets?
5. What other changes would you recommend in Dave's marketing strategy?

Source: Adapted from "Sound strategy," *INC.*, May 1991:46–56. © 1991 by Goldhirsh Group, Inc. Used with permission. Dave Fokos also provided information to support development of this case.

video case 11

SELLING EARTH'S SOUNDS

Kevin O'Leary, a sound engineer, is hoping to gain a piece of the annual $100 million nature recordings industry. He is the founder and president of Earth Noise, an independent record label that features recordings of various nature sounds. The Earth Noise recordings have very high sound quality, and Kevin is convinced that they could capture a significant share of the market. But Kevin is having trouble getting the recordings to customers. Identifying and securing distribution channels has been difficult, and Kevin is considering how he can ensure that his product reaches potential customers.

Earth Noise began in 1995 with its first recording, *The Sounds of Algonquin*. Then Kevin immediately made plans to leave for Guatemala and the Queen Charlotte Islands in British Columbia to make two more recordings. His goal was to produce as many CDs as possible to get a catalogue of recordings together. He felt that the way to make profits in this industry was to establish a good distribution network for the label, but getting distribution with just one recording was virtually impossible. Distributors were more interested in selling an entire product line.

Making more recordings was necessary, but expensive. Travel and equipment costs required that Kevin get cash from investors. He hired Kathy Meisler, a sales and marketing manager, to, among other things, arrange for an outside investor. The result was an alliance with Audio Products International (API), the makers of Mirage audio speakers, who provided $28 000 to finance Kevin's trip to Guatemala in return for the use of Kevin's recordings to demonstrate their speakers. Kevin was positioning his recordings as audiophile quality recordings. This distinguished his label from most of his competitors and was an excellent fit with API's positioning of its high-end speakers.

The other way that Kevin distinguished his recordings was by packaging them with a travel guide, including photos and artwork from the recording location. While other nature recordings have mixed nature sounds with music, he is more interested in providing a realistic recreation of the environment where the recordings were made. He plans to call his series of CDs *A Day in the Life of. . .* and promote the fact that they are not generic recordings but rather relate to a specific place.

The recording sessions in Guatemala and BC went very well. In fact, in Guatemala, Kevin recorded sounds for an unplanned CD: He met a family of drummers and recorded what will be sold as a world music CD in addition to his nature recording. However, when the mixing of the CDs was done back in Canada, some interference on the recordings meant that more money and time were spent getting the recordings ready for launch.

To continue to finance the mixing of the Guatemala CDs and a launch party for them, Kathy went back to API for more money. Although they had originally said they would not provide more cash until the CDs were ready, they agreed to invest another $10 000 to ensure the project's completion. Both Kathy and Kevin were anxious for the CDs to be launched before the Christmas season, the busiest time for CD sales. They set the launch party for late October 1996 and invited industry representatives, media people, and potential investors. The response to the recordings was very positive.

While the launch was seen as a way to get the product out into distribution, it wasn't successful. Earth Noise missed the Christmas season and, in January 1997, still had no distributor. In addition, Kathy left the company, and Kevin was back to doing everything himself. Short of cash to complete the mixing of the BC recording, Kevin began to try to find other investors. He visited The Upper Canada Brewing Company to explore the idea of a cross-promotion.

With no distribution arrangements in place yet, Kevin approached Page Distribution in late January 1997. Page Distribution, which supplies about 1000 stores, agreed to take 100 CDs. Denon, an even larger distributor, showed some interest but wanted to wait until March to distribute the CDs, arguing that stores are not interested in anything new until then. So two years after its initial recording was ready, Earth Noise was just starting to be distributed to customers. As Kevin waited for customer response to his CDs, he continued looking for investors and continued to plan still other CDs for the Earth Noise product line.

Questions

1. What are the options available to Kevin for getting the Earth Noise CDs distributed?
2. What would you recommend that Kevin do to increase the distribution of his products?

Source: This case was prepared by Auleen Carson and is based on "CD Man," *Venture* (February 9, 1997).

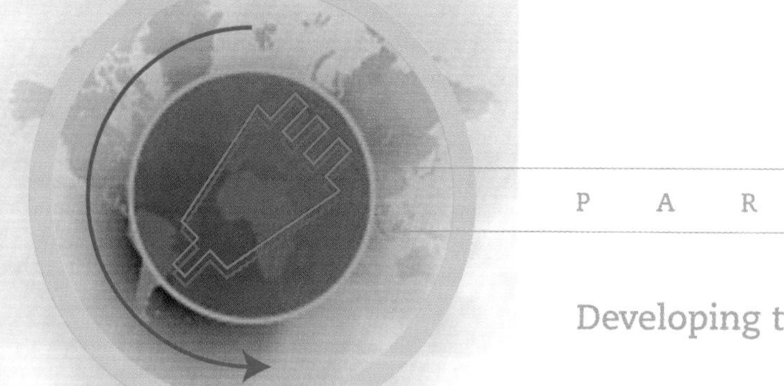

PART 1 2 3 4

Developing the Marketing Mix

Concept Connections

When you finish this chapter, you should be able to

1. Explain the roles of retailers and wholesalers in the distribution channel.
2. Describe the major types of retailers and give examples of each.
3. Identify the major types of wholesalers and give examples of each.
4. Explain the marketing decisions facing retailers and wholesalers.

chapter 12
Retailing and Wholesaling

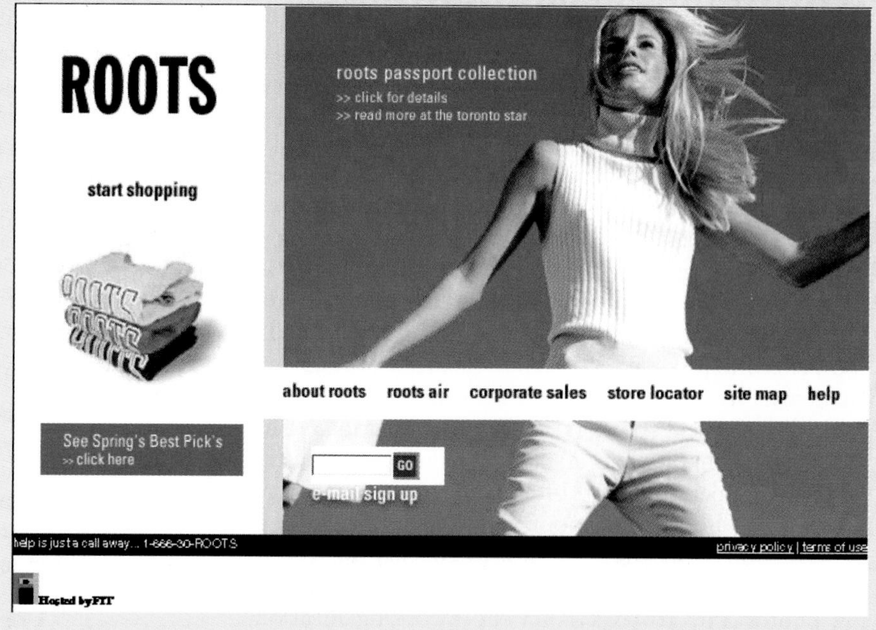

"Take hard-as-nails consumers. Add murderous competition. What do you get? Some sizzling opportunities for radical retailers." There is no doubt that Canada has a turbulent retail environment: an environment marked by some dramatic failures—such as the bankruptcy of Eaton's and subsequent sale of the chain to Sears—but also some dramatic successes. Take Roots, for example, the little leather goods firm that has managed to become associated with what it means to be Canadian. Currently, there are over 150 exclusive Roots stores in Canada, the United States, Japan, Korea, and Taiwan.

Roots and other retailers that have thrived in this difficult era all share one distinguishing feature—the ability to anticipate what their customers want and provide that product or service before their competitors. But product selection alone isn't enough. Consumers also want outstanding service and stimulating retail environments, provided at a reasonable price. Retailing expert Dr. Len Berry puts it this way: Successful retailers are committed to "the creation of a compelling value for their target customers." Value is created by pricing products and services fairly, providing exciting merchandising, offering respectful service, saving customers' time and energy, and making shopping more fun. Creating stores that both entertain and provide goods and services is important since "shopping is both a rational and an emotional experience." Retailers must understand how to stimulate consumers' senses to make shopping a more enjoyable and satisfying experience.

Even this may not be enough. One Toronto retailing analyst notes, "More specialty clothing stores are selling items that encompass an entire lifestyle." This is certainly what Roots Canada has done. New-style retailers, like Roots, have been able to capture their customers' way of looking at the world. As the people at Roots note, "We don't want to just sell you clothes and athletic gear and shoes and bags—although it's obviously important that we do. We want to help you embrace a lifestyle, a culture that will change the way you look at the world . . . and yourself."

It hasn't taken Canadians long to embrace such lifestyle marketers—Roots, Chateauworks, Club Monaco, and Urban Outfitters. These retailers sell an array of goods ranging from fashion items

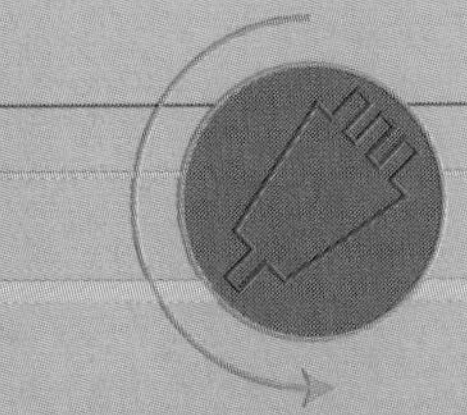

to perfume, furniture, housewares, stationery, clothing, candy, makeup, and more in large, open-concept stores based around a single lifestyle theme. Club Monaco, for example, sells housewares and furniture that match its minimalist brand positioning. Roots, describing itself as "eclectic," offers leather goods, casual clothing, perfume, household goods, and furniture with what it calls "a retro feel" linked to its Canadian outdoor heritage.

Randy Scotland of the Retail Council of Canada believes the popularity of lifestyle stores "makes perfect marketing sense," especially if the retailers' product lines are in sync with the feel of the store and are "true to the feeling, ethics and culture of brand." Alan Gee of Gee Jeffery & Partners Advertising agrees. He says that fashion retailers can be very successful at selling products for homes and lifestyles if they truly understand the meaning of their brand in consumers' lives. "Once you have brand understanding, you can leverage that code into [all] areas of a person's life." Today's powerful retailers realize that they are no longer distributors of manufacturers' brands: Instead, they are developing and positioning their own brands and products that fit more diverse aspects of consumers' lives.

Years before it thought about lifestyle marketing, Roots worked long and hard to build its unique brand equity. Founders Michael Budman and Don Green, two Detroit-reared hippies who loved Canada and its outdoors, were among the first to understand the marketing potential of Canadiana. They founded more than a store: They built a brand using this theme. They brought it to life with symbols of pristine blue lakes, summer camps, blood red sunsets, towering green forests, and canoes. Thus the Roots brand was born in the early 1970s with a single product—a negative-heel "earth" shoe. In the 1980s, it became identified even more with Canadian symbolism when Roots began to feature its beaver-logoed sweatshirts. Today Geoff Pevere, author of a book on Roots, describes the firm as the "quintessential Canadian success story. . . . It is successful but not overtly so, understated but immensely popular—in other words, good clean Canadian fun [yet a] high flyer of international fashion. The secret to their success? Hard work, an uncanny ability to predict and ride trends, quality products, and unabashed enthusiasm for that good ol' Canadian backwoods myth."

Building a brand is one thing. Successfully extending it without diluting its meaning for consumers is quite another. So far, Roots has managed to maintain its brand integrity. It has extended its brand from leather goods and casual clothing to fragrances. Roots offers *For Her* fragrance, a unisex product called *UniScent,* and *MiniScent,* a cologne for children. Forging ahead, Roots took advantage of the growing strength of its brand and expanded into the home furnishing market. It opened *Roots Home* in November 1998. In addition to furniture, these stores carry such items as pillows and bedding, luggage, jewellery, and desk accessories as well as "relaxed-style" clothing. We've had "a great response, [and] the furniture has done phenomenally," says Rima Biback, director of home operations. She describes the concept as "furniture for keeps." Roots also opened a lodge in British Columbia, which features Roots products as well as its lifestyle experience.

Some marketing analysts have started to wonder just how far Roots can extend its brand. When it announced "Roots Air" in June 2000, some wondered if "The beaver could fly." Roots decided to partner with Skyservice Airlines to offer business travellers an alternative to Air Canada on routes between Toronto and Montreal, Calgary, Edmonton, and Winnipeg. It remains to be seen whether the airline can get off the ground.

Never a company to rest on its laurels, Roots works continually to build its brand. It has leapt beyond simply having Canadians wear its clothes to having Canadian Olympians don them. Roots became a "Canadian brand" as our athletes stood in the global spotlight sporting their official red and white Roots gear that became as tied to the country as it was to the company. Canadians weren't the only ones to pick up on the brand. Roots Canada gained worldwide recognition through its presence at the 1998 Nagano Winter Olympics. Not only did Roots Canada gain world recognition by providing Canadian Olympians with distinctive uniforms, it "saw the power of television" as a tool to communicate its brand values and build global presence. Using the theme, "these are my roots," a national television campaign featuring Canadian gold-medal-winning snowboarder and counter-culture icon Ross Rebagliati was launched across Canada and the US. As Roots' strategists noted, however, "It's not just the advertising, it's the whole thing about sponsorship and the Olympics. . . . It's the constant overlapping of the brand into a wide range of categories" that helps make the Roots brand name powerful and distinctive."

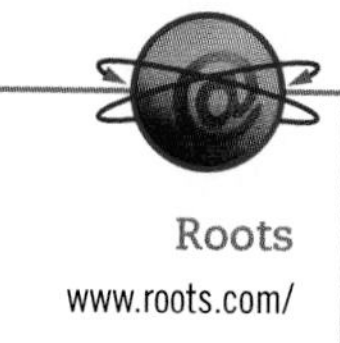

Roots
www.roots.com/

In addition to the brand value, lifestyle retailers like Roots offer their customers convenience. Linking together diverse products under a common brand theme simplifies consumer decision making. For those consumers who find time a key factor, lifestyle collections mean consumers no longer have to "go to 15 stores to find everything they want . . . they can do better things with their lives." To provide an even better response to the needs of time-pressed consumers, Roots was one of the first Canadian retailers to set up an e-commerce operation.

Like any vendor that takes its business online, Roots wanted to provide its customers with 24/7 service availability—in other words, give consumers convenient access 24 hours a day, seven days a week. Roots knew it had a globally recognized brand name thanks in part to its Olympic sponsorships. It could fulfill orders through its two Canadian state-of-the-art manufacturing facilities. A no-brainer—right? Just set up an e-commerce site, have the inventory on hand, fulfill the orders, and voilà—instant riches!

As Roots discovered, however, nothing is ever easy in practice. First, setting up an e-commerce operation meant it was, in effect, going global. Suddenly it had to serve people who were paying for orders in guilders, drachmas, francs, shillings, pounds and US dollars. Not surprisingly, "The whole process of building the site was slower than we thought," says Roots co-founder Michael Budman. Roots turned to IBM's Global Merchant program for help. Global Merchant enabled Roots to provide secure, real-time credit card processing in 30 different currencies; handle sales tax and value-added tax calculations; fulfill orders through multi-location warehousing; and distribute internationally.

While important, these features pale in comparison to other demands of online customers. Relationship management is the key, and Roots knew it had to care about the customers' total online experience just as it did in its bricks-and-mortar stores. As Ken Cassar, an analyst with Jupiter Communications' digital commerce strategy practice, warns, the "greatest challenge is living up to the expectations that consumers have toward their brands. Nailing the basics such as site performance, inventory, fulfillment management, and customer service becomes more crucial than ever."

Since ordering online involves more perceived risk, customers expect a confirmation e-mail within 15 minutes of placing their order. They also want to know they can contact a real person if they have a problem. Therefore, Roots provides a toll-free number as well as e-mail contact points. Finally, its developers stress that Root's Web site is more than a simple online store: "It's a coming together of strong brand and strong commerce." Roots seems to have tapped one of the secrets to online success. "It's not the pure e-businesses, and it's not the bricks-and-mortar companies that will be successful. It will be the companies that combine both of them," an experienced e-business analyst notes. Even more importantly, Roots founder Michael Budman believes, "Web surfers from around the world will—whether they buy or not—get a great sense of who Canadians are and what our lifestyle is through this site." Go have a look for yourself to see if you agree.[1]

The Roots story provides many insights into the workings of one of Canada's most successful retailers. This chapter looks at retailing and wholesaling. In the first section of this chapter, we look at the nature and importance of retailing, major types of store and non-store retailers, the decisions retailers make, and the future of retailing in Canada and abroad. In the second section, we discuss these same topics as they relate to wholesalers.

Retailing

Retailing
All activities involved in selling goods or services directly to final consumers for their personal, non-business use.

Retailers
Businesses whose sales come primarily from retailing.

What is retailing? We all know that Wal-Mart, Sears, and The Bay are retailers, but so are Avon representatives, the local Holiday Inn, and Internet marketers. **Retailing** includes all the activities involved in selling goods or services directly to final consumers for their personal, non-business use. Many institutions—manufacturers, wholesalers, and non-profit organizations—do retailing. But most retailing is done by **retailers,** businesses whose sales come *primarily* from retailing—reselling goods to end consumers.

Although most retailing is done in retail stores, non-store retailing has been growing much faster than has store retailing. Non-store retailing includes selling to final consumers through direct mail, catalogues, telephone, home TV shopping shows, home and office parties, door-to-door contact, vending machines, online services and the Internet, and other direct retailing approaches. We discuss such direct marketing approaches in detail in Chapter 16. In this chapter, we focus on store retailing. Although we have separated the types of retailing, research has shown that customers who use multiple channels spend ten times more than shoppers who use a single channel. Specifically, Digitrends.net found that one retailer's Web-only customers spent $181 per year; those buying in stores spend $291 annually; while catalogue customers spent $438 yearly. However, customers who shopped all three channels spent $1575.[2]

Types of Retailers

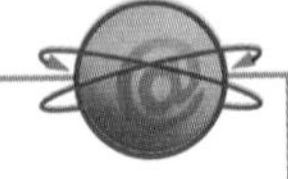

Retail Council of Canada
www.retailcouncil.org/

Retailing is an important sector in the Canadian economy. The Retail Council of Canada reports that retailing accounts for 6.2 percent of our total gross domestic product, and creates two percent of the country's employment or about 1.7 million jobs.[3]

Retail stores come in all shapes and sizes, and new retail types keep emerging. The most prevalent types of retail stores are described in Table 12-1 and discussed in the following sections. Retail establishments can be classified in terms of several characteristics, including the amount of service they offer, the breadth and depth of their product lines, the relative prices they charge, and how they are organized. Table 12-2 lists some of Canada's major retailers along with their revenues. Three major types of retailers dominate the Canadian retailing landscape: department stores equal 6.8 percent of the mix, chain stores make up 31.7 percent of the total, and independent stores account for the remaining 61.5 percent. Note that independence reflects store ownership, not the banner that the store operates under. And percentages of chains versus independents vary by retail category. A major trend in Canada is that in some sectors, retailing has become highly concentrated. In the supermarket and grocery store category, chain stores account for 52.6 percent of total revenue. In fashion retailing, chains account for 61.3 percent of the revenues earned by women's clothing stores, and 68.8 percent for men's. Shoe retailing is even more concentrated, with chains making up 74.4 percent of sales. Another trend marking retailing in Canada is the decline of department stores. While they made up 11 percent of retailers in the 1980s, their percentage fell to 6.6 percent of the mix during the 1990s.

TABLE 12-1 Major Types of Retailers

Type	Description	Examples
Specialty stores	Carry a narrow product line with a deep assortment within that line; apparel stores, sporting goods stores, furniture stores, florists, and bookstores. Specialty stores can be subclassified by the degree of narrowness in their product line. A clothing store would be a *single-line store;* a men's clothing store would be a *limited-line store;* and a men's custom-shirt store would be a *superspecialty store.*	Tall Men (tall men's clothing); The Limited (women's clothing); The Body Shop (cosmetics and bath supplies)
Department stores	Carry several product lines—typically clothing, home furnishings, and household goods—with each line operated as a separate department managed by specialist buyers or merchandisers.	Sears, The Bay
Supermarkets	Relatively large, low-cost, low-margin, high-volume, self-service operations designed to serve consumers' total needs for food, laundry, and household maintenance products.	Safeway Foods, A&P, Loblaws, Sobeys, Thrifty
Convenience stores	Relatively small stores that are located near residential areas, operate long hours seven days a week, and carry a limited line of high-turnover convenience products. Their long hours and their use by consumers mainly for "fill-in" purchases make them relatively high-price operations.	7-Eleven, Beckers, Mac's, Couche-Tard, Provi-Soir
Superstores	Larger stores that aim to meet consumers' total needs for routinely purchased food and non-food items. They include *supercentres,* combined supermarket and discount stores, which feature cross-merchandising. They also include *category killers* that carry a very deep assortment of a particular line. Another superstore variation is the *hypermarket,* a huge store that combines supermarket, discount, and warehouse retailing to sell routinely purchased goods as well as furniture, large and small appliances, clothing, and many other items.	*Supercentres:* Wal-Mart Supercentres; *Category killers:* Toys 'R' Us (toys), Petsmart (pet supplies), Chapters (books), Home Depot (home improvement), Best Buy (consumer electronics); *Hypermarkets:* Carrefour (France); Pycra (Spain), Meijer's (Netherlands)
Discount stores	Sell standard merchandise at lower prices by accepting lower margins and selling higher volumes. A true discount store *regularly* sells its merchandise at lower prices, offering mostly national brands, not inferior goods. Discount retailers include both general merchandise and specialty merchandise stores.	*General discount stores:* Wal-Mart, Zellers; *Specialty discount stores:* Future Shop (electronics), Crown Bookstores (books)
Off-price retailers	Sell a changing and unstable collection of higher-quality merchandise, often leftover goods, over-runs, and irregulars obtained at reduced prices from manufacturers or other retailers. They buy at less than regular wholesale prices and charge consumers less than retail. They include three main types:	
Independent off-price retailers	Owned and run by entrepreneurs or by divisions of larger retail corporations.	T.J. Maxx, Winners
Factory outlets	Owned and operated by manufacturers and normally carry the manufacturer's surplus, discontinued, or irregular goods. Such outlets increasingly group together in *factory outlet malls,* where dozens of outlet stores offer prices as much as 50 percent below retail on a broad range of items.	Dansk (dinnerware), Dexter (shoes), Ralph Lauren and Liz Claiborne (upscale apparel)
Warehouse (or wholesale) clubs	Sell a limited selection of brand name grocery items, appliances, clothing, and a hodgepodge of other goods at deep discounts to members who pay $25 to $50 annual membership fees. They serve small businesses and other club members out of huge, low-overhead, warehouse-like facilities and offer few frills or services.	Wal-Mart-owned Sam's Club, Max Clubs, Price-Costco, BJ's Wholesale Club

Amount of Service

Different products require different amounts of service, and customer service preferences vary. Retailers may offer one of three levels of service—self-service, limited service, and full service.

Self-service retailers increased rapidly in Canada during the Great Depression of the 1930s. Customers were willing to perform their own "locate-compare-select" process to save money. Today, self-service is the basis of all discount oper-

TABLE 12-2 Canada's Top Retailers by Category

Sector	Company	1999 Revenues
Supermarkets and food distribution	Loblaw Companies	$18 810 000
	Empire Co.	6 414 938
	Sobeys Inc.	6 230 721
	Provigo	5 874 400
	Canada Safeway	3 324 600
Department stores	The Hudson Bay Co.	7 295 751
	Sears	6 131 200
	Zellers	4 598 000
	Costco Canada	3 087 962
	Jean Coutu Group	2 289 370
Clothing stores	Dylex Ltd.	1 081 767
	Reitmans (Canada)	526 811
	Suzy Shier	357 733
	Mark's Work Wearhouse	321 187
	Boutiques San Francisco	226 769
Banks, trusts, credit unions, caisses populaires	Royal Bank of Canada	19 683 000
	Bank of Montreal	16 685 000
	Bank of Nova Scotia	16 654 000
	TD	15 683 000
	CT Financial Services	4 154 000
Speciality stores	Canadian Tire Corp.	4 728 259
	Future Shop	1 960 274
	Katz Group	1 700 000
	Rona Inc.	988 385
	Hartco Enterprises	850 279

Source: Compiled from "The top 1000: Canada's power book," *Report on Business Magazine,* July 2000:126–8.

ations and typically is used by sellers of convenience goods (such as supermarkets) and nationally branded, fast-moving shopping goods (such as the Future Shop).

Limited-service retailers, such as Sears, provide more sales assistance because they carry more shopping goods about which customers need information. Their increased operating costs result in higher prices. In *full-service retailers,* such as specialty stores and first-class department stores, salespeople assist customers in every phase of the shopping process. Full-service stores usually carry more specialty goods for which customers like to be "waited on." They provide more liberal return policies, various credit plans, free delivery, home servicing, and extras such as lounges and restaurants. More services result in much higher operating costs, which are passed along to customers as higher prices.

Product Line

Specialty store
A retail store that carries a narrow product line with a deep assortment within that line.

Department store
A retailer that carries a wide variety of product lines—typically clothing, home furnishings, and household goods; each line is operated as a separate department managed by specialist buyers or merchandisers.

Retailers can also be classified by the length and breadth of their product assortments. **Specialty stores** carry a narrow product line with a deep assortment within that line. Examples are stores that sell sporting goods, furniture, books, electronics, flowers, or toys. Specialty stores are flourishing as the use of market segmentation, market targeting, and product specialization has created a greater need for stores that focus on specific products and segments.

In contrast, **department stores** carry a wide variety of product lines. In recent years, department stores have been squeezed between more focused and flexible specialty stores on the one hand, and more efficient, lower-priced discounters on the other. In response, many have added "bargain basements" and promotional

Specialty stores are flourishing with their offering of high-quality products, convenient locations, good hours, and excellent service.

events to meet the discount threat. Others have set up store brand programs, "boutiques" and "designer shops" (such as Tommy Hilfiger or Polo shops within department stores), and other store formats that compete with specialty stores. Still others are trying mail-order, telephone, and Web site selling. Service and outstanding product assortments remain the key differentiating factors.

Supermarkets
Large, low-cost, low-margin, high-volume, self-service stores that carry a wide variety of food, laundry, and household products.

Supermarkets are large, low-cost, low-margin, high-volume, self-service stores that carry a wide variety of food, laundry, and household products. Chains account for most of the supermarket sales in Canada, and this channel is rapidly consolidating. In 1998, Empire, owner of Atlantic Canada's Sobeys, purchased the Oshawa Group for $1.44 billion, adding banners like IGA and Price Chopper to its shopping cart. The purchase gave it roughly a 20 percent share of the Canadian grocery market. Rival Loblaw Companies countered by snapping up Provigo, boosting its share of the Canadian supermarket business to about 40 percent.[4] Despite ongoing consolidation, supermarkets continue to look for new ways to build their sales. Most chains now operate fewer but larger stores. They practise "scrambled merchandising," and carry many non-food items—beauty aids, housewares, toys, prescriptions, appliances, video cassettes, sporting goods, garden supplies—hoping to find high-margin lines to improve profits. They also are improving their facilities and services to attract more customers. Many supermarkets are "moving upscale," providing "from-scratch" bakeries, gourmet deli counters, and fresh seafood departments. Others are cutting costs, establishing more efficient operations, and lowering prices to compete more effectively with food discounters.

Convenience store
A small store located near a residential area that is open long hours seven days a week and carries a limited line of high-turnover convenience goods.

Convenience stores are small stores that carry a limited line of high-turnover convenience goods. These stores locate near residential areas and remain open long hours, seven days a week. When supermarkets won the right to open for business on Sundays, and drugstore chains and gas station boutiques began selling groceries and snack foods, convenience stores lost their monopoly on their key differentiating variable—*convenience*. The result has been a huge industry shakeout. While many of the "mom-and-pop" stores that once dominated the industry are closing, others are being opened by the huge chains. For example, while Couche-Tard may not exactly be a household name, with 1600 outlets it is Canada's largest operator of convenience stores. It owns stores from Victoria, BC to Sept-Iles, Quebec—stores that operate under the Couche-Tard name as well as such banners as Mac's, Becker's, Mike's Mart, and Daisy Mart. The chain has been growing in both size and profitability at a time when convenience stores' share of Canadian food and grocery items fell from 2.1 to 1.7 percent. How has Couche-Tard done this? By positioning its stores as destination outlets. Whereas once these stores sold overpriced emergency goods, they now offer a wide range of convenience items that are competitively priced, as well as ATMs, fax machines, photocopiers, and stamp

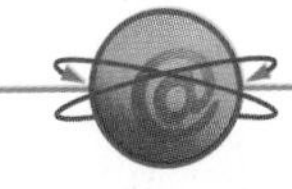

Couche-Tard
www.couche-tard.com/

machines. Moreover, there are gas bars at 435 outlets. Like their larger rivals, Couche-Tard convenience stores have started branding their own food items. They are investing heavily to redesign their stores to match the needs of their local neighbourhoods. Those in upscale areas offer such high-margin, mouth-watering, fresh-baked goods as croissants that customers can eat at in-store cafés. Those in areas frequented by male, blue collar workers stock meat-laden Subway sandwiches. Like many savvy marketers, Couche-Tard also knows that employee ability and satisfaction is highly correlated with customer satisfaction. Therefore, it invests heavily in employee training so that its stores can offer the service and merchandising that rival their larger competitors.[5]

Superstore
A store almost twice the size of a regular supermarket that carries a large assortment of routinely purchased food and non-food items and offers such services as dry cleaning, post offices, photo finishing, cheque cashing, bill paying, lunch counters, car care, and pet care.

Superstores are much larger than regular supermarkets and carry a large assortment of routinely purchased food and non-food items. Supervalu, which even calls itself "the real Canadian Superstore," has locations from Thunder Bay, Ontario west to Vancouver, BC, with stores in all of western Canada's major cities, including Whitehorse in the Yukon. Supervalu stores carry everything from telephones and children's apparel to fresh fruits and seafood.

Recent years have seen the advent of superstores that are actually giant specialty stores, the so-called *category killers*. These "big-box" retailers are the megastores that have crossed the border from the US. As big as airplane hangars, the stores carry a wide assortment of a particular line and have a knowledgeable staff. Home Depot Canada, Chapters, Office Depot, The Sports Authority, and Michaels Arts and Crafts are among the many recent entrants into the Canadian marketplace.

Another superstore variation is *hypermarkets,* huge superstores perhaps as large as six football fields. Although hypermarkets have been very successful in Europe and other world markets, they have met with little success in North America. Despite their size, most hypermarkets have only limited product variety, and many people balk at the serious walking required to shop in them.

Service retailers
Retailers that sell services rather than products.

Finally, for some businesses, the "product line" is actually a service. **Service retailers** include hotels and motels, banks, airlines, universities, movie theatres, tennis clubs, bowling alleys, restaurants, repair services, hair-care shops, and dry cleaners. Service retailers in Canada are growing faster than product retailers, and each service industry has its own retailing drama. Banks look for new ways to distribute their services, including online banking, automated tellers, direct deposit, and telephone banking. Professional service providers—firms composed of lawyers,

Turning many of its convenience stores into destination outlets featuring branded products has enabled Couche-Tard to achieve superior profitability.

architects, chartered accountants, physiotherapists, or dentists—are just beginning to understand the importance of marketing. And universities are battling as never before to attract students into their programs.

Relative Prices

The third way retailers can be classified is according to the prices they charge. Most retailers charge regular prices and offer normal-quality goods and customer service. Some offer higher-quality goods and service at higher prices. The retailers that feature low prices are discount stores, off-price retailers, and catalogue showrooms.

Discount store
A retail institution that sells standard merchandise at lower prices by accepting lower margins and selling at higher volume.

A **discount store** sells standard merchandise at lower prices by accepting lower margins and selling at higher volume. The early discount stores cut expenses by operating in warehouse-like facilities in low-rent, heavily travelled districts. In recent years, facing intense competition from other discounters and department stores, many discount retailers have "traded up." They have improved decor, added new lines and services, and opened suburban branches, which has led to higher costs and prices.

Off-price retailers
Retailers that buy at less than regular wholesale prices and sell at less than retail. They include factory outlets, independents, and warehouse clubs.

When the major discount stores traded up, a new wave of **off-price retailers** moved in to fill the low-price, high-volume gap. Ordinary discounters buy at regular wholesale prices and accept lower margins to keep prices down. In contrast, off-price retailers buy at less than regular wholesale prices and charge consumers less than retail. Off-price retailers have made the biggest inroads in clothing, accessories, and footwear, but they can be found in all areas, from discount brokerages to food stores and electronics.

Factory outlets
Off-price retailing operations that are owned and operated by manufacturers and that normally carry the manufacturer's surplus, discontinued, or irregular goods.

The three main types of off-price retailers are *factory outlets, independents,* and *warehouse clubs.* **Factory outlets** are owned and operated by manufacturers and normally carry the manufacturer's surplus, discontinued, or irregular goods. Examples are Arrow Shirts, the Nike Factory Outlet, and the Danier Leather Factory outlet. Such outlets sometimes group together in *factory outlet malls,* where dozens of outlet stores offer prices as low as 50 percent below retail on a wide range of items.

Independent off-price retailers
Off-price retailers that are either owned and run by entrepreneurs or are divisions of larger retail corporations.

Independent off-price retailers are either owned and run by entrepreneurs or are divisions of larger retail corporations. Although many off-price operations are run by smaller independents, most large off-price retailer operations are owned by bigger retail chains. Examples include Winners, which is owned by US-based TJX.

Warehouse club (wholesale club)
Off-price retailer that sells a limited selection of brand-name grocery items, appliances, clothing, and a hodgepodge of other goods at deep discounts to members who pay annual membership fees.

Warehouse clubs (or *wholesale clubs,* or *membership warehouses*) such as Price-Costco sell a limited selection of brand name grocery items, appliances, clothing, and a hodgepodge of other goods at deep discounts to members who pay annual membership fees. They operate in huge, warehouse-like facilities and offer few frills. Such clubs make no home deliveries and accept no credit cards, but they do offer rock-bottom prices. Warehouse clubs took the country by storm in the 1980s, but their growth slowed considerably in the 1990s as a result of growing competition among warehouse store chains and effective reactions by supermarkets.

In general, although off-price retailing blossomed during the 1980s, competition has stiffened as more off-price retailers have entered the market. The growth of off-price retailing slowed a bit recently because of effective counterstrategies by department stores and regular discounters. Still, off-price retailing remains a vital and growing force in modern retailing.

Retail Organizations

Although many retail stores are independently owned, an increasing number are banding together under some form of corporate or contractual organization. The major types of retail *organizations—corporate chains, voluntary chains* and *retailer cooperatives, franchise organizations,* and *merchandising conglomerates*—are

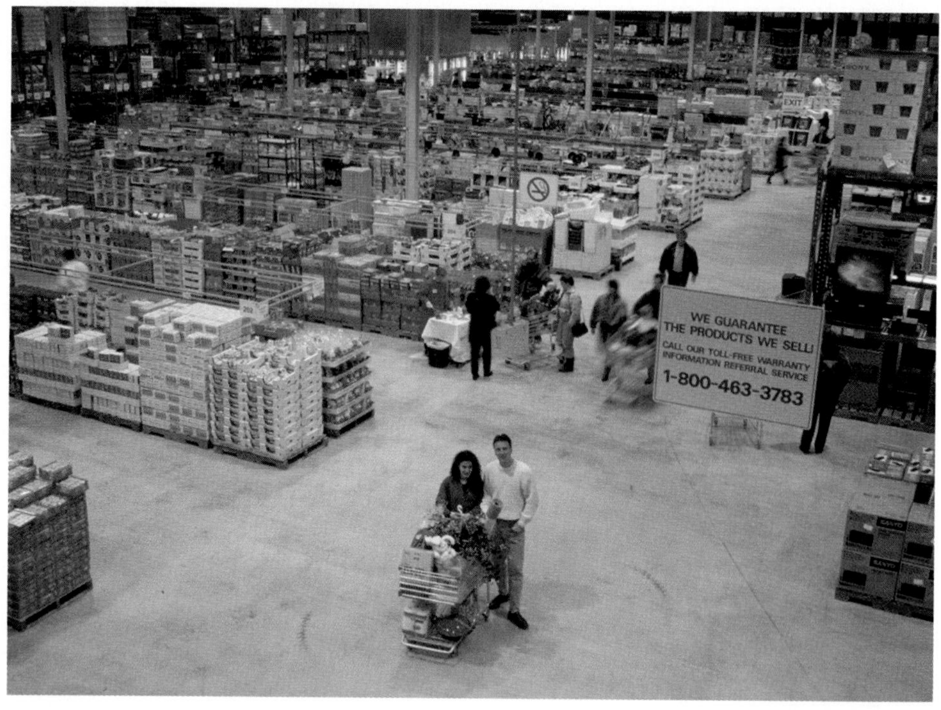

Warehouse clubs operate in huge, low-overhead, warehouse-like facilities, where customers must wrestle large items to the checkout line. But such clubs offer low prices.

described in Table 12-3. Retailing is more concentrated in Canada than it is in the US, with 40 percent of Canadian retailers belonging to some type of chain compared with 20 percent of their US counterparts.

Chain stores are two or more outlets that are commonly owned and controlled. Many US-based chain stores have invaded Canada, and more are on the way. For example, Old Navy (the discount division of Gap), American Eagle Outfitters, and Skechers USA Inc. (a trendy California-based shoe store) plan to enter in the spring of 2001.[6] While many of these operations are welcomed by consumers, they threaten to take business away from their Canadian rivals. Chains have many advantages over independents. Their size allows them to buy in large quantities at lower prices. They can afford to hire corporate-level specialists to deal with pricing, promotion, merchandising, inventory control, and sales forecasting. Corporate chains gain promotional economies because their advertising costs are spread over many stores and over a large sales volume. Since the US chains have even deeper pockets and a broader scope of operations, they have even greater advantage with regard to the above factors. To fight this invasion, Canadian chains often consolidate even further.

Chain stores
Two or more outlets that are commonly owned and controlled, have central buying and merchandising, and sell similar lines of merchandise.

The great success of corporate chains has also caused many independents to band together in contractual associations. One form is the **voluntary chain**—a wholesaler-sponsored group of independent retailers that engages in group buying and common merchandising. The most recognizable examples of this form are the Independent Grocers Alliance (IGA) and Western Auto. The other form of contractual association is the **retailer cooperative**—a group of independent retailers that band together to set up a jointly owned central wholesale operation and conduct joint merchandising and promotion efforts. True Value Hardware is an example of this contractual association. These organizations give independents the buying and promotion economies they need to meet the prices of corporate chains.

Voluntary chain
A wholesaler-sponsored group of independent retailers that engages in group buying and common merchandising.

Retailer cooperative
A group of independent retailers that band together to set up a jointly owned central wholesale operation and conduct joint merchandising and promotion efforts.

A **franchise** is a contractual association between a manufacturer, wholesaler, or service organization (the franchiser) and independent businesspeople (the franchisees), who buy the right to own and operate one or more units in the franchise

Franchise
A contractual association between a manufacturer, wholesaler, or service organization (a franchiser) and independent businesspeople (franchisees), who buy the right to own and operate one or more units in the franchise system.

TABLE 12-3 Major Types of Retail Organizations

Type	Description	Examples
Corporate chain stores	Two or more outlets that are commonly owned and controlled, employ central buying and merchandising, and sell similar lines of merchandise. Corporate chains appear in all types of retailing, but they are strongest in department stores, variety stores, drugstores, shoe stores, and women's clothing stores.	La Senza (lingerie), Sports Experts (sports goods), Loblaws (grocery)
Voluntary chains	Wholesaler-sponsored groups of independent retailers engaged in bulk buying and common merchandising.	Independent Grocers Alliance (IGA), Western Auto, True Value Hardware
Retailer cooperatives	Groups of independent retailers that set up a central buying organization and conduct joint promotion efforts.	Calgary Group (groceries), ACE (hardware), Mountain Equipment Co-op (outdoor goods)
Franchise organizations	Contractual association between a *franchiser*—a manufacturer, wholesaler, or organization—and *franchisees*—independent businesspeople who buy the right to own and operate one or more units in the franchise system. Franchise organizations are normally based on some unique product, service, or method of doing business, or on a trade name or patent, or on goodwill that the franchiser has developed.	McDonald's, Subway, Pizza Hut, Jiffy Lube, 7-Eleven, Yogen Früz
Merchandising conglomerates	A free-form corporation that combines several diversified retailing lines and forms under central ownership, along with some integration of their distribution and management functions.	The Venator Group (owner of Foot Locker, Lady Foot Locker, Northern Reflections, Northern Traditions)

system. The main difference between a franchise and other contractual systems (voluntary chains and retail cooperatives) is that franchise systems typically are based on some unique product or service; on a method of doing business; or on the trade name, goodwill, or patent that the franchiser has developed. Franchising has been prominent in fast-food companies, motels, gas stations, video stores, health and fitness centres, auto rentals, hair-cutting salons, real estate and travel agencies, and dozens of other product and service areas. Franchising is described in detail in Marketing Highlight 12-1.

Venator Group
www.venatorgroup.com/

Merchandising conglomerates are corporations that combine several retailing forms under central ownership and share some distribution and management functions. The Venator Group operates a number of specialty chains including Northern Reflections, Northern Traditions, Northern Elements, and Northern Getaway as well as Kinney Shoe Stores and Foot Locker (sports shoes). Diversified retailing, which provides superior management systems and economies that benefit all the separate retail operations, is likely to increase.

Retailer Marketing Decisions

Retailers are searching for new marketing strategies to attract and hold customers. In the past, retailers attracted customers with unique products, more or better services than their competitors offered, or credit cards. Today, national brand manufacturers, in their drive for volume, have placed their branded goods everywhere. Therefore, stores offer similar assortments—national brands are found not only in department stores, but also in mass-merchandise and off-price discount stores. As a result, stores are looking more alike: They have become "commodified." In any city, a shopper can find many stores, but few variations in products.

Service differentiation between retailers has also eroded. Many department stores have trimmed their services, whereas discounters have increased theirs. Customers have become smarter and more price sensitive. They see no reason to pay more for identical brands, especially when service differences are shrinking. And

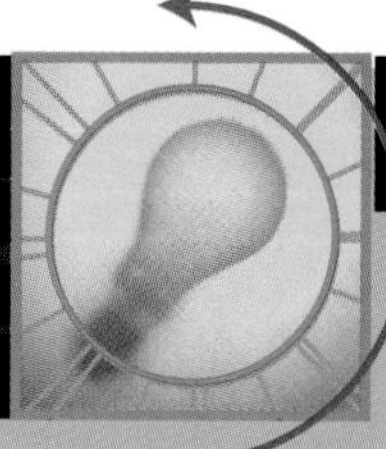

marketing highlight 12-1

Franchise Fever

Once considered upstarts among independent businesses, there are now 65 000 franchised businesses operating in Canada, with a new Canadian franchise opening every hour and forty-five minutes. Generating over $90 billion in sales, franchises account for 48 percent of all service and retail sales in Canada, compared to 35 percent in the United States. The franchise industry directly employs more than one million Canadians. According to Francon, Canada's sole franchise research company, Canadians have embraced franchising as a means of self-employment to a far greater extent than the populace of any other country. This isn't hard to believe in a society where it's nearly impossible to stroll down a city block or drive on a suburban thoroughfare without seeing a Tim Hortons, McDonald's, Midas Muffler, or 7-Eleven. In fact, you might be forgiven for thinking every possible corner in Canada is occupied by a Tim Hortons. The TDL Group Ltd., which operates the franchises, had 1700 locations in Canada and 100 in the US in 2000, when sales for the chain topped $1.6 billion.

While not as developed in other countries as in Canada, franchising is nonetheless a global phenomenon. Take McDonald's, for example: One of the best-known and most successful franchisers, it now has 24 500 stores in 116 countries and racks up more than $54 billion in system-wide sales. Over 80 percent of McDonald's restaurants worldwide are owned and operated by franchisees. Gaining fast is Subway Sandwiches and Salads, one of the fastest-growing franchises, with nearly 14 000 shops in 71 countries.

A number of Canadian franchise operations are also reaching beyond their domestic borders and trying to hook the world on the baked goods that have expanded our waistlines. Cinnaroll Bakeries Ltd. (www.cinnzeo.com), which operates 25 Cinnzeo outlets in Western Canada selling decadent fresh-baked cinnamon buns, currently has 10 Cinnzeo franchises in the Philippines, with an additional 30 expected to open by 2002. Cinnaroll has ambitious international marketing plans and has its eye on further expansion into South America, Australia, Eastern Canada, and the US. Says Cinnaroll president and CEO, Brian Latham: "We're not ruling out any area of the world." Similarly, The Great Canadian Bagel Co. of Markham, Ontario, founded in 1993, now operates nearly 160 stores across Canada, while its sister company, The Great American Bagel, has 58 outlets in the US. Both are owned by the same Canadian family, the Flatleys. In 1997, it launched a new venture—The Great International Bagel. The division currently markets their particular brand of doughy goodness in both the UK and Russia.

How does a franchising system work? The individual franchises are a tightly knit group of enterprises whose systematic operations are planned, directed, and controlled by the operation's founder, called a *franchisor*. Generally, franchises are distinguished by three characteristics:

1. *The franchisor owns a trade or service mark and licenses it to franchisees in return for royalty payments.*
2. *The franchisee is required to pay for the right to be part of the system.* Yet this initial fee is only a small part of the total amount that franchisees invest when they sign a franchising contract. Start-up costs include rental and lease of equipment and fixtures, and sometimes a regular licence fee. McDonald's franchisees may invest as much as $864 000 in initial start-up costs. The franchisee then pays McDonald's a service fee and a rental charge that equal 11.5 percent of the franchisee's sales volume. Subway's success is partly due to its low start-

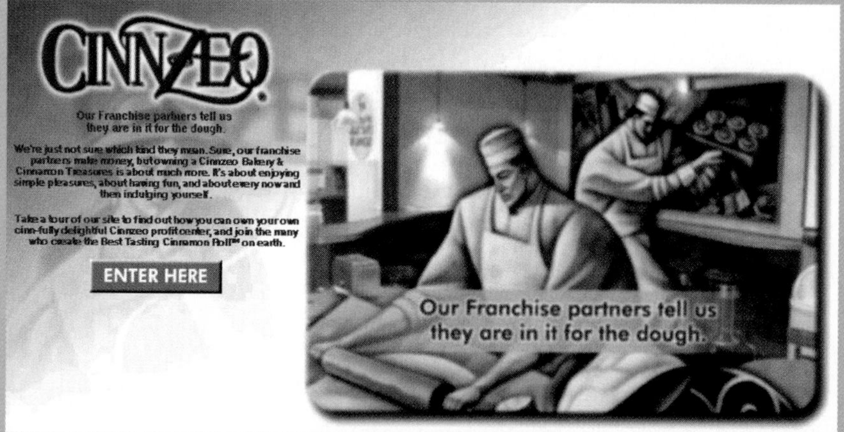

Canada's Cinnaroll Bakeries, which operates the Cinnzeo chain of outlets, has ambitious plans for overseas expansion.

because bank credit cards are now accepted at most stores, consumers no longer need credit from a particular store. For all these reasons, many retailers are rethinking their marketing strategies.[7]

As Figure 12-1 shows, retailers face major marketing decisions about their *target markets and positioning, product assortment and services, price, promotion,* and *place.*

up cost of $65 000 to $100 000, which is lower than 70 percent of other franchise system start-up costs.

3. *The franchisor provides its franchisees with a marketing and operations system for doing business.* McDonald's requires franchisees to attend its "Hamburger University" in Oak Brook, Illinois, for three weeks to learn how to manage the business. Franchisees must also adhere to certain procedures in buying materials.

In the best cases, franchising is mutually beneficial to both franchisor and franchisee. Franchisors can cover a new territory in little more than the time it takes the franchisee to sign a contract. They can achieve enormous purchasing power. (Consider the purchase order that Holiday Inn is likely to make for bed linens, for instance.) Franchisors also benefit from the franchisee's familiarity with local communities and conditions, and from the motivation and hard work of employees who are entrepreneurs rather than "hired hands." Similarly, franchisees benefit from buying into a proven business with a well-known and accepted brand name. And they receive ongoing support in areas ranging from marketing and advertising to site selection, staffing, and financing.

As a result of the franchise explosion in recent years, many types of franchisors are having difficulty. John Lorinc, author of *Opportunity Knocks: The Truth about Canada's Franchise Industry,* says 35 percent of all franchises fail and 80 percent may only break even. Subway, in particular, has been criticized for misleading its franchisees by telling them that it has only a two percent failure rate when the reality is much different. Some franchisees also believe that they've been misled by exaggerated claims of support, only to feel abandoned after the contract is signed and $100 000 is invested. Difficulties may arise due to hidden costs imposed on franchisees or the signing up of people who lack the resources to get the business off the ground. The most common complaint: Franchisors focused on growth who "encroach" on existing franchisees' territory by bringing in another store. Or franchisees may object to parent-company marketing programs that may adversely affect their local operations. For instance, franchisees strongly resisted a McDonald's promotion in which the company reduced prices on Big Macs and Egg McMuffins in an effort to revive stagnant sales. Many franchisees believed that the promotion would cheapen McDonald's image and unnecessarily reduce their profit margins.

There will *always* be a conflict between the franchisors, who seek system-wide growth, and the franchisees, who want to earn a good living from their individual franchises. Some new directions that may deliver both franchisor growth and franchisee earnings are:

- *Strategic alliances, co-branding, and twinning.* The newest trend in franchising is the marriage between two independent franchises at a single location. Tim Hortons, for example, often shares facilities with Wendy's; Baskin-Robbins teams up with Dunkin Donuts; Second Cup partners with Harvey's. Since the largest costs borne by franchisees are for land and staff, forming an alliance with another franchisee to share a location makes economic sense and can draw a more broad-based market to the joint outlets.
- *Code of ethics.* Each member of the Canadian Franchise Association (www.cfa.ca) is bound by a code of ethics designed to overcome some areas of difficulty. The code stipulates these conditions: There will be a full and accurate written disclosure of all information considered material to the franchise relationship; the company selling the franchise will provide reasonable guidance, training, and supervision for franchisees; fairness shall characterize all dealings between the franchisor and its franchisees; and the franchisor shall make every effort to resolve complaints, grievances, and disputes through fair and reasonable negotiation.
- *Non-traditional site locations.* Franchises have opened in airports, sports stadiums, university campuses, hospitals, gambling casinos, theme parks, convention halls, and even river boats.

Franchise fever is unlikely to cool down soon. Canadian franchisors like Uniglobe Travel International, Speedy Muffler King, Priority Management Systems Inc., and Manchu Wok are not only growing in Canada, they are conquering international markets as well.

Sources: David North, "King cruller," *Canadian Business,* 31 December 1999; David Todd, "Great Canadian Bagel makes slow but sure gains in Moscow," *Strategy,* 14 February 2000:27; Norma Ramage, "Canadian cinnamon buns savoured in Asia," *Marketing On-Line,* 19 June 2000; Norman D. Axelrad and Robert E. Weigand, "Franchising—A marriage of system members," in Sidney Levy, George Frerichs, and Howard Gordon, eds., *Marketing Managers Handbook,* 3rd ed., Chicago: Darnell, 1994:919–34; Lawrence S. Welch, "Developments in international franchising," *Journal of Global Marketing,* 6(1–2), 1992:81–96; Andrew E. Serwer, "McDonald's conquers the world," *Fortune,* 17 October 1994:103–16; "Trouble in franchise nation," *Fortune,* 6 March 1995:115–29; Robert Maynard, "The decision to franchise," *Nation's Business,* January 1997:49–53; Cliff Edwards, "'Campaign 55' flop shows growing power of franchisees," *Marketing News,* 7 July 1997:9; "Canadian Franchise Association Code of Ethics," Advertising Supplement, *Globe and Mail,* 18 September 1996:6; Jennifer Lanthier, "How franchises seduce those with the most to lose," *Financial Post,* 22 April 1997:28, Susan Noakes, "Creating marriages of convenience," *Financial Post,* 14 February 1997:16; Industry Canada "Canadian capabilities: Key facts about Canadian franchise expertise," strategis.ic.gc.ca/SSG/dm01301e.html; www.cfa.ca/.

Target Market and Positioning Decision

A retailer first must define its target market and decide how it will position itself in this market. Should the store focus on upscale, midscale, or downscale shoppers? Do target shoppers want variety, depth of assortment, convenience, or low prices? Until it defines and profiles its markets, a retailer cannot make consistent

FIGURE 12-1 Retailer marketing decisions

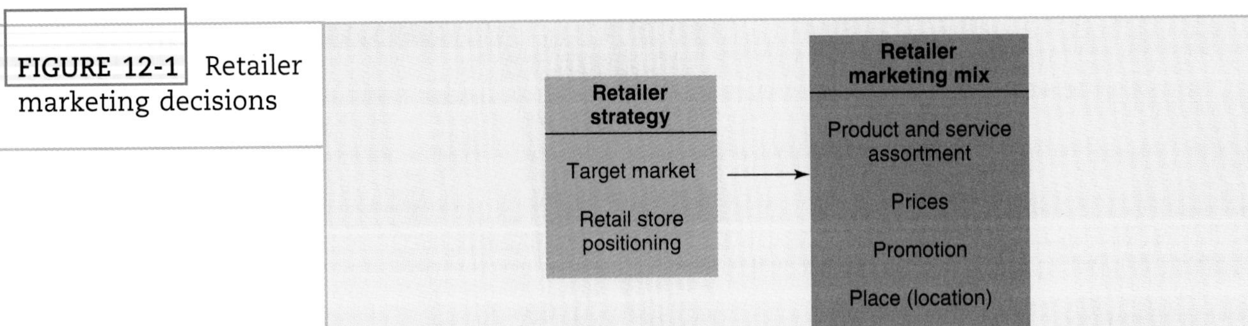

decisions about product assortment, services, pricing, advertising, store decor, or anything else that must support its position.

Too many retailers fail to define their target markets and positions clearly. They try to have "something for everyone" and end up satisfying no market well. In contrast, successful retailers define their target markets well and position themselves strongly. In 1963, Leslie H. Wexner borrowed $7000 to create The Limited, which started as a single store targeting young, fashion-conscious women. All aspects of the store—clothing assortment, fixtures, music, colours, personnel—were orchestrated to match the target consumer. He continued to open more stores, but a decade later his original customers were no longer in the "young" group. To catch the new "youngs," he started the Limited Express. Over the years, he started or acquired other highly targeted store chains, including Lady Bryant and Victoria's Secret, to reach new segments. Today The Limited, Inc. operates more than 5300 stores in seven different segments of the market, with sales of more than $15 billion.

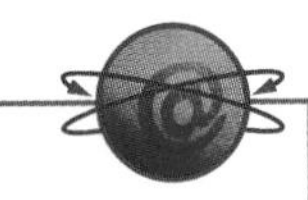

The Limited
www.thelimited.com/

Even large stores like Wal-Mart and Sears must define their major target markets to design effective marketing strategies. In recent years, thanks to strong targeting and positioning, Wal-Mart has expanded to the point where its sales almost equal those of General Motors (see Marketing Highlight 12-2).

Product Assortment and Services Decision

Retailers must decide on three major product variables: *product assortment, services mix,* and *store atmosphere.*

The *retailer's product assortment* must match target shoppers' expectations. The retailer must determine both the product assortment's *width* and its *depth.* Thus, a restaurant can offer a narrow and shallow assortment (small lunch counter), a narrow and deep assortment (delicatessen), a wide and shallow assortment (cafeteria), or a wide and deep assortment (large restaurant). Another product assortment element is the *quality* of the goods: The customer is interested not only in the range of choice but also in the quality of the products available.

No matter what the store's product assortment and quality level, there always will be competitors with similar assortments and quality. Therefore, the retailer must find other ways to *differentiate* itself from similar competitors. It can use any of several product differentiation strategies. For one, it can offer merchandise that no other competitor carries—its own private brands or national brands on which it holds exclusives. Many of Canada's best-performing fashion retailers—Club Monaco, Roots Canada, and the Venator Group—not only stock their stores with their own brands of clothing, but also extend these brands into new lines of accessories and cosmetic products. Items such as jewellery, belts, backpacks, perfume, and toiletries are used to reinforce the store's brand image.[8] Second, the retailer can feature blockbuster merchandising events—Ben Moss Jewellers is known throughout Western Canada for their promotions involving celebrities. Finally, the

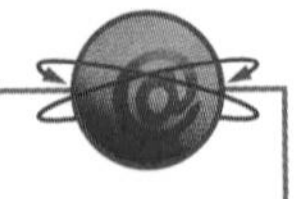

Club Monaco
www.clubmonaco.com/

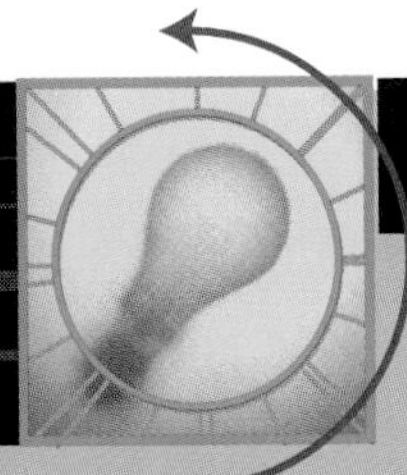

marketing highlight 12-2

Wal-Mart Canada—Distinguished Marketer of the Year 2000

Dave Ferguson, president and CEO of Wal-Mart Canada Inc., was named the Distinguished Canadian Retailer of the Year for 2000. The annual award, presented by the Retail Council of Canada, honours outstanding achievement and leadership in retailing. This award follows his 1999 acclaim when *Marketing Magazine* named him "Marketer of the Decade."

In presenting the 2000 award, Retail Council of Canada president Diane Brisebois exclaimed, "Dave Ferguson's pace-setting contributions to the retailing industry more than qualify him for this tribute. Under his accomplished leadership, Wal-Mart Canada has become a shining star not only in the Canadian retail marketplace, but in the international Wal-Mart organization as well." She went on to note that Wal-Mart Canada has had a great impact on the Canadian retailing scene by pushing itself and other retailers to improve customer service, competitive product offerings, and supply chain management. In addition to its retailing prowess, Wal-Mart Canada believes strongly in giving back to the community. It has built one of the country's strongest ongoing community involvement programs, donating over $6 million to local charities and causes.

Wal-Mart has come a long way since its founding in 1962 by Sam Walton and his brother in small-town Rogers, Arkansas. Most experts believed that the big, flat, warehouse-type store that sold everything from apparel to automotive supplies at very low prices was doomed to failure. Yet, from its modest beginnings, the chain expanded rapidly throughout the US.

The company entered Canada in 1995, when it purchased 122 Woolco stores. Today, it operates 166 stores nationwide and has created more than 14 000 quality retail and construction jobs. Furthermore, Dave Ferguson stresses that Wal-Mart Canada is much more than just Canadian outlets for American products. "Through our 'buy Canadian' merchandising program we continue to source more than 80 percent of our merchandise from Canadian businesses." And Wal-Mart recently entered into an agreement with Canada Post that gives Wal-Mart the exclusive rights to launch a unique line of Canadian collectible items developed and supplied by Canada Post Corporation. The first product—the Canada Day Millennium Keepsake—was made available on Canada Day, 2000.

Wal-Mart's phenomenal growth shows few signs of slowing, either in Canada or overseas. It has expanded into Latin and South America as well as Asia. Within only a few years of entering the grocery business with its supercentres—and more recently with its smaller Neighbourhood Market stores—Wal-Mart has become North America's number two grocery retailer.

Wal-Mart is beginning to flex its cybermuscles. The retailing giant already sells a selection of merchandise on its Web site (www.wal-mart.com). Many industry experts believe that Wal-Mart will soon dominate Internet marketspaces in the same way that it now dominates the physical marketplace. "At the end of the next four years," predicts one retailing industry consultant, "Wal-Mart will be number one on land and online."

As a result of these combined efforts, Wal-Mart is now the world's fourth largest company. Its performance has rewarded investors handsomely. An investment of $2300 in Wal-Mart stock in 1970 is worth $7.5 million today.

What are the secrets behind this spectacular success? Wal-Mart listens to and takes care of its customers, treats employees as partners, and keeps a tight rein on costs.

Listening to and Taking Care of Customers

Wal-Mart positioned itself strongly in a well-chosen target market. Initially, Sam Walton focused on value-conscious consumers in small towns. The chain built a strong everyday low-price position long before it became fashionable in retailing. It grew rapidly by bringing the lowest possible prices to towns ignored by national discounters.

Wal-Mart knows its customers and takes good care of them. As one analyst puts it, "The company gospel . . . is relatively simple: Be an agent for customers, find out what they want, and sell it to them for the lowest possible price." So the company listens carefully. For example, all top Wal-Mart executives go where their customers hang out, each spending at least two days a week visiting stores, talking directly with customers, and getting a first-hand look at operations. Then, Wal-Mart delivers what customers want—a broad selection of carefully selected goods at unbeatable prices.

But the right merchandise at the right price isn't the only key to Wal-Mart's success. Wal-Mart also provides outstanding service that keeps customers satisfied. A sign reading "Satisfaction Guaranteed" hangs prominently at each store's entrance. Another sign inside the store reads "At Wal-Mart, our goal is: You're always next in line!" Customers are often welcomed by "people greeters" eager to lend a helping hand or just to be friendly. And, sure enough, the store opens extra checkout counters to keep waiting lines short.

Wal-Mart not only cares for customers in its stores, but it also supports their communities. The company supports everything from local sporting events to local charities. According to Steve Arnold, a marketing professor at Queen's University, being a good corporate citizen reinforces consumers' attachment to the retailer. And he should know. He's conducted over 400 studies on Wal-Mart.

Treating Employees as Partners

Wal-Mart believes that, in the final accounting, the company's people are what really makes it better. Thus, it works hard to show employees that it cares about them. Wal-Mart calls employees "associates," a practice now widely copied by competitors. The associates work as partners, become deeply involved in operations, and share rewards for good performance.

> Everyone at Wal-Mart [is] an associate—from [the CEO] . . . to a cashier. . . . "We," "us," and "our" are the operative words. Wal-Mart department heads, hourly associates who look after one or more of 30-some departments ranging from sporting goods to electronics, see figures that many companies never show general man-

To keep customers satisfied, Wal-Mart has "people greeters" who are eager to lend a helping hand.

agers: costs, freight charges, profit margins. The company sets a profit margin for each store, and if the store exceeds it, the hourly associates share part of the additional profit.

The partnership concept is deeply rooted in the Wal-Mart corporate culture. It is supported by open-door policies and grassroots meetings that give employees a say in what goes on and encourage them to bring their problems to management. Wal-Mart's concern for its employees translates into high employee satisfaction, which in turn translates into greater customer satisfaction.

Keeping a Tight Rein on Costs

Wal-Mart has the lowest cost structure in the industry: Operating expenses amount to only 16 percent of sales, compared to 23 percent at Kmart. Thus, Wal-Mart can charge lower prices but still reap higher profits, allowing it to offer better service. This creates a "productivity loop." Wal-Mart's lower prices and better service attract more shoppers, producing more sales, making the company more efficient, and enabling it to lower prices even more.

Wal-Mart's low costs result in part from superior management and sophisticated technology. Its Bentonville, Arkansas headquarters contains "a computer-communications system worthy of the Defense Department," giving managers instant access to sales and operating information. And its huge, fully automated distribution centres employ the latest technology to supply stores efficiently. Wal-Mart also spends less than competitors on advertising—only 0.5 percent of sales, compared to 2.5 percent at Kmart and 3.8 percent at Sears. Because Wal-Mart has what customers want at the prices they'll pay, its reputation has spread rapidly by word of mouth. It has not needed more advertising.

Finally, Wal-Mart keeps costs down through good old "tough buying." Whereas the company is known for the warm way it treats customers, it is equally well known for the cold, calculating way it wrings low prices from suppliers. The following passage describes a visit to Wal-Mart's buying offices.

> Don't expect a greeter and don't expect friendly. . . . Once you are ushered into one of the Spartan little buyers' rooms, expect a steely eye across the table and be prepared to cut your price. "They are very, very focussed people, and they use their buying power more forcefully than anyone else . . . ," says the marketing vice-president of a major vendor. "All the normal mating rituals are [forbidden]. Their highest priority is making sure everyone at all times in all cases knows who's in charge, and it's Wal-Mart. They talk softly, but they have piranha hearts, and if you aren't totally prepared when you go in there, you'll have your [head] handed to you."

Some observers wonder whether Wal-Mart can continue to grow at such a torrid pace and still retain its focus and positioning. They wonder if an ever-larger Wal-Mart can stay close to its customers and employees. The company's managers are betting on it. Says one top executive: "We'll be fine as long as we never lose our responsiveness to the consumer."

Sources: Quoted material from Randy Scotland, "Wal-Mart Canada's Dave Ferguson named Distinguished Retailer of the Year," press release, Retail Council of Canada, 18 April 2000; Wal-Mart Canada press release, 29 June 2000; Bill Saporito, "Is Wal-Mart unstoppable?" *Fortune,* 6 May 1991:50–9; and John Huey, "Wal-Mart: Will it take over the world?" *Fortune,* 30 January 1989:52–61. Also see Christy Fisher, "Wal-Mart's way," *Advertising Age,* 18 February 1991:3; Bill Saporito, "David Glass won't crack under fire," *Fortune,* 8 February 1993:75–80; Bill Saporito, "And the winner is still . . . Wal-Mart," *Fortune,* 2 May 1994:62–70; and www.wal-mart.com/.

retailer can differentiate itself by offering a highly targeted product assortment—Penningtons and Cotton Ginny Plus carry goods for larger women; The It Store offers an unusual assortment of gadgets in what amounts to a toy store for adults.

Retailers also must decide on a *services mix* to offer customers. The old "mom-and-pop" grocery stores offered home delivery, credit, and conversation—services that today's supermarkets ignore. The services mix is one of the key tools of non-price competition for setting one store apart from another.

The *store's atmosphere* is another element in its product arsenal. Every store has a physical layout that makes moving around in it either hard or easy. Paco Underhill, a retailing consultant, captured the importance of perceived crowding in a store with his "bum-brush" theory. He suggests that the possibility of a shopper making a purchase decreases significantly every time his or her posterior is accidentally brushed by another passerby.[9] Every store has a "feel": One store is cluttered, another charming, a third plush, a fourth sombre. The store must have a planned atmosphere that suits the target market and moves customers to buy.

Virgin Group
www.virgin.com/

Increasingly, retailers are turning their stores into theatres that transport customers into unusual, exciting shopping environments. New York's famous toy store, F.A.O. Schwartz, has customers lining up to get in. Customers ride escalators through a toy kingdom, and make their way through various boutiques with elaborate animated displays and spectacular exhibits, featuring Lego toys, Barbie dolls, giant stuffed zoo animals, and even a talking tree. Virgin Group (the company that includes Virgin Atlantic Airways, Virgin Hotels, Virgin Megastore, and Virgin Communications) has just entered retailing. The new music and entertainment Virgin Megastore in downtown Vancouver is the epitome of stores combining shopping and entertainment. The 40 000-square-foot facility has a wealth of interactive features including an in-store DJ booth, individual listening stations, booths for viewing movies, and a café where people can sip espresso. In-store performances encourage shoppers to spend more time and, of course, more money. Careful attention was paid to store design. Wide aisles, escalators, and careful signage allow for easy movement throughout the store. Metal and marble are used in some sections to give them a modern look; fresco-like murals are used in others to create a completely different atmosphere.[10]

Many of today's successful new retailers, like Virgin, offer entertaining shopping experiences in addition to deep product selection.

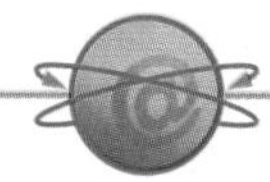

Indigo Books and Music
www.indigo.ca/

Indigo Books and Music, the Canadian upstart bookseller that was founded to take on big-box retailers Barnes & Noble and Chapters, uses atmospherics to turn shopping for books into entertainment. It knows that shopping is a social activity for many consumers: People shop not only to make purchases, but also to mingle with others, see what's new, and treat themselves to something interesting or unexpected. Thus, Indigo stores feature rich colours and wood accents. They hold special events and appearances by authors. They also offer plenty of space, where people can meet and feel at home.[11]

All of this confirms that retail stores are much more than simply assortments of goods. They are environments to be experienced by the people who shop in them. Store atmospheres offer a powerful tool by which retailers can differentiate their stores from those of competitors.

Price Decision

A retailer's price policy is a crucial positioning factor that must be decided in relation to its target market, its product and service assortment, and its competition. All retailers would like to charge high markups and achieve high volume, but the two seldom go together. Most retailers seek *either* high markups on lower volume (most specialty stores) *or* low markups on higher volume (mass merchandisers and discount stores). Thus, Winnipeg-based Hanford Drewitt prices men's suits starting at $1000 and shoes at $400—it sells a low volume but makes a hefty profit on each sale. At the other extreme, Winners sells brand-name clothing at discount prices, settling for a lower margin on each sale but selling at a much higher volume.

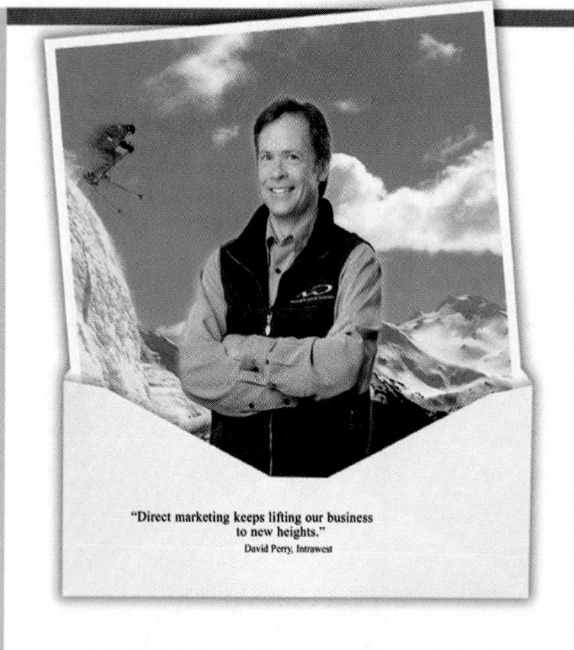

"Direct marketing keeps lifting our business to new heights."
David Perry, Intrawest
Intrawest is discovering higher ground with the power of direct mail.
Intrawest is in the business of offering exhilarating outdoor fun, with eleven mountain resorts across North America, including the number-one rated Whistler-Blackcomb. It relies on direct mail to reach its core customers and get them on the mountains to enjoy the high alpine experience. "Direct mail is the most dominant element in our marketing mix. We acquire over half our annual Express Card memberships through direct mail alone!" says David Perry, Vice-President of Marketing and Sales for Whistler-Blackcomb. Intrawest has a mountain of experience in direct mail, which now also prominently features its Web site address to generate traffic and enable potential visitors to utilize their extensive on-line sevices. With the power of direct mail behind them, Intrawest is at the summit of success.
Put the power of direct marketing to work for you too!
Call 1 888 280-3101 to find out about Canada Post's complete line of free direct marketing tools that will help you deliver success for your business.
CANADA POST
POSTES CANADA

This ad sponsored by Canada Post and Intrawest shows how retailers and manufacturers often cooperate to jointly advertise products and outlets for them.

Promotion Decision

Retailers use such promotion tools as advertising, personal selling, sales promotion, and public relations, as well as cooperative advertising and promotions. They cooperate with product manufacturers to share the cost of materials. They advertise in newspapers and magazines, and on radio, television, and the Internet. Advertising may be supported by circulars and direct-mail pieces. Personal selling requires careful training of salespeople in how to greet customers, meet their needs, and handle their complaints. Sales promotions may include in-store demonstrations, displays, contests, and visiting celebrities. Such public relations activities as press conferences and speeches, store openings, special events, newsletters, magazines, and public service activities are always available to retailers.

Place Decision

Retailers often cite three critical factors in retailing success: *location, location,* and *location!* A retailer's location is key to its ability to attract customers. And the costs of building or leasing facilities have a major impact on the retailer's profits. Therefore, site location decisions are among the most important the retailer makes. Small retailers may have to settle for whatever locations they can find or afford. Large retailers usually employ specialists who select locations using advanced methods.

One of the savviest location experts in recent years has been toy-store giant Toys 'R' Us. Most of its new locations are in rapidly growing areas where the population closely matches its customer base. In an ever-intensifying war for the grocery consumer, even Canada's leading supermarket chain, Loblaws, continues to battle the franchised independent supermarkets—Foodland, Fortinos, Freshmart, IGA, Metro, Your Independent Grocer—for the best locations to pre-empt each other's expansion plans. The undisputed winner in the "place race" has been Wal-Mart, whose strategy of being the first mass merchandiser to locate in small and rural markets has been one of the key factors in its phenomenal success.

Most stores today cluster together to increase their customer pulling power and to give consumers the convenience of one-stop shopping. The main types of store clusters are the *central business district* and the *shopping centre.*

Central business districts
Clusters of businesses and retail outlets, usually in the city core.

Central business districts were the main form of retail cluster until the 1950s. Every large city and town had a central business district. When people began to move to the suburbs, however, these central business districts began to lose business. In recent years, many cities have joined with merchants to try to revive downtown shopping areas.

Shopping centre
A retail location planned, developed, owned, and managed as a unit.

A **shopping centre** is a retail location that is planned, developed, owned, and managed as a unit. A *regional shopping centre,* the largest and most dramatic type, contains from 40 to over 200 stores. The Eaton Centre in Toronto, Place Ville Marie in Montreal, and West Edmonton Mall are shopping centres, featuring a mix of large department stores and many small specialty stores. They attract customers from a wide area. A *community shopping centre* contains 15 to 40 retail stores. It normally contains a branch of a department store or variety store, a supermarket, specialty stores, professional offices, and sometimes a bank. Most shopping centres are *neighbourhood shopping centres* or strip malls that generally contain five to 15 stores. They are close and convenient for consumers. They usually contain a supermarket, perhaps a discount store, and several service stores—dry cleaner, self-service laundry, drugstore, video rental outlet, barber or beauty shop, and hardware store.

All the shopping centres combined in North America account for about one-third of all retail sales; however, they may have reached their saturation point. Through the past decade, on average, consumers have been going to traditional malls less often, staying a shorter period of time, and visiting fewer stores. Why are people using shopping malls less? First, with more dual-income households, people have less time to shop. "You have two workers in every family and no one has time to go to the mall for four hours anymore," observes one industry analyst. "People who used to go to the mall 20 times a year now go two or three times." Second, a recent survey of BC shoppers revealed that 58 percent of consumers now find shopping more of a chore than they did in the past. Listed as the top three reasons for their frustration were long line-ups at checkouts, poor service, and lack of assistance in stores.[12]

Furthermore, shoppers appear to be tiring of traditional malls, which are too big, too crowded, and too much alike. Today's large malls offer great selection but are less comfortable and convenient. Finally, today's consumers have many alternatives to traditional malls, ranging from online shopping to *power centres,* which are presenting a new challenge to traditional malls. These unenclosed shopping centres consist of a long strip of retail stores, including large, free-standing anchors such as Wal-Mart, Home Depot, Staples, Michaels, and Danier Leather Outlet. Each store has its own entrance with parking directly in front for shoppers who wish to visit only one store. Add to all this the emergence of Internet shopping, and you can see why some retail analysts believe the concept of the shopping mall is beginning to look dated.

The West Edmonton Mall is the largest mall in the world. Besides containing over 800 shops and services, it features the world's largest indoor amusement park and the world's largest indoor lake.

The Future of Retailing

Retailers operate in a harsh and fast-changing environment that offers both threats and opportunities. For example, the industry suffers from chronic overcapacity resulting in fierce competition for customer dollars. Consumer demographics, lifestyles, and shopping patterns are changing rapidly, as are retailing technologies. Moreover, quickly rising costs make more efficient operation and smarter buying essential. To be successful, then, retailers will have to choose target segments carefully and position themselves strongly. They will have to take into account the following retailing developments as they plan and execute their competitive strategies.

New Retail Forms and Shortening Retail Life Cycles

New retail forms continue to emerge to meet new situations and consumer needs. But the life cycle of new retail forms is becoming shorter. Department stores took about 100 years to reach the mature stage of the life cycle; more recent forms, such as furniture warehouse stores, reached maturity in about 10 years. Internet retailing is still an environment where seemingly solid retail positions can crumble quickly. One of Canada's most venerable retailers, Eaton's, knows this only too well. The fall of the 127-year-old retailing veteran "serves as a stark reminder to mass-market retailers that past success means little in a fiercely competitive and rapidly changing industry."[13] Retailers can no longer sit back and rely on a once-successful formula—they must keep adapting.

Wheel of retailing concept
A concept of retailing that states that new types of retailers usually begin as low-margin, low-price, low-status operations but later evolve into higher-priced, higher-service operations, eventually becoming like the conventional retailers they replaced.

Many retailing innovations are partially explained by the **wheel of retailing** concept.[14] According to this concept, many new types of retailing forms begin as low-margin, low-price, low-status operations. They challenge established retailers that have become "fat" by letting their costs and margins increase. The new retailers' success leads them to upgrade their facilities and offer more services. In turn, their costs increase, forcing them to increase their prices. Eventually, the new retailers become like the conventional retailers they replaced. The cycle begins again when still newer types of retailers evolve with lower costs and prices. The wheel of retailing concept seems to explain the initial success and later troubles of department stores, supermarkets, and discount stores and the recent success of off-price retailers.

Growth of Non-Store Retailing

Although most retailing still takes place the old-fashioned way—across countertops in stores—consumers now have an array of alternatives, including mail-order, television, phone, and online shopping.

Despite all the talk about the Internet sounding the death knell of bricks-and-mortar retail operations, online shopping and retailing is still in its infancy and currently represents less than three percent of retail sales. While Canadians are one of the most "wired" populations in the world, and declare themselves ready, willing, and able to shop online, they often find that there are few Canadian Web sites on which to make their purchases. Canadian retailers have been somewhat slow in entering the e-tailing race for a number of reasons. First, many don't see e-tailing as a significant competitive threat even though 63 percent of the dollars Canadian e-shoppers spend go to the United States. Other barriers to e-tailing development include lack of senior executive commitment, challenges of order fulfillment, lack of resources, and the complexity of measuring online performance.[15] However, e-tailing is expected to grow rapidly since Canadians have a history of being rapid adopters of new technologies and more and more Canadian retailers are starting to enter cyberspace using their sites to complement their store sales or provide consumers with product information.

Increasing Intertype Competition

Competition is increasing from many different types of retailers. A consumer can buy CDs at specialty music stores, discount music stores, electronics superstores, general merchandise discount stores, video-rental outlets, and through dozens of mail-order and Web sites. They can buy books at stores ranging from independent local bookstores to discount stores such as Wal-Mart, superstores such Chapters or Indigo, or Web sites such as Amazon.com. When it comes to brand-name appliances, department stores, discount stores, off-price retailers, or electronics superstores all compete for the same customers. Industry experts note that there is a trend toward more cross-shopping—consumers buying one item at upscale retailers like Holt Renfrew and another from the Dollar Store.

Competition between chain superstores and smaller, independently owned stores has become particularly heated. Because of their bulk buying power and high sales volume, chains can buy at lower costs and thrive on smaller margins. The arrival of a superstore can quickly force nearby independents out of business. Yet the news is not all bad for smaller companies. Many small independent retailers are thriving. Independents are finding that sheer size and marketing muscle are often no match for the personal touch that small stores can provide or the specialty niches that small stores fill for a devoted customer base.

The Rise of Mega-Retailers

The rise of huge mass-merchandisers and specialty superstores, the formation of vertical marketing systems and buying alliances, and a rash of retail mergers and acquisitions have created a core of superpower mega-retailers. Through their superior information systems and buying power, these giant retailers can offer better merchandise selections, good service, and large price savings to consumers. As a result, they grow even larger by squeezing out their smaller, weaker competitors. The mega-retailers also are shifting the balance of power between retailers and producers. A relative handful of retailers now control access to enormous numbers of consumers, giving them the upper hand in their dealings with manufacturers. For example, Wal-Mart's revenues are more than three times those of Procter & Gamble. Wal-Mart can, and often does, use this power to wring concessions from P&G and other suppliers.[16]

Growing Importance of Retail Technology

Retail technologies are becoming critically important as competitive tools. Progressive retailers are using computers to produce better forecasts, control inventory costs, order electronically from suppliers, send e-mail between stores, and even sell to customers within stores. They are adopting checkout scanning systems, online transaction processing, electronic funds transfer, electronic data interchange, in-store television, and improved merchandise-handling systems.

Technology helped the managers of the newly renovated A&P in Hamilton, Ontario to unravel a mystery. Their scanner data revealed that the five percent of the store clientele who used frequent-buyer cards were purchasing less. A follow-up survey revealed that although most people like the store's new look, they didn't like the new self-serve deli. As a result of this customer feedback, the store was remodelled again, purchasing levels went back up, and A&P avoided making a chain-wide blunder.[17]

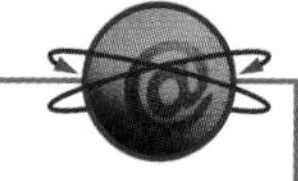

Pier 1 Imports
www.pier1.com/

One innovative scanning system now in use is the shopper scanner, a radar-like system that counts store traffic allowing retailers to better understand hours when their store traffic surges and plan their staffing accordingly. Pier 1 Imports uses the same system to test, among other things, the impact of newspaper ads on store traffic. Moreover, by combining traffic and sales data, retailers say they can find out how well the store converts browsers into buyers.[18]

Perhaps the most startling advances in retailing technology concern the ways in which today's retailers are connecting with customers:[19]

> In the past, life was simple. Retailers connected with their customers through stores, through their salespeople, through the brands and packages they sold, and through direct mail and advertising in the mass media. But today, life is more complex. There are dozens of new ways to attract and engage consumers. . . . Indeed, even if one omits the obvious—the Web—retailers are still surrounded by technical innovations that promise to redefine the way they and manufacturers interact with customers. Consider, as just a sampling, touch screen kiosks, electronic shelf labels and signs, handheld shopping assistants, smart cards, self-scanning systems, virtual reality displays, and intelligent agents. So, if we ask the question, Will technology change the way [retailers] interface with customers in the future? The answer has got to be yes.

Retail Stores as "Communities" or "Hangouts"

With the rise in the number of people living alone, working at home, or living in isolated and sprawling suburbs, there has been a resurgence of establishments that, regardless of the product or service they offer, also provide a place for people to meet. These places include cafés, tea shops, juice bars, bookshops, superstores, children's play spaces, brew pubs, and urban greenmarkets. This is a North America–wide phenomenon. Brew pubs such as the Kingston Brew Pub offer tastings and a place to pass the time. The Discovery Zone, a chain of children's play spaces, offers indoor spaces where kids can go wild without breaking anything while stressed-out parents exchange stories. And, of course, there are the now-ubiquitous coffee houses and espresso bars, such as Starbucks, whose numbers have grown from 2500 in 1989 to over 10 000 today.

marketers speak out

Stephen Arnold: The Meaning of Retail Globalization

Stephen Arnold, a Queen's University professor renowned throughout the world for his expertise with regard to retail patronage, provided the following insights about global retail trends.

Several meanings are associated with the term "retail globalization." In one context, it refers to the decision of the international retailer to either standardize or adapt its format throughout the world. For example, US-based Wal-Mart wishes to see its name on each store in every world market—a veritable McDonald's of retailing. It acquired the Woolco chain in Canada and changed the name to Wal-Mart within 10 months. Germany's Wertkauf became Wal-Mart once the store conversions were completed. This "globalization" approach contrasts with a "multinational" strategy whereby the retailer adapts to each national market. For example, Netherlands retailer Royal Ahold purchased the eastern US Stop & Shop, Giant, BI-LO and Tops food chains but maintained their original names.

A second meaning of retail globalization relates to the predicted dominance of world markets by three or four retailers pursuing growth strategies. For instance, some observers predict that Wal-Mart, Ahold and France's Carrefour will soon dominate world markets for frequently-purchased food and non-food merchandise. Wal-Mart is already the world's largest retailer with $287 billion at 2001 fiscal year end. Carrefour is the world's second largest retailer with slightly less than half of Wal-Mart's volume. Ahold is in the top 10 and rapidly climbing. In contrast, Canada's largest and second largest home-grown retailers are Loblaws and The Bay. They sold, respectively, $19.5 billion and $7.5 billion worth of goods in 1999. These much smaller national chains could either be acquired by one of the retail giants or forced out of business. They have little or no international experience to draw upon. They're not unlike members of the university downhill ski team who entered the Ontario winter games to find themselves competing against the French, Italian and US Olympic teams.

The impact of these global retailers on Canadian markets to date may predict the future. Within four years of entering Canada, Wal-Mart became this nation's largest department store. Its sales exceeded those of Zellers, Sears and The Bay. Eaton's went bankrupt and Kmart withdrew from the Canadian market. In three surveys conducted 1.5 years apart tracking the Kingston, Ontario market, Wal-Mart's share of shoppers rose from seven percent to 22 percent to 30 percent. This gain was at the expense all other competitors. Similarly, Home Depot's share of shoppers in the Kingston market was 27 percent six months after the store's grand opening and 36 percent after 18 months. Cashway's share of shoppers was halved and Beaver Lumber closed its doors.

It is anticipated that Wal-Mart will introduce its supercentre stores to Canada and add food to its non-food offering. It uses this hypermarket format in every one of its other world markets except Canada and Puerto Rico. Predictions are that the number of stores will rise from 174 to 300 and that Canadian sales will reach $24 billion. Wal-Mart will dwarf every other Canadian retailer.

How should Canadians respond to the dominance of its retail system by an oligopoly of international retailers? In fact, they already acted and "voted" with their shopping dollars. Consumers cannot resist the convenient store locations, everyday low prices, wide assortments and friendly service.

Stephen Arnold.

The final meaning of retail globalization relates to the potential outcomes of world dominance by a small number of retail firms. One issue is whether retail globalization equates to retail homogenization and, in the long run, reduced choice and a sameness of offerings. For example, in a typical Canadian market, one will find A&P, Costco, Home Depot, Sears and Wal-Mart, all US-based retailers. A related issue concerns the transformation of the choice process by the global retailers. Is the relative importance shoppers attach to store choice attributes fixed or does the market entry of a global retailer change the manner in which consumers shop for frequently purchased products? A non-traditional view is that preferences evolve and that a new competitor can enter an existing retail market and alter consumer preferences toward the combination of attributes that the competitor represents. The new entrant is referred to as a "market spoiler," meaning that the characteristics considered ideal for this market have changed from those that favour existing competitors. Wal-Mart's propensity for changing consumer preferences for store choice attributes in its own favour was identified in studies conducted in Kingston, Atlanta and Chicago. The importance of low prices and good service went up and the determinacy of sales and promotions fell.

Sources: S.J. Arnold and J. Fernie, "Wal-Mart in Europe: Prospects for the UK," *International Marketing Review,* 17 (4/5), 2000:433–453; S.J. Arnold, J. Handelman, and D.J. Tigert, "The Impact of a Market Spoiler on Consumer Preference Structures (or, What Happens When Wal-Mart Comes to Town)," *Journal of Retailing and Consumer Services,* 5(1), 1998:1–13; *Chain Store Age,* "World's 100 largest retailers," December 2000:121; J. Simmons and T. Graff (1998), *Wal-Mart Comes to Canada,* Toronto: Centre for the Study of Commercial Activity, Ryerson Polytechnic University; Neil Wrigley, "The Globalisation of Retail Capital: Themes for Economic Geography," in *Handbook of Economic Geography,* G. Clark, M. Gertler and M. Feldman, eds., Oxford University Press, 2000:292–313.

Bookstores have become part bookstore, part library, and part living room. Chapters and Indigo feature not only shelves stacked with books and speedy computerized checkouts, but also rich wood-panelled reading rooms, cushy chairs, and coffee bars. They offer literary events and book signings. There are daily newspapers from around the world and endless racks of magazines. You'll find everyone there from backpack-toting high school students, to retirees thumbing through the gardening books, to parents accompanying their toddlers at reading circles. In addition to books, these retailers offer comfort, relaxation, and community.

Wholesaling

Wholesaling includes all activities involved in selling goods and services to those buying for resale or business use. A retail bakery is engaging in wholesaling when it sells pastry to the local hotel. We call **wholesalers** those firms engaged *primarily* in wholesaling activity. Vancouver-based Group Telecom (GT), for example, is a telecommunications services wholesaler that targets Canada's 2.5 million small and medium-sized businesses. These independent business firms are price sensitive and demand a high level of service from their wholesaler. This market is one GT believes has been "underserved," so it offers customized bundles of services—all on a single bill and with one customer service number to phone.[20]

Wholesaling
All activities involved in selling goods and services to those buying for resale or business use.

Wholesaler
A firm engaged primarily in wholesaling activity.

Wholesalers buy mostly from producers and sell mostly to retailers, industrial consumers, and other wholesalers. But why are wholesalers used at all? For example, why would a producer use wholesalers rather than selling directly to retailers or consumers? Quite simply, wholesalers are often better at performing one or more of these channel functions:

- *Selling and promoting.* Wholesalers' sales forces help manufacturers reach any small customers at a low cost. The wholesaler has more contacts and is often more trusted by the buyer than the distant manufacturer.
- *Buying and assortment building.* Wholesalers can select items and build assortments needed by their customers, thereby saving the consumers much work.
- *Bulk breaking.* Wholesalers save their customers money by buying in carload lots and breaking bulk (breaking large lots into small quantities).
- *Warehousing.* Wholesalers hold inventories, thereby reducing the inventory costs and risks of suppliers and customers.
- *Transportation.* Wholesalers can provide quicker delivery to buyers because they are closer than the producers.
- *Financing.* Wholesalers finance their customers by giving credit, and they finance their suppliers by ordering early and paying bills on time.
- *Risk bearing.* Wholesalers absorb risk by taking title and bearing the cost of theft, damage, spoilage, and obsolescence.
- *Market information.* Wholesalers give information to suppliers and customers about competitors, new products, and price developments.
- *Management services and advice.* Wholesalers often help retailers train their sales clerks, improve store layouts and displays, and set up accounting and inventory control systems.

Today's bookstores offer something greater than just books and magazines—they're selling comfort, relaxation, and community.

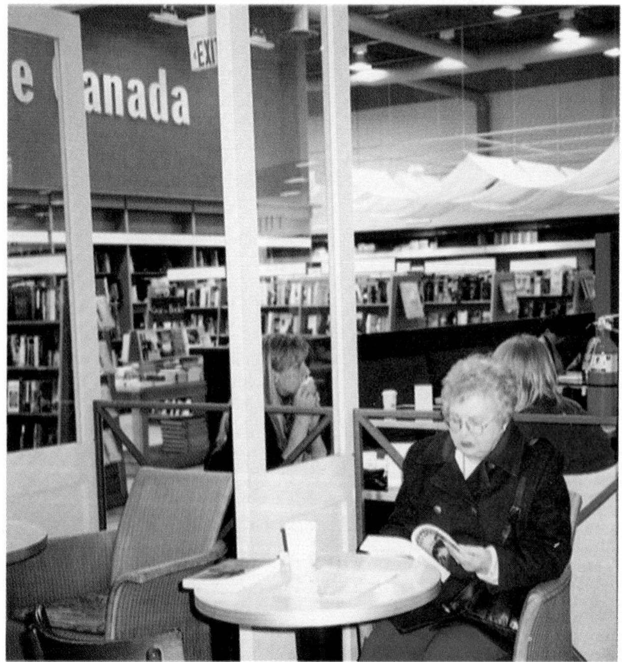

Types of Wholesalers

Merchant wholesalers
Independently owned businesses that take title to the merchandise they handle.

Broker
A wholesaler who does not take title to goods and whose function is to bring buyers and sellers together and assist in negotiation.

Agent
A wholesaler who represents buyers or sellers on a relatively permanent basis, performs only a few functions, and does not take title to goods.

Manufacturers' sales branches and offices
Wholesaling by sellers or buyers themselves rather than through independent wholesalers.

Wholesalers fall into three major groups (see Table 12-4): *merchant wholesalers, brokers and agents,* and *manufacturers' sales branches and offices.*

Merchant wholesalers, independently owned businesses that take title to the merchandise they handle, account for about 50 percent of all wholesaling. Merchant wholesalers include two broad types: *full-service wholesalers* and *limited-service wholesalers.* Full-service wholesalers provide a full set of services, whereas the various limited-service wholesalers offer fewer specialized services to their suppliers and customers.

Brokers and agents differ from merchant wholesalers in two ways: They do not take title to goods and they perform only a few functions. Like merchant wholesalers, they generally specialize by product line or customer type. A **broker** brings buyers and sellers together and assists in negotiation. **Agents** represent buyers or sellers on a more permanent basis. *Manufacturers' agents* (also called manufacturers' representatives) are the most common type of agent wholesaler. Together, brokers and agents account for 11 percent of the total wholesale volume.

The third major type of wholesaling is that done in **manufacturers' sales branches and offices** by sellers or buyers themselves rather than through independent wholesalers. Manufacturers' offices and sales branches account for about 31 percent of all wholesale volume.

Wholesaler Marketing Decisions

Wholesalers have experienced mounting competitive pressures in recent years. They have faced new sources of competition, more demanding customers, new technologies, and more direct-buying programs on the part of large industrial, institutional, and retail buyers. As a result, they have had to improve their strategic decisions on target markets and positioning, and on the marketing mix—product assortments and services, price, promotion, and place (see Figure 12-2).

Target Market and Positioning Decision

Like retailers, wholesalers must define their target markets and position themselves effectively—they cannot serve everyone. They can choose a target group by size of customer (only large retailers), type of customer (convenience food stores only), need for service (customers who need credit), or other factors. Within the target group, they can identify the more profitable customers, design stronger offers, and build better relationships with them. They can propose automatic reordering systems, set up management-training and advising systems, or even sponsor a voluntary chain. They can discourage less profitable customers by requiring larger orders or adding service charges to smaller ones.

Marketing Mix Decisions

Again like retailers, wholesalers must decide on product assortment and services, prices, promotion, and place. The wholesaler's "product" is the assortment of *products and services* that it offers. Wholesalers are under great pressure to carry a full line and to stock enough for immediate delivery. But this practice can damage profits. Wholesalers today are cutting down on the number of lines they carry, choosing to carry only the more profitable ones. Wholesalers also are rethinking which services count most in building strong customer relationships and which should be dropped or charged for. The key is to find the mix of services most valued by their target customers.

Price is also an important wholesaler decision. Wholesalers usually mark up

TABLE 12-4 Major Types of Wholesalers

Type	Description
Merchant Wholesalers	Independently owned businesses that take title to the merchandise they handle. In different trades, they are known as *jobbers, distributors,* or *mill supply houses.* Include full-service wholesalers and limited-service wholesalers:
Full-service wholesalers	Provide a full line of services: carrying stock, maintaining a sales force, offering credit, making deliveries, and providing management assistance. There are two types:
Wholesale merchants	Sell primarily to retailers and provide a full range of services. *General-merchandise wholesalers* carry several merchandise lines, while *general-line wholesalers* carry one or two lines in greater depth. *Specialty wholesalers* specialize in carrying only part of a line. (Examples: health-food wholesalers, seafood wholesalers.)
Industrial distributors	Sell to manufacturers rather than to retailers. Provide several services, such as carrying stock, offering credit, and providing delivery. May carry a broad range of merchandise, a general line, or a specialty line.
Limited-service wholesalers	Offer fewer services than full-service wholesalers. Limited-service wholesalers are of several types:
Cash-and-carry wholesalers	Carry a limited line of fast-moving goods and sell to small retailers for cash. Normally do not deliver. Example: A small fish store retailer may drive to a cash-and-carry fish wholesaler, buy fish for cash, and bring the merchandise back to the store.
Truck wholesalers (or truck jobbers)	Perform primarily a selling and delivery function. Carry a limited line of semi-perishable merchandise (such as milk, bread, snack foods), which they sell for cash as they make their rounds of supermarkets, small groceries, hospitals, restaurants, factory cafeterias, and hotels.
Drop shippers	Do not carry inventory or handle the product. Upon receiving an order, they select a manufacturer, who ships the merchandise directly to the customer. The drop shipper assumes title and risk from the time the order is accepted to its delivery to the customer. They operate in such bulk industries as coal, lumber, and heavy equipment.
Rack jobbers	Serve grocery and drug retailers, mostly in non-food items. They send delivery trucks to stores, where the delivery people set up toys, paperbacks, hardware items, health and beauty aids, or other items. They price the goods, keep them fresh, set up point-of-purchase displays, and keep inventory records. Rack jobbers retain title to the goods and bill the retailers only for the goods sold to consumers.
Producers' cooperatives	Owned by farmer members and assemble farm produce to sell in local markets. The co-op's profits are distributed to members at the end of the year. They often attempt to improve product quality and promote a co-op brand name, such as Sun Maid raisins, Sunkist oranges, or Diamond walnuts.
Mail-order wholesalers	Send catalogues to retail, industrial, and institutional customers featuring jewellery, cosmetics, specialty foods, and other small items. Maintain no outside sales force. Main customers are businesses in small outlying areas. Orders are filled and sent by mail, truck, or other transportation.
Brokers and Agents	Do not take title to goods. Main function is to facilitate buying and selling, for which they earn a commission on the selling price. Generally specialize by product line or customer types.
Brokers	Chief function is bringing buyers and sellers together and assisting in negotiation. They are paid by the party who hired them, and do not carry inventory, get involved in financing, or assume risk. Examples: food brokers, real estate brokers, insurance brokers, and security brokers.
Agents	Represent either buyers or sellers on a more permanent basis than brokers do. There are several types:
Manufacturers' agents	Represent two or more manufacturers of complementary lines. A formal written agreement with each manufacturer covers pricing, territories, order handling, delivery service and warranties, and commission rates. Often used in such lines as apparel, furniture, and electrical goods. Most manufacturers' agents are small businesses, with only a few skilled salespeople as employees. They are hired by small manufacturers who cannot afford their own field sales forces, and by large manufacturers who use agents to open new territories or to cover territories that cannot support full-time salespeople.
Selling agents	Have contractual authority to sell a manufacturer's entire output. The manufacturer either is not interested in the selling function or feels unqualified. The selling agent serves as a sales department and has significant influence over prices, terms, and conditions of sale. Found in such product areas as textiles, industrial machinery and equipment, coal and coke, chemicals, and metals.
Purchasing agents	Generally have a long-term relationship with buyers and make purchases for them, often receiving, inspecting, warehousing, and shipping the merchandise to the buyers. They provide helpful market information to clients and help them obtain the best goods and prices available.
Commission merchants	Take physical possession of products and negotiate sales. Normally, they are not employed on a long-term basis. Used most often in agricultural marketing by farmers who do not want to sell their own output and do not belong to producers' cooperatives. The commission merchant takes a truckload of commodities to a central market, sells it for the best price, deducts a commission and expenses, and remits the balance to the producer.

TABLE 12-4 *Continued*

Type	Description
Manufacturers' and Retailers' Branches and Offices	Wholesaling operations conducted by sellers or buyers themselves rather than through independent wholesalers. Separate branches and offices can be dedicated to either sales or purchasing.
Sales branches and offices	Set up by manufacturers to improve inventory control, selling, and promotion. *Sales branches* carry inventory and are found in such industries as lumber and automotive equipment and parts. *Sales offices* do not carry inventory and are most prominent in dry goods and notions industries.
Purchasing offices	Perform a role similar to that of brokers or agents but are part of the buyer's organization. Many retailers set up purchasing offices in such major market centres as New York and Chicago.

the cost of goods by a standard percentage—say, 20 percent. Expenses may run 17 percent of the gross margin, leaving a profit margin of three percent. In grocery wholesaling, the average profit margin is often less than two percent. Wholesalers are trying new pricing approaches. They may cut their margin on some lines to win important new customers. They may ask a supplier for special price breaks when they can turn them into an increase in the supplier's sales.

Although *promotion* can be critical to wholesaler success, most wholesalers are not promotion minded. Their use of trade advertising, sales promotion, personal selling, and public relations is largely scattered and unplanned. Many are behind the times in personal selling—they still see selling as a single salesperson talking to a single customer instead of as a team effort to sell, build, and service major accounts. Wholesalers also need to adopt some of the non-personal promotion techniques used by retailers. They need to develop an overall promotion strategy and to make greater use of supplier promotion materials and programs.

Finally, *place* is important—wholesalers must choose their locations and facilities carefully. Wholesalers typically locate in low-rent, low-tax areas and tend to invest little money in their buildings, equipment, and systems. As a result, their materials-handling and order-processing systems are often outdated. In recent years, however, large and progressive wholesalers are reacting to rising costs by investing in automated warehouses and online ordering systems. Orders are fed from the retailer's system directly into the wholesaler's computer, and the items are picked up by mechanical devices and automatically taken to a shipping platform where they are assembled. Winnipeg-based Coghlan's Limited provides camping accessories to the largest retailers in Canada, including Canadian Tire and Wal-Mart. To continue supplying these firms, it has had to invest in several technology and efficiency measures. Coghlan's electronic data interchange (EDI) system allows its customers to electronically submit orders, thus shortening the retailer's reorder time. It has also invested in a quick response (QR) system that allows Coghlan's

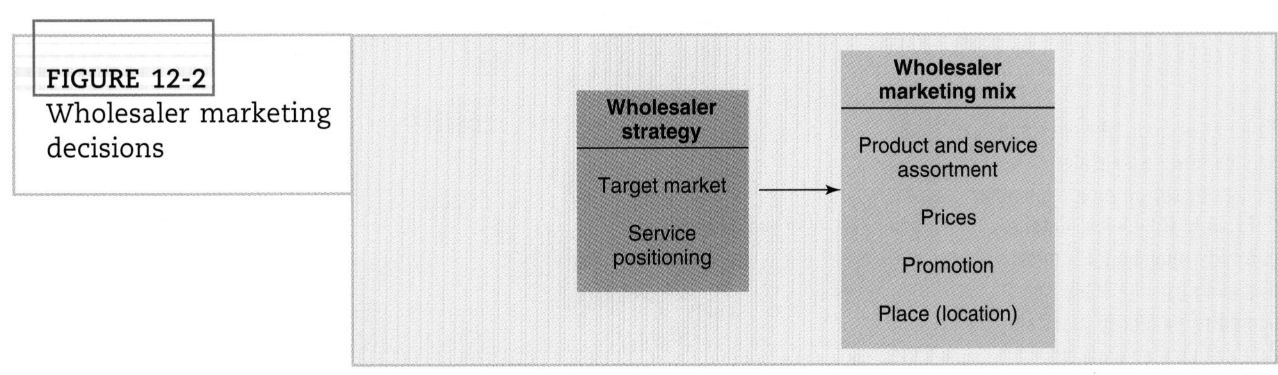

FIGURE 12-2 Wholesaler marketing decisions

to fill an order and have it on the customer's loading dock within 72 hours. Most large wholesalers use computers to carry out accounting, billing, inventory control, and forecasting. Modern wholesalers are adapting their services to the needs of target customers and finding cost-reducing methods of doing business.

Trends in Wholesaling

The thriving wholesaling industry is facing considerable challenges. The industry remains vulnerable to one of the most enduring trends of the past decade—fierce resistance to price increases and the winnowing-out of suppliers based on cost and quality. Progressive wholesalers constantly watch for better ways to meet the changing needs of their suppliers and target customers. They recognize that, in the long run, their only reason for existence comes from adding value by increasing the efficiency and effectiveness of the entire marketing channel. To achieve this goal, they must constantly improve their services and reduce their costs.

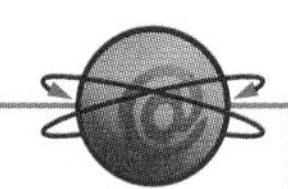

McKesson
www.mckesson.com/

McKesson, North America's leading wholesaler of pharmaceuticals and healthcare products, provides an example of progressive wholesaling. To survive, McKesson had to remain more cost effective than manufacturers' sales branches. Therefore, it automated its 36 warehouses, established direct computer links with 225 drug manufacturers, designed a computerized accounts receivable program for pharmacists, and provided drugstores with computer terminals for ordering inventories. Retailers can even use the McKesson computer system to maintain medical profiles on their customers. Thus, McKesson has delivered better value to both manufacturers and retail customers.

One study predicts several developments in the wholesaling industry.[21] Geographic expansion will require that distributors learn how to compete effectively over wider and more diverse areas. Consolidation will significantly reduce the number of wholesaling firms. Surviving wholesalers will grow larger, primarily through acquisition, merger, and geographic expansion. The trend toward vertical integration, in which manufacturers try to control their market share by owning the intermediaries that bring their goods to market, remains strong. In the health-

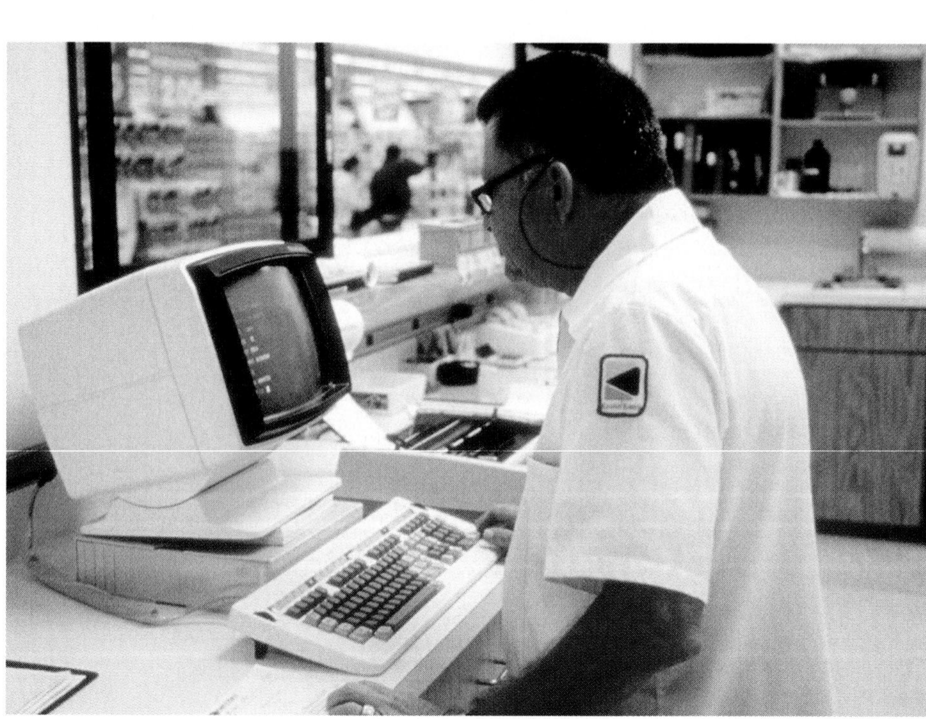

To improve both efficiency and service, drug wholesaler McKesson set up direct computer links with drugstores. Retailers can order merchandise directly and even use the McKesson computer system to maintain medical profiles on their customers.

care sector, for instance, drug manufacturers have purchased drug distribution and pharmacy management companies. This trend began in 1993 when drug-industry giant Merck acquired Medco Containment Services, a drug-benefits manager and mail-order distributor. The surviving wholesaler-distributors in this sector and in others will be bigger and will provide more services for their customers.[22]

The distinction between large retailers and large wholesalers continues to blur. Many retailers now operate wholesale clubs, and hypermarkets perform many wholesale functions. In return, many large wholesalers are setting up their own retailing operations. Supervalu, a leading food wholesaler, now operates its own retail outlets.

Wholesalers will continue to increase the services they provide to retailers—retail pricing, cooperative advertising, marketing and management information reports, accounting services, online transactions, and others. Rising costs on the one hand and the demand for increased services on the other will put the squeeze on wholesaler profits. Wholesalers who do not find efficient ways to deliver value to their customers will soon drop by the wayside. However, the increased use of computerized and automated systems will help wholesalers to contain the costs of ordering, shipping, and inventory holding, boosting their productivity. By 1990, more than 75 percent of all wholesalers were using online order systems.

Finally, facing slow growth in their domestic markets and such developments as the North American Free Trade Agreement, many large wholesalers are now going global and will begin to generate much of their revenue outside their home country.

Review of Concept Connections

Although most retailing is conducted in retail stores, in recent years non-store retailing has increased rapidly. In addition, although many retail stores are independently owned, an increasing number are now banding together under some form of corporate or contractual organization. Wholesalers have also experienced recent environmental changes, most notably mounting competitive pressures. They have faced new sources of competition, more demanding customers, new technologies, and more direct-buying programs on the part of large industrial, institutional, and retail buyers.

1. Explain the roles of retailers and wholesalers in the distribution channel.

Retailing and wholesaling consist of many organizations bringing goods and services from the point of production to the point of use. Retailing includes all activities involved in selling goods or services directly to final consumers for their personal, non-business use. Wholesaling includes all the activities involved in selling goods or services to those who are buying for the purpose of resale or for business use. Wholesalers perform many functions, including selling and promoting, buying and assortment building, bulk breaking, warehousing, transporting, financing, risk bearing, supplying market information, and providing management services and advice.

2. Describe the major types of retailers and give examples of each.

Retailers can be classified as store retailers and non-store retailers. Store retailers can be further classified by the amount of service they provide (self-service, limited service, or full service); product line sold (specialty stores, department stores, supermarkets, convenience stores, superstores, and service businesses); and relative prices (discount stores, off-price retailers, and catalogue showrooms). Today, many retailers are banding together in corporate and contractual retail organizations (corporate chains, voluntary chains and retailer cooperatives, franchise organizations, and merchandising conglomerates).

3. Identify the major types of wholesalers and give examples of each.

Wholesalers fall into three groups. Merchant wholesalers take possession of the goods: They include full-service wholesalers (wholesale merchants, industrial distributors) and limited-service wholesalers (cash-and-carry wholesalers, truck wholesalers, drop shippers, rack jobbers, producers' cooperatives, and mail-order wholesalers). Brokers and agents do not take possession of the goods but are paid a commission for aiding buying and selling. Manufacturers' sales branches and offices are wholesaling operations conducted by non-wholesalers to bypass the wholesalers.

4. Explain the marketing decisions facing retailers and wholesalers.

Each retailer must make decisions about its target markets, product assortment and services, price, promotion, and place. Retailers must choose target markets carefully and position themselves strongly. Today, wholesaling is holding its own in the economy. Progressive wholesalers are adapting their services to the needs of target customers and are seeking cost-reducing methods of doing business. Facing slow growth in their domestic markets and developments such as the North American Free Trade Association, many large wholesalers are also now going global.

Key Terms

Agent *(p. 523)*
Broker *(p. 523)*
Central business districts *(p. 517)*
Chain stores *(p. 508)*
Convenience store *(p. 505)*
Department store *(p. 507)*
Discount store *(p. 504)*
Factory outlets *(p. 507)*
Franchise *(p. 508)*
Independent off-price retailers *(p. 507)*
Manufacturers' sales branches and offices *(p. 523)*
Merchant wholesalers *(p. 523)*
Off-price retailers *(p. 507)*
Retailer cooperative *(p. 508)*
Retailers *(p. 502)*
Retailing *(p. 502)*
Service retailer *(p. 506)*
Shopping centre *(p. 517)*
Specialty store *(p. 504)*
Supermarkets *(p. 505)*
Superstore *(p. 506)*
Voluntary chain *(p. 508)*
Warehouse club (or wholesale club) *(p. 507)*
Wheel of retailing concept *(p. 518)*
Wholesaler *(p. 522)*
Wholesaling *(p. 522)*

Discussing the Issues

1. Convenience stores have lost their monopoly on convenience. Explain what you would do to increase a convenience store's sales.
2. Warehouse clubs that are restricted to members only, such as Price/Costco, are growing rapidly. They offer a very broad but shallow line of products, often in institutional packaging, at very low prices. Some members buy for resale, others buy to supply a business, and still others buy for personal use. Decide whether these stores are wholesalers or retailers. How can you make a distinction?
3. Answer the following questions about category killers: (a) How is a category killer different from other types of retailers? (b) Why has this form of retailing grown so rapidly? (c) What types of retailers are most threatened by category killers, and why? (d) How will online retailing affect category killers? Give an example of a category killer that has been affected by online marketing.
4. In the past few years, online retailing has boomed. (a) How will retailers going online change the competitive balance between retailers, direct and catalogue marketers, wholesalers, and manufacturers? (b) What are the major advantages of online retailing? The pitfalls? (c) What do you think is the future of online retailing?
5. Many Canadian and US retailers are significantly behind European and Asian retailers when it comes to global expansion. (a) Why is this so? (b) Which Canadian retailers are positioned for global expansion? Explain. (c) How will online retailing affect global retail expansion? (d) Study Sweden's IKEA home furnishings stores (www.ikea.com). Why has IKEA been so successful in expanding into the North American market?
6. List and describe each of the channel functions that have been traditionally assigned to wholesalers. How must wholesalers change to meet the threat of increasing competition from larger retailers? From direct marketers?

Marketing Applications

1. As consumers demand more and more service and customization, virtual retailing seems to have a brighter future. Through virtual retailing, a seller can come directly into your home, at your convenience, and allow you to participate in designing your own personalized product and shopping experience. This sounds great—no more ill-fitting bathing suits or greeting cards that seem like they were written for someone else, no high-pressure salespeople, no congested parking lots. At virtual retail sites, you can spend as much or as little time as you need to make up your mind. Virtual retailing has made mass customization a reality. All you have to do is point and click. Look at the following Web sites for more information on customizing clothing products: Gap (www.gap.com), Interactive Custom Clothes (www.ic3d.com), Lands' End (www.landsend.com), QVC's Fashion Advisor (www.QVC.com), and Macy's (www.macys.com). Then answer the following questions.
   a. How does virtual retailing compare with more traditional shopping formats? What are its primary advantages and disadvantages for consumers?
   b. What target markets would be most interested in virtual retailing? Do the Web sites you just visited appear to be appealing to those segments? Explain.
   c. Compare the marketing strategies of the Web retailers you just visited.
   d. Pick one of the Web sites and design your own article of clothing. Discuss the pros and cons of your experience. How was this experience different from buying in a retail store? Would you be willing to purchase the item you designed?
   e. While some Canadian retailers like Grocery Gateway, Chapters, Roots, and Danier Leather have online virtual stores, others have been reluctant to take on the challenges of virtual retailing? What explains this reluctance? What advice would you give to a Canadian retailer thinking of taking the online plunge?

Internet Connections

Online Store

In this exercise you are going to build your own online store. Yahoo! Store is a comprehensive solution for small businesses seeking to establish an online storefront. Visit Yahoo! Store at **store.yahoo.com.** Go ahead and create a free online store (it expires in 10 days). You can sell anything you want at your store—but don't worry, no one can place a real order. Looking for ideas? How about some stuff you have lying around your room? Once you have created the store make a printout of the home page and give it to your professor along with the URL. The URL will read like this: store.yahoo.com/yourusername. Now complete the following chart listing the retail functions provided by Yahoo! Store.

For Discussion

1. What type of retail operation defines your store (e.g., department store)? Explain in terms of amount of service and product line.
2. Who is your target market and what position will this store occupy?
3. What is the cost of running a store on Yahoo! Store?
4. Who are some of Yahoo! Store's more prominent clients?
5. What steps would you take to advertise your store?
6. Yahoo! Store domain names are store.yahoo.com/mystore. For an additional charge you can register a domain name such as www.mystore.com. Which approach would be better for your business? Why?

	Function Provided by Yahoo! Store? (y/n)
Web store design	
Web store hosting	
Order processing	
Electronic shopping cart	
Secure order form	
Credit authorization	
Warehouse notification	
Order fulfillment	
Merchandising	
Relationship marketing	
Data warehousing and data mining	
Customer service	

Savvy Sites

Visit these sites to see some cool trends in online retailing.

- Lands' End (www.landsend.com), the catalogue retailer, allows Internet shoppers to build a model according to their own body shape and colouring, and then dress the model with recommended outfits.
- The award-winning Virtual Reality Mall (www.vr-mall.com) gives Internet shoppers something they miss from bricks-and-mortar malls: ambiance. Note you'll need a VRML plug-in for your Web browser to get the best effects.
- The Sharper Image (www.sharperimage.com) offers three-dimensional views and animations for selected products.
- The Retail Council of Canada (www.retailcouncil.org) posts a wealth of information online about Canadian retailing. Click on the *Retailer Resources* tab to review the reports it posts.

Notes

1. Quotes taken from Sonja Rasula, "Beyond clothes: Fashion retailers are evolving into lifestyle merchandisers—clothing the home as well as the body," *Marketing On-Line,* 10 May 1999; David Eggleston, "New Web site gets to Roots of e-commerce," *Strategy,* 3 January 2000:D14; and Natalie Bahadur, "Roots rolls out inaugural television campaign," *Strategy,* 12 October 1998:10. Also see Natalie Bahadur, "Roots extends to home furnishings," *Strategy,* 9 November 1998:9; Julie McCann, "Tip of the hat to the Roots boys," *Marketing On-Line,* 21/28 December 1998; www.Roots.com.
2. Nathan Rudyk, "Multi-channel customers spend 10 times more," *Strategy,* 6 November 2000:D6.

3. Retail Council of Canada, "The Retail Sector in Canada," April 1999:6–9.

4. Sinclair Stewart, "Sobeys shops for agency: Grocer preparing to fend off aggressive foes," *Strategy,* 6 December 1999:1.

5. Brian Dunn, "The king of bread, butts and beer," *Marketing,* 25 October 1999:23; Anita Lahey, "Cornered stores," *Marketing,* 4 August 1997:10–1; Luis Millan, "King of the corner store," *Canadian Business,* 26 September 1997:101–3.

6. Marina Strauss, "New wave of U.S. retailers advance on Canada," *Globe and Mail,* 12 January 2001:M1.

7. For an in-depth discussion, see Lawrence H. Wortzel, "Retailing strategies for today's mature marketplace," *Journal of Business Strategy,* Spring 1987:45–56.

8. Mariam Mesbah, "Special report: Fashion retailers branch into cosmetics," *Strategy,* 20 January 1997:20.

9. Wendy Cuthbert, "Environment plays major role in purchase decision: Expert," *Strategy,* 29 September 1997:14.

10. Erica Zlomislic, "Special report: Store-level marketing: Virgin's megahit," *Strategy,* 26 May 1997:24.

11. Laura Campbell, "Ending not yet written in cutthroat bookstore war," *Financial Post,* 7 October 1997:10; Myron Magnet, "Let's go for growth," *Fortune,* 7 March 1994:60–72; Val Ross, "Indigo Books stakes out Kingston," *Globe and Mail,* 7 February 1997: C3. Also see Dierdre Donahue, "Bookstores: A haven for the intellect," *USA Today,* 10 July 1997:D1,D2.

12. See Joanna Dale, *Consumer Attitudes towards Retail in BC,* Retail Council of Canada, 21 September 2000, www.retailcouncil.org/research/bcretail/sld026.htm. Steven Bergsman, "Slow times at Sherman Oaks: What's ailing the big malls of America?" *Barron's,* 17 May 1999:39.

13. Amy Barrett, "A retailing pacesetter pulls up lame," *Business Week,* 12 July 1993:122–3.

14. See Malcolm P. McNair and Eleanor G. May, "The next revolution of the retailing wheel," *Harvard Business Review,* September–October 1978:81–91; Stephen Brown, "The wheel of retailing: Past and future," *Journal of Retailing,* Summer 1990:143–7; Stephen Brown, "Variations on a marketing enigma: The wheel of retailing theory," *Journal of Marketing Management,* 7(2) 1991: 131–55; and Stanley C. Hollander, "The wheel of retailing," *Marketing Management,* Summer 1996:63–6.

15. IBM and the Retail Council of Canada, *E-Retail: The Race Is On,* June 1999:3–7.

16. See Nirmalya Kumar, "The power of trust in manufacturer-retailer relationships," *Harvard Business Review,* November–December 1996:92–106.

17. David Menzies, "Retail and high-tech," *Marketing On-Line,* 5 August 1996.

18. "Business bulletin: Shopper scanner," *Wall Street Journal,* 18 February 1995:A1,A5; Kenneth Labich, "Attention shoppers: This man is watching you," *Fortune,* 19 July 1999:131–4.

19. Regina Fazio Maruca, "Retailing: Confronting the challenges that face bricks-and-mortar stores," *Harvard Business Review,* July–August 1999:159–68.

20. Lara Mills, "GT pursues 'underserved' telco market," *Marketing On-Line,* 25 October 1999.

21. See Arthur Andersen & Co., *Facing the Forces of Change: Beyond Future Trends in Wholesale Distribution,* Washington, DC: Distribution and Education Foundation, 1987:7; Joseph Weber, "It's 'like somebody had shot the postman,'" *Business Week,* 13 January 1992:82; and Michael Mandel, "Don't cut out the middleman," *Business Week,* 16 September 1996:30.

22. Richard A. Melcher, "The middlemen stay on the march," *Business Week,* 9 January 1995:87.

Company Case 12

Hitting the Sweet Spot with Tweens

Philip Kotler often makes the point that the most important thing for marketers is to forecast where customers are moving, and to be in front of them. Anyone trying to market to Canada's 2.5 million tweens should keep this mandate top of mind. This echo boom market is grabbing marketers' attention not only because of its size but also because of its spending power. It is estimated that young Canadian girls alone have over $700 million in disposable income. And they are twice as likely as boys the same age to spend it on clothes. Even more notable is that the tween market is 10 times larger in the US.

Marketers are rushing to build brand loyalty among this wired and media-savvy group by creating new brands they might regard as "cool." Firms as disparate as YTV, Schneider Corporation, and Bank of Montreal are scrambling to keep pace with them. An open audience for branded products, they are lovers of brand icons like Coke and Nike, as well as new products that are being developed just for them—GT Global Mutual Funds for Kids, Pillsbury's Pizza Pops, portable milkshakes called Milk Mania, L'Oreal Kids Shampoo and Conditioner, and Bonne Bell Lip Smackers. Specialty retailers like Le Chateau Junior Girl, GUESS?, and La Senza are opening stores to serve them or have included tween sections in their stores.

One of the most successful Canadian tween retailers is Nancy Dennis, founder of Toronto's Ch!ckaboom (216.162.231.34/stores/170.html). Ch!ckaboom specializes in serving girls 5 to 13 years of age, providing them with a venue where they can drop in, meet friends, fiddle with accessories, and shop to their hearts' content without having to deal with snobby salespeople breathing down their necks.

What has Ch!ckaboom done that has made it stand out from this growing crowd? "The best practice in retail is to respect my customer," says Nancy Dennis. She knows that the tween girl wants to have fun just as much as she wants to find the 'in' clothes in her size. Therefore, the stores offer events such as Spice Girl Days, birthday clubs, and Valentines and Halloween parties. An advocate of relationship marketing, Ch!ckaboom leverages its database to keep in contact with its diminutive customers. Ch!ckaboom hopes to expand across the country. You can bet there are many tweens hoping it does just that.

Christopher Edgar and Steve Kahn, founders of Delia's, are two more entrepreneurs who know that hitting the right target market makes all the difference. The two roommates started a catalogue business selling to female university students. Sales were at best ho-hum until they realized that it was actually the little sisters of the university students who were buying the merchandise. Sensing an opportunity, they shifted targets and aimed their catalogue, named Delia's, at the 12- to 24-year-old market. Since that decision in 1994, Delia's has become *the* shopping place for American teens. According to teen shopper Addie, "If it's in Delia's, it's all right to wear, but if it's not in Delia's, you take a chance in wearing it."

How does Delia's hit the teens' sweet spot? Primarily through its edgy image. It uses fresh-faced, wide-eyed models with whipped-up hair that is sometimes green and sometimes blue. No glam dolls here! Styles include wide-legged pants, clunky shoes, baby-doll dresses, ankle-length skirts, striped T-shirts, and the like—all very hip and high-spirited, but not overly sexy. Even the order form at Delia's is something special. There you can find tips on how to order pants so that they droop well below the hips with hems dragging. The under-16 crowd, especially 12-year-olds, find the catalogue most appealing, but their older sisters look at it, too—just to see what's there. You never know what you may find.

When their catalogues arrive, teens haul them to school to giggle over new styles and decide what they really need. In their own minds they identify strongly with the models, so Delia's can become very special to them. The company encourages this attitude by hiring high school and college girls to answer the telephones, chat, answer questions, and provide shoppers with fashion tips. In turn, Delia's customers are fanatically loyal. They send the cataloguers photos of themselves, letters, critiques of the clothes, suggestions for new merchandise, and tons of e-mail. Specially designated Delia's employees answer each letter and e-mail, a major investment in relationship building with what is often a very fickle market. Staying in touch with the market is extremely important when the target is so young and fast changing.

Delia's hits the sweet spot in other ways, including its brand portfolio and ever-widening merchandise assortment, plus multiple paths to market. Only about 30 percent of the merchandise sold through the catalogue carries the Delia's label. Eager readers find a host of other desirable brands such as Roxy by Quiksilver, Free People, Dollhouse, 26 Redsugar, Sugartooth, and Greed Girl. With each brand, Delia's spreads its risk. If one brand doesn't appeal, others might, so the catalogue does not depend solely on Delia's buyers and designers guessing right on the market's fashion wants.

Initially, Delia's catalogue was passed around from hand to hand but by 1996, the catalogue retailer had developed a stable database, which has become one of its key strengths. Over the years, the company has compiled the database from telephone requests (sometimes 5000 a day). By mid-1999, Delia's had a database of 11 million individuals, including more than one million actual buyers. To maintain the loyalty of its customers, Delia's does not sell or share the database. Communications and transactions with Delia's are kept private and confidential.

To expand their market, Steve and Chris have pursued two additional strategies. First, they moved into bricks-and-mortar retailing by acquiring TSI Soccer Corp., a soccer apparel and equipment retailer. Purchasing TSI Soccer achieved placement in malls, exposure to the male half of the teen market, and a broadened merchandise assortment that includes items associated with teens' primary sport—soccer. Later, Delia's purchased Screeem!, giving it outlets across the US. Finally, Delia's opened its first branded Delia's store in New York in February 1999. The merchandise assortment included not only clothing but also cosmetics, bath products, posters, candy, novelty home accessories, and underwear. The store looked like a three-dimensional version of the catalogue. The Delia's logo was featured throughout, ceilings were festooned with pink parachute fabric, and inflatable pink and yellow armchairs hang from the walls. From the start, products flew off Delia's shelves. Satisfied that sales revenues had exceeded targets, the company opened eight more Delia's stores before the end of

1999 and began to convert its Screeem! stores to the Delia's format.

Delia's second major new strategy was adding Internet services to its arsenal of direct-marketing weapons. All Internet activities are grouped under a subsidiary called ITurf. First, Delia's purchased gURL.com, a Web site for teenage girls that features news, chat rooms, and a link to the new Delia's Web site. The Delia's.com site mostly entertains, but it also sells some merchandise. The print catalogue remains the main selling vehicle. By 1999, only three to four percent of sales were made online.

Delia's has also introduced contentsonline.com, a home furnishings Web site, and droog.com, a boys' Web site. These were paired with *Contents,* a print furnishings catalogue aimed primarily at girls, and *Droog,* a catalogue for young males. According to Delia's founders, young girls like to furnish their own rooms, so a furnishings catalogue that includes inflatable and bean bag chairs and throw rugs should appeal to loyal Delia's customers. The latest Internet launch is dotdotdash.com, which is aimed at 7- to 11-year-olds. As if all this Internet activity were not enough, Delia's is also available in the teen shopping category on Yahoo!.

Delia's rapid expansion comes at a high price. Stores are much more capital-intensive than direct-sales channels. They require major up-front investments in leases, furnishings, inventory, and sales personnel. A catalogue with slow-selling merchandise can be quickly replaced, but a store with slow-selling merchandise suffers from the sales and markdowns needed to move inventory. The Internet operations are another drain on resources. The ITurf subsidiary required building an expensive infrastructure. Although investors seem willing to let Internet companies spend millions to build customer bases and infrastructure, the lack of sales (remember the three to four percent?) is an important issue. However, even with the losses in late 1998 and 1999, Delia's continued to be a darling of the stock market.

Still, there are serious problems in dealing with this fickle market that can turn on a retailer instantly. Even young Addie, who was so sold on Delia's, is becoming disillusioned. She says, "Having all my friends dress out of the same catalogue ended up meaning that everybody has the same stuff. . . . I bought this sweater and six people in my school had it, and they all wore it on the same day, and I'd rather be original with my clothes."

Interviews with teens reveal that they frequently pore over catalogues and then tell their mothers what to order for them. Some say it's too much trouble to order over the Internet. In addition, this is a market that is highly sociable—teens like to hang out in groups and visit stores. The Internet may not offer the social interaction that going to the mall or sharing catalogues does. Because of these concerns, Ch!ckaboom has decided to expand slowly, has limited itself to mall operations, and has shunned the Internet. Delia's, on the other hand, is betting heavily on a marketing channel that may not provide sufficient return on equity. Tracking the future of these two tween retailers may provide us all with an insightful lesson.

Questions

1. Check out the many Delia's Web sites. How are they similar? How do they differ?
2. Does expanding to the male market using catalogues or the Internet make sense? Do boys want to shop in those media?
3. From a consumer's viewpoint, what advantages does the Internet offer? What disadvantages?
4. What are the advantages of retail stores? The disadvantages?
5. Is a firm likely to be successful in selling to multiple targets, such as 7- to 11-year-olds and then 12- to 24-year-olds? Will customers grow out of the Delia's catalogue when they turn 12?
6. Which retailer has made the right moves in your opinion, Ch!ckaboom or Delia's?

Sources: Mikala Folb, "Totally girl," *Marketing,* 4/11 January 1999:10–2; Shawna Steinberg, "Have allowance will transform economy," *Canadian Business,* 13 March 1998:59–71; "ITurf IPO lifts Delia's profits," *WWD,* 10 June 1999:9; "Delia's 2nd quarter loss deepens," *WWD,* 2 September 1999:5; "We are going to own this generation," *Business Week,* 15 February 1999:88; "Delia's Screeem! and Jeans Country acquisition a done deal," *Daily News Record,* 3 August 1998:8; "Gullemin promoted to president of Delia's," WWD, 22 March 1999:44; "Internet, retail costs dampen Delia's 3rd quarter earnings," *WWD,* 10 December 1998:15; Catherine Curan, "Delia's buys TSI Soccer, WWW site," *WWD,* 31 December 1997:3; Thomas Cunningham, "Internet may spur more fashion IPO's," *WWD,* 19 July 1999:24; Yolanda Gault, "Market drops as Delia's shops, but analysts stand by cataloger: Marketer to teens makes move to stores," *Crain's New York Business,* 8 June 1998:23; Lawrence Gould, "How 2 grown men mastered girl talk: Apparel catalog for Generation Y producing totally awesome results," *Crain's New York Business,* 27 October 1997:4; Denise Lavoie, "Agency aims to get inside minds of teens during shopping spree," *Greensboro News and Record,* 7 September 1999:B6,B7; Patricia McLaughlin, "12-year-olds dig Delia's look," *St. Louis Post-Dispatch,* 18 September 1997:2; Karen Parr, "New catalogs target Gen Y," *WWD,* 24 July 1997:12; Cynthia Redecker, "Delia's opens first retail unit," *WWD,* 25 February 1999:11; Cynthia Redecker, "Delia's widens Web effort," *WWD,* 3 December 1998:13.

video case 12

SHELF WARS

For years, when analysts considered the question of who had the power in a channel of distribution, the answer always was the manufacturer. Today, however, especially in the food industry, packaged goods firms across Canada are being squeezed by consolidation among retailers. In Canada the top six retail food chains control almost 75 percent of the outlets. Compare this figure to the US where the top six chains control around 24 percent of the marketplace.

The trend toward retail concentration is amplified by a number of accompanying trends. Mass merchandisers, club stores, and wholesalers are also consolidating. Thus, the grocery chains are snapping up acquisitions partly as a defensive measure. For example, there is evidence that Wal-Mart, the biggest retailer in the world, and Zellers will move into the grocery business in Canada in a big way. "Wal-Mart is twice the size of the entire Canadian grocery industry in size, so you have to pay attention," says Nick Gennery of the Canadian Council of Grocery Distributors. "You're going to get casualties."

Furthermore, many good retailers also offer their own store brands and private label brands that compete directly with manufacturers' brands. In many cases, manufacturers' brands are being taken off the shelves to make way for private label products, which may be more profitable for the grocery chains. This is possible because many food products are in the maturity stage of the product life cycle and in consumers' eyes many brands appear equal.

Therefore, it isn't surprising that the big grocery chains are putting pressure on suppliers' profit margins. One consequence of this is that Canadian packaged good firms allocate a much higher portion of their marketing budgets (approximately 24 percent) on trade-focused promotions, compared to 13 percent in the US. While such trade spending may help manufacturers keep shelf space, the spending takes away from manufacturing firms' abilities to invest to build their brands.

Joelle Verdon, a retail analyst who works for CIBC World Capital, says, "I think the people who are most at risk are the small suppliers." Verdon tracks Loblaws and Sobey's, the two grocery giants leading the consolidation trend. While there is widespread grumbling about the situation among food suppliers in Canada, few are willing to air their complaints publicly, for fear of retaliation. "Right now, the only choice the manufacturers have is to not say a word, to accept with resignation," says Gerald Ponton of the Alliance des manufacturiers et exportateurs du Quebec. The association says an ombudsman may be needed to settle disputes between suppliers and the grocery chains.

But having a dispute resolution mechanism may only be a temporary solution. Former Nabob Foods CEO John Bell advocates having senior management become passionately involved in product and brand innovation. "CEOs," he notes, "must recognize that the marketing responsibility spreads far beyond the marketing department. Marketing is a vital culture that must be re-engineered back into the total business. Few leaders are creating environments that encourage marketing innovation in the consumer packaged-goods industry." Bell goes on to say that while many Canadian corporate leaders have embraced numerous cost-cutting initiatives as a means of offsetting store brand gains, this move won't save their firms. The leaders of Canada's consumer-goods companies need to recognize that their own personal attention to their brands holds the key to long-term profitability. He thinks senior managers at other Canadian firms can learn from the example he set. "During my years as a CEO, I kept my eye on brand equity. I knew that we had to continually differentiate to develop premium prices and margins. And I was confident that the consumer would reward us with more inherent brand value than our competition."

Questions

1. Why have government officials and market regulators long been concerned with the issue of growing concentration in some industries?
2. Private label brands have been in the marketplace for many years, yet it wasn't until recently that they began to be perceived as a threat by manufacturers of nationally branded food products. What explains this change?
3. If you were a marketer working for a manufacturer of a nationally branded food product, what would you do to offset the power of retailers?

Sources: This case was prepared by Peggy Cunningham and is based on "Shelf Wars," *Venture* (March 7, 2000); John Bell, "Be a Brand Surgeon," *Marketing On-Line,* January 22, 2001.

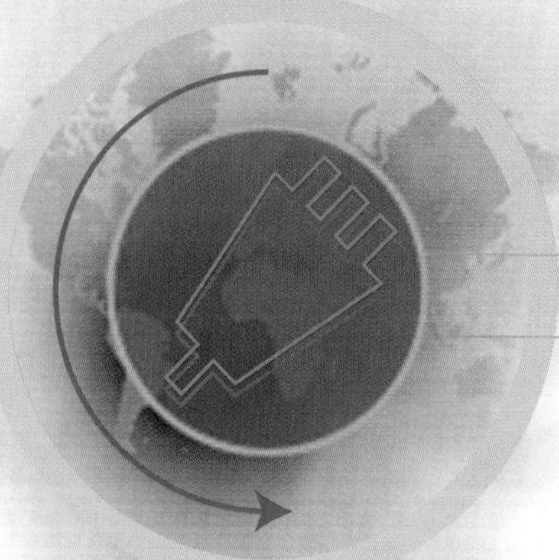

PART 1 2 3 4

Developing the Marketing Mix

Concept Connections

When you finish this chapter, you should be able to

1. Name and define the five tools of the promotion mix.
2. Discuss the process and advantages of integrated marketing communications.
3. Outline the steps in developing effective marketing communications.
4. Explain the methods for setting the promotion budget and factors that affect the design of the promotion mix.

chapter 13
Integrated Marketing Communication Strategy

Jim Lesinski, director of marketing communications and research for Volvo Trucks North America, first proposed putting an ad for Volvo's heavy-duty trucks on the Super Bowl in 1994. His bosses at Swedish parent AB Volvo, who were not familiar with the hype and frenzy that surrounds North American football, must have thought he'd gone a little ditzy. "How much will it cost?" they asked. "About $1.9 million in media costs," replied Lesinski. "Plus another $750 000 or so to produce the ad." "And how long and how often will the ad run?" they asked. "Just once," said Lesinski, "for 30 seconds." With eyebrows raised and mouths agape, Volvo's top management respectfully rejected Lesinski's proposal.

In fact, early on, Lesinski himself had some doubts. Did it make sense to spend almost a third of his annual marketing budget on a single ad? Given the narrow target market for Volvo's huge, $180 000 trucks, was it wise to advertise in the granddaddy of mass-media spectacles, amidst the glitzy showcase ads run by big-spending consumer product companies selling to the masses? Volvo Trucks' target market constituted a mere one percent of the total Super Bowl audience. Moreover, no other heavy-duty truck manufacturer was advertising on television, let alone on the Super Bowl.

But the more he thought about it, the more convinced Lesinski became. Volvo had been selling heavy trucks in North America since 1981 under a variety of nameplates, including Volvo, Autocar, and White/GMC. Its early trucks lacked quality, sold at relatively low prices, and had gained a reputation as low-status "fleet trucks." In recent years, however, Volvo Trucks had consolidated its nameplates under the Volvo brand and had developed a new line of premium trucks—the VN Series. These new Volvo trucks were superior to competing premium brands in overall quality, design, safety, and driving comfort. Now, all that remained was to raise Volvo Trucks' old low-status image to match the new high-quality reality. That task, Lesinski knew, would take something dramatic—something like the Super Bowl. He persisted and finally won approval to place a single ad in the 1998 Super Bowl.

The target market for heavy-duty trucks is truck fleet buyers and independent owner-operators. However, truck drivers themselves are perhaps the most important buying influence. The industry faces a severe driver shortage, and firms perceived as having

better-performing, more comfortable, higher-status trucks have a big edge in attracting and holding good drivers. As a result, truck buyers are swayed by driver perceptions. Therefore, Lesinski's communications goal was to improve the image of Volvo's VN Series trucks not just among truck buyers but also among drivers. No other event reaches this audience more completely than the Super Bowl. In fact, nearly 70 percent of all truck drivers watch some or all of an average Super Bowl game.

Still, Jim Lesinski knew that a single Super Bowl ad, by itself, wasn't likely to have much lasting impact on buyer and driver perceptions. Instead—and this is the real story—he designed a comprehensive, carefully targeted, four-month integrated promotional campaign, with Super Bowl advertising as its centrepiece (see figure below). Called The Best Drive in the Game Sweepstakes, the promotion offered truck drivers a chance to win a new Volvo VN770 truck. Lesinski began promoting the Best Drive sweepstakes in September 1997, using a wide range of carefully coordinated media, including trucker magazines and radio stations. Drivers could enter the sweepstakes by responding to print or radio ads, by visiting a Volvo Truck dealer or participating truck stop, or by clicking onto the Volvo Trucks Web site (a large proportion of truckers use the Internet regularly to schedule loads). To create additional interest, Volvo Trucks sponsored a North American truck tour, consisting of two caravans of three VN770s each, which visited major truck stops, encouraging truck drivers to enter the Best Drive sweepstakes and giving them a chance to experience a new Volvo VN770 first-hand.

The campaign attracted more than 48 700 entrants. Each entrant received a wallet-size entry card with one of 40 "Volvo Truths" printed on it—each emphasizing a key VN770 positioning point. If the phrase on a driver's card matched the winning phrase revealed in the Super Bowl commercial, the driver became a finalist eligible for the grand prize. To further encourage drivers to watch the commercial, Volvo Trucks sponsored Super Bowl parties at 40 Flying J truck stops. It also had Volvo VN770s at each truck stop so that drivers could see the truck that was causing all the commotion.

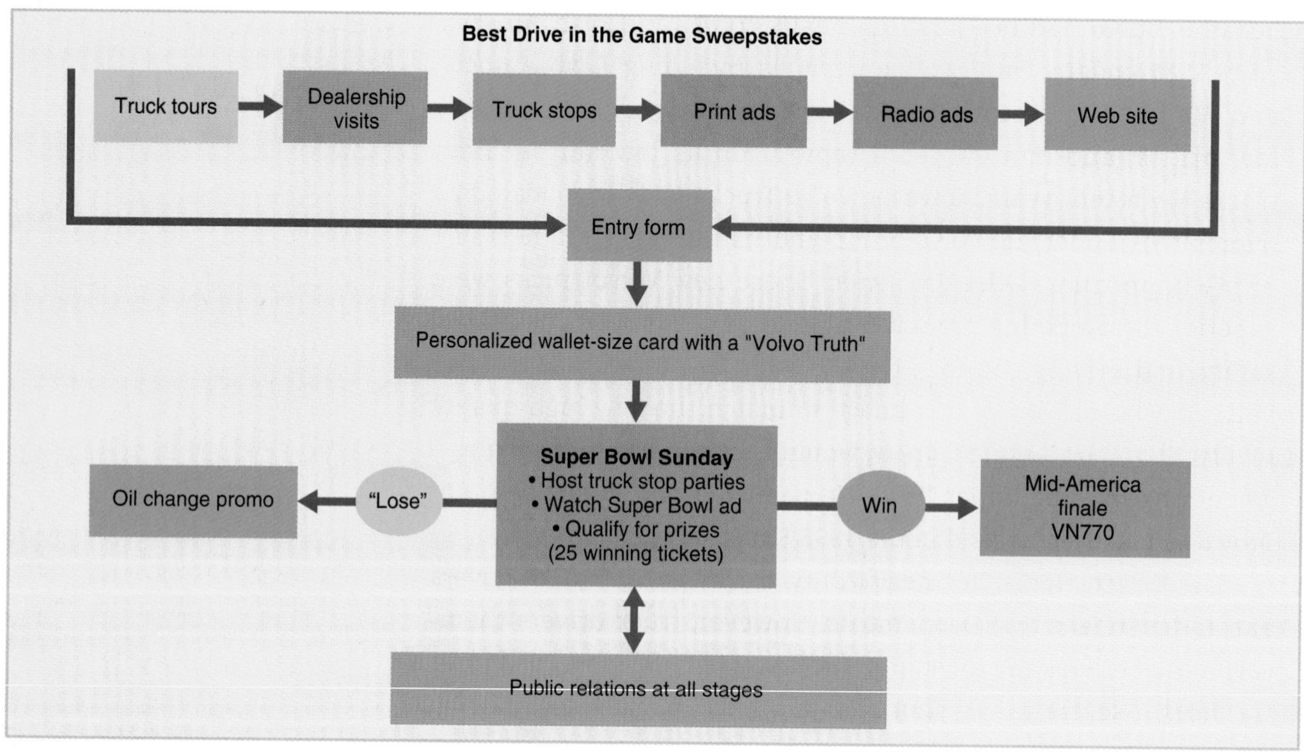

Volvo Trucks
www.volvotrucks.volvo.com/

On Super Bowl Sunday 1998, Jim Lesinski found himself at a Greensboro, North Carolina, truck stop, anxiously awaiting the fourth-quarter airing of his ad. He sat shoulder to shoulder with a standing-room-only crowd of truckers, clustered around a lounge television with their Best Drive wallet cards in hand. To Lesinski's dismay, a clever ad for Tabasco Sauce preceded the Volvo ad (remember the exploding mosquito?) and the crowd was still laughing as the Volvo commercial began. Lesinski still remembers counting off the missed seconds (at a cost of some $60 000 apiece!) waiting for the group to settle their attention on his ad.

The Volvo Trucks ad itself used soft humour to make the quality point. It featured an experienced and approachable professional driver named Gus, driving a new Volvo VN770 down a desert highway. Gus talked sagely about "what 30 years on the road have taught me" and advised "always run the best truck you can." During the 30-second spot, the scenes shifted to show both the sleek, handsome exterior of the truck and its luxurious interior. "But success hasn't spoiled me," Gus concluded. "I still put my pants on one leg at a time." As Gus delivered this last line, a uniformed butler approached from the sleeper area of the truck, presenting a small silver box on a pillow. "Your toothpick, sir," he intoned. The winning phrase, "Volvo—Drive Safely," appeared on the screen as the commercial ended.

To Jim's enormous relief, the drivers at the truck stop seemed to really like the commercial. They were pleased that it portrayed professional truck drivers and their huge, sometimes scary trucks in a positive light. More importantly, the ad got the drivers buzzing about the VN770 truck and the winning phrase. In the month following the Super Bowl, the 10 finalists holding winning phrases received all-expense-paid trips to the trucking industry's premier trade show, the Mid-America Truck Show in Louisville, Kentucky. Volvo stole the show, sponsoring a Brooks and Dunn concert at which company officials held an on-stage drawing in front of 20 000 truckers to select the grand prize winner.

In all, the Best Drive in the Game Sweepstakes cost Volvo Trucks North America $3.6 million—$2.7 million for the ad alone. Was it worth the cost? Lesinski and his bosses at AB Volvo certainly think so. Later research showed that the campaign had a sizeable, positive impact on both trucker and public perceptions. More than 30 million adults recalled seeing the Super Bowl ad. Just that one ad created a 98 percent increase in the general public's awareness of Volvo trucks and significantly improved public perceptions of Volvo drivers as intelligent, safe, successful, and friendly.

Perhaps more importantly, the ad was viewed by 1.4 million truck drivers, almost half the target market.

Twenty-three percent of these drivers talked about the ad with someone else, generating more than 325 000 conversations about the commercial. After the Best Drive campaign, substantially higher proportions of drivers and buyers perceive the Volvo VN770 as being like a "Hilton" rather than a "Motel 6," and as a "sleek, aerodynamic, friendly vehicle" versus a "work truck." The campaign created 30 percent driver preference for Volvo trucks, higher than preferences for competitors Freightliner (25%), Peterbilt (23%), and Kenworth (16%). By the end of 1998, sales of Volvo trucks were up by 44.5 percent over the previous year, and market share had risen 2.5 points to 12 percent. Based on these results, Volvo Trucks North America sponsored a repeat promotion, The Best Drive in the Game II, the following year, including a brand new ad in the 1999 Super Bowl.

Why did the Best Drive promotion work so well? Success resulted from much more than just a single Super Bowl ad. "The ad was definitely the main attraction," says Jim Lesinski. "But it was really just the lure that pulled drivers into the full Best Drive promotion and got them into our trucks." By blending Super Bowl advertising with a full slate of other carefully targeted ads, promotions, and events, Lesinski created a complete integrated marketing communications campaign that had a larger and more lasting impact than any single ad could ever have achieved.[1]

Modern marketing calls for more than just developing a good product, pricing it attractively, and making it available to target customers. Companies also must *communicate* with their customers, and what they communicate should not be left to chance. For most companies, the question is not *whether* to communicate, but *how much to spend* and *in what ways.*

The Marketing Communications Mix

Marketing communications mix (or promotion mix)
The specific mix of advertising, personal selling, sales promotion, and public relations a company uses to pursue its advertising and marketing objectives.

Advertising
Any paid form of non-personal presentation and promotion of ideas, goods, or services by an identified sponsor.

Personal selling
Personal presentation by the firm's sales force to make sales and build customer relationships.

Sales promotion
Short-term incentives to encourage purchase or sale of a product or service.

Public relations
Building good relations with the company's publics by obtaining favourable publicity, building up a good "corporate image," and handling or heading off unfavourable rumours, stories, and events.

Direct marketing
Direct communications with carefully targeted individuals to obtain an immediate response.

A company's total **marketing communications mix,** or **promotion mix,** consists of the specific blend of advertising, personal selling, sales promotion, and public relations tools that the company uses to pursue its advertising and marketing objectives. The five major types of promotion are:[2]

- **Advertising:** Any paid form of non-personal presentation and promotion of ideas, goods, or services by an identified sponsor.
- **Personal selling:** Personal presentation by the firm's sales force to make sales and build customer relationships.
- **Sales promotion:** Short-term incentives to encourage the purchase or sale of a product or service.
- **Public relations:** Building good relations with the company's publics by obtaining favourable publicity, building up a good "corporate image," and handling or heading off unfavourable rumours, stories, and events.
- **Direct marketing:** Direct communications with carefully targeted individual consumers to obtain an immediate response—the use of mail, telephone, fax, e-mail, and other non-personal tools to communicate directly with specific consumers or to solicit a direct response.

Each type of promotion has its own tools. Advertising includes print, broadcast, outdoor, and other forms. Personal selling includes sales presentations, trade shows, and incentive programs. Sales promotion includes point-of-purchase displays, premiums, discounts, coupons, specialty advertising, and demonstrations. Direct marketing includes catalogues, telemarketing, fax transmissions, and the Internet. Thanks to technological breakthroughs, marketers can now communicate through traditional media (newspapers, radio, telephone, and television), as well as its newer forms (fax machines, cellular phones, pagers, and computers). These new technologies have encouraged more companies to move from mass communication to more targeted communication and one-on-one dialogue.

At the same time, communication goes beyond these specific promotion tools. The product's design, its price, the shape and colour of its package, and the stores that sell it—*all* communicate something to buyers. Thus, although the promotion mix is the company's primary communication activity, the entire marketing mix—promotion *and* product, price, and place—must be coordinated for greatest communication impact.

In this chapter, we begin by examining the rapidly changing marketing communications environment, the concept of integrated marketing communications, and the marketing communication process. Next, we discuss the factors that marketing communicators must consider in shaping an overall communication mix. Finally, we summarize the legal, ethical, and social responsibility issues in marketing communications. In Chapter 14, we look at mass-communication tools—advertising, sales promotion, and public relations. Chapter 15 examines the sales force as a communication and promotion tool.

Integrated Marketing Communications

Over the past few decades, companies around the world perfected the art of mass marketing—selling highly standardized products to masses of customers. In the process, they developed effective mass-media advertising techniques to support their mass-marketing strategies. These companies routinely invested millions of dollars in the mass media, reaching tens of millions of customers with a single ad. However, as we move into the twenty-first century, marketing managers face some new marketing communications realities.

The Changing Communications Environment

Two major factors are changing the face of today's marketing communications. First, as mass markets have fragmented, marketers are shifting away from mass marketing and developing focused marketing programs, designed to build closer relationships with customers in more narrowly defined micromarkets. Second, vast improvements in information technology are speeding the movement toward segmented marketing. Today's information technology helps marketers to keep closer track of customer needs—more information about consumers at the individual and household levels is available than ever before. New technologies also provide new communications avenues for reaching smaller customer segments with more tailored messages.

The shift from mass marketing to segmented marketing has had a dramatic impact on marketing communications. Just as mass marketing gave rise to a new generation of mass-media communications, the shift toward one-on-one marketing is spawning a new generation of more specialized and highly targeted communications efforts.[3]

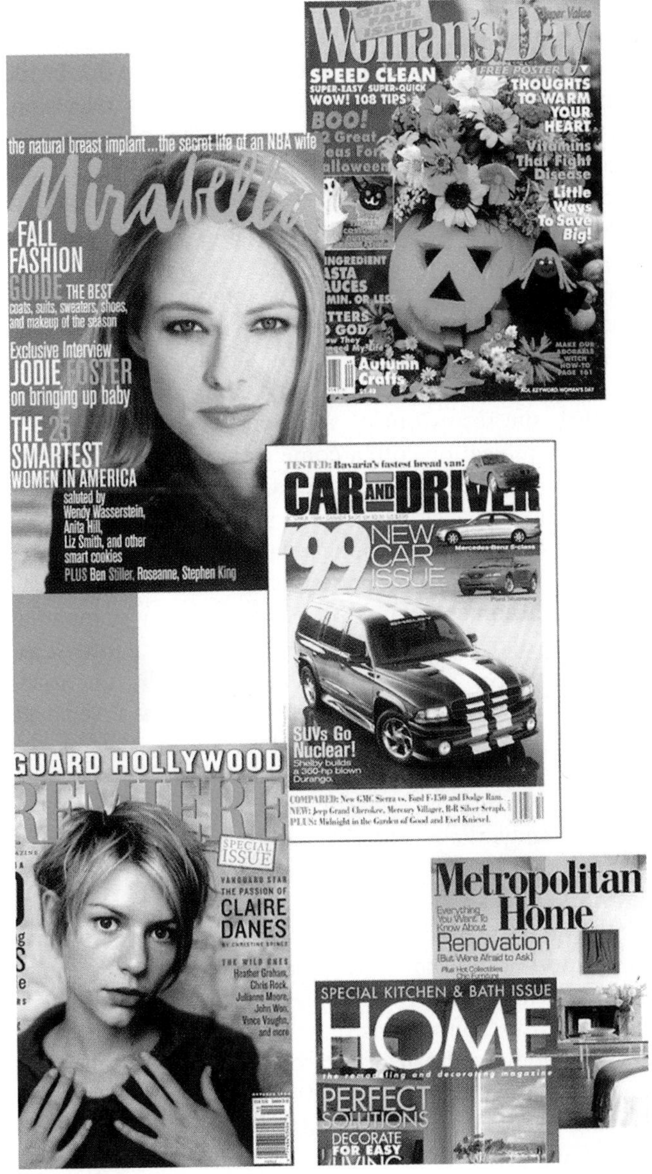

The relatively few mass magazines of the mid-twentieth century have been replaced by thousands of special-interest magazines. HMF alone publishes these and more than 20 other magazines reaching 17 different markets and more than 47 million readers, not to mention a wide range of online, broadcast, outdoor, and other media.

Given this new communications environment, marketers must rethink the roles of various media and promotion mix tools. Mass-media advertising has long dominated the promotion mixes of consumer product companies. However, although television, magazines, and other mass media remain very important, their dominance is now declining. Market fragmentation has resulted in media fragmentation into more focused media that better match today's targeting strategies. For example, in 1975, what were the three major US TV networks (ABC, CBS, and NBC) attracted 82 percent of the 24-hour viewing audience. By 1995, that number had dropped to only 35 percent, as cable television and satellite broadcasting systems offered advertisers dozens or even hundreds of alternative channels, which reach smaller, specialized audiences. It's expected to drop even further, down to 25 percent by the year 2005. Similarly, the relatively few mass magazines of the 1940s and 1950s—*Look, Life, Maclean's, Saturday Evening Post*—have been replaced by more than 18 600 special-interest magazines, reaching more focused audiences. Beyond these channels, advertisers are making increased use of new, highly targeted media, ranging from video screens on supermarket shopping carts to CD-ROM catalogues and Web sites on the Internet.[4]

More generally, advertising appears to be giving way to other elements of the promotion mix. In the glory days of mass marketing, consumer product companies spent the lion's share of their promotion budgets on mass-media advertising. Today, media advertising captures only about 26 percent of total promotion spending.[5] The rest goes to various sales promotion activities, which can be focused more effectively on individual consumer and trade segments. Marketers are using a richer variety of focused communication tools in an effort to reach their diverse target markets. In all, companies are doing less broadcasting and more narrowcasting.

The Need for Integrated Marketing Communications

The shift from mass marketing to targeted marketing, with its corresponding use of a richer mixture of communication channels and promotion tools, poses a problem for marketers. Consumers are being exposed to a greater variety of marketing communications from and about the company from an array of sources. However, customers don't distinguish between message sources the way marketers do. In the consumer's mind, advertising messages from different media—such as television, magazines, or online sources—blur into one. Messages delivered via different promotional approaches—such as advertising, personal selling, sales promotion, public relations, or direct marketing—all become part of a single message about the company. Conflicting messages from these different sources can result in confused company images and brand positions.

All too often, companies fail to integrate their various communications channels. The result is a hodgepodge of communications to consumers. Mass advertisements say one thing, a price promotion sends a different signal, a product label creates still another message, company sales literature says something altogether different, and the company's Web site seems out of sync with everything else.

The problem is that these communications often come from different company sources. The advertising department or advertising agency plans and implements advertising messages. Sales management develops personal selling communications. Other functional specialists are responsible for public relations, sales promotion, direct marketing, online sites, and other forms of marketing communications. Such functional separation has recently become a major problem for many companies and their Internet communications activities, which are often split off into separate organizational units. "These new, forward-looking, high-tech functional groups, whether they exist as part of an established organization or as a separate new business operation, commonly are located in separate space, apart from the traditional operation," observes one integrated marketing communications expert. "They generally are populated by young, enthusiastic, technologically proficient people with a burning desire to 'change the world,'" he adds, but "the separation and the lack of cooperation and cohesion" can be a disintegrating force in marketing communications (see Marketing Highlight 13-1).

In the past, no one person was responsible for thinking through the communication roles of the various promotion tools and coordinating the promotion mix. Today, however, many companies are adopting the concept of **integrated marketing communications (IMC)**. Under this concept, as illustrated in Figure 13-1, the company carefully integrates and coordinates its many communications channels to deliver a clear, consistent, and compelling message about the organization and its products.[6] As one marketing executive puts it, "IMC builds a strong brand identity in the marketplace by tying together and reinforcing all your images and

Integrated marketing communications (IMC)
The concept under which a company carefully integrates and coordinates its many communications channels to deliver a clear, consistent, and compelling message about the organization and its products.

messages. IMC means that all your corporate messages, positioning and images, and identity are coordinated across all [marketing communications] venues. It means that your PR materials say the same thing as your direct mail campaign, and your advertising has the same 'look and feel' as your Web site."[7]

The IMC solution calls for recognizing all contact points at which the customer may encounter the company, its products, and its brands. Each brand contact will deliver a message, whether good, bad, or indifferent. The company must strive to deliver a consistent and positive message at all contact points.

To help implement IMC, some companies appoint a marketing communications director, or marcom manager, who has overall responsibility for the company's communications efforts. Compaq Canada, for example, has a vice-president of integrated marketing communications. IMC produces better communications consistency and greater sales impact. It places the responsibility in someone's hands—where none existed before—to unify the company's image as it is shaped by thousands of company activities. It leads to a total marketing communication strategy aimed at showing how the company and its products can help customers solve their problems.

A View of the Communication Process

IMC involves identifying the target audience and shaping a well-coordinated promotional program to elicit the desired audience response. Too often, marketing communications focus on overcoming immediate awareness, image, or preference problems in the target market. But this approach to communication has limitations: It is too short term and too costly, and most messages of this type fall on deaf ears. Marketers are moving toward viewing communications as *managing the customer relationship over time,* during the preselling, selling, consuming, and postconsumption stages. Because customers differ, communications programs need to be developed for specific segments, niches, and even individuals. Given the new interactive communications technologies, companies must ask not only "How can

FIGURE 13-1
Integrated marketing communications

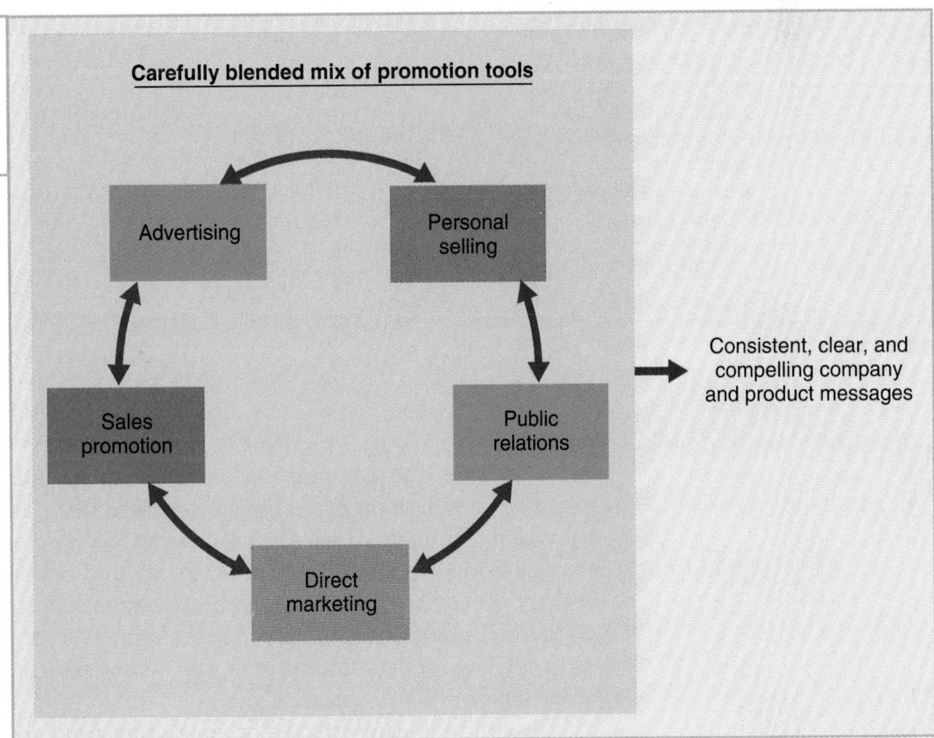

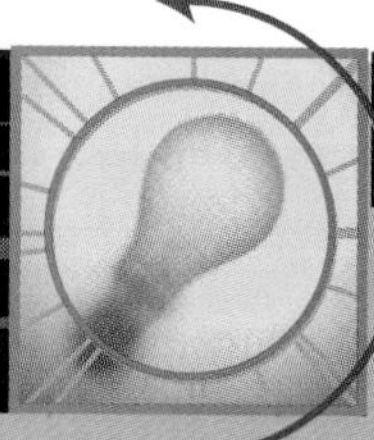

marketing highlight 13-1

The Internet, Interactivity, and All Those Nets and Dot-Coms: Disintegrated Marketing Communications?

Ever have a day when you couldn't get a TV commercial out of your head? Or do ad jingles from yesteryear sometimes stick in your cranium, like "I'd like to buy the world a Coke," or "Plop, plop, fizz, fizz. Oh what a relief it is"? Or do long lost words like "Two all beef patties, special sauce, lettuce, cheese, pickles, onions, on a sesame seed bun" suddenly and inexplicably burst from your mouth? If you're like most people, you sop up more than a fair share of TV advertising.

Now, try to remember the last ad you saw while surfing the Internet. Drawing a blank? That's not surprising. The Web's ineffectiveness as a major brand-building tool is one of today's hottest marketing issues, even though spending on Internet advertising by Canadian marketers grew by 126 percent between 1998 and 1999. Despite its growth, Internet advertising ($55.5 million) represents only a small portion of Canadian advertising expenditures. Television still represents 34.1 percent of total spending at $2.36 billion, followed by daily newspapers (25.1% at $1.7 billion), radio (13.8% at $952 million), weekly newspapers (11.4% at $788 million), magazines (10.8% at $747 million), and outdoor signage (4.1% at $287 million). Still, some firms are treating the Internet as if it were the "one and only" communication medium of the future.

The problem? According to integrated marketing communication guru Don Schultz, all the special attention this new medium is getting may be resulting in disintegrated marketing communications. Says Schultz:

> My mailbox has filled with brochures, invitations, meetings, get-togethers, and debates all promising to explain interactivity, new media, e-commerce and electronic media. Each . . . promises to give me the full picture of how to do the Internet, the Web, extranets, intranets, and all the other "nets" that are popping up everywhere. Not one has even suggested how all this new stuff might fit with, coordinate alongside, relate to, or be integrated with the existing media systems. Nothing on how to combine or bring together existing programs and existing customers with the brave new world of the 21st century.

Most troubling is that many firms are organizing their new e-communications operations into separate groups or divisions, isolating them from mainstream marketing activities. "It is . . . the apartness that concerns me," Schultz observes. "We seem to be creating the same problems with new media, new marketing, and new commerce that we created years ago when we developed separate sales promotion groups, separate direct-marketing activities, separate public relations departments, separate events organizations, and so on. . . . In my view, we are well on the way to disintegrating our marketing and communication programs and processes all over again." However, whereas companies appear to be compartmentalizing the new communications tools, customers won't. According to Schultz:

> New media, the Internet, interactivity and all the Nets and "dot-coms" are critical to marketing and communication practice, but they are not the be-all-and-end-all of marketing and marketing communication. They . . . are not going to instantaneously replace all our current techniques, approaches or media systems. . . . The real issue for most [marketers] and consumers is transition, from what they do now to what they likely will do in the future. And, the truth is, most [consumers] won't compartmentalize their use of the new systems. They won't say, "Hey, I'm going off to do a bit of Net surfing. Burn my TV, throw out all my radios, cancel all my magazine subscriptions, and, by the way, take out my telephone and don't deliver any mail anymore." It's not that kind of world for consumers, and it shouldn't be the kind of world for marketers either.

To be sure, the new Internet promises exciting marketing communications potential. However, marketers trying to use the Web to build brands face many challenges. One limitation is that the Internet doesn't build mass brand awareness. Instead, it's like having millions of private conversations. The Web simply can't match the impact of the Super Bowl, where tens of millions of people see the same 30-second Coca-Cola or Hallmark ad at the same time. Thus, using the Internet, it's hard to establish the universal meanings—like "Always Coca-Cola" or "When you care enough to send the very best"—that are at the heart of brand recognition and brand value. That's why tactics that have worked on TV have failed on the Web. For example, Bell Atlantic developed an online soap opera that re-

we reach our customers?" but also "How can we find ways to let our customers reach us?"

Therefore, the communications process should start with an audit of all the potential interactions that target customers may have with the product and company. For example, someone purchasing a new computer may talk with others, see television commercials, read articles and ads in newspapers and magazines, and try out computers in the store. Marketers must assess the influence that each of these communications experiences will have at different stages of the buying process. This understanding will help them allocate their communication dollars more efficiently and effectively.

To communicate effectively, marketers need to understand how communica-

volved around yuppie newlyweds Troy and Linda. Although the site won raves from critics and had lots of fans, Bell Atlantic's research showed it did little to boost the brand.

Another Internet limitation is format and quality constraints. Web ads are still low in quality and impact. Procter & Gamble and other large advertisers have been pushing to get Internet publishers to allow larger, more complex types of ads with high-quality sound and full-motion video. So far, however, ads on the Internet are all too ignorable. Even if advertisers could put larger, richer ads on the Web, they would likely face a consumer backlash. In the digital world, consumers control ad exposure. Many consumers who've grown up with the Internet are sceptical of ads in general and resentful of Web ads in particular. Internet advertisers face an uphill battle in getting such consumers to click onto their ads. In fact, a recent survey found that 21 percent of Internet users polled said they never clicked on Internet ads and another 51 percent said they clicked only rarely.

Facing such realities, most marketers opt for fuller promotion campaigns to build their brands. Even companies that rely primarily on e-commerce for sales are conducting most of their branding efforts offline. Business-to-business e-commerce star Cisco Systems spends ad money on full-page ads in the *Wall Street Journal* rather than on Web banners. Dell Computer is one of the largest ad spenders in tech trade magazines and runs a $150-million-plus branding campaign almost entirely on TV. Dell hopes to conduct 50 percent of all transactions online and contends that it can't generate that kind of volume with Web advertising.

Similarly, most traditional marketers are adding the Web as an enhancement to their more traditional communication media. They wed the emotional pitch and impact of traditional brand marketing with real service offered online. For example, television ads for Saturn still offer the same old-fashioned humorous appeal. But now they point viewers to the company's Web site, which offers lots of help and very little hype. The site helps serious car buyers select a model, calculate payments, and find a dealer online. Even marketers that can't really sell their goods via the Web are using the Internet as an effective customer communication and relationship enhancer. For example, Procter & Gamble has turned Pampers.com into the Pampers Parenting Institute, addressing various issues of concern to new and expectant parents.

The Internet can rarely stand alone as a brand-building tool. Even companies that rely primarily on e-commerce for sales are conducting most of their branding efforts offline.

Thus, although the Internet offers electrifying prospects for marketing communication, it can rarely stand alone as a brand-building tool. Instead, it must be carefully integrated into the broader marketing communications mix. Schultz makes this plea: "My cry is to integrate, not isolate. Yes, we need to explore and develop the new media and new approaches, but we need to . . . integrate [them] with the old, melding e-commerce and across-the-counter commerce. There never has been a greater need for integration than there is today. Let's recognize and develop the new electronic forms on the basis of what they are—alternatives and perhaps enhancements for the existing approaches presently in place—and nothing more. Then again, they are nothing less, either."

Sources: Quotes and excerpts from Don E. Schultz, "New media, old problem: Keep marcom integrated," *Marketing News*, 29 March 1999:11. Also see "Net leads the way in spending," *Marketing On-Line*, 25 September 2000; Jeffrey O'Brien, "Web advertising and the branding mission," *Upside*, September 1998: 90–4; Saul Hansell, "Selling soap without the soap operas, mass marketers seek ways to build brands on the Web," *New York Times*, 24 August 1998:D1–2; Ellen Neuborne, "Branding on the Net," *Business Week*, 9 November 1998:76–86; and Bradley Johnson, "Boom or bust?" *Advertising Age*, 1 November 1999:1,52.

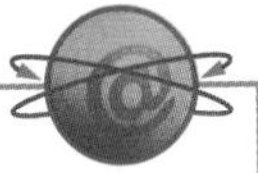

Hewlett-Packard
www.hp.com/

tion works. Communication involves the nine elements shown in Figure 13-2. Two of these elements are the major parties in a communication—the sender and receiver. Another two are the major communication tools—the message and the media. Four more are major communication functions—encoding, decoding, response, and feedback. The last element is noise in the system. Definitions of these elements are applied to an ad for Hewlett-Packard colour multifunction machines:

- *Sender:* The party sending the message to another party—here, Hewlett-Packard.
- *Encoding:* The process of putting thought into symbolic form—HP's advertising agency assembles words and illustrations into an advertisement that will convey the intended message.

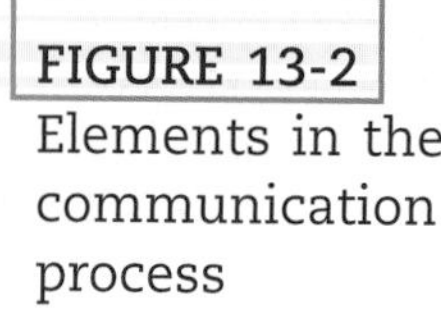

FIGURE 13-2
Elements in the communication process

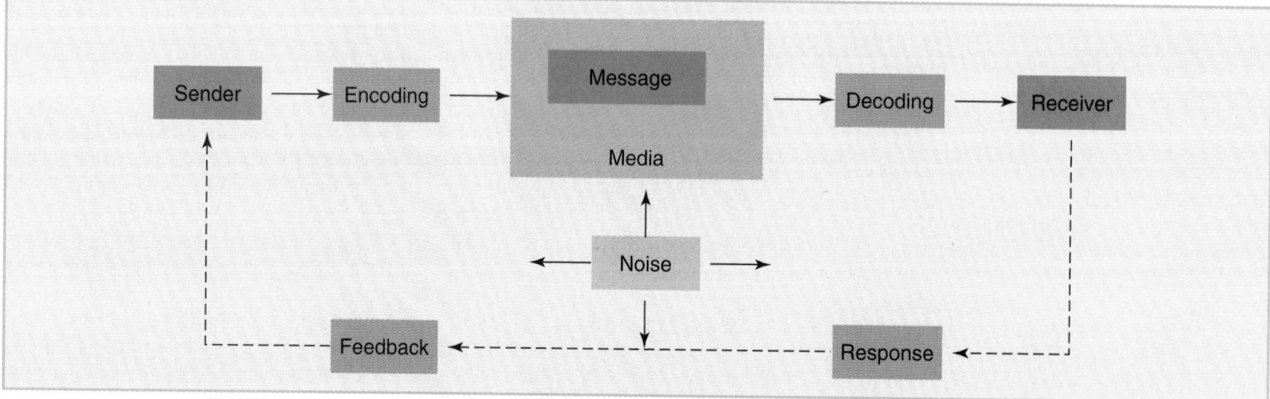

An understanding of the concerns of home-business owners helps Hewlett-Packard communicate effectively.

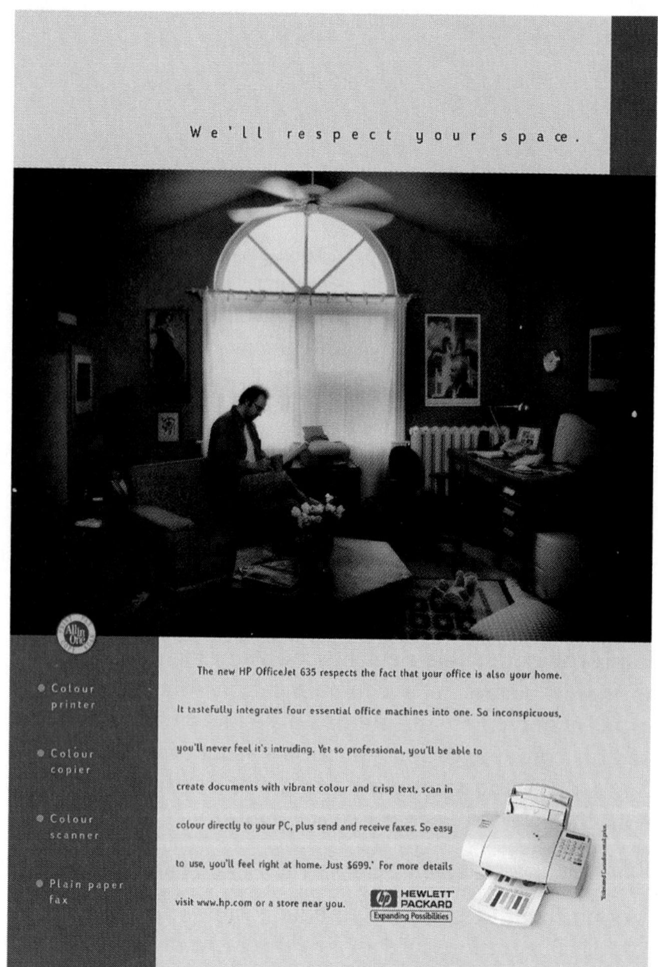

- *Message:* The set of symbols that the sender transmits—the actual HP multifunction machine ad.
- *Media:* The communication channels through which the message moves from sender to receiver—in this case, the specific magazines that HP selects.
- *Decoding:* The process by which the receiver assigns meaning to the symbols encoded by the sender—a consumer reads the HP multifunction machine ad and interprets the words and illustrations it contains.
- *Receiver:* The party receiving the message sent by another party—the home office or business customer who reads the HP multifunction machine ad.
- *Response:* The reactions of the receiver after being exposed to the message—any of hundreds of possible responses, such as the consumer is more aware of the attributes of HP multifunction machines, actually buys an HP multifunction machine, or does nothing.
- *Feedback:* The part of the receiver's response communicated back to the sender—HP research shows that consumers are struck by and remember the ad, or consumers write or call HP praising or criticizing the ad or HP's products.
- *Noise:* The unplanned static or distortion during the communication process, which results in the receiver's getting a different message than the one the sender sent—the consumer is distracted while reading the magazine and misses the HP ad or its key points.

For a message to be effective, the sender's encoding process must mesh with the receiver's decoding process. Therefore, the best messages consist of words and other symbols that are familiar to the receiver. The more the sender's field of experience overlaps with that of the receiver, the more effective the message is likely to be. Marketing communicators may not always share their consumer's field of experience. For example, an advertising copywriter from one social stratum might create ads for consumers from another stratum—say, blue-collar workers or wealthy business owners. However, to communicate effectively, the marketing communicator must understand the consumer's field of experience.

This model points out several key factors in good communication. Senders need to know what audiences they wish to reach and what responses they want. They must be good at encoding messages that take into account how the target audience decodes them. They must send messages through media that reach target audiences, and they must develop feedback channels so that they can assess the audience's response to the message.

Steps in Developing Effective Communication

We now examine the steps in developing an effective integrated communications and promotion program. The marketing communicator must: identify the target audience; determine the response sought; choose a message; choose the media through which to send the message; select the message source; and collect feedback.

Identifying the Target Audience

A marketing communicator starts with a clear target audience in mind. The audience may be potential buyers or current users, those who make the buying decision or those who influence it. The audience may be individuals, groups, special publics, or the general public. The target audience will affect the communicator's decisions on *what* will be said, *how* it will be said, *when* it will be said, *where* it will be said, and *who* will say it.

Determining the Desired Response

After defining the target audience, the marketing communicator must decide what response is desired. In most cases, the final response is *purchase*. But purchase is the result of a long process of consumer decision making. The target audience may be in any of six **buyer readiness stages,** the stages that consumers typically pass through on their way to making a purchase. These stages are *awareness, knowledge, liking, preference, conviction,* and *purchase* (see Figure 13-3). The marketing communicator needs to know where the target audience is now and to what stage it needs to be moved.

Buyer readiness stages
The stages consumers typically pass through on their way to purchase: awareness, knowledge, liking, preference, conviction, and purchase.

The marketing communicator's target market may be totally unaware of the product, know only its name, or know little about it. The communicator must first build *awareness* and *knowledge*. When Nissan introduced its Infiniti automobile line, it began with an extensive "teaser" advertising campaign to create

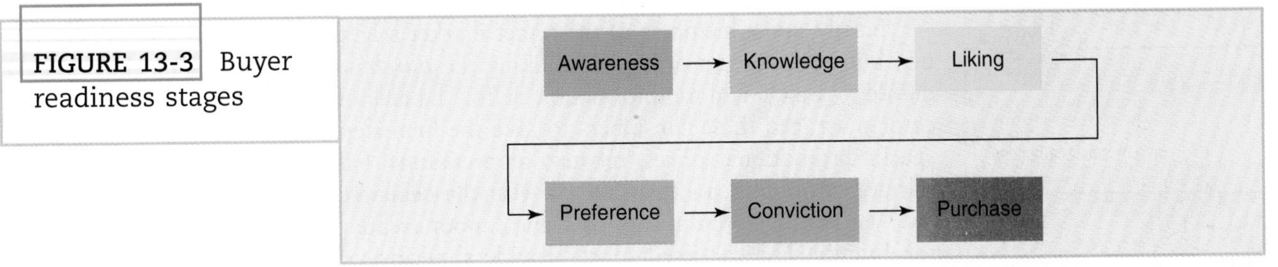

FIGURE 13-3 Buyer readiness stages

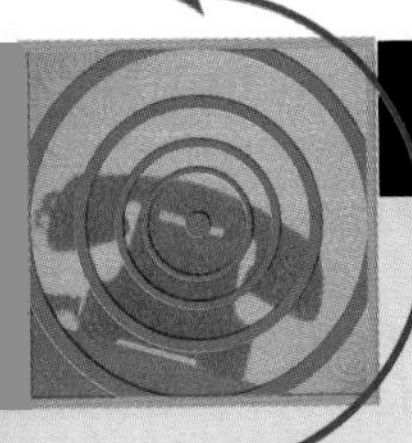

marketers speak out

Alan Quarry, President of Quarry Integrated Communications

"Clients count on us to help build their business, build their brands, build their customer relationships and build their profits . . . and we deliver," states Alan Quarry, "head coach" of Quarry Integrated Communications, a firm based in Waterloo, Ontario, with offices in Toronto, Dallas, and Japan. The hand-lettered signs posted all around Quarry's premises capture their essence: "Our mission is to help our clients build their businesses through integrated communications." Quarry's clients—firms like Nortel Networks, Hewlett-Packard, Royal Bank, Cyanamid Crop Protection, Clarica Life, Hoffmann-la Roche, Elanco Animal Health, FedEx, Merck Frosst, and Sprint Canada—all agree that Quarry has helped them accomplish this objective.

It's hard to catch up with Alan Quarry. A person with seemingly endless energy, he not only is the president of Quarry Integrated Communications, but he also finds time to teach marketing communications to fourth-year honours business students at Wilfrid Laurier University. When he isn't teaching, travelling, working with his clients, or sharing a laugh with his family, he has his head in a book. He is a strong believer that continuous learning is the key to success in the modern economy. "As communicators, we can never stop increasing our knowledge about consumer motivation and how effective communications work," states Quarry.

Quarry Integrated focuses on building demand for considered-purchase goods and services in the information technology, financial services, agribusiness, and health care industries. But, as Quarry notes, "Advertising doesn't work like it used to. People have grown sceptical, info-saturated, atomized in their interests, and now wired to the Internet." So how do you reach your customers in such a jaded marketplace? Quarry asks. We know that advertisers can't simply deliver a snappy selling message and expect results. Increasingly, the challenge is to understand the lifestyles, attitudes, and motivations of individual customers, and find a way to reach them with a consistent, relevant message. In other words, you have to use integrated communications where integration means consistency of brand contacts. Even more importantly, Quarry notes, "Consistency means trust. Trust means better relationships with your customers."

As you may gather from the last statement, Quarry Integrated Communications is a values-led company. Three core values guide its actions: integrity, relevance, and achievement. Visit Quarry's Web site to understand fully the importance of these guiding principles for the firm (www.quarry.com/culture/values). Integrity means that Quarry conducts its business honestly and fairly with its clients, associates, suppliers, and the marketplace. In terms of relevance, Quarry works to anticipate and identify critical success factors for clients and then exceed their expectations by delivering on its commitments in a creative, timely, and cost-effective manner. To Quarry, achievement is successfully building the businesses of its clients and their brands.

In addition to being values-led, Quarry Integrated is a highly innovative firm, which broke the traditional adver-

name familiarity. Initial ads for the Infiniti created curiosity and awareness by showing the car's name but not the car. Later ads created knowledge by informing potential buyers of the car's high quality and many innovative features.

Assuming target consumers *know* the product, how do they *feel* about it? Once potential buyers know about the Infiniti, Nissan's marketers want to move them through successively stronger stages of feelings toward the car. These stages include *liking* (feeling favourable about the Infiniti), *preference* (preferring Infiniti to other car brands), and *conviction* (believing that Infiniti is the best car for them). Infiniti marketers can use a combination of the promotion mix tools to create positive feelings and conviction. Advertising extols the Infiniti's advantages over competing brands. Press releases and other public relations activities stress the car's innovative features and performance. Dealer salespeople tell buyers about options, value for the price, and after-sale service.

Nissan Canada
www.nissancanada.com/

Finally, some members of the target market might be convinced about the product, but not quite get around to making the *purchase*. Potential Infiniti buyers may decide to wait for more information or for the economy to improve. The communicator must lead these consumers to take the final step. Actions may include offering special promotional prices, rebates, or premiums. Salespeople may call or write to selected customers, inviting them to visit the dealership for a special showing.

Marketing communications alone cannot create positive feelings and purchases for Infiniti. The car itself must provide superior value for the customer. In fact, tising agency model in the early 1990s and developed a new model for doing business. "The structure of the traditional ad agency seemed dysfunctional and almost anti-client to me," states Alan Quarry. "All the internal politics and focus on driving mass-media spending was not the kind of organization we wanted to be. We couldn't be the type of strategic ally that our clients need to be successful in the future.

"We believe that mass media advertising is communications 'at' the consumer. Integrated marketing communications (IMC) is a conversation 'with' the consumer. There will be a lot less marketing in the future and a lot more 'customerizing' as IMC guru Don Schultz has pointed out. We believe that relationship-building dialogue with the customer strengthens and can even improve products and brands."

To help make this all happen, Quarry Integrated is wired. No, not from three-martini lunches, but by the ethernet hubs, Internet routers, T-1 lines, video conferencing, and leading edge telephony and software, which they use to improve communications between Quarry and its clients. This "technology-enhanced communications" approach is another difference between Quarry and many of its competitors. "Lots of ad agencies seem to think of buying technology as being an 'expense'. . . we think of acquiring the tools we use as an 'investment,'" explained Alan Quarry. "It's a mindset thing. We know that we cannot be a successful, global organization and help our clients build without being tech-savvy."

In an industry characterized by disturbingly high staff turnover rates, Quarry Integrated has had one of Canada's best track records for continuity. Many think that Quarry's high retention rate has a lot to do with the environment created at the workplace. It's an environment without corner offices. (In fact, Alan Quarry, the president, does not have an assigned office at all. Instead he pushes his mobile work surface around and answers to the nickname 'Virtu-Al.') It has idea rooms named the Eureka Room and the Kaboom Room. There's a 1950s-style diner, called Al's Diner (in honour of Albert Einstein), where the Quarry team and guests meet, work, and have access to a free supply of fruit, veggies, and other brain food. It's an environment that offers at least one view of the outside world no matter where you stand. The workplace motto—"Think like the customer, Always anticipate, And have fun!"—is posted all around.

Alan Quarry.

Quarry Integrated Communications has been incredibly successful in an industry where many believe starting new communication agencies, let alone independent Canadian-owned agencies, is next to impossible. However, Quarry continues to grow. Not content to rest on its laurels, Quarry Integrated Communications has a remarkable growth objective: To be the best integrated communications organization in the galaxy! Seeing the incredible commitment and energy in this firm can convince anyone that it is well on its way to accomplishing this aim.

Sources: Information provided to Peggy Cunningham by Alan Quarry. Also see www.quarry.com.

outstanding marketing communications can actually speed the demise of a poor product. The more quickly potential buyers learn about the poor product, the more quickly they become aware of its faults. Thus, good marketing communication calls for "good deeds followed by good words."

Designing a Message

Having defined the desired audience response, the communicator turns to developing an effective message. Ideally, the message should get *attention*, hold *interest*, arouse *desire*, and obtain *action* (a framework known as the *AIDA model*). In practice, few messages take the consumer all the way from awareness to purchase, but the AIDA framework suggests the qualities of a good message.

In putting together the message, the marketing communicator must solve three problems: what to say (*message content*), how to say it logically (*message structure*), and how to say it symbolically (*message format*).

Message Content

The communicator must identify an appeal or theme that will produce the desired response. There are three types of appeals: rational, emotional, and moral.

Rational appeals
Message appeals that relate to the audience's self-interest and show that the product will produce the claimed benefits; for example, product quality, economy, value, or performance.

Rational appeals relate to the audience's self-interest. They show that the product will produce the desired benefits. Rational appeal messages may show a prod-

To move consumers toward purchase of the Infiniti, Nissan created a multi-phase promotion campaign. The first teaser ads, which did not even show the car, built awareness. Later ads created liking, preference, and conviction by comparing Infiniti's features with those of competitors.

INTRODUCING A NEW CONCEPT IN LUXURY FROM JAPAN.

There is a new line of luxury cars available soon. A new concept, based on the ancient Japanese notion of simplicity, beauty and tranquility. It's called Infiniti.

It is a concept and philosophy that places the driver as more important than the car, and reduces the layers of ornamentation and distraction that can keep you from fully enjoying yourself as you drive.

You'll find this philosophy beautifully expressed in the new Infiniti Q45 luxury sedan and M30 sports coupe. The stylish Q45, for example, offers a large, comfortable interior with such amenities as leather upholstery, Bose® Audio System, and power windows and door locks.

But while the feeling is luxurious, the attention is on the driver and the driving experience. Large, easy-to-read analog gauges, carefully positioned switches and controls that provide a unified tactile feedback so you know by feel and sound that they've engaged. And power, from an advanced 4.5-liter four cam, 32-valve V8 that will take you from 0-60 mph in just over seven seconds or to a top speed limited to 150 mph.

The exciting Infiniti M30 sports coupe is also a true driver's car, with a responsive 162-horsepower V6, anti-lock braking, Sonar Suspension™ and leather-trimmed interior.

It's an expression of luxury based on the sheer pleasure of driving. Infiniti.

For more information or for the name of the Infiniti dealer nearest you, call 1-800-826-6500.

Thank you.

created by Nissan

INFINITI.

uct's quality, economy, value, or performance. In its ads, Mercedes offers cars that are "engineered like no other car in the world," stressing engineering design, performance, and safety. Buckley's Mixture took its most recognizable quality, the bad taste of its cough syrup, and turned it into an award-winning campaign linked by the tag line, "It tastes awful. And it works."

Emotional appeals
Message appeals that attempt to stir up negative or positive emotions—for example, fear, guilt, shame, love, humour, pride, and joy—to motivate purchase.

Emotional appeals attempt to stir up either negative or positive emotions that can motivate purchase. Communicators can use such positive emotional appeals as love, pride, joy, and humour. Advocates for humorous messages claim that they attract more attention and create more liking and belief in the sponsor. Cliff Freeman, the advertiser responsible for Little Caesars' humorous "Pizza, Pizza" ads, contends that: "Humour is a great way to bound out of the starting gate. When you make people laugh, and they feel good after seeing the commercial, they like the association with the product." But others maintain that humour can detract from comprehension, wear out its welcome fast, and overshadow the product.[8]

Consider some recent ads from Telus:[9]

For the Christmas 2000 shopping season, Telus Corporation, one of Canada's leading telecommunications companies, launched a new series of 12 ads for Telus Store products using humour to draw attention to its products. In one ad, a woman overhears Christmas carolers approaching

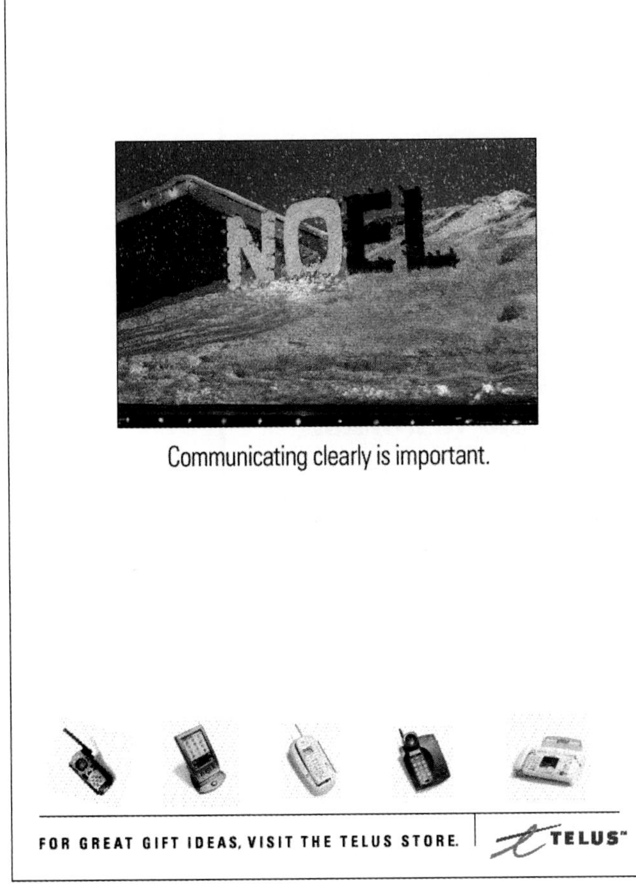

NOEL
Communicating clearly is important.
FOR GREAT GIFT IDEAS, VISIT THE TELUS STORE.
TELUS

Telus Corporation successfully used humour as a way to convey otherwise dry product benefits and to generate traffic in its stores.

her home on a snowy festive night. She cheerfully opens the door, only to find the group singing loudly but totally unintelligibly through the mufflers wrapped up to their eyeballs. The ad then cuts to the headline, "Communicating clearly is important," and then quickly features some key products. As the "Creative Eye" section of *Marketing Magazine* notes, "Great work—fresh and memorable. Fun and well produced, [in fact] the second Telus campaign is brilliant. It's a fresh way to convey otherwise dry product benefits. It also creates a very smart, approachable brand character." Humour helped the ads break through the clutter of competitors' Christmas campaigns and accomplished their purpose of getting people to think of the variety of gifts they can buy at the Telus Store when doing their Christmas shopping expeditions. Palmer Jarvis DDB, of Vancouver created the campaign.

Communicators can also use negative emotional appeals such as fear, guilt, and shame, which get people to do things they should (brush their teeth, buy new tires), or to stop doing things they shouldn't (smoke, drink too much, eat fatty foods). One Crest ad invokes mild fear of cavities when it claims: "There are some things you just can't afford to gamble with." Etonic ads ask: "What would you do if you couldn't run?" and go on to note that Etonic athletic shoes are designed to avoid injuries—they're "built so you can last." A Michelin tire ad features cute babies and suggests, "Because so much is riding on your tires."

Moral appeals are directed to the audience's sense of what is "right" and "proper." They often are used to urge people to support such social causes as a cleaner environment and aid to the needy, or combat such social problems as drug abuse, discrimination, sexual harassment, and spousal abuse. An example of a moral appeal is the March of Dimes appeal: "God made you whole. Give to help those He didn't."

Moral appeals
Advertising messages directed to the audience's sense of what is "right" or "proper."

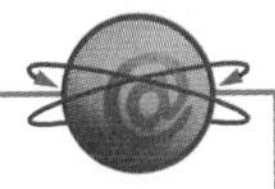

March of Dimes
www.modimes.org/

Message Structure

The communicator must decide which of three ways to use to structure the message. The first is whether to draw a conclusion or leave it to the audience. Early research showed that drawing a conclusion was usually more effective; however, more recent research suggests that the advertiser is often better off asking questions and letting buyers draw their own conclusions. The second structure issue is whether to present a one-sided argument—mentioning only the product's strengths—or a two-sided argument—touting the product's strengths while also admitting its shortcomings. Buckley's Mixture built its entire business around this technique:[10]

Buckley's Mixture was first developed in 1919 by pharmacist William Knapp Buckley in his Toronto drug store. W.K. was a pioneer, not only in terms of developing a highly effective product, but also because he was one of the first to recognize the power of catchy copy. He used both print and radio at a time when advertising, especially radio advertising, was a relatively new and a poorly understood phenomena. Advertising made the product a hit, despite its taste. It wasn't long before W.K. extended his success overseas. By the late '30s, Buckley's had introduced itself to cold sufferers in the United States and Caribbean, and to New Zealand, Australia, and Holland by the '40s. The company roared along until the 1960s. Suddenly, pharmacies started to be bought up by chains and other cough medicines started to advertise. The creative advertising strategies that had made Buckley's so successful and unique among the rest of the category were now being used by everyone, and sales began sliding. It wasn't until the 1980s that the company hit on its 'the back to basics' strategy. Buckley's Mixture possessed two strong characteristics: lousy taste and tremendous efficacy. Using these two points of difference, Buckley's produced an award-winning advertising campaign that made Buckley's Mix-

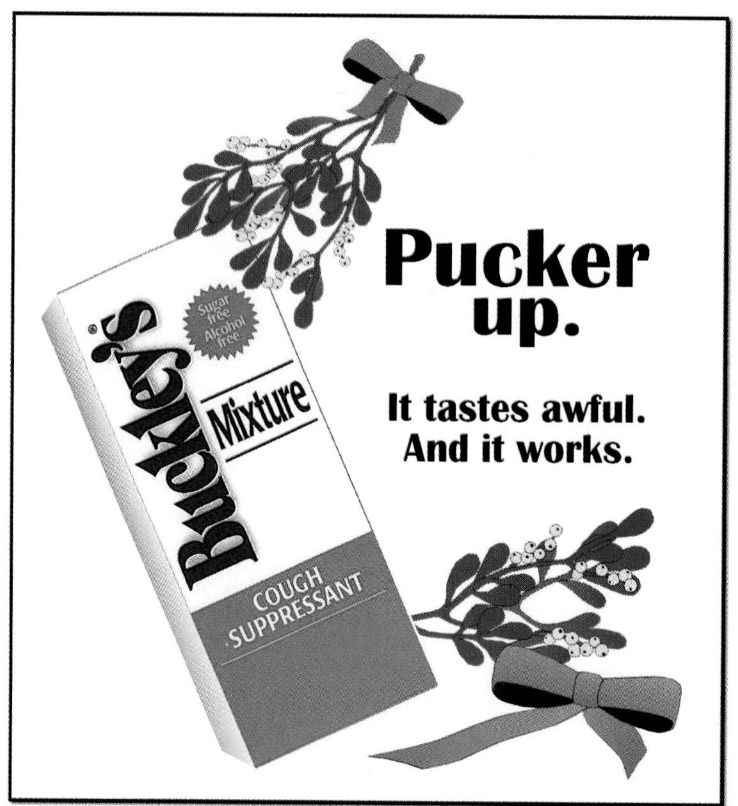

Buckley's Mixture has won world renown by using simple and humorous two-sided advertising—"It tastes awful, and it works."

ture and Frank Buckley (W.K.'s son) household names in Canada. The company's simple, honest, and humorous approach to advertising and its famous tag line, "It tastes awful, and it works," attracted attention, praise, and advertising awards. More importantly it brought in new users. Today, Buckley's Mixture is the top-selling cough syrup in Canada by volume, commanding a 10 percent share of the market. The 'bad taste' campaign also solidified its position in the Caribbean, Australia, New Zealand, and the US. If, like other Canadians, you regard Buckley's as part of your Canadian heritage, you can join other fans and view Buckley's current and historical advertising at www.buckleys.com/Cdn/Cdn%20Frames/cdn_main_page.htm.

Usually, a one-sided argument is more effective in sales presentations—except when audiences are highly educated, negatively disposed, or likely to hear opposing claims. In these cases, two-sided messages can enhance the advertiser's credibility and make buyers more resistant to competitor attacks. The third message structure issue is whether to present the strongest arguments first or last. Presenting them first gets strong attention, but may lead to an anti-climactic ending.[11]

Message Format

The marketing communicator needs a strong *format* for the message. In a print ad, the communicator has to decide on the headline, copy, illustration, and colour. To attract attention, advertisers can use novelty and contrast; eye-catching pictures and headlines; distinctive formats; message size and position; and colour, shape, and movement. If the message will be carried over the radio, the communicator must choose words, sounds, and voices. The "sound" of an announcer promoting banking services, for example, should be different from one promoting quality furniture.

If the message is to be carried on television or in person, then all these elements plus body language have to be planned. Presenters plan their facial expressions, gestures, dress, posture, and hair style. If the message is carried on the product or its package, the communicator has to watch texture, scent, colour, size, and shape. Colour plays a major communication role in food preferences. When consumers sampled four cups of coffee that had been placed next to brown, blue, red, and yellow containers (all the coffee was identical, but the consumers did not know this), 75 percent felt that the coffee next to the brown container tasted too strong; nearly 85 percent judged the coffee next to the red container to be the richest; nearly everyone felt that the coffee next to the blue container was mild; and the coffee next to the yellow container was seen as weak. Therefore, if a coffee company wants to communicate that its coffee is rich, it should probably use a red container along with label copy boasting the coffee's rich taste.[12]

Choosing Media

The communicator now must select *channels of communication*. There are two broad types of communication channels—*personal* and *non-personal*.

Personal Communication Channels

Personal communication channels
Channels through which two or more people communicate directly with each other, including face to face, person to audience, over the telephone, or through the mail or e-mail.

In **personal communication channels**, two or more people communicate directly with each other. They can communicate face to face, over the telephone, or even through the mail or e-mail. Personal communication channels are effective because they allow for personal addressing and feedback.

The company controls some personal communication channels directly; company salespeople, for example, contact buyers in the target market. But other personal communications about the product may reach buyers through channels not directly controlled by the company. These may be independent experts—consumer advocates, consumer buying guides, and others—making statements to target buyers. Or they may be neighbours, friends, family members, and associates talking to target buyers. This last channel, known as **word-of-mouth influence**, has considerable effect in many product areas.

Word-of-mouth influence
Personal communication about a product between target buyers and neighbours, friends, family members, and associates.

Personal influence carries great weight for products that are expensive, risky, or highly visible. For example, buyers of automobiles, home decor, and fashion often go beyond mass-media sources to seek the opinions of knowledgeable people.

Companies can take several steps to put personal communication channels to work for them. They can devote extra effort to selling their products to well-known people or companies, who may, in turn, influence others to buy. They can create *opinion leaders*—people whose opinions are sought by others—by supplying certain people with the product on attractive terms. For example, companies can work through community members such as local radio personalities, class presidents, and heads of local organizations. And they can use influential people in their advertisements or develop advertising that has high "conversation value."

Non-Personal Communication Channels

Non-personal communication channels
Media that carry messages without personal contact or feedback, including major media, atmospheres, and events.

Non-personal communication channels are media that carry messages without personal contact or feedback. They include major media, atmospheres, and events. *Major media* include print media (newspapers, magazines, direct mail); broadcast media (radio, television); and display media (billboards, signs, posters). *Atmospheres* are designed environments that create or reinforce the buyer's leanings toward buying a product. Thus, lawyers' offices and banks are designed to communicate confidence and other qualities that might be valued by their clients. *Events* are staged occurrences that communicate messages to target audiences, such as press conferences, grand openings, shows and exhibits, public tours, and other events arranged by public relations departments. Many Canadian companies sponsor sporting events that draw audiences that match the firm's target market. The

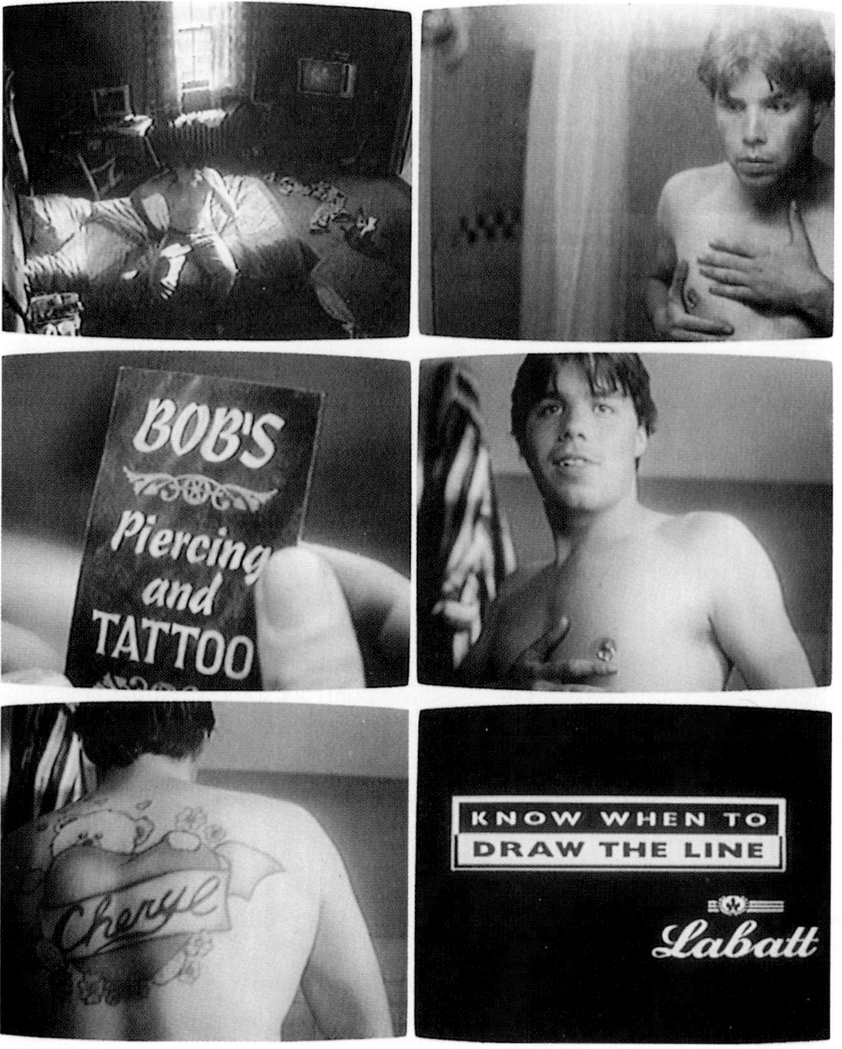

Labatt used non-personal communication channels for its award-winning "Know When to Draw the Line" campaign.

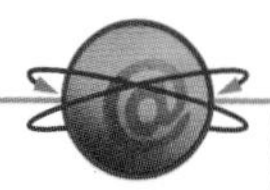

Molson Indy
www.molsonindy.com

Bank of Montreal, for example, is the lead sponsor for equestrian events held at Spruce Meadows in Calgary and at the Royal Winter Fair in Toronto. Molson Breweries holds two annual Indy races: one in Vancouver, the other in Toronto.

Non-personal communication affects buyers directly. It also often affects them indirectly by causing more personal communication. Communications first flow from television, magazines, and other mass media to opinion leaders and then from these opinion leaders to others. Thus, opinion leaders step between the mass media and their audiences and carry messages to people who are less exposed to media. This suggests that mass communicators should aim their messages directly at opinion leaders, letting them carry the message to others.

Selecting the Message Source

In either personal or non-personal communication, the message's impact on the target audience is affected by how the audience views the communicator. Messages delivered by highly credible sources are more persuasive. Therefore, marketers hire celebrity endorsers—well-known athletes, actors, and even cartoon characters—to deliver their messages (see Marketing Highlight 13-2).

Many food companies promote to doctors, dentists, and other health care providers to motivate these professionals to recommend their products to patients.

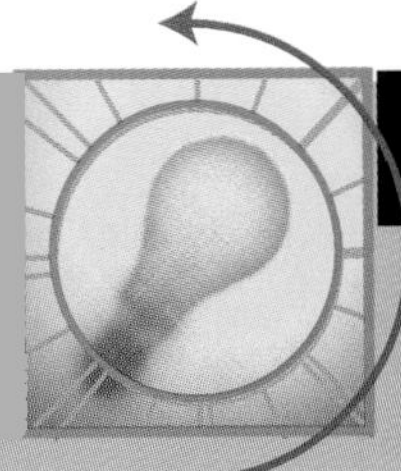

marketing highlight 13-2

Celebrity Endorsers

"Kid, you've got the talent, but you've got a problem," barks Bill Laimbeer, one of basketball's all-time dirtiest players, at young superstar Grant Hill during a commercial for Fila. "You're too nice." A series of drills follows in which Laimbeer tries to teach Hill elbowing, tripping, referee abuse, cameraman pushing, nose piercing—all the skills needed for today's modern athletes to make big money off the court and playing field. But the joke is on Laimbeer. A follow-up spot shows Hill calling his mom, asking her to rescue him. The next commercial in the series depicts Hill finally breaking free of Laimbeer's hold, despite 52 days of brainwashing at "Camp Tough Guy." "I've got to play with decency, honesty," he says as a ray of light dawns upon him. "I've got to play clean." Clean is now cool. Clean is also lucrative. For endorsing Fila's running shoes, Hill received about $36 million over five years.

Teams, as well as individual athletes, are attracting sponsorship dollars. In a landmark deal, TD Waterhouse Investor Services, the Toronto-based discount brokerage, signed on as title sponsor for the next three Toronto Maple Leafs and Toronto Raptors seasons, 2001–2004.

Choosing the wrong salesperson can result in embarrassment and a tarnished image. Hertz discovered this when it entrusted its good name to the care of O.J. Simpson. Kellogg Canada Inc. is still feeling the agony over its sponsorship of sprinter Ben Johnson, who was stripped of his gold medal after the 1988 Olympics for taking an illegal substance.

Manufacturers and advertisers seek an endorser's "halo effect"—the positive association that bathes the product in good vibes after a popular sports celebrity has pitched it. The trend toward nice is very good news for brand names that are marketed globally. Tennis star Michael Chang has emerged as the most popular athlete in Asia by far. Reebok is basing its entire Asian strategy around him, as is Procter & Gamble's Rejoice (Pert Plus) shampoo line. What makes Asia so crazy about Chang? It's not just his heritage. It's also his persona. On a continent where family is considered paramount, Chang is coached by his brother, and they travel frequently with their parents. He's properly humble and soft-spoken as well. "We've always been a very close-knit family, and I think that's pretty characteristic of Asian families, period," says Chang.

Professional athletes aren't the only ones drawing sponsorship dollars. Amateur athletes, especially those training for the Olympics, are receiving increased attention. Olympic sponsorship is a significant marketing vehicle, whether it is of the Games themselves, the teams that compete in them, or individual athletes. People aren't as jaded in their views of Olympic athletes as they are about their professional counterparts. Although Olympic athletes may not be household names, people believe that these athletes compete for the love of the sport. Thus, the goodwill that adheres to a company that supports Olympic athletes is greater than that associated with support of a professional sports celebrity. Since the Olympics draw both international and national audiences, they provide sponsoring companies with the opportunity to speak to the world.

The power of the Games led Kellogg to re-enter the sponsorship game. Runner Donovan Bailey graced the front of the Corn Flakes box. Swimmer Joanne Malar, who projects an image of fitness and health-consciousness, was chosen as the perfect fit for Special K. Divers Anne Montminy and Annie Pelletier also receive Kellogg's support.

Kellogg certainly isn't alone in its sponsorship of Canadian Olympic athletes. Home Depot Canada has a unique program in which it provides jobs for 10 Olympians in training. Panasonic runs breakthrough advertising showing the women's rowing team tearing up the pavement of Canadian cities. Nike Canada supports the snowboarding and hockey teams. Roots Canada was one of Canada's official clothing providers for the Games, and also sponsors individual athletes such as skater Elvis Stojko. Tim Hortons supports the Canadian Cycling Association, while Procter & Gamble supports the Spirit of Sport Foundation.

Olympic sponsorship is not without risks, however. When firms endorse an individual athlete, they run the risk that the person might not perform as well as hoped. They may say something unfortunate in their excitement over victory. They may even bring disrepute, as when Canadian snowboarder Ross Rebagliati was temporarily stripped of his win after testing positive for marijuana. Many sponsors are now making their sponsored athletes sign codes of conduct and morality.

Rather than sponsoring individual competitors, many firms are now endorsing teams. Ken McGovern, a Vancouver researcher who specializes in sponsorship, says, "When you're endorsing a team, what you're really doing is endorsing the spirit of the Games, the excitement of competition and the national pride that comes with that." Corporations that help make all this happen reap a tremendous harvest of goodwill.

Although the sponsorship arena has long been dominated by male athletes, not only men's teams are drawing sponsorship dollars. In 1998, women's hockey was an Olympic event for the first time, and the Canadian team attracted a number of sponsors including Imperial Oil.

While some corporations focus their sponsorship efforts on just the athletes, other firms, such as McDonald's of Canada, take a more integrated approach. Around the 2000 Olympics season, the company began by sponsoring the CBC, the official broadcaster of the games. Each of its hundreds of Canadian restaurants was designated an "official headquarters." All of McDonald's in-restaurant materials featured Olympic themes—from tray liners to sandwich wraps to a special magazine touting Olympic values. Olympic watches were offered as the featured premium, and the company sent coupon booklets bearing Olympic logos to every Canadian household. Sales of the watches alone raised $1 million for the Canadian Olympic team. So that people watching the television coverage of the Games didn't get bored with watching a single ad aired again and again, McDonald's created 11 commercials. McDonald's believed that it was better to be associated with the spirit of the Games than to sponsor an individual athlete.

Sources: Portions adapted from Lane Randall, "Nice guys finish first," *Forbes,* 16 December 1996:236–42. Also see Susan Chandler, "Michael Jordan's full corporate press," *Business Week,* 7 April 1997; Roy S. Johnson, "Tiger!" *Fortune,* 12 May 1997:73–84; John Heinzl, "Logos an Olympic event," *Globe and Mail,* 20 October 1997:B1,B4; Lara Mills, "Women get in the Game," *Marketing,* 7 April 1997:10–1; James Walker, "Ben Johnson on their minds," *Financial Post,* 13 July 1996; Patti Summerfield, "TD Waterhouse makes landmark sports deal," *Strategy,* 23 October 2000:4; and www.kelloggs.com/index_nite.html.

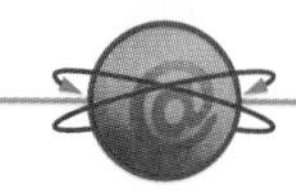

Becel Canada
www.becelcanada.com/

This has been an important strategy for Lipton's Becel margarine, since research showed that health professionals were important influencers on their patients' dietary choices. In addition to award-winning advertising that helped the brand grow throughout the 1990s, Becel developed its Becel Heart Health Information Bureau. This "educational arm" of the brand provides health care professionals and the public with current information on nutrition and the scientific issues affecting heart health. While maintaining its objectivity, the bureau strives to disseminate both key scientific facts about heart health and key brand messages, primarily on the Becel Canada Web page.[13]

Collecting Feedback

After sending the message, the communicator must research its effect on the target audience. This involves asking the target audience members whether they remember the message, how many times they saw it, what points they recall, how they felt about the message, and their past and present attitudes toward the product and company. The communicator also wants to measure behaviour resulting from the message—how many people bought a product, talked to others about it, or visited the store.

Feedback on marketing communications may suggest changes in the promotion program or in the product offer itself. For example, when the new Boston Market restaurant chain enters new market areas, it uses television advertising and coupons in newspaper inserts to inform area consumers about the restaurant and to lure them in. Suppose feedback research shows that 80 percent of all consumers in an area recall seeing Boston Market ads and are aware of what the restaurant offers. Sixty percent of those who are aware of it have eaten at the restaurant, but only 20 percent of those who tried it were satisfied. These results suggest that although the promotion program is creating *awareness,* the restaurant isn't giving consumers the *satisfaction* they expect. Therefore, Boston Market needs to improve its food or service while staying with the successful communication program. In contrast, suppose the feedback research shows that only 40 percent of area consumers are aware of the restaurant, that only 30 percent of those aware of it have tried it, but 80 percent of those who have tried it return. In this case, Boston Market needs to strengthen its promotion program to take advantage of the restaurant's power to create customer satisfaction.

Setting the Total Promotion Budget and Mix

We have examined the steps in planning and sending communications to a target audience. But how does the company decide on the total *promotion budget* and its division among the major promotional tools to create the *promotion mix?* We now look at these questions.

Setting the Total Promotion Budget

One of the hardest marketing decisions facing a company is how much to spend on promotion. John Wanamaker, the department-store magnate, once said: "I know that half of my advertising is wasted, but I don't know which half. I spent $2 million for advertising, and I don't know if that is half enough or twice too much." Therefore, it is not surprising that industries and companies vary widely in how much they spend on promotion. Promotion spending may be 20 to 30 percent of sales in the cosmetics industry and only two or three percent in the industrial machinery industry. Within any industry, both low and high spenders can be found.

How does a company decide on its promotion budget? We look at four common methods used to set the total budget for advertising: the *affordable method,* the *percentage-of-sales method,* the *competitive-parity method,* and the *objective-and-task method.*[14]

Affordable Method

Affordable method
Setting the promotion budget at the level management thinks the company can afford.

Some companies use the **affordable method:** They set the promotion budget at the level they think the company can afford. Small businesses often use this method, reasoning that the company cannot spend more on advertising than it has. They start with total revenues, deduct operating expenses and capital outlays, and then devote some portion of the remaining funds to advertising.

Unfortunately, this method of setting budgets completely ignores the effects of promotion on sales. It tends to place advertising last among spending priorities, even in situations in which advertising is critical to the firm's success. It leads to an uncertain annual promotion budget, which makes long-range market planning difficult. Although the affordable method can result in overspending on advertising, it more often results in underspending.

Percentage-of-Sales Method

Percentage-of-sales method
Setting the promotion budget at a certain percentage of current or forecasted sales or as a percentage of the sales price.

Other companies use the **percentage-of-sales method,** setting their promotion budget at a certain percentage of current or forecasted sales. Or they budget a percentage of the unit sales price. The percentage-of-sales method has a number of advantages. First, using this method means that promotion spending is likely to vary with what the company can "afford." It also helps management think about the relationship between promotion spending, selling price, and profit per unit. Finally, it supposedly creates competitive stability because competing firms tend to spend about the same percentage of their sales on promotion.

Despite these claimed advantages, however, the percentage-of-sales method has little to justify it. It wrongly views sales as the *cause* of promotion rather than as the *result.* "A study in this area found good correlation between investments in advertising and the strength of the brands concerned—but it turned out to be effect and cause, not cause and effect. . . . The strongest brands had the highest sales and could afford the biggest investments in advertising!"[15] The budget is based on availability of funds rather than on opportunities. It may prevent the increased spending sometimes needed to turn around falling sales. Because the budget varies with year-to-year sales, long-range planning is difficult. Finally, the method does not provide any basis for choosing a *specific* percentage, except what has been done in the past or what competitors are doing.

Competitive-Parity Method

Competitive-parity method
Setting the promotion budget to match competitors' outlays.

Still other companies use the **competitive-parity method,** setting their promotion budgets to match competitors' outlays. They monitor competitors' advertising or get industry promotion spending estimates from publications or trade associations, and then set their budgets based on the industry average.

Two arguments support this method. First, competitors' budgets represent the collective wisdom of the industry. Second, spending what competitors spend helps prevent promotion wars. Unfortunately, neither argument is valid. There are no grounds for believing that the competition has a better idea of what a company should be spending on promotion than does the company itself. Companies differ greatly, and each has its own special promotion needs. Finally, there is no evidence that budgets based on competitive parity prevent promotion wars.

Objective-and-Task Method

Objective-and-task method Developing the promotion budget by defining specific objectives; determining the tasks that must be performed to achieve these objectives; and estimating the costs of performing these tasks. The sum of these costs is the proposed promotion budget.

The most logical budget setting method is the **objective-and-task method,** whereby the company sets its promotion budget based on what it wants to accomplish with promotion. This budgeting method entails defining specific promotion objectives; determining the tasks needed to achieve these objectives; and estimating the costs of performing these tasks. The sum of these costs is the proposed promotion budget.

The objective-and-task method forces management to spell out its assumptions about the relationship between dollars spent and promotion results. But it is also the most difficult method to use. It is often hard to determine which specific tasks will achieve specific objectives. For example, suppose Sony wants 95 percent awareness for its latest camcorder model during the six-month introductory period. What specific advertising messages and media schedules should Sony use to attain this objective? How much would these messages and media schedules cost? Sony management must consider such questions, even though they are hard to answer.

Setting the Overall Promotion Mix

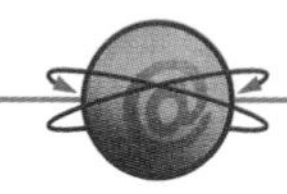

MAC Cosmetics
www.maccosmetics.com/

The company now must divide the total promotion budget among the major promotion tools—advertising, personal selling, sales promotion, and public relations. It must blend the promotion tools carefully into a coordinated *promotion mix*. Companies within the same industry differ greatly in the design of their promotion mixes. For example, Avon spends most of its promotion funds on personal selling and direct marketing, whereas Revlon spends heavily on consumer advertising, and Toronto-based M•A•C (Make-up Art Cosmetics) has rocketed onto the world stage with almost no traditional advertising. We now look at the many factors that influence the marketer's choice of promotion tools.

The Nature of Each Promotion Tool

Each promotion tool—advertising, personal selling, sales promotion, public relations, and direct marketing—has unique characteristics and costs. Marketers must understand these characteristics in selecting their tools.

Advertising. Advertising can reach masses of geographically dispersed buyers at a low cost per exposure and enables the seller to repeat a message many times. Television advertising, for example, reaches huge audiences. On an average day, 77 percent of Canadians view television at least once. This viewership may be split between Canadian national networks (19.5%), French networks (17.7%), Canadian Global and independents (17.6%), and US conventional and superstations (17.4%). More than 127 million North Americans tune in to the Super Bowl, and about 78 million people watched at least part of the past Academy Awards broadcast. "If you want to get to the mass audience," says a media services executive, "Broadcast TV is where you have to be." He adds, "For anybody introducing anything who has to lasso an audience in a hurry—a new product, a new campaign, a new movie—the networks are still the biggest show in town."[16]

Beyond its reach, large-scale advertising says something positive about the seller's size, popularity, and success. Because of advertising's public nature, consumers tend to view advertised products as more legitimate.

Advertising is also very expressive. It allows the company to dramatize its products through the artful use of visuals, print, sound, and colour. On the one hand, advertising can be used to build a long-term image for a product (such as Coca-Cola ads). On the other hand, advertising can trigger quick sales (such as Sears' weekend sale ads).

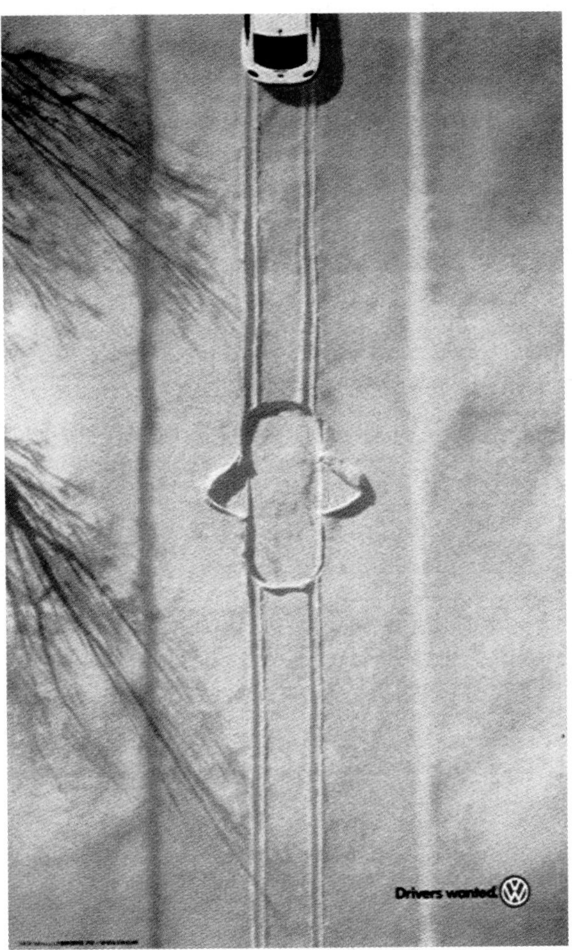

Advertising is an important part of Volkswagen's promotion mix. This award-winning, distinctive, eye-catching ad helped Volkswagen grab consumers' attention.

Advertising also has shortcomings. Although it reaches many people quickly, advertising is impersonal and cannot be as persuasive as company salespeople. For the most part, advertising can carry on only a one-way communication with the audience, and the audience does not feel that it must pay attention or respond. In addition, advertising can be very costly. Although some advertising forms, such as newspaper and radio advertising, can be done on small budgets, other forms, such as network TV advertising, require very large budgets.

Personal Selling. Personal selling is the most effective tool at certain stages of the buying process, particularly in building up buyers' preferences, convictions, and actions. Compared to advertising, personal selling has several unique qualities. It involves personal interaction between two or more people, so each person can observe the other's needs and characteristics and make quick adjustments. Personal selling also allows all kinds of relationships to develop, ranging from a matter-of-fact selling relationship to a deep personal friendship. The effective salesperson keeps the customer's interests at heart to build a long-term relationship. Finally, with personal selling, the buyer usually feels a greater need to listen and respond, even if the response is a polite "no thank you."

These qualities come at a cost, however. A sales force requires a longer-term commitment than does advertising: A company can turn on and off its advertising, but it is hard to change the size of a sales force. Personal selling is also the company's most expensive promotion tool, costing industrial companies an average of over $275 per sales call.[17] North American firms spend up to three times as much on personal selling as they do on advertising.

Sales Promotion. Sales promotion includes a wide assortment of tools, including coupons, contests, cents-off deals, and premiums such as "buy 10 products, and get one free." These attract consumer attention and provide information that may lead to a purchase. They offer strong incentives to purchase by providing inducements or contributions that give additional value to consumers. And sales promotions invite and reward quick response. Where advertising says, "Buy our product," sales promotion says, "Buy it now."

Companies use sales promotion tools to create a stronger and quicker response. Sales promotion can be used to dramatize product offers and to boost sagging sales. Sales promotion effects are usually short lived, however, and are not effective in building long-run brand preference.

Public Relations. Public relations offers several benefits. It is very believable: news stories, features, and events seem more real and believable to readers than ads do. Public relations also can reach many prospects who avoid salespeople and advertisements—the message gets to the buyers as "news" rather than as a sales-directed communication. And, like advertising, public relations can dramatize a company or product. Marketers tend to underuse public relations or to use it as an afterthought. Yet a well-planned public relations campaign used with other promotion mix elements can be very effective and economical.

Direct Marketing. The many forms of direct marketing—direct mail, telemarketing, electronic marketing, online marketing, and others—share four distinctive

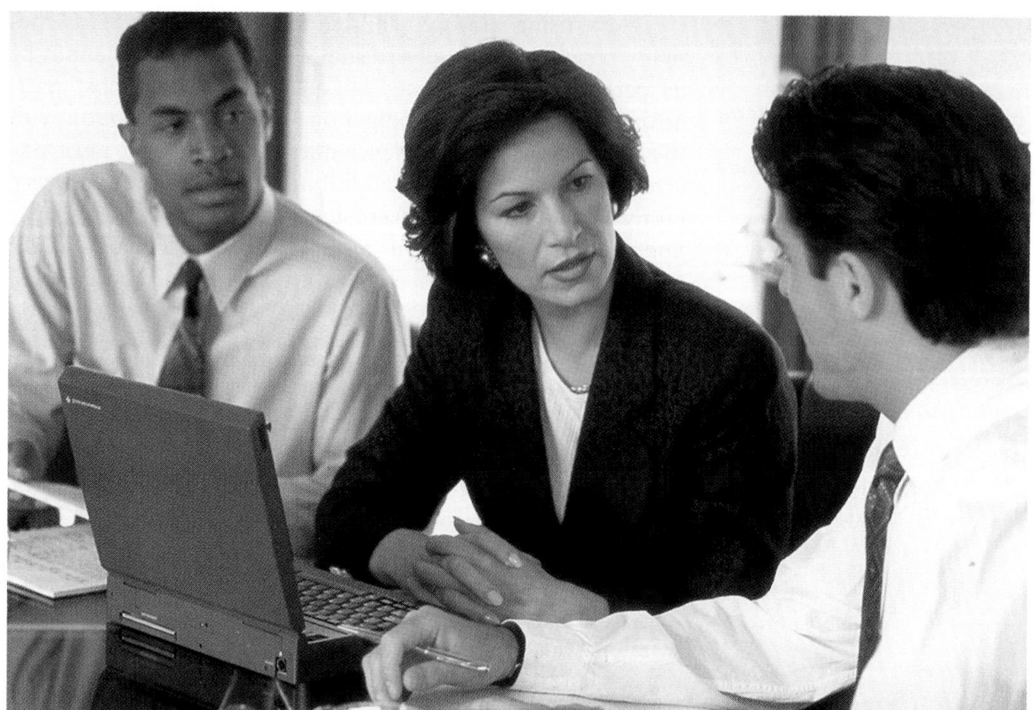

With personal selling, the customer feels a greater need to listen and respond, even if the response is a polite "no thank you."

characteristics. Direct marketing is non-public: The message is normally addressed to a specific person. Direct marketing is also immediate and customized: Messages can be prepared very quickly and can be tailored to appeal to specific consumers. Finally, direct marketing is interactive: It allows a dialogue between the marketer and consumer, and messages can be altered depending on the consumer's response. Therefore, direct marketing is well suited to highly targeted marketing efforts and to building one-on-one customer relationships.

Promotion Mix Strategies

Push strategy
A promotion strategy that calls for using the sales force and trade promotion to push the product through channels. The producer promotes the product to wholesalers, the wholesalers promote to retailers, and the retailers promote to consumers.

Pull strategy
A promotion strategy that calls for spending a lot on advertising and consumer promotion to build up consumer demand. If the strategy is successful, consumers will ask their retailers for the product, the retailers will ask the wholesalers, and the wholesalers will ask the producers.

Marketers can choose from two basic promotion mix strategies—*push* promotion or *pull* promotion. Figure 13-4 contrasts the two strategies. A **push strategy** involves "pushing" the product through distribution channels to final consumers. The producer directs its marketing activities (primarily personal selling and trade promotion) toward channel members to induce them to carry the product and to promote it to final consumers. Using a **pull strategy,** the producer directs its marketing activities (primarily advertising and consumer promotion) toward final consumers to induce them to buy the product. If the pull strategy is effective, consumers then will demand the product from channel members, who will in turn demand it from producers. Thus, under a pull strategy, consumer demand "pulls" the product through the channels.

Some small industrial goods companies use only push strategies; some direct-marketing companies use only pull. Most large companies use some combination of both. For example, Frito-Lay uses mass-media advertising to pull its products, and a large sales force and trade promotions to push its products through the channels. In recent years, consumer goods companies have been decreasing the pull portions of their promotion mixes in favour of more push.

Companies consider many factors when developing their promotion mix strategies, including *type of product-market* and the *product life cycle stage.* For example, the importance of different promotion tools varies between consumer and busi-

FIGURE 13-4 Push versus pull promotion strategy

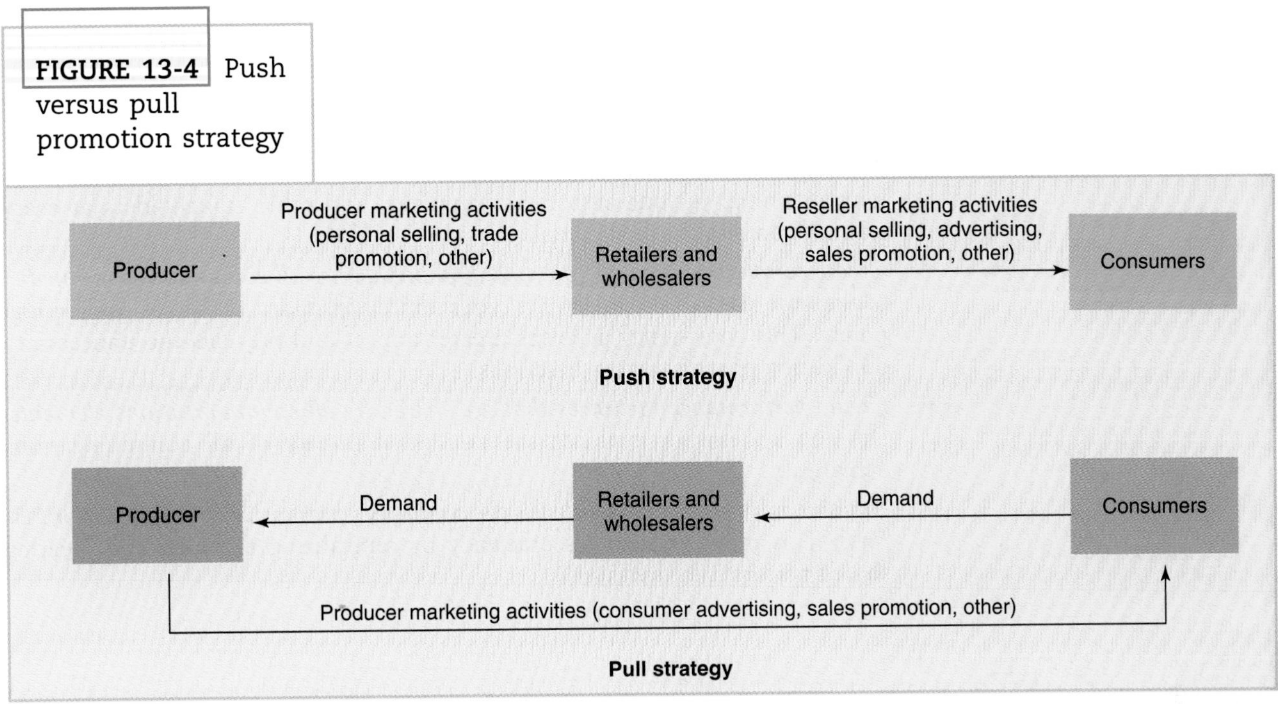

ness markets. Consumer goods companies usually "pull" more, putting more of their funds into advertising, followed by sales promotion, personal selling, and then public relations. In contrast, business-to-business marketers tend to "push" more, putting more of their funds into personal selling, followed by sales promotion, advertising, and public relations. In general, personal selling is used more heavily with expensive and risky goods and in markets with fewer and larger sellers.

The effects of different promotion tools also vary with stages of the product life cycle. In the introduction stage, advertising and public relations are good for producing high awareness, sales promotion is useful in promoting early trial, and personal selling must be used to get the trade to carry the product. In the growth stage, advertising and public relations continue to be powerful influences, whereas sales promotion can be reduced because fewer incentives are needed. In the mature stage, sales promotion again becomes important relative to advertising: Buyers know the brands, and advertising is needed only to remind them of the product. In the decline stage, advertising is kept at a reminder level, public relations is dropped, and salespeople give the product only a little attention; however, sales promotion might continue to be strong.

Integrating the Promotion Mix

Having set the promotion budget and mix, the company must take steps to see that all of the promotion mix elements are smoothly integrated. This is a checklist for integrating the firm's marketing communications.[18]

- *Analyze trends—internal and external—that can affect your company's ability to do business:* Look for areas where communications can help the most. Determine the strengths and weaknesses of each communications function. Develop a combination of promotional tactics based on these strengths and weaknesses.
- *Audit the pockets of communications spending throughout the organization:* Itemize the communications budgets and tasks and consolidate these into a single budgeting process. Reassess all communications expenditures by product, promotional tool, stage of the life cycle, and observed effect.

- *Identify all contact points for the company and its brands:* Work to ensure that communications at each point are consistent with your overall communications strategy and that your communications efforts are occurring when, where, and how your customers want them.
- *Team up in communications planning:* Engage all communications functions in joint planning. Include customers, suppliers, and other stakeholders at every stage of communications planning.
- *Create compatible themes, tones, and quality across all communications media:* Make sure each element carries your unique primary messages and selling points. This consistency achieves greater impact and prevents the unnecessary duplication of work across functions.
- *Create performance measures that are shared by all communications elements:* Develop systems to evaluate the combined impact of all communications activities.
- *Appoint a director responsible for the company's persuasive communications efforts:* This move encourages efficiency by centralizing planning and creating shared performance measures.

Socially Responsible Marketing Communication

People at all levels of the organization must be aware of the growing body of legal and ethical issues surrounding marketing communications. Most marketers work hard to communicate openly and honestly with consumers and resellers. Still, abuses do occur, and public policy makers have developed a substantial body of laws and regulations to govern advertising, personal selling, and direct marketing activities. In this chapter, we discuss issues regarding advertising and personal selling. Issues relating to direct marketing are addressed in Chapter 16.

Advertising and Sales Promotion

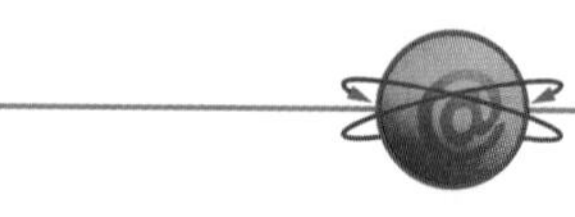

Canadian Radio-television and Communications Commission
www.crtc.gc.ca/

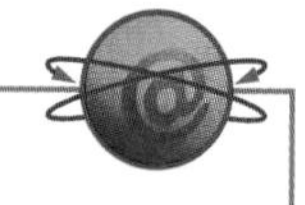

Advertising Standards Canada
www.adstandards.com/

The advertising industry in Canada is controlled both by the Canadian Radio-television and Telecommunications Commission (CRTC) and by voluntary industry codes administered by Advertising Standards Canada. The CRTC, which independently governs broadcast licensing, is itself governed by the *Broadcasting Act* of 1991 and the Telecommunications Act of 1993. The primary objective of the *Broadcasting Act* is to ensure that all Canadians have access to a wide variety of high-quality Canadian programming. The main objective of the *Telecommunications Act* is to ensure that Canadians have access to reliable telephone and other telecommunications services at affordable prices. The CRTC also has the mandate to ensure that programming in the Canadian broadcasting system reflects Canadian social values, creativity, and talent, the country's linguistic duality, its multicultural diversity, and the special place of aboriginal people within Canadian society. The CRTC regulates over 5900 broadcasters, including television, cable distribution, AM and FM radio, pay and specialty television, direct-to-home satellite systems, multipoint distribution systems, subscription television, and pay audio, as well as 61 telecommunications carriers including major Canadian telephone companies. The CRTC also administers several codes that have a particular impact on certain categories of advertising. For example, the Code for Broadcast Advertising of Alcoholic Beverages governs advertising of alcoholic beverages with over seven percent alcohol.

Advertising Standards Canada (ASC), established as the Canadian Advertising Foundation in 1963, is a national industry association committed to assuring the integrity and viability of advertising through industry self-regulation. Its members

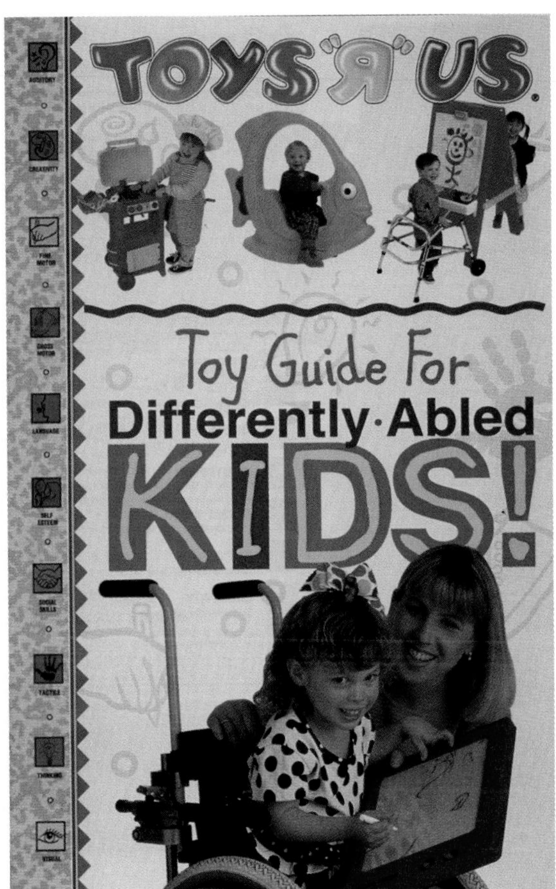

Toys 'R' Us helped both parents and disabled children with its new toy guide.

include advertisers, agencies, media organizations, and suppliers to the advertising sector. ASC receives, reviews, adjudicates, and reports on complaints about advertising. Industry codes and guidelines administered by ASC include the Canadian Code of Advertising Standards, the Gender Portrayal Guidelines, Broadcast Code for Advertising to Children, the Guide to Food Labelling and Advertising, Advertising Code of Standards for Cosmetics, Toiletries & Fragrances, Guidelines for the Use of Comparative Advertising in Food Commercials, Tobacco Voluntary Packaging, and the Advertising Industry Code. Details of these codes can be found on the ASC Web site.

A company's trade promotion activities are also closely regulated. Under the *Competition Act,* sellers cannot favour certain customers through their use of trade promotions. They must make promotional allowances and services available to all resellers on proportionately equal terms.

Beyond simply avoiding legal pitfalls, such as deceptive or bait-and-switch advertising, companies can use advertising to encourage and promote socially responsible programs and actions. For example, Toys 'R' Us (Canada) was praised by a number of groups for its new *Toy Guide for Differently Abled Kids!* This 16-page catalogue, featuring 50 toys designed for disabled children, was distributed through the company's 56 Canadian locations as well as through such agencies as Easter Seals and the Canadian National Institute for the Blind. Although none of the toys displayed in the catalogue was specifically designed for disabled children, the publication informed parents about which toys were suitable for their children and how the toys might help their children develop certain skills.[19]

Personal Selling

A company's salespeople must follow the rules of "fair competition." For example, salespeople may not lie to consumers or mislead them about the advantages of buying a product. To avoid bait-and-switch practices, salespeople's statements must match advertising claims.

Different rules apply to consumers who are visited by salespeople at home than to those who go to a store in search of a product. Because people called on at home may be taken by surprise and may be especially vulnerable to high-pressure selling techniques, most provincial governments have stipulated a *three-day cooling-off rule* to give special protection to customers who are not seeking products: Under this rule, customers who agree in their own homes to buy something have 72 hours in which to cancel a contract or return merchandise and get their money back, no questions asked.

Much personal selling involves business-to-business trade. In selling to businesses, salespeople may not offer bribes to purchasing agents or to others who can influence a sale. They may not obtain or use technical or trade secrets of competitors through bribery or industrial espionage. Finally, salespeople must not disparage competitors or competing products by suggesting things that are not true.[20]

Review of Concept Connections

Modern marketing calls for more than just developing a good product, pricing it attractively, and making it available to target customers. Companies also must communicate with current and prospective customers, and what they communicate should not be left to chance. For most companies, the question is not whether to communicate, but how much to spend and in what ways.

1. Name and define the five tools of the promotion mix.

A company's total marketing communications mix—also called its promotion mix—consists of the specific blend of advertising, personal selling, sales promotion, public relations, and direct marketing tools that the company uses to pursue its advertising and marketing objectives. Advertising includes any paid form of non-personal presentation and promotion of ideas, goods, or services by an identified sponsor. In contrast, public relations focuses on building good relations with the company's various publics by obtaining favourable unpaid publicity. Firms use sales promotion to provide short-term incentives to encourage the purchase or sale of a product or service. Personal selling is any form of personal presentation by the firm's sales force for the purpose of making sales and building customer relationships. Finally, firms seeking immediate response from targeted individual customers use non-personal direct marketing tools to communicate with customers.

2. Discuss the process and advantages of integrated marketing communications.

Recent shifts in marketing strategy from mass marketing to targeted or one-on-one marketing, coupled with advances in information technology, have had a dramatic impact on marketing communications. Although still important, the mass media are giving way to a profusion of smaller, more focused media. Companies are doing less broadcasting and more narrowcasting. As marketing communicators adopt richer but more fragmented media and promotion mixes to reach their diverse markets, they risk creating a communications hodgepodge for consumers. To prevent this, companies are adopting the concept of integrated marketing communications, which calls for carefully integrating all sources of company communication to deliver a clear and consistent message to target markets.

To integrate its external communications effectively, the company must first integrate its internal communications activities. The company then works out the roles that the various promotional tools will play and the extent to which each will be used. It carefully coordinates the promotional activities and the timing of when major campaigns take place. Finally, to help implement its integrated marketing strategy, the company appoints a marketing communications director who has overall responsibility for the company's communications efforts.

3. Outline the steps in developing effective marketing communications.

In preparing marketing communications, the communicator's first task is to identify the target audience and its characteristics. Next, the communicator must define the response sought, whether it be awareness, knowledge, liking, preference, conviction, or purchase. Then a message should be constructed with an effective content and structure. Media must be selected, both for personal and non-personal communication. Finally, the communicator must collect feedback by watching how much of the market becomes aware, tries the product, and is satisfied in the process.

4. Explain the methods for setting the promotion budget and factors that affect the design of the promotion mix.

The company must decide how much to spend on promotion. The most popular approaches to making this decision are to spend what the company can afford, to use a percentage of sales, to base promotion on competitors' spending, or to base it on an analysis and costing of the communication objectives and tasks.

The company must divide the promotion budget among the major tools to create the promotion mix. Companies can pursue a push or a pull promotional strategy, or a combination of the two. What specific blend of promotion tools is best depends on the type of product-market, the desirability of the buyer's readiness stage, and the product life cycle stage.

Key Terms

Advertising *(p. 540)*
Affordable method *(p. 557)*
Buyer readiness stages *(p. 547)*
Competitive-parity method *(p. 557)*
Direct marketing *(p. 540)*
Emotional appeals *(p. 550)*
Integrated marketing communications *(p. 542)*
Marketing communications mix (promotion mix) *(p. 540)*
Moral appeals *(p. 551)*
Non-personal communication channels *(p. 553)*
Objective-and-task method *(p. 558)*
Percentage-of-sales method *(p. 557)*
Personal communication channels *(p. 553)*
Personal selling *(p. 540)*
Public relations *(p. 540)*
Pull strategy *(p. 560)*
Push strategy *(p. 560)*
Rational appeals *(p. 549)*
Sales promotion *(p. 540)*
Word-of-mouth influence *(p. 553)*

Discussing the Issues

1. Name which form of marketing communications each of the following represents: (a) a U2 T-shirt sold at a concert, (b) a *Rolling Stone* interview with Nelly Furtado arranged by her manager, (c) a scalper auctioning tickets via e-Bay (ebay.com) for a Pearl Jam concert, and (d) a record store selling Our Lady Peace albums for $2 off the week their latest music video debuts on MuchMusic, and (e) Shania Twain's development of a Web page to keep fans aware of her concert tours, latest recordings, and line of signature clothing products.
2. The shift from mass marketing to targeted marketing, and the corresponding use of a richer mixture of promotion tools and communication channels, poses problems for many marketers. Using all of the promotion mix elements suggested in the chapter, propose a plan for integrating marketing communications at one of the following: (a) your university or college, (b) McDonald's (see www.mcdonalds.com), (c) Burton Snow Boards (see www.burton.com), or (d) a local zoo, museum, theatre, or civic event. Discuss your plan in class.
3. Many firms advertising in Canada use American rather than Canadian celebrities to endorse their products. For example, Sprint Canada uses Candice Bergen (who plays Murphy Brown on the self-titled sitcom) to promote its service. Why do you think they made this choice? Identify a product or service that has made effective use of a celebrity endorser. Identify another in which you think the use of a celebrity endorser was inappropriate. What criteria did you use to differentiate between a successful and unsuccessful use of a celebrity endorser?
4. Using Figure 13-2, describe the communications process for (a) a local newspaper ad for new cars, (b) a phone call from a representative of MCI requesting service sign-up, (c) a salesperson in Sears attempting to sell you a television set, and (d) Microsoft's Web page (www.microsoft.com) allowing you to ask questions about products.
5. The marketing communicator can use one or more types of appeals or themes to produce a desired response. (a) What are these types of appeals? (b) When should each be used? (c) Provide an example of each type of appeal using three different magazine ads.
6. Celebrity endorsers like Wayne Gretzky, Michael Jordan, and Tiger Woods, and numerous Olympic athletes like Marnie McBean, Simon Whitfield, Emilie Heymans, Anne Montminy, and Ian Millar have had a huge impact on advertising and endorsements. Explain the positive and negative consequences of using celebrity sports figures to promote a company's products. What impact does the use of sports celebrity endorsers have on the average person? Is this different from the impact of other types of celebrity endorsers?
7. Decide which of the promotional budget models described in the text would be most appropriate for (a) a small retail gift store, (b) an office supply company that has had a consistent sales and promotion pattern during each of the past five years, (c) a grocery store that has faced intense competition from three competitors in its immediate market area, and (d) an electronics manufacturer that is seeking to expand its market base and national appeal. Explain.

8. Each promotional tool has its own characteristics. Marketers must understand these characteristics in selecting their tools. Using Coca-Cola as an example, demonstrate how each of the promotional tools might be used to create an integrated marketing communications approach for the upcoming year.

Marketing Applications

1. The markets for personal and handheld computers are exploding. It seems that there will soon be a PC for every desk or pocket. However, tomorrow's computers will probably be as different from today's as today's laptops are from yesterday's old "punch card" machines. But how do you tell consumers in plain terms what they need to know about new generations of products without boring them? Computer manufacturers have learned that most consumers do not respond well to the detailed descriptions that are often needed to explain complex technological features and differences. The answer may be as close as the computer company's Web site. Experts predict that more and more consumers will be surfing the Web for product information and that fewer will use traditional information sources. Examine these Web sites: Sharp (www.sharp.ca), IBM (www.can.ibm.com), NEC Computer Systems (www.nec.com), Casio (www.casio.com), Apple (www.apple.com/ca/), and Sony (www.sony.ca).
   a. How are the marketing communications at these Web sites different from those found in traditional advertising media? Develop a grid that compares and critiques the two forms of marketing communication. Assess the advantages and disadvantages of each form.
   b. Which of these Web sites is the most effective? Explain.
   c. After reviewing each site, pick a product that you might like to own (such as a laptop or handheld computer). Based solely on the Web sites above, which company and product most grabs your attention and purchasing interest? Critique your information-gathering experience: What information was most useful? How could the communication be improved? Would you be willing to purchase the product via the Internet? Why or why not?

2. In five short years, Charles Brewer turned MindSpring Enterprises (www.mindspring.com) from a one-room operation into one of North America's largest Internet service providers (ISP). When Mindspring recently merged with EarthLink Network, it jumped past such industry giants as Microsoft, AT&T, and Prodigy to become the number two US ISP behind mammoth AOL (www.aol.com). However, with three million customers versus AOL's 20 million, catching up will take careful strategic planning—and a bit of luck. MindSpring/EarthLink plans to spend $300 million (half of its annual revenues) on promotion to encourage AOL customers (approximately one million defect from AOL each month) to join the ISP "with better service." EarthLink also plans to attack AOL's small business market by offering customized e-mail addresses, home pages, and applications that AOL doesn't currently provide. Will these moves move MindSpring/EarthLink closer to the top, or will the AOL juggernaut continue to roll unchecked? Only time will tell.
   a. What successful communications strategies does MindSpring/EarthLink appear to be using now? How could MindSpring/EarthLink use integrated marketing communications (IMC) to challenge AOL?
   b. What other areas of AOL vulnerability might MindSpring/EarthLink attack?
   c. If you were AOL's CEO, what would you do to meet the threat?
   d. If you were to give one piece of advice to an ISP that wanted to get your business, what would the advice be? What would be the best way for MindSpring/EarthLink to communicate in response to your advice?

Internet Connections

Integrated Marketing Communications

McDonald's is one of the most powerful brands in the world. In addition to its product mix, wide distribution of restaurants, and value pricing, McDonald's has extremely effective communications with important audiences. The concept of integrated marketing communications recognizes that customers are only one group to whom a firm wants to disseminate persuasive information. In addition to targeting kids and their parents, McDonald's is concerned with shareholders, potential franchisees, potential employees, and the communities in which the restaurants reside. Visit McDonald's online (www.mcdonalds.com) and see how it communicates to various audiences. View each page named in the table and then formulate a sentence to describe your opinion about the overall communication content and desired response

For Discussion

1. Why do you think McDonald's wants to communicate with each of the non-customer groups?
2. Although the specific messages may differ, is the overall appeal of its messages consistent to all audiences (rational or emotional tone, visuals, colour, brand name, and image)? What is the overall feeling you get from viewing its site?
3. Is McDonald's online message to consumers consistent with what you've seen on TV and elsewhere?
4. Have you seen any of McDonald's promotions or packages that direct consumers to the Web site? Specify where you've seen them.

Audience	One-sentence message to this audience	Desired response from this audience
Customer: Kids		
Customer: Adults		
Investors		
Potential franchises (corporate)		
Potential employees		
Community		
Other (specify)		
Other (specify)		

Savvy Sites

- Want to see some Web sites that don't do a good job at attracting and keeping visitors? Visit Web Pages That Suck (www.webpagesthatsuck.com) for an interesting and humorous look at the Web's worst.
- Check out the Advertising Age (www.adage.com) and AdWeek (www.adweek.com) online editions to learn more about what is happening in integrated marketing communications worldwide.
- Want to see an ad you loved again and again? Go to AdCritic (www.adcritic.com) and check out their weekly videos of new ads as well as your favourites.

Notes

1. Based on information supplied by Jim Lesinski at Volvo Trucks North America.
2. For these and other definitions, see Peter D. Bennett, *Dictionary of Marketing Terms,* Chicago: American Marketing Association, 1988.
3. For more discussion, see Don E. Schultz, Stanley I. Tannenbaum, and Robert F. Lauterborn, *Integrated Marketing Communication,* Chicago: NTC, 1992:11,17; Larry Percy, *Strategies for Implementing Integrated Marketing Communication,* Chicago: NTC, 1997; and James R. Ogdan, *Developing a Creative and Innovative Integrated Marketing Communications Plan,* Upper Saddle River, NJ: Prentice Hall, 1998.
4. Michael Kubin, "Simple days of retailing on TV are long gone," *Marketing News,* 17 February 1997:2,13; Elizabeth Lesly Stevens and Ronald Glover, "The entertainment glut," *Business Week,* 16 February 1998:88–95; Ronald Glover, "If these shows are hits, why do they hurt so much?" *Business Week,* 13 April 1998:36; Stuart Elliott, "Fewer viewers, more commercials," *New York Times,* 8 June 1999:1; Joe Mandese, "Networks facing a most uncertain fate," *Advertising Age,* 14 February 2000: 54,516; www.magazine.org, March 2000.
5. "Promotion practices condensed," *Potentials,* November 1998:6.
6. See Schultz, Tannenbaum, and Lauterborn, *Integrated Marketing Communication:* Chapters 3, 4.
7. P. Griffith Lindell, "You need integrated attitude to develop IMC," *Marketing News,* 26 May 1997:6.
8. Kevin Goldman, "Advertising: Knock, knock. Who's there? The same old funny ad again," *Wall Street Journal,* 2 November 1993:B10; Marc G. Weinberger, Harlan Spotts, Leland Campbell, and Amy L. Parsons, "The use and effect of humour in different advertising media," *Journal of Advertising Research,* May–June 1995:44–55.
9. "The creative eye," *Marketing On-Line,* 11 December 2000.
10. The history of Buckley's Mixture can be found online at www.buckleys.com.
11. For more on message content and structure, see Leon G. Schiffman and Leslie Lazar Kanuk, *Consumer Behavior,* 5th ed., Englewood Cliffs, NJ: Prentice Hall, 1994:Chapter 10; Alan G. Sawyer and Daniel J. Howard, "Effects of omitting conclusions in advertisements to involved and uninvolved audiences," *Journal of Marketing Research,* November 1991:467–74; Cornelia Pechmann, "Predicting when two-sided ads will be more effective than one-sided ads: The role of correlational and correspondent inferences," *Journal of Marketing,* November 1992:441–53; and Ayn E. Crowley and Wayne D. Hoyer, "An integrative framework for understanding two-sided persuasion," *Journal of Consumer Research,* March 1994:561–74.
12. Philip Kotler, Peggy Cunningham, and Ronald E. Turner, *Marketing Management: Analysis, Planning, Implementation, and Control,* 10 ed., Scarborough, ON: Prentice Hall Canada, 2000: 612–3.
13. Phil Connell and Peggy Cunningham, *Becel Margarine: Meeting Expectations,* case, Queen's University, January 2001.
14. For a more comprehensive discussion on setting promotion budgets, see J. Thomas Russell and W. Ronald Lane, *Kleppner's Advertising Procedure,* Englewood Cliffs, NJ: Prentice Hall, 1993: 138–41.
15. David Allen, "Excessive use of the mirror," *Management Accounting,* June 1966:12. Also see Laura Petrecca, "4A's will study financial return on ad spending," *Advertising Age,* 7 April 1997:3,52.
16. For more on Canadian viewing habits, see Canadian Media Directors' Council, *1999–2000 Media Digest.* Quote from Stuart Elliott, "Fewer viewers, more commercials," *New York Times,* 8 June 1999:1.
17. See "Median costs per call by industry," Sales & Marketing Management, 28 June 1993:65.
18. Based on Matthew P. Gonring, "Putting integrated marketing communications to work today," *Public Relations Quarterly,* Fall 1994:45–8.
19. James Pollock, "Toys 'R' Us reaches out to differently-abled kids," *Marketing,* 16 October 1995:2.
20. For more on the legal aspects of promotion, see Louis W. Stern and Thomas I. Eovaldi, *Legal Aspects of Marketing Policy,* Englewood Cliffs, NJ: Prentice Hall, 1984:Chapters 7,8; Robert J. Posch, *The Complete Guide to Marketing and the Law,* Englewood Cliffs, NJ: Prentice Hall, 1988:Chapters 15–17; and Kevin Kelly, "When a rival's trade secret crosses your desk . . ." *Business Week,* 20 May 1991:48.

Company Case 13

Fierce Creatures: Insects, Dogs, and Other Amigos Work to Ring Up PCS Sales

In 1997, the sector that spent the most on advertising was the telecommunications industry. A record number of primetime ads were run as the telecommunications giants fought new market entrants. Canada's largest advertiser, BCE, parent of the Bell companies, spent a cool $99 million on advertising. Rogers Cantel dug deep and found $35.5 million for its communications budget. Sprint Canada splurged with another $17.6 million. AT&T budgeted $16.6 million. And Unitel coughed up an additional $13.8 million. Even the newest players had huge expenditures: Microcell and Clearnet spent $400 000 and $800 000, respectively.

Part of these expenditures went to support the launch of the industry's newest products—personal communications services or PCS—those funky little handsets that handle everything from e-mail to voice-mail to actual telephone calls. The fight for market share is being fought with a vengeance and, if this market follows the history of cell phones, it won't be an easy battle. Even after years on the market, cell phones have penetrated a meagre 12 to 15 percent of the Canadian market.

It may not be surprising that consumers have been so slow on the uptake. They have been barraged with ads and sales pitches, yet they find it impossible to compare prices and total costs of the services since most of the companies were subsidizing the cost of the phone by making consumers sign long-term service contracts and charging them premium per-minute usage rates. At least, that was the case until Clearnet, of Pickering, Ontario, entered the scene.

Clearnet is one of the four firms vying for share in this superheated market. While the telecommunications giants, Bell and Rogers Cantel, are marketing their PCS products to existing customers as upgrades for their current products, the upstarts, Clearnet and Microcell, want consumers to see PCS as a totally new product class that will give consumers control over their personal and business communications. Thus, Rogers Cantel used promotions that extended the Amigo brand into the PCS arena shouting, "Let's get digital!" and Bell used the same 12-year-old spokesperson for both its Bell Mobility and PCS spots to tie the two product lines together. Microcell built its strategy around faithful FIDO.

When planning its strategy, Clearnet believed it faced a three-fold challenge: Introduce a completely new technology; establish a unique brand identity for its product; and provide potential buyers with enough information so that they would be comfortable making a purchase decision.

Research conducted by Clearnet and its agency, TAXI Advertising and Design, showed that consumers were concerned about rampant technological change and the constant product variations it created. Therefore, the team knew that focusing on the technology itself would be a mistake. Unlike the other companies, Clearnet decided to offer national coverage from day one instead of rolling out its products on an area-by-area basis. It also decided to simultaneously aim its product at both the end-consumer and the business marketplaces. Unlike the other competitors, Clearnet's pricing strategy is simplicity itself. Consumers pay $149.99 for their PCS phone and sign up for one of two talk-time plans. George Cope, Clearnet president, says, "We've finally made wireless telephoning accessible and affordable. No more 60¢-a-minute charges." In addition to simplicity in pricing, Clearnet made its phones widely available. Customers can use one of over 600 outlets across Canada as well as such non-traditional phone sales outlets as Blockbuster Video, Business Depot, Future Shop, Grand & Toy, Battery Depot, and The Telephone Booth.

Given Clearnet's cross-country launch and non-traditional distribution channels, it needed a communications strategy that would be as meaningful in Amherstview as it was in the Okanagan. Moreover, Clearnet, a small player facing industry giants, had only a small communications budget to launch the product, $800 000 compared to the $10 million used by Bell to launch its PCS service. Therefore, Clearnet had to carefully integrate its efforts so that it could speak to consumers with one voice.

In the face of these daunting challenges, Clearnet decided to create a human face for its brand that would link all of the elements of their campaign. This thinking gave birth to Mike, the "buddy" who can handle all forms of communication including two-way radio. Mike is an unassuming guy meant to typify to potential users that the service is a practical way to save users both time and money. Clearnet put Mike everywhere. Clearnet decided it was important to use a shotgun approach, believing it could only reach key buyers with this type of campaign. Thus, Mike appeared in a teaser campaign placed in newspapers, on television, in direct-mail pieces, at special events, and in news releases.

Clearnet's initial campaign was aimed at generating awareness. Its next task was to provide potential buyers with more information to move them through the decision-making process. This is where newspaper advertising really came into its own. According to Rick Seifeddine, Clearnet's director of communications and advertising, "Newspapers allow you to touch a lot of people, but [they] give you a little more time to deliver a complex message."

The secondary objective of the campaign was to generate leads about people most interested in the product so that Clearnet could follow up with more personal, targeted sales methods. Being able to explore niche markets overlooked by the two big players is an important part of Clearnet's strategy. It plans to use a direct marketing program that will target small firms and home businesses in which internal and external communications is essential to getting their work done. As part of its direct marketing efforts, Clearnet will make use of the Web, telemarketing, direct mail, and direct television.

Clearnet's "Mike" campaign helped turn the company into the mouse that roared. It became the industry leader, selling 30 000 units and growing its staff from 11 employees to over 1600. To sustain this remarkable growth, Clearnet launched a second campaign late in 1997. All of the ads featured nature-based images—everything from dung beetles to fly-catching plants. Clearnet chose the images to convey its positioning as the "simple" choice—one that wouldn't ensnare customers in complex contracts. Ads contained the message that buying PCS technology was as hassle-free as buying a toaster.

Were the ads enough to help Clearnet reign supreme in the competitive jungle? They certainly turned the small firm into a force to be reckoned with. In October 2000, Clearnet was acquired by TELUS Corporation, western Canada's leading telecommunications company, and a new company, TELUS Mobility, was born. It has since moved quickly to the forefront of Canada's wireless marketplace. Go to the Clearnet website (www.clearnet.com/english/pcs) to learn more about its current advertising campaigns and the Telus merger.

Questions

1. When launching a new product based on a new technology, is competition a good or bad thing?
2. Which strategy do you think is most viable for the PCS product launch—the one followed by the big telecommunications companies that position their products as line extensions, or the one used by the upstart firms that position their products as breakthrough, new-to-the world offerings? Which one is easier to communicate to prospective customers? Which one offers the biggest payback?
3. Describe the unique selling proposition around which Clearnet's integrated communication program was built.
4. While Clearnet's shotgun approach may give the firm the volume it needs to cover the huge costs of launching the product, do you think this strategy is viable for the future?
5. The communications task facing marketers of the new PCS technology is complex. They have to convey messages to consumers that range from the benefits associated with the product to the capabilities of the new technologies. They must explain how PCS differs from cell phones and what the various price-points will be. The firms also have to move consumers step-by-step through the decision-making process. What media vehicles would you recommend for people at different decision-making stages? Can you use the same media for end-consumers and business customers?
6. The huge amount of ad spending in the telecommunications market may have caused considerable consumer confusion. Did Clearnet's advertising campaign differentiate the firm from its competition? Before you read this case, did you recall Clearnet's ads? Did you understand the benefits of its products?
7. As consumers become more comfortable with PCS technology, what communication challenges will Clearnet face in the future?

Sources: Quotes from Terence Belford, "Dial-up goes digital," *Financial Post,* 20 November 1997:P5; and David Bosworth, "Special report: Mike packs wallop with media splash," *Strategy,* 3 March 1997:30. Also see David Chilton, "Clearnet—Meet Mike," *Strategy,* 30 September 1996:5; Lesley Daw and Bobbi Bulmer, "The Telco barrage," *Marketing,* 20 October 1997:22–5; Mark De Wolf, "PCS products a natural for direct marketing," *Strategy,* 21 July 1997:DR1; Lara Mills, "Clearnet PCS adopts 'natural' strategy," *Marketing,* 6 October 1997:3; Patti Summerfield, "Bell Mobility launches PCS Plus," *Strategy,* 13 October 1997:2; www.clearnet.com/.

video case 13

Infomercials: Brand Building Tools or Disguised Advertising?

Turn on your TV late at night or in the early morning hours and you'll see that infomercials are everywhere. The word alone conjures up images of washed-up TV stars hawking everything from thigh-masters to spray-on hair. But what's this . . . a 30 minute, prime-time spot featuring the upscale Land Rover? Another for the services offered by the Bank of Montreal and a third for Sprint Canada. Why are these national brand advertisers using what was once regarded as the cheesiest form of advertising?

Infomercials are the fastest growing sector in advertising and more and more infomercials are appearing on Canadian prime-time television. Infomercials are television commercial messages promoting products or services that are more than 12 continuous minutes in length. Infomercials are exempt from the CRTC-imposed 12-minutes-per-hour ceiling on advertising time. Sometimes called direct response television, infomercials attempt to elicit a measurable audience response in the form of an order or request for further information. This is usually done by placing a toll-free number in the commercial.

In 1995, the Telecaster Committee of Canada reported that there were two infomercials approved for broadcast, but by 1999 more than 600 infomercials had been approved. The increased numbers of infomercials are only one change affecting the industry. Today, infomercials are being aired by some of Canada's most prestigious companies as well as its charitable organizations. The number of really successful, long-running infomercials has also dramatically increased. Sprint Canada, for example, sponsored an infomercial that ran almost 4000 times, and Look Communications broadcast an infomercial for close to two years. Cantel AT&T has found infomercials so effective that it produced ten between 1995 and 2000. Recently it adopted a MuchMusic-style infomercial to hawk its "Pay as You Go" service to teens.

Today, the only stations that cannot air infomercials are those that receive public funding, such as CBC or TVOntario. All other channels, including specialty channels, can broadcast infomercials whenever they please. One station, Toronto's Star Television, runs nothing but infomercials 24 hours a day, seven days a week. Despite the concern about audience fragmentation, television still reaches more Canadians than any other medium. The 2000/2001 Television Bureau of Canada's audience statistics show that 85 percent of Canadian adults over 18 watch television daily. This compares to the 66 percent who read newspapers, the 42 percent who read magazines, and the 34 percent who use the Internet. And as products and services become increasingly complex, consumers may need more information than ever before to optimize their choices. Producers of such products have recognized the power of infomercials to deliver needed information to target audiences.

The arrival of big business has transformed infomercials. They no longer use tacky pitches where people scream at you to buy their products. Instead, many infomercials today have high production values. For instance, the Bank of Montreal's "Matchmaker" RSP infomercial employed experts and customer testimonials to increase believability. Others use "mini-dramas" that viewers can identify with. One thing is certain: when infomercials are of high quality, they bring in new customers. Cantel's "Pay as You Go" infomercial not only generated direct sales, but helped in-store sales as well since teens who viewed the infomercial were more predisposed to buy.

Producing high quality programming takes deep pockets, talented producers and expensive actors. The key to getting people to watch is that infomercials must be entertaining as well as informative. The transformation of infomercials has been so profound that even the name is starting to change. Producers like Ian French call them "direct response programming." They are also known as documercials, edumercials, and storymercials. Many look more like soap operas than half-hour commercials.

What concerns advertising critics is that the line between regular programming and commercial time is becoming increasingly blurred. They contend that viewers may not know they are watching a "product pitch" if they happen to tune in late and miss the opening disclaimer, which states that the program is paid-for, commercial material. Some formats have drawn more criticism than others, especially those infomercials that look just like news talk shows. No matter what they are called, infomercials seem here to stay. The debate rages, however, about whether they are deceptive advertising.

Questions

1. Why are large companies that sell national brands turning to infomercials?
2. Some sponsors defend the discreet approach to selling taken by some infomercials, claiming fewer ads today hit people over the head with commercial claims. They ask "So what?" when it is claimed people may not know they are watching a long commercial. Is it important that people know they are viewing commercial programming? Are there certain groups who may be harmed by not knowing they are viewing a commercial?
3. If you were a brand manager for a nationally recognized brand, would you use an infomercial? Why or why not?

Sources: Peggy Cunningham prepared this case based on "In Disguise," *Undercurrents,* October 19, 1999; James Careless, "Blue-Chip Marketers Join the Ranks of the Infomercial True Believers," *Marketing On-line,* November 1, 1999; Ian French, "Finding the Time," *Marketing On-line,* October 16, 2000; Media Digest, "Direct Response Television," *Marketing On-line,* September 11, 2000.

P A R T 1 2 3 4

Developing the Marketing Mix

Concept Connections

When you finish this chapter, you should be able to

1. Define the roles of advertising, sales promotion, and public relations in the promotion mix.
2. Describe the major decisions involved in developing an advertising program.
3. Explain how sales promotion campaigns are developed and implemented.
4. Explain how companies use public relations to communicate with their publics.

chapter 14

Advertising, Sales Promotion, and Public Relations

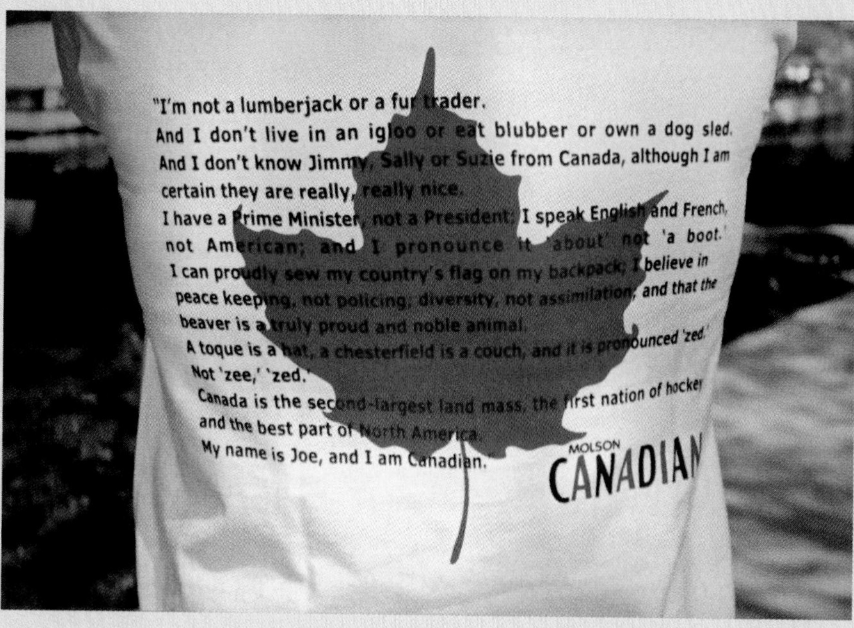

"I'm not a lumberjack or a fur trader.
And I don't live in an igloo or eat blubber or own a dog sled.
And I don't know Jimmy, Sally or Suzie from Canada, although I am certain they are really, really nice.
I have a Prime Minister, not a President; I speak English and French, not American; and I pronounce it 'about' not 'a boot.'
I can proudly sew my country's flag on my backpack; I believe in peace keeping, not policing; diversity, not assimilation; and that the beaver is a truly proud and noble animal.
A toque is a hat, a chesterfield is a couch, and it is pronounced 'zed.'
Not 'zee,' 'zed.'
Canada is the second-largest land mass, the first nation of hockey and the best part of North America.
My name is Joe, and I am Canadian."
MOLSON
CANADIAN

"I Am Marketer of the Year" trumpeted the headline in *Marketing Magazine,* announcing the honour recently bestowed on Molson Canada. Not bad for a company that tagged the year 2000 as the "year of the comeback!" Molson had been suffering from flat or sinking sales. Its profits had fallen: In one year alone, Molson's profitability was reported to be $100 million lower than that of its main competitor, Labatt Breweries. So getting the Marketer of the Year award is nothing short of astounding, given the hurdles Molson had to overcome to reach the podium.

Molson's marathon began with a total overhaul of its marketing strategies. It hired two marketing "top guns" from packaged goods firms rather than the "beer guys" who had long paced its halls. Their first mandate was to regain control of Molson's brands. One initiative saw Molson seizing control of sales and marketing for its Canadian brand in the Maritimes, where its market share had been slipping. Then in October, it spent $200 million to buy back its US beer sales, which had taken a nose-dive by a whopping 35 percent since 1993 when Molson first entered a partnership with Milwaukee-based Miller Brewing. Molson passed the baton to Coors Brewing of Golden, Colorado in an effort to improve the marketing of Molson brands south of the border. In November, Molson moved to strengthen its international position by jumping into the Brazilian beer market. Why Brazil? It's the fourth largest market for beer in the world, with Brazilians downing 4.5 times more beer than Canadians.

Molson's next task was to totally revamp its advertising and sales promotion efforts. This was critical for a company that spends over $48 million annually on measured media advertising alone. The brewer was beginning to suspect that this spending wasn't producing the results it should. Molson took the drastic measure of firing its agency of 42 years, MacLaren McCann of Toronto, and hired three new agencies to handle its key brands—Canadian, Export, and lesser-known Rickard's Red.

Bensimon Byrne D'Arcy of Toronto was put in charge of advertising for Canadian. The agency decided to return the "I Am" tag line that had been dropped from recent advertising, believing that this slogan still had great equity among beer drinkers. However, the new campaign was far from "more of the same" advertising.

"The original campaign wasn't 'I Am Canadian.' It was 'I Am' and this is my attitude," explains Alan Middleton, a professor of marketing at York University's Schulich School of Business in Toronto. This time around, the spotlight was thrown onto a flannel-shirted Joe Canadian, and "The Rant" was born. Joe's witty one-liners—"Canadians have a prime minister, not a president" "We pronounce it 'about,' not 'aboot' " "The beaver is a truly proud and noble animal"—tapped into many Canadians' frustrations with being inextricably linked to the US. Suddenly it was okay not to be a wannabe American.

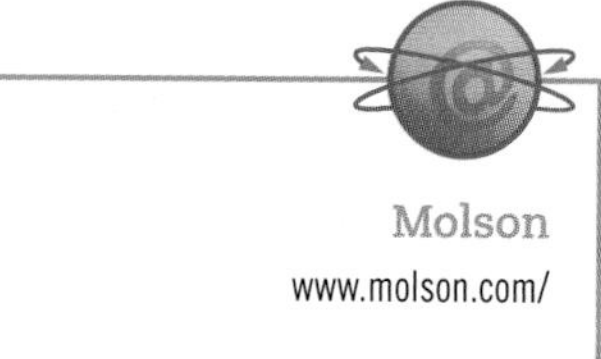
Molson
www.molson.com/

The Rant was a huge move away from traditional beer advertising, which had long relied on scenes of people partying with their not too subtle message that it was your brand of beer that made you attractive to the opposite sex. The new "I Am" creative made many Molson executives' hands sweat. There wasn't a beer bottle or a woman in sight! But focus groups had shown that Canadians valued the differences between themselves and Americans. They also suggested that Canadians had a unique way of expressing these differences. "Many [participants] would start off slowly when asked what it means to be a Canadian, but by the end of the interview, they had worked themselves up emotionally." Thus, the structure of the final commercial reflected this insight as well.

Needless to say, Molson was delighted when it became the campaign of the year, won a Bronze Lion at Cannes, generated word-of-mouth communication among practitioners and consumers alike, and inspired copycat work from a variety of imitators, including US network NBC and Australia's Foster's Brewing.

Even the most jaded of advertising critics admitted that The Rant was "pretty darn good advertising. It drove the old I Am Canadian positioning to a new level, where it seemed smarter, more empathetic than the juiced-up lager louts with leaves painted on their faces." There was just enough truth in the barbs "aimed at our hotshot American cousins to cheer us up and make us feel smug and righteous and superior. And yet it wasn't mean or vicious or hateful." Everyone watching just couldn't help puffing up their chest a little and enjoy being a Canadian. The campaign "contained those magic elements of good advertising—emotion, relevance and surprise. And, it was funny."

Despite this string of successes, though, industry observers say Molson still has some work to do. Labatt and Molson began the race for share in the year 2000 neck and neck. Both held about 45 percent of the market. However, Molson's share has only begun to inch upwards as a result of increased sales of Canadian. It still hadn't realized the higher sales targets the brewer had hoped for. Thus, while launching strong ad campaigns and regaining brand control were certainly steps in the right direction, Molson also has to get a grip on its sales promotion efforts. Much of Molson's sales promotions are handled by Molstar Sports and Entertainment. This division manages such events as the Molson Indy and its cross-country music concerts. However, there was a growing belief that these efforts weren't linked sufficiently to the brewer's key brands.

Molson decided that although these "big name" venues were important, it also needed grassroots efforts to bring the Canadian brand closer to consumers and build excitement around the campaign. Therefore, it started to stage live performances of The Rant at movie theatres and hockey games. It dispatched "I Am" summer patrols to hand out tattoos and sew flags on backpacks at Canada Day events across the country. The brewer also organized the Molson Canadian Rocks Simulbash—five concerts in five cities that were simulcast to clubs across the country via closed-circuit TV.

Giveaways, bundled products, and contests are other sales promotion weapons Molson has deployed to win over consumers. Many of these are featured on its I

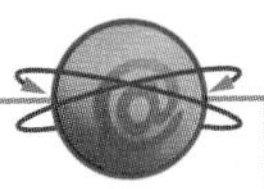

I Am Canadian
www.iam.ca/promos/

Am Canadian Web site. For example, to build winter season excitement, Molson launched its online hockey pool promotion for the NHL playoffs, partnering with Faceoff.com to create the "I Am a Hockey Millionaire" hockey pool. In a joint effort with its new American partner, Molson is also offering "Warm-Up Gear," Molson merchandise offered in specially marked cases of 24 that contain 12 Canadian and 12 Coors Light. To generate traffic to its site and improve its 'stickiness,' Molson also provides information on Canada's music scene under its famous banner, "Molson Canadian Rocks."

There is no doubt that winning the "beer wars" will be tough. Will these integrated communication efforts pay off for Canadian and generate both sales and improved profitability for Molson? As with all marketing investments, the outcome is never guaranteed, but there is no doubt that the contest will be fun to watch.[1]

Companies, like Molson, must do more than make good products: They must inform consumers about product benefits and carefully position products in consumers' minds. To do this, they must skillfully use the mass-promotion tools of a*dvertising, sales promotion,* and *public relations.* We take a closer look at each of these tools in this chapter.

Advertising

Advertising can be traced to the very beginnings of recorded history. Archeologists working in the countries around the Mediterranean Sea have dug up signs announcing various events and offers. The Romans painted walls to announce gladiator fights, and the Phoenicians painted pictures promoting their wares on large rocks along parade routes. A Pompeii wall painting praised a politician and asked for votes. During the Golden Age in Greece, town criers announced the sale of cattle, crafted items, and even cosmetics. An early "singing commercial" went as follows: "For eyes that are shining, for cheeks like the dawn / For beauty that lasts after girlhood is gone / For prices in reason, the woman who knows / Will buy her cosmetics from Aesclyptos."

Modern advertising, however, is a far cry from these early efforts. It is a highly sophisticated tool that works to inform and persuade us, whether the purpose is to sell Coca-Cola worldwide, increase our giving to the United Way, or get us to drink more milk or practise safe sex. According to a recent report commissioned by the Institute of Canadian Advertising, advertising is a significant industry in Canada. The advertising sector includes firms that create and support advertising (advertising services); the media that produce and carry advertising; and advertising-related work in industries whose output is not advertising (for example, animation firms). The industry accounts for about 212 000 jobs, or 1.7 percent of all jobs in Canada. That's bigger than either the insurance or real estate agent industry and the accounting and legal services industry.[2]

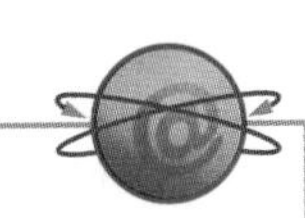

Institute of Canadian Advertising
www.ica-ad.com/

The aggregate expenditure of the Canadian advertising industry was $14.5 billion. US advertisers spent $318 billion; worldwide ad spending exceeded $621 billion. In Canada, expenditures on media account for the largest portion of aggregate spending ($6.9 billion in 1999), according to a study by the media analysis firm Carat Expert in Montreal. Growth in media expenditures is slowing, however. This is due to two trends in Canadian businesses: mergers that have resulted in the disappearance of some advertising budgets and decreased spending by the telecommunications sector, which believes massive new investments to educate consumers are no longer required. Some experts believe this trend will soon be reversed. The Canadian Marketing Association, for example, estimates that $10 billion will be spent on advertising in various media in Canada in 2001. In 1999, television represented 34.1 percent of total media spending at $2.36 billion, followed by daily

marketers speak out

Peter Elwood, Former CEO of Thomas J. Lipton Inc.

What does a former CEO of one of Canada's packaged goods companies know about advertising, you might ask. Plenty, if that former CEO is Peter Elwood, a man who recently retired after a long career with Thomas J. Lipton Inc. and Lever Canada. These companies, both divisions of Unilever, a giant international marketer, sell such well-known brands as Lever 2000; Becel and Imperial margarines; Red Rose, Salada, and Lipton teas; Sunlight detergent; Ragu sauces; and Lipton soups.

In the last 12 years, Peter and his team created two award-winning campaigns judged the best in Canada. They also won three CASSIE (Canadian Advertising Success Stories) awards. Working with Peter were three top Canadian agencies: Ammirati Puris Lintas, Ogilvy & Mather, and MacLaren McCann.

Peter Elwood has an eclectic background as well as years of marketing experience. Before joining Lipton, he worked for S.C. Johnson. He joined Lipton as a brand manager in 1974, became the marketing director in 1981, and rose to be vice-president of marketing (food and drinks division) by 1984. He worked for Lipton's parent, Unilever, in the UK, became the president of Lever in 1993, and assumed the presidency of Lipton in 1996. Peter Elwood took a few minutes away from arranging his next golf game to speak with Peggy Cunningham about what makes great advertising.

In Peter's view, there is a great need today to develop breakthrough marketing communications. Although speaking effectively about brands and products is as old a problem as advertising itself, Peter notes that marketers have long known that over half of their advertising dollars are wasted. The critical question is: "Which half?"

In our highly competitive marketplace, consumers are exposed to more advertising messages than ever before. Peter knows only too well that marketers have to justify every expense. But justifying advertising budgets is getting harder than ever before since the number of media outlets (including the Internet) used to carry commercial messages is growing rapidly. Moreover, Peter notes, consumers are empowered and have the technological capability to screen out many messages by using televisions that skip through advertisements. Furthermore, today's buyers are highly educated and cynical consumers. If messages are boring, uninteresting, or aren't brilliantly targeted, consumers just tune out, and those precious advertising dollars might as well have been flushed down the drain.

Some firms have reacted by just eliminating advertising. Why take the risk of using such a difficult, inefficient tool, they ask. But this isn't the solution in Peter's view. In fact, it may begin a "spiral of doom." Without advertising that builds brand positioning in the hearts and minds of consumers, firms cannot differentiate products and are forced to sell on price.

Therefore, Peter stresses, the need to develop advertising platforms that work is more important than ever. Firms need advertising that connects to consumers. However, the old ways of developing copy—determining who you are talking to, establishing the unique selling proposition, selecting effective media to convey the message—is just not good enough anymore. As a recent article in *Marketing Magazine* proclaimed, "Clients get the advertising they deserve!" Watchers of Canada's advertising industry contend that most marketers are unwilling to venture beyond the comforting den of "safe" advertising and marketing. But when it comes to taking a risk in pursuit of a innovative idea, few will reach for the brass ring. Peter Elwood is viewed as one marketer who holds that ring firmly in both hands.

Peter is adamant that there are two absolutely critical things that have to be placed front and centre in the development of effective communications. First, advertisers have to develop a deep consumer insight. Such an insight is a universal truth—not yet recognized—that is relevant to the brand. Second, they have to work as a team with their agencies, al-

newspapers (25.1% at $1.7 billion), radio (13.8% at $952 million), weekly newspapers (11.4% at $788 million), magazines (10.8% at $747 million), outdoor signage (4.1% at $287 million), and the Internet (0.8% at $55.5 million).[3]

Although advertising is used mostly by business firms, it is also used by a wide range of non-profit organizations, professionals, and social agencies that advertise their causes to various target publics. The top three industries in terms of advertising expenditures in Canada, which account for 39 percent of all ad spending, are retail, automobile manufacturing, and business equipment and services. These categories are followed by food manufacturing, financial and insurance services, and entertainment. Despite your perceptions that beer ads are everywhere, brewers rank number 12 in terms of ad spending. While government advertising falls into fifteenth place, there has been a recent trend toward increased government spending on advertising both at the federal and provincial levels, as governments lowing all members to contribute what they do best.

What does developing this insight involve? To answer, we look to Peter's experience at Lipton. First, Peter stresses, you have to dive deep into the psyche of the consumer. You have to find out from consumers what they are thinking and saying to themselves as they use your products and services in situ. Rather than using traditional research, you need one-on-one interviews and the help of ethnographers and psychologists who observe and interpret the meanings of products in people's lives.

Take the work that Peter authorized when Lipton sought to develop a new campaign for its chicken noodle soup. Lipton had long known that kids liked their chicken noodle soup, and moms knew this, too. But why weren't they serving the soup more often? They knew it was good for their kids. If Peter had been content to use the old, simple way of advertising, he could have just instructed his agency to develop ads that would just tell moms their kids liked the soup, so go buy it. But Peter knew this just wasn't enough in today's marketplace.

Lipton's research revealed that moms did not understand their children. Moms were often afraid their kids would get bored with food. Think back. If you were like 99.9 percent of Canada's kids, you found meals boring activities that just kept you from doing other more fun things. Therefore, moms worked to serve their children lunches that would expose them to a variety of foods and nutritionally balanced meals. But what wasn't clear in their minds was that kids don't get bored doing the things they like. In fact, if they like it, they will do it over, and over, and over again. Like having the same story read every night, or watching the same movie or playing video games over and over.

Kids also like to get attention or cause a reaction. It's all part of growing up. These insights led to a series of ads including the recent "whoopee cushion" spot, the ice ad where a child repeatedly presses the ice cube maker on the fridge, and the drums ad where a repeated drum beat disturbs a father just trying to read his paper. Not only did these ads break through and speak to consumers, they drove sales.

The second route to success for great advertising, which is often given lip service in companies but is rarely followed, is taking a team approach to advertising development. To develop breakthrough campaigns, Peter stresses, you not only need the marketing strategists who want to take the brand forward, you need a team with people who can write and draw. These are the strong right-brained people. Where many companies go wrong, Peter believes, is confusing the roles of the different players. While your brand people may be intelligent and strategically insightful, they aren't the people you want writing your copy. You have to leave that to the creative people. And you will know when they have it right. The idea will be insightful, easily noticeable and exciting. In fact, Peter notes, it may even be risky. But if that is the case, Peter recommends that is exactly what you should go with. How else will you get the communications program that will really break through?

Peter Elwood.

As Peter Elwood knows, perhaps better than any other Canadian marketer, the use of consumer insight integrated into advertising in a very entertaining and appealing way can be highly effective. It put the old favourite Lipton's Chicken Noodle Soup back on Canada's lunch tables; and Canada's moms, still smiling after viewing Lipton's ads, don't feel at all guilty serving it more often.

Sources: Peggy Cunningham talked with Peter Elwood on December 1, 2000. Also see Lara Mills, "Tough times for heroic marketers: Where have all the larger-than-life leaders gone?" *Marketing On-Line,* 24 January 2000; Doug Robinson, "When yuck doesn't suck: Lipton knew kids liked its chicken noodle soup . . . the challenge was convincing their parents," *Marketing On-Line,* 29 March 2000; "Marketing awards: Television campaign," *Marketing On-Line,* 27 March 2000.

work to communicate directly with Canadians. In 1998 alone, Ottawa spent a total of $89.1 million on advertising, 43 percent over the previous year. The Ontario government topped the list in terms of provincial ad spending, allocating $50.6 million to advertising in 1998. The Quebec government also increased its spending to $39.2 million, while BC's advertising budget rose to $31.2 million.[4]

Major Decisions in Advertising

Marketing management must make four important decisions when developing an advertising program (see Figure 14-1): *setting advertising objectives, setting advertising budgets, developing advertising strategy* (message decisions and media decisions), and *evaluating advertising campaigns.*

FIGURE 14-1 Major advertising decisions

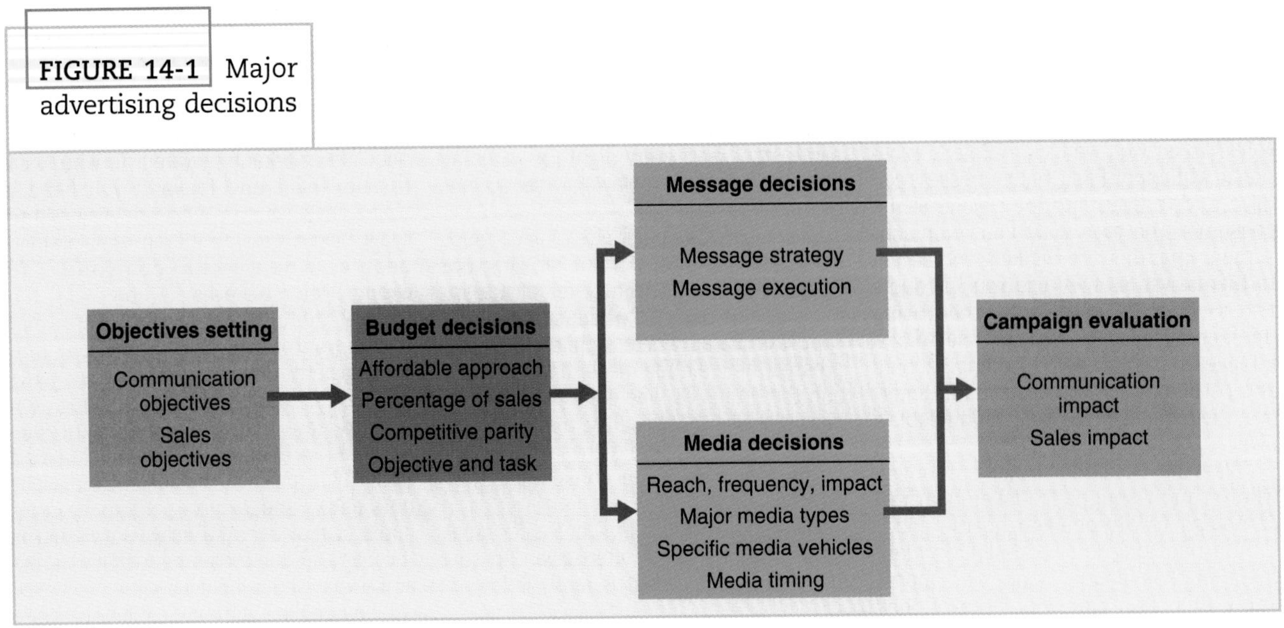

Setting Advertising Objectives

The first step in developing an advertising program is to set *advertising objectives.* These objectives should be based on past decisions about the target market, positioning, and marketing mix. The marketing positioning and mix strategy define the job that advertising must do in the total marketing program.

Advertising objective
A specific communication *task* to be accomplished with a specific *target* audience during a specific period of *time.*

Informative advertising
Advertising used to inform consumers about a new product or feature and to build primary demand.

Persuasive advertising
Advertising used to build selective demand for a brand by persuading consumers that it offers the best quality for their money.

Comparison advertising
Advertising that compares one brand directly or indirectly to one or more other brands.

An **advertising objective** is a specific communication *task* to be accomplished with a specific *target* audience during a specific period of *time.* Advertising objectives can be classified by primary purpose—whether the aim is to *inform, persuade,* or *remind.* Table 14-1 lists examples of each of these objectives.

Informative advertising is often used in introducing a new product category; in this case, the objective is to build primary demand. For example, producers of compact-disc players first informed consumers of the sound and convenience benefits of CDs. **Persuasive advertising** becomes more important as competition increases. Here, the company's objective is to build selective demand. When compact-disc players became established, Sony began trying to persuade consumers that its brand offered the best quality for their money.

One form of persuasive advertising is **comparison advertising,** in which a company directly or indirectly compares its brand with one or more other brands. In its classic comparison campaign, Avis positioned itself against market leader Hertz by claiming, "We're number two, so we try harder."

Rogers @Home, a service that provides cable access for Internet users, launched an aggressive comparative campaign to protect its market share. In the spring of 2000, telephone companies began offering Canadian consumers high-speed Internet services. Using TV, print, radio, online advertising, posters, and print inserts, Rogers @Home's integrated communications were designed

Rogers @Home launched an aggressive comparative campaign to protect its market share.

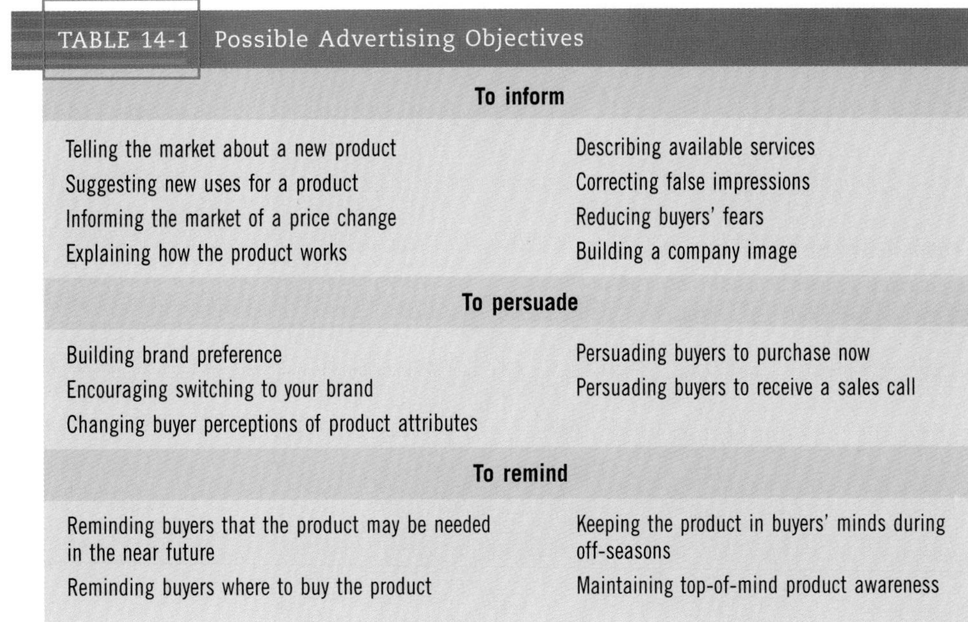

TABLE 14-1 Possible Advertising Objectives

To inform	
Telling the market about a new product	Describing available services
Suggesting new uses for a product	Correcting false impressions
Informing the market of a price change	Reducing buyers' fears
Explaining how the product works	Building a company image
To persuade	
Building brand preference	Persuading buyers to purchase now
Encouraging switching to your brand	Persuading buyers to receive a sales call
Changing buyer perceptions of product attributes	
To remind	
Reminding buyers that the product may be needed in the near future	Keeping the product in buyers' minds during off-seasons
Reminding buyers where to buy the product	Maintaining top-of-mind product awareness

to cast doubt on the efficiency of high-speed Internet connection over telephone lines. Mass media were used to break through to consumers. Direct mail was selected as the means to explain telephone's failings in greater detail. Aiming at the target audience of savvy surfers who value speed above all else, the campaign used the motif of "download rigor mortis"—a condition from which one would presumably suffer if not using cable. The humorous ads showed patients being rushed to hospitals, their frozen, claw-like hands rising from their gurneys. The campaign was so successful that it doubled the number of subscribers over the numbers gained during the same period the previous year despite the increased competition.[5]

Firms using comparative claims must exercise caution, however. The *Competition Act* stipulates that an advertisement using competitive claims must be based on an adequate and proper test that supports it. A case between Duracell and its arch-rival, Eveready, resulted in Duracell having to change its advertising. Even though Duracell had performed advanced tests on both companies' batteries, the tests were deemed to be inadequate since they hadn't included Eveready's newest battery, which was on retailers' shelves when the ad aired.[6]

Reminder advertising
Advertising used to keep consumers thinking about a product.

Reminder advertising is important for mature products: It keeps consumers thinking about the product. Stanfield's reminded consumers about the benefits of their long underwear in an award-winning outdoor campaign.

Setting the Advertising Budget

After determining its advertising objectives, the company next sets its *advertising budget* for each product. Chapter 13 discussed four common methods for setting promotion budgets. Here we discuss some specific factors that the company should consider when setting the advertising budget.

A brand's advertising budget often depends on its *stage in the product life cycle*. New products typically need large advertising budgets to build awareness and to gain consumer trial. Mature brands usually require lower budgets as a ratio to sales. *Market share* also affects the amount of advertising needed. Because building the market or taking share from competitors requires larger advertising spending than does simply maintaining current share, high-share brands usually need more advertising spending as a percentage of sales. Also, brands in a market with many *competitors* and high advertising *clutter* must be advertised more

THE ASHANTIS OF GHANA THINK A WOMAN'S BODY GETS MORE ATTRACTIVE AS SHE AGES.
Please contact your travel agent for the next available flight.
A 50 year old's body more attractive than a 20 year old's? Why not? It's only perception, after all. In every culture, our bodies change as we age. Wouldn't it be nice if ours were to celebrate the process? Exercise. Establish a healthy routine. Start with a balanced breakfast every morning and go from there. Kellogg's Special K cereal is fat free and a source of nine essential nutrients so it's a light, sensible way to help start your day. At any age, looking your best is about being strong and healthy. Which is important if you expect to be travelling in the near future.

Kellogg developed a campaign that broke through the advertising clutter and repositioned Special K® as a food that is part of a balanced diet.

heavily to be noticed above the noise. *Undifferentiated brands*—those that closely resemble other brands in their product class (beer, soft drinks, laundry detergents)—may require heavy advertising to set them apart. When the product differs greatly from competitors, advertising can be used to point out the differences to consumers.

No matter what method is used, setting the advertising budget is a difficult task. How does a company know if it is spending the right amount? Some critics charge that large consumer packaged goods firms tend to spend too much on advertising while business-to-business marketers generally underspend on advertising. They claim that, on the one hand, the large consumer companies use a lot of image advertising without really knowing its effects, and overspend as a form of "insurance" against not spending enough. On the other hand, business advertisers tend to rely too heavily on their sales forces to bring in orders, and underestimate the power of company and product image in preselling to industrial customers; therefore, they do not spend enough on advertising to build customer awareness and knowledge.

Some companies such as Coca-Cola and Kraft have built sophisticated statistical models to determine the relationship between promotional spending and brand sales, and to help determine the "optimal investment" across various media. Still, because so many factors affect advertising effectiveness, some controllable and others not, measuring the results of advertising spending remains an inexact science. In most cases, managers must rely on large doses of judgment along with more quantitative analysis when setting advertising budgets.[7]

Developing Advertising Strategy

Advertising strategy consists of two major elements—creating advertising *messages* and selecting advertising *media*. In the past, most companies developed messages and media plans independently. They often viewed media planning as secondary to the message creation process. The creative department first created good advertisements; then the media department selected the best media for carrying these advertisements to desired target audiences. This often caused friction between creatives and media planners.

Today, however, media fragmentation, soaring media costs, and more focused target marketing strategies have promoted the importance of the media-planning function. In some cases, an advertising campaign might start with a great message idea, followed by the choice of appropriate media. In other cases, however, a campaign might begin with a good media opportunity, followed by advertisements designed to take advantage of that opportunity. Increasingly, companies are realizing the benefits of planning these two important elements *jointly*. Therefore, advertisers are orchestrating a closer harmony between their messages and the media that deliver them. Media planning is no longer an after-the-fact complement to a new ad campaign. Media planners are now working closely with creatives to allow media selection to help shape the creative process, often before a single ad is written. In some cases, media people even initiate ideas for new campaigns.

Among the more noteworthy ad campaigns based on tight media–creative partnerships is the pioneering campaign for Absolut vodka, marketed by Seagram.[8]

> For years, Seagrams Canada of Montreal has worked closely with a slew of magazines to set Absolut's media schedule. The schedule consists of up to 100 magazines, ranging from consumer and business magazines to theatre playbills. The agency's creative department is charged with creating media-specific ads. The result is a wonderful assortment of very creative ads for Absolut, tightly targeted to audiences of the media in which they appear. For example, Seagrams has long been an avid supporter of the gay community, and it wanted to develop ads specifically geared to gays and lesbians. Working closely with niche publication *Xtra!* magazine staff, it developed the concept for "Absolut Pride," "Absolut Out" (aptly featuring a closet), and "Absolut Commitment" (showcasing two grooms on a wedding cake). Brand manager, Holly Wyatt, believed the partnership with *Xtra!* made sense because the magazine's staff were in tune with trends in the gay and lesbian community. "Absolut Pride," in particular, received a lot of extra media coverage including a feature on *Entertainment Tonight*. When asked why she targeted the gay and lesbian community, Wyatt noted that the market is the best representation of Absolut's target audience, regardless of sexual orientation. "They're young, sophisticated, somewhat upscale. And Absolut consumers do tend to swing towards the arts," she says. "It just makes sense for us." In all, Absolut has developed more than 500 ads for the almost two-decade-old campaign. At a time of soaring media costs and cluttered communication channels, a closer cooperation between creative and media people has paid off handsomely for Absolut. Largely as a result of its breakthrough advertising, Absolut now captures a 63 percent share of the imported vodka market in North America.

Absolut Vodka
www.absolut.com/

Creating the Advertising Message

No matter how high the budget, advertising can succeed only if commercials gain attention and communicate well. Good advertising messages are especially important in today's costly and cluttered advertising environment. About 99 percent of Canadian households are equipped with a television, and over 77 percent of Canadians watch television at least once a day. However, the number of television channels beamed into Canadian homes has skyrocketed from two in the 1950s to over 70 today—one national English channel, one national French channel, 18 regional channels, 39 specialty networks, and 12 pay TV offerings. Add to this the growing number of American signals that are picked up by Canadians who, in 2000, spent 24 percent of their viewing time watching US stations. Canadian media

Absolut Vodka works closely with specific media to develop targeted ads such as "xxxxx" aimed at the gay and lesbian market.

options also include 910 radio stations, 108 daily newspapers, and 1600 magazines. The clutter is made worse by a continuous barrage of catalogues, direct-mail and online ads, and out-of-home media.[9]

If all this advertising clutter bothers some consumers, it also causes big problems for advertisers. Take the situation facing network television advertisers. They regularly pay $300 000 or more for 30 seconds of advertising time during a popular prime time program, even more if it's an especially popular program such as *ER* ($817 000 per 30-second spot), *Friends* ($765 000), *Frasier* ($699 000), *The Drew Carey Show* ($555 000), or a mega-event such as the Super Bowl (more than $2.4 million).[10] Then, their ads are sandwiched in with a clutter of some 60 other commercials, announcements, and network promotions per hour.

Television viewers used to be pretty much a captive audience for advertisers when they had only a few channels from which to choose. But with cable and satellite TV, VCRs, and remote-control units, viewers now have many options. They can avoid ads by watching commercial-free cable channels. They can "zap" commercials by pushing the fast-forward button during taped programs. With remote control, they can instantly turn off the sound during a commercial or "zip" around the channels to see what else is on. One study found that half of all television viewers switch channels when the commercial break starts.[11]

Therefore, just to gain and hold attention, advertising messages must be better planned, more imaginative, more entertaining, and more rewarding to consumers. "Today we have to entertain and not just sell, because if you try to sell directly and come off as boring or obnoxious, people are going to press the remote on you," points out one advertising executive. "When most TV viewers are armed with remote channel switchers, a commercial has to cut through the clutter and seize the viewers in one to three seconds, or they're gone," comments another.[12] Some advertisers even create intentionally controversial ads to break through the clutter and gain attention for their products (see Marketing Highlight 14-1).

Message Strategy. The first step in creating effective advertising messages is to decide what general message will be communicated to consumers—to plan a *message strategy*. The purpose of advertising is to get consumers to think about or react to the product or company in a certain way. People will react only if they believe that

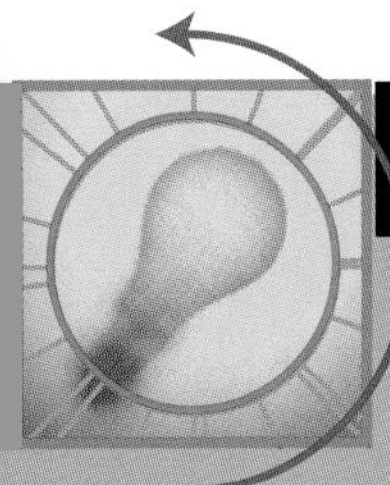

marketing highlight 14-1

Advertising on the Edge: You Either Hate 'em or Love 'em

You may remember the ad. It opens with a calm, deep-voiced announcer sitting comfortably in a leather chair in a library setting. The spot cuts to a concrete wall with "Outpost.com" emblazoned on it. "Hello," he intones, "we want you to remember our name—Outpost.com." To the shock of some viewers and to the surprised delight of others, he continues, "That's why we've decided to fire gerbils out of this cannon through the 'O' in Outpost." He gives a nod, and his assistant fires a nearby cannon. "Boom!" The cannon hurls a gerbil toward the hole. "Splat!" A near miss—the gerbil hits the wall, then falls to the ground and scurries away. "Cute little guy," says the announcer, smiling warmly. "Again," he instructs. "Boom!" This time, a gerbil sails high over the wall. "Boom!" "Splat!" "Boom!" "Splat!" "So close," affirms the announcer. Finally, the cannon blasts a gerbil cleanly through the "O," setting off a fanfare of sirens, buzzers, and flashing lights. The ad closes with an invitation to viewers to "Send complaints to Outpost.com—the cool place to buy computer stuff online."

It was all pretend, of course, but complain people did. These ads by Outpost.com—the Internet company that sells computer technology products and consumer electronics online—set off a flurry of controversy among ad agencies and animal protection groups alike. "They do a slick job of depicting violence to animals . . . it's heinous," says an ASPCA spokesperson, who led a letter-writing effort against the campaign. PETA (People for Ethical Treatment of Animals) called it "one of the most reckless ad campaigns in years." Despite the criticism, however, the ads did draw attention—Outpost.com rocketed from near obscurity into the national spotlight in a matter of weeks.

Outpost.com's commercials are examples of a new genre of irreverent, cutting-edge advertising—commercials that intentionally create controversy, even if it means turning off some potential customers. In today's cluttered advertising environment, these ads go to extremes to get attention—you either love 'em or hate 'em. "It's the age-old question of breaking through the clutter," says the creative director of the ad agency that developed the Outpost.com ads. You turn to "anything you can to get noticed," he says. The ads follow a series of movie and television hits that feature crudeness, lewdness, black humour, or violence—*There's Something about Mary, American Pie, South Park.* "With such entertainment fare pushing the limits of bad taste, increasingly rude, nasty, or just plain boorish behavior is showing up in advertising campaigns as well," notes one analyst.

Indeed, the Outpost.com campaign is just one of many controversial ad efforts. Other examples abound. While flipping through your favourite magazine, you might encounter a Toyota ad targeting echo boomers with the headline "Attention nose pickers. . . ." On the next page is a boundary-pushing ad from Candies, featuring company spokesmodel Jenny McCarthy sitting on a toilet with her pants around her calves, wearing little more than her bright orange Candies shoes. In November 2000, Labatt Breweries was criticized by Bob Runciman, Ontario Minister of Consumer and Commercial Relations, for going too far in linking sex and drinking in its "Knowledge" TV spot for Carlsberg. The ad featured three women discussing one's new boyfriend and using a gesture to allude to the fact that the boyfriend enjoys performing oral sex.

In 1999, Palmer Jarvis DDB was severely criticized for a print ad it created for Vancouver's KOKO Productions Inc. that ran in *Marketing Magazine.* The ad featured a blood-covered baseball bat and the tag line, "Disappointed Coach" as well as a reference to the Dunbar Little League. A seemingly endless stream of complaints poured in to *Marketing's* editor including: "Whatever was in the agency's mind, the client's mind and your publication's mind to run this ad is beyond me. A baseball bat with the blood and matted hair of a child is meant to be funny? Shocking? Distasteful? Relevant? With the deaths of Reena Virk in Victoria, Matt Baranovski in a Toronto park late last year and the Columbine tragedy, I am left shaking my head in disbelief." The president of Palmer Jarvis published an apology stating, "While we are always trying to create communication messages that are impactful, this particular ad was in bad taste. We make ads which we hope people will find entertaining, exciting and memorable. In this case, we demonstrated a lack of judgment and for this we are truly sorry."

Outpost.com's marketers knew that the ads would be controversial: That was the point. "Our intent was to create memorable ads that would force people to remember our name," says an Outpost.com spokesperson. The agency creative director adds, "We told the people at Outpost that we didn't know if these ads were good or bad. What we

they will benefit from doing so. Therefore, developing an effective message strategy begins with identifying customer *benefits* that can be used as advertising appeals. In the search for benefits to feature, many creative people start by talking with consumers, dealers, experts, and competitors. Others try to imagine consumers buying or using the product to figure out the benefits they seek. Ideally, advertising message strategy will follow directly from the company's broader positioning strategy.

Ads on the edge: These ads go to extremes to bust through the clutter—either you love 'em or you hate 'em.

told them was that they were memorable—they'll get people to your Web site."

Mission accomplished. Outpost.com received 13 000 e-mails during the 10-week campaign; a surprising 60 percent of them were positive. More important, by the end of the campaign, business was booming. Outpost.com signed 15 000 new customers in the two weeks after the commercials first aired, and 30 000 new customers by the end of the campaign. At the end of the fiscal year, the company had nearly quadrupled its sales over the previous year. Moreover, as a testament to its cutting-edge creativity, the campaign amassed more than a dozen of the ad industry's highest awards and spawned many competitors.

Some industry critics questioned the campaign's long-term effectiveness. It appealed to only a narrow segment of viewers, they claimed, and did little to position Outpost.com or to tell people what it had to sell. In fact, Outpost.com shifted to a more informational campaign, which positions the company more firmly on its products and free overnight delivery policy.

When Canadian consumers believe that ads violate the Canadian Advertising Code or cross the boundary of good taste, they can file a complaint with Advertising Standards Canada (ASC). The foundation publishes an annual report that provides statistics on such complaints and reports about those complaints that were upheld. In 1999, for example, ASC received 1075 complaints. Seventeen percent of these complaints were upheld. Complaints centred on issues as diverse as concern about ads that showed random acts of violence directed at young children (the KOKO ad, for example), the use of nudity, and images or language suggestive of sexual activity.

Ads for which complaints were upheld in 1999 include a KIA Canada television ad that showed two women drivers aggressively competing for the same parking spot. The complaint stated that the commercial displayed a disregard for safety and could encourage unsafe or dangerous behaviour. Another ad that had to be withdrawn because it sexually objectified women was for Escape Lofts. The print ad showed a segmented, nude female body to promote apartments. Thus, while "on the edge ads" can undoubtedly attract attention, they can also offend and bring censure to both the firm and its agency.

Sources: Astrid Van Den Broek, "Gov't comes down on Carlsberg ad," *Marketing On-Line,* 27 November 2000; "Letters to the editor: The KOKO onslaught continues," *Marketing On-Line,* 10 January 2000; Advertising Standards Canada, *1999 Complaints Report,* www.adstandards.com/en/Standards/AdComplaintsReport.html; Melanie Wells, "Wanted: Television ad complaints," *USA Today,* 11 January 1999:4B; Dottie Enrico, "Creature feature," *TV Guide,* 23 January 1999:13; Hank Kim, "Creature feature," *Adweek,* 23 November 1998:20; Anthony Vagnoni, "'Something about this advertising," *Advertising Age,* 8 February 1999:30; Sara Sellar, "Pop goes the gerbil," *Sales & Marketing Management,* May 1999:15; Tom Kurtz, "Unsettling TV commercials: And now, a gross-out from our sponsor," *New York Times,* 25 July 1999:7; Stephanie Eads, "Eighty-six the flying gerbils," *Business Week,* 6 December 1999:52; and Debra Ako Williamson, "Outpost.com drops gerbils and wolves, touts free shipping," *Advertising Age,* 31 January 2000:70.

Message strategy statements tend to be plain, straightforward outlines of benefits and positioning points that the advertiser wants to stress. These strategy statements must be turned into advertisements that will persuade consumers to buy or believe something. The advertiser must develop a compelling *creative concept*—or *big idea*—that will bring the message strategy to life in a distinctive and memorable way. At this stage, simple message ideas become great ad campaigns. Usually, a copywriter and art director will team up to generate many creative concepts, hoping that one of these concepts will turn out to be the big idea. The creative concept may emerge as a visualization, a phrase, or a combination of the two.

The creative concept will guide the choice of specific appeals to be used in an advertising campaign. Advertising appeals should have three characteristics. First, they should be *meaningful,* pointing out benefits that make the product more desirable or interesting to consumers. Second, appeals must be *believable*—consumers must believe that the product or service will deliver the promised benefits. *Marketing Magazine* reports that only one-third of Canadians trust advertising.[13] If advertising is to be effective, viewers must view it as a credible source that communicates to them with integrity. Appeals should also be *distinctive*—they should tell how the product is better than the competing brands. For example, the most meaningful benefit of owning a wristwatch is that it keeps accurate time, yet few watch ads feature this benefit. Instead, based on the distinctive benefits they offer, watch advertisers might select any of a number of advertising themes. For years, Timex has been the affordable watch that "Took a lickin' and kept on tickin'," while Swatch has featured style and fashion, whereas Rolex stresses luxury and status.

Message Execution. The impact of the message depends not only on *what* is said, but also on *how* it is said. The advertiser has to turn the big idea into an actual ad execution that will capture the target market's attention and interest. The creative people must find the best style, tone, words, and format for executing the message. Any message can be presented in different *execution styles:*

- *Slice of life.* This style shows one or more "typical" people using the product in a normal setting. For example, Electric Library shows the face of a frustrated student trying to get a term paper completed.
- *Lifestyle.* This style shows how a product fits in with a particular lifestyle. For example, the Ontario Milk Marketing Board shows how active Canadians get their energy.

Electric Library uses slice-of-life advertising to target students with an image anyone writing a term paper can relate to.

- *Fantasy.* This style creates a fantasy around the product or its use. Perfume ads are famous for this type of advertising. The Gap even introduced a perfume named Dream: Ads show a woman sleeping blissfully and suggests that the scent is "the stuff that clouds are made of."
- *Mood or image.* This style builds a mood or image around the product, such as beauty, love, or serenity. No claim is made about the product except through suggestion. Bermuda tourism ads create such moods.
- *Musical.* This style shows one or more people or cartoon characters singing a song about the product. One of the most famous ads in history is a Coca-Cola ad built around the song, "I'd like to teach the world to sing."
- *Personality symbol.* This style creates a character that represents the product. The character can be *animated* (the Jolly Green Giant, Cap'n Crunch, Garfield the Cat) or *real* (Morris the 9-Lives Cat).
- *Technical expertise.* This style shows the company's expertise in making the product. Thus, Maxwell House shows one of its buyers carefully selecting the coffee beans, and Titleist explains its ability to make a better golf ball.
- *Scientific evidence.* This style presents survey or scientific evidence that the brand is better or better liked than one or more other brands. For years, Crest toothpaste has used scientific evidence to convince buyers that Crest is better than other brands at fighting cavities.
- *Testimonial evidence.* This style features a highly believable or likeable source that endorses the product. It could be celebrities, like Canadian figure skating pair Brasseur and Eisler (beef), or ordinary people saying how much they like a given product ("My doctor said Mylanta").

The advertiser also must choose a *tone* for the ad. Procter & Gamble always uses a positive tone: Its ads say something very positive about its products and avoid humour that might detract from the message. In contrast, Little Caesars' "pizza, pizza" ads use humour—in the form of the comical Little Caesars character—to drive home the advertiser's "two for the price of one" message.

The advertiser must use memorable and attention-getting *words* in the ad. For example, rather than claiming simply that "a BMW is a well-engineered automobile," BMW uses more creative and higher-impact phrasing: "The ultimate driving machine." London Life could promise prospective customers that it will help them plan for their retirement, but this would not have the impact of promising "Freedom 55."

Finally, *format* elements make a difference on an ad's impact as well as its cost. A small change in ad design can make a big difference on its effect. The *illustration* is the first thing the reader notices—it must be strong enough to draw attention. Next, the *headline* must effectively entice the right people to read the copy. Finally, the *copy*—the main block of text in the ad—must be simple but strong and convincing. Moreover, these three elements must effectively work *together*.

Short Man by Brown's, a specialty clothing retailer for the "vertically challenged," successfully followed these lessons in a recent award-winning series of magazine ads. The goal of the campaign was to attract new customers and infuse more life, notoriety, and personality into the brand. Before launching the ads, owner Lou Brown, the consummate Short Man, had reminded agency Holmes & Lee of Toronto that, "It had goddamn well better work, or you're dead."[14]

Selecting Advertising Media

The major steps in media selection are deciding on *reach, frequency,* and *impact;* choosing among major *media types;* selecting specific *media vehicles;* and deciding on *media timing.*

Ad agency Holmes & Lee took a stereotypical fashion standard and twisted it to develop arresting illustrations that made consumers laugh while looking at Short Man by Brown's in a fresh way.

Deciding on Reach, Frequency, and Impact. To select media, the advertiser must decide what reach and frequency are needed to achieve advertising objectives. **Reach** is a measure of the *percentage* of people in the target market who are exposed to the ad campaign over a given period of time. For example, the advertiser may try to reach 70 percent of the target market during the first three months of the campaign. **Frequency** is a measure of how many *times* the average person in the target market is exposed to the message. For example, the advertiser may want an average exposure frequency of three. The advertiser also must decide on the desired **media impact**—the *qualitative value* of a message exposure through a given medium. For example, for products that need to be demonstrated, messages on television may have more impact than messages on radio because television uses sight *and* sound. The same message in one magazine (say, *Maclean's*) may be more believable than in another (say, *The National Enquirer*). In general, the more reach, frequency, and impact the advertiser seeks, the higher the advertising budget will have to be.

Reach
The percentage of people in the target market exposed to an ad campaign during a given period.

Frequency
The number of times the average person in the target market is exposed to an advertising message during a given period.

Media impact
The qualitative value of a message exposure through a given medium.

Choosing among Major Media Types. The media planner must know the reach, frequency, and impact of each of the major media types. Table 14-2 summarizes the advantages and limitations of each of the major media types—newspapers, television, direct mail, radio, magazines, and outdoor.

Media planners consider many factors when making their media choices. The *media habits of target consumers* affect media choice—radio and television are the best media for reaching teenagers, for example. So will the *nature of the product*—fashions are best advertised in colour magazines, and Polaroid cameras are best demonstrated on television. Different *types of messages* may require different media. A message announcing a major sale tomorrow will require radio or newspapers; a message with a lot of technical data may require magazines or direct mailings. *Cost* is also a major factor in media choice. Television is very expensive; newspaper advertising costs much less. The media planner considers both the total cost of using a medium and the cost per thousand exposures—the cost of reaching 1000 people using the medium.

Media impact and cost must be re-examined regularly. For a long time, television and magazines dominated in the media mixes of national advertisers, with other media often neglected. However, the costs and clutter of these media have gone up, audiences have dropped, and marketers are adopting strategies beamed

TABLE 14-2 Profiles of Major Media Types

Medium	Advantages	Limitations
Newspapers	Flexibility; timeliness; good local market coverage; broad acceptability; high believability	Short life; poor reproduction quality; small pass-along audience
Television	Good mass-market coverage; low cost per exposure; combines sight, sound, and motion; appealing to the senses	High absolute costs; high clutter; fleeting exposure; less audience selectivity
Direct mail	High audience selectivity; flexibility; no ad competition within the same medium; allows personalization	Relatively high cost per exposure, "junk mail" image
Radio	Good local acceptance; high geographic and demographic selectivity; low cost	Audio only, fleeting exposure; low attention ("the half-heard" medium); fragmented audiences
Magazines	High geographic and demographic selectivity; credibility and prestige; high-quality reproduction; long life and good pass-along readership	Long ad purchase lead time; high cost; no guarantee of position
Outdoor	Flexibility; high repeat exposure; low cost; low message competition; good positional selectivity	Little audience selectivity; creative limitations
Internet	High selectivity; low cost; immediacy; interactive capabilities	Small, demographically skewed audience; relatively low impact; audience controls exposure

at narrower segments. As a result, advertisers are turning toward alternative media, ranging from cable TV and outdoor advertising to parking meters and shopping carts (see Marketing Highlight 14-2).

Media vehicles
Specific media within each general media type, such as specific magazines, television shows, or radio programs.

Selecting Specific Media Vehicles. The media planner next chooses the best **media vehicles**—specific media within each general media type. For example, television vehicles include *This Hour Has 22 Minutes*, *ER*, *Venture*, *Friends*, and *Hockey Night in Canada*. Magazine vehicles include *Maclean's*, *Equinox*, and *Chatelaine*. The media planner ultimately decides which vehicles give the best reach, frequency, and impact for the money.

Media planners also compute the cost per thousand persons reached by a vehicle. For example, if a full-page, four-colour advertisement in *Maclean's* costs

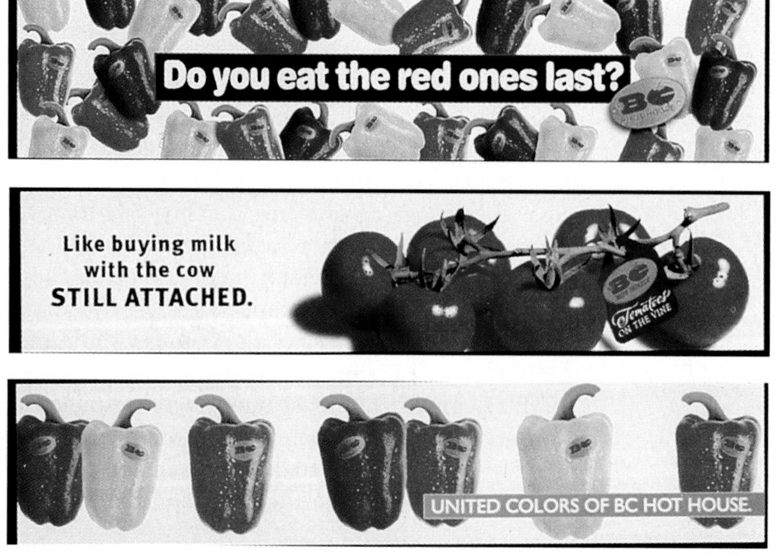

The media buyer for BC Hot House made it impossible to miss these ads placed on every bus within 300 kilometres of Vancouver.

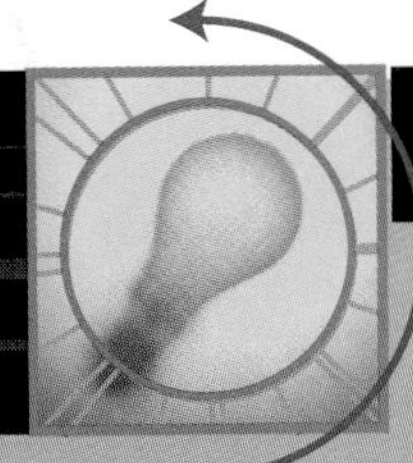

marketing highlight 14-2

Advertisers Seek Alternative Media

As network television costs soar and audiences shrink, many advertisers are looking for new ways to reach consumers. And the move toward micromarketing strategies, focused more narrowly on specific consumer groups, also has fuelled the search for alternative media to replace or supplement network television. Advertisers are shifting larger portions of their budgets to media that cost less and target more effectively.

The two media benefiting most from the shift are outdoor advertising and cable television. Billboards have undergone a resurgence in recent years. Although outdoor advertising spending recently levelled off, advertisers now spend more than $813 million annually on outdoor media, a 68 percent increase over a decade ago. Gone are the ugly eyesores of the past; in their place, we now see cleverly designed, colourful attention grabbers. Outdoor advertising provides an excellent way to reach important local consumer segments.

Cable television is also booming, with over 76 percent of all Canadian households subscribing. The launch of specialty channels has dramatically changed Canadian broadcasting: While the major channels still earn 90 percent of advertising revenues, such specialty channels as Bravo, the Discovery Channel, Life Network, the New Country Music, Showcase Television, and WTN are each now earning revenues in excess of $5 million. Moreover, they are continuing to attract an ever-larger audience and, even more importantly, their ad revenue growth is increasing at a rate of 9.3 percent compared to the three percent gain experienced by conventional TV. These channels are expected to penetrate 60 percent of Canadian households in the near future. Not only do these stations offer the benefit of delivering highly targeted audiences, but their audiences may also have been difficult to reach by traditional means. MuchMusic, for example, presents an avenue to communicate with hard-to-reach teens, while stations like Bravo attract upscale female audiences.

Specialty channels are a bargain compared to many other forms of media advertising. Not only are they 25 to 50 percent cheaper than national television, but they are also giving magazines a run for their money. An advertiser can run a month-long campaign on a specialty channel for about the price of buying a full-page colour ad in some print media. These low prices have attracted many new advertisers to television. YTV, for example, has begun targeting small toy manufacturers that previously could not consider television advertising because of its prohibitive costs.

Cable television and outdoor advertising seem to make good sense. But, increasingly, ads are popping up in far less likely places. In their efforts to find less costly and more highly targeted ways to reach consumers, advertisers have discovered a dazzling collection of "alternative media." As consumers, we're used to ads on television, in magazines and newspapers, on the radio, and along the roadways. But these days, no matter where you go or what you do, you probably will run into some new form of advertising.

You escape to the ballpark, only to find billboard-size video screens running Labatt Blue ads, while a blimp with an electronic message board circles lazily overhead. You pay to see a movie at your local theatre, but first you see a two-minute science fiction fantasy that turns out to be an ad for General Electric portable stereo boxes. Then the movie itself is full of not-so-subtle promotional plugs for Pepsi, Domino's Pizza, Alka-Seltzer, MasterCard, Fritos, or any of a dozen other products. You sit down to rest your weary feet in the eating area of your local mall only to find the table top covered by an ad. An even bigger surprise is that the sponsor is The Body Shop, which, up until now, has avoided advertising and relied on publicity. In Guelph, Ontario, you pass school buses carrying exterior ads with social messages. Boats cruise along public beaches flashing advertising messages for Sundown Sunscreen or Gatorade to sunbathers. Advertisers seeking a really out-of-this-world alternative can pay $500 000 for 58 feet of prime advertising space on the hull of a Conestoga 1620 expendable rocket launched by NASA.

Some of these alternative media seem a bit far-fetched, and they sometimes irritate consumers. But for many marketers, these media can save money and provide a way to hit selected consumers where they live, shop, work, and play.

Marketers have discovered a dazzling array of "alternative media."

This may leave you wondering if there are any commercial-free havens remaining for ad-weary consumers. Forget it! Even the back seat of taxis, public elevators, and stalls in public restrooms have been invaded by innovative marketers.

Sources: See Alison Leigh Cowan, "Marketers worry as ads crop up in unlikely places," *Raleigh News and Observer*, 21 February 1988:11; Kathy Martin, "What's next? Execs muse over boundless ad possibilities," *Advertising Age*, 27 August 1990; John P. Cortez, "Ads head for the bathroom," *Advertising Age*, 18 May 1992:24; Ronald Grover, Laura Zinn, and Irene Recio, "Big brother is grocery shopping with you," *Business Week*, 29 March 1993:60; Richard Szathmary, "The great (and not so great) outdoors," *Sales & Marketing Management*, March 1992:75–81; Riccardo A. Davis, "More ads go outdoors," *Advertising Age*, 9 November 1992:36; "Special report: Cable TV," *Advertising Age*, 27 March 1995:51–3; "Redrawing the TV map," *Marketing*, 30 October 1995:13; Jim McElgunn, "Who's watching what?" *Marketing*, 29 May 1995:14–15; Andrea Haman, "Boom still on for specialties," *Marketing*, 30 October 1995:30–1; Marina Strauss, "Is there no hiding place left?" *Globe and Mail*, 18 January 1996:B12; and Canadian Media Directors' Council *95–96 Media Digest*.

$30 563 and *Maclean's* readership is 510 319 people, the cost of reaching each group of 1000 persons is about $60. The same advertisement in *Shift Magazine* may cost only $8125 but reach only 68 012 persons—at a cost per thousand of about $119. The media planner would rank each magazine by cost per thousand and favour those magazines with the lower cost per thousand for reaching target consumers.

The media planner must consider the costs of producing ads for different media. Whereas newspaper ads can cost very little to produce, flashy television ads can cost millions. On average, advertisers pay $450 000 to produce a single 30-second television commercial, though Nike paid a cool $2.8 million to make a single ad called "The Wall."[15]

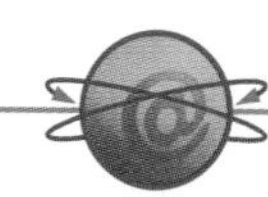

Nike Canada
www.nike.com/canada/

In selecting media vehicles, the media planner must balance media cost measures against several media impact factors. First, the planner must balance costs against the media vehicle's *audience quality*. For a baby lotion advertisement, for example, *New Mother* magazine would have a high-exposure value; *The Hockey News* would have a low-exposure value. Second, the planner must consider *audience attention*. Readers of *Flare*, for example, typically pay more attention to ads than do *The Economist* readers. Third, the planner must assess the vehicle's *editorial quality*—*Maclean's* and *Canadian Business* are more believable and prestigious than *The National Enquirer*.

Deciding on Media Timing. The advertiser also must decide how to schedule the advertising over the course of a year. Suppose sales of a product peak in December and drop in March. The firm can vary its advertising to follow the seasonal pattern, to oppose the seasonal pattern, or to be the same all year. Most firms do some seasonal advertising. Some do *only* seasonal advertising: For example, Hallmark advertises its greeting cards only before major holidays.

Finally, the advertiser must choose the pattern of the ads. *Continuity* means scheduling ads evenly within a given period. *Pulsing* means scheduling ads unevenly over a given time period. Thus, 52 ads could either be scheduled at one per week during the year or pulsed in several bursts. The idea is to advertise heavily for a short period to build awareness that carries over to the next advertising period. Those who favour pulsing feel that it can be used to achieve the same impact as a steady schedule, but at a much lower cost. However, some media planners believe that although pulsing achieves minimal awareness, it sacrifices depth of advertising communications.

Recent advances in technology have had a substantial impact on the media planning and buying functions. New computer software applications—optimizers—allow media planners to evaluate many combinations of television programs and prices. This helps them make better decisions about which mix of networks, programs, and day parts will yield the highest reach per ad dollar.[16]

Evaluating Advertising

The advertising program should regularly evaluate both the *communication effects* and the *sales effects* of advertising. Measuring the communication effect of an ad—*copy testing*—tells whether the ad is communicating well. Copy testing can be done before or after an ad is printed or broadcast. Before the ad is placed, the advertiser can show it to consumers, ask how they like it, and measure recall or attitude changes resulting from it. After the ad is run, the advertiser can measure how the ad affected consumer recall or product awareness, knowledge, and preference.

But what sales are caused by an ad that increases brand awareness by 20 percent and brand preference by 10 percent? The sales effect of advertising is harder to measure than the communication effect. Sales are affected by many factors besides advertising—such as product features, price, and availability.

One way to measure the sales effect of advertising is to compare past sales with past advertising expenditures. Another way is through experiments. For example, to test the effects of different advertising spending levels, Pizza Hut could vary the amount it spends on advertising in different market areas and measure the differences in the resulting sales levels. It could spend the normal amount in one market area, half the normal amount in another area, and twice the normal amount in a third area. If the three market areas are similar and all other marketing efforts in the area are the same, then differences in sales in the three cities could be related to advertising level. More complex experiments can include other variables, such as difference in the ads or media used.

Other Advertising Considerations

In developing advertising strategies and programs, the company must address two additional questions: First, how will it organize its advertising function—who will perform which advertising tasks? Second, how will it adapt its advertising strategies and programs to the complexities of international markets?

Organizing for Advertising

Companies organize in different ways to handle advertising. In small companies, someone in the sales department may handle advertising. Large companies set up advertising departments whose job it is to set the advertising budget, work with the ad agency, and handle direct-mail advertising, dealer displays, and other advertising not done by the agency. Most large companies use outside advertising agencies because they offer several advantages.

Advertising agency
A marketing services firm that assists companies in planning, preparing, implementing, and evaluating their advertising programs.

How does an **advertising agency** work? Advertising agencies were started in the 1800s by salespeople and brokers who worked for the media and received a commission for selling advertising space to companies. As time passed, the salespeople began to help customers prepare their ads. Eventually, they formed agencies and grew closer to the advertisers than to the media. Today's agencies employ specialists who often perform advertising tasks better than the company's own staff. Agencies also bring an outside perspective to solving the company's problems, along with a lot of experience from working with different clients and situations. Therefore, even companies with strong advertising departments use advertising agencies.

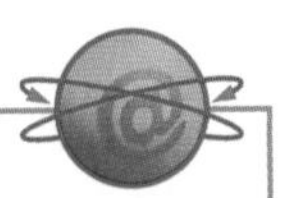

Cossette Communication Group
www.cossette.com/

Some ad agencies are huge. Take Canada's top three agencies. Cossette Communication Group Inc., headquartered in Quebec City, is Canada's largest agency with revenues exceeding $94 million. Toronto's MacLaren McCann Canada Inc. takes second place with $71 million in revenues. The Young & Rubicam Group of Companies, also headquartered in Toronto, has revenues of almost $69 million. Other agencies operate on a much smaller scale, but can still win big accounts. TAXI Advertising & Design, for example, lists Chapters, Clearnet, Pfizer, and

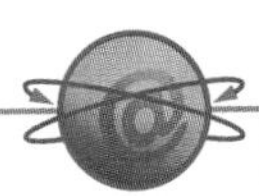

MacLaren McCann
www.maclaren.com/

Young & Rubicam
www.yr.com/

TAXI Advertising and Design
www.taxi.ca/

Unilever among its clients.[17] Having Canadian agencies with insight into our unique marketplaces is important. A recent survey revealed that 45 percent of English Canada say they care a lot about whether the commercials they view on television are created in Canada. This percentage is even higher in Quebec, where 58 percent of the respondents stressed that they want commercials especially designed for them. Canadian viewers also believe that they can tell whether a commercial is Canadian made.[18]

Most large advertising agencies have the staff and resources to handle all phases of an advertising campaign for their clients, from creating a marketing plan to developing ad campaigns and preparing, placing, and evaluating ads. Agencies usually have four departments: creative, which develops and produces ads; media, which selects media and places ads; research, which studies audience characteristics and wants; and business, which handles the agency's business activities. Each account is supervised by an account executive, and people in each department are usually assigned to work on one or more accounts.

Ad agencies traditionally have been paid through commissions and fees. In the past, the agency typically received 15 percent of the media cost as a rebate. Therefore, an agency that bought $60 000 of magazine space for a client would be billed $51 000 ($60 000 less 15 percent) by the magazine, and would in turn bill the client for $60 000, keeping the $9000 commission. If the client purchased space directly from the magazine, it would have paid $60 000 because commissions are only paid to recognized advertising agencies.

However, both advertisers and agencies have become increasingly dissatisfied with the commission system. Larger advertisers complain that they pay more for the same services received by smaller ones simply because they place more advertising. Advertisers also believe that the commission system drives agencies away from low-cost media and short advertising campaigns. Agencies are dissatisfied because they perform extra services for an account without receiving additional pay.

As one advertising analyst notes, "The commission formula tends to encourage costly media buys and has been criticized for overlooking important emerging mediums such as the Internet. . . [Therefore] the 15 percent commission on media spending that . . . was once standard in the advertising business . . . is about as dead as the three-martini lunch." New agency payment methods include anything from fixed retainers or straight hourly fees for labour to incentives keyed to performance of the agencies' ad campaigns, or some combination of these.[19]

Another trend affecting the advertising agency business is increased polarization of agencies—some are becoming more diversified, others are becoming more specialized. The new diversified agencies offer a complete list of integrated marketing and promotion services under one roof, including advertising, sales promotion, marketing research, public relations, and direct and online marketing. Some have even added marketing consulting, television production, and sales training units in an effort to become full "marketing partners" to their clients. Other specialized and focused "creative boutiques" are smaller and offer limited services.

International Advertising Decisions

International advertisers face many complexities not encountered by domestic advertisers. The most basic issue is the degree to which global advertising should be adapted to the unique characteristics of various country markets. Some large advertisers have attempted to support their global brands with highly standardized worldwide advertising, with campaigns that work as well in Bangkok as they do in Burlington. For example, Jeep created a worldwide brand image of ruggedness and reliability. Gillette's ads for its Sensor Excel for Women are almost identical worldwide, with only minor adjustments to suit the local culture. Ericsson, the Swedish telecommunications giant, spent $150 million on a standardized global

Gillette's Sensor Excel for Women ads are almost identical worldwide, with only minor adjustments to suit the local culture.

television campaign with the tag line "make yourself heard," which featured Agent 007, James Bond.

Standardization produces many benefits—lower advertising costs, greater global advertising coordination, and a more consistent worldwide image. But it also has drawbacks. Most importantly, it ignores the fact that country markets differ greatly in their cultures, demographics, and economic conditions. Therefore, most international advertisers "think globally but act locally." They develop global advertising strategies that make their worldwide advertising efforts more efficient and consistent. Then they adapt their advertising programs to make them more responsive to consumer needs and expectations within local markets.

Coca-Cola, for example, has a pool of commercials that can be used in or adapted to several international markets. Some can be used with only minor changes—such as language—in several countries. Local and regional managers decide which commercials work best for which markets. Recently, in a reverse of the usual order, a series of Coca-Cola commercials developed for the Russian market, using a talking bear and a man who transforms into a wolf, was shown in the United States. "This approach fits perfectly with the global nature of Coca-Cola," says the president of Coca-Cola's Nordic division. "[It] offers people a special look into a culture that is different from their own."[20]

Global advertisers face some special problems. Advertising media costs and availability differ greatly between countries. Countries also differ in the extent to which they regulate advertising practices. Many countries have extensive systems of laws restricting how much a company can spend on advertising, the media used, the nature of advertising claims, and other aspects of the advertising program. Such restrictions often require advertisers to adapt their campaigns from country to country.

For example, alcoholic products cannot be advertised or sold in Muslim countries. Tobacco products are subject to strict regulation in many countries—Canada and the United Kingdom, for example, ban all tobacco advertising, including sports sponsorships by tobacco companies.

Regulations on advertising to children also vary widely. While in some countries, like the US, there are no restrictions, in others, like Norway and Sweden, for example, no TV ads may be directed at children under 12. In Canada, Quebec forbids advertising aimed at children under 13. To play it safe, McDonald's advertises itself as a family restaurant in countries with these restrictions.

Adjust decision & chip focus.

Comparative ads, while acceptable and even common in the US and Canada, are less commonly used in the United Kingdom, unacceptable in Japan, and illegal in India and Brazil. PepsiCo found that its comparative taste test ad in Japan was refused by many television stations and actually led to a lawsuit. China has restrictive censorship rules for TV and radio advertising; for example, the words "the best" are banned, as are ads that "violate social customs" or present women in "improper ways." Coca-Cola's Indian subsidiary was forced to end a promotion that offered prizes, such as a trip to Hollywood, because it violated India's established trade practices by encouraging customers to buy to "gamble."[21]

Thus, although advertisers may develop global strategies to guide their overall advertising efforts, specific advertising programs are usually adapted to meet the requirements of local cultures, customs, media characteristics, and regulations.

Sales Promotion

Sales promotion
Short-term incentives to encourage purchase or sale of a product or service.

Advertising and personal selling often work closely with another promotion tool—sales promotion. **Sales promotion** consists of short-term incentives to encourage the purchase or sale of a product or service. Whereas advertising and personal selling offer reasons to buy a product or service, sales promotion offers reasons to buy now. It includes a variety of promotion tools designed to stimulate this earlier or stronger market response.

Sales promotions are found everywhere. A free-standing insert in the Sunday newspaper contains a coupon offering 50 cents off President's Choice coffee. An e-mail from CDNow offers $5.00 off your next CD purchase over $9.99. The end-of-the-aisle display in the local supermarket tempts impulse buyers with a wall of Coke cartons. An executive who buys a new Compaq laptop computer gets a free carrying case. A family buys a new Taurus and receives a rebate cheque for $500. A hardware store chain receives a 10 percent discount on selected Black & Decker portable power tools if it agrees to advertise them in local newspapers.

Rapid Growth of Sales Promotion

Consumer promotion
Sales promotion designed to stimulate consumer purchasing.

Trade promotion
Sales promotion designed to gain reseller support and to improve reseller selling efforts.

Sales force promotion
Sales promotion designed to motivate the sales force and make its selling efforts more effective.

Business promotion
Sales promotion designed to generate business leads, stimulate purchase, reward customers, and motivate salespeople.

Sales promotion tools are used by most organizations, including manufacturers, distributors, retailers, trade associations, and non-profit institutions. **Consumer promotions** are targeted toward final buyers, **trade promotions** to retailers and wholesalers, **sales force promotions** to members of the sales force, and **business promotions** to business customers. In the average consumer packaged goods company, sales promotion accounts for 74 percent of all marketing expenditures.[22]

Several factors have contributed to the rapid growth of sales promotion, particularly in consumer markets. Inside the company, product managers face greater pressures to increase their current sales, and promotion now is accepted more by top management as an effective sales tool. Externally, the company faces more competition, competing brands are less differentiated, competitors are using more promotions, and consumers have become more deal-oriented. Advertising efficiency has declined because of rising costs, media clutter, and legal restraints. Finally, retailers are demanding more deals from manufacturers.

The growing use of sales promotion has resulted in *promotion clutter,* similar to advertising clutter. Consumers are increasingly tuning out promotions, weakening their ability to trigger immediate purchase. To rise above the clutter, therefore, manufacturers are offering larger coupon values or creating more dramatic point-of-purchase displays.

In developing a sales promotion program, a company must first set sales promotion objectives and then select the best tools for accomplishing these objectives.

Sales Promotion Objectives

Sales promotion objectives vary widely. Sellers can use consumer promotions to increase short-term sales or to help build long-term market share. The objective may be to entice consumers to try a new product, lure consumers away from competitors' products, get consumers to "load up" on a mature product, or hold and reward loyal customers. Objectives for trade promotions include getting retailers to carry new items and more inventory, getting them to advertise the product and give it more shelf space, and getting them to buy ahead. For the sales force promotions, objectives include getting more sales force support for current or new products or getting salespeople to sign up new accounts.

Kraft Canada
www.kraftfoods.com/canada/

In general, sales promotions should aim at *consumer relationship building.* Rather than creating only short-term sales volume or temporary brand switching, they should help to reinforce the product's position and build long-term relationships with consumers. This is what Kraft Canada has done with its magazine, *What's Cooking.* Included in newspapers as a free-standing insert, the booklet contains letters from consumers, cooking tips, information on maintaining a healthy diet, recipes using Kraft products, and Kraft's toll-free number, which consumers can call to get more "good food ideas." Consumers look forward to receiving the magazine, and many keep it and refer to it for years to come. In such a way, marketers avoid "quick-fix," price-only promotions in favour of promotions designed to build brand equity.

The "loyalty marketing programs" that have mushroomed in recent years are other examples of sales promotions used to solidify relationships with customers. For instance, the Second Cup sponsors a "frequent buyer" program whereby regular customers receive free cups of coffee as well as coffee beans.

Major Sales Promotion Tools

Many tools are available to accomplish sales promotion objectives.

Consumer Promotion Tools

The main consumer promotion tools are samples, coupons, cash refunds, price packs, premiums, advertising specialties, patronage rewards, point-of-purchase displays and demonstrations, and contests, sweepstakes, and games.

Samples
Offers to consumers of a trial amount of a product.

Samples are offers of a trial amount of a product. Sampling is the most effective—but most expensive—way to introduce a new product. Some samples are free; for others, the company charges a small amount to offset its cost. The sample might be delivered door-to-door, sent by mail, handed out in a store, attached to another product, or featured in an ad. Sometimes, samples are combined into sample packs, which can then be used to promote other products and services. Procter & Gamble has even distributed samples via the Internet:[23]

When Procter & Gamble decided to relaunch Pert Plus shampoo, it extended its $30 million ad campaign by constructing a new Web site (**www.pertplus.com**). P&G had three objectives for the Web site: Create awareness for reformulated Pert Plus, get consumers to try the product, and gather data about Web users. The site's first page invites visitors to place their heads against the computer screen in a mock attempt to measure the cleanliness of their hair. After "tabulating the results," the site tells visitors that they "need immediate help." The solution: "How about a free sample of new Pert Plus?" Visitors obtain the sample by filling out a short demographic form. The site offers other interesting features as well. For example, clicking "get a friend in a lather" produces a template that will send an e-mail to a friend with an invitation to visit the site and receive a free sample. How did the sampling promotion work out? Even P&G was shocked by the turnout. Within just two months of launching the site, 170 000 people visited and 83 000 requested samples. More surprising, given that the site is only 10 pages deep, the average person visited the site 1.9 times and spent a total of 7.5 minutes each visit.

Sampling has grown rapidly in Canada. Recent research has shown that when given a choice between a free sample and a coupon, 92 percent of consumers prefer a sample. Since aging consumers are less likely to try new products, manufacturers like sampling because it provides a risk-free way for consumers to try a new product. Since a person is hired to conduct most in-store sampling programs, consumers can also ask for more information about a product. Retailers also like sampling programs because they add excitement to the in-store shopping experience. Sampling is becoming so popular, however, that manufacturers must become increasingly creative and targeted with their sampling programs. Grocery shoppers, for example, may be offered up to 10 samples each time they enter a store.[24]

Coupons
Certificates that give buyers a saving when they purchase a specified product.

Coupons are certificates that give buyers a saving when they purchase specified products. They are supposed to generate excitement and competition among brands, but an increasing number of manufacturers believe that couponing is expensive and inefficient. To improve efficiency, many manufacturers and retailers are turning to e-coupons. Toronto-based Val-Pak of Canada, whose direct mail blue envelopes are ubiquitous across the country, recently launched **ValPak.com** to distribute coupons electronically. "What's really good is people can go on there whenever they want, print when they want and print off what they may use versus receiving coupons that they won't use," says Stany Bergeron, director of operations at Val-Pak.[25]

Heaviest coupon users in Canada tend to be women, between the ages of 35 and 49, with families and incomes over $35 000. Quebec residents use more coupons than do consumers in the other provinces.

Within just two months, the P&G Pert Plus Web site received 170 000 visitors and 83 000 sample requests.

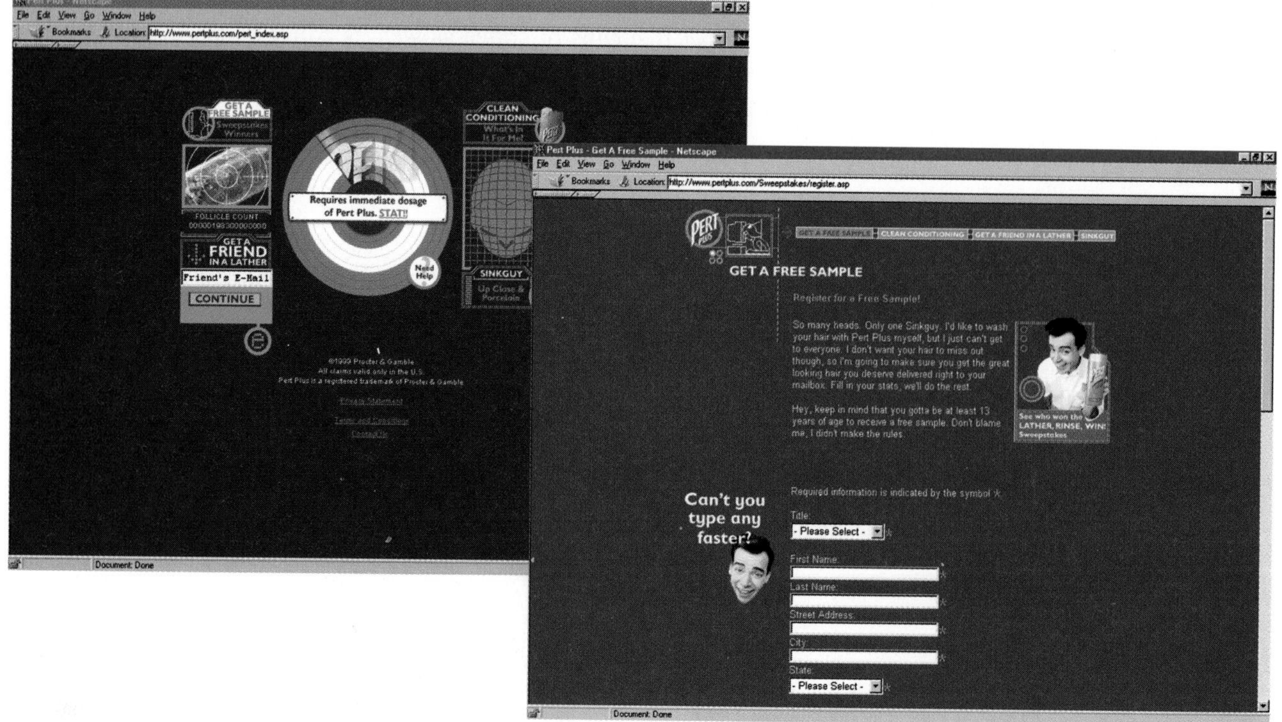

Cash refund offers (rebates)
Offers to refund part of the purchase price of a product to consumers who send a "proof of purchase" to the manufacturer.

Cash refund offers, or **rebates**, are like coupons except that the price reduction occurs after the purchase rather than at the retail outlet. The consumer sends a "proof of purchase" to the manufacturer, who then refunds part of the purchase price by mail. Toro ran a clever pre-season promotion on some of its snow blower models, offering a rebate if the snowfall in the buyer's market area turned out to be below average. Competitors were not able to match this offer on such short notice, and the promotion was very successful.

Price packs (cents-off deals)
Reduced prices that are marked by the producer directly on the label or package.

Price packs (also called **cents-off deals**) offer consumers savings off the regular price of a product. The reduced prices are marked by the producer directly on the label or package. Price packs can be single packages sold at a reduced price (such as two for the price of one), or two related products banded together (such as a toothbrush and toothpaste). Price packs are very effective—even more so than coupons—in stimulating short-term sales.

Premiums
Goods offered either free or at low cost as an incentive to buy a product.

Premiums are goods offered either free or at low cost as an incentive to buy a product. A premium may come inside the package (in-pack) or outside the package (on-pack). If reusable, the package itself may serve as a premium—such as a decorative tin. Premiums are sometimes mailed to consumers who have sent in a proof of purchase, such as a box top. "Drink it. Get it." was the slogan for the Pepsi Stuff premium offer that one industry analyst called the "most successful promotion run in Canada in the last 40 years." Pepsi added value to a purchase of their product in a highly "youth-relevant" way by letting people redeem points of specially marked packages for "must-be-seen" merchandise from the Pepsi stuff catalogue. Eighty-one percent of soft-drink users were aware of the offer. The promotion increased Pepsi's market share by seven percent. While 53 percent of the gain came from people switching brands, the remainder came because heavy Pepsi drinkers consumed more product. Although the share gains are impressive, the program also improved consumer attitude and imagery measures of Pepsi.[26]

Advertising specialties
Useful articles imprinted with an advertiser's name, given as gifts to consumers.

Advertising specialties are useful articles imprinted with an advertiser's name given as gifts to consumers. Typical items are baseball caps, pens, calendars, key rings, matches, shopping bags, T-shirts, caps, nail files, and coffee mugs. Such items can be very effective promotions. In a recent study, 63 percent of all consumers surveyed were either carrying or wearing an ad specialty item. More than three-quarters of those who had an item could recall the advertiser's name or message before showing the item to the interviewer.[27]

Patronage rewards
Cash or other awards for the regular use of a certain company's products or services.

Patronage rewards are cash or other awards offered for the regular use of a certain company's products or services. Airlines offer "frequent flyer plans," awarding points for miles travelled that can be turned in for free airline trips. Marriott Hotels adopted an "honoured guest" plan that awards points to users of their hotels. Baskin-Robbins offers frequent-purchase awards—for every 10 purchases, customers receive a free litre of ice cream.

Point-of-purchase (POP) promotions
Displays and demonstrations at the point of purchase or sale.

Point-of-purchase (POP) promotions include displays and demonstrations at the point of purchase or sale, such as the five-foot-high cardboard display of Cap'n Crunch next to Cap'n Crunch cereal boxes. Unfortunately, many retailers do not like to handle the hundreds of displays, signs, and posters they receive from manufacturers each year. Manufacturers have responded by offering better POP materials, tying them in with television or print messages, and offering to set them up.

Contests, sweepstakes, games
Promotional events that give consumers the chance to win something—such as cash, trips, or goods—by luck or through extra effort.

Contests, sweepstakes, and **games** such as Tim Hortons' "roll up the rim to win" give consumers the chance to win something, such as cash, trips, or goods, by luck or through extra effort. A *contest* calls for consumers to submit an entry—a jingle, guess, suggestion—to be judged by a panel that will select the best entries. A *sweepstakes* calls for consumers to submit their names for a drawing. A *game* presents consumers with something—bingo numbers, missing letters—every time they buy, which may or may not help them win a prize. A sales contest urges dealers or the sales force to increase their efforts, with prizes going to the top performers.

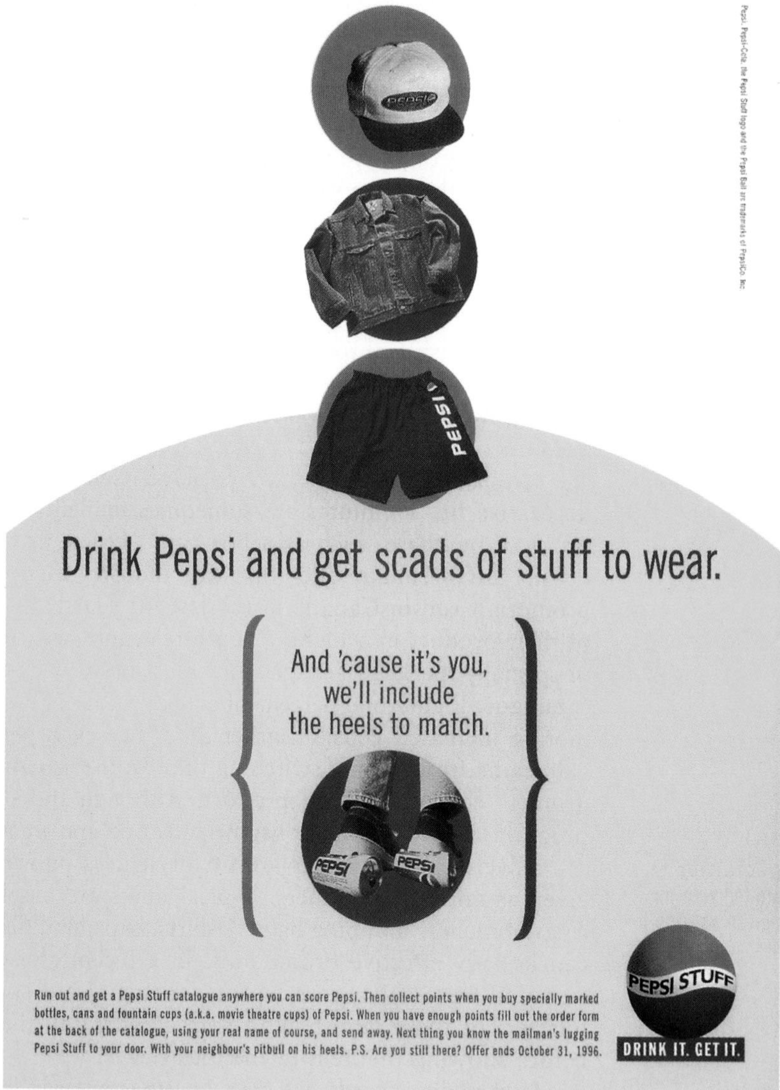

The Pepsi Stuff program was heralded as the most successful promotional campaign to run in Canada in 40 years.

Trade Promotion Tools

More sales promotion dollars are directed to retailers and wholesalers (68%) than to consumers. Trade promotion can persuade retailers or wholesalers to carry a brand, give it shelf space, promote it in advertising, and push it to consumers. Shelf space is so scarce these days that manufacturers often have to offer price-offs, allowances, buy-back guarantees, or free goods to retailers and wholesalers to get on the shelf and, once there, to stay on it.

Manufacturers use several trade promotion tools. Many are the same tools used for consumer promotions—contests, premiums, displays. Or the manufacturer may offer a straight **discount** off the list price on each case purchased during a stated period of time (also called a *price-off, off-invoice,* or *off-list*). The offer encourages dealers to buy in quantity or to carry a new item. Dealers can use the discount for immediate profit, advertising, or price reductions to their customers.

Discount
A straight reduction in price on purchases during a stated period of time.

Manufacturers also may offer an **allowance** (usually so much off per case) in return for the retailer's agreement to feature the manufacturer's products in some way. An *advertising allowance* compensates retailers for advertising the product. A *display allowance* compensates them for using special displays.

Allowance
Promotional money paid by manufacturers to retailers in return for an agreement to feature the manufacturer's products in some way.

Manufacturers may offer *free goods*—extra cases of merchandise—to intermediaries who buy a certain quantity or who feature a certain flavour or size.

They may offer *push money*—cash or gifts—to dealers or their sales force to "push" the manufacturer's goods. Manufacturers may give retailers free *specialty advertising items* that carry the company's name, such as pens, pencils, calendars, paperweights, matchbooks, and memo pads.

Business Promotion Tools

Companies spend billions of dollars each year on promotion to industrial customers. They use these business promotions to generate business leads, stimulate purchases, reward customers, and motivate salespeople. Business promotion includes many of the same tools used for consumer or trade promotions. Here, we focus on two major business promotion tools—conventions and trade shows, and sales contests.

Many companies and trade associations organize *conventions and trade shows* to promote their products. Firms selling to the industry show their products at the trade show. Every year, over 4300 trade shows worldwide draw about 85 million people. John Treleaven, director of trade planning and operations for the International Business Development Bureau at the Department of Foreign Affairs and International Trade in Ottawa says, "Trade fairs are the most powerful marketing tool at the disposal of Canadian exporters."[28] The success of trade shows is revealed in the bottom lines of many Canadian companies. Recently, the 400 Canadian firms that displayed their wares at the 40 largest German trade fairs rang up more than $250 million in sales. Vendors receive many benefits, such as opportunities to find new sales leads, contact customers, introduce new products, meet new customers, sell more to present customers, and educate customers with publications and audiovisual materials. Trade shows also help companies reach many prospects not reached through their sales forces. In emerging economies, such as Russia, where conventional marketing and media channels are underdeveloped, trade fairs are the only means of reaching potential buyers. Business marketers may spend as much as 35 percent of their annual promotion budgets on trade shows.

A *sales contest* is a contest for salespeople or dealers to motivate them to increase their sales performance over a given period. Called "incentive programs,"

At this consumer electronics trade show, 2000 exhibitors attracted over 91 000 professional visitors.

these contests motivate and recognize good company performers, who may receive trips, cash prizes, or other gifts. Some companies award points for performance, which the receiver can turn in for any of a variety of prizes. Sales contests work best when they are tied to measurable and achievable sales objectives, such as finding new accounts, reviving old accounts, or increasing account profitability.

Developing the Sales Promotion Program

The marketer must make several decisions to define the full sales promotion program. First is the *size of the incentive:* A minimum incentive is necessary if the promotion is to succeed; a larger incentive will produce more sales response. The marketer also must set *conditions for participation.* Incentives may be offered to everyone or only to select groups.

The marketer must decide how to *promote and distribute the promotion* program itself. A 50-cents-off coupon could be given out in a package, at the store, by mail, or in an advertisement. Each distribution method involves a different level of reach and cost. Increasingly, marketers are blending several media into a total campaign concept. The *length of the promotion* is also important. If the sales promotion period is too short, many prospects (who may not be buying during that time) will miss it. If the promotion runs too long, the deal will lose some of its "act now" force. Finally, the marketer must determine the *sales promotion budget.* The most common way is to use a percentage of the total budget for sales promotion. A better way is the objective-and-task method discussed in the previous chapter.

Evaluation is very important, yet many companies fail to evaluate their sales promotion programs, and others evaluate them only superficially. The most common evaluation methods is to compare sales before, during, and after a promotion. Suppose a company has a six percent market share before the promotion, which jumps to ten percent during the promotion, falls to five percent right after, and rises to seven percent later on. The promotion seems to have attracted new users and more buying from current customers. After the promotion, sales fell as consumers used up their inventories. The long-run rise to seven percent means that the company gained some new users. If the brand's share had returned to the old level, then the promotion would have changed only the *timing* of demand rather than the *total* demand.

Consumer research also would show the kinds of people who responded to the promotion and what they did after it ended. *Surveys* can provide information on how many consumers recall the promotion, what they thought of it, how many took advantage of it, and how it affected their buying. Sales promotions also can be evaluated through *experiments* that vary such factors as incentive value, length, and distribution method.

Clearly, sales promotion plays an important role in the total promotion mix. To use it well, the marketer must define the sales promotion objectives, select the best tools, design the sales promotion program, pre-test and implement the program, and evaluate the results.

Public Relations

Public relations
Building good relations with the company's various publics by obtaining favourable publicity, building up a good "corporate image," and handling or heading off unfavourable rumours, stories, and events.

Another major mass promotion tool is **public relations**—building good relations with the company's various publics by obtaining favourable publicity, building up a good "corporate image," and handling or heading off unfavourable rumours, stories, and events. Public relations (PR) departments may perform any or all of the following functions:

- *Press relations or press agentry:* Creating and placing newsworthy information in the media to attract attention to a person, product, or service. The Canada

Canada NewsWire
www.newswire.ca/

NewsWire Web site has many examples of different firms' press releases.

- *Product publicity:* Publicizing specific products.
- *Public affairs:* Building and maintaining national or local community relations.
- *Lobbying:* Building and maintaining relations with legislators and government officials to influence legislation and regulation.
- *Investor relations:* Maintaining relationships with shareholders and others in the financial community.
- *Development:* PR with donors or members of non-profit organizations to gain financial or volunteer support.

Public relations is used to promote products, people, places, ideas, activities, organizations, and even nations. Marketing boards have used PR to rebuild interest in declining commodities such as eggs, apples, milk, and potatoes. The Canadian Dietetic Association credits effective PR for the nearly 15 000 calls it received during one March Nutrition Month program—34 percent more than expected.[29] New York City turned around its image when its "I Love New York" campaign took root, attracting millions more tourists to the city. Johnson & Johnson's masterly use of PR played a major role in saving Tylenol from extinction after its product-tampering scare. Nations have used PR to attract more tourists, foreign investment, and international support.

Public relations can have a strong impact on public awareness at a much lower cost than advertising (see Marketing Highlight 14-3). The company does not pay for the space or time in the media. Rather, it pays for a staff to develop and circulate information and to manage events. If the company develops an interesting story, it may be picked up by several media, having the same effect as advertising that would cost millions of dollars. And it would have more credibility than advertising. Public relations results can sometimes be spectacular.

Public relations can also be used to help overcome corporate crisis. Whistler Mountain Resort Association faced such a crisis when its Quicksilver chair failed, detaching several chairs from the cable and injuring several skiers and killing one. Whistler's marketing director David Perry's first priority was to manage informa-

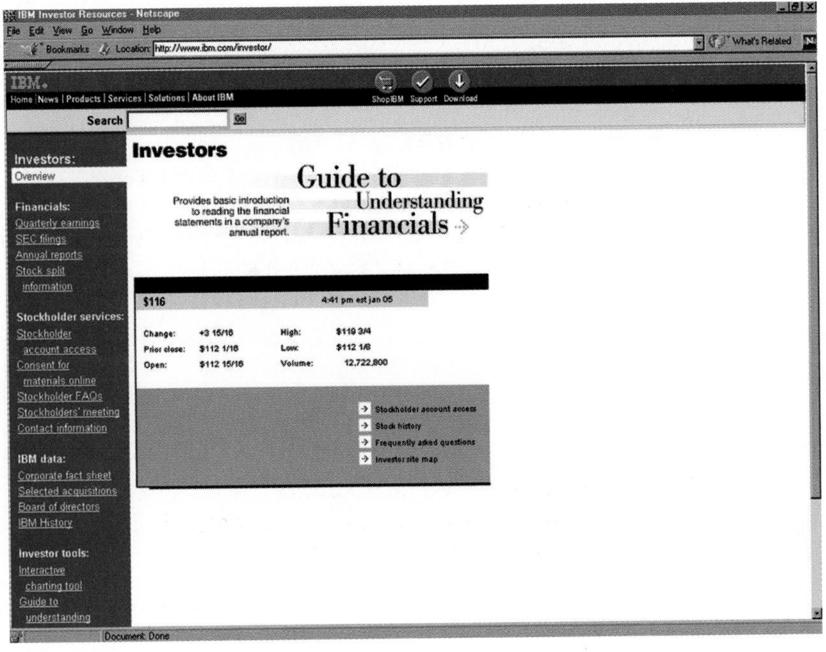

One function of public relations is investor relations. The IBM Web site features a special section for current and potential investors.

marketing highlight 14-3

Public Relations: Stretching the Marketing Budget

Italian sports-car maker Lamborghini sells fewer than 100 of its cars each year in North America. Marketing Lamborghinis is no simple matter. The car is pure poetry in motion—but at a steep price. The Diablo VT's 492-horsepower engine delivers a top speed of 323 km/hr and goes from 0 to 95 km/hr in just 4.1 seconds. The price: $344 000. Just to lease a Diablo VT runs $4318 a month with a $74 000 down payment. Moreover, because so few Lamborghinis are sold, most people rarely see one. Therefore, to gain exposure and persuade would-be buyers, the company must invest its modest US$ 850 000 marketing budget carefully.

According to one journalist who test drove the $295 000 Lamborghini Diablo VT, "On the beauty meter . . . [it] rates right up there with a roomful of Matisse originals."

Lamborghini's eventual goal is to sell 1500 to 2000 units a year in North America. This goal is based partly on expanding its product line-up to include a sport-utility vehicle priced in the $110 000 to $145 000 range. To reach this ambitious sales goal, however, the car maker will need to increase its exposure and awareness. It currently advertises in several select business, travel, and lifestyle magazines, emphasizing the car's speed and sensual beauty. In addition, the company fielded a direct-mail campaign to 50 000 prospective buyers with a median household income of $2 million.

When it comes to advertising, however, $850 000 doesn't go far. So Lamborghini stretches its limited marketing budget with an assortment of less expensive public relations efforts. The company actively courts the press. For example, it makes the car available to auto journalists for test drives. This resulted in one *New York Times* review describing the car as "kinetic sculpture, proof of affluence, and amusement-park ride wrapped into one." After a test drive, a *Fortune* journalist wrote, "On the beauty meter, the screaming lemon-yellow Diablo rates right up there with a roomful of Matisse originals. . . . Neighbors I have never met come rushing out of their homes to get a closer look." And after riding with Lamborghini's chief US test driver, another journalist reported, "He fired up the engine and shot out of Lamborghini's vast and immaculate garage. He slammed the car sideways through the parking lot [and] a split second later straightened the Diablo out with a snap and hammered ahead. No swaying, no rolling, no hesitation, just unadulterated energy. It was an all-sensory extravaganza." Lamborghini also sponsors tasteful PR events. For example, it held a cocktail party for 200 people at a Giorgio Armani store in Boston, with an invitation list put together by the store and *The Robb Report,* a publication devoted to the lifestyles of the wealthy.

Lamborghini is constantly seeking new ways to expose the car to its affluent audience. As a result of good public relations efforts, the Lamborghini Diablo VT was designated as a pace car for the 1995 PPG Indy Car World Series. This gave Lamborghini exposure at 15 race sites and allowed local dealers to give prospective buyers a ride around the track in the days before a race. Says a Lamborghini executive, "We sold three cars by doing that last year at the Detroit Grand Prix." Lamborghini is also making a demonstrator available to its North American dealers, so that prospects can test-drive the car without the dealer worrying about kilometrage and insurance costs.

Lamborghini's total annual sales amount to only a tiny fraction of the advertising budgets of the major car makers. However, through the innovative use of PR, the company successfully stretches its modest marketing budget to gain exposure among affluent buyers.

Sources: Quotes from Raymond Serafin, "Even Lamborghini must think marketing," *Advertising Age,* 1 May 1995:4; Faye Rice, "Lamborghini's sales drive," *Fortune,* 12 June 1995:13; and Sue Zesiger, "Driving with the devil," *Fortune,* 17 February 1997:170–1; home.lamborghini.com/

tion flow and keep panic under control. He quickly informed parents waiting at the bottom of the hill that their kids were safe. Perry also opened up a media centre from which reporters could work. He recruited senior managers to call all of the skiers who had been on the lift that day and arranged for counselling for employees affected by the stress of the accident. Whistler ran ads thanking the community for its support during the crisis and conducted technical investigations to prevent such a failure from occurring in the future. It also adjusted its PR policies based on this experience to ensure that they were even more effective.[30]

Despite its potential strengths, public relations is often described as a marketing stepchild because of its limited and scattered use. The PR department is usually located at corporate headquarters. Its staff is so busy dealing with various publics—shareholders, employees, legislators, city officials—that PR programs to support product marketing objectives may be ignored. And marketing managers and public relations practitioners do not always talk the same language. Many PR practitioners view their job as simply communicating. In contrast, marketing managers tend to be much more interested in how advertising and PR affect sales and profits.

This situation is changing, however. Many companies now want their PR departments to manage all of their activities with a view toward marketing the company and improving the bottom line. They know that good public relations can be a powerful brand-building tool. Two well-known marketing consultants provide the following advice, which points to the potential power of PR as a first step in building brands:[31]

> Just because a heavy dose of advertising is associated with most major brands doesn't necessarily mean that advertising built the brands in the first place. The birth of a brand is usually accomplished with [public relations], not advertising. Our general rule is [PR] first, advertising second. [Public relations] is the nail, advertising the hammer. [PR] creates the credentials that provide the credibility for advertising. . . . Anita Roddick built The Body Shop into a major brand with no advertising at all. Instead, she traveled the world on a relentless quest for publicity. . . . Until recently Starbucks Coffee Co. didn't spend a hill of beans on advertising, either. In 10 years, the company spent less than $10 million on advertising, a trivial amount for a brand that delivers annual sales of $1.3 billion. Wal-Mart Stores became the world's largest retailer . . . with very little advertising . . . In the toy field, Furby, Beanie Babies, and Tickle Me Elmo became highly successful . . . and on the Internet, Yahoo!, Amazon.com, and Excite became powerhouse brands, [all] with virtually no advertising.

Therefore, some companies are setting up special units called *marketing public relations* to support corporate and product promotion and image making directly. Many companies hire marketing public relations firms to handle their PR programs or to assist the company PR team.

Major Public Relations Tools

One of the major tools that public relations professionals use is news. PR professionals find or create favourable news about the company and its products or people. Sometimes news stories occur naturally, and sometimes the PR person can suggest events or activities that would create news. *Speeches* can also create product and company publicity. Increasingly, company executives must field questions from the media or give talks at trade associations or sales meetings, and these events can either build or hurt the company's image. Another common PR tool is *special events*—ranging from news conferences, press tours, grand openings, and fireworks displays to laser shows, hot-air balloon releases, multimedia presentations, and star-studded spectaculars designed to reach and interest target publics. Levi-Strauss & Company launched this interesting PR program:[32]

> In the increasingly more casual business world, as companies relax their dress codes, they are often dismayed to find employees showing up at the office in anything from sweatsuits to torn jeans. Where can they turn for a little fashion advice? Levi-Strauss & Company to the rescue! The world's largest apparel maker has put together an elaborate and stealthy program to help companies advise

The birth of a brand is often accomplished with public relations, not advertising. Beanie Babies have been highly successful with virtually no advertising.

their people on how to dress casually without being sloppy. To promote the program initially, Levi mailed a newsletter to 65 000 human resource managers and sent videos to some 7000 companies. Since 1992, the company has provided information and advice to more than 30 000 companies, including Charles Schwab & Company, IBM, Nynex, and Aetna Life & Casualty. Through the program, Levi offers snazzy brochures and videos showing how to dress casually. Other activities range from putting on fashion shows and manning a toll-free number for employees who have questions about casual wear to holding seminars for human resource directors. Levi also created a Web page from which human resources managers can obtain advice and Levi's Casual Businesswear Kit, a detailed guide for starting and maintaining company dress policies. Levi's avoids outright product pitches. Instead, the company explains, it's simply "trying to create a dress code for dress-down wear." Of course, it wouldn't hurt if that wear had the Levi label attached.

Public relations people also prepare:

- *written materials* to reach and influence their target markets, including annual reports, brochures, articles, and company newsletters and magazines
- *audiovisual materials,* such as films, slide-and-sound programs, and video and audio cassettes, as communication tools
- *corporate identity materials* to help create a corporate identity that the public immediately recognizes: logos, stationery, brochures, signs, business forms, business cards, buildings, uniforms, and company cars and trucks—all become marketing tools when they are attractive, distinctive, and memorable.

Companies can improve public goodwill by contributing money and time to *public service activities.* For example, Procter & Gamble and Publishers Clearing House held a joint promotion to raise money for the Special Olympics. The Publishers Clearing House mailing included product coupons, and P&G donated 10 cents per redeemed coupon to the Special Olympics.

A company's Web site can also be a good PR vehicle. Consumers and members of other publics can visit the site for information and entertainment. Such sites can be very popular. For example, Butterball's site, which features cooking and carving tips, received 500 000 visitors on one day during US Thanksgiving week in 1998. Web sites can also be ideal for handling crisis situations. For example, when several bottles of Odwalla apple juice sold on the West Coast were found to contain *E. coli* bacteria, Odwalla initiated a massive product recall. Within just three hours, the company set up a Web site laden with information

Butterball
www.butterball.com/

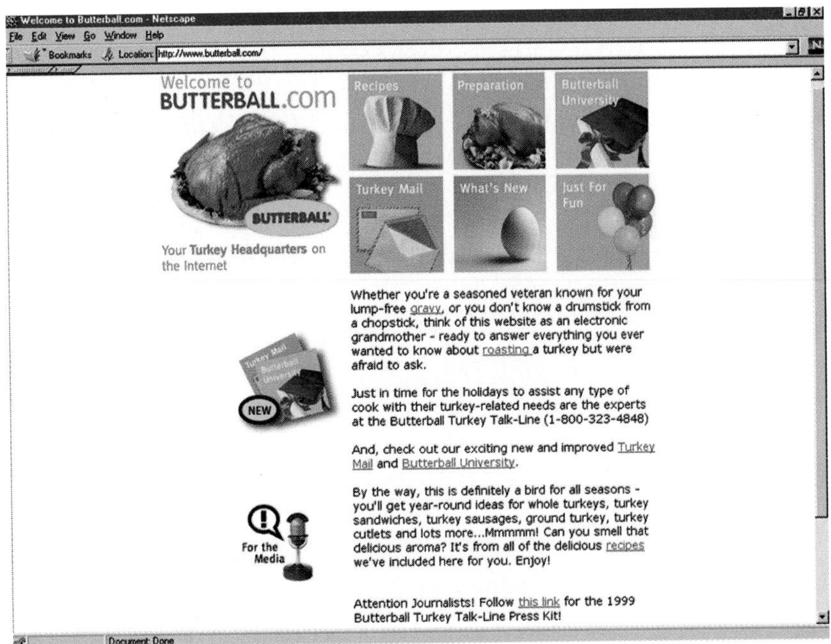

A company's Web site can be a good public relations tool: Butterball's site, which features turkey cooking and carving tips, received over 500 000 visits in one day during US Thanksgiving week.

about the crisis and Odwalla's response. Company staffers also combed the Internet looking for newsgroups discussing Odwalla and posted links to the site. In all, notes one analyst, "Today, public relations is reshaping the Internet, and the Internet, in turn, is redefining the practice of public relations." Says another, "People look to the Net for information, not salesmanship, and that's the real opportunity for public relations."[33]

As with the other promotion tools, in considering when and how to use product public relations, management should set PR objectives, choose the PR messages and vehicles, implement the PR plan, and evaluate the results. The firm's public relations should be blended smoothly with other promotion activities within the company's overall integrated marketing communications effort.

Review of Concept Connections

Companies must do more than make good products—they must inform consumers about product benefits and carefully position products in consumers' minds. To do this, they must skillfully use three mass-promotion tools in addition to personal selling, which targets specific buyers. These tools are advertising, sales promotion, and public relations.

1. Define the roles of advertising, sales promotion, and public relations in the promotion mix.

Advertising—the use of paid media by a seller to inform, persuade, and remind about its products or organization—is a strong promotion tool. Canadian marketers spend more than $8 billion each year on advertising, which takes many forms and has many uses. *Sales promotion* covers a variety of short-term incentive tools—coupons, premiums, contests, buying allowances—designed to stimulate final and business consumers, the trade, and the company's own sales force. In recent years, sales promotion spending has been growing faster than advertising spending. *Public relations*—gaining favourable publicity and creating a favourable company image—is the least used of the major promotion tools, although it has great potential for building consumer awareness and preference.

2. Describe the major decisions involved in developing an advertising program.

Advertising decision making involves decisions about the objectives, the budget, the message, the media, and, finally, the evaluation of results. Advertisers should set clear *objectives* as to whether the advertising is intended to inform, persuade, or remind buyers. The advertising *budget* can be based on sales, competitors' spending, or the objectives and tasks.

The *message decision* calls for planning a message strategy and executing it effectively. The *media decision* involves defining reach, frequency, and impact goals; choosing major media types; selecting media vehicles; and deciding on media timing. Message and media decisions must be closely coordinated for maximum campaign effectiveness. Finally, *evaluation* calls for evaluating the communication and sales effects of advertising before, during, and after the advertising is placed.

3. Explain how sales promotion campaigns are developed and implemented.

Sales promotion campaigns call for setting sales promotion objectives (in general, sales promotions should be *consumer relationship building*); selecting tools; developing and implementing the sales promotion program by using trade promotion tools (*discounts, allowances, free goods, push money*) and business promotion tools (*conventions, trade shows, sales contests*) as well as deciding on such elements as the size of the incentive, the conditions for participation, how to promote and distribute the promotion package, and the length of the promotion. After this process is completed, the company evaluates the results.

4. Explain how companies use public relations to communicate with their publics.

Companies use public relations to communicate with their publics by setting PR objectives; choosing messages and vehicles; implementing the plan; and evaluating results. To accomplish these goals, PR professionals use several tools, including *news, speeches, and special events*. They also prepare written, audiovisual, and corporate identity materials and contribute money and time to public relations activities.

Key Terms

Advertising agency *(p. 593)*
Advertising objective *(p. 580)*
Advertising specialties *(p. 599)*
Allowance *(p. 600)*
Business promotion *(p. 596)*
Cash refund offers (rebates) *(p. 599)*
Comparison advertising *(p. 580)*
Consumer promotion *(p. 596)*
Contests, sweepstakes, games *(p. 599)*
Coupons *(p. 598)*
Discount *(p. 600)*
Frequency *(p. 589)*
Informative advertising *(p. 580)*
Media impact *(p. 589)*
Media vehicles *(p. 590)*
Patronage rewards *(p. 599)*
Persuasive advertising *(p. 580)*
Point-of-purchase promotions (POP) *(p. 599)*
Premiums *(p. 599)*
Price packs (cents-off deals) *(p. 599)*
Public relations *(p. 602)*
Reach *(p. 589)*
Reminder advertising *(p. 581)*
Sales force promotion *(p. 596)*
Sales promotion *(p. 596)*
Samples *(p. 597)*
Trade promotion *(p. 596)*

Discussing the Issues

1. Advertising objectives can be classified by primary purpose: to inform, to persuade, or to remind. In your local newspaper, find examples of ads pursuing each of these objectives. Use Table 14-1 to explain your answers.
2. What are the benefits and drawbacks of comparison advertising? Find a comparison ad in your favourite magazine. (a) Which has more to gain from using comparison advertising—the leading brand in a market or a lesser brand? Why? (b) In the ad you found, what is the relative market position of the ad's sponsor? (c) Is it an appropriate use of comparison advertising? Explain.
3. Surveys show that many Canadians are sceptical

of advertising claims. (a) Do you trust advertising? Explain. (b) What types of advertising do you trust the most? The least? (c) Suggest how the advertising industry could increase advertising credibility.

4. Advertisers must develop compelling creative concepts, or big ideas, that will bring their message strategies to life in a distinctive way. Sony recently developed a robot pet dog. Priced at $3750, the robopet can bark for attention, sit up, lie down, scratch its face, wag its tail, play ball, express emotion through changing eye colours, and learn. Sony is betting that robopets will soon be as hot as video games. Name Sony's new robopet and develop a compelling message strategy and creative concept that will aid Sony (www.sony.com) in developing a nationwide advertising campaign for the next Christmas season.

5. Pick one of the execution styles suggested in the chapter that best fits the following situations and explain your choice: (a) Schwinn bicycles wishes to demonstrate the pleasure and freedom found in trail riding; (b) Lexus wants to demonstrate the benefits of leasing over purchasing one of its cars; (c) Caterpillar wishes to demonstrate the quality and maintenance-free benefits of its huge earth-moving machines; and (d) CIBC wants to demonstrate the security and ease of using its online banking services.

6. Which factors call for more frequency in an advertising media schedule, and which factors call for more reach? Can you increase one without sacrificing the other or increasing the advertising budget?

7. Which of the sales promotion tools described in the chapter would be best for stimulating sales of the following products and services? (a) A dry cleaner that wishes to emphasize low prices on washed and pressed dress shirts; (b) Gummi Bears' new black cherry flavour; and (c) Procter & Gamble's efforts to bundle laundry detergents and fabric softeners together in a combined marketing effort.

8. The Internet is the latest public relations frontier. Web users now routinely share their experiences and problems with a company's products, service, prices, and warranties on electronic bulletin boards and chat rooms and at various Web sites. What kinds of special PR problems and opportunities does the Internet present to marketers? How can companies use their own Web sites to deal with these problems and opportunities? Find a good example of a company that uses its Web site as a PR tool.

Marketing Applications

1. Total toothpaste's market-leading position has many people at Colgate-Palmolive smiling these days. Almost four out of 10 people across the globe use Total. However, achieving this position was not easy. To move to number one in the huge toothpaste market, Total had to unseat Procter & Gamble's long-time market-leading Crest brand. Colgate spent $180 million launching Total. Perhaps more importantly, beyond obtaining the usual American and Canadian Dental Association's seal of approval, Total was the first toothpaste to earn the US Food and Drug Administration's permission to claim that it could prevent gingivitis, the early stages of gum disease. When first introducing the brand, Colgate skipped its warehouses and shipped 46 million tubes of Total to 13 000 stores in just three days. It shipped the product directly to 130 000 promotional displays (about five times the usual amount) strategically placed in retail outlets. At the same time, it blitzed the market with billboards, transit posters, television commercials, print ads, and coupons, announcing that Total was "so advanced it even works when you're not brushing." Colgate is now beginning to use the Total name on line extensions. For example, it now has Colgate Total Fresh Stripe Toothpaste. Together Colgate toothpaste brands now capture almost 30 percent of the world market, and, for the year ending January 2000, Colgate controlled 39.7 percent of the $124.2 million Canadian toothpaste market, compared to Crest's share of 26.7 percent. Colgate is betting that consumers will keep smiling over Total for many years to come.

a. Evaluate Total's integrated marketing communication strategy. What has been the secret to Colgate's success with Total?

b. Visit the Colgate Web site (www.colgate.ca) and evaluate the company's efforts to extend its communications efforts to the Internet.

c. As a competitor, how would you respond to Colgate's success with Total? (See Procter & Gamble's Web site at www.pg.com and its Crest site at www.crestsmiles.com for additional information.) What media would you use? Explain.

2. Philip Morris Company is the world's largest tobacco company. It's also one of the most controversial. Philip Morris is full of apparent contradictions. For example, it recently spent $150 million to persuade children not to smoke; it contributes $90 million in cash and $22.5 million in food each year to fight hunger, combat domestic violence, and support the arts; and it has paid $US 8.5 billion to reimburse states for the costs of treating smoking-related illnesses. Even its employees have given $7.5 million to charities. Such numbers are impressive by any standard. So why is Philip Morris on every social crusader's hit list? The answer: the tobacco culture that engulfs the organization. For years Philip Morris operated under a siege mentality, closing itself off from the questions and criticism coming from the outside world. Recently, however, this culture has slowly begun to change. The $111 billion company is now renewing its efforts to change its image. However, being a responsible corporate citizen and changing the company's culture, products, and image will not be easy.

a. What public relations issues does Philip Morris face?

b. On its Web site (www.philipmorris.com), Philip Morris admits that "cigarette smoking is addictive." What kind of public relations advantages does this admission create? What problems?

c. Outline a public relations program for gaining public trust and shareholder interest.

d. Visit the Web sites of other Philip Morris companies (e.g., Kraft Canada). What public relations synergies do you see? What problems might these synergies create?

Internet Connections

Online Advertising

Diverse content and advertising on the Web make it similar to television, magazines, and other traditional media. Web advertising comes in many forms such as banners and sponsorships. The online advertising market has grown quickly but still represents a small proportion of all media advertising expenditures. Content providers sell online advertising to businesses that wish to target a particular audience. DoubleClick, one of the largest online advertising firms, specializes in targeted advertising. It even holds patented techniques for targeting ads online. Visit the Web site at www.doubleclick.com and complete the following table to indicate seven of the possible ways DoubleClick targets ads using audience psychographics and behaviour. Hint: Look for this information in the section for advertisers.

For Discussion

1. If you were buying ad space for your college or university to increase enrolment, which DoubleClick market/method would you use? Justify.
2. For your college or university ad, would you rather buy a banner or a sponsorship? Explain.
3. For the college or university ad, would you rather buy an online ad or place a magazine or radio ad? Explain.
4. What type of targeting are you able to do with DoubleClick's Boomerang service?
5. How does DoubleClick monitor the performance of your ad? What type of information can they provide?
6. DoubleClick claims to be able to target to an audience of one person. Explain how they do this.

Targeting Method (Market description)	Definition/Option

Savvy Sites

- The Web is becoming a great place for sales promotions. Check out Playhere's giveaway page (www.playhere.com) for coupons, contests, and sweepstakes.
- NetRatings (www.netratings.com), in association with A.C. Nielsen, provides statistics on the top banner ads online.
- For a killer media property, visit ZDNet (www.zdnet.com): This media firm has over seven million unique visitors a month and sells a lot of advertising.

Notes

1. Quotes from Barry Base, "Molson Canadian rant is darn good advertising," *Strategy,* 3 July 2000:16; John Heinzl, "Molson: I am Canadian once more, and proud of it," *Globe and Mail,* 17 March 2000. Also see Astrid Van Den Broek, "I am marketer of the year: Under the leadership of Dan O'Neill, Molson creates some stellar ads, regains control of its brands and is poised for the future," *Marketing On-Line,* 18/25 December 2000; David Bosworth, "My name is Molson. I am top client of the year," *Strategy,* 31 July 2000:15; Craig Saunders, "Molson Canadian: The sequel," *Strategy,* 19 June 2000:3; www.iam.ca/promos.
2. Institute of Canadian Advertising, *Economic Impact Report,* 1998, www.ica-ad.com/new/sub_main.cfm.
3. "Net leads the way in spending," *Marketing On-Line,* 25 September 2000; "2001: A Marketing Odyssey: Seven association leaders predict the challenges the next year may bring," *Marketing On-Line,* 18/15 December 2000; Robert J. Coen, "Spending spree," *Advertising Age Special Issue: The Advertising Century,* 1999: 126.
4. Jim McElgunn, "Canada's top 25 advertising categories," *Marketing On-Line,* 27 September 1999; Astrid Van Den Broek, "Government ad spends soared in '98," *Marketing On-Line,* 19 April 1999.
5. "The 2000 RSVP Awards, winners by category—communication products & services," *Strategy,* 24 November 2000:20.
6. See Donald E. Schultz, Dennis Martin, and William P. Brown, *Strategic Advertising Campaigns,* Chicago: Crain Books, 1984:192–7; and Philip Kotler, *Marketing Management: Analysis, Planning, Implementation, and Control,* 8th ed., Englewood Cliffs, NJ: Prentice Hall, 1994: 630–1.
7. See Andrew Ehrenberg, Neil Barnard, and John Scriven, "Justifying our advertising budgets," *Marketing & Research Today,* February 1997:38–44; and Dana W. Hayman and Don E. Schultz, "How much should you spend on advertising?" *Advertising Age,* 26 April 1999:32.
8. Information from Rosalind Stefanac, "Corporate ads in rainbow colours: Big mainstream marketers are crafting innovative adver-

tising strategies in a bid to get closer to gay and lesbian consumers," *Marketing On-Line,* 1 May 2000; Gary Levin, "'Meddling' in creative more welcome," *Advertising Age,* 9 April 1990:S4,S8; Lynne Roberts, "New media choice: Absolut Vodka," *Marketing,* 9 April 1998:12; Eleftheria Parpis, "TBWA: Absolut," *Adweek,* 9 November 1998:172; and the Q&A section at www.absolutvodka.com, March 2000.

9. *1999–2000 Media Digest,* Canadian Media Directors' Council.
10. "1999–2000 network TV price estimates," *Advertising Age,* 20 September 1999:12.
11. Richard Cook, "Tackling the problem of increased TV zapping," *Campaign,* 25 September 1998:16.
12. Edward A. Robinson, "Frogs, bears, and orgasms: Think zany if you want to reach today's consumers," *Fortune,* 9 June 1997: 153–6. Also see Marc Gunther, "What's wrong with this picture?" *Fortune,* 12 January 1998:107–14; John Consoli, "A crescendo of clutter," *Mediaweek,* 16 March 1998:4–5; and Chuck Ross, "TV commercial clutter has ad buyers worried," *Advertising Age,* 6 December 1999:77.
13. Sarah Smith, "Advertising success stories," *Marketing On-Line,* 22 November 1999.
14. "Holmes & Lee, Award Winners 2000," *Strategy,* www.strategymag.com/aoy/1999/holmesandlee.
15. See *Television Production Cost Survey,* New York: American Association of Advertising Agencies, 1998; and the 4A's Web site at www.aaaa.org/resources.
16. See Gary Schroeder, "Behavioral optimization," *American Demographics,* August 1998:34–6; and Erwin Ephron, "Ad world was ripe for its conversion to optimizers," *Advertising Age,* 22 February 1999:S16.
17. "Canada's top marketing communications services companies," *Marketing Magazine,* 26 June 2000:23–32.
18. Jim McElgunn, "Who cares where an ad's made?" *Marketing Magazine,* 8 May 1995:20; "Canada's top agencies," *Marketing,* 24 July 1995:11.
19. Patricia Winters Lauro, "New method of agency payments drive a stake through the heart of the old 15% commission," *New York Times,* 2 April 1999:2.
20. Patti Bond, "Today's topic: From Russia with fizz, Coke imports ads," *Atlanta Journal and Constitution,* 4 April 1998:E2. Also see Jack Neff, "P&G hammers last nail into commission coffin," *Advertising Age,* 20 September 1999:4.
21. See "UK tobacco ad ban will include sports sponsorship," AdAgeInternational.com, May 1997; "Coca-Cola rapped for ruining competition in India," AdAgeInternational.com, February 1997; Naveen Donthu, "A cross-country investigation of recall of and attitude toward comparative advertising," *Journal of Advertising,* June 1998:111; John Shannon, "Comparative ads call for prudence," *Marketing Week,* 6 May 1999:32; and "A Trojan horse for advertisers," *Business Week,* 3 April 2000:10.
22. "Promotion practices condensed," *Potentials,* November 1998:6.
23. Debra Aho Williamson, "P&G's reformulated Pert plus builds consumer relationships," *Advertising Age,* 28 June 1999:52.
24. Lesley Daw, "The tasting race," *Marketing Magazine,* 18/25 August 1997:S1–2; David Mudie, "The sampling menu," *Marketing Magazine,* 18/25 August 1997:S3.
25. Raju Mudhar, "Print and redeem," *Marketing On-Line,* 22 November 1999.
26. Jeff Lobb, "Stuff-ing it to Coke," *Marketing Magazine,* 27 January 1997:15.
27. See "Power to the key ring and T-shirt," *Sales & Marketing Management,* December 1989:14; and J. Thomas Russell and W. Ronald Lane, *Kleppner's Advertising Procedure,* 12th ed., Englewood Cliffs, NJ: Prentice Hall, 1993:408–10.
28. "International trade fairs," advertising supplement to *Canadian Business,* January 1994.
29. "The agency perspective," *Marketing Magazine,* 13 February 1995:16–7.
30. Gail Chiasson, "PR in action: When the media come calling," *Marketing Magazine,* 12 February 1996:23.
31. Al Ries and Laura Ries, "First do some publicity," *Advertising Age,* 8 February 1999:42.
32. Linda Himelstein, "Levi's vs. the dress code," *Business Week,* 1 April 1996:57–8; "Dressing for success," *IAB Online Advertising Guide,* Spring 1998:29A: and www.levistrauss.com/casual/casual.html, December 1999.
33. Mark Gleason, "Edelman sees niche in Web public relations," *Advertising Age,* 20 January 1997:30; Michael Krauss, "Good PR critical to growth on the Net," *Marketing News,* 18 January 1999:8.

Company Case 14

University of Ottawa Intercollegiate Sports

The phone rang in the office of Luc Gelineau, the director of sports services at the University of Ottawa. He had just finished a meeting with the sports services advisory council outlining the recent budget cuts to the "Big 5" [basketball (male and female), hockey, football, and volleyball] intercollegiate programs and strategies to acquire alternative funding. On the line was John Goldfarb, the manager of the local branch of the Royal Bank of Canada. The bank was recently approached as a potential sponsor of intercollegiate sports, and Goldfarb was calling to update Gelineau on the reaction of the bank executives. He summarized the situation:

"Well Luc, I've spoken to several of the executives and it seems like we might be interested in getting involved. We're excited at the possibilities and would like to sit down and discuss the details. Specifically, we would like to know what type of exposure your teams can offer us."

Gelineau understood what Goldfarb was getting at but, after recently attending a football game and being surrounded by empty seats, he realized that he could provide few of the exposure incentives that he felt the bank was looking for (see Exhibit 1 for attendance records). He got off the phone, turned to his MBA interns and said:

"Dammit guys, we have a quality product! Our soccer team won the national championships, our football team is ranked third in the nation, we've produced athletes that have competed internationally at the Olympics and professionally. How come we still can't get fans out to watch these stars of tomorrow! Set up another meeting with the advisory council. We need to look at intercollegiate sports and investigate ways we can increase attendance at games and make it more attractive for sponsors to become involved."

Background

Established in 1976, sports services at the University of Ottawa is a subsidiary of student affairs. They manage and operate all of the sporting facilities on campus, including the university's gymnasiums, hockey arena, and football field. In addition to offering recreational, instructional, and intramural activities to students, Sports Services provides the necessary training environment for student athletes, enabling them to represent the university on an intercollegiate level. Eight men's and seven women's teams compete at Canadian Intercollegiate Athletic Union (CIAU) or Ontario University Athletic Association/Ontario Women's Intercollegiate Athletic Association (OUAA/OWIAA) events. Of these 15 intercollegiate teams, the five highest-profile sports are classified as the "Big 5."

Historically, sports services relied on money raised through their recreational, instructional, and intramural programs, along with funds from student auxiliary fees, to operate each of the intercollegiate teams effectively. The 1994–95 overall intercollegiate budget was about $650 000.

The budgets for the Big 5 teams were more than adequate to run their programs effectively prior to and including the 1994–95 season. However, more recently, several factors caused significant reductions to each of the team's operating budgets and raised the need to investigate alternative methods of funding.

Gender Equity

The issue of gender equity in sports has become a "hot" topic, not only on the campuses of Canadian universities, but across the United States as well. In March 1994, then director of sports services, Michel Leduc, appointed a committee on gender equity to study the status of women's involvement in sports services. To establish a policy of gender equity in intercollegiate sports, the committee recommended that financing and membership in men's and women's interuniversity programs should reflect the gender distribution of the student population: women = 56%; men = 44%. In response to this recommendation, sports services granted intercollegiate status to women's soccer and reduced the ratio of men's to women's financing from 2.66:1 in 1994–95 to 1.96:1 for the 1996–97 season. This decrease in funding for male-dominated teams (e.g., football) led to a chain of events that resulted in decreases to all intercollegiate teams.

Mass Participation

Increased enrolment in sports services is transforming the traditional competitive environment into a more recreational atmosphere; that is, more participation in recreational activities is occurring instead of traditional competitive intercollegiate sports.

Financial Constraints

In January 1996, the University of Ottawa outlined proposed cuts to the 1996–97 budget that would eliminate over $7 million from university services including

Exhibit 1 Ticket Sales Analysis Seasons 1991–1996 (Average Attendance)

	1991–92	1992–93		1993–94		1994–95		1995–96	
Team	Tickets	Tickets	%	Tickets	%	Tickets	%	Tickets	%
Football	970	1163	20%	815	−30%	531	−35%	625	18%
Hockey	103	189	46%	196	4%	228	17%	180	−21%
Volleyball	58	138	140%	147	7%	124	−16%	181	14%
Basketball	154	281	82%	213	−24%	220	3%	201	−9%
Total Tickets	1312	1771	35%	1371	−23%	1103	−20%	114	74%

a 14 percent or $435 000 reduction to the budget of student affairs. Increases in students' tuition fees and resulting demonstrations held by the Student Federation Union Organization (SFUO) have made it unrealistic for sports services to increase athletic auxiliary fees to compensate for the budget cuts. In addition, recent renovations to sports services' athletic facilities have resulted in a further strain on funds.

Environment

Student Life at the University of Ottawa

The University of Ottawa, North America's oldest and largest bilingual university, is located in the downtown core of the city. Student enrolment for the 1996–97 academic year totalled nearly 25 000 full time and part time (see Exhibit 2 for breakdowns). In addition, 77 percent of the university's graduates remain in the Ottawa area.

The university school year begins with one week of activities for the first-year students. These activities are organized by senior students, who serve as floor reps in the residences, and executives of the faculty associations. Recently, these activities have included games, pub crawls, talent contests and other events. These new students look to their senior peers for guidance and direction. At the same time, they are looking to maximize their freedom and explore new activities and interests. Although the transition to university life can be rough, active involvement can smooth out the bumps in the adjustment period.

At the end of this week, students move to the usual routine of courses and homework. About 2000 students live in the university residences. Events are sporadically planned throughout the year, arranged by various associations and clubs, coinciding with such calendar events as Halloween, Christmas, and Valentines Day. Most of these activities are organized by the faculty associations and are extremely popular with the students. However, faculty activities are rarely directed to the intercollegiate sports program. Currently there are nine faculties at the University of Ottawa (see Exhibit 2 for more details), each of which has its own student association.

The school year is divided into two semesters, fall and winter. The fall semester is broken up by the Thanksgiving long weekend in early October and University of Ottawa Day (when regular students have the day off and prospective students visit the campus) in late October. The Christmas break ends the month of December. The winter semester is highlighted by the study break in late February and the four-day weekend in the beginning of April before exams. The typical student has 15 hours of class time a week plus additional homework time. In general, students usually have some time to participate in extracurricular activities during the week.

Exhibit 2 Student Composition at the University of Ottawa

	Graduate	Undergraduate	Total
Full time	2147	14 150	16 297
Part time	1378	6074	7452
Total	3525	20 224	23 749

	Graduate	Undergraduate	Total
English program	2363	12 350	14 713
French program	1162	7874	9036
Total	3525	20 224	23 749

	Graduate	Undergraduate	Total
Female	1759	11 985	13 744
Male	1766	8239	10 005
Total	3525	20 224	23 749

	Graduate	Undergraduate	Total
Graduate students	3525		3525
		22	22
First year		8480	8480
Second year		4511	4511
Third year		4846	4846
Fourth year		2365	2365
Total	3525	20 224	23 749

	Full Time	Part time	Total
	Age	Age	Age
	Mean	Mean	Mean
Graduate students	32.0	35.5	33.4
Undergraduate students	24.2	33.7	27.1
Total	25.2	34.0	28.0

	Graduate	Undergraduate	Total
Faculty of Administration	861	2199	3060
Faculty of Arts	500	4873	5373
Common Law	561		561
Civil Law	67	516	583
Faculty of Education	541	1503	2044
Faculty of Engineering	372	1357	1729
Faculty of Medicine	232	852	1084
Faculty of Science	359	2031	2390
Registrar's Office	30		30
Faculty of Health Sciences	152	1781	1933
Faculty of Social Science	441	4521	4962
Total	3525	20 224	23 749

Activities in Ottawa/Hull Region

A relatively small and young population, the people of Ottawa have traditionally been strong supporters of all sporting events and activities. In 1996, the region was home to two major junior hockey teams (Hull Olympiques, Ottawa 67s); three interuniversity athletic programs (Algonquin College, Carleton University, University of Ottawa); a triple A baseball team (Ottawa Lynx); and three other professional sports franchises (Ottawa Rough Riders Football Club, Ottawa Senators Hockey Club, and Ottawa Loggers Roller Hockey Club).

Although all of the professional teams have been well supported in the past, recently they have experienced significant attendance problems. The decline in attendance is threatening the very existence of the 126-year-old tradition of Rough Rider Football in Ottawa. As of November 4, 1996, the Canadian Football League revoked the Ottawa Rough Riders franchise. Although there is talk of starting a new franchise, Ottawa fans are still left without football to satisfy their gridiron needs. Similarly, after initial enthusiasm for the introduction of the Senators in 1991, filling the newly constructed 19 000-seat Corel Centre has become a problem. Many of the supporters of these teams cite the high ticket prices and poor competitive performance as reasons for their absence.

Although attendance has sharply declined, there is still a strong base of potential supporters in the region. Ottawa residents are very active and, according to the last census, spend more money on entertainment than the average Canadian. Instead of sporting events, people have turned to other entertainment options such as the numerous local theatres, museums, and art galleries.

The Game Experience

The Big 5 varsity teams compete throughout the school year, with the seasons of different teams beginning and ending at different times. The football team kicks off the varsity season usually with the first game taking place at the end of the first week of class. While the football season ends in November, the hockey, basketball, and volleyball teams compete throughout the fall and winter semesters.

Getting Students to Attend

Before deciding what should be done to alleviate the problem, the group of MBA interns decided to go to a game themselves.

Jeff, the most outgoing of the group, attempted to encourage some of his classmates to come. He approached them with: "Hey guys, a bunch of us are going to the game this weekend. Why don't you come?"

Tara, usually a sports enthusiast, responded: "What game? I haven't heard a thing about it!"

Jeff exclaimed: "How can you say that? There are posters in every building on campus, and a pep rally was held at the campus bar."

"Oh. Is that what that was?" asked Adam sarcastically. "I thought it was a little get-together for the physics club."

"Okay, Okay!, so a lot of people didn't show up, but I heard other promotions such as ticket giveaways and Rowdy Challenges are being attempted to bring more fans out," responded Jeff. (He didn't need to say that a Rowdy Challenge was a competition between two groups on campus, usually within residence, to see who had more spirit at a sporting event.)

In an attempt to stay away from the game, Adam interjected: "I was at a game last year and although the play was exciting, it just wasn't made into an event."

Jeff replied: "Well guys, sports services apparently hires students to run promotions during the game, and they hold contests at half-time. You can win a pizza or even drive home with a new car for a year."

"Hey! I like pizza," exclaimed Tara enthusiastically. "I'm willing to give the game a chance if the price is right. What is it going to cost us?"

"Well," Jeff explained. "There are different ticket prices depending on whether you are a student and whether you're interested in seeing more than one game." (See Exhibit 3 for a description of ticket prices.)

Tara replied: "You know, I've always wanted to go to a Gee-Gees game, but I never know where the games are played. Where are the games played and how do you get. . . ."

Interrupting Tara, Adam began to chuckle and said: "Yeah, the reason you don't know where to go is

Exhibit 3 Intercollegiate Ticket Price Structure

	Students	Adults
Regular season:		
Hockey	$2	$4
Basketball		
Volleyball		
Football	$4	$7
Playoffs:		
Hockey	$3	$5
Basketball		
Volleyball		
Football	$4	$7
Season pass:		
(Admit individual to all home games)	$20	$30

because the football games are a half-hour walk from campus."

Jeff acknowledged the distance to the football stadium but said: "All of the other teams play their games right on campus, so there's no excuse!"

Finally, after realizing that the game might be an opportunity to have a good time and meet new people, Adam agreed to go to the game with Jeff and some of his classmates.

The Game as an Event

In the spring of 1994, a marketing survey was conducted in an attempt to understand students' perceptions of sports services. As part of the survey, an analysis of intercollegiate sports revealed that while the majority of students were interested in sports, only a small percentage were drawn into supporting the Gee-Gees. With regard to those students who attended football games, the highest proportion of respondents (31%) answered that they went to the games to be with their friends. Interestingly, only 15 percent of the respondents who attended did so to see the game.

In addition to these findings, an informal survey conducted by the promotions officer of sports services revealed that more than just the game would need to be offered to make the games more attractive. In fact, this finding was consistent with past attendance records: Games with high attendance were often associated with an event outside of the game itself. The survey also identified that students have the perception that the quality of the games is poor, even though past successes are numerous.

The annual Panda Game between Ottawa and Carleton is a good example of game-related events resulting in elevated attendance. This historic game always attracts a large number of students, as events leading up to the game promote rivalries between the two universities. While attendance for the Panda game has ranged from 2000 to 5000 in recent years, sports services has had a difficult time carrying these numbers over to other regular season games. In contrast, several other Canadian universities have been able to maintain a respectable number of spectators at all of their games by making them an event and part of the university tradition. However, this has not occurred at the University of Ottawa.

Sports Services' Dilemma

Back in his office, Luc Gelineau was getting ready for the meeting with the advisory council when he turned to his interns:

"You know, guys, I am so damn frustrated! I have been working like mad to get a sponsorship deal with the Royal Bank and I'm not sure if it is going to happen. I would love to invite some of their managers out to the game on Saturday and show them the outstanding product that we have to offer. However, how could I if our fan support is typical of most games? They would probably no longer be interested in working out a deal! How do I get more people to attend our games?"

Gelineau reflected on a game he had attended at the University of Michigan between the Wolverines and the Buckeyes from Ohio State, where the stands were filled to the rafters with over 100 000 fans. He thought how nice it would be to get even a small percentage of those numbers to come out to a game. If only the University of Ottawa could cultivate this type of environment, then attaining the support of students, alumni, local residents, companies, and sponsors would be easy.

Although Gelineau knew what they wanted, he did not know how it should be accomplished. Out of frustration he turned to his interns and said: "What should we do?"

QUESTIONS

1. What must Luc Gelineau do before a sponsorship deal with the Royal Bank (or another firm) can be undertaken? When developing your answer, think about the things that make a sponsorship attractive for a corporation.
2. Corporate sponsorship of educational programs in public schools and universities has been a controversial topic. What are the pros and cons of entering into a sponsorship arrangement?
3. What market segments does Gelineau have to consider when developing his plans? Which is the most important segment? Can he attract multiple segments to the games? Will the presence of one segment detract from the experience of the others?
4. What role will the different elements of the promotion mix play in helping Gelineau revitalize sports services at the University of Ottawa?
5. Design a promotion plan that will help Gelineau solve his problems. Be specific about the objectives of your plan, the target audience, the media you will use, and the creative strategy you will employ.

Source: This case was written by David S. Litvack, University of Ottawa. It was reproduced with permission of the author.

video case 14

IMAGE MAKING: THE CASE OF HARRY ROSEN

When Harry Rosen, men's clothing retailer, decided to remake the image of his stores to attract a new target market, he chose Roche Macaulay and Partners, an ad agency in Toronto, to help him. Considered a "hip" agency in the industry, Roche Macaulay and Partners bills approximately $50 million a year. Since the Harry Rosen account could be worth $1 million a year, it represented a substantial account. The agency was therefore anxious to provide a compaign that was acceptable to the Harry Rosen management team within the eight-week deadline they had been given.

There are 22 Harry Rosen stores in Canada, which together generate $100 million in sales a year. Although successful at serving existing customers, Harry Rosen was concerned that the business was not attracting young men, which could have serious implications for the future of his business. While the new image was necessary to attract new clients, Rosen wanted to ensure that this new image would be acceptable to his existing, core customers. The first task for the ad agency then, was to compare customers to non-customers to determine why younger men were not shopping at Harry Rosen stores. To do this they used one of the most common research methods in advertising: focus groups. Three groups, costing $10 000, were run. One group was composed of regular Harry Rosen customers, the other two of young men who don't shop at Harry Rosen.

The focus groups revealed that younger men associated Harry Rosen stores with their fathers, not themselves. They viewed themselves as individuals and did not believe that Harry Rosen could outfit them to maintain that individuality. Among the questions asked in the focus groups was, "If Harry Rosen was a car, what type of car would it be?" The answers to this question included adjectives like, "bigger and conservative." Participants also thought the Harry Rosen "car" would be driven by a 55-year-old, confirming the association of the stores with older men. While each group was in session, Harry Rosen and his management team, along with agency personnel, were watching behind a one-way mirror to try to better understand the younger demographic group they hoped to target.

One goal of focus groups is to identify what is known in advertising as the "consumer insight." If properly identified, this consumer insight can be used to develop a powerful advertising campaign that is meaningful to targeted consumers. In this case, two of the key insights from the focus groups, as identified by the agency personnel, were that time was a precious commodity for the younger demographic group and that they had to shop. The agency people tried to develop a campaign to build on these findings, including tag lines such as, "The average man would rather get out than shop for clothes," "When you shop at Harry Rosen it is time well spent," and "Harry Rosen takes the hassle out of shopping." After Harry Rosen saw these initial ideas, he was unconvinced. He questioned the findings of the focus groups and did not believe that time was an important enough issue to focus on. Additionally, he believed that the campaign focused too much on negative concepts such as "hassle."

The Roche Macaulay team started again from scratch to develop another series of ad ideas. This time they developed a campaign that focused on recognizable people wearing clothes from Harry Rosen. The headline of the ad would include the person's name and proclaim that the outfit they were shown in is what they will be wearing on a particular day. These ads would then be run in newspapers across Canada on the date mentioned in the ad. The people used in the ads would be an eclectic mix of personalities such as sports figures, authors, artists, and business people. They would also represent different styles and sizes to emphasize the fact that Harry Rosen can help customers maintain their individuality.

Harry Rosen was pleased with this new idea. He felt that the campaign built a strong identity that would bring in new customers but would also be meaningful to his existing customers. In the fall of 1996, the campaign was run in newspapers across Canada.

Questions

1. Describe the characteristics of the agency-client relationship in this case. Based on this case, what observations would you make about the way this relationship works?
2. Discuss the advantages and disadvantages of using focus-group research to develop advertising. What role did the focus play in developing the campaign for Harry Rosen?

Source: This case was prepared by Auleen Carson and is based on "Harry Rosen," *Venture* (September 22, 1996).

P A R T 1 2 **3** 4

Developing the Marketing Mix

Concept Connections

When you finish this chapter, you should be able to

1. Discuss the role of a company's salespeople in creating value for customers and building customer relationships.
2. Explain how companies design sales force strategy and structure.
3. Explain how companies recruit, select, and train salespeople.
4. Describe how companies compensate and supervise salespeople, and how they evaluate sales force effectiveness.
5. Discuss the personal selling process, distinguishing between transaction-oriented marketing and relationship marketing.

chapter 15

Personal Selling and Sales Management

When someone says " salesperson," what image comes to mind? Perhaps it's the stereotypical "travelling salesman"—the fast-talking, ever-smiling peddler who travels his territory and foists his wares on reluctant customers. Such stereotypes, however, are out of date. Today, most professional salespeople are well-educated, well-trained women and men who work to build long-term, value-producing relationships with their customers. They succeed not by taking customers in but by helping them out—by assessing customer needs and solving customer problems.

Consider Lear Corporation, one of the largest, fastest-growing, and most successful automotive suppliers in the world. Every year, Lear produces more than $18 billion worth of automotive interiors—seat systems, instrument panels, door panels, floor and acoustic systems, overhead systems, and electronic and electrical distribution systems. Its customers include most of the world's leading automotive companies, including Ford, General Motors, Fiat, Volvo, Mercedes-Benz, Ferrari, Rolls-Royce, and Toyota. Lear operates more than 300 facilities in 33 countries around the globe, including nine in Canada. During the past few years, Lear has achieved record-breaking sales and earnings growth. During the past five years, Lear's sales have more than tripled, and its "average content per car" in North America has increased over four-fold since 1990. It currently owns about a 30-percent share of the North American interior components market.

Lear Corporation owes its success to many factors, including a strong customer orientation and a commitment to continuous improvement, teamwork, and customer value. But perhaps more than any other part of the organization, Lear's outstanding sales force makes the company's credo, "Consumer driven. Customer focused," ring true. In fact, Lear's sales force was recently given top ranking by *Sales & Marketing Management* magazine. What makes this an outstanding sales force? Lear knows that good selling these days takes much more than just a sales rep covering a territory and convincing customers to buy the product. It takes teamwork, relationship building, and doing what's best for the customer. Lear's sales force excels at these tasks.

Lear's sales depend completely on the success of its customers. If the automakers don't sell cars, Lear doesn't sell interiors. So the Lear sales force strives to create not just sales, but customer success. In fact, Lear salespeople aren't "sales reps," they're "account managers," who function more as consultants than as order getters. "Our salespeople don't really close deals," notes a senior marketing executive. "They consult and work with customers to learn exactly what's needed and when."

Lear Corporation
www.lear.com/

To more fully match up with customers' needs, Lear has diversified its product line to become a kind of "one-stop shopping" source. Until a few years ago, Lear supplied only seats; now it sells almost everything for a car's interior. Providing complete interior solutions for customers also benefits Lear. "It used to be that we'd build a partnership and then get only a limited amount of revenue from it," the executive says. "Now we can get as much as possible out of our customer relationships."

Lear is heavily customer focused, so much so that it's broken up into separate divisions dedicated to specific customers. For example, there's a Ford division and a General Motors division, and each operates as its own profit centre. Within each division, high-level "platform teams"—made up of salespeople, engineers, and program managers—work closely with their customer counterparts. These platform teams are closely supported by divisional manufacturing, finance, quality, and advanced technology groups. Lear's limited customer base, consisting of only a few dozen customers in all, allows its sales teams to get very close to their customers. "Our teams don't call on purchasers; they're linked to customer operations at all levels," the marketer notes. "We try to put a system in place that creates continuous contact with customers." In fact, Lear often locates its sales offices in customers' plants. For example, the team that handles GM's light truck division works at GM's truck operation campus. "We can't just be there to give quotes and ask for orders," the marketing executive says. "We need to be involved with customers every step of the way—from vehicle concept through launch."

Lear's largest customers are worth billions of dollars in annual sales to the company. Maintaining profitable relationships with such large customers takes much more than a nice smile and a firm handshake. Certainly there's no place for the "smoke and mirrors" or "flimflam" sometimes mistakenly associated with personal selling. Success in such a selling environment requires careful teamwork among well-trained, dedicated sales professionals who are bent on profitably taking care of their customers.[1]

Robert Louis Stevenson noted that "everyone lives by selling something." While everyone has experience with the sales personnel they meet in every retail establishment, they are probably less familiar with the sales forces used by business organizations to sell products and services to customers around the world. In fact, companies such as IBM Canada and Xerox are famous for the quality of their sales staff. Procter & Gamble, Warner-Lambert, and Wrigley's Canada all hire university graduates into sales jobs, since having highly educated, professional sales personnel is essential for building strong relationships with channel members. Sales forces are also found in many other kinds of organizations. Canada Post uses an extensive sales force to help launch new products such as its direct-mail offerings and courier services. Universities use recruiters to attract new students. Agriculture Canada sends specialists into the field to convince farmers to use new agricultural methods and products. You will have to take on a sales role when you have to sell your knowledge and expertise to prospective employers.

The Role of Personal Selling

There are many types of personal selling jobs, and the role of personal selling can vary greatly from one company to another. Here, we look at the nature of personal selling positions and at the role the sales force plays in modern marketing organizations.

The Nature of Personal Selling

Selling is one of the oldest professions in the world. The people who do the selling go by many titles, including: *salespeople, sales representatives, account executives, sales consultants, sales engineers, agents, district managers,* and *marketing representatives.* Modern salespeople are well-trained professionals who work to build and maintain long-term relationships with customers: They build these by listening to their customers, assessing customer needs, and organizing the company's efforts to solve customer problems and satisfy customer needs. Consider Boeing, the aerospace giant that dominates the worldwide commercial aircraft market with a 55 percent market share. It takes more than a friendly smile and a firm handshake to sell expensive airplanes:[2]

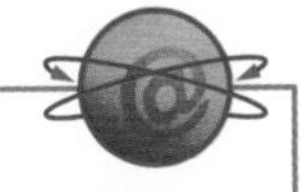

The Boeing Company
www.boeing.com/

> Selling high-tech aircraft at $70–$90 million or more a copy is complex and challenging. A single big sale can easily run into the billions of dollars. Boeing salespeople head up an extensive team of company specialists—sales and service technicians, financial analysts, planners, engineers—all dedicated to finding ways to satisfy airline customer needs. The salespeople begin by becoming experts on the airlines, much like Wall Street analysts would. They find out where each airline wants to grow, when it wants to replace planes, and details of its financial situation. The team runs Boeing and competing planes through computer systems, simulating the airline's routes, cost per seat, and other factors to show that their planes are most efficient. Then the high-level negotiations begin. The selling process is nerve-rackingly slow—it can take two or three years from the first sales presentation to the day the sale is announced. Sometimes top executives from both the airline and Boeing are brought in to close the deal. After getting the order, salespeople then must stay in almost constant touch to keep track of the account's equipment needs and to make certain the customer stays satisfied. Success depends on building solid, long-term relationships with customers, based on performance and trust. According to one analyst, Boeing's salespeople "are the vehicle by which information is collected and contacts are made so all other things can take place."

Salesperson
An individual acting for a company by performing one or more of these activities: prospecting, communicating, servicing, and information-gathering.

The term **salesperson** covers a range of positions. At one extreme, a salesperson might be largely an *order taker,* such as the department store salesperson standing behind the counter. At the other extreme are *order getters*—salespeople whose positions demand the *creative selling* of products and services, ranging from appliances, industrial equipment, or airplanes to insurance, advertising, or consulting services. Other salespeople engage in *missionary selling:* These salespeople are not expected or permitted to take an order, but only build goodwill or educate buyers. One example is the salesperson for a pharmaceutical company who calls on doctors to educate them about the company's drug products and to urge them to prescribe these products to their patients. In this chapter, we focus on the more creative types of selling and on the process of building and managing an effective sales force.

The Role of the Sales Force

Personal selling is the interpersonal arm of the promotion mix. Advertising consists of one-way, non-personal communication with target consumer groups. In contrast, personal selling involves two-way, personal communication between salespeople and individual customers—whether face to face, by telephone, through video conferences, or by other means. This means that personal selling can be more effective than advertising in more complex selling situations. Salespeople can probe customers to learn more about their problems. They can adjust the marketing offer to fit the special needs of each customer and can negotiate terms of sale. They can build long-term personal relationships with key decision makers.

The role of personal selling varies from company to company. Some firms have no salespeople at all—for example, companies that sell only through mail-order

The term "salesperson" covers a wide range of positions, from the clerk selling in a retail store to the engineering salesperson who consults with client companies.

catalogues or those that sell through manufacturer's representatives, sales agents, or brokers. In most firms, however, the sales force plays a major role. In companies that sell business products, such as Xerox or DuPont, the company's salespeople work directly with customers. In fact, to many customers, salespeople may be the only contact. To these customers, the sales force *is* the company. In consumer product companies such as Procter & Gamble or Wilson Sporting Goods that sell through intermediaries, final consumers rarely meet salespeople or even know about them. Still, the sales force plays an important behind-the-scenes role. It works with wholesalers and retailers to gain their support and to help them be more effective in selling the company's products.

The sales force serves as a critical link between a company and its customers. In many cases, salespeople serve both masters—the seller and the buyer. First, they *represent the company to customers.* They find and develop new customers and communicate information about the company's products and services. They sell products by approaching customers, presenting their products, answering objections, negotiating prices and terms, and closing sales. In addition, salespeople provide services to customers, carry out market research and intelligence work, and fill out sales call reports.

At the same time, salespeople *represent customers to the company,* acting inside the firm as "champions" of customers' interests. Salespeople relay customer concerns about company products and actions back to those who can handle them. They learn about customer needs and work with others in the company to develop greater customer value. Thus, the salesperson often acts as an "account manager" who manages the relationship between the seller and buyer.

As companies move toward a stronger market orientation, their sales forces are becoming more market focused and customer oriented. The old view was that salespeople should worry about sales and the company should worry about profit. The current view holds that salespeople should be concerned with more than just producing *sales*—they also must know how to produce *customer satisfaction* and *company profit.* They should be able to examine sales data, measure market potential, gather market intelligence, and develop marketing strategies and plans. In other words, the sales force must help the company create long-term, profitable relationships with customers.

Managing the Sales Force

Sales force management
The analysis, planning, implementation, and control of sales force activities. It includes designing sales force strategy and structure and recruiting, selecting, training, compensating, supervising, and evaluating the firm's salespeople.

We define **sales force management** as the analysis, planning, implementation, and control of sales force activities. It includes designing sales force strategy and structure and recruiting, selecting, training, compensating, supervising, and evaluating the firm's salespeople. These major sales force management decisions, shown in Figure 15-1, are discussed in the following sections.

Designing Sales Force Strategy and Structure

Marketing managers face several sales force strategy and design questions. How should salespeople and their tasks be structured? How large should the sales force be? Should salespeople sell alone or work in teams with other people in the company? Should they sell in the field or by telephone?

Sales Force Structure

A company can divide sales responsibilities along any of several lines. The decision is simple if the company sells only one product line to one industry with customers in many locations. In that case the company would use a *territorial sales force structure.* However, if the company sells many products to many types of customers, it might need a *product sales force structure,* a *customer sales force structure,* or a combination of the two.

Territorial sales force structure
A sales force organization that assigns each salesperson to an exclusive geographic territory in which that salesperson carries the company's full line.

Territorial Sales Force Structure. In the **territorial sales force structure,** each salesperson is assigned to an exclusive geographic territory and sells the company's full line of products or services to all customers in that territory. This sales organization has many advantages. It clearly defines the salesperson's job, and because only one salesperson works the territory, he or she gets all the credit or blame for territory sales. The territorial structure also increases the salesperson's desire to build local business relationships that, in turn, improve selling effectiveness. Finally, because each salesperson travels within a limited geographic area, travel expenses are relatively small.

A territorial sales organization often is supported by many levels of sales management positions. Campbell Soup, for example, recently changed from a product sales force structure to a territorial one, whereby each salesperson is now responsible for selling all Campbell Soup products. Starting at the bottom of the organization, *sales merchandisers* report to *sales representatives,* who report to *retail supervisors,* who report to *directors of retail sales operations,* who report to *regional sales managers.* Regional sales managers, in turn, report to *general sales managers,* who report to a *vice-president and general sales manager.*

Product Sales Force Structure. Salespeople must know their products, especially when the products are numerous and complex. This need, together with the

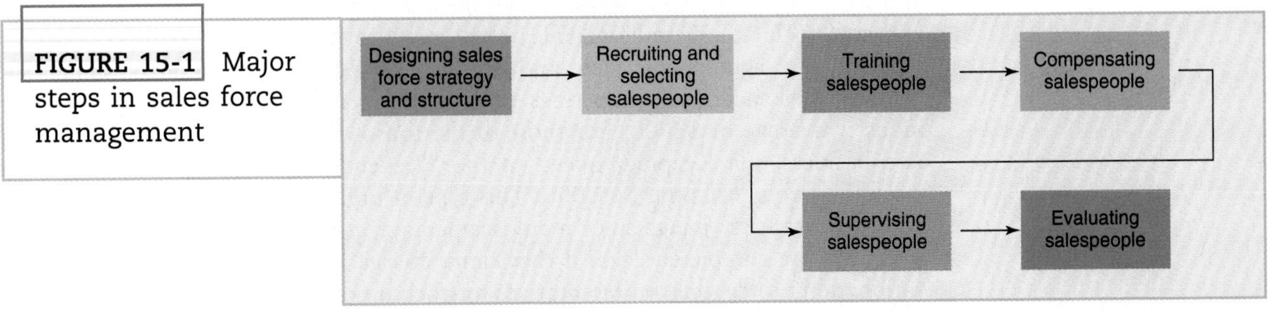

FIGURE 15-1 Major steps in sales force management

Product sales force structure
A sales force organization under which salespeople specialize in selling only a portion of the company's products or lines.

Kodak Canada
www.kodak.ca

trend toward product management, has led many companies to adopt a **product sales force structure,** in which the sales force sells along product lines. Kodak uses different sales forces for its film products than for its industrial products. The film products sales force deals with simple products that are distributed intensively, whereas the industrial products sales force deals with complex products that require technical understanding.

The product structure can lead to problems, however, if a single large customer buys many different company products. For example, Baxter International, a hospital supply company, has several product divisions, each with a separate sales force. Several Baxter salespeople might end up calling on the same hospital on the same day. This means that the salespeople travel over the same routes and wait to see the same customer's purchasing agents. These extra costs must be compared with the benefits of better product knowledge and attention to individual products.

Customer sales force structure
A sales force organization under which salespeople specialize in selling to specific customers or industries.

Customer Sales Force Structure. More and more companies are using a **customer sales force structure,** in which they organize the sales force along customer or industry lines. Separate sales forces may be set up for different industries, for serving current customers versus finding new ones, and for major accounts versus regular accounts.

Organizing the sales force around customers can help a company become more customer focused and build closer relationships with important customers. For example, giant ABB, the $30-billion-a-year Swiss-based industrial equipment maker, changed from a product-based to a customer-based sales force. The new structure resulted in a stronger customer orientation and improved service to clients:[3]

> Until four months ago, David Donaldson sold boilers for ABB. . . . After 30 years, Donaldson sure knew boilers, but he didn't know much about the broad range of other products offered by ABB's Power Plant division. Customers were frustrated because as many as a dozen ABB salespeople called on them at different times to peddle their products. ABB's bosses decided that this was a poor way to run a sales force. So [recently], David Donaldson and 27 other power plant salespeople began new jobs. [Donaldson] now also sells turbines, generators, and three other product lines. He handles six major accounts . . . instead of a [mixed batch] of 35. His charge: Know the customer intimately and sell him the products that help him operate productively. Says Donaldson: "My job is to make it easy for my customers to do business with us. . . . I show them where to go in ABB whenever they have a problem." The president of ABB's power plant businesses [adds]: "If you want to be a customer-driven company, you have to design the sales organization around individual buyers rather than around your products."

Pyramid sales force structure
A sales force organization under which salespeople recruit others into the network so that the organization constantly expands.

Pyramid Structures. Some successful firms, such as Amway, Tupperware, and Mary Kay, use **pyramid sales force structures,** or multi-level plans. In Canada alone, these organizations generate $1.3 billion in annual sales and employ 600 000 salespeople. Pyramid firms rely on current salespeople to recruit others into the network so that the organization constantly expands. When a salesperson recruits a new sales rep, the recruiter receives a small commission on all the sales that the new recruit generates. Weekenders of Toronto is one of the most successful organizations of this type. Boasting a sales force of 15 000, it rang up sales of $70 million, and as it expands into new territories such as Chile, Germany, and Australia, is expected to hit $250 million. Sales reps convince their friends to hold "parties" where six to eight people view and buy a line of coordinated knit clothing. The average Weekenders sales rep rings up $17 000 per year in sales compared to an industry average of $2000. For those at the top of the pyramid, it can be a lucrative business. Lia Keeping, queen of the Weekenders sales force, takes home a monthly cheque of about $64 000. This type of organization has long been tainted with an unsavoury image since many scams have used this type of structure. However, they are completely legal if they don't charge an entry fee to join the organization, don't force sales representatives to stock up on products at rates above those it costs plan operators, and are honest about what a typical salesperson earns.[4]

Complex sales force structure
A sales force organization that combines several types of sales force structures.

Complex Sales Force Structures. When a company sells a wide variety of products to many types of customers over a broad geographical area, it often combines several types of sales force structures. Salespeople can be specialized by customer and territory, by product and territory, by product and customer, or by territory, product, and customer. No single structure is best for all companies and situations. Each company should select a sales force structure that best serves the needs of its customers and fits its overall marketing strategy.

Sales Force Size

Since salespeople constitute the company's most productive but most expensive asset, companies must next consider sales force size. In recent years, sales forces have been shrinking in size. One study revealed that, in just the two years from 1996 to 1998, the average company's sales force decreased by a whopping 26 percent. Advances in selling technology, such as selling on the Internet or the use of account management software, which make salespeople more efficient, is one cause of sales force reduction. Merger mania, on both the seller and customer sides, has also led to fewer salespeople. Merged firms rarely need a double sales force. "When you merge two sales forces, you'll have about one and a half sales forces when you're done," says a sales consultant. Similarly, the merging of two customer firms means fewer customers, and fewer customers means that fewer salespeople are needed to call on them.[5]

Workload approach
An approach to setting sales force size in which the company groups accounts into different size classes and then determines how many salespeople are needed to call on them the desired number of times.

Many companies use some form of **workload approach** to set sales force size. A company first groups accounts into different classes according to size, account status, or other factors related to the amount of effort required to maintain them. It then determines the number of salespeople needed to call on each class of accounts the desired number of times. The company might think as follows: Suppose we have 1000 Type A accounts and 2000 Type B accounts. Type A accounts require 36 calls a year, and Type B accounts require 12 calls a year. In this case, the sales force's *workload*—the number of calls it must make per year—is 60 000 calls [(1000 × 36) + (2000 × 12) = 36 000 + 24 000 = 60 000]. Suppose our average salesperson can make 1000 calls a year. Thus, the company needs 60 salespeople (60 000 ÷ 1000).

Other Sales Force Strategy and Structure Issues

Sales management must also decide who will be involved in the selling effort and how various sales and sales-support people will work together.

Outside sales force (or field sales force)
Outside salespeople who travel to call on customers.

Inside sales force
Salespeople who conduct business from their offices via telephone, e-mail, and fax or visits from prospective buyers.

Outside and Inside Sales Forces. The company can have an **outside sales force** (or *field sales force*), an **inside sales force,** or both. Outside salespeople travel to call on customers. Inside salespeople conduct business from their offices via telephone, e-mail, and fax or visits from prospective buyers.

To reduce time demands on their outside sales forces, many companies have increased the size of their inside sales forces. These include technical support people, sales assistants, and telemarketers. *Technical support people* provide technical information and answers to customers' questions. *Sales assistants* provide clerical backup for outside salespeople: They call ahead and confirm appointments, conduct credit checks, follow up on deliveries, and answer customers' questions when outside salespeople cannot be reached. *Telemarketers* use the phone to find new leads and qualify prospects for the field sales force, or to sell and service accounts directly.

Telemarketing
Using the telephone to sell directly to consumers.

The inside sales force frees outside salespeople to spend more time selling to major accounts and finding new major prospects. Depending on the complexity of the product and customer, a telemarketer can make from 20 to 33 decision maker contacts a day, compared to the average of four that an outside salesperson can see. And for many types of products and selling situations, **telemarketing** can be as effective as a personal call but much less expensive. Whereas a typical personal sales call can cost well over $250, a routine industrial telemarketing call costs only about $7.50 and a complex call about $30.[6] Telemarketing can be used successfully by both large and small companies:

> Kodak Canada recently began placing new emphasis on telemarketing. While it has always employed an inside sales staff to serve small or distant customers, it has now begun encouraging customers to call its telemarketers to receive faster service—whether it be improved inventory replenishment or updates on upcoming special offers and events. To retain the personal touch with customers using telemarketing services, Kodak has begun sending its customers photographs of its telesales reps along with flow charts so that customers can better understand how requests for service move through the company.
>
> Similarly, Molson Breweries has hired six telesales people to manage inventory, promotions and merchandising for its smaller clients, allowing it to shrink its Ontario sales force from 125 salespeople to 70. Canadian telemarketing guru Jim Domanski stresses that telemarketing costs about one-tenth the rate for making a personal sales call and that a good telemarketer can reach as many companies in a day as a field sales rep can contact in a week.[7]
>
> Climax Portable Machine Tools has proven that a small company can use telemarketing to save money and still lavish attention on buyers. Climax sales engineers, who once spent one-third of their time on the road, training distributor salespeople and accompanying them on four calls a day, now service about 30 prospects a day, following up on leads generated by ads and direct mail. Because it takes about five calls to close a sale, the sales engineers update a prospect's computer file after each contact, noting the degree of commitment, requirements, next call date, and personal comments. For example, "If anyone mentions he's going on a fishing trip, our sales engineer enters that in the computer and uses it to personalize the next phone call," says Climax's president, noting that's just one way to build good relations. Another is that the first mailing to a prospect includes the sales engineer's business card with his picture on it. Of course, it takes more than friendliness to sell $15 000 machine tools over the phone (special orders may run $200 000), but the telemarketing approach is working well. When Climax customers were asked, "Do you see the sales engineer often enough?" the response was overwhelmingly positive. Obviously, many people didn't realize that the only contact they'd had with Climax had been on the phone.[8]

Thus, while some marketers have shunned telemarketing, equating it with the annoying calls they get at dinner, others are leveraging the concept. Instead of operating call centres (centres managing outgoing sales calls), they have developed *contact centres* that are the hub of the enterprise. Through the use of sophisticated technology, contact centres leverage existing customer information to enhance, maintain, and manage customer relationships throughout their life cycles. Contact centres can be accessed through the Internet as well as the more traditional vehicles of telephone, e-mail, and fax. Contact centres also integrate the customer service centre with the sales centre.

Experienced telemarketers sell complex chemical products by phone at DuPont's corporate telemarketing centre. Says one: "I'm more effective on the phone . . . and you don't have to outrun the dogs."

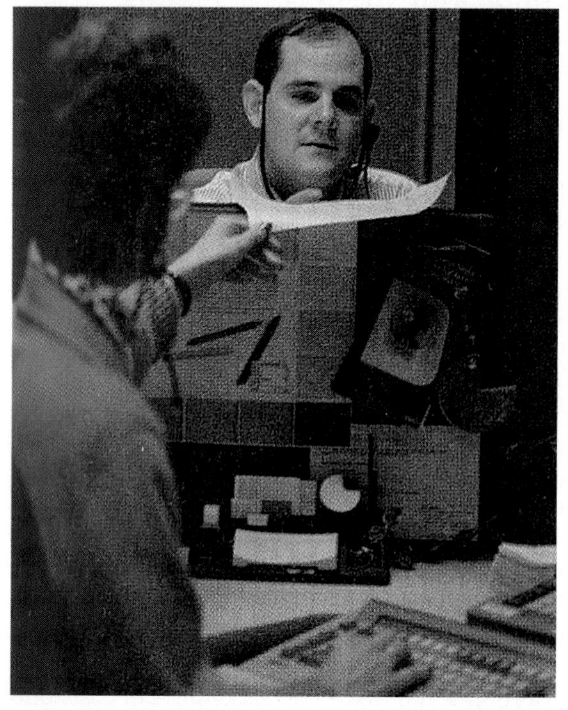

Say a customer gets frustrated while trying to find information about a replacement part on a company's Web site. He clicks a live help icon and immediately receives assistance from the first available representative in the contact centre. The person can guide him verbally through the Web site or can take over the screen and show him specific pages or options. Now imagine a customer on an automotive manufacturer's Web site. She drills down several pages to a point in the site where she's calculating her financing options for a new Corvette. Such behaviour indicates that she is not just browsing, but is close to making a buying decision. Web-enabled contact centres use this type of click stream data as cues to trigger action by a sales representative, who can approach the customer online and help her through the buying process just as in a traditional retail environment.[9] As these examples show, the Internet offers great potential for restructuring sales forces and conducting sales operations—not just for selling, but for everything from training salespeople to conducting sales meetings and servicing accounts (see Marketing Highlight 15-1).

Team Selling. For years, the customer has been solely in the hands of the salesperson. The salesperson identified the prospect, arranged the call, explored the customer's needs, created and proposed a solution, closed the deal, and turned cheerleader as others delivered what he or she promised. For selling relatively simple products, this approach can work well. But if the products are more complex and the service requirements greater, the salesperson simply can't go it alone. Instead, most companies now are using **team selling** to service large, complex accounts.

Team selling
Using teams of people from sales, marketing, engineering, finance, technical support, and even upper management to service large, complex accounts.

Companies are finding that sales teams can unearth problems, solutions, and sales opportunities that no individual salesperson can. Such teams may include experts from any area or level of the selling firm—sales, marketing, technical and support services, R&D, engineering, operations, finance, and others. In team selling situations, the salesperson shifts from "soloist" to "orchestrator."[10]

In many cases, the move to team selling mirrors similar changes in customers' buying organizations. According to the director of sales education at Dow Chemical, over 80 percent of purchasing decisions are now being made by multifunctional buying teams, including purchasing, engineering, and financial management staff. To sell effectively to such selling teams, he states, "Our sellers . . . have to captain selling teams. There are no more lone wolves."[11]

Some companies, including IBM Canada, Xerox, and Procter & Gamble, have used teams for a long time. Others have only recently reorganized to adopt the team concept. Cutler-Hammer, which supplies circuit breakers, motor starters, and other electrical equipment to heavy industrial manufacturers such as Ford Motor, recently developed "pods" of salespeople that focus on a specific geographical region, industry, or market. Each pod member contributes unique expertise and knowledge about a product or service that salespeople can leverage when selling to increasingly sophisticated buying teams.[12]

Team selling has some pitfalls. Selling teams can confuse or overwhelm customers who are used to working with only one salesperson. Salespeople who are used to having customers all to themselves may have trouble learning to work with and trust others on a team. Finally, difficulties in evaluating individual contributions to the team selling effort can create some sticky compensation issues.

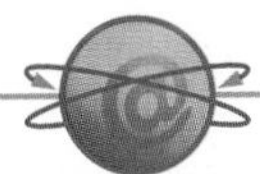

Dun & Bradstreet
www.dnb.com/

Still, team selling can produce dramatic results. Dun & Bradstreet, the world's largest marketer of business information and related services, recently established sales teams made up of representatives from its credit, collection, and marketing business units, which up to then had worked separately. Their mission was to work as a team to call on senior executives in customer organizations, learn about customer needs, and offer solutions. The teams concentrated on D&B's top 50 customers.

When one of the D&B sales teams asked to meet with the chief financial officer of a major telecommunications company, the executive responded, "I'm delighted you asked, but why talk?" He found out after a one-hour meeting. The D&B team listened as he discussed problems facing his organization, and by the end of the information-seeking session, the team had come up with several solutions for the executive and had identified $2.25 million in D&B sales opportunities from what had been a $1 million customer. More teams met with more clients, creating more opportunities. About a year after the program started, D&B's marketing department had targeted $300 million in sales opportunities, about half of which would not have been found under the old system. Now these teams are getting together with D&B's top 200 customers.[13]

Warner-Lambert
www.warner-lambert.com/

Recruiting and Selecting Salespeople

At the heart of any successful sales force operation is the recruitment and selection of good salespeople. To "weed out mediocrity," Warner-Lambert Canada is

marketing highlight 15-1

Point, Click, and Sell: Welcome to the Web-Based Sales Force

There are few rules at Fisher Scientific International's sales training sessions. The chemical company's salespeople are allowed to show up for new workshops in their pyjamas. No one flinches if they stroll in at midnight for their first class, take a dozen breaks to call clients, or invite the family cat to sleep in their laps while they take an exam. Sound unorthodox? It would be if Fisher's salespeople were trained in a regular classroom. But for the past year and a half, the company has been using the Internet to teach the majority of its salespeople in the privacy of their homes, cars, hotel rooms, or wherever else they bring their laptops.

To get updates on Fisher's pricing or refresh themselves on one of the company's highly technical products, all salespeople have to do is log on to the Web site and select from the lengthy index. Any time of the day or night, they can get information on a new product, take an exam, or post messages for product experts—all without ever entering a corporate classroom. Welcome to the new world of the Web-based sales force.

In the past few years, sales organizations around the world have begun saving money and time by using a host of new Web approaches to train reps, hold sales meetings, and even conduct live sales presentations. "Web-based technologies are becoming really hot in sales because they save salespeople's time," says technology consultant Tim Sloane. Web-based technologies help keep reps up to speed on their company's new products and sales strategies. Fisher Scientific's reps can dial up the Web site at their leisure, and whereas newer reps might spend hours online going through each session in order, more seasoned sellers might just log on for a quick refresher on a specific product before a sales call. "It allows them to manage their time better, because they're only getting training when they need it, in the doses they need it in," says John Pavlik, director of the company's training department. If salespeople are spending less time on training, Pavlik says, they're able to spend more time on what they do best—selling.

Training is only one of the ways sales organizations are using the Internet. Many companies are using the Web to make sales presentations and service accounts. For example, Digital Equipment Corporation's salespeople used to spend a great deal of time travelling to the offices of clients and prospects. But since 1997, the company (now a division of Compaq) has been delivering sales pitches by combining teleconferences with Web presentations. For example, when Digital's account team in Calgary needed to see what their marketing manager in Toronto had prepared for a client, they just logged on to the PowerPoint presentation and uploaded it using Internet Conference Center, Web-based software. Once everyone was logged on, the marketing manager was able to take control of the browsers and lead the reps through the presentation in real time, highlighting and pointing out specific items as he went. The account reps added their comments, based on their more detailed knowledge of the client, and the revised presentation was then shown online to the client. The beauty of the whole process? It's so fast. "The use of [the Web] clearly helps shorten our sales cycle." Presentations are created and delivered in less time—sometimes weeks less than the process would take face-to-face—and salespeople are able to close deals more quickly.

Other companies are using Web-based sales presentations to find new prospects. Oracle Corporation, the $12-billion software and information technology services company, conducts online, live product seminars for prospective clients. Prospects can scan the high-tech company's Web site to see which seminars they might want to attend, then dial in via modem and telephone at the appropriate time (and Oracle pays for the cost of the phone call). The seminars, which usually consist of a live lecture describing the product's applications followed by a question-and-answer session, average about 125 prospective clients apiece. Once a seminar is completed, prospects are directed to another part of Oracle's Web site, from which they can order products. "It costs our clients nothing but time," says Oracle's manager of Internet marketing programs, "and we're reaching a much wider audience than we would if we were doing in-person seminars."

The Internet can also be a handy way to hold sales strategy meetings. Consider

one firm that has begun hiring undergraduate and graduate students to improve the skill level of those people it sends into the field. The performance difference between an average salesperson and a top salesperson can be substantial. In a typical sales force, the top 30 percent of the salespeople bring in 60 percent of the sales. Thus, careful salesperson selection can greatly increase overall sales force performance. Beyond the differences in sales performance, poor selection results in costly turnover. One study found an average annual sales force turnover rate of 27 percent for all industries. The costs of high turnover can be great. When a salesperson quits, the costs of finding and training a new salesperson—plus the costs of lost sales—can run as high as $75 000 to $125 000. And a sales force with many new people is less productive.[14]

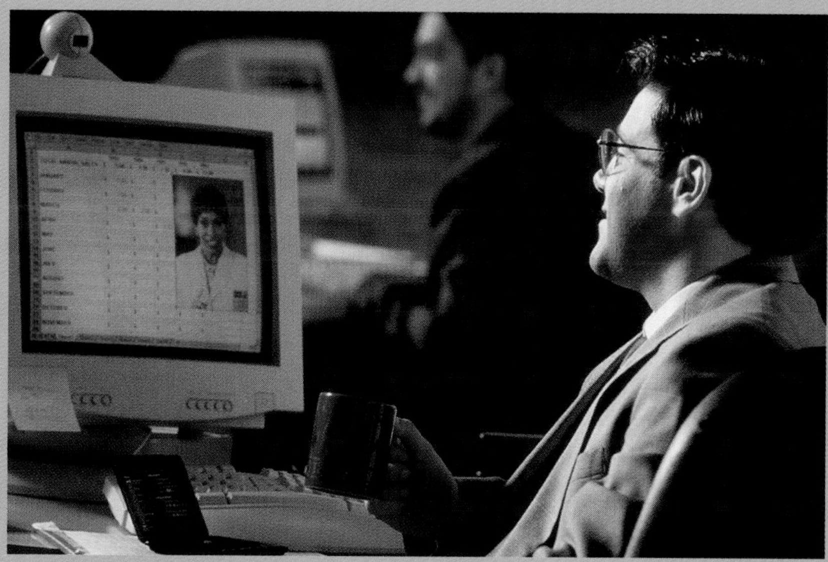

Sales organizations around the world are now using the Internet to train salespeople, hold sales meetings, and even conduct live sales presentations.

Cisco Systems, which provides networking solutions for the Internet. Sales meetings used to take an enormous bite out of Cisco's travel budget. Now the company saves about $1.5 million a month by conducting many of those sessions on the Web. Whenever Cisco introduces a new product, it holds a Web meeting to update salespeople in groups of 100 or more on the product's marketing and sales strategy.

Usually led by the product manager or a vice-president of sales, the meetings typically begin with a 10-minute slide presentation that spells out the planned strategy. Then, salespeople spend the next 50 or so minutes asking questions via teleconference. The meeting's leader can direct attendees' browsers to competitors' Web sites or ask them to vote on certain issues by using the software's instant polling feature. "Our salespeople are actually meeting more online then they ever were face to face," says Mike Mitchell, Cisco's distance learning manager, adding that some salespeople who used to meet with other reps and managers only a few times a quarter are meeting online nearly every day. "That's very empowering for the sales force, because they're able to make suggestions at every step of the way about where we're going with our sales and marketing strategies."

Thus, Web-based technologies can produce big organizational benefits for sales forces. They help conserve salespeople's valuable time, save travel dollars, and give salespeople a new vehicle for selling and servicing accounts. But the technologies also have some drawbacks. For starters, they're expensive. Setting up a Web-based system can cost up to several hundred thousand dollars. Such systems also can intimidate low-tech salespeople or clients. "You must have a culture that is comfortable using computers," says one marketing communications manager. "As simple as it is, if your salespeople or clients aren't comfortable using the Web, you're wasting your money." Also, Web tools are susceptible to server crashes and other network difficulties, not a happy event when you're in the midst of an important sales meeting or presentation.

For these reasons, some high-tech experts recommend that sales executives use Web technologies for training, sales meetings, and preliminary client sales presentations, but resort to old-fashioned, face-to-face meetings when the time draws near to close the deal. "When push comes to shove, if you've got an account worth closing, you're still going to get on that plane and see the client in person," says sales consultant Sloane. "Your client is going to want to look you in the eye before buying anything from you, and that's still one thing you just can't do online."

Source: Adapted from Melinda Ligos, "Point, click, and sell," *Sales & Marketing Management*, May 1999:51–5. Also see Chad Kaydo, "You've got sales," *Sales & Marketing Management*, October 1999:29–39; and Ginger Conlon, "How to move customers online," *Sales & Marketing Management*, March 2000:27–8.

What Makes a Good Salesperson?

Selecting salespeople would not be a problem if the company knew what traits to look for. If it knew that good salespeople were outgoing, aggressive, and energetic, for example, it could simply check applicants for these characteristics. But many successful salespeople are bashful, soft-spoken, and laid-back. Some are tall and others are short; some speak well and others poorly; some dress fashionably and others shabbily.

Still, the search continues for the magic list of traits that spells sure-fire sales success. One survey suggests that good salespeople have a lot of enthusiasm, persistence, initiative, self-confidence, and job commitment. They are committed to sales as a way of life and have a strong customer orientation. Another study suggests that good salespeople are independent and self-motivated, and are excellent listeners. Still another study advises that salespeople should be a friend to the customer as well as persistent, enthusiastic, attentive, and—above all—honest. They must be internally motivated, disciplined, hard-working, and able to build strong relationships with customers. Finally, studies show that good salespeople are team players rather than loners.[15]

How can a company determine what traits salespeople in its industry should have? The *duties* of the job suggest some of the traits a company should look for. Is a lot of planning and paperwork required? Does the job call for much travel? Will the salesperson face a lot of rejections? Will the salesperson be working with high-level buyers? The successful salesperson should be suited to these duties. The company also should look at the characteristics of its most successful salespeople for clues to needed traits.

Recruiting Procedures

Once management has decided on needed traits, it must *recruit* salespeople. The human resources department looks for applicants by getting names from current salespeople, using employment agencies, placing classified ads, and contacting university students. Until recently, companies sometimes found it hard to sell university students on selling. Many thought that selling was a job and not a profession, that salespeople had to be deceitful to be effective, and that selling involved too much insecurity and travel. In addition, some women believed that selling was a man's career. To counter such objections, recruiters now offer high starting salaries and income growth. For example, in its *1999/2000 Sales Compensation* report, the Canadian Professional Sales Association noted that junior sales representatives can earn up to $54 000 a year, while key account representatives can pull in over $95 000. Divisional or regional sales managers have earnings as high as $113 400.[16] Recruiters also tout the fact that many of the presidents of large North American corporations started out in marketing and sales. They point out that more than 28 percent of the people now selling industrial products are women. And women account for a much higher percentage of the sales force in some industries, such as textiles and apparel (61%), banking and financial services (58%), communications (51%), and publishing (49%).

Selecting Salespeople

Recruiting will attract many applicants, from which the company must select the best. Selection procedures range from a single informal interview to lengthy testing and interviewing. Many companies give formal tests to sales applicants. Tests typically measure sales aptitude, analytical and organizational skills, personality traits, and other characteristics. Test results count heavily in such companies as IBM, Prudential, Procter & Gamble, and Gillette. Gillette claims that tests have reduced turnover by 42 percent, and that test scores have correlated well with the later performance of new salespeople. But test scores provide only one piece of information in a set that includes personal characteristics, references, past employment history, and interviewer reactions.[17]

Training Salespeople

Many companies used to send their new salespeople into the field almost immediately after hiring them. They would be given samples, order books, and general instructions ("Sell in Manitoba and Saskatchewan"). Training programs were luxuries. To many companies, a training program translated into much expense for instructors, materials, space, and salary for a person who was not yet selling, and a loss of sales opportunities because the person was not in the field.

Today's new salespeople, however, spend anywhere from a few weeks or months to a year or more in training. Rob Granby, vice-president of sales at Cadbury Beverages Canada, believes that ongoing training and a supportive corporate culture are essential: "If your corporate culture isn't one that nourishes and helps salespeople flourish, then no matter what you layer on in terms of bonus programs and special incentives, it won't make a difference."[18]

Although training can be expensive, it can also yield dramatic returns on the training investment. Nabisco did an extensive analysis of the return on investment of its two-day professional selling program, which teaches sales reps how to plan for and make professional presentations to their retail customers. Although it cost about $1500 to put each sales rep through the program, the training resulted in additional sales of more than $183 000 per rep and yielded almost $31 000 of additional profit per rep.[19] While some firms do their sales training in-house, others send their representatives to executive education programs or turn to the Canadian Professional Sales Association for help.

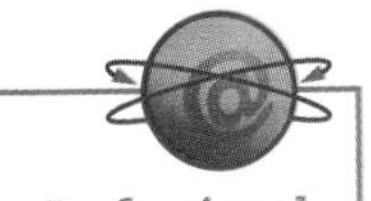

Canadian Professional Sales Association
www.cpsa.com/

Training programs have several goals. Since salespeople need to know and identify with the company, most training programs begin in describing the company's history and objectives, its organization, its financial structure and facilities, and its chief products and markets. Because salespeople also need to know the company's products, sales trainees are shown how products are produced and how they work. Since they also need to know customers' and competitors' characteristics, the training program teaches them about competitors' strategies and about different types of customers and their needs, buying motives, and buying habits. Because salespeople must know how to make effective presentations, they are trained in the principles of selling. Finally, they need to understand field procedures and responsibilities. They learn how to divide time between active and potential accounts and how to use an expense account, prepare reports, and route communications effectively.

Compensating Salespeople

To attract salespeople, a company must have an appealing compensation plan. These plans vary greatly by industry and by companies within an industry. The level of compensation must be close to the "going rate" for the type of sales job and needed skills. To pay less than the going rate would attract too few quality salespeople; to pay more would be unnecessary.

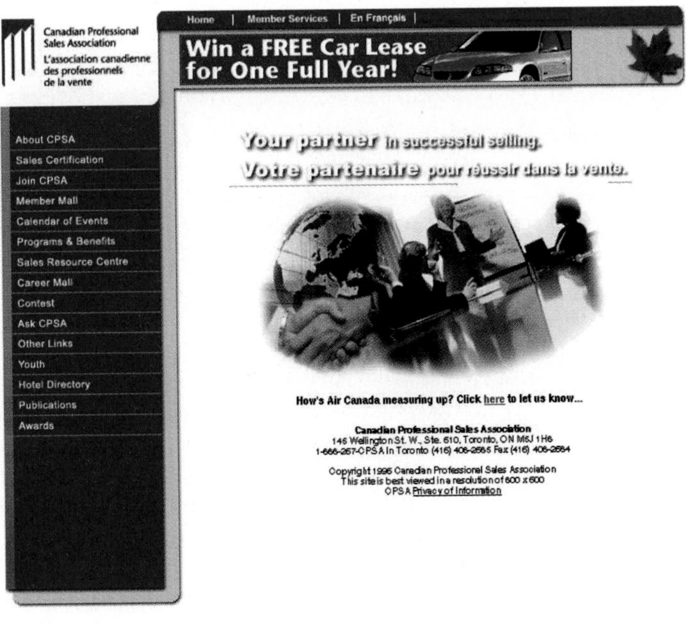

Many firms turn to the Canadian Professional Sales Association for help with sales training.

Compensation comprises several elements—a fixed amount, a variable amount, expenses, and fringe benefits. The fixed amount, usually a salary, gives the salesperson some stable income. The variable amount, which may be commissions or bonuses based on sales performance, rewards the salesperson for greater effort. Expense allowances, which repay salespeople for job-related expenses, let salespeople undertake needed and desirable selling efforts. Fringe benefits, such as paid vacations, sickness or accident benefits, pensions, and life insurance, provide job security and satisfaction.

Management must decide what *mix* of these compensation elements makes the most sense for each sales job. Different combinations of fixed and variable compensation give rise to four basic types of compensation plans—straight salary, straight commission, salary plus bonus, and salary plus commission. A study of sales force compensation plans showed that 70 percent of all companies surveyed use a combination of base salary and incentives. The average plan consisted of about 60 percent salary and 40 percent incentive pay.[20]

The sales force compensation plan can be designed to both motivate salespeople and direct their activities. For example, if sales management wants salespeople to emphasize new account development, it may pay a bonus for opening new accounts. The compensation plan should direct the sales force toward activities that are consistent with overall marketing objectives.

Table 15-1 illustrates how a company's compensation plan should reflect its overall marketing strategy. If the overall strategy is to grow rapidly and gain market share, the compensation plan should reward high sales performance and encourage salespeople to capture new accounts. This may suggest a larger commission component coupled with new account bonuses. However, if the marketing goal is to maximize profitability of current accounts, the compensation plan may contain a larger base salary component, with additional incentives based on current account sales or customer satisfaction.

In fact, companies are moving away from high commission plans that can drive salespeople to make short-term grabs for business (see Marketing Highlight 15-2). Notes one sales force expert: "The last thing you want is to have someone ruin a customer relationship because they're pushing too hard to close a deal." Companies are designing compensation plans that reward salespeople for building customer relationships and growing the long-run value of each customer.[21] Astra Pharma has not used a commission plan for some time; instead, it rewards its representatives for their level of understanding of their industry, gained through com-

TABLE 15-1 The Relationship between Overall Marketing Strategy and Sales Force Compensation

	STRATEGIC GOAL		
	To Rapidly Gain Market Share	**To Solidify Market Leadership**	**To Maximize Profitability**
Ideal salesperson	• An independent self-starter	• A competitive problem solver	• A team player • A relationship manager
Sales focus	• Deal making • Sustained high effort	• Consultative selling	• Account penetration
Compensation role	• To capture accounts • To reward high performance	• To reward new and existing account sales	• To manage the product mix • To encourage team selling • To reward account management

Source: Adapted from Sam T. Johnson, "Sales compensation: In search of a better solution," *Compensation & Benefits Review,* November–December 1993:53–60.

pany training and outside courses, and their involvement in it. And this involvement means more than a "nine-to-five" job. Reps offer evening presentations to groups that influence patients' treatment decisions, such as the Heart and Stroke Foundation and the Canadian Lung Association. They work with hospitals and drug stores to organize patient seminars.[22]

Supervising Salespeople

New salespeople need more than a territory, compensation, and training—they need *supervision*. Through supervision, the company *directs* and *motivates* the sales force to do a better job.

Directing Salespeople

How much should sales management be involved in helping salespeople manage their territories? Since it depends on many things, from the company's size to the experience of its sales force, companies vary widely in how closely they supervise their salespeople.

Many companies help their salespeople in identifying customer targets and setting call norms. In addition, they may specify how much time their sales forces should spend prospecting for new accounts. Companies may also direct salespeople in how to use their time efficiently. One tool is the *annual call plan,* which shows which customers and prospects to call on in which months and which activities to carry out. Activities include taking part in trade shows, attending sales meetings, and carrying out marketing research. Another tool is *time-and-duty analysis*. In addition to time spent selling, the salesperson spends time travelling, waiting, eating, taking breaks, and doing administrative chores.

Figure 15-2 shows how salespeople spend their time. On average, actual face-to-face selling time accounts for only 30 percent of total working time. If selling time could be raised from 30 to 40 percent, this would be a 33 percent increase in the time spent selling. Companies are always looking for ways to save time—using phones instead of travelling, simplifying record-keeping forms, finding better call and routing plans, and supplying more and better customer information.

Many firms have adopted sales force automation systems that computerize sales force operations for more efficient order-entry transactions, improved customer service, and better salesperson decision making. Salespeople use computers to profile customers and prospects, analyze and forecast sales, manage accounts, schedule sales calls, enter orders, check inventories and order status, prepare sales and expense reports, process correspondence, and carry out many other activities. Sales force automation not only lowers sales force costs and improves productivity, but also improves the quality of sales management decisions. Here is an example of successful sales force automation:[23]

Owens Corning
www.owenscorning.com/

> Owens-Corning recently put its sales force on line with FAST—its newly developed Field Automation Sales Team system. This system provides Owens-Corning salespeople with a constant supply of information about their company and the people they're dealing with. Using laptop computers, each salesperson can access three types of programs. First, FAST gives them a set of generic tools, with everything from word processing to fax transmission to creating presentations online. Second, it provides product information—tech bulletins, customer specifications, pricing information, and other data that can help close a sale. Finally, it offers up a wealth of customer information—buying history, types of products ordered, and preferred payment terms. Reps previously stored such information in loose-leaf books, calendars, and account cards. FAST makes working directly with customers easier than ever. Salespeople can prime themselves on backgrounds of clients; call up pre-written sales letters; transmit orders and resolve customer-service issues on the spot during customer calls; and have samples, pamphlets, brochures, and other materials sent to clients with a few keystrokes.

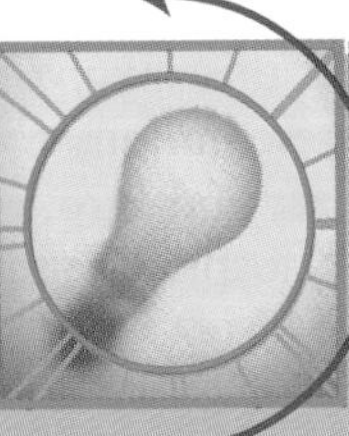

marketing highlight 15-2

Paying for Customer Value

For years, companies have paid their salespeople based on sales volume and dollar sales. Both are worthy goals, as long as the primary objective is selling the product. However, as the emphasis shifts to adding customer value, retaining customers and building strong relationships, and building "share-of-customer" (percentage of the customer's total business captured), companies are adding a new set of measures to their sales compensation equations. Increasingly, salespeople are being evaluated and compensated based on these kinds of measures:

Long-term customer satisfaction. This requires a salesperson to not oversell customers in the short run to satisfy a sales quota, but to look out for customers' best interests and focus on helping them achieve their goals.

Full customer service. This requires that the salesperson provide whatever customers need by working within the firm as well as building alliances with other companies that offer complementary products and services needed by customers. The goal is to never send a customer out the door to become someone else's customer.

Retention rates. Salespeople strive to ensure that once customers buy from the company, they don't buy from anyone else.

Growth of customer value. This involves increasing each customer's value to the company by increasing the customer's overall volume of business and capturing a greater share of that business. To make this happen, salespeople must build strong relationships based on real value and customer success.

To understand how including such measures in the compensation formula can affect a salesperson's performance, imagine rewarding a car salesperson in different ways. Most car dealerships reward salespeople for moving cars. Each car sale results in a commission. Once the commission is paid, the salesperson turns to finding a new customer for the next sale. But what if, in addition to a token commission, the dealership rewarded the sales associate for long-term customer satisfaction, measured by, say, high 18-month satisfaction scores? Such rewards would motivate the salesperson to follow up with the customer, to ensure that the service department was handling the customer well, and to identify and resolve a host of other problems that might upset the customer.

Suppose the dealership further rewarded the sales associate for share-of-customer. The associate would then find out what else is in the customer's garage and concentrate on ways to use the dealership's products to build "share-of-garage." If rewarded for such smart selling, the associate would find service, repair, and accessories for a customer, and get them all under the dealership's roof. The dealership would know what the customer wanted next, and when. In addition, the sales associate would feed customer information into the dealership's database, so that the customer would be served well even when the associate was on a well-earned vacation. Then, the dealership and the associate could work together to track customer needs electronically.

Most importantly, suppose that the dealership rewarded this salesperson for increasing long-term customer value to the dealership—perhaps by paying a tiny percentage of every dollar ever spent at the dealership by the customer on cars, financing, insurance, service, and repair. The salesperson would thus be motivated to not just make the sale, but to ensure that each customer returned to this dealership for everything, forever.

To be sure, reaching this level of sophistication in sales force compensation will not be easy. Such measures are difficult to track and apply. However, salespeople usually do what they are rewarded for doing. Sales compensation plans can help motivate salespeople to build real relationships between customers and the company, increasing the value of each customer to the company.

Source: Adapted from Don Peppers and Martha Rogers, "The money trap," *Sales & Marketing Management,* May 1997:58–60.

Compensation plans are being redesigned to motivate salespeople to build real relationships with customers.

FIGURE 15-2 How salespeople spend their time

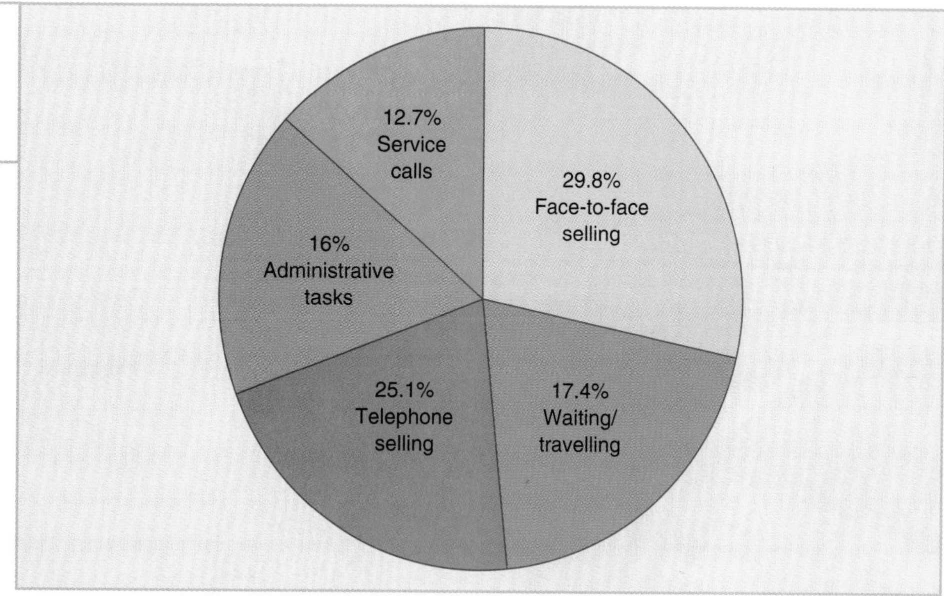

Source: Dartnell Corporation, *30th Survey of Sales Force Compensation.* © 1998 Dartnell Corporation.

Perhaps the fastest-growing sales force technology tool is the Internet. In a recent survey by Dartnell Corporation of 1000 salespeople, nearly 61 percent reported using the Internet regularly in their daily selling activities. Common uses include gathering competitive information, monitoring customer Web sites, and researching industries and specific customers. More than half of those not yet online reported that they soon would be. As more companies provide their salespeople with Web access, experts expect explosive growth in sales force Internet usage.[24]

Motivating Salespeople

Some salespeople will do their best without any special urging from management. To them, selling may be the most fascinating job in the world. But selling can also be frustrating. Salespeople often work alone, and they must sometimes travel away from home. They may face aggressive, competing salespeople and difficult customers. They sometimes lack the authority to do what is needed to win a sale and may thus lose large orders they have worked hard to obtain. Therefore, salespeople often need special encouragement to do their best.

Management can boost sales force morale and performance through its *organizational climate, sales quotas,* and *positive incentives.* Organizational climate describes the feeling that salespeople have about their opportunities, value, and rewards for a good performance within the company. Some companies treat salespeople as if they are not very important; other companies treat their salespeople as their prime movers and allow virtually unlimited opportunity for income and promotion. Not surprisingly, a company's attitude toward its salespeople affects their behaviour. If they are held in low esteem, there is high turnover and poor performance; if they are held in high esteem, there is less turnover and higher performance.

Sales quotas
Standards set for salespeople, stating the amount they should sell and how sales should be divided among the company's products.

Many companies set **sales quotas** for their salespeople—standards stating the amount they should sell and how sales should be divided among the company's products. Compensation is often related to how well salespeople meet their quotas.

Companies also use several positive incentives to increase sales force effort. *Sales meetings* provide social occasions, breaks from routine, chances to meet and talk with "company brass," and opportunities to air feelings and to identify with a larger group. Companies also sponsor *sales contests* to spur the sales force to make a selling effort above what would normally be expected. Pierre Généreux of

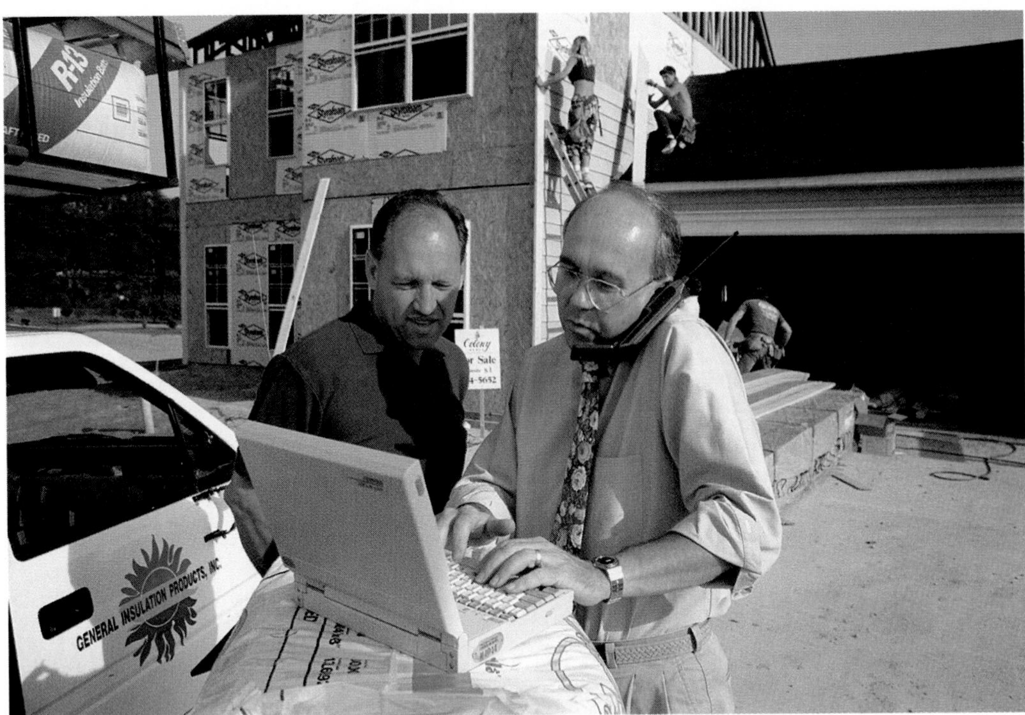

Owens-Corning's FAST sales force automation system makes working with customers easier than ever.

St-Jean de Matha, in a unique manner, won a continent-wide sales contest at the annual Ski-Doo dealers' convention. He made a presentation in French to several hundred American and English-Canadian colleagues, none of whom understood anything he said. Généreux, who is a unilingual francophone, used a combination of showmanship, authoritative tone, and passion to "bring the heart out" of his product. His "romancing of the machine" was so convincing that he won the "best salesperson" competition. Other incentives include honours, merchandise and cash awards, trips, and profit-sharing plans.[25]

Evaluating Salespeople

We have described how management communicates what salespeople should be doing and how it motivates them to do it. This process requires good feedback. And good feedback means getting regular information from salespeople to evaluate their performance. Management gets information about its salespeople in several ways. The most important source is the *sales reports,* including weekly or monthly work plans and longer-term territory marketing plans. Salespeople also write up their completed activities on *call reports* and turn in *expense reports* for which they are partly or wholly repaid. Additional information comes from personal observation, customer surveys, and talks with other salespeople.

The sales manager might begin with a *qualitative evaluation,* looking at a salesperson's knowledge of the company, products, customers, competitors, territory, and tasks. Personal traits—manner, appearance, speech, and temperament—can be rated. The sales manager can also review any problems in motivation or compliance. Each company must decide what would be most useful to know. It should communicate these criteria to salespeople so that they understand how their performance is evaluated and can make an effort to improve it.

Using sales force reports and other information, sales management can also conduct a more *formal evaluation* of members of the sales force. Formal evaluation produces four benefits. Management develops and communicates clear standards for

For a sales force incentive, American Express suggests that companies reward outstanding sales performers with high-tech Persona Select cards, prepaid electronic reward cards that allow recipients to purchase what they want.

judging performance. Management gathers well-rounded information about each salesperson. Salespeople receive constructive feedback that helps them to improve future performance. Salespeople are motivated to perform well because they know they will have to sit down with the sales manager and explain their performance.

One type of evaluation compares and ranks the sales performances of different salespeople. Such comparisons can be misleading, however. Salespeople may perform differently because of differences in territory potential, workload, level of competition, company promotion effort, and other factors. Furthermore, sales are not usually the best indicator of achievement. Management should be more interested in how much each salesperson contributes to net profits—a concern that requires looking at each salesperson's sales mix and expenses.

Another type of evaluation compares a salesperson's current performance with past performance. Such a comparison should directly indicate the person's progress. Table 15-2 provides an example. The sales manager can learn many things about Chris Bennett from this table. Bennett's total sales increased every year (line 3), though this does not necessarily mean that he is doing a better job. The product breakdown shows that Bennett has been able to push the sales of product B further than those of product A (lines 1 and 2). According to the quotas for the two products (lines 4 and 5), the success in increasing product B sales may be at the expense of product A sales. According to gross profits (lines 6 and 7), the company earns twice as much gross profit (as a ratio to sales) on A as it

TABLE 15-2 Evaluating a Salesperson's Performance

Territory: Midland	1997	Salesperson: Chris Bennett 1998	1999	2000
1. Net sales product A	$251 300	$253 200	$270 000	$263 100
2. Net sales product B	$423 200	$439 200	$553 900	$561 900
3. Net sales total	$674 500	$692 400	$823 900	$825 000
4. Percent of quota product A	95.6	92.0	88.0	84.7
5. Percent of quota product B	120.4	122.3	134.9	130.8
6. Gross profits product A	$ 50 260	$ 50 640	$ 54 000	$ 52 620
7. Gross profits product B	$ 42 320	$ 43 920	$ 53 390	$ 56 190
8. Gross profits total	$ 92 580	$ 94 560	$109 390	$108 810
9. Sales expense	$ 10 200	$ 11 100	$ 11 600	$ 13 200
10. Sales expense to total sales (%)	1.5	1.6	1.4	1.6
11. Number of calls	1675	1700	1680	1660
12. Cost per call	$ 6.09	$ 6.53	$ 6.90	$ 7.95
13. Average number of customers	320	324	328	334
14. Number of new customers	13	14	15	20
15. Number of lost customers	8	10	11	14
16. Average sales per customer	$ 2108	$ 2137	$ 2512	$ 2470
17. Average gross profit per customer	$ 289	$ 292	$ 334	$ 326

does on B. Bennett may be pushing the higher-volume, lower-margin product at the expense of the more profitable product. Although Bennett increased total sales by $1100 between 1997 and 1998 (line 3), the gross profits on these total sales actually decreased by $580 (line 8).

Sales expense (line 9) shows a steady increase, although total expense as a percentage of total sales seems to be under control (line 10). The upward trend in Bennett's total dollar expenses does not seem to be explained by any increase in the number of calls (line 11), although it may be related to success in acquiring new customers (line 14). However, there is a possibility that in prospecting for new customers Bennett is neglecting present customers, as indicated by an upward trend in the annual number of lost customers (line 15).

The last two lines on the table show the level and trend in Bennett's sales and gross profits per customer. These figures become more meaningful when they are compared with overall company averages. If Bennett's average gross profit per customer is lower than the company's average, he may be concentrating on the wrong customers or may not be spending enough time with each customer. The annual number of calls (line 11) indicates that Bennett may be making fewer calls than the average salesperson. If distances in the territory are not much different, this may mean he is not putting in a full workday, is poor at planning routing or minimizing waiting time, or spends too much time with certain accounts.

Principles of Personal Selling

We now turn from designing and managing a sales force to the actual personal selling process. Personal selling is an ancient art that has spawned a large literature and many principles. Effective salespeople operate on more than just instinct—they are highly trained in methods of territory analysis and customer management.

The Personal Selling Process

Most companies take a *customer-oriented approach* to personal selling. They train salespeople to identify customer needs and to find solutions. This approach assumes that customer needs provide sales opportunities, that customers appreciate good suggestions, and that customers will be loyal to salespeople who have their long-term interests at heart.

The problem solver salesperson fits better with the marketing concept than does the hard-sell salesperson or the glad-handing extrovert. Buyers today want solutions, not smiles; results, not razzle-dazzle. They want salespeople who listen to their concerns, understand their needs, and respond with the right products and services.

Steps in the Selling Process

Selling process
The steps that the salesperson follows when selling, which include prospecting and qualifying, pre-approach, approach, presentation and demonstration, handling objections, closing, and follow-up.

Most training programs consider that the **selling process** comprises several steps that the salesperson must master (see Figure 15-3). These steps focus on the goal of getting new customers and obtaining orders from them. However, most salespeople spend much of their time maintaining existing accounts and building long-term customer *relationships*. We discuss the relationship aspect of the personal selling process in a later section.

Prospecting and Qualifying

Prospecting
The step in the selling process in which the salesperson identifies qualified potential customers.

The first step in the selling process is **prospecting**—identifying qualified potential customers. Approaching the right potential customers is crucial to selling success. As one expert puts it: "If the sales force starts chasing anyone who is breathing and seems to have a budget, you risk accumulating a roster of expensive-to-serve, hard-to-satisfy customers who never respond to whatever value proposition you have." He continues, "The solution to this isn't rocket science. [You must] train salespeople to actively scout the right prospects. If necessary, create an incentive program to reward proper scouting."[26]

The salesperson must often approach many prospects to get just a few sales. Although the company supplies some leads, salespeople need skill in finding their own. They can ask current customers for referrals. They can build referral sources, such as suppliers, dealers, non-competing salespeople, and bankers. They can join organizations to which prospects belong or can engage in speaking and writing activities that will draw attention. They can search for names in newspapers or directories and use the telephone and mail to track down leads. Or they can drop in unannounced on various offices—the practice of *cold calling*.

Salespeople need to know how to *qualify* leads—that is, how to identify the good ones and screen out the poor ones. They can qualify prospects by evaluating their financial ability, volume of business, special needs, location, and possibilities for growth.

Preapproach

Preapproach
The step in the selling process in which the salesperson learns as much as possible about a prospective customer before making a sales call.

Before calling on a prospect, the salesperson should learn as much as possible about the organization (what it needs, who is involved in the buying) and its buyers (their characteristics and buying styles). This step is known as the **preapproach.** The salesperson can consult standard sources (*Scott's Directory, Moody's, Standard & Poor's, Dun & Bradstreet*), acquaintances, and others to learn about the company. The salesperson should set *call objectives,* which may be to qualify the prospect, to gather information, or to make an immediate sale. Another task is to decide on the best approach, which might be a personal visit, a phone call, or a letter. The best timing should be considered carefully because many prospects are busiest at certain times. Finally, the salesperson should consider an overall sales strategy for the account.

FIGURE 15-3 Major steps in effective selling

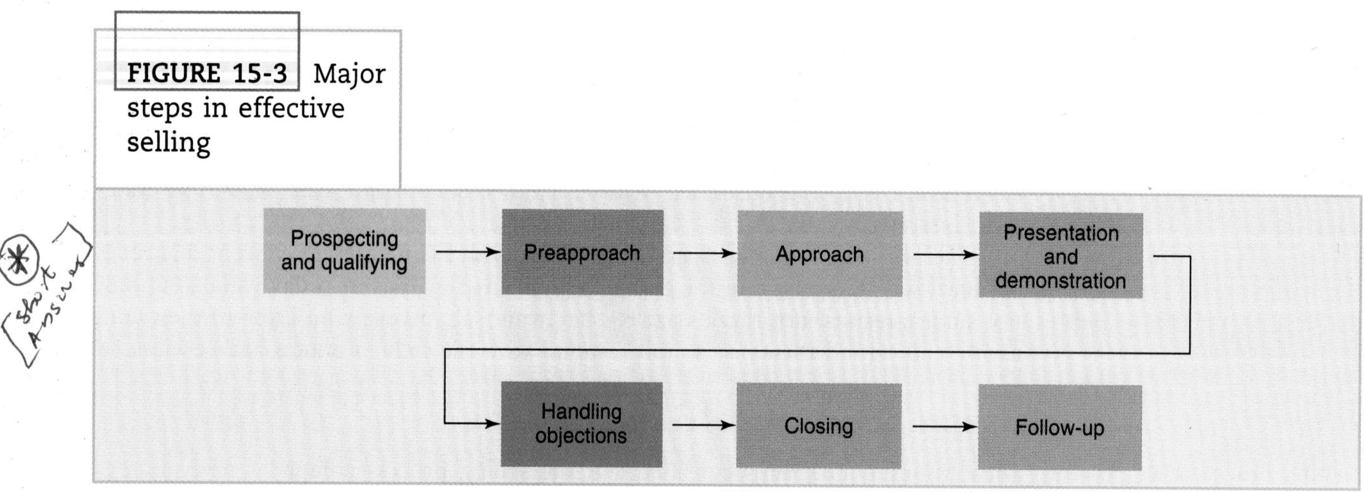

Approach

Approach
The step in the selling process in which the salesperson meets and greets the buyer to get the relationship off to a good start.

In the **approach** step, the salesperson meets and greets the buyer and gets the relationship off to a good start. The success of the approach depends on the salesperson's appearance, opening lines, and follow-up remarks. Opening lines should be positive, such as "Mr. Johnson, I am Chris Bennett from the Alltech Company. My company and I appreciate your willingness to see me. I will do my best to make this visit profitable and worthwhile for you and your company." This opening might be followed by some key questions to learn more about the customer's needs or the showing of a display or sample to attract the buyer's attention and curiosity.

Presentation and Demonstration

Presentation
The step in the selling process in which the salesperson tells the product "story" to the buyer, showing how the product will make or save money for the buyer.

In the **presentation** step of the selling process, the salesperson tells the product "story" to the buyer, showing how the product will make or save money. The salesperson describes the product features but concentrates on presenting customer benefits. Using a *need-satisfaction approach,* the salesperson starts with a search for the customer's needs by getting the customer to do most of the talking.

This approach calls for good listening and problem-solving skills:[27]

> "I think of myself more as a . . . well, psychologist," notes one experienced salesperson. "I listen to customers. I listen to their wishes and needs and problems, and I try to figure out a solution. If you're not a good listener, you're not going to get the order." Another salesperson suggests, "It's no longer enough to have a good relationship with a client. You have to understand their problems. You have to feel their pain."

The qualities that purchasing agents dislike most in salespeople include being pushy, late, and unprepared or disorganized. The qualities they value most include empathy, honesty, dependability, thoroughness, and follow-through.[28] Sales presentations can be improved with product samples or demonstrations: If buyers can see or handle the product, they will better remember its features and benefits. Visual aids, such as booklets, flip charts, slides, and videotapes or videodiscs, can show how a product performs and provide other information about it. Booklets and brochures remain useful as "leave behinds" for customer reference. Today, advanced presentation technologies allow for full multimedia presentations to only one or a few people. Audio and videocassettes, laptop computers with presentation software, and online presentation technologies have replaced the flip chart. Advanced Sterilization Products, a Johnson & Johnson company, even provides its sales force with a virtual reality presentation—the STERRAD Experience. Originally designed for use at conferences, the presentation equipment has been redesigned for sales calls and consists of a small video player with five headsets, all easily transported in an ordinary-size briefcase. Prospects don a helmet for a virtual reality tour of the inner workings of the STERRAD Sterilization System for medical devices and surgical

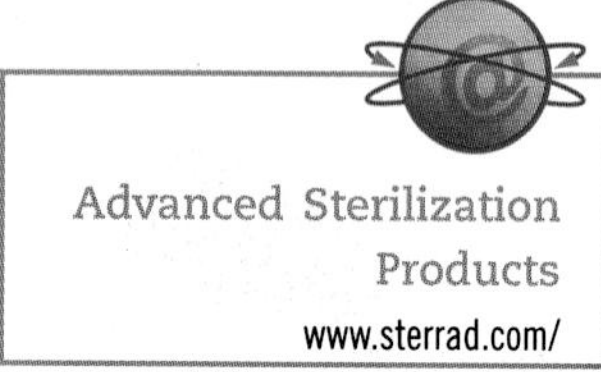

Advanced Sterilization Products
www.sterrad.com/

In the sales presentation, the salesperson tells the product story to the buyers.

instruments. The presentation provides more information in a more engaging way than could be done by displaying the actual machinery.[29]

Handling Objections

Handling objections
The step in the selling process in which the salesperson seeks out, clarifies, and overcomes customer objections to buying.

Customers almost always have objections during the presentation or when asked to place an order. The problem can be either logical or psychological, and objections are often unspoken. In **handling objections,** the salesperson should use a positive approach, seek out hidden objections, ask the buyer to clarify any objections, take objections as opportunities to provide more information, and turn the objections into reasons for buying. Every salesperson needs training in the skills of handling objections.

Closing

Closing
The step in the selling process in which the salesperson asks the customer for an order.

After handling the prospect's objections, the salesperson now tries to close the sale. Some salespeople do not get around to **closing** or do not handle it well. They may lack confidence, feel guilty about asking for the order, or fail to recognize the right moment to close the sale. Salespeople should know how to recognize closing signals from the buyer, including physical actions, comments, and questions. For

Advanced Sterilization Products provides its sales force with a presentation in which prospects don a helmet for a virtual reality tour of the inner workings of the STERRAD Sterilization System for medical devices and surgical instruments.

example, the customer may sit forward and nod approvingly or ask about prices and credit terms. Salespeople can use one of several closing techniques. They can ask for the order, review points of agreement, offer to help write up the order, ask whether the buyer wants this model or that one, or note that the buyer will lose out if the order is not placed now. The salesperson may offer the buyer special reasons to close, such as a lower price or an extra quantity at no charge.

Follow-up

Follow-up
The last step in the selling process in which the salesperson follows up after the sale to ensure customer satisfaction and repeat business.

The last step in the selling process—**follow-up**—is necessary if the salesperson wants to ensure customer satisfaction and repeat business. Right after closing, the salesperson should complete any details on delivery time, purchase terms, and other matters. The salesperson then should schedule a follow-up call when the initial order is received to ensure that there is proper installation, instruction, and servicing. This visit would reveal any problems, assure the buyer of the salesperson's interest, and reduce any buyer concerns that might have arisen since the sale.

Relationship Marketing

The principles of personal selling just described are *transaction oriented*—their aim is to help salespeople close a specific sale with a customer. But in many cases, the company is not seeking simply a sale: It has targeted a major customer that it would like to win and serve. The company would like to show the customer that it has the capabilities to serve the customer's needs in a superior way over the long haul, in a mutually profitable *relationship*.

Relationship marketing
The process of creating, maintaining, and enhancing strong, value-laden relationships with customers and other stakeholders.

Most companies today are moving away from transaction marketing, with its emphasis on making a sale. Instead, they are practising **relationship marketing,** which emphasizes building and maintaining profitable long-term relationships with customers by creating superior customer value and satisfaction. Recognition of the importance of relationship marketing has increased rapidly in the past few years. Companies are realizing that when operating in maturing markets and facing stiffer competition, it costs a lot more to wrest new customers from competitors than to keep current customers.

Today's customers are large and often global. They prefer suppliers who can sell and deliver a coordinated set of products and services to many locations, who can quickly solve problems that arise in their different parts of the nation or world, and who can work closely with customer teams to improve products and processes. For these customers, the sale is only the beginning of the relationship.

Unfortunately, some companies are not set up for these developments. They often sell their products through separate sales forces, each working independently to close sales. Their technical people may not be willing to lend time to educate a customer. Their engineering, design, and manufacturing people may have the attitude that "it's our job to make good products and the salesperson's to sell them to customers." However, companies increasingly are recognizing that winning and keeping accounts requires more than making good products and directing the sales force to close lots of sales. It requires a carefully coordinated, whole-company effort to create value-laden, satisfying relationships with important customers.

Relationship marketing is based on the premise that important accounts need focused and continuous attention. Studies have shown that the best salespeople are those who are highly motivated and good closers, but more than this, they are customer-problem solvers and relationship builders (see Marketing Highlight 15-3). Good salespeople working with key customers do more than call when they think a customer may be ready to place an order. They also study the account and understand its problems. They call or visit frequently, work with the customer to help solve the customer's problems and improve its business, and take an interest in customers as people.

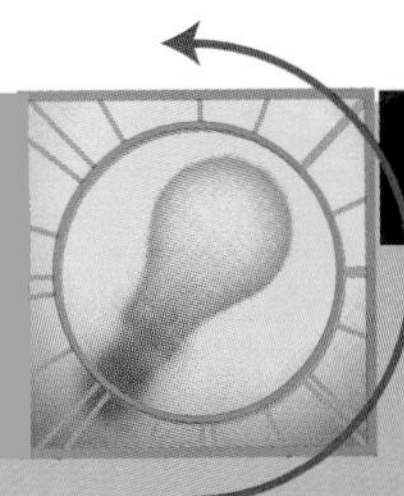

marketing highlight 15-3

Great Salespeople: Drive, Discipline, and Relationship-Building Skills

What sets great salespeople apart from all the rest? What separates the masters from the merely mediocre? In an effort to profile top sales performers, Gallup Management Consulting, a division of the Gallup polling organization, has interviewed around half a million salespeople. Its research suggests that the best salespeople possess four key talents: intrinsic motivation, disciplined work style, the ability to close a sale, and, perhaps most importantly, the ability to build relationships with customers.

Intrinsic Motivation

"Different things drive different people—pride, happiness, money, you name it," says one expert. "But all great salespeople have one thing in common: an unrelenting drive to excel." This strong, internal drive can be shaped and moulded, but it can't be taught. The source of the motivation varies—some are driven by money, some by hunger for recognition, some by a yearning to build relationships. The Gallup research revealed four general personality types, all high performers, but each with different sources of motivation. *Competitors* are people who not only want to win, but crave the satisfaction of beating specific rivals—other companies *and* their fellow salespeople. They'll come right out and say to a colleague, "With all due respect, I know you're salesperson of the year, but I'm going after your title." The *ego-driven* are salespeople who just want to experience the glory of winning. They want to be recognized as being the best, regardless of the competition. *Achievers* are a rare breed who are almost completely self-motivated. They like accomplishment and routinely set goals that are higher than what is expected of them. They often make the best sales managers because they don't mind seeing other people succeed, as long as the organization's goals are met. Finally, *service-oriented* salespeople are those whose strength lies in their ability to build and cultivate relationships. They are generous, caring, and empathetic. "These people are golden," says the national training manager of Minolta Corporation's business equipment division. "We need salespeople who will take the time to follow up on the 10 questions a customer might have, salespeople who love to stay in touch."

No one is purely a competitor, an achiever, ego-driven, or service-driven. There's at least some of each in most top performers. "A *competitor* with a strong sense of *service* will probably bring in a lot of business, while doing a great job of taking care of customers," observes the managing director of Gallup Management Consulting. "Who could ask for anything more?"

Disciplined Work Style

Whatever their motivation, if salespeople aren't organized and focused, and if they don't work hard, they can't meet the ever-increasing demands that customers are making. Great salespeople are tenacious about laying out detailed, organized plans, then following through in a timely, disciplined way. There's no magic here, just solid organization and hard work. "Our best sales reps never let loose ends dangle," says the president of a small business equipment firm. "If they say they're going to make a follow-up call on a customer in six months, you can be sure that they'll be on the doorstep in six months." Top sellers rely on hard work, not luck or gimmicks. "Some people say it's all technique or luck," notes one sales trainer. "But luck happens to the best salespeople when they get up early, work late, stay up till two in the morning working on a proposal, or keep making calls when everyone is leaving at the end of the day."

The Ability to Close a Sale

Other skills mean little if a seller can't ask for the sale. No close, no sale. Period. So what makes for a great closer? For one thing, an unyielding persistence, say managers and sales consultants. Claims one, "Great closers are like great athletes. They're not afraid to fail, and they don't give up until they close." Part of what makes the failure rate tolerable for top performers is their deep-seated belief in themselves and what they are selling. Great closers have a high level of self-confidence and believe that they are doing the right thing. And they've got a burning need to make the sale happen—to do whatever it takes within legal and ethical standards to get the business.

The Ability to Build Relationships

Perhaps most important in today's relationship-marketing environment, top salespeople are customer problem solvers and relationship builders. They have an instinctive understanding of their customers' needs. Talk to sales executives, and they'll describe top performers in these terms: Empathetic. Patient. Caring. Responsive. Good listeners. *Honest.* Top sellers can put themselves on the buyer's side of the desk and see the world through their customers' eyes. Today, customers are looking for business partners, not golf partners. "At the root of it all is an integrity of intent," says a Dallas sales consultant. "High performers don't just want to be liked, they want to add value." High-performing salespeople, he adds, are "always thinking about the big picture, where the customer's organization is going, and how they can help them get there."

Source: Adapted from Geoffrey Brewer, "Mind reading: What drives top salespeople to greatness?" *Sales & Marketing Management,* May 1994:82–8.

Review of Concept Connections

Selling is one of the world's oldest professions. Regardless of their title—salesperson, sales representative, account executive, sales consultant, sales engineer, agent, district manager, marketing representative—members of the sales force play a key role in modern marketing organizations.

The term salesperson covers a wide spectrum of positions. Salespeople may be order takers—the department store salespeople who stand behind the counter. Or they may be order getters—salespeople engaged in the creative selling of products and services such as appliances, industrial equipment, advertising, or consulting services. Other salespeople perform missionary selling, in which they are not involved in taking an order but in building goodwill or educating buyers. To be successful in these more creative forms of selling, a company must first build and then manage an effective sales force.

1. **Discuss the role of a company's salespeople in creating value for customers and building customer relationships.**

   Most companies use salespeople, and many companies assign them an important role in the marketing mix. In companies selling business products, salespeople work directly with customers: Often the sales force is the customer's only direct contact with the company and may be viewed by customers as representing the company itself. For consumer product companies that sell through intermediaries, consumers usually do not meet salespeople or even know about them; the sales force works behind the scenes, dealing with wholesalers and retailers to obtain their support and help them become effective in selling the firm's products.

   As an element of the marketing mix, the sales force is very effective in achieving certain marketing objectives and carrying out such activities as prospecting, communicating, selling and servicing, and information gathering. But with companies becoming more market oriented, a marketed-focused sales force also works to produce customer satisfaction and company profit. To accomplish these goals, the sales force needs not only the traditional sales skills but also skills in marketing analysis and planning.

2. **Explain how companies design sales force strategy and structure.**

   In designing a sales force, sales management must address such issues as what type of sales force structure will work best (territorial, product, customer, pyramid, or complex); how large the sales force should be; who will be involved in the selling effort; and how its various sales and sales support people will work together (inside or outside sales forces and team selling).

3. **Explain how companies recruit, select, and train salespeople.**

   To hold down the high costs of hiring the wrong people, companies must recruit and select salespeople carefully. In recruiting, a company may look to job duties and the characteristics of its most successful salespeople to suggest the traits it wants in its sales force and then look for applicants through recommendations of current salespeople, employment agencies, classified ads, and university employment offices. The selection process can be as short as a single informal interview or as long as involved testing and interviewing. Once selection is complete, training programs familiarize new salespeople not only with the art of selling, but also with the company's history, its products and policies, and the characteristics of its market and competitors.

4. **Describe how companies compensate and supervise salespeople, and how they evaluate sales force effectiveness.**

   The sales force compensation system helps to reward, motivate, and direct salespeople. In compensating salespeople, companies try to offer an appealing compensation plan that is close to the going rate for the type of sales job and needed skills. In addition to compensation, all salespeople need supervision, and many need continuous encouragement because they must make many decisions and face many frustrations. Furthermore, the company must evaluate their performance periodically to help them do a better job. In evaluating salespeople, the company relies on receiving regular information gathered through sales reports, personal observations, customers' letters and complaints, customer surveys, and conversations with other salespeople.

5. **Discuss the personal selling process, distinguishing between transaction-oriented marketing and relationship marketing.**

   The art of selling involves a seven-step selling process: prospecting and qualifying; preapproach; approach; presentation and demonstration; handling objections; closing; and follow-up. These steps help marketers to close a specific sale and as such are transaction oriented. However, a seller's dealings with customers should be guided by the larger concept of relationship marketing. The company's sales force should help to orchestrate a whole-company effort to develop profitable long-term relationships with key customers based on superior customer value and satisfaction.

Key Terms

Approach *(p. 640)*
Closing *(p. 641)*
Complex sales force structure *(p. 625)*
Customer sales force structure *(p. 624)*
Follow-up *(p. 642)*
Handling objections *(p. 641)*
Inside sales force *(p. 625)*
Outside sales force (field sales force) *(p. 625)*
Preapproach *(p. 639)*
Presentation *(p. 640)*
Product sales force structure *(p. 624)*
Prospecting *(p. 639)*
Pyramid sales force structure *(p. 624)*
Relationship marketing *(p. 642)*
Sales force management *(p. 623)*
Salesperson *(p. 621)*
Sales quotas *(p. 635)*
Selling process *(p. 639)*
Team selling *(p. 627)*
Telemarketing *(p. 625)*
Territorial sales force structure *(p. 623)*
Workload approach *(p. 625)*

Discussing the Issues

1. More than 60 pyramid companies operate in Canada, selling everything from vitamins to cleaning products. Many people are attracted to these organizations because there are no costs to join, they have no educational requirements, and no sales experience is necessary. As pyramid selling becomes more competitive, what will these types of firms have to do to be successful? What training methods would work best for these types of organizations? If they are going to invest in training, what can pyramid organizations do to reduce turnover, which currently averages 75 percent?
2. The term "salesperson" covers a range of positions. List and briefly describe the positions that are normally filled by a salesperson. Provide an example of each of these positions. State what your career ambition is and briefly describe how you might be involved in selling.
3. One of the most pressing issues that sales managers face is how to structure the sales force and salespeople's tasks. Evaluate the methods described in the text. For each method, provide (a) a brief description of its chief characteristics, (b) an example of how it's used, and (c) a critique of its effectiveness.
4. Telemarketing and Web-based selling (see Marketing Highlight 15-1) provide marketers with opportunities to reach customers at work and in their homes. Critique each of these approaches, discussing the advantages and disadvantages of each. Provide an example of product or service marketing that uses each approach and discuss how the selling process works in these examples.
5. What is team selling and what are its advantages and disadvantages? How would recruiting and training for a sales team differ from recruiting and training for individual selling?
6. Many people think that they do not have the attributes and abilities required for successful selling. What role does training play in helping a person develop selling skills and ability?
7. List and briefly describe the steps involved in the personal selling process. Which step do you think is most difficult for the average salesperson? Which step is the most critical to successful selling? Which step do you think is usually done most correctly? Explain each of your choices.

8. Explain the meaning of relationship marketing. Describe how relationship marketing might be used in (a) selling a personal computer to a final consumer, (b) selling a new car, (c) providing a student with a college education, and (d) selling season tickets to a local drama theatre.

Marketing Applications

1. Being a stock broker can be an exciting and challenging occupation. In years past, young broker trainees received extensive training on the technical workings of the stock market and the characteristics of potential clients. One of the most difficult tasks for new brokers was finding and developing clients. This involved long and often discouraging hours on the telephone "prospecting" and "cold-calling" potential clients. Today, however, things are changing. The rapid expansion of investment and information alternatives have made the broker's job more challenging. Most major investment services brokerages are now online, and brokers can now help information-hungry investors in ways that would have been unimaginable only a few years ago. Visit the following Web sites: E*Trade (www.etrade.com), TDWaterhouse (www.tdwaterhouse.ca), Charles Schwab (www.schwab.com) and *The Globe and Mail* (www.globeinvestor.com).
   a. How have such sites changed the brokerage business? How is the selling function in the brokerage business changing?
   b. How can online brokerage services help the average broker to be a more effective salesperson? What sales strategies appear to be most appropriate for the broker who wishes to use personal contact and online connections to do business?
   c. Which Web site did you find to be the most user friendly? Why? Which of the sites would make it easiest for you to get in touch with a broker in your local area? How could the local broker find out that you had been using his or her company's online service?
   d. Prepare an analysis grid that compares the above sites on sales stimulation, information services, cost, graphic design, responsiveness, security, and relationship marketing. Which site is best? Why?

2. Jonathan Ellermann was excited about his new job as a personal communication consultant for Nokia (www.nokia.com), the phone producer that captures a quarter of the global market and half the profits. Rivals such as Ericsson (www.ericsson.se), Vodafone (www.vodaphone.com), Panasonic (www.panasonic.com), and Motorola (www.motorola.com) have vowed to make things tougher for Nokia in the coming year. They've developed new designs, communications applications, and strategic alliances between hardware and software makers in an effort to lure fickle consumers away from Nokia.
   a. Ellermann is attempting to sell Nokia's latest model personal communication device to Shell Oil's Houston branch (about 5000 phones). What sales strategy and plan should Ellermann recommend? In your answer, consider the advantages and disadvantages of Nokia's product.
   b. Would you recommend that Nokia employ individual selling or team selling? Explain.
   c. Which step of the sales process do you think will be most critical to Ellermann's success?
   d. What could Ellermann do to establish a strong relationship with local Shell representatives?

Internet Connections

Prospecting Online

An interesting way to build a prospect list online is to find out which Web sites are linked to your site. By placing a link to your site, the business has demonstrated an interest in your product and, therefore, is a potential customer. The AltaVista search engine (www.altavista.ca) provides a feature that automatically constructs this list. Herman Miller, Inc. sells office furniture and systems to businesses, and it might use this feature to develop leads for the salespeople. In the Alta Vista search box type "link:www.hermanmiller.com" to find out which sites are linked to Herman Miller's home page. From that list, select four sites that might be good prospects, and explain why you chose them.

For Discussion

1. How could Herman Miller use the same search feature to find out which prospective customers have an interest in competitive office furniture stores? Would these constitute good prospects for Herman Miller? Why or why not?
2. What is the next step after building the prospect list?
3. How could Herman Miller identify prospects directly on its own Web site?
4. How could Herman Miller use e-mail to move prospects closer to purchase?

Company	Web Address	Reason for Inclusion

Savvy Sites

- *Sales & Marketing Management* (www.salesandmarketing.com) is a "magazine for executives who want to build sales, stay ahead of the competition, keep up with technology, and market their companies to today's tough customers."
- Looking for a job in sales? Some of the best sites for finding jobs in any field are www.monster.com, www.strategymag.com/careers.asp, globecareers.workopolis.com.
- Dale Carnegie (www.dalecarnegie.com) is the master of sales training. At this site you can get tips as well as take some interesting tests such as "Are you a workaholic?" Also check out the Canadian Professional Sales Association (www.cpsa.com).

Notes

1. Quotes from Andy Cohen, "Top of the charts: Lear Corporation," *Sales & Marketing Management,* July 1998:40. Also see Sarah Lorge, "Better off branded," *Sales & Marketing Management,* March 1998:39–42; Terril Yue Jones, "The Forbes Platinum: Consumer durables: Low-cost supplier," *Forbes,* 11 January 1999:156–8; "Lear Corporation," *Sales & Marketing Management,* July 1999:62; and "This is Lear," www.lear.com/d.htm, March 2000.
2. See Bill Kelley, "How to sell airplanes, Boeing-style," *Sales & Marketing Management,* 9 December 1985:32–4; Andy Cohen, "Boeing," *Sales & Marketing Management,* October 1997:68; and Laurence Zukerman, "On center runway, Boeing's little 717," *New York Times,* 15 June 1999:6.
3. Patricia Sellers, "How to remake your sales force," *Fortune,* 4 May 1992:96. Also see Charles Fleming and Leslie Lopez, "The corporate challenge—no boundaries: ABB's dramatic plan is to recast its business structure along global lines," *Wall Street Journal,* 28 September 1998:R16; and "Employing 200,000 people in over 100 countries," www.abb.com, September 1999.
4. Kenneth Kidd, "Clothes encounters," *Report on Business,* October 1996:58–71.
5. Melinda Ligos, "The incredible shrinking sales force," *Sales & Marketing Management,* December 1998:15.
6. See Rudy Oetting and Geri Gantman, "Dial 'M' for maximize," *Sales & Marketing Management,* June 1991:100–6; and "Median costs per call by industry," *Sales & Marketing Management,* 28 June 1993:65.
7. Mark Stevenson, "The lean, mean sales machine," *Canadian Business,* January 1994:34,36.
8. See "A phone is better than a face," *Sales & Marketing Management,* October 1987:29; Brett A. Boyle, "The importance of the industrial inside sales force: A case study," *Industrial Marketing Management,* September 1996:339–48; Victoria Fraza, "Upgrading inside sales," *Industrial Distribution,* December 1997:44–9; and Michele Marchetti, "Look who's calling," *Sales & Marketing Management,* May 1998:43–6.
9. Lorraine Neal, "Live from your Web site, it's CRM time!" *Marketing On-Line,* 21 August 2000; Susan Leigh, "Customer contact centres a tool for growth," *Strategy,* 7 June 1999:D14.
10. Richard C. Whiteley, "Orchestrating service," *Sales & Marketing Management,* April 1994:29–30.
11. Rick Mullin, "From lone wolves to team players," *Chemical Week,* 14 January 1998:33–4.
12. Robert Hiebeler, Thomas B. Kelly, and Charles Ketteman, *Best Practices: Building Your Business with Customer-focused Solutions,* New York: Arthur Andersen/Simon & Schuster, 1998: 122–4. Also see Whiteley, "Orchestrating Service": 29–30; Mark A. Moon and Susan Forquer Gupta, "Examining the formation of selling centers: A conceptual framework," *Journal of Personal Selling and Sales Management,* Spring 1997:31–41; and Donald W. Jackson Jr., Scott M. Widmier, Ralph Giacobbe, and Janet E. Keith, "Examining the use of team selling by manufacturers' representatives: A situational approach," *Industrial Marketing Management,* March 1999:155–64.
13. See Christopher Meyer, "How the right measures help teams excel," *Harvard Business Review,* May–June 1994:95–103; Michele Marchetti, "Why teams fail," *Sales & Marketing Management,* June 1997:91; Melinda Ligos, "On with the show," *Sales & Marketing Management,* November 1998:70–6; and Jackson, Widmier, Giacobbe, and Keith, "Examining the use of team selling by manufacturers' representatives":155–64.
14. See George H. Lucas Jr., A. Parasuraman, Robert A. Davis, and Ben M. Enis, "An empirical study of sales force turnover," *Journal of Marketing,* July 1987:34–59; Lynn G. Coleman, "Sales force turnover has managers wondering why," *Marketing News,* 4 December 1989:6; Thomas R. Wotruba and Pradeep K. Tyagi, "Met expectations and turnover in direct selling," *Journal of Marketing,* July 1991:24–35; and Chad Kaydo, "Overturning turnover," *Sales & Marketing Management,* November 1997:50–60.
15. See Geoffrey Brewer, "Mind reading: What drives top salespeople to greatness?" *Sales & Marketing Management,* May 1994: 82–8; Barry J. Farber, "Success stories for salespeople," *Sales & Marketing Management,* May 1995:30–1; Roberta Maynard, "Finding the essence of good salespeople," *Nation's Business,* February 1998:10; and Jeanie Casison, "Closest thing to cloning," *Incentive,* June 1999:7.
16. The Canadian Professional Sales Association, *1999/2000 Sales Compensation report,* www.cpsa.com/html/src_reference_and_research.asp.
17. See "To test or not to test," *Sales & Marketing Management,* May 1994:86.
18. Mark De Wolf, "Special report: Motivating the sales force," *Strategy,* 18 August 1997:19.
19. Robert Klein, "Nabisco sales soar after sales training," *Marketing News,* 6 January 1997:23.
20. Christen P. Heide, "All levels of sales reps post impressive earnings," press release, www.dartnellcorp.com, 5 May 1997.
21. Geoffrey Brewer, "Brain power," *Sales & Marketing Management,* May 1997:39–48; Don Peppers and Martha Rogers, "The money trap," *Sales & Marketing Management,* May 1997: 58–60.
22 "Editorial: New motivational ideas reflect new breed of rep," *Strategy,* 21 August 1995:14.
23. Tony Seideman, "Who needs managers?" *Sales & Marketing Management,* June 1994:15–7. Also see Tim McCollum, "High-tech marketing hits the target," *Nation's Business,* June 1997: 39–42; Ginger Conlon, "Plug and play," *Sales & Marketing Management,* December 1998:64–7; and Erika Rasmusson, "The 5 steps to successful sales force automation," *Sales & Marketing Management,* March 1999:34–40.
24. Christen Heide, "Rep use of the Internet up 226 percent in 2 years," *Sales & Marketing Management Executive Report,* 19 August 1998:8–9; Melinda Ligos, "Point, click, and sell," *Sales & Marketing Management,* May 1999:51–6.
25. B.J. Del Conte, "Language is no barrier when it comes to sales," *Financial Post Magazine,* April 1996:14.
26. Bob Donath, "Delivering value starts with proper prospecting," *Marketing News,* 10 November 1997:5. Also see Sarah Lorge, "The best way to prospect," *Sales & Marketing Management,* January 1998:80.
27. David Stamps, "Training for a new sales game," *Training,* July 1997:46–52.

28. Brewer, "Brain power":42; Rosemary P. Ramsey and Ravipreet S. Sohi, "Listening to your customers: The impact of perceived salesperson listening behavior on relationship outcomes," *Journal of the Academy of Marketing Science,* Spring 1997:127–37.

29. "Briefcase full of views: Johnson & Johnson uses virtual reality to give prospects an inside look at its products," *American Demographics,* April 1997.

Company Case 15

CDW: Restructuring the Sales Force

The Third Interview

Brady Hilshire stared at the pages before him and sighed. The interview process had gone very well so far. In fact, he was beginning the third step in the interview process with CDW Computer Centers, Inc. The company had just moved up to number 11 from number 36 on *Fortune* magazine's list of the "100 best companies to work for in America," and he wanted a job offer. This interview, he believed, would be the clincher.

To begin this third step, the CDW recruiter had given Brady a brief case study on the company. His instructions were to read the case carefully, identify a crucial problem facing CDW, develop several solutions to the problem, pick the best solution, and write up his recommendation to the company. Brady took a deep breath and began to read.

A Shooting Star

Things had gone very well for CDW since its humble beginnings on CEO Michael Krasny's kitchen table in 1982. Krasny sold his first computer, a used IBM PC, through a classified ad, discovering in the process that he could add value and make money by reselling computers. Over the years, CDW gradually transformed into a direct marketer of brand-name computers, accessories, peripherals, and software from such companies as Compaq, IBM, Hewlett-Packard, Microsoft, and Toshiba. By 1988, the company's growth dictated a move to a new 28 000-square-foot facility in Northbrook, Illinois; and by 1991, it had 143 employees. In May 1993, CDW successfully went public, ending the year with $270 million in sales and 247 employees. That was only the beginning.

Each year following its initial public offering, CDW set new performance records. In 1995, CDW was among the first US companies to launch an e-business Web site. In 1996, the company won *Computer Shopper's* Best Buy award for Best Vendor Web Site. In 1997, CDW reached $1 billion in sales; *Fortune* recognized it as one of "America's 100 fastest-growing companies," and *Computer Retail Week* selected it as the Retailer of the Year. In 1998, CDW joined the *Fortune 1000* at number 868, and *PC Magazine* recognized it as one of America's "100 most influential companies." Analysts estimated that CDW, a company that started with a single man and a single computer, finished 1999 with an estimated $2.5 billion in sales, more than 2000 employees, some 600 000 customers, thousands of products, and a sales growth rate more than twice that of the industry.

A Successful Corporate Strategy

Glancing over his case study, Brady noted that from the beginning, CDW had held fast to its CEO's original business model—what the company called a win–win philosophy among CDW's co-workers, customers, vendors, and shareholders. The company expressed this philosophy in its mission statement: "To be one of the nation's highest-volume computer resellers selling brand-name products; to provide a fun and challenging work environment and above-average earnings; and to maintain a high net profit by running a lean, highly automated, systems-oriented company." Brady reflected that the mission statement was supported by a dozen or so "philosophies of success" that he had seen posted throughout the colourful work areas in the 318 000-square-foot facility in Vernon Hills, Illinois—sayings such as "It's only good if it's win–win!" and "Smile! People can hear your smile through the phone."

The company's true basis for its success, however, rested on CDW's circle of service, meaning that everything CDW did revolved around providing the best customer service possible. That meant the right support and excellent execution—as defined by the customer. To this end, CDW had invested in warehouse automation, in-depth training of its sales force, sales force automation, and other innovations to provide unparalleled expertise and unmatched response time focused on relevant customer concerns. The company's goal was to "treat every customer as if they were your only customer." CDW refined that treatment on an ongoing basis by following the philosophy that "success means never being satisfied."

The Sales Force Structure

Analysts attributed much of CDW's success to a highly trained, highly competent inside sales force that reached customers through inbound/outbound calling and direct-mail catalogues. CDW targeted its selling efforts toward business clients, maintaining a core strength in small and medium-size businesses and continued growth and concentration in large business customers. The sales force worked out of the Chicago area with all operations and shipping handled out of their headquarters in Vernon Hills. The company trained its sales force of about 850 account managers as generalists to assist virtually any customer, drawing where necessary on technical support from dedicated vendor hotlines, vendor representatives, electronic information available on the Web, and dedicated presales network technicians. The company trained each of its account managers to take a proactive, entrepreneurial selling approach—but maintained its goal of cooperation and a fun work environment by assigning account managers to teams with street, city, and state names. For example, one team was Fisherman's Wharf, a part of the San Francisco group, which was part of California state. There were typically eight or fewer salespeople in a "street," three to four streets in a "city," and three to four cities in a "state." "Street contests" pitted street against street in a variety of lively competitions, such as company- or vendor-sponsored sales contests to promote new products or to increase attention on company focus areas.

CDW's customers interfaced with the sales force in several ways. The company assigned call-in customers to the account manager who answered the customer's original call. Additionally, account managers proactively developed accounts by profiling business needs and providing business assistance through a broad range of technical products and value-added services. Account managers picked up Internet customers via random assignment; that is, once a new customer (a new company) made its first purchase on the Web site, the CDW information system automatically posted the company and contact person's name and randomly assigned the company to a salesperson who was Web certified (had passed the tests on basic CDW Web page use). Typically, developing a profitable account base took an account manager between 6 and 18 months, depending on account complexity and account manager tenure. Account managers maintained account ownership as long as the customer was satisfied and actively purchasing. No matter what the type of initial contact, account managers worked to identify short- and long-term opportunities, building strong relationships with their customers and seeking to provide full solutions.

CDW recruited both experienced salespeople and recent college graduates. To hire experienced salespeople, the recruiting staff generated a résumé stream through an Internet presence, local job fairs, and newspapers. The staff recruited on college campuses fall and midwinter seeking to build long-term relationships with a select group of schools. New hires, after three to six months of intensive training, began as account managers. The company assigned them randomly, or based on need, to one of the street teams. After two years of selling experience, account managers could earn the right to be "street leaders."

CDW paid its account managers on a monthly commission basis. The company guaranteed each account manager a minimum predetermined commission level and a substantial draw. An account manager earned commission based on his or her gross profit shipped. Within guidelines, each account manager could control profit margins based on customer volume and needs. However, although CDW wanted to offer competitive prices, it did not want to compete based on price alone. The commission rate could increase significantly based on sales goals achieved, certification, and the ability to act as a value-added business consultant for the client. Successful salespeople could move out of direct selling and into sales management. Sales managers assumed responsibility for all streets within a given city. Senior sales managers assumed responsibility for all cities within a given state, and the general sales manager coordinated the entire sales force, reporting to the vice-president of sales.

Brady noted that the company emphasized technical training for the sales force, establishing its own CDW University in 1990. Furthermore, it focused on personal development of its salespeople through a variety of certifications, ongoing training, and development of management skills. Brady also noted that in 1998, CDW had modified its selling structure by creating CDW-G, a subsidiary focused exclusively on meeting the needs of government and education customers.

Analysts predicted that CDW would increase the total number of account managers by more than 40 percent by the end of 2000.

A Web Presence

In 1995, CDW developed its Web site, www.cdw.com, to support the sales force's efforts to provide excellent customer service. The company maintained a focus on e-business, which it defined as providing added value for its business partners through a variety of Web support services—moving beyond the traditional e-commerce models that often amounted to unassisted retail sales on the Web. Although any individual or company could go to the site and make a purchase, CDW believed that if a customer did any significant business with the company, it would have to have the technical assistance that its salespeople and technical specialists could offer. CDW wanted to build relationships with its customers.

The company's early entry into e-business started with Web site access to consumer product information and specifications. Later in 1995, CDW added other site capabilities to allow consumers to track the status of orders placed through account managers; and in 1996, the company expanded its Web site's capabilities to include direct sales. At that time, the company added online account creation and ordering capabilities to the existing advertising and marketing information.

Late in 1996, without restructuring its sales force, the company made a strategic push toward focusing on business customers. To complement the focus, CDW enhanced its Web site to focus on business-to-business relationships. The company improved the Web site's functionality by introducing new tools for business customers. For example, the site notified buyers of pertinent price cuts, provided support for direct returns to vendors, and listed full product catalogues. At the end of 1998, CDW introduced extranets—direct, secured links between the customer and CDW, which facilitated the customer's procurement process. The extranets provided customers with better access to critical business information, including more detailed order status information, serial-number tracking, and purchase acquisition summaries. A staff of 25 IT support people worked continuously on enhancing and perfecting Web site support for CDW's business customers. In 1999, direct Web sales averaged about six percent of total sales, and *PC Week* ranked CDW's Web site as the number one e-commerce site for IT buyers.

The Challenge

Brady sat back and looked at the case study, considering the dilemma of finding a problem with a company that seemed to have done just about everything right. Nonetheless, he thought, the challenges for all companies involved with computers were very real. Industry issues for CDW would have to include such problems as margin erosion in high-technology goods, limited product availability as a result of vendor production capabilities, volatile overseas markets, new entrants into the computer reselling business, and a growing interest in direct Internet sales. Direct challenges within the company itself would likely include recruiting, training, and developing hundreds of account managers, meeting continued needs for increased capacity, maintaining superior customer service, and keeping a sales force structure supportive of CDW's goals.

After reviewing the case information one last time, Brady decided to focus on the issue of sales force structure for his interview question. As he began to think about CDW's customers and to envision himself as a member of one of CDW's street teams, he wondered what sales force strategy CDW should use to sustain its phenomenal growth and earnings while still maintaining outstanding customer service and a highly motivated sales force.

Questions

1. What problems do you see with CDW's current sales force strategy and structure?
2. What blend of inside selling and Web site support would generate the most customer satisfaction for CDW's business customers? Would you recommend encouraging e-commerce rather than e-business as the case defines the two terms?
3. What impact would the upcoming rapid increase in the size of CDW's sales force have on your recommendations for a sales force strategy and structure?
4. Given your recommendations, what actions would you take to ensure a highly motivated sales force?

Sources: Dr. Barbara Dyer, Assistant Professor, Ohio University, developed this case in cooperation with CDW.

video case 15

SHIFTING INTO THE BIG TIME

In New York City, the centre of the media universe, you'll find newsstands crammed with magazines. A thousand new publications begin in the United States every year, and if they manage to survive, they soon surface in the Big Apple. Knowing that New York is the lifeblood of the industry, publisher Andrew Heinzman is taking his seven-year-old Canadian magazine, *Shift*, south of the border. He knows the risks and the rewards. If *Shift* can make it here, the world will be its oyster and he admits he's already eyeing the British and Asian markets.

Shift is about the collision between technology and culture. It examines the often overlooked human side of technology and how technology changes how we live. *Shift* was the Canadian magazine success story in the 1990s. It started as an obscure literary journal in 1992 but became a quasi-mainstream consumer title with a paid circulation of 70 000. *Shift* created its own buzz and won an audience. Check it out at www.shift.com.

Heinzman believes there's an empty niche in the US market that his magazine can perfectly fill. *Shift* is about living in a digital culture. It takes the position that technology and the Internet have affected the way we work, play, shop, and communicate. But *Shift* isn't a first mover into this marketspace. US-based *Wired, Spin* and *Details* magazines target people with the same lifestyle. But the folks at *Shift* feel that *Wired* has become more of a business technology magazine, while *Spin* and *Details* are youth oriented titles. *Shift* plans to target the 25- to 35-year-old urban, computer-literate reader. *Wired*'s average reader is 43 years old. The result? A huge opportunity in the eyes of Heinzman and his backers.

Heinzman's mantra might be, "You have to spend money to make money!" *Shift's* owner, Normal Net Canada of Montreal, expects to invest $5 million to $10 million to make the magazine fly on a worldwide level. Rents for midtown Manhattan office space are exorbitant and landlords can demand a seven-year lease. Heinzman also knows he needs help from people who are familiar with the US scene. He needs to hire a newsstand consultant, PR specialist, direct-mail experts, and a new associate publisher. He had to plan a really big launch party in New York as well as arrange for the placement of banner ads on hip Web sites. However, Heinzman and his crew manage what first seemed impossible—the magazine reaches US newsstands on time with a launch date of October 7, 1999.

Shift hoped to achieve US circulation of 80 000 by featuring stories and editorial content from both sides of the border. The magazine sought sponsorship from US advertisers of technology, fashion, cigarettes, alcohol and video game products. Success seemed assured since advertiser response was good and circulation increased from 70 000 to 150 000 copies. But a dark cloud soon appeared on the horizon. Distribution and operating costs soared and attempts were made to sell *Shift* to a publisher with deeper pockets. To keep the magazine afloat, the employees finally took charge, accepting a cut in pay in exchange for an equity stake in the magazine. Undaunted, Heinzman retrenched and not only worked to return the magazine to its Canadian roots, but he developed a television spinoff of the magazine—Shift TV, a half-hour digest airing on the Life Network. Despite these changes, it may be some time before the magazine can change gears and shift into success.

Questions

1. What elements of the communication mix were used to help launch *Shift* into the US marketplace?
2. Why have so many successful Canadian companies failed when they entered the US market?
3. If you were Andrew Heinzman, what would you do next to try and ensure *Shift*'s success?

Sources: Peggy Cunningham prepared this case based on "Shifting into the Big Time," *Venture*, October 5, 1999; Stan Sutter, "You go, *Shift*, you go," *Marketing On-Line*, October 11, 1999: "Media Briefs: Publisher plans a *Shift* in New York," *Marketing On-Line*, May 31, 1999; Ken Fasciano, "*Shift* magazine lays off entire staff," CBC News, October 31, 2000.

PART 1 2 3 4

Developing the Marketing Mix

Concept Connections

When you finish this chapter, you should be able to

1. Discuss the benefits of direct marketing to customers and companies and the trends fuelling its rapid growth.
2. Define a customer database and list the four ways that companies use databases in direct marketing.
3. Identify the major forms of direct marketing.
4. Compare the two types of online marketing channels and explain the effect of the Internet on electronic commerce.
5. Identify the benefits of online marketing to consumers and marketers and the four ways that marketers can conduct online marketing.
6. Discuss the public policy and ethical issues facing direct marketers.

chapter 16

Direct and Online Marketing

When 19-year-old Michael Dell began selling personal computers from his university dorm room in 1984, few would have bet on his chances for success. In those days, most computer makers sold their PCs through an extensive network of all-powerful distributors and resellers. Even as the fledgling Dell Computer Corporation began to grow, competitors and industry insiders scoffed at the concept of mail-order computer marketing. PC buyers, they contended, needed the kind of advice and handholding that only full-service channels could provide. Mail-order PC sales, like mail-order clothing, would never amount to more than 15 percent of the market.

Yet young Michael Dell has proved the sceptics wrong. In little more than a decade, he turned his dorm-room mail-order business into a $33 billion computer empire. Dell Computer is now the world's largest direct marketer of computer systems and the world's fastest-growing computer manufacturer. Over the past three years, Dell's sales have increased at an average of 53 percent per year, twice as fast as any competitor and five times the industry average. Profits have skyrocketed 89 percent per year, and, since 1990, Dell's stock has risen an incredible 29 600 percent. Dell Canada has moved into the number one position in overall PC sales in Canada, up from number three: Dell now has 13.9 percent of the total Canadian computer systems market, which includes desktop, workstation, server, and notebook sales. Not bad for a Canadian subsidiary with only 460 employees working from offices located in Halifax, Montreal, Ottawa, Toronto, and Vancouver.

Lawrence Pentland, president of Dell Canada, notes: "This growth shows that Canadian businesses and consumers are embracing Dell's direct model, leading-edge technology, competitive pricing, and services and support." Direct buyers now account for nearly a third of all PC sales, and Dell's once-sceptical competitors are now scrambling to build their own direct marketing systems.

What's the secret to Dell's stunning success? Anyone at Dell can tell you without hesitation: It's the company's radically different business model—the direct model. "We have a tremendously clear business model," says Michael Dell. "There's no confusion about what the value proposition is, what the company offers, and why it's great for customers. That's a very simple thing, but it has tremendous power and appeal." It also garners tremendous suc-

cess for the company. Dell's direct marketing approach delivers greater customer value through an unbeatable combination of product customization, low prices, fast delivery, and award-winning customer service. A customer can talk by phone with a Dell representative on Monday morning; order a fully customized, state-of-the-art PC to suit his or her special needs; and have the machine delivered to his or her doorstep by Wednesday—all at a price that's 10 to 15 percent below competitors' prices. Dell backs its products with high-quality service and support. As a result, Dell consistently ranks among the industry leaders in product reliability and service, and its customers are routinely among the industry's most satisfied.

Dell customers receive exactly the machine they need. Michael Dell's initial idea was to serve individual buyers by allowing them to customize machines with the special features they wanted at low prices. However, this one-to-one approach also appeals strongly to corporate buyers, because Dell can easily preconfigure each computer to precise requirements. Dell routinely preloads machines with a company's own software and even undertakes such tedious tasks as pasting inventory tags on each machine so that computers can be delivered directly to an employee's desk. As a result, about 90 percent of Dell's sales are to large corporate, government, and educational buyers.

Direct selling results in more efficient selling and lower costs, which translate into lower prices for customers. Because Dell builds machines to order, the company carries little inventory. Dealing one-to-one with customers helps the company to react immediately to shifts in demand, so Dell doesn't get stuck with PCs no one wants. Finally, by selling directly, Dell has no dealers to pay. As a result, on average, Dell's costs are 12 percent lower than those of Compaq, its leading PC competitor.

Dell knows that time is money, and the company is obsessed with "speed." For example, Dell has long been a model of just-in-time manufacturing and efficient supply-chain management. It has also mastered the intricacies of today's lightning-fast electronic commerce. This combination makes Dell a lean and very fast operator. "Dell calls it 'velocity'—squeezing time out of every step in the process—from the moment an order is taken to collecting the cash. [By selling direct, manufacturing to order, and] tapping credit cards and electronic payment, Dell converts the average sale to cash in less than 24 hours. By contrast, Compaq Computer Corp., which sells primarily through dealers, takes 35 days, and even mail-order rival Gateway 2000 takes 16.4 days." Such blazing speed results in more satisfied customers and still lower costs: Customers are often delighted to find their new computers arriving within as few as 36 hours of placing an order. And because Dell doesn't order parts until an order is booked, it can take advantage of ever-falling component costs. On average, its parts are 60 days newer than those in competing machines, and hence 60 days further down the price curve. This gives Dell a six percent profit advantage from parts costs alone.

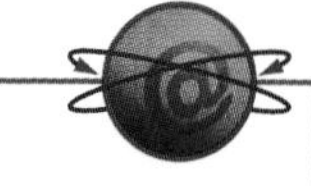

Dell Computer Corp.
www.dell.ca/

Flush with success, Dell is taking its direct marketing formula a step further. It's again doing what once seemed impossible—selling PCs on the Internet. Now, by simply clicking the "Buy a Dell" icon at Dell's Web site, customers can design and price customized computer systems electronically. Then, with a click on the "purchase" button, they can submit an order, choosing from online payment options that include credit card, company purchase order, or corporate lease. Dell dashes out a digital confirmation to customers within five minutes of receiving the order. After receiving confirmation, customers can check the status of the order online at any time.

The Internet is a perfect extension of Dell's direct marketing model. Customers who are already comfortable buying direct from Dell now have an even more powerful way to do so. "The Internet," says Michael Dell, "is the ultimate direct model. . . . [Customers] like the immediacy, convenience, savings, and personal touches that the [Internet] experience provides. Not only are some sales done completely online, but people who call on the phone after having visited dell.ca are twice as likely to buy."

Today, its more than 50 country-specific sites account for over 50 percent of Dell's sales. In addition, 70 percent of Dell's technical support is handled through online service tools, without dispatching a service representative. In just a single quarter in one year, Dell.com received some 25 million visits. Buyers range from individuals purchasing home computers to large business users buying high-end $45 000 servers. Michael Dell sees online marketing as the next great conquest in the company's direct marketing crusade. "The Internet is like a booster rocket on our sales and growth," he proclaims. "Our vision is to have all customers conduct all transactions on the Internet, globally."

As you can imagine, competitors are no longer scoffing at Michael Dell's vision of the future. It's hard to argue with success, and Dell has been very successful. By following his hunches, at the tender age of 35 he has built one of the world's hottest computer companies. In the process, he's amassed a personal fortune exceeding $6.2 billion.[1]

Many of the marketing tools we examined in previous chapters were developed in the context of *mass marketing*—targeting broadly with standardized messages and marketing offers. Today, with the trend toward more narrowly targeting or one-to-one marketing, companies are adopting *direct marketing* as a primary marketing approach or as a supplement to other approaches. Increasingly, companies are turning to direct marketing in an effort to reach carefully targeted customers more efficiently and to build stronger, more personal, one-to-one relationships with them.

In this chapter, we examine the nature, role, and growing applications of direct marketing and its newest form—online, or Internet, marketing. We address these questions: What is direct marketing? What are its benefits to companies and their customers? How do customer databases support direct marketing? What channels do direct marketers use to reach individual prospects and customers? What marketing opportunities do online channels provide? How can companies use integrated direct marketing for competitive advantage? What public and ethical issues do direct and online marketing raise?

What Is Direct Marketing?

Mass marketers have typically sought to reach millions of buyers with a single product and a standard message delivered through the mass media. For example, Procter & Gamble originally launched Crest toothpaste in one version with a single message—"Crest fights cavities"—hoping that 300 million North Americans would learn the message and buy the brand. P&G did not need to know its customers' names or anything else about them, only that they wanted to take good care of their teeth. Most marketing communications consisted of one-way communication directed *at* consumers, not two-way communication *with* them.

Direct marketing
Direct communications with carefully targeted individual consumers to obtain an immediate response.

In contrast, **direct marketing** consists of direct communications with carefully targeted individual consumers to both obtain an immediate response and cultivate lasting customer relationships. Direct marketers communicate directly with customers, often on a one-to-one, interactive basis. Using detailed databases, they tailor their marketing offers and communications to the needs of narrowly defined segments or even individual buyers. Beyond brand and image building, they usually seek a direct, immediate, and measurable consumer response. Dell Computer, for example, interacts directly with customers, by telephone or through its Web site, to design built-to-order systems that meet customers' individual needs. Buyers order directly from Dell, and Dell quickly and efficiently delivers the new computers to their homes or offices.

The New Direct Marketing Model

Early direct marketers—catalogue companies, direct mailers, and telemarketers—gathered customer names and sold goods mainly through the mail and by telephone. However, fired by rapid advances in database technologies and new marketing media—especially the Internet and other electronic channels—direct marketing has undergone a dramatic transformation.

In previous chapters, we've discussed direct marketing as direct distribution, as marketing channels that contain no intermediaries. We've also included direct marketing as one element of the marketing communications mix—as an approach for communicating directly with consumers. In fact, direct marketing is both these things. Most companies still use direct marketing as a supplementary channel or medium for marketing their goods. Thus, Lexus markets mostly through mass-media advertising and its high-quality dealer network but also supplements these channels with direct marketing. Its direct marketing includes promotional videos and other materials mailed directly to prospective buyers and a Web page that provides consumers with information about various models, competitive comparisons, financing, and dealer locations. Similarly, although Zellers and The Bay conduct most of their business through bricks-and-mortar stores, their Web initiatives, launched in November 2000, allow customers great choice on how and when to shop. "The ability to be a true cross-channel retailer is crucial in today's environment, and we believe that customers really will reward retailers who offer them the most choice," says Michael LeBlanc, director of customer retention at The Hudson's Bay Company.[2]

Lexus Canada
www.lexuscanada.com/

However, for many companies, direct marketing is much more than just a supplementary channel or medium. For these companies, direct marketing—especially in its newest transformation, Internet marketing and e-commerce—constitutes a new and complete model for doing business. "The Internet is not just another marketing channel; it's not just another advertising medium; it's not just a way to speed up transactions," says one strategist. "The Internet is the foundation for a new industrial order. [It] will change the relationship between consumers and producers in ways more profound than you can yet imagine."[3] This new direct model, suggests another analyst, is "revolutionizing the way we think about . . . how to construct relationships with suppliers and customers, how to create value for them, and how to make money in the process; in other words, [it's] revolutionizing marketing."[4]

Whereas most companies use direct marketing and the Internet as supplemental approaches, other firms such as Dell Computer, Amazon.com, and the so-called e-corporations like eBay and E*TRADE use it as the only approach. Other companies, such as Nortel, Charles Schwab, IBM, and many others, are rapidly transforming themselves into direct marketing superstars.

As our chapter opener story suggests, perhaps the company that best exemplifies this new direct marketing model is Dell Computer. On its Web page, Dell explains its direct model this way:

> Dell's award-winning customer service, industry-leading growth, and financial performance continue to differentiate the company from competitors. At the heart of that performance is Dell's unique direct-to-customer business model. "Direct" refers to the company's relationships with its customers, from home-PC users to the world's largest corporations. There are no retailers or other resellers adding unnecessary time and cost, or diminishing Dell's understanding of customer expectations. Why are computer-systems customers and investors increasingly turning to Dell and its unique direct model? There are several reasons: (1) *Price for performance:* By elim-

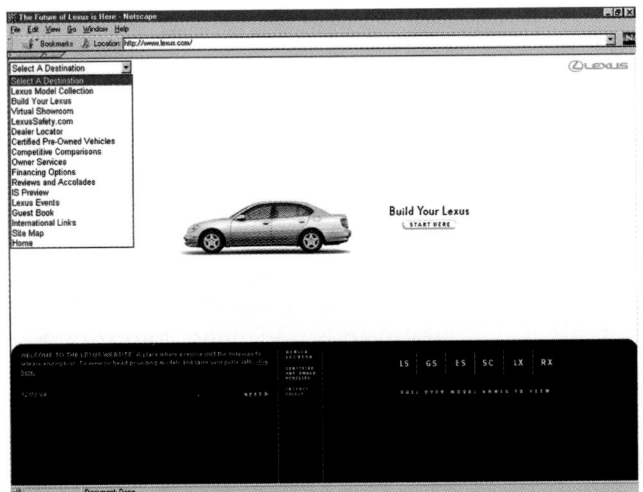

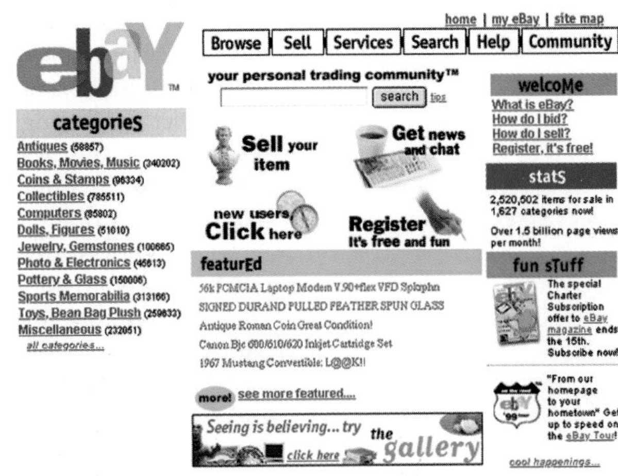

For companies like Lexus, direct marketing and the Web supplement other marketing efforts. However, for the so-called e-corporations like online auctioneer eBay, they constitute a complete model for doing business.

inating resellers, retailers, and other costly intermediary steps, together with the industry's most efficient procurement, manufacturing, and distribution process, Dell offers its customers more powerful, more richly configured systems for the money than competitors. (2) *Customization:* Every Dell system is built to order—customers get exactly, and only, what they want. (3) *Service and support:* Dell uses knowledge gained from direct contact before and after the sale to provide award-winning, tailored customer service. (4) *Latest technology:* Dell's efficient model means the latest relevant technology is introduced in its product lines much more quickly than through slow-moving indirect distribution channels. Inventory is turned over every 10 or fewer days, on average, keeping related costs low.

Thus, Dell has built its entire approach to the marketplace around direct marketing. This direct model has proven highly successful, not just for Dell, but for the fast-growing number of other companies that use it.

Many strategists have hailed direct marketing as the marketing model of the twenty-first century. They envision a day when all buying and selling will involve direct connections between companies and their customers. According to one account, the new model "will fundamentally change customers' expectations about convenience, speed, comparability, price, and service. Those new expectations will reverberate throughout the economy, affecting every business." Comparing the adoption of the Internet and other new direct marketing technologies to the early days of the airplane, Amazon.com CEO Jeff Bezos says, "It's the Kitty Hawk era of electronic commerce." Even those offering more cautious predictions agree that the Internet and e-commerce will have a tremendous impact on future business strategies.

Benefits and Growth of Direct Marketing

Whether used as a complete business model or as a supplement to a broader integrated marketing mix, direct marketing brings many benefits to both buyers and sellers. As a result, direct marketing is growing very rapidly.

Benefits to Buyers

Direct marketing benefits buyers in many ways. It is *convenient:* Customers don't have to battle traffic, find parking spaces, and trek through stores and aisles to find and examine products. They can do comparative shopping by browsing through mail catalogues or surfing Web sites. Direct marketers never close their doors. Buying is *easy and private:* Customers encounter fewer buying hassles and don't have to face salespeople or open themselves up to persuasion and emotional pitches. Business buyers can learn about available products and services without waiting for and tying up time with salespeople.

Direct marketing often provides shoppers with greater product access and selection. For the Web, the world's the limit: Unrestrained by physical boundaries, cyberstores can offer an almost unlimited selection. Try comparing the incredible selections offered by Web merchants such as HMV.com or Wine.com to the more meagre assortments of their counterparts in the bricks-and-mortar world.

Beyond a broader selection of sellers and products, online and Internet channels also give consumers access to a wealth of comparative information about companies, products, and competitors. Good sites often provide more information in more useful forms than even the most solicitous salesclerk can. Villa.ca, the home and garden store operated by Chapters.ca, for example, offers gardeners information on everything from their new garden furniture to the best way to arrange various types of cut flowers.

Finally, online buying is *interactive and immediate.* Consumers often can interact with the seller's site to create exactly the configuration of information, products, or services they desire, then order or download them on the spot. Moreover, the Internet and other forms of direct marketing give consumers a greater measure of control. "The Internet will empower consumers like nothing else ever has," notes one analyst. "Think about this: Already 16 percent of car buyers shop online before showing up at a dealership, and they aren't comparing paint jobs—they're arming themselves with information on dealer costs. . . . The new reality is consumer control."[5]

Benefits to Sellers

Direct marketing yields many benefits to sellers. First, direct marketing is a powerful tool for *customer relationship building.* Direct marketers build or buy databases containing detailed information about potentially profitable customers. Using these databases, they build strong, ongoing customer relationships. With today's technology, a direct marketer can select small groups or even individual consumers, personalize offers to meet their special needs and wants, and promote these offers through individualized communications. Consider the award-winning campaign by ClubLink, a recreational resort company that owns and operates 30 golf courses in Ontario and Quebec, including Glen Abbey, home to the PGA Tour's Bell Canadian Open:[6]

> In their drive for new, younger members, ClubLink wanted to show that golf is fun. They developed a list of prospective members by segmenting their in-house database according to several factors, such as age and the number of times played at a ClubLink course. They sent out three mailings, each with a different promotion. To emphasize the "fun" attitude of ClubLink, the first mailing suggested the excuses a golfer might offer in order to get out of work for the day. The second mailing included a set of ear plugs golfers could give to friends who were bored hearing golf stories, and the third took a more serious tone, outlining the many resorts around the world at which members could play. The campaign was a "hole-in-one" for the firm resulting in sales over 600 percent greater than the previous years' efforts.

Direct marketing can also be timed to reach prospects at just the right moment. Because they reach more interested consumers at the best times, direct marketing materials receive higher readership and response. Direct marketing also permits easy testing of alternative media and messages.

Because of its one-to-one interactive nature, the Internet is an especially potent direct marketing tool. Companies can interact online with customers to learn more about specific needs and wants. In turn, online customers can ask questions and volunteer feedback. Based on this ongoing interaction, companies can increase customer value and satisfaction through product and service refinements.

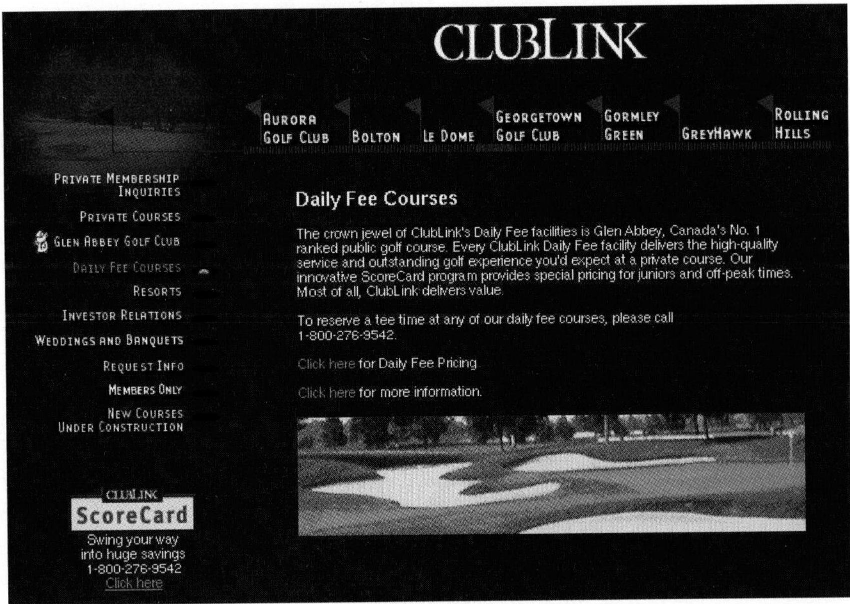

In an award-winning campaign, ClubLink used direct mail to boost its membership.

Direct marketing via the Internet and other electronic channels yields additional advantages, such as *reducing costs* and *increasing speed and efficiency.* Online marketers avoid the expense of maintaining a store and the accompanying costs of rent, insurance, and utilities. Online retailers reap the advantage of a negative operating cycle. Amazon.com, for example, receives cash from credit card companies just a day after customers place an order. Then it can hold the money for 46 days until it pays suppliers, the book distributors and publishers.

By using the Internet to link directly to suppliers, factories, distributors, and customers, businesses like Dell Computer and General Electric are wringing waste out of the system and passing on savings to customers. Because customers deal directly with sellers, online marketing often results in lower costs and improved efficiencies for channel and logistics functions such as order processing, inventory handling, delivery, and trade promotion. Finally, communicating electronically often costs less than communicating on paper through the mail. For instance, a company can produce digital catalogues for much less than the cost of printing and mailing paper ones.

Online marketing also offers greater *flexibility,* allowing the marketer to make ongoing adjustments to its offers and programs. For example, once a paper catalogue is mailed, the products, prices, and other catalogue features are fixed until the next catalogue is sent. However, an online catalogue can be adjusted daily or even hourly, adapting product assortments, prices, and promotions to match changing market conditions.

Purdy's Chocolate Shops
www.purdys.com/

Finally, the Internet is a *global* medium that allows buyers and sellers to click from one country to another in seconds. Web surfers from Eastern Canada, Paris, or Istanbul can access Purdy's Chocolate Shops as easily as can chocolate lovers in Alberta and British Columbia, where Purdy's operates its 44 stores. Thus, even small online marketers find that they have ready access to global markets.

The Growth of Direct Marketing

Sales through traditional direct marketing channels (catalogues, direct mail, and telemarketing) have been growing rapidly. Whereas North American retail sales grow by about six percent annually, direct marketing sales have been growing by about eight percent. John Gustavson, president of the Canadian Direct Marketing

Association, notes that the direct response industry, which generated $50 billion in sales in the year 2000, is now one of the top five industry sectors in the Canadian economy. Revenues generated by direct marketing are expected to increase by 60 percent over the next five years to $81.7 billion. Take a look at some other compelling statistics about the importance of Canadian direct marketing:[7]

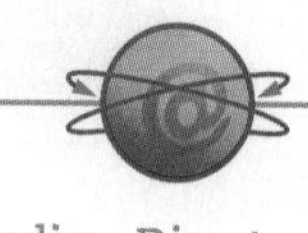

Canadian Direct Marketing Association
www.cdma.org/

- Addressed advertising mail generated $14.7 billion in sales in 2000 and is forecast to rise by 63 percent to $26.2 billion in 2005.
- Telemarketing sales will rise by 51 percent to $24.3 billion in 2005.
- Compare these figures to sales generated by direct-response television ads—a 52-percent increase is forecast in sales generated through television over the next five years to $6.7 billion.

While direct marketing through traditional channels is growing rapidly, online marketing is growing explosively. With 65 percent of Canadians now able to access the Internet, up from 29 percent two years earlier, few marketers can ignore its potential. Statistics Canada reports that 19 percent of the households with home Internet access used the medium to purchase goods or services. Another 28 percent used it for electronic banking, while 9 of 10 households used e-mail last year. Canadian sales generated through the Internet will more than double, going from $2.3 billion in the year 2000 to $5.5 billion in 2005. While Canadian e-commerce still lags that in the US, the 2000 Canadian e-Business Roundtable meeting projected that the Canadian e-business sector will grow at an annual rate of 75.5 percent, with total Canadian e-business spending reaching $150 billion by 2004.[8] We will examine online and Internet marketing more closely later in this chapter.

In the consumer market, the extraordinary growth of direct marketing is a response to the new marketing realities discussed in previous chapters. Market fragmentation has resulted in an ever-increasing number of market niches with distinct preferences. Direct marketing allows sellers to focus efficiently on these mini-markets with offers that better match specific consumer needs.

Other trends have fuelled the rapid growth of direct marketing in the consumer market. Higher costs of driving, traffic congestion, parking headaches, lack of time, a shortage of retail sales help, and lines at checkout counters all encourage at-home shopping. Consumers are responding favourably to direct marketers' toll-free phone numbers, their willingness to accept telephone orders 24 hours a day, seven days a week, and their growing commitment to customer service. The growth of 24-hour and 48-hour delivery via Purolator, CanPar, Federal Express, UPS, DHL, and other express carriers has made direct shopping fast and easy. Finally, the growth of affordable computer power and customer databases has enabled direct marketers to single out the best prospects for any product they wish to sell.

Direct marketing has also grown rapidly in business-to-business marketing, partly in response to the ever-increasing cost of reaching business markets through the sales force. Since personal sales calls often cost $250 per contact, they should be made only when necessary and to high-potential customers and prospects. Lower cost-per-contact methods—such as telemarketing, direct mail, and the newer electronic media—often prove more cost effective in reaching and selling to more prospects and customers.

Customer Databases and Direct Marketing

Table 16-1 lists the main differences between mass marketing and *one-to-one marketing.*[9] Companies that know about individual customer needs and characteristics can customize their offers, messages, delivery modes, and payment methods to maximize customer value and satisfaction. And today's companies have a very pow-

TABLE 16-1 Mass Marketing Versus One-to-One Marketing

Mass Marketing	One-to-One Marketing
Average customer	Individual customer
Customer anonymity	Customer profile
Standard product	Customized market offering
Mass production	Customized production
Mass distribution	Individualized distribution
Mass advertising	Individualized message
Mass promotion	Individualized incentives
One-way messages	Two-way messages
Economies of scale	Economies of scope
Share of market	Share of customer
All customers	Profitable customers
Customer attraction	Customer retention

Source: Adapted from Don Peppers and Martha Rogers, *The One-to-One Future,* New York: Doubleday/Currency, 1993.

erful tool for accessing the names, addresses, preferences, and other pertinent information about individual customers and prospects—the customer database.

Customer database
An organized collection of comprehensive data about individual customers or prospects, including geographic, demographic, psychographic, and behavioural data.

A **customer database** is an organized collection of comprehensive data about individual customers or prospects, including geographic, demographic, psychographic, and behavioural data. The database can be used to locate good potential customers, tailor products and services to the special needs of targeted consumers, and maintain long-term customer relationships. *Database marketing* is the process of building, maintaining, and using customer databases and other databases (products, suppliers, resellers) for the purpose of contacting and transacting with customers.

Many companies confuse the customer mailing list with the customer database. A customer mailing list is simply a set of names, addresses, and telephone numbers. A customer database contains much more information. In business-to-business marketing, the salesperson's customer profile may contain such information as the products and services the customer has bought; past volumes and prices; key contacts (and their ages, birthdays, hobbies, and favourite foods); competitive suppliers; status of current contracts; estimated customer expenditures for the next few years; and assessments of competitive strengths and weaknesses in selling and serving the account. In consumer marketing, the customer database may contain a customer's demographics (age, income, family members, birthdays), psychographics (activities, interests, and opinions), buying behaviour (past purchases, buying preferences), and other relevant information. The catalogue company Fingerhut maintains a database containing some 1300 pieces of information on each of 30 million households (see Marketing Highlight 16–1). And Ritz-Carlton's database holds more than 500 000 individual customer preferences.

Database marketing is most frequently used by charities and non-profit marketers, business-to-business marketers, and service retailers (hotels, banks, and airlines). Increasingly, however, consumer packaged goods companies and retailers are also using it. A recent survey found that almost two-thirds of all large consumer product companies are currently using or building such databases for targeting their marketing efforts.[10] Armed with the information in their databases, these companies can identify small groups of customers to receive fine-tuned marketing offers and communications. Kraft Foods has amassed a list of more than 30 million users of its products who have responded to coupons or other Kraft

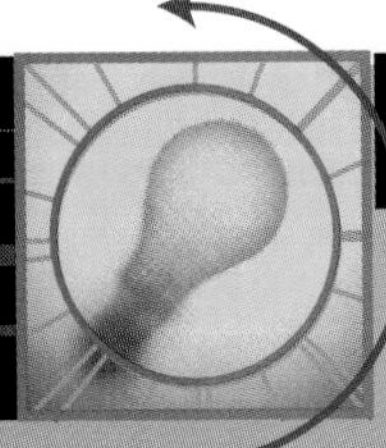

marketing highlight 16-1

Database Marketing: Fingerhut Builds Strong Customer Relationships

As Betty Holmes sifts through the day's stack of mail, one item catches her eye. It's only a catalogue, but it's speaking directly to her. A laser-printed personal message on the catalogue's cover states: "Thank you, Mrs. Holmes, for your recent purchase of women's apparel. To show our thanks, we are offering you up to five free gifts, plus deferred payment until July 31." The note goes on, with amazing accuracy, to refer Betty to specific items in the catalogue that will likely interest her.

The catalogue is from Fingerhut, the giant direct-mail retailer and master database marketer. A typical Fingerhut catalogue offers products ranging from $20 toy phones to $2000 big-screen televisions. Fingerhut operates on a *huge* scale: It sends out some 558 million mailings each year—more than 1.5 million per day. When new customers first respond to a direct-mail offer, Fingerhut asks them to fill out a questionnaire about the kinds of products that interest them. Using information from this questionnaire and from other sources, along with information about later purchases, Fingerhut has built an impressive marketing database. The database contains about 1300 pieces of information on each of 30 million active and potential customers. It's filled with the usual demographic details such as address, age, marital status, and number of children, but it also tracks hobbies, interests, birthdays, and seemingly obscure facts.

The database allows Fingerhut to target the most likely buyers with products that interest them. Instead of sending out the same catalogues and letters to all of its customers, Fingerhut tailors its offers based on what each customer is likely to buy. Moreover, promotions such as the Birthday Club provide opportunities to create special offers that sell more products. A month before a child's birthday, Birthday Club customers receive a free birthday gift for their child if they agree to try any one of the products Fingerhut offers in an accompanying mailing. A customer who responds to these and other offers may become one of millions of "promotable" customers who receive Fingerhut mailings. As a result of such skillful use of its database, Fingerhut achieves direct-mail response rates that are three times the industry average. Says one retailing consultant, "Fingerhut is one of those pioneering companies that is making intense knowledge of their customer a core competency."

Fingerhut uses its database to build long-term customer relationships that go well beyond its merchandise. It stays in continuous touch with preferred customers through regular special promotions—an annual sweepstakes, free gifts, a deferred-billing promotion, and others. These special offers are all designed with one goal in mind: to create a reason for Fingerhut to be in the customer's mailbox. Once in the mailbox, the personalized messages and targeted offers get attention.

Credit is a cornerstone of Fingerhut's relationship with customers. The average Fingerhut customer has a household income of just around $35 000. Whereas many retailers and credit companies are reluctant to extend credit to this moderate-income group, Fingerhut encourages credit. Catalogues list monthly payments in bold type and actual prices in fine print. Customers can spread a $40 running shoe purchase over 13 months with payments of just $4.79 per month. Fingerhut regularly extends credit to people who would otherwise have to pay cash. "When I started out, Fingerhut was the only place that would give me credit," says Marilyn Gnat, a loyal Fingerhut customer who raised nine children on a modest income.

Despite selling to consumers of mod-

promotions. Blockbuster, the massive entertainment company, uses its database of 36 million households and two million daily transactions to help its video-rental customers select movies and to steer them to other Blockbuster subsidiaries.

American Express uses its database to tailor offers to cardholders. In Belgium, it is testing a system that links cardholder spending patterns with postal-zone data. If a new restaurant opens, for example, the company may offer a special discount to cardholders who live within walking distance and who eat out a lot. And FedEx uses its sophisticated database to create 100 highly targeted, customized direct-mail and telemarketing campaigns each year to its nearly five million customers shipping to 212 countries. By analyzing customers carefully and reaching the right customers at the right time with the right promotions, FedEx achieves response rates of 20 to 25 percent and earns an 8-to-1 return on its direct-marketing dollars.[11]

Smaller companies can also make good use of database marketing:[12]

> HSBC faced just a small challenge—a new name, low brand awareness, and a budget significantly lower than that of other Canadian financial institutions targeting high-net-worth, educated, savvy investors during the cluttered RRSP period. Needless to say, it had to come up with a breakthrough campaign. Its solution—a teaser campaign promoting a fictional dot.com,

est means, Fingerhut turns credit into a competitive advantage by using its huge database to effectively control credit risks. Some 40 percent of Fingerhut customers have had so little credit that they don't even have credit reports. The company's extensive database helps it to do a better job than competitors can of predicting customers' creditworthiness. Fingerhut further controls credit risks by what it offers to whom. When a new customer makes a first order, the amount of credit allowed may be limited to $50. If the customer pays promptly, the next mailing offers higher-ticket items. Good customers, who pay their bills regularly, receive cards and rewards to reinforce this behaviour. For example, an award envelope cheers "Congratulations! You've been selected to receive our 'exceptional customer award!'" and contains a certificate suitable for framing.

Fingerhut has begun applying its database touch to the Internet. Customers can now log on to the Fingerhut Online Web site (www.fingerhut.com) and order products from the catalogue using an online order form. The company's popular Andy's Garage Sale site (www.andysgarage.com) even customizes its interactions with Web customers. "If you are repeatedly buying golfing equipment and I'm buying boat supplies, it'll show you golf bags and it'll show me life jackets," explains Fingerhut's vice-president of marketing.

Fingerhut's database stores millions of facts on tens of millions of consumers.

The skillful use of database marketing and relationship building have made Fingerhut one of the largest direct-mail marketers in the United States. Founded in 1948 by brothers Manny and William Fingerhut, it now sells more than $2.8 billion worth of mail-order merchandise each year, making it the second largest consumer catalogue company in the US behind J.C. Penney. In fact, one in every six US households has *bought* something from the company. Fingerhut's success is no accident. "Most of our competitors use a full catalogue; they could care less about what the individuals want," notes a Fingerhut executive. "Fingerhut finds out what each customer wants and builds an event around each promotion."

Sources: Quotes from Eileen Norris, "Fingerhut gives customers credit," *Advertising Age,* 6 March 1986:19; Susan Chandler, "Data is power. Just ask Fingerhut," *Business Week,* 3 June 1996:69; and Mitch Wagner, "Repeat traffic is goal of customerized Web sites," *Computer World,* 25 November 1996:48. Also see John N. Frank, "A finger in the card pie," *Credit Card Management,* July 1996: 22–8; and Rob Yoegel, "Fingerhut's penny mailing," *Target Marketing,* April 1997:53–5.

www.invest-the-world.com. Knowing sophisticated investors took pride in knowing each and every investment opportunity, HBSC bet that an unknown site would spark investors' fear of missing out on a great opportunity. Using its customer database, HSBC sent a direct mail piece to 95 400 potential investors that directed them to the site. Once there, HSBC's RRSP products were presented along with the chance to win a free trip for two anywhere in the world HSBC mutual funds were managed. The direct mailing was cleverly supported by print, outdoor, online banner ads, newspaper wraps, and even Post-it notes that also grabbed attention. The campaign not only won awards, it resulted in a flood of new clients who opened up new accounts in one of the worst RRSP seasons in more than a decade.

A company can use its database in four ways:

1. *Identifying prospects.* Many companies generate sales leads by using advertising that has some sort of response feature, such as a business reply card or toll-free number. The database is built from these responses. The company identifies the best prospects, then reaches them by mail, phone, or personal calls in an attempt to convert them into customers.
2. *Deciding which customers should receive a particular offer.* A company identifies the profile of an ideal customer for an offer. It then searches its databases for

Many non-profits, such as the Canadian Wildlife Federation, use database marketing to raise funds.

individuals most closely resembling the ideal type to improve its targeting precision over time. Following a sale, it can set up an automatic sequence of activities: one week later, send a thank-you note; five weeks later, send a new offer; 10 weeks later (if customer has not responded), phone the customer and offer a special discount.

3. *Deepening customer loyalty.* Companies can build customers' interest and enthusiasm by remembering their preferences and by sending appropriate information, gifts, or other materials. For example, Mars, a market leader in pet food as well as candy, compiled the names of almost every German family that owns a cat by contacting veterinarians and by offering the public a free booklet, *How to Take Care of Your Cat.* People who request the booklet, fill out a questionnaire, providing their cat's name, age, birthday, and other information. Mars then sends a birthday card to each cat along with a new cat food sample and money-saving coupons for Mars brands. The result is a lasting relationship with the cat's owner.
4. *Reactivating customer purchases.* The database can help a company make attractive offers of product replacements, upgrades, or complementary products just when customers may be ready to act. For example, a General Electric customer database contains each customer's demographic and psychographic characteristics along with an appliance purchasing history. Using this database, GE marketers assess how long specific customers have owned their current appliances and which past customers may be ready to purchase again. A rich customer database allows GE to build profitable new business by locating good prospects, anticipating customers' needs, cross-selling products and services, and rewarding loyal customers.

Like many other marketing tools, database marketing requires a special investment. Companies must invest in computer hardware, database software, analytical programs, communication links, and skilled personnel. The database system also must be user friendly and available to various marketing groups, including those in product and brand management, new-product development, advertising and promotion, direct mail, telemarketing, field sales, order fulfillment, and customer service. A well-managed database should lead to sales gains that will more than cover its costs.

Forms of Direct Marketing Communication

The major forms of direct marketing, shown in Figure 16-1, are *face-to-face selling, telemarketing, direct-mail marketing, catalogue marketing, direct-response television marketing, kiosk marketing,* and *online marketing.*

Face-to-Face Selling

The original and oldest form of direct marketing is the sales call, which we examined in Chapter 15. Most business-to-business marketers rely heavily on a professional sales force to locate prospects, develop them into customers, build lasting relationships, and grow the business. Or they hire manufacturers' representatives and agents to carry out the direct selling task. In addition, many consumer companies use a direct selling force to reach final consumers: insurance agents, stockbrokers, and salespeople working part or full time for direct sales organizations such as Avon, Amway, Mary Kay, and Tupperware.

FIGURE 16-1 Forms of direct marketing

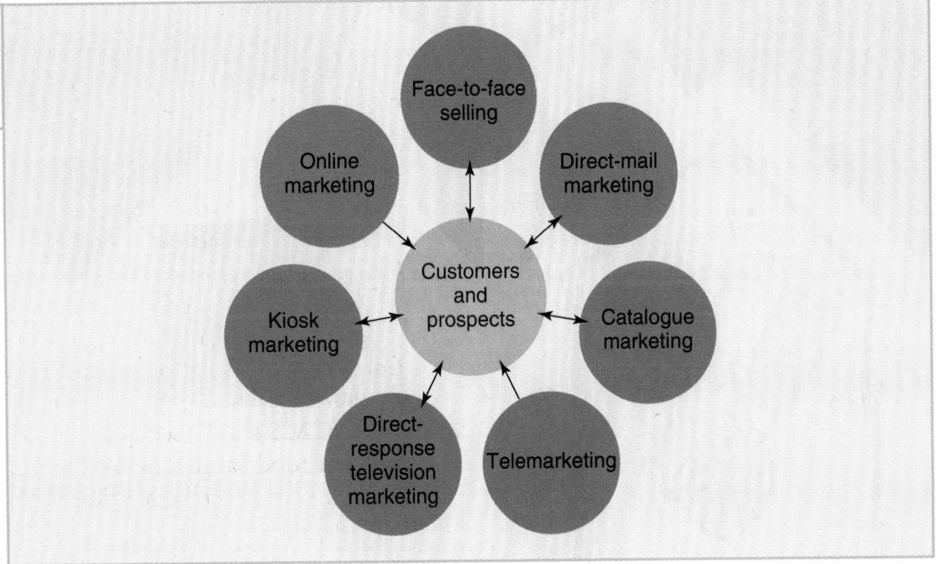

Telemarketing

Telemarketing
Using the telephone to sell directly to consumers.

Telemarketing—using the telephone to sell directly to consumers—has become the major direct marketing communication tool. Telephone marketing now accounts for over 38 percent of all direct marketing media expenditures.[13] We're all familiar with telemarketing directed toward consumers, but business-to-business marketers also use telemarketing extensively.

Marketers use outbound telephone marketing to sell directly to consumers and businesses. Inbound toll-free numbers are used to receive orders from television and radio ads, direct mail, or catalogues. The use of toll-free numbers has taken off in recent years as more companies have begun using them and as current users have added new features such as toll-free fax numbers. Residential use has also grown. To accommodate this rapid growth, new toll-free area codes (888, 877, 866) have been added. After the 800 area code was established in 1967, it took almost 30 years before its eight million numbers were used up. In contrast, 888 area code numbers, established in 1996, were used up in only two years.[14]

Other marketers use 900 numbers to sell consumers information, entertainment, or the opportunity to voice an opinion on a pay-per-call basis. For example, for a charge, consumers can obtain weather forecasts from American Express (900-WEATHER at 75¢ a minute), pet care information from Quaker Oats (900-990-PETS at 95¢ a minute), or golf lessons from *Golf Digest* (900-454-3288 at 95¢ a minute). In addition to its 800 number and Internet site, Nintendo offers a 900 number for $1.50 per minute for game players wanting assistance with the company's video games. Ronald McDonald House Charities uses a 900 number to raise funds. Each call to 900-CALL-RMHC results in a $15.00 contribution, which is simply charged to the caller's local phone bill. Overall, the use of 900 numbers grew by more than 10 percent a year in five years.[15]

Many consumers appreciate many of the offers they receive by telephone. Properly designed and targeted telemarketing provides many benefits, including purchasing convenience and increased product and service information. However, the recent explosion in unsolicited telephone marketing has annoyed many people who object to the almost daily "junk phone calls" that pull them away from the dinner table or fill their answering machines. To help overcome this problem, "Do not call" lists are maintained by the Canadian Direct Marketing Association, where one executive notes, "We want to target people who want to be targeted."

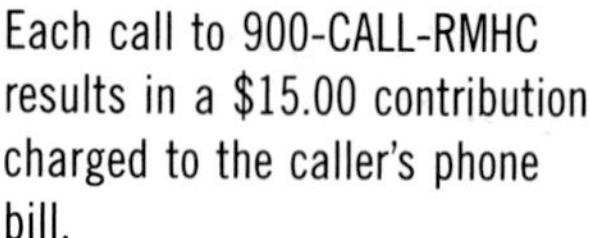
Each call to 900-CALL-RMHC results in a $15.00 contribution charged to the caller's phone bill.

Direct-Mail Marketing

Direct-mail marketing
Sending an offer, announcement, reminder, or other item to a person at a particular address.

Direct-mail marketing involves sending an offer, announcement, reminder, or other item to a person at a particular address. Using highly selective mailing lists, direct marketers send out millions of mail pieces each year—letters, ads, samples, foldouts, and other "salespeople with wings." Direct mail is well suited to direct one-to-one communication. It permits high target market selectivity, can be personalized, is flexible, and allows easy measurement of results. Whereas the cost per thousand people reached is higher than with mass media such as television or magazines, the people who are reached are much better prospects. Direct mail has proven successful in promoting all kinds of products, from books, magazine subscriptions, and insurance to gift items, clothing, gourmet foods, and industrial products. Direct mail is also used heavily by charities, which use it to raise billions of dollars each year.

The direct-mail industry always seeks new methods and approaches. For example, videocassettes have become one of the fastest-growing direct mail media: With VCRs in most North American homes, marketers mailed out an estimated 85 million tapes in 1995. For instance, to introduce its *Donkey Kong Country* video game, Nintendo created a 13-minute MTV-style video, which it sent to two million avid video-game players. This direct-mail video helped Nintendo sell 6.1 million units of the game in only 45 days, making it the fastest-selling game in industry history.[16] Some direct marketers even mail out computer disks. For example, Ford sends a computer disk called "Disk Drive Test Drive" to consumers responding to its ads in computer publications: The diskette provides technical specifications and attractive graphics about Ford cars and answers frequently asked questions.

Until recently, all mail was paper based and handled by Canada Post, telegraphic services, or for-profit mail carriers such as Purolator, Federal Express, DHL, or Airborne Express. Recently, however, three new forms of mail delivery have become popular:

- *Fax mail.* Fax machines allow delivery of paper-based messages over telephone lines. Fax mail has one major advantage over regular mail: The message can be sent and received almost instantaneously. Marketers now routinely send fax mail announcing offers, sales, and other events to prospects and customers with fax machines. Fax numbers of companies and individuals are now available through published directories. However, some prospects and customers resent receiving unsolicited fax mail, which clutters their machines and consumes their paper.

- *E-mail.* E-mail allows users to send messages or files directly from one computer to another. Messages arrive almost instantly and are stored until the receiving person retrieves them. Many marketers now send sales announcements, offers, product information, and other messages to e-mail addresses—sometimes to a few individuals, sometimes to large groups. However, as people receive more unimportant e-mail messages that they can ignore or discard, they may look for an "agent" software program to sort these out from the more important messages. Unsolicited e-mail may anger some users so much they *spam* the sender by sending a return message designed to jam the sender's system.
- *Voice mail.* Voice mail is a system for receiving and storing oral messages at a telephone address. Telephone companies sell this service as a substitute for answering machines. The person with a voice-mail account can check messages by dialing into the voice-mail system and punching in a personal code. Some marketers have set up programs that will dial a large number of telephone numbers and leave the selling messages in the recipients' voice mailboxes.

These forms deliver direct mail at incredible speeds, compared to the post office's "snail mail" pace. Yet, much like mail delivered through traditional channels, they may be resented as junk mail if sent to people who have no interest in them. For this reason, marketers must carefully identify appropriate targets so they don't waste their money and the recipients' time (see Marketing Highlight 16–2).

Catalogue Marketing

Rapid advances in technology, along with the move toward personalized, one-to-one marketing, have resulted in dramatic changes in catalogue marketing. *Catalog Age* magazine used to define a catalogue as "a printed, bound piece of at least eight pages, selling multiple products, and offering a direct ordering mechanism." This definition is out of date: Although printed catalogues remain the primary medium, with the stampede to the Internet, catalogues are going electronic. Many traditional print cataloguers have added Web-based catalogues to their marketing mixes and a variety of new Web-only cataloguers have emerged.

Catalogue marketing
Selling through catalogues mailed to a select list of customers or made available in stores.

Catalogue marketing has taken off in the past 25 years. Annual catalogue sales in North America (both print and electronic) are expected to grow from a current $120 billion to more than $160 billion by 2002.[17] Some huge general merchandise retailers, including Sears and Canadian Tire, sell a full line of merchandise through catalogues. More recently, the giants have been challenged by thousands of specialty catalogues that serve highly specialized market niches. Consumers can buy just about anything from a catalogue. Sharper Image sells $3600 jet-propelled surfboards. Ikea Canada can help you furnish almost any living space with style. Harry Rosen can dress you for any occasion: While customers get its catalogue (which combines feature articles and fashion advice) for free, others can buy it on newsstands for $6. Tilley Endurables, Mountain Equipment Co-op, and the Banana Republic Travel and Safari Clothing Company feature everything you would need to go hiking in the Sahara or the rain forest. Some larger retailers are taking on these specialty retailers with their own niche catalogues. Zellers, for example, recently launched its new *Special Delivery Baby* catalogue and online baby-gift registry. It targets "tweens" with its *Gen Z* catalogue.

Specialty department stores, such as Holt Renfrew, Ashley China, and Neiman Marcus use catalogues to cultivate upper-middle-class markets for high-priced, often exotic, merchandise. Several major corporations have also developed or acquired catalogue divisions. Avon now issues 10 women's fashion catalogues along with catalogues for children's and men's clothes. Walt Disney Company

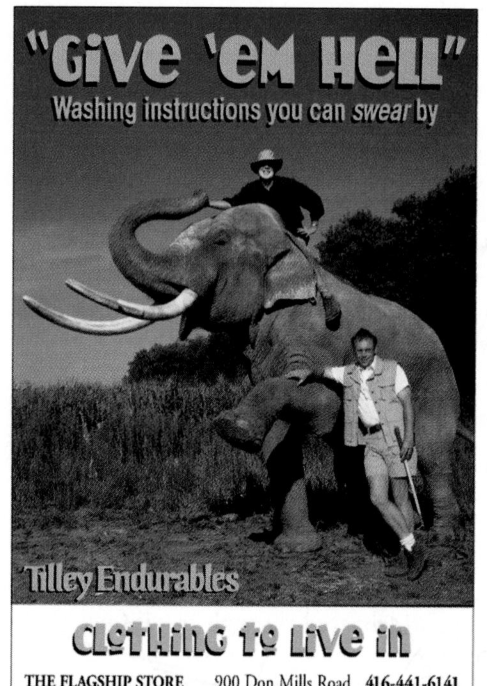

Tilley Endurables uses a tri-channel strategy: bricks and mortar, catalogue, and the Web.

mails out over six million catalogues each year featuring videos, stuffed animals, and other Disney items.

The Internet has had a tremendous impact on catalogue selling. In the face of increasing competition from Internet retailing, one expert even predicts "catalogues are doomed . . . mail-order catalogues as we know them today won't even survive."[18] Therefore, even traditional cataloguers are adding Web-based catalogues. In fact, more than three-quarters of all catalogue companies now present merchandise and take orders over the Internet. For example, the successful marriage of Sears' old-style catalogue with its new-style Web site generated over $100 million in revenues in 2000, making it one of the most successful e-tail sites in Canada.[19] Sears' success is partly due to its ability to leverage its skills and infrastructure developed with its traditional catalogue. Sears is also relaunching eatons.com, a site carrying a more limited selection targeting higher-income consumers. The Lands' End Web site, which debuted in 1995, gets around 180 000 e-mail queries a year, surpassing its print mail response.[20]

Along with the benefits, Web-based catalogues present challenges. Whereas a print catalogue is intrusive and creates its own attention, Web catalogues are passive and must be marketed. "Attracting new customers is much more difficult to do with a Web catalogue," says an industry consultant. "You have to use advertising, linkage, and other means to drive traffic to it." Kevin Bartus, president of Blue*Spark, a Toronto-based Web development firm, says, "Retailers are learning an online business is not, in most cases, big enough to support a complete business offering. Retailers are turning to a tri-channel: bricks and mortar, catalogue, and Web."[21] Take the case of La Senza, the Montreal-based lingerie retailer. It first launched a Web site featuring a separate line of merchandise to avoid cannibalizing store sales, but finally had to relaunch the site as an arm of its existing business. To further integrate, customers can return items bought online in stores and sign up for the e-mail club there as well. Thus, even cataloguers who are sold on the Web are not likely to abandon their print catalogues completely.

Sears used the skills and infrastructure it developed using traditional catalogues to launch one of Canada's most successful e-tailing sites.

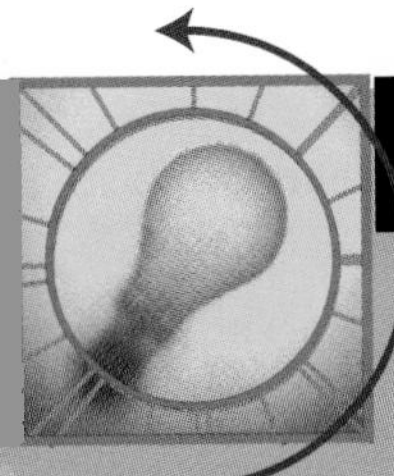

marketing highlight 16-2

Misdirected Marketing: My Dead Dog May Already Be a Winner!

Poor database management and wrongly targeted direct marketing not only aggravates consumers, it costs companies millions of dollars each year and sometimes makes them look downright foolish. Take the following account, written by Lee Coppola, the bemused recipient of some of this misdirected mania:

> Ever wonder what happens when a pet takes on a persona? Ashley could have told you, if he could have talked. Ashley was the family mutt, an SPCA special, part beagle and part spaniel. For years, most of them after he died, he also served as the family's representative in the local telephone book. He was picked for the role quite haphazardly one day when I tried to keep my number out of the book to avoid getting business calls at home. When I balked at the $60-a-year fee, the cheery telephone company representative suggested I list the number in one of my children's names.
>
> I was munching on a sandwich at the time and Ashley followed me around the kitchen waiting for a crumb to fall. "Can I put the phone in any name?" I asked the rep as I sidestepped Ashley. "Certainly," she answered. So I listed the number under Ashley's name and therein gave birth to 10 years of telephone calls and mail to a dog.
>
> "A remarkable new book about the Coppolas since Confederation is about to make history—and you, Ashley Coppola, are in it," touted one letter asking Ashley to send $10 right away for "this one-time offer." Ashley received hundreds of pieces of mail, the bulk soliciting his money.
>
> The most ironic pitches for cash were from the SPCA and the local zoo, a kind of animal-helping-animal scenario. And we wondered how the chief executive of a local cemetery might react if he knew he was asking a canine to buy a plot to give his family "peace of mind." Or a local lawn service's thoughts about asking a dog who daily messed the grass, "Is your lawn as attractive as it could be?" Then there was the letter offering Ashley "reliable electronic security to protect your home." One of the kids asked if that wasn't Ashley's job.
>
> The kids soon got into the swing of having their dog receive mail and telephone calls. "He's sleeping under the dining room table," one would tell telemarketers. "He's out in the backyard taking a whiz," was the favourite reply of another. My wife would have nothing of that frivolity, preferring to simply reply, "He's deceased."
>
> But that tack backfired on her one day when our youngest child took an almost pleading call from a survey company employee looking for Ashley. "I'm Ashley," the 17 year old politely replied, taking pity on the caller. He dutifully gave his age and answered a few questions before he realized he was late for an appointment and hurriedly cut short the conversation. "Can I call you again?" the surveyor asked. "OK," our son said as he hung up.
>
> Sure enough, the surveyor called again the next day and asked for Ashley. But this time Mom answered and gave her standard reply. "Oh, my God," exclaimed the caller. "I'm so, so sorry." The surveyor's horrified grief puzzled my wife until our son explained how he had been a healthy teenage Ashley the day before.
>
> Sometimes we worried about our dog's fate. You see, he broke several chain letters urging him to copy and send 20 others or risk some calamity. After all, Ashley was warned, didn't one person die nine days after throwing out the letter?
>
> Did I mention credit cards? Ashley paid his bills on time, judging from the $5000 lines of credit for which he "automatically" qualified. Made us wonder about the scrutiny of the nation's credit card industry.
>
> Of course, Ashley was no ordinary dog. He was an Italian dog. How else to explain the solicitation to Mr. Coppola Ashley that came all the way from Altamura, Italy, and sought donations to an orphanage? Then there was the offer to obtain his family's cherished crest, "fashioned hundreds of years ago in Italy," and purchase the Coppola family registry that listed him along with all the other Coppolas in America.
>
> Is there some message to all this? Think of the saplings that were sacrificed to try to squeeze money from a canine. Or the time, energy, and money that were wasted each time a postage or bulk-mail stamp was affixed to an envelope being sent to a mutt. We did feel sheepish about the deception when the mail came from the self-employed trying to make a buck. We wondered if a local dentist really would have given Ashley a "complete initial consultation, exam, and bitewing X-rays for *only three dollars*." And what might have been the expression on the saleswoman's face if Ashley had shown up for his complimentary Mary Kay facial?
>
> Ashley did appreciate, however, the coupon for dog food.

Source: Lee Coppola, "My dead dog may already be a winner!" *Newsweek*, 5 July 1999:11.

Direct-Response Television Marketing

Direct-response television marketing
Television spots that persuasively describe a product and give customers a toll-free number for ordering.

Direct-response television marketing takes one of two major forms. With *direct-response advertising*, direct marketers air commercials, often 60 or 120 seconds long, that persuasively describe a product and give customers a toll-free number for ordering. Television viewers also encounter 30-minute advertising programs, or *infomercials*, for a single product.

Some successful direct-response ads run for years and become classics. For example, Dial Media's ads for Ginsu knives ran for seven years and sold almost three mil-

The infomercial for George Foreman's Lean Mean Fat-Reducing Grilling Machine has not only racked up $300 million in sales, it has also become a classic.

lion sets of knives, worth more than $60 million in sales; its Armourcote cookware ads generated more than twice that much. The current infomercial champ:[22]

> It's three o'clock in the morning. Plagued with insomnia, you grab the remote and flip around until a grinning blonde in an apron catches your attention: "I'm going to show you something you won't believe! Juicy meals in minutes! Something else you won't believe . . . George Foreman!" The studio roars, and boxing's elder statesman, in a red apron, shows off his Lean Mean Fat-Reducing Grilling Machine and highlights the grease caught in the pan below. "Eew!" the audience screams. It can be yours for three easy payments plus shipping and handling. Don't laugh. [This infomercial has] notched $300 million in sales of Foreman grills in less than four years.

For years, infomercials have been associated with somewhat questionable pitches for juicers, get-rich-quick schemes, and nifty ways to stay in shape without working very hard at it. Recently, however, a number of top marketing companies—GTE, Johnson & Johnson, MCA Universal, Sears, Procter & Gamble, Revlon, Apple Computer, Toyota, and others—have begun using infomercials to sell their wares over the phone, refer customers to retailers, or send out coupons and product information.[23]

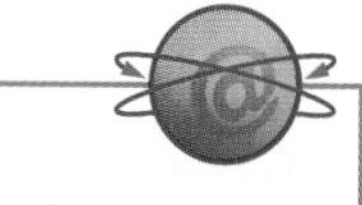
The Shopping Channel
www.tsc.ca/

Home shopping channels, another form of direct-response television marketing, are television programs or entire channels dedicated to selling goods and services. Some home shopping channels, such as The Shopping Channel, broadcast 24 hours a day. The program's hosts offer bargain prices on such products as jewellery, lamps, collectible dolls, clothing, power tools, and consumer electronics—usually obtained by the home shopping channel at closeout prices. The Shopping Channel's savvy customer-centred marketers didn't take long to add the Web to their marketing mix. Long accustomed to providing consumers with the convenience of shopping at any time, day or night, in the medium of their choice, they launched in May 1999. The site presents browsers with a full selection of all of its products, spanning nine product categories—jewellery, health and beauty, fashions, fitness, at home, electronics, toys, crafts, and collectibles. The site allowed the television retailer to break free of the limitations inherent in using TV, which can focus on only one product at a time. TV did not allow shoppers to browse through the channel's full offerings. tSc's online customers can now have access to a full assortment of its products at any time without having to wait for the information on these products to appear in shows on television. tSc's best customers, those with higher income and education, have naturally gravitated to tSc.ca, but, more importantly, the site has attracted a significant number of new customers. Moreover, the average order value is 27 percent higher than that of television-only users. View and click obviously makes a dynamic marketing option.[24]

Kiosk Marketing

Some companies place information and ordering machines—called *kiosks* (in contrast to vending machines, which dispense actual products)—in stores, airports, and other locations. Hallmark and American Greetings use kiosks to help customers create personalized cards. Lee jeans stores use a kiosk called Fit Finder to provide women with a quick way to determine the size and style of Lee jeans that fit their personal preference. Toyota Canada used kiosks to target younger buyers. The Liquor Control Board of Ontario installed interactive kiosks to run advertisements for featured products and to enhance customer service. Ikea Canada allows UNICEF to set up fundraising kiosks in its stores.[25]

Business marketers also use kiosks. Investment Canada placed a kiosk at an Atlanta trade show to introduce Canadian telecommunications and computer products to international buyers. Dow Plastics places kiosks at trade shows to collect sales leads and to provide information on its 700 products. The kiosk system reads customer data from encoded registration badges and produces technical data sheets, which can be printed at the kiosk or faxed or mailed to the customer. The system has resulted in a 400-percent increase in qualified sales leads.[26]

Online Marketing and Electronic Commerce

Online marketing The use of interactive online computer systems, which link consumers with sellers.

Commercial online service Provider of online information and marketing services to subscribers who pay a monthly fee.

Internet (or the Net) A vast and global web of computer networks.

Online marketing is conducted through interactive online computer systems, which link consumers with sellers electronically. There are two types of online marketing channels: commercial online services and the Internet.

Commercial online services offer online information and marketing services to subscribers who pay a monthly fee. The best-known online service provider is giant America Online, which has more than 21 million subscribers. Microsoft Network (MSN) and Prodigy trail far behind AOL with 2.45 million and one million subscribers, respectively. In contrast, Sympatico, which is the most popular portal in Canada, has only 896 000 users.[27] These online services provide subscribers with information (news, libraries, education, travel, sports, reference), entertainment (fun and games), shopping services, dialogue opportunities (bulletin boards, forums, chat boxes), and e-mail.

After growing rapidly through the mid-1990s, the commercial online services are now being overtaken by the **Internet** as the primary online marketing channel. In fact, all of the online service firms now offer Internet access as a primary service. Created by the US Defense Department during the 1960s, initially to link government labs, contractors, and military installations, the Internet is now a huge public computer network that links computer users of all types all around the world. Anyone with a PC, a modem, and the right software can browse the Internet to obtain or share information on almost any subject and to interact with other users.[28]

Internet usage surged with the development of the user-friendly World Wide Web access standard and Web browser software such as Netscape Navigator, Microsoft Internet Explorer, and Mosaic. Even novices surf the Net with fully integrated text, graphics, images, and sound. Users can send e-mail, exchange views, shop for products, and gain access to news, recipes, art, and business information. The Internet itself is free, although individual users usually must pay a commercial Internet service provider (ISP) to be hooked up to it.

Sympatico is Canada's largest provider of commercial online services.

marketers speak out

Nick Jones, Internet Evangelist

Yes, Nick's official business title is "Internet evangelist." He has the business card to prove it, but it is somewhat of an understatement to say that Nick Jones took an indirect route into business and marketing. After all, Nick pursued an undergraduate degree in fine arts.

Since he thought his best career bet would be in administrating an arts organization, and unable to tear himself away from campus life, Nick decided to take an MBA. He did a summer internship with Warner-Lambert only to be convinced that he wasn't the packaged goods type. He shifted gears again and took a masters of public administration only to discover that he was not destined to be a bureaucrat, but was very much a businessperson after all.

Nick's first job after graduation brought him to Toronto, where he joined a friend who was running a fledgling baseball magazine. Nick took on the role of marketing and sales manager. He did everything from developing advertising to running events. He even developed their award-winning *Dugout* Web site, writing the code by hand. Nick learned that the big trick to being successful in publishing is getting what you print to people who will pay for it. Like many start-up organizations, the magazine was incurring heavy production and distribution costs. Although the magazine had national and international subscribers, there just weren't enough buyers, and the magazine went into bankruptcy.

Nick moved on to Incontext, a software company that specialized in HTML editing software. The company was doing well, until Microsoft came on the scene and merged with one of Incontext's chief competitors. The result: closure number two.

Undaunted, Nick moved on to Southam New Media, the interactive media arm of Southam newspaper group. Southam's president gave the group the mandate to experiment and learn about new media and find new ways to deliver information to consumers in a profitable manner. Southam's president was convinced that just being a newspaper company wouldn't be sufficient to allow the firm to survive into the twenty-first century. Nick was in heaven. He could freely explore an array of services just to learn what they were doing and how they were doing it. But, the summer of 1996 brought Conrad Black onto the scene. He purchased Southam and had quite a different view of new media. He saw the new media group as a "figment of previous management's overheated imagination." Surprise: Nick was dehired once again.

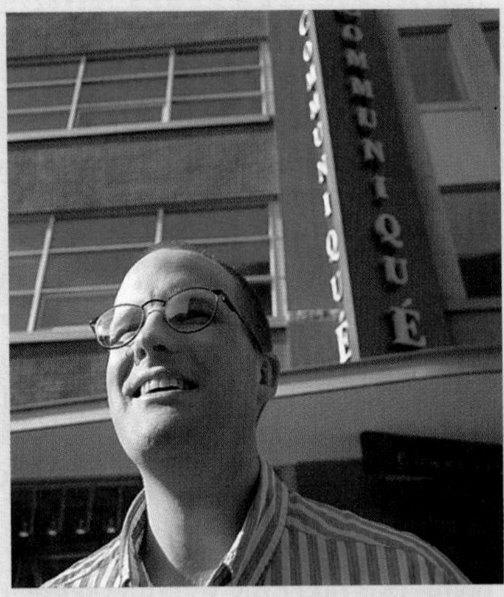

Nick Jones.

He landed briefly at Grey Advertising's interactive group, but when things didn't work out, Nick decided to take a time-out. Although he did some consulting, he spent most of his time biking, sailing, and reading. He sat down and wrote a personal mission statement to clarify his goals and then set out to find the position that would meet the mission statement. He found it at Communiqué, an integrated communications company formed by the union of several independent companies. Communiqué is a highly entrepreneurial firm full of energy, karma, and excitement. It is a very technology-driven company—one that uses technology to drive performance. If employees need a tool to better perform their job, they get it along with the training required to use the technology effectively.

When Communiqué takes on a client, it first does a communications audit. It looks at everything the client uses to communicate to its publics, from its letterhead to its Web site. The aim of the audit is to determine if the company is using the right tools to create the integrated image and position that the client desires. This approach has given Communiqué an edge—so much that it recently won the Microsoft and A&W accounts.

Now for Nick's role as the Internet evangelist. Communiqué's clients know about TV and radio and what these media can do for them, but they are uncomfortable with newer technologies like interactive kiosks, e-mail, and Web sites. Nick attends presentations to prospective clients to assess which vehicles are the best ones to obtain the results that client wants to achieve. He sells the necessity of having a Net presence with religious zeal.

Taking advantage of Internet marketing opportunities is no easy task, however. Creating a Web site takes a lot of insight and analysis. The design, function, and aesthetics of the site have to be carefully planned and integrated. The client has to think carefully about what services it wants to provide and what the potential interaction with its customer will be. In addition, firms using the Internet have to understand that while Canada is a very regional country, they are communicating to the planet when they post a site on the Internet. Firms have to build a Web site where anyone in the world can comfortably get information about what the company does.

But the job doesn't stop there. Even though you have to think globally, you can't forget about the local, home market. You have to balance the content of your site: If there is too much local content, it is perceived as hokey and unsophisticated; if there is too much global emphasis, you create the impression you don't care about local customers. No longer content to act just as a consultant, Nick moved on again in 1998 and became the general manager of the Chapters Internet group. In 2000, his entrepreneurial spirit took over once again, and he founded the Canadian Bootcamp for Internet Start-ups to provide information, contacts, and resources for Canadian businesses venturing onto the Web. If you ever have any doubt about the faith this evangelist has in the Internet, just watch for one of the sessions Nick gives across Canada.

Rapid Growth of Online Marketing

Although still in their infancy, Internet usage and online marketing are growing fast. In 2000, more than 170 countries were connected to the Internet, and 327 million people had access through over 100 million computers. At the end of the last millennium, Canadian e-commerce totalled about $11 billion or 6.8 percent of the world share. Global Internet commerce is expected to grow to an astounding $3.9 trillion by 2004. While Canadian e-commerce revenues are expected to grow to $151.5 billion by 2004, our world share may drop to as low as 3.9 percent, as other countries start to use e-commerce more heavily. Web sites emerge so quickly that no one knows how many exist today, but at the beginning of 2001 the search engine Google noted that its database contained over 1.3 billion pages.[29]

Internet access varies by region. British Columbia and Ontario have the most connected populations, at 53 percent. Alberta follows closely with 52 percent of its residents connected. Forty-eight percent of people in Manitoba and Saskatchewan are online, while Atlantic Canada has 43 percent. Quebec trails the rest of the country with only 40 percent of its citizens having Internet access.

While business-to-consumer e-commerce is growing rapidly, business-to-business Internet commerce is exploding. Business buyers are by far the largest Web users, accounting for more than 90 percent of all e-commerce. While almost 70 percent of Canadian public sector businesses have Web sites, only 14.5 percent use their sites to sell goods, but 44.2 percent use the Internet for procuring them.[30]

Electronic commerce
A buying and selling process that is supported by electronic means.

This explosion of Internet usage heralds the dawning of a new world of *electronic commerce*. **Electronic commerce** is the general term for a buying and selling process that is supported by electronic means. *Electronic markets* are "marketspaces" in which sellers offer their products and services electronically, and buyers search for information, identify what they want, and place orders using a credit card or other means of electronic payment.

The electronic commerce explosion is all around us:

- A reporter wants to buy a 35-mm camera. He logs on to the Shopper's Advantage Web site (www.cuc.com/ctg/cgi-bin/sashopper/), clicks on cameras, then

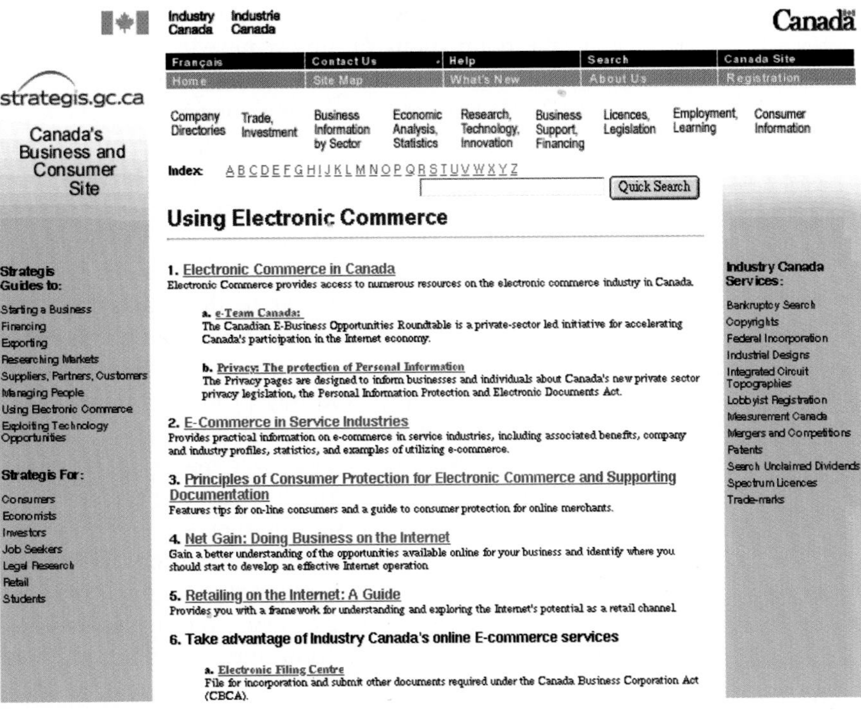

Industry Canada has designed its Electronic Commerce Web site to boost Canada's e-businesses.

clicks on 35-mm cameras. A list of all the major brands appears, along with information about each brand. He can retrieve a photo of each camera and reviews by experts. Finding the camera he wants, he places an order by typing in his credit card number, address, and preferred shipping mode.

- An executive is planning a trip to London and wants to locate a hotel that meets her needs. She signs on to the Travelocity Web site (www.travelocity.com) and inputs her criteria (rate, location, amenities, safety). The computer produces a list of appropriate hotels, and she can book a room once she has made her choice.

Canadians are leaders in the use of this new medium. A recent survey by A.C. Neilsen found that 53 percent of Internet users in Canada used information they found on the Internet before making a purchase, compared to 39 percent in the United States.[31]

The Online Consumer

The Internet population differs demographically from the general population. As a whole, the Internet population is younger, more affluent, better educated, and more male than the general population. Fifty-five percent of Canadians with household incomes of $80 000 or greater use the Web at least once a week. However, the cyberspace population is becoming more mainstream and diverse. For example, while 42 percent of Canadian weekly Web users are 18 to 34 years old, 16 percent are people aged 55 to 64. Men still make up the majority of weekly Web users at 58 percent, but women are getting online fast and account for 42 percent of weekly users. A recent study of Internet "newbies"—those who started using the Internet in the past year—found that Canadians aged 35 to 54 were the fastest-growing group.[32] An industry analyst summarizes:[33]

> The Internet isn't just a geek's playground anymore. These days, everybody's logging on. . . . Doral Main, a 51-year-old mother of two and office manager of a low-income property company . . . saves precious time by shopping on the Internet for greeting cards and getaways. Her Net-newbie father, Charles, 73, goes online to buy supplies for his wood-carving hobby. Even niece Katrina, 11, finds excitement on the Web, picking gifts she wants from the Disney.com site. "It's addictive," Main says of the Net. [Indeed,] the Web isn't mostly a hangout for techno-nerds anymore.

Increasingly, the Internet provides online marketers with access to a broad range of demographic segments. Internet users come from all age groups. For example, the populations of almost nine million "Net kids" and more than eight million teens (predicted to reach almost 22 million and 17 million, respectively, by the year 2002) have attracted a host of online marketers. America Online offers a Kids Only area, featuring homework help and online magazines along with the usual games, software, and chat rooms. The Microsoft Network site carries Disney's Daily Blast, which offers kids games, stories, comic strips with old and new Disney characters, and current events tailored to preteens. Nickelodeon offers Natalie's Backseat Traveling Web Show, which includes games based on a Nickelodeon character named Natalie. "Similar to the offline market," observes one expert, "kids and teens have a profound impact on online purchasing decisions. . . . Instead of grabbing parents' coat sleeves, today's kids ask parents for credit card numbers in place of an allowance and buy products online."[34]

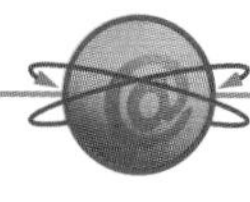

Nickelodeon
www.nick.com/

Although Internet users are younger on average than the population as a whole, seniors aged 55 and over make up around 24 percent of today's online users, and that number will grow to 40 percent by 2003. Whereas younger groups are more likely to use the Internet for entertainment and socializing, older Net surfers go online for more serious matters. For example, 24 percent of people in this age group use the Internet for investment purposes, compared with only three percent of those 25 to 29. Thus, older Netizens make an attractive market for Web businesses, ranging from florists and automotive retailers to financial services providers.[35]

SRI Consulting VALS2
www.future.sri.com/

Internet users also differ psychographically from the general consumer population. As discussed in Chapter 5 (see Marketing Highlight 5–1), Forrester Research and SRI Consulting have developed approaches for measuring attitudes, preferences, and behaviour of online service and Internet users. SRI Consulting's Web site allows visitors to take the VALS2 questionnaire and get immediate feedback on their VALS2 type. The firm has identified 10 psychographic segments ranging from Wizards, skilled users who identify strongly with the Internet, to Socialites, who are strongly oriented toward social aspects of the Internet.[36]

Finally, Internet consumers differ in their approaches to buying and in their responses to marketing. They are empowered consumers who have greater control over the marketing process. People who use the Internet place greater value on information and tend to respond negatively to messages designed only for selling. Whereas traditional marketing targets a somewhat passive audience, online marketing targets people who actively select which Web sites they will visit and which ad banners they will click on. They decide what marketing information they will receive about what products and services and under what conditions.

Internet search engines such as Yahoo!, Google, and Excite give consumers access to varied information sources, making them better informed and more discerning shoppers. In fact, online buyers are increasingly creators of product information, not just consumers of it. As greater numbers of consumers join Internet interest groups that share product-related information, "word of Web" is joining "word of mouth" as an important buying influence. Therefore, the new world of e-commerce will require new marketing approaches.

Conducting Online Marketing

Marketers can conduct online marketing in four ways: creating an electronic presence online; placing ads online; participating in Internet forums, newsgroups, or "Web communities"; or using online e-mail or Webcasting.

Creating an Electronic Online Presence

A company can establish an electronic online presence by buying space on a commercial online service or by setting up its own Web site. Buying a location on a

Richmond BC Savings Credit Union knows that offbeat humour appeals to many Web users.

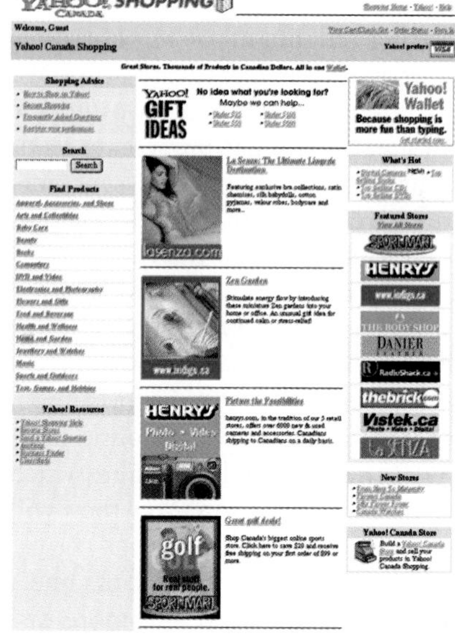

Many retailers use such commercial service providers as Yahoo! Canada to help them create an online presence.

commercial online service involves either renting storage space on the online service's computer or establishing a link from the company's own computer to the online service's shopping mall. Yahoo! Canada's shopping page, for example, has links to Danier Leather, The Body Shop, Indigo, Radio Shack, and Sports Mart, to name a few. Such links help direct the millions of consumers who use these search engines to these retail services. The online services may even design the storefront for the company and introduce it to their subscribers. For these services, the company pays the online service an annual fee plus a small percentage of the company's online sales.

In addition to buying a location on an online service, or as an alternative, many companies have created their own Web sites. These sites vary greatly in purpose and content. The most basic type is a **corporate Web site,** which is designed to handle interactive communication *initiated by the consumer.* The objective of this site is to build customer goodwill and to supplement other sales channels rather than to sell the company's products directly. For example, you can't buy ice cream at www.benjerrys.com, but you can learn all about Ben & Jerry's company philosophy, products, and locations; send a free e-card to a friend; or subscribe to the Chunk Mail newsletter. Similarly, Nabisco's LifeSavers Candystand Web site doesn't sell candy but does generate consumer excitement and goodwill, as well as valuable feedback to LifeSavers brand managers:[37]

Corporate Web site
Site designed to handle interactive communication initiated by the consumer.

> Nabisco's highly-entertaining LifeSavers Candystand Web site (www.candystand.com) features a rich variety of more than 27 interactive games, along with a variety of informational features and promotions, primarily designed to interest children and teenagers. Candystand contains 11 themed sections, each dedicated to a particular LifeSavers brand. "Our philosophy is to create an exciting online experience that reflects the fun and quality associated with the LifeSavers brands," says Silvio Bonvini, senior manager of new media at LifeSavers Company. "For the production cost of about two television spots we have a marketing vehicle that lives 24 hours a day, 7 days a week, 365 days a year." Candystand attracts more than 300 000 unique visitors a month. The site also offers LifeSavers an efficient channel for gathering customer feedback. Its "What Do You Think?" feature has generated 180 000 responses since the site launched in March 1997. "It's instant communication that we pass along directly to our brand people," Bonvini says. "It's not filtered by an agency or edited in any way." Comments collected from the Web site have resulted in improved packaging of one LifeSavers product and the resurrection of the abandoned Wintergreen flavor in the Carefree sugarless gum line.

Corporate Web sites typically offer a rich variety of information and other features in an effort to answer customer questions, build closer customer relationships, and generate excitement about the company. They generally provide information about the company's history, its mission and philosophy, and the products and services that it offers. They might also tell about current events, company personnel, financial performance, and employment opportunities. Most corporate Web sites also provide entertainment features to attract and hold visitors. Finally, the site might also provide opportunities for customers to ask questions or make comments through e-mail before leaving the site.

Marketing Web site
A site designed to engage consumers in an interaction that will move them closer to a purchase or other marketing outcome.

Other companies create a **marketing Web site,** which is designed to engage consumers in an interaction that will move them closer to a purchase or other marketing outcome. With a marketing Web site, communication and interactions are *initiated by the marketer.* Such a site might include a catalogue, shopping tips, and such promotional features as coupons, sales events, or contests. Companies aggressively promote their marketing Web sites in print and broadcast advertising, and through "banner-to-site" ads that pop up on other Web sites. Consumers can find a Web site for buying almost anything. Wal-Mart Canada established a site so that people living in remote areas in Canada could have access to some of its products. The Bank of Montreal's electronic arm, mbanx, gives people nationwide access to all of the bank's services. IBM Canada encourages people to think of them when they do "e-business." For the Royal Canadian Mint, Internet marketing makes sense since 60 percent of its sales come from outside Canada.

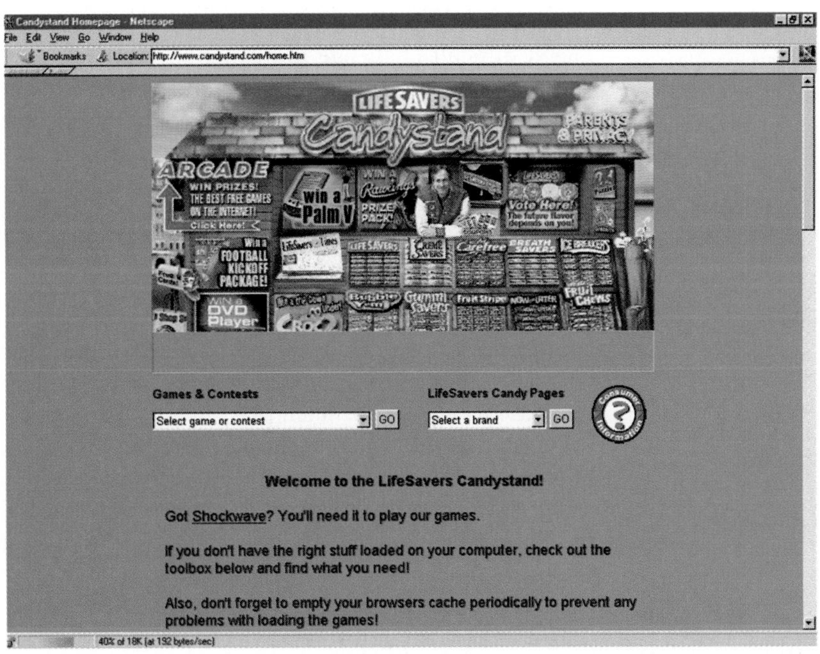

The Candystand Web site doesn't sell LifeSavers products: The corporate Web site offers online entertainment and information and gathers consumer feedback.

Toyota operates marketing Web sites nationally and internationally (www.toyota.ca, www.toyota.com). Once a potential customer clicks in, the automaker wastes no time in trying to turn the inquiry into a sale. The site offers plenty of entertainment and useful information, from cross-country trip guides and tips for driving with kids to events such as a Golf Skills Challenge and a Bike Express. But the site is also loaded with more serious selling features, such as detailed descriptions of current Toyota models and information on dealer locations and services, complete with maps and dealer Web links. Visitors who want to go further can use the Shop@Toyota feature to choose a Toyota, select equipment, and price it, then contact a dealer and even apply for credit. Or they fill out an online order form (supplying name, address, phone number, and e-mail address) for brochures and a free, interactive CD-ROM that shows off the features of Toyota models. The chances are good that before the CD-ROM arrives, a local dealer will call to invite the prospect in for a test drive. Toyota's Web site has now replaced its toll-free number as the number one source of customer leads.

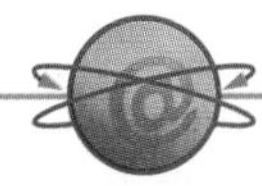

Sun Microsystems
www.sun.com/

GE Plastics
www.ge.com/plastics/

FedEx
www.fedex.com

Business-to-business marketers also make good use of marketing Web sites. Corporate buyers can visit Sun Microsystems' Web site, for example, select detailed descriptions of Sun's products and solutions, request sales and service information, and interact with staff members. Customers visiting GE Plastics' Web site can draw on more than 1500 pages of information to get answers about the company's products anytime and from anywhere in the world. The FedEx Web site allows customers to schedule their own shipments, request a courier, and track their packages in transit.

Creating a Web site is one thing; getting people to visit the site is another. The key is to create enough value and excitement to get consumers to come to the site, stick around, and come back again. This means that companies must constantly update their sites to keep them fresh and exciting. Doing so involves time and expense, but the expense is necessary if the online marketer wishes to cut through the increasing online clutter. In addition, many online marketers spend heavily on good old-fashioned advertising and other offline marketing avenues to attract visitors to their sites. Says one analyst, "The reality today is you can't build a brand simply on the Internet. You have to go offline."[38]

For some types of products, attracting visitors is easy. Consumers buying new cars, computers, or financial services will be open to information and marketing initiatives from sellers. Marketers of lower-involvement products, however, may face a difficult challenge in attracting Web site visitors. As one veteran notes, "If you're shopping for a computer and you see a banner that says, 'We've ranked the top 12 computers to purchase,' you're going to click on the banner. [But] what kind of banner could encourage any consumer to visit dentalfloss.com?"[39] For such low-interest products, the company should create a corporate Web site to answer customer questions and build goodwill, using it only to supplement selling efforts through other channels.

Placing Advertisements Online

Online ad
An advertisement that pops up while subscribers are surfing online services or Web sites.

Companies can use online advertising to build their Internet brands or to attract visitors to their Web sites. **Online ads** pop up while Internet users are surfing online services or Web sites. Such ads include banner ads, pop-up windows, "tickers" (banners that move across the screen), and "roadblocks" (full-screen ads that users must pass through to get to other screens they wish to view). A Web user or America Online subscriber who is looking up airline schedules or fares might find a flashing banner on the screen exclaiming, "Rent a car from Alamo and get up to two days free!" To attract visitors to its own Web site, Toyota sponsors Web banner ads on other sites, ranging from ESPNet SportZone to Parent Soup, a kind of online coffee klatch through which moms and dads exchange views. Another form of Web advertising is content sponsorships. Advil, for example, sponsors ESPN SportZone's Injury Report, and Oldsmobile sponsors AOL's Celebrity Circle.

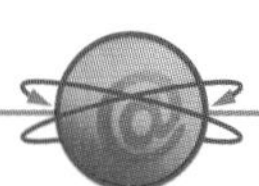

ESPNet Sport Zone
www.espn.com/

Parent Soup
www.parentsoup.com/

Companies spent almost $40 million in Canada on Web advertising in 1999 (compared to $3 billion allocated to Web advertising by US firms). This spending, however, represents only a tiny fraction of overall advertising media expenditures, and it still plays only a minor role in their promotion mixes. Many marketers still question the value of Internet advertising as an effective tool. Costs are reasonable compared with those of other advertising media. For example, Web advertising on ESPNet SportZone, which attracts more than 500 000 Web surfers and 20 million "hits"—the number of times the site is accessed—per week, costs about $300 000 per year. However, Web surfers can easily ignore these banner ads and often do. Moreover, the industry has yet to come up with good measures of Web advertising impact—of who clicks on Web ads and how the ads affect them.

Participating in Forums, Newsgroups, and Web Communities

Companies may decide to participate in or sponsor Internet forums, newsgroups, and bulletin boards that appeal to specific special interest groups. Such activities may be organized for commercial or non-commercial purposes. *Forums* are discussion groups located on commercial online services. A forum may operate a library, a chat room for real-time message exchanges, and even a classified ad directory. America Online boasts about 14 000 chat rooms, which account for a third of its members' online time.[40] Most forums are sponsored by interest groups. Therefore, as a major musical instruments manufacturer, Yamaha might start a forum on classical music.

Newsgroups are the Internet version of forums, where people post and read messages on a specific topic. Internet users can participate in newsgroups without subscribing. There are thousands of newsgroups dealing with every imaginable topic, from healthful eating and caring for your Bonsai tree to collecting antique cars or exchanging views on the latest soap opera happenings.

Bulletin board systems (BBSs) are specialized online services that focus on a specific topic or group. There are over 60 000 BBSs in North America, dealing with such topics as vacations, health, computer games, and real estate. Marketers might want to identify and participate in newsgroups and BBSs that attract subscribers who fit their target markets. However, newsgroups and BBS users often

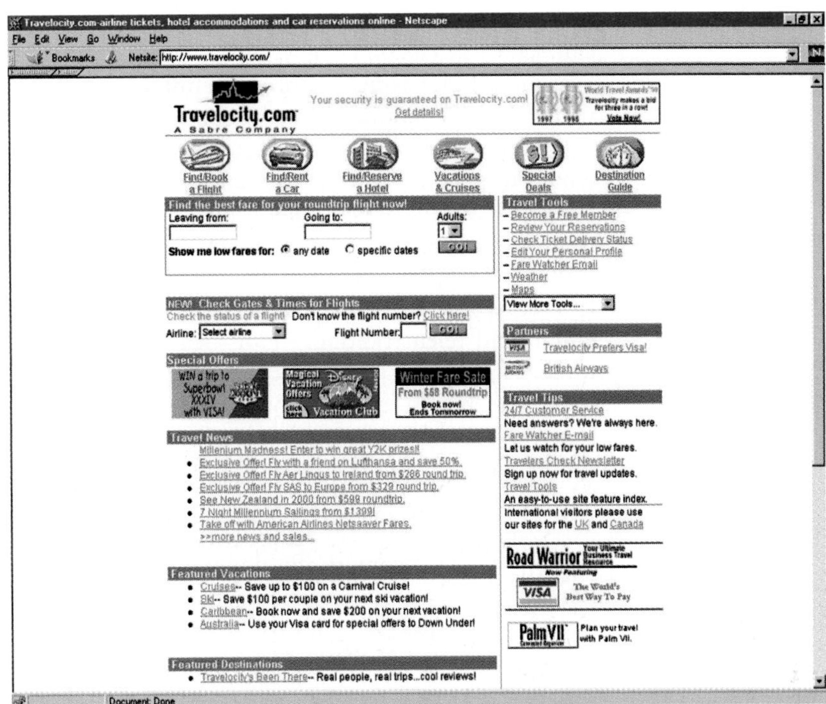

While booking airline tickets on Travelocity.com, site visitors are exposed to banner ads from VISA, Disney Vacation Club, and others; however, such ads are easily overlooked.

resent commercial intrusions on their Net space, so marketers must tread carefully, participating in subtle ways that provide real value to participants.

The popularity of forums and newsgroups has resulted in a rash of commercially sponsored Web sites called *Web communities*. Such sites allow members to congregate online and exchange views on issues of common interest. They are the cyberspace equivalent to a Starbucks coffeehouse, a place where everybody knows your e-mail address. For example, iVillage is a Web community in which "smart, compassionate, real women" can obtain information and exchange views on families, fitness, relationships, travel, finances, or just about any other topic. The site reaches 7.3 million unique visitors per month, greater than the combined monthly average paid circulation of *Cosmopolitan, Glamour, Chatelaine, Vogue,* and *Marie Claire* magazines. Tripod is an online hangout for twenty-somethings, offering chat rooms and free home pages for posting job résumés.

Visitors to these Internet neighbourhoods develop a strong sense of community. Such communities are attractive to advertisers because they draw consumers with common interests and well-defined demographics. Parent Soup, where 200 000 users discuss kid-related issues, provides an ideal environment for the Web ads of Johnson & Johnson, Gerber's, Wal-Mart, and other companies targeting family audiences. Moreover, cyberhood consumers visit frequently and stay online longer, increasing the chance of meaningful exposure to the advertiser's message.

Web communities can be either social or work related. One successful work-related community is Agriculture Online (@griculture Online). This site offers commodity prices, recent farm news, and chat rooms of all types. Rural surfers can visit the Electronic Coffee Shop and pick up the latest down-on-the-farm joke or join a hot discussion on controlling soybean cyst nematodes. @griculture Online has been highly successful, attracting as many as five million hits a month.[41]

Using E-Mail and Webcasting

A company can encourage prospects and customers to send questions, suggestions, and even complaints to the company via e-mail. Customer service representatives can quickly respond to such messages. The company can also develop Internet-based electronic mailing lists of customers or prospects. Such lists provide an excellent opportunity to introduce the company and its offerings to new customers and to build ongoing relationships with current ones. Using the lists, online marketers can send out customer newsletters, special product or promotion offers based on customer purchasing histories, reminders of service requirements or warranty renewals, or announcements of special events.

3Com Corporation, a computer hardware manufacturer, made good use of e-mail to generate and qualify customer leads for its network interface cards. The company used targeted e-mail and banner ads on 18 computer-related Web sites to attract potential buyers to its own Web site featuring a "3Com Classic" sweepstakes, where, by filling out the entry form, visitors could register to win a 1959 Corvette. The campaign generated 22 000 leads, which were further qualified using e-mail and telemarketing. "Hot" leads were passed along to 3Com's inside sales force. "[Sales reps] were very skeptical," says a 3Com marketing manager, "but they were blown away by how well the contest did." Of the 482 leads given to reps, 71 turned into actual sales that totalled $3.75 million. What's more, states the manager, "Now I've got 22 000 names in my e-mail database that I can go back and market to."[42]

Webcasting service
A service that automatically downloads customized information to recipients' PCs.

Companies can also sign on with a **Webcasting service,** such as PointCast and Ifusion, which automatically download customized information to recipients' PCs. For a monthly fee, subscribers to these services can specify the channels they want—news, company information, entertainment, and others—and the topics they're interested in. Then, rather than spending hours scouring the Internet, they can sit back while the Webcaster automatically delivers information of interest to their desktops.[43]

Webcasting, also known as "push" programming, affords an attractive channel through which online marketers can deliver their Internet advertising or other information content. The major commercial online services are also beginning to offer Webcasting to their members. For example, America Online offers a feature called Driveway that will fetch information, Web pages, and e-mail based on members' preferences and automatically deliver it to their PCs.

As with other types of online marketing, companies must be careful that they don't cause resentment among Internet users who are already overloaded with "junk e-mail." Warns one analyst, "There's a fine line between adding value and the consumer feeling that you're being intrusive."[44] Companies must beware of irritating consumers by sending unwanted e-mail to promote their products. Netiquette, the unwritten rules that guide Internet etiquette, suggests that marketers should ask customers for permission to e-mail marketing pitches—and tell recipients how to stop the flow of e-mail promotions at any time. This approach, known as permission-based marketing, is emerging as a new model for e-mail marketing (see Marketing Highlight 16–3).

The Promise and Challenges of Online Marketing

How does the demographic and psychographic profile of this group of online users at an Internet café differ from that of the general population?

Its most ardent apostles envision a time when the Internet and e-commerce will replace magazines, newspapers, and even stores as sources of information and buying. Yet, despite all the hype and promise, online marketing may be years away from realizing its full potential. Even then, it is unlikely to fulfill such sweeping predictions. To be sure, online marketing will become a full and complete business model for some companies—Internet firms such as Chapters.ca, eBay, Yahoo!, E*TRADE, and Netscape; and direct marketing companies such as Dell Computer. But for most companies, online marketing will remain just one important approach to the marketplace that works alongside other approaches in a fully

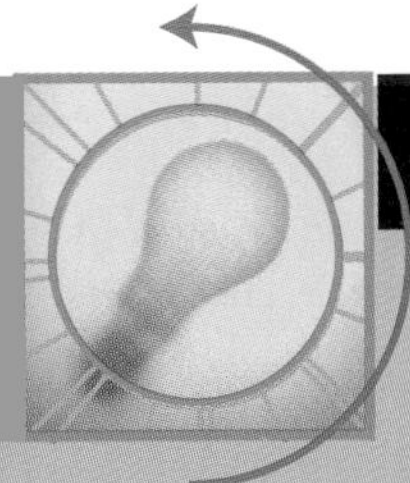

marketing highlight 16-3

Permission-Based Marketing: Click Here for Our Pitch

Companies that send marketing pitches via e-mail walk a fine and dangerous line. One false move—such as sending e-mail to a customer who didn't request it—can quickly damage a company's reputation. Yet, more and more companies are now walking that fine line, and for good reason. Done right, an e-mail campaign can build profitable customer relationships at a fraction of the cost of a "d-mail" (direct-mail) campaign.

E-mail marketing offers several benefits. The Internet gives marketers immediate access to millions of customers and prospects. Studies show that 80 percent of Internet users respond to e-mail within 36 hours, compared with a two percent response rate for the average direct-mail campaign. There is a catch, though. To achieve stellar click-throughs and to get recipients to respond quickly—or even at all—marketers must follow the cardinal rule of e-mail marketing: Get the consumer's permission. In fact, Seth Godin, a pioneer of direct marketing on the Web and CEO of Yoyodyne Entertainment Inc. (recently acquired by Yahoo!), has even come up with a term—"permission-based marketing"—to define the new e-mail marketing model. According to Godin, whose company specializes in developing Web-based marketing relationships for its clients, consumers are weary of unwanted marketing pitches. Permission-based marketing provides the perfect remedy by using the interactivity of the Internet to let consumers have a say in what is sent to them. Godin compares permission-based marketing to dating; if a company conducts itself well in its first contact with consumers, it will build up trust that encourages them to open up to subsequent offers.

Compared to other forms of online promotion, e-mail is usually a hands-down winner. In fact, as Peter Evans, vice-president of marketing with Toronto-based e-mail marketing service provider FloNetwork, reports: "Permission-based e-mail dramatically surpasses all customer contact methods, including traditional mail, as the preferred way for online buyers to learn about new products and services. Online buyers were asked, 'If you were to be contacted directly by your favourite online merchant regarding new products, services or promotions, which one of the following methods would you prefer?' A whopping 73 percent said their preferred contact method is permission-based e-mail, compared with regular mail (21%), "spam" (4%), in-person sales calls and telemarketing (both under 1%)."

Then there's cost. With 'snail mail' there's paper, printing, and postage expenses that are growing every year. In contrast, e-mail costs almost nothing to produce and send. Microsoft used to spend about $105 million a year on paper-driven campaigns. Now, the software giant sends out 20 million pieces of e-mail every month at a significant savings over the costs of paper-based campaigns.

One company that has been successful in using permission-based e-mail marketing campaigns is Iomega Corporation, which markets computer storage devices such as the popular Zip drive. Iomega always starts its e-mail campaigns with its base of registered customers. From this select list, it mails only to those who have given Iomega permission to send them e-mail. By targeting customers who actively agree to receive e-mail, companies can increase their chances of getting a positive response or sale and avoid being blackballed on the Internet. BMW Canada is another firm that successfully integrated permission-based marketing, event marketing, and the Internet as it geared up for the re-introduction of the MINI planned for 2002.

Whereas most consumers who are peeved at getting junk mail simply toss it in the trash, angry consumers can strike back online in new, alarmingly effective ways. With just a quick e-mail to friends, to a listserv, or to other Web sites—or by setting up an anti-company Web site—an irate consumer can give offending companies a bad reputation almost instantaneously. For this reason, effective e-mail marketers not only restrict their mailings to those who "opt in" but also offer recipients the chance to "opt out" at every turn. At Iomega, for instance, every single e-mail, even those sent to people on record as consenting to additional mailings, provides customers with an easy opt-out option.

Yet, it takes much more than asking permission and providing an opt-out escape to craft a successful e-mail marketing campaign. Most important: As in any direct marketing offer, you must offer something of value. Second, the value you offer must be tailored to the buyer. A recent survey revealed that relevance of

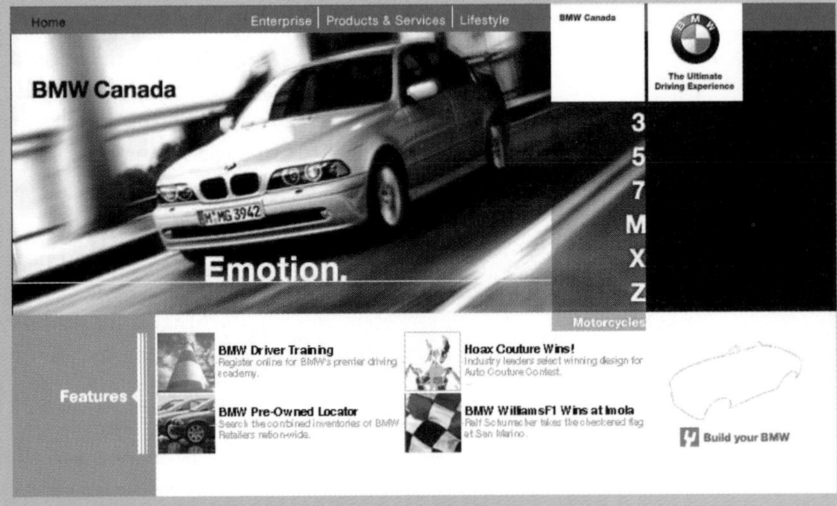

BMW Canada is using permission-based marketing in its prelaunch campaign for the MINI.

the message is the key ingredient in determining whether an e-mail was "good" or "bad." Nearly six in ten respondents said that the best permission-based e-mails are targeted to their individual interests.

These are some other important guidelines followed by pioneering e-mail marketers:

Give the customer a reason to respond: Yoyodyne offers surfers powerful incentives for reading e-mail pitches and online ads. The innovative direct marketing firm uses e-mail trivia games, scavenger hunts, and instant-win sweepstakes to lure customers. So far, more than a million Internet surfers have agreed to wade through product information from companies such as Sprint, Reader's Digest, and Major League Baseball to become eligible for prizes such as a trip to the Caribbean or a bag of gold.

Personalize the content of your e-mails: The Web allows companies to personalize e-mails based on past interactions, and customers are more receptive to personalized pitches. Cyberstore Chapters.ca has gained a loyal following by sending willing customers personalized recommendations based on past purchases. IBM's "Focusing on You News Digest" is distributed directly through customers' office e-mail, delivering to them only "the news they choose." Customers who agree to receive the newsletter select from topics listed on an interest profile.

Offer something the customer can't get via direct mail: Direct-mail campaigns take a lot of time to plan, carry out, and mail. Because e-mail campaigns can be carried out more quickly, they can offer time-sensitive information. Travelocity, a travel site on the Web, sends frequent e-mails called Fare Watchers, which pitch last-minute cheap airfares. Club Med uses e-mail to pitch unsold, discounted vacation packages to the 34 000 people in its database.

Playing by such rules, many direct marketers have turned e-mail into a hot new marketing media. Rather than resenting it, many customers and prospects actively seek to be put on the e-mail lists of their favourite companies.

Sources: Quotes from Peter Evans, "Going beyond 'yes,'" *Strategy*, 14 August 2000:D14. Also see Nicole Harris, "Spam that you might not delete," *Business Week*, 15 June 1998:115–8; Bernadette Johnson, "BMW preps for Mini," *Strategy*, 9 October 2000:13; Matt Barthel, "Marketer: Banks miss Web's real strength—relationships," *American Banker*, 21 October 1998:19; Jay Winchester, "Point, click, sell," *Sales & Marketing Management*, November 1998:100–1; Michelle L. Smith, "One to one: Put the customer in the information driver seat and build better relationships," *Direct Marketing*, January 1998: 37–9; Roberta Fusaro, "More sites use e-mail for marketing," *Computerworld*, 19 October 1998:51–4; and Mary Kuntz, "Point, click—and here's the pitch," *Business Week*, 9 February 1998:ENT8–10.

integrated marketing mix. For many marketers, the Web is still not a money-making proposition. According to one report, less than half of today's Web sites are profitable.[45] These are some of the challenges that online marketers face:

- *Limited consumer exposure and buying:* Although expanding rapidly, online marketing still reaches only a limited marketspace. Moreover, many Web users do more window browsing than actual buying. One source estimates that, although 65 percent of current Internet users have used the Web to check out products and compare prices before a purchase decision, only 14 percent of Internet users have actually purchased anything online. Still fewer have used their credit card.[46]
- *Skewed user demographics and psychographics:* Although the Web audience is becoming more mainstream, online users still tend to be more upscale and technically oriented than the general population. This makes online marketing ideal for marketing computer hardware and software, consumer electronics, financial services, and certain other classes of products. However, it makes online marketing less effective for selling mainstream products.
- *Chaos and clutter:* The Internet offers millions of Web sites and a staggering volume of information. This can make navigating the Internet frustrating, confusing, and time consuming for consumers. In this chaotic and cluttered environment, many Web ads and sites go unnoticed or unopened. Even when noticed, marketers will find it difficult to hold consumer attention. One study found that a site must capture Web surfers' attention within eight seconds or lose them to another site. That leaves very little time for marketers to promote and sell their goods.
- *Security:* Consumers still worry that unscrupulous snoopers will eavesdrop on their online transactions or intercept their credit card numbers and make unauthorized purchases. In turn, companies doing business online fear that others will use the Internet to invade their computer systems for the purposes of commercial espionage or even sabotage. Online marketers are developing solutions

to such security problems. However, there appears to be an ongoing competition between the technology of Internet security systems and the sophistication of those seeking to break them.

- *Ethical concerns:* Privacy is a primary concern. Marketers can easily track Web site visitors, and many consumers who participate in Web site activities provide extensive personal information. This may leave consumers open to information abuse if companies make unauthorized use of the information in marketing their products or exchanging electronic lists with other companies. Canada's new *Electronic Privacy Act* should allay some of these concerns for consumers using Canadian Web-based businesses. There are also concerns about segmentation and discrimination. The Internet currently serves upscale consumers well. However, poorer consumers have less access to the Internet, leaving them increasingly less informed about products, services, and prices.[47]

Despite these challenges, companies large and small are quickly integrating online marketing into their marketing mixes. As it continues to grow, online marketing will prove to be a powerful tool for building customer relationships, improving sales, communicating company and product information, and delivering products and services more efficiently and effectively.

Integrated Direct Marketing

Too often, a company's individual direct marketing efforts are not well integrated with one another or with other elements of the marketing and promotion mixes. For example, a firm's media advertising may be handled by the advertising department working with a traditional advertising agency, whereas its direct-mail and catalogue business efforts may be handled by direct marketing specialists, and its Web site is developed and operated by an outside Internet firm.

Within a direct marketing campaign, too many companies use only a "one-shot" effort to reach and sell a prospect or a single vehicle in multiple stages to trigger purchases. For example, a magazine publisher may send a series of four direct-mail notices to a household to get a subscriber to renew before giving up. A more powerful approach is **integrated direct marketing,** which involves carefully coordinated multiple-media, multiple-stage campaigns. Such campaigns can greatly improve response. Whereas a direct-mail piece alone may generate a two percent response, adding a Web site and toll-free phone number may raise the response rate by 50 percent. Then, a well-designed outbound telemarketing effort may lift response by an additional 500 percent. Suddenly, a two percent response has grown to 15 percent or more by adding interactive marketing channels to a regular mailing.

Integrated direct marketing
A direct marketing approach that involves multiple-vehicle, multiple-stage campaigns.

More elaborate integrated direct marketing campaigns can be used. Consider the multimedia, multistage campaign shown in Figure 16-2. Here, the paid ad creates product awareness and stimulates inquiries. The company immediately sends direct mail to those who inquire. Within a few days, the company follows up with a phone call seeking an order. Some prospects will order by phone; others may request a face-to-face sales call. In such a campaign, the marketer seeks to improve response rates and profits by adding media and stages that contribute more to additional sales than to additional costs (see Marketing Highlight 16–4).

Public Policy and Ethical Issues in Direct Marketing

Direct marketers and their customers usually enjoy mutually rewarding relationships. Occasionally, however, a darker side emerges. The aggressive and sometimes shady tactics of a few direct marketers bother or harm consumers, casting a shadow over the entire industry. Abuses range from simple excesses that irritate consumers

FIGURE 16-2 An integrated direct marketing campaign

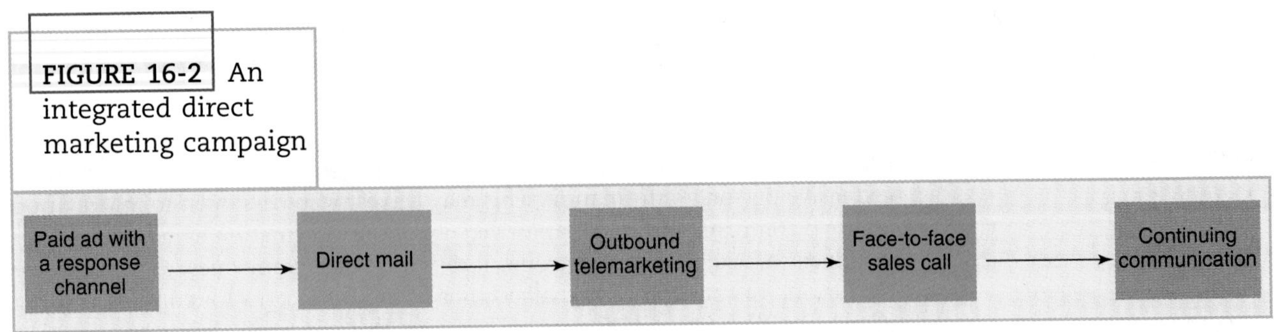

to instances of unfair practices or even outright deception and fraud. During the past few years, the direct marketing industry also has faced growing concerns about invasion of privacy issues.[48]

Irritation, Unfairness, Deception, and Fraud

Direct marketing excesses sometimes annoy or offend consumers. Most of us dislike direct-response TV commercials that are too loud, too long, and too insistent. Especially bothersome are dinnertime or late-night phone calls. Beyond irritating consumers, some direct marketers have been accused of taking unfair advantage of impulsive or less sophisticated buyers. Television shopping shows and program-long "infomercials" seem to be the worst culprits. They feature smooth-talking hosts, elaborately staged demonstrations, claims of drastic price reductions, "while they last" time limitations, and unequalled ease of purchase to inflame buyers who have low sales resistance.

Worse yet, so-called "heat merchants" design mailers and write copy intended to mislead buyers. Other direct marketers pretend to be conducting research surveys when they are actually asking leading questions to screen or persuade consumers. Fraudulent schemes, such as investment scams or phony collections for charity, have also multiplied in recent years. Crooked direct marketers can be hard to catch. Direct marketing customers often respond quickly, do not interact personally with the seller, and usually expect to wait for delivery. By the time buyers realize that they have been bilked, the thieves are usually somewhere else plotting new schemes.

Invasion of Privacy

Invasion of privacy is perhaps the toughest public policy issue now confronting the direct marketing industry. Privacy is defined as the right to be left alone. Information privacy, which is at the heart of many concerns about direct marketing practices, refers to individuals' rights to determine when, how, and to what extent they will share personal information about themselves with others. These days, it seems that almost every time consumers order products by mail or telephone, enter a sweepstakes, apply for a credit card, or take out a magazine subscription, their names are entered into some company's already bulging database. Using sophisticated computer technologies, direct marketers can use these databases to "micro-target" their selling efforts.

Consumers often benefit from such database marketing—they receive more offers that are closely matched to their interests. However, many critics worry that marketers may know *too* much about consumers' lives, and that they may use this knowledge to take unfair advantage of consumers. At some point, they claim, the extensive use of databases intrudes on consumer privacy. For example, they ask, should Bell be allowed to sell marketers the names of customers who frequently

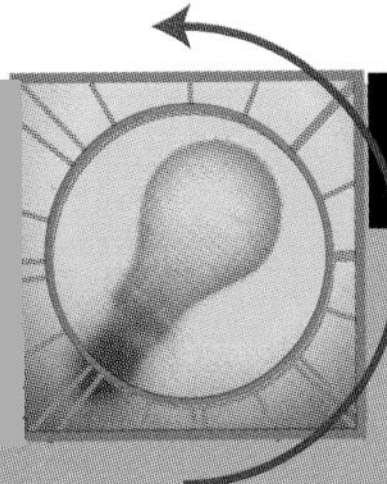

marketing highlight 16-4

American Standard's Integrated Direct Marketing: Anything but Standard

You probably haven't thought much about your bathroom: It's not something that most of us get all that inspired about. But as it turns out, you probably have a relationship with your bathroom unlike that with any other room in your house. It's where you start and end your day, primp and preen and admire yourself, escape from the rigours of everyday life, and do some of your best thinking. The marketers at American Standard, the plumbing fixtures giant, understand this often-overlooked but special little room. And they've set out upon a mission to help people design bathrooms worthy of their finest moments.

Working with its ad agency, Carmichael Lynch, American Standard has created a wonderfully warm and highly effective but not-so-standard integrated marketing campaign. The campaign, called "We want you to love your bathroom," targets men and women aged 25 to 54 from households planning to remodel bathrooms or replace fixtures. The campaign uses a carefully integrated mix of brand image and direct-response media ads, direct mailings, and personal contracts to create a customer database, generate sales leads, gently coax customers into its retail showroom, and build sales and market share.

The campaign begins with a series of humorous, soft-sell brand image ads in home and shelter magazines like *Home, House Beautiful,* and *Country Living,* which have a high percentage of readers undertaking remodelling products. Featuring simple but artistic shots of ordinary bathroom fixtures and scenes, the ads position American Standard as a company that understands the special relationships we have with our bathroom. For example, one ad shows a white toilet and a partially unwound roll of toilet paper, artfully arranged in a corner against plain blue-grey walls. "We're not in this business for the glory," proclaims the headline. "Designing a toilet or sink may not be as glamorous as, say, designing a Maserati. But to us, it's every bit as important. After all, more people will be sitting on our seats than theirs."

Another ad shows a man's feet in goofy floppy-eared dog slippers on a white tile bathroom floor. "The rest of the world thinks you're a genius," notes the ad. But "after a long day of being brilliant, witty, and charming, it's nice just to be comfortable. The right bathroom understands. And accepts you unconditionally." Each simple but engaging ad includes a toll-free phone number and urges readers to call for a free guidebook "overflowing with products, ideas, and inspiration."

The brand image ads position American Standard and its products, but when it comes to generating inquires, the real workhorses are the one-third-page, coupon-like "direct-response" ads that run in the same magazines. One such ad notes, "You will spend seven years of your life in the bathroom. You will need a good book." Readers can obtain the free guidebook by mailing in the coupon or calling the toll-free number listed in the ad.

Consumers who respond find that they've taken the first step in a carefully orchestrated relationship-building venture. First, they receive the entertaining, highly informative, picture-filled 30-page guidebook *We Want You to Love Your Bathroom,* along with a folksy letter thanking them for their interest and noting the locations of nearby American Standard dealers.

The guidebook is full of helpful tips on bathroom design. It starts with answers to some simple questions: What kind of lavatory—what colour? The bathtub—how big, big enough for two? The toilet—sleek one-piece or familiar two-piece? The faucet—you'll fumble for it every morning, so be particular about how it operates. To spice things up, the guidebook also contains entertaining facts and trivia. An example: "During the Middle Ages, Christianity preached that to uncover your skin, even to bathe, was an invitation to sin. Thank heavens for perfume. These days, we average about four baths or 7.5 showers a week." And, of course, the booklet contains plenty of information on American Standard products, along with a tear-out card that prospective customers can return to obtain more detailed guides and product catalogues.

In addition to the guidebook, customers receive a carefully coordinated stream of communications from American Standard, starting with a series of

American Standard has created a wonderfully warm and effective but not-so-standard integrated marketing campaign, starting with ads like this.

"Bathroom Reading" bulletins, each containing information on specific bathroom design issues. One issue contains information and tips on how to make a bathroom safer; another issue offers "10 neat ways to save water."

Meanwhile, information about prospective customers and their remodelling projects collected by the toll-free operator or from the coupon goes into American Standard's customer database. The database generates leads for salespeople at American Standard's showrooms throughout North America. The company markets the program to key distributors and kitchen and bath dealers, motivating them to follow up on leads and training them how to do it effectively. The key is to get customers who've made inquiries to come into the showroom. Not long after making their inquiries, prospective customers typically receive a hand-written postcard—or perhaps even a phone call—from a local dealer's showroom consultant, who extends a personal invitation to visit, see American Standard products first hand, and discuss bathroom designs. In this way, the integrated direct marketing program builds relationships not just with buyers, but with dealers as well.

American Standard's integrated direct marketing campaign has done wonders for the company's positioning and performance. Since the campaign began, American Standard's plumbing division has experienced steady increases in sales and earnings: Earnings were triple those of the previous year. The campaign generates tens of thousands of qualified leads a year for local showrooms—more than a half million qualified leads so far. Research confirms significant shifts in consumer perceptions of American Standard and its products—from "boring and institutional" to well designed and loaded with "personal spirit." According to Bob Srenaski, group vice-president of marketing at American Standard, the campaign has "totally repositioned our company and established a momentum and winning spirit that is extraordinary. . . . The campaign has been incredible. It's given American Standard and its products a more personal face, one that's helped us to build closer relationships with customers and dealers."

call the toll-free numbers of catalogue companies? Is it right for credit bureaus to compile and sell lists of people who have recently applied for credit cards—people who are considered prime direct marketing targets because of their spending behaviour? Or is it right for provinces to sell the names and information of driver's licence holders? In their drive to build databases, companies sometimes get carried away. In one survey of consumers, 79 percent of respondents said that they were concerned about threats to their personal privacy.

Governments around the world have been exploring the question of whether to institute privacy legislation. The first major step was taken by the European Union. In 1995, it issued a directive on the protection of personal data, which provides a framework for collecting and processing personal data. Predictably, the US and Canada have responded to the whole privacy issue differently. While the US opted for industry self-regulation, Canadian governments believed more controls were needed. Until recently, Quebec was the only province with legislation dealing with the privacy of personal information. On 1 January 2001, the Canadian *Personal Information Protection and Electronic Documents Act* (formerly Bill C6) came into effect. For full details on the act, visit the Privacy Commissioner of Canada Web site. The privacy act governs all federally regulated industries and businesses that operate interprovincially. Provinces have until 2004 to develop their own legislation to regulate businesses that operate solely within their boundaries. The new legislation uses a number of guiding principles to protect consumers and control how firms gather and use their personal information:

Privacy Commissioner of Canada
www.privcom.gc.ca/

- *Consumer consent:* Knowledge and consent must be obtained from consumers before a firm can collect, use, or disclose consumers' personal information.
- *Limitations:* A firm may collect only the information appropriate for the purposes for which it is being gathered: For example, if it needs to mail you something, the firm can ask for your home mailing address, but not any additional, unnecessary information beyond what it needs to address the mailing. Furthermore, a firm may use the information only for the purpose for which it was gathered. To make additional use of the information, it must get permission from the individual. Finally, a firm may not transfer the information to a third party without the permission of the individual.

- *Accuracy:* A firm must ensure that the information it gathers is recorded accurately, and it must appoint an employee to be responsible for this. For example, to comply with this portion of the legislation, Peter Cullen was recently designated as the new corporate privacy officer at the Royal Bank of Canada.
- *Right to access:* Individuals have the right to know what information is being held about them. They can also demand that errors in their personal information be rectified and may request that their personal information be withdrawn from a firm's database.

The direct marketing industry is addressing issues of ethics and public policy. Direct marketers know that, left untended, such problems will lead to increasingly negative consumer attitudes, lower response rates, and calls for more restrictive provincial and federal legislation. Most direct marketers want the same things that consumers want: honest and well-designed marketing offers targeted only toward consumers who will appreciate and respond to them. Direct marketing is just too expensive to waste on consumers who don't want it.

Review of Concept Connections

Mass marketers have typically tried to reach millions of buyers with a single product and a standard message communicated via the mass media. Consequently, most mass marketing communications were one-way communications directed *at* consumers rather than two-way communications *with* consumers. Today, many companies are turning to direct marketing in an effort to reach carefully targeted customers more efficiently and to build stronger, more personal, one-to-one relationships with them.

1. Discuss the benefits of direct marketing to customers and companies and the trends fuelling its rapid growth.

Customers benefit from direct marketing in many ways: Home shopping is fun, convenient, and hassle free, saves time, and gives them a bigger selection of merchandise. It allows them to comparison shop, using mail catalogues and online shopping services, and then order products and services without dealing with salespeople. Sellers also benefit. Direct marketers can buy mailing lists containing names of nearly any target group, customize offers to special wants and needs, and then use individualized communications to promote these offers. Direct marketers can also build a continuous relationship with each customer; time offers to reach prospects at the right moment, thereby receiving higher readership and response; and easily test alternative media and messages. Finally, direct marketers gain privacy because their offer and strategy are less visible to competitors.

Some trends have led to the rapid growth of direct marketing. Market fragmentation has produced an increasing number of market niches with specific preferences. Direct marketing enables sellers to focus efficiently on these mini-markets with offers that better match particular consumer wants and needs. Also encouraging at-home shopping are the higher costs of driving, traffic congestion, and parking headaches, lack of time, a shortage of retail sales help, and long lines at checkout counters. Consumers like the convenience of direct marketers' toll-free phone numbers, their acceptance of orders around the clock, and their commitment to customer service. The growth of quick delivery via express carriers has also made direct shopping fast and easy. The increased affordability of computers and customer databases has allowed direct marketers to single out the best prospects for each of their products. Finally in business-to-business marketing, lower-cost-per-contact media have proven more cost-effective in reaching and selling to more prospects and customers than if a sales force were used.

2. Define a customer database and list the four ways that companies use databases in direct marketing.

A *customer database* is an organized collection of comprehensive data about individual customers or prospects, including geographic, demographic, psychographic, and behavioural data. Companies use databases to identify prospects, decide which customers should receive a particular offer, deepen customer loyalty, and reactivate customer purchases.

3. **Identify the major forms of direct marketing.**

The main forms of direct marketing are *face-to-face selling, telemarketing, direct-mail marketing, catalogue marketing, direct-response television marketing, kiosk marketing,* and *online,* or *Internet, marketing.* Most companies continue to rely heavily on *face-to-face selling* through a professional sales force, or they hire manufacturers' representatives and agents. *Direct mail marketing* is sending an offer, announcement, reminder, or other item to a person at a specific address. Recently, three forms of mail delivery have become popular—*fax mail, e-mail,* and *voice mail.* Some marketers rely on *catalogue marketing,* selling through catalogues mailed to a select list of customers or made available in stores. *Telemarketing* is using the telephone to sell directly to consumers. *Direct-response television marketing* has two forms—*direct-response advertising,* or *infomercials,* and *home shopping channels. Kiosks* are information and ordering machines that direct marketers place in stores, airports, and other locations. *Online marketing* involves online channels and electronic commerce and is usually conducted through interactive online computer systems, which electronically link consumers with sellers.

4. **Compare the two types of online marketing channels and explain the effect of the Internet on electronic commerce.**

The two types of online marketing channels are *commercial online services* and the *Internet. Commercial online services* provide online information and marketing services to subscribers for a monthly fee. The *Internet* is a vast global and public web of computer networks. Unlike commercial online services, use of the Internet is free—anyone with a PC, a modem, and the right software can browse the Internet to obtain or share information on almost any subject and to interact with other users.

The explosion of Internet usage has created a new world of *electronic commerce,* the buying and selling process that is supported by electronic means. In this process, *electronic markets* become "marketspaces" in which sellers offer products and services electronically, while buyers search for information, identify their wants and needs, and then place orders using a credit card or other form of electronic payment.

5. **Identify the benefits of online marketing to consumers and marketers and the four ways that marketers can conduct online marketing.**

Online marketing benefits consumers in many ways: It is *interactive, immediate,* and provides access to an abundance of comparative *information* about products, companies, and competitors. Marketers also benefit from online marketing: It helps consumer relationship building, reduces costs, increases efficiency, provides more flexibility, and is, in the form of the Internet, a global medium that enables buyers and sellers in different countries to interact with each other in seconds. Marketers can conduct online marketing by creating an electronic storefront; placing ads online; participating in Internet forums, newsgroups, or "Web communities"; or by using e-mail or Webcasting.

6. **Discuss the public policy and ethical issues facing direct marketers.**

Direct marketers and their customers have typically forged mutually rewarding relationships. However, there remains a potential for customer abuse, ranging from irritation and unfair practices to deception and fraud. In addition, there have been growing concerns about invasion of privacy, perhaps the most difficult public policy issue currently facing the direct marketing industry.

Key Terms

Catalogue marketing *(p. 669)*
Commercial online service *(p. 673)*
Corporate Web site *(p. 678)*
Customer database *(p. 663)*
Direct marketing *(p. 657)*
Direct-mail marketing *(p. 668)*
Direct-response television marketing *(p. 671)*
Electronic commerce *(p. 675)*
Integrated direct marketing *(p. 685)*
Internet (or the Net) *(p. 673)*
Marketing Web site *(p. 678)*
Online ad *(p. 680)*
Online marketing *(p. 673)*
Telemarketing *(p. 667)*
Webcasting service *(p. 682)*

Discussing the Issues

1. This chapter suggests that a new direct marketing model has been created. Answer the following questions: (a) What is direct marketing? (b) How is it different from other forms of marketing delivery? (c) How will the new direct marketing model affect the emerging electronic marketplace?
2. As part of an integrated marketing mix, direct marketing brings many benefits to both buyers and sellers. Describe these benefits. Provide three examples of direct marketing firms that demonstrate strong marketing benefits for their customers. Describe and explain the benefits fully.
3. Companies that know about individual customer needs and characteristics can customize their offers, messages, delivery modes, and payment methods to maximize customer value and satisfaction. Pick two of these organizations and answer the following questions about them: (a) Your college or university's alumni association, (b) IBM Canada, (c) the Stratford Shakespeare Theatre, (d) the Canadian Cancer Society, and (e) Lexus. What information should these companies keep in their customer database? Where would they get this information? How might they use the database? How much would it cost to build such a database?
4. List and briefly describe each of the major forms of direct marketing. Pick one of the following companies and demonstrate how it could use each form of direct marketing to sell its products and services: (a) Microsoft, (b) General Motors, or (c) Gap.
5. Direct-mail marketing used to mean sending an offer, announcement, reminder, or item to a person through the mail. Today, however, new forms of direct communication are emerging. Critique (a) fax mail, (b) e-mail, and (c) voice mail as forms of direct mail. Discuss the advantages, disadvantages, customer profiles, costs, and future of each form.
6. Contact a personal computer direct marketer, such as Dell Computer at www.dell.ca or Gateway at www.gateway.com. (a) How does the company make it easy to order its products? (b) What differentiates this company from traditional retailers or manufacturers? (c) What are the company's chief advantages and disadvantages? (d) How does it provide security (or not)? (e) Based on this experience, what is your opinion of online marketers?
7. In the past year there has been a dramatic increase in the number of Web communities (commercially sponsored Web sites). If you were (a) Nike, (b) the Royal Bank, (c) British Airways, or (d) Fuji, what type of Web communities would you be interested in sponsoring? What would be the possible advantages and disadvantages of doing this? Find a Web community and evaluate its site. Discuss your conclusions in class.
8. Online marketing offers great promise for the future. Assume that you are the sales manager for a local travel agency. Make a case that would persuade your superiors that going online would be a good investment. Cite the potential positive and negative outcomes.

Marketing Applications

1. Many consumers used to dread anniversaries, birthdays, Mother's Day, Valentine's Day, and seemingly countless other gift-giving occasions because of the hassles associated with trying to find the perfect gift. E-commerce is beginning to change all that. Today, when you need to send flowers or small gifts at the last minute, the Internet is definitely the way to go. For example, a fast-growing number of florist Web sites provide the e-shopper with a convenient way to search by price, occasion, or types of flowers. Last-minute gift givers no longer have to rely on the florist's judgment or even to visit the florist to pick out arrangements. The florist Web sites let buyers make their own selections without leaving home or the office. Most of these Web retailers offer event reminder services via e-mail so that buyers will never forget important dates and occasions. Visit these Web sites for more information: 1-800-Flowers (www.1800flowers.com), Flowers Canada (shop.store.yahoo.com/flowerscanada-ca), and FTD's Flower Power (shop.store.yahoo.com/flower power-ca).

a. How does purchasing floral arrangements via the Internet compare with buying them by telephone or in person? Compare these channels in terms of cost, speed of delivery, selection of merchandise, freshness, dependability, ease of ordering, and ability to personalize requests.

b. What are the difficulties in using the Internet for this type of purchasing? How could these difficulties be overcome?

c. Which of these Web sites seems to be the most user friendly? Why? Which site would you be most willing to use? Why?

d. What future do you see for marketing flowers and gifts via the Internet? If you were a local florist, would you invest in a Web page? Why or why not? If you did invest in a Web page, how would you get old and new customers to use it?

2. Do you hate bulky PCs and laptops? Do you want something more mobile? Japanese camera maker Olympus (www.olympus.com) and computer maker IBM (www.ibm.com) have developed a computer you can wear. The screen is a monocle that fits over one eye, and the computer itself is a pocketbook-size box with two buttons. This wearable PC weighs only 13 ounces, has an Intel Pentium processor and 64 megabytes of memory, and runs the Microsoft Windows operating system. To use the system, the wearer flips out the tiny eye screen from a headset and manipulates a banana-shaped handle with a touchpad and two buttons to select icons on the "Eye Trek" virtual screen. Keyboards are under development, although not currently available. Users can open and look at files and play audio and video. The wearable PC seems to be a step in the right direction for accomplishing Olympus's objective of getting in on the ground floor of the "virtual world" that is overtaking our society.

a. What is the target market for the wearable PC? What uses do you foresee for the device? What would you name it?

b. How might such a device advance society's use of the Internet? The use of online purchasing?

c. Propose an integrated direct marketing campaign for introducing the wearable PC to the target market.

d. What opportunities should an e-marketer see in such a device?

e. Would you buy one of these PCs? Explain.

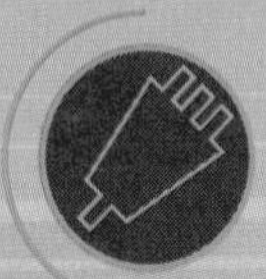

Internet Connections

Online Marketing

Online marketing can bring benefits to customers that other channels cannot. One example is the online music store, where customers can listen to clips of selected tracks before buying a CD. Other online benefits are ease of communication with customers and adaptability to marketplace changes. Visit CDNow (www.cdnow.com) and look up three CDs of your choosing. For each CD, record below the total number of tracks on that CD and the number of tracks that CDNow will let you sample.

For Discussion

1. Does CDNow offer other benefits that you might not find at a traditional retail music store? If so, what are they?
2. If you were to purchase a CD, how could CDNow use the information from your visit to develop a one-to-one relationship with you?
3. Are CDNow's prices competitive?
4. How could traditional music stores offer some of the same benefits as CDNow? Would it be cost-effective for them to do so?
5. Do you think CDNow should open a traditional store in addition to its online store? Why or why not?
6. Visit www.bizrate.com and see how CDNow rates against the competition. How do they place?

Savvy Sites

- Did-it (www.did-it.com) gives Webmasters many ways to publicize their new Web sites, including 50 e-mail lists that target either consumers or businesses—the cyberspace version of direct mail.
- Direct Marketing World (www.dmworld.com) is an information centre for the direct marketing industry.
- IBM has a great site for people thinking of starting an e-business (advisor.internet.ibm.com/inet.nsf). Visit the site and evaluate several options for your Internet business plan.

Notes

1. Quotes and Dell performance statistics from "Dell Canada no. 1 in overall PC sales," press release, Toronto, 1 May 2000, www.dell.ca/en/gen/corporate/press/pressoffice_ca_2000-05-01-tor-000.htm); Gary McWilliams, "Whirlwind on the Web," *Business Week,* 7 April 1997:132–6; Bill Robbins and Cathie Hargett, "Dell Internet sales top $1 million a day," press release, Dell Computer Corp., 4 March 1997; "The *InternetWeek* interview—Michael Dell," *InternetWeek,* 13 April 1999:8; and www.dell.com/corporate/access/factpak/index.htm, January 2000. Also see "Nerdy like a fox," *Business Week,* 11 January 1999:74; James Cox, "Technology, stock market click for world's richest," *USA Today,* 21 June 1999:2A; Melanie Warner, "The young and the loaded," *Fortune,* 27 September 1999:S12; and David Rynecki, "Has Dell become just another growth stock?" *Fortune,* 21 February 2000:317–8.
2. Bernadette Johnson, "HBC.com aims to give customers another reason to shop," *Strategy,* 1 January 2001:D1.
3. Gary Hamel and Jeff Sampler, "The e-corporation: More than just Web-based, it's building a new industrial order," *Fortune,* 7 December 1998:80–92.
4. Alan Mitchell, "Internet zoo spawns new business models," *Marketing Week,* 21 January 1999:24–5.
5. Hamel and Sampler, "The e-corporation":82.
6. "The 2000 RSVP Awards: Winners by category—direct mail," *Strategy,* 24 November 2000:23.
7. David Eggleston, "Technology takes spotlight at CMA summit," *Strategy,* 22 May 2000:D1.
8. Canadian Marketing Association, "CMA study forecasts strong growth in marketing industry," news release, 11 December 2000; Lori Enos, "Report: Canadian e-commerce gaining ground," *E-Commerce Times,* 9 November 2000; Statistics Canada, "Plugging in: Household Internet use," *The Daily,* 4 December 2000; "Internet marketing survey in Canada," *24/7 Media Report,* January 2001, ads.fp.sandpiper.net/adserver.247canada.com/survey.pdf.
9. See Don Peppers and Martha Rogers, *The One-to-One Future,* New York: Doubleday/Currency, 1993.
10. Carol Wright Promotions Inc., *18th Annual Survey of Promotional Practices,* Naperville, IL, 1999:36.
11. For these and other examples, see Jonathan Berry, "A potent new tool for selling: Database marketing," *Business Week,* 4 September 1994:56–62; Weld F. Royal, "Do databases really work?" *Sales & Marketing Management,* October 1995:66–74; Daniel Hill, "Love my brand," *Brandweek,* 19 January 1998:26–9; and "FedEx taps into data warehousing," *Advertising Age's Business Marketing,* January 1999:25.
12. "The 2000 RSVP Awards: Winners by category—financial services & insurance: wealth management," 24 November 2000:34.
13. See *Economic Impact: U.S. Direct Marketing Today,* Direct Marketing Association, 1999, accessed online at www.the-dma.org/services/libres-ecoimpact1b1a.shtml.
14. Matthew L. Wald, "Third area code is added in the land of the toll-free," *New York Times,* 4 April 1998:10.
15. Kevin R. Hopkins, "Dialing in to the future," *Business Week,* 28 July 1997:90; Holly McCord, "1-900-CALL-AN-RD," *Prevention,* August 1997:54.
16. Junu Bryan Kim, "Marketing with video: The cassette is in the mail," *Advertising Age,* 22 May 1995: S-1.
17. *Economic Impact: U.S. Direct Marketing Today.*
18. Irwin Helford, "Your catalogs are doomed!" *Catalog Age,* August 1999:101,106.
19. Scott Gardiner, "The marketing side of Sears," *Marketing On-Line,* 18 December 2000.
20. Bruce Horovitz, "Catalog craze delivers holiday deals," *USA Today,* 1 December 1998:3B.
21. Andrea Zoe Aster, "Deciphering the new e-retail," *Marketing On-Line,* 20 November 2000.
22. Erika Brown, "Ooh! Aah!" *Forbes,* 8 March 1999:56.
23. Ted Starkman, "Attention television shoppers," *Marketing On-Line,* 22 November 1999.
24. Jim Auchmute, "But wait, there's more!" *Advertising Age,* 17 October 1985:18; Kathy Haley, "Infomercials lure more top marketers," *Advertising Age,* 9 May 1994:IN2,IN8; Chad Rubel, "Infomercials evolve as major firms join successful format," *Marketing News,* 2 January 1995:1,36; Jacqueline M. Graves, "The Fortune 500 opt for infomercials," *Fortune,* 6 March 1995:20.
25. M.R. Kropko, "Card markers struggling with computer kiosks," *Marketing News,* 3 June 1996:6; David Chilton, "LCBO installs interactive kiosks," *Strategy,* 24 January 1997:13; Wendy Cuthbert, "Cineplex gets ad kiosks," *Strategy,* 31 March 1997:4;

"For the record: UNICEF kiosks at IKEA," *Strategy*, 24 November 1997:15.

26. "Interactive: Ad age names finalists," *Advertising Age*, 27 February 1995:12–4.

27. See Andrea Zoe Aster, "Fast company," *Marketing On-Line*, 20 November 2000; Matt Richtel, "Small Internet providers survive among giants," *New York Times*, 16 August 1999:1; Dean Foust and David Ricks, "In a squeeze at Mindspring," *Business Week*, 20 September 1999:139–42; and Timothy J. Mullaney, "AOL rules!" *Business Week*, 3 April 2000: EB134–6.

28. For more on the basics of using the Internet, see Raymond D. Frost and Judy Strauss, *The Internet: A New Marketing Tool—2000*, Upper Saddle River, NJ: Prentice Hall, 2000.

29. Industry Canada, *Internet Commerce Statistics*, summary sheet, e-com.ic.gc.ca/using/en/e-comstats.pdf http://e-com.ic.gc.ca/using/en/e-comstats.pdf, 7 November 2000; Canadian Media Directors' Council, *Media Digest 1999–2000*:50.

30. Industry Canada, *Internet Commerce Statistics*, summary sheet, e-com.ic.gc.ca/using/en/e-comstats.pdf http://e-com.ic.gc.ca/using/en/e-comstats.pdf, 7 November 2000. Information also provided by Forrester Research, August 1999. Also see Laura Cohn, "B2B: The hottest Net bet yet?" *Business Week*, 17 January 2000:36–7.

31. Brendan Christie, "Sympatico: The Internet service for everyone," *Strategy*, 26 May 1997:SS1.

32. Canadian Media Directors' Council, *Media Digest 1999–2000*:50–1

33. Roger O. Crockett, "A Web that looks like the world," *Business Week*, 22 March 1999:EB46–7.

34. "Kids and teens to spend more online," accessed online at www.cyberatlas.com, 7 June 1999. Also see Roger O. Crockett, "Forget the mall. Kids shop the Net," *Business Week*, 26 July 1999:EB14; Eryn Brown, "The future of Net shopping? Your teens," *Fortune*, 12 April 1999:152; and "Just surfin' through," *American Demographic*, January 2000:12.

35. See Canadian Media Directors' Council, *Media Digest 1999–2000*:50–1, Crockett, "A Web that looks like the world":EB47; and Joanne Cleaver, "Surfing for seniors," *Marketing News*, 19 July 1999:1,7.

36. See Rebecca Piirto Heath, "The frontiers of psychographics," *American Demographics*, July 1996:38–43; Paul C. Judge, "Are tech buyers different?" *Business Week*, 26 January 1998:64–5,68; and future.sri.com, June 1999.

37. Don Peppers and Martha Rogers, "Opening the door to consumers," *Sales & Marketing Management*, October 1998:22–9.

38. Laurie Freeman, "Why Internet brands take offline avenues," *Marketing News*, July 1999:4; Paul C. Judge, "The name's the thing," *Business Week*, 15 November 1999:35–9.

39. John Deighton, "The future of interactive marketing," *Harvard Business Review*, November–December 1996:154.

40. Robert D. Hof, "Internet communities," *Business Week*, 5 May 1997:64–80.

41. See Ian P. Murphy, "Web 'communities' a target marketer's dream," *Advertising Age*, 7 July 1997:2; Patricia Riedman, "Web communities offer shopping options for users," *Advertising Age*, 26 October 1998:S10; Neil Cross, "Building global communities," *Business Week*, 22 March 1999:EB42–3; and Richard Siklos, "Weaving yet another Web for women," *Business Week*, 17 January 2000:101.

42. Erika Rasmusson, "Tracking down sales," *Sales & Marketing Management*, June 1998:19.

43. See Mary J. Cronin, "Using the Web to push key data to decision makers," *Fortune*, 19 September 1997:254; and Tim McCollum, "All the news that's fit to print," *Nation's Business*, June 1998:59–61.

44. Amy Cortese, "It's called Webcasting, and it promises to deliver the info you want, straight to your PC," *Business Week*, 24 February 1997:95–104. Also see Kenneth Leung, "Marketing with electronic mail without spam," *Marketing News*, 19 January 1998:11; Philip M. Perry, "E-mail hell: The dark side of the Internet age," *Folio*, June 1998:74–5; and Chad Kaydo, "As good as it gets," *Sales & Marketing Management*, March 2000:55–60.

45. Heather Green, "Cyberspace winners: How they did it," *Business Week*, 22 June 1998:154–60; and "Believe it or not, Web stores can make money," *Computerworld*, 7 December 1998:4. Also see Michael D. Donahue, "Adapting the Internet to the needs of business," *Advertising Age*, 2 February 1998:26; Shikhar Ghosh, "Making business sense of the Internet," *Harvard Business Review*, March–April 1998:126–35; and Lisa Bransten, "E-commerce (A special report)—A new model—The bottom line: If they built it, will profits come?" *Wall Street Journal*, 12 July 1999:R8.

46. "eCommerce: Consumers and shopping online," accessed online at www.emarketer.com/estats/ec_shop.html, September 1999.

47. See "Digital divide persists in the U.S.," obtained online at www.cyberatlas.com, July 8, 1999; "Privacy: On-line groups are offering up privacy plans," *Wall Street Journal*, 22 June 1998:B1; Edward C. Baig, Marcia Stepanek, and Neil Gross, "Privacy: The Internet wants your personal information. What's in it for you?" *Business Week*, 5 April 1999:84–90; and Marcia Stepanek, "A small town reveals America's digital divide," *Business Week*, 4 October 1999:188–98.

48. Portions of this section are based on Terrence H. Witkowski, "Self-regulation will suppress direct marketing's downside," *Marketing News*, 24 April 1989:4. Also see Katie Muldoon, "The industry must rebuild its image," *Direct*, April 1995:106; Jim Castelli, "How to handle personal information," *American Demographics*, March 1996:50–7; and Elyssa Yoon-Jung Lee, "How do you say 'Leave me alone?' " *Money*, June 1998:140.

Company Case 16

CarsDirect.com: Shaking up the Competition

Not long ago, buying a car was an onerous task. When consumers visited a dealership, they were at a disadvantage. Not only did they have little information, they also couldn't negotiate. Because consumers buy cars infrequently, few develop strong negotiation skills and most forget what they learned the last time.

Even consumers who took the time and effort to gather information and who were skillful negotiators found the process long and tedious. They visited the car lot, haggled with the salesperson, and then haggled more with the business manager over financing. The process could take hours, even days. At the end, many consumers believed that they had been taken advantage of by the dealer, who had all the power.

Along Comes the Internet

The Internet let consumer-oriented organizations distribute information easily. Consumer Reports (www.consumerreports.com), AutoSite (www.autosite.com), Consumer's Digest (www. consumersdigest.com), Car and Driver (www.caranddriver.com), Kelley Blue Book (www.kbb.com), and Edmund's (www.edmunds.com) quickly set up Web sites offering consumers performance, pricing, and dealer information. Carforums.com (www.carforums.com) even offered model-specific chat rooms so that consumers could talk with one another about their cars and car problems.

Although helping consumers get more information was fine, savvy e-commerce entrepreneurs saw that the Internet offered a way to begin to change the car-buying process itself. Autobytel (www.autobytel.ca) was one of the first companies to offer car-buying assistance. Other companies, such as Cost Finder Canada (www.costfindercanada.com), AutoConnect (www.autoconnect.com), AutoWeb (www.autoweb.com), and AutoVantage (www.autovantage.com) quickly followed. In fact, analysts estimated that there were soon more than 100 automotive Web sites offering some type of car-shopping help. Autobytel and similar services signed up dealers who agreed to participate and pay fees for referrals. The sites helped consumers identify dealers in their areas who had the cars they were seeking. The services would either notify the dealer about an interested consumer or simply let the consumer know where to find the dealer. Some sites allowed consumers to submit electronic, "no-haggle" bids to dealers. Using these services, however, the consumer still had to visit the dealer to conclude the negotiations and take possession of the car.

Cars Delivered Fresh Daily

It was only a matter of time before some bold entrepreneur took the next logical step. As a result of having gone through the traditional car-buying process himself, Internet entrepreneur Bill Gross realized there had to be a better way. Gross had previously founded the Pasadena, California–based Internet incubator Idealab!, which had already spawned such companies as eToys, GoTo.com, and Free-PC. Gross and other investors, including Michael Dell of Dell Computer, established CarsDirect.com (www.carsdirect.com).

Rather than just serving as an electronic intermediary, CarsDirect actually closes the sale and delivers the car to the consumer. A consumer visiting the CarsDirect Web site finds a simple, three-step process to follow. First, the site guides the consumer through the process of selecting the vehicle. Using information and guidance that the site provides, consumers can choose from a complete selection of production vehicles available in the United States. Consumers who want a specialty vehicle, such as a Ferrari, or who don't find the vehicle they are seeking, can e-mail the company directly. A service advisor contacts them within 24 hours.

Once a consumer selects a car, CarsDirect negotiates with the 1700 dealers in its network to find it. CarsDirect tries to set a price to the consumer that is in the bottom 10 percent of the market price range for the particular vehicle. Its substantial buying power allows CarsDirect to get the vehicle from the dealer at an even lower price, then make a profit on the difference between what it pays the dealer and what it charges the consumer. One dealer reported selling 53 cars to CarsDirect over a three-month period. Selling to CarsDirect lowers the dealer's costs because the dealer doesn't have to pay the sales commission it would normally pay to salespeople.

Having found a car and set a price, CarsDirect offers the car to the consumer. Consumers can lock in the price by making a fully refundable $50 deposit. They can pay cash; use their own financing, such as through a local bank; or select a lease or loan package that CarsDirect.com offers. Consumers who want to use a

CarsDirect financing package can fill out an application online.

Finally, the consumer decides how to take delivery. The company offers consumers the option of going to a local CarsDirect Priority Dealer to pick up the vehicle. Or, depending on where they live and the vehicle purchased, CarsDirect will deliver the vehicle to a consumer's home or office. (In Los Angeles, CarsDirect delivery trucks display the slogan, "Cars Delivered Fresh Daily.") No matter which option consumers select, they will be able to inspect their vehicles, find out about service options, and ask questions.

CarsDirect was the first company to offer the consumer the opportunity to purchase a vehicle, finance the purchase, and take delivery without ever leaving home.

Will This Work?

Although CarsDirect sold its first car in December 1998, its official launch was in May 1999. By August 1999, total sales had topped $100 million and the company was reaping daily revenues of more than $1.5 million. The company projected total revenues would top $400 million in its first year.

Although these numbers are impressive, especially for an Internet-based company, the average daily rate of $1.5 million represents only about 52 vehicles per day, given the average vehicle price of about $29 000. CarsDirect gets only about two percent of this amount to cover its expenses and generate a profit.

CarsDirect raised $30 million in its first two rounds of start-up funding and expects to raise another $150 million. Like other e-commerce ventures, it remains in the red, and the founders don't anticipate profits until 2001.

Profits or not, CarsDirect is shaking up the car-buying industry. Microsoft's CarPoint.com responded by joining forces with Ford Motor Company. Together, they are developing a site that would allow consumers to order cars online directly from the factory. Trilogy Software of Austin, Texas, is funding CarOrder.com, a company that intends to spend up to $600 million to buy under-performing dealerships in smaller markets. CarOrder.com will then use these dealerships to create regional distribution centres, transforming these dealers into online retailers to serve large territories. Like CarsDirect, CarOrder would take online orders. However, it would ship the cars to its own dealerships and deliver them to customers from those dealerships.

Another competitor, AutoNation of Fort Lauderdale, Florida, is putting the inventory of its 270 dealerships online and encouraging other independent dealers to sell on its Web site. Autobytel reported that it is also testing a direct sales method. Even Ford and GM have launched new units that will buy dealerships and operate them as factory-owned stores, allowing them to test Internet selling.

Moreover, several companies are experimenting with e-commerce car-buying strategies in foreign markets. GM is testing strategies in Taiwan, where it already sells 10 percent of its vehicles via the Internet. It began building cars to order in 2000. Ford has set up a seamless e-commerce system in the Philippines that links consumers, dealers, Ford, and its suppliers. Meanwhile, Autobytel has moved into Europe. There, European Union laws enable manufacturers to restrict new car sales to captive dealers. Such laws have led to inflated prices in many markets, as much as 25 percent higher on average than in the United States. When this exemption expires in 2002, Autobytel hopes to be able to offer direct sales over the Internet.

Where to from Here?

Where will this lead? No one's sure. An analyst for one company argues that, "All [CarsDirect has] is motivated salespeople in a call centre" who try to get dealers to sell cars for less than CarsDirect's customer is paying. Other analysts note that although the number of new vehicle buyers using the Internet to shop has risen from 25 percent in 1998 to 40 percent in 1999, the number of people using the Internet to actually buy a vehicle is still relatively small. Further, CarsDirect and other online vehicle retailers face restrictive state franchise laws, some of which ban Internet sales. They also face political and legal actions by some of the 20 000 established dealers and complicated ordering systems by which automakers require dealers to take unwanted cars to get hot-selling models.

Finally, CarsDirect has proven that some consumers will make a five-figure purchase over the Internet without having seen the car. However, some analysts still wonder: Are there enough such consumers out there for CarsDirect to become profitable?

Questions

1. How do customers and CarsDirect each benefit from online marketing?
2. Outline CarsDirect's marketing strategy. What problems do you see with its strategy?
3. What marketing recommendations would you make to CarsDirect? Specifically, how can CarsDirect get more people to visit its site and purchase cars using its service?

4. What advantages or disadvantages will CarsDirect and its competitors face in foreign markets? How are Canadian auto dealers preparing for the entry of firms like CarsDirect?

5. What ethical issues does CarsDirect face? How should it deal with those issues?

Sources: CarsDirect.com home page, **www.carsdirect.com**; Edward Harris, "Web car-shopping puts buyers in driver's seat," *Wall Street Journal,* 15 April 1999:B10; Daniel Taub, "Firm proves people are ready to buy cars on the Web," *Los Angeles Business Journal,* 23 August 1999:5; John Couretas, "CarsDirect tops online buying list from Gomez," *Automotive News,* 20 September 1999:10; Fara Warner, "Internet auto retailer CarOrder.com receives funds to acquire dealerships," *Wall Street Journal,* 29 September 1999:B2; Tim Burt, "Autobytel to push online car sales in Europe," *Financial Times,* 8 October 1999:30; Fara Warner, "New tactics shake up online auto retailing," *Wall Street Journal,* 18 October 1999:B1; and Fara Warner, "GM tests e-commerce plans in emerging markets," *Wall Street Journal,* 25 October 1999:B6.

video case 16

E-Tailing: Tales of Profit and Loss

Over the last few years, many bricks and mortar retailers have attempted to transform themselves into clicks and mortar retailers. While some rushed into the e-commerce world, others were more reluctant. When Internet shopping first started, it looked like God's gift to retail. Not only was there no sales staff to pay, there was no physical space to rent. Many thought that e-tailing just meant hooking up that website and watching the dollars come rolling in. There was a lot of talk about new rules of business and the e-revolution that would overturn traditional business models.

In 1999, the Internet was seen by many as the world's newest and biggest mall. Many retailers, both giants with world-renowned brands and tiny specialty stores, began to set up virtual shops. The problem was, however, no one knew exactly how much money you could make selling online or what it would cost you to set up a virtual presence. Some small retailers established a web presence for just a few hundred dollars but many larger retailers spent hundreds of thousands of dollars establishing their e-stores.

Larry Stevenson, former Chapters CEO, spent a whopping $22 million just setting up operations for his Internet division. Chapters wanted to be the leading Canadian e-tailer and it knew it had to spend big to get there. The first expense was technology: the credit card capabilities, the security features, and the website itself. Chapters wanted a site that would offer an experience consistent with the one that customers have when they enter a Chapters store. The site plus the staff costs cost eight million dollars. Then there was distribution. Anyone who intends to fill thousands of Internet orders a day needs a serious system. Chapters built its own highly automated warehouse. Price tag? Ten million dollars. And don't forget the advertising and marketing. Larry Stevenson spent $3.7 million on that.

Even with a well-known brand stemming from its physical stores, Chapters.ca had to convince consumers to go online. It knew costs would long exceed revenues and told shareholders not to hold their breath waiting for early profits. To help bring customers to the site, Chapters forged a number of strategic alliances. Chapters.ca has a presence on a number of leading Canadian portal sites, including Yahoo.ca, AOL.ca, MSN.ca, Canada.com and Canoe in addition to a network of more than 9000 affiliated sites, both large and small. Each receives a commission for linking customers to Chapters.ca. However, as David Pecaut of the Boston Consulting Group notes, companies had better have deep pockets and lots of support from their investors and venture capitalists if they plan to stay the course.

By the end of 2000, Chapters.ca was attracting more than two million hits per week. The site enjoys the highest consumer awareness of any Canadian e-commerce site, according to research by Toronto-based Kubas Consultants. The site claims more than 820 000 customers, 63 percent of whom are repeat buyers. Despite all the sales and traffic the site generated, it was still an e-business where every dollar of sales cost $1.12 to produce. Chapters predicted that it would be profitable by 2002, but in 2001 it was brought out by the rival Indigo chain and Heather Reisman replaced Larry Stevenson as CEO of the chain.

In sharp contrast to Chapters, Toronto-headquartered Danier Leather had reservations about going online and didn't want to bet the firm to establish a web presence. Found in 1972, Danier is a "vertically integrated" operation that sources raw materials as well as designing, manufacturing, distributing and retailing its own line.

Danier turned to IBM's e-business team for advice. IBM presented e-business models varying in cost from $250 000 to $450 000. For a retailer with 1999 sales totaling $109 million, this was a major investment. IBM encouraged Danier to follow in the footsteps of American retailing giants like Eddie Bauer, the Gap and L.L. Bean. But Danier's chief operating officer wasn't entirely sold. He was worried about the ongoing operating costs. Canadian Internet guru Jim Carroll, who has written 22 handbooks on how to use the Internet, noted, "I think they will discover that the majority of people are still gonna want to buy leather products in a real store because they want to try it on and see that it fits. I think there is almost an aura out there amongst a lot of retailers that this is something magic, you know. That all they need to do is create a store and something magic happens, and the orders flow in. I think there is a bit of excessive hype out there that is overinflating their expectations."

Danier's Jeffery Wortsman believed he didn't have much choice about establishing a web presence. Part of Danier's strategy was to transform itself from a mass merchant retailer into a high-fashion label. This was no small task given Danier was more likely to be confused with the Olde Hide House than with Club Monaco or Roots. Moreover, Danier's shoppers were demanding service in three retail channels: stores, catalogues, and the Internet. So Danier launched itself into cyberspace, but took a cautious approach. Wortsman had already waited two years for technology prices to come down, and he chose the lowest priced package IBM offered. He also set modest objectives for his web business hoping the new website would generate one to two percent of Danier's sales.

In 2001, retailers are poorer and wiser about e-tailing ventures. While web commerce accounted for $3.7 billion in consumer sales in 2000, it still accounts for less than two percent of every dollar of retail spending. E-tailers also discovered that acquiring new online customers was far more costly than anyone imagined. While it costs traditional retailers approximately $3 to get a new customers in the door, or $4.50 to get someone to buy from a retail catalogue, it costs $23.50 to get new customers for "bricks and click" operations and an astounding $39.00 to acquire a new customer if the company operates only in cyberspace. Thus, it is not surprising that ad spending as a percentage of sales can be as high as 65 percent for dot.com companies, while it is only four percent for traditional firms. E-tailers also discovered they couldn't operate with virtual inventory. Online consumers just weren't willing to wait for goods to be ordered and then delivered. Finally, many consumers are still nervous about shopping online. Privacy and security concerns still haunt cyberspace merchants. There is no doubt that e-tailing is here to stay, but models of success remain elusive!

Questions

1. Visit Danier's e-tailing site at www.danier.com and Chapters site at www.chapters.ca. Which site is more user friendly? Which one would you shop at? Which one would you more likely use just to gather information?
2. Chapters took a very aggressive approach to building an online presence. Danier Leather took a more conservative approach. Compare and contrast the strengths and weaknesses of the two approaches. Which approach best positioned the company for long-term success?
3. Web retailers that also have a bricks and mortar presence face the challenge of creating the same level of service quality no matter what channel the shopper chooses to use. Describe some of the tactics you might use to help a "bricks and clicks" company achieve consistent service quality.

Sources: Peggy Cunningham prepared this case based on "E-Commerce: Retail's Risky Venture?" *Venture*, October 5, 1999: Patrick Brethour, "Bricks and clicks the new e-bus model," *Globe and Mail*, March 10, 2001, p. B1, B6; Terry Poulton, "Chapters.ca plots category domination," *Strategy*, January 15, 2001, p. 22; Justin Smallbridge, "The Midas touch," *Marketing On-Line*, February 26, 2001; Peter Vamos, "Danier Leather plans to shed old skin," *Strategy*, July 31, 2000, p. 7.

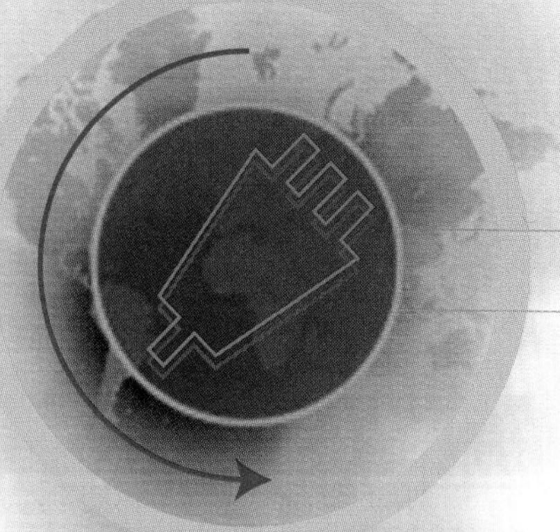

P A R T 1 2 3 **4**

Managing Marketing

Concept Connections

When you finish this chapter, you should be able to

1. Discuss how the international trade system, economic, politico-legal, and cultural environments affect a company's international marketing decisions.
2. Describe three key approaches to entering international markets.
3. Explain how companies adapt their marketing mixes for international markets.
4. Identify the three major forms of international marketing organization.

chapter 17 The Global Marketplace

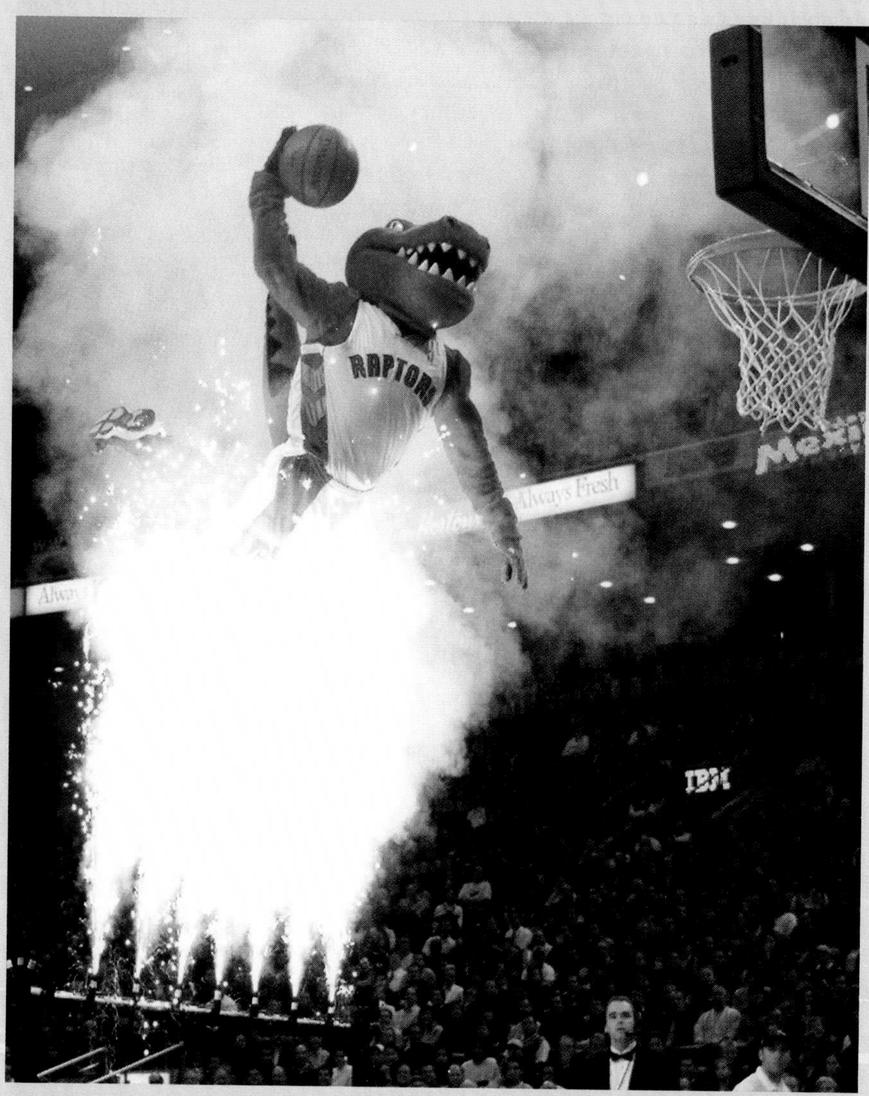

Basketball, the quintessential North American game, is rapidly becoming a worldwide craze. A *New York Times* survey of over 45 000 teenagers on five continents asked: "What are your favourite entertainment pursuits?" The top two answers: watching television and basketball. If you ask Canadian teenagers aged 12 to 17 to name their favourite athletes, Wayne Gretzky loses out to Michael Jordan, Shaquille O'Neal, and Damon Stoudamire. And no organization is doing more to promote worldwide basketball than the National Basketball Association (NBA), a truly global marketing enterprise. NBA games are televised around the world, and the league with its partners sells millions of dollars worth of NBA-licensed basketballs, backboards, T-shirts, and other merchandise both inside and outside North America every year. The NBA is now a powerful worldwide brand. A recent *Fortune* article summarizes:

> Deployed by global sponsors Coca-Cola, Reebok, and McDonald's, these well-paid travelling salesmen will hawk soda, sneakers, burgers, and basketball to legions of mostly young fans. That they are recognized from Santiago to Seoul says a lot about the soaring worldwide appeal of hoops—and about the marketing juggernaut known as the NBA. After watching their favourite stars swoop in and slam-dunk on their local TV stations, fans of the league now cheer the mate in Latin America, the trofsla in Iceland, and the smash in France. Care to guess the most popular basketball team in China? Why, it's the "Red Oxen" from Chicago, of course.

Like many other businesses, the NBA's primary motive for going global is growth. In the US, the league now sells out most of its games, and licensing revenues have flattened in recent years. According to NBA commissioner David Sterns, "There are just so many seats in an arena and so many hours of television programming, period. The domestic business is becoming mature. That's why we're moving internationally." Compared with the NBA's overall yearly revenues of $3 billion, current international revenues are modest—estimated at a little more than $90 million from TV rights fees, sponsorships, and the league's share of licensing sales. But worldwide potential is huge, and the league is investing heavily to build its popularity and business abroad.

The NBA's success abroad is primarily a result of the league's strong marketing efforts. Entry into the Canadian market was a natural for the NBA since basketball, originally invented by a Canadian, was already a popular sport. Examining how the NBA built its Canadian fan base is like reading a case study on the tactics the organization has used around the world. The NBA rolled out a marketing machine that's been fine-tuned for a decade in the United States. Television programming leads the way—not just broadcasts of games but an array of NBA-produced programs, mostly targeting children and teenagers, which promote the league and its players. Given the popularity of hockey, just getting Canadian television coverage was a major challenge. Ken Derrett, managing director of NBA Canada Inc., notes: "Providing access to NBA games on television is an essential foundation for growth."

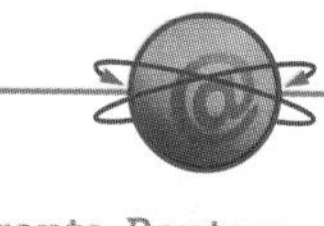

Toronto Raptors
www.nba.com/raptors/

Vancouver Grizzlies
www.nba.com/grizzlies/

Before the Toronto Raptors and Vancouver Grizzlies began playing in the league in 1995, broadcast coverage of the NBA in Canada was sparse. Since NBA basketball is as much about spectacle and entertainment as it is about sport, having televised games is only one part of the mix. NBA-based programs were also used to promote the league and its players: *NBA in the Paint* and YTV's *Dunk Street,* a half-hour hoop show with a Canadian slant, for example, drew an average of 204 000 weekly viewers. NBA Canada also ran two advertising spots "I love this game," designed to further educate Canadians about basketball, and "I love this stuff," focused on promoting merchandise sales. The ads ran on TV shows popular among young fans, like Much Music. And the tactics worked. After one year, research revealed that 57 percent of NBA fans in English Canada were more interested in the NBA than they had been previously.

Once television has pried open the new foreign market, the NBA and its partners move in with an array of live events, attractions, and grassroots activities. For example, McDonald's and the NBA sponsor a program called 2Ball that teaches basic basketball skills to thousands of kids in its international marketplaces. Coca-Cola, meanwhile, targets basketball-crazed teenagers by putting NBA and team logos on Sprite soft-drink cans sold in 30 countries. "We're using the NBA and their players to help sell Sprite, but at the same time it does a lot for the NBA," says Coca-Cola's director for worldwide sports.

Since live fans are important to the excitement of the game, the NBA and its Canadian sponsors knew it must draw teens to the games. However, how do you make the game more accessible and exciting, given the limited income of most teens? Raptors sponsor Sprite found one key when it created the Sprite Zone at the Air Canada Centre. The Sprite Zone is a special section of 1442 seats where tickets cost only $10 (less than half the regular $24 ticket price). The Zone is also a fun, dynamic place for Sprite's teen target audience to watch the game, spurred on by six "Sprite Zone leaders," theme nights, and chances to win Raptor merchandise or upgraded courtside tickets.

Merchandise sales and selling corporate sponsorships are the final tactics used in new international markets to help build loyalty and generate revenues for the teams' coffers. For example, NBA Canada has issued over 60 licences to date. Air Canada, Shoppers Drug Mart and Nestlé Canada were quick to jump on board. Kellogg Canada was another eager partner, putting the phone number for season tickets on its boxes of Rice Krispies. Kellogg's Joanne Doyle, manager of product communications, went with NBA sponsorship because "the demographics of the [NBA] broadcasts also show a good female viewership, important to us since most grocery shoppers are women." Despite skillful marketing, however, the NBA's success in Canada is far from assured.

Similar tactics to those used in Canada were used to "slam-dunk" the European and Asian marketplaces, where amateur basketball had been thriving since the 1936 Olympics. To help build the market for professional basketball in these areas, the NBA also leveraged the Internet. The NBA's site (www.NBA.com) offers materials in several languages and draws almost a third of its visitors from outside North America. A survey of 28 000 teenagers in 45 countries by [a global ad agency] found that Jordan was the world's favourite athlete by far. In China, which has its own professional basketball leagues, boys on the streets of Beijing and Shanghai wear Bulls gear because they want to be like Mike.

The NBA recently encountered a rash of problems—Michael Jordan's retirement and the end of the Chicago Bulls dynasty, negative publicity surrounding several high-profile players, and a prolonged players' strike that cut the 1998–1999 season in half. These and other events present fresh challenges to the league's marketing prowess. Still, the future looks bright. The NBA emerged from the potentially disastrous players' strike nearly unscathed, and although TV ratings for the NBA finals dipped, games still top the Nielsen ratings. Most experts expect more high flying from the NBA as it continues to extend its international reach. One sustaining factor in the NBA's global appeal is the continuing presence of foreign-born players. Almost every team roster includes one: Toni Kukoc from Croatia, Luc Longley from Australia, Georghe Muresan from Romania, Arvydas Sabonis from Lithuania, Detlef Shrempf from Germany. Such players attract large followings in their home countries. As *Fortune* concludes:

> Imagine, then, the impact in China if a promising 18-year-old, seven-foot-one centre named Wong Zhizhi, who played for that country's . . . Olympic team, develops into an NBA star. Basketball's popularity is already exploding in China, one of the very few nations where the NBA gives away its TV programming because [it] is determined to make inroads there. Nearly all of China's 250 million TV households get the NBA Action highlights show and a game of the week on Saturday mornings; this year China Central TV broadcast the NBA all-star game live for the first time. Winning the loyalty of two billion Chinese won't be a kou qui—a slam-dunk—but Stern is, well, bullish. "The upside is tremendous," he says. Can Ping-Pong survive an NBA invasion? Stay tuned.[1]

Given our small domestic marketplace, the ability to trade internationally has long been important to Canadian citizens and businesses. Today, more than 40 percent of everything that Canadians produce is exported. This figure equates into $12 145 of internationally traded goods and services for every Canadian—kids, youth and retirees included. Trade means imports as well as exports bringing in technology and materials needed to create exports while offering Canadians a wider range of purchase choices for everything from oranges to cars to medication. It encourages competitive pricing, creates jobs, stimulates technological advances and promotes ever increasing knowledge and skills. It can't be denied, however, that trade, like any opportunity, involves risk, especially in today's highly complex, globally competitive marketplace.[2]

Global Marketing in the Twenty-First Century

The world is shrinking rapidly with the advent of faster communication, transportation, and financial flows. Products developed in one country—Gucci purses, Mont Blanc pens, McDonald's hamburgers, Japanese sushi, Pierre Cardin suits, German BMWs—are finding enthusiastic acceptance in other countries. We would not be surprised to hear about a German businessman wearing an Italian suit and meeting an English friend at a Japanese restaurant and who later returns home to drink Russian vodka and watch Canada's *The Air Farce* on television.

International trade is booming. Since 1969, the number of multinational corporations in the world's 14 richest countries has more than tripled, from 7000 to 24 000. Experts predict that, by 2005, world exports of goods and services will reach 28 percent of world gross domestic product, up from only nine percent 20 years ago. With $412 billion in exports of goods and services in 1999, Canada is one of the world's leading trading nations and the most export-oriented of the G7 industrialized economies. In fact, one in three jobs in Canada can be tied to trade. We export more, proportionally, than the US or Japan. More than 43 percent of Canada's GDP is linked to trade. Since exports are expected to increase by 10 percent in 2001, half of Canada's output will be sent overseas. Compare these figures with those of the US, where international trade now accounts for a quarter of GDP. While Canadian companies have long been criticized for depending excessively on the easily accessible US market, more firms are broadening their trade horizons. Companies exporting to both the US *and* other countries increased by 53 percent in 2000.[3]

True, many companies have been carrying on international activities for decades: Nortel, Bell, McCain, Bata, Coca-Cola, IBM, Kodak, Nestlé, Shell, Bayer, Nokia, Sony, and other companies are familiar to most consumers around the world. But global competition is intensifying. Foreign firms are expanding aggressively into new international markets, and domestic companies that never thought about foreign competitors suddenly find these competitors in their own backyards. The firm that stays at home to play it safe may not only lose its chance to enter other markets but also risk losing its home market.

In North America, such names as Sony, Toyota, Nestlé, Norelco, Mercedes, and Panasonic have become household words. Products and services that appear to be domestic really are produced or owned by foreign companies: Bantam books, Cadbury chocolate, Baskin-Robbins ice cream, GE and RCA televisions, Firestone tires, Kiwi shoe polish, Lipton tea, Carnation milk, and Pillsbury products, to name a few. North America also has attracted huge foreign investments in such basic industries as steel, petroleum, tires, and chemicals, and in tourist and real

Many companies have made the world their market.

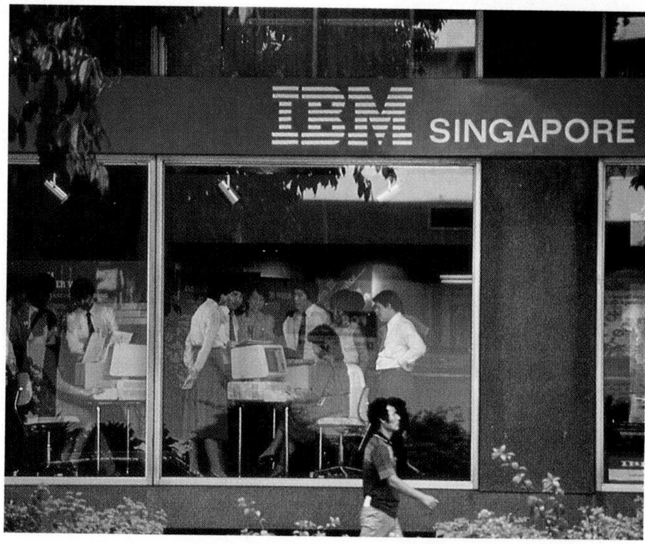

estate ventures, illustrated by Japanese land purchases in British Columbia and California. Few North American industries are now safe from foreign competition.

In an era of free trade, firms must learn how to enter foreign markets and increase their global competitiveness. Many Canadian companies have been successful at international marketing: Nortel, Mosaid, Corel, IMAX, Bombardier, CAE, Labatt, Moosehead, Northern Reflections, Alcan, Magna International, Barrick Gold Corp., Nova Corp., Newbridge Networks, and Atco, to name a few. Order some french fries in Thailand, Russia, Costa Rica, Tunisia, Vietnam, or Syria, and chances are you will be biting into a product manufactured by McCain International Inc. of Florenceville, New Brunswick. But you don't have to be an industry giant to venture into overseas markets. Blitz Design Corp. of Langley, British Columbia, developed and markets "power" sugar-free breath mints to more than 15 countries around the world. Its largest market is the United States, where it is among the top 10 in sales—not a bad accomplishment, considering it took on such giant brands as Breathsavers, Tic Tac, Certs, and Clorets.[4]

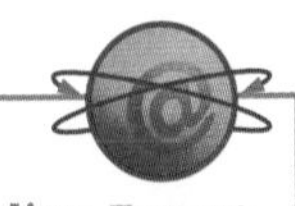

Canadian Export Development Corp.
www.edc-see.ca/

Department of Foreign Affairs and International Trade
www.dfait-maeci.gc.ca./

Many firms are still hesitant about testing foreign waters. However, the federal government and its "Team Canada" approach, the Canadian Export Development Corp., and the Department of Foreign Affairs and International Trade are helping Canadian businesses, both large and small, make inroads in overseas markets.

The longer companies delay taking steps toward internationalizing, the more they risk being shut out of growing markets in Western Europe, Eastern Europe, the Pacific Rim, and elsewhere. All companies first have to answer some basic questions: What market position should we try to establish in our country, in our economic region, and globally? Who will our global competitors be and what are their strategies and resources? Where should we produce or source our products? What strategic alliances should we form with other firms around the world?

Although the need for companies to go abroad is great, so are the risks. Companies that go global confront several major problems. High debt, inflation, and unemployment in many countries have resulted in highly unstable governments and currencies, which limits trade and exposes global firms to many risks. For example, in 1998 Russia created a global economic crisis when it devalued the ruble, effectively defaulting on its global debts. A more widespread Asian economic downturn had a far-reaching impact on Western firms with significant markets or investments there.

Governments are placing more regulations on foreign firms, such as requiring joint ownership with domestic partners, mandating the hiring of nationals, and limiting profits that can be taken from the country. Moreover, foreign governments often impose high tariffs or trade barriers to protect their own industries. Finally,

Many small Canadian firms are successful international marketers. Feathercraft exports kayaks to Japan and Blitz Design Corp. is a winner selling breath mints to 15 countries.

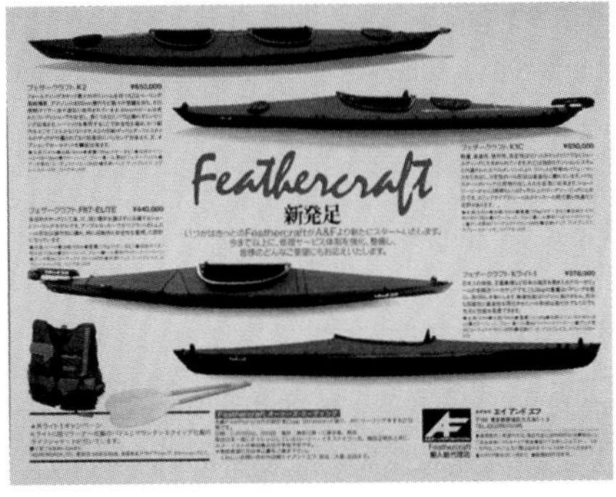

corruption is an increasing problem: Officials in several countries often award business not to the best bidder but to the highest briber.

Global industry
An industry in which the strategic positions of competitors in given geographic or national markets are affected by their overall global positions.

Global firm
A firm that, by operating in more than one country, gains R&D, production, marketing, and financial advantages that are not available to purely domestic competitors.

Still, companies selling in global industries have no choice but to internationalize their operations. A **global industry** is one in which the competitive positions of firms in given local or national markets are affected by their global positions. A **global firm** is one that, by operating in more than one country, gains marketing, production, R&D, and financial advantages that are not available to purely domestic competitors. The global company sees the world as one market. It minimizes the importance of national boundaries and raises capital, obtains materials and components, and manufactures and markets its goods wherever it can do the best job. Global firms gain advantages by planning, operating, and coordinating their activities on a worldwide basis. For example, Ford's "world truck" sports a cab made in Europe and a chassis built in Canada; it is assembled in Brazil and imported to the United States for sale. Otis Elevator gets its elevators' door systems from France, small geared parts from Spain, electronics from Germany, and special motor drives from Japan. It uses the United States only for systems integration.

Because firms around the world are going global at a rapid rate, domestic firms in global industries must act quickly before the window closes. This does not mean that small and medium-size firms must operate in a dozen countries to succeed: These firms can practise global niching. In fact, companies marketing on the Internet may find themselves going global whether they intend it or not (see Marketing Highlight 17-1). But the world is becoming smaller, and every company operating in a global industry—whether large or small—must assess and establish its place in world markets.

As Figure 17-1 shows, a company faces six major decisions in international marketing. Each decision will be discussed in detail in this chapter.

Looking at the Global Marketing Environment

Before deciding whether to operate internationally, a company must thoroughly understand the international marketing environment. That environment has changed a great deal over the last two decades, creating both new opportunities and new problems. The world economy has globalized. World trade and investment have grown rapidly, with many attractive markets opening up in Western and Eastern Europe, China, India, the Pacific Rim, Russia, and elsewhere. There has been a growth of global brands in automobiles, food, clothing, electronics, and many other categories. The international financial system has become more complex and fragile, and North American companies face increasing trade barriers erected to protect domestic markets from outside competition.

The International Trade System

A company looking abroad must first understand the international *trade system*. When selling to another country, the firm faces various trade restrictions. The most

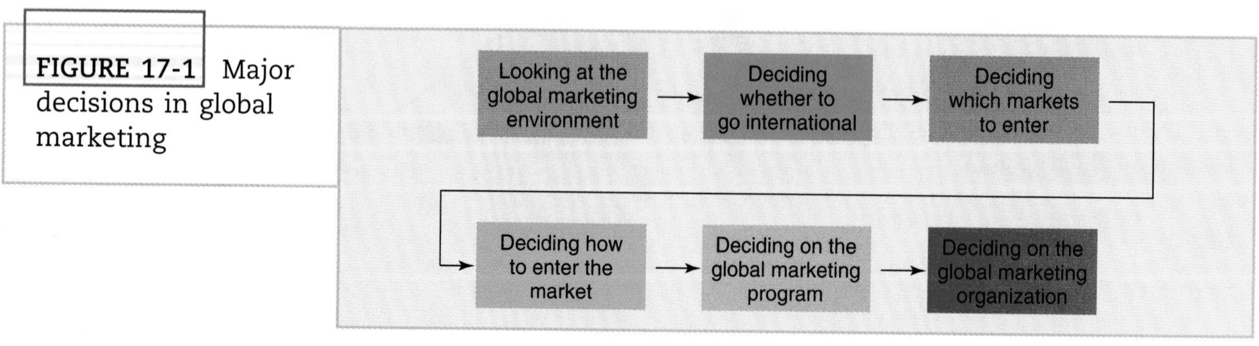

FIGURE 17-1 Major decisions in global marketing

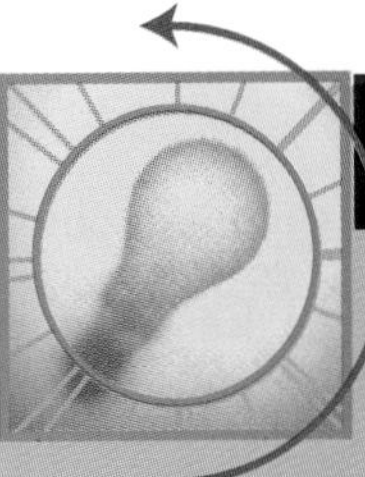

marketing highlight 17-1

WWW: The World Is Your Oyster.com

As the Internet and online services attract more users around the world, many marketers are taking advantage of the Internet's global reach. Major global marketers already on the Net range from automakers (General Motors) to publishers who put their magazines online (Brunico Inc.), to retailers who put catalogues online (J. Crew), to global wine shippers (Virtual Vineyards), to compact disc marketers (CDNow), to banks (ING). All are taking advantage of cyberspace's making national boundaries trivial.

Companies that sell or promote on the Internet have the whole world for a market. For some of these companies, the global market has largely been a hit-or-miss affair. They present their content in English for the North American market; and, if any international users stumble across it and end up buying something, so much the better.

Other marketers have made a more strategic decision to enter the global market. They're using the Web and online services to reach new customers outside their home countries, support existing customers who reside abroad, and build global brand awareness.

Many companies have adapted their Web sites to provide country-specific content and services to their best potential international markets, often in the local language. For example, in an attempt to increase brand awareness in individual European markets, Reebok has launched a multilingual European Web site—available in English, French, Italian, Spanish, Greek, and Turkish. The site (www.europe.reebok.com) targets sports and fitness enthusiasts and includes local events in each market. Similarly, Dell Computer offers dozens of country-specific, local-language Web sites for such markets as France, Germany, Belgium, China, Japan, and Brunei.

For the most part, marketers have zeroed in on the countries or regions with the largest potential online populations. Europe and Japan are prime targets. Although European and Japanese online usage has lagged behind that in North America, it is catching up quickly. Online subscribers are expected to grow from seven percent of Europe's population in 1998 to 13 percent in 2001. The Japanese Internet user population was expected to double by the year 2001, with e-commerce jumping to $12.5 billion from $2.5 billion in 1998.

Despite encouraging e-commerce developments in Europe and Asia, Internet marketers sometimes overstate seemingly surefire global opportunities. The reality of the global Internet market depends on each country's economic, technical, cultural, political, and regional dynamics. Technological challenges abound. While telecommunications channels, the backbone of the Internet, are ubiquitous in Canada and the US, response times overseas can be dismal. Many countries remain technologically underdeveloped and have a low-income citizenry lacking PCs or even phone connections. Other countries have acceptable phone and PC penetration, but high subscription and connection costs sharply restrict such casual uses as surfing on the Internet. For example, in Europe, net subscriptions typically run $105 a month, more than triple North American rates. In the United Kingdom, connection rates can run over $5 per hour, with long-distance calling and data surcharges in rural areas running as high as $24 per hour.

In addition, the global marketer may run up against governmental or cultural restrictions. France, for instance, has laws against providing encrypted content. In Germany, a vendor can't accept payment via credit card until two weeks after an order has been sent. Privacy regulations also vary. Europe and Canada have strict codes limiting direct marketing firms from gathering certain types of data. Furthermore, underdeveloped banking systems have limited credit card usage in many countries. The issue of who pays taxes and duties on global e-commerce is even murkier. Therefore, marketers outside North America sometimes have to find alternative marketing and collection approaches.

Businesses need to realize that the Web does not offer complete solutions for transacting global busines—and it probably never will. Most companies will always find it difficult to complete a big business-to-business deal via e-mail. The Internet will not overcome customs red tape or local regulations regarding import or export of certain goods. The Web can't guarantee that goods will arrive in perfect condition. Despite the barriers, however, global Internet enterprise is growing rapidly. In fact, 83 per-

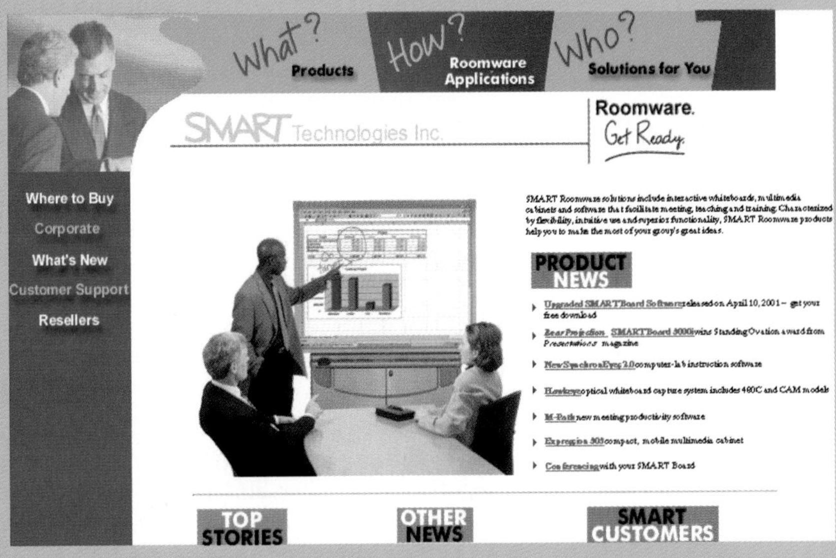

SMART Technologies, a winner of the 2000 Canada Export Awards, uses its Web site to serve both domestic and international clients.

cent of managers surveyed recently by consulting firm KPMG Peat Marwick said that e-commerce would be a major export vehicle beyond the year 2000. For companies that wish to go global, the Internet and online services can represent an easy way to get started or to reinforce other efforts.

For larger companies, casting an international web is a natural. For example, Hewlett-Packard uses a Web site to deal with its resellers Europe-wide, offering information in many languages. Nestlé's Web site links to company sites for Taiwan, Australia, Brazil, Chile, New Zealand, Switzerland, Spain, Germany, France, Japan, Sweden, Greece, and the United Kingdom. Texas Instruments' European Semiconductor group uses a "TI & Me" site to sell and support its signal processors, logic devices, and other chips across Europe.

But small companies can also market globally on the Web. Calgary's SMART Technologies Inc. was named the 2000 Exporter of the Year by the Department of Foreign Affairs and International Trade, which has given the Canada Export Awards for the past 17 years to Canadian companies that demonstrate excellence in competing internationally. SMART uses the Internet to promote sales of its Canadian-made products to over 50 countries. Visit its Web site and click on the "Where to buy" button, and you will find a list of SMART's international distributors. Upscale retailer and cataloguer The Sharper Image now gets 25 percent of its online business from overseas customers. Online music marketer CDNow, which stumbled onto global markets almost by accident, now actively develops its global business. So get online and see if the world can be your oyster.

Sources: Peter Krasilovsky, "A whole new world," *Marketing Tools supplement, American Demographics,* May 1996:22–5; "2000 Canada export awards," *Canadian Business,* 5 February 2001:61; Richard N. Miller, "The Year Ahead," *Direct Marketing,* January 1997:42–4; Jack Gee, "Parlez-vous Inter-Net?" *Industry Week,* 21 April 1997:78–9; Michelle V. Rafter, "Multilingual sites give companies access to global revenue sources," *Business Section, Chicago Tribune,* 11 May 1998:9; "Reebok targets its new Web site at Euro markets," *Marketing,* 1 October 1998:16; Shannon Oberndorf, "Europe jumps online," *Catalog Age,* June 1999:10; Bill Spindle, "E-commerce (A special report)," *Wall Street Journal,* 12 July 1999:R22; Erika Rasmusson, "E-commerce around the world," *Sales and Marketing Management,* February 2000:94.

Tariff
A tax levied by a government against certain imported products to either raise revenue or protect domestic firms.

Quota
A limit on the amount of goods that an importing country will accept in certain product categories to conserve on foreign exchange and to protect local industry and employment.

Embargo
A ban on the import of a certain product.

Exchange controls
Government limits on the amount of its foreign exchange with other countries and on its exchange rate against other currencies.

Non-tariff trade barriers
Non-monetary barriers to foreign products, such as biases against a foreign company's bids or product standards that go against a foreign company's product features.

common is the **tariff,** which is a tax levied by a foreign government against certain imported products. The tariff may be designed either to raise revenue or to protect domestic firms. The exporter also may face a **quota,** which sets limits on the amount of goods the importing country will accept in certain product categories. The purpose of the quota is to conserve on foreign exchange and to protect local industry and employment. An **embargo,** or boycott, totally bans some kinds of imports.

Firms may face **exchange controls,** which limit the amount of foreign exchange and the exchange rate against other currencies. They also may encounter **non-tariff trade barriers,** such as biases against bids or restrictive product standards that go against North American product features. The Japanese have found a clever way to keep foreign manufacturers out of their domestic market: They plead "uniqueness." Japanese skin is different, the government argues, so foreign cosmetics companies must test their products in Japan before selling there. The Japanese say their stomachs are small and have room for only the *mikan,* the local tangerine, so imports of US oranges are limited. Now the Japanese have come up with what may be the flakiest argument yet: Their snow is different, so ski equipment should be too.[5] At the same time, certain forces *help* trade between nations. Examples are the General Agreement on Tariffs and Trade and various regional free trade agreements.

The World Trade Organization and GATT

The World Trade Organization (WTO) is a global organization that deals with the rules of trade between nations. As of November 2000, the WTO had 140 member countries that account for over 90 percent of world trade. Other countries are negotiating membership. The WTO works to ensure that trade among the world's nations flows as smoothly and freely as possible. It administers trade agreements, provides a forum for trade negotiations, and handles trade disputes. The WTO was established on 1 January 1995 as the successor to the General Agreement on Tariffs and Trade (GATT) that had been in effect since 1948.

The GATT set up the basis for a multilateral trading system that was designed to promote world trade by reducing tariffs and other international trade barriers. Since the signing of GATT, world trade has grown significantly. Member nations have met in eight rounds of GATT negotiations, designed to reassess trade barriers and set new rules for international trade. The first seven rounds of negotiations reduced the average worldwide tariffs on manufactured goods from 45 to 5 percent. The most recently completed GATT negotiations, dubbed the Uruguay Round, dragged on for seven long years, from 1986 to 1994. The benefits of the Uruguay Round will be felt for many years, as the accord promotes long-term global trade growth. It reduced the world's remaining merchandise tariffs by 30 percent. The new agreement also extended GATT to cover trade in agriculture and a wide range of services and it toughened international protection of copyrights, patents, trademarks, and other intellectual property. It was the Uruguay Round that established the WTO to enforce GATT rules.[6]

World Trade Organization
www.wto.org/

Negotiations to further liberalize world trade continued after the end of the Uruguay Round. In 1997, agreement was reached on further liberalization measures for trading telecommunication services, information technology products, banking, insurance, securities, and financial information. In 1998, WTO members agreed to study trade issues arising from global electronic commerce. In 2000, talks focused again on agriculture and services. The WTO also works with other organizations on a number of special issues. For example, in early 2001, it participated in a joint workshop with the World Health Organization to discuss how to improve poor countries' access to essential drugs.

Economic community
A group of nations organized to work toward common goals in the regulation of international trade.

Regional Free Trade Zones

Some countries have formed *free trade zones* or **economic communities**—groups of nations organized to work toward common goals in the regulation of international trade. One community is the *European Union (EU)*. Formed in 1957, the European Union—then called the Common Market—set out to create a single European market by reducing barriers to the free flow of products, services, finances, and labour among member countries and developing policies on trade with nonmember nations. Today, the European Union represents one of the world's single largest markets. Its 15 member countries—Belgium, Germany, France, Italy, Luxembourg, Netherlands, Denmark, Ireland, the United Kingdom, Greece, Spain, Portugal, Austria, Finland, and Sweden—contain over 376 million consumers and account for 20 percent of the world's exports. As more European nations seek admission, the EU could contain as many as 450 million people in 28 countries. The EU imports $15.6 billion of goods and services from Canada—almost five percent (4.71%) of our export trade. However, we import almost twice as many goods and services from Europe than we export ($31.8 billion).

The Department of Foreign Affairs and International Trade and its trade commissioners help Canadian businesses penetrate world markets.

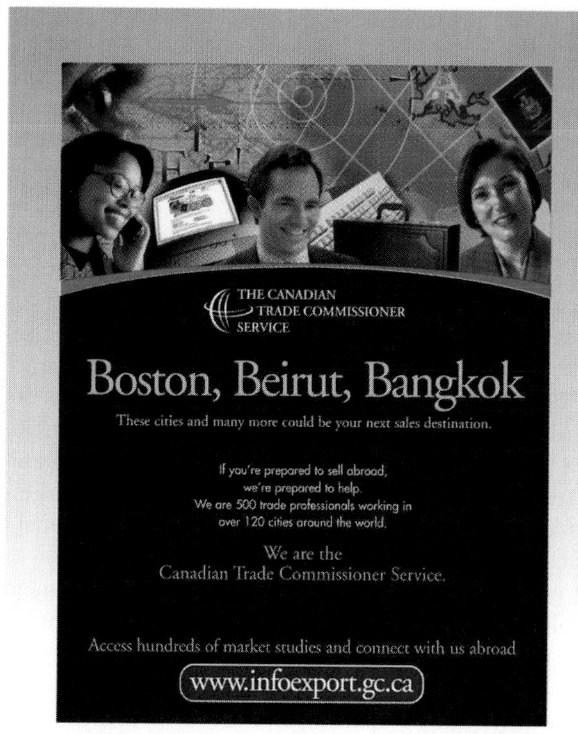

European unification offers tremendous trade opportunities for North America and other non-European firms. However, it also poses threats. As a result of increased unification, European companies will grow bigger and more competitive. Perhaps an even greater concern is that lower barriers inside Europe will only create thicker outside walls. Some observers envision a "Fortress Europe" that heaps favours on firms from EU countries but hinders outsiders by imposing such obstacles as stiffer import quotas, local content requirements, and other non-tariff barriers.

Progress toward European unification has been slow: Many doubt that complete unification will ever be achieved. However, on 1 January 1999, 11 of the 15 member nations took a significant step toward unification by adopting the euro as a common currency. These 11 nations represent 290 million people and a $10 trillion market. Currencies of the individual countries will be phased out gradually until 1 January 2002, when the euro will become the only currency. Adoption of the euro will decrease much of the currency risk associated with doing business in Europe, making member countries with previously weak currencies more attractive markets. In addition, by removing currency conversion hurdles, the switch will likely increase cross-border trade and highlight differences in pricing and marketing from country to country.[7]

Even with the adoption of the euro as a standard currency, from a marketing viewpoint, creating an economic community will not create a homogeneous market. As one international analyst suggests, "Even though you have fiscal harmonization, you can't go against 2000 years of tradition."[8] With 14 languages and distinctive national customs, it is unlikely that the EU will ever become one unified whole. Although economic and political boundaries may fall, social and cultural differences will remain, and companies marketing in Europe will face a daunting mass of local rules. Still, even if only partly successful, European unification will make a more efficient and competitive Europe a global force with which to reckon.[9]

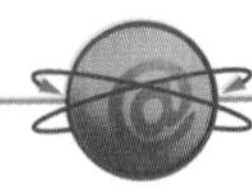

NAFTA Secretariat
www.nafta-sec-alena.org/

In North America, the United States and Canada phased out trade barriers in 1989. In January 1994, the *North American Free Trade Agreement (NAFTA)* established a free trade zone with the United States, Mexico, and Canada. The agreement created a single market of 360 million people producing and consuming $10 trillion worth of goods and services. Within its first 15 years, NAFTA will eliminate all trade barrier and investment restrictions among the three countries.

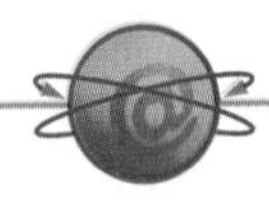

APEC Secretariat
www.apecsec.org.sg/

Canada is also a member of APEC—the Asian-Pacific Economic Cooperation. The 21 member economies began their association in 1989. The other APEC members are Australia, Brunei, Chile, China, Hong Kong, Indonesia, Korea, Japan, Malaysia, Mexico, New Zealand, Peru, the Philippines, Papua New Guinea, Russia, Singapore, Taiwan, Thailand, the United States, and Vietnam. As part of Canada's year of Asia Pacific, these economies met in Vancouver in 1997. The association hopes to foster free trade in a region that now accounts for 45 percent of world trade. While the more developed countries want to set a timeline for the implementation of tariff reductions, less developed countries, such as Indonesia, Malaysia, and Thailand, have been more cautious, fearing that such actions will harm industries just in their infancy.[10]

Other free trade areas are forming in Latin America. MERCOSUR links six full members—Argentina, Brazil, Paraguay, and Uruguay—and associate members—Bolivia and Chile. With a population of more than 200 million and a combined economy of over $1.5 trillion a year, these countries make up the largest trading bloc after NAFTA and the EU. There is talk of a free trade agreement between the EU and MERCOSUR.[11]

Although the recent trend toward free trade zones has caused great excitement and new market opportunities, it also raises some concerns. For example, many North American unions fear that NAFTA will lead to the further exodus of manufacturing jobs to Mexico, where wage rates are much lower than in Canada and the US. Environmentalists also worry that companies that are unwilling to play by the strict environmental protection rules will relocate in Mexico where pollution regulation has been lax.

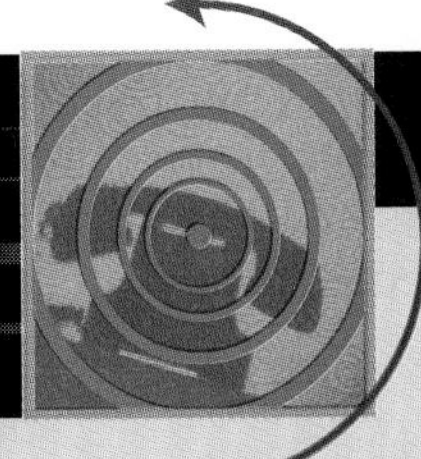

marketers speak out

Arthur Soler, President
Cadbury Chocolate Canada Inc.

Even though Arthur Soler, the president of Cadbury Chocolate Canada Inc., won't tell us the "Caramilk secret," he can tell us a lot about the challenges associated with Canadian marketing.

Arthur did not begin his career as a marketer. He graduated from Ryerson Polytechnical Institute in 1965 and went to work at Procter & Gamble as a financial analyst. In 1970, he joined Warner-Lambert as a financial planning manager, but soon moved into marketing with Adams Brands, the division that markets Trident Gum, Halls, and Clorets. In 1990, he ended his 20 years with Warner-Lambert to become the president of Neilson Cadbury, Canada's largest chocolate-bar manufacturer. In January 1996, the firm was acquired by Cadbury Schweppes UK, making it part of the world's sixth largest confectionery company. It is from this position that Arthur speaks to us.

The Challenges of Marketing to Trade Customers

Arthur Soler has no doubts about what constitute the major challenges facing marketers today. Marketers must do at least as good a job of marketing to the trade as they do marketing to final consumers. Whereas we can segment consumers into relatively homogeneous groups and then market to them using one program, no similar strategy is possible with trade customers, Arthur stresses. Thus, programs must be tailored to meet the needs of each retailer.

Another lesson to be learned when marketing to the trade, Arthur stresses, is understanding that it is not brands that are important to trade customers, but rather the category that they care about. Trade customers do not care if you sell a lot of just one brand or divide the sales among 10 brands; what they want is the best means to improve their business.

This need to understand the trade, in addition to marketing to final consumers, has changed the way marketing departments operate and the way marketers and salespeople are trained. Arthur's marketing vice-president has two years in sales, and his sales VP has eight years in marketing. This cross-training is important because sales needs to understand the consumer element, and marketing needs to appreciate the complexities of marketing to the trade.

Today's reality is that the trade is driving the business. If you want to have a powerful retailer, like one of the warehouse clubs, carry even one of your major brands, you have to package the product in the manner dictated by the retailer.

The mind-boggling power of the trade in Canada arises from high levels of concentration. Arthur makes the point that you no longer sell to the retailers—they sell to you. Manufacturers are asked to buy end-of-aisle displays, space in the retailer's flyers, a portion of the retailer's cooperative advertising, and a position on the shelf. Paying so much attention to the trade has resulted in many marketers losing their focus on the consumer, Arthur believes, but this can be a fatal mistake.

Despite the dire predictions several years ago that brands were dying, this has not happened. Brands have sometimes become weaker: Some marketers became arrogant about the power of their brands, believing that consumers would always pay more for branded products. The introduction of high-quality private-label products belied this assumption. Consumers quickly saw that they could get good value for lower prices.

The inability to raise prices has resulted in a renewed focus on controlling costs. When prices could go up indiscriminately, marketers became lazy about monitoring overhead expenses and waste. This is not the case today. The focus at Cadbury Chocolate has been to eliminate waste right across the supply chain. Concentrating on achieving greater efficiency has allowed Cadbury to use less working capital, carry less inventory, and still improve customer service.

Global Marketing?

Changing tack, Arthur moved our discussion along to the issue of global marketing. While he notes that competition is global, brands aren't. He thinks there is too much emphasis on global competition. While companies may have global power in terms of the resources, knowledge, and research that they can bring to the marketplace, market competition is fought at the brand level. To make his point, Arthur stresses that there are only a few truly global brands—McDonald's, Coca-Cola, Gillette—but there are many powerful domestic brands.

Arthur Soler.

Whether marketing globally or domestically, you still use the same fundamentals—establishing clear objectives, linking consumer behaviour to strategy, segmenting the market, and integrating the elements of the marketing mix. In other words, you have to get the fundamentals right on a region-by-region basis. Arthur makes his point by noting that, while CrispyCrunch is the number one brand in English Canada, it is number 23 in Quebec, where consumers just do not like its peanut butter taste. Cadbury is also beginning to think more about segmenting further to meet the needs of multicultural segments, especially those of the Asian market. In addition to regional and cultural differences, you also must understand the trade.

In closing, Arthur stresses his optimism about marketing in Canada. While many bemoan the difficulties of marketing here, Arthur notes that it is a country that has stable growth, consumers with disposable income, and a number of companies that are growing even though others are going. The trick, he advises, is to know the difference between the two.

Source: Peggy Cunningham interviewed Arthur Soler on 18 April 1996 for *Principles of Marketing.* We sincerely thank him for the insights he provided on the practice of marketing.

Whether conducting business in North America or venturing further afield, Canadian businesspeople must realize that each nation has unique features that must be understood. A nation's readiness for different products and services and its attractiveness as a market to foreign firms depend on its economic, politico-legal, ethical, and cultural environments.

Economic Environment

The international marketer must study each target country's economy. Two economic factors reflect the country's attractiveness as a market—the country's industrial structure and its income distribution. The country's *industrial structure* shapes its product and service needs, income levels, and employment levels. The four types of industrial structures are:

- *Subsistence economies.* In a subsistence economy, the vast majority of people engage in simple agriculture. They consume most of their output and barter the rest for simple goods and services. They offer few market opportunities.
- *Raw-material-exporting economies.* These economies are rich in one or more natural resources but poor in other ways. Much of their revenue comes from exporting resources. Examples are Chile (tin and copper); Zaire (copper, cobalt, and coffee); and Saudi Arabia (oil). Canada's "old economy" is as a major exporter of raw materials of softwood lumber, paper, petroleum, coal, and fish. These countries are good markets for large equipment, tools and supplies, and trucks. If there are many foreign residents and a wealthy upper class, they are also a market for luxury goods. For example, the Canadian firm Crystal Fountains has received orders of about $1 million from the United Arab Emirates, where people are willing to pay $150 000 to $200 000 for fountains.
- *Industrializing economies.* In an industrializing economy, manufacturing accounts for 10 to 20 percent of the country's economy. Examples include Egypt, the Philippines, India, and Brazil. As manufacturing increases, the country needs more imports of raw textile materials, steel, and heavy machinery, and fewer imports of finished textiles, paper products, and automobiles.
- *Industrial economies.* Industrial economies are major exporters of manufactured goods and investment funds. They trade goods among themselves and also export them to other types of economies for raw materials and semifinished goods. The varied manufacturing activities of these industrial nations and their large middle class make them rich markets for all sorts of goods. Canada's "new economy" is made up of manufacturing, service, and high-tech firms, which export a large portion of their output. The transportation-equipment industry (autos, railway equipment, aircraft) accounts for 26 percent of our exports. The communications sector, led by such giants as Nortel and BCE, also accounts for much of our international trade. Canada is also an exporter of many services. SNC-Lavalin, located in Montreal, is one of the world's largest consulting engineering firms. Our banks are heavily involved in international markets. When Canadian Pacific Hotels & Resorts bought a majority interest in the US-based Fairmont Hotels chain in 1999, it became a dominant player in the luxury hotel market, with 36 properties and more than 18 000 rooms in the US, Canada, Mexico, and the Caribbean.[12]

The second economic factor is the country's *income distribution.* Countries with subsistence economies may consist mostly of households with very low family incomes. In contrast, industrialized nations may have low-, medium-, and high-income households. Still other countries may have only households with either very low or very high incomes. However, marketers must not form stereotypes based on average income alone. Even people in low-income countries may find ways to buy products that are important to them:[13]

> Philosophy professor Nina Gladziuk thinks carefully before shelling out her hard-earned zlotys for Poland's dazzling array of consumer goods. But spend she certainly does. Although she earns just $750 a month from two academic jobs, Gladziuk, 41, enjoys making purchases: They are changing her lifestyle after years of deprivation under communism. In the past year, she has furnished a new apartment in a popular neighbourhood near Warsaw's Kabaty Forest, splurged on foreign-made beauty products, and spent a weekend in Paris before attending a seminar financed by her university. . . . Meet Central Europe's fast-rising consumer class. From white-collar workers like Gladziuk to factory workers in Budapest to hip young professionals in Prague, incomes are rising and confidence surging as a result of four years of economic growth. In the region's leading economies—the Czech Republic, Hungary, and Poland—the new class of buyers is growing not only in numbers but also in sophistication. . . . In Hungary, ad agency Young & Rubicam labels 11 percent of the country as "aspirers," with dreams of the good life and buying habits to match. Nearly one-third of all Czechs, Hungarians, and Poles—some 17 million people—are under 30 years old, eager to snap up everything from the latest fashions to compact discs.

Thus, international marketers face many challenges in understanding how the economic environment affects decisions about which global markets to enter and how.

Politico-Legal and Ethical Environment

Nations differ greatly in their politico-legal environments. A company must consider at least four politico-legal factors in deciding whether to do business in a given country: attitudes toward international buying, government bureaucracy, political stability, and monetary regulations.

In their attitudes toward international buying, some nations are quite receptive to foreign firms, but others are quite hostile. For example, India has bothered foreign businesses with import quotas, currency restrictions, and limits on the percentage of the management team that can be non-nationals. As a result, many North American companies left India because of all the hassles. In contrast, such neighbouring Asian countries as Singapore, Thailand, Malaysia, and the Philippines woo foreign investors and shower them with incentives and favourable operating conditions.

A second factor is *government bureaucracy*—the extent to which the host government runs an efficient system for helping foreign companies: efficient customs handling, good market information, and other factors that support conducting business. North Americans are often shocked by demands for bribes to make these trade barriers disappear even though such demands are illegal and unethical. These issues are discussed in Marketing Highlight 17-2.

Ads appearing in Hungarian magazines cater to a new class of buyer with dreams of the good life and buying habits to match, eager to snap up everything from jewellery to the latest cell phones.

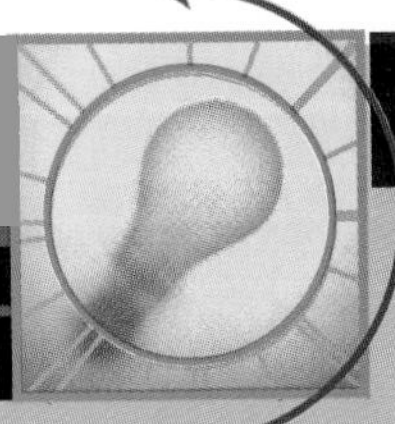

marketing highlight 17-2

The Grey Zone: International Marketing Ethics

Well-known business ethics scholar Richard De George wrote: "Business ethics is as national, international, or global as business itself, and no arbitrary geographical boundaries limit it." International business ethics is increasingly becoming front-page news, but the topic isn't a new one or even one born in modern times. For centuries, trade has brought people and cultures into direct conflict. The exploitation of numerous countries in the colonial periods of France, England, and Spain illustrate extreme cases of unethical marketing practice. Exchanges in which worthless beads were traded for gold and silver make some of the scandals presented in the modern press pale in comparison.

Marketing has long been associated with questions of ethics, both nationally and internationally. Marketing and ethics are closely aligned since the element of trust is inherent in the creation of the ongoing exchange relationships that lie at the heart of marketing. It cannot be denied that firms operating in international markets face a growing number of ethical issues. Business is increasingly global in nature: Firms operate in multiple national markets and they seek to raise capital from multiple international sources. Moreover, since foreign market growth outpaced North American market growth, the mandate for understanding how to manage international ethical behaviour is growing.

Decisions that marketers must make while working within the context of any corporation are complex and are often fraught with conflicts of values. Such conflicts are at the heart of many ethical dilemmas even in national business enterprises. They become seemingly insurmountable problems in the arena of international businesses, where people from different cultures, political systems, economies, value systems, and ethical standards must interact. In other words, ethical concerns involve more than black-and-white decisions; they involve many shades of grey, where the values of people from one country conflict with those from another. For example, in some countries, giving and receiving gifts is customary at the close of business transactions. However, for many North American firms, acceptance of gifts, other than mere tokens of appreciation such as chocolates or flowers, is viewed as unethical or may even be illegal.

Ethical issues arise in all of the functional areas of international business and centre on such business strategy questions as market-entry decisions, bribery and gift giving, contract negotiations, human resource issues, crisis management situations, product policy, advertising practices, pricing and transfer pricing, information systems management and privacy, grey markets, environmental concerns, accounting, finance and taxation, and production. Many of these areas are of specific concern to marketers. International advertising, for example, often raises ethical concerns. While many European countries use nudity and sexual innuendo in their advertising, some North Americans find this offensive. In some countries, such as India, even showing people kissing is objectionable.

Offering certain products for sale in some countries has also raised ethical criticism. North American companies have been criticized for marketing harmful chemicals overseas, chemicals that are banned from use in their home markets. Avon has been criticized for selling cosmetics to people in countries where many people cannot afford enough food. Even though a product itself may not be inherently harmful, ethical criticism has been directed at companies that did not take measures to prevent harm arising to consumers who incorrectly used products (like baby formula, drugs, or pesticides) due to high rates of illiteracy and inability to understand product-use instructions. There are also ethical issues associated with packaging in international markets. In some countries, such as Germany, manufacturers must recycle all packaging. In others, due to lack of disposal facilities, packaging adds to pollution problems.

Pricing raises yet another set of ethical concerns. Sometimes, higher prices must be charged due to the increased costs of marketing overseas, but when overly high prices are levied just because a firm has a monopoly in a foreign country, ethical questions have to be asked. Ethical criticism has been levied at firms for their refusal to send female sales representatives or managers into countries with adverse gender stereotypes even though this hampers women's chances for advancement or higher earnings.

Bribery is always a thorny issue in international markets. While it is undeni-

Political stability is another issue. Governments change hands, sometimes violently. Even without a change, a government may decide to respond to new popular feelings. The foreign company's property may be taken, its currency holdings may be blocked, or import quotas or new duties may be set. International marketers may find it profitable to do business in an unstable country, but the unsteady situation will affect how they handle business and financial matters.

Finally, companies must consider a country's *monetary regulations*. Sellers want to take their profits in a currency of value to them. Ideally, the buyer can pay in the seller's currency or in other world currencies. Short of this, sellers may accept a blocked currency—one whose removal from the country is restricted by the buyer's government—if they can buy other goods in that country that they able that in some countries it is viewed as a "normal" way of doing business, this is not universally the case. Marketers should be aware that in most countries, bribery is an illegal practice. And because North Americans hold the stereotypical belief that bribes are expected overseas, we often make the mistake of offering such a payment when we perceive the slightest hesitation in signing a business deal. Rather than expecting a bribe, the foreign official may just be more risk averse or want more information. The offering of a bribe, in these cases, will not only cause offence but will often terminate the relationship.

When discussing international business ethics, North Americans believe that we take the moral highroad. We've all read reports of companies being blocked from doing business in South America because of rigged bidding systems, or losing sales in China or Korea because firms cannot legally pay the bribes necessary to get the business. However, we have to be aware that some countries may have higher moral standards than we do. For example, one survey showed that fewer Japanese executives will cheat on their expense sheets than will a comparable group of North American executives. Other surveys of Canadian businesspeople have shown that most ethical problems arise not in doing business in exotic locales, but rather in dealing with our closest neighbour, the United States. While this may be due to the fact that we do more business with the US than with any other country, problems such as industrial espionage, product safety concerns, sales practices, and hiring practices have been areas of growing ethical concern.

Despite the number of ethical issues marketers face, there are often few guidelines to help them come to terms with these issues. International marketers must be aware, however, that they have multiple responsibilities to the firms and their customers. They must avoid knowingly harming any of their constituents. They must sell safe products, ensure truthful advertising, and charge fair prices. As a minimum, marketers working for Canadian companies must abide by the laws of the countries in which they operate. However, being an ethical marketer often means going beyond the mere provisions of a legal system. Marketers also must consider what is right or wrong. Such considerations involve respecting the human rights of people, no matter what country they reside in. It involves avoiding the exploitation of individuals or their environment.

Many companies, such as Imperial Oil and Warner-Lambert, have developed codes of ethics to guide their employees' decisions. A 1995 survey of the CEOs of the top 500 companies in Canada revealed that 80 percent of these firms had codes of ethics. Many of these firms require that the principles outlined in the code be applied wherever the firm is operating. In other words, the rules applying to conducting business in Canada also apply to subsidiaries of the business operating overseas.

In Canada, top levels of management are responsible for setting ethics policy and ensuring its implementation throughout the firm. Leading scholars in the field of marketing ethics emphasize that planning for ethical behaviour must begin at the same time as the rest of the strategic international market planning effort. Ethics cannot be an afterthought. This type of planning includes making such decisions as which international markets to enter, since some areas are known for their inherent ethical challenges. For example, does the firm want to enter markets dominated by totalitarian and military regimes, or those known for their record of human rights violations or ongoing environmental damage? Other questions include what types of products to market. The marketing of pesticides, tobacco, liquor, and pharmaceuticals, for example, all have unique ethical questions associated with them.

In addition to having a code of ethics, a firm must actively train its employees to be more sensitive to ethical issues, especially as it sends them overseas. While fewer than 40 percent of firms offer ethics training, surveys indicate that employees want this type of training, that it has a positive effect in reducing unethical behaviour, and that it heightens ethical issue recognition and sensitivity.

In the end, although international marketing can be one of the most exciting and rewarding areas of the profession, be aware that it also presents some of the most difficult ethical problems and issues.

Source: This highlight is based on Peggy Cunningham's article "Managing marketing ethics in international business: Literature review and directions for future research," published in the Proceedings of the ASAC Conference, Windsor, June 1995.

need themselves or can sell elsewhere for a needed currency. Besides currency limits, a changing exchange rate also creates high risks for the seller.

Most international trade involves cash transactions. Yet many nations have too little hard currency to pay for their purchases from other countries. They may want to pay with other items instead of cash, which has led to the practice of **countertrade.** Countertrade takes several forms. *Barter* involves the direct exchange of goods or services. Another form is *compensation* (or *buyback*), whereby the seller sells a plant, equipment, or technology to another country and agrees to take payment in the resulting products. *Counterpurchase* occurs when the seller receives full payment in cash but agrees to spend some portion of the money in the other country within a stated time period. Countertrade deals can be very complex. For

Countertrade
International trade involving the direct or indirect exchange of goods for other goods instead of cash. Forms include barter, compensation (buyback), and counterpurchase.

example, Daimler-Benz once sold 30 trucks to Romania in exchange for 150 Romanian jeeps, which it then sold to Ecuador for bananas, which were in turn sold to a German supermarket chain for German currency. Through this roundabout process, Daimler-Benz finally obtained payment in German money.[14]

Cultural Environment

Each country has its own folkways, norms, and taboos. The seller must examine the way consumers in different countries think about and use certain products before planning a marketing program. There are often surprises. For example, the average French man uses almost twice as many cosmetics and beauty aids as his wife. The Germans and the French eat more packaged, branded spaghetti than do Italians. Italian children like to eat chocolate bars between slices of bread as a snack. Japanese people will not eat chocolate and peanuts together because they believe that it will cause nose bleeds. Companies that ignore such differences can make some very expensive and embarrassing mistakes:[15]

> McDonald's and Coca-Cola managed to offend the entire Muslim world by putting the Saudi Arabian flag on their packaging. The flag's design includes a passage from the Koran (the sacred text of Islam), and Muslims feel very strongly that their Holy Writ should never be wadded up and tossed in the garbage. Nike faced a similar situation in Arab countries when Muslims objected to a stylized "Air" logo on its shoes that resembled "Allah" in Arabic script. Nike apologized for the mistake and pulled the shoes from distribution.

Business norms and behaviour also vary among countries. Business executives need to be briefed on these factors before conducting business in another country. These are some examples of differing global business behaviour:

Overlooking cultural differences can result in embarrassing mistakes. When it learned that the stylized "Air" logo on its shoes resembled "Allah" in Arabic script, Nike apologized and pulled the shoes from distribution.

- South Americans like to sit or stand very close to each other when they talk business; in fact, almost nose to nose. The North American business executive tends to keep backing away as the South American moves closer. Both may end up being offended.
- In face-to-face communications, Japanese business executives rarely say no, leaving North Americans frustrated and not knowing where they stand. However, when North Americans come to the point quickly, Japanese business executives may find this behaviour pushy and offensive.
- In France, wholesalers don't want to promote a product. They ask their retailers what they want and deliver it. If a company builds its strategy around the French wholesaler's cooperation in promotions, it is likely to fail.
- When North American executives exchange business cards, each usually gives the other's card a cursory glance and stuffs it in a pocket for later reference. In Asia, however, executives dutifully study each other's cards during a greeting, carefully noting company affiliation and rank. They use both hands to give their card to the most important person first.

Therefore, marketers must study the cultural traditions, preferences, and behaviours of each country and region they want to enter. An understanding of key differences in consumer and distributor behaviour kept Vogue Pools from falling off the deep end.

> LaSalle, Quebec's Vogue Pools sells backyard swimming pools—virtually the same products around the world. However, the firm realized that it needed

very different product and distribution strategies to meet the needs of customers in different countries. For example, in Canada, 90 percent of pools are sold through specialized pool retailers, which offer their customers installation service. In Europe, however, just the opposite is true. Ninety percent of people buying pools do their own installation. Therefore, Vogue realized, these consumers would need help. Since Vogue representatives couldn't join buyers in their backyards to offer a helping hand, they did the next best thing. Pools were redesigned to simplify the installation process. In fact, Vogue took the "Ikea approach." Customers must still dig a hole, but they can use a single tool to assemble their Vogue pool and no longer need to use a confusing array of nuts and bolts. Differences in behaviour didn't stop with customers. Distributors had unique perspectives as well. Gilles Lebuis, VP of marketing, notes, "A distributor in France will know his market much better . . . than someone from Switzerland. . . ." Thus, even though it might have been cheaper to use a single European distributor, Vogue chose different distributors for each country. It sells through major do-it-yourself chains in France and pool distributors in Belgium, Switzerland, Germany, and Austria. Sales have topped $11 million using these strategies, keeping Vogue stroking along.[16]

Deciding Whether to Go International

While many firms view themselves as local businesses serving their immediate communities, they must become aware of the globalization of competition even if they never plan to go overseas themselves. Too many companies have recognized the dangers too late and have gone out of business when faced with new competitors such as the category killers from the United States or abroad. Companies that operate in global industries, where their strategic positions in specific markets are affected strongly by their overall global positions, have no choice but to think and act globally. Thus, Nortel must organize globally if it is to gain purchasing, manufacturing, financial, and marketing advantages. Firms in a global industry must be able to compete on a worldwide basis if they are to succeed.

Several factors may draw a company into the international arena. Global competitors may attack the company's domestic market by offering better products or lower prices. The company may want to counterattack these competitors in their home markets to tie up their resources. Or it may discover foreign markets that present higher profit opportunities than the domestic market does. The company's domestic market may be shrinking, or the company may need a larger customer base to achieve economies of scale. Or it may want to reduce its dependence on any one market to reduce its risk. Finally, the company's customers may be expanding abroad and require international servicing.

Before going abroad, the company must weigh the risks and assess its ability to operate globally. Can the company learn to understand the preferences and buyer behaviour of consumers in other countries? Can it offer competitively attractive products? Will it be able to adapt to other countries' business cultures and deal effectively with foreign nationals? Do the company's managers have the necessary international experience? Has management considered the impact of regulations and the political environments of other countries?

Because of the risks and difficulties of entering international markets, most companies do not act until some situation or event thrusts them into the global arena. Someone—a domestic exporter, a foreign importer, a foreign government—may ask the company to sell abroad. Or the company may be saddled with overcapacity and must find additional markets for its goods.

Deciding Which Markets to Enter

Before going abroad, the company must set its international *marketing objectives and policies*. First, it must decide what *volume* of foreign sales it wants. Most companies start small when they go abroad. Some plan to stay small, seeing international sales as a small part of their business. Other companies have bigger plans, seeing international business as equal to or even more important than their domestic business.

The company must choose *how many* countries it wants to market in. Generally, it makes sense to operate in fewer countries with deeper commitment and penetration in each. The Bulova Watch Company decided to operate in many international markets and expanded into over 100 countries; unfortunately it had spread itself too thin, made profits in only two countries, and lost around $55 million.

In contrast, although consumer-product company Amway is now breaking into markets at a furious pace, it is doing so only after decades of gradually building up its overseas presence. Known for its neighbour-to-neighbour direct-selling networks, Amway expanded into Australia in 1971, a country far away but similar to its North American market. Then, in the 1980s, Amway expanded into 10 more countries, and the pace increased rapidly from then on. By 1994, Amway was firmly established in 60 countries, including Hungary, Poland, and the Czech Republic. Following its substantial success in Japan, China, and other Asian countries, the company entered India in 1998. Entering the new century, international proceeds account for over 70 percent of the company's overall sales.[17]

Next, the company must decide on the *types* of countries to enter. A country's attractiveness depends on the product, geographical factors, income and population, political climate, and other factors. The seller may prefer certain country groups or parts of the world. In recent years, many major markets have emerged, offering both substantial opportunities and daunting challenges (see Marketing Highlight 17-3).

After listing possible international markets, the company must screen and rank each one. Consider this example:[18]

> Many mass marketers dream of selling to China's more than 1.2 billion people. For example, Colgate is waging a pitched battle in China, seeking control of the world's largest toothpaste market. Yet, this country of infrequent brushers offers great potential. Only 20 percent of China's rural dwellers brush daily, so Colgate and its competitors are aggressively pursuing promotional and educational programs, from massive ad campaigns to visits to local schools to sponsoring oral care research. Through such efforts, in this $350 million market dominated by local brands, Colgate has expanded its market share from seven percent in 1995 to 24 percent today.

Colgate's decision to enter the Chinese market seems fairly straightforward: China is a huge market without established competition. Given the low rate of brushing, this already huge market can grow even larger. Yet we still can question whether market size *alone* is reason enough for selecting China. Colgate must also consider other factors. Will the Chinese government remain stable and supportive? Does China provide for the production and distribution technologies needed to produce and market Colgate's products profitably? Will Colgate be able to overcome cultural barriers and convince Chinese consumers to brush their teeth regularly? Can Colgate compete effectively with dozens of local competitors? Colgate's current success in China suggests that it could answer yes to all of these questions. Still, the company's future in China is filled with uncertainties.

A company should rank possible global markets on several factors, including market size, market growth, cost of doing business, competitive advantage, and risk level. It can use indicators like those shown in Table 17-1 to determine the potential of each market, and then decide which ones offer the greatest long-run return on investment.

General Electric's appliance division uses what it calls a "smart bomb" strategy for selecting global markets to enter. GE executives microscopically examine each potential country, measuring such factors as strength of local competitors, market growth potential, and availability of skilled labour. The company then targets only markets where it can earn more than 20 percent on its investment. The

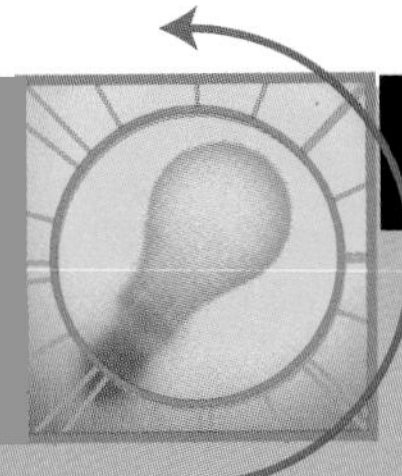

marketing highlight 17-3

The Last Marketing Frontiers: Eastern Europe, China and Vietnam, and Cuba

As communist and formerly communist countries reform their markets, and trade barriers are dismantled, North American companies are eagerly anticipating the profits that await them. Here are "snapshots" of the opportunities and challenges that marketers face in three of the world's global marketing frontiers.

Eastern Europe: A Market Ready to Harvest

As Central and Eastern Europe continue the transition to free-market economies, the market for Canadian goods and services is expanding. Rapid economic growth and the privatization of state-owned companies point the way to increasing opportunities. The Canadian Development Corporation (CDC), a Crown corporation, has helped Canadian firms expand into the region by providing them with financial and risk management services. The Canadian International Development Agency (CIDA) runs other federal government programs designed to help firms ease their way into these markets.

Russia, a challenging market, boasts 250 Canadian companies that have thrived in the oil and gas, agricultural, housing and construction, and telecommunications markets. However, as Russia's economy struggles, Canadian exports have been falling: In 1997, Canada exported $379 million to Russia, but in 1999 (the most recent data available) exports fell to $174 million. Poland is Canada's second largest trade partner in the area. Canada has long enjoyed an excellent reputation in Poland. While charting a course through Poland's business channels is no easy task, perseverance pays, and Canadian firms exported $205 million to the country in 1999. Since the Czech Republic is one of the most stable and fastest-growing former communist countries in Europe, Canadians firms have been working diligently to build relationships there. Hungary is another target of Canadian firms. The new airport in Budapest, built by a Canadian-led consortium, bears witness to the country's open and friendly business environment. Canadian exports to Hungary increased by 500 percent over a 10-year period.

China: 1.2 Billion Consumers

In Guangdong province, Chinese "yuppies" walk department-store aisles to buy $140 Nike or Reebok running shoes or think nothing of spending $6 on a jar of Skippy peanut butter in the supermarket section. Although Chinese consumers make as little as $190 a month, they still have plenty of savings and spending money because of subsidized housing and health care. In Shenzen, Guangdong's second largest city, consumers have the highest disposable income in all of China—$5600 annually. With purchasing power like this, a population of 1.2 billion, and the fastest-growing economy in the world, China is encouraging companies from around the world to set up shop there. Instead of the communist propaganda of yore, modern Chinese billboards exclaim, "Give China a chance."

Since the prime minister's first highly publicized "Team Canada" trade delegation to China in 1994, Canadian exports to China have grown tremendously. The most recent mission, Team Canada 2001, to Beijing, Shanghai, and Hong Kong, wrapped up 27 new business for Canadian enterprises totalling $5.7 billion. Hong Kong is a major financial and high-technology hub and a key gateway for Canadian companies doing business in Asia. It is already home to the largest Canadian business community in Asia.

Yet for all its market potential, there are many hurdles to jump in entering mainland China and marketing to the Chinese. Even firms that have been highly successful in the Chinese market, such as Nortel or Bombardier, still face prolonged and difficult negotiations. Firms are often unsure about who has the authority to close a deal or make a final decision. Moreover, China is not one market, but many, and regional governments may discriminate against certain goods. Distribution channels are undeveloped, consisting of thousands of tiny mom-and-pop stores that can afford to stock only a few bottles or packages at a time. And China's dismal infrastructure can turn a rail shipment travelling from Guanzhou to Beijing into a month-long odyssey. As Canadian firms expand from Hong Kong into mainland China, *guanxi*, or connections, have become one of the keys to doing business. Many believe that businesses will need a Chinese partner with local political connections to be successful. Others acquire Chinese business partners who can help them penetrate distribution channels and hire experienced personnel. Another major concern is China's distressing human rights record. Levi Strauss has turned its back on China's vast market for blue jeans because of such concerns. But other firms counter that industry can be part of the solution. "Supporting the business sector will result in economic and political freedoms for the Chinese people," says a 3M spokesperson.

Vietnam: An Untapped Market Vietnam seems like a marketer's dream: 72 million consumers, 80 percent of whom are under 40 years old; loads of natural re-

Pepsi in China—a huge marketing opportunity?

sources, including oil, gold, gas, and timber; and a coastline of pristine beaches that could turn out to be the hot new tourist spot. Vietnam is the world's twelfth most populous nation and southeast Asia's second largest market.

Amid all the excitement, however, are some notes of caution. The per-capita income of most Vietnamese is $280 a year, and Vietnam's transportation and communication systems rank among the world's worst. While the country and its markets develop, marketers are spending their money cautiously. Because most consumers are seeing products for the first time, companies are investing most of their marketing dollars in very simple advertising campaigns. For this reason, radio and billboards are fruitful venues for advertising. One billboard in Ho Chi Minh City boasts a single word: Sony.

Cuba: Watching and Waiting

Cuba is an important emerging market with considerable potential for Canadian exporters and investors. It comprises half the land mass of the Caribbean, and with a population of about 11 million, it is the largest market in the region. Canada and Cuba have a long history of trade. Today, Cuba is Canada's first trading partner in the Caribbean, while Canada is Cuba's second largest trading partner globally; Russia is still number one. Tourism, mining, and agriculture are the main areas of trade focus. Twenty-six Canadian import and export companies have registered as operating offices in Cuba, and over 200 000 Canadians visited the island in 1999. Two-way trade in 1999 totalled $701.8 million. Canadian exports to Cuba were $396.0 million in 1999. As with the emerging markets of China and Vietnam, Cuba's infrastructure needs years of rebuilding. Some places have no running water, gasoline, sewer systems, and energy sources. "They'll have to take care of the basic concept of survival before they can think about pizza and Pepsi," says Joe Zubizarreta, a Cuban-born advertising executive. Thus, it isn't surprising that Canada's main exports to Cuba are metal structures and hardware, industrial machinery and parts, motor vehicles and parts, electrical equipment, and fertilizers.

Not only has the US-led embargo against Cuba dampened the country's economic prospects, but American political pressure has also caused problems for Canadian firms that do business in Cuba. However, while these American laws increase the risk for Canadian companies, they also prevent American competitors from entering the market. Instead of having to challenge entrenched American competitors as Canadian firms do in other Latin American markets, the principal competitors in Cuba are mostly from Latin America (especially Mexico) and Europe (especially Spain, Italy, and France), as well as from Asia.

Sources: Melana Zyla, "Polish your connections to prosper in business," *Globe and Mail,* 1 July 1997:C13; "Central and Eastern Europe: A market ready to harvest," *Advertising Supplement, Canadian Business,* July 1997; Nattalia Lea, "Passage to the China market," *Marketing,* 12 September 1994:8; Marlene Piturro, "Capitalist China?" *Brandweek,* 16 May 1994:24–7; Mark L. Clifford, "How you can win in China," *Business Week,* 26 May 1997:66–9; "Hong Kong means business," *Financial Post,* 30 June 1997:HK4; Department of Foreign Affairs and International Trade, "Team Canada 2001 concludes with $5.7 billion in new deals," news release, 17 February 2001; Cyndee Miller, "U.S. firms rush to claim share of newly opened Vietnam market," *Marketing News,* 14 March 1994:11; Thomas A. Kissane, "What are we doing in Vietnam?" *Sales & Marketing Management,* May 1996:96–7; Christy Fisher, "U.S. marketers wait for opening in Cuba," *Advertising Age,* 29 August 1994:1,6; Sean Mehegan, "Is Castro convertible?" *Restaurant Business,* 1 May 1996:36–8; Department of Foreign Affairs and International Trade, *Cuba: A Guide for Canadian Businesses,* 2nd ed., June 1999, www.infoexport.gc.ca/docs/view-e.asp?did=214&gid=193.

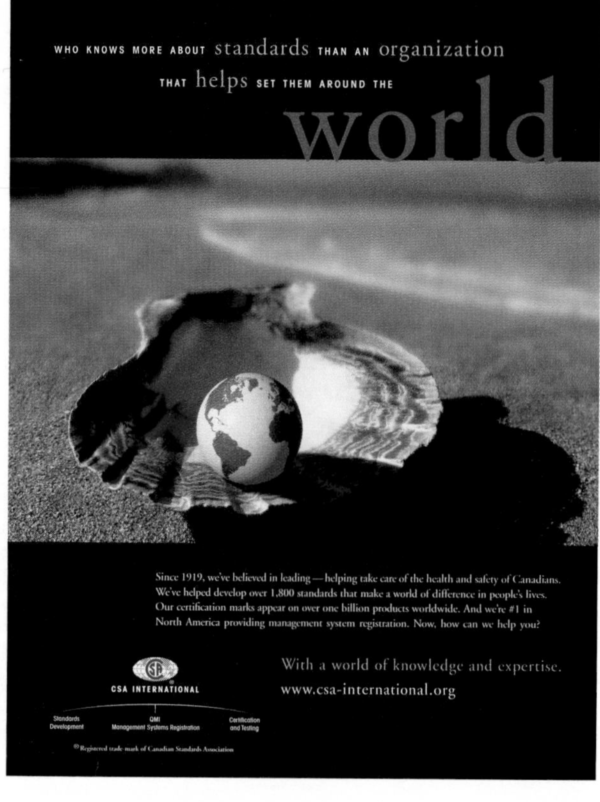

The Canadian Standards Association International can help firms with their market-entry decisions.